The Management of Telecommunications

Business Solutions to Business Problems Enabled by Voice and Data Communications

Second Edition

Houston H. Carr
Auburn University

Charles A. Snyder
Auburn University

Boston   Burr Ridge, IL   Dubuque, IA   Madison, WI   New York   San Francisco   St. Louis
Bangkok   Bogotá   Caracas   Kuala Lumpur   Lisbon   London   Madrid   Mexico City
Milan   Montreal   New Delhi   Santiago   Seoul   Singapore   Sydney   Taipei   Toronto

McGraw-Hill Higher Education

*A Division of The **McGraw-Hill** Companies*

THE MANAGEMENT OF TELECOMMUNICATIONS: BUSINESS SOLUTIONS TO BUSINESS PROBLEMS ENABLED BY VOICE AND DATA COMMUNICATION

Published by McGraw-Hill/Irwin, a business unit of The McGraw-Hill Companies, Inc., 1221 Avenue of the Americas, New York, NY, 10020. Copyright © 2003, 1997 by The McGraw-Hill Companies, Inc. All rights reserved. No part of this publication may be reproduced or distributed in any form or by any means, or stored in a database or retrieval system, without the prior written consent of The McGraw-Hill Companies, Inc., including, but not limited to, an any network or other electronic storage or transmission, or broadcast for distance learning.

Some ancillaries, including electronic and print components, may not be available to customers outside the United States.

This book is printed on acid-free paper.

domestic   1 2 3 4 5 6 7 8 9 0 DOW/DOW 0 9 8 7 6 5 4 3 2
international   1 2 3 4 5 6 7 8 9 0 DOW/DOW 0 9 8 7 6 5 4 3 2

ISBN 0-07-248931-6

Publisher: *George Werthman*
Senior sponsoring editor: *Rick Williamson*
Developmental editor: *Kelly L. Delso*
Manager, Marketing and Sales: *Paul Murphy*
Marketing manager: *Greta Kleinert*
Media producer: *Greg Bates*
Senior project manager: *Pat Frederickson*
Production supervisor: *Debra R. Sylvester*
Senior designer: *Jennifer McQueen*
Photo research coordinator: *Jeremy Cheshareck*
Photo researcher: *Connie Gardner*
Senior supplement producer: *Rose M. Range*
Senior digital content specialist: *Brian Nacik*
Cover design: *Kiera Cunningham*
Typeface: *10/12 Palatino*
Compositor: *Carlisle Communications, Ltd.*
Printer: *R. R. Donnelley & Sons Company*

Library of Congress Cataloging-in-Publication Data

Carr, Houston H., 1937-
    The management of telecommunications : business solutions to business problems enabled by voice and data communications / Houston H. Carr, Charles A. Snyder.— 2nd ed.
        p. cm.
    Includes index
    ISBN 0-07-248931-6 (alk. paper) - ISBN 0-07-119928-4 (alk. paper)
    1. Business—Communication systems. 2. Telecommunication systems. I. Snyder, Charles A. II. Title.
HD30.335 .C36 2003
384'.068–dc21

                                    2002071850

INTERNATIONAL EDITION ISBN 0-07-119928-4

Copyright © 2003. Exclusive rights by The McGraw-Hill Companies, Inc. for manufacture and export. This book cannot be re-exported from the country to which it is sold by McGraw-Hill. The International Edition is not available in North America.

www.mhhe.com

This book is dedicated to . . .

- Our students who made the text necessary and worthwhile

- Managers who must have this knowledge to be competitive

and above all

- Our wives, *Genyth* and *Margrit*, who gave us the time and support to make the book a reality.

Preface

In the economy of the 21st century, almost everything is both global and mobile.

Telecommunications technology has become much more than a business tool. It has now become an essential feature of the business environment and is embodied in both operations and the products of organizations.

We are living in an age of *convergence*. That is, we have witnessed the coming together of computing and telecommunications so that many would describe the present as having moved from being systems-centric (mainframe computer), through personal computer–centric, to network-centric, and now to Internet or Web-centric. Some predict that the future (starting around the year 2010) will become more content-centric. Businesses are in a state of evolution that has been both caused and enabled by technology and a technology-based infrastructure.

This is a book about the use and management of telecommunications resources that support the business of the organization, that is, business telecommunications. It provides the information at a level that will be understandable to the student new to telecommunications while still providing essential and in-depth knowledge to satisfy the need for specificity and technological knowledge for the subject. We discuss data and computer communications in some detail as this is where much of the efficiency and effectiveness of business telecommunications take place. We also address that other side of telecommunications, the worldwide telephone system and its impact on local interorganizational human communications. All of the discussion takes place within the management and decision-making environment of running a business that grows in size and telecommunications sophistication.

While information (and data) may be the lifeblood of the organization, telecommunications is the circulation system. Just as the organism cannot exist without its lifeblood, it cannot exist without it being distributed properly. Telecommunications is central to how organizations conduct their business in that it is the conduit for vital organizational information flows. Therefore, a knowledge of telecommunications is essential to students or anyone who will be part of any organization that is decentralized and dispersed, shares resources, and communicates. An understanding of the vocabulary, technology, and use of telecommunications is critical to business/organizational decision makers.

The changed nature of the business environment means that managers can no longer rely on technical specialists to provide them with all telecommunications decisions. Business students must understand how telecommunications in general and telecommunications-intensive information systems in particular are part of the strategic, tactical, and operational decision processes of an organization. The nature of the evolving environment means that a knowledge of telecommunications can mean the difference between achieving competitive advantage and failure. In the 21st century, almost everything will be both global and mobile. Therefore, the organization's telecommunications infrastructure will be vital to its success.

Don't buy technology! Buy resolution to a problem or opportunity! The final determinant is, "What are the *management implications* for choosing a given solution?"

A BOOK FOR BUSINESS STUDENTS

The essentials for a business book on telecommunications, by the global nature of the business market, must be based on management decision making in an environment of competition. The existing texts on telecommunications were generated primarily from an engineering perspective. This text presents the essentials of telecommunications for business decision making around a building-block approach, from the very simple to the global and very complex. Other texts immerse the student in the technology without relating that technology to the business requirements for it. Our approach systematically builds a business and its information and telecommunications systems so that the reader can easily understand relevant issues and be introduced to the technology at a point where the technology makes business sense.

COURSES IN THE CURRICULUM

Courses in telecommunications are now a normal part of Schools of Business curricula. The view that telecommunications is vital to MIS and to business education is widely recognized. This trend will continue as we more fully absorb and integrate the technology of microcomputers, electronic and voice mail, teleconferencing, multimedia, facsimile, distributed processing, the computer integrated enterprise, electronic commerce, wireless and mobile commerce, especially on the Internet's World Wide Web, and communications in general. We believe the need for understanding business telecommunications and courses in business schools will continue to grow at an increasing rate. The growth should be spurred by the radical changes in organizations as the result of reengineering of processes, reliance on teams, and increased dispersion of operations made possible by broad bandwidth, wireless, and mobile technologies.

The objective of this text is to provide the student sufficient vocabulary, technical understanding, and alternatives to be an effective business telecommunications decision maker. In addition the student should become "snowproof," which means to be insulated from being overpowered by vendors and highly technology-based colleagues. Many, if not most, of the students using this text will have limited technological backgrounds, but will be placed in situations to make or support decisions on the use of telecommunications. These students must internalize knowledge and understanding so as to deal effectively with vendors and "techies" who may attempt to overwhelm them with a strange vocabulary and the self-evident merits of telecommunications technology. Students armed with the tools contained in this book will be able to lead the decision process because they understand the technology trade-offs in relation to costs, marketing, customer service, and competition.

The book includes additional material in the chapters and at the end of the chapters that will carry undergraduate students, graduate students, managers, and executives to a deeper and richer understanding of technological concepts. Where some books concentrate only on data communications, we cover both voice and data systems. While others give only broad coverage, we complement breadth with optional depth. While others concentrate on the technology, we support an understanding of technology and the need to manage it. This book provides several levels of understanding: the technology, the vocabulary, the management issues, and the decision environment.

> Bringing technology to bear on a process yields richer dividends if one is willing to consider reengineering the process.

Part of our thrust is to use real and created cases to demonstrate the concepts of the chapters and to show the decision process that is occurring. We provide problems that allow the students to demonstrate understanding of the decision processes, such as when to consider bypass; the economics of a VAN or organizational networks; use of real and virtual networks; the lingering implications of the AT&T divesture, telecommunications regulation, telecommunications deregulation, and privatization; twisted-wire versus fiber optic cable versus wireless; telecommunications as an investment rather than a cost; and the economic value of truly managing the organization's voice and data systems.

Students in a two-year program other than an associate degree in telecommunications will probably take the course in the second year. Those in a telecommunications program will likely use the book the first year. Students in a four-year college will take the course their junior or senior year regardless of their program. The students will most likely be MIS/CIS or computer science majors, although we believe the book should have appeal to engineering management curricula. The students may include this as an elective course, taking it to strengthen their technical backgrounds. Most students will realize that taking a business telecommunications course was one of their better decisions when they are faced with a myriad of telecommunications choices in the organizational environment.

> From a management perspective, the primary focus is on the *level of quality* and the *level of service* rather than on the technology itself.

ENGINEERING OR BUSINESS

We focus on business applications and provide examples that are relevant to business rather than concentrating primarily on the technology as do most of the books on networking and data communications. Our aim is to provide the essential information that will enable students to make a smooth transition to managerial roles. Engineering students should find that this book will provide needed managerial topics and issues that many of them will encounter as they transition to project leadership and supervisory positions in their organizations. We attempt to make the subject real and referent to everyday life so it becomes something students will want to know about.

Major telecommunications companies have found this book useful in bringing new managers up to speed quickly, especially if they come from a nontechnology background. The book reads easily for managers from other disciplines and allows them to learn at a quick pace.

Many students from a nontechnical curriculum who take a traditional telecommunications course will rapidly encounter what may appear to be high-level electrical engineering material. To avoid this, we introduce the technology within the more comfortable context of the business needs for communications. The book has a strong management tone and decision thrust; therefore the instructor must be aware that the technology itself may not be self-evident. To aid this process, we explain technical subjects through analogous comparison to familiar subjects.

We have applied this method to teaching with considerable success. When students discover that technology can be learned, they have fun with many of the analogies. The students' success rate will depend on the expectations and proper presentation sequencing of the instructor. Business students should learn an appropriate level of the material and achieve success levels comparable with those attained in average business courses.

This book is designed for a pragmatic, nontheoretical approach to telecommunications. The *management and use of* telecommunications systems and equipment involve large expenditures and require understanding of the dimensions of the relevant decisions. The vocabulary is elementary, the technical content is understandable, the methods are applied, and the subject is comprehensive.

> The value of any telecommunications technology is measured in its contribution to the firm's business objectives.

AIDS TO LEARNING

To aid in the learning process, we use a developing, although contrived, business case throughout the book. By addressing technology within the environment of business needs, the reader develops an appreciation for the *business need* for the technology. The continuing case threaded throughout the chapters accentuates the concepts and provides a building-block approach that integrates each new facet and tenet of telecommunications into a coherent business application.

A computer-based graphing tool, netViz®, is optionally packaged with each text to aid the student in visualizing network problems and solutions. Finally, there are cases and papers as well as recommended readings at the end of most chapters that further discuss relevant topics.

INTRODUCTION TO THE CONTINUING CASE
Johnson Enterprises, Inc.

We begin each chapter with a portion of a continuing case in which we describe the evolution and development of a small business. **Johnson Enterprises, Inc.**, the organization in question, is a successful business now headed by Carlton Johnson. His father, Michael, started the company in 1951 that is today **JEI.** What was a one-person operation in a small building on East Oak Street in Denver, Colorado, has grown into a multidivision and multinational corporation with several manufacturing sites and many customers.

Johnson Lighting Company, like the majority of companies started each year, began life as an idea. Resources, other than a motivated owner, were scarce. Michael opened business with an office and a telephone. He had the capital to carry him through the first two years of business, during which time he established a reputation as a reliable firm with which to do business. He relied on his suppliers to warehouse his inventory, selling his services out of a group of catalogs. He also relied on these suppliers to provide him short-term credit. He demonstrated his value to his suppliers by a willingness to do quality work and paying his bills on time.

As we follow the daily adventures of **Johnson Lighting Company,** we will introduce business decision opportunities, some brought about because of telecommunications technology and some that would require new capabilities. In each case, we will show that the use of the technology is to solve a business problem or capitalize on an opportunity. Additionally, you should be aware that this company, like many in the world today, often stumbles into opportunities, and it is only astute awareness or luck that prevents future problems.

Look here for questions and answers that help you learn.

To enforce and reinforce topics, we use *marginal notes* on many pages, as a way to highlight items in the margins. Within the body of the text, and even in the case, we use *information windows* and *technology notes* to bring more lengthy items to the forefront. Finally, we include articles about how companies are using the technology under discussion in *real-world windows*. The use of real-world examples throughout sets this book apart from those that focus primarily on technology.

INFORMATION WINDOW, TECHNOLOGY NOTE, OR REAL WORLD

For example, as we discuss the evolution of Johnson Lighting, we introduce various technologies. Some of this technology requires explanation because it is new, or because it is old and no longer in use. The point of these *technology notes* is to bring the explanation of the technology close to its introduction in the text. The purpose of describing antiquated technology is to show the roots of what we use today. While you may not be as interested in this old stuff as some new hot technology, remember that this is what many people with whom you will work grew up with. This is also where the vocabulary we use today comes from. This is all a point of reference and a reminder of just how far we have come in a short time.

CHAPTER SUMMARIES

The book is composed of 16 chapters divided into seven topic areas. A brief description of each follows.

Part I—Communications Basics

This opening section discusses the analog part of our world, that is, the basic communications model, voice systems, and media. This sets the environment for the digital portion that follows in Part II.

Chapter 1—What Is Technology? What Is Telecommunications?

Telecommunications is a special form of technology. This chapter reminds the reader that s/he is familiar and comfortable with much technology in the home and office, paying special attention to the telecommunications-based technology. This is followed with the basic model of communication and telecommunications. The chapter includes a brief overview of the major types of information systems.

Chapter 2—Where Did the Telephone Come From and How Does It Work?

This chapter reviews the analog and voice world. It begins by describing the plain old telephone system (POTS) that was in place before data communications. While this is historical, it's where we came from and provides a valuable frame of reference to explain the evolution to the present environment. We concentrate on voice telephone communications, and such concepts therein as analog wave forms, telephone channels, switch and instrument capabilities, and private branch exchanges.

Chapter 3—What Technologies and Media Do We Use for Voice and Data Systems?

Channels are paths over which signals travel; media are the physical circuits on which channels reside. This chapter reviews wired and wireless media. Although wired media, in general, have greater bandwidth, the wireless domain is growing rapidly because it frees us to be more productive and competitive. Wireless covers the spectrum of radio, microwave, satellite; GPS and infrared (IR); IEEE 802.11b and *Bluetooth*; fixed, movable, and moving.

Part II—Data Communications and Networks

This section takes the reader through the basics of digital data communications, beginning with codes and modems. This is followed by digital-to-analog (D/A) conversion, modulation, multiplexing, topology, protocols, and network equipment. This covers complex material, but is broken into five chapters for ease of learning.

Chapter 4—Data Communications: The Basics

Beginning with the telegraph, we introduce the reader to the digital world and its coding schemes, and serial and parallel circuits. Next are discussions of modems, compression, and attenuation. The chapter ends with error detection and correction.

Chapter 5—Data Communications: Conversion, Modulation, and Multiplexing

For data communications, we want to work in a digital environment. We cover the analog-to-digital conversion and how to put multiple signals on a single circuit, that is, modulation and multiplexing. It ends with our first look at ISDN and expands on compression standards. In the end, we are looking for as much bandwidth as we can muster, which takes into account the native bandwidth of the channel, noise, and compression.

Chapter 6—Networks by Topology and Protocols

This is a discussion of possible shapes and layouts of networks, for example, topologies, and their merits plus the protocols that accompany the topologies. The chapter ends with a discussion of the ports of a computer through which we communicate with the outside world.

Chapter 7—Telecommunications Architectural Models

Architectural models provide frameworks for understanding telecommunications systems interconnectivity. This brings us to the Open Systems Interconnect (OSI) seven-layer model established so that equipment will interoperate.

Chapter 8—LANs, WANs, Enterprise Networks, and Network Equipment

Networks are composed of components to enable connectivity from small, local area to large, even global, networks. This chapter begins with a discussion of networks as to geography and security, from LANs to WANs and VPNs. It ends with equipment from the simplest repeater and goes through routers to gateways.

Part III—Uses of Networks

This section discusses uses of connectivity, starting with the Internet and moving to business applications, such as teleconferencing, telecommuting, and other ways to support dispersed operations.

Chapter 9—The Internet Connects to the World; the Intranet Connects the Organization

The Internet is about connectivity. This chapter discusses this ultimate WAN and its primary applications that are based on the Internet browser and the World Wide Web. This is where the reader will likely be in sync with the material relating to eCommerce and eBusiness. Concepts of net storage and B2B/B2C are discussed. A major example of national connectivity is provided by JANET, which covers most of the United Kingdom. Finally, the intranet, Internet technologies inside the organization, is discussed.

Chapter 10—Business Applications of Telecommunications

There are thousands of applications for telecommunications. We chose to consolidate them here as opposed to placing them within chapters. Now that the reader is familiar with voice and data systems, s/he can appreciate these and other applications that may produce competitive advantage. These applications range from the familiar ATM to teleconferencing, telecommuting, EDI, and military uses of telecommunications.

Part IV—Legislation and Global Issues

This part concentrates on the legal and regulatory sides of telecommunications. The world's telecommunications industry has been shaped by laws, regulations, and deregulation.

Chapter 11—How Do Legislation and Regulation Affect Telecommunications?

Telecommunications in the United States of America has developed in an environment of laws, rules, and regulations. We discuss the major legislative acts and their implications to the telecommunications industry and the managers who must work within it. The Telecommunications Act of 1996 updates the Telecommunications Act of 1934. While these events seem particular to this one nation, all countries must deal with regulation, deregulation, privatization, and control and the U.S. experience can serve as an example to be followed or avoided. This is followed by a discussion of the special telecommunications needs for those needing accommodation.

Part V—Managing Telecommunications

Here we stress the area of the management of telecommunications, how we organize to make it all work, and how we control projects. Probably one of the most important issues for the telecommunications managers today is the area of security, which is expanded upon here.

Chapter 12—Management of Voice and Data Systems in Organizations

The management of telecommunications involves the management of groups of people and their tasks. We develop an understanding of the organization and supervision of people required: (1) the group who creates, installs, and maintains the systems; (2) the oversight issues such as performance and configuration management; (3) security and privacy; and (4) quality-of-service (QoS) strategies.

Chapter 13—How Do You Manage Telecommunications Projects? SDLC for Telecommunications

All organizations will need to install, update, and add capabilities to the telecommunications infrastructure. We take a systems development life cycle approach to the projects that will effect these changes. It is vital for anyone involved in projects to understand the phases of the project and how they and the component resources can be managed to create the needed telecommunications capabilities.

Part VI—The Need for Bandwidth

This final section discusses high speed, broadband needs, and capabilities. First we contend that one can do a lot with a little bandwidth. Then we review the possibilities of technology to use in those cases where you need a lot of bandwidth. This is addressed for both the office and the home.

Chapter 14—Bandwidth for the Office

Once we have determined that wide bandwidth is required, we discuss some of the alternatives, in this chapter and the next. The more bandwidth we have, the greater are the growth possibilities and the greater the flexibility. This all, however, comes with an attendant cost. This chapter introduces the lower- and high-bandwidth technologies appropriate for the office.

Chapter 15—Bandwidth for the Home

The home and SOHO generally have differing bandwidth than does the traditional office. This chapter discusses the possibilities, ranging from ISDN to DSL and cable modems. It ends with a discussion of various wireless technologies.

Part VII—The Future

We close the book with a look to the future. As the reader should now appreciate, the technology changes almost daily.

Chapter 16—Epilogue

We discuss those forces that will drive the adoption of technology and what will cause it to be constrained. One way is to ask people what they can envision in the presence of free computing, global connectivity, and unlimited, low-cost bandwidth.

DISTINGUISHING FEATURES AND BENEFITS

Our book provides students with the following features and benefits:

Telecommunications is placed in the context and environment of the business.

- Communications is at the heart of business transactions.
- Voice and data communications support business.
- Most business functions depend on telecommunications.
- Most information systems are telecommunications-intensive information systems.
- The historical review of voice and data communications is thorough and understandable.
- Relevant legislation and regulation are covered.
- Coverage of business applications directly relates learning to the future activities of the student.

Technology is explained, but in relation to management decision making.

- The value and merit of technology is not self-evident.
- The creation of telecommunications capabilities requires trade-offs.
- The use of technology like telecommunications may be a cost or an investment.
- Differences between analog and digital cellular are covered.
- Both wired and wireless systems are covered.

The management of telecommunications is a part of business strategy.

- Telecommunications, properly utilized, can give a competitive advantage.
- Telecommunications, like MIS, is vital to the conduct of business.
- Telecommunications allows decentralization of the decision process.
- Coverage is provided on management of telecommunications projects.

INSTRUCTOR SUPPORT MATERIALS

A comprehensive instructor support package will be available to adopters of the text.

- *Instructor's Manual* includes solutions to end-of-chapter questions, teaching suggestions, lecture outlines, and suggestions for using the PowerPoint classroom presentation software.
- *Testbank and computerized testbank*, prepared by Gerald Canfield of the University of Maryland, contains true-false, multiple choice, and other test questions. Also available in computerized form.

- *PowerPoint Classroom Presentation Software* contains lecture presentation slides of key topics and graphics from each chapter as well as lecture outlines and other teaching tips.

Caveat

Technology in general and telecommunications technology in particular are evolving so rapidly that you will likely become aware of capabilities that are not covered in this text. In our chapter on telecommunications in the future we may well be talking about your present. By the time this book is published, the future may have arrived. We have, however, covered the important facts and features of telecommunications that allow you to work effectively in the industry, even one that is evolving so rapidly. Though you may be using higher-speed, greater-bandwidth channels; more powerful switches; better computers; and even media unheard of in the 1990s, the tenets of telecommunications management remain unchanged. These are that business managers, not technicians or engineers, must make the decisions about technology that provide a business solution to a problem, opportunity, or threat from the environment. This book was developed and dedicated to allow you to do this, with an awareness that the technology and the environment are rapidly evolving.

ACKNOWLEDGMENTS

We would like to express our gratitude to the reviewers of this project who gave us their suggestions for improving the final text:

Kemal Altinkemer
Purdue University

Ralph Annina
Keller Graduate School of Management

Robert Burnside
DeVry Institute of Technology

Gerald C. Canfield
University of Maryland–Baltimore County

Robert P. Cerveny
Florida Atlantic University

James S. Cross
Michigan Technological University

Art Dearing
Tarleton State University

Omar A. El Sawy
University of Southern California–Los Angeles

K. Dale Foster
Memorial University of Newfoundland

Varun Grover
University of South Carolina

Michael Henson
BellSouth Telecommunications

Bhushan L. Kapoor
California State University–Fullerton

George D. Kraft
Illinois Institute of Technology

Kuber Maharjan
Purdue University School of Technology

Denise J. McManus
Wake Forest University

Sabyasachi Mitra
Georgia Institute of Technology

Marianne Murphy
Northeastern University

J. David Naumann
University of Minnesota

Ram Pakath
University of Kentucky

Roger Alan Pick
University of Missouri–Kansas City

Hasan Pirkul
The Ohio State University

Jim Quan
Florida Atlantic University

Chetan Sankar
Auburn University

Neal G. Shaw
University of Texas at Arlington

Siva Viswanathan
University of Maryland–College Park

Michael E. Whitman
Kennesaw State University

We wish to acknowledge the contributions of others in compiling this book: **Dr. Denise J. McManus** of Wake Forest University for her help with the Glossary and risk management; **Justin Williams** for his help with TCP/IP; **Dafni Greene** for her help with network hardware; **James Ryan** for his help on Quality of Service; **Steve Guendert** for his aid with SAN and NAS systems; **Ken Liang** for his help with customer relationship management; **Heath Campbell** for general help in moving from 1/e to 2/e; **Stephen Kirkemeir,** Sr. Vice President of *BellSouth* for his guidance and encouragement in this endeavor; and to our many colleagues who added their talent by way of cases at the end of chapters.

Our thanks also go out to the book team at McGraw-Hill/Irwin: Rick Williamson, Kelly Delso, Pat Frederickson, Jennifer McQueen, along with many others who contributed their ideas and hard work to the project.

Houston H. Carr

Charles A. Snyder

URL for the book: http://telecom.business.auburn.edu/jei

Brief Contents

Contents

**PART V
Managing Telecommunications**

**Chapter 12
Management of Voice and Data Systems
in Organizations   512**

The Management of Telecommunications

Business Solutions to Business Problems Enabled by Voice and Data Communications

Second Edition

Chapter **One**

What Is Technology?
What Is
Telecommunications?

CONTINUING CASE—PART 1

The Creation of a Small Business and Its Need for Telecommunications

Johnson Enterprises, Inc., is a successful business now headed by Carlton Johnson. His father, Michael, started the company in 1951 that is today called JEI (see Figure 1.1). What was a one-man operation in a small building on East Oak Street in Denver, Colorado, has grown to several hundred employees, global operations, and annual sales of $263 million. The company began by selling lighting systems to secure parking lots and building entrances and expanded to include a large variety of security and allied services. Started as *Johnson Lighting,* it evolved into *Johnson Lighting and Security (JL&S)* as security operations were added. JL&S was eventually turned over to Michael's son, Carlton, who rapidly expanded the firm and its lines of business.

Michael Johnson opened *Johnson Lighting* selling pole-mounted mercury vapor lights for parking lots and building entrances. He rented a small office in a shopping center and moved in a desk, chair, and a few tables to display his product line. One of his first acts was to obtain telephone service from the local telephone company. The telephone company installed a single line and a black rotary dial instrument, the standard of the time. It should be noted that Michael, like most businessmen, considered the telephone a necessity. He also took for granted the local telephone company service.

Michael knew that a telephone was absolutely essential for doing business as it was the primary link to his customers and suppliers. To emphasize this point, try to imagine Michael or any other person doing business without telephone services. It would mean that business could only be conducted with the customer or supplier physically present in Michael's office or with Michael visiting each supplier or customer site.

To increase his volume and diversity, Michael added a line of security locks, hiring a locksmith, Fred Fox, to handle this portion of the business. When Michael increased his organization from one to two people, he went from doing all work himself to having to include the effort of another person. He found that he could do most of the coordination on a face-to-face basis. It was nice to have another person in the office, but the office was a bit small for conducting both the lock and lighting businesses simultaneously when customers were present. Michael thought he should expand his office space and place security locks in one office and lighting in an adjoining office. He rented the space next door, which had been a shoe store, putting

FIGURE 1.1   Organization and Facilities of Johnson Lighting, Circa 1951

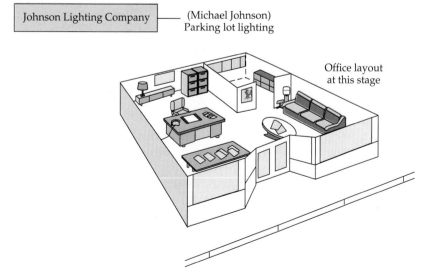

Johnson Lighting Company —— (Michael Johnson)
Parking lot lighting

Office layout at this stage

FIGURE 1.2   Organization and Facilities of Johnson Lighting, Circa 1964

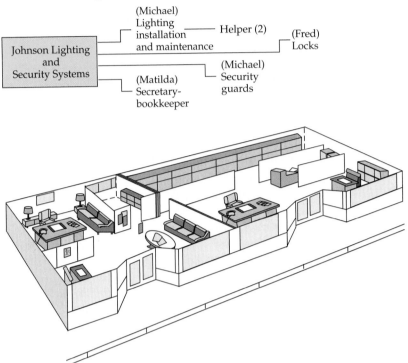

a door in the wall between the two offices. The security lock office used the same telephone number, but Michael had a second instrument installed by the local telephone company. He put in a buzzer at each desk whereby the person answering the phone could alert the other to a call. The new telephone instrument was the same type as the previous one.

With his experience and new knowledge of the security marketplace, Michael saw the opportunity to use local college students as temporary employees and provide security patrols for office buildings.

He placed advertisements at the local college and hired four students to provide walking patrols at two building complexes downtown. Thus, over a short period, Johnson Lighting was providing lighting, locks, and security patrols. With this new and expanded vision of his business, Michael changed the company title to **Johnson Lighting and Security.** (See Figure 1.2.) Michael also hired a part-time secretary and bookkeeper and two men to help with equipment installation and maintenance. He now had three people in the office, two doing outside work, and four on scheduled patrols.

LOOK AROUND YOU

technology
You find it in your home, car, school, and office. It changes the way you work and how you live. It affects much of your life, yet you are so familiar with it, you hardly notice it at all.

Technology in general, and telecommunications technology in particular, permeates your life. If you watched a movie last night, either on airwaves broadcast television, on a movie channel on cable or satellite television, or on a videocassette recorder (VCR), digital video recorder (DVR), or digital versatile disk (DVD), when you adjusted the volume of the movie or started the VCR or DVD with a remote control, you were employing several technologies. You also routinely use a cordless or cellular telephone. While you will find telecommunications technology in the office and while shopping, you are likely most familiar (and comfortable) with it in the home.

Most of us take technologies that surround us for granted. We have homes equipped with some of these: a television; videocassette recorder (VCR); video or audio disk player; microwave oven; automatic coffee maker; food processor; trash compactor; vacuum cleaner; whirlpool tub; man-made fiber carpeting; plastic utensils and furniture; a heat pump for climate control; automatic dishwasher; refrigerator with ice maker and freezer; rheostat-controlled lighting; automatic clothes washer and dryer; stereo sound system; home computer; automatic garage-door opener; fire/smoke alarm; home intercommunications system; and multiple telephones. We would probably only take note of many of these embodiments of technology if we were denied them. As we will note later in the chapter, our working lives also are greatly influenced by multiple technologies.

technology awareness
Some technologies are so ubiquitous we tend to forget they surround us.

The technologies mentioned above are some of the more obvious in your surroundings. They are all examples of technology that most of us live with on a daily basis. Our focus is on the telecommunications technologies, and many of them also go unnoticed because we are so accustomed to them.

From a news or entertainment point of view, we have near real-time reporting of events that occur halfway around the globe. In the spring of 1991, millions watched the war in the Persian Gulf (Desert Storm) as it happened. Television networks brought the news in real-time via satellite circuits, showed you analyses via computer-generated graphics, and let you be part of the daily battle status briefing transmitted via satellite or fiber-optic cable. In fact, the coverage of the news was so complete, CNN had to be cautioned as to content as it was believed that CNN's coverage was Iraq's primary source of intelligence. The Persian Gulf War has been characterized as the first technology-based war—the first high war routinely using "smart" weapons.[1] Subsequently, the anti-terrorist war (Enduring Freedom) has seen a further evolution of technology-based war. For example, the use of GPS-guided munitions, night-vision devices, and remotely-piloted air vehicles has fundamentally changed the equation of military advantage. The commander was able to direct operations from 7,000 miles away on a near real-time basis.

telecommunications technology
The means employed to effect communications of voice, data, and image *over a distance.*

As a further example of how you are surrounded by technology in general and telecommunications technology in particular, consider this scenario. Next door, your stockbroker neighbor drives up in her new BMW, talking on a cellular phone as she uses the remote door opener to open her garage. In her car she has an AM-FM-satellite radio stereo system with a compact disk player. She had a CB (citizens band) radio in a previous car, but the advent of the cellular phone has allowed her to replace it and its bulky 36-inch antenna with in-car telephone service. Her previous car cellular telephone allowed her to maintain contact with her office and her clients as she drove to an appointment or to the golf course. The new one incorporates a palm device by which she can display email and websites from the Internet, with constant wireless connectivity. Another neighbor returns from work in his '57 DeSoto. This car is the love of his life and the bane of your portable television because the DeSoto's ignition system causes your TV to crackle. You also can hear interference from his ignition system over your portable telephone, so when he is working on the engine you always use the old standby, the ordinary plug-in-the-wall phone. While the technology employed in the BMW and in your house have progressed, the older technology remains useful, despite inherent weaknesses.

---

[1] *Smart* means the embodiment of computer systems and telecommunications technology. Without telecommunications to provide feedback of data to the control and guidance computer, the system does not work.

telecommunications technology devices
Many of the day-to-day technologies we take for granted incorporate telecommunications technologies.

point-of-service or -sales (POS)
Systems that automate the sales transaction data to a large extent. The universal product code (UPC) is an example of a technology used by POS.

universal product code
Michael Newman/PhotoEdit

The **office** traditionally has meant a desk in an office building, downtown. Today, due to telecommunications technology, the office may be your home or even your car.

Meanwhile, your younger sister is in her room, using the computer to do homework assignments. She has connected to America Online® through an ISP, over a cable modem, to scan the Internet to find information for the paper she is writing. As she works, the system tells her that she has new electronic mail from a friend. She flips to the mail section and learns there is a concert on satellite channel 134 of DirecTV®.

In the above scenario, the cellular, portable, and wall-mounted telephones; the garage-door controller; the cable modem; satellite TV; and AM-FM-satellite radio are all devices that contain or depend on telecommunications technology. These and the other technologies discussed in the scenario are only some of the obvious surface-level technologies. They do not include many technologies that are hidden from view—those required to control or manufacture the more obvious technologies. We use a lot of technology, especially electronic computer-based technology and telecommunications equipment.

Another place we come in contact with technology is where we make purchases, for example, at checkout counters in stores. At the check-out at the grocery store, the goods are laser-scanned by the point-of-sale (POS) device, recorded on the cash register tape, and noted in the store computer's real-time inventory system. When you buy a hamburger, your order is taken on a computer terminal and displayed to the cook. At the department store, the labels are scanned and the information is used not only for your purchase and for inventory replenishment, but for marketing campaigns. (Waldenbooks® goes one step further and stores scanned data on purchases to profile its customers for future direct-mail marketing and Barnes and Noble will display books of your liking when you browse or order online.) The potential of point-of-sale data collection has only begun to be realized. Clothing stores, for example, are using the scanned data to send to the apparel makers and thread and textile suppliers for replenishment; the stores also are using these data for electronic bill payment. Since some of these last technologies are just beginning to be employed, the potential payoff has yet to be widely accepted. However, they promise to become ubiquitous in the business environment of the 21st century.

The office is another center of technology. In the scenario, the stockbroker called her office from her car on the cellular phone to check her voice mail-box for messages. At the office and in the car, she routinely uses a computer or wireless palm device for near real-time stock quotations, stock market news, and data from financial services such as Reuters Money Network®. She has many clients who also have computers that monitor stock movements and some automatically generate buy and sell orders. She carries a Quotrek® FM radio in her pocket to receive stock quotes whenever she is in a city with transmission services. Her Skytel® personal two-way pager will alert her to telephone messages when she is away from the office or car, and give her the ability to respond to questions. In the office, she relies on facsimile, workstations, a sophisticated voice (telephone) system, and electronic mail. Other nontelecommunications–based technology in the office includes copy and dictation equipment, scanners to input data to her workstation, and laser printers for quick, high-quality reports. Her computer allows her to tailor information about her clients' portfolios, providing them better service and enhancing her reputation.

Whether you are at home, shopping, or at the office, technology serves and surrounds you. It is important for you to recognize and understand it, so you can be more effective in your daily life. The more you become aware of the technology around you, the greater its value will be to you.

THIS BOOK

technology applications
The purpose of technology for this book is to provide *business solutions*.

This book is about telecommunications equipment, capabilities, systems, and, most of all, management. We describe the equipment and capabilities within a business context, and discuss systems and management of telecommunications as a major way to provide solutions to significant business problems and to take advantage of opportunities. Our objective is to educate you in this technology and, more importantly, to instill in you the importance of the use of telecommunications technology for business solutions. Peter Keen, a noted consultant to senior management, says, "Senior management will learn a lot about telecommunications over the next few years. If they don't they are virtually guaranteeing their firm will be at a competitive disadvantage . . . decisions about technology are not technological decisions, they are business decisions. We can not leave technological decisions to the engineers."[2] Keen's insights reinforce our purposes in building this book: to discuss telecommunications technologies from a business point of view as opposed to an engineering one.

competitive advantage
That feature, any feature, of your organization that causes a customer to choose you over a competitor.

We will be discussing telecommunications so that you, as a present or future end-user or manager, can consider its utility in communicating, collaborating, and sharing resources. You generally use telecommunications to perform dispersed functions as if you were physically close, to reduce costs, and to obtain and maintain a competitive advantage in the marketplace. If you compete outside your city, state, country, or continent, you must use telecommunications daily to operate. If you are to stay current with your customers or competitors, you must use telecommunications in today's fast-paced business environment.

telecommunications utility
The ability to leverage resources to remote locations.

Up to this point, we have mentioned technology without trying to explain how it works. Because we felt you were familiar with most of the systems we mentioned, we used them to help set the stage. In this process, however, we have introduced several terms that will be essential for further understanding of telecommunications. Specifically, since this is a book about communications using telecommunications technology, it is appropriate to begin with a discussion of what communications is. First, there are four very important definitions (see Information Window 1–1).

We next present a general model of communications. The model is one that underlies all of the systems that will follow. It provides the conceptual basis for all of our systems regardless of the technologies employed.

THE COMMUNICATIONS MODEL

channel
The communications *path* between a sender and receiver(s).

To send data over a distance, you must have a **sender** (the **source**), a communications medium and telecommunications (**channel**), and a **receiver** (the **destination**). Figures 1.3 and 1.4 depict these models of communications. Note, in the case of human communications, the sender takes an idea or information, encodes[3] it into speech, and transmits it over the air-medium channel. The receiver must receive

---

[2] Peter G. W. Keen, *Competing in Time* (Cambridge, MA: Ballinger Publishers, 1988).
[3] Encoding means to change the idea or information into symbols that represent it during transmission. For audible conversations, the ideas and information are encoded into the words we use to express ourselves. As we will develop later, machines encode letters, characters, and symbols into numeric ones and zeros (binary code) for transmission.

Information Window   1–1

Data are abundant; **information,** the stuff with which decisions are made, is scarce.

Communications is a *human* process.

electromagnetic The use of radio waves to carry data.

Photonic systems use light to carry data.

data communications That part of telecommunications dealing with the movement of data between machines, usually computers.

Data and information are, for our intent, the same thing. Technically, information is processed or meaningful data, while data are unprocessed. Data become information when they are processed so a human may act upon them. However, for simplicity, we will use the terms *data* and *information* interchangeably in our discussion of telecommunications.

Communications is a process that allows information to pass between a sender and one or more receivers . . . the transfer of meaningful information or ideas from one location to a second location. Communications is a human process; humans communicate by sending information (about ideas) between themselves.

Telecommunications is the transmission of data, or information, over a distance. *Tele* is the Greek word meaning *at a distance, far off.* Thus, we can classify smoke signals, semaphore flags, lanterns and signal flares, telegraph systems, televisions, telephones, written letters, and hand signals as capabilities that support telecommunications. The problems with these communications forms include reliability, speed of transmission, and comprehension. For our purposes, we will define *telecommunications* only *to be communication by electrical, electromagnetic, or photonic means, over a distance.*

Data communications is the specialized transmission of data between machines, using a code, and is generally not understandable to people in its transmitted form. It is useful to differentiate *data communications* from *telecommunications* as the former is a specialized function. Telecommunications is the more general term and involves the transmission of information or ideas over a distance between humans or machines.

FIGURE 1.3
The Basic Communications Model

Sender — Medium — Receiver

Source   Channel   Destination

the **message** from the air, decode the words, and receive the original idea or information. Meanwhile, there is an opportunity for noise to be introduced at each step of the communications process.

The basic communications model we describe in Figure 1.3 is called a **transport model,** a simplistic mode of moving data from one source to one or more destinations. The environment and model become more complicated such as in Figure 1.5 but often more useful when we move to a **data-sharing model** where we move the data back and forth or, better, share the data simultaneously between two or more people or devices.

medium The *means* of movement of signals from node to node. Any material used for propagation or transmission of signals.

When we communicate, we must consider the following: the intent of the sender (what is being communicated); the encoding of the message (language, code, etc.); the channel (the **medium**); the ability of the receiver to decode the message; and, finally, the way the receiver interprets the transmitted message. Human-to-human interaction is the concern of "simple communications." For example, two people need to use the same spoken or written language and have a similar background of experiences and knowledge to interpret messages in

FIGURE 1.4
An Expanded Communications Model

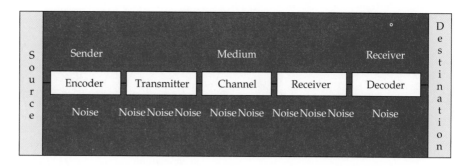

noise
Any unwanted signal that interferes with the desired signal.

a similar fashion. Additionally, each of the five processes contains **noise** in many forms. These noises range from incorrect language syntax (he ain't goin' to do that thing), to the effect of "bad" telephone circuits, to loud background music.

In Figure 1.5 we illustrate voice communications by various media. First, we show that even in the simplest case of communications without any devices to augment transmission, a sender communicates to a receiver by transmitting sound waves through the air medium. When we consider cans connected by a taut string, a common communications toy used by children, we see the employment of another medium, the string. In the bottom of the figure, we see simple telephone communications using conducted **copper wire**—the common medium known as **twisted-pair.** Other media are coaxial cable, radio waves through space (generally called wireless), and optic fibers.

Encoding signals onto or into a format for transmission is required *in all cases.*

Decoding of signals is required so the true data can be removed from the envelope they were sent in.

Figure 1.6(a) illustrates a telecommunications system that incorporates many of the previously mentioned concepts. In this illustration, we can see the essentials of an idea being converted into a message, spoken (**encoded**) into a transmitter at the source, and then being transported over a distance by a medium to a receiver (the destination), where the message is **decoded** by the receiver so the sender's idea is replicated in the receiver's mind. This entire process is usually taken for granted by individuals conversing on the telephone. The process may be diagrammed according to our communications model as shown in Figure 1.6(b).

Fortunately, in data communications we are not usually as concerned with the intent of the message as we are only interested in ensuring the message is accurate and complete. In other words, we generally are concerned that the proper characters were sent and received exactly in the correct sequence. The data communications process is shown in a simplified illustration in Figure 1.7.

With an understanding of communications in its basic form, you begin to develop a mental model of its value and use. The better we can understand the process of communications, especially telecommunications, the more we can use the technology to solve business problems and exploit opportunities.

BUSINESS TELECOMMUNICATIONS

The goal of telecommunication systems is the reliable movement of data over a distance.

Telecommunications can be used for convenient or necessary business functions, such as telephone communications to accept and transmit orders. Its use can change the very nature of business; for example, from a rudimentary viewpoint, the telephone is seen as an essential business tool. However, from the perspective of an innovative businessperson, telephone telecommunications can be viewed as an important means for gaining and maintaining competitive advantage.

FIGURE 1.5   Voice Communications by Various Media

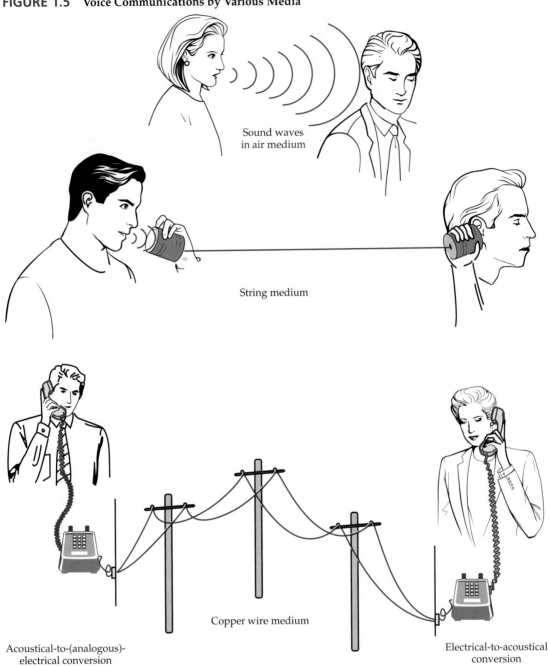

Sound waves
in air medium

String medium

Copper wire medium

Acoustical-to-(analogous)-
electrical conversion

Electrical-to-acoustical
conversion

Objectives of Telecommunications from a Business Viewpoint

We have discussed a number of uses of telecommunications. Now it is necessary
to understand the basic objectives of telecommunications to provide a framework for the material presented in the following chapters. By putting these
objectives into their simplest form, we provide the foundation to apply the

FIGURE 1.6(a)   A (Voice) Telecommunications Process

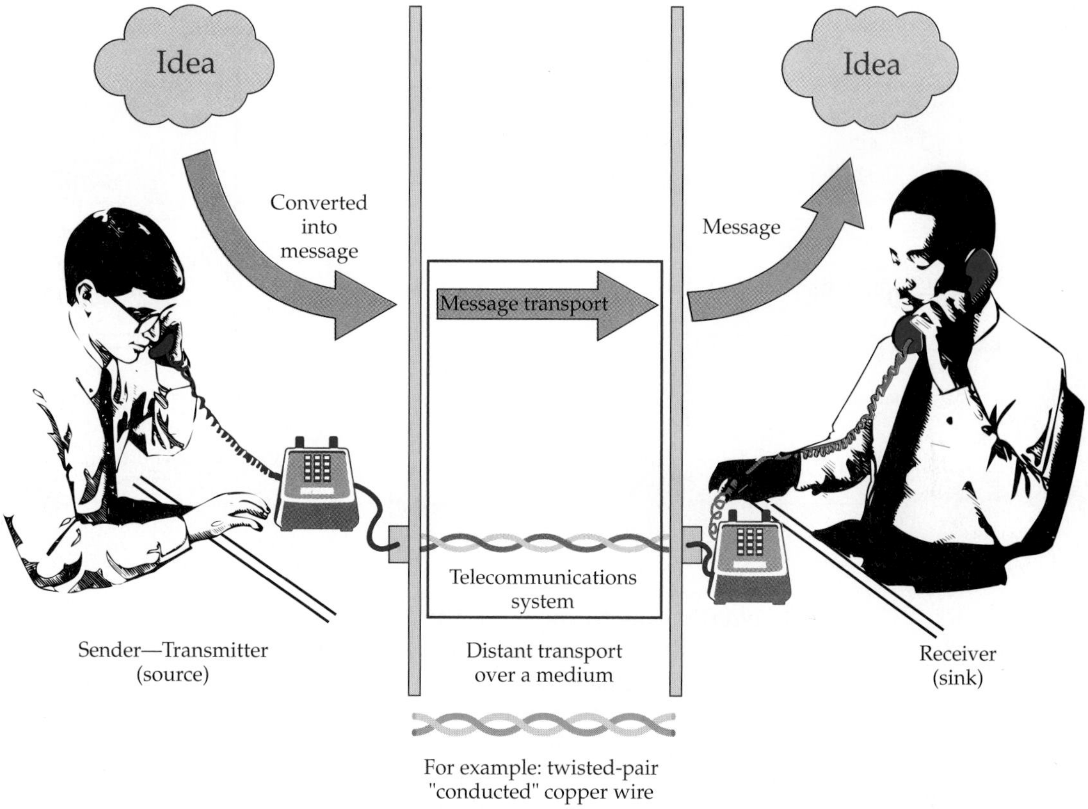

Idea

Idea

Converted
into
message

Message

Message transport

Telecommunications
system

Sender—Transmitter
(source)

Distant transport
over a medium

Receiver
(sink)

For example: twisted-pair
"conducted" copper wire

FIGURE 1.6(b)   A Telecommunications Model

| Source | Encoder | Transmitter | Channel | Receiver | Decoder | Destination |

appropriate technology to solve business problems. The four objectives we present demonstrate the way telecommunications supports the functions of the business and its goals.

The first objective of telecommunications is to **communicate:** to exchange ideas or information between humans or between machines. With telecommunications technology, we extend the ability of humans to communicate between themselves or between their machines by overcoming time and distance. The need for a channel or medium between machines is more obvious as they cannot communicate by air as humans can. Since only a small proportion of human communications is face-to-face, there is a great need to be able to communicate over a distance. The greater your ability to communicate over a distance, the greater your ability to expand your influence and market.

The second objective of telecommunications is to allow organizations and individuals to **distribute and share information.** The very nature of organizations calls for sharing information. Organizations are populated with specialists who

**Information and
resource sharing**
increase their value
and reduce cost.

FIGURE 1.7   **Data Communications Process**

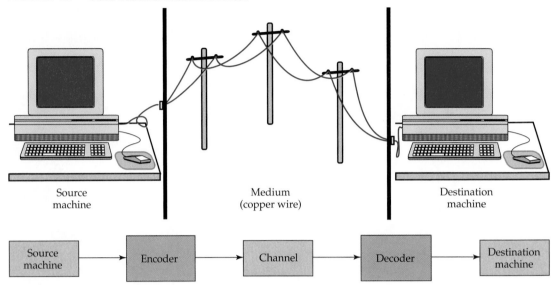

must communicate to carry out the functions of the organization, for example, production, sales, and accounting. As organizations increase in size and complexity, there is a greater need to specialize functions and communicate between these functions. The accounting department now has specific and separate functions of accounts receivable, accounts payable, payroll, and so forth. In the emerging organizational structure using cross-functional teams to perform projects, there is increased need for team members to collaborate. Telecommunications make this collaboration possible and effective without regard to geographical dispersion of the participants. The greater your ability to share information, the greater your ability to control your organization and react to new information and conditions in the marketplace.

The third objective of telecommunications is to allow organizations to **operate with dispersed or distant functions as if they were centrally located.** Think of any organization (company, church, government, military unit, or university) and you will realize that as it expands to more than one location, it needs to communicate more and over a greater distance. The organization needs to be located in several places to do business yet needs to act as if it were one closely located function. The greater the ability to disperse operations, the greater the ability to expand the organization physically and still maintain control over the organization.

Finally, organizations need to **share resources.** The resources may be a central repository of information, a computer, a printer, or an idea. Telecommunications allow people and machines to share resources regardless of their proximity. This enables the organization to avoid the cost of redundancy (duplicate equipment, information, or services) and simplifies the management of information. For example, this means that a dispersed organization does not have to duplicate its databases and other resources if it uses telecommunications to share them. The greater your ability to share resources, the greater your efficiency (reduced cost) and effectiveness (best performance or productivity) in the use of these resources. This ability to disperse yet control allows you to place the resource, for example,

The ability to decentralize and operate as if centrally located is paramount to any distributed organization.

shared server, in the most secure and maintainable location, yet be accessible from many places and controlled from the central or yet another location. Connectivity allows for control and dispersion at the same time.

Why Is It Important to Achieve the Objectives of Telecommunications?

Any company, organization, or enterprise that enters the marketplace with products or services must offer their products or services in such a way that they will attract customers. Whether you consider a person selling apples on the street, IBM introducing a new personal computer, or the federal government instituting universal health care, the provider of these products or services must offer the customers something special. The something special can take several forms. Orville Redenbacher's strategy for attracting customers is to "do one thing and do it better than anyone else." When the something special attracts customers and causes them to remain customers, we call it a competitive advantage.

COMPETITIVE ADVANTAGE

Telecommunications in many organizations is the basis for competitive advantage.

The term **competitive advantage** means anything that favorably distinguishes a firm, its products, or services from those of its competitors in the eyes of its customers or end-users in such a way that the consumer chooses to purchase that product or service over another. A monopoly has absolute competitive advantage. A firm[4] operating in pure competition has none. One objective of any firm competing in the marketplace is to have a product, service, or strategy that makes the market choose that firm over all others.

Organizations gain and sustain a competitive advantage via four basic strategies: (1) low-cost leadership, (2) focus on market niche, (3) product and service differentiation, and (4) linkages to partners. If an organization chooses to compete on

[4] The term *firm* in this book is intended to mean any formal organization, whether educational, governmental, private, public, profit-making, or nonprofit. In like manner, we consider that all organizations, or firms, must consider the idea of competitive advantage. Many would say that organizations such as governmental, religious, philanthropic, and other not-for-profit groups do not address competitive advantage. We contend that in these organizations, just as in the profit-oriented firms, there is competition for each budget dollar. Therefore, any project must show an advantage or reason why the dollars should be spent for it and not other projects.

cost, it must reduce its costs, relative to perceived benefits, farther than its competitors. Telecommunications can aid in this by reducing the time to process transactions; supporting just-in-time delivery of materials, which reduces inventory costs; and moving information to aid and hasten the decision process. As we will show in later chapters as well as the paragraphs that follow, organizations that compete on service and product differentiation can use telecommunications effectively in their strategy. Customer service, once made possible by the tried-and-true technology in toll-free telephone numbers, and now provided via Internet websites, assists the customer in choosing one organization's product over another's. We discuss the (800) WATS services and Internet and Web connectivity in great detail later.

Competitive advantage is absolute for a monopoly and zero in the environment of pure competition.

Companies have only recently realized that computer-based management information systems (MIS) can be used for competitive advantage by providing information vital to the decision and competitive process. The application of telecommunications technology enhances the use of information systems for competitive advantage. A classic though early and now simplistic example is the case of Baxter Health Care, formerly American Hospital Supply (AHS) Company, placing terminals in customer's facilities (hospitals) that were connected via telecommunication linkages to the mainframe computer of AHS. When customers (hospital purchasing agents) were ready to place an order for supplies, they had only to enter the data into the terminal at their facility as opposed to filling out an order form and mailing it. This system reduced the amount of work required of the customer and time delays and provided better service. In doing so, it created a significant competitive advantage for its owner through the innovative application of telecommunications. The technology used was not new; the technology of terminals connected to computers via telephone lines had existed for many years. What was new was the business decision to place the input devices (terminals) on the customer's premises and give the customer access privileges to the AHS[5] computer and data. Thus, as we will emphasize many times in this book, what seemed like a technology decision was a business decision.

The Ford Motor Company installed a cellular telephone in its Lincoln, not for the driver, but so the car could call the factory to order parts when one failed.

Two other examples of using telecommunications for competitive advantage are those offered by American Airlines (AA) and Otis Elevator Company (OEC). AA had to stretch technological frontiers to create an information system that gained them first place in airline reservations systems and sales. Their SABRE® reservation system is recognized as having created a significant competitive advantage for the company; telecommunications made this system possible. OEC, on the other hand, used existing technology to allow its elevators to run system tests and, using the public telephone system, to call for repair personnel and order replacement parts, all without the knowledge of the owner of the equipment. OEC, like AA, used telecommunications to change the perception of its products and services, thus creating a competitive advantage. As competitors catch up, as in the case of AA, competitive advantage becomes *competitive necessity*. Today most other players, such as United Airlines, offer services on the Internet, while AA moves to counter with EasySabre® via America Online and other direct-access providers.

The competitive advantage that American Airlines created with *Sabre* has been diluted by such services as Travelocity, Expedia, and Orbitz.

---

[5] This American Hospital Supply example illustrates a simple use of telecommunications. A newer system, the $50 million Singapore TradeNet System, links all components of a system, resulting in clearing a vessel in or out of the world's largest port in 20 minutes as opposed to four days.

COMPUTERS AND TELECOMMUNICATIONS

An early question an organization faces as it buys microcomputers is how their value can be enhanced by connecting them as opposed to letting them stand alone. The answer entails additional questions of costs versus benefits.

Stand-Alone Computers

Stand-alone, nonnetworked computers are self-contained and self-sufficient.

If you have a **microcomputer (PC[6])** at home or at school, is it connected to anything other than the printer? If not, you have a self-sufficient, stand-alone computer. It can operate by itself. However, when you want to use data from somewhere else, you have to key in the data or copy it in from a diskette or some other medium. If you want to send data somewhere else, you have to print it out or store it on a diskette and mail it. While this may all sound simplistic and out of touch, it is the standard technology of just a decade or so ago.

Connectivity

connectivity
The value of computers is leveraged, and thus enhanced, by networking them.

If the computer you use connects via wires, telephone lines, or even coaxial cable, you have physical connectivity. (The ultimate objective is often application-to-application connectivity in order to exchange data. Telecommunications support this via the physical conduit.) This simply means you can receive data from outside sources and send data from the computer to other places. If you start looking around, especially in the business world, you will find that many, if not most, computers are connected in some way to outside sources or destinations of data. The cash register in the department store and the checkout stand in the grocery store are prime examples of computer systems that are connected to other devices or systems.

network
A group of nodes (computers) that can communicate among themselves because they are connected via channels.

In today's business environment, one has to think of telecommunications and computers in the same context. Although many classifications of computers exist, from palm-top to **supercomputers,** it is appropriate to consider computers existing in two basic environments: micro or small computer and mainframe or large computer classifications. Then, regardless of their size and function, computers increase in value when we connect them to communicate and share resources.

In the early days of microcomputers, all systems were stand-alone units; they were not connected to other computers. Users quickly realized that these autonomous units needed connectivity to access data that resided elsewhere. This realization has led to the almost universal connection of computers to share and to communicate. When you send email, go to a website, or download a computer game, you take advantage of connectivity.

The use of large computers is totally dependent on telecommunications. Early **mainframe computers** (circa 1950–1965) used devices directly connected to the computer to input data and commands and receive output. Today's computers allow the user to be located at a distance from the mainframe and accomplish input, output, and command by using a telecommunications-connected video

---

[6] Most people use the abbreviation *PC* interchangeably with the term *microcomputer*. As a point of historical reference, IBM created the abbreviation PC when it created the IBM Personal Computer® (IBM/PC) in August 1981 and Apple used the phrase "The Personal Computer" for its Apple IIe® in 1983. Like the terms *cellophane* and *zipper*, personal computer and PC have come into the public domain. We will use it in this manner to refer to desktop and laptops microcomputers.

display terminal or a microcomputer acting as a terminal. The mainframe requires telecommunications in some form for access.

A relatively new use of telecommunications, for support systems, allows the presence of a human maintenance person's expertise without that person being present. This ranges from computers calling personnel when required to come and make repairs, to the technician accessing a malfunctioning machine from a remote site. A specific example is the elevator company mentioned earlier that includes a small computer in the elevator control system to continuously test the elevator and its controls and to make a telephone call when necessary to order new parts and a technician to install these parts. The company uses a technology feature and a telecommunications circuit for competitive advantage. The advantage: their elevators are less likely to be inoperative due to need for repair.

Why Is It All Important?

Can you imagine organizations being effective and competitive without telecommunications technologies?

The concepts of telecommunications are simple. The conceptual model of communications remains the same regardless of the technologies we have employed to enhance the capabilities. *In a basic communications system there is always a sender, a message, a medium, and a receiver (in an environment of noise).* The technology of telecommunications appears to consist of **electrical** and **electromagnetic** or radio optical (**photonic**) engineering. The important point is that this complex technology, generally handled by engineers and their technical staff, continues to perform the same function for the organization: send communications over a distance. For example, the telephone does the same thing it did when Bell developed a working model: it allows people at remote distances to communicate verbally. The same is true today whether we are using electrical energy over copper wires, electromagnetic radiation over cellular telephones, or light waves over fiber-optic light guides. (The new technologies have been overlaid on the same, basic conceptual model. The technologies represent the physical model.)

A modern manager needs to know the technologies that can help exploit business opportunities. For example, an understanding of telephone repeaters provides a better appreciation for the underlying technology and what is possible with the technology. It is not only important but essential to understand that a variety of technological alternatives exist to solve a business problem. Managers need to be able to judge the alternative that is most suitable, based on cost–benefit trade-offs, rate of information transfer (speed), reliability, error rate, and other dimensions of suitability and feasibility.

Managers must understand sufficient technology to make the correct business decisions. One cannot leave telecommunications decisions to the engineers because they are business decisions. The value of telecommunications is not self-evident. *Technology does not exist for itself. The value of technology lies only in its ability to solve a business problem* or take advantage of an opportunity in a cost-beneficial manner.

Storage versus Transport

It's easy to get so involved in the technology of computer-based systems that we don't place them in the right perspective. Remember that we define *management information systems* as "all systems and capabilities necessary to manage, process, transport, and use information as a resource in the organization." This definition indicates that there are several different areas or categories of interest. For

Real World 1–1

Today, businesses realize the true value of their data and the necessity for reliable storage technology. Key drivers of the massive growth in storage demand are the Internet, eCommerce, and personalized Web services. It is estimated that by 2003, 75 percent of IT (information technology) spending will be on storage.

"Bruce Albertson, CEO of Iomega, maker of computer memory storage devices, has an Internet problem. His company's flagship product, the Zip drive, once the must-

have PC accessory, is no longer an absolute necessity, now that storage is available free on the Internet."[1]

Authors' note: This is true if, and only if, the place of availability and the place of need for the data in question have connectivity to the Internet and sufficient bandwidth to make the transfer in a reasonable time.

[1] David Kirkpatrick, "Epocalypse! Now!" *eCommerce*, September 2000.

Information Window 1–3

For an example of how fast new telecommunications technologies are accepted, look at the following. It took 30 years for radio to reach 50 million people; television

only took 13 years for this goal. The WWW reached 250 million users in only four years.

example, to manage information we need to capture, categorize, and store data. With transaction processing systems and database management systems, we capture data and store it. Thus, data capture and **storage** are categories of interest.

Once we have captured data, we can process it into information. **Processing** may range from simple Visual Basic programs to complex statistical analysis. The objective of processing is to take data and convert or transform those data into a form that will increase the knowledge of the recipient.

Finally, the area of **transport,** which is what the rest of this book is about, is a category of interest. Whether you store or use information, you generally want to either move it to somewhere else or access it from a remote location, which requires conduit and transport capabilities, that is, telecommunications.

One can argue that without transport or telecommunications, the other categories of MIS are severely limited. The focus of our book is on the transport of information throughout the organization for business needs.

Who Are the Players?

This book is written for business managers or those who plan to become business-managers, individuals who face problems or opportunities in a competitive environment. The technology may be viewed from different perspectives depending on what you do. For example, WorldCom sells MCI long-distance services; therefore, telecommunications is the product. For DuPont, MCI's long-distance services are the medium for selling products, and are absolutely transparent as long as they allow the caller to communicate clearly with the receiver about chemical and fiber opportunities and problems. For the one, telecommunications is the product; for the other, it is the tool.

FIGURE 1.8
**The Players in the
Telecommunications
Environment**

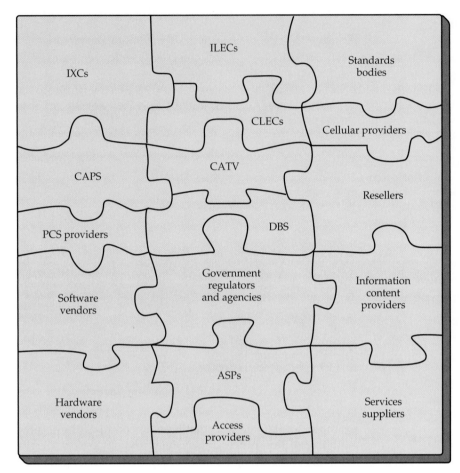

The **players**
that affect
telecommunications
decisions are the
results of laws
imposed to level
the playing field.

Many of the other players in telecommunications are quite visible to you, such as the local telephone provider (e.g., Bell South) and the long-distance provider (e.g., AT&T). Others have a strong influence but are not as visible, such as the standards-setting organizations, the governmental and regulatory agencies and legislative bodies, the vendors and suppliers of equipment and software, and the access and information providers. These players, shown in Figure 1.8, are all important to telecommunications and to decision makers. We will discuss all of them in turn, focusing on technology first to set the stage. Recent developments in the U.S. market, for example, the Telecommunications Act of 1996 and the results of its enforcement, mean the list of players is evolving (see Figure 1.8). This act is discussed in a later chapter.

MANAGEMENT INFORMATION SYSTEMS (MIS)—A MAJOR REASON WE NEED TELECOMMUNICATIONS

Systems are
composed of
equipment, software,
people, and
procedures to achieve
a stated goal.

Classification of Systems

Since we discuss telecommunications systems, it is useful to briefly discuss systems in general. A **system,** as shown in Figure 1.9, *is a group of interrelated and interdependent parts working together to achieve a common goal.* This is as true for a manual system as it is for one that is computer-based. Thus, when we refer to systems, we are addressing not a single entity but a collection of components that work together to achieve an objective or goal. The system of interest (the focal system) contains processes over which we have control that are related to the goal and other parts of the system. If there are items of interest that affect the system but are beyond its control, those items are, by definition, in the *environment,* that is, outside the system. We do not ignore the environment, as that is where many problems, threats, and opportunities originate, such as government regulations, new technology, and aggressive competitors. We can, and often must, react to the environment but sometimes we can exercise significant influence over these forces through proactive strategies.

FIGURE 1.9
**Elements of
a System**

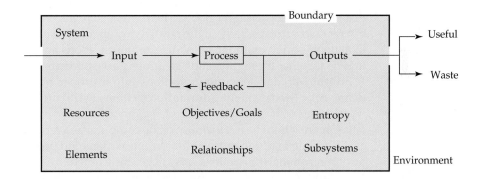

Information Window   1–4

Most urban dwellers are familiar with **electronic** *entertainment*. It started with AM radio and expanded into broadcast television and single-channel FM radio. Then we got cable-delivered television and FM radio moved to stereo (two-channel) mode. Shortly before the Hughes Corporation began to deliver direct broadcast television to the home, sound in TV was upgraded to stereo and surround (three-channel) mode, and next Dolby Digital® was introduced. Although the Internet started to spread in the major industrial nations in the late 1980s, it was not until the rapid spread of personal computers and the advent of the *World Wide Web* that it became a must-have technology. Networked services started with Prodigy® and CompuServe®, but when America Online® (AOL) and, subsequently, Microsoft Network® (MSN) hit the market, email and surfing the Net or Web became a common practice (circa 1995).

The advent of the World Wide Web brought retail *electronic commerce*. Attributes of electronic commerce that had existed for some time include electronic data interchange, just-in-time inventory, bar coding, imaging, and

similar technologies. In order to take advantage of the technologies embodied in electronic commerce, management must understand their possibilities and uses. If electronic commerce is to be pervasive in the industrial nations of the world, business managers and workers must understand the technologies. We believe this is the reason that you are reading this book and/or taking a course about the management of telecommunications.

With the availability of the graphical user interface (GUI) and the World Wide Web, the Internet has become the global information highway for commerce and entertainment. It took the killer application of the Web and its browsers to give life to the technology of the Internet, and this combination has spawned growth in computer-based entertainment, communications, and commerce never before experienced. Internet connectivity provides the retail interface to the users in business-to-consumer applications and to other firms in business-to-business communications. The global connectivity provided by the Internet is driving much of what happens in commerce today.

Is your computer a system; does it have parts that work together to achieve a common goal?

The computer has caused us to focus our attention on systems because it functions as a system and supports the functioning of systems. A **computer** is a digital, internally stored program device that uses binary instruction and logic to store, retrieve, and manipulate numbers and textual data. In the age of global competition, telecommunications is an integral part of computer systems. Thus, the use of the term *computer* or *computer systems* generally implies a telecommunications component by which the user or the computer communicates with parts of the system. In this text, we focus on *telecommunications-intensive computer-based information systems*.

Information systems have become essential to the modern organization and promise to become even more critical as time progresses. This is substantiated by the fact that most organizational theorists refer to our current organizations as competing in the *knowledge society* or *information society*. Not only is the organization competing in an information-intense environment, but also in one that is geographically dispersed and increasingly global. There is a need to make decisions at the local level but retain control centrally, in the new environment. One cannot effectively compete in a global society without sound telecommunications and networking capabilities that tie together the organization's various parts, partners, and markets.

knowledge society (information society)
More people are now involved in knowledge and information jobs than any other type.

MIS are computer-based capabilities employed to collect, store, process, manage, and distribute information for the organization.

To put MIS and telecommunications into a proper relationship, it is useful to define MIS. **Management information systems (MIS)** *are all systems and capabilities necessary to manage, process, transport, and use information as a resource to the organization.* Organizations began their use of the computer as a replacement for devices such as the adding machine in accounting computations and processing numbers created by organizational transactions. Organizations wanted to exploit the computer's ability to accurately and rapidly process large amounts of transaction data. This ability of computers led to an *emphasis on cost-saving* data capture and storage. This phase of computer application may be labeled as the *transaction processing phase*.

The early view of mechanizing or automating part of the business process (business, used here, means the business of the organization, which may not be profit-oriented) focused on efficiency and had a data orientation. This view began to change quickly as the possibility of support to management and the decision process became evident. The advent of management information systems brought an *information perspective*. Although the first attempts at creating MIS (circa 1965) were less than exciting successes, the idea that data and information were high-cost, high-value resources came to be accepted. This management perspective accompanied the introduction of data-intensive entities, such as individual databases, consolidated databases, database management systems, database administrators, and data dictionaries. With the new perspective, managers came to realize that data and information could and should be used to support decision making. All of these developments occurred in a *centralized mainframe environment*, the only environment that was then possible. This environment allowed several people to remotely access the computer from multiple points. However, the true environment was that of a single user and a centralized computer. (As a point of reference, we are describing the personal computer concept, one user at a time, but not a desktop model!)

centralized computing
The environment where computing resources are in a central location and under central control.

In the centralized mainframe environment, multiple users were primarily connected by a **remote job entry (RJE) terminal.** This means that several people, taking turns, could provide data entry and receive printout in a batch mode. In **batch processing,** jobs are entered into a queue as a whole block and wait their turn for complete access to the computer. In the early batch environment, users had to wait for job completion and output, often requiring two hours to two weeks for turnaround. Frustration at delays led to the concept of multiprogramming, several

Timeshare of computers is like timeshare of condominiums: it allows multiple usage and lower cost.

users sharing concurrent access on a very short time-slice basis so that it appeared to the user as if he/she were the only user. This concept became known as **time-sharing.** Along with timesharing came a more sophisticated operating system, the program that controls the way the computer processes its jobs.

Since both RJE and timesharing required that the operating system of the central processor manage more than one job internally, **telecommunications** became recognized as an essential part of computer processing. In order for organizations to use RJE and terminals, wires or cables had to be strung and software had to be created to allow the connection of a remote device. Data communications became an important subject for those who were charged with making the connections effective and efficient.

As a result of the ability to remotely access a mainframe computer and share its resources, *commercial timeshare* became a reality. This business is an extension of the *service bureau* concept. A service bureau was a business established to provide computer processing for noncomputer owners. Originally, users had to bring their data to the bureau and jobs were run in the batch mode. Commercial timeshare allowed noncomputer owners to enter jobs from a remote entry device, such as a terminal, and access the computational power of the bureau's computer. This, obviously, required a telecommunications capability.

Distributed computing moves the power of the computer and its resident data close to the activities that require them.

Eventually, companies began to realize the value of **distributed computing,** the ability to locate mainframes at organizational subdivisions and share data among the machines. Distributed computing allowed processing to be close to the organization's activities and provided a way to consolidate the data and resultant information for overall control. Distributed computing required a telecommunications environment to move the data and computer applications among the processing sites.

Mainframe, mini, and microcomputer are descriptions that try to differentiate capabilities and size, but this differentiation is now of less consequence.

By the mid-1970s, the **minicomputer** concept was well proven and desk-size systems with 1960s mainframe power were being delivered. The potential for distributed processing continued to grow with much less expensive processing. **Decision support systems (DSS),** computer-based capabilities that provided support for unstructured problems, were being developed and technology support for the office (**office automation systems** or **OAS**) was becoming well accepted. Initially both DSS and OAS were localized environments with DSS using mainframes for support and OAS using dedicated word processors. Telecommunications enabled the localized environment to change rapidly, especially in the office. For example, telecommunications allowed *electronic mail* to add a new dimension to the office environment, replacing paper copies, reducing time of transmittal, and soon supporting *facsimile* transfer of any document one could put on a copier.

The IBM-PC, which started the present personal computer environment, was born in August 1981.

The introduction of the IBM **Personal Computer (PC)** in August 1981 had a significant impact. Although Apple Computers and the Tandy Corporation had shown the world that personal **microcomputers** were possible in the late 1970s, it took IBM's entry to legitimize the concept for business. With the adoption of the microcomputer by business came a new view of the management, processing, and use of information as a resource to the organization. Microcomputers brought significant computer power to the desktop and made interaction with the organization's data more personal. With easy-to-use, powerful telecommunications software and a low-cost modem, the PC became a terminal device, allowing the user to access other microcomputers, share commercial timeshare services and databases, and send electronic mail and facsimile. With telecommunications, users had a window on Main Street; without it, they were locked in a closet.

TABLE 1.1
Characteristics of Information Systems Capabilities

Capability	Orientation	Level	Focus	Nature
TPS	Data	Operational	Task, efficiency	Structured
MIS	Information	Management control	Resource	Structured
DSS	Decision	All, strategic	Alternatives	Unstructured
OAS	Productivity	Operational	Task, efficiency	Structured
EIS	Problem	Executive	Status, problem	Flexible, easy
AI/ES	Knowledge	Operational, tactical	Problem	Structured
EPSS	Knowledge	Organizational	Task performance	Unstructured

While this is a book about telecommunications, much of the technology we discuss will be used by other computer-based systems. As we discuss data communications, we describe the connectivity between computer-based applications whose purpose is to aid in decision making. Therefore, it is appropriate to review these information systems to be sure we all have a common point of reference.

The name given to the information system describes its activities, output, or intent. Table 1.1 lists the major categories of information systems, ranging from those that collect and store data to those that house the experience of experts and attempt to emulate their decision processes.

The IBM/PC had a CPU processing speed of 4.7 MHz. We passed 2,000 MHz in late 2001. Is there an upper limit?

The basis of most information systems is **TPS (transaction processing systems),** which are designed to capture and store data on the activities of the organization. These were the first systems to be computerized. Initially this was done to reduce clerical effort and the cost of data collection and to improve data accuracy. With the expansion of computer-based systems, TPS were installed to capture and store the basic activity of the organization in a way that was readily accessible by individuals and other systems. *The focus of TPS is data* and short-term events of the organization. For example, the payroll system is used to collect labor hours expended by person and by project. These are the basic data of the system, which are generally used at the operational level of management to direct the day-to-day operations of the organization. From this processing and storage of data come summary reports and the information needed to produce paychecks and income tax withholding (W-2[7] in the United States) forms. These same data also might be used by another system to determine charges for the products created. An example of another TPS is the capability that allows you to use your credit cards to pay for a gasoline purchase at the pump, with no human intervention.

Management Information Systems (MIS) take data from TPS and transform them into information to support the basically structured decision process. These systems produce scheduled reports and provide the information used by middle and upper management for the management control function. Where the focus of TPS was data, *the focus of MIS is information.* An example is an MIS that uses the payroll system data to produce a report for each department showing the costs by project, indicating overruns and schedule slippages.

Data are facts about the entities and activities of the organization. *Information* is processed or meaningful data. Table 1.2 describes the attributes of information and Table 1.3 displays information attributes by organizational level. MIS tend to produce standardized, structured reports. The focus is on information content to support the management control function of the organization.

[7] The W-2 is a U.S. Internal Revenue Service (tax) form. Obviously, it is representative of any governmental requirement.

TABLE 1.2
Attributes of
Information

Attribute	Definition
Accuracy	Information is true or false, accurate or inaccurate. The main question is: Does the information portray the situation or status as it really is? Inaccurate information may be treated by the user as if it were accurate.
Form	Distinctions of form are qualitative and quantitative, numeric and graphic, printed and displayed, summary and detail. Often a selection of one or the other alternative form is dictated by the situation.
Frequency	A measure of how often information is needed, collected, or provided.
Origin	Information may originate from sources in or outside the organization.
Time horizon	Oriented toward the past, current events, or future activities and events.
Relevance	Information is relevant if it is needed for a particular situation. Information needed at one time may not be relevant now. Likewise, information obtained "just in case it is needed" is not relevant.
Completeness	Complete information provides the user with all that needs to be known about a particular situation.
Timeliness	Information that is available when it is needed, not outdated through delay.

TABLE 1.3
Information Attributes versus Level within the Organization

Organization Level Information Attributes	Clerical, Operational People	Supervisor	Staff	Manager	Executive
Accuracy	High	High	High	Moderate	Low
Timeliness	Current	Current	Current	Moderate	Not timely
Breadth, scope	Narrow	Moderate	Moderate	Wide	Very wide
Time horizon	Immediate	Near term	Near term	Mid-term	Long-term
Relevance	Complete	High	High	Moderate	Varying
Level of detail	High	High	High	Moderate	Low
Level of aggregation	Low	Added summary	Added summary	Moderate	High
Orientation	Task	Operational decision	Problem	Resource allocation	Strategic decision
	Task	Group	Analysis	Department	Enterprise
Source	Operational system	Operational system	Operational system	Reports, MIS	Staff
Quantifiability	High	High	High	Moderate	Low
Use	Frequent	Frequent	Frequent	Moderate	Infrequent
	Data	Information	Data	Information	Knowledge
Perspective	Internal	Internal	Internal	Internal	External
Type of system	TPS	MIS	MIS	MIS, DSS	DSS, EIS

DSS (decision support systems) may be any capabilities that aid or assist the decision process, but more specifically they provide access to data and models to support solving unstructured problems. *The focus here is on the decision process* involving planning and troubleshooting. It is often believed that DSS are used most at the executive levels for strategic planning. In reality, decision support is of significant value in any situation and at any management level where the problem being addressed is not well defined and where the answer to one question may prompt other questions.

In the payroll example, it may have been suggested that department 10 is undeservedly paid more than department 18. A DSS would provide ready access to the database from payroll to display a mean and a standard deviation of the pay rates of each department and even a statistical analysis (from a model base) to determine if indeed one department was higher paid. Once this question was answered, the user could query the DSS using the same data to determine if one department has greater overtime, absenteeism, or missed schedules. None of these questions were expected at the time that the present MIS was created, and some questions are the result of previous answers. Thus, DSS are decision-oriented and are designed to answer impromptu questions in a style suiting the user.

OAS (office automation systems) bring technology to the office and to knowledge workers. As drill presses and cutting machines have aided factory workers and increased their productivity, word processing, facsimile, and electronic mail increase the productivity of knowledge workers. These technologies affect not only the way jobs are performed but also what is done. They support the effective use of information. One classic example of the purpose of such technology is to increase the efficiency of office tasks while enabling a "paperless" office. For example, instead of an individual creating a memo, giving it to a secretary to type on a typewriter, making changes, retyping it, and putting it in the mail, an organization using OAS would have the originator create the memo on a word processor and distribute it via electronic mail. Even quicker for a single recipient, the creator could write the memo by hand and send it via facsimile, much like a copy machine with output at a remote location. The evolution of office automation has proceeded to the point of *groupware*, incorporating more functionality for improving group processes. Lotus Notes® is an example of this development. Users of these systems are provided connectivity that allows them to work remotely, as if they were in the same room. The principle of these systems is information sharing and work collaboration, dominant forces in modern business.

EIS (executive information systems) are MIS and DSS designed with the executive in mind. They provide very easy access to current information needed by these top managers. The presentations may be used in planning or in following progress. Information content is high and data content is low. Managers at the executive level are interested in receiving up-to-date information with a minimum of effort. Since these systems are designed for high-level executives, they are generally easy to use; they do not require extensive training to gain full value of the system. The initial display from our payroll example might be used in one EIS screen to show progress on one program, total cost in another, and overtime by department in a third. The subsequent displays would be drill-downs to the data that comprised the upper levels, giving the executive an ability to view any area of interest at the level of detail desired.

AI/ES (artificial intelligence/expert systems) add the personal knowledge of an expert to computer systems, thereby allowing the system to make decisions similar to those made by the expert. Where TPS and MIS might provide the generally available data required for solving a problem, the knowledge base of the AI/ES capability and its inferencing ability allow wide use of expertise not available through other means. Such systems tend to be difficult and expensive to build, and many people are hesitant to rely on them due to the critical nature of some problems. For example, medical diagnostic expert systems are just now being accepted by physicians, although the ability is not new. With an expert system and a telecommunications link, a physician in a small town can have remote access to specialized diagnostic expertise and counseling that would generally be beyond his knowledge, without requiring travel or the physical presence of a specialist.

Electronic performance support systems (EPSS) are special systems designed to capture knowledge of experts so that the relevant knowledge may be called on by a person needing just-in-time expert advice. Some **knowledge management (KM)** systems employ EPSS and distribute them via company intranets to people in the firm on an as-needed basis. These systems do not make decisions, but they provide expert advice to those performing critical processes. Some have referred to these EPSS as an "expert in a box."

In addition to EPSS, KM systems also include "best practices databases" and employ software to enable employees access to the best practices stored in so-called knowledge bases. Many professional services organizations find these systems valuable in showing the codified experiences of their best performers in order to speed learning to recent hires.

Case 1-1

Competitive Advantage Through Telecommunications

A New Opportunity through Intranets

Susan Blocker and En-Lin Chen

To survive in the business world today, companies need to develop some kind of unique characteristic to remain competitive. Each company uses a different strategy to gain their competitive advantage; some companies emphasize time delivery, others may stress product safety, product differentiation, or customer services. Telecommunications, defined as the transmission of data or information over a distance, is one of the tools that companies can use to gain that competitive advantage. One very popular telecommunications tool is the computer network. Many computer networks have been installed, but among them, the Internet is one of the widest that connects computers around the world.

The Internet provides users an effective method for extracting information from a remote place without physically visiting it. By using web browsers, users can get their information not only in textual form but also in graphical and audio forms. Supported by the Internet, the World Wide Web (WWW) is comprised of servers that provide information on sites. When users request the information from the WWW, the server sends the data. The idea behind the WWW was to share information. Now companies use the WWW to provide information to their customers and for their advertisements. However, companies are taking the Internet concept a bit further to what is called "Intranet." *An intranet is an Internet inside a company.* "New computer networks called internal webs make it easy for employees at companies like US West, Morgan Stanley, and Turner Broadcasting to share information and collaborate on projects." [3]

When a corporation uses Web servers for their groupware platform and isolates that server from the Internet's World Wide Web by corporate firewalls, an intranet is formed. The firewall is necessary to prevent outside unauthorized access to the information that belongs to the organization. When anyone on the Internet tries to get into the company's internal web, the firewall mechanism requests a password and/or other forms of identification before entry is allowed. Intranets are being used inside corporations to enhance internal communication, boost employee satisfaction, and save money, says the Business Research Group. Of the 170 medium to large-sized companies interviewed, the group estimates that 23 percent of the companies have already begun or plan to begin using an internal web. An additional 20 percent of sites are studying the use of web servers inside the corporation. [2] Another indication of the popularity of intranets is Netscape Communications' announcement in October 1995 that it had experienced record third-quarter revenues of $20.8 million. Netscape, the leading provider of web browsers, states that more than half of those revenues came from sales to corporations that are setting up their own internal webs.[3]

The intranet changes the way companies do their business and the way they communicate. Companies want the technology of the web because it makes it easier for employees to get the information they want and need. The web provides employees easy access to text, graphics, audio, and video, all organized into colorful documents called home pages. The intranet allows employees to call up internal company information such as customer profiles and product inventory—valuable information that was once untapped because it was buried in databases that could only be accessed by the computer specialists in the company.

Another benefit of an intranet is that it can connect different types of computers on the network such as PCs, Macintoshes, and workstations. This is a solution to the incompatibility between departments within and between companies. Employees don't need to worry about where or how the information is stored, further reducing a previous complexity in the information organization of a company.

One of the biggest advantages of intranets is the cost savings. Using the connection provided by the Internet, the implementation of an intranet requires two key things: browser programs which allow people to search the network and view the information and the server programs which store, organize, and manage the information. Because of the wide area of coverage of the Internet, companies can exchange information with different divisions, even divisions in different countries. US West has implemented a global village which connects 15,000 people in 14 states. Employees meet in online "chat rooms" to exchange information and computer documents. They also discuss ongoing projects. US West salespeople use the web to keep in touch with managers back in Denver. A rumor mill will soon be added to allow employees to anonymously question senior executives. Customers may soon benefit from US West's internal web when the company plans to let service representatives use their intranet to fill orders online.[3]

The Intranet concept will greatly influence various industries in the future. The potential is great. Determining the strategy that is best suited for a particular company must be determined, but telecommunications has made the choices now feasible. Management is the value-added aspect, not the technology, as it is easily copied. How the technology is used to support the key business factors will be where the competitive advantage is derived. Thus, telecommunications has provided the means that management must understand and utilize to their best ability.

REFERENCES

1. Keen, Peter G.W. *Shaping the Future: Business Design Through Information Technology,* Cambridge: Harvard Business School Press, 1991.

2. Millison, Doug. "Intranet Wave is Coming, says BRG Report." *Digital Pulse,* October 1995, p. xx.

3. Sprout, Alison L. "The Internet inside your company." *Fortune Magazine,* December 1995, p. xx.

Summary

Telecommunications is the process that allows information to pass between a sender and one or more receivers by electrical, electromagnetic, or photonic means over a distance. This book is about telecommunications in a business environment. More specifically, this is a book about management and decision processes in a business that are part of and result from the use of computer-based information systems and telecommunications technologies.

More computers are used for telecommunications than for computing. Should we rename them?

We focus on *telecommunications-intensive, computer-based information systems* for business. Modern organizations are increasingly information dependent, and their various computer systems are of limited usefulness unless they are linked by telecommunications.

Engineers study telecommunications to be able to address technical issues involved in the movement of voice and data. Business managers should study telecommunications in order to make business decisions about the use of technology: to solve business problems and to take advantage of business opportunities. Both areas of study have their place, but neither replaces the other. A better understanding of the technology of telecommunications should enable managers to make sound business decisions. Without this knowledge, managers will be at a competitive disadvantage in a globally competitive world that is dependent on effective and efficient telecommunications.

Key Terms

artificial intelligence (AI), *24*

batch processing, *20*

centralized computing, *20*

channel, *7*

communicate, *11*

communications, *8*

competitive advantage, *7*

connectivity, *15*

data, *8*

data communications, *8*

data-sharing model, *8*

decision support systems (DSS), *21, 23*

decode, *9*

destination, *7*

distributed computing, *21*

electrical, *16*

electromagnetic, *8*

electronic, *19*

electronic performance support systems (EPSS), *25*

encode, *9*

executive information systems (EIS), *24*

expert systems (ES), *24*

goal of telecommunications systems, *9*

information, *8*

knowledge management (KM), *25*

mainframe computer, *15, 21*

management information systems (MIS), *20, 22*

medium, *8*

message, *8*

microcomputer, *15*

minicomputer, *21*

network, *15*

noise, *9*

office automation systems (OAS), *21*

personal computer (PC), *21*

photonic, *8*

point-of-service or -sales (POS), *6*

processing, *17*

receiver, *7*

remote job entry (RJE) terminal, *20*

sender, *7*

Recommended Readings

Network Magazine—a monthly managerial and technical publication on data communications.

Wall Street Journal **Reports on Technology**—a periodic insert in the *WSJ* on the fields of technology, often telecommunications.

Communications News—a monthly periodical covering all aspects of networking decisions.

Discussion Questions

1.1. Compare and contrast the terms **communications, telecommunications,** and **data communications.**

1.2. Consider your home environment and add to the list of technologies used in the home.

1.3. Consider the technological differences between the neighbor's '57 DeSoto and the new BMW. What technologies are you looking for in your next new car?

1.4. Provide examples of noise in your daily life, especially as it deals with communications.

1.5. Examples of data communications that might be found in the home are AOL® and CompuServe® or MSN® as they are used with home computers. What capabilities do these services offer? Does noise affect these services?

1.6. Why is it essential for managers to understand telecommunications? Answer in terms of (a) local, (b) regionally dispersed, and (c) global operations.

1.7. Do you agree that the sender and receiver of ideas must have a common background or level of understanding for communications to take place?

1.8. What is the basic difference between the voice communications and data communications model?

1.9. Can you cite examples of how companies have used telecommunications or data communications for competitive advantage?

1.10. How can a decentralized organization operate without telecommunications?

1.11. Compare and contrast the telecommunications equipment and media of Dick Tracy, Maxwell Smart, Napoleon Solo, James Bond, James T. Kirk, and Jean Luc Picard.

1.12. Many individuals and groups start new companies each year. What are the major considerations for such a venture? What role does telecommunications play in start-up companies?

1.13. Can you name and explain the alternatives for communicating between Johnson's home office and their major suppliers?

1.14. What are some of the differences between the telephone equipment in the simple versus the complex office?

1.15. Describe how telecommunications is necessary for doing business and how telecommunications can become a part of the product or service of a business.

1.16. When does telecommunications become a major factor in the business?

1.17. How are sound waves transmitted from a sender to a receiver over distance?

1.18. How can Michael Johnson use telecommunications to support growth strategies? What are the implications of his *not* using telecommunications?

1.19. How did Johnson's original line of business tie in with his new line of locksmithing? Did this combination cause any problems?

1.20. At the time that Johnson started the walking guard service, were there technology alternatives?

Projects

1.1. Bring to class major articles or publication issues that deal with technology in general and telecommunications in particular.

1.2. Bring an article to class that shows how an organization uses telecommunications to carry on its core business.

1.3. Bring an article to class that shows how an organization uses telecommunications for competitive advantage.

1.4. Bring to class examples of technologies being used at points-of-service.

1.5. Have one member of the class write down a two-sentence message. Then, have the originator whisper the message to one other member of the class. Have this member whisper it to another member until it goes all around the class and back to the originator. Compare the original message and the final message. Discuss the implications of this exercise.

1.6. The following telecommunications trivia, though historical, provide an indication of telecommunications activity and dollar value. The trivia were compiled by Karin DeVenuta and presented in "Facts and Figures," *The Wall Street Journal Reports—Technology*, Friday, November 9, 1990. Consider the implications for (a) the business, (b) the consumer, (c) the local telephone company, and (d) the long-distance carriers. A valuable exercise would be to update these statistics to the present time and see the change.

One in four consumers surveyed plans to buy a cellular phone in the next five years. The reasons: business (41 percent), convenience (26 percent), personal calls (7 percent), emergencies and safety (6 percent).

Average monthly bill for cellular-phone subscribers: $83.95, a decline of $13 from three years ago.

The Yellow Pages were consulted 17.4 billion times in 1989. People in Des Moines, Iowa, made the most use of the Yellow Pages with 2.9 references a week. New Yorkers average less than one reference per week.

In the first six months of 1990, AT&T, MCI, and Sprint together spent an average of $1.1 million a day on advertising.

On the typical business day, 58 million calls originated in New York City. The busiest pay phone in the state is at the Marcy Correction Facility. The phone gets continuous use about seven hours a day.

A three-minute, station-to-station, daytime call from New York to San Francisco costs 75 cents today. In 1915, the same call—in today's dollars—cost $20.70.

Herbert Hoover was the first U.S. president to have a telephone on his desk. Prior to 1929, the president used a telephone booth outside his office.

Americans made 48.5 billion long-distance calls in 1989, followed by the British (26.3 billion), Chinese (22.8 billion), Japanese (20.9 billion), and Germans (12.6 billion). Americans make over one billion international calls a year, most frequently to Canada, Mexico, the United Kingdom, and Germany.

Who has a fax machine? Four percent of home-based workers, 8 percent of telecommuters, and 31 percent of small businesses.

The typical household generates 3.5 calls a day lasting a mean time of 6.17 minutes.

Teenagers do not make more calls than adults. But they talk longer. Teenage girls spend about 25 percent more time on the phone than do adults; boys, about 15 percent more.

Of the people who own answering machines, more than one-third use them to screen calls.

About 31 percent of Americans have unlisted phone numbers; the highest concentration is in Las Vegas, where more than 61 percent of the numbers are unlisted.

Chapter **Two**

Where Did the Telephone Come From and How Does It Work?

CONTINUING CASE—PART 2
Johnson Lighting and Security Systems

The next expansion Michael undertook was to provide small businesses deterrence and enhanced protection against forced entry, through the installation of sensors and alarms. Not only was the addition of good door locks important, but also the addition of metal strips to windows to detect opening and breakage, sounding an alarm outside the building. The strips also acted as visible evidence of entry protection.

The business rapidly expanded with the appearance of larger shopping centers and office buildings. His first big contract came in 1964 with a large-scale shopping mall (the Italian Mall), for which he contracted to install a standard parking lot lighting system. Because of an increase in attempted robberies in parking lots, Michael saw a need to provide greater security for mall patrons. He also believed that the issue of security could be used in marketing the mall. Michael approached the mall developer and presented a proposal for 24-hour security by way of enhanced lighting and a walking security patrol, recommending that this service be included in the mall development and promotion campaign.

Despite the expansion, Michael still had a small organization. He had hired two lighting installer-maintenance personnel, a secretary-bookkeeper, a locksmith, and a group of part-time guards. His office was in a small building that now contained three telephone instruments. When he opened the business he simply went to the local phone company and signed up for a single-line, single-instrument phone service. Both arrived in three weeks and were installed by Mountain Bell, the part of AT&T responsible for local services in the Denver, Colorado, area. With his latest expansion, Michael saw a need for better telephone service. He called on the local Telco to provide a second telephone number/line and to install both numbers on each of the phone instruments. This meant that he had to rent new phones from the local telephone company, each having a switch to go from line to line.

Like most organizational managers, Michael made his telecommunications decision on an ad hoc basis. That is, he had no plan, no architecture for guiding his telecommunications configuration in accordance with the organization's objectives. The term that has come into use for such a comprehensive telecommunications plan for the organization is **telecommunications architecture.** As the organization grows and increases its telecommunications complexity, the term *telecommunications architecture* will be revisited, and you will see its vital role in today's networked environment.

With the successful implementation of security at the Italian Mall in 1964 and expanded security services, Michael realized that he had an opportunity to service that and other malls with even more security products and services. He thought there was a need for foot patrol services in addition to alarm systems and for remote monitoring systems. He decided to investigate the regulations that governed operation of a bonded guard service in the state and municipality. As it turned out, he could establish a guard service with little difficulty. After filing the appropriate documents, he called the local newspaper to place an advertisement for his first complement of permanent guard personnel. It was his intention to seek a total contract with the Golden West Shopping Mall, the newest and largest mall in the city. As he had already established a solid reputation with the mall's developer, he felt that he had the inside track to obtain a contract for external lighting, security guards, and locks for the mall. His proposal was accepted in 1971.

The Golden West Mall contract in hand, Michael hired four security guards immediately and renewed his advertisement for more personnel. He now dreamed of a "full service" security services company, but first had to deal with more immediate problems. He had to make office arrangements, obtain a patrol car, expand the telephone system, and advertise the new security services.

Michael pondered the communications requirements for his mushrooming business and realized that the existing system would have to be expanded to support the new lines of business. He was thankful to have AT&T as his telephone company, his Telco. AT&T could help him define his requirements and install the equipment needed to complement the service that would replace the simple system presently in place.

The Telco had provided Michael with very good service. He quickly found that he not only used the Telco for equipment and local service, but for all his telecommunications services. The Telco provided dial-tone service at a flat rate plus long-distance charges for any call outside of the local calling area. The local calling area consists of those **telephone**

number prefixes to which a caller on flat rate can call without a toll.

In 1974, the foot patrol security personnel had only to punch a clock to show that a guard had inspected a certain point at a given time. With the introduction of new and less expensive hand-held radios, the foot patrol personnel were in constant contact with the base station. This provided the guard with added personal security and allowed the guard much faster notification of and response to an incident. The vehicle patrol personnel also were provided car radios for constant contact with guards and the dispatcher. As the number of guards increased and the need for communications and control was more obvious, a central control point was needed. (See Figure 2.2 for basic elements of the radio dispatch system.) Michael added a security chief to his organization (see Figure 2.1) to

FIGURE 2.1 **Johnson Security Services Organization, circa 1974**

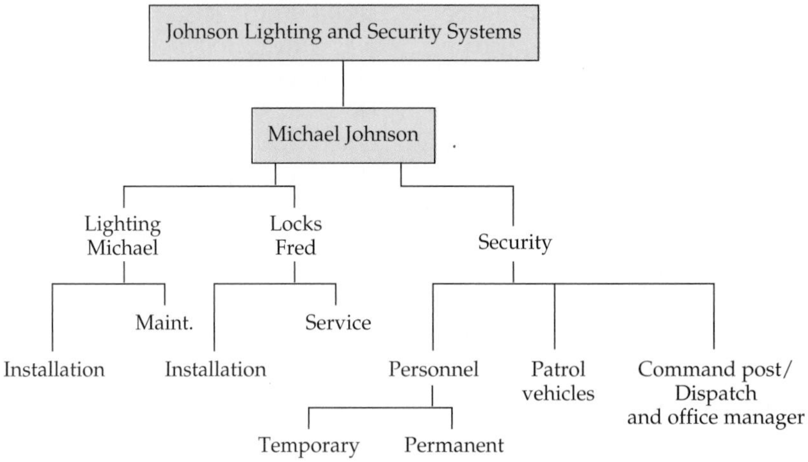

Johnson Lighting and Security Systems

Michael Johnson

Lighting Michael — Locks Fred — Security

Maint. — Service

Installation

Installation

Personnel — Patrol vehicles — Command post/ Dispatch and office manager

Temporary — Permanent

FIGURE 2.2 **Johnson Lighting and Security Systems Basic Radio Dispatch**

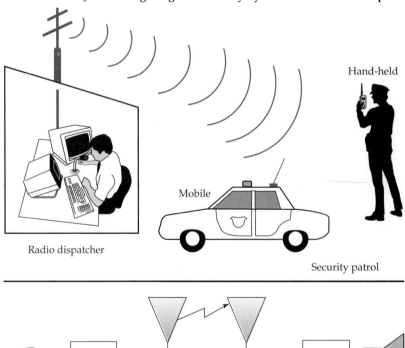

Radio dispatcher

Mobile

Hand-held

Security patrol

Microphone — Radio Transmitter — Transmitting antenna — Receiving antenna — Radio Receiver — Speaker

supervise and coordinate this new functional area of the business.

With experience in mall and small company security, the time seemed right to move into industrial security services. About 70 miles away in Colorado Springs, a government facility released a proposal for a security system requiring foot patrol and fire protection. Michael believed he was ready to expand his business, but also saw that the remote location would require the maintenance of an office in that city as well as a different communications system. For the time being, every time he called the distant location there was a toll charge.

Awarded the government contract, Michael decided to establish an area office in Colorado Springs as the contract ultimately required 23 guards on a rotating schedule. With an area office, Michael received inquiries about providing services to several malls and businesses in the city. Instead of having interested parties call into the area office, which necessitated a person at that office who could make commitments and contracts, he approached the Telco about an inward-WATS capability so callers from Colorado Springs could reach the Denver home office toll-free. The

Telco recommended a foreign exchange (FX) leased line (a virtual extension of the local loop) instead (see Figure 2.3). Thus, when the home office picked up the phone for one of their lines, it received a dial tone from Colorado Springs. When Colorado Springs customers called Johnson Lighting and Security in Denver, they used a local number and invoked no toll charge. Thus customers in the Colorado Springs local area could call the main office as though it were within the local calling area. Also, the Denver office could use the line to call the Colorado Springs office and local calling area without toll charges.

Michael realized that he had a large number of people to manage and probably needed a manager for the Colorado Springs operation. Upon reflection, however, Michael realized that he had the choice of either finding such a manager or operating the office remotely with good telecommunications.

A point to be stressed is that Michael now had to be as concerned with the management of people as with the installation of security systems. He had become a manager. Management is the control of the work of others. An important aspect of management here is that it requires communications to effect this

FIGURE 2.3   FX Line Effect
FX line means call to distant location is same as in local calling area.

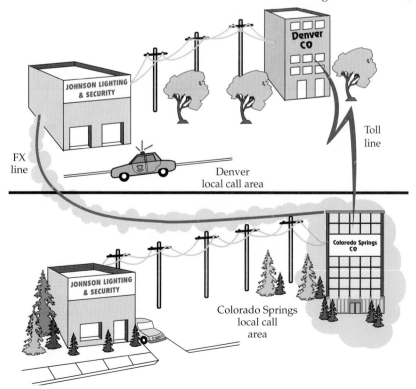

control. If the people being managed are nearby, communications may be verbal and in person. If the people are dispersed, the manager is dependent on telecommunications both to operate the business and to manage others responsible for operating parts of it.

Telecommunications technologies may have dictated the way Michael dealt with his employees, as well as with suppliers, customers, and vendors. The concepts of distance and time have shrunk as telecommunications technology has made it possible to control organizational activities at a distance. The change has come at the price of increased complexity.

Telecommunications technologies presented new commercial opportunities. Michael extended his expertise in security to take advantage of new opportunities through the use of telecommunications. The expansion would not have been feasible without the telecommunications mentioned, that is, telephone communications between distant offices and radio contact with foot and vehicle patrols. However, Michael did not consider the technology and the organizational infrastructure of the vendors of the technology as he purchased more services. Michael still simply called the local arm of AT&T to meet his new needs. We will see later that the AT&T organizational structure came under attack from the Justice Department of the U.S. government and that this changed not only how companies obtain telecommunications services but the entire telecommunications environment in the United States.

With the growth and success of the business, Michael had come to understand that he had (1) grown a group of businesses with little planning, (2) expanded his reliance on telecommunications but with no strategy or plan, and (3) gained a lot of people to manage. He saw continued growth in the security field and the addition of allied fields. However, a major aspect that allowed him this vision was his reliance on communications and other people.

With the addition of the distant subsidiary, Michael had significantly expanded his employment of telecommunications in his business. He had progressed from having only the simplest telephone service to the use of multiple telephone lines and instruments. Also, he had added radio communications systems in two locations and had become a subscriber to a foreign exchange service. In addition to how he previously used the telephone for customer and supplier contact, Michael now used radio telecommunications as a part of the service provided.

Michael now realized that he had a large number of people to manage (see Figure 2.4). Instead of being just a security and lighting company, Johnson Lighting and Security was in the people business as well. Michael wondered if this was a good time to turn the direction of the security and lighting company over to his son so he could concentrate on the planning of a larger vision for his business.

FIGURE 2.4   Johnson Lighting & Security Services with Subsidiary Office, circa 1974

Note: Numbers refer to quantity of telephone instruments.

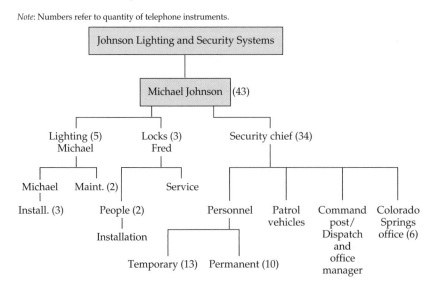

INTRODUCTION

In this chapter we introduce the basic concepts of voice communications and the analog voice network. Voice communications is the mainstay of most organizations, a technology that has advanced greatly during its short existence. Our focus is the channel for human communications, that is, the media and the attendant noise environment. The modern press is filled with articles and news about multimedia, hypertext, video conferencing, and the information superhighway, with an emphasis on data communications. *Voice technology*, however, remains the largest segment of telecommunications and continues to be vital in the conduct of modern organizations, commanding the larger share of telecommunications expenditures. As the title to a section in the May 1991 issue of *The Office* announced, and which remains as true today, "Without Telephones, the World's Out of Business."

voice telephone
The user-oriented technology that now connects most of the world.

Technology Note   2–1
Telephones and Switching Equipment

The *rotary phone* mentioned is the third generation telephone instrument. The first instrument hung on the wall and had a hand-crank electric generator to get the attention of the telephone operator. Next, the instrument was made into a candlestick and the attention of the operator was obtained when the caller lifted the ear piece off of the hook (phone going "**off hook**"). The instrument was then changed to the present handset, incorporating mouth and ear peices. (See Figure 2.5.) In these cases, the operator sat at a switchboard panel and *manually* connnected the called to the calling party by plugging a connecting wire from one jack to an-

other. She then would make the called party's phone ring and listen until the party answered the phone. In the case of *party lines,* multiple residences were connected to a single wire and each party on the line had a distinctive ring, for example, two longs and one short. One member of a party line could eavesdrop on another simply by picking up the phone when it stopped ringing. Though not intended to be used in this manner, members of a party line could also have a multiple party conference by just picking up their phones at the same time. This is similar to the (900) 970-XXXX phone circuits available today.

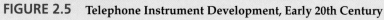

FIGURE 2.5   Telephone Instrument Development, Early 20th Century

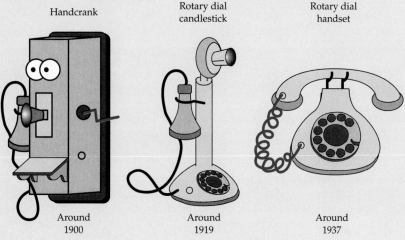

Handcrank	Rotary dial candlestick	Rotary dial handset
Around 1900	Around 1919	Around 1937

Technology Note
The Bell System

2–2

At this point in history, AT&T's **Bell System** was the major supplier of local telephone services, but there were over 1,000 other, generally small, local telephone companies (Telcos). Western Electric, the manufacturing arm of AT&T, was the supplier of all equipment used by the Bell System and made one telephone instrument for single-line telecommunications environments, the black telephone. (GTE, one of the major Telcos, also made and supplied telephones for their system, as did ITT. These suppliers were small compared to the total business of the Bell System and Western Electric.)

At this time, the Bell System had a granted monopoly to provide telephone service within specified areas. It was illegal to use any equipment other than Bell-supplied

(rented) equipment in a Bell System area. It was the opinion of its management that the Bell System could guarantee integrity of the telephone system *only* by ensuring proper equipment was used . . . their equipment.

The connection from the telephone instrument to the switching equipment, located at the Telco's *central office,* is called the **local loop** (see Figure 2.6). This local loop is a pair of wires, that is in reality a single (conducted) wire that forms an electrical path, a loop, from the telephone to the connect point at the switching equipment. The switch makes the proper connections to continue this loop to the receiver's telephone, effectively making a continuous loop of wire from the sender to the receiver and back.

FIGURE 2.6   The Local Loop

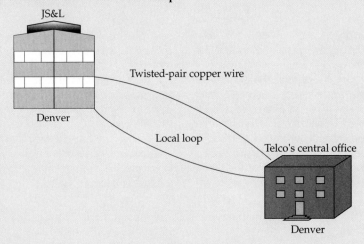

Technology Note
The Central Office and Local Loop

2–3

The Telco's central office is the connection point for all local loops. In this building, the local loops terminate on the **line termination equipment (wiring frame)** and are then connected to the switches that make the loop-to-loop connections. If the call goes to a customer that is not connected to the same central office as the calling party, the switch connects to a trunk cable to another central office. There is a toll for the connection between

central offices if they are not in the same **local calling area.**

Area calling services offered by Telcos provide two alternatives to the normal fixed rate service. The area of local calls can be expanded to include those frequent exchanges that would otherwise be a local toll call. Secondly, charges are calculated on a lower fixed rate plus a small charge per minute.

In the Continuing Case, we see how a small business manager makes telecommunications decisions that affect his business—decisions that we have reported surround voice telecommunications only. The telecommunications technologies that have been introduced are voice technologies. In this chapter we explain voice telecommunications in more detail so you will understand the technologies that our case firm has employed. In order to provide a foundation for understanding voice communications and technology, we discuss some relevant historical developments and their evolution. You may think it a bit archaic to devote a chapter to voice communications, and to the tried-and-true telephone, but this area and this instrument are at the heart of most business activity.

Technology Note
Switching Equipment

2–4

The next major improvement of telephone technology, generation two, was the creation of *switching equipment* to make telephone connections, thus replacing the operators. It was predicted that if switching equipment had not been developed; ALL employable females would be needed as telephone operators to handle the traffic. (This is historical fact and in no way intended to be gender-specific. As an aside, AT&T used young boys to handle the multiple connection in long-distance connections in large central offices, but found them to be far less capable than the woman who replaced them.)

The first telephone switching equipment was invented by an undertaker, Alan B. Strowger, who thought the telephone operator was diverting his business to the competition. This invention used a rotary dial on the instrument to send out electrical pulses that stepped a series of switches according to the telephone number. This set up a path from the sender to the receiver. Thus, the terms **step-by-step,** or **stepper, switch,** and **rotary dial telephone** came into use. The technology was first commercially used in 1919. The rotary phone is shown in Figure 2.7.

FIGURE 2.7   **Telephone Handset and Rotary Dial Telephone**
Adapted from Misra and Belitsos.

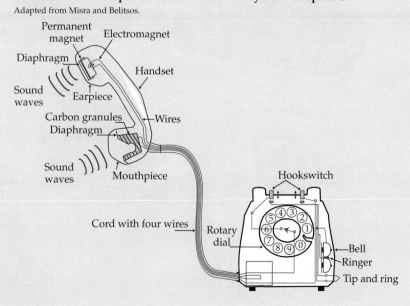

INTEROFFICE COMMUNICATIONS

interoffice communications
The more people are involved in any work assignment, such as in the office, the greater is the need for and dependence on rapid, easy, and effective communications.

For the business, the absence of telephone communications has a severe impact. The telephone is now routinely used to take orders, call for service, check on invoices or deliveries, order lunch, contact prospective customers, or call the bank to arrange an increase in a line of credit. Obviously, there are a myriad of other business uses of the telephone that firms, both small and large, would be hard-pressed to do without. All of the cited uses involve contact with external entities. Almost every organization of any size relies on the telephone for internal communications as well [see Figure 2.8(a)]. If you did not have telephone service inside the organization, your trips, as shown in Figure 2.8(b), to other people's desks and offices would increase significantly, breaking your train of thought and your ability to be productive. Consider for a moment the multiple internal communications requirements to operate a large firm. There is a need to coordinate plans, report deviations from schedules, inform superiors and subordinates of progress, verify bills, confirm receipt of shipments, arrange meetings, and so forth. Internal management of the modern organization has become reliant on the existence of ubiquitous telephone capability.

To effectively use and manage an organization's **telephone service,** you need to understand the technology involved. We start with a bit of history and then delve into the technology. The point of doing this is to provide some idea of how we got to where we are today and to reinforce the point that telephone service is vital to

FIGURE 2.8(a)
Interoffice Communications with Telephone

FIGURE 2.8(b)
Interoffice
Communications
without Telephones

the organization. Telephone service is often considered simply a necessity for doing business with cost of service taken for granted. Businesses with this view are often just "bill payers," who take little action to manage their telephone service. This service is frequently a significant expense to an organization. We are talking about tens or hundreds of thousands of dollars each month for many firms, an amount that should be a subject of management concern. Since *telephone service and costs can be effectively managed*, it is important for managers to understand the technologies and alternatives so that they can make logical decisions. We will discuss these costs and alternative pricing after we discuss the basic voice technologies. Only then can you consider a price-performance trade-off.

A QUICK HISTORY OF TELECOMMUNICATIONS

The path to modern telecommunications began with the invention and widespread use of the landline telegraph, radio telegraph, and teletypewriter. Because these are data communications technologies, and we want to concentrate on voice telecommunications in this chapter, a detailed discussion will be delayed until later. We will cover these technologies briefly as a historical point of reference. Included in this history is the important role of legislation and regulation.

The telegraph was
the first form of
electrical data
communications, but
used specially trained
operators at each end.

The Telegraph and Morse Code

The telegraph uses a code created by Samuel Morse in 1837 consisting of long and short electrical signals, much like the actions of an electric door buzzer. The sending operator taps the key to send the dots and dashes and the receiving operator listens

Information Window   2–1

From a recent *Fortune* comes the following quote that indicates the importance of internal communications. "Meet three exemplars of effective intra-corporate communications. They have already learned a key lesson of the Nineties. The lesson Internal communications—talk back and forth within the organization, up and down the hierarchy—may well be more important to a company's suc-cess than external communications, what PR types loftily used to style 'dialogue with major constituencies.' It is the free flow of information inside the company that enables you to identify and attack problems fast, say, when customer service representatives first get an earful about some quality glitch, or salesmen in the field encounter a new competitor."

Morse code
Unique in that it was designed for human operators' use. Other codes were designed for machines.

to the sounds and writes down the characters of the message (see Figure 2.9). This same basic concept holds true for either landline-based telegraph or radio telegraph, which sends the signals from radio transmitter to receiver. In each case the operator must convert the message to or from **Morse code.** The teletypewriter adds a typewriter-like device at each end that converts the code, provides message storage, and prints the final message. These concepts will be elaborated on when we discuss data communications in detail.

Two uses of Morse code that many people will recognize are "V" for victory and "SOS." The first was the employment of the opening stanza of Beethoven's 5th Symphony, coincidentally the letter "V" in Morse code (ta, ta, ta, dah), in radio broadcasts by the BBC (British Broadcasting Corporation) during World War II. This symbolic use of the "V" for victory became a trademark with special connotation. The second use is dot-dot-dot, dash-dash-dash, dot-dot-dot for "SOS." While many people readily recognize these sounds and believe they mean "save our ship (or souls)," these letters were chosen due to their distinct sound pattern and ease of transmission in an emergency situation.

Landline-based telegraphs, radio telegraphs, and teletypewriters are all digital data communications devices. Each depends on the use of a standard code. All three devices rely on conversion of written words to code, transmission of the coded message, and translation of the code back into writing. Each of these communications systems requires that the sender compose his or her thoughts in writing and that someone trained in machine use and codes convert the message for transmission. See Figure 2.9(b). The destination receives only what has been initially written. Senders and receivers (the originating and receiving humans) are intermediaries in this process and are seldom end users when they employ these communications media. The capabilities of each of these technologies require professional key or teletypewriter operators. However, Mr. Bell and his telephone changed all of that (circa 1876). The telephone and voice communications are the basis for the following discussions.

The telephone is one of the very few communications devices designed for end-users, without assistance except, in some cases, to make initial connections.

The Telephone

The **telephone** is an analog device that takes the sender's spoken words in the form of acoustic energy, converts the acoustic signals to equivalent (analogous) electrical signals, sends them over a medium (usually a copper wire), converts them back from electrical to acoustic energy in the receiving unit, and lets the receiver hear a reproduction of the sender's voice and the original message. (See Figure 2.10.) Thus, the sending and receiving people are end users who do not require professional

FIGURE 2.9
Morse Telegraph

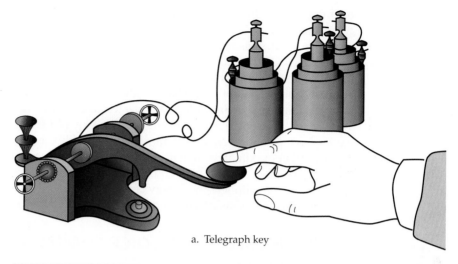

a. Telegraph key

■ is a short signal/sound or "dot"
— is a long signal/sound or "dash"

Character	Morse Code	Character	Morse Code
A	■ —	T	—
B	— ■ ■ ■	U	■ ■ —
C	— ■ — ■	V	■ ■ ■ —
D	— ■ ■	W	■ — —
E	■	X	— ■ ■ —
F	■ ■ — ■	Y	— ■ — —
G	— — ■	Z	— — ■ ■
H	■ ■ ■ ■	,	■ ■ — — ■ ■
I	■ ■	.	■ — ■ — ■ —
J	■ — — —	1	■ — — — —
K	— ■ —	2	■ ■ — — —
L	■ — ■ ■	3	■ ■ ■ — —
M	— —	4	■ ■ ■ ■ —
N	— ■	5	■ ■ ■ ■ ■
O	— — —	6	— ■ ■ ■ ■
P	■ — — ■	7	— — ■ ■ ■
Q	— — ■ —	8	— — — ■ ■
R	■ — ■	9	— — — — ■
S	■ ■ ■	0	— — — — —

b. Codes for numbers, letters, and punctuation

FIGURE 2.10
Acoustic-to-Electrical-to-Acoustic Transformation of a Telephone Call

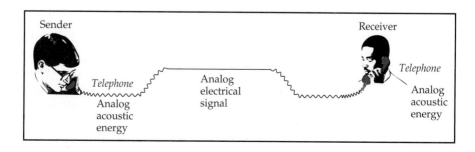

Sender

Telephone

Analog
acoustic
energy

Analog
electrical
signal

Receiver

Telephone

Analog
acoustic
energy

operators or machines. This advance allows the users to have direct access to the communications device and offers them the opportunity to compose the message as they send it. This type of communications is interactive whereas the previous modes, for example, telegraph, were not interactive and did not provide rapid response because intermediary operators were required.

The telephone not only has changed the way people interact, but has changed our concept of time and distance. We can now feel as close to others as the nearest phone. The American Telephone and Telegraph Company (AT&T) and many smaller companies have provided circuits to most homes and businesses in the United States. As of 1991, approximately 92 percent of the U.S. population had telephone service, providing connections to similar equipment throughout the industrialized world and giving everyone with telephone service a truly global reach. In the next section we describe some of the basic terms and technological foundations of telephony.

THE TECHNOLOGY OF VOICE COMMUNICATIONS

We will now introduce the underlying technologies that support the telephone system and voice communications. Managers need to be familiar with these concepts and associated terminology in order to make informed business decisions.

Analog Signals

All signals in nature, such as vision and hearing, appear as analog signals.

Before we get to the telephone and voice signals, let us look at **analog** signals in general. The sound coming from the speaker is continuously varying **acoustic** energy. The telephone instrument converts this acoustic energy to analogous electrical energy. If, instead of speaking, we were hearing a single tone from a tuning fork, the signal would be a simple *sine wave,* as shown in Figure 2.11(a). A simple sine wave is a regular repeating wave, represented by crests and troughs around a midpoint. A single repetition of a crest and trough is a cycle. The number of repetitions or cycles that occur within a second of time is the **frequency** of the signal and is termed **hertz** [Figure 2.11(b)]. We think of frequency as the pitch of a signal. The distance from the trough to the top of the crest is the **amplitude** of the signal or its volume; the greater the amplitude, the "louder" the signal. The third parameter of an analog signal is its *phase*, which describes the point to which the signal has advanced in the cycle. Phase will be important to us later in this book as it is used in putting data on analog signals.

hertz
The technical term for analog frequency and bandwidth, e.g., cycles per second. The greater the hertz (Hz), the higher the pitch of an audible signal.

In the human voice, we have a combination of many simple sine waves. The resultant signal looks like the *voice print* in Figure 2.12. This voice print is a combination of frequencies from the lowest to the highest that the circuit can carry. Circuits that have a narrow bandwidth can only carry a small range of frequencies, and, therefore, the richness of the resultant voice print is limited, as is the trueness of the representation of the signal.

Bandwidth

Bandwidth is the carrying capability of the channel. The more you have, the better.

While electrical signals travel at about the speed of light (186,292 miles per second = 299,654 km/sec), the quantity of information we can pass during a given amount of time is of prime interest to us. If we are talking about digital signals (such as the telegraph characters), speed is measured in characters per second. With analog signals, however, our concern is the ability to pass a given spectrum of tone, an amount of frequency, that is, the **bandwidth** of the circuit (see Figure 2.14). For normal telephone circuits we need to pass a signal of only 4,000 cycles per second,

FIGURE 2.11
Amplitude **of the sine waves is** *measured.* **When sound waves have been converted to electrical energy for transmission, we use an electrical measure such as** *volts.* **A strong wave is relatively high, while a high wave is relatively low.**

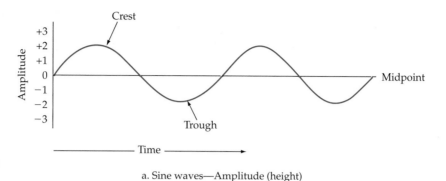

a. Sine waves—Amplitude (height)

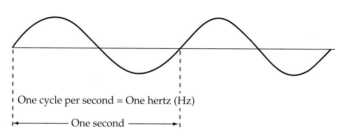

b. Sine waves—Frequency (width)

FIGURE 2.12
Voice Print

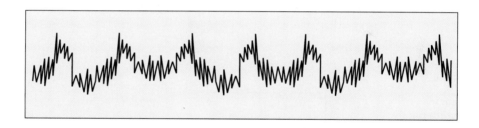

or hertz, to communicate the total telephone signal. (The 300–3,000 hertz portion of the frequency spectrum contains the actual voice.) If we want to use one circuit to pass several such telephone signals, we would need a bandwidth several times 4 KHz (kilohertz) wide. As the amount of desirable bandwidth increases, the limits of a given medium are reached, some much sooner than others. See Figure 2.13.

voice spectrum
The part of the telephone frequency range (300–3,000 Hz) used for voice transmission. This is a limit of the end points, not the medium.

TELEPHONE CHANNEL CAPACITY

A circuit carries or is the medium for a telephone channel. The *analog bandwidth (the range of frequencies) for a telephone channel is 4,000 hertz (Hz),* or 4 kilohertz (KHz). As Figure 2.14 shows, the **voice spectrum** within the telephone channel covers the frequencies from 300 to 3,000 Hz[1] and is 2,700 Hz wide, with the remainder of the channel space being allocated to guard bands that provide separation space. Note that the

[1] If you read other telecommunications books, you will likely find differing views on the frequency bandwidth of the telephone voice spectrum. Most agree that the lower limit is 300 Hz, but the upper limit is stated to be 3,000, 3,100, or 3,400 Hz. Even a member of a Telco did not know the bandwidth because it was not a limiting feature for them. It is a limiting feature for companies like Hayes Corporation who make modems. The important point is that the bandwidth is very limited.

Information Window   2–2

The maximum human acoustic (hearing) ability is in the range of 20 cycles per second (hertz), which is lower than the lowest note on a pipe organ, to about 20,000 hertz, though this high note is often heard only by dogs. (The note A below middle C on a piano is tuned to 440 hertz.) The AM radio transmits on a 10,000 hertz wide band with a frequency response of 100 to 4,000 hertz and is considered adequate for talk programs and most popular music. For the real music lover, FM radio covers a 200,000 hertz band and transmits from 50 to about 15,000 hertz and is considered of excellent quality. (Television sound has only recently tried to rival FM radio.) Meanwhile, we need only the range from 300 to 3,000 hertz to transmit human voice conversations. Although the typical voice frequency range is 100 to 10,000 hertz, the restricted telephone bandwidth is adequate to not only provide intelligible speech, but also communicate the characteristics of the speaker's voice, that is, we can recognize the person speaking and pick up his or her mood through voice and tone inflections.

FIGURE 2.13
Acoustic Frequency Bandwidth of Various Devices

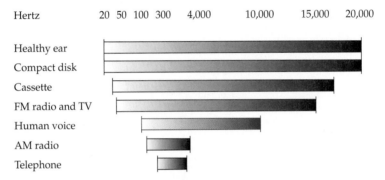

FIGURE 2.14
Frequency Bandwidth for a Voice Channel

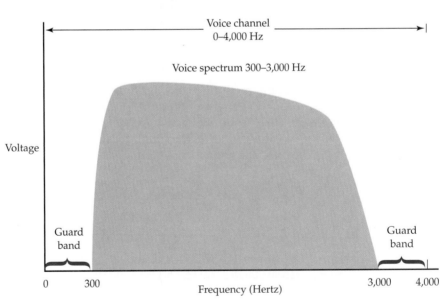

bandwidth is not related to the actual frequencies used for voice transmission, only with the difference between the upper and lower limits of the range. This range of 2,700 Hz is adequate for voice communications but becomes a limit when we wish to carry more analog or digital information, such as high fidelity music or digital data at a high rate of speed. While the **public switched telephone network** provides access

public switched (voice) network
The total *analog* telephone network that allows connectivity over the entire country and much of the world via an array of switches and media.

to almost every home and office in the developed world, the size of this *information pipeline* is restricted, and, thus, so is the speed or quantity of information flow. (As with the garden hose, you can pump only so much volume though a small pipe.) In addition, much of the spectrum is not available due to the equipment and not the medium. Twisted-pair wire can handle a greater bandwidth, but the equipment limits it.

CENTRAL OFFICE, SWITCH, AND INSTRUMENT CAPABILITIES

central office
The place into which all local loops terminate; the place housing the switch. Previously, the location of the operator, thus the name "Central."

The very first telephones were directly connected from one person's instrument to another. This meant you had to have a phone for each person to whom you talked. Then a switching office was developed so that local loops went from residences and offices to the **wiring frames**[2] in the switching office, called the **central office (CO)**. A person would make the connection of one local loop to another in the central office by physically plugging a short wire from the connector attached to one local loop to the other. This required one or more human operators to make all connections. (Since the operators were often located in the central office, they were referred to as Central.) Table 2.1 is a list of telephone companies in one state, Alabama, in the early 1990s. This state of 3.5 million people had four major cities, 34 telephone companies, 364 central offices, 307 exchanges, 106,431 miles of aerial and buried copper cable and fiber, and 20,211,245 access (subscriber) lines.

When the sender is connected to one central office and the receiver to another, the call goes between the two COs via a **trunk line** or trunk cable. If the two COs

---

Information Window   2–3

Less than 1.0

Milli—1/1000—as in a milliwatt is one one-thousandth of a watt. A 100-watt light bulb uses 100,000 times as much power as this.

Micro—1/1,000,000—as in a microsecond is one one-millionth of a second; there are one million microseconds in a second. A micro-century is five minutes.

Nano—1/1,000,000,000—as in one nanosecond is one one-billionth of a second. Computer memory speed is measured in nanoseconds; microcomputer memory has a speed of about 60 nanoseconds to complete a store or retrieve function.

Pico—1/1,000,000,000,000—1 trillionth.

Greater than 1.0

Kilo—1,000—as in 1 kilowatt (KW) is one thousand watts. Since BPS is bits-per-second of digital data transfer, 10K BPS would be 10,000 bits-per-second.

Mega—1,000,000—as in 1 megabyte of disk storage is one million bytes. A small hard drive on a microcomputer held 40 megabytes (40 million characters) of storage in the late 1980s, and now holds tens of gigabytes of storage.

Giga—1,000,000,000—as in 1 giga BPS is one billion bits-per-second digital data speed. Compact disks can hold 0.8 gigabyte.

Tera—1,000,000,000,000—1 trillion. A specific project of the computing industry is to create a computer that operates at a speed of 1 teraFLOP (where FLOP is floating-point operations per second).

---

[2] A wiring frame is the physical structure that holds the end of the local loops. The circuit is then connected to the switch. Changing locations of telephone instruments without changing telephone numbers previously necessitated moving the connections from the switch to the proper local loop on the wiring frame. This is now done with software in the switch.

TABLE 2.1 Alabama Telephone Companies, circa 2001

Company	No. Exchanges	Access Lines	To. C.O.	Dig. C.O.	Aerial	Buried	Fiber	1-Pty	Eqa	Class	ISDN	SS7
Ardmore	3	8,999	3	3	21.00	817.00	43.00	8,744	YES	YES	NO	YES
Blountsville	0	4,394	2	2	171.43	169.66	20.41	4,278	YES	YES	NO	YES
Brin. Mtn.	0	12,724	4	4	957.70	126.30	33.10	12,614	YES	YES	YES	YES
Butler	3	5,140	4	4	15	557	70	5,140	YES	YES	NO	YES
Castleberry	0	990	1	1	0	167	0	973	YES	YES	NO	YES
Cherokee	2	2,382	3	3	16	213	20	2,334	YES	YES	NO	YES
Elmore-Coosa	0	5,968	3	3	303	340	4	5,096	YES	Y/N	Y/N	Y/N
Farmers	6	18,605	8	7	917	1200	79	18,356	YES	YES	NO	YES
GT Com	1	2,363	2	2	9	241	2	2,275	YES	YES	NO	YES
GTE	90	297,993	91	91	5839	15624	1503	229,353	YES	Y/N	Y/N	Y/N
Goshen	0	964	1	1	0	142	8	964	YES	YES	NO	YES
Graceba	2	5,784	3	3	29	575	55	5,658	YES	YES	NO	YES
Grove Hill	0	2,617	1	1	1	206	8	2,617	YES	YES	YES	YES
Gulf	0	44,231	13	13	0	2010	290	51,522	YES	YES	YES	YES
Hayneville	2	2,657	4	4	1	325	93	2,568	YES	YES	NO	YES
Hopper	0	3,897	2	2	88	332	43	3,845	YES	YES	NO	NO
Interstate	0	8,517	4	4	237	74	39	8,407	YES	YES	YES	YES
Lamar	0	2,491	2	2	23	597	0	2,372	YES	NO	NO	NO
Leeds	0	23,088	5	5	1041	669	74	11,514	YES	YES	YES	YES
Millry	0	6,805	5	5	0	1022	108	6,766	YES	YES	NO	YES
Mon-Cre	0	3,570	3	3	1	347	130	3,199	YES	YES	NO	YES
Monroeville	1	13,681	10	10	94	1486	37	11,748	YES	YES	NO	YES
Moundville	0	1,865	1	5E CD	4	201	7	1,833	YES	YES	YES	YES
New Hope	0	6,300	3	3	165	237	55	6,220	YES	YES	NO	YES
Oakman	0	2,634	4	4	135	251	23	2,634	YES	YES	NO	YES
Oneonta	0	7,783	1	1	575	12	62	8,031	YES	YES	YES	YES
Peoples	4	16,268	11	11	105	2435	102	16,268	YES	YES	NO	YES
Pine Belt	3	2,674	4	4	0	387	38	2,522	YES	YES	NO	YES
Ragland	0	1,423	1	1	8	96	8	1,398	YES	NO	NO	NO
Roanoke	0	5,427	2	2	200	236	13	5,334	YES	YES	NO	YES
S.C.B.	96	19,666,168	151	125	26696	37010	4427	1,410,793	YES	Y/N	Y/N	Y/N
Southland	0	12,446	5	7	11	1052	69	10,366	YES	YES	NO	YES
Union Springs	0	4,812	4	4	38	477	87	4,706	YES	YES	NO	YES
Valley	0	5,586	1	1	161	61	21	5,579	YES	YES	YES	YES
Total	213	20,211,245	362	336	37,861.24	69,694.42	7,572.63	1,876,027	Y/N	Y/N	Y/N	Y/N

FIGURE 2.15 **Strowger Step-by-Step Switch**

Source: Stan Schatt and Steven Fox, *Voice/Data Telecommunications for Business* (Englewood Cliffs, NJ: Prentice Hall, 1990), p. 23.

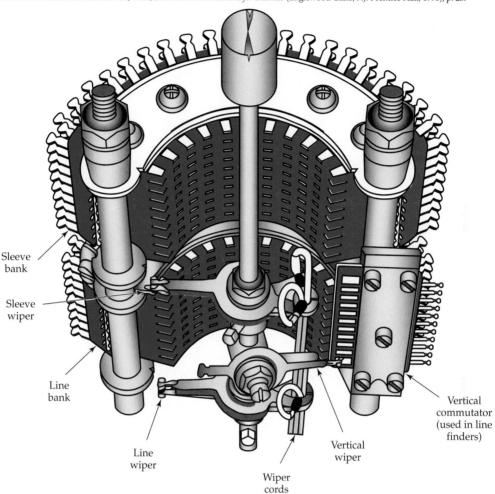

Sleeve
bank

Sleeve
wiper

Line
bank

Line
wiper

Wiper
cords

Vertical
wiper

Vertical
commutator
(used in line
finders)

A toll is a charge
made for a service.
Long-distance voice
calls have a toll.

The switch takes the
place of the operator
to connect the calling
party to the called.

are in the same calling area, there is no charge **(toll)** for this connection; otherwise the call is subject to a *long-distance toll* and the circuit is called a *toll trunk*.

With the invention of the Strowger step-by-step switch (see Figure 2.15), human operators were replaced by switches for local connections. **Long-distance** connections continued to be made by human operators. It was this use of switch technology that allowed telephone systems to expand quickly while reducing costs. This use of switching technology continues to develop today, having gone through five distinct generations (see Table 2.2): manual switchboard, step-by-step technology, crossbar technology, solid-state technology, and digital switching.

The switching equipment in the CO is activated and operated in conjunction with the telephone instrument. The first instrument using the switch was the **rotary dial telephone,** which created electrical pulses by opening and closing a contact in the phone when the round dial was twisted and released. The second

TABLE 2.2
Switch Technology Progression

Direct connection, no switch (1st telephone)	1876
Manual switching of mechanical connections	1878
Electromechanical:	
a. Step-by-step (Strowger) switching	1919
b. Panel switching (Strowger extension)	1921
c. Cross-bar (hermetically sealed relays)	1938
Solid state switching	1965
Digital (electronic switching) system (ESS)	1970

FIGURE 2.16
Dual-Tone Multifrequency (DTMF) Touchpad

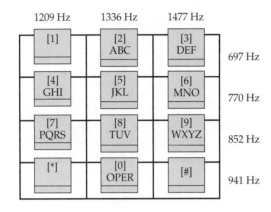

TouchTone pads turn the "dumb" telephone instrument into a computer terminal.

and current equipment, called **TouchTone**® by AT&T, generates tones that operate the switches. The importance of this change in technology is that this equipment is really a small 12-key terminal attached to the (now digital) central office switch. The digital switch is really a special-purpose computer; therefore, you have a small terminal on your phone connected directly to the computer. The **touchpad** telephone also allows you to command the telephone switch or other computers, using the 10 digits and the * and # keys. (See Figure 2.16.) This has significant implications to telephone systems since the caller can now command the system to perform functions, such as entering an account number and responding to computer-generated questions. This increased functionality, discussed later in this chapter, enables the so-called *intelligent telephone system*. Rotary phones generally cannot perform this same function because the switch does not easily interpret the pulses as codes, rotary phones do not include the # and * keys (e.g., function keys), and they are far slower. (As shown in Figure 2.16, the DTMF [dual-tone multifrequency] touchpad uses one tone for each column and one for each row: two per code. This is a total of seven tones to create twelve codes.)

Dial tone means the availability of audio channels.

Whether you access the central office (wired) switch by pulse or tone handsets, the result of the connection is a dial tone. A **dial tone** is a sound you hear on the telephone instrument when you pick up the handset (going off hook), indicating that the **CO switch** has acknowledged your request for a circuit and is ready to make the connection you request. **Dialing** is a process that signals the **network** by sending pulses or tones to the CO equipment, where they are interpreted and the proper circuit is established. This circuit connects the calling and the called telephone instruments. With a cellular telephone, there is no dial tone. This is because the cell

FIGURE 2.17 **The Basic Telephone Voice System**

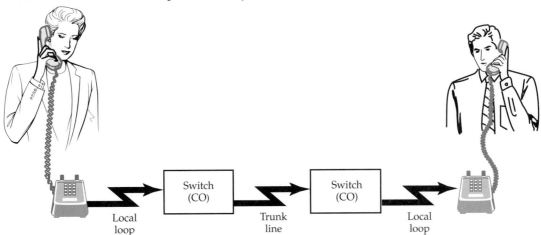

Local loop Trunk line Local loop

phone sends a data packet with the desired information to the cellular switch over a data channel before a voice channel is established. On the other hand, the wired system gets the attention of the switch, which sends the dial tone.

An example of how the basic wired telephone circuit operates is depicted in Figure 2.17. The calling party received a dial tone, indicating access to the network via the local loop to her CO switch. The CO-to-CO trunk is representative of any number of connections necessary to connect one CO to another. If the call is out of the local calling area, this trunk will be long distance and incur a toll. If the two parties are connected to the same CO, there is no trunk used at all. The sequence of numbers she has dialed has caused the switch in her CO to pass the connection via a trunk to another CO that is connected to the called party's local loop and telephone. In the second CO, based on the numbers she has dialed, the equipment determines that the called party's telephone is available or not available and responds accordingly. If the called line is busy, a busy tone is generated and returned to the calling party. If the called party is available, the caller will hear a ring that is generated by the second CO switch and the calling party also will hear the phone ringing. The two sounds are generated by separate equipment and the called party can actually pick up before the calling party hears a ring. When the called party takes his/her instrument off hook, the network connection is completed and the calling party may converse. Both individuals are able to hear themselves as well as the other party by way of *sidetone*, which is normal speech returned for hearing yourself as you talk. On the telephone, sidetone provides feedback on how you sound. Without sidetone, your speech will become garbled because there is no feedback.

The **plain old telephone system (POTS),** using the *Signaling System Seven* protocol, includes the telephone number of the calling party between the first and second ringing signals. If the receiving party has arranged for Caller ID®, s/he will intercept this information and the telephone number of the calling party may be displayed, along with other information. It is possible to block this information at the sending end. Some people will not accept any calls that do not include Caller ID.

FIGURE 2.18
Key System
Instrument

The old Bell System, through its manufacturing division Western Electric, took great care to develop a reliable and humanly compatible telephone instrument. It evolved from the wall-mounted instrument, to the candlestick model, and then to several versions of the tabletop model. All of these were simple, or dumb, instruments as they had no switching capability within the physical telephone instrument. The exception is a **key instrument** (see Figure 2.18) that has the ability to switch between several lines coming to the telephone. With changes in AT&T and the Bell System, the ownership of the physical instrument became the responsibility of the user. The ability to incorporate extra features into the telephone has changed the nature of the instrument. You now have a choice in price, quality, and features, allowing customers to choose a low-priced, simple instrument or one with many added features.

Capabilities of telephone instruments now include redial of the last number called, storage of often-called numbers, display of the number called and the time, the ability of several people to hear the conversation through a speaker in the phone, placement of the caller on hold, and automatic retry of a busy number. While some of these features are also available for a fee in the switch, many telephone instruments now have a high level of capability and intelligence and provide greater flexibility; however, they are usually much more difficult to use.

As the signal propagates along the twisted-wire circuit, whether the local loop or a trunk, the circuit experiences signal *attenuation* (reduction in strength). This means that the **voltage** level of the signal is lowered as the signal moves down the wire. To keep the signal at an acceptable level, amplifiers, or repeaters, are installed about every mile of the circuit. These repeaters amplify the signal and keep it at the predetermined level. However, any induced noise is also amplified, reducing the **signal-to-noise ratio.** Thus, in an analog system, the farther the voice communications signals travel, the more noise and, consequently, the lower the signal-to-noise ratio. The objective of a voice circuit is to minimize noise and have the desired signal strength be much greater than any noise, for example, a high signal-to-noise ratio. Therefore, it is not difficult to understand why long-distance calls were of lower quality than local calls. (When we discuss digital transfer of voice communications, we will learn that this does not have to be true.)

AT&T and other companies have created a vast telephone network in the United States. A signal can be sent from any phone to any other phone in the United States

Signal-to-noise ratio is the relationship of the strength of the desired signal on the circuit to the strength of the noise. The higher the S-to-N ratio, the better.

Technology Note
Keeping Signals at the Desired Level

2–5

Because signals lose their strength or are deformed as they travel along the path, it is necessary to take action to counter these conditions. As analog signals weaken with distance, we use amplifiers, often called repeaters, to make the signal stronger. We do somewhat the same with digital signals. The point is that distance weakens all signals and we must apply technology to keep the signal within bounds.

FIGURE 2.19   **Possible call circuit from Atlanta to Eugene via the telephone network—dashed lines represent some alternative routes**

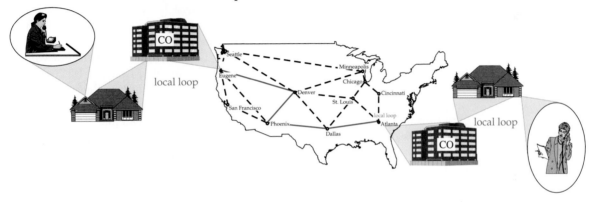

and much of the rest of the world. In creating the path from one phone to another, the network connects many links. To give you an idea of how this process works, assume that you want to call from Atlanta, Georgia, to Eugene, Oregon. (See Figure 2.19.) Here is what happens: The telephone is dynamically switched based on the number dialed. Even though the call could be routed different ways each time the call is made, you are not charged for incremental distances. *(Voice traffic is charged [tariffed] based on distance.)*

- When you pick up the phone in Atlanta, you connect your instrument to the local loop running from your residence or office to the local telephone company's central office.

- A switch at the central office connects you with a line to the long-distance system (LDS) in much the same way you would be connected to another phone for a local call. (There may be a connection from the initial central office to another before connecting to the long-distance service. This cable is called a trunk.)

Telephone switching hierarchy, circa 1970—regional center; sectional center; toll office; end-office.

- The long-distance system provides a circuit of one or more links to a central office in or near Eugene, Oregon. Because of the vast voice communications network, your circuit may not be the most direct but simply the most available at the moment of your call. This ensures a minimum delay and the greatest probability of getting a circuit. For example, Figure 2.19 shows that this long-distance connection goes from Atlanta, to Dallas, to Phoenix, to Denver, and then to Eugene. However, there are literally thousands of other possible connections, including going through Chicago, Minneapolis, or Seattle. Furthermore, each point-to-point circuit may be any of the possible media.

- A line connects you from the long-distance system to the local telephone company central office wiring frame.

- Finally, a connection is made to the local loop running to the receiving instrument.

Telco
Your local telephone service provider; the telephone company.

With the evolution of switching equipment (now called *the switch*) to digital-controlled computers, enhanced services not possible before can be provided. Many of the services are made possible by storing data in permanent memory in the switch. For example, the *last number calling* your number is kept in storage, and you can call this number by commanding the switch to access the memory and place the call by pressing * 69. Such commands would generally be generated with codes from your touchpad phone starting with a *. Similarly, you can have a list of numbers give distinctive sounds, keep a list of numbers you do not want to receive calls from, and have your *calls forwarded* to another number. With *call waiting,* you can connect your instrument to a waiting call and place the present caller on hold. You can make conference calls and even a record of nuisance calls that will stand up in court. For a complete list of these services available from your local Telco,[3] consult your telephone directory.

911 Emergency

In the U.S., most communities have a simplified emergency telephone number. In order to help with speed dialing, the sequence 9-1-1 is employed. A 911 call is automatically routed to emergency response units: police, fire, and ambulance. If the call is made to a PBX (private branch exchange), using either 911 or 9-911, the PBX is smart enough to know whether to forward the call to an interior phone or outside to the standard 911 destination, even when the 900 area code is blocked.

Reverse 911

In an extension of the emergency 911 call-in capability, there is a move to employ the system in reverse. In the case of an emergency situation such as an impending flood, storm, etc., emergency units can notify a large percentage of the population to take appropriate measures. This is in addition to other warning methods. This was done in smaller U.S. towns in the 1930s and 1940s when the local operator would manually connect a large number of phones and continue to repeat the message. This is how one of the authors learned of the end of World War II in Europe.

Both of the above are reliable because POTS and cellular systems work even during power outages. This is called a *life line.* Cordless phones on POTS do not.

---

[3] The term *Telco* is used to mean any local telephone services provider.

COMMUNICATIONS CIRCUITS AVAILABLE

POTS (plain old telephone system) The basic analog voice capability put in place by AT&T and other local providers over the past century.

WATS (wide area telecommunications service) Basically discount bulk pricing of long-distance service.

The most obvious choice of a communications circuit for end users is the local **telephone system (POTS[4]).** If the number you are calling is within your local calling area, you simply dial the number and make the connection at no additional cost. If the number you are calling is not in your local calling area, you have several choices. First, you may choose to dial direct and pay for the phone call at normal **"long-distance"** rates, which are generally lower after business hours and on weekends. An alternative for businesses that utilize the telephone heavily is to contract for **WATS (wide area telecommunications service).** The premise of WATS is that the business pays a fixed charge for a specific number of hours of phone services per month to a select group of states plus a reduced cost per minute of actual use. The total cost is lowered through this high-quantity discount method. A variation on this theme is **in-WATS** service. In this case, the receiver pays all toll charges. This is the well-known 800 (and the new 888 and 877) area code and provides what appears to be a local call for a long-distance connection. It would be difficult to find a business today that does not have in-WATS for its customers. Alternately, individuals can get in-WATS service so their friends and family can call them and pay no fee.

Another area code that has special connotations is the 900 area code. While the 800, 888, and 877 codes reverse charges, the 900 area code adds extra fees on the call. One valuable use of this feature is to allow customers whose equipment is out of warranty to call a 900 area code number for assistance, knowing they will be charged a fee for service, say $1.00/minute. As the 800, 888, and 877 numbers are all allocated, new in-WATS area codes must be created.

line conditioning A means for providing higher-quality communications on a channel or circuit by adjusting parameters, thus reducing noise.

If your business is located in a town outside of a major city's local calling area and you have heavy telephone traffic, you can lease a telephone line (a circuit) that connects your switchboard to the city's central office switch. This procedure entails a fixed rate for the leased line but incurs no usage cost. This type of line may even be *conditioned* to provide a higher-quality, cleaner communications environment. Conditioning is important to data communications by reducing the noise environment and providing greater speed. The lessee can achieve higher quality by renting a known permanent circuit rather than utilizing a temporary, pieced-together, dial-up circuit. Replacing switched connections with permanent connections and tuning the circuit to specific electrical values achieves additional quality (a cleaner circuit). The leased circuit may offer the exclusive use of a twisted-pair circuit or microwave channel,[5] which gives you the total capability of that physical medium, or just a single 4 KHz analog channel or 32-to-64 Kbps circuit of any physical medium. The greater the capability and the cleaner the environment, the greater the cost. The total cost of the leased circuit, however, will generally be much lower than the equivalent dial-up circuit *if* it supports a high volume of traffic.

[4] POTS stands for the plain old telephone system, which is the nationwide voice capability often referred to as the Bell System. It is envied by less-developed nations and provides connectivity and communications between almost any home and businesses in the United States. We will use the term *POTS* in this book to refer to this public switched telephone (voice) network.

[5] As we will cover in more detail in the next chapter, a circuit is the physical medium, such as a twisted-pair link. When you have a circuit, it is assumed that you have the total bandwidth it has to offer. A channel can be either the total circuit or a portion of it. Thus, you can divide a circuit into several channels. Any microwave channel is generally only a part of the circuit.

Private Branch Exchange (PBX) versus Centrex

private branch exchange (PBX)
A telephone switch on the organization's premises. When you have a PBX, you are your own Telco internally.

Centrex services are PBX services offered by a common carrier.

A **private branch exchange** is a multiple-line business telephone system that resides on the company premises and either supplants or supplements the Telco local services. To an extent it is in competition with the services provided by the central office, for example, **Centrex**®. Centrex services are PBX services offered by a common carrier, that is, a group of lines and services owned, provided by, and located in the **CO switch** in a way that makes them appear as a separate facility for the customer. The Telco maintains the equipment and charges the customer for this service. In reality, Centrex service may be little different than standard local service except for a few added features and possibly quantity discounting. Both Telco services are regulated by state and federal agencies. In contrast, a PBX is **customer premises equipment (CPE),** is unregulated, and is owned and maintained by the customer. A company with 100 local telephone lines, standard telephone equipment, and either standard or Centrex service runs 100 lines from the CO switch to instruments on the premises. When a PBX is involved, fewer lines to the CO switch can be used. The result is lower costs for lines but a customer investment and cost in PBX equipment and maintenance. Because a large portion of an organization's communications are interior to the organization, most of the communications do not go beyond the PBX, which reduces the need for outside lines to the CO switch. There may be fewer than 30 lines running from the PBX on the premises to the CO switch, with 100 lines radiating out from the PBX to the telephone instruments. It is estimated that as of the beginning of the millennium, there are in excess of 30 million local lines terminated in PBXs. (See Figure 2.20.)

least-cost routing
One feature of a PBX is the ability to include intelligence that, upon a request for a long-distance call, determines the lowest-cost route and uses that vendor.

A significant feature of the PBX is its ability to record call activity and create reports. For example, the equipment makes records of all calls and callers, giving an accurate account of this expense. Additionally, the reports show times of high activity and inward call blocking, noting the need for additional equipment or outside lines.

CPE (customer premises equipment)
The instruments and equipment on the customer's premises.

The business alternative to a PBX is to have the local telephone company provide the service. Such service can range from simple enhanced phone capabilities, such as **multiple lines,** intercommunication **(intercom),** and speaker phones, to Centrex. In Centrex service, the Telco owns and maintains the equipment, but it dedicates the capability to your business. An advantage of using the phone company and Centrex is that a third party is responsible for all service. It should be noted that some Telcos have their own registered names for Centrex; for example, BellSouth calls their service Essex®.

When a company progresses to a point of making a PBX-versus-Centrex decision, management must be aware of having growth built into the choice. For example, purchasing a nonexpandable PBX locks the company into a specific technology with finite limits. *Leasing Centrex means someone else (the local Telco) maintains the equipment and manages expansion and growth. Purchasing your own PBX means YOU provide this maintenance and management,* hopefully at a cost savings. This operation and maintenance, however, can be purchased from the vendor or a third-party firm. If you are risk averse, buy expertise by choosing Centrex.

Automatic call distribution (ACD) and voice mail enhance voice communications.

Important features that could be a part of or ancillary to a PBX are **automatic call distribution (ACD)** and **voice mail.** The former adds intelligence to the receipt of incoming phone calls to channel them to a vacant instrument, often with announcements (the familiar menu you hear when calling a business). The latter is used with or without ACD to allow reception of a phone call when the recipient is busy or absent. Voice mail can be viewed as an intelligent answering machine.

FIGURE 2.20   **Various Forms of Phone Lines**

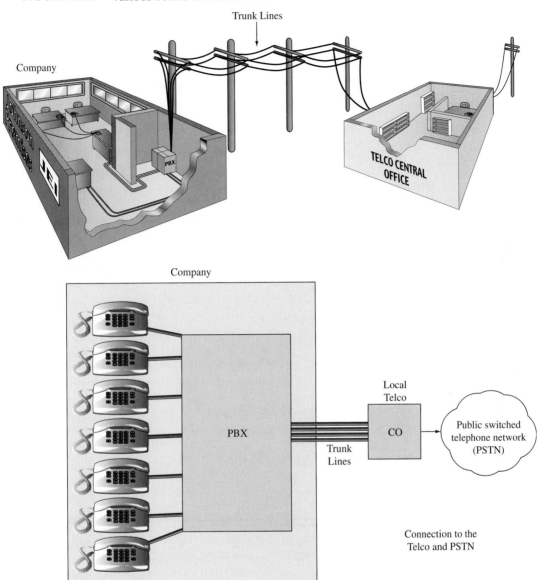

A PBX Network

Since we are studying the management of telecommunications, you should remember that the use of ACD and voice mail is first a management decision before it is a technical decision. Both features place a machine between the caller and the called party.

Have you called an airlines reservation telephone number, or the IRS, or a computer software discount house, or some other merchant lately and had the computer tell you that all agents were busy, but please stay on the line for the next available

ACD gives airlines the ability to place their agents in Kansas and Montana and provide reservation services to all of the nation.

agent? You called into an automatic call distribution (ACD) computer that was controlling the instruments of a number of people. For example, when you call (800) 433–7300 for American Airlines or (800) 221–1212 for Delta Airlines, the ACD system does the following just prior to answering your call:

- Determines which reservation center around the country (Atlanta or Salt Lake City) is lightly loaded and most likely to have an available agent.

- Determines if there is an available agent at that center.

- Connects you with the agent or answers your call and gives you a message to wait on the line.

Telecommunications trade-off considerations are reliability, cost, maintenance, features, speed, vendor support, and flexibility.

If you called into Microsoft Corporation, developer of the disk operating system (DOS) and the developer of the Windows operating system for IBM and compatible computers, the ACD always answers the phone and gives you choices as to how your call is transferred. You have to answer four questions by pressing numbers on the touchpad to finally get to the human of your choice, unless you already know the person's telephone extension. This may seem like a lot of work up front, but Microsoft is using telephone technology to ensure that its customers receive the best and quickest assistance possible. If you interact with the computer to get more information, you enter the more sophisticated realm of **interactive voice response (IVR).** As an example of IVR, let's examine a bank service of checking an account further. First the customer dials the number of the bank and the recorded voice asks that a choice be made from a menu that may include determining the account balance. If you respond by pressing the appropriate number key on your telephone, the computer asks for your account number and usually a **PIN (personal identification number).** Once the PIN is entered, the computer accesses the proper information and passes it through a voice response capability to speak the amount of the balance. The customer then may be asked to return to the menu for additional options, such as last deposit. In this case, the touchpad on the telephone is an input device, so the telephone is like a terminal and the computer uses data-to-voice translation to provide voice response in an interactive mode.

interactive voice response (IVR) Allows 24/7 operation from a bank.

personal identification number (PIN) Is a number known to the user that authenticates access.

A cost consideration offered by PBX systems, and by outside vendors, is least-cost routing. With this service, the PBX connects to points-of-presence of several long-distance providers, for example, AT&T, MCI WorldCom, or Sprint. The PBX will determine the lowest-cost route depending on the destination of the call and time of day. The person placing the call is unaware of this decision process at the PBX. Alternatively, DeltaCom®, a private corporation, provides much the same service. The customer places the call through DeltaCom, and its switch determines the lowest-cost route. DeltaCom is able to do this through negotiating rates with multiple long-distance providers, passing these rates, plus commission, to the customer.

Centrex vs. PBX In addition to costs, a most powerful feature of Centrex over PBX is that you can configure a single system over multiple locations in a metropolitan area. It will look and feel like a single PBX over multiple locations.

Remember, Centrex services are not always equal. If your Telco has an AT&T 5ESS, System 85, or equivalent *CO switch*, the switch already has the ability to offer significant flexibility and services. You may have seen advertisements for the services offered by Telcos, especially the Bell System, on television. You already may have call waiting, call forwarding, call blocking, distinctive ringing, last caller, and Caller ID, features previously offered only on PBXs. (Caller ID is available only with digital PBXs and CO switches like the digital 5ESS.) Thus, when considering Centrex versus PBX, you must first determine the capabilities or generation of the CO switch. A second consideration is the nature of regulation imposed on your Telco. If the local phone company is not authorized to offer tariffed services, you have little choice.

TABLE 2.3
Centrex versus PBX Considerations

Feature	Centrex	PBX
Initial cost	Low	High
Leasing cost > 500 lines	High	Attractive
Maintenance cost	None	All
Cost to move instruments	High	Low
Local control	Low	High
Selection (least-cost) routing of long-distance calls	None	Option
Software upgrades and costs	None	User responsibility
Changes to new equipment	Telco provides	Fixed
Ability to change	Telco decides	Customer decides
Move to ISDN	Telco provides	Customer funds
Insurance	Telco provides	Customer pays
Power consumption and costs	Telco provides	Customer pays
Capacity to grow	High	Low (limited)
Back-up power/processor	Telco provides	Customer responsibility
Housing space	Telco provides	Customer provides
Service mileage charge	None	Customer pays
Reliability (MTBF)	Highest	Medium-to-high

When choosing between Centrex and PBX, areas of concern include reliability, cost, maintenance, features, speed, vendor support, and flexibility. Table 2.3 shows some of the differences between Centrex services and a PBX. Managers must carefully examine the trade-offs to make the *correct business decision.* Certainly, the actual cost figures should be used within the analysis! The value of the qualitative aspects must be assigned by the manager, based upon the specific situation.

Digital PBX

Although we discuss digital equipment and transmission in later chapters, we cannot leave the topic of private branch exchanges without discussing the trend toward **digital**[6] **PBX** equipment.

The cost of Centrex may be higher than a PBX for a single location. With multiple locations, cost effectiveness makes Centrex a competitive alternative. In the latter case, it will appear that the company is in one location to the callers.

An advantage of the PBX, in addition to increased control and lower cost, is that some systems are entirely digital. Thus, you can plug your terminal or computer into the telephone instrument and communicate with devices under the control of the PBX without using the intermediary equipment, such as modems (to be explained later). With this capability in-house, you could connect to a digital telecommunications network and never convert the signal. As we will discuss in later chapters, this capability would provide the cleanest and fastest switched circuit available.

Rolm, formerly a part of IBM and now part of Siemens, produces one of the few digital PBX systems. When connected to a digital switch at the CO, such as AT&T's 5ESS switch, a digital path is provided through the switch, but the remainder of the local loop is analog. The Rolm system, on the other hand, provides a digital path from voice handset or computer at one end to similar equipment at the other end. This is a relatively recent improvement of equipment; the PBX has traditionally been separate from data communications. As the world moves to digital channels in order to reduce noise, increase control, and combine voice, data, image, video, and text,

[6] Briefly, digital signals are discrete values, such as +5 volts and zero volts, to represent units, for example, 1s and 0s. This is a different way to transmit information and provide control. Analog signals, on the other hand, are continuous in value.

digital PBXs will become very important. An example of further adaptation is the connection of the PBX to local area networks (LANs), giving a digital path and control from computer to computer via the network. The extension of this is *ISDN (Integrated Services Digital Network)*, which will be discussed in more detail later.

Size matters! When switches were first installed, they occupied large rooms. You can now buy a 12-line PBX that is a circuit board and will fit in a server computer. Thus, small companies can have the value of a PBX and install it in a computer, providing additional features of computer-telephony integration, to be discussed next.

Computer-Telephony Integration (CTI)

The objective of Centrex and PBX switches is to add the decision-making ability of the computer to the switching capability of the telephone. The term **computer-telephony integration (CTI)** has been used to describe this trend. The simplest form is to have the PBX extract the Caller ID signal as it forwards the call to the appropriate person. At the same time, it sends the caller's telephone number to a computer where it is compared to a customer database. By the time the phone is answered, the computer has sent the customer's file to the computer at the same desk, giving the customer service representative knowledge of the account. Taking this further, Siemens Rolm Communications and Aspect Telecom offer products that allow monitoring of remote workers, offer advanced automated call distribution, and so forth. The Siemens Rolm software allows the using firm to track up to 250 skills and assign each a proficiency level and preference rating, so when callers indicate a problem, the system will route the call, based on information provided to the agency, to the appropriate skill level.

Leased versus Switched Lines

When determining whether to use standard, Centrex, or PBX services, consideration also must be given to which types of lines to use in high-volume situations. This is not in reference to high-volume WATS service, but to whether a leased line can reduce your cost. For example, in the JL&S case, Michael is considering installing a leased (foreign exchange) line to a nearby major city so his customers in that city would not have to pay long-distance charges. This means that the customer dials a local number that is connected to a distant central office. This gives you an idea of the cost trade-off of fixed-cost leased line versus switched variable cost line. Although, in the JL&S case, Michael could have used in-WATS to achieve the same objective, an FX line gives the appearance that the organization is located locally, which could be a competitive advantage.

Depreciation and Other Concerns

Many decisions are made based on accounting standards and tax considerations as opposed to technology features. This is particularly true for the Centrex–PBX decision. If the decision is made for Centrex services, there is no concern for amortization or depreciation of equipment. The vendor, not the organization, purchases all Centrex equipment. However, with a purchased PBX, the equipment must be depreciated over its useful lifetime. While the time period for depreciation for telecommunications equipment in general formerly was 10 to 15 years, it is now from three to five years. The depreciation time or, more accurately, the useful lifespan for PBXs is presently from four to seven years. While the equipment may easily last several times that number of years, its technological usefulness does not.

The different effects of different depreciation schedules are important due to the time value of money.

Software upgrade and costs can be very significant with PBXs. In one case with which the authors are familiar, the firm had to pay over $30,000 for upgrade of a $70,000 PBX simply to accommodate new area codes.

In the modern era of rapidly evolving technology, the useful lifespan of telecommunications equipment continues to shorten. As new features are developed, they replace older ones. Staying with older technology may be cost-conscious while moving to new technology keeps you current with customers and competitors, possibly resulting in cost-effectiveness. Additionally, in a dynamic market, many vendors will fail, often leaving you with equipment that can no longer be readily supported and maintained. This may cause you to seek third-party suppliers who support such equipment at premium prices. This further presses the telecommunications manager to purchase from established suppliers, hurting the chances of new entrants in the market. Further, if you purchase new systems that do not have the ability to grow and be upgraded, you will find that you have bought into a dead-end position as the market moves. As many organizations have found, they live with their decisions for a long time.

The choice between (1) the acquisition (lease) of standard lines from the local Telco, (2) the contractual agreement with that same Telco for dedicated Centrex services, and (3) the purchase of a PBX is a management decision. It revolves around two concerns: which systems best provide the services you need now and in the near future and which systems cost least. A hidden part of this decision is the need for maintenance and upgrade. When management chooses to lease services from the local Telco, it leaves maintenance and upgrade in the hands of the lessor. When it chooses to purchase a PBX, it assumes all responsibility for, not only installation, but repair, maintenance, and upgrade. Where a PBX may indeed provide greater services at a lower cost, it does mean a greater responsibility and added cost in the form of repair and maintenance.

Looking Ahead—Voice over the Internet Protocol (VoIP)

One of the problems with any book on telecommunications is that it may be best to present the information in a simplified step-by-step manner, but readers who know enough technology would like to jump ahead to more modern technical material. Wireless cellular phones and voice over IP networks (private and the Internet) are presently expanding at very rapid rates. These technologies are discussed next.

As we discuss in a later chapter, the Internet provides global connectivity. It is a data network, different from the largely analog voice network. It, however, can carry voice communications once converted into digital format, which we will explain later. In any case, with a personal computer with (*a*) an Internet service and (*b*) a multimedia board—that is, sound input and output—voice calls can be made over the Internet. It's generally a bit more complex than just dialing a telephone number, but is far cheaper.

For example, to make a call on the Internet, software, such as Internet Phone, a part of Microsoft's Netmeeting, is required. Next a microphone must be connected to the soundboard and the speakers should be working. To call someone, you activate the Internet Phone program, which gets a connection to the Internet through an Internet service provider (ISP). Using your calling directory, you may

The useful lifespan of telecommunications equipment continues to decrease. This means that upgrades and replacement are a way of life.

waiting for Godot syndrome That often paralyzing feeling that you keep waiting for the next improvement before you buy. With this attitude, no one would ever purchase a microcomputer!

The ratio of expenses for voice and data is moving from 80% : 20% in large organizations. At the same time, the ratio on long-distance lines is about 50% : 50%.

Technology Note   2–6

IP telephones originally came to market as client software running on PCs to provide low-cost, consumer-oriented, PC-to-PC communications over the Internet. However, quality of service (QoS) issues delayed this implementation's widespread acceptance and, today, most of the focus on IP phones is centered on private business network applications.

In this context, an enterprise IP phone is a desktop business telephone that delivers enhanced, low-cost telephony services by leveraging the corporate data networking infrastructure (LAN). Within an IP-PBX, the telephones utilize standards such as H.323, SIP, and Megaco. Additionally, the enterprise IP telephone is backwards compatible with existing PBXs. Businesses are driving the demand for IP phones (also known as LAN-based telephony) due to the cost and network management savings this new technology can deliver. Cost savings can be realized through the migration of separate networks for both voice and data to one unified voice over data network, and through avoidance of carrier access charges and settlement fees. These charges are particularly expensive for corporations with multi-international sites.

Businesses benefit from these cost savings without sacrificing voice quality (as with earlier PC implementations) because managed corporate intranets do not have the QoS issues that plague the public Internet. In order for enterprise IP phones to supplant traditional PBX or key-system phones in the kind of volume necessary to allow for their survival in the marketplace, they must achieve toll quality or better. LAN-based IP phones are not limited to the traditional 8 KHz telephony voice sampling rate, which limits voice bandwidth to 4 KHz. Therefore, wideband voice codecs, which afford a higher voice quality than can be obtained in current telephony systems, can be employed. These wideband codecs will allow IP phones to achieve better than toll quality voice. Today, LAN-based IP phones can deliver voice quality approaching toll quality. As VoIP solution deployments expand, it is expected that high-fidelity voice will become widespread.

IP telephones are initially appearing as a low-cost solution for small businesses that would otherwise require a key system or low-end PBX. The advantage of an IP telephone includes having one wiring system for both voice and data, better scalability as additional stations are added, and the ability to mix and match IP telephones from different manufacturers.

A prominent example of IP phone deployment is the Unified PBX (UnPBX) model. UnPBXs enable the upgrading of existing enterprise PBX systems, allowing additional users to be added to the system via a data network connection. This allows the use of a common, low-cost LAN in place of an often proprietary PBX network interface. Additional branch offices can be added in a simple manner by installing a homogeneous ethernet-based IP phone.

Though VoIP will cannibalize some of the telecommunications carriers' existing POTS (plain old telephone service) services, the carriers have determined that they must compete in this rapidly growing marketplace. The market projections cannot be ignored: according to IDC, by 2002 the Internet could carry 11 percent of U.S. and international long-distance traffic.

Over time, improvements in the Internet's QoS will precipitate change. Infrastructure improvements such as faster backbone links and switches, faster end-user connections such as xDSL and cable modems, and new protocols like RSVP and techniques like tag switching (which give priority to delay-sensitive data such as voice and video) will make their mark. In conjunction with improvements in quality, other factors will propel the introduction and success of IP phones into the consumer environment. These factors include the proliferation of home LANs, an increasingly sophisticated user base desirous of better voice quality and more data-convergent features, and, not the least, the creeping obsolescence of the traditional voice network.

Still, the current lack of consumer-oriented network infrastructure necessary to facilitate IP telephones dictates that at least in the near term, the primary field of deployment for these devices will occur in the business environment, where LANs and PBXs are the norm.

Source: http://www.telogy.com/ipphone/overview.html.

locate the computer of a friend with a similar Internet Phone capability and you "make a call," which means your computer sends a ringing signal to the other computer. If the computer is on and your friend is there, the computer will "ring" and your friend can activate Internet Phone and answer the call. If your friend is somewhere else or the computer is not active, the call does not go through.

Some parts of the country have added technology that provides an answering computer that dials a local telephone number to make the final call. In this case, the friend would not know the difference between an Internet call and a regular call, except for quality. The quality of an Internet call will tend to degrade faster due to greater delays than that provided by a long-distance provider.

Voice over the Internet Protocol
Unlike POTS, VoIP is message-switched (as explained in a later chapter). POTS is circuit-switched.

If we can make calls over the Internet, we can do the same over private networks. Although local area and wide area networks are discussed later, they are generally privately owned data networks that we can use for analog telephone calls, just like we can with the Internet. The objective is to reduce long-distance calling charges. A major problem is that managers want to use the telephone on the desk in the usual manner but avoid long-distance lines. This choice of IP versus tolled lines is done by the telephone switch within the organization. The PBX receives the dialed number and determines if it must connect with the POTS network, the long-distance network, or the IP network (public or private). To make the use of the private network viable, there must be a computer and PBX at the other end to operate the reverse way, making the final connection to the receiving telephone. Additionally, as discussed later, the network must not have delays in transmission that would make the conversation of unacceptably poor quality.

Case 2-1

Work of a Telephone Operator in the 1940s

Mrs. Eloise B. Brown
Operator #21
Selma, Alabama, Telephone Exchange, Southern Bell Telephone Company

INTRODUCTION

The television program "Laugh-In"® was popular in the 1970s. One of the skits they included starred comedian Lily Tomlin as a telephone operator (Ernesteen) who had her own view of customer service. Hopefully, you realize the skit was a farce and the success of the U.S. telephone system is due in no small part to those women who faithfully operated the manual switchboards and answered questions as part of their daily chores.

What follows are the memoirs of one such lady, the mother-in-law of one of the authors, who was a telephone operator in Selma, Alabama, during the 1940s, 50s, and 60s, while raising four sons and a daughter, and caring for a husband, the manager of an 8,000-acre farm. The story is not fictional; it is an accurate account of how she worked in the Bell System.

One of the authors grew up in the town of Boyce, in Clarke County, Virginia, population 346. He can still remember one of the town's wealthiest residents driving around to take up a collection for the telephone operator when her house burned to the ground. She was known and loved by all, and this was one way the community could show how important she was. This occurred in the late 1940s; the author's family telephone number was 49W; the telephone did not have a dial.

THE EARLY YEARS

I began work at the Selma Telephone Exchange of the Southern Bell Telephone Company in the mid 1940s, 60-plus years after it was founded. When I went to apply for a job, I walked in without an appointment. I just told them I was looking for a job with the Telephone Company. After taking a written and oral test, which the instructor graded at once, I was hired. Then I was trained on the old local board, which consisted of 12 or 14 sets of cords.

The board itself was made up of panels of numbers which repeated themselves for the length of the room. The board was like a desk. The bottom back part held the cords and switches; the top part had the numbers of all of the telephones in Selma.

In order to establish a connection for people to talk, you had to use a matching pair of cords: the back one to answer with and the front one to ring the number they were calling. The ringing was done with a key in front of the cords, which also had to match the cords. Some of the telephones were private lines (one home on a connection), and some were party lines (more than one home on a connection). If it was a two-party line, you would ring a certain way. If it was a four-party line, you would ring a different way.

There was a light for every telephone (private or party line). When the party picked up the telephone at home, it activated a light on the board, which was answered by an operator with one of the back cords, which we held in our hands at all times.

If I remember correctly, we used *J* and *W* and would ring once for *J* and twice for *W*. We used a black and orange sleeve to help us to remember what ring to use. If it was one ring *(J)*, the cord would be orange, and if *W* (black) turned over it meant two rings.

TRAINING AND EQUIPMENT

In the early years, operators were usually friends or relatives of those already working. They would come in and be shown what to do by their friend or relative. When they came in, it was without pay. Then, when an operator was needed, the friend or relative would tell the person, and she would be hired and then, of course, paid. No test was required for those with the informal training.

The official training of a new operator lasted 10 to 14 days; usually two people were trained at the same time. After the instructor explained a few things about the equipment, she assigned a headset and an operator number. My number was 21 for all the years I worked.

We each wore our own headset all the time, except when some repair was required. The headset attached to a triangular piece of metal that sat on your chest and the speaker came up to your mouth and was held around your neck by belting. An earpiece was held to your ears by two (heavy) wires that went over your head. The whole thing was pretty heavy to wear eight hours a day. These headsets were replaced with lighter and lighter ones over the years. Because the wires were always very fragile, we had specific instructions on how to wear the headset.

We also had specific instructions on how to relieve an operator when we went into the chair at the board to start our shift. There were two jacks on the board at each chair. As we went to relieve the operator, we put one plug into the jack on the left, coming into the position standing. The operator then unplugged her headset from the jack on the right, sliding out of the chair into a standing position. We then moved our plug from the jack into the right position, and we sat down as she stood in order to continue handling the call that was in progress. The keys were closed while this took place, which was a very short time, especially after we were trained.

One of the first things we did while training was to plug into a position with an experienced operator and listen to her and watch her cord handling, which was most important. Also, after answering a signal, we learned to say, "Thank you." Usually, about the second day, the trainee was allowed to answer a few signals which the instructor plugged in with her. After three or four days, if the trainee was doing OK, she was left by herself. The rest of the training period was mostly for us to gain speed in our work. During training, the first week the hours were usually 8:00 AM to 5:00 PM. The second week was split hours, 8:00 AM to 12:00 PM and 4:00 PM to 8:00 PM. After training, we would go to the bottom of the schedule. Telephone people worked according to seniority.

LONG DISTANCE

After about six months working on the local boards, most of the operators were trained for information or long distance (LD). I begged to be trained for all of it. My supervisors, Ruth Watkins and Louise Cox, obliged. The LD (toll) board was similar to the local board except smaller in size. Cords and ringing keys were in matched pairs as on the local board. When taking a LD call, we recorded the details on a ticket so it could be timed on a calculagraph. The details had to be perfect so your customer would get a correct number and be billed correctly. Also, the timing had to be watched: you had to stamp the ticket in and out to get the correct time the customer was billed for. Also, the time of the call was important because night and evening rates were different.

We had direct circuits to Atlanta, Birmingham, Mobile, and Montgomery. If calls were placed to these places, we rang on the first available circuit, always going from left to right. An operator answered, we passed the number to her, and she would ring it for us. But if we had a call to, say, Chicago, we would ring Birmingham and ask her to connect us with that city. This was referred to as a built-up switch, and we were responsible for clearing the line or circuit at the end of the conversation. To remember to do that, we attached a cord clip to the front cord, rang, and released the circuit. If the call was to a place beyond Chicago, it was a multiswitch and when the conversation ended we rang and stayed on the line until the Birmingham operator answered and said, "Clear to Muncie, Indiana."

All during this work, we overlapped with other work, cutting out of one call when necessary and getting back to the one waiting. On the local board in my earlier years, the work was less mental and more physical. At first, the board was not really overloaded or too high to reach while seated. When the U.S. Army Air Corps built Craig Field in Selma in the early 1940s, the city grew and so did that board. We sat in chairs that were like bar stools with rungs where our feet rested. As the board grew upward, we would literally stand on the rungs to reach the higher numbers.

As my expertise and curiosity grew, I wanted to be trained for the different positions that make up a telephone company office. We had a rate clerk for customer rates and for pay stations. The information operator intercepted when numbers had been changed or disconnected. The B board was for incoming and outgoing long distance. Then, wonder of wonders, a new telephone office was built, and we moved over to it. We then were all trained for long distance, which is much less physical and much more mental. The calculagraph was the timer for LD calls. It was not too difficult. The call tickets went through several changes during my time on LD. I mastered all the differences fairly well except the mark-sense card; very small marks were made with a pencil for each number. I almost despaired but finally I got the hang of that system, but not too much later they changed to a more comfortable way to write tickets for calls. I'm sure though that I would probably not know which way to go in a new office now.

I really enjoyed my years of work with the telephone company. It was a good place to work; I made a lot of friends over the years. I enjoyed fair pay and very good relations with almost all the management and workers. So now, I'm retired and getting better benefits than most people. I am a member of the Telephone Pioneers, and we still have a lot of good times together.

Eloise B.

Summary

This chapter began your venture into telecommunications using voice technology. Voice communication is not a new subject, but it is a vital subject in the arena of competition. Few organizations today can survive without their telephone system, whether it is individual lines from a local provider, Centrex, or an internal PBX. A major portion of the business expense of telecommunications is still voice communications. While the proportion of voice versus data is changing, the number of dollars in voice is far from insignificant.

Telecommunications managers must now plan, organize, staff, control, and coordinate voice communications in their organizations. Money can be saved with good management, but far more importantly, communications can be enhanced, leading to a competitive advantage. These managers must understand voice technologies to support their organization's business. Whether you evaluate Telco-provided or company-provided lines, voice mail, ACD, or WATS service, these technologies support communications with customers, suppliers, and even competitors.

Because there are many solutions to voice communications from many vendors, the implications of a given choice should be obvious. That is to say, when a manager chooses a specific technology from a specific vendor, the consequences will be long lived. The cost–benefit analysis in this situation will often concentrate on the technical aspects of the choices. Of equal if not greater import are the implications of the choices to the ongoing operation of the organization. If you choose a vendor with proprietary standards, you lock your organization into that vendor's view of the future. If, however, you take into account the architecture of the system into which the new application will fit, for example, the new PBX, you will ensure that it is interoperable with present capabilities and future additions. This gives you significant future alternatives, not found in all choices.

Key Terms

acoustic, *44*
amplitude, *44*
analog, *44*
area calling service, *38*
automatic call distribution (ACD), *56*
bandwidth, *44*
Bell System, *38*
central office (CO), *47*
Centrex, *56*
Centrex vs. PBX, *56*
CO switch, *50*
computer-telephony integration (CTI), *60*
customer premises equipment (CPE), *56*
dial tone, *50*
dialing, *50*
digital PBX, *59*
frequency, *44*
hertz, *44*
interactive voice response (IVR), *58*
intercom, *56*
interoffice communications, *40*

in-WATS, *55*
IP telephony, *62*
key instrument, *52*
least-cost routing, *56*
line conditioning, *55*
line termination equipment, *38*
local calling area, *38*
local loop, *38*
long distance, *49*
Morse code, *42*
multiple lines, *56*
network, *50*
off hook, *37*
personal identification number (PIN), *58*
plain old telephone system (POTS), *51*
private branch exchange (PBX), *56*
public switched telephone network, *46*
rotary dial telephone, *39*
signal-to-noise ratio, *52*
step-by-step (stepper) switch, *39*

telco, *54*
Telecommunications architecture, *33*
telecommunications trade-off considerations, *58*
telegraph, *41*
telephone, *42*
telephone number prefix, *33*
telephone service, *40*
toll, *49*
touchpad, *50*
TouchTone, *50*
trunk line, *47*
voice mail, *56*
Voice over the Internet Protocol (VoIP), *61*
voice spectrum, *45*
voice telephone, *37*
voltage, *52*
wide area telecommunications service (WATS), *55*
wiring frame, *47*

Discussion Questions

2.1. What is meant by **telecommunications architecture**?

2.2. What is the function of the central office? What happens if the central office is destroyed?

2.3. Why is it important to examine telecommunications even for the simple business?

2.4. What telecommunications alternatives exist today that were not available to Michael Johnson in the early 1950s?

2.5. Do you think the training methods of the Telco in the 1930s would work today? (Case 2.1)

2.6. JL&S chose an FX line to Colorado Springs. What other options would they have today?

2.7. What communications would you choose today for Michael's foot patrol?

Projects

2.1. Take your telephone directory and look up the service options available to a simple business (fixed service, measured service, multiparty). What services should Johnson Lighting install? Find the prices associated with each alternative and develop a price–performance matrix.

2.2. Call the 800 information number and find the telephone number for a PBX vendor, for example, Nortel, AT&T, Rolm, Hitachi. Call the vendor and order information on their products. Determine the PBX features and costs and compare these features and costs to your local Telco's Centrex service.

2.3. Determine the cost (tariff) and waiting time to get a 900 telephone number.

2.4. Determine the cost (tariff) and alternative features of getting WATS service.

2.5. Choose teams of five people and select a nontelecommunications project. Spend the next 48 hours working on the project without use of any voice telecommunications equipment or service. Was it possible to work without use of voice telecommunications equipment?

2.6. Visit the library and view issues of *Enterprise Communications* and *Computer Telephony* magazines to learn the strength of voice communications via the telephone in the conduct of business. List the development and products that are used with voice communications.

2.7. Go to several businesses in your city and find the percent of revenues that are spent on telecommunications. What type industry do you expect to have the largest budgets?

2.8. What are the pros and cons of running your own telephone company, for example, a PBX?

2.9. Who in the community provides bypass services?

Chapter **Three**

What Technologies and Media Do We Use for Voice and Data Systems?

CONTINUING CASE—PART 3

Johnson Lighting and Security Enters Data Communications

Business Growth Calls for Better Management

Johnson Lighting and Security (JL&S) had experienced significant growth over the past few years. Michael Johnson noted that a greater and greater amount of his time is required to keep records, attend to bookkeeping, and maintain inventory records. (See Figure 3.1.) Michael comes into the office on weekends to try to keep current on record keeping and correspondence. While he expected this extra work in the early days of his small company, and even found it exciting, the long hours and weekend work are taking their toll on Michael and his family.

Because of his expanded business and his policy of providing a high level of service, Michael has a very large amount of his assets tied up in inventory. His storage space is jammed with inventory since he tries to keep sufficient product on hand so he can compete on a service basis. His inventory is expensive, and he buys everything from his suppliers on credit. Presently, he has an opportunity to expand into an additional line of business. But because he has expended his existing credit, he realizes that a line of credit at the bank has become a necessity. He approaches his account executive, John Keller, at the bank where he has been using primarily a checking account and asks about such a line of credit.

John welcomes this new business and asks Michael to give him his current financial status in the form of income statements and balance sheets for the most recent four quarters and for the last year. Michael spends the weekend creating these statements from his manual bookkeeping system. Upon reviewing these statements and discussing with Michael how he generated the report, John

FIGURE 3.1   **Johnson's Manual Accounting System Was No Longer Adequate**

says that Johnson Lighting & Security has inadequate record keeping for its level of business activity. Johnson is stretching its ability to keep current on financial information. John says that for the bank to feel secure about Johnson Lighting & Security as an extended credit customer, Michael must either (a) hire a full-time bookkeeper, (b) retain an accounting firm to do this work, or (c) put his accounting system on a computer.

In the past, Michael had done part of the bookkeeping so he could be aware of what was happening. He also had used a part-time bookkeeper, Matilda Simmons. While the idea of employing an accounting firm has occurred to him, he does not want to obligate himself to the cost. Since he wants to continue to maintain personal control as well as minimize costs, he does not want to hire a full-time bookkeeper. With all of this in mind, Michael chooses to explore a computer-based accounting system. Because he is unfamiliar with anything other than his home-grown manual accounting system, he asks John for advice.

"The bank uses a Burroughs mainframe computer for its own systems," John tells Michael. "Since it has excess processing capability, especially after normal banking hours, the bank has created a service bureau that provides primarily accounting services to other firms. We would be happy to let you use this system, for a fee of course. I think you will find the system very friendly and easy to use. Let me take you down to the computer department and introduce you to our manager there. I think you will find doing business with our computer a pleasant experience."

John takes Michael to the computer department and introduces him to the manager of the service bureau, Nancy Rose. John leaves them to discuss the bank's services and heads for an appointment on the golf course.

Nancy explains to Michael that the bank's computer has an accounting system that is tailored for small businesses. It is designed for the user to enter all bills, invoices, deposits, and checks, and will create financial statements and keep a balanced set of accounts. She will have one of her accountants go over the forms for data entry with Michael. Michael will fill out the forms and deliver them to the bank each week. The bank's personnel will enter the data, process it, and produce output reports that

Michael can pick up at the bank. This way, Michael can continue to maintain his level of understanding and control over costs. The bank will maintain security of the forms, reports, and stored data, and provide the services outlined in the contract. With these services, Michael should have better financial information regularly with significantly less effort. In addition, the bank will be able to respond more quickly to his needs because he will have the financial data in the required form with no additional effort.

"Now, how do I learn to use the system?" asked Michael, a bit afraid that getting computer processing for his business might be a headache.

"Our account supervisor will show you the forms today, and I will arrange for you to attend a two-day class next week. You can start to fill out the forms right away if you wish, using the manuals we will give you, or you can wait for the classes. In any case, we will guarantee you will have the reports within 48 hours after you give us the forms for processing."

Michael chooses not to wait for the class and spends the weekend poring over the manuals and learning how to use the bank's system. Since all of the work is pencil and paper, he requires no new equipment. By Sunday afternoon, he has entered all of the accounting data for the first three months of the previous year. However, he realizes that he does need to be sure he did it right and decides to go to the training class. He shows up on Monday morning, after giving instructions to his crews, and begins the training.

By Tuesday afternoon, Michael is convinced he has entered the data correctly and understands the use of the system. He takes the forms he has completed to the bank just before the data entry department closes. (See Figure 3.2.) Michael picks up the reports Friday morning and hurries back to the office to study them. After an hour of poring over the reports, he realizes that, except for the five mistakes he made in writing down the figures, he has much better information than with his old system. He corrects the entries and returns to the bank to ask Nancy if they can enter the data and have new reports by the next morning. She says that because these are error corrections, they will give him the quick response, but normally it takes 48 hours to produce the reports.

FIGURE 3.2   **Johnson's Data Are Delivered to the Bank before Data Communications Are Added**

The next morning (Saturday) Michael gets the reports and balances them against his manual reports. The numbers still don't balance with his manual system, and he realizes that it is now the manual system that has the errors. With this success attained, he spends the afternoon showing his part-time bookkeeper, Matilda, how to enter the data. He goes over the entries for the first three months of the previous year and asks her to spend any extra time she has during the next weekend entering data for the rest of that year and then to continue working on the current year. He then wants her to go back and write down the data for the previous three years when she can find the time.

Matilda is somewhat apprehensive about dealing with a computer-based system and responds, "This is a lot of work, Mr. Johnson. Are you sure I can do it right?"

"Tell you what, Matilda. I will get you into a class at the bank this afternoon, and you can have the same training I had. I know that you can do it correctly with a little training. And I'll give you time-and-a-half for the weekend!"

When the current year's data are entered, checked, and corrected, Michael takes the financial reports to the bank and discusses a line of credit with John. John easily finds from the reports that Michael is a good credit risk and makes arrangements for Michael to have the money he wants as a line of credit. Michael leaves the bank with the financial backing that will allow him to expand his business. Even more important is his new computer-based accounting system that frees his weekends and gives him better information.

In time, Matilda entered all of the data for the current and previous four years. Michael uses the bank's system for several months with the handwritten forms and a lot of travel back and forth to the bank. He then asks Nancy if it would be possible to enter the data and print out the reports at his office to eliminate the manual effort,

FIGURE 3.3 Hardcopy Terminal and Video Terminal

Source: Mary E. S. Loomis, *Data Communications*

travel expense, and time delays. Nancy explains that the bank will lease JL&S a DECWriter® terminal (see Figure 3.3) on which Michael can enter the data directly, give a command for processing, and receive his weekly reports on demand. (A DECWriter is a 30-characters-per-second, typewriter-like terminal that can be used as a remote terminal to a computer.) Nancy explains that Michael will need a telephone line and modem for the equipment.

"What is a modem?" asks Michael.

"A modem stands for MOdulator-DEModulator. (See Figure 3.4.) It is a piece of equipment that converts the digital codes of the DECWriter terminal to audible tones that can be carried by the voice telephone system. You will need one installed at your business, and we have one at this end. You will make a telephone call and connect your modem-terminal when you hear our computer answer the call."

"One thing more, Michael: the bank's computer is unavailable on Sundays as that is the only time we can do maintenance on the equipment. Also, our experience shows that we have equipment interruptions for about two hours a week. This means that on some occasions, you will not be able to use

FIGURE 3.4 **AT&T Dataphone 2112 Direct Connection Modem**

Courtesy of AT&T

the computer exactly when you want it. Also, the computer will be very busy at the end of the month, so it may run a bit slow."

"Thanks. I am glad you told me that. I have trained my part-time bookkeeper to enter data for me and print reports, so if I am called away for business, there is someone to be sure the system works."

"That's a good idea, Michael. Many people forget that adding a computer increases your risk just a little because it means that if either the computer, the people who use it, or the telecommunications lines are not available, the system is not available."

Michael leased a DECWriter from the bank and carried it to his office in the back of one of his installation trucks. He called his local Telco representative, Harry Peterson, and discussed leasing a modem. Harry tells him he can lease an acoustic coupler and modem, either a Bell Model 103A that works at 300 baud or a Bell Model 205B, a 1200-bits-per-second modem. The model 103A is $100 per month, and the Model 205B is $300 per month. (This is the early 1970s.) Because Michael does not know what a baud is or what difference speed will make, and since 300 of anything sounds like a lot, he leases the 300 baud modem. Harry gets

the acoustic coupler modem installed, uses one of Johnson's phone lines, and shows Michael how to make the connection to the bank's computer. (See Figure 3.5.) Since Michael doesn't expect to use the DECWriter a lot during business hours, thereby tying up the phone line, he does not think he will need an additional phone line for the terminal. He begins to use the new equipment, getting Matilda to enter the data each day. He finds he can get reports almost anytime he wants and realizes he has even better record keeping with this system. (See Figure 3.6.) At the end of the month, he sees the bills for the modem, DECWriter, and computer time and agrees that, although the total cost is more than he expected, the books have never been in better shape and he can spend the weekend at his lake cabin with his family—for the first time in two years. In addition, Michael finds that he can stay on top of his business better and with less effort. One discovery due to more current information is that his large inventory is costing more than the additional incremental customer service is worth. Michael discovered to his chagrin that his inventory turnover ratio was not within an acceptable range. By reducing this inventory, and thus improving inventory turnover, he more than offsets the cost of the service bureau.

FIGURE 3.5   **Johnson Lighting & Security Data Communications**

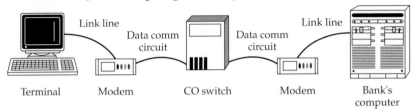

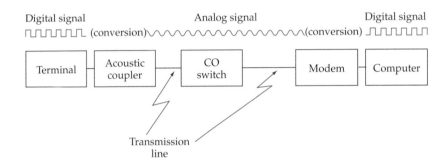

FIGURE 3.6   **Johnson's Data Processing Connection to the Bank**

Stepping back from Michael and his day-to-day problems for just a moment, we see a small business person discover that technology has influenced the operation of his business. Thus, we come again to the goal of this book, of telecommunications, and of technology in general: the purpose of any technology is to solve a business problem or capitalize on an opportunity.

As Michael becomes more familiar with the accounting system, he begins to experiment with the computer and the program. He finds a "what-if" feature where he can temporarily change values and see the financial effect of the change. He is considering buying another truck, so he uses the program to see what the added expenses will do to his profit position, taking into account that his crews could respond more quickly to new clients as well as present customers. He also finds that printing out reports at 300 baud (which we will find is about 30 characters per second, just like the speed of the DECWriter) is a bit slow. He has two ways around this problem: (1) buy more expensive equipment or (2) print summary reports most of the time and only print the long reports at the service bureau. Opting for printing summary reports, he finds that the DECWriter spends less time connected to the phone line. He prints out full reports at the service bureau only at the end of each month and picks them up two days later.

The bank has other programs in addition to accounting, and Michael finds several that would be of use to him at his Denver office. One program would help schedule the guard patrols at the Colorado Springs office. He leases another DECWriter and acoustic coupler-modem, placing them at the Colorado Springs office, and arranges to use the additional programs. Since the bank has a branch office in Colorado Springs, Johnson Lighting does not have to use the company's leased FX line to Denver to dial up the computer, but can dial up a local Colorado Springs line for connection. Michael sends the senior guard at the Colorado Springs facility to a training class to learn to use the terminal to input data and print reports and guard schedules. Since the program stores anticipated schedules as well as actual tours of patrol, Michael can call up the reports at his office to see how well his guards are meeting their schedules.

With experience at the Denver and Colorado Springs offices, Michael starts to use the terminals to send data between the offices. At first, one office would call the computer and leave messages and data in a file. The other office would dial into the computer and print the file. One day, a new guard mistakenly called the Denver office line on which the DECWriter was attached. Not realizing what was happening, Matilda connected the modem to the line, and the guard started to type data into his DECWriter and out on the Denver DECWriter, with no use, or charge, of the computer. Michael quickly realized the value of this form of data and message sending and wrote up instructions for using the system. He called Harry at the Telco and asked if there was anything special they should be doing when they connected the two terminals and Harry said that they might want to lease punched paper tape machines and input the data off-line before sending it. This way, they could be sure the data were correct before sending them to the other office. Michael leased two punch machines and took one to Colorado Springs. Both offices could enter data and messages and check them before sending to the other office or before connecting to the computer. Since the bank charges for computer connect time as well as for computer processing time, the cost of using the computer decreases with less connect time.

By establishing the data communications link to the bank's bureau, Michael has entered the domain of teleprocessing. Teleprocessing is the processing of data at a distant or remote location by using data communications circuits. These circuits and the system configuration are shown in Figure 3.7. The basic equipment is shown as well as the concept of conversion of digital-to-analog signals by the modems. (See Figure 3.5.) The telephone line is connected to the bank exactly like the voice link (indeed, it is the same line or circuit).

In the process of creating this network configuration, Michael has, again, established an ad hoc, piecemeal architecture. Like many organizations, Michael has let the immediate problem and its solution dictate how he does business as opposed to deciding on a basic business strategy and a corresponding network architecture. This is typical of organizations that have built so-called legacy networks (terminals connected to computers via modems and multiplexers). Today, organizations are faced with many more choices, such as different kinds of connectivity from the Telcos and alternate providers. We will discuss the importance of systems and network architectures later.

FIGURE 3.7
JL&S's
Teleprocessing
Network

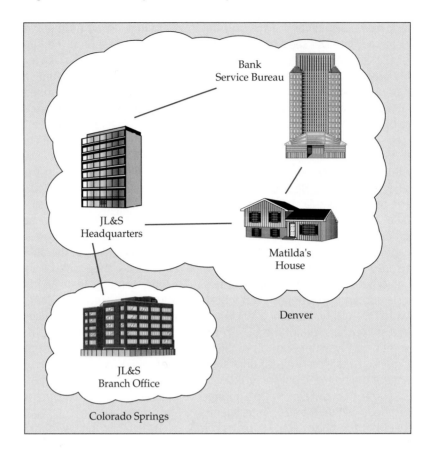

INTRODUCTION

In this chapter, we introduce basic telecommunications technology in the form of voice communications and its media. All transmission must be carried by some **medium**, whether it be copper, glass, or radio or light waves in space. Each has a **capacity** and each has a susceptibility to noise. [Although much of the technology may seem outdated, to understand the value of the technology we use today one should understand the historical background.]

In this chapter, we also continue the discussion of the components of the communications model presented in Chapter 1. In Chapter 2, we discussed the nature of the signals from sender to receiver. Here, we concentrate on the channel between sender and receiver and the media used therein.

When we discuss voice transmission in this chapter, the emphasis is on analog. However, today most voice transmissions use some digital circuits. We will discuss digital technology in Chapter 4 and concentrate on analog concepts here. Thus, the mixing of analog and digital subjects and then their separation for explanation is intentional. We also mix analog and digital modes while describing a technology instead of separating all of the analog technology into one chapter and all of the digital technology into another chapter.

Technology Note 3–1
Vehicle Radio

The **radio** system employs electromagnetic radiation for wireless transmission of communications, whereas the telephone of the era uses twisted-pair copper wires. Michael has a base station with a transmitter-receiver. The car has a similar transmitter-receiver in the trunk of the vehicle. The microphone changes the acoustic energy of sound waves into analog (low frequency) electrical energy. The radio transmitter adds the low frequency to a high-frequency carrier radio frequency for transmission. The receiver reverses this process by subtracting out the carrier frequency and converting the electrical energy to acoustic energy in the form of sound waves in the earpiece.

ALTERNATE TRANSMISSION TECHNOLOGIES AND MEDIA

Circuit versus Channel

circuit
The path followed by a signal.

channel
All or a part of a circuit.

A communications **circuit** is a path over which a signal can travel. Circuits are generally thought of as something physical, like wire or a radio wave. A **channel** is the actual path for the signal and may occupy the total circuit or be a portion of it. Thus, a TV cable is a circuit (physical coaxial cable) and has many channels for the TV channels. Some media include paths in both directions, either simultaneously or in one direction at a time. A circuit for a voice channel can be established using several media. We discuss each medium fully as we progress through the book, but it is prudent to show the alternative media available at this point.

Electrical

electrical
Using direct or alternating current to carry a signal on a conductive medium.

Twisted-pair wire is the simplest circuit for carrying an electrical signal; it is a pair of wires, lightly twisted to reduce noise. The other electrical circuit, coaxial cables, are logically the same as twisted-pair wire except one (ground) wire surrounds the second wire.

Electromagnetic[1]

electromagnetic
Using rapidly varying (high-frequency) current to carry another signal.

Electromagnetic circuits use radio in some form. **Microwave radio** channel circuits are provided over radio channels between line-of-sight transmitters and receivers. **Satellite** circuits are the same as microwave channels except that the signal is received, repeated, and forwarded to the receiving unit by a receiver-transmitter (satellite transponder) located in space. **Omnidirectional radio** systems use transmitters that radiate (transmit) in all directions.

Light (Photonic)

photonic
Light is the data carrier on a transparent medium.

Infrared systems use space as the medium and light as the carrier. Fiber optic cable uses glass or plastic as the medium and light waves as the carrier. Each medium

---

[1] Alternating current electricity, radio waves, and light are all electromagnetic waves. We differentiate them here to indicate that electromagnetic waves are electrical in nature while photonic waves are not electrical in nature. This is significant when it comes to noise, interference, crosstalk, and splicing medium.

Technology Note   3–2
Circuits and Pricing

WATS (wide area telecommunications service) offers bulk pricing for high-volume telephone service. It involves a fixed charge for a specified number of calling hours per month and a variable charge for each minute called, with the result of a lower total cost. The first zone for WATS is inside the state in which the organization is located. The second zone is the group of states surrounding the home state. There are a total of five classes of WATS service, level 5 service including the entire United States.

A special case of WATS is in-WATS, where the receiver of the call pays the charge. This is the familiar 800 area code. When the caller places a call, such as 1(800)321–1223, a switch redials the real telephone number and the receiver pays the charges.

1	(Direct distance dialing)
800 or 888	(In-WATS area code)
321	(Prefix = central office exchange)
1223	(Extension)

Foreign exchange (FX) leased line—In this case, a company leases a line from a local Telco or long distance carrier, or both, from the firm's location to the switch of a distant central office. Thus, when the user picks up his phone, he receives a dial tone of the distant central office, avoiding a long-distance charge. Physically, the Telco permanently makes connections through the two central offices to allow the circuit to appear as a direct line from one CO to the leaser's instrument.

Trunks between COs—When a caller connected to his local Telco's central office wishes to talk with a person connected to another central office, the call goes over a trunk line between the two facilities. The trunk may be any medium and may be free or toll, depending on whether the central offices are in the same local calling areas.

Information Window   3–1

Bandwidth is the information-carrying capacity of a channel.

Analog bandwidth is a range of frequencies and is measured in hertz. For example, the bandwidth of the voice spectrum of a telephone channel is 2,700 Hz. Because this is not a high bandwidth, modems have a limited analog bandwidth to encode with digital information, making 56 Kbps an apparent upper limit at this time on a circuit with an inherent analog bandwidth of 1 MHZ.

Digital bandwidth is measured in bits per second.

We speak of a digital channel's speed, meaning its bandwidth. The greater the bandwidth, the greater the speed in delivering a specified amount of data. The data don't travel faster; the amount of data per unit of time is increased.

has different characteristics and capacity. We discuss photonic media later as they are used primarily as data communications and control systems.

WIRED MEDIA AND TECHNOLOGIES

Twisted-Pair

A circuit of *copper wires* is a loop with a single wire going from the sender to the receiver and back. This single loop is seen as a pair of wires, but a complete loop out and back is required for electrical conductivity.[2] If the pair of wires is free from electromagnetic interference, it can carry a frequency bandwidth of about 1 megahertz analog. Thus, a telephone system copper wire circuit would seem to be able to carry a very large number of analog conversations. Noise, however, is a problem that affects the capacity of copper wire circuits, especially as distance increases. One primary method of reducing susceptibility to noise occurring in the form of injected, unwanted electrical signals is to twist the wire, producing the popular term **twisted-pair.** The twisting causes cancellation of the injected signal. (See Figure 3.8.) In other words, the noise signal is induced onto portions of wires that twisting has placed in reverse order, canceling the noise signals because they are out of phase with each other. This procedure also prevents the copper pair from radiating signals that would cause interference with nearby circuits.

We constantly encounter wires carrying electrical current. The wire on the hair dryer we use, the speaker wires on the stereo, the toaster cord, the lamp cord, the long cord on the vacuum cleaner, the power cord on the television, and the cord on the clothes washer, dryer, and iron are just a few. All but one of these carry current at 110–220 volts potential and result in electrical power being conveyed to a device to do work. The amount of power in the devices mentioned ranges from 2 watts for the stereo speakers, to 60–100 watts for the lamp, 1,200 watts for the hair dryer, and 5,000 watts for the electric clothes dryer. These wires, except for those of the stereo speakers, carry sizeable amounts of electrical power, at dangerous voltage levels.

Telecommunications and data communications circuits carry information via electrical voltage and current. The levels of voltage and current in the circuit, however, are very small compared with power devices in the home. The voltage used by communications networks is in the range of 0 to ± 20 volts. This is the same voltage range used by the telephone system except there is a 90-volt ringing voltage. These circuits carry micro- to milliamperes of current and convey micro- to milliwatts of power. This is the same *voltage range* as a stereo speaker system and

twisted-pair copper wire
The most-used, lowest-cost medium.

Media
Twisted-pair
  copper
Coaxial cable
Radio
  Microwave
  Satellite
  Omni-
  directional Photonic
  Fiber optic
  Infrared

Information Window   3–2
What to Watch Out for after the Hurricane

Going outside after a storm often reveals a mess. There may be fallen wires on the ground. The question is, *which wires are dangerous?* If you look at the shape of the wire and the color of insulation, you can reduce your risk of touching the wrong one.

First, cable TV wires are coaxial cable; they are round single wires and the insulation is black. These are not dangerous because the shielding under the insulation is grounded. Next, the UTP of the telephone local loop have black insulation and are flattened single round cables. They are not dangerous. Next are the power lines from the

transformer on the utility pole to the residence or office. The bundle here is generally two black insulated round wires, about the size of your thumb, and a non-insulated aluminum wire. While the voltage can be 220 Vac, leave them alone because they can be fatal.

Finally, the most dangerous are the high-voltage lines that run through the neighborhood. They can carry voltages from 7 kV to 25 kV and, if still active, will turn you into a crispy critter; that is, they will kill you quickly. These have *no* insulation; they are silver (aluminum) wires about the size of your finger and are deadly.

---

[2] The twisted-wire circuit is, as noted, a single wire making a complete loop. One leg of the loop can be an earth path, as in the telegraph. For the telephone, the loop is interrupted with each switch. The use of wire instead of the earth return path has less attenuation and lower noise, thus the use of twisted pair.

even an automobile battery (pre-42 volt adoption). The point is that telecommunications circuits have the same voltage and current characteristics as devices in the home, but the voltage level is not dangerous. In the home, the danger of having too much power in a given wire (too many devices plugged into one extension cord) always exists. Such a condition can cause the wire to overheat and eventually can

Technology Note   3–3
Stranded versus Solid Wires and Cables

Electrical wires (see Figure 3.8), by themselves or grouped in a cable, can be either solid material or stranded (see Figure 3.9). **Solid wire** is a single thread of wire the size, or gauge, stated. Solid wire is the least expensive to make, but its stiffness increases as its size increases. For our purposes, a solid wire is made as a pair of wires, with each wire covered by insulation and the

wire group surrounded by an insulation jacket. You find solid wire used where it is handled only once and carries sizeable amounts of currents. An example is the wiring in the walls of a home or office. This wire, often called romex, consists of two solid 10- to 14-gauge conductors (0.064 to 0.102 inch, or 1.63 to 2.59 mm in diameter) for carrying high currents and a third, smaller solid wire

FIGURE 3.8   **Some Wire/Cable Types**

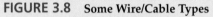

Single conductor wire   Twisted pair

Multiple conductors

Shielded twisted-pairs

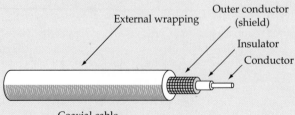

External wrapping   Outer conductor (shield)

Insulator
Conductor

Coaxial cable

Technology Note (*Continued*)   3–3
Stranded versus Solid Wires and Cables

for a system ground. **Stranded wire** is a single wire that is composed of a group of smaller solid wires. The objective of stranding is to make the wire flexible and easy to handle. All of the cords attached to appliances are stranded wire. The power cord going to a small stereo system is a pair of 18-gauge wires composed of nineteen, 31-gauge, twisted strands (each 0.007 inch or 0.227 mm in diameter). A heavier power or extension cord might be 14-gauge stranded wire, composed of nineteen, 26-gauge strands (each 0.047 inch or 0.404 mm in diameter). Stranded wire and solid wire of the same gauge are electrically equivalent. Some wires are also shielded to reduce electromagnetic interference. **Shielding** is a protective enclosure that surrounds a transmission medium. It is designed to protect and to minimize electromagnetic leakage and interference.

FIGURE 3.9 **Solid and Stranded Wire with Identical Capacities**

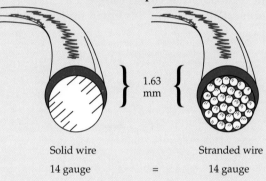

Solid wire		Stranded wire
14 gauge	=	14 gauge

1.63 mm

Technology Note   3–4
Voltage and Current

Voltage is like the water pressure in a garden hose. The greater the pressure, the harder the water will be forced out of the nozzle. Current, on the other hand, is like the amount of water coming out of the hose. High pressure or voltage will perform certain tasks well, such as shooting a small water stream a long distance or creating a spark across an automobile spark plug. A large volume of water or current will perform a totally different task, such as quickly filling a swimming pool or charging an automobile battery. Taken together, voltage and current produce power, defined as the ability to do work. For the home, you need a sizeable water pressure and volume of flow to get the water sprinkler to work. For the hair dryer, you also need a sizeable voltage (120 volts) and current (10 amperes) to produce the 1200 watts of heat (power). But for data communications, we work in the 0 to ± 20 volt range, with milliamperes of current to work at the 1 milliwatt power level with good results. When the voltage level diminishes over a long distance, we amplify it back to the original level (like a water pump would) and send it on its way.

result in a fire. Communications circuits, on the other hand, are designed to transmit low voltage over a long distance with the absence or minimum of noise.

Looking Ahead—xDSL

Unshielded twisted pair (UTP) is still a valuable resource. Its native analog bandwidth is about one megahertz, although POTS uses only a small part of that. Since there is UTP running from the central office to nearly every home and office in developed countries, the opportunity is present to use the greater analog bandwidth to create wide digital bandwidth. That's what **digital subscriber line (DSL)** does. DSL, in several forms, takes advantage of the total bandwidth of the circuit and gives great digital bandwidth, often with several channels in that bandwidth.

As is discussed later, the first mode of DSL is **integrated services digital network (ISDN)** or digital telephone. By placing ISDN technology on each end on the local loop, we can turn the analog circuit into a digital multichannel telephone capability and provide two channels for voice or computer connectivity and one for data and control.

The next capability involves different technology and creates a broader digital bandwidth called xDSL. In this environment, three channels are created, one for

digital subscriber line
Allows more of the POTS bandwidth to be used.

The Real World   3–1

By the year 2005, industry analyst Gartner predicts that *13 million* people in the United States will be connected by cable modem and *10 million* in the United States will be connected by DSL services.

Source: AT&T ad in *Fortune*, October 9, 2000.

The Real World   3–2

HomePortal™ 1500 Residential Gateway supports ADSL speeds of up to 8 megabits per second (Mbps) when used in conjunction with ADSL service of the same rate. This model combines a DSL modem, router, hub, firewall, and Web console to turn your existing phone lines into a secure, high-speed home network.

Source: http://www.2wire.com/products/products.asp.

The Real World   3–3

Local telephone companies currently offer residential ISDN services that provide connection speeds up to 128 Kbps and they are looking to digital subscriber line (DSL) technologies that can provide downstream speeds beyond 1.5 Mbps. Other alternatives include fast downstream data connections from direct broadcast satellite (DBS), fixed wireless providers, and, of course, high-speed cable modems.

Source: http://www.cabledatacomnews.com/cmic/cmic1.html.

full-time telephone and two for data transport, such as Internet access. One data channel is generally slow-speed upstream and the other is for fast-speed downstream. We discuss the particulars later, but this technology allows a resource that is in place to be used in competition with high-speed cable modem access to the Internet and multiple voice and data channels to a **small or home office (SOHO).**

Dealing with Noise

The total circuit from your telephone instrument to the receiver consists of a number of parts with connections and switches at each junction. The combination of long lines and connections makes the circuit susceptible to noise and loss of signal strength. For these reasons, the phone companies must keep the lines and switches of good quality to make analog signal transmission acceptable.

Circuits, especially metal wires, that are not protected from their environment are susceptible to noise from a variety of sources. Some environments are cleaner than others, but all are potential sources of error-producing noise. One of the greatest sources of noise inside a residence is the induction motor in refrigerators and air conditioners. For this reason, wire-pairs are twisted, and coaxial cables and some twisted-pairs use an outer, shielded covering. (See Figure 3.10.)

Wire circuits can act as interference transmitters as well as receivers. As the frequency of the signal in the circuit increases, the circuit tends to radiate the signal. Twisting the wire-pair reduces the effect of this transmission, as does twisting the other wires that are potential receivers. It is the tendency of circuits to become radiators or transmitters that limits the frequency the circuit can pass, as well as increasing **attenuation.** Thus, as analog frequencies go above 1 MHz, shielding *may* have to be used around the wire to meet **FCC (Federal Communications Commission)** standards of **RFI (radio frequency interference)** or **EMI (electromagnetic interference).**

Figure 3.11 shows three effects taking place in an analog environment: attenuation of a signal over distance, noise on the medium, and amplification of

Voltage levels in telecommunications and computer equipment, except for monitors and power supplies, are not generally dangerous.

Current is what kills.

Telephone voltages are safe except for the 90-volt ringing voltage.

noise
Any unwanted, detectable signal that coexists with the intended signal.

FIGURE 3.10
Cable Shielding Guide

How much shielding is right for your environment:

Unshielded: Conductors are tinned, so that they're easier to solder, and so they're more resistant to error-causing oxidation. Use in quiet offices where there is little electrical interference.

Single Shield: Use single copper braid for low-frequency devices such as terminals. Use single foil shield with printers and other parallel devices in "low-noise" environments.

Double Shield— Foil and Braid: Mylar-backed aluminum foil protects against high-frequency noise and tinned copper braid blocks low-frequency noise. Together they provide 100% data protection in very noisy offices.

Individually Shielded Pair: Each pair of conductors has its own mylar/ aluminum foil shield. Use in environments where there is excessive interference from heavy-duty equipment.

FIGURE 3.11   Three Effects in Analog Environment

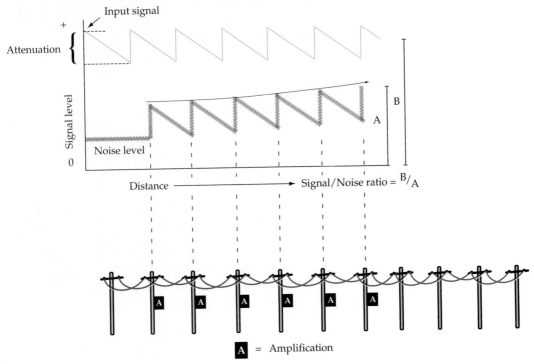

signal attenuation
The loss of signal strength over distance or through distortion.

signals to keep them at the desired level. Since the noise is amplified along with the desired signal, and may increase relatively due to noise in the **amplifier,** the signal-to-noise ratio will tend to deteriorate with distance and repeating amplifiers.

Coaxial Cable

coaxial cable (coax)
What you get cable TV on.

A **coaxial cable** is similar to a pair of copper wires with the exception that one wire is a braided or solid sheath that encompasses (shields) the other wire. Insulation material separates the two wires, the center wire is at high signal level, and the shield wire is at ground (zero volts) potential. The grounding of the outer shielding wire means that interference cannot penetrate the coaxial cable and induce noise onto the circuit. Shielded/coaxial cables also do not radiate signals to other circuits as nonshielded circuits may. Using a coaxial cable provides a much larger analog bandwidth and digital transmission speed. The cable does cost significantly more, however, and the signal attenuation per mile is much greater than twisted-pair circuits. Tables 3.1 and 3.2 show characteristics of various media.

CATV
Cable or community television using coaxial cable is the way over 65 million homes in the United States receive television.

Coaxial cables became increasingly common through their use in **cable television (CATV),** which sends 50 or more full-color television channels to both homes and offices. The CATV coaxial cable that extends from the sending station to the receiving areas uses a moderately large diameter solid aluminum shielding. This distribution cable is more expensive due to materials but provides a larger bandwidth and lower signal attenuation. Special connections are used to tap into the cable

TABLE 3.1
Bandwidth and Speed of Telecommunications Media

Circuit Media	Analog Bandwidth (MHz)
Twisted-pair	1
Coaxial cable	350, 500, and 750
Microwave radio	30 (1 channel)
Satellite radio	6 (per channel)
Omni-radio	0.010 AM, 0.2 FM
Television	6 (per channel)
Telephone channel	0.004

TABLE 3.2
Characteristics of Circuit Media

Wire
  1. 22–26 gauge copper
  2. Low bandwidth
  3. Used for virtually all local loops
  4. Low installation cost
  5. Susceptible to noise
Coaxial Cable
  1. Ground is shielded (immune to interference)
  2. Bandwidth of 350 MHz, 500 MHz, 750 MHz
  3. Up to 10,800 voice conversations
  4. Amplifiers every mile
  5. 50–100 analog TV channels/cable
  6. Cable tapped easily; low to medium security
Microwave Radio Terminal
  1. 4–28 GHz frequency range
  2. Up to 6,000 voice circuits in a 30-MHz-wide channel
  3. Line of sight—20–30 miles between towers
  4. Mostly used for analog
  5. Subject to interference by rain
  6. Must have FCC license, regulated
  7. No right-of-way permit required; great for building-to-building within city
Satellite Radio
  1. Uplink and downlink each 22,300 miles (geosynchronous orbit)
  2. Footprint is one-third of earth
  3. Propagation delay = 44,600 miles/186K mps = .2398 second
  4. Most common carriers have left satellite for terrestrial
  5. Only security is encryption
Omni-Directional Radio
  1. Wireless—replaces wires and cables
  2. Passes thru walls
  3. Very localized
  4. Easy to install; easy to move
Infrared (Photonic)
  1. Within a set of walls (room)
  2. Omnidirectional
  3. Low speed
  4. Easy to install; easy to move
  5. Not secure
  6. Very localized
Fiber Optic Cables
  1. Made of glass or plastic
  2. Difficult to splice
  3. Secure due to #3 & #4
  4. Very high speed
  5. Unidirectional strand
  6. Difficult to split signal
  7. Immune to RFI, EMI, crosstalk
  8. Most expensive, greatest bandwidth = low $/bit

Information Window   3–3
AT&T Wireless

John Zeglis of AT&T Wireless Group (established in 1994; went public in 2000 as a tracking stock) stated that they have 13.5 million subscribers. In mid-2000 AT&T had a cable footprint covering one-third of the United States and 80 million wired customers.

The Real World   3–4
Set-Top Boxes Could Control Your Life

It's more than a channel changer—utility companies are developing energy management service through a TV set-top box. A pilot program offered by Pacific Gas & Electric, TCI, and Microsoft allows customers to program the system to run the dishwasher or turn on the pool cleaning system during off-peak hours to conserve energy. The system is being designed to offer two-way communications, and customers will be able to pay their bills electronically. If the system is successful, PG&E may license it to other utilities.

Source: *Investor's Business Daily.*

with smaller coaxial cables[3] that run to individual residences or offices. As these coaxial networks spread out over cities, the potential for their use as private telecommunications circuits rises. For example, an organization could rent a part of the bandwidth to send signals from one point to another (we will discuss this later under the subject of frequency division multiplexing). The signal propagates to all parts of the network, but only the renting organization has access to it. Presently, such use is limited.

Cable Modem for Internet Access

Probably nothing has captured the imagination of people like the Internet and the World Wide Web. We discuss the Internet in more detail in Chapter 9. Next we present a discussion of cable modems for Internet access.

When computers were first introduced in the home, the only external access was via modems to **electronic bulletin board systems (BBS).** These electronic bulletin boards were other computers set up to hold shareable programs and information in small DOS files. Once the Internet and its graphical access through the WWW and the browser became popular, far more bandwidth was required to download the Windows files, text pages, and graphics. Text requires little bandwidth, while graphics and large files are bandwidth hogs. Where a 2,400 **baud** modem was sufficient for a BBS, the Internet requires 100 times that for the high graphical content.

baud
A measure of the number of analog signal changes per second.

[3] The coaxial cables that distribute signals to the neighborhood are generally silver and 1 inch in diameter. The standard types are 550 MHz and 750 MHz. The range to 50 MHz is presently unused, but will likely be used for reverse channel.

The Internet was not very interesting in the beginning. It took the "killer application" of the World Wide Web to make a difference. This, however, created a significant demand for high bandwidth access.

The introduction of cable modems for Internet access was quite natural because, as of mid-2000, of the 105 million homes in North America that are passed by CATV coaxial cable, more than 75 million were cable TV subscribers. Since one in two homes in the United States now had a microcomputer, a ready market existed with the addition of the modem and the digital infrastructure.

Cable modem technology includes a box that replaces or supplements the computer's modem. The allocation of one or more channels for upload and download of data is provided by the CATV company. In the primary format, the cable provider requires use of a standard modem and POTS line for data upload since the bandwidth requirement is small and allocates a common, "digital" channel for download. The download channel is simply an analog television channel that carries all of the data in digital format. Like the telephone modem, the cable modem uses an analog carrier onto which digital data are encoded. Thus, one logs onto the Internet with a standard modem and POTS line and receives the pages requested on the download channel. A single CATV 6 MHz channel converts to a digital bandwidth of 27 Mbps. This is enough to carry three **National Television Standards Committee** TV channels, one HDTV and one NTSC channel, or Internet traffic. A cable modem and internal network interface card work at speeds of 10 Mbps, much like a local area network at work. Much more on this in later chapters.

NTSC is the standard for the television sets from 1937–2006, then replaced by HDTV.

The actual speed on a cable modem system is dependent on the inherent speed of the download channel and the number of users online, because users *share* this bandwidth. While the speed is superior to a standard modem, sometimes 100 times faster, users may experience much less bandwidth during times of heavy use. Cable modem bandwidth is shared by up to 5,000 users, on an on-demand basis. Although several hundreds (or thousands) of users may be active, if a request occurs during a lull, very high bandwidth will be available.

Full duplex is what makes the telephone so easy to use.

Full duplex systems allocate an upload channel, generally in a lower frequency, for digital uploads. This eliminates the need for POTS and a standard modem. This upload channel is generally much slower than the download channel.

Broadband means high speed or wide bandwidth.

Baseband uses all the bandwidth of a circuit as one channel.

Fiber Optic Cable

Two media use light as the data-carrying mechanism: the space medium for infrared signals (see below) and fiber optic strands. We will now discuss a new medium, **fiber optic cable,** that exists primarily for digital data.[4] Optical fiber can be used in both the analog **broadband**[5] and digital **baseband**[6] modes, but in the telecommunications arena it is used almost exclusively in the baseband mode for digital communications. **Fiber optic circuits** are one-way communications paths, with a light source (laser or light-emitting diode) at one end that pulses on and off and a light detector at the other end. The medium is a very thin, high-quality glass or plastic fiber, wrapped with protective coverings (see Figure 3.12). The speed of communications is extremely high, potentially

Fiber optic cables are made up of very small one-way glass strands that have the greatest bandwidth of any media used.

---

[4] Two uses of fiber optic cable you will find close to home are for (1) cable television distribution cables and (2) exchange-to-exchange telephone service. In the former, the glass medium is used in an analog mode where the television signal is modulated onto (carried by) the analog carrier wave. In the latter, the phone companies use a digital form.

[5] Transmission equipment and media that can support a wide range of electromagnetic or photonic frequencies. Generally meaning an analog path that is frequency division multiplexed to create several channels.

[6] A narrow band circuit, generally not subdivided into channels. Often describing a digital circuit.

FIGURE 3.12
Fiber Optics

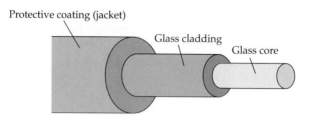

Protective coating (jacket)

Glass cladding

Glass core

Fiber optic cable

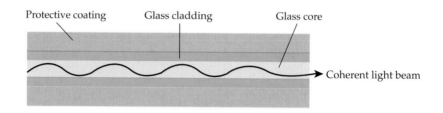

Protective coating   Glass cladding   Glass core

→ Coherent light beam

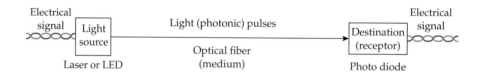

Electrical signal — Light source — Light (photonic) pulses — Destination (receptor) — Electrical signal

Laser or LED   Optical fiber (medium)   Photo diode

one terabit per second, and the circuit is impervious to electromagnetic noise. Since this medium uses light as opposed to electrical signals, it neither radiates nor receives electromagnetic interference. **Crosstalk** (radiation of signals from one circuit to another) from cable to cable that occurs in twisted-pair circuits is nonexistent. As noted in advertisements for long-distance telephone carrier services, fiber optic circuits are being installed wherever possible, often replacing microwave and satellite circuits, to improve transmission quality and bandwidth.

Circuits that use fiber optic capabilities often begin and end with some other media. For example, if you have a computer or terminal on a network that uses optical fiber as the medium, the signals originate as electrical pulses. They would then be passed as parallel signals on the originator's data bus to a device that transforms them into a serial stream, still electrical. These serial electrical pulses activate a laser or light-emitting diode that sends pulses of light onto the fiber media. At the other end of the fiber, a light-sensitive element detects the presence or absence of light at precise times and generates electrical pulses accordingly. Thus, until the originating and receiving units are photonic devices, there must be an electrical-to-light-to-electrical transformation.

Fiber optic cables are small, sometimes being added as a part of larger twisted-pair or coaxial cable bundles. Reduction of production costs, coupled with high quality and fast transmission, makes it an excellent medium. The difficulty in splicing to itself and to other media, however, increases cost of use. Fiber optics will become the medium of choice for high bandwidth requirements of the future as all telecommunications convert from analog to digital modes.

Fiber optic circuits use a laser or light-emitting diode (LED) as the source end and a light detector at the receiving end. There must be a light-to-electrical signal conversion at each end.

Technology Note 3–5
Optical Fiber Characteristics

1. Uses light source, LED or laser, instead of electrical; analog and digital.
2. Unidirectional—used in pairs.
3. Bandwidth/speed = 135 Mbps over 40 miles; going to 155 Mbps and on with ATM and SONET.
4. Difficult to splice and interconnect.
5. Difficulty in splicing adds security.
6. Does not radiate or receive electromagnetic signals; immune to radiated signals (crosstalk) and other noise.

Information Window 3–4

Fiber optic cable has been laid undersea for several years, replacing the twisted-pair Trans-Atlantic Cable of the 1950s and satellite communications. One of the most ambitious projects is the worldwide FLAG (fiber optic link around the globe) telecommunications system. Upon completion, FLAG will connect 12 countries and link the United Kingdom to Japan through 30,000 kilometers of undersea fiber optic channels.

Dense Wave Division Multiplexing (DWDM)

DWDM
A fiber optic transmission technique that employs multiple light wavelengths to transmit data parallel-by-bit or serial-by-character. Source: http://www.iec.org.

We normally assume that there is a single "pipe" of light on a single strand of fiber. With such an environment, the prediction is that we can achieve a bandwidth of about one terabit per second, or one thousand gigabits per second, which is a million megabits per second. That seems like a lot of bandwidth. However, in high-traffic channels, the demand actually may exceed this bandwidth. What would you do in this situation? You either have to have spare (dark) strands or you must install new strands at a cost of $330,000 per kilometer, or you can use technology to enhance the bandwidth you have.

DWDM allows you to make better use of the full bandwidth of a fiber strand.

With different technology at each end of the fiber strand, pipes of different light can be added to the same strand, presently up to 64 different light waves, to increase the bandwidth of a single strand by 64 times. Now there is a predicted bandwidth of 64,000,000,000,000 bps. This would be sufficient bandwidth to carry 3.2 million HDTV channels simultaneously. While you might not find 3.2 million channels you wish to transport, you might, as indicated in the section that follows, wish to narrowcast one of 100,000 prerecorded programs to each of 3.2 million viewers.

Hybrid Fiber/Coax (HFC)

As noted in the Real World 3–6, fiber was used initially as a hybrid combination with coaxial cable, called **hybrid fiber/coax(HFC).** Consider that CATV companies had strung coaxial cable to millions of homes in the United States but that the bandwidth of coaxial cable is small compared with optic fiber strands. The combination of the two media allows for high bandwidth to the neighborhood and use of existing coaxial cable from the neighborhood to the home, providing a good trade-off between the cost of installation of new media and the exploitation of present media. (See Figure 3.13.)

Wire-based CATV systems presently use coaxial cables with frequency bandwidths of either 50–350 MHz or 50–750 MHz. This limits the number of analog

FIGURE 3.13
Hybrid Fiber/Coax Services

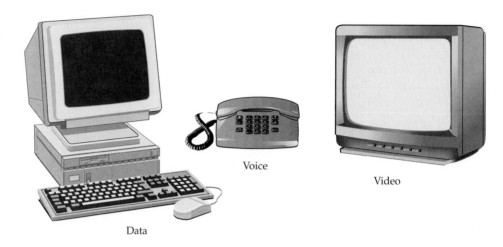

Voice

Video

Data

The Real World   3–5

1st Qtr 1999—AT&T closes merger with TCI.
2nd Qtr 1999—AT&T deploys a coast-to-coast OC-48 Internet backbone.
4th Qtr 1999—AT&T announces a major network expansion that will add 16,500 route-miles of the latest-generation fiber optic cable to supply customers with OC-192 (10 gigabit) service. This network expansion will

be capable of supporting OC-768 (40 gigabit) service when that technology becomes commercially available. AT&T is the first carrier to have live OC-192 Internet traffic on its backbone.

Source: AT&T ad in *Fortune*, October 9, 2000.

The Real World
NY Superhighway Trial   3–6

Time Warner Cable and Time are testing a fast online service in Elmira, New York, that will run at 1,000 times modem rates. The fiber/coaxial service will be run by Hewlett-Packard.

HP's Broadband Interactive Data Solution (BIDS) for hybrid fiber/coax networks will provide the server complex, network backbone, signal conversion system, cable modem, and PC software. The server complex includes servers to manage subscriber lists and content, a broadband Internet server, and a fire-wall.

Services including news, weather, local information, multimedia content, and the Internet will initially reach 500 homes, schools, libraries, and government offices picked from Time Warner's 27,000 Elmira customers. The service will start at a lower rate and build up to full speed later in 1995, with a cable modem providing 30 Mbps// upstream and 3 Mbps//downstream.

Source: Telecoms Newsline.

FIGURE 3.14
HFC Architecture

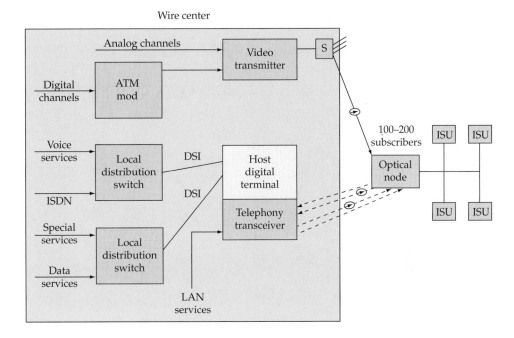

Bandwidth, for digital channels, is measured in bits per second.

channels that can be delivered to 50 and 100, respectively. To increase the number of channels, there are two choices: (1) use a medium with greater bandwidth or (2) digitize the signals and multiplex three digital channels into one analog channel.

The first choice of medium would seem to be optical fiber cable, as its bandwidth is, for all intents and purposes, unlimited. All new cable, however, would have to be installed from the signal source to each receiving residence. This is a very expensive, though desirable, alternative. The competing alternative, the one that is being considered first, is to install optical fiber from the signal source to neighborhoods of from 200 to 1,200 houses and then distribute the signal to the residence via the existing coaxial cable. (See Figure 3.14.) This creates a hybrid installation of fiber optic stands and coaxial cables. When the length of the coaxial cable is limited to a thousand feet or less and is in good shape, a greater bandwidth can be achieved. This is part of what gives HFC greater ability. (See Figure 3.15.)

Hybrid fiber/coax (HFC) makes use of the installed CATV network and uses fiber for high-speed, high-quality distribution to the neighborhood.

The advantage of HFC to the CATV company is lower cost by using the part of the existing system that would be the most expensive to replace, while delivering more services and channels via the new fiber distribution cables. (See Figure 3.16.) Additionally, the newly installed fiber optic cables negate the need for most amplifiers in the distribution cables and are far less susceptible to disruption by electrical storms. The hybrid configuration provides a higher-quality signal and lower maintenance costs. A bidirectional signal is provided for (interactive) commands from the users. (See Figure 3.17.)

Fiber to the Curb (FTTC)

FTTC has greater bandwidth and lower noise than HFC, but will be very expensive to run all the way to the premises.

As HFC and digital channels and compression (discussed later) increase the number of channels in existing systems, the ultimate circuit to the curb is a pair of fiber optic strands from the source to a point very near each residence. Connectivity from that point into the residence will be less important but generally more expensive. This will provide significantly greater bandwidth in both directions and make the services' offerings restricted only by the imagination of the providers and the purses of the receivers.

FIGURE 3.15   Basic HFC for Video and Voice

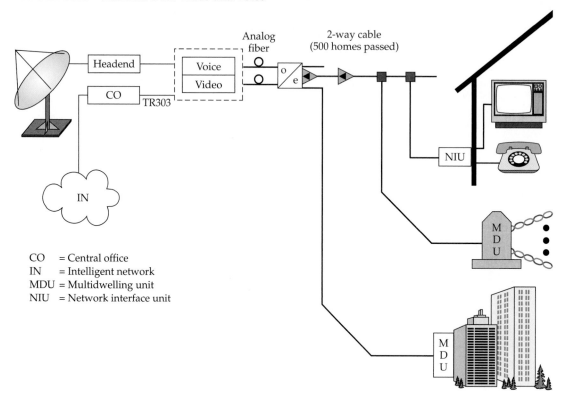

CO   = Central office
IN   = Intelligent network
MDU = Multidwelling unit
NIU = Network interface unit

**FIGURE 3.16
HFC Bandwidth**

Downstream bandwidth = 700 MHz = 110
Analog channels (50–750)

Upstream bandwidth = 37 MHz (5–42 MHz)

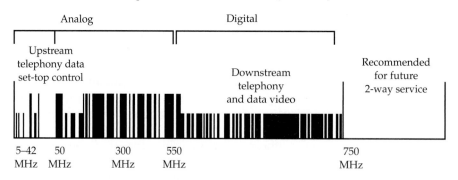

WIRELESS TECHNOLOGIES AND MEDIA

Wired connectivity, as we have been discussing previously, means a physical electrical or photonic channel. **Wireless** is the absence of such physical channels. Wireless generally takes two forms: electromagnetic (radio) waves and light (infrared) waves.

We are accustomed to **wireless communications** meaning mobile communications, specifically pagers and cellular telephones. While wireless makes mobility

Wireless
is the driving
technology of the
21st century.

FIGURE 3.17
Broadband Signal Multiplexing Combining Signals on Shared Links

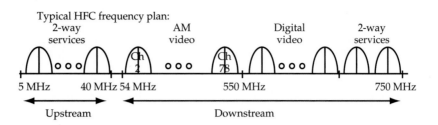

- HFC: Different frequencies for different services
  — Transparency of services, formats, modulation (AM, digital)
  — Upstream spectrum ~ 5–40 MHz

The Real World   3–7

For $67 a month in Fort Worth, Texas, AT&T Fixed Wireless customers can get two phone lines and high-speed Internet access, plus an Angel box that doubles as a receiver and a hub for a home computer network that can support as many as five PCs.

Source: "On the Net without a Wire," *eCommerce*, September 2000.

1.3 billion wirelessly connected people by 2004—Intel® leads the way.
Source: Intel ad, *Fortune*, October 9, 2000.

Fixed wireless is a direct replacement for a wired circuit.

possible and offers significant value, the potential of fixed wireless also has great value.

Fixed wireless is a **wired** replacement in that it is from point to point and is not designed to be movable. One specific use is to replace, or compete with, POTS UTP local loops. While local Telcos have UTP providing service to the home, new providers do not have such access and must rent access from the Telco or install the last mile, which is generally very expensive due to the cost of stringing wire or digging trenches for cable. Fixed wireless offers the potential to bypass this expense. One simply installs an omnidirectional antenna at a central point and a unidirectional antenna on the side of the residence or office and is in business. It is a good business decision if the provider can (1) create the network for less than renting local loops and (2) achieve sufficient bandwidth to provide the desired service, generally Internet access. Given that these conditions are met, it is much faster to install fixed wireless.

Meanwhile, other companies are using different portions of the spectrum and different technology to provide broadband fixed wireless service to businesses. A big reason is that connecting a building in a major city with fiber costs about $400K, while fixed wireless can do it for $50K.

We must remember, however, that most data and voice access is bidirectional. Where cable modem delivery of entertainment used to be concerned with only one-way delivery, Internet access now requires bidirectional communications even if the bandwidth is asymmetric, that is, higher downstream than upstream.

The first form of connectivity is **fixed node,** generally wired connectivity. This connectivity would be for desktop machines and servers. Although wireless channels will suffice, we generally see LANs implemented via UTP cables. Radio

Technology Note   3–6

What started as a clandestine project at McCaw Cellular is now a major exercise at AT&T as the scientists move to create an economical fixed wireless capability. The objective initially was to bypass the Telco's high charges for carrying long-distance traffic; now the data market is as large a market. AT&T spent $100 billion to purchase CATV facilities with the access to 50 million homes. With fixed wireless capabilities, they believe they can access 15 million more for only $3 billion.

Author's note: Things change very rapidly, as AT&T sold its CATV service to Charter in Fall 2001.

Source: *eCommerce*, September 2000.

Information Window   3–5

Fixed nodes support the user who works at a specific location, generally doing a select group of tasks. The movable node supports the user who may have more than one fixed location. With a wide coverage, moving connectivity satisfies this need, as long as the bandwidth is not too great, and allows the user to be where s/he needs to be, not where the supporting technology is located.

frequencies and infrared light (IR) wireless networks (discussed in the following pages) could perform the same function. Advantages of wireless, in addition to the absence of cables, would be going through walls for multiroom connectivity for RF and not going through walls for limited area coverage for IR. Disadvantages include a small area of coverage and, for the time being, limited bandwidth.

A wired circuit means the user is tethered to the point of connection.

The second form is **movable node,** that is, laptop computers that are carried from point to point. These devices can be supported with wired media, but wireless media would allow the machines to be at any of a number of locations and be connected as long as there is a connection point within a few hundred feet. Additionally, the connection does not require any effort; it is made when the laptop computer comes within range and is active. This form is also called fixed wireless. A form of this just coming on the market is fast-access Internet access from cell towers.

The third form is **moving node** such as wireless *PDAs. Palm Pilot*®*, Handspring*®*, and Blackberry*®, as well as palmtop computers and connected machines in the factory or warehouse, provide the user with information while actually moving. Thus, wireless connectivity for these computers means that they need a wide area of connectivity, require no effort involved in the connectivity, and continuously provide information exchange as the user roams.

radio
A medium that has become more valuable for new wireless applications.

Radio (Air Medium)[7]

Omnidirectional **air-medium radio** transmitters and receivers, like those used for AM and FM radio and television programs, are indeed telecommunications

---

[7] When we discuss radio and television, we think of the medium as the air between the transmitter and receiver. We actually use the *space,* not the air. The electromagnetic waves travel just as well in (outer) space as they do in air. The use of the term *air medium* is for convenience.

Information Window   3–6
Sports Firsts in Television

1. First televised baseball game: Columbia University hosting Princeton at Baker Field in New York City on May 17, 1939.
2. First major league game on TV: August 26, 1939; NBC televised a doubleheader from Ebbetts Field between the Brooklyn Dodgers and the Cincinnati Reds.
3. First coast-to-coast heavyweight title fight: Jersey Joe Walcott vs. Ezzard Charles from Municipal Stadium in Philadelphia, June 5, 1952.
4. First professional football game telecast: October 22, 1939, Brooklyn Dodgers over the Philadelphia Eagles.
5. First network world series telecast: 1947, Brooklyn Dodgers vs. New York Yankees on NBC.

capabilities. While we do not consider them prime candidates for many data communications systems, they are used for such systems as stock market quotations and personal pagers, along with taxi companies and police and fire departments, and cellular telephones. With AM/FM radio and television through an air medium, we are interested in transmitting from one source to as many receivers within the local areas as possible. Whether the radio/TV is for private consumption, such as taxi, fire, police, pager, stock quotation, or subscriber music, or public consumption (entertainment) as with commercial radio and television, the transmitter has a reliable receiving range that is selected at the time the license is given. Range for radio is a function of the power of the transmitter (radio ranges from 50 to 50,000 watts of power), the height of the antenna above the terrain (mountain tops are excellent), the terrain itself (mountains are terrible), and the weather conditions.

the spectrum
The broad spectrum chart shows that the radio frequency bands are limited and, thus, have high value.

When we transmit radio or television signals, the source is at a point and the destinations are in a large circle around the source. This is broadcasting. When we use microwave transmission from one tower to another tower (line-of-sight), this is narrowcasting. The two modes of transmission are based on the size and location of the audience.

The frequency range for commercial AM radio is 550 KHz to 1.6 MHz. The variables are the same for commercial air-medium television, except that the frequency range is 50 to 212 MHz for VHF (channels 1 thru 13) and 400 to 950 MHz for UHF (channels 14 thru 84). Because of the higher frequencies for TV, higher power (100,000+ watts) is allowed in the VHF bands, and antennas are usually located on very high structures. UHF stations, on the other hand, are often licensed to provide very localized coverage and may have lower power, for example, 100 to 5,000 watts, so as to minimize interference in the receiving area. FM radio uses the frequency range of 88 MHz to 108 MHz, which falls between TV channels 6 and 7. See Figure 3.18 for the broad spectrum.

You will see an example of the use of air-medium radio at your local McDonald's restaurant or other fast-food establishment. McDonald's uses technology to allow the person handling the drive-thru window mobility. The person at the window has a mobile radio pack on his/her waist and can walk around the store, while answering the requests from the drive-thru lane.

NTSC Television Bandwidth and Spectrum

When television was introduced in New York in 1937[8], it was via omnidirectional broadcast over the air. Since then it has changed, in many cases, to coaxial cable and direct broadcast satellite. However, the format has remained basically the same. Color video and stereo, as well as surround sound, have been added; each requires more bandwidth or a more judicious use of the existing bandwidth. The total bandwidth has remained at six megahertz since inception. The information content, which equates to picture quality, remains at 400 lines vertically, with a picture rate of 30 frames per second. European standard TV has more definition.

The improved color picture and enhanced sound of present TV are the result of viewers wanting more. MTV and its presentation of stereo music was a prime reason that sound improved. With stable color came a desire for better definition under all conditions. As personal computers gained sharper definition on their monitors, consumers wanted the same or better picture definition on television. In response to consumer demand, high definition television was created.

Technology Note   3–7

Television is also primarily an analog medium. The system we use today was established in the 1930s. Color was grafted onto it in the early '50s. This is when American television picked up its name, NTSC. The initials stand for National Television Standards Committee. This is the committee that established the standards for our television system. The problem is that NTSC is an analog system. In computer video, colors and brightness are represented by numbers.

But with analog television, everything is just voltages, and voltages are affected by wire length, connectors, heat, cold, video tape, and on and on. This is why most engineers today claim that NTSC stands for Never Twice the Same Color!

Source: http://www.seanet.com/Users/bradford/ntscvideo.html.

FIGURE 3.18   The Broad Spectrum

Source: Adapted from Avery L. Jenkins, "Catch the Wave," *PC Week.*

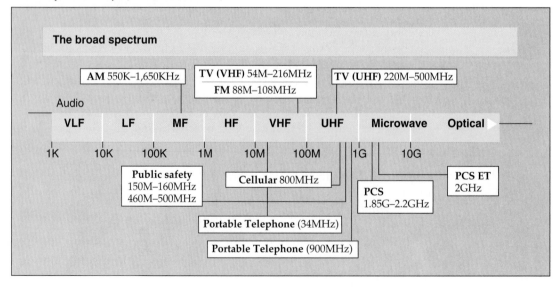

---

[8] The first regularly scheduled radio broadcast service was KDKA in Pittsburgh, Pennsylvania, in 1920.

FIGURE 3.18
The Broad Spectrum—
continued Joseph Sohm/Stock Boston

High Definition Television (HDTV)

HDTV increased the information-carrying capacity of the TV channel and uses digital technology in the United States.

HDTV can be in an analog or digital environment. Japan chose analog and the United States chose digital for HDTV. The objective in each case is to provide greater picture information and quality and better sound bandwidth. In order to achieve the desired outcome, there must be changes. One must either allocate more analog bandwidth, for example, twice as much as an NTSC channel, or convert to digital and use compression to reduce the bandwidth requirements. In either case, the detail of the picture is greater with better clarity and the sound quality has moved from that of FM radio to that of compact disks.

The 1080i-format high-definition digital TV (HDTV), on cable or satellite direct broadcast, will be the U.S. primary standard in 2006. This standard requires new

Technology Note   3–8

The original impetus for HDTV came from wide-screen movies. Soon after wide-screen was introduced, movie producers discovered that individuals seated in the first few rows enjoyed a level of participation in the action not possible with conventional movies. Evidently, having the screen occupy a great field of view (especially peripherally) significantly increases the sense of "being there."

Early in the 1980s, movie producers were offered a high-definition television system developed by Sony and NHK in the late 70s. This system (called NHK Hi-vision) and its variants are capable of producing images having essentially the same detail as 35-mm film. With these systems, a scene could be recorded, played and edited immediately, and then transferred to film. As a consequence, many of the intermediate delays in conventional film production were eliminated. The new medium also offered a number of possibilities for special effects not possible in conventional film production.

Following the introduction of HDTV to the film industry, interest began to build in developing an HDTV system for commercial broadcasting. Such a system would have roughly double the number of vertical lines and horizontal lines when compared to conventional systems.

Now, the most significant problem faced with HDTV is exactly the same problem faced with color TV in 1954. There are approximately 600 million television sets in the world and approximately 70 percent of them are color TVs. An important and critical consideration is whether the new HDTV standard should be compatible with the existing color TV standards, supplant the existing standards, or be simultaneously broadcast with the existing standards (with the understanding that the existing standards would be phased out over time).

Source: http://www.ee.washington.edu/conselec/CE/kuhn/hdtv/95×5.htm.

"Tonight's regularly scheduled programming will be preempted for a special episode of whatever the hell you want." *Replay TV®* ad from October 2000 issue of *Sound & Vision.*

television sets to decode the 1080i format and/or new set top boxes for the TV. HDTV sets are being produced to also convert NTSC signals into a 480P format. Where NTSC TV in digital format requires about 8 Mbps bandwidth, HDTV requires 19.2 Mbps.

Entertainment-on-Demand

Recorded or transmitted entertainment comes in three primary forms or modes. audio, video, and gaming. Entertainment also comes in four forms or schedules: periodic scheduled, special events, near-on-demand, and on-demand.

How many channels do you really want? You can watch only one channel at a time; two with P-I-P.

We are accustomed to periodic scheduled events as that is the general format of radio and television. Special events on TV are becoming more commonplace and are often pay-per-view as opposed to being part of the generalized subscription of cable TV or premium channels. We only get near-on-demand entertainment in places like hotels where they may have a sizable list of movies one can order and the hotel staff inserts the appropriate cassette that is ordered. The format we are moving to is *on-demand radio and television.*

Video-on-Demand (VoD)

Television in the home and movies in the theater are forms of entertainment on demand. Historically, most people have had to depend on advertised schedules of events, whether on television or at public places, and then bend their schedules to accommodate the fixed schedules of the events. With technology, this dependence on a fixed schedule can change.

Wouldn't you like to watch anything, anytime, anywhere?

The first way to have scheduled entertainment accommodate the viewer was to videotape programs (storing) using a programmable video cassette recorder (VCR). This required the viewer to determine when the program was aired, place

Information Window   3–7

An advertisement in the July 2000 issue of *Phone+*® magazine by Qwest shows the marquee of Roy's Motel and Café reading, "Every room has every movie ever made in every language day or night." This is possible, in this view of the near future, when you have enough bandwidth to access servers around the world that have stored all the music, or even movies and television shows, ever made. As the ad asks, "What could you do with the bandwidth to change everything?"

a tape in the machine, and program the machine correctly. Next came pay-per-view movies on premium TV channels that were aired several times a day. The newest entrant accommodating viewers is the digital video recorder (DVR), which uses a hard drive for digital storage and a downloaded schedule of events to find the programs of interest and automatically record them. With DVR, the television viewer's first option is to watch what was recorded that fell in his/her area of interest, as opposed to just watching what is being broadcast at the current time.

Another level of user-controlled entertainment is video-on-demand (VoD). This means that the user thinks up what s/he wants and it is provided. VoD requires more bandwidth and a server that contains a lot of programs. Ultimately, it means that there will be digital video servers that contain all programs of interest, old and new, from which the viewer can choose. It also means a high bandwidth channel is required to the user's television and, potentially, pay-per-view for everything. If the program is NTSC television, only about 6–8 Mbps is required; if HDTV format is used, 19.2 Mbps is required.

Internet Broadcast TV

Internet TV means you could see any station's programming anywhere on the globe.

The Internet means connectivity; the **World Wide Web (WWW)** and browsers give a graphical user interface. The uses of the Internet have increased rapidly. First there was special radio broadcast of sports over the Internet and now there is continuous broadcast of hundreds of radio stations over the Internet 24 hours, 7 days per week (24*7). This means that the audience of a particular radio station is not limited by the reach of its air-broadcast signal; it has a global reach. Just as the small UHF television station WTBS in Atlanta, Georgia, became a major player due to the use of satellite delivery, other radio and television stations can achieve a national or even global presence as the bandwidth of the Internet accommodates their signal. As the bandwidth of the Internet increases and the delays decrease, the use of this "free" resource continues to evolve and can make even a local provider into a global competitor.

Enhanced TV

The American Broadcasting Company describes enhanced TV as a live interactive TV experience, converging on-air and online programming. It does not replace on-air programming; the added computer information is available to make the viewer's experience more interesting. Included are games, viewer opinion polls, and chat sessions, adding involvement to the viewing.

To use Enhanced TV, you must have both your online computer and your television in the same room. While a program, such as "Monday Night Football," is in progress, ETV allows viewers to test their play-calling skills and, during commercials,

Drawing by W. Miller, © 1993. The New Yorker Magazine, Inc.

ETV asks trivia questions. Viewer polls also are displayed when an instant replay is in progress, giving the armchair quarterback much more power.

Another form of ETV is when it is used with *Web-TV*®. For example, a chef on the Food Channel prepares a specialty item and clicking on the screen brings up the recipe for printing.

Cellular Radio

Cellular phones
Mean that you call the person, not the place.

A specific use of air-medium radio that has recently[9] regained significant popularity is for mobile telephones. This is due to the use of **cellular radio.** Formerly, circa 1980, mobile radiotelephone meant that there were one or two transmitters for a medium-size city, limited to only a few hundred FCC-assigned frequencies. Each telephone permanently had one of the frequencies; therefore, you could have only a few hundred vehicles with telephones. (Mobile radiotelephone systems, like cellular systems, connect with the local Telco switch via landlines from base stations.) With cellular radio telephones, the area is divided into cells of about five miles in diameter, although the size is dependent on the density of telephone traffic and physical terrain. Each cell has a base station with a computer-controlled transmitter-receiver, each of which is connected to a master switching center, called a Mobile Telephone Switching Office (MTSO). As a vehicle places a call within a cell or enters the cell while talking, the vehicle phone communicates to the cellular station on a frequency selected at the moment. When the vehicle leaves the cell and enters another cell, or the computer determines that another cell receiver-transmitter can provide better-quality service, the computer, with the aid of the MTSO, will hand off the vehicle transmission to the transmitter-receiver in the new cell and clear the fre-

---

[9] Cellular telephone first came into use in October 1983. However, it was more than 10 years before it was widely used.

Cell phone, pager, PDA, Internet access all in one device. **Now, that's connectivity.**

Cellular phones, combined with global positioning systems and on-board computers, alert the Lincoln Warning System in case your car is disabled, dispatching help based on the location provided by the GPS.

PCS (personal communications system) is digital telephone plus paging.

quency in the old cell for a new caller. If the receiver of the conversation is also a cellular customer and in the same cell as the sender or any cell connected to the sender's MTSO, which is not likely or required, the call potentially bypasses the local phone company's CO. However, most of the time, the call goes to the local phone company's switch and on to either a terrestrial phone or out of another MTSO's cellular transmitter to the receiving vehicle phone. The caller can be in Atlanta, and the receiver can be in New York City, and the call can continue as long as each participant is within a cell. However, if one participant enters an area not covered by cellular radio, the conversation stops. The vehicle can be an airplane, and the conversation can continue up to about a half hour's distance beyond the coastline or, using satellite, can continue as long as it is in the cone of coverage. (See Figures 3.19 and 3.22.) A sample of cellular coverage is provided in Figure 3.20. Note how it defines the local calling area.

In the case of cellular telephones, the cellular switching computer and MTSO act as a CO switch. The local loop is the radio connection between the transmitter tower and the vehicle or portable cellular unit. The switch in this instance not only creates the path, it also allocates radio frequencies. Unlike a local CO, the cellular switch knows a hand-off of the call will occur within a small amount of time.

FIGURE 3.19   Mobile Cellular Telephone System

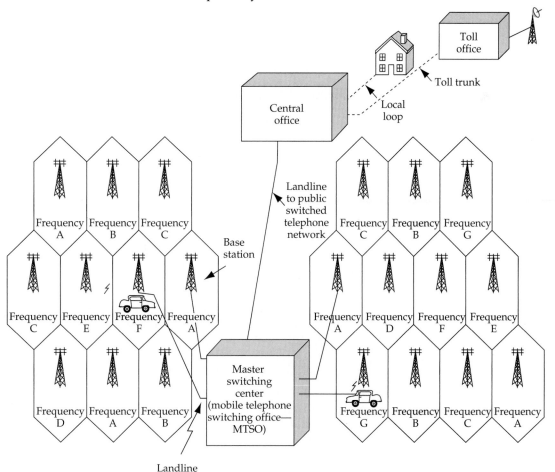

FIGURE 3.20
ALLTEL
Montgomery's Local
Coverage Area

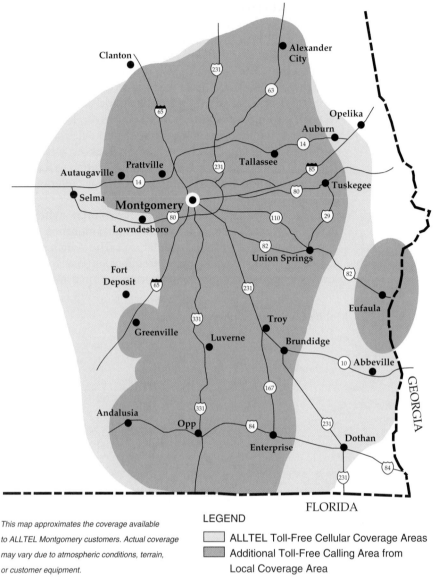

*This map approximates the coverage available
to ALLTEL Montgomery customers. Actual coverage
may vary due to atmospheric conditions, terrain,
or customer equipment.*

LEGEND

☐ ALLTEL Toll-Free Cellular Coverage Areas
▨ Additional Toll-Free Calling Area from
  Local Coverage Area

The Real World   3–8

Ten thousand miles above the earth, satellites orbit silently through space, waiting for the owner of a Lincoln Continental who might someday require emergency assistance. With the push of a button, the available RESCU system (Remote Emergency Satellite Cellular Unit) uses global positioning satellites to determine your location. Your position is then relayed via your cellular phone to the Lincoln Security Response Center, which will dispatch assistance and keep you informed (subject to cellular area limitations).

Source: Lincoln advertisement in *Architectural Digest.*
http://www.lincolnvehicles.com.

Six weekends a year, Auburn, a college town of 35,000, becomes the third largest city in Alabama as fans flock in to watch SEC football. Due to the increased number of cars, vans, and RVs with cellular phones, blocking is severe.

As we create this second edition of the text, one state, New York, and one nation, Japan, have made it a finable offense to talk on a cellular phone while driving. The assumption is that the driver will be distracted by the call. Thus, hands-free talking is becoming important.

cellular blocking BellSouth Mobility added many mini-cells and mobile towers to provide coverage for the 1996 Summer Olympics.

Advanced mobile phone service (AMPS) was the evolution from mobile radiotelephone service.

Analog and digital cellular both use analog radio wave carrier.

Most cellular telephones initially used analog radio as the medium, in the frequency range of 850–900 MHz. In high-density areas, the traffic is too great, and it is not unusual for a call to be blocked: no frequencies are available for a new call or a hand-off. Use of digital technology relieves this in all but the highest-density areas by providing more frequencies, less noise, and a better environment for data communications. Digital cellular protocols are discussed in the following pages.

While some contend that the costs of a cellular telephone are high relative to a landline system (monthly costs of US$200 are not unusual), the value to the business often surpasses the cost. People who spend a large amount of time traveling in their cars can now utilize this time to make contacts with customers, receive and give information to their secretaries, or check their voice mail. An example of the acceptance of the "mobile" market is that total sales for 1994 were stated to be US$26.3 billion and rising to US$92.5 billion by the year 2001. A feature of cellular phone systems is that phone numbers are not generally available via the information directory. This will likely change with the deregulation of the industry and the enforcement of number portability: the ability to move a specific number from switch to switch and system to system.

Caveat—This discussion centers around the U.S. deployment of cellular telephones. The United States has different cellular standards than Europe, but the concepts remain the same. As service is put in new areas, the choice of equipment will be somewhat standards-based driven. Thus, as services are introduced into the former Eastern Bloc of Europe and developing countries of Asia and South America, standards will come into play.

Cellular Radio (Telephone) Protocols

There are a confusing number of cellular standards, protocols, and technologies. In the next sections, we provide some basics to help in understanding the differences. Table 3.3 showing timelines and generations summarizes the major differences.

Advanced Mobile Phone Service (AMPS)

AMPS started as an analog system using the 800 Mhz frequency band. AMPS is widely deployed in the United States, Canada, and Mexico. It is also a de facto standard in Central and South America and is used in the Pacific Rim, Russia, and Africa.

The analog version was deployed by AT&T in 1983 before divestiture. Early estimates were drastically short of the actual subscriber rates achieved. Part of the market penetration came as a result of technological advances in handsets, the electronic components, and mass market economies of scale that brought prices down.

The Real World   3–9

By the year 2010, there will be one billion wireless subscribers worldwide on 3G networks. (Source: Strategis Group.)

On January 1, 2000, the worldwide penetration of wireless service was approximately 7 $\frac{1}{2}$ percent. Penetration will exceed 32 percent, on a global basis, in the first decade of the new millennium. (Source: Cahners In-Stat Group.)

By the year 2004, revenue from wireless data will reach $33.5 billion globally. (Source: Strategis Group.)

Source: http://www.uwcc.org/.

TABLE 3.3   Timeline of Cellular

Source: *Wired,* June 2001, p. 87.

Generation	Rollout	Data Rate Mbps	Uses	Component Technologies
1G	1981–83	Analog	Early car phones	AMPS, TAC, NMT
2G	1991–95	10 Kbps	Mass-market cell phones	GSM, TDMA, CDMA
2.5G	1999	.064–.144	Wireless net access	Same + GPRS, EDGE, IS-95B
3G	2001–2005	.348–2.0	Location-based service	WCDMA
4G	2010	10–100	Video	OFDM

Technology Note   3–9

The **AMPS** family of wireless standards was intended to be just another analog radiotelephone standard (e.g., **advanced mobile phone service** followed IMTS: improved mobile telephone service). However, due to the high capacity allowed by the cellular concept, the lower power that enabled portable operation, and its robust design, AMPS has been a stunning success. Today, about half the cellular phones in the world operate according to AMPS standards, which, since 1988, have been maintained and developed by the Telecommunications Industry Association (TIA). From its humble beginnings, AMPS has grown from its roots as an 800 MHz analog standard to accommodate TDMA and CDMA digital technology, narrowband (FDMA) analog operation (NAMPS), in-building, and residential modifications. Most recently, operation in the 1800 Mhz (1.8–2.2 GHz) PCS frequency band has been added to standards for CDMA and TDMA. All of these additions have been done while maintaining an AMPS compatibility mode (known as BOA: boring old AMPS). It might be boring, but it works, and the AMPS compatibility makes advanced digital phones work everywhere, even if all their features are not available in analog mode. TACS (or ETACS) is a close relative, basically being AMPS in the 900 MHz frequency band.

Source: http://www.cnp-wireless.com/amps.html.

Time Division Multiple Access (TDMA)

who pays—Calls to ordinary (landline) telephones do not cost the receiver, but cellular calls do.

In **TDMA,** a single channel is divided into several timeslots. Multiple users get one of every few slots so that a small amount of voice from a user is transmitted, then the next user's voice slot is transmitted, and so on until all the users on a channel have a chance to transmit, then the cycle repeats. Voice conversations are compressed with TDMA.

Global System for Mobile Communications (GSM)

GSM is a digital implementation of TDMA that is operational all over Europe. GSM is also more and more popular in the United States and Canada as well as Asia and other parts of the world although at a different frequency range.

One of the advantages of GSM is its digital nature. One can connect a GSM cellular phone to a notebook computer to access a full range of email, fax, Internet, intranet, and short messaging services (an integrated paging service) without adapters, cables, and telephone jacks. Another advantage of GSM is the ability to roam very widely and still have services because of liberal roaming agreements.

The GSM phone has a smart card called a Subscriber Identity Module (SIM) that is installed in the instrument. This card provides identification, authentication, and the basis for billing.

Code Division Multiple Access (CDMA)

CDMA is a spread spectrum technology. By using spread spectrum, CDMA achieves a capacity increase over analog AMPS of 8 to 10 times and 4 to 5 times over GSM. Call quality also is improved and there is enhanced privacy. The technology allows for better coverage, resulting in fewer cell sites and the ability to use the same frequency in every cell sector. CDMA also offers improved talk time and bandwidth on demand.

Personal Communications

Cloning of cellular phones is a process of duplicating the identification of a supposedly unique identifier and then making calls that are charged back to the original device.

Nationwide paging is a reality in the United States. Many people feel lost without these devices.

The first radio device that showed the way for **personal communications** was the **pager.** This device began as a small radio receiver carried on the person that gave a beeping sound (hence the pager was called a beeper), notifying the user to call a specified telephone number for a message. This device progressed to the point where a short audible announcement could be sent to the pager. The present digital technology sends textual information that is stored in the receiver and notifies the user of a new message either by making a sound or silently vibrating. Pagers can be as small as pencils, and some can store pages of textual messages. SkyTel® pagers use a satellite network to locate the receiving pager in thousands of cities and towns across the United States. Their latest pagers feature two-way capabilities, for example, the ability to respond to a page with a preprogrammed or customized response. Meanwhile, newer cellular telephones and laptop computers are including paging capabilities. See Figure 3.21 for a SkyTel pager.

While the pager capability will probably be merged into the PDA and even the cellular telephone, text messages will likely be a lasting requirement. Often we want to be informed, but not to carry on a conversation.

The domain of personal communications has expanded far beyond the simple pager. This category now includes the pocket or purse-size cellular telephone that uses cellular radio towers for communications. Next are pocket telephones that use one of several satellites (to be explained later) for their signals. With capabilities such as the Iridium® satellite-based systems, you will never be away from the phone, as one of 66 low-orbit satellites will find you.

Most new cellular phones are digital, providing enhanced clarity and noise rejection, security, and an increased number of numbers. People interested in switching

FIGURE 3.21
A SkyTel Pager
Steve Marcus/Reuthers

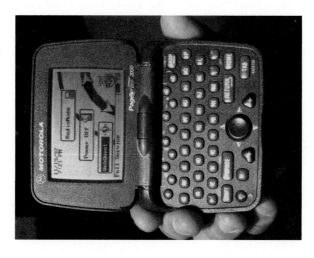

The Real World   3–10
I'm Not Only Mobile, I'm Unstoppable—
Interactive Messaging PLUS by BellSouth

Unstoppable is exactly what you and your team can be with Interactive Messaging PLUS from BellSouth MyBiz Interactive. You can receive messages and quickly respond to one person or several people at once, whether they're across the hall or across the country. Our special confir-mation feature tells you that messages between users have been *delivered* and *read*. You can even receive and respond to Internat email when you're on the go.

Source: Ad in September 2000 *SKY Magazine*, p. 50.

Technology Note   3–10

Interactive Messaging

Get email all over the place with new Arch Webster 100 Interactive Messaging Service. Arch Webster 100 Interactive Messaging Service, featuring the Motorola T900 device, makes it easy to keep up with your email when you're on the go. The new Arch Webster 100 offers you the simplest, smallest, lightest, and most affordable two-way messaging solution for sending and receiving email from virtually anywhere. It also allows you to receive timely information—such as weather, news, and stock quotes, along with alpha-numeric messages and voice mail notification.

Source: http://content.arch.com/products/advanced.html.

from analog to digital cellular phones will have to purchase new equipment except for a few dual-mode instruments. (Remember, the carrier signal from the phone to the tower remains analog; the voice is converted and carried as digital codes.)

Radio and POTS

The telephone system that Alexander Graham Bell and others developed has tra-ditionally been a wire-based system for most homes. Radiotelephones were for business vehicles, and cellular began there also. What broke this tradition was the introduction of the **portable (or cordless) telephone.**

Cordless telephones use two FM radio transmitter-receivers to replace the wire from the handset to the base station. The transmitters operate at different fre-quencies, to provide full duplex, just like on a wire. These systems use analog car-rier waves and originally carried the voice as analog waves modulated onto the 34 MHz carrier. Therefore, it was easy to detect and extract the voice signal. Four developments have made the cordless telephone of better quality and more secure:

Do you really need a wired telephone or will cordless do?

1. The first change seen on the original 34 MHz phones was the use of multiple channels. This meant that you could change the frequency of the channel of transmission from the base station to the handset to get away from noise or an eavesdropping neighbor. Present phones have from 2 to 40 channels.

2. Next came the movement to the 900 MHz portion of the radio spectrum. This is a cleaner (less noise) frequency than the lower frequency. Operation in the 900 MHz radio band allows the signal to penetrate walls and other physical barriers more easily. The mode is still analog, but techniques are added to either change channels, offset channel frequencies, or partially encrypt the voice for security.

3. Next, the providers digitized the voice and carried it as digital data on the analog carrier. This makes interception of the voice much more difficult and provides better voice quality.

4. Fourth, some phones use **spread spectrum,** which is a technology that constantly changes channels (frequencies) between the handset and the base station on a predefined frequency shift. If the eavesdropper does not know the allocations and timing, the results will appear as noise, making detection almost impossible. Thus, the change of frequency, digitizing the voice, and adding spread spectrum give a higher-quality signal that is very secure. Encryption adds even more security.

The latest change in the cordless systems is the movement to the 2,400 MHz (2.4 Ghz) frequency. While the phones are advertised as having greater reach, the primary advantage is clarity and less interference from other phones.

Microwave and Satellite Radio

Microwave radio circuits are special air-medium, high-frequency, line-of-sight radio systems that send signals from one transmitting station to one receiving station, generally 20 to 30 miles apart. Where twisted-wire and coaxial circuits could operate bidirectionally by taking turns or using different parts of the bandwidth, the microwave radio system is unidirectional (simplex) because one station is a transmitter and the other is a receiver. Because of this, a separate microwave radio link is required for the return path. (In reality all media are one-way due to the need to add directional amplifiers to overcome attenuation. Two paths are required where two-way communications are needed.)

Satellite radio is logically the same as a microwave radio circuit except that the sending station transmits to a satellite relay station 22,300 miles above the earth. The signal is relayed down to another earth station. The satellite is in a geosynchronous orbit, causing it to appear stationary above the earth. Three satellites can cover the earth's surface (see Figure 3.22). The major drawback to satellite communications is the time delay in the uplink to the satellite and the downlink to earth. The total propagation delay is about half a second. While satellite transmission allows communication across bodies of water and difficult terrain, the delay is generally difficult for people to tolerate in voice communications. We continue a discussion of satellite communications used by business in later chapters on data communications.

Until the early 1990s, satellite TV transmission was analog, using C and K bands, which meant ground antennas of at least 6, preferably 10, feet in diameter for home reception. In the early 1990s, the Hughes Corporation allocated US$2 billion to make three TV broadcast satellites, two for orbit and one spare, at a cost of US$200 million each. The difference in these satellites is that they had a higher power output and transmitted a digitally encoded signal. Additionally, the ground home antennas were only 18 inches in diameter and could be installed by the user. Because of the digital signal, the picture quality was better and the sound quality compared

Microwave is always line-of-sight, whether terrestrial or satellite.

FIGURE 3.22
Full Communi-
cations Coverage
Provided by Three
Geostationary
Satellites Photo
courtesy of Tony
Freeman/PhotoEdit

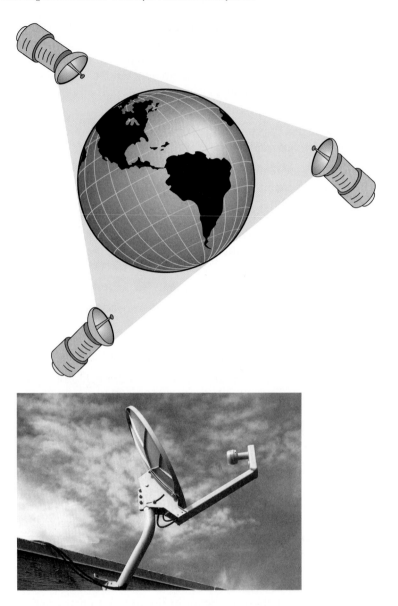

with that of a compact disk. This service, called DirecTV®, was soon followed by PrimeStar® and EchoStar®. (DirecTV has absorbed PrimeStar and is seeking to acquire EchoStar.) The latter services had slightly larger antennas (for example, 36 inches in diameter) and leased the equipment, whereas DirecTV began service by having the user purchase the equipment, which consisted of an antenna, lead-in coaxial cable, amplifier/descrambler, and remote. These services, although initially thought to be mostly for rural and remote viewers, saw wide acceptance in urban areas as the first competition to CATV. With digital satellite-delivered television, users had relatively small and inexpensive equipment, a wide choice of alternatives to choose from for varying fees, digital uninterrupted music, movies-on-demand, and special pay-per-view from up to 75 channels. (See Table 3.4.)

In mid-1996, Hughes began another offering, called DirecPC, which offed Internet downloads of 400 Kbps to a PC and the capacity for multimedia services. Initial

TABLE 3.4
Satellites Used by CNN

Satellite Designation	Coverage
Galaxy5	North America
Soledaridad1	Central America
Panamasat1	South America
Brazilsat	Brazil
Thor	Scandinavia
Arabsatic	North Africa
Astra1B	UK & Western Europe
Panamsal4	Eastern Europe & SE Asia
ISNAL2-B	
Palapa B2P	Japan, Korea, SE Asia
INSAL2-B	
Superbird B	
Panamsat2	
Apetor1	SE Asia & Australia
N O N E	China and Russia

calls for service are made by the modem and then uplinked to the DirecPC Network Operations Center to the Galaxy IV satellite. While more expensive than services by Internet providers, this system provides coverage of the 48 contiguous states of the United States at a significantly higher bandwidth.

Microwave and satellite radio systems, which had such great promise for voice communications, have been replaced with other media in many instances. Fiber optic (digital) technology has replaced microwave technology for most long-distance systems. Microwave technology still finds use in local, short-haul environments such as in cities between buildings, for ease of installation, and for precludence of right-of-way permits in congested areas.

Very small aperture terminals (VSAT) have relatively smaller (approximately 8 to 16 inches = 20–40 cm) antennas than satellite earth station dishes. A VSAT network has many of these terminals linked through the satellite to a central control station on the ground. For example, the next time you pass by a major new car dealer, note the satellite antenna on the roof. If it is less than 1.5 feet in diameter, it is VSAT.

Direct Broadcast Service TV

Direct broadcast satellites using VSAT (very small aperture terminal) antennas allow competition on the turf of CATV providers.

With the advent of low-cost electronics and lower-cost satellite launching facilities, several companies have placed geosynchronous satellites in place for direct broadcast of digital television programming and data. Satellite direct broadcast is not a new idea, but having a small, very low cost installation that doesn't take up the whole back yard is. This fixed wireless system is the first major competitor to cable TV. The new direct broadcast service (DBS) TV providers choose to send the signals in digital form from the beginning as opposed to the original service, which, like original cable, was analog. Digital transport increases quality and adds enhanced features such as HDTV and AC3 sound while making the best use of the frequency spectrum. The cable companies are coming to this same conclusion as they convert upper channels to digital.

Synchronous versus Low Orbit Satellites

Direct broadcast satellite can be called wireless cable TV; usually all digital.

Direct broadcast service television uses geosynchronous satellites that appear to be stationary in orbit. This gives them the same coverage of the earth's surface at all times. However, they must be located 22,300 miles above the earth's surface and, thus, their power is dissipated during transmission. Recent entrants into satellite broadcast, both voice and data, are choosing to put up not just one geosynchronous satellite but a number of low earth orbit (LEO) satellites; 77 were planned in the case of the original *Iridium* system. LEOs are in low earth orbit only several hundred miles above the planet. This means they will be in constant motion, being in view of an earth station for only minutes at a time. This requires that the satellite control system switch the user from satellite to satellite as they go out of and come into view. It also means that the amount of power required for broadcast is less for the same reception. While geosynchronous satellites have limited areas for parking to see the optimal portions of the earth and have long expected lifespans, the low-orbit satellites have almost unlimited orbit locations but very limited lifespans.

Wireless Cable Television (LMDS, MMDS)

The title of this section seems to be contradictory, that is, how can you have cable-less cable? The terminology may be unfortunate, but the idea was that wireless technology could offer similar functionality to conventional cable.

When the alternative to on-air broadcast TV was launched, it used the cheapest, low-noise medium available, that is, coaxial cable. Therefore, it was called cable television. The title has stuck, so when the medium changed, the title was simply extended.

Coaxial cable transport of cable TV uses the same standards and frequencies as on-air broadcast. The signal is modulated onto a carrier wave of the same frequency that would be used for omnidirectional broadcast. In extreme cases, the channels are changed, but the technology is the same.

Wireless cable systems use protocols called MMDS and LMDS to place multiple channels of television and Internet access on a frequency spectrum that is wirelessly broadcast. Generally, they use a single omnidirectional broadcast antenna and broadcast to 36-inch conical microwave antenna located on the wall of a building, much like direct satellite broadcast television. In this case, LMDS and MMDS don't use a satellite transponder; they send their signals line-of-sight from their antenna to yours. The lesser capability has a total bandwidth less than coaxial cable and satellite, about 25 TV channels, and the distance covered is about a 25-mile radius. The quality competes nicely with cable, it can be installed much faster, and the cost is less because there is no need to run the cables and rent or install utility poles. Newer systems have far greater bandwidth, are bidirectional, and are digital.

LMDS and MMDS are quick ways to install Internet access in a city.

Technology Note   3–11

Multipoint microwave distribution system, also known as multichannel multipoint distribution system and wireless cable, is another wireless broadband technology for Internet access. MMDS channels come in 6 MHz chunks and run on licensed and unlicensed channels. Each channel can reach transfer rates as high as 27 Mbps (over unlicensed channels: 99 MHz, 2.4 GHz, and 5.7 to 5.8 GHz) or 1 Gbps (licensed channels). MMDS is a line-of-sight service (see Fresnel Zone definition), so it won't work as well around mountains, but it will work in rural areas, where copper lines are not available.

Source: http://webopedia.internet.com/ TERM/M/MMDS.html.

Technology Note   3–12

LMDS is an acronym for **local multipoint distribution service.** This service can provide two-way digital communication. Applications of LMDS include voice, video, and high-speed data communication. The bandwidth of LMDS is more than twice the total bandwidth of AM/FM radio, VHF/UHF TV, and cellular telephone combined. Using LMDS, transmission speeds of several gigabits per second are possible along line-of-sight distances of several miles.

LMDS has a range of the communication spectrum regulated by the FCC in the United States. In 1998, the FCC auctioned licenses to LMDS for the first time. Licenses are geographically divided into local regions called BTAs (basic trading areas). LMDS licenses also are divided into two blocks of frequencies: the A block and the B block (licensed separately). They are located in the 28 to 31 GHz range of the spectrum. Because the frequencies are high,

they have a short wavelength. This means they can't bend around obstacles the way longer waves (like FM radio waves) do. You must have a permanent line of sight between an LMDS transmitter and receiver. Because of this, applications are best suited for communication between a transmission site and building (with a permanent antenna). LMDS technology can be combined with other fiber or wired networking technology to extend LMDS-based services. LMDS is a cost-effective solution to the last mile problem: connecting net users to large capacity network connections without the prohibitive installation costs of fiber to the home and without the transmission limitations of copper lines.

Source: http://www.lmds.vt.edu/. Also see http://www.mm-tech.com/lmds.htm.

Technology Note   3–13

KANSAS CITY—Sprint Corp. will gain a wireless component for its highly touted Integrated On-Demand broadband network, through the acquisition of American Telecasting Inc. (Colorado Springs, Colo.), announced Tuesday (April 27). ATI, a specialist in **Metropolitan Multipoint Distribution Service (MMDS),** holds licenses covering a potential 10 million households in Denver; Portland, Oregon; Seattle; and Las Vegas.

MMDS, known informally as "wireless cable," is a service occupying bands between 5 Ghz and 10 GHz. Originally used only for one-way private broadcast of cable

signals, MMDS has been promoted as a wideband Internet access service, though its capacity is not as great as the 28-GHz LMDS service. ATI and other companies promoting MMDS have been in a financial slump in recent months, and the Sprint acquisition follows similar MMDS service acquisitions, such as MCI WorldCom's purchase of CAI Wireless Systems Inc.

Source: http://www.eet.com/story/OEG19990428S0012.

Wireless Internet Access

Television has many advertisements for wireless Internet access. Wireless Internet access allows getting information from the Internet on cellular telephones, pagers, or PDAs, for example, *Palm Pilot*® or *Blackberry*®. There are two aspects of wireless Internet access: (1) information to a portable device and (2) wireless access to a stationary computer.

This environment will be competition for Internet access, competition with standard modem, cable modem, and xDSL access. With new cellular and other wireless technologies and protocols, it soon will be possible and economically feasible for the local wireless provider to provide a 128-to-767 Kbps wireless channel to the Internet from the home or hotel by way of existing cell towers. Wireless

The Real World   3–11

This week (February 2001) Novatel Wireless finally released the Minstrel S modem, the first Springboard module that offers wireless WAN access to email and the Web. Like the other Novatel Minstrel modems for the Palm family, the Minstrel S uses the CDPD (Cellular Digital Packet Data) network, which supports data transfers at speeds up to 19.2 Kbps.

Source: http://www.zdnet.com/products/stories/reviews/0,4161,2649483,00.html.

The Real World   3–12
Get Things Done in a Meeting. Imagine That.

Another endless meeting where more gets said than done? Not if you've got the wireless convenience of SkyTel service with a Motorola Timeport™ interactive communicator. With SkyTel wireless email, you're connected with the world outside the conference room. And with our InfoBeam™ Internet search features, you have a wealth of information in the palm of your hand. So you can get things done while others simply talk about it.

Source: Ad in September 2000 *SKY Magazine*, p. 11.

technologies are developing so rapidly that they are beginning to compete effectively with wired technologies.

Mobile Wireless—Person-to-Person versus Point-to-Point

From the alley to the valley, and everywhere in between, business is becoming truly mobile—and the demand for information and access, immediate. It's a new-age reality and it's creating the need for a virtual office—one that's wireless and ready for business anyplace, anytime, and anywhere. **WorldCom** Source: Worldcom ad, *Fortune,* October 9, 2000.

When telephones were first introduced into homes and offices, they had a special place. For example, in many old homes, there was a telephone alcove or a telephone desk. When one received or wished to place a telephone call, one went to the alcove or desk and talked. It was a special event.

Today, most homes in developed nations have a number of telephones. Many have cordless phones with which the user can walk around while talking. The cellular telephone is the extreme case because the phone can always be with the person. This means that the perception of the call is no longer place-to-place, as it is with stationary telephones, but person-to-person. This perception changes the nature of telecommunications and relationships. The ability to always be in touch changes the way we live.

Many lesser-developed nations have large numbers of their population who have never made a telephone call. These nations lack what is known as teledensity and this presents a challenge to their governments and to the developed nations as well.

While the above example is for the telephone, the following paragraphs describe other wireless environments. As wireless technologies have greater bandwidth and become less expensive, they will become a preferred medium because they allow mobility.

Global Positioning System (GPS)

Knowing where you are and directions to where you need to go via **GPS** has changed the way we travel and find our destination. Airlines, trucking firms, express delivery vans, military aircraft, submarines, soldiers in the field, hikers, and tourists who once referred to maps or used a compass now rely on a small handheld GPS receiver. This technology receives signals from several of 22 orbiting satellites to calculate precise location, altitude, and speed. The signals also are used by other equipment for exact time synchronism. When combined with D-GPS, the location is so precise that mining companies use it to determine boundary locations.

When the location data of the GPS circuitry is combined with charting information, like in the *eMap Deluxe*® by Garmin (see Figure 3.23), the users have a visual display of where they are, what is around them, and a map of directions. This device, the size of a small, flat calculator, contains a 12-parallel-channel GPS receiver and weighs a mere six ounces.

GPS and a mapping program get you from here to there and tell you where you are all the time.

Infrared

Another air-medium technology used for control, with which you are most likely familiar, is *infrared (IR)*, such as that used in the TV, VCR, CD player, and stereo remote controls. This technology and fiber optics use light waves instead of electricity. They are used almost exclusively for digital signals and will be covered in a later chapter. The remote control used to command your TV transmits invisible light pulses that the detector in the TV interprets as commands to change channels, volume, and so on. A very different use of this form of data transmission is in the IR data links used by IBM and Texas Instruments in their laptop computers and Hewlett-Packard in their LaserJet® printers. The laptops send data in IR form at a rate of about 115 Kbps over an IrDA channel, and the printers or any IR receivers accept the data without the use of wiring. The IrDA 1.0 channel is specified at 115 Kbps, whereas the new IrDA 2.0 channel has transfer speeds of 1.152 Mbps, with a new goal of 10 Mbps being researched. Most laptop and notebook computers began to include this IR link as of the end of 1996.

infrared
A technology that has become more important for telecommunications in the wireless arena.

FIGURE 3.23
GPS Receiver
Vincent Dewitt/Stock Boston

DIGITAL WORLD

If you have made a long-distance telephone call recently, you were using a **digital** circuit to communicate. We are deferring the discussion of digital voice and analog-to-digital conversion until later as the concept fits better with data communications. However, it suffices to say at this point that where analog waves are continuous in nature, digital circuits use discrete, digital 1s and 0s to carry the information.

The telephone system we have been discussing is an *analog* capability. The connection between two users, via the switch in the central office, carries analog electrical energy that is analogous to the acoustic energy of the speaker's voice. There is but one channel on the wire. One replacement for this technology, called *integrated services digital network (ISDN)* does several things. First, the path for communications is digital. By this we mean that the channels carry digital codes. Next, the path of communications is divided into several channels, some for communications of either voice or data and one for control. Finally, the analog voice energy is converted to an analog electrical equivalent and then converted again to a digital equivalent, to be discussed later. This means that ISDN telephones send the voice energy as digital data over one channel on a digital circuit. The other channel may be used simultaneously to send digital data, allowing the users to speak to a person and communicate computer-to-computer at the same time and on the same line.

Prepaid Wireless

40 percent of the people in the United States don't have checking or credit accounts and rely on prepaid services.

IDC predicts that cellular usage in South America will double by the end of 2004 and that data will increase tenfold by then.

It is estimated that 40 percent of the people living in the United States do not have checking or credit accounts. Some choose to do this overtly, but some are "credit challenged" or have no established credit history, such as younger people. If one doesn't have the credit rating to get an account, the alternative to a contract is prepaid service. (See Figure 3.24.) In the case of cellular telephone providers, one purchases a telephone and prepays for a number of minutes of talk time. In some cases, one can purchase the telephone and minutes as a package in a gasoline service station. Once the number is activated, the system is used just as any other cellular phone. However, when all of the prepaid minutes are used, or the life of the prepaid minutes expires, one has to buy more minutes. This way, you pay-before-you-go, but a poor credit rating does not prevent the use of this technology.

Changing Use of Existing Services

GTE's *Airfone*® is a service on airliners that allows passengers to telephone from their seat. The first installation had one or two cordless phones per airplane. The

Information Window   3–8

One of the features of a new technology is that it generally has features or early uses that may go against established social, civil, or safety issues. The telephone's normal use is for communications but can be used for (social) phone sex. Caller ID provided knowledge of who was calling but was taken to court (civil) by the ACLU as violating the caller's option to make the called individual answer the phone. Now, states (New York) and nations (Japan) are banning the use of cell phones while driving a car due to safety concerns. And many see the Internet's World Wide Web, not as a retail market, but as a place that distributes hate literature and pornography.

FIGURE 3.24
Prepaid Calling Card

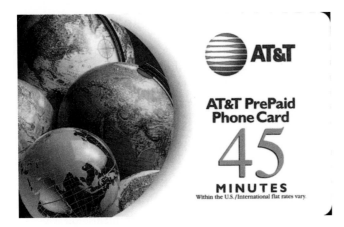

Technology Note   3–14
Telecommunications at Mercedes-Benz

The Mercedes-Benz (MBUSI) manufacturing facility in Vance, Alabama, is located approximately 20 miles southwest of Birmingham on 966 acres. The site includes a 1.1-million-square-foot manufacturing facility that produces 80,000 sport utility vehicles annually. The workforce consists of 1,900 employees on site. The company is part of a global area network that extends to six continents. The telephone system utilizes Lucent Technology Definity G3R hardware; BellSouth provides the local calling service via four ISDN PRI T-1 lines. AT&T provides long-distance service via three PRI T-1 lines. There is one ISDN PRI T-1 line (24 channels) for dial on demand directly on the DaimlerChrysler Corporate Network. Additionally, there are 16 voice channels on an ATM 1-MB bandwidth from Vance to Germany, with additional channels for data connection. The company utilizes fiber SMARTRing technology. The MBUSI/IT department also maintains the five video conferencing rooms at the facility.

Another mission-critical service provided by the IT department is the management of the two-way radio trunk. I once read that communications is the "glue" of the organization. This is absolutely true! In order for MBUSI to build the 21 M Class sport utility vehicles an hour, there have to be lots of people communicating with each other. I previously described how the organization communicates with the world outside of the plant via tele-phone services and EDI. The communications within the plant are imperative. Two-way radios, in addition to pagers and cellular phones, provide a cost-effective way for people involved in building the SUVs to communicate with each other. Each engineer, maintenance person, floor supervisor, and production manager has a two-way radio. Currently, there are 275 mobile radios used at the facility. The trunking system permits a large number of users to share a relatively small number of communication paths (trunks). At MBUSI, this sharing of communications is managed automatically by computer. Channel selections are made by a central controller that makes other decisions normally made by the radio user. The advantages of trunking are faster system access, better channel efficiency, user privacy, and scalability (expansion flexibility). The previous line is a commercial endorsement of Motorola. Some of our Motorola MTX radios have dial pads with which we can connect to the PBX and make phone calls. It is not an ideal practice, but if you do not have a cell phone at your immediate disposal, it is functional.

Dave Hauer, DC employee

Author's note: MBUSI has made plans since this note was written to double the size of the plant, and thus increase the need for communications.

users would go to the station and bring the handset back to their seat. Now you find them on every row of seats, sometimes on the back of each seat.

Airlines found that they could charge for services such as telephone and Internet access as an alternative to a movie.

Originally, Airfone provided only voice service, now (circa 2001) costing $2.99 connection fee and $3.28 per minute for a domestic call.[10] The service was pricey, so they realized that the connectivity they already had was usable with data service. Now you can use their instrument or your laptop to check your email, send facsimiles, get stock quotes from Bloomberg network, and check on weather from the *Weather Channel*®. During the promotion period, you could check your email for $1.99 per minute and no connection charge.

Ubiquitous Wireless Network

The tools of business evolved rapidly during the last quarter of the 20th century. When first available, the mobile telephone and analog pager were expensive perks for the businessperson on the move. The late 1970s saw paging service become low cost and commonplace. The year 1983 ushered in cellular telephones with a prediction of 1,000,000 units in the United States by the end of the century. This prediction missed the number by several million as the Chicago area itself had 900,000 cell phones in 1999. We now have wireless PDAs that connect to the Internet and other wireless services, giving stock and sports quotes to people on the move. Where is this heading? Predictions abound; however, it is dangerous to predict, as indicated above.

Consider the possibilities with a personal appliance, such as the present *Palm Pilot*®, *Blackberry*®, or *Handspring*® PDA *and* connectivity everywhere, for example, a ubiquitous wireless network. One can always be in touch, always be able to make inquiries, and have data at one's disposal, without having to be at a designated spot. As with every new technology, this appliance and ubiquitous connectivity will change the way we live and work. A person can access a store's newspaper advertisements as s/he stands outside the store. Better still, if one tells the appliance what is an interesting purchase, its search engine will find the nearest store that has this item. All of this can take place very rapidly.

Email in the Air

Mobile Computing indicated in its October 2000 issue that AT&T would be offering wireless email access on airliners and at the gate. About the same time *Wayport* is offering a service in Texas airports whereby members can access the Internet wirelessly, using the 11 Mbps IEEE 802.11b wireless LAN standard.

Wireless LANS are finally catching up with ethernet speeds, thanks to the new IEEE 802.11b standard that runs at up to 11 Mbps. IEEE 802.11b broadcasts in the

Information Window   3–9
Looking Ahead—Wireless LANs

We cover data communications and networks in the next chapter, but we add a note here about the wireless possibilities of this environment. A data network is simply two or more computers connected by one or more channels. The channels can be UTP, fiber, or wireless.

---

[10] GTE Airfone advertisement in September 2000 *SKY Magazine*.

Technology Note Compaq: Wireless LAN	3–15

Cut the strings that bind you with the wireless LAN. Use technology that frees you from technology. Total, wireless access to your company's local area network with no wires attached. You'll be working when and where you are most inspired.

Source: http://www5.compaq.com/inspiration/experience.

unlicenced 2.4 Ghz industrial, scientific, and medical (ISM) waveband, meaning it can be used worldwide without special permission.

Wireless Developments

First it was cellular voice; now it is anywhere data.

A significant amount of business is being conducted in a wireless environment and the trend appears to be accelerating. Several firms have reported that their agents now have totally substituted wireless palm-held devices for the notebooks and laptops used just a short time ago. This conversion has contributed to the success of Research In Motion Ltd., a formerly obscure Canadian company. During their first two years after they introduced their *BlackBerry*® device, about 800,000 were sold. The device has been called essentially a pager that can link to corporate email servers to send and receive email. The *BlackBerry* still has a long way to go to equal the *Palm Pilot*®'s success, as they have sold an estimated 10 million handheld computers. The European introduction is expected to provide another boost in *Black-Berry* sales and popularity.

The impact of such wireless devices on the conduct of business is likely to grow as many mobile workers discover the advantages of connectivity. Legal firms are especially pleased with their ability to communicate with their attorneys while they are out of the office.

Satellite Radio and Television

Sirus Satellite Radio®, as of mid 2000, has launched the first of three earth orbit satellites to provide 50 channels of commercial-free music and up to 50 channels of commercial programming, in digital format. Soon you will be able to drive coast-to-coast, listening to the same radio program.

satellite radio
100 radio channels coast-to-coast; 61 music, 39 talk shows.

The satellite radio market, according to investment bank Merrill Lynch, consists of 200 million motorists, including 3 million truckers, 9 million RVs, and more than 22 million consumers underserved by radio.[11]

According to the January 22, 2001, issue *of Autoweek*, the Datron Cruise TV was displayed at the 2001 Consumer Electronics Show, allowing users to receive DirecTV® in their car. So, along with VHS VCR or DVD in the back for the kids, now you can receive live video, movies, and music via DirecTV as you "see the USA in your Chevrolet."

[11] Sirus 1999 Annual Report.

Information Window
Effective Bandwidth

3–10

We know that the actual *maximum* bandwidth of a modem is that which is advertised or less. For example, a 33.6 Kbps modem can pass a maximum of 33,600 bps or less, depending on connectivity. The *effective* rate can be higher. Thus, the effective bandwidth of any channel can be the advertised, less, or more.

First, any given channel has a native bandwidth. For example, a DS0 is designated to have a 64 Kbps bandwidth, with about 56 Kbps as being usable and the other being overhead. If the circuit on which the DS0 resides is noisy, the effective bandwidth will be less due to either retransmission or the system slowing down to work better in the noise. The effective bandwidth however, can, be increased via compression. So the resultant effective bandwidth of a channel is dependent on the native structure, noise environment, and compression.

Wireless Bandwidth

The amount of bandwidth we can achieve on any medium, wired or wireless, is dependent on the native bandwidth available, the congestion of the spectrum, the noise environment, and the amount of compression possible. For UTP, coaxial cable, and fiber strands, the user is in a baseband mode and has all of the native bandwidth unless there are active devices in the line. With IR wireless, a limited portion of the light spectrum is available. With radio wireless, the spectrum is congested and there are many requests for all frequencies. This means that the use of digital modulation onto the analog radio carrier is even more important because significant compression ratios are possible. As noted with the cellular telephone, the various protocols offer different forms of compression and spectrum sharing, thus providing greater bandwidth.

It is predicted that cellular bandwidth for data will reach full-motion, full-color video by 2006.

How Do We Connect All Those Wireless Devices?

A person on the move will likely have a laptop computer, a personal digital assistant for scheduling, a cellular telephone, and possibly a pager. These devices often carry copies of the same data. Until the advent of *Bluetooth*® you would have to use a cable to make connections, if connectivity between devices was supported, and then move or synchronize the data on the different machines. In order to take advantage of the technology, Toshiba became the first to debut *Bluetooth*-ready notebook computers with built-in antenna, for both long- and short-range wireless networks. The *Bluetooth* capability offers the ability to do this wirelessly and automatically, as Technology Note 3.16 indicates.

The Last Mile Considerations

The distance from the junction point of POTS, CATV, or even power service to the home is referred to as the *last mile*. Here is where single circuits must be installed and often it means adding poles in neighborhoods or digging up the street, sidewalks, and yards. It's the most expensive portion of the total circuit.

Telephone companies have local loops of UTP for the last mile to most homes and offices; CATV companies have coaxial cable; power companies have electrical circuits. As the need for greater bandwidth grows, the question arises as to whether the present last mile circuit can transport greater bandwidth or if new media must be installed. For example, technology in Europe provides the possibility of using the power circuits for data, although not a wide bandwidth due to noise. POTS UTP can be converted to xDSL with only the addition of technology at each end, providing the

Technology Note   3–16

Bluetooth wireless technology will enable users to connect a wide range of computing and telecommunications devices easily and simply, without the need to buy, carry, or connect cables. It delivers opportunities for rapid ad hoc connections, and the possibility of automatic, unconscious, connections between devices. It will virtually eliminate the need to purchase additional or proprietary cabling to connect individual devices. Because *Bluetooth* wireless technology can be used for a variety of purposes,

it will also potentially replace multiple cable connections via a single radio link. It creates the possibility of using mobile data in a different way, for different applications such as "surfing on the sofa," "the instant postcard," "three in one phone," and many others. It will allow them to think about what they are working on, rather than how to make their technology work.

Source: http://www.bluetooth.com/bluetoothguide/faq/1.asp.

Technology Note   3–17

Time Domain has developed the *PulsON™* chipset based upon time modulated–ultra wideband (TM-UWB). TM-UWB is the underlying architecture behind PulsON technology that has the potential to enable entirely new wireless applications and products, magnitudes of improvement to existing wireless applications, and tremendous consumer and public safety benefits. Instead of traditional sine waves, Time Domain's PulsON sends millions of low-power coded pulses per second across an ultra wideband of spectrum producing high speed and high performance for communications, radar, and precise positioning/tracking.

Ultra wideband uses extremely low-power radio pulses (50 millionths of a watt) that extend across a large portion of the spectrum, from 1 gigahertz to 4 gigahertz. Because UWB sends the pulses at such low power and across such

a broad frequency range—and because the pulses are so short (half a billionth of a second)—receivers listening for transmissions at specific frequencies perceive them as mere background noise—as the low-level signals that exist almost everywhere and that are almost universally ignored as long as they don't interfere with reception.

Time Domain's system sends out 40 million pulses a second at differing, but precisely defined, intervals. Delaying or advancing a pulse by a few trillionths of a second defines it as a digital 1 or 0, creating a short-range data carrier capable of transmitting up to 10 megabits per second or more (depending on the protocol used and other factors) at distances up to 150 feet.

Source: http://www.timedomain.com.

present voice channel and higher bandwidth data channels. A question that remains is whether utility companies will install fiber circuits to the home or go wireless.

The last mile is the most expensive portion of a voice, video, or data circuit.

The decision to provide fiber or a wireless environment is dictated by several considerations. First, what is the total bandwidth required? Second, what amount of compression is available, for example, is it enough to use existing channels? Third, will switching be done at a central office or in the home? These last two considerations can be demonstrated by television. Do you want to deliver and receive 300 channels simultaneously, requiring fiber, or just one or two channels at a time, like satellite DBS, with the channel switching done at a central office? This latter is possible via xDSL over POTS local loops.

As a reminder, we discussed LMDS and MMDS in the category of wireless CATV. These are ready candidates for wireless last mile considerations. The new entrant to this arena is the technology of *time modulated–ultra wideband architecture*. As described in Technology Note 3.17, this emerging technology allows for high bandwidth wireless digital communications over a finite distance to the home from a central neighbor podium.

Wireless Point-to-Point and Multipoint

Figures 3.25 and 3.26 illustrate two types of wireless connectivity. The first is *point-to-point* and, in this case, represents a wireless T-1 circuit. This shows two simplex circuits, one in each direction, providing good connectivity without requiring right-of-way or construction, as long as the two buildings can see each other. The second shows the use of *point-to-multipoint* radio, providing bidirectional, omnidirectional service to several buildings. This instance is described as a MAN (metropolitan area network), providing services to business or SOHOs in an area of town.

Business Decisions about Wireless Technology

Can you afford for a businessperson to be out of touch?

In our age of frequent business restructuring, wireless technologies seem to offer a great deal of promise to improve efficiencies in business processes. In essence,

FIGURE 3.25
Wireless T-1
(Point-to-Point)

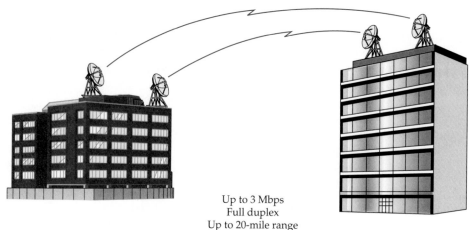

Up to 3 Mbps
Full duplex
Up to 20-mile range
Point-to-point transmission of synchronous data

FIGURE 3.26
Wireless MAN

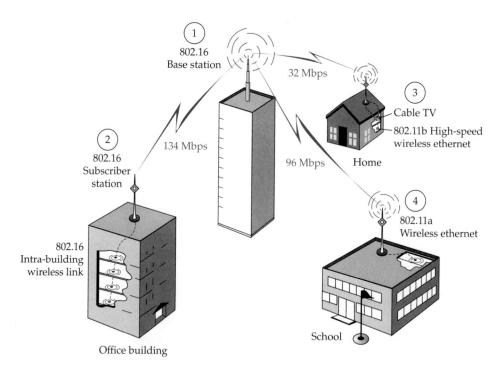

these technologies enable businesses to innovate and change the conventional wisdom about where and how business should be done.

Business managers need to be able to evaluate the candidate processes that can benefit from wireless solutions. Below are some considerations that should help in the evaluation.

One of the first questions is whether there are instances where immediate action needs to be taken on high-value information. Wireless can provide the means to speed up the decision process and the responsiveness to customer needs and other critical issues.

Wireless technologies also can help track assets and people. This feature enables the monitoring of shipments, people's locations, equipment, and so forth. Can knowing the locations of employees and assets provide value? FedEx and United Parcel Service (UPS) have been using wireless for years to track shipments and deliveries.

Wireless devices free employees to spend more time on tasks at customer premises and other mobile jobs such as remote repairs, sales, meeting of potential customers, and so on. Business managers need to determine if greater mobility will enhance productivity or work performance of mobile workers.

Can the provision of access to data be a means of providing enhanced customer service? One airline has been experimenting with a system that would provide wireless notification of its customers of changes in flight schedules. This could reduce aggravation when delays or cancellations can be communicated before the customer departs for the airport. Such applications could contribute to competitive advantage.

An ability to provide data or information at a location where it is needed might enable process streamlining. Many firms find it desirable to move functions closer to the customer, and wireless supports this concept. Empowered employees could do invoices and billing on customer premises. This application could shorten billing cycles and improve cash flow.

Anywhere that data are captured in a field location and later entered elsewhere may become candidates for using wireless. Wireless devices can enable direct data collection and entry. This can be a cost savings from eliminating re-entry expense. In addition, utility companies can reduce costs using wireless. These companies can set up wireless meter readers that do not require humans in the field.

Clarity Consulting has developed a list of key questions to ask in selecting a wireless strategy. They are summarized below:

WHO will use the application?

Device and application needs should be tailored to the user's requirements. Characteristics such as processing power, displays, data entry/capture capability, portability, and ease of use should be viewed from the user's perspective.

HOW will the application be used?

Immediacy, data source and volume, and processing are considerations here.

WHERE will the application be used?

Proximity or range needed, coverage area, and bandwidth are factors to consider.

WHAT data are required?

Would a business-person need video on his/her cell phone or wireless PDA?

What data sources, degree of confidentiality, formatting, synchronization with others, and processing requirements should be assessed.

Managers must be aware that there are several constraints and issues regarding the deployment of wireless solutions. Many of these issues will be mollified as the 3G systems are made widely available. Certainly, managers must be concerned with standards, coverage, bandwidth, security, and support tools available. Constraints such as device size, ease of use, display size and resolution, keyboard size, portability, and useful battery life are clearly to be evaluated. One consideration that management must acknowledge is the susceptibility to loss. This includes interception of data as well as high rates of theft and loss of the devices themselves.

Case 3-1
Analog versus Digital Cellular

Heath Campbell

INTRODUCTION

An estimated 100 million people in the United States have a cell phone and the number is increasing every day [8]. However, very few people truly understand the technology behind these devices that have revolutionized our lives. The purpose of this case is to explain the technology and standards in use today in simple, easy-to-understand terms.

TECHNOLOGY BASICS

A cell phone is basically a two-way radio that acts like a telephone. Currently there are two distinct types of cell phones available: digital and analog. Most people are aware of the two types of cell phones available, but aside from the price difference do not understand the true technological differences. Basically, analog or digital refers to the method used to convert information into an electrical signal.

Analog cell phones, besides being cheaper, are based on an older technology. In analog systems, an electrical voltage or current is generated that is proportionate to the sound (i.e., voice) being observed. For example, when you speak, your voice creates sound waves that oscillate at certain frequencies. An analog telephone creates a voltage that goes up and down in unison with the sound your voice creates, that is, the voltage is "analogous" to the tone. These signals are then transmitted to the base station by modulating the audio directly onto a carrier much like FM radio is transmitted through the air by converting the music to an RF signal.

In a digital system the "oscillations" are expressed as a number. A digital phone converts the audio to digital "ones (1's)" and "zeros (0's)" through sampling. These digital samples are numbers that represent varying voltage levels at specific points in time. At the receiving end, the digital systems convert the voltage signals back to analog, or sound wave, form.

WHY IS DIGITAL BETTER?

By now you are wondering, "What makes digital better (and more expensive) than analog?" A digital system may be more complex than an analog system; however, there are a number of advantages to digital systems. The primary advantage is that once the signal is in digital form, it can be processed and manipulated to gain a number of improvements. One such improvement is the ability for error detection and correction through the use of extra data that are added to the signal and then checked at the reception point to ensure accurate transmission [7]. Analog systems, on the other hand, are more susceptible to interference in the transmitted signal. This interference is then converted directly back into the recovered signal.

One example of analog interference is the static heard on an AM radio during a thunderstorm or noisy FM reception from a car radio when stopped at a red light in a dead spot or behind a hill. In the digital systems, the equipment examines the voltage being sent and determines if it is a zero or a one. The testing point is halfway between zero volts (the signal for sending a zero "0") and five volts (the signal for sending a one "1"), or 2.5 volts. For example, when sending a zero, the noise or static must be substantial enough to reach a level of 2.6 volts before it would be misinterpreted as a one. Thus, in the digital system, the noise must be 50 percent of the signal level or greater to be detected at all. In an analog signal, noise of 1 to 10 percent can easily be detected. This is just one reason why digital systems are generally less noisy than analog systems.

Another advantage of digital is increased call capacity. Cell phones use frequency modulation as a carrier signal to transmit messages. This radio signal only allows one conversation per radio channel, so call capacity is limited to the number of frequencies in use. Analog systems use high-power base stations that require large areas between towers. This limits the availability of each frequency and causes analog networks to be easily overloaded. Digital systems use multiple low-power base stations to alleviate this problem. By using low-power base stations, digital systems are able to increase the number of cells within a certain perimeter. Frequencies can be duplicated by base stations that are just a few cells away. This frequency duplication is one method that allows for increased call capacity. Others will be described later.

IF DIGITAL SYSTEMS ARE SO MUCH BETTER, WHY DO WE HAVE ANALOG TODAY?

There are two primary reasons why we still have the old analog phone systems. First is the large investment necessary to convert the analog infrastructure currently in the United States to a digital system. In addition to converting the carrier's equipment to digital, the users of cellular service will have to discard their old analog cell phones and purchase newer and more expensive digital phones. The other reason is the need to decide on an accepted digital standard.

CELL PHONE STANDARDS

"Cell phone standards" refers to the digital encoding format of the signal being processed and transmitted. Currently there are several standards generally accepted in the industry: TDMA (time division multiple access), CDMA (code division multiple access), NAMPS (advanced mobile phone service), and GSM (Global System for Mobile Communications).

TDMA

Time division multiple access, as suggested by the name, divides a channel into separate time slots to allow for multiple conversations on the same frequency. This is done through compression of the voice, which is then transmitted in a regular series of bursts. These bursts of data are sent in a cycle and interspersed with other users' conversations, with each user getting an equivalent time slot in each cycle. TDMA allows for a three-to-one improvement in call capacity over the existing analog system. TDMA was the first digital system developed and implemented in the United States and it reached a high level of market penetration before the development of CDMA.

CDMA

Code division multiple access uses spread spectrum technology to scatter the transmission over a range of frequencies as opposed to sending it down a single channel. Theoretically, this would allow for 10 to 20 times higher capacity than the current analog system. CDMA offers many other benefits including improved call quality, simplified system planning through the use of the same frequency in every sector of every cell, enhanced security and privacy, improved coverage allowing for fewer cells, and increased bandwidth. Due to the added benefits of CDMA, many cellular companies are researching it as the possible standard of the future.

NAMPS

The controversy over CDMA and TDMA has led to the development of NAMPS. NAMPS (advanced mobile phone service) is an improvement of the current analog system format used in the United States. *NAMPS is not a digital format;* instead it uses digital encoding to boost call capacity by about three-to-one over the existing analog system. NAMPS was developed in order to allow cellular providers greater capacity while the benefits of TDMA and CDMA are being evaluated.

GSM

In Europe, the controversy over digital standards was resolved by designating a "board" to select a standard for communications protocol. This board was called the GSM (Global System for Mobile Communications) board and developed the GSM standard. GSM is a TDMA standard currently being used in Europe. GSM also is used in the United States, Canada, and other parts of the world, although employing different frequencies than the European standard.

SUMMARY AND CONCLUSION

The comparisons in this case clearly reveal two distinct advantages of digital cell phone systems over analog cell phone systems. These advantages are improved voice quality and increased call capacity. Among the digital standards currently available, CDMA is superior in sound quality, calling capacity, and available bandwidth and is a candidate to become the digital standard of the future.

BIBLIOGRAPHY

1. Houston Carr and Charles Snyder, *The Management of Telecommunications: Business Solutions to Business Problems* (Burr Ridge, IL: Irwin/McGraw-Hill, 1997) pp. 199–203.

2. Benjamin Lange, "A Virtual PBX.com Tech Tutorial—Analog vs. Digital Systems Explained," March 1999. http://www.virtualpbx.com/ana_vs_dig.html.

3. http://www.virtualpbx.com/what_is_c_ph.html.

4. http://.iit.edu/~diazrob/cell.

5. http://www.iit.edu/~diazrob/cell/basics.html.

6. http://www.iit.edu/~diazrob/cell/analogDigital.html.

7. http://www.wow-com.com.

Case 3-2
Cellular Technology

John Matlock

INTRODUCTION

NTT DoCoMo, Japan's leading mobile operator, launched its commercial 3G (third-generation wireless) service on Monday, October 1, 2001. Known as Freedom of Mobile multimedia Access (FOMA), NTT DoCoMo is using industry standard IMT-2000 to achieve downlink speeds of 384 Kbps, enabling fast and smooth video streaming and wireless data communications for customers. [1] In contrast, companies in the U.S. wireless market are unlikely to launch commercial 3G anytime soon given the current economic slowdown and ongoing military operations worldwide. Negotiations between U.S. Federal Communications Commission, Commerce Department, Department of Defense, Federal Aviation Administration, other government agencies, and wireless providers are on hold pending the "war on terrorism." "As a country we're all worried about the most basic human need for security," said Blair Levin, an analyst for Legg Mason in Washington, DC. "That's going to take priority over mobile data needs by civilians so we can watch movies on our cell phones." [2]

MOBILE COMMUNICATIONS CONCEPT

Mobile communications embrace two key concepts. The primary concept is that smaller is better. Cellular companies break a large area down into adjacent hexagonal cells of roughly equal area. Radio towers, known as base stations, occupy the center of each cell and communicate with wireless devices. The second concept is that less is better. This concept diminishes transmission power from base station towers. Applying both concepts simultaneously enables reduced transmission power and reduced cell areas to allow for reuse of radio frequencies (in nonadjacent cells). These concepts allow for many more users of the service compared to one frequency over a larger area. [3]

WIRELESS/CELLULAR FUNDAMENTALS

The key to wireless/cellular networks is the mobile switching center (MSC) or mobile telephone switching office (MTSO). The MSC connects smaller cells into a larger networked system. The mobile communications network looks like this diagram [3]:

Mobile Communications Network [3]

Source: R. Costello, *Basic Concepts of Communications: An Introduction*, available at http://www.gartner.com (October 15, 2001).

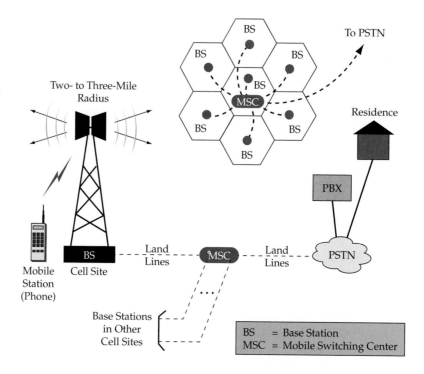

1G FIRST GENERATION (ANALOG) WIRELESS

Better known as analog cellular, first generation wireless uses technology known as advanced mobile phone system (AMPS) to optimize use of transmission frequencies. AMPS devices connect to a base station using a specific frequency. Approximately 1,000 frequencies are available for use at any particular time and two cells are able to use the same frequency for a voice call if they are not adjacent to each other. [4] Erricson AMPS uses a frequency range of 850–900 MHz. Digital TDMA standards (known as D-AMPS) provide the evolutionary path to a digital environment. [5] See Evolutionary Path of Wireless Technology at Appendix A.

1.5G (DIGITAL WIRELESS)

During the mid 1990s, providers introduced digital wireless service. These devices were based on a variety of standards including TDMA, GSM, and CDMA. GSM is by far the leading standard with 220 million handsets shipped in 2001, compared to 49 million and 72 million handsets shipped for TDMA and CDMA respectively. [6] This wireless technology provides digital voice service, 9.6 to 14.4 Kbps data service, and enhanced calling features such as call waiting, Caller ID, and voice mail. However, 1.5G does not provide the customer with always-on data connection. Time division multiple access (TDMA) communication technology divides a single radio frequency channel into six unique time slots, allowing a number of users to access a single channel at one time without interference. By dividing the channel into slots, three signals (two time slots for each signal) can be transmitted over a single channel. Thus, TDMA technology, also referred to as ANSI-136, provides a three-to-one gain in capacity over analog technology. Each caller is assigned a specific time slot for transmission. [7]

GSM, or Global System for Mobile Communications, is a digital cellular or PCS network used throughout the world that shares the same time division multiple access transmission method as TDMA. CDMA is a spread spectrum technology, spreading the information contained in a particular signal of interest over a much greater bandwidth than the original signal. [8] TDMA and CDMA are used primarily in the Americas, while GSM is used primarily in Europe and Asia, although GSM has a wide user base in the United States, for example, Voice Stream.

3G (THIRD-GENERATION HIGH-SPEED DIGITAL WIRELESS)

Competing companies worldwide are migrating to 3G wireless as fast as possible. Most firms are preparing to migrate to 3G in various steps. In Europe GSM will migrate to Universal Mobile Telecommunications System (UMTS) using Enhanced Data Rates for Global Evolution (EDGE), which in essence bumps data rates up to 384 Kbps. EDGE also is used on TDMA networks to migrate to 3G. Another technology, general packet radio service (GPRS) will enable GSM networks to transfer data and wireless Internet content over the network at 115 Kbps. Using a packet data service, subscribers are always connected and always online, so services will be easy and quick to access. Finally, CDMA competitors will migrate to cdma2000, an additional standard under IMT-2000 (International Telecommunication Union [ITU], a UN agency). Cdma2000 enables providers to use existing hardware to initially migrate to 3G 1x, providing data rates of 144 Kbps and doubling the voice capacity of the network. The follow-on evolution for cdma2000 is to migrate to 3G 1xEV with data rates capable of 2.4 Mbps.

Other technologies for migration include wideband code division multiple access (WCDMA). In WCDMA voice, images, data, and video are first converted to a narrowband digital radio signal. The signal is assigned a marker (spreading code) to distinguish it from the signal of other users. WCDMA uses variable rate techniques in digital processing and can achieve multirate transmissions. WCDMA has been adopted as a standard by the ITU under the name IMT-2000 direct spread. [7] This is the technology in use by NTT DoCoMo in the Japanese market. Below is an overview of potential bandwidth for each technology standard:

Comparison of 3G Technology Speeds

Source: "Leading the Evolution to 3G," available at http://www.sprintpcs.com/about sprint pcs/Cdma_3g/index.html (October 15, 2001).

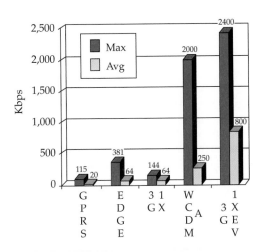

SUMMARY

Undoubtedly, migration to G3 will be slow and evolutionary here in the United States but potentially very fast and efficient once issues related to frequency management are resolved. Europe has adopted a standard with limited bandwidth in its migration to G3. Finally, Asia is moving quickly to adopt IMT-2000/WCDMA standards to achieve exceptional bandwidth now. Sprint PCS perceives the threat from existing/new entrants versus bandwidth to look like the chart below:

The Race to Reach 3G

Source: "Leading the Evolution to 3G," available at http://www.sprintpcs.com/aboutsprintpcs/Cdma_3g/index.html (October 15, 2001).

	2000	2001	2002	2003	2004
Sprint PCS CDMA 2000 path:	1S-95A 14.4 kbps	3G1X 144 kbps Field Trial 4Q	3G1X 144 kbps Nationwide mid 2002	3G1X 288 kbps 3G1xEV-DO 2.2Mbps	3G1xEV-DV 3 to 5 Mbps
GSM:	GSM 9.5 kbps	GPRS 115 kbps	EDGE 384 kbps	W-CDMA 2 Mbps	?
TDMA:	CDPD 19.2 kbps	GSM GPRS 115 kbps	EDGE 364 kbps	W-CDMA 2 Mbps	?

APPENDIX A

Evolutionary Path of Wireless Technology

	Technology	Pros and Cons
1G	AMPS (advanced mobile phone service)	■ Analog voice service only
1.5G	CDMA (code division multiple access) TDMA (time division multiple access) GSM (Global System for Mobile Communications)	■ Digital voice service ■ 9.6-Kbps to 14.4-Kbps data service ■ Enhanced calling features (such as Caller ID) ■ No always-on data connection ■ Superior voice quality
3G	W-CDMA (wideband code division multiple access) cdma2000 (based on the IS-95 CDMA standard)	■ Always-on data connection up to 2 Mbps ■ Broadband data services (such as streaming audio and video)

BIBLIOGRAPHY

1. FOMA, NTT DoCoMo. Retrieved October 15, 2001, from http://www.NTTDo CoMo.com.

2. "U.S. Taking the Slow Road to 3G." Retrieved October 15, 2001, from http://www.zdnet.com/zdnn/stories/news/0,4586,2815630,00.html? chkpt=zdnn_rt_latest.

3. R. Costello. *Basic Concepts of Communications: An Introduction.* Retrieved October 15, 2001, from http://www.gartner.com.

4. *Technology A–Z.* Retrieved October 15, 2001, from http://www.ericsson.com/ technology.

5. H. Carr and C. Snyder. *The Management of Telecommunications.* Burr Ridge, IL: Irwin/McGraw-Hill, 1997.

6. B. Baxter. *Wireless Update.* Half Moon Bay, CA: Murenove, Inc., 2001.

7. "Frequently Asked Questions." Retrieved October 15, 2001, from http://www. uwcc.org/edge/tdma_faq.html.

8. "Leading the Evolution to 3G." Retrieved October 15, 2001, from http://www. sprintpcs.com/aboutsprintpcs/Cdma_3g/index.html.

Summary

This chapter discussed the channels of telecommunications. More specifically, it addressed the circuit media of these channels, the physical paths on which the data ride. Whether it be the twisted-pair of the telephone local loop, the coaxial cable of CATV, or space for radio, television, and satellite, all channels must have a circuit medium.

Voice communications have historically used analog signals and the media of copper wire and microwave and satellite radio. This remains true today for the Telcos, but most of the long-distance traffic rides on fiber cables. The use of radio in cellular systems has gained great acceptance and could even threaten the existence of wired switched telephone systems. Cellular technology has such value to businesses that the seemingly high costs are readily accepted as the best alternative available. Meanwhile, this original analog technology is giving way to the newer PCS digital mode to provide greater clarity and security.

Recent changes in legislation in the United States (see Chapter 9 for details) have allowed many more operators to provide telecommunications services. Some, like the CATV and phone companies, have large investments in coaxial and twisted-pair cable plants. It is financially prudent to use the installed physical plant, so the CATV companies are working to make use of their coaxial cable in the neighborhood while distributing the signals there via fiber cables. As we discuss in a later chapter, the Telcos are finding that their twisted-pair circuits have the ability to carry significant bandwidth, giving them new uses for this old technology.

Wireless technology, radio, microwave, satellite, and infrared are finding new uses in the area of data communications. These media allow channels without a need for right-of-way and expensive digging. They offer the potential to change the way the business operates as they give convenient and low-cost connectivity.

The subject of media is one of technology, of bandwidth, and of connectivity. As with all choices, the one you make may be low cost but managerially constraining. The question will always arise whether to use an existing medium or install a new one. The one you have may be a low-cost good, but the new one offers new opportunities. Thus, the choice always has management implications.

Key Terms

advanced mobile phone service (AMPS), *105*
air-medium radio, *96*
amplifier, *86*
attenuation, *85*
bandwidth, *80-93*
baseband, *89*
baud, *88*
broadband, *89*
cable modem, *89*
cable television (CATV), *86*
capacity, *78*
cellular blocking, *105*
cellular phone, *102*
cellular radio, *102*
channel, *79*
circuit, *79*
coaxial cable, *86*
code division multiple access (CDMA), *107*
crosstalk, *90*
dense wave division multiplexing (DWDM), *91*
digital, *116*
digital subscriber line (DSL), *84*
electrical, *79*
electromagnetic, *79*
electromagnetic interference (EMI), *85*
electronic bulletin board systems (BBS), *88*
Federal Communications Commission (FCC), *85*

fiber optic cable, *89*
fiber optic circuit, *89*
fiber to the curb (FTTC), *93*
fixed node, *95*
fixed wireless, *95*
full duplex, *89*
global positioning system (GPS), *115*
Global System for Mobile Communications (GSM), *106*
high definition television (HDTV), *99*
hybrid fiber/coax (HFC), *91-93*
infrared, *115*
integrated services digital network (ISDN), *84*
local multipoint distribution service (LMDS), *113*
medium, *78*
microwave radio, *79*
movable node, *96*
moving node, *96*
multipoint microwave distribution system (MMDS), *112*
National Television Standards Committee (NTSC), *89*
noise, *85*
omnidirectional radio, *79*

pager, *107*
personal communications, *107*
personal communications system, *103*
photonic, *79*
portable telephone, *108*
radio, *79*
radio frequency interference (RFI), *85*
satellite, *79*
shielding, *83*
small or home office (SOHO), *85*
solid wire, *82*
spectrum, *97*
spread spectrum technology, *109*
stranded wire, *83*
time division multiple access (TDMA), *106*
twisted-pair, *81*
unshielded twisted pair (UTP), *84*
wide area telecommunications service (WATS), *80*
wired, *95*
wired connectivity, *94*
wireless, *94*
wireless communications, *94*
World Wide Web (WWW), *101*

Recommended Readings

Gartner.com
MetaGroup.com
TECHRepublic.com

Discussion
Questions

3.1. What effect will cellular phones have on small business in the next 10 years?

3.2. How feasible do you think it is for every employee of a firm to have a portable telephone?

3.3. What transmission media would you expect to dominate in voice communications in the 21st century?

3.4. Are personal communications devices, in general, and cellular telephones, in particular, safe?

3.5. Do you think there is a viable career in being a telecommunications manager in an organization?

3.6. Discuss some of the cost–benefit categories that a manager must understand in making the voice telecommunications decisions for an organization.

3.7. How is Michael's business similar to other small businesses in its need for accounting information?

3.8. What advantages does the service bureau afford Michael's business over the manual system?

3.9. What are the telecommunications issues involved in the decision to use a service bureau?

3.10. If Michael places a terminal in the home of an employee, what are some of the business concerns he should consider? Consider costs, benefits, and risks in your answer.

3.11. How can a business be operated by employees who remain at home most of the work week?

Projects

3.1. Visit a simple business in your community and determine its telecommunications profile. What telecommunications equipment is employed, what vendors or sources are used, and what services are used? What telecommunications problems does the business encounter?

3.2. Take your telephone directory and look up the services available to a simple business. List the alternatives the business manager should be aware of.

3.3. Go to the Yellow Pages of your phone book and identify businesses and their telecommunications needs, rating them on a continuum from high need to low need, noting why the need is as you say. Do you expect the businesses on the low end have any reason to move towards the high end?

3.4. What can the small, rapidly expanding business do to *properly* plan its telecommunications expansion to keep from buying too small or too large? Take an example of such a business and develop a telecommunications plan for an anticipated 30 percent growth rate per year.

3.5. Contact your local telephone provider and determine services offered to small businesses. What are the gaps in needed services?

3.6. Using Case 3.1, choose an organization and determine if they are candidates for cellular service. Describe how a cost–benefit analysis could be conducted for adopting cellular service and allocating service among employees. Use the who, how, where, and what key questions in your evaluation. What recommendations would you make for choosing a cellular protocol?

Chapter **Four**

Data Communications: The Basics

CONTINUING CASE—PART 4

Michael Finds a New Business

Michael had come a long way in just six months. He now spent more time at home and had a better record-keeping system than before. One day, as he enjoyed lunch at a nearby restaurant, instead of gulping down a sandwich at the office, he told a friend who had an office nearby of his new capability. His friend, Lewis Johns, was in the home appliance business with his two sons and admitted quickly that he also was spending too much time on paperwork and not enough time selling or fixing equipment (producing income) or at home. Lewis said he could not afford, or really did not want, to hire even a part-time bookkeeper, so Michael asked if he could set him up on Michael's accounting system and let him pay Matilda to input the data. Because of their friendship, Lewis agreed to let Michael try. They further settled on Lewis paying Michael for all of his costs plus a 20 percent fee.

Michael had not intended to expand his business beyond security patrols, lines of security, and lighting equipment, but this venture seemed like a way to pay for some of his computer costs. He told Lewis that he would ask Matilda if she would like to work extra time for him and that he would arrange with the bank to establish a new system for Lewis. Michael told Matilda of the opportunity, and she readily agreed to input the data and print off the reports at night, for the usual hourly wage. She received last year's data from Lewis and started the job.

Michael invited Lewis to lunch a month later to discuss how his bookkeeper was doing on the computer system. Lewis was very pleased with the service and told Michael that he had told two friends about the service. Michael had not expected more business so quickly, but immediately wrote down the names that Lewis gave him. After lunch Michael called the two small companies and arranged to show them his capability and talk prices. Since he had a month's computer experience behind him, he decided that a 30 percent fee above expenses was in order. He signed up both accounts and told Matilda later that day of his new line of business: ***Johnson Information Services (JIS)***.

"And do I do all of the work?" she asked.

"I have an idea I think you will really like, Matilda," Michael responded. "How about placing a DECWriter and modem in your home, and you work there. That way you won't have to commute to the office or even stay late to do the work you do now. The firms will deliver the data to you, and I will bring our sales slips, bills, and invoices to your house on my way home each day. You enter the data for each account and print the reports. Keep records of how much time you spend on each account, and give them to me each week. What do you think?"

"I think you are brilliant, boss! When do we start?"

"Let me call the bank to set up more accounting systems and lease two more DECWriters, no, make that three—we need one for your home. Then I will call Harry for three more **acoustic coupler** modems. I guess we should put in another telephone line at your home so you can talk on the phone while on the computer. Maybe you should tell your family tonight as I think the equipment will arrive soon."

"Great, I should go home and clean up the extra bedroom. That will be my office. Can I write off some expenses for using it as an office?"

"Well, I think we had better ask the IRS, but I am pretty sure you can. To be sure we are in agreement, you will have the data delivered to you at your home and do most of your work there. I think you will need to come to the office once or twice a week to be sure our records are in shape here. I will pick up my reports when I drop by to give you our data. The other companies will pick up their reports when they want them. By the way, I've raised your compensation by 10 percent."

"Sounds neat, Mr. Johnson. And I can work any time I want?"

"Yes, any time you want, as long as you get the data entered and the reports produced on time. I want you to learn as much about the bank's computer as you can and see if there are more ways to use their system. Meanwhile, I am pretty sure I can get a few more clients. Make sure I don't give you more work than you can handle. When we start to overload you, we will need to find other people to work for you entering data."

"Uhm, it sounds like I will be a supervisor. I'll ask my sister if she wants to do some work when the time comes. I think she is still pretty good at typing and could learn data entry quickly. If we hire her, would we put a terminal in her home or an extra in mine?"

"It's up to you, but we will talk about it when it happens."

What Michael has introduced for Matilda is telecommuting. Instead of driving to the office, Matilda has "virtual presence." More organizations will face this issue as people in the workforce prefer to stay at home or are unable to commute, for example, workers with disabilities or parents of young children. Telecommuting has become extremely important and is a growing phenomenon. We will discuss it in more detail later.

Michael went home early that day, planning to drive up to the lake for dinner. He was pleased about his new venture, **Johnson Information Services**, and was beginning to see how telecommunications was making a difference. Without having to be there more than once a week, he was managing the Colorado Springs office from a distance because of the telephone and new terminals. The telephone was an asset, extending the range of his business. Now, with the bank's computer, he was able to use the phone lines and terminals to both improve his own business and enter a new one. All of these changes happened because he needed a line of credit; they happened without any formal planning.

Michael now has established a data communications network. The network is composed of several nodes, or terminal points. For example, Michael's terminal is a node, as is the bank's computer. There are nodes at the JL&S main office, the bank service bureau, and the home of Matilda in Denver, as well as at the JL&S office in Colorado Springs. This sort of network is a predecessor of the more elaborate networks that have evolved today, which we discuss in subsequent chapters. But it is also only a precursor of the JL&S expanding network.

"I am not sure all this success is good," Michael thought. "Maybe I should spend part of this weekend thinking about what business I want to be in and how I should manage it. I also should find out where I can learn more about computers and communications, as that seems to be a source of a lot of money."

He absentmindedly turned on the radio as he drove and hummed along with the music. "Another form of telecommunications," he thought, looking at the radio.

Expansion at JL&S

Michael and Carlton had enjoyed another good year. Their services were well accepted in Denver and Colorado Springs, and profits were higher than expected. The companies were generating a substantial amount of cash, some of which Michael invested in small improvements, but most of which he placed in certificates of deposit (CDs). Even after giving all of his employees a nice raise, there was a large surplus for investment. Michael was alert for new opportunities to expand the operations of JEI and JL&S. One of his pet ideas was to move JL&S into a wider territory. It seemed natural to investigate Colorado's Rocky Mountain Front Range area for opportunities.

Michael found that Woodie Van Allen, the owner of Mile High Security, was having marital problems and was planning on leaving the state to pursue a new opportunity. Mile High offered a line of services in Boulder and Fort Collins, Colorado, that were similar to those marketed by JL&S in Denver and Colorado Springs. Woodie called Michael and offered to sell the company very reasonably if Michael could make up his mind quickly.

As Michael hung up the phone, he realized that this was the opportunity to expand JL&S and to move into more cities in the Front Range area of Colorado. He wanted to talk with both Woodie and Carlton about this, and even include Bill for strategy as well as his Colorado Springs security chief, Tom Marshall, for operational considerations. All of this would take more time, and Woodie had said time was of the essence in this deal.

"Telephone conferencing!" thought Michael out loud. He picked up the phone and called the telephone operator.

"Operator."

"How do I make a conference call with Boulder, Colorado Springs, and three phones here in Denver?"

"All you have to do is give me the phone numbers, and I will make the connections for you. You will be the last number I connect."

"Great, here are the numbers."

After 25 minutes on the phone with all of the people involved, Michael was convinced that this was a good deal, pending his careful evaluation of the financial condition of the company. He had long coveted the Boulder and Fort Collins market due to its proximity to Denver and the potential of two additional university customers (Figure 4.1). Now he had a real chance to expand there with a head start. He jumped into one of the new patrol cars and drove to Boulder, taking along a portable terminal and modem. After summarizing the terms of sale, he dialed up his computer from Boulder and loaded Woodie's financial statements into his accounting system. Michael then produced reports that gave him a familiar view of Woodie's company and the possibilities when he totaled the two companies' assets and liabilities. With this knowledge, and the belief that Carlton could work closely with Woodie's employees, the two men shook hands and agreed on the purchase price and terms of the acquisition. Michael went to the bank the next day to arrange for the purchase of Mile High Security.

With the acquisition of Mile High Security, JEI had doubled the number of facilities to four locations. This meant greater dispersion of facilities, people, and control. As control extends geographically, the ability to manage from a central location becomes stretched. Therefore, his need for good managers at each location had now become more critical as he had to share his time between more products, services, and locations. This meant relin-

quishing or delegating some authority and control. Michael believed that he would also have to rely far more on his telecommunications capability to manage the company than in the past. Although many facilities were under Carlton's direction, Michael believed that he must stay in close touch. He must now reexamine his telephone capability, the ability of his MIS to handle the additional firms, and his belief in the competencies of the key people. Michael's euphoria at gaining the new territory and market was tempered by the realization that management had become more complex. He decided that he must review policy to ensure he wouldn't lose control. However, he had to put all of this in the back of his mind as he headed home to the prospect of visitors.

Michael's brother, Hugh, had arrived to visit Denver for a week. After dinner, Hugh took the floor to expound on his strongly held views on how to run a business. He was convinced that he had the answers to almost all of the real business questions! He declared that he was buying a PBX for his business in Sarasota, Florida, and that Michael really should investigate the advantages of this technology. Michael stated that he was heretofore satisfied with the local Telco's central office service. However, he also thought the idea of adding a PBX might possibly be valuable. The question of how valuable was one

FIGURE 4.1   Major Universities in JL&S Service Area

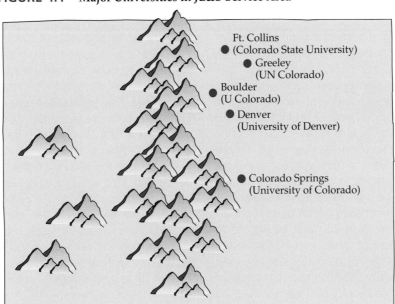

that needed answering, as Michael now addressed each new business venture and each new technology from a viewpoint of value and integration.

Policy

Since telecommunications costs were becoming a significant part of the cost of doing business, Michael needed a means of identifying and evaluating telecommunications alternatives. In the past, telecommunications costs had not been carefully analyzed, so no model existed for the firm. Michael decided to call a meeting with Bill Bolton and Carlton to discuss the need for closer analysis of telecommunications alternatives and decisions.

On the following Monday, after a full weekend with Hugh, Michael, Bill, and Carlton met in Michael's office to discuss JEI's telecommunications capabilities and policies. Michael outlined his concerns and stated that he wanted to develop a minimum set of specific telecommunications policies. One policy should be a proper course of action to follow when making decisions about customer premises equipment (CPE) and services. Michael said it would make sense if they had such policies so that proper analysis was followed before any major decisions were made. He pulled out his book on economic decisions and said that something like the guidance in it should be a good starting point.

One of the results of this meeting was the discussion of just what dimensions of telecommunications decisions were relevant in making choices. For example, in looking at the local exchange company's latest recommendations that Michael lease a high-speed line between Denver and Colorado Springs, he decided that the decision centered around the following dimensions: (1) speed, (2) capacity, (3) cost, and (4) service. He also believed that the capacity dimensions should include some projections for future growth. Now Michael was considering a PBX and needed a policy, or at least a viewpoint, from which to make this decision. This was especially relevant in view of the new organizational expansion. He decided, with Bill, that he should at least answer questions of speed, capacity, cost, and service before he made any particular decision on a PBX or other equipment. The concern for control of the business weighed heavily on his mind, but he was not sure how it fit the criteria.

PBX or Centrex for JEI

Michael's analysis showed that Centrex service, a group of switch services dedicated to his needs, had advantages for the growing company in that he could make additions at any time with a guaranteed, currently existing rate. He saw that JEI could have exactly the capacity needed at the present time, with no need for "overbuy" in anticipation of future growth. In addition, he found it difficult to forecast capacity needs and saw that several PBX vendors would impose contractual termination penalties. There was further difficulty for Michael in understanding the component needs such as circuit packs, cabinets, and the best array of features to procure. (Michael is buying technical expertise along with Centrex capabilities from the Telco.)

Michael thought about the nature of his business and decided to place a high degree of importance on reliability and maintenance. He could ill afford downtime as he was guaranteeing his customers a reliable security service, 24-hour access to their computer accounts, and disaster recovery capability. A system for JEI required 24-hour maintenance, and this meant the redundancy offered by Centrex was very important. The Telco expected less than one outage per year of less than two minutes. They were able to do this because of redundant processors, back-up power systems, and very high security. In a way, the Centrex system reflected JEI's major business in the security and reliability areas. Also, there was no need to have any equipment on JEI's premises other than telephones. Michael was mildly surprised to find out that a PBX could also be a significant power user as well as increase his insurance costs.

As shown in Figure 4.2, JEI presently had 41 telephone lines. Michael read that one author says that a PBX is not cost-effective under 100 lines. After considering this fact, coupled with the dispersion of JEI, and speed, capacity, cost, and service, Michael opted to remain with the Telco. He did not have a significant demand for high-data speed, 41 lines gave him adequate voice capacity, and the percentage of internal calls was low. Staying with the Telco, as an alternative to buying a PBX, gave a lowest-cost (e.g., investment) decision, and the Telco promised to continue their present level of service. Additionally, the Telco had profiled JEI as a high-growth customer and agreed to a list of no-cost enhancements as they became available. Further, Michael believed that the future growth

FIGURE 4.2   JEI Expanded Organizational Chart (circa 1987)

(Number of telephone lines shown with [#])

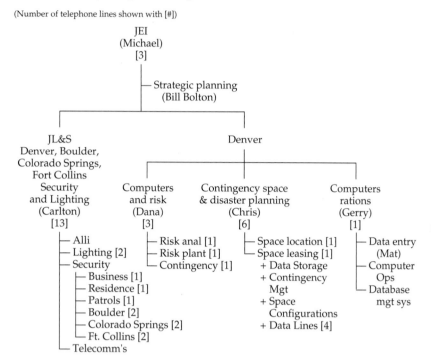

forecast for JEI could be handled adequately by local service or enhanced Centrex services. At this time, a PBX for JEI was not a good decision. Thus, Michael concluded that Centrex services were more cost-effective given specific conditions at JEI and JL&S at the time of analysis. Michael realized, however, that as he added more lines, gained more customers who required long distance calls, incoming WATS service, and a significant amount of digital communications, he must reevaluate this decision.

As Michael wrestled with the decision about PBX equipment, he remembered his early experiences with a key system. When he had expanded into the lock business and needed an additional line, he first installed standard phones and just pressed a buzzer to tell the other person to answer the call. Later he changed the phones to instruments that could tie into both lines and switch between them with a small rotary switch on the phone instrument. With the addition of even more lines into JL&S, he installed four-button telephones that allowed each user to see which lines were in use, by the lighted buttons on the phones, and select a line by pressing one of the buttons. This simple key system equipment gave Michael greater control of his communication lines, but did not provide any of the services available with a PBX or Centrex services. With time and the introduction of new technology, the distance between the key system and a PBX grew shorter as the former included features of the latter. Additionally, the hardware features of the earlier equipment were now provided with software capabilities. See Figure 4.3 for PBX diagrams.

By going through the evaluation process, Michael had come to realize that the environment (his business environment plus the local telecommunications environment) plays a large part in a PBX-versus-Centrex decision. He now realized that the telecommunications decision process must be recurring because circumstances of the business and technology environments are dynamic and evolving. The decision that once lasted for 10 years must now be revisited annually. Thus, just as he considers business opportunities frequently, he must do the same with the technology that supports his ability to expand and compete. Of possibly even greater value was that Michael had seen that there was a way to address problems and opportunities much more systematically than he had in the past. He also had developed a much better set of business-related telecommunications evaluation criteria by going through the Centrex-versus-PBX analysis.

FIGURE 4.3   **Proposed PBX (Voice) for JEI**

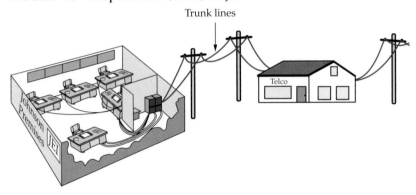

INTRODUCTION

Data communications is changing the industrialized world today. It connects machines together to increase the reach of the humans that rely on them to make decisions.

This chapter expands on the basic concepts of telecommunications. The focus of the chapter is that part of telecommunications called *data communications*. As small organizations grow, they enter this phase of telecommunications usage that is increasingly important to their business. Although voice communications continue to be the greater part of telecommunications expense, data communications is the fastest growing part of telecommunications. Data communications touches our

Technology Note   4–1
Service Bureau and Timeshare

A **service bureau** is a concept that had great popularity and promise in the earlier days of MIS. The premise of this service was that many smaller companies had the desire to have computer-based systems but did not have the ability to manage a large computer or did not want the financial responsibility associated with buying or leasing and running a mainframe computer. The giants of the computer industry, IBM and Control Data, both had the ability and resources for such a capability and created a business of providing fee-based services to other companies. One method of operation was for the smaller company to bring the data forms to the bureau. The bureau performed data entry, provided processing, and returned output reports to the client. Other companies, such as banks and insurance companies, began to provide a similar service by taking advantage of nighttime excess capability of their mainframe computers. In some cases, individuals would approach several companies that had small amounts of excess capacity, combine these capacities, and sell the service. In this case, the selling organization had no resources, only those they leased and resold.

With the advent of economical telecommunications capabilities, the service bureaus provided the services by way of dial-up and leased telephone lines. Timeshare services are presently provided by companies such as Boeing Computer Service (BCS), McDonnell-Douglas (McAuto), and Computer Services Corporation (CSC). **Timeshare** means a business can have at its disposal almost unlimited computer processing and storage, output report printing or printing at their premises, fee-based programming services, and the use of a wide variety of royalty-based programs. For example, a company could contract with McAuto to lease a video display terminal, a 100-line-per-minute line printer, a 4800-bits-per-second modem, mainframe processing, blocks of disk storage, and a variety of accounting, finance, inventory, and engineering programs. There would be a monthly fixed fee for equipment and a variable charge for processing, storage, and program use. The computer services from a bureau are an expense as opposed to being an incurred liability.

lives in many ways. We use it daily to access our bank through an **automated teller machine (ATM)**[1] transaction, buy gas, or access the World Wide Web. It is inconceivable for the economy of the United States to operate without reliable and readily available data communications links.[2] We discuss some of the systems, such as the airline reservations system, the banking system, and so on, that are dependent on the underlying data communications systems as examples of what is done to create a competitive advantage by exploiting telecommunications (specifically data communications) technologies. In our continuing case, we have the protagonists encounter the business need for data communications. The case example is typical of many growing businesses as they become more sophisticated.

THE HISTORY OF DATA COMMUNICATIONS

Data communications began with the telegraph on copper wire and has progressed to digital video via satellite and fiber optic cable.

We review the history of data communications in more detail here than we did in the voice telecommunications chapter. Several technical aspects of data communications are introduced in order to provide you with the basic understanding needed to make business decisions and to follow the rationale used (the same as used by Johnson Lighting and Security in the case) in adopting data communications systems.

There are two reasons for starting our discussion of data communications from a historical setting. First, although we readily understand the older technology, we may not realize that it *is* data communications. Additionally, we have a greater appreciation for the present technology when we understand the path leading to it and realize what a short time it has taken to travel this path (see Figure 4.4).

THE TELEGRAPH

Telegraphy was not user-oriented; it depended on skilled intermediaries.

The evolution of modern telecommunications equipment began with the first electrical means of communications over a distance: the telegraph (circa 1837). This device consists of a long distance loop of wire that has an electric storage battery for energy, a key to open and close the circuit, and a sounding unit that responds to the electrical current with a noise. See Figures 4.5(a) and 4.5(b). A home door

FIGURE 4.4
Timeline of Early Telecommunications Development

Telegraph invented by S. Morse	Western Union started	A. G. Bell patents telephone	Bell Company founded	AT&T created	Marconi wireless telegraphy	Vacuum tube developed
1837	1856	1876	1877	1885	1886	1913

[1] As you enter the business world of telecommunications, a new technology is being introduced with the same initials, ATM. This technology, which we will discuss in later chapters, is asynchronous transfer mode, a form of high-speed switching and data transport. Our point is to call this to your attention because ATM in each of its forms will be important to your life and career.

[2] As we update this book, the World Trade Center in New York City, New York, was destroyed by a terrorist attack. While a number of businesses had headquarters there and many telecommunications lines ran through this structure, the infrastructure of U.S. business was not significantly altered. As we discuss in a later chapter, management has come to realize the vital importance of a disaster recovery plan and business continuity planning.

FIGURE 4.5 The Telegraph

a. Telegraph key

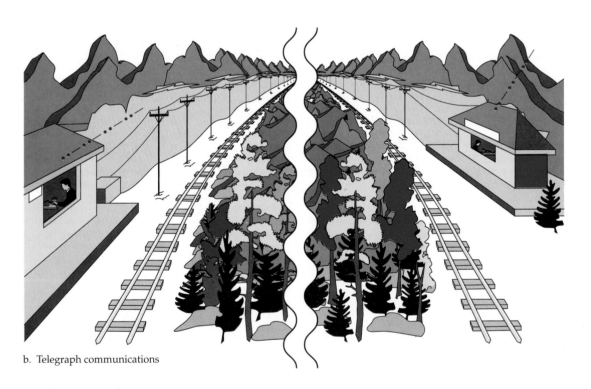

b. Telegraph communications

buzzer is an equivalent system. The telegraph operator sends the message in a code that bears the name of the equipment's originator, Samuel Morse. The capability requires an operator who understands how to mentally translate (encode) the message into **Morse code** (Figure 4.6) and tap the code on the key at a reasonable speed. In this case the medium is copper wire that is strung from the sending station to the receiving station and back (although the return "wire" or path may be the earth). Potentially, a number of receiving stations can be connected along the route, and each would hear all messages sent on the wire. (We will see later that a more

FIGURE 4.6
Morse and Computer Codes for Letters, Numbers, and Punctuation

■ is a short signal/sound or "dot"
— is a long signal/sound or "dash"

Letter	Morse telegraph code	Equivalent digital bits	7-bit ASCII (computer) code
A	■ —	0 1	1 0 0 0 0 0 1
B	— ■ ■ ■	1 0 0 0	1 0 0 0 0 1 0
C	— ■ — ■	1 0 1 0	1 0 0 0 0 1 1
D	— ■ ■	1 0 0	1 0 0 0 1 0 0
E	■	0	1 0 0 0 1 0 1
F	■ ■ — ■	0 0 1 0	1 0 0 0 1 1 0
G	— — ■	1 1 0	1 0 0 0 1 1 1
H	■ ■ ■ ■	0 0 0 0	1 0 0 1 0 0 0
I	■ ■	0 0	1 0 0 1 0 0 1
J	■ — — —	0 1 1 1	1 0 0 1 0 1 0
K	— ■ —	1 0 1	1 0 0 1 0 1 1
L	■ — ■ ■	0 1 0 0	1 0 0 1 1 0 0
M	— —	1 1	1 0 0 1 1 0 1
N	— ■	1 0	1 0 0 1 1 1 0
O	— — —	1 1 1	1 0 0 1 1 1 1
P	■ — — ■	0 1 1 0	1 0 1 0 0 0 0
Q	— — ■ —	1 1 0 1	1 0 1 0 0 0 1
R	■ — ■	0 1 0	1 0 1 0 0 1 0
S	■ ■ ■	0 0 0	1 0 1 0 0 1 1
T	—	1	1 0 1 0 1 0 0
U	■ ■ —	0 0 1	1 0 1 0 1 0 1
V	■ ■ ■ —	0 0 0 1	1 0 1 0 1 1 0
W	■ — —	0 1 1	1 0 1 0 1 1 1
X	— ■ ■ —	1 0 0 1	1 0 1 1 0 0 0
Y	— ■ — —	1 0 1 1	1 0 1 1 0 0 1
Z	— — ■ ■	1 1 0 0	1 0 1 1 0 1 0
,	— — ■ ■ — —	1 1 0 0 1 1	0 1 0 1 1 0 0
.	■ — ■ — ■ —	0 1 0 1 0 1	0 1 0 1 1 1 0
1	■ — — — —	0 1 1 1 1	0 1 1 0 0 0 1
2	■ ■ — — —	0 0 1 1 1	0 1 1 0 0 1 0
3	■ ■ ■ — —	0 0 0 1 1	0 1 1 0 0 1 1
4	■ ■ ■ ■ —	0 0 0 0 1	0 1 1 0 1 0 0
5	■ ■ ■ ■ ■	0 0 0 0 0	0 1 1 0 1 0 1
6	— ■ ■ ■ ■	1 0 0 0 0	0 1 1 0 1 1 0
7	— — ■ ■ ■	1 1 0 0 0	0 1 1 0 1 1 1
8	— — — ■ ■	1 1 1 0 0	0 1 1 1 0 0 0
9	— — — — ■	1 1 1 1 0	0 1 1 1 0 0 1
0	— — — — —	1 1 1 1 1	0 1 1 0 0 0 0

effective way to communicate to multiple receiving nodes on a circuit is to place the address of the receiving station on the message so that all other nodes will ignore it.) The agent at the receiving station must be able to follow the clicks (dots and dashes) of Morse code; decode the taps into the receiver's language (expanding abbreviations); and write down the message. The agent must accomplish all of these tasks at the (real-time) speed of the sender's transmission since there is no storage capability. What we have described here is the earliest electrical transmission of data—a topic that we deal with extensively in later chapters.

The telegraph was the first data communications device, providing messages over great distances with minimum time.

The **telegraph** was a significant advance in communications technology as it allowed long distance communications in hours that had previously taken days and weeks. The process and medium were reliable as long as lines stayed intact. (Problems were encountered during the U.S. Civil War and in the days of the Old West when the lines were cut.) The main disadvantage of the telegraph is that only stations on the line can send and receive messages. The network of lines extended

Information Window   4–1

When we discuss the telegraph, we think of the *electric* telegraph, invented by Samuel Morse. The telegraph is actually a mechanical device out of history. During the Napoleonic Wars, telegraph towers using signaling arms were spaced on hilltops for line-of-sight signaling. A well-known vineyard in France got its name from the telegraph tower once on its hilltop.

to most medium and large cities and even some small towns, depending on rail transportation and business activity. Of note is the fact that the network did not extend to the customer as user. That is, the telegraph is designed for specially trained operators, not the originator or receiver of its information. Eventually, the telegraph system and its replacement systems did extend into businesses. They did not, however, have the extensive reach of the modern telephone network.

Code Length

The Morse code is *variable* in length: the number of bits per character (dots and dashes) varies by character. For comparison, a true digital (binary) representation of this code is shown in Figure 4.6. One advantage of the Morse code's variable length is that it uses a minimum of signals or bits (dots and dashes) to send a word, as some letters require only one dot or dash. The code was designed to take advantage of the frequency of occurrence of letters in words; for example, the letter *e* appears often and was given a code of one dot, the shortest signal possible. Since humans were interpreting the signals, this was efficient and effective. Fixed-length codes are much preferable for machine-to-machine communications because then there is no question when a character is complete.

All communications, whether between humans or machines, require the use of a *protocol.* This simply means *rules for communications.* In the case of the telegraph system, the protocol is the code used, that is, the meaning of each group of dots and dashes, and agreement as to who can transmit and when.

There must be a compromise between the number of code places (characters) in the code versus the amount of signals or, as in the digital codes, bits[3] required for a character. An early code system, the Baudot code, has five bits to represent a character[4] and can, therefore, represent 32 unique code points, enough only for capital letters and *some* numbers. Allocating one or more codes as an *escape* or shift key allows additional code points to be designated. Baudot uses two escape characters and represents 58 characters. The exact code set, for example, letters represented, is dependent on the Baudot standard utilized. The intent usually is to represent at least all capital letters, numbers, some punctuation marks, and some effector codes that cause the machine to take action, such as go to top-of-page.

The 7-bit **ASCII code (American Standard Code for Information Interchange),** sponsored by the American National Standards Institute (ANSI), Figure 4.7(a), has become a widely used standard.[5] It can represent 128 characters ($2^7 = 128$): all capital and lowercase letters, numbers, special symbols such as punctuation, and

code length
The more bits per character in a code, the longer the time to transmit or the wider the required bandwidth (greater speed).

Computer keyboards generally have 110 keys with Shift, Ctrl, and Alt special keys. How many characters can it represent?

7-bit and 8-bit codes
Seven-bit codes define 128 characters ($2^7 = 128$). Eight-bit codes define 256 characters.

[3] A *bit* is a binary digit, the basic building block for digital representation of data.
[4] Baudot, ASCII, and EBCDIC are digital coding schemes to represent data.
[5] Standards are critical to the success of data communications. Without standards, one machine could not understand another.

FIGURE 4.7

From Figure 4.7(a), letter "A" is binary 1000001 or decimal "65."
From Figure 4.7(b), letter "A" is decimal "65."

First Three Bit Positions (Bits 7,6,5)								
	000	**001**	**010**	**011**	**100**	**101**	**110**	**111**
0000	NUL	DLE	SP	O	@	P	`	p
0001	SOH	DC1	!	1	A	Q	a	q
0010	STX	DC2	"	2	B	R	b	r
0011	ETX	DC3	#	3	C	S	c	s
0100	EOT	DC4	$	4	D	T	d	t
0101	ENQ	NAK	%	5	E	U	e	u
0110	ACK	SYN	&	6	F	V	f	v
0111	BEL	ETB	'	7	G	W	g	w
1000	BS	CAN	(	8	H	X	h	x
1001	HT	EM	)	9	I	Y	i	y
1010	LF	SUB	*	:	J	Z	j	z
1011	VT	ESC	+	;	K	[	k	{
1100	FF	FS	,	<	L	\	l	|
1101	CR	GS	—	=	M	]	m	}
1110	SO	RS	.	>	N	^	n	~
1111	SI	US	/	?	O	–	o	DEL

(Left vertical label: LAST FOUR BIT POSITIONS)

a. ANSI ASCII 7-bit binary code for telecommunications

000	(Graphics	010 (Graphics
020	characters)	030 characters)
040	( )*+, -./01	050 23456 789:;
060	<=>?@ ABCDE	070 FGHIJ KLMNO
080	PQRST UVWXY	090 Z[\]^_`abc
100	defgh ijklm	110 nopqr stuvw
120	xyz{| }~Çü	130 éâäàå çêëèï
140	îïÄÅE æÆôöò	150 ûùÿjÖÜ ¢£¥P█
160	áíóúñ Ñªº¿⌐	170 ¬½¼i « » ▇▇|
180	╡╢╖╕╣║╗╝	190 ╞╟╚╔╩╦╠═╬
200	╚╔╩╦╠	210 ╤╥╙╘╒╓╫╪┘┌
220	█▄▌▐▀ ßΓπΣσ	230 µτ ΦΘΩ δ∞φε∩
240	≡±≥≤⌠⌡	250 ·√ⁿ²■

b. Eight-bit (256) ASCII characters with decimal codes

transmission control characters. Adding an eighth bit to the ASCII doubles the number of code points. The 8-bit ASCII code, Figure 4.7(b), is used for most microcomputers to represent the characters noted plus graphic characters. IBM continues to utilize their mainframe-originated 8-bit **Extended Binary Coded Decimal Interchange Code (EBCDIC)** in some of their PC-based programs. This difference in code representations necessitates an EBCDIC–ASCII code conversion in many cases. Fortunately, there is a direct relationship between the codes and conversion is quick.

When a code is devised, the originator must compromise between the possible number of code points, or characters, and the number of bits it takes to represent a code point. This relates to speed of transmission, which is equivalent to analog bandwidth. For example, to send the short imperative sentence "please help me" (three words = 14 characters and spaces) would require 41 dots or dashes or dash-equivalent pauses (between words). The rule of thumb was that a dash has a sound three times as long as a dot and that the space between words was two dashes or more in time duration. Thus, the time to send these 41 bits (a total of 16 dashes and 19 dots) would be the time required to send 67 dots. Sending the same by 7-bit

8-bit ASCII
The exact codes in a code set depend on the use of the code. Code sets used for graphics will differ from the same code when used for data communications.

ASCII code would take $7 \times 14 = 98$ 1s or 0s. In this case, ASCII took one-third greater speed of transmission (sending 98 bits in the time it takes to send 67 dots). However, machines have the ability to interpret the 1s and 0s at higher and higher rates of speed, whereas humans have an upper limit.

The effect of the size of the code is again apparent when you send text faster via 5-bit Baudot code than 8-bit ASCII code because of the fewer bits required per unit of time. Organizations are finding that they need to send more and more data, which requires either that there is greater bandwidth or that the data must be made "smaller." We discuss making data smaller (compression) later.

The codes above encode specific groups of characters. Suppose you have more characters than you have places in the code, such as in European and Oriental languages. For this situation, a 16-bit code, called the Unicode, has been developed that can represent 65,536 ($2^{16} = 65,536$) characters, believed to be sufficient for any occasion. Because there is backing from a group of significant companies in the field of computers, the Unicode may become a standard, replacing even ASCII and EBCDIC codes.

Radio Telegraph (Wireless Telegraphy)

Wireless telegraphy was as amazing in its time as the first satellite communications were later.

The first of the two primary improvements to the telegraph was the use of radio waves to send the message through an air medium (**wireless telegraphy** by Guglielmo Marconi, circa 1886). This capability allowed any two radios (one transmitter and one receiver) that could "hear" each other to communicate messages via Morse code. The wireless telegraph system created an electromagnetic pulse on the radio's antenna when the operator pressed the key. The receiving set intercepted the pulse that was radiated through the air medium and generated a sound that represented the sent pulse. This advance made wireless transcontinental communications possible and ushered in electronic ship-to-ship and ship-to-shore communications. (See Figure 4.8.) Users of radio communications encountered two problems. Both weather conditions

FIGURE 4.8 Wireless Telegraphy

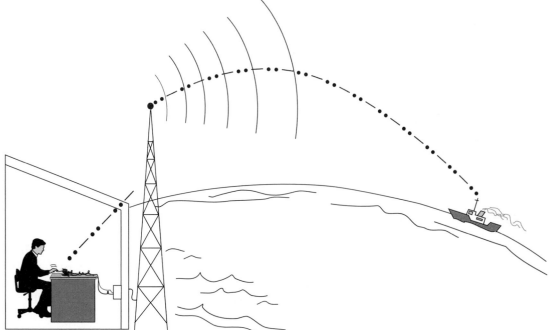

and the distance between stations affected the quality of the transmissions. However, considering the alternatives, radio telecommunications was a significant advance. Although the vacuum tube was not invented until later, ushering in the radio as we know it today, the use of simple electrical technology for wireless telegraphy was quite important to advancing communications. Recall that the wire-medium telegraph used a key to open and close a circuit, which caused electrical current to flow and activate a sounding device at the receiving end. Thus, the first improvement in the telegraph permitted wireless telecommunications over considerable distance as well as over water, although the basic code and keying devices were unchanged. The teletypewriter discussed next changed the basics of telegraphy more.

The Teletypewriter Adds Storage

The teletypewriter ushered in the era of machine-based communications, as it provided storage, switching, and machine encoding.

The second improvement on the telegraph principle was the **teletypewriter.** This device replaced both the single coding key used by human operators when sending messages and the sounding unit used for receiving them. The operator typed the message onto a full alphanumeric keyboard. The equipment, not the operator, converted the message to a code somewhat like Morse code, and either transmitted the message to a receiving unit or punched it onto paper tape (see Figure 4.9). (The medium for the teletypewriter circuit could be either wire or air.) If the message was recorded onto tape, the task could be accomplished "**off line**" (the teletypewriter was not connected to the communications line), and the message could be transmitted later when the system established a circuit with the receiving unit. This meant that the actual typing of the message could be done slower than transmission

FIGURE 4.9

 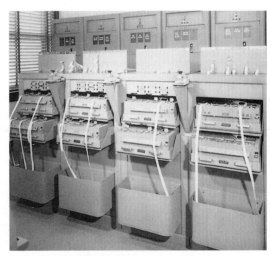

a. An early message switching center in a large industrial company. Short sections of punched paper tape can be seen in the rack in the foreground. Storage bins of punched tape are on the back wall. (Photo courtesy of Dow Chemical Company)

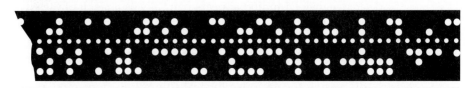

b. Five-level band of coded paper type from a teletypewriter

speed and that corrections could be made before a connection was made, increasing the message's reliability and transmission speed.

Thus, the teletypewriter introduced a machine that accomplished the code encryption for the operator, allowing companies to use less-skilled personnel. This advance increased process reliability and speed, and provided for decryption and printing of the message. Even more important, the teletypewriter provided message storage. Further, one station could send messages to a second that could store the message for later forwarding to a third, and so on. These innovations were very important and provided the basis for a widespread telecommunications industry that was to flourish for years. But gone are the days of Western Union's dominance of (telegraph) telecommunications and the myriad of delivery boys on bicycles.

By now, you should understand the *concept* of **data communications**. This concept, embodied in the teletypewriter system just discussed, includes an encryption and sending device, a medium, a decryption and receiving unit, and the ability to store the message at either end. What the teletypewriter system does not include, as we will discuss later, is an automated method of message handling, a way to switch circuits, and a form of error detection and correction. Also, the telegraph and teletypewriter systems were devices designed for humans to be the ultimate senders and receivers of messages, though not the ultimate originators and destinations. Today, human operators often act merely as facilitators for the sending and receiving computers. The telephone's development marked the beginning of user-to-user connections.

THE TELEPHONE SYSTEM

Public switched (voice) telephone network
The simple instrument Bell invented spawned the network that now connects most home and businesses in the industrial world.

It is significant that Alexander Graham Bell's patent for the first telephone was entitled "Improvement in Telegraphy." In reality, the telephone system developed by AT&T and others (there are still over one thousand local non-Bell telephone companies) provides a tremendous potential for machine-to-machine communications as well as human-to-human communications. The potential of machine-to-machine communications, of data communications, is realized due to the vast network created for voice communications. This network goes from and to basically every home and office in the industrialized world. Where the telegraph network went from town-to-town, the telephone network goes from user-to-user. It is this network that makes the voice capability network so attractive for data communications.

The voice network was designed to carry analog voice signals. When two people talk, they are sending continuously varying signals. Should there be noise on the line, such as that produced by a lightning storm or a dirty switch, the people know it is noise. **Noise** generally adds to the background environment in which the conversation takes place and does not change the sounds being transmitted. This is not true with data communications. As we will see in the following section, noise can be the source of great problems for the transmission of digital data.

In addition to noise, signals are subject to distortion, which is a natural phenomenon that is very critical to digital signals. It is totally separate from the effects of noise. Noise appears as an external influence; it is an extraneous signal that is added to the desired signal. Distortion appears naturally as a result of the environment through which the signal must pass. Both must be countered in order to pass data correctly.

MODES (DIRECTIONS) OF TRANSMISSION

In discussing the various physical communications media, we noted that some were **simplex,** meaning one-way communications, all the time, like AM or FM

Information Window
Noise on Purpose

4–2

Some years ago, an enterprising group transformed an old warehouse into the world's largest honky-tonk, and Billy Bob's Texas® was born. This 4.5-acre "watering hole," situated in the old stockyard district in Cowtown (Fort Worth, Texas), sported 14 bars at which you could get a cool Lone Star Longneck or a bottle of Colorado Coolaid (Coors beer). You could have a meal at the Greasy Spoon Restaurant, your new reptile skin boots shined, or, of course, your car parked by a valet.

On occasion some gentlemen would stay at Billy Bob's longer than anticipated, or pay a visit without informing "the significant other," necessitating a phone call to calm

any fears. To help this precarious situation, a special phone had been installed. It was in a phone booth that had been padded to keep out unwanted background noise from Billy Bob's. The special feature of the phone was that when you put an extra $2 into the slot, the *environmental noise* of your choice would be heard in the background. There were such choices as a busy office, an airport, and a department store. The point of this noise on purpose? To create additional information for the call's recipient for the protection of the call's originator. (Our intent in this example is not to condone the actions but to show a novel use of noise.)

FIGURE 4.10   **Communications Channels**

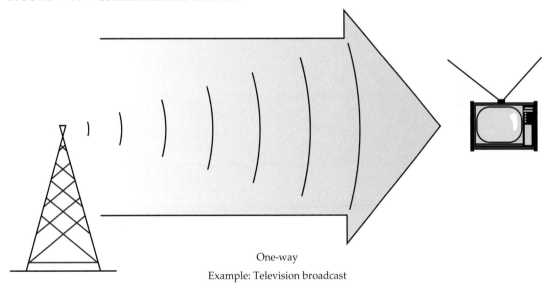

One-way
Example: Television broadcast

a. Simplex transmission

(*continued*)

radio, air-broadcast TV, and cable television. (See Figure 4.10.) Others were one way at a time, but with a bidirectional capability through circuit reversal, which is called a **half-duplex** operation. This is the mode used by many terminals and microcomputers. A noncomputer example of a half-duplex operation would be Michael's patrol cars that kept in contact with the base radio station. The third mode is **full-duplex,** or simultaneous bidirectional communications. This mode, for example, makes use of a single twisted-pair circuit and frequency division to divide the communications channel into two parts, that is, forward and reverse channels. An original use of full-duplex is to echo (repeat back) the characters

FIGURE 4.10 **Communications Channels**—*concluded*

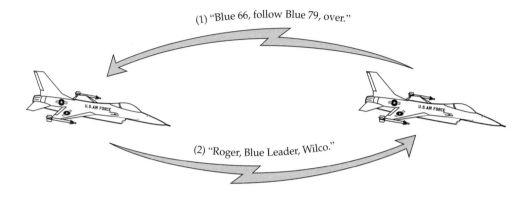

(1) "Blue 66, follow Blue 79, over."

(2) "Roger, Blue Leader, Wilco."

Example: Radio between aircraft

b. Half-duplex transmission (one way at a time)

"I've really won the prize!" "Yes!"
"Oh no, not the two million!" "No"
"Yes!" "WOW!" "Paris" "Oh, boy!"

Example: Telephone with both speaking at once.

c. Full-duplex transmission (both directions simultaneously)

sent from a terminal to a computer to display exactly what the computer received as opposed to just repeating what was transmitted from the source. A more relevant use of full-duplex is to have a small reverse channel to communicate back to a sending node that data were received correctly, without interrupting the forward channel. This is discussed later in the chapter under error detection.

Simplex transmission occurs when the path is always in one direction, as with commercial air-medium or cable TV. In this case, the TV set is a receive-only unit. Half-duplex operation is possible when each end of the medium can transmit and receive. A CB or aircraft radio does this, activating a change in modes by a switch on the microphone. Modems do this when they recognize that a message being received has ended and it has data waiting to be sent.

Both units on a full-duplex system transmit and receive all the time. Part of the channel bandwidth is allocated for one unit to send (and the other unit to receive), and part is for the other unit to send. As we will see later in error detection, full-duplex allows for a fast response to the correctness of sent data but reduces the bandwidth of either direction. Thus, when the primary movement of data is in one direction, the circuit can either be half-duplex or allocate the greater bandwidth to the forward channel and a minimum bandwidth to the reverse (response) channel. This makes the forward channel fast and the reverse channel slow. This is often done in cable modems and DSL Internet access as users' upload is generally small in comparison to download.

DIGITAL DATA

Digital data
are literally data represented by combinations of numbers, for example, 1s and 0s. They can be text, voice, images, video, or facsimile. Having all of these in a digital form means we can use the same network to carry them all, simultaneously.

Digital computers employ **binary** (bi-state) codes to represent data: every piece of data that a computer processes or stores is encoded into a series of 1s and 0s in accordance with some standard convention, called a **code.** We discussed some familiar codes earlier. To transmit digital codes you must have a channel that does not contain noise that appears as digital data.

Voice signals are **analog** signals, continuously varying waves of energy. Digital data use **discrete** levels of voltage (e.g., +5 volts for a 1 and 0 or −5 volts for a zero). Noise on a circuit can appear like digital data because many devices such as those with motors produce voltage spikes (see Figure 4.11). While there are many advantages in having any signal in a digital form, digital data are much more susceptible to noise; therefore, we must use circuits that avoid noise. The selection of the medium is very important. Fiber circuits are the best as a noise-free environment.

Data Signals

As data communications is the transmission and receipt of binary codes (electrical pulses or light representing 1s and 0s) between terminals and computers, any injected signal that appears to be like the binary codes will distort the information being sent. Injected noise does appear much like binary bits and can either add to the transmitted bits or change them. It is for this reason that we must either change the binary signals from terminals and computers to be impervious to noise or change the medium to exclude noise. The first situation occurs when we use modems, and the second occurs when we use shielded wires, coaxial cables, fiber-optic strands, or conditioned[6] data networks. Much of what we will discuss in the area of data communications addresses either of these two situations. In order for us to

FIGURE 4.11
Effect of Noise on Digital Data Transmission

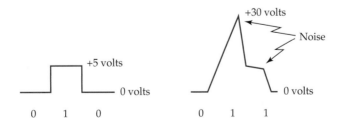

[6] Typically, this is a nonswitched voice-grade channel with the addition of equipment to provide minimum values of line characteristics for data transmission; that is, to add devices to a line to reduce the noise environment and/or to increase its bandwidth.

understand the nature of data communications, we need to understand the alternative circuit forms and their importance. They are discussed in the next section.

Serial versus Parallel Circuits

serial versus parallel
Telephone lines are serial channels; PC printer cables are usually parallel.

The two circuit forms for sending coded messages are parallel and serial circuits. In a **parallel** circuit the number of wires from sender to receiver is equal to or greater than the number of bits for a character. Thus, for an 8-bit character, which is what most microcomputers use, the parallel medium from one point to another would have eight or more wires or paths. In such a parallel circuit, each bit of the character travels down its own wire simultaneously with the other bits of the character on other wires. This mode provides fast communications, such as on the data bus[7] within the PC or from computer to the printer or secondary storage, but this mode requires eight or more wires. The alternative, which is used for most data communications, is the **serial** circuit. In this mode, the bits of the character follow each other down a single wire or its equivalent. This form takes eight times as long as parallel communications, but requires only one wire-pair. Obviously, the telegraph, which was discussed earlier, used serial communications. (Oftentimes, the originating system generates the code in a parallel circuit and sends it over a serial circuit. Obviously, this procedure requires a conversion device at each end. This conversion is the task of the modem, to be discussed further later.)

Figure 4.12 shows that in a given amount of time, a serial circuit will transport a bit while a parallel circuit will transport the total character, which is seven or eight times as much data. Parallel circuits, however, are seldom used for long-haul circuits because of cost (eight wires versus two) and complexity of synchronizing bits.

BASIC DATA COMMUNICATIONS LINKS

If you want to send data from one terminal or computer to another you are dealing with **data terminating equipment (DTE).** (See Figure 4.13.) DTEs are noncommunications-oriented components of a data communications environment. In order for the data transfer to work, you need some sort of **data communications equipment (DCE).** DCEs are communications-oriented components of a network, such as telephone switching equipment, media, modems, and so on. For a total point-to-point network, you will connect the DTEs via DCEs.

Information Window   4–3

The computerized reservation system developed by American Airlines parent, AMR Corporation, has received widespread acclaim. This system, called SABRE, is cited as one of the first computer and telecommunications systems used for gaining competitive advantage. SABRE was deployed to travel agents nationwide so that instant reservations could be made after the agent was able to browse through a wide variety of schedule, expense, and package options at the terminal. It is difficult to imagine what sort of chaos would result if the airline reservation networks were out of service! Each time you make an airline reservation a great deal of data communications must take place.

[7] A data bus is a transmission path or channel where all attached devices receive all transmission at the same time.

sender to receiver. (We also call this **bandwidth.**) An asynchronous network that sends 10-bit characters at a rate of 300 bits per second (bps) will transmit 30 characters per second. The term **baud,** which we often use interchangeably with bps, *refers to the number of times a change of analog signal occurs in the circuit.* If one signal change occurs per bit, then baud and bps measure the same rate. However, as the data transfer rate increases above 600 bps over 4 KHz telephone circuits, the bandwidth limit of the circuit is reached. For FSK modulation to work, the circuit must have a bandwidth of 1.5 times the baud rate. Thus, at 1200 baud, 1800 Hz would be required for transmission in each direction, requiring a total analog bandwidth of 3600 Hz, which exceeds the voice spectrum of a POTS line. Therefore, when FSK is used at or above 1200 baud, the transmission is limited to half-duplex modems that are 600- or 1200-baud modems.

Caveat—When you acquire a POTS line from your local telephone company, you are only acquiring an analog voice channel that can be switched to another telephone. You are not buying or being guaranteed bandwidth. Because of noise, the shiny new 28.8 Kbps modem you just purchased may be communicating at 9.6 Kbps. Some Telcos will condition your line, for a fee, giving you higher bandwidth.

Faster Modems

To achieve a greater speed, the modem must use some technique to encode more than one bit per baud. If we can assume that we are actually pushing the envelope and running at 1200 baud, we must be able to encode 12 bits per baud at 14.4 Kbps and 24 bits at 28.8 Kbps. To do this, the machine must use one of the three parameters to encode more than one bit per baud. As we noted with FSK, we have reached the limit of frequency modulation. Amplitude modulation, by itself, is not often used. The technique most used because the equipment has the highest probability of detecting a change is **phase shift modulation.**

If an analog sine wave starts at zero degrees and continues through its form, a phase shift is said to occur if the instantaneous phase of the wave is set to something new. For example, if the wave entering 90 degrees is abruptly shifted to 180 degrees, a phase shift has occurred and can be readily detected. Plus, you have just created a way to place a bit on the waveform due to the shift in phase. If you shift every 90 degrees, you have two bits encoded on the baud (e.g., $4 \times 90° = 360°$). Thus, in this simple case, a 1200-baud wave, with shifts at 90 degrees, could carry two digital bits and create 2400 bps. Taking this further, shifting at 45 degrees gives you three bits, or 3600 bps. Adding amplitude shift with phase shift, as in *quadrature amplitude modulation (QAM),* you could have the possibilities shown in Table 4.1, which is four bits. *Trellis code modulation,* called such because the form of the bits on an oscilloscope resembles the trellis used in rose gardens, uses QAM but marks specific codes as unusable to improve reliability.

Using these techniques, one way to encode data is to shift when there is a change from 1 to 0 or 0 to 1. This is referred to as phase shift keying (PSK) (see Figure 4.15[a]). Thus, the measuring device will detect each time period and assume that the new time slot is the same digit as the last if there is no shift. Using **differential phase shift keying (DPSK),** a shift occurs when a 1 is sent (see Figure 4.15[b]).

Compression

We have noted how it is possible to have more than one bit represented in each baud. Thus, with these techniques, you can presently have 14.4 Kbps, 28.8 Kbps,

Modems use amplitude, frequency, or phase shift to encode more than one bit per baud.

Modems, regardless of the stated bandwidth, are 600- or 1200-baud devices.

TABLE 4.1
Example of Phase Changes Possible by Use of QAM

Phase Change (Degrees)	Relative Amplitude	Quadbit
0	3	001
0	5	1001
45	$\sqrt{2}$	0000
45	$3\sqrt{2}$	10000
90	3	0010
90	5	1010
135	$\sqrt{2}$	0011
135	$3\sqrt{2}$	1011
180	3	0111
180	5	1111
225	$\sqrt{2}$	0110
225	$3\sqrt{2}$	1110
270	3	0100
270	5	1100
315	$\sqrt{2}$	0101
315	$3\sqrt{2}$	1101

FIGURE 4.15

Source: Adapted from Stanford Rowe, *Telecommunications for Managers,* 3rd ed. (Englewood Cliffs, NJ: Prentice Hall, 1995), p. 297–98.

a. Phase shift modulation

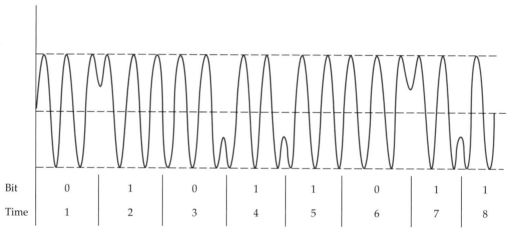

Bit	0	1	0	1	1	0	1	1
Time	1	2	3	4	5	6	7	8

b. Differential phase shift modulation

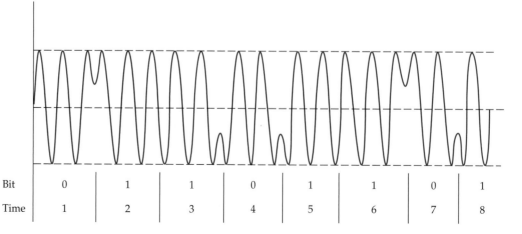

Bit	0	1	1	0	1	1	0	1
Time	1	2	3	4	5	6	7	8

33.6, and 56 Kbps. This is the *actual* bit rate. Using compression, the encoding of redundant characters allows for a greater *effective* bit rate. Using V-34*bis* modem standards, 4:1 compression can be achieved for files that are mostly text. This means that the effective bit rate can range from 55 Kbps to an advertised 288 Kbps.

Caveat—True V-34 modems perform the compression and decompression with hardware on the modem. Some low-priced modems do this with software (on the processor in the computer, resulting in a slower rate). See Cases 5–1 and 5–2 for more on compression and modem capabilities.

Modem Standards

A standard is a definition or format that has been approved by a recognized standards organization or is accepted as a de facto standard by the industry. It is a set of rules covering equipment and software. Recall that protocols are sets of rules governing how equipment and software applications interoperate. The capabilities of and standards for modems have evolved greatly over the past 25 years. One standard is based on the way modems communicate with each other; another, the form of compression they use; and the third, and oldest, the instruction set used. This later standard is called *Hayes-compatibility*, meaning it responds to a standard set of commands originated and standardized by Hayes Microcomputer Products, a major modem manufacturer of the 1980s and 1990s. When you purchase a modem that meets certain standards, you most likely can communicate with any modem that meets the same standards. For example, all *v90* modems should be able to *interoperate,* that is, work with each other.

What you can't ignore is software. The final value of your modem purchase will depend on getting a communications program that's both sophisticated and easy to use. Many modems come bundled with simple software. In any case, the software will hide the modem's complexity behind simple commands and screen displays that will let you roam the world by phone from your desk.

Modems in Direct Connection

When modems are used for connection of dumb terminals or PCs emulating terminals, then the **terminal** is directly connected to an application running on a computer, such as a **mainframe**. The modems create a **path** between terminal and applications. This is because of the software running the modems. The software uses AT commands[8] to instruct the modems to make the connection, and then the application takes over. At this point, the modem does all the work for the user.

Modems in Enhanced Connection

With different software, the connection changes from direct "dumb" connection to that of a PC as a node on a network. The software is SLIP/PPP software.

SLIP or *serial line internet protocol* is a communications protocol that supports an Internet connection (using TCP/IP) over a dialup line. There is also a common variant of SLIP called *compressed SLIP* or *CSLIP*; it can be somewhat faster in operation than standard SLIP. *PPP* or *point-to-point protocol* is a newer protocol that does essentially the same thing as SLIP or CSLIP; however, it's better designed and more acceptable to the sort of people who like to standardize protocol specifications. When using the Internet or online services, especially when graphical data such as interfaces are involved, SLIP and PPP are a must.

---

[8] AT commands are standard modem commands from the Hayes Company.

Forms of Data Transmission: Asynchronous versus Synchronous Communications

Terminals and computers generate streams of characters, composed of bits. The modem converts the digital signal stream to an analog signal stream. The two forms of data communications are asynchronous and synchronous streams. During **asynchronous** communications, *each character* is considered by itself with no relation to the character sent before or after it. All timing and error checking are within the bits of the character. See Figure 4.16(a). In asynchronous communications, a group of 10 bits makes up a character. The heart of the group, assuming use of the ASCII code, is either 7 or 8 bits for the data (letter, number, etc.) being sent. Following the data *may* be 1 bit for error checking (called parity checking) and 1 or 2 bits for character stop bits, making 10 bits in all. The modems operate on one 10-bit character at a time with no apparent control between characters: No timing is maintained.[9] At the time communications is established, the sending and receiving machines agree on the bit pattern, for example, 7 or 8 bits for data; even, odd, or no parity; 1 or 2 stop bits; and speed of communications. The slowest device will set the speed. If the line is noisy, the two DTEs will slow down to a speed of transmission that is reliable.

FIGURE 4.16
Data Transmission

Source: Stanford Rowe, *Telecommunications for Managers*, 3rd ed. © 1995. Reprinted by permission of Prentice Hall, Inc.

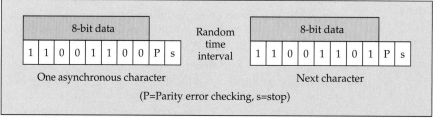

a. Asynchronous data transmission

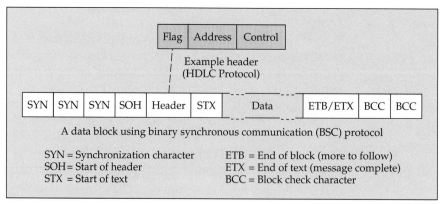

b. Synchronous data transmission

[9] In a later chapter, we will discuss a high-speed digital technology called asynchronous transfer mode (ATM). Although the initials also are used for automated teller machine in banking, this technology is used for high-speed communications. The unit of measure is a cell, which contains a total of 53 bytes. It is referred to as asynchronous because there is no control maintained from cell to cell, as there is no control from character to character therein.

With **synchronous** communications, the unit of control is a *block of data:* a group of text, numbers, or binary characters. See Figure 4.16(b). Header characters, which include timing and possibly address information, begin the block and are added in front of the real data being sent. The data group is a number of characters (more than 1 but generally less than 1,025 characters) that are sent with minimum or no error checking bits among them. Finally, the modem software adds trailer characters to the end of the block of data that include comprehensive error checking (called *block check characters [BCC]*) for the total block of data and an end-of-block and/or end-of-message indication. Often, this block of data is referred to as a *packet.*

What would happen if you sent executable code in a data packet and *did not* have the capability of transparency?

Most communications with terminals and microcomputers acting as terminals use the ASCII code and asynchronous communications (although the data may then be put into data blocks for further error checking). The reason for this is that most modems are low-cost asynchronous devices. In many instances, managers make a choice based on the availability of existing devices rather than a cost–benefit analysis. The communications circuit is direct (point-to-point) from sender to receiver. Thus, if you are using a terminal or employing your PC as a terminal, you would have a hard-wired connection or dial a computer (mainframe or microcomputer) and make a direct temporary connection.

Usually, to send a large amount of data from one computer to another, you would use synchronous communications to achieve a more rapid and reliable transfer. This mode results in greater accuracy and speed, and more efficient use of the network. The two forms of synchronous communications are continuous and packet switching. In *continuous synchronous* communications, the sender or receiver establishes a dedicated (dialup or leased) point-to-point connection and the source sends data to the destination. The sender transmits a number of blocks of data, containing say 128, 256, or 1,024 characters each. For the transmission of an 85-page document (about 256,000 text characters), the system would transmit 1,000 blocks of 256 characters each. This transmission would take about 50 seconds on a 56 Kbps circuit.

The alternative form of synchronous communications is called *packet switching.* Like continuous communications, this mode may use the ASCII or EBCDIC coding scheme and sends the data as blocks of characters. This is covered later in the book.

If faced with a need to move data and unsure of what type environment is needed, the first choice is to do what is cheap and easy, that is, an asynchronous modem and POTS line. This is exactly what a large textile firm did when it needed to download sales data each week from a major discount retail chain. Since they did not know the quantity of data or the cost, they chose to use a 9.6 Kbps asynchronous modem and dial into the network where the data were stored. The end result was a four-hour phone call once a week to download the data.

In the above example, the pure asynchronous protocol would add 30 percent overhead to the data if 7-bit ASCII with parity check was used and 20 percent overhead if 8-bit ASCII without parity check was used. However, most file transfer protocols block (e.g., packetize) the asynchronous data and achieve efficiencies of about 88 percent. If the organization determined that this was to be a normal task and that they would be downloading more data from the one retailer plus from other retailers, they might move to a digital network and synchronous communications. Such an environment might be a switched-56 Kbps line from the Telco. Although the line would be quite a bit more expensive than a POTS line, it would be, in this case, six times as fast. With synchronous protocols requiring less than 4 percent overhead, the end result would be a speed differential of:

$$9,600 \times 0.88 = 8,448$$
$$56,000 \times 0.96 = 55,760$$
$$55,760 \div 8,448 = 6.4 \text{ times faster}$$

Thus, if the switched-56 line cost less than six times as much as the dialup POTS line, the company would be better off. In reality, it would have to cost a bit less because new, expensive, synchronous modems would be required at each end.

The ultimate objective of a data communications system is throughput of useful information. As we add signal control, designation addressing, and error control bits and characters to communications units and blocks, the number of useful bits relative to total bits transmitted decreases. Thus, our objective of accurate communications is in conflict with rapid communications, and we must have a trade-off. The use of synchronous (block-oriented) communications is an attempt to increase the speed possible with asynchronous (character-oriented) communications by reducing the relative amount of control and error check. In any case, as we strive for reliability and accuracy, we sacrifice speed.

Security

We note later that there are four parameters for data communications: performance, accessibility, reliability, and security (PARS). From the preceding discussion, we see that reliability is of the utmost importance. Based on recent and continuing problems with viruses and intrusions, **security** would seem to be the next most important parameter. Security not only ensures that the message is kept from unauthorized eyes, it ensures that the data are not changed or destroyed, elements of reliability.

Keeping Signals at the Required Level

A characteristic of electrical and photonic signals is that they diminish, or weaken, as they travel away from their source. For example, the light from a flashlight is blinding at the bulb but is barely visible a mile away. This phenomenon is called **attenuation.** In the case of the flashlight, the attenuation is caused by the divergence of the signal. One of the more common forms of attenuation in telecommunications is the case of microwave transmission in storms where the signal is attenuated by deflection by rain and snow particles. Our interest in attenuation lies in the fact that all telecommunications signals suffer from it and that we must take specific and frequent action to counter its effect.

For analog signals, **amplifiers** (repeaters) are used to increase the signal strength. A weak signal is boosted to a strong signal, just as in a stereo amplifier. For telephone circuits, repeaters are placed about a mile apart on twisted-pair wire circuits to keep the signal strength at the predetermined level. While this continuous amplification of the signal does indeed keep the signal at the proper level, thus allowing us to hear the conversation, the process picks up and amplifies noise at the same time. Electrical circuits receive noise from outside sources and even generate noise within themselves. While the noise signal is usually at a very low level relative to the intended signal, the noise will be significant if it is amplified enough times. The relationship between the level of the desired signal and the level of the undesirable noise is called the **signal-to-noise ratio.** We want a very good, or large, signal-to-noise ratio, indicating that the signal is significantly louder than the noise that accompanies it.

To place this in perspective, AM radio broadcast suffers most from poor signal-to-noise ratios. If you are attempting to listen to a distant station, the noise in the

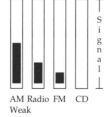

AM Radio FM CD
Weak

Signal-to-noise ratio
(Blue is noise.)

atmosphere will soon be loud relative to the radio station's program. FM radio improves greatly on this ratio because frequency modulation inherently clips the noise from the signal. (The noise appears as amplitude modulation and the receiver cuts off, or clips, the amplitude changes and converts only the frequency changes.) Tape cassettes are the medium of choice for many music fans and offer a reasonable signal-to-noise ratio, until they are compared to compact disks (CDs). Tapes have a reasonable frequency response but have tape hiss. When CDs have been created with the digitizing of the music at the source (as opposed to recording it on analog tape), there is almost a total absence of noise, producing the ultimate in signal-to-noise ratios. In all cases, CDs have the best signal-to-noise ratio because they do not add any noise at playback time as do tapes.

Where analog channels simply amplify the attenuated signals, digital channels use *signal regeneration* to overcome attenuation and noise. The digital regenerator receives a low, often misshaped, signal and recreates the signal as a strong and perfect digital wave form. Therefore, no noise is amplified, reproduced, or recreated if the regeneration occurs before the signal is too distorted. Therefore, the repeating regenerators must be properly positioned. For this reason, long distance telephone carriers convert the analog signals to digital forms and regenerate them all along the channel, providing a signal at the receiving telephone "clear enough to hear a pin drop."

SIGNAL RELIABILITY

The purpose of data communications is to transport digital data over a distance with speed and reliability. (Data signals are converted to analog if a nondigital network is being used.) A chance exists, however, that the digital bits of the data message will be changed by the noise environment of the circuit. Thus, we must have at least error checking and notification, and preferably error correction, to ensure that the message received is the message sent. In all but the simplest cases, this procedure involves putting extra bits or characters in the data stream that can be used by the receiving unit to detect the presence or absence of changed data.

Error Detection

Error detection means you know if the data have been corrupted by noise.

The simplest mode of error checking is called *echo checking*. This process involves echoing each transmitted character back from the receiving unit to the sending operator, generally via a full-duplex capability. The system relies on the terminal operator visually checking the returned data and confirming that they are what were sent. This obviously requires a human at the terminal to see the echo and detect errors. It also assumes transmitting only humanly recognizable characters.

Parity checking is the simplest error detection scheme for asynchronous data, but it is of low reliability.

Since the characters in data communications are often unintelligible to humans, that is, executable programs, database fields, and so on, or a human is not present or cannot read fast enough, a different form of error checking is used. The simplest form used in asynchronous communications is called *vertical redundancy checking (VRC)* or **parity checking** and adds a parity bit in each character to validate that the character was received correctly. See Figure 4.17(a). When the system uses even parity, the sending modem sums the number of 1s in the character being sent and places a 0 or 1 in the parity bit position to make the total number of 1s an even quantity. (Odd parity does the same to create an odd number of 1s.) The receiving modem performs the same count and compares the result with the value of the parity bit. Noise often changes an even number of bits at the same time, however, and the error condition is not detected. While this method of error checking is used almost universally, its use alone carries some risk.

FIGURE 4.17(a)
Asynchronous
Data = One
Character

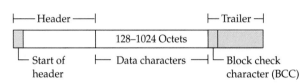

FIGURE 4.17(b)
Synchronous Data =
One Block

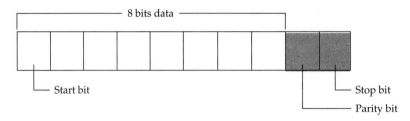

An error detection scheme similar to VRC that is used on blocks of data is *longitudinal redundancy check (LRC)*. This protocol adds a byte of data, the block check character, and puts as bit one the parity check bit of all first bits of all bytes of the data in the block. Bit two is the parity of all of the second bits of all bytes of the block of data, and so on. Thus, LRC increases the probability that an error in a block of data will be detected.

Another simple form of error checking for blocks of data is *checksum.* In this mode, the sending unit sums the data block to produce a number that is placed in the checksum BCC byte. See Figure 4.17(b). The receiving unit makes the same computation and compares it with the **block check character (BCC)** byte. If the two numbers do not match, a negative acknowledgment (NAK) is sent to the receiving unit to retransmit the data block. Checksum is a simple calculation and is the method used first in the blocked asynchronous communications called XMODEM. Most communications software can handle checksum.

Cyclic redundancy checking (CRC) is the most complex, the most common, and the most reliable error checking mode used for synchronous communications. This method is based on dividing the block of data by a polynomial and producing a value and a remainder based on a coefficient k, which is the degree of the polynomial. The CRC character(s) transmitted as the BCC code(s) is the remainder computed. The receiving unit performs a similar division procedure. The receiving unit then compares the remainder it produced with the remainder transmitted. If the two remainders are the same, the system assumes no errors were introduced. For an error to be undetected it must add enough change so the remainder computed at the receiver is equal to the original remainder transmitted. Induced noise often appears as a burst of bits, and the check method must be able to detect a number of changes that seem to escape detection in simpler schemes. This method will reliably detect error patterns of k or fewer bit changes. Since the coefficient $k = 16$ is often used, CRC will detect up to 16-bit changes in a block of data. This gives an overall reliability, using $k = 16$, of 0.99999997, one part error in 10^8 data bits.

Block check characters (BCC) are bytes in the trailer that are used to determine that the block of data was received as sent.

Cyclic redundancy checking (CRC) is the error detection scheme of choice. CRC-32 is better than CRC-16.

Error Correction

Once the receiving unit detects an error, it should take action to correct the data in question. Only systems that have little or no chance of retransmission include additional data that can determine which bits were changed. Such codes are called **Hamming codes.** An example system using this code would be a space probe at the reaches of our solar system, where the time for the data to reach the receiver is hours to days. If, however, you are transmitting data in a purely asynchronous mode and an error is detected via VRC parity checking, the receiving modem may notify the ultimate receiving unit that an error occurred or most likely it will continue processing data and just discard the bad character. If the receiving unit attempted to correct a single corrupted character through character retransmission, as we will explain in synchronous communications, the network would suffer an intolerable amount of idle time. With modern software and hardware, however, you usually send asynchronous data as groups so that block error checking ensures a more reliable result.

For synchronous communications, the units are working with blocks of data. When the receiving unit detects an error in the block or packet, it requests that the sending unit retransmit the total data block in question. Commonly, retransmission involves an **automatic repeat request (ARQ).** The receiving unit checks the block of data and informs the source whether the block was good or bad. The data being transmitted are held in a buffer at the source unit until the receiving unit confirms, by reverse communications, that the block of data was good (positive acknowledgment = ACK). If an error was detected and a negative acknowledgment (NAK) sent, the data are retransmitted.

Digital Data Communications

All communications media that we discussed in the previous chapter are capable of transmitting information in either digital or analog form. Recall that computer data are represented in digital form. In spite of these two facts, computer data have been transmitted mostly in analog form. The primary reason for this is that the providers of communications facilities had historically established analog facilities. The facilities were created for analog voice transmission, even though the telegraph was digital. However, advances in digital technology and lower prices for digital electronics are bringing about a change from analog transmission to digital transmission. As we have illustrated, the primary reason for this is greater reliability, lower noise, and more control; that is, computers can work with and on digital data better than analog signals. Digital **compression** techniques have allowed significantly greater amounts of data to be passed.

Cities now see that the existence of digital communications capabilities provide them with a competitive advantage in attracting industry. Within several decades most major metropolitan areas probably will have made the transition from relying on the local providers to investing in strategic facilities that include digital transmission and storage. Where a city once improved the navigational ability of a nearby river or built roads, it now invests in information highways. Were it not for the considerable existing investment in analog transmission facilities and the tax laws that make transition costly, the transition might happen even sooner.

Case 4-1

Internet Banking

Julie Watson

Partly because of consumer demand and partly because of a highly competitive environment, the banking industry has taken its products and services online to the Internet. Currently there are approximately 789 online banks: some are

Internet-only, others are subsidiaries of existing banks [2]. Throughout the banking industry's emergence onto the Web, there have been several questions concerning its viability, business structure, available services, the convenience factor of banking via the Internet, and security.

According to a recent article in *The Atlanta Journal and Constitution*, "An estimated 10.5 million households used online banks last year for bill-paying, checking accounts, credit cards and loans, buying certificates of deposits and other financial services" [2]. A recent report by IDC, "U.S. Online Banking Market Forecast Analysis, 2000–2004," predicts that almost 23 million Americans will be banking online by 2004 [7]. The trend toward online banking is increasing at a fast pace; however, there are still several problems the banking industry and consumers face as this growth continues.

Banks are spending increasingly more on new technology and implementation of Internet-based banking services. According to a report by TowerGroup, Needham, Massachusetts, U.S. banks are projected to spend $2.1 billion on e-banking technology in 2005. This is a fourfold increase from the $500 million they are spending this year. "The 2.1 billion will be divided among channel management ($1.2 billion), electronic bill payment and presentment ($470 million), wealth management ($380 million), end user access ($65 million), and network access ($40 million). By 2005, it is also projected that more than 3,000 banks will offer e-banking with transactional capabilities" [6].

The problem banks face with this investment is uncertainty—uncertainty of how much they need to invest and uncertainty of when the investment will pay off. It is noted that banks have been reluctant to sell the technology and their services and that they need to do a better job of marketing e-banking to their customers [6].

E-BANK BUSINESS STRUCTURES

There are three basic types of Internet banking "business models." The first is the Internet-only bank, which exists only online such as Net.Bank, Telebank, Security First Network Bank, and CompuBank. The second group is the traditional bricks-and-mortar banks that have already established themselves in the banking industry, but seek to get some of the online banking marketspace. These include banks such as Wells Fargo, Bank of America, and Citibank. The last group is those that are already established, but have set up an Internet-only bank that is a separate entity from its parent. The perfect example of this type of model is BancOne's Wingspan.

To date, Internet-only banks have attracted only 225,000 customers, representing 2 percent of the customers who manage their accounts online [8]. There are several drawbacks to this form of banking over the others. True online banks have no branch offices where customers can talk to real people when they have problems. Another disadvantage is online banks rarely provide ATM machines for their customers—forcing customers to use other banks' ATM machines and paying transaction fees. In addition, customers are unable to make cash deposits. They can make direct deposits of paychecks, but have to mail in all other checks [2].

One way National InterBank and Juniper Financial Corp. have solved this problem is to partner with Mail Boxes Etc. and allow customers to make deposits to their online accounts from any of Mail Boxes Etc.'s 3,400 locations. The next step is to put ATMs in Mail Boxes Etc. stores so customers can make cash withdrawals [9].

Internet-only banks are not all bad, however. There are a few marked advantages to using companies of this type. Besides the absence of ATM machines, they provide anytime, anywhere access wherever a computer terminal and Internet access is available—there are no constraints such as banking hours and holidays. Since the Internet is the only branch for Internet-only companies, these companies have focused on the customer when creating their Web interfaces and are much more user-friendly compared to bricks-and-mortar banks. With lower overhead costs, these institutions are able to remove traditional fees for good customers. Bill paying is easy and convenient with electronic bill-paying services. It also must be noted that Internet-only banks must meet the same regulatory requirements and monitoring criteria as traditional banks [4].

The traditional "bricks and mortar" turned "clicks and mortar" companies are having considerably more success at attracting online users. As a matter of fact, 95 percent of online bank customers use the online services of a traditional bank [2]. These companies, like Wells Fargo, see the Internet as just another medium for them to deliver bank services to traditional banking customers. The customers who opt for banking online still have the use of ATMs and can go into any bank branch, plus they have the option of managing and tracking their accounts online. It is obvious Wells Fargo has a competitive advantage because of its "clicks and mortar" structure; however, it loses some of its competitive advantage by charging its customers $5 for using its bill-paying service [8].

The last model is illustrated in BancOne's new addition, Wingspan. This model is different from the others in that while the companies are separate entities, some of BancOne's services are available to Wingspan customers. An interview from *Business Week* indicates that the only way for old economy companies to compete in the Internet Age is to "set up a completely independent organization and let that organization attack the parent" [1]. BancOne has done this with Wingspan. For starters, Wingspan has its own advisory board. Wingspan's computer system processes account transactions immediately, whereas BancOne and others use older systems that update customer records overnight. A special search capability allows customers to search the Internet for the lowest mortgage rate and e-mails the customer when it is found, even if it's not through BancOne. Wingspan's certificates of deposit have interest rates that are at least half a percentage point higher than those available through BancOne. One of the shared services is that BancOne allows Wingspan customers the use of its ATMs. Even if Wingspan customers choose not to use BancOne ATMs, Wingspan will reimburse up to $5 of the ATM fees incurred [8].

SECURITY AND SAFETY ISSUES

Recently, an online banking customer mistakenly typed in the wrong address for Bank of America—instead of www.bankofamerica.com, she typed www.wwwbankofamerica.com. A bank site opened up and she was asked to log on, only it wasn't Bank of America's website. It made people wonder if the site had been set up to pry into bank customer's bank accounts. Unfortunately this was not the only "mistaken-identity" case involving bank sites. Several national banks have recently discovered that their banks' website had a twin site. This activity of "spoofing" has become quite a problem for online banks. The Office of the Comptroller of the Currency (OCC) issued a regulatory alert on the subject to the banks under its supervision in July.

One of the solutions offered for this problem is for digital certification of customers by use of "smart cards." Users would stick these cards into computers and use them much the same way as they insert debit cards into ATMs. Passwords would still be required, but the smart card would verify that the cardholder is the real bank customer and assure customers that the site belongs to a real bank [5].

In the meantime, to avoid having any more problems, the OCC officials encourage banks to better communicate their exact Web addresses to customers and to check the Web for similar domain names and disclose those to their customers. Also, banks are using security seals, which are little logos that, when clicked on, verify the site's authenticity to the users [5].

SECURITY AND SAFETY MEASURES FOR THE USER

Though the Internet offers ease of use and convenience, it is important for consumers to research a prospective bank and make decisions that will prevent possible fraudulent activity. The FDIC has compiled a list of "Tips for Safe Banking over the Internet."

The first recommendation is to confirm that an online bank is legitimate and that all deposits are insured. A possible place to look would be at www.fdic.com to get some basic information about a bank [3]. Gomez.com offers a discussion on online banking as well as rankings by various attributes [2]. It is also possible to look at the bank's website to find any brief history, the official name, and headquarters and to verify its insurance status—"Member FDIC" [3].

Second, it is important for consumers to keep their personal information private and secure. It is important for consumers to know how their bank uses their personal information and whether it is shared with affiliates of the bank or other parties [3].

Starting July 2001, banks are required to give customers a copy of their privacy policy once they become customers, regardless if they are conducting business online or offline [3].

Because the Internet is a public network, consumers need to learn how to safeguard their banking information, credit cards numbers, Social Security number, and other personal data. It is a good idea to look at the bank's website for information about its security practices, or contact the bank directly [3].

Consumer Action recommends looking for "128-bit encryption," which is the standard in the industry [2].

CONCLUSION

Just as electronic commerce has changed our way of doing business, electronic banking is the natural evolution in the banking industry. It is still debatable which banks will stay on top and which banks will die out. Of the three models, the "clicks and mortars" seem to be the consumers' choice because of their established physical presence, customer service, and ease of use. The downside for these banks is that it is expensive for them to establish Internet marketspace while maintaining their old economy core business.

Internet-only companies are in a risky position in that consumers expect to be satisfied upon their first experience. These banks are the ones that cause most debate in the banking industry. The positive side to these banks is that the technology to set up an Internet bank is inexpensive and easily available—there is no reputation on the line.

As with electronic commerce, the ones that stay on top are usually the ones that got there first. It can be assumed that Internet banking is the same.

Not only do banks have to market their services more and to perfect their systems, consumers must get comfortable with entrusting their money to e-banks before this sector of the banking industry will succeed—customers' trust is paramount for it to succeed. Great strides are being made to make security as perfect as possible, but consumers must exercise caution as well when using online banking services.

REFERENCES

1. Christenson, Clayton M., and Paul C. Judge. "A Brutal Survival Plan." *BusinessWeek Online,* June 28, 1999. http://www.businessweek.com.

2. Ezell, Hank. "Online Banking Growing Rapidly; Interest Rates Are Great, but Sometimes the Service Isn't. . ." *The Atlanta Journal and Constitution,* August 13, 2000, p. G:3.

3. FDIC Safe Internet Banking. http://www.fdic.gov. Last updated September 15, 2000.

4. "Bank: Internet Banking." http://www.gomez.com.

5. Kharif, Olga, "Sounding the Alarm over Fake Bank Sites." *BusinessWeek Online,* August 7, 2000. http://www.businessweek.com.

6. Marlin, Steven. "Study: 3,000 U.S. Banks Will Offer E-Banking Services by 2005." *Bank Systems & Technology* 37, no. 9 (September 2000), p. 10.

7. Murray, Michael. "Online Banking Will Soar, Study Predicts." *Real Estate Finance Today* 17, no. 13 (August 28, 2000), p. 9.

8. Rainer, R. Kelly. MNGT 600 Final Exam, Summer 2000.

9. Trombley, Maria. "Internet Banks Establish Physical Presence." *Computerworld* 34, no. 32 (August 7, 2000) p. 41.

Summary

In this chapter, we have expanded on the basic telecommunications concepts with a focus on data communications. We introduced the concepts by examining the telegraph, the earliest electrical telecommunications system for data. The use of Morse code led to the discussion of other codes, code lengths, and so on. The use of some sort of code for data communications is essential and requires standards. We saw that most data communications focus on the transmission of computerized data. We have discussed some other historical developments including radio telegraphy (wireless), the teletypewriter, and the telephone system to introduce the data communications concept in a stepwise fashion. As the world of data communications expands, managers need to understand the development and the basic technology that inundate them.

In our examination of data communications, much of the discussion surrounds the transmission of data over a network designed for the analog world. Consequently, we have covered the impact of noise on data transmission in the analog network as it is always with us until we move to a clean environment, that is, fiber circuits. Again, there is a need to understand the existing communications infrastructure because it presents certain technological and economic constraints on data communications.

Our examination of data communications looked at data signals and the basic forms of circuits for transmission: serial and parallel circuits. Also, we learned that in establishing basic data communications links, we need to understand data terminating equipment (DTE) and data communications equipment (DCE) and their very different roles. The modem is one of the rather ubiquitous DCE devices, and managers should understand its functions.

The movement of digital data via analog channels requires the use of modems at each end. There are varying techniques employed in modems, such as frequency shift keying (FSK) to phase shift keying. These devices can be asynchronous or synchronous, which have direct consequences for speed and error detection. The manager must consider not only the efficiency of the alternatives, but the cost and reliability as well.

The concept of signal attenuation, or weakening, was discussed in more detail. The means of dealing with attenuation vary with the type of circuit: analog amplification or digital regeneration. We noted the importance of the signal-to-noise ratio in keeping the signals at the desired level absolutely and relative to noise.

The notation of speed of data transmission as either bits per second or baud was covered, as was the vital nature of error detection and correction. Again, the method used for error detection depends on the nature of the circuit, asynchronous or synchronous. Methods of increasing the speed of data transmission also were introduced.

This chapter initiated our discussion and coverage of the important topic of data communications. There were several key terms and definitions that are necessary for a manager to understand as data communications concepts are expanded. The topic is of such great importance and scope that we will continue it in the next two chapters and pick it up again at the end of the book.

Key Terms

acoustic coupler, *135*
American Standard Code for Information Interchange (ASCII), *144*
amplifier, *160*
analog, *151*
asynchronous, *158*
attenuation, *160*
automatic repeat request (ARQ), *163*
automated teller machine (ATM), *141*
bandwidth, *155*
baud, *155*
binary, *151*
bits per second (BPS), *154*

block check characters (BCC), *162*
code, *151*
compression, *155*
cyclic redundancy checking (CRC), *162*
data communications, *140*
data communications equipment (DCE), *152*
data terminating equipment (DTE), *152*
demodulation, *153*
differential phase shift keying (DPSK), *155*
digital, *151*
discrete, *151*
error correction, *162*

error detection, *161*
Extended Binary Coded Decimal Interchange Code (EBCDIC), *145*
frequency shift keying (FSK), *153*
full-duplex, *149*
half-duplex, *149*
Hamming codes, *162*
mainframe, *157*
modem, *153*
modulation, *153*
Morse code, *142*
noise, *148*
off line, *147*
parallel, *152*
parity checking, *161*

Recommended Readings

Infoworld

Internet Week

Network Magazine

Network World

Discussion Questions

4.1. Why is it necessary to employ a modem when transmitting data via the voice telephone network?

4.2. Would you have to employ modems between computers in the same room or building?

4.3. What effect can the introduction of extraneous noise have on the quality of data at the receiving equipment?

4.4. Describe the differences among the various modes of transmission. Explain the difference between DCE and DTE and give examples of each.

4.5. A textile company in the Southeast connects to a VAN for download of retail sales information. It does this each week for four hours on a 9.6 Kbps modem. Does this make economic sense?

Projects

4.1. Determine if a bank in your neighborhood provides service bureau services. Check to determine if there are similar data services available from other sources and list them and their services along with relevant costs and telecommunications requirements.

4.2. What sort of data processing capabilities do small and medium-sized businesses in your locale employ? Do a small survey and report the alternatives used and list the cost/risk associated with each.

4.3. What telecommunications facilities are most frequently employed by smaller businesses for data communications in your vicinity? How are they comparable in terms of cost and performance? What data communications configurations are most popular?

4.4. Visit a bank and find out the data communications used and determine the importance of each to the bank's businesses.

Bibliography

Foskett, Charles. "The Plain Truth About ISDN." *Telephony* 219 (September 10, 1990), pp. 41–43.

Hicks, William, telecommunications employee. Interview in Huntsville, Alabama, December 1991.

Jarmon, Don, telecommunications employee. Interview in Huntsville, Alabama, December 1991.

Paludan, Mike. "Computer Alliances: Firms Working Together to Compete and Survive." *The Huntsville Times*, December 8, 1991, sec. C, p. 1.

Rowe, Stanford H. *Business Telecommunications.* New York: Macmillan Publishing Company, 1991.

Ryan, Robert J. "Back to the Future." *Telephony* 220 (January 21, 1991), pp. 30–32.

Chapter Five

Data Communications: Conversion, Modulation, and Multiplexing

CONTINUING CASE—PART 5

Meanwhile, Back at JL&S

As the manager and chief engineer of JL&S for several years, Carlton had gained expertise in evaluating lighting and alarm systems. He had evolved the company to the point where it was largely dependent on Herbert Controls, of Kansas City, Missouri, a manufacturer of top-quality security system components. Tom Herbert, its founder and president, started a company making very high quality environmental sensors and controls, as well as computer peripherals. The demand for his sensors and controls diminished as increased competition provided comparable functionality at lower cost. Tom had made a point of providing the very best in his products through engineering enhancements. Unfortunately, this led to high costs and restricted markets. Carlton had been an early customer and, as a competent electrical engineer himself, valued the quality of Tom's products, especially in security installations where a long mean-time-before-failure was required. Carlton believed that high cost for high quality was necessary for low risk. He also enjoyed a close personal relationship with Tom and several other Herbert Controls personnel.

While the control and sensor market languished, Tom's line of computer peripherals had met with great demand. Low-cost Hayes-compatible modems and uninterruptable power supplies (UPS) continued to be eagerly sought in the industrial and consumer markets. Michael was a customer of Herbert's UPS in his disaster recovery and computer operations. While Herbert's line of peripherals was quite profitable, his line of controls was not. Tom was convinced that if he kept enhancing the controls, they would be recognized as the best, and profits would follow. He could not take the advice of several advisors to dispose of this part of the business because it had given him his start. He concentrated on his line of controls to the extent that he siphoned significant profits from the peripherals to fund continued enhancement, manufacture, and marketing of the controls. This led him to the brink of bankruptcy.

Facing the alternatives, Tom called Carlton, his most loyal customer and good friend, and offered to sell him all rights and assets of the controls division at under 40 cents on the dollar if Carlton would keep his employees and continue the product line

for a specified time period. Tom said that his creditors had agreed that if he could find a solvent recipient for the control line facility, they would allow them to develop a normal debt service and allow Tom to reorganize the remainder of the company under Chapter 11 protection.

Carlton called his dad and told him they needed to talk about a fantastic opportunity. He explained the situation on the phone and asked Michael to meet him at the lake to discuss the possibilities and the risk. Michael agreed to discuss the venture, but cautioned Carlton that he had been down the opportunity road before and was being very cautious about new ventures. After all, hadn't Carlton just nearly doubled his JL&S responsibilities with the addition of facilities from Mile High Security? It seemed as though expansion was getting out of hand.

Michael and Carlton met at the lake. The fishing rods continued to gather dust as they tried to consider all of the alternatives of the venture. First, if they did not take over the sensors and controls lines of this failing company, it would cease and JL&S would have to find another line of products that might be less reliable. Since JL&S had a large installed base of this equipment, failure to get replacement parts would mean that they would have to use different or substitute parts at time of failure, necessitating reengineering and additional costs. Carlton was very satisfied with the products, as were his customers. Thus, this was a point in favor of the venture. Carlton also thought that even though he could tolerate the high cost of the controls, he would be able to work with the manufacturing engineers at Herbert to reduce this cost without reducing quality.

Another issue that loomed was the management of the recently expanded security business, now even further geographically dispersed. Did Carlton's assistant and marketing relations director, Alli Harrison, have the skills and degree of experience needed to become the overall marketing manager of JEI? Alli had joined JL&S the previous year in the capacity of market analyst. It was to her credit that JL&S had waited to enter into the residential market as her analysis had highlighted important factors that did not exist for business in the commercial market. She had seemed to fit into the firm very well, and her MBA from a major state university appeared to be excellent preparation for a management position.

Carlton was confident that Alli could handle more responsibility. He was somewhat afraid that he would lose some of his objectivity, because he really was excited about Herbert. Carlton rationalized that if he had the right telecommunications system, he could still participate in JL&S's Colorado activities, even if he was in Missouri, 600 miles away. (Figure 5.1.)

The next two considerations were the availability of cash or credit for the funding of the new venture and the skills necessary for managing the facility. JL&S had become a "cash cow," generating funds held in reserve by JEI. It appeared that JL&S did have sufficient financial backing for the takeover. This could be confirmed with a meeting with their banker. Of course, they had to be able to predict a favorable return on investment, but they knew that the banks were very impressed by their lack of debt and strong cash flow.

The second consideration, that of Carlton's skills in operating a manufacturing facility, was a different matter. He had shown great expertise in the design and installation of systems composed of purchased parts, but he had no direct manufacturing experience. The facility was located in Kansas City, Missouri. Carlton had become friends with the manager of operations at the facility and felt he could work closely with him. He called his friend, Doug Turner, to discuss the possibility.

After a quick outline of the possibilities, Carlton asked Doug about remaining with the firm. He added, "Hey, Doug, if we buy your facility from Tom, can I count on you staying there and running the operations . . . as plant manager?"

"Well Carlton, I never turned down a promotion. I believe that with the proper management, we can return to profitability. I must warn you, however, that the plant will be back in bankruptcy court within a year if you don't implement several cost-cutting measures that were needed for some time that Tom would never approve. We probably are producing the most overengineered products in our market, using some outdated processes."

"Doug, you know manufacturing and I know engineering. I have learned to trust your judgment. Let's meet next Tuesday and discuss both the overall design of the controllers and your suggestions. My guess is that I can live with your changes, if you can live with my ignorance of manufacturing. In addition, I've got several ideas about improving the controllers I've gained from our experience in installing and servicing them."

After a series of meetings with the bankers in Denver and Kansas City, Michael and Carlton arranged for the purchase of the controls part of Herbert Controls at a very favorable price. They had pro forma predictions of returning the manufacturing of controllers to profitability within two years. Alli's marketing analysis showed that the potential was very strong for sales to accelerate rapidly if high

FIGURE 5.1(a)   Growth of Johnson's Expanding Territory

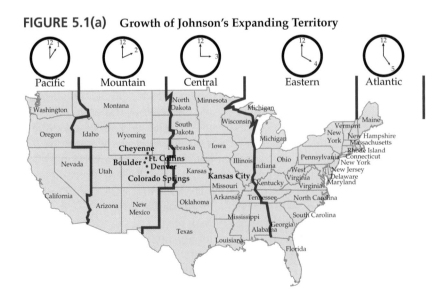

FIGURE 5.1(b) **Facilities**

Fort Collins

Greeley

Boulder

Bank

Bank

Disaster recovery
site

Denver— Headquarters

Matilda

Colorado Springs

Kansas City
office tower and plant

FIGURE 5.1(c) **JEI Organizations**

JEI

| JL&S | Johnson Security Controls (JSC) (manufacturing) | Shared Tenant Services (STS) | Security International, Inc. (SII) | Computer operations | Computers and risk | Contingency space and disaster planning |

value could be maintained while costs were made more competitive since customers perceived the high quality favorably. As shown in Figure 5.1, Johnson had now become a much more widely dispersed organization. The firm had a new set of operational characteristics, strategies, and telecommunications needs. Management had become more complex with facilities in two time zones and 600 miles apart.

Johnson Specialty Controls (JSC)

It was decided that Carlton would take over responsibility for manufacturing in the new company. The new name for the company was Johnson Specialty Controls, or JSC. All product brand names became JSC's, and thus the goodwill from Herbert Controls was transferred along with the other assets. As part of this move, Michael asked his Colorado Springs

FIGURE 5.1(d) **Communication between Facilities**

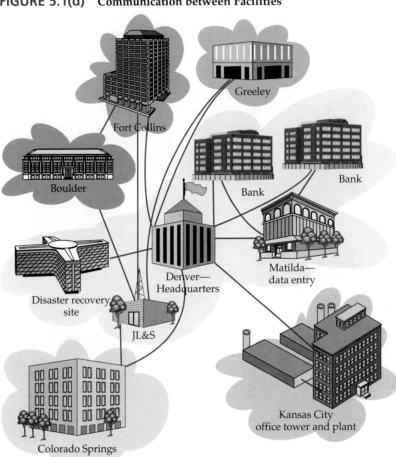

security chief, Tom Marshall, to head up JL&S and for Alli to become part of his JEI staff as marketing manager for the total organization. Tom said he understood security but would have to be guided in his new job as JL&S manager.

Carlton spent the next few months learning about the manufacture of control products. He and Doug found ways to reduce the cost of manufacturing of the controllers, while keeping their historically high quality. They did this by reengineering the product for manufacturability as opposed to total functionality and changed the factory process of assembly. As a result of changing the manufacturing line, he found that the facility had vacant space and unused plant capacity, and saw that he could use it to design and manufacture other specialized security equipment cost-effectively. The equipment lines to be developed further were motion and intrusion detection, fire and water sensors, remote alarms, and alarms and fire suppression for computer rooms and other special

environments. He felt he now had a market niche that worked well with JL&S's market and that he also could sell a product superior to that of companies similar to JL&S. Along with the manufacturing facility came the office building with some new features that presented Carlton with some management challenges. The office situation was, however, secondary to getting the plant on track. See Figure 5.2 for some items manufactured by Specialty Controls.

The Kansas City Facility

The newly acquired Kansas City plant was quite large, with approximately 30,000 square feet of production floor space and an attached six-story office building. The production lines consisted primarily of three areas for assembly and insertion of circuit boards for the controllers. About one-half of the production was automated, using Digital Equipment

FIGURE 5.2   Some Items Manufactured by Specialty Controls

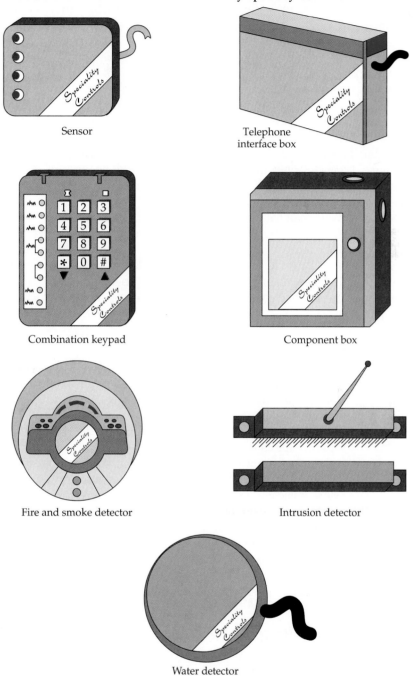

Sensor

Telephone interface box

Combination keypad

Component box

Fire and smoke detector

Intrusion detector

Water detector

Corporation (DEC) VAX computers. The entire Kansas City plant used DEC computers in both the direct production and administration. Doug had excellent relations with DEC, so he was fully confident of their support when needed. The plant's automated systems directly reported critical infor-mation to the administrative system, so Doug could monitor status fairly well by perusing reports generated by the central system. Doug had long desired to increase the degree of automation and to implement a more nearly real-time capacity for monitoring the entire production sequence. He was especially interested in gaining more status information of the work-in-process inventory, but Tom had seen little advantage to introducing change in the way he had been operating for many years.

Doug had joined the American Production and Inventory Control Society (APICS) and had become certified by passing the examinations in all areas. Through his APICS activities, he became aware of the latest trends in manufacturing and was anxious to prove that he could implement the right systems to turn the production of controllers around. Doug was enthusiastic about a new evolution in manufacturing systems: enterprise resource planning (ERP). The concept seemed even more promising than the systems that were widely used called materials requirements planning (MRP) and the broader version, MRP II.

In the first few weeks of intense review and audit, Carlton and Doug evaluated each of the major products from both an engineering and production viewpoint. They together had discovered several ways to reengineer most circuit boards as well as points at which they could increase machine insertion. Many of the improvements came from Doug's previous suggestions as well as from production workers who had a stake in making the JSC operation successful.

While Carlton and Doug were focused on the engineering and production aspects, Alli was busy doing an expanded marketing analysis. She conferred regularly with Carlton and Doug via conference call to ensure that she was up-to-date on all proposed changes in the product. Alli was excited about the new tasks and was particularly gratified to see her preliminary optimism more than justified. Her careful analysis revealed that there was a great deal of price elasticity in the products. She predicted that if a target of a 30 percent price reduction could be achieved, there would be greater than a 100 percent increase in demand and sales, if her aggressive marketing plan was executed.

INTRODUCTION

In the previous chapter, we introduced asynchronous and synchronous transmission of data, modems and the encoding of bits into analog signals, and error detection and correction. Data communications is important and somewhat complex. In order to cover this topic adequately, we have devoted four chapters to the topic. In this chapter we expand upon the discussion of data communications with the topics of modulation, multiplexing, data compression, protocols, and ISDN digital telephone. We now move further into the digital realm. Until the early 1990s, voice and fax were serviced by one network, data by another, television by another, and so on. By moving all of these to a digital mode, we have the potential to serve them *all* with a single transport capability: a single network.[1] We are headed toward that single transport ability, one providing great speed and reliability with little noise or delay.

DIGITAL REPRESENTATION OF AN ANALOG SIGNAL

Digital Voice

We have noted that the public switched telephone network is an **analog** network developed to handle voice traffic. As the signal travels down the wire, it loses strength and attenuates. Recall that line **amplifiers**[2] are placed every mile or so to

---

[1] A network is two or more nodes connected by one or more channels. They will be discussed further later.

[2] By convention, devices that amplify analog signals are called **repeaters**, whereas devices that regenerate and amplify digital signals are call **regenerators**, though they could be referred to as regenerative repeaters.

The Real World 5–1

We talk about the electric telegraph being the first instance of data communications, circa 1857. However, in the late eighteenth century (1790s), data communications systems were in place in Europe. "Right about the time the Bastille was being stormed in France and one coup followed another in Sweden, French clergyman Claude Chappe and Swedish nobleman Abraham Niclas Edel-

crantz were building the first two systems. Within a few years, many European nations had fully operational, nationwide **optic telegraph networks**, each with hundreds of 'stations' with semaphore towers."

Source: Gerald J. Holzmann and Bjorn Pehrson, *The First Data Networks*.

---

boost the signal strength, keeping the volume at a predefined level. One problem with boosting analog signals through **repeaters** is that they amplify all parts of the signal including any noise that is picked up along the way. A method of avoiding this problem is to convert the analog voice signal to a **digital** form, transmit it digitally, and then transform it back to analog at the receiving end. Although this signal also will attenuate over distance, the digital signal is *regenerated and amplified* instead of just being amplified when required, leaving the noise behind. Thus, transmitting voice as data communications instead of analog voice signals means a cleaner signal at the destination. In addition, we can handle digital voice in the same way as data, with the exception that reception delays are less tolerated for voice than data. In other words, transmitting voice and data via direct circuit will work well, but if the digitized data are then separated into blocks, or packets, such as with a packet-switching network (to be discussed later), the transfer of data may not meet the time constraints of digitized voice. See Figure 5.3 for a diagram illustrating signal regeneration.

To convert an analog signal to a digital form, equipment must sample the signal many times a second, convert the measured analog signal to a digital (integer) figure, and encode the digital figure as a digital code. In Figure 5.4(a), the sine wave represents a simple analog signal, much like a voice conversation. A device samples the signal strength at each point, *a* through *n*, and measures the values of 1 through 5 volts (analog). The analog values are represented as **binary** numbers (see Figure 5.4[b]) and transmitted over a network as digital data. The equipment at the receiving end of the digital circuit converts the binary numbers back to analog signals, to voltage levels, using the same timing as the original sampling device. Thus, a spoken analog signal is represented by a digital signal, transmitted, and then converted back to its original analog form for playback (hearing). The fidelity of reproducing the analog signal is dependent on the sample rate and the number of integer sample points. A rate of 8,000 times per second is required for a good representation of telephone conversation. Also, the system requires 256 integer values of measurement, which can be represented with 8 digital bits ($2^8 = 256$). This combination necessitates a digital signal of 8 bits, 8,000 times per second, or a digital speed of 64,000 bps. The standard that employs these rates is called **pulse code modulation (PCM).** Thus, PCM samples the level of a voice conversation 8,000 times per second using a scale of 256 integer points, converts each integer measurement into an 8-bit code, and transmits the resultant information

Pulse code modulation (PCM) uses a scanning rate twice the highest frequency.

FIGURE 5.3 Digital Signal Regeneration

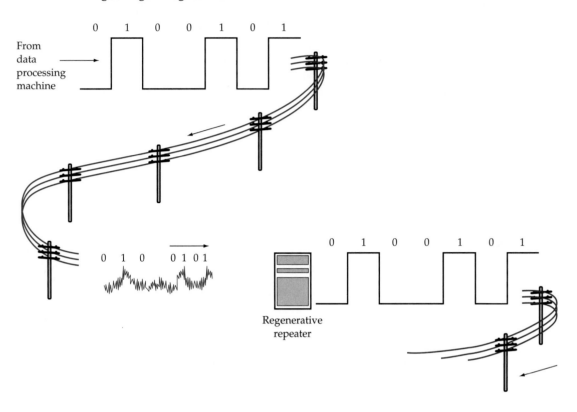

FIGURE 5.4(a)
Converting an
Analog Signal to
Digital (Binary)

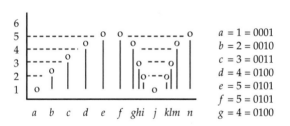

$a = 1 = 0001$
$b = 2 = 0010$
$c = 3 = 0011$
$d = 4 = 0100$
$e = 5 = 0101$
$f = 5 = 0101$
$g = 4 = 0100$

at a speed of 64,000 bps. The receiving unit reverses the process and a voice conversation is reproduced.

A variation of this method is **adaptive differential pulse code modulation (ADPCM),** which measures the signal just like the PCM method but transmits the difference between successive measured values instead of the value itself. ADPCM allows the use of a 4-bit code to represent the difference value and reduces the signal requirement to 32,000 bps. The system uses 3 bits to represent 8 integer values and 1 bit to note whether the change was positive or negative. By additional compression (leaving out the silence periods and sending redundant data as multiples) and encoding techniques, the digital rate can be further reduced without sacrificing quality. Equipment is available that reduces voice to 16,000 bps with no discernable loss of quality, and AT&T uses a proprietary method to compress to 8,000 bps in its nationwide long-distance

Multimedia
applications are
including ADPCM
technology.

Off-the-shelf
components can
provide PCM
(64 Kbps), ADPCM
(32 Kbps), and 16
Kbps D-to-A and A-to-D conversion without
loss of sound quality.

FIGURE 5.4(b)
Binary Equivalent
Numbers

Decimal	Binary
0	0 0000
1	0 0001
2	0 0010
3	0 0011
4	0 0100
5	0 0101
6	0 0110
7	0 0111
8	0 1000
9	0 1001
10	0 1010
11	0 1011
12	0 1100
13	0 1101
14	0 1110
15	0 1111

service. The importance of analog-to-digital (A–D) conversion at this point is that almost all long-distance carriers use A–D and D–A conversion and move analog telephone conversations as digital data. One result is noise-free, clear conversations.

If we convert real-time analog signals, such as telephone conversations and television programs, to digital signals, we must not delay their transmission and conversion back to analog or a disturbing result will occur. When using the satellite medium, there is a delay caused by the long distance the signal must travel and the transponder's switching time. This is annoying for voice conversations because they are two-way, back-and-forth, but completely transparent to TV broadcast because it is unidirectional and continuous. Delay due to satellite transmission would seem to be irrelevant to data communications. The problem in the latter case, however, is that delays are imposed by responses from the receiving station in noting errors in transmission. This delay translates into significant amounts of wait time and, thus, nonuse of the circuit during the reversal of a **half-duplex** circuit.

SIGNAL TRANSMISSION AND CHANNELS

Circuits, Channels, and Networks

Channels
are logical paths for communicating data.

Circuits
are physical connections and can be divided into channels.

A **channel** is a path, not necessarily a pair of wires, for transmission between two or more nodes or points. The channel connects the source to the receiver or destination. It is thought of as a one-way communications path, and although the transmission is usually electrical, it also may be photonic (see Figure 5.5).

A **circuit** is a means of connecting two points for communications. It is thought of as the physical connection between the points, as well as a two-way communications path, and can be divided into multiple channels.

Information Window   5–1

Compact disk players read the data from the disks and move the data instantly to the D-to-A converters. The use of compact disk players portably and in cars was delayed because jarring the reader would cause it to lose data and stop playing. This problem has been solved by reading the digital data well ahead of its playback speed, storing the digital data in RAM memory, and converting it to analog as appropriate. Up to 10 seconds of data are read; meaning that you can jar the reader and lose track for up to 10 seconds and not interrupt playback. This method could be used for any simplex mode, but would not work for interactive modes, such as voice communications.

FIGURE 5.5
Simple and Complex Networks

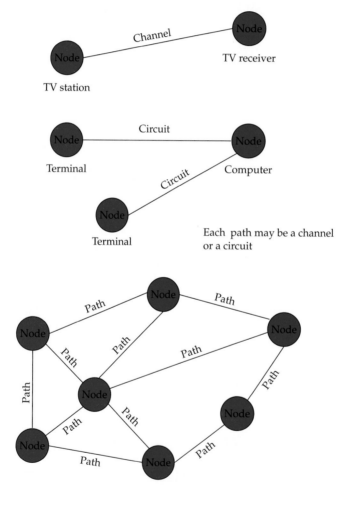

There are various *data paths* over which communications takes place. (See Figure 5.5.) A **path** is the route between any two nodes. A **network**, therefore, consists of a pattern of paths and associated equipment that establish connections between nodes. We will discuss various classifications and patterns of networks in a later chapter.

Do you remember the definition of a network?

Modulation

We have mentioned amplitude modulation and frequency modulation radio several times. Because these forms of signal modification are two major examples of signals that share channels and circuits, let's stop a moment and discuss them.

The premise for this discussion is that we have a signal, such as voice or music, that we wish to communicate to a remote place. As in the case of radio, when we broadcast from the sending station, we cannot broadcast the voice or music directly. Therefore, we must superimpose the desired signal onto a carrier signal. For example, if you are listening to AM station WREL in Lexington, Virginia, you have tuned your radio to a carrier frequency of 1180 kilohertz. Superimposed onto this (single frequency) carrier is the music. In the case of **amplitude modulation (AM),** the music is superimposed, or modulated, onto the carrier wave by varying the amplitude of the carrier wave in correlation to the music signal. As shown in Figure 5.6, an analog signal, such as music, is combined with an analog carrier wave as variations in amplitude to create an amplitude modulated signal. The music signal we show as an example is vastly simplified. Music and voice signals are combinations of hundreds of frequencies, resulting in a wave that is very complex.

Modulation places payload signals onto carrier signals.

Nodes are end or switching points on a path.

FIGURE 5.6
Modulation

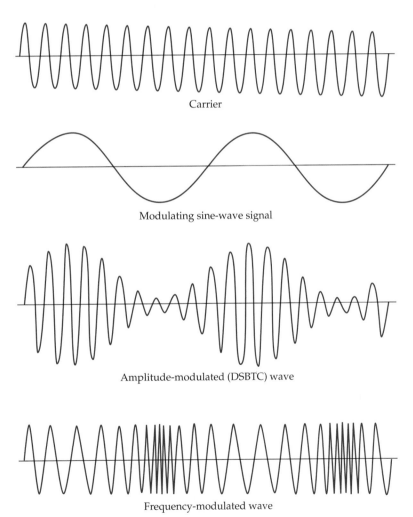

Carrier

Modulating sine-wave signal

Amplitude-modulated (DSBTC) wave

Frequency-modulated wave

In the case of **frequency modulation (FM),** such as 96 ROCK in Atlanta, Georgia, the analog music signal varies the frequency, not the strength (amplitude), of the carrier wave. Where the AM receiver (550–1680 KHz carrier) simply reproduces a signal that is the amplitude variation of the broadcast signal, the FM receiver (88–108 MHz carrier) reproduces a signal that follows the frequency variation of the broadcast signal.

Television uses both amplitude and frequency modulation to transmit the picture and sound to your home. Each TV channel has a 6 MHz bandwidth, superimposed onto a carrier wave in the range of 50–212 MHz for **very high frequency (VHF)** channels 2–13 and 450–900 MHz for **ultrahigh frequency (UHF)** channels 14–84. The audio signal occurs at 5.75 MHz, using frequency modulation. The black-and-white video signal uses amplitude modulation in the range of 0.5 to near 5.75 MHz, with color information being coded at 3.6 MHz using other AM techniques.

Neither analog nor digital signals can be transmitted directly because of the noise environment or, as in the case of radio and television, the distance required. Therefore, we modulate the desired signals, such as voice or music in the case of analog signals, onto a carrier frequency, which can be transmitted farther. See Figure 5.6. The process of modulation bypasses much of the noise interference. Because the frequency bands are much wider than required to carry one signal, we divide the frequency into multiple channels. This process will be discussed next.

Circuit Sharing (Multiplexing)

Multiplexing shares circuits by allocating multiple channels by either frequency or time.

Any of the media we use for communications circuits can handle a wider analog **bandwidth** or higher digital speed than one communications signal requires. For example, a twisted-pair line can accommodate a one megahertz bandwidth, and a telephone conversation on the local loop and over the long-distance carrier's channel requires only 2,700 Hz bandwidth. To make efficient use of circuits, carriers would want to transmit more than one conversation over a circuit. This is especially true with circuits having large volumes of traffic, such as between central offices in the same calling areas and between calling areas (a toll trunk call). Two basic methods, frequency division multiplexing (FDM) and time division multiplexing (TDM) of the primary circuit, accommodate circuit sharing. While used in different environments, FDM and TDM perform the same basic function, the sharing of a circuit. FDM is used on analog broadband circuits and TDM is used on digital baseband circuits.

Broadband generally refers to wide analog circuits, often divided into channels via FDM.

Baseband means a single channel, usually with digital data.

Frequency division multiplexing (FDM) places several signals onto one channel or circuit by placing each at a different part of the (analog) frequency spectrum. For example, 12 continuous telephone circuits are required between Atlanta and Savannah, Georgia, and there is only one twisted-pair wire circuit. Instead of stringing 11 additional twisted-pair wire circuits, we can use frequency division multiplexing to share the existing one circuit by stacking the conversations on top of each other. (See Figure 5.7.) In a simplistic illustration, the first conversation occupies the frequency between 0 and 4,000 hertz, as it would on a simple local loop. Assuming we needed no buffer zone between conversations other than that provided within the 4,000 hertz envelope, the second conversation would be shifted up 4,000 hertz and occupy the frequency between 4,001 and 8,000 hertz. The signal actually being transmitted would occur in the band between 4,001 and 8,000 hertz, but it would be converted back to 0 to 4,000 hertz before being sent to the local loop. The third conversation would be at 8,001 and 12,000, and so on. These 12 conversations could be accommodated by a single circuit with a bandwidth of only 48 KHz. A normal twisted-wire circuit could potentially handle

FIGURE 5.7
Multiplexed Circuit

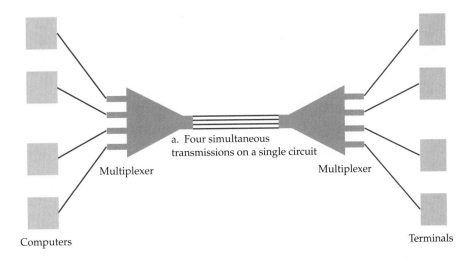

a. Four simultaneous
transmissions on a single circuit

Multiplexer   Multiplexer

Computers   Terminals

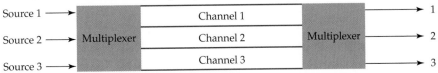

b. Frequency division multiplexing

Source 1 →   → 1
Source 2 →   Multiplexer | Channel 1 | Multiplexer → 2
Source 3 → | Channel 2 | → 3
                          | Channel 3 |

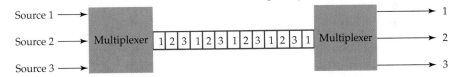

c. Time division multiplexing

Source 1 →   → 1
Source 2 →   Multiplexer | 1 2 3 1 2 3 1 2 3 1 2 3 1 | Multiplexer → 2
Source 3 →   → 3

250 conversations (250 × 4,000 hertz = 1 megahertz) but is usually limited to 48 4-KHz channels or less. In this example, the Telco could increase the number of telephone channels between two cities hundreds of miles apart 5,000 percent by adding multiplexing equipment at each end.

When the first transatlantic telephone cables were laid, ships carried several thousand miles of large expensive cable and dropped it gently to the ocean floor. By the time demand generated the need for additional transatlantic circuits, technological advances negated the need for laying much additional cable. By multiplexing the existing physical circuits, the communications companies could meet the increased need quickly and at a low cost. Later, cableless satellite circuits provided the additional circuits. Still later, digital **fiber optic** circuits were put under the sea from continent to continent to provide new and greatly increased bandwidth and reliability, replacing their analog twisted-pair ancestors. Remember that fiber cables from the United States to Australia are less than 12,000 miles (19,320 km) in length and therefore have a total distance delay of 6.4 milliseconds. A satellite channel of one transponder has a 47,000-mile (75,670-km) path and adds to the transponder delay to create a one-half-second delay in the circuit. Thus, for voice communications, the fiber cables are much preferred. Both media were used in live news broadcasts of Operation Desert Storm in 1991 as well as in Enduring Freedom in 2002.

The Real World   5–2

1874. That Was Then.

Braving a hostile ocean, the men of the *Faraday* laid the first transatlantic cable between Ireland and America. That cable was manufactured by Siemens. It could carry 22 messages at one time, and it carried the world into a new area of communications.

1994. This Is Now.

The digital telephone switch Siemens manufactures today handles 1,000,000 calls an hour. It can even carry data, text, and voice simultaneously on a single phone line. And private telephone systems from ROLM®, a Siemens company, deliver voice and data solutions that help both large corporations and small businesses improve productivity.

Advertisement by Siemens Corporation in *Telecommunication* issue, *The Wall Street Journal*, February 11, 1994, p. 8.

We are accustomed to frequency division in our daily lives. For example, broadcast television transmits 12 VHF channels via the air medium over six megahertz channels (channels 2–13 broadcast on a frequency band of 50–212 MHz with FM radio channels or stations occupying 200 KHz each in the 88–108 MHz frequency range between channels 6 and 7). Many additional channel slots are also available in the 450–900 megahertz UHF spectrum, and satellites have several hundred more. We use a filter to select the channel of choice from the large number being received, and the TV converts the signal to video and corresponding audio. With a cable TV (CATV) network, the coaxial cable coming to the home or office can carry over 50 TV channels[3] multiplexed on the one circuit. Once the viewer determines the one channel desired, the receiver selects the signal for that channel alone and the TV converts it to video and audio.

As a different way to view this, the portion of the total electromagnetic spectrum set aside for television programming has a number of discrete channels occupying the spectrum. The same is true for CATV. In our TV set, the RF (radio frequency) receiver selects the desired frequency bandwidth (channel) and converts the signal by subtracting out the frequency that had been added to move the "real" frequency to the allocated slot. This signal, in turn, is converted to video and corresponding audio.

Examples of Divided Channels

Subchannel is a division of a channel, which may be a division of a circuit.

When a channel is established, but not totally utilized, the potential exists to further divide the channel for additional uses. Such is the case in **subsidiary communications authorization (SCA)** subchannel transmission over the FM radio spectrum. Although a commercial FM channel is 200 KHz wide (100 KHz useful), the spectrum used for stereo broadcast occupies frequencies of 20–15,000 Hz for the primary channel, 19 KHz for the stereo pilot signal, and 23–53 KHz for the stereo subchannel. The spectrum from 53 KHz to 100 KHz is unused. SCA uses the 53 KHz to 92 KHz band for either analog or digital transmission. For example, an FM music station in Atlanta, Georgia, leases a small bandwidth at the 67 KHz frequency to Lotus Information Service to broadcast

[3] As noted previously, the number of channels that a coaxial cable can deliver is dependent on (1) the analog bandwidth of the cable (e.g., 350, 550, or 750 MHz), (2) the analog bandwidth of the channel (standard or HDTV), and (3) whether the channel is carried as uncompressed analog (6 MHz) or compressed digital (3–10 channels per 6 MHz bandwidth).

Information Window   5–2

In 1970, the Club of Rome published a report that estimated that the world's supply of petroleum, above and below ground, would last only 40 years. In 1990, when asked about their prediction that there should be only 20 years' supply left, the Club said that the reserves at that point would last 90 years. The basis for the change in predictions was that we now had the *technology* to explore further and deeper, *and* the addition of new technology such as computers in cars and other efficiency measures would significantly stretch the existing supply. Thus, technology effectively increased the supply of what appeared to be a scarce resource.

Thus it is with technology and telecommunications. Where we once used one twisted-pair circuit for one channel, frequency division multiplexing technology allows the physical media to increase to the equivalent of 12, 24, or 48 physical channels. Technology, in this case FDM, increased the supply of scarce resources.

(simplex) its stock market quote service, digitally and encrypted at about 8 Kbps. Subscribers in the city can receive updated stock market quotes on specially designed FM radio receiving units. Additionally, some subscribers attach this unit to a microcomputer for computer-based monitoring of stock activity. The second leaser of a subchannel from this radio station is a digital paging service that uses the 57 KHz frequency to broadcast a very narrow signal to portable paging units.

On the analog side, the background music service *Muzak*® typically will lease the 67 KHz frequency with a 6 KHz bandwidth for transmitting specially arranged music to subscribers from commercial FM stations. Some grocery stores in Atlanta receive music via another mode at the 92 KHz frequency, called AM double sideband suppressed carrier. This technique uses sideband carriers with bandwidths of 10 KHz each to send two channels of high-quality music. All of this activity is occurring in addition to the commercial FM broadcast.

Another service using multiplexed transmission occurs when CATV networks transmit news and stock market data in digital form in addition to the usual analog signals. Usually, CATV subscribers connect the cable to a television set or decoder and receive analog TV programs. In some areas, subscribers pay for a special attachment device (modem equivalent) and software for their microcomputers and receive the transmitted text data from the CATV cable. While commercial online stock quote services operate bidirectionally, allowing subscribers such as stockbrokers to ask for specific information, both the CATV and SCA services are simplex. Some CATV systems update the data only three times daily.

A final example of FDM that uses digital data is the Hughes Communications direct satellite TV broadcast, begun in the United States in 1994. This satellite transmits 75 channels on each of two satellites in analog form to 18" house-mounted satellite antennas. The signals have compressed digital TV signals, which are uncompressed, decoded, and unscrambled for premium channels, and played on the TV set. The audio is compact disk quality and the video is considered of higher quality and lower noise than commercial air-medium or CATV equivalent.

Time division multiplexing (TDM) shares the circuit's time allocation instead of the frequency allocation. (See Figure 5.8.) A simplistic, but seldom used, form of TDM physically switches from originator to originator to share the time available, and the receiving unit does the same in synchronism. If the signals change slowly

FIGURE 5.8
Statistical Time Division Multiplexing

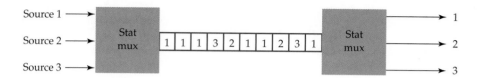

or they can be stored, this method will work well. The master controlling unit may mechanically switch among slave units on a scheduled basis, giving each slave unit a predetermined portion of time, or provide a nonequal amount of time based on past need, called statistical multiplexing (see below). An alternative method is for the controller to *poll* the slaves to see if each wishes to be connected. **Polling** provides more control and requires more overhead, but as with statistical methods, active devices have more access time.

The transmission of digital data, which can be stored, makes the best use of time division multiplexing. The originating sending computers or terminals store their outgoing messages until the originating multiplexer (MUX) connects to each for a short time period. Part of the connected sender's message is transmitted, and the MUX switches to the next sender. Since the sending unit can store its message, any timing problem is eliminated. Another logical view of this capability is that the time-division-multiplex sending modem stores the message of each of the terminals or computers to which it is attached and interleaves their messages into one long string, a portion at a time. If you have four slow, 2,400 bps computers communicating over a single 9,600 bps circuit, the computers will notice no delay because the total speed of the four input signals sums to the speed of the communications circuit. In the case of very high speed circuit media such as fiber optic cables capable of a transmission speed of 100+ Mbps, a large number of the slower-sending units can share one circuit with no waiting.

A specific use of TDM was in an office that uses video display terminals connected to a remote computer. In the 1970s, organizations installed coaxial cables from a controller near the computer to each terminal and transmitted at a high digital speed (10+ Kbps). In reality, the terminal operators were inputting data at a speed of much less than 10 characters per second, requiring a speed of less than 100 bps (using 10 bits per character). Further, it is unlikely that the operators could sustain even this speed, so the combined speed of 10 operators would average less than 1,000 bps. A circuit capable of maintaining 1,200 bps TDM, therefore, could support these 10 terminals, replacing 10 coaxial cables. If this equipment were installed today, the most cost-effective configuration would be use of a single 1,200 bps modem and a phone line or a statistical multiplexer, to be discussed below. Most offices have extra twisted-pair circuits that are part of the phone line cables and, therefore, require no extra installation cost. Today, TDM speeds are much higher than discussed as modem speeds have increased. This trend is expected to continue.

A special form of time division multiplexing is **statistical multiplexing.** The most common use of this technology has been the terminal-host configuration, where the terminals attached to the CPU are not always transmitting. The technology is very cost-effective in an environment where multiple computers must communicate directly to other computers but only a single communications channel is available (non-LAN environment). The time during which the terminals or computers are idle is a lost resource if you are using TDM and multiple lines.

Statistical TDM shares a single line among multiple sources on a nonuniform basis.

Statistical time division (STDM) multiplexers are intelligent devices capable of identifiying which terminals are idle and which terminals require transmission, and allocating line time only when it is required. This means line time is provided only when a terminal is transmitting, making much more efficient use of the line resource, which is often the scarce and expensive resource. There is no allocation of units to channels; however, the identification of the transmitting terminal must be sent with the data.

This is the beginning of the *bandwidth-on-demand* capability. For example, suppose you have 10 terminals each connected via 5 kbps modems (requiring 10 modems at each end). These modems are not expensive, say $30 each. Twenty of them, however, cost $600. If you use them at a rate of 10 characters per second input (keyboarding) and 1,000 characters per second output (to display a page of a document), you would have a lot of wasted time on each circuit. You could replace all modems and lines with two synchronous statistical modems running at 56 Kbps (costing about $200) and one line and have sufficient bandwidth. Efficiency is gained at a lower total cost because less equipment is required and there is less idle time. Newer STDM units provide additional capabilities, such as data compression, line prioritization, mixed-speed lines, host-port sharing, network port control, automatic speed detection, internal diagnostics, memory expansion, and integrated modems.

Data communications networks can use either of the two methods of sharing the bandwidth. **Broadband** networks generally utilize frequency division multiplexing for video, data, and/or audio. They divide the frequency bandwidth into multiple analog channels. **Baseband** networks generally use time division multiplexing, dividing the digital bandwidth into multiple logical channels. Whether the network is a *local area network* providing service to a small number of units (2–50) over a radius of one-half mile distance or to a large commercial network, the considerations are the same. In all of the instances discussed, we shared the frequency or time allocation of a circuit to increase the circuit's utilization and/or reduce cost.

Integrated Services Digital Network (ISDN)

ISDN is being used extensively in Western Europe and Japan by businesses. In Germany, more than one million ISDN basic rate interface (BRI) lines were installed in 1996. At the same time, another one million lines were deployed in France and the U.K. Over half a million ISDN BRI lines were deployed in Japan. In these instances, ISDN offers the equivalent bandwidth and reliability of leased lines at significant cost savings.

In Chapter 3 we introduced ISDN as the digital replacement of the analog POTS telephone. In this technology, we bring together several of the technologies discussed above. First, the circuit for the call is digital, as it is directed by a digital switch. Next, the circuit (e.g., local loop) is time division multiplexed into three channels. These are two bearer (B) channels of 64 Kbps each for voice or data and one delta (D) channel of 16 Kbps for control, resulting in a circuit of 144 Kbps bandwidth. (An additional 16 Kbps of bandwidth are allocated for maintenance, bringing the actual total bandwidth to 160 Kbps.) When a B channel is used for voice, the analog voice is converted to an electrical analog equivalent and then converted as described above to its PCM digital equivalent. While this is being sent on one B channel, the other B channel may be used for computer-to-computer communications. This latter capability is as simple as plugging the serial port of a computer into the serial port on the ISDN telephone and bringing up the software to cause communications, all while you speak on the phone. ISDN phones are special; they can receive Caller ID® and can handle Call Waiting®, among a long list of other services.

Figure 5.9 shows the comparison of analog POTS and digital ISDN telephone communications. In each case, the local loop is a single twisted-pair copper pair from the switch to the premise wall. For POTS, an analog bandwidth of 4 KHz is used,

FIGURE 5.9
POTS versus ISDN Telephone

Characteristic	POTS	ISDN
Local loop	Twisted-pair, copper	Twisted-pair, copper
Channels	1	3
Bandwidth	2,700 Hz analog	160 Kbps digital
Noise level	Medium	Low and controllable
Signaling	Touch-Tone®	Data channel

with a voice channel inside of 2,700 Hz. This voice channel, when used for data communications, can be multiplexed via a modem and carry 28.8 Kbps. ISDN has a bandwidth of 144 Kbps, which is multiplexed into three channels, two of which have a bandwidth of 64 Kbps. Although there is some overhead and most computer serial ports are limited to 32.4 Kbps,[4] the *two B channels* provide a much wider bandwidth.

For managers wishing to evaluate ISDN, the information about ISDN products is available through the World Wide Web. *Network Computing's* ISDN Web page lists every ISDN vendor as well as product reviews and other useful technical information. Figure 5.10 compares ISDN primary rate interface (PRI), basic rate interface (BRI), and T1 leased lines.

Compression

Compression increases the bandwidth of a channel without adding or replacing circuits or channels.

As the amount of data needed to be sent over a channel increases, as with video teleconferencing, you must either acquire a higher bandwidth channel or reduce the amount of data to be transferred. Reducing the amount of data by not sending redundant data is called **compression.** *Compression is used to reduce the amount of storage required and the amount of bandwidth required in transport.* One way is to determine what symbols appear many times in the file or frame. Text files contain many occurrences of blanks and words like "the." It is possible to encode the occurrence of a series of blanks as a much smaller amount of data, or the often occurring words as single characters. As noted in the cases at the end of this chapter, this is called using a dictionary and provides compression ratios of up to 2-to-1. At the other end, the process is reversed, recreating the file as it was originally. With still images or video, you often have part of each frame or picture that is the same, such as the blue sky. The compression program scans along each line of the frame, from line-to-line, and frame-to-frame, and sends only the data that have changed, to reduce by as much as 250-to-1 the amount of data sent.

Bandwidth of a channel is determined by the native bandwidth of that channel plus the level of data compression.

Compression is becoming a very important issue as an alternative to large storage devices and wide bandwidth channels. With compression, it is possible to send color television in a reduced form over two 64 Kbps ISDN channels, where a 45 Mbps T3 channel is required without it. However, another phenomenon is occurring that is outpacing the ability of the receiving unit to uncompress the data in real time. As DSL and cable modems become commonplace, greater requirements for decompression are being placed on the receiving computers. This trend will continue, requiring receiving units to have more powerful decompressing abilities as users and vendors move toward the transmission of full-color live video, and *Dolby Digital*® signals.

[4] When the standard was established for RS-232C serial communications in 1969 (prior to the development of the personal computer), the stated speed was 20 Kbps. A new serial communications standard is being developed for personal computers at a speed of 10 Mbps.

FIGURE 5.10
**Comparison of
ISDN (PRI) and
BRI with T1**

23 B Channels

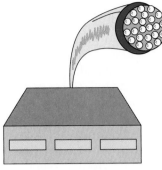

- twenty-three 64 Kbps channels

- 1.472 Mbps total bandwidth

- Tariffs range (1996) from $300 to $2,000 per
  month. (More than 11 times BRI bandwidth.)

PRI concentrator
(also one D channel for call setup and control)

Two B Channels

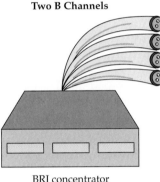

- Two 64 Kbps channels per BRI line

- 128 Kbps maximum bandwidth per BRI line.

- Service tariffs can average (1996) from $30 to
  $100 per circuit.

BRI concentrator
(also one D channel)

24 Channels

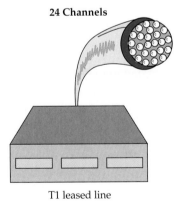

- Twenty-four 64 Kbps channels

- 1.544 Mbps total bandwidth

- Service prices (1996) range from $600 to $750
  per month with some drops as low as $300
  per month.

T1 leased line

A specific benefit of compression technology is in the storing and moving of
graphics. The two primary formats used are **GIF (CompuServe Graphics Interchange Format**, .GIF) and **JPEG (Joint Photographic Experts Group**, .JPEG).
Graphic file formats incorporate compression and decompression algorithms as part
of the file open/save or import/export operations. The GIF and JPEG formats both
use sophisticated compression algorithms, but they differ in that the GIF format

incorporates a lossless compression method and JPEG a lossy method. *Lossless* compression preserves all of the visual data in a picture: no information is discarded or altered during compression/decompression operation. The compression scheme looks for complex repeated patterns within an image. In contrast, JPEG is a *lossy* compression scheme. It achieves very high compression ratios by discarding data.

GIF can achieve a 2:1 compression ratio and has no loss of data or quality. JPEG can achieve compression ratios up to 17:1, but at a sacrifice of image quality. JPEG compression has another significant disadvantage; that is, compressed data take longer to decompress before they can be displayed on the screen.

It is possible to have a compromise. You can tweak your graphics files to make it seem as if the images are downloading faster than normal through GIF's feature called *interlacing*. This format keeps track of the odd-numbered and even-numbered scan lines in a picture separately. At download time, all of the odd-numbered scan lines are transmitted first. To the viewer, it appears as if the download is much faster, although it takes the same or slightly longer to get the rest of the picture. Netscape® Navigator uses this scheme. A new version of JPEG will have the same format.

Effective bandwidth is equal to the channel's native bandwidth, minus the effects of noise, plus that gained due to compression.

A format with which many are familiar is the **Motion Picture Experts Group (MPEG)**. It was originally designed for compressing digitized versions of movies, resulting in the MPEG1 and MPEG2 formats, the latter of which is used widely today, especially in satellite direct broadcast. The extension of MPEG2 is the MPEG3 format, used primarily for audio. It is a lossy format but takes advantage of the characteristics of the human ear, meaning that there are times that the ear cannot distinguish certain sounds, so they are discarded. This is unlike MPEG1 and MPEG2, which are lossless formats.

NETWORK MEDIA

Just as the differentiation of the naming of a network—**local area networks (LAN), metropolitan area networks (MAN), wide area networks (WAN)**—tends to be artificial, the media used by the network are highly dependent on the circumstances and are not related to the type of network. (Please see Chapter 6 for greater details.) We note that almost any media can be used for almost any network, although LANs most often use twisted-pair wire and coaxial cable. As the cost of technology declines, the use of higher-speed media will become prevalent. For example, MANs are adopting fiber digital data interface (FDDI) with its 100 Mbps speed on fiber optic strands. With time and price reductions, this same technology is an obvious choice for LANs and WANs as organizations move larger files, images, and even real-time voice and data. Thus, it is not the geographic coverage that specifies medium, it tends to be cost and, to some extent, the maturity of technology. Ethernet® first used thick coax and then thin-ax (small, thin coaxial cable); it now uses unshielded twisted-pair copper wire as the technology has evolved to support that medium and the cost is less. The cost of fiber optic cables continues to decline, as is the cost of making connections with this medium; it will soon be the medium of choice for all new installations. Additionally, most nodes, especially switches and interconnects, use conducted electricity for analog and digital communications and logic. As photonic switches become cost-feasible, it will be most cost-effective to get the digital data into a photonic form as soon as possible and leave it there. This will make fiber optic cable the medium of choice in all circumstances, including the voice local loop, when the connecting hardware for fiber drops in price below other media.

Until photonic switches and computers become commonplace, we will continue to use unshielded and shielded twisted-pair copper wire and braided copper and solid aluminum sheathed coaxial cable. Where there is an obstacle, such as a need for a right-of-way, a building, a mountain, or an ocean, we will use microwave and satellite radio. Where wires and cables are in the way within rooms, we will use radio-based and infrared wireless networks. All of these media have their place in networks and each is cost-effective under specific circumstances. But it is not the medium, the topology, the protocol, or the manufacturer that is of primary importance; it is the availability of reliable communications to solve a business problem or exploit an opportunity.

Case 5-1

Data Compression

Len Barker

INTRODUCTION

Data compression consists of reducing storage requirements by eliminating redundancy (repetitive patterns in data). It is used in a variety of applications including sector-oriented disk compression and compression of large data files, data being communicated over networks, backup or distribution files, and sampled voices and graphic data. The technology is advancing quickly, but problems exist, such as the plethora of incompatible and nonstandard compression products, the increased demand on the host processor, and the greater hardware and software complexity it requires. This case helps make sense out of all of this by examining the basics of data compression, data compression applications, and data compression techniques.

THE BASICS

Data compression works because a block of data has an information content substantially smaller than the block itself. For example, you could use an infinite number of bits trying to express π as the decimal number 3.14159265 . . . or you can use just a few bits and represent the value as π. Both the symbol and the decimal number represent the same value, but the character π provides a shorthand for expressing it. You also can use an equation to represent π, once again using far fewer bits than might have once seemed necessary.

The concept of data compression is not new. A familiar example is the system employed in Morse code. Each letter is encoded using a sequence of dots and dashes. The simplest approach would be to specify the 26 letters of the alphabet using a five bit binary code, with each bit consisting of a dot or a dash. Instead of assigning the same number of bits to each letter, Morse code performs some very simple data compression by using a variable length code. Samuel Morse knew that the bottleneck to information flow was the speed with which human operators could send messages using this code. By assigning fewer bits to more frequently used letters, he minimized the number of bits that had to be used to encode messages.

Other examples of data compression existing long before computers include

- Secretarial shorthand, where entire words or phrases are condensed to a single symbol.

- Classified newspaper ads, where "DWM seeks SWF" shortens the message.

- Signal flags on ships, where a single pennant can indicate "divers over the side" or "ammunition being loaded."

Data compression has been used for years; however, the techniques and applications used as a result of the computer age are recent inventions.

APPLICATIONS

Data compression is used in many applications, but its use is not always beneficial. Complex hardware and software are required to run the compression algorithms, which also use extra CPU time. Compression is beneficial if a large amount of data is to be communicated over a path that either is very expensive or has low bandwidth. Likewise, if storage space is limited or expensive, compression would be appropriate. Finally, data are often compressed if they either are used frequently or need to be accessed only at human speeds (rather than at database-access speeds). Typical data compression applications in use include

- Sector-oriented disk compression, such as that found in the Double-Space feature of MS DOS 6.0.

- Compression of large data files where appropriate. A good example is the compression of help files in Windows.

- Compression of files for backup or distribution. Programs such as PKZIP often are used to compress files before they are downloaded over phone lines or stored on floppy disk.

- Compression of sampled data in graphics data. Graphics data in particular can effectively overwhelm any system's online storage capability very quickly. Compression techniques designed especially for graphics reduce storage requirements by a factor of 100 and can help with the flood of data.

- Compression of data being transmitted over low-speed networks. V.42bis compression in modems, as well as proprietary techniques used by routers, can help alleviate the bottleneck created when sending data over phone lines.

TECHNIQUES

Data compression techniques are either lossy or lossless. Most compression methods in the past were lossless, which means that the original data can be reproduced entirely from the compressed data. However, the best compression ratio that can be expected from this technique is about 2 to 1. Lossless compression is a necessity for some forms of data, like spreadsheets, where any loss in accuracy is unacceptable.

Lossy compression means that a given set of data will undergo a loss of accuracy or resolution after a cycle of compression and decompression. This fast-growing discipline is usually performed only on sampled voice or graphics data. Lossy compression algorithms typically have a compression factor that can be modified to allow more or less compression of data. By giving up varying degrees of resolution, compression ratios of as much as 250 to 1 are possible. While this generally results in a loss of resolution, the loss of resolution can be adjusted to be completely undetectable.

ENTROPY ENCODING

Entropy encoding is an early lossless technique developed by information theorists. It attempts to do exactly what Morse did by devising coding schemes that use varying numbers of bits depending on the probability that a given piece of data will appear.

The most well-known form of entropy encoding is Huffman encoding. Huffman encoding uses a simple algorithm to develop an encoding scheme for a given block of data, once the probabilities of its various bytes are known. Many variations on Huffman encoding exist, including adaptive schemes that continually modify the encoding scheme based on the character's changing probabilities. Huffman's encoding scheme has been proven to be optimal for fixed-length binary codes. For other types of encoding, better compression methods may exist. But if you are using fixed-length codes for a block of data, the Huffman algorithm will provide you with the best-possible encoding scheme.

DICTIONARY-BASED METHODS

Dictionary-based compression was developed in the early 1980s, supplanting entropy encoding as the most popular encoding technique. Lempel and Ziv developed the two most popular techniques, known as LZ77 and LZ78.

Dictionary-based compression takes a completely different approach to compression than entropy encoding does. Instead of trying to efficiently encode each character of a message as entropy encoding schemes do, dictionary-based schemes try to build a code book of commonly seen strings of bytes. Whenever one of these strings appears in a message, the encoder can substitute a simple reference to that string in the dictionary table.

LZSS data compression uses a simple dictionary technique. Its dictionary consists of a window into the previously seen text. Window sizes of 4 KB or 8 KB are typical. Whenever a string of bytes in a message is identical to a string that appears in the window of previously seen data, a pointer to the previously seen block is passed, along with its length.

LZW data compression operates somewhat differently. Instead of using only the last 4 KB or 8 KB of the message to form a dictionary, LZW compressors build a dictionary that uses strings of bytes from the entire file or message being compressed. Managing the dictionary may require more work but potentially offers a more comprehensive dictionary of byte sequences.

STANDARDS

Two international standards for lossy graphics compression are known as MPEG, for the Motion Picture Experts Group, and JPEG, for Joint Photographic Experts Group. As the names imply, JPEG is used to compress single graphics images, while MPEG is used for motion pictures. These algorithms are capable of compressing photographic images to ratios of 10 to 1 or greater with no visible loss of resolution. By giving up varying degrees of resolution, compression ratios of as much as 250 to 1 or greater are possible.

Many different schemes have been developed over the past few years by industry associations and individual vendors. The following is a partial list: Motion JPEG, MPEG (I, II, III, IV), Indeo (by Intel), Cinepak, Microsoft Video 1, Fractal (used by Microsoft Encarta), and a revolutionary compression technique by Digital Compression Technology (DCT) that promises to send multimedia data across copper wire at 16 Mbps.

SUMMARY

Data compression will be very important to the future of computing. Increasing hard disk capacity using compression is common as is the compression of commercial software before distribution. However, data compression will play its biggest role in bringing video to the desktop, because of the volume of data involved in capturing, storing, and displaying video. The industry is struggling to define standards for compression so that large volumes of information can be delivered to the masses.

REFERENCES

1. "Data Compression, Part Three." *Computer Shopper* 14, no. 2 (February 1994), p. 636.
2. "Fractal Image Compression." *Byte* 18, no. 11 (October 1993), p. 195.
3. *Infoworld* 16, no. 10 (March 1994), p. 82.
4. "Just One Word: Compression." *Windows Sources* 1, no. 10 (November 1993), p. 103.
5. "Small Firm Delivers Big on Digital Compression." *Computer Shopper* 14, no. 5 (May 1994), p. 61.
6. "The Squeeze on Data." *Lan Magazine* 9, no. 5 (May 1994), p. 129.

Case 5-2

Current Issues in Data Compression

Matt Reed

In 1956, IBM introduced the first large-capacity disk drive. The capacity of this disk drive was five whopping megabytes, and this oversized storage unit was available to rent for a mere $3,200 per month. Outrageous? Guess again. EMC Corp. leader Michael Ruettgers estimates that worldwide sales of hard drive storage will top $31 billion this year. With Federal Express already at over 100 terabytes (mid-2000) and NTT Docomo, a Japanese wireless Web service, at over 265 terabytes, it is apparent that storage space has become an expensive issue to many businesses. [6]

Issue number two: With the average home Internet user connecting at about 52 Kbps, waiting for a one megabyte file to download in less than 45 seconds is not yet a mainstream reality, although it is not unreasonable to expect the same download to take less than a second or two within the next 10 years. A "Web snob" might choose only to check email from home, opting instead to wait to browse the Internet until the next day at work where connection speeds might be dozens, even hundreds of times faster.

How do we speed up the delivery from one computer to another, easing the wait times for users? How can the needs of the recipient be met more efficiently, given the same bandwidth or the existing storage space? Compression is the solution to both problems. WhatIs.com defines compression as the reduction in size of data in order to save space or transmission time. Tech TV, formerly ZDTV, continues to say that compression uses algorithms to scan a file for repeating patterns in the data. Then it replaces the data with smaller codes that take up less room. This holds true for text compression and multimedia compression, with multimedia compression having the greatest impact. Currently there are hundreds of compression techniques available with more on the horizon. This paper will discuss the types of compression, as well as purposes for compression. Furthermore, current trends and issues with compression will be addressed.

LOSSY VERSUS LOSSLESS COMPRESSION

While the universal goal of compression is to conserve on file size, there are different methods of achieving this goal. One method, called lossless compression, is to use algorithms that will allow the file to appear in its original form, even when compressed from its original state. Lossless compression is necessary when working with files that have no tolerance for data loss. Lossless compression can achieve compression ratios of roughly 2:1 or 3:1, depending on the format used. On the other hand, there are files such as graphics, video, and audio that can sustain loss with little discernible net effect, often with a great reduction in file size. This is called lossy compression. Lossy compression, depending on the algorithm used, can compress a file up to 1/1500 of its original size.

AUDIO COMPRESSION

While text compression is simple to understand, audio, photo, and video compression formats make a more significant impact on computing. Take the following audio example: the compact disc has been in use since the 1980s, and for over a decade, home users had neither the technology nor the savvy to pirate music. If some industrious doctoral student figured out a way to transfer the data from a CD to a computer, it would serve little purpose, considering that the average hard drive purchased in the 80s would have been enough to hold only a fraction of a single song! Today, the technology to compress the data at least tenfold from a music CD exists as freeware to the public. The result is that many users now store dozens of CDs in a compressed MP3 format on their high-capacity hard drives. Furthermore, the flexibility of the Internet allows users to freely, although mostly illegally, trade music as compressed files. However there is an additional factor to consider with the MP3 format. Licensing.

For a software company to create an MP3 encoder, the licensing fees are $15,000 up front plus $2.50 per unit distributed. Similarly, a playback device of any sort will set the creator back $15,000 plus 50 cents per unit distributed. [3] While MP3 is the most common format for sound compression, it is not the only game in town. One of the other formats is WMA, a Microsoft audio compression format that achieves greater compression ratios than MP3. Dolby Laboratories has released AAC, the Advanced Audio Coding format, which compresses nearly 30 percent more than MP3 with less data loss. [1] Both formats are lossy compression formats (as opposed to lossless formats), which means that while they are both capable of sampling music at a rate higher than the human ear can discern, in the conversion from an analog sound to a digital sound, small amounts of data are left out, because they are deemed unnecessary. Another very exciting system of compression is Ogg Vorbis, an open-source format that is available to anyone in the public domain who chooses to take advantage of it. An MIT student who believes that licensing fees and patents have no business in the industry created Ogg Vorbis. [3]

IMAGE COMPRESSION

Images have a great need for compression, as uncompressed file sizes can be quite large. On the Internet, it is usually not possible to view image formats other than JPEG, GIF, and PNG without plug-ins. There are other options imminent, as we see JPEG2000 and DjVU, among other lossy compression formats, on the horizon. JPEG2000 allows the viewer to toggle between different resolutions of the same image, without reloading the page or using thumbnails at up to 200 times compression, with negligible data loss. [4] The initial image might be roughly 4K, but by right-clicking on the image, the user may select a higher resolution view of the image. One immediate benefit would be that a Web page filled with 10 JPG2000 images would load much quicker than a Web page with a single 50K image of equal dimensions on it, but the resolution would still be of higher quality and the overall file size much smaller. DjVU, a standard developed by AT&T, achieves compression ratios up to 1500:1, which is 5 to 10 times as high as current methods. (DjVU.com) DjVU has a look and functionality similar to Adobe Acrobat but with significantly more compression. One example shown on the DjVu website has a 110-page annual report in both PDF and DjVu formats. The PDF file is 147 MB, while the DjVu file is a mere 2.5 MB! Compare the high ratios offered by lossy compression methods with a brand new lossless format called PhotoJazz by BitJazz, which offers ratios between roughly 2:1 and 3:1. [5] Impressive, but nothing compared to the 1,000:1 ratio achieved with a high-quality lossy algorithm.

VIDEO COMPRESSION

Arguably the most significant form of compression is video compression. Combining audio compression and dynamic imaging leads us to video compression. With competition for delivery of video signals through cable, Internet, phone line, and satellite channels, the video sent must be more versatile than in years past. The goal is to use lower amounts of bandwidth to deliver video with no perceived loss in quality, more compactly than ever before. Consider QuickTime and RealPlayer, competitors for years until their recent landmark agreement to combine efforts and encode data under the same compression standards. Before this arrangement, RealPlayer had the upper hand after years of use with their streaming media player. QuickTime was a more recent competitor in the streaming media market, and its success was somewhat limited due to marketing strategies aimed chiefly at Apple users. Real Networks, on the other hand, had licensing agreements with Microsoft and Netscape to include RealPlayer as part of a standard browser installation, which gave it a serious competitive advantage over Apple's QuickTime product. The two joined forces over the summer of 2000, combining CODEC research and earning potential. Both products offer a similar service: on demand, instant video delivery, live or previously recorded, over the Internet, either streaming or by download. This offers us a glimpse into the (not so distant) future when televisions and computers will each be capable of the same media broadcasts at times that suit the user, not the sender.

There is a long way to go before this technology is strong enough to be considered fully reliable over a slow-speed, non-frame-relay connection, and resolutions of streaming broadcasts are often limited to one-eighth of the screen size to limit the amount of data to be sent. On another video front is MPEG-4, a revolution in video compression that allows the encoder to compress a full-length movie to roughly 600 megabytes, small enough to be pressed on a CD. This remarkable compression is considered the frontrunner to replace MPEG-2 as the industry standard for video. [7] In standard video there are limitations that have plagued hardware manufacturers for some time. One limitation is that decoders such as the ones used in satellite and digital cable homes have decoding capabilities built in to the hardware. [8] Hardware decoders, although generally faster than software decoders, cannot update decoding software easily at this time. The result is that the entire industry, from satellite companies and cable companies to the Motion Picture Association of America, has to agree on a single standard that will allow all parties to have the same capabilities and limitations. It is difficult to determine what is "too good to be true" and what is true. One young developer in 1998 boasted a revolutionary 1,000:1 ratio of video compression. He claimed that he could fit a 1.3-gigabyte video on a single floppy disk. [2] Since the May 1998 article, there has been no information on any further development of this story. True or not, could ratios of 1,000:1 for video compression be possible? What would the implications be on society?

CONCLUSIONS

There is a downside to these fantastic strides in technology. Two issues we face with compression are fraud and copyright violations. Research for this paper discovered multiple instances of companies making fraudulent claims. Some of these claims, even though unsubstantiated, resulted in large investments for these companies. The most outrageous was a scam artist whose claims about a new technology for compression brought in millions of dollars that were promptly spent on frivolities.

The copyright violations resulting from compression are alarming. In all digital formats, there is a way to copy, pirate, trade, and redistribute (copyrighted) material. Napster is the first of its kind in the music industry, but imitations have cropped up, allowing anyone access to a free-for-all forum in which any connected user can download any other user's music at no cost. Similar trading environments have come to life in the movie-trading end. Everything from popular commercials to television excerpts to full-length motion pictures can be traded, albeit at a much slower rate due to larger file sizes. Much of the full-length film trading is prohibitive for the time being, because many users find it difficult to sacrifice 600 megabytes of disk space for a film they can only watch on their computer with a software decoder.

Besides audio and video files, most images from the Internet can be copied with little effort. Any Internet user might right-click on an image and set it as wallpaper or save it to the desktop and email it to a friend, both of which may very well violate a company's copyright agreement. Compression techniques open a whole host of issues for which precedents have not been set.

The compression formats have been in place for some time, and improvements are both anticipated and expected. The average person can already receive data to their satellite decoder, TiVo, Palm VII, Visor, laptop, desktop, car, cell phone, and virtual pet. The data that are transmitted have been passed through many hands as they have been optimized, compressed, encrypted, and retransmitted. Through what media will the data travel? What kinds of decoding or decompression devices will the recipient need to use the data? Rest assured that the channels through which the data travel will increase in speed and reliability, but increases in compression will make a significant impact as well.

BIBLIOGRAPHY

1. Arnold, Jim. "AAC Audio Format Selected by BMG and Universal Music Group for Commercial Music Downloads. http://www.dolby.com/press/m.pr.0008.AAC. BMGUMG.html.August 28, 2000.

2. Cochrane, Nathan, and Mike Van Niekerk. "Sending TV Down the Phone Line." http://www.theage.com.au/daily/980519/infotech/infotech1.html. May 19, 1998.

3. Dvorak, John C. "MP3 Gives Way to Ogg Vorbis." http://forbes.com/columnists/ dvorak. September 21, 2000.

4. Johnson, R. Colin. "JPEG2000 Wavelet Compression Spec Approved." http://www.eetimes.com/story/OEG19991228S0028. December 29, 1999.

5. Johnson, R. Colin. "Lossless Image Compression Algorithm Harnesses Entropy." http://www.eetimes.com/story/OEG19981113S0040. November 13, 1998.

6. Lyons, Daniel. "BOOM! Cover Story on Storage." *Forbes*, October 2, 2000, pp. 146–53.

7. Ward, Mark. "Video Shrinks with MP4." http://news.bbc.co.uk/hi/english/ sci/tech/newsid 774000/774615.stm. June 8, 2000.

8. Yoshida, Junko. "Cable Carries MPEG-4 Flag in Codec War." http://www. techweb.com/wire/story/TWB20000512S0015. May 12, 2000.

Summary

We have continued our exploration of data communications in this chapter, expanding on the concepts surrounding the digital telecommunications world. We discussed the measures taken to transmit digital data over the public switched telephone network, an analog network designed for voice, including amplifiers and regenerators. We examined how an analog signal is converted to digital form and reconverted for voice fidelity. In looking at the methods, the standard called pulse code modulation (PCM) for 8-bit coding was described. In addition, a variation of PCM called adaptive differential pulse code modulation (ADPCM) that allows use of a 4-bit code was discussed. The field of analog-to-digital conversion has gained importance as most long-distance carriers now use it for converting voice (analog) to digital data for transport because voice and other analog signals can be transmitted more clearly and efficiently in digital form.

In this chapter, the concepts of circuits, channels, and networks were clarified. A channel is a path between nodes. While the channel is a logical path, a circuit is a physical connection between two points. When we consider the multiple alternative paths in a pattern between several nodes, we refer to it as a network. The network provides a multitude of possible connections between nodes in its more complex configuration.

The concept of modulation as a way to transmit a signal via a carrier was introduced. The techniques of amplitude modulation (AM) and frequency modulation (FM) illustrate the concepts of modulation in familiar examples.

Proceeding from the idea of modulation, the concept of circuit sharing by means of multiplexing shows how multiple signals can share a primary circuit. The two basic methods of multiplexing were described. First, frequency division multiplexing (FDM) places several signals on the circuit by putting each signal in a different point of the frequency spectrum. FDM is used with analog transmission. On the other hand, time division multiplexing (TDM) uses time internal allocation to share the circuit instead of making frequency allocations. TDM efficiency is greatest when transmitting digital data, where the storage of messages can eliminate timing problems. TDMs are easier to operate and less expensive than FDMs.

The special version of TDM called statistical multiplexing also was discussed. The stat-MUX allocates circuit space on time based on statistical need. This concept is based on the fact that all terminals (nodes) are not always transmitting data. The downtime (time a node is not transmitting) of an idle node is allocated by the stat-MUX to nodes that need the time for transmitting. Thus, many more devices can be connected than with FDM or TDM.

The standards embodied in Integrated Services Digital Network (ISDN) were expanded upon to incorporate the digital and data communications aspects. Primary rate ISDN has two bearer (B) channels of 64 Kbps each for either voice or data and one delta (D) channel of 16 Kbps for control. The two B channels allow for simultaneous voice conversation and digital data communications between computers. ISDN is now readily available in many parts of the world and offers several advantages for users of the World Wide Web. Pricing is quite variable, but as more demand is generated, pressure should mount to lower costs. As more people use ISDN, the original dream of a unified communications network tying together every business, home, and computer becomes closer to reality.

One of the techniques that helps us transmit greater amounts of data over a channel without increasing the channel's bandwidth is called compression.

Compression techniques vary, but they reduce the amount of data by eliminating redundant data. Compression, therefore, appears to increase the bandwidth of a channel.

The media used in a network may place constraints on the network. Media can be of almost any type from twisted-pair copper wire to fiber optic strands. Often the media in a network were specified at different times and may have been selected based on costs and/or the maturity of the technology at the time of construction. Managers of networks need to know the media deployed and the impact of the media on the utility of their networks.

We have now covered the basics of data communications. We have begun our exploration and adventure into the world of digital communications, just touching on some subjects, leaving further discussion to later chapters. Our objective is to introduce new technology and vocabulary at the same pace that Michael discovers it. Where Michael uses telecommunications technology to solve problems and opportunities associated with his growing business, information in these chapters expands on the technologies and ideas to give you the background needed to avoid Michael's mistakes. By the time we finish, you will understand the technology, its architecture, and its management. Of even greater importance, you will understand the business case for using it.

Key Terms

adaptive differential pulse code modulation (ADPCM), *178*
amplifier, *176*
amplitude modulation (AM), *181*
analog, *176*
bandwidth, *182*
baseband, *182*
broadband, *182*
channel, *179*
channel bandwidth, *188*
circuit, *179*
compression, *188*
CompuServe Graphics Interchange Format (GIF), *189*
digital, *177*
fiber optic, *183*

frequency division multiplexing (FDM), *182*
frequency modulation (FM), *182*
half-duplex, *179*
Joint Photographic Experts Group (JPEG), *189*
local area network (LAN), *190*
metropolitan area network (MAN), *190*
Motion Picture Experts Group (MPEG), *190*
multiplexing, *182*
network, *180*
node, *181*
path, *180*
polling, *186*

pulse code modulation (PCM), *177*
regenerator, *176*
repeater, *176*
statistical multiplexing, *186*
subchannel, *184*
subsidiary communications authorization (SCA), *184*
time division multiplexing (TDM), *185*
ultrahigh frequency (UHF), *182*
very high frequency (VHF), *182*
wide area network (WAN), *190*

Discussion Questions

5.1. How is data communications from a computer to a terminal similar to the early telegraph? How is it different?

5.2. Why is the voice telephone network used for data communications since the data cannot be transmitted in their original digital form?

5.3. If you buy an article at a grocery store and its UPC bar code is read at the checkout point-of-sale (POS) terminal, how is data communications being used?

5.4. Visit a bank and determine how its ATMs are connected to the bank and to the telecommunications networks such as AVAIL, CIRRUS, HONOR, ALERT, and others, that provide access to other banks. What type of media, protocol (rules or standards of communications), and speed does each use?

5.5. If your state has a lottery, what type of communications does it use to the ticket outlets? First ask the local ticket seller and then the central lottery agency for the state.

Projects

5.1. List all of the data communications that you have employed in the past week.

5.2. Research the sampling rates and bandwidth requirements for the following disk protocols: CD, SACD, and DVD-A.

5.3. Investigate the compression method for MP3 music. Is it lossy or lossless?

5.4. Compare and contrast the modulation used in television audio: stereo versus surround sound.

5.5. Determine the multiplexing used in television and radio.

5.6. Call the cable TV provider and determine all of its services. Does it have digital radio, stock quotes, bidirectional communications? What media does it use?

5.7. Does your local exchange carrier (LEC) provide ISDN service? How is it priced?

5.8. Find a geographically dispersed retailer using multiple POS terminals and determine bandwidth requirements for collection of sales data.

Chapter **Six**

Networks by Topology and Protocols

CONTINUING CASE—PART 6

More Managers Require More Systems

Michael sat on his patio swing, thinking about business. His thoughts were interrupted by his oldest son, Carlton. Carlton had recently graduated with a BS in Electrical Engineering and had taken time off as a reward for a job well done. He had several companies interested in hiring him and even had a job offer in hand. Carlton had two weeks to accept the offer and intended to use the time to relax and also see if the other firms might offer a better opportunity. Meanwhile, he wanted to kick back for a while and not worry too much about the work-a-day world.

"What are you thinking about, Dad?"

"Oh, taking mental stock of the company's direction," Michael replied. "I was wondering if I am doing as well as I seem to be doing and if I should expand into a new line of business. Here it is 1981, and the business environment seems ripe for expansion. Of course, I've done pretty well with JL&S, but this time I'm not sure how much room for expansion exists in this line of work. It seems good, but I doubt if I can consider it a super-growth business. I've been considering some way to really grow as opposed to just growing at a slow rate. Since I've started using the computer service, I've been considering some new angles. My first thought was to build on my new computer business. What do you think of that?"

"Well, computer systems are here to stay. Have you considered moving from the bank's service bureau to a computer of your own? Perhaps you could provide a better service than the bank if you had the computer business as a main business. It seems to me that there is a big opportunity here."

"That's very interesting. I think it's a distinct possibility. Can you give me any more ideas?"

"Well, you remember I was telling you about the new microcomputers that seem to be gaining a foothold, especially the IBM Personal Computers? We used minicomputers in our university program, and they were good. I don't recommend PCs (the IBM Personal Computer) because they are too limited for a business as big as JL&S, but I was thinking you might consider a minicomputer for the lighting and security business now that you have several lines. If it has the right capacity, you could do all of your business as well as the other companies' service with a higher profit."

"That's right in line with my thinking. I just don't understand enough to make up my mind yet. I need

some time to do more evaluations. Tell you what, let's pack up our gear, and you and I spend the weekend at the lake cabin and think this through. If you don't have any conflicting plans, we can get in some good fishing while we are thinking."

"Well, I haven't got any heavy plans, but how about Mom and sis?"

"They are going to her mother's, and I was going to be all alone anyway. I'll leave her a note. It's a shame we don't have a phone at the cabin, so I could call her later."

Michael and Carlton drove to the lake cabin, discussing the idea on the way. Carlton already knew a fair amount about the business, but mainly the technical side. Carlton had never really paid much attention to the profits and losses, inventory turnover, cash flow, market share, overhead, and so on. He knew how to do standard mark-up and figured that if the customers paid, the firm would make a profit. He had worked with his father's business during several summers and was fairly good at lighting planning, but his main interest has been working with the radio and the remote computer terminals.

After two hours, they arrived at the cabin and settled in for the weekend. Normally, Michael would have headed for the boat with a rod in hand, but today his mind was working overtime on business matters. After only a few minutes he asked Carlton to join him on the porch.

"Let me tell you what I really have been thinking about, son. To put all my cards on the table, how about you taking over the JL&S business and letting me work on new ventures? You know the JL&S business and that it's going to be good, and you can have security if only you manage it well."

Michael sat quietly as Carlton grasped what he had just heard. "Me, take over YOUR business? Run it all? But what would you do? What would I do? I don't know all that you know."

"I know you feel you know the technical side of the business and not the business side, but I have a good feeling about this. Let's see just what the business involves now and what I think it would take for you to run it. Then we can discuss what I want to do with my time. I'm nowhere near retiring and plan to keep an eye on you until you are ready to fly alone.

I have been thinking about new ventures that should be a wonderful addition. If you take over the day-to-day operations of JL&S, I'll be able to work on the new ventures. We are profitable enough and have good cash flow now. I'm convinced we have become the leader in our market area and will have steady growth. I predict that we can expand and still spin off enough capital for some new ventures."

For the next two days, Michael and Carlton discussed the lighting and security business, JIS, and even managed to catch a dozen fish. Carlton did seem to have a very good knowledge of the technical side of each line of business, but Michael had to caution him as to the management and business decision issues at hand. As the sun was setting Sunday, Michael decided he was very comfortable with Carlton becoming the general manager of Johnson Lighting and Security Company. This meant that Carlton had no small task; he had to develop a business sense and understanding of the important management issues.

"The reason I want to step aside from the day-to-day operations of JL&S is that I need to consider not only the new ventures I mentioned but also the structure and strategy of JIS and JL&S. I think we should rename our business **Johnson Enterprises, Inc.**, or **JEI** for short. The actual businesses we have are on good footings and are sound in operation. I am much more concerned that the basic financial strategy and the information system are in need of attention. I thought I was doing a good job before the bank forced me into a computer-based system, but now I know that loan was the best move I ever made. If the bank had not forced me to organize my accounts for the computer, I would have no idea of the financial traps I would be facing. With the data on the computer, I have seen my overall trends, found the slow-moving product lines as well as the slow-paying customers, and even have found a way to compare the product lines for contribution to profit. And with our communications link I can keep my finger on the pulse of the Colorado Springs operation by getting their figures about as fast as I can for the local operations."

"What do you mean by contribution to profitability, Dad?"

"You know the new residential halogen lights we just began to install? Well, after running the numbers from six installations, it seems that the vendor grossly underestimated the installation time and cost

and we are just breaking even on these jobs, although his original figures said these jobs would be high-profit-margin jobs. I would never have been able to see this in a timely fashion without computer-resident data. I have a hunch that I have several other dogs hiding as well. I plan to spend the next month making sure the data files are set up so our actual operations and profitability are visible. Meanwhile, I want you to spend part of your time making sure our different jobs seem complementary; that is, they don't have conflicting objectives. Then, after I feel comfortable about our present computer-based system on the service bureau, I plan to find a good small computer system to move to. As you said, we can probably save a fair amount of money by moving to our own computer. I also believe that I can convince the people I got to use the bank's service to allow me to be their service provider. I think I can set up my own service bureau and let my customers pay for my equipment."

"I like the idea already, Dad. You work on the computer angle, and I will learn the business. Let's see if I can be doing a good enough job within a month so you only check in with me on Fridays as to daily operations. That way, you will soon be free from worrying about JL&S and can concentrate on JEI and new ventures. I might be able to enroll in a basic management class in the evenings, so I can get a better foundation in business."

Johnson's Business Strategy

Michael had started his business and seen it grow, but had no plan or strategy as to its development. He added lines of business as the opportunities presented themselves, never really considering how the lines fit into a general strategy or business vision. However, he had made money. In fact, he made money in spite of his lack of a clearly stated strategy. He just seemed to do the right thing or have the right opportunity forced upon him at the right moment. He was not kidding about the value of having to install the computer system to get the loan. Changing from a manual method of operation to a computer-based system had been much work and caused many anxious nights and days, but the move was well worth the effort. What was most valuable was that he now had a good feeling for the operation and control of the business due to the organization of the data in the computer-based system. His ability to coordinate all of the Colorado Springs duties via telephone, do scheduling on the computer, and send or receive messages via the teletypewriter meant he saved two hours' driving time on any day he did not have to go to that site. Having a Colorado Springs number ring on his Denver phone meant his new and old customers in Colorado Springs did not hesitate to call as there was no expense to them. He had become a serious competitor in that city, and did it from his office in Denver.

"If I can expand my business to Colorado Springs by using telecommunications, is there no limit to expansion with this technology?" he asked himself. "Well, this is because all of my people who work in Colorado Springs live there, and I only do the control and administration here in Denver. Now if I can find a line of business that does not take people, I can operate it by telephone or data lines."

Michael worked for the next two months to improve his accounting system on the service bureau while his son took over most of the management of JL&S. In the meantime, he bought six books on computers and enrolled in a course at the community college. He found he knew enough to finish the course in two weeks and asked the instructor to let him join the following class. Michael quickly realized that these classes were teaching him computer languages, not about computer systems. He looked at the books and realized he needed to learn something about how he should organize his data and create systems to present management information for decision making. During the time he had been working with the service bureau, he had come to realize that there were many good computer systems for sale and that it was much easier to buy one than build one. He also realized the importance of telecommunications in providing connectivity between the remote terminals and the computer. He had gained the knowledge to give him a new perspective and a final realization that he now needed professional advice.

Time to Ask for Help

Michael visited the offices of the IBM Corporation in Denver and began asking questions about computers for small businesses. He found that the sales-

people were very willing to take time to talk with him and did not seem intent on selling him anything right away. They kept asking one question, to which he did not have as good an answer as he wished he had, "What is your objective in learning about computers?"

One of the IBM people, Nowell Loop, invited Michael to lunch, where they continued to discuss Michael's plans and needs. Michael told Nowell of his history with the service bureau and remote terminals and how he had come to believe he could save money and add new lines of business with the addition of his own computer. He was, however, hesitant to jump into a large financial obligation and wanted to be very sure that he could handle the technical side of a small computer, if a suitable one existed.

"We have several computers that have proven very productive and cost-effective for small businesses," Nowell assured Michael. "Let's discuss the System 34 as a point of reference and see if it will fit your needs."

Aha! thought Michael, here comes the sales pitch. Two hours later he was still looking for the sales pitch and finally realized that it was to Nowell's best interest to be sure the System 34 solution was the right solution before trying to sell anything. The two men moved back to Nowell's office, where Michael was shown the physical equipment.

"Tell you what," commented Nowell, "you give me written permission to access your accounts at the service bureau and I will download the data to the System 34. After my systems analyst, Sally Belle, does a little data manipulation, I will load your accounts into one of our accounting systems and let you compare the System 34 and the service bureau for capability."

Nowell used the modem connected to the System 34 and dialed into Michael's account on the service bureau computer. Two hours later all of the data had been moved to the System 34 and Michael was printing out operating reports. Nowell created command files on the System 34 that let Michael do the same reports as the service bureau. Then he showed Michael how to use other commands to work with the data to do just what Michael wanted to do all along: see how different lines of business contributed to the profitability of the firm. Nowell even showed Michael how his Colorado Springs office could dial into the System 34 and access files as they did with the present computer. Nowell also showed Michael the software library that was available for the computer. He explained the advantages of packaged software for several potential applications at JL&S and the new JEI organization.

"OK, Nowell, you have done quite a number on me. How much will a System 34 cost me, and what kinds of terms can we work out?"

An hour later, Michael was convinced that the move to the System 34 was a good and cost-effective one. The system Nowell priced for JEI would have the same ability as the service bureau to be accessed from remote sites. This had been an especially important feature for Michael as he was convinced that it was not just the power of the computer that was his future but the access of properly stored and displayed data from various remote sites.

He returned to his office, or rather to Carlton's office, to discuss the final decision with his son, the JL&S general manager. He really knew he would sign with IBM; he just wanted to let Carlton be part of the process. Nowell had shown him that he could move to his own computer and reduce his costs while giving him added visibility of his operations and financial status from remote sites. However, the new system would be more expensive unless he could convince his friends to move to his system. Nowell showed him a new way for charging his customers for service and reporting how much business he would need to make the profit level he wanted. Nowell had firmly convinced him that the System 34 required no full-time operator, that Michael could easily operate the machine himself. Additionally, Nowell demonstrated an estimating program for bidding large projects. Not only would this allow JEI to bid this type of contract with greater assurance, it would give an aura of sophistication from the use of computer printouts.

Of even greater interest to Michael was that Nowell taught him about the organization of data and how the remote terminals connected to the computer. Michael still did not have a specific strategy, but he knew a lot more about how to think about data and the total system.

INTRODUCTION

In discussing networks, we need to describe how they are physically created, physically joined, and electrically connected. This is called the topology of the network. Additionally, all networks must have rules that control communications. Recall that the sets of rules are called protocols. While it is useful to separate the two concepts for initial discussion, we intertwine them for greater clarity.

Although it would be very useful to work with discrete networks in isolation, it often is valuable to describe them all and then take one for further discussion. Thus, we start by showing how they are similar, but differ, and then discuss classes of networks.

CONNECTIVITY BASICS

The way that networks are constructed and connected is called **topology.** For a network, topology means how the connections are physically and electrically made. The simplest network is one where there are only two computers (called an N = 2 network, the "N" meaning the number of **nodes**). If both nodes are computers, you have a point-to-point topology. (See Figure 6.1.) Most likely the medium remains UTP, from

FIGURE 6.1
**Point-to-Point
(N=2) Network**

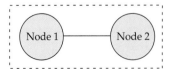

one machine to the other. This is the physical topology, simply meaning how we lay the wires from node-to-node. Its electrical topology would be the communications path between machines and, in this case, each machine can share the other's resources or, at least, can send messages and data to the other. This is much like the connection between your computer and its printer. Refer to Technology Note 6–2 (p. 225) for a discussion of how computers are connected to each other and to networks.

Peer-to-Peer

In considering the relationship between connected nodes, we have two relationships. One is where, in this N = 2 network, both computers are of the same standing: neither is a master and neither is a slave or client. This would be a peer-to-peer network. Windows operating systems include peer-to-peer networking. All connected computers are equal. We will consider a different relationship later.

The alternative to point-to-point topology is multipoint topology, the environment where many computers are connected to a common communications channel. (See Figure 6.2.) We should add that this means connected locally. When we describe widely dispersed nodes, our view will be different than multipoint connectivity because the way we send messages will be different. Thus, multipoint access, one of the primary aspects of the network protocol, or rules of communications, provides for multiple nodes to access the network channel and how they communicate.

shared resource
Any device such as a hard drive or printer that can be accessed and used by all nodes on the network.

server
A dedicated resource (microcomputer or mainframe) that shares disk space and serves the other nodes on the network.

Client/Server Architecture

Let's return to the relationship between nodes. When the nodes on the network are not equal, we have a different environment. For example, let's assume you have a network of 15 computers. (See Figure 6.3.) All but one of the computers are user workstations and one provides services to the rest. You now have a **client/server architecture (C/SA).** As it implies, the workstations are clients of the **server.** The clients request services from the server, such as shared file space, common printers, and shared processing. This requires the connectivity of a network and creates an environment where updates for all clients can be as simple as updating a single application on the server. This avoids going to each client for such a software

FIGURE 6.2
How Computers Are Connected to Networks

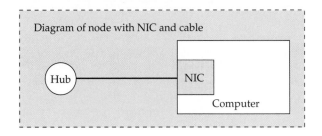

Diagram of node with NIC and cable

Hub —— NIC

Computer

FIGURE 6.3
Multipoint (N>2) Network

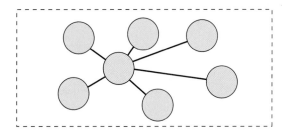

TABLE 6.1
**Potential Benefits
of Networks**

I. Cost Savings
  A. *Reduced number of peripherals,* such as printers, application and file storage, and facsimile modems, as the network allows sharing of peripherals among users on the network.
  B. *Less storage space required per workstation,* as only one copy of software is stored on the publicly accessible file server.
  C. *Reduced software costs for workstations,* since the LAN keeps the only copy of the software. This generally means that although there must be a license and a number of copies to cover the number of users who use the software at any *one time,* the number of copies is generally less than the total number of users.
  D. *Single-network communications,* reducing the cost of redundant networks. Thus, as more users are connected to one network or as smaller networks are interconnected, communications and sharing increase.
  E. *Savings in installation and maintenance.*
    1. New stations are easy to install and existing stations can be moved without substantial cost.
    2. *Only one copy of each software package must be installed or updated.*
II. Sharing of Resources
  A. *Reduced cost per resource item* as peripherals, applications, and files are shared.
  B. *Potential availability of more expensive peripherals* that would not be justified for single users (for example, plotters or expensive printers).
  C. *Greater use of resources* as they are shared.
  D. *Reduced redundancy* as only single application resources are required to be maintained/updated.
III. User Interface
  A. *Interface with the network* is transparent.
  B. *Less or no involvement by users in operational tasks* such as backup and recovery. This is true only for files and applications stored on shared devices on the network. Generally, this does not include private workstation storage.
  C. *Capability of sharing data and text for joint work* or review by management, where software exists that allows for joint access to a file or application.
  D. *Added functionality* provided by the network in terms of electronic mail. One of the prime values of telecommunications is facilitation of human communications; networks enable more effective communications.
IV. Encourages Management Control
  A. *Control of the introduction of new technology* by imposition of network standards.
  B. *One network management environment* may be established versus managing multiple network environments at the same time.
  C. *Equipment compatibility* by requiring a single protocol.
  D. *Uniformity of communication and resources* as all users are accessing and sharing the one network.

update, but remember, you must have licenses for all users. See Table 6.1 for potential benefits of networks.

PROTOCOLS

Protocol
Determines how data
move on the network.

A **protocol** is a standard, or set of rules or guidelines, that governs the interaction between people, between people and machines, or between machines. More specifically, a protocol is a set of procedures or conventions used routinely between equipment such as terminals or computers. For our purposes, we have protocols (a) for using data communications circuits; (b) for communicating between DTEs, such as terminals and computers; (c) for communicating on networks; and (d) for specific data exchange such as handshaking, that is, signal exchange at initiation between devices that establishes a logical communications channel for information transmissions. (See Figure 6.4.)

A protocol is implemented by transmitting specific characters on the telecommunications line, or by the switches in equipment or software. Generally, we are interested in methods of line access and collision avoidance, as well as line format.

We noted earlier that one purpose of the protocol was to provide and control access in a multipoint network. The second primary service is collision avoidance or control. A **collision** is the case when two nodes transmit at the same time. The result is unintelligible to all, so something must be done. Some systems make collisions impossible; others have rules that react to them. Thus, collision prevention or resolution is a part of the concept of network protocol.

The simplest method of collision control is **polling.** In this environment, a central node has ultimate control, like a teacher in the second grade of a primary school or the POTS switch in the Central Office. Polling takes two forms; first, the central node asks each receiving node, in turn, if it has something to send. At the same time, it will determine if the central node has something to give to the receiving node. In this way, two nodes cannot interfere with each other. A variation of this is that the central node waits for a signal from a node wishing to transmit and then recognizes that node. This is the case of wired POTS as it waits for you to lift the receiver, at which time it determines if it can service the phone and returns a dial tone if it can. In either case, the transmitting node must have the unique attention of the central node, thus making a collision impossible. That's the good side of polling; the bad side is the amount of time it takes to poll. This is overhead and considered wasteful. Overhead means it is using up a resource without doing what we consider useful work. Although polling is valuable, it is not the purpose for which the network was created. Useful work is the transfer of information, not the effort of access and control, or even security.

The second method of avoiding a collision is the one used in the **ring topology.** One way to connect nodes is to make them into a ring, with each node connected to one computer above (or to the left of) it and one below (or to the right of) it. Any data are passed from one node to the next; thus, everyone receives all messages. A node, however, only reads the messages destined for it. This is multipoint connectivity, so how do we control collisions?

In the ring topology we continuously pass a data packet, called a **token,** around the ring from one node to the next. When a node wishes to transmit, it must first

Collisions
occur when two nodes transmit at the same time.

Collisions
result in all communications being unintelligible.

Collisions
cause everyone to lose, as all transmissions are destroyed.

FIGURE 6.4
Some Consideration of Device-to-Device Handshaking, a Function of Protocol

A. **Communications startup**—communications initiated.
B. **Character identification and framing**—determine text characters and which are control characters
C. **Message identification**—separate characters into messages.
D. **Line control**—receiving unit says data were good, by turnaround, and requests next block.
E. **Error control**—what to do in case of error (retransmit), what to do when communications breaks and is reestablished.
F. **Termination**—normal and abnormal.

take possession of the token. If another node has possession of the token, it must wait. The node with the token then attaches the message or file to the end of the token and sends it on its way. Only one node can possess the token at a time, thus avoiding collisions. Think of a relay runner who must have a baton before starting. The token is analogous to the baton.

The final method of collision control is to react to, as opposed to avoiding, collisions. In the systems that choose to react to collisions, some method must exist to recognize that a collision has taken place and then there must be rules for how to react. This is a primary method in the Ethernet bus network. The network allows multiple computers to access the common channel (multiple access). Any node may transmit when it thinks it is permissible. This means there is no recurring overhead, as in the case of polling or token passing. The nodes use carrier sense technology to listen to the common channel. When one believes all is quiet, it can transmit. If more than one node transmits at a time, a collision takes place. The network protocol has collision detection capabilities, causing the offending nodes to stop transmitting. They wait a random amount of time and try again. While there is no constant overhead, as in the case of polling and token passing protocols, there is overhead in the form of wasted time in reacting to the collisions by retransmitting the message.

ACCESS TO WIDE AREA NETWORKS

The previous discussion focused on computers that are closely located. When we get to users who may be hundreds to thousands of miles apart, the need for access and collision control are the same, but the solution is very different. For widely dispersed users, long paths exist that connect the various parts. Generally, a user at one location will send the desired message to a network entry point. We think of this wide area network as a cloud. That is, we don't know what is going on inside, but we know that there are ways to get the message from here to there. The network will determine how the message passes through all the paths, based on protocol and lists of transport. For example, one protocol creates virtual channels or temporary paths through the maze. When a message arrives, it flows through that prescribed path. The path can change if a link is busy or broken, but the end and switching points place the message packets onto the links, one at a time, to ensure that no other packets interfere with it. There may be packets from many sources on the link at one time, but they are in sequence and do not create collisions.

TOPOLOGY

topology
The electrical or channel configuration.

There are two types of **topology,** physical and electrical (logical). For local networks, the physical topology is almost always a star. This means the cables from the end node, the user workstation client or the server, run from that computer to a central point. Thus, they star out of the point, the telecommunications closet (see Figure 6.5).

The reason for the star network is simple: it is much easier to make the connections and troubleshoot a network in a single place than to go to the locations of the computers. Also, there is likely a need for air conditioning to cool and electrical power to run the equipment of the network. Thus, the equipment is located in the closet with appropriate power, cooling, and security.

FIGURE 6.5
Telecommunications Closet

ELECTRICAL TOPOLOGY

When you walk into an office and see a local area network, you will find wires running from each client to the central telecommunications closet. In that closet is a piece of equipment that connects all of the wires and makes the electrical topology. One of the simplest electrical topologies is the **star network** (see Figure 6.6). As in the case of POTS, all channels terminate into a computer (or switch). In the star electrical topology, the nodes at the end of the channels request the attention of the central node and communication takes place.

The second way to connect the nodes electrically is to make them all multipoints on a single, shared channel. As Figure 6.7 shows, we logically connect each connecting wire to a central wire, making a **bus network.** This is done in the telecommunications closet by using a **hub** (see Figure 6.8). All of the wires are plugged into the ports of the hub, which appears as a small box. Inside of the hub, the wires are connected together like the diagram of the logical bus. The physical topology is still a star, but the electrical connectivity provided by the hub makes it into an electrical bus.

The third kind of local connectivity is the **ring network.** As we said previously, and as shown in Figure 6.9, each computer is connected to one computer above (or to its left) and one below (or to its right). This means that all messages pass around the ring and each transited node will see part of each message. Again, the physical topology is a star, but the hub, called an **MSAU** or **multiple-station access unit,** will connect the wires as a ring. (See Figures 6.10 and 6.11.)

PROTOCOLS EXPANDED

We will have a different protocol for each configuration of network. This applies for local connectivity and for wide area connectivity. The simplest protocol is for the local $N = 2$, point-to-point network, well represented by your computer and its printer. When the computer wishes to send information to the printer, it begins to transmit over its parallel port, through the cable, to the printer. The printer buffer (memory) receives

FIGURE 6.6(a)   Electrical and Physical Star Topology

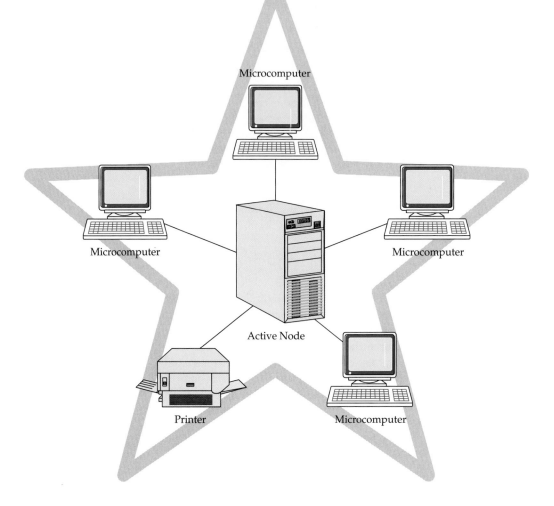

Microcomputer

Microcomputer

Microcomputer

Active Node

Printer

Microcomputer

FIGURE 6.6(b)
Electrical and
Physical Star
Network

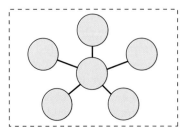

data until the buffer is full, at which time the protocol controlling communications sends an X-OFF message to the computer, signaling the computer to stop transmitting. As the buffer empties, it sends an X-ON signal, and data flow begins. These X-ON/X-OFF signals continue until all of the message is transmitted to the printer. All protocols contain some method of data flow control. X-ON/X-OFF is the simplest method. Each of the protocols that follows has its own method of flow control.

FIGURE 6.7(a)
Bus Topology

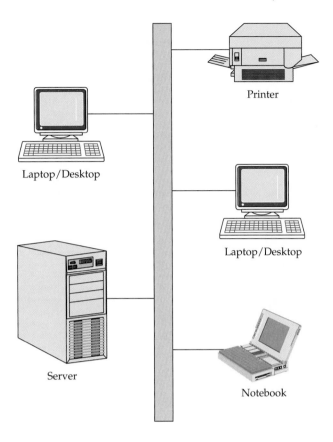

Printer

Laptop/Desktop

Laptop/Desktop

Server

Notebook

FIGURE 6.7(b)
Logical Bus
Network

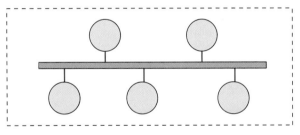

FIGURE 6.8
Electrical Network
Using a Hub

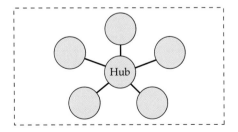

Hub

More sophisticated protocols are required for more complex networks. Such is the case in a multipoint network such as a bus. Here, there are no masters or slaves as all nodes are considered equal, though one node may have the network software resident—and act as a server. With a bus, such as an Ethernet bus using IEEE 502.3 **CSMA/CD (Carrier Sense Multiple Access/Collision Detection)**

FIGURE 6.9(a)
Ring Topology

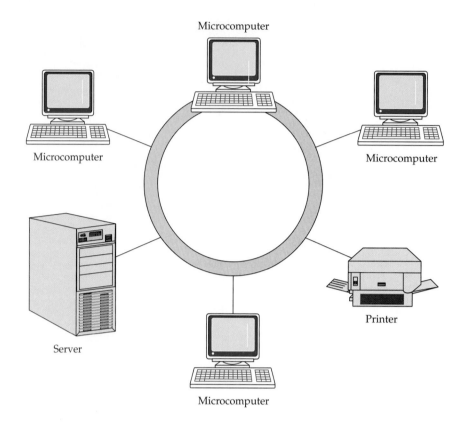

FIGURE 6.9(b)
Logical Ring
Network

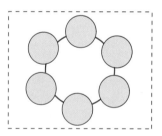

FIGURE 6.10
Electrical Ring
Network

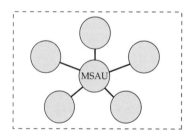

protocol, *multiple access* of many nodes is possible because each single node uses *carrier sense* to determine that the network is quiet. If no signals are heard, for example, no one else is transmitting, the node in question broadcasts a message on the network that all nodes hear. (This is called *broadcasting,* as opposed to narrow-casting or unicasting.) Under normal conditions, every node receives and reads the header of the message and only the named recipient reads the actual message.

FIGURE 6.11
Physical (Star-Connected) Token-Passing Ring Architecture

This LAN does not require a dedicated server, but 'it just communicates' and does not share resources. Making one of these devices a print-and-file server, while not requiring added hardware, software, or cost, would remove it from use as a user device. Any node could be designated to be a file and/or a print server.

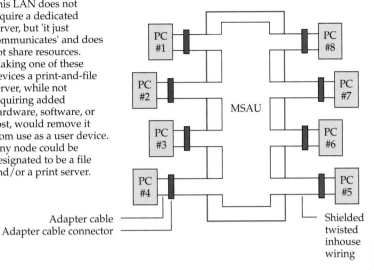

Adapter cable

Adapter cable connector

Shielded twisted inhouse wiring

Technology Note   6–1

Network operating systems (NOS) determine how the network treats resources and their contention for access. The simplest is a peer-to-peer network, where the NOS has few features. Procomm, for example, supports password protected access, allows viewing the directory of the other machine, and allows file transfer. Novell NetWare, at the other extreme, allows hundreds of nodes, manages collisions, allows the attachment of analysis tools, and has servers for common storage. NetWare NOS is significantly more complex and capable than Procomm, and, of course, more expensive. The NOS determines what can be done technically and, even more important, what user functions and controls are provided. The NOS decision is both technical and managerial as it determines the environment of connectivity for the organization for a long time to come.

Initially, NOS were applications in and of themselves, either residing on the server as in Ethernet or distributed across the nodes as in token passing. Microsoft's Windows 95 and 98 and Windows NT each has NOS capabilities, as does IBM's OS/2. This means that the NOS is being distributed and the number of entrants has increased. By choosing any of these latter interfaces and NOS, you are choosing that vendor's view of the interface and network.

If a second node broadcasts at the same time, a collision occurs, making all transmission unintelligible. Each node is intelligent enough to allow *collision detection* and stops transmitting for an individual random amount of time. When the timer for each offending mode expires, they try to transmit again, using the same quiet channel rule.

The use of carrier sense is a primary way of gaining line access in a bus topology, though it is not the only way (token-passing is another bus protocol). CSMA/CA (Carrier Sense Multiple Access/Collision Avoidance), like token-passing and polling, precludes collisions. However, the greater possibility of collisions during periods of high use causes throughput to decrease. Thus, in choosing between a collision detection and a collision avoidance protocol, the level of busy conditions must be considered. For example, a 10 Mbps CSMA/CD bus will be faster than a 4 Mbps token-passing ring in light loads, but the reverse may well be true in heavy traffic due to the overhead of a bus network.

The *message format* of the protocol defines the location and amount of true data contained in the message and the overhead necessary to ensure that the destination receives the data as they were sent. To do this, the message format of synchronous protocol usually has *header, text or data,* and *trailer* sections, and possibly synchronization characters.

An example and the one that is so often used for PC-to-PC communications and file transfer is the **XMODEM** protocol. This protocol was defined by Ward Christensen and placed in the public domain. It is designed for one sender and one receiver. The roles of the two units change during the conversation as they take turns transmitting. The basic protocol is asynchronous communications, but the data characters are sent in block as opposed to character-by-character. This allows excellent error detection, not available in simple asynchronous communications. XMODEM requires an 8-bit data code and may use checksum or cyclical redundancy check (CRC) error detection. The original block size was 128 bytes, but modern versions use 1,024 bytes for greater throughput. The sender sends a block of characters surrounded by a header and trailer. The header consists of an SOH (start of header) character, followed by a block number character, followed by the same block number with each bit inverted. The trailer contains a checksum character, which is the sum of the ASCII values of all of the 128 data characters added together and divided by 255, with remainder retained.

XMODEM is simple, but was limited as to error checking until the use of CRC became common. It is designed for **half-duplex** and waits for acknowledgement (ACK) at each block.

With **synchronous communications,** shown in Figure 6.12(a), protocols define the content of the packet, including a header that may include a large amount of information. The actual content is protocol specific as well as connection dependent. That is to say, more information is required for some networks than for others where the sender and destination are known. Data that *may* be

**FIGURE 6.12(a)
Synchronous Data =
One Block**

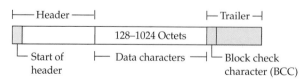

included in the header section are as follows (please see the following chapter for more details):

- Start of header (SOH) character.

- Address of the destination.

- Address of the sender.

- Block number of this block of data (e.g., sequence number).

- Possibly the block number in reverse for reliability.

- Other administrative information such as a time stamp.

The protocol will define the header as fixed length or variable length. Thus, for a fixed-length protocol, the receiving node knows when the header stops and the data fields begin. Should the data field be *variable* length, there must be a *framing* field in the header noting the data length. For a *fixed-length* data field, this is not necessary as the end of fixed data, like the length of a fixed header, is *positional* in nature.

Following the data field is the trailer, containing the *block check character (BCC)* for error detection, such as CRC (see previous chapter), and possibly characters denoting end of transmission with a number of blocks. (If the header includes the total number of blocks, a frame noting the last block is not necessary, although it may be more efficient than having the receiving node determine this.) The larger the BCC field, the greater the probability of error detection.

The final consideration of synchronous transmission of blocks of data is keeping the sending and receiving nodes in time synchronization. During handshaking, the two units determine the speed of transmission and, therefore, the receiving node knows when to sample the line to detect a bit. Should the synchronization of the two nodes slip in time, the receiving node will sample at the wrong time and miss a bit. Therefore, synchronous protocols often call for placing multiple synchronization characters within the blocks of data.

Synchronous data link protocols, designed to handle blocks of data, have several formats. Some are *character-oriented,* using special characters to indicate the beginning and end of messages. An example is the Binary Synchronous Communications (BISYNC) protocol by IBM. Others are *byte-count-oriented,* using special characters to mark the beginning of the header, followed by a count field that indicates how many characters are in the data portion, followed by block control characters. An example is DEC's DDCMP. *Bit-oriented* protocols use one flag character to mark the beginning and end of a message. The header and its fields are of predefined length and the header is followed by data with no intervening control character. An example of this protocol is Synchronous Data Link Control (SDLC) used by IBM (see Figure 6.12[b]).

All of the synchronous protocols have structures that contain information as to the destination and length of the message (header), the payload (data section), and

FIGURE 6.12(b)
Synchronous Data Link Control (SDLC) Packet

8 Bits	8 Bits	8 Bits	Variable	16 Bits	8 Bits
Flag 01111110	Address	Control	Data (Octets)	Frame Check	Flag 01111110

methods for error detection (trailer). Additionally, a protocol must have a feature called *transparency* if it is to carry executable code as the payload. That is, if the data portion could be interpreted as commands to the receiving node, there must be a feature that tells the receiving node to treat any of the data as binary units and not interpret them.

LAN versus WAN Protocols

Protocols are selected based on the job they must perform and the environment they will be operating in. LAN protocols are continuous in nature, such as CSMA/CD on a bus network, or block as in token-passing rings. WAN traffic, on the other hand, often travels significant distances and is continuous in a virtual channel or packet over a cloud. The LAN traffic on a bus will be in contention with other traffic, but the other methods, either on a LAN or WAN, have protocols that preclude contention, and thus collisions.

Internet Protocols

Computers can't just throw data at each other any old way. Because so many different types of computers and operating systems connect to the Internet via modems or other connections, they have to follow protocols. The Internet is a very heterogenous collection of networked computers and is full of different protocols, including the following:

TCP/IP (transmission control protocol/Internet protocol)[2]—These two protocols were developed by the U.S. military to allow computers to talk to

The Real World   6–1
A Quick Look at Ethernet

Ethernet was first developed by DEC, Intel, and Xerox in 1980. Based on Carrier Sense Multiple Access with Collision Detection (CSMA/CD), Ethernet stations "listen" on the shared network cable prior to transmission. If stations attempt to transmit at the same time, a "collision" is detected—during which time no station can transmit. Bad network cable or faulty equipment also can contribute to excessive collisions. With its relatively simple and direct medium access control, today's Ethernet is the choice for 70 percent of all LAN installations.

While five specifications share the CSMA/CD architecture, the media type (i.e., cabling), media connector, and, perhaps most importantly, transmission speeds can differ.

The most popular choice for Ethernet is 10BaseT:

- The hub-based star configuration is more reliable than the older bus topology.

- The network is easy to install, maintain, and expand.

- There is a large selection of equipment from multiple vendors.

NEW ADVANCES

Although the performance of standard 10BaseT is 10 Mbps, vendors and users have applied new technology to improve this transmission rate with

- 100BaseT (Fast Ethernet), which uses 4-pair Category 3 cable, 2-pair Category 5 cable, or fiber to deliver 10 times the base transmission rate (100 Mbps).

[2] Please see http://coverage.cnet.com/Resources/Information/Glossary/Terms/tcpip.html for these and other definitions.

The Real World (Continued) A Quick Look at Ethernet

6–1

- **Full-Duplex Ethernet (FDE)** to effectively double the base transmission rate when used with full-duplex switching hubs (to 20 or 200 Mbps).

- Switches that replace the shared media approach of standard hubs and concentrators, providing each connection with the full transmission rate, both increasing performance and decreasing the number of collisions by providing each node with its own transmission channel.

- Fiber cabling, which delivers superior performance by removing the impact of EMI and increasing the maximum segment length to 2,000 meters.

COMMON ETHERNET EQUIPMENT

A **transceiver** (transmitter/receiver) is either built into an Ethernet port or must be attached via an **Attachment Unit Interface (AUI)** connector. An external transceiver is usually only required when connecting an Ethernet port to a medium that is not supported by the network card. For example, a card with an AUI and BNC connector cannot be attached to a fiber or unshielded twisted pair (UTP) Ethernet network unless an AUI-to-Fiber (ST) or AUI-to-RJ45 transceiver is used.

REPEATERS

A repeater simply electronically boosts and amplifies the signal to increase the transmission distance. Depending on your network's configuration, only a certain number of repeaters may be used to a maximum distance.

CONCENTRATORS AND HUBS

The simplest way to build an Ethernet network, **concentrators** and hubs are common on small 10BaseT networks. The hubs and concentrators serve as the central connection points for an Ethernet network.

INTELLIGENT HUBS/STACKABLES

Intelligent hubs allow a network administrator to effectively monitor and control each individual port on a hub. The limits of the monitoring and control are dependent on the available software and the hubs. Stackables, or modular hubs, typically offer the management capabilities of intelligent hubs as well as mixed-media support and easy network expansion.

BRIDGES, SWITCHES, AND ROUTERS

Ethernet **bridges** are commonly used to partition network segments to reduce the number of collisions, increase end-to-end distance (beyond that of repeaters), or improve performance. Ethernet **switches** are essentially high-speed bridges that maintain individual connections for improved performance (see diagrams).

Routers like bridges are also used to segment Ethernet networks. Routers filter and forward network traffic based on information other than the Ethernet destination address (MAC), such as the IP addresses contained in TCP/IP packets.

Source: "Ethernet Tutorial," Industrial Computer Source, p. 3.

Ethernet Specifications

	Media Type	Media Connector	Maximum Segment Length	Maximum Number of Nodes per Segment
10Base5	Thick coax	AUI (TNC)	500m	100[†]
10Base2	Thin coax	BNC	185m	30[†]
10BaseT	UTP	RJ45	100m	1[‡]
10BaseF	Fiber optic	ST or SMA	2,000m	1[‡]
100Base-TX	Cat. 5 UTP	RJ45	100	1[‡]
100Base-FX	(62.5/125)MM Fiber	SC, MIC, ST	412	1

† Bus Topology—where stations are serially attached along a length of cable.
‡ Star Topology—where each station is connected to an individual port on a hub or concentrator.

(continued)

a. Bus topology

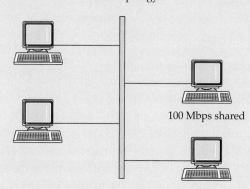

100 Mbps shared

b. Star topology

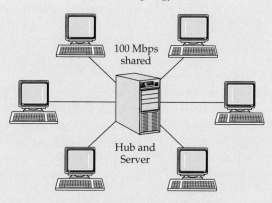

100 Mbps shared

Hub and Server

c. Switch based

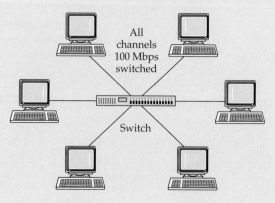

All channels 100 Mbps switched

Switch

The Real World
What Is Fast Ethernet?

6–2

In response to the growing needs of users interested in more performance, two new 100 Mbps LAN standards were drafted. The first, and the one described here, is the **100BaseT Fast Ethernet** standard. Drafted as part of the 802.3 Ethernet specification, 100BaseT Fast Ethernet is similar to the Ethernet standard in that it relies on the same CSMA/CD media access control (MAC) mechanism. The other competing standard was defined separately under a new group, as the IEEE 802.12 standard. With a media access control that is based on an entirely new "demand-priority" mechanism instead of CSMA/CD, the 802.12 standard is capable of transporting not only Ethernet frames, but also token-ring frames as well. As a result, this standard is called 100VG-AnyLAN. Because 100VG-AnyLAN is drastically different from Ethernet, it is not discussed in this section unless within the context of the 100BaseT Fast Ethernet standard.

Fast Ethernet is essentially a boost of Ethernet's speed of 10 Mbps to 100 Mbps—a 10-fold increase. As described as part of the original IEEE 802.3, 100BaseT Fast Ethernet is 10 times as fast as standard Ethernet, but is the same with regard to the frame format and the MAC mechanism. The reason this is possible is because the MAC layer for Ethernet was specified to be speed-independent. So despite that Fast Ethernet is 10 times faster than Ethernet, both use the same MAC layer.

For 100BaseT Fast Ethernet there are three types of media that are supported: 100BaseT4 for 4-pair twisted-pair Cat. 3 (or above) cable, 100Base-FX for two-stranded optical fiber, and 100Base-TX for 2-pair twisted-pair, Category 5–grade cable. The FX and TX standards are sometimes also known collectively as 100Base-X. Rather than create new media standards for 100Base-X, the Fast Ethernet committee used the standards originally developed by ANSI for the FDDI standard (ANSI X3T9.5). The T4

specification is provided as an alternative to users with lower-grade twisted-pair cabling. Of the three, the most prevalent is the 100Base-TX standard.

The TX media standard is based on the ANSI TP-PMD physical media specifications (FDDI over STP or UTP wiring). For the common UTP wiring, two pairs of wires (pin-pairs 1.2 and 3.6) are used, one to receive and the other to transmit data signals. This is different from the pairs selected for the TP-PMD standard in order to comply with the 10BaseT standard. The wiring requirements for 100Base-TX are different from 10BaseT because the signal frequency of the network is much higher than for standard Ethernet. For proper operation of 100Base-TX, users are required to use 100-ohm, Category 5–grade UTP cable and cannot use Category 3 or Category 4. Like 10BaseT, 100Base-TX has a hub-to-end station limit of 100 meters. With the use of repeaters, users can extend the single-segment distance to 200 meters. Users must be careful to calculate round-trip times, as meeting the minimum specification is crucial to proper operation.

KEY BENEFITS

While the implementation of Fast Ethernet is still new, the underlying basis is the same that has been used in Ethernet for the past decade—the same technology that is used at over 30 million nodes all over the world. This has immediate benefits: (1) Convenient migration for most users; (2) a 10-fold performance increase over standard Ethernet; (3) easy expansion of networks due to passive media access techniques; (4) broad vendor support, which means more product selection; (5) Fast Ethernet products that are usually less expensive than competing products based on alternative technology.

Source: "100BaseT Tutorial," Industrial Computer Source, p. 9.

100Base-X Technical Specifications

Technology	Wiring	Topology	Connector	Length
100Base-TX	Cat. 5 UTP/STP, 2 pair	Star	8-pin (RJ45) 9-pin ("D-type")	100m
100Base-FX	62.5/125 MM fiber	Star	SC, MIC, ST	412m
100Base-T4	Cat. 3 or above, 4 pair	Star	8-pin (RJ45)	100m

(continued)

The Real World (*Continued*)   6–2
What Is Fast Ethernet?

a. Star topology

100 Mbps
shared

Hub

b. Physical — MAC layer

MAC

100Base-TX   100Base-T4

100Base-FX

c. Easy migration

Model
28115

10 Mbps   100 Mbps

PC   PC/Server

each other over long-distance networks. IP is responsible for moving packets of data between nodes. TCP is responsible for verifying delivery from client to server. TCP/IP forms the basis of the Internet and is built into every common modern operating system (including all flavors of Unix, the Mac OS, and the latest versions of Windows). TCP/IP is covered in more detail in a later chapter.

SLIP (serial line Internet protocol)—SLIP is a standard for connecting to the Internet with a modem over a phone line. It has serious trouble with noisy dial-up lines and other error-prone connections, so look to higher-level protocols like PPP for error correction.

PPP (point-to-point protocol)—PPP is the Internet standard for serial communications. Newer and better than its predecessor SLIP, PPP defines how your modem connection exchanges data packets with other systems on the Internet.

CONNECTIVITY IN NETWORKS

A primary form of local (area) networks is the bus, using the CSMA/CD protocol. The trade name for this environment is generally **Ethernet.** The standard speed for Ethernet in the early 1990s was 10 Mbps. The common channel medium for this was Category 3 UTP wiring. Category 3 is a standard for wiring that specifies the gauge size and number of twists per foot, determining the native bandwidth and the radiation to be expected. This wiring allowed networks with specified link lengths to be constructed with two pairs of wires for a 10 Mbps bandwidth. This was called **10BaseT** (bandwidth, mode of transmission, and medium). With different electronics on the ends of the links and using four wire pairs, it is possible to extend the bandwidth to 100 Mbps, called **Fast Ethernet.**

10BaseT means a speed of 10 Mbps, running on baseband type 3 twisted-pair wire. 100BaseT is the same but faster, generally requiring a better grade of wire (type 5).

The predecessor of 10BaseT networks has bandwidth of 1-to-2 Mbps, called 10Base2. With the addition of nodes and the use of networks for more than text-based email, the need for greater bandwidth became evident. In addition, there was a need for more sophisticated access and control. The same thing happened as 10BaseT networks matured; nodes used up all of the bandwidth and many organizations moved to **100BaseT** networks. When installing new media in a building that anticipates a 100BaseT network, it is best to install Category 5 wiring. Although it is a bit more expensive than Category 3 wiring, it requires cheaper node equipment and uses only two pairs of wires. Meanwhile, some organizations see the handwriting on the wall and are installing fiber instead of even Category 5 wiring, knowing that the need for bandwidth will continue. A 100 Mbps network, running on fiber, would be called a 100BaseFX network.

Meanwhile, a new entrant to the wired area (circa 2001) is **Giga-Ethernet,** designated as **1000BaseT.** This can be run over Category 5 or 6 wiring or fiber (**1000BaseFx**). With the consideration of adding large file transfer, images, and even video conferencing to local networks, the need for bandwidth is apparent. (One of the authors recently experienced a 10BaseT Novell NetWare network with 2,500 nodes. This would be a great place for 1000BaseT or FX.)

Windows-Based Network

Ever since version 3.11, Microsoft's Windows operating system has included networking capabilities. You can use the serial ports for an N = 2 network; you must install **network interface cards (NICs)** and use a hub for networks with more than two nodes. The network operating system uses the CSMA/CD protocol.

network operating systems
The supervisors of networks.

The use of Windows as your **network operating system (NOS)** becomes important as you find you have more than one computer at home or you live close to a colleague, for example, in an apartment. Also, the addition of a high-speed access to the Internet, such as a cable modem or DSL, will allow you to share the bandwidth if you have a network. It is possible, even easy, to install a hub that connects the several computers together and to the modem, creating a network with Windows with all units having modem access. (Apple computer's Appletalk was one of the first peer-to-peer-capable networking protocols.)

Ring Network

The final protocol is **token passing,** used primarily on ring networks. As noted earlier, a data packet (token) passes around the network continuously. Transmission is only possible for the node that captures the token. It then attaches the data to it and sends it on its way. Each node reads the packet header, but only the designated recipient reads the message. The recipient then adds a message noting correct receipt and sends it back to the source. All nodes read the token header but only the original sender reads the message. It then clears the token and releases it. This protocol has a constant overhead required by the token. Therefore, users will perceive less difference in a lightly or heavily loaded ring, whereas a heavily loaded bus will slow down significantly due to recovering from collisions.

Figure 6.13 shows how LANs of varying topologies and protocols can be connected. The connecting device shown is a gateway, which will be described later. The gateway has the intelligence to translate among or between LANs and to wide area networks (WANs).

Later, we will discuss larger networks, one of which is a metropolitan area network (MAN). A MAN is installed around a city or portion thereof to provide common access to shared resources. The most common topology for a MAN is a counter rotating ring. This means two rings with the tokens passing in opposite directions. The redundancy is installed to allow the network to self-heal in case of a medium cut. The protocol most used is token passing is the form of **Fiber Distributed Data Interface (FDDI),** running at 100 Mbps, which would be described as 100BaseFx. While the speed of the network may increase with changes, the environment infrastructure remains the same.

FIGURE 6.13
LAN/WAN
Interconnectivity

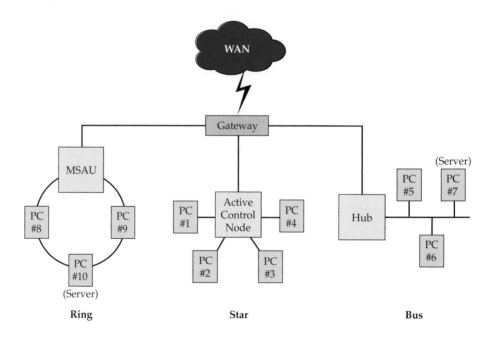

Technology Note   6–2
Connecting to and from a Personal Computer

We call the end and switching points of networks nodes. For the users, this means a computer on which s/he can do some work. PCs come with several ports, that is, places where cables with connectors can be inserted. This allows the user to make connections from the computer to another computer or network. (See Figure 6.14.) These ports also are used to connect to peripherals by which the user controls the PC, but these are not our primary interest.

Inside of the PC, on the motherboard, is the internal bus, which connects all of the communicating parts of the

FIGURE 6.14 **Back View of Computer**

Source: http://www.gateway.com/consumer/matrix/hm_sel_Matrix.shtml.

Mid Tower Rear

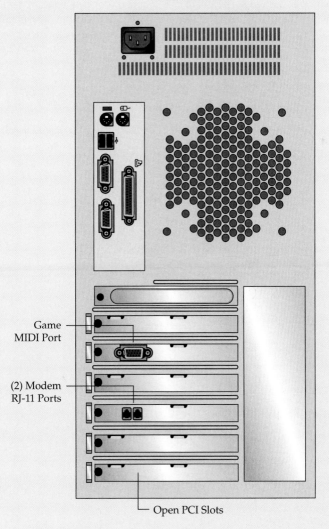

Game
MIDI Port

(2) Modem
RJ-11 Ports

Open PCI Slots

(continued)

Technology Note (*Continued*)   6–2
Connecting to and from a Personal Computer

computer. It is the connections from this bus to the out-side world that interests us. While users will have a video card connected directly to the motherboard and, thus, to the bus, this is not our interest. We want to know how to get data to and from the computer to another computer or network.

The first connector of interest is the **serial port** (see Figure 6.15). This nine-pin female connector is designed to use just two pins and, therefore, transfer all data se-quentially, or serially, to the UTP connected to it. All PCs have serial ports, noted as COM1 and/or COM2. Although they may be used for peripherals such as the keyboard or mouse, we can use them for external connectivity. For ex-ample, although it is preferable to have an internally in-stalled modem, connected directly to the motherboard

and bus, we can have an externally serial port–connected modem. The good thing about the serial port is that it is on all machines and can be used for a variety of connec-tions. The weak point is that it is limited to 32 Kbps. Therefore, if you connect a 56K modem externally, you will be restricted to 32 Kbps. However, using the Win-dows network operating system or other software, you can connect two or more computers via their serial ports and communicate at this slow speed.

A connector found on all PCs is the **parallel port.** This 25-pin male connector is designed to communicate on eight or nine wires in parallel, thus conveying a full byte at a time. The parallel port, designated as LPT1 or PRN, is generally used to communicate on an N = 2 net-work to the printer. It can be used for multiple tasks

FIGURE 6.15   Connector Panel of Computer

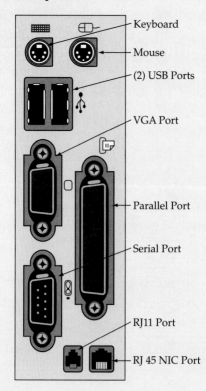

Keyboard
Mouse
(2) USB Ports
VGA Port
Parallel Port
Serial Port
RJ11 Port
RJ 45 NIC Port

Technology Note (*Continued*)   6–2
Connecting to and from a Personal Computer

simultaneously, such as adding an Iomega Zip drive. This port is most often used for peripherals and not for network communications.

One communications avenue that is installed when the computer is constructed is the **universal serial bus (USB)** port. This small, rectangle connector in its initial form has a speed of 12 Mbps; USB-2 has a speed of 480 Mbps. As the name implies, it is designed to overcome the bandwidth restriction of the RS-232C standard serial port. An additional feature of the USB port is that it can be connected to a USB hub, allowing multiple connections to the computer. The connection can be expanded, possibly by daisy-chaining to a total of 127 lines into one USB connector. The USB protocol is such that when a device is connected to a USB port, the systems automatically recognize one another and begin operation. Due to its expanded bandwidth, manufacturers are routinely including USB ports on printers, cameras, and other user peripherals.

The **IEEE 1394,** or **FireWire standard external bus,** supports data transfer rates of up to 400 Mbps. These ports are found on devices that, like USB, wish to communicate at near hard drive speeds. FireWire requires a 1394 port and can, like USB, extend this single port to up to 63 devices.

Users can add a **network interface card (NIC)** that connects on the interior to the PC directly to the motherboard and internal bus. This connection provides the maximum bandwidth to the NIC, with the NIC determining the bandwidth to the external world. Presently, NICs

operate at 10 and 100 Mbps. The above are wired ports; we now describe a wireless port, followed by descriptions of other wireless connectivity.

The **infrared (IR)** port is covered with plastic and has no way to insert a connector. The port first appeared on laptops and other portable devices as a way to connect wirelessly to printers. IR ports have became standard on all portable and moveable devices, allowing users to communicate with and synchronize PDAs, laptops, and desktops. An important protocol in this area is *Bluetooth,* which can communicate with a number of wireless devices.

Just a we can add a modem for POTS communications and have an IR port for wireless data transfer, users can add a wireless modem, which is really a wireless network interface card. Where a standard NIC uses UTP for the channel, the wireless NIC uses radio frequencies. The IEEE 802.11b wireless modems, also known as **WiFi,** operate in the 2.4 GHz spectrum and have bandwidth of about 11 Mbps at distances from several dozen to several hundred feet. Their obvious advantage is that they can roam within their area of coverage and remain connected. The other end of the wireless connection is often a wireless adapter that then connects to a wired network. Thus, the wireless unit is an extension of a standard wired network.

Back to the NIC, just as you can attach a wired hub to the NIC port, you can attach a wireless adapter, which is a wireless hub. Then other devices with wireless NICs can attach via the adapter with no wires.

Information Window   6–2

Bluetooth and IEEE 802.11b standards are of great importance as predictions indicate that by the end of 2005 there will be almost one billion handheld devices used by enterprise employees. The employees are expected to gain increased productivity by scheduling, email access,

m-commerce, GPS, and other applications that enable the "wireless workforce."

Source: information@tmcnet.com, October 3, 2001.

Case 6-1

How do You Choose between Token Passing Ring, Ethernet, Fast Ethernet, or Gigabit Ethernet Protocols?

Ron Davis

A computer network is simply a system that connects multiple computers together. These computers then have the ability to communicate with each other and are allowed to share both information and resources across the network. The proliferation of computer networks has been accelerated by the advent of the client/server architecture and by the increase in demand for Internet and World Wide Web access. Computer networks have even expanded into small businesses and into the home due to the relatively low costs associated with installation and maintenance of small networks.

Over the past 30 years, numerous networking protocols (Ethernet, token ring, domain, Cambridge ring, ProNET-10) have been developed and marketed. Of these, Ethernet and token ring remain the two dominant protocols available today. Each protocol is subdivided based on its operating speed. Ethernet is classified as standard Ethernet (10Base-X), Fast Ethernet (100Base-X), or Gigabit Ethernet (1000Base-X). A token ring network may operate at speeds of either 4 mbps or 16 mbps.

NETWORK BASICS

Computer networks are composed of several components. A basic network consists of four separate items: a network interface card, a medium connecting the computers (typically copper or fiber cable), a hub, and a network protocol or operating system. Each node shares the networking cable and has access to all of the resources available on the network. Since the network is a shared resource, generally only one node may send information across the network at a time. (There are exceptions to this rule.) The primary role of the network protocol is to determine exactly how the nodes will share the network cable. Token ring, for example, mandates an orderly one-directional flow of data. Token ring controls *access* to the network. Ethernet, on the other hand, is similar to a group of third graders all raising their hands and yelling "me, me, me" at the same time. Ethernet operates on a *first-come, first-served* basis. There is no right or wrong protocol. Each one just does its job in a different manner that brings its own advantages, disadvantages, costs, and benefits.

TOKEN RING

A token ring network is somewhat similar to and yet remarkably different from Ethernet. Under token ring, nodes are not allowed to compete for access to the network. Instead, token ring controls access to the network through

FIGURE 1
Token Ring with
Four Nodes

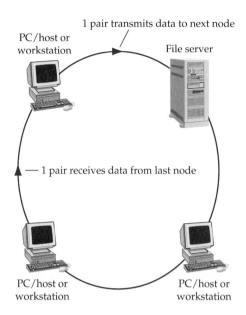

1 pair transmits data to next node

PC/host or
workstation

File server

— 1 pair receives data from last node

PC/host or
workstation

PC/host or
workstation

the use of a token. A node must capture the token prior to accessing the network.
(See Figure 1.) By controlling the token, the node prevents other nodes from
accessing the network. For example, imagine a network of three nodes (A, B,
and C) and node C wants to send a file to node B. As the token passes node A, it
is allowed to pass since node A does not need to use the network. The token also
passes node B for the same reason. As the token passes node C, it is captured by
the node. Node C then transmits packets onto the ring containing the destination
address, source address, error checking information, and the data. These data
then travel around the ring to node A. Node A looks at the destination address and
then allows the information to pass since the data are not intended for node A.
Node B then examines the destination address and realizes that it is the target.
Node B then copies the data to memory and releases the packets back to the network. Node C then receives the packets, releases the token, and performs an error-
checking function. If the transmission has been performed incorrectly, node C will
recapture the token and resend the information.

Throughout this process, network managing software will monitor the ring
for errors. If an error occurs, the software will attempt to correct the problem.
However, serious errors may cause the ring to beacon and bring down the network. The networking manager software will attempt to correct the problem by
issuing a "times-out," which will clear the ring and generate a new token. Critical
problems may be caused by faulty wire or by a bad network interface card. This is
one of the major disadvantages of the token ring protocol; a failure of one piece of
hardware may disrupt or disable the entire network.

TOKEN RING (16 MBPS)

Token ring is able to quadruple its speed to 16 mbs by permitting early token
release. Early token release permits a node to release the token after transmission but prior to receiving confirmation of a successful transfer from the ring.
This is possible because all of the packets flow in one direction around the ring.

FIGURE 2
Token Ring Using
Early Token Release
at 16 Mbps

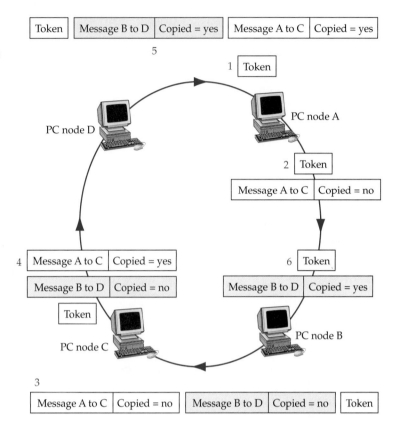

(See Figure 2.) This process also allows multiple packets onto the ring. This in effect allows multiple users to access the ring at the same time. However, each transmission is separated by a minute amount of time.

The token ring network in Figure 2 consists of four nodes and requires six steps to complete two separate transmissions. (Step 1) Node A begins the sequence by receiving and holding the token. (Step 2) Node A then transmits a message to node C and releases the token. (Step 3) Node B allows the transmission to continue but grabs and holds the token. Node B transmits a message to node D and releases the token. (Step 4) Node C then copies the transmission from node A, confirms successful receipt, and then releases the transmission and token. (Step 5) Node D also copies the transmission from node B, confirms successful receipt, and then releases the transmission and token. (Step 6) Node A removes its original transmission from the ring and releases the token. Node B also strips its transmission from the ring and releases a now free token. This process is now ready to be duplicated by another transmitting node on the ring.

ETHERNET (10BASE-X)

Ethernet derives its name from the Greek word *aether*. The 18th- and 19th-century scientific community viewed *aether* as a "ubiquitous force . . . flowing through walls and around corners . . . an invisible, almost magical, presence that went everywhere and connected everything." As Bob Metcalfe, a young engineer at Xerox in the early 1970s, was developing his networking system, he envisioned it functioning in the same manner as *aether*. Therefore, he christened his prototype "Ethernet." (See Figure 3.)

Rather than controlling access to the network via a token, Ethernet allows nodes to compete for access to the network. (See Figure 4.) Whichever node can transmit first has control of the network. To maintain order under this system, an Ethernet node listens before it sends and also listens while it sends. This principal is called carrier sense multiple access/collision detect (CSMA/CD). A node is not allowed to transmit while another node is broadcasting over the network. If two

FIGURE 3
Metcalfe's Original Ethernet Design

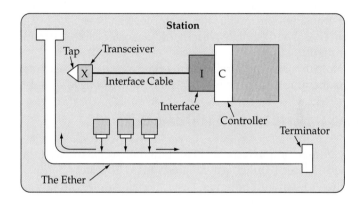

FIGURE 4
Ethernet Network with Bus Topology

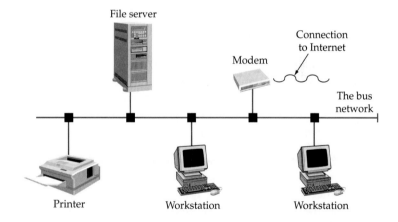

Standard	Speed	Media
10Base5	10 Mbps	Thick coaxial
10Base2	10 Mbps	Thin coaxial
10Broad36	10 Mbps	Thick coaxial
10Base-T	10 Mbps	Twisted pair
10Base-F	10 Mbps	Fiber optic
100Base-TX	100 Mbps	Twisted pair
100Base-FX	100 Mbps	Fiber optic
1000Base-CX	1000 Mbps	Copper cable
1000Base-LX	1000 Mbps	Fiber optic
1000Base-SX	1000 Mbps	Fiber optic

nodes do transmit at the same time, this results in a collision. If a collision is detected, both nodes stop transmitting and listen for the network to become available again.

The advantages of Ethernet include lower hardware costs and faster speeds. Disadvantages include reduced security, media distance limitations, and network congestion due to collisions.

Ethernet nomenclature can be somewhat confusing. The Institute of Electrical and Electronic Engineers (IEEE) has developed standards for both Ethernet and token ring networks. The Ethernet standard is maintained under IEEE 802.3 guidelines. Ethernet nomenclature is based on three factors: speed, number of signals, and transmission media. For example, 1000Base-SX is Gigabit Ethernet running over a baseband (shortwave length) fiber optic cable. Currently, there are 10 defined standards.

Note that baseband refers to media that can only carry one signal at a time while broadband refers to media that can handle multiple signals.

FAST ETHERNET (100BASE-X)

The primary improvement of Fast Ethernet over standard Ethernet is speed. Fast Ethernet operates 10 times faster than standard Ethernet while maintaining a similar connection to standard Ethernet. Fast Ethernet requires an upgrade to both 100-megabit hubs and 100-megabit network interface cards. The media for the network must be category 3 UTP (although category 5 UTP is preferred) or optical cable.

GIGABIT ETHERNET (1000BASE-X)

Gigabit Ethernet is designed primarily to function as a backbone of a network by removing most bandwidth bottlenecks. It operates at 1000 megabits per second or one billion bits per second. Gigabit Ethernet operates 100 times faster than standard Ethernet. Gigabit Ethernet requires upgrades to 1000-megabit hubs and network interface cards and will function on category 5 UTP or optical cable.

At this time, it is not practical to run individual clients at gigabit speeds. Therefore, hybrid Ethernet systems are becoming more commonplace. For example, a small business might connect its servers to each other with Gigabit Ethernet while connecting to clients with standard or Fast Ethernet. Internet connectivity could be maintained with several T1 or T3 lines. This example offers the impressive speed while reducing hardware costs. This example also reveals the flexibility of a system that incorporates standard, Fast, and Gigabit Ethernet technologies.

CONCLUSION

Over the past couple of years, it is obvious that Ethernet has been winning the war for network domination and has become the standard for network protocols. A survey taken by *Computerworld* in early 1998 stated, "more than 60 percent of Token Ring users said they were migrating toward Ethernet . . . Ethernet would seem to be pushing Token Ring out of the running." Zdnet.com described token ring in even gloomier terms by stating that "[token ring is] fading into oblivion, done in by its high price and lack of a high speed migration path."

Despite the fact that token ring obviously offers greater reliability, stability, and bandwidth efficiency, Ethernet continues to dominate due to its higher speeds and lower costs of installation. Hardware costs are often quite dramatic between Ethernet and token ring. Ethernet network interface cards are priced in the $20 to $90 range. However, many computer manufacturers are now routinely including an Ethernet NIC with the base price of the PC. An Ethernet 10BaseT hub usually ranges between $100 and $400. In contrast, a token ring adapter sells in the $200 to $400 range while a token ring switch may sell for $800 to $1,000. These differences in costs really escalate when all of the components for a network with hundreds or thousands of nodes are considered.

In addition, IBM has made no move to accelerate token ring beyond its current 16 Mbps operating speed. Considering that it is economically feasible to design and implement an Ethernet hybrid network operating anywhere between 6 and 60 times faster than token ring's 16 Mbps speed, consumers have seen no reason to pay more for token ring and receive a lot less.

In 1985, IBM promised to support token ring technology for 10 years and it has fulfilled that promise. But in that 10 year period, token ring has been outclassed by Ethernet in terms of both speed and cost. The Ethernet standard will remain the networking protocol of choice for the immediate future.

REFERENCES

1. Bird, D. *Token Ring Network Design*. Wokingham, England: Allison-Wesley Publishers Company, 1994.

2. Carr, H., and C. Snyder. *The Management of Telecommunications*. Burr Ridge, IL: McGraw-Hill, 1997.

3. Harrington, J. *Ethernet Networking Clearly Explained*. San Diego: Morgan Kaufmann, 1999.

4. Johnson, H. *Fast Ethernet—Dawn of a New Network*. Upper Saddle River, NJ: Prentice Hall, 1996.

5. Korzeniowski, P. "Token Ring's Death Watch." Available at www.zdnet.com/eweek/reviews/0526/26token.html, 1997.

6. Saunders, S. *Gigabit Ethernet Handbook*. New York: McGraw-Hill, 1998.

Summary

This chapter has discussed a logical model for constructing networks, the physical construction of networks (topology), and the standards for moving data across networks (protocols) and has given definition to them based on use. Protocols govern the internal workings of the telecommunications system and deal with how the network operating system handles high traffic, contention, and congestion. Methods of line access, such as polling, were discussed. We noted other means of collision detection and avoidance such as carrier sense and token passing. The message format protocols include asynchronous (character-oriented) and synchronous, designed to handle blocks of data. Regardless of message format, we need to have reliable error detection and avoidance. Topology addresses the consideration of pattern of connection, size, and distance. Protocols and topology are interrelated and are used to create networks to support business needs, that is, local and wide area networks.

This material tends to be fairly technical, but necessary to understand so you can participate on a team determining whether and how to implement and use a network. Additionally, managers who make network decisions must understand such technology and terminology to be effective in their decisions. The classic problem encountered when the project team members and the ultimate decision makers do not understand the alternatives is that they buy based on lowest cost and constrain their ability to modify and upgrade. Careful evaluation of the features of the alternatives can help avoid major problems and constraints.

Networks provide significant benefits, but often at significant prices. Obviously, you must measure the costs against the benefits. The cost of network cards, lines, and a few printers and shared disk drives is easy to compare to the cost of no connectivity and multiple printers and large data storage. However, the cost of substandard communications versus the benefit of rapid and easy electronic communications and collaborative workgroups is harder to quantify and judge.

Understanding the technology of networks gives you a proper place on the project team and supports you in making business decisions. Use of engineers for the truly technical parts of the network is appropriate. The final decision, however, remains a business decision, based on good engineering and business information.

Key Terms

10BaseT, 223
100BaseT, 223
100BaseT Fast Ethernet, 221
1000BaseFx, 223
1000BaseT, 223
Attachment Unit Interface (AUI), 219
bridge, 219
bus network, 211
Carrier Sense Multiple Access/Collision Detection (CSMA/CD) protocol, 213
client/server architecture (C/SA), 207
collision, 209
concentrator, 219
Ethernet, 223
Fast Ethernet, 223
Fiber Distributed Data Interface (FDDI), 224
FireWire standard external bus (IEEE 1394), 227

Full-Duplex Ethernet (FDE), 219
Giga-Ethernet, 223
half-duplex, 216
hub, 211
infrared (IR), 227
multiple-station access unit (MSAU), 211
network interface card (NIC), 223-227
network operating system (NOS), 223
node, 206
parallel port, 226
point-to-point protocol (PPP), 223
polling, 209
protocol, 208-215
ring network, 211
ring topology, 209
router, 219

serial line Internet protocol (SLIP), 223
serial port, 226
server, 207
shared resource, 207
star network, 211
switch, 219
synchronous communications, 216
token, 209
token-passing protocol, 224
topology, 206-210
transceiver, 219
transmission control protocol/Internet protocol (TCP/IP), 218
universal serial bus (USB), 227
WiFi, 227
XMODEM, 216

Discussion
Questions

6.1. What peripherals can be shared?

6.2. Discuss the pros and cons of the three major network topologies.

6.3. How can a 4 Mbps token-passing ring outperform a 10 Mbps CSMA/CD bus?

6.4. Discuss the means used on various networks to ensure collision avoidance and minimization of interference.

6.5. Why have LANs become so popular?

6.6. What legal questions would Michael face as he moved to absorb SII into JEI? Are these of concern to the telecommunications manager or just the CEO?

Projects

6.1. Go to several businesses in your city and find the percent of revenues that are spent on telecommunications. What type of industry do you expect to have the larger budgets?

6.2. Design a telecommunications network for a state lottery system.

6.3. Find an organization that has a complex network. What are the protocols that govern the network? Are there problems involved because of differing protocols?

6.4. Determine various data communications services and characteristics available from your telephone company.

6.5. Develop a list of industries that have become dependent, in a competitive sense, on data communications for their survival.

6.6. Can you determine the firms that have data communications as the basis for their business? Is there an industry that exists because of data communications?

6.7. Determine the data communications used in your organization or school. List the uses and the transmission media, for example, twisted-pair wire, coaxial cable, microwave, fiber optics, and so on.

6.8. Divide the class into groups of two or three people. Each group is to find a local company that uses MIS and telecommunications. Write a three-page report on this company, describing its product or service and the use of MIS and, especially, telecommunications capabilities.

Chapter Seven

Telecommunications Architectural Models

CONTINUING CASE—PART 7

Time for a Look at Telecommunications between Kansas City and Colorado

As Alli reached for the phone to start another conference call with Kansas City, she realized this was the fifth one this week. She put the phone down and turned to her desktop computer, using it to call up the accounting program on the JEI System 38. Using a high-level language, she isolated and downloaded to her PC all of the phone charges for the first six months of the calendar year. Then she segregated the costs between Denver and Kansas City.

"Zowie," she thought. "It's worse than I realized." The conference calls between the two facilities had grown to over $500 per week. She looked at the accounting program again and found that the FX line between Denver and Colorado Springs cost far less. Even with a longer distance, a leased line between the two facilities should not be near $500 per week.

When Michael walked into the office, she told him she had discovered a way to reduce some costs. "Did you know we were spending over $500 a week on calls between Denver and Kansas City? I bet we could lease a line for less."

"I forgot all about our expenses in that area. Get with Carlton and the AT&T representative, and let's see if you are right."

"I understand that when you go around the local Telco to get a telecommunications service you are using *bypass*. We are bypassing the local Telco and going directly to the long-distance provider. The FX line to Colorado Springs uses the COs in both cities, so the Telco is involved at both ends. In this case, however, we will be bypassing the Telco and going directly to the long-distance provider, assuming they think we are a large enough customer to bring a line to our office."

Shared Tenant Services

The acquisition of the Kansas City manufacturing plant (Johnson Specialty Controls) also had provided another small business for Carlton in the shared tenant services (STS) that was a part of the deal. This business was bundled with 30,000 square feet of space in a six-story office building that came along with the plant. Tom Herbert had built the office

building in order to have his own offices and to provide space for the rapidly growing businesses in an area that had been extremely short of modern office space. Tom had opted to employ the concept of STS in order to add to the income from leased space.

Under the STS arrangement, the building owner provided several services (and charged fees for them). Chief services were the telecommunications and computing services that the tenants were obligated to purchase. There was, in essence, a miniature telephone company on the premises. The Telco brought its connections to the premises boundary via a trunk cable, but on the premises Tom had a PBX and coin-operated public telephones, and even provided telephone instruments for all tenants. Of course, the Telco perceived this STS arrangement as a form of bypass, since the Telco's services were replaced by Tom's on the building premises. It was of interest to Carlton that an additional aspect of the STS arrangement was the provision of a computer-controlled environmental system governing the climate for each office and a security system. The computer service of the STS arrangement was only a hint of future enhancements for service. For example, the system could provide a backbone for security monitoring. Carlton stuck this idea in the back of his mind as an attractive venture for JEI.

Sue High was in charge of STS for Tom and came to work for Carlton. (See Figure 7.1.) She spent most of her time finding tenants to keep the building filled as her arrangement with Tom had consisted of a base salary plus commissions based on occupancy and STS activity level. Meanwhile, Matilda began data entry in Denver for the KC office building, tenants, and factory, moving the data sheets, by U.S.P.S. mail or overnight carrier when required. The resultant data were uploaded back to the KC computer via commercial telephone line and then over the leased line pending the acquisition of a data circuit between the Denver and KC offices.

With the purchase of the Johnson Security Controls (JSC) plant, JEI got a manufacturing facility and office space that was much too large. Carlton got the facility as part of the deal, and Tom leased back part of the office space. Meanwhile, Sue attempted to fill the rest. Tom had recently purchased a PBX for the

FIGURE 7.1   JEI Expanded Organizational Chart (circa 1987)

Numbers are quantities of telephone instruments.

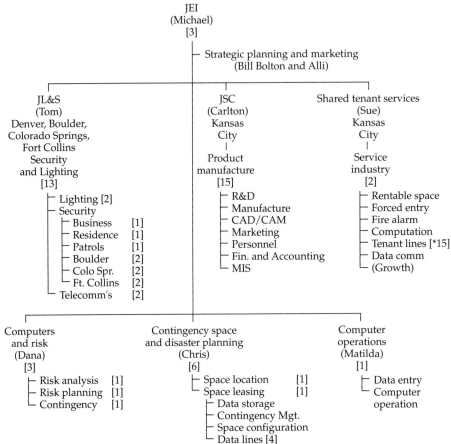

new office building, with lines supporting the factory. The extra office space, above Tom's needs, had been a venture of Tom's—shared tenant services, without the services. Now, Carlton could move the PBX to the building, move the administrative computer from the factory to the office building, and provide the services to the tenants and the factory.

Management Discussions

Michael leaned back in his new leather executive chair and allowed his thoughts to trace the rapid-fire developments of the past few weeks. He felt somewhat chagrined that he had only recently become concerned about the firm's development and maintaining a unifying thread to his businesses. It seemed like growth was inevitable and that he might get caught up to the point that he would lose control of the

direction of the organization. Michael decided that it was time to call together Carlton, Bill, Alli, Dana, and Chris as a minimum number of key players and review the bidding. He feared that the company might easily get overextended and end up in serious trouble unless growth was properly controlled.

As Michael waited for his newly hired secretary to coordinate the meeting, he jotted down some of his concerns. His list looked like this:

1. Do we have enough competence to run all of the businesses?

2. What are the qualifications of my people?

3. What is the best way for us to organize the "new" JEI?

4. How can we continue to grow in our existing markets at an adequate rate?

5. What do we need to be able to manage our dispersed organization?

6. How can we keep the Johnson reputation of service alive if we are so widespread?

7. What are the implications for strategy?

Michael decided to have his key people meet at the lake cabin instead of the office to seriously reflect and get some consensus on their new organization. He was already leery of the connection between his own IBM shop and the DEC system in Kansas City. It seemed that the telecommunications architecture had taken on a major degree of importance and that they might need a consultant to help sort out how to tie the two systems together.

As he drove home, his head was full of topics that he might place on the meeting's agenda. He thought, "It used to be so easy when I was aware of everything and understood every aspect of the business." His roots were in lighting and security, but the newest business was pure manufacturing. Meanwhile, new opportunities in computer services and shared tenant services seemed to have nothing in common with these two ventures. He needed to understand the difference between what he wanted to do and what he needed to do.

Disaster Recovery at JSC

Michael woke earlier than usual and decided to read the newspaper outside. He usually slept easily and only woke early when something was bothering him. As he sipped his coffee, he realized what was wrong—there was no disaster recovery for JSC. He had purchased the division and had it up and running and had not stopped long enough to assess the risk of operations and what to do in case of a disaster.

"Chris," Michael started, "how would you like to spend a week in Kansas City? I need you to go there and do a risk assessment on the new division and come up with a disaster recovery plan. Work it in your schedule over the next four weeks, and let me know the outcome. My guess is that this assessment will be an easy one. And by the way, pick out an office for yourself in the tower while you're at it and draw up plans for me to review for a branch of your group there. I want to start offering disaster planning in that area, and I am sure they will need your help in coordinating the rental of the unused factory and office space there."

"You want me to move there?"

"No, I want you here. Just set up an office, and let me know the market and how we can manage it."

"No problem," Chris said. "I'll be back to you with a formal report within four weeks."

Revisiting the Telecommunications Architecture

Michael met Carlton, Alli, Dana, Chris, and Bill for a working weekend at the lake. JL&S had expanded to two new cities, both out of the Denver local calling area, and Carlton had acquired a manufacturing plant in another local access transport area (LATA). It was time to review the telecommunications architecture.

The FX line to Colorado Springs worked well and was very cost effective. Meanwhile, the Boulder office concentrated on a very local business and had not purchased any discounted long-distance service. The Fort Collins office had developed its market well in that city and, at the time that the business was acquired by JL&S, had plans to expand into Cheyenne, Wyoming, only 25 miles away. A specific problem, in addition to the federal consideration of doing business across state lines, was the cross-LATA consideration. Michael saw this as more complexity than he wanted, and asked Bill to look into this. He also asked Alli to look into the cost and benefit of a leased line between Fort Collins and Denver.

"And while you're at it, Alli, how can we determine if we need more lines in Colorado Springs. How do we know if the lines are busy too much of the time?"

"Funny you should ask, Michael. I was wondering about that last week and called the Telco. They gave me two answers. First, the easiest way to learn how many times a call comes in when you are on the phone is to put in call-waiting. That way you would not miss answering the call, and you could count the number of times it happened. Second, the Telco can do a study, for example, set the switch to count the number of busy occurrences."

Carlton sat impatiently, drawing on a pad of paper, as his dad spoke with Bill and Alli.

"What's that you're drawing, Son?"

"I'm trying to locate the center of a new line of business for us," he replied.

"What? Another line of business?"

"It's OK, Dad. This one is just an extension of JL&S's security lighting business. Look at this map. We are in the middle of six college campuses. If you are attuned to what's happening on these campuses, you will know that physical security is becoming newsworthy. Specifically, there is real concern about attacks on female students at night, as they walk home from class. Also, all colleges are installing an evergrowing number of computers that are choice targets for thieves."

"So, you feel there is a market in supplying and installing campus lighting and security systems?"

"Yes! I took the day off yesterday and walked around three of the campuses. The lighting is very old, and in many cases the campus has expanded past any planned lighting at all. I got the names of the procurement officers and have been thinking how to formulate a coordinated plan."

"Is there a universitywide system in Denver that we could go after for a coordinated approach?" asked Bill.

"Good idea, Bill," said Michael. "Carlton, find out if there is a single administrative body to present our plan to; otherwise we will have to go after each one individually. Also, what about selling our walking and vehicle patrol services to these same campuses until the lights are in?"

After the Meeting

As his staff slept, Michael walked along the edge of the lake, mulling over recent events. He had picked up a book in Denver about Apple Computer and how they averted disaster. The author made the point that there comes a time when an entrepreneur's creation outgrows its creator's ability to manage. Apple Computer was started by two young, creative engineers. They had developed the right product at the right time. As their success grew, so did the company, until it reached a point that required not the creativity of its developers but the vision and consistency of a professional manager. Steve Wozniak was the first to leave, and Steve Jobs left only after John Scully pushed him out, for all the right reasons.

Michael wondered if he was at his limits as an entrepreneur. Was it time to hire professional management? He had begun to do so when he hired Tom in the area of risk analysis and management.

Well, hiring Tom actually had been to create a new line of business, not to reorganize or totally direct JEI. Bill Bolton, on the other hand, was a true professional manager, hired to develop strategy for JEI. He and Bill had discussed informally how they might recognize Michael's limits at management, but the conversation had not gone too far. "Maybe now was the time, and the place, to revisit the idea," thought Michael, as he walked back to the cabin.

The next day, everyone but Michael and Bill left after lunch. The two men then spent the afternoon discussing the totality of JEI and Michael's wishes for the future. Along about dusk, they agreed that it was time for Michael to step down as president of JEI and take the position of chairman of the board, but give the position of CEO and COO to the new president. Then, Michael could concentrate on vision and strategy and leave the operations to the president.

Michael, as head of JEI, had created the Denver-based security organizations that purchased piece parts and installed assembled systems. With the acquisition of Security Controls in Kansas City, Kansas, JEI had done two things new: (1) they had ventured into manufacturing of parts, and were meeting their needs plus making a surplus, and (2) they were operating remotely from the Front Range of the Colorado foothills. With the Kansas City facility came a need to communicate requirements and inventory levels of production at Kansas City. When the level of data communications was low, use of modems on POTS was adequate and inexpensive. Additionally, fax was coming in as a feasible way to communicate paper-based ideas. However, as Alli found out, the cost of telephone communications had increased dramatically, and the firm's real needs to move data had not been addressed.

The FX line from Denver to Kansas City both reduced their voice call expense and gave them a base from which to consider data communications. When Matilda had files to download after data entry, the cost of the circuit was a fixed charge when the FX line was available. She was now inputting the data into JEI's System 38 and then moving the data from the System 38 to the VAX in Kansas City. With the lower cost of the FX line, all agreed that more data needed to be moved in each direction. At first, it was only a matter of connecting the two computers via modem and letting them run, even though the 2400 bits per second speed seemed frightfully slow for such fast computers. The use of 2400 bps was based on not having to purchase new modems when the data transfer began. As the volume increased, Michael purchased two 9600 bps modems. Alli questioned the need for the faster speed since the line cost was not an issue, but Michael said the amount of data being moved was just the tip of the iceberg, and they needed the extra capacity if they were to move test results, WIP inventory levels, and requirements data. The 9600 bps modems arrived, along with MNP-5 compression software, which gave them an effective rate, when using text files, of about 14,400 bps. Alli realized they now had a resource of great value, even if she did not yet know exactly what to do with it.

Michael Meets SII

As the Kansas City facility stabilized its production and got costs under control, the firm found that they had a significant surplus of production capability and produced inventory. Michael looked at the major trade journals in security and made a list of suppliers for equipment in his field and providers of security installations. He noticed that a company named Security International, Inc. (SII), operated out of Kansas City, Missouri, and was reported to have 42 district or franchise offices in the West and Midwest. Because the offices all used local names, Michael had not encountered their competition on a large scale. What he did notice was that they used a consistent logo on their equipment, a logo that was gaining recognition. However, when Michael investigated SII in Dun & Bradstreet's credit database, he found an over-the-counter traded company with poor stock performance, less than expected return on sales and equity, and high debt. He believed SII could add a large market for JL&S and was, itself, ripe for takeover. The large market potential and growing recognition made Michael eager to evaluate the possibilities.

Michael made a point of meeting Gary Smythe, the founder and CEO of SII, at a security installation conference in Dallas. They had dinner on several occasions and walked through the vendor display area together. Later, over, drinks, Gary approached Michael about joining SII and gaining from their wide operations and visibility. He began a hard sell on how he had developed SII into a high-visibility

home and office security installation firm, one that could give JL&S an entrée into wider areas of business. He showed Michael how he had developed the company, leveraging all of its assets to buy up small security firms. While this left him with a large debt service, he was now poised to become a high-visibility, nationwide service provider.

Michael listened patiently and with great interest as Gary outlined his plans for the combined corporation. He then countered Gary's effusive sales pitch with an in-depth recitation that revealed his understanding of SII's financial problems, comparing SII's plight with JEI's sound financial situation. As a final response, he offered to purchase SII and meld it into JL&S, absorbing the SII debt and holding the creditors at bay. Gary was taken aback, first thinking he was talking to a newcomer to the business but finding that he was talking to a master. Michael told Gary outright that his skills were obviously in building up and expanding a business, but not in running it or even financing it. He then offered Gary a position in JEI of looking for potential new acquisitions, both companies and franchises.

"If the takeover is consummated," Michael told Gary, "my staff will continue in their present assignments. Doug is in charge of engineering and manufacturing, Alli heads marketing, Carlton monitors communications and all costs, and Bill continues to develop strategy. Gary, you will be in charge of new acquisitions and franchising development. All offices of the new corporation will use equipment manufactured by the Kansas City plant."

Gary was happy with the final proposal and was eager to lend his expertise to the new enterprise. He was relieved to be released from the onerous aspects of daily budgets and management. He had tried to outmaneuver one with greater skills than his and had come out of the encounter outmaneuvered, but with a far more secure future than when he entered the engagement.

By merging SII with JL&S, Michael now had more than 45 locations to coordinate. When Michael and Carlton had offices only in the Front Range to manage, the telephone and its connectivity to the bank's, and then JEI's, computer were adequate. Most of their communications were voice, with only about 30 percent data. With the acquisition of Security Controls in Kansas City, the need to communicate at a greater distance and in another timezone developed. The primary point for establishing communications was between the manufacturing plant in Kansas City and its suppliers; they needed to establish data communications to coordinate requirements and supply, while maintaining a minimum of inventory. Specifically, JL&S and JSC found value in using communications wire from a firm in Atlanta; plastic boxes from Minneapolis; metal boxes from Birmingham; power supplies from San Diego; batteries from Columbus, Georgia; cable from Dallas; lighting fixtures from St. Louis; and touchpads from a firm in Groton, Connecticut.

Before joining JEI, SII had handled all of their suppliers by telephone and manual cardex files. Carlton and Doug decided they could not work in this environment, and respectfully demanded that Michael find a telecommunications manager to control costs and make telecommunications more computer-based. They told Michael that if JEI could develop a stable system, it should be able to reduce inventory to less than three days, a 75 percent reduction over what was in place when they bought the operations in Kansas City and a 98 percent reduction over what SII was experiencing.

With the suppliers using some form of computer-based communications to receive requirements and confirm shipments, JSC manufacturing in Kansas City was assured of adequate inventory with minimum surplus. Therefore, the computer at Kansas City became the central hub for what was now a star network to the suppliers. Each supplier communicated directly to the single computer in Kansas City. Meanwhile, JEI's computer in Denver managed all other enterprises.

JEI Looks for a Telecommunications Manager

Michael called Nowell Loop at IBM and found he had been promoted and moved to the Dallas Education Center. After two transfers of his phone call, the old friends brought each other up to date. Michael told Nowell of his new acquisitions and his son's insistence on hiring someone experienced in the technology and management of telecommunications.

"Just what do you want this person to do, Michael?"

"It appears that we are at a point in our company where we need to establish tight communications between the parts of the company and between our manufacturing branch and its suppliers. What we don't need is a highly qualified and focused engineer, but rather a person to guide us in our thinking and then direct the installation of the ultimate architecture and technology we select."

"Are you looking to implement CIM?"

"What's that, Nowell?"

"**CIM** stands for **computer integrated manufacturing,** the application of information and manufacturing technology, plans, and resources to improve the efficiency and effectiveness of a manufacturing enterprise through vertical, horizontal, and external integration. A primary goal of CIM is global optimization. So, are you interested in CIM?"

"Not initially, my friend. We just want to get connectivity, so we can manage better. From what you say about CIM, I think it should be a part of our long-term strategy, so I don't want to discount it altogether. But first, I need to get organized and stable with my having a manufacturing facility a time-zone away and newly acquired offices all over the western part of the United States."

"Hey, I know what you mean. It's like the old adage of crawling before walking. Tell you what, why don't you spend a little money and come to one of my CIM courses here in Dallas and see if it doesn't get you thinking. Even better, bring Bill and Carlton with you, and you can use this time to start changing your strategy and developing a telecommunications architecture."

"I agree! It sounds like I need to bring my whole staff. How about sending me information on the classes, schedule, and cost, and I will find a way to be in Dallas soon."

"Look for a package containing particulars on the CIM course in the mail this week."

Michael looked out his window at Pikes Peak and realized that Nowell was right. It was time to get going. Buying Security Controls was an important step, but it was acquiring SII that put the frosting on the cake, a cake that would spoil if he did not get his strategy working for him, not against him. He reached for the phone to set up lunch with Bill to start the talks. As he did, the multibuttoned instrument on his desk rang first.

"Mr. Johnson, my name is Scott Engle," started the voice on the other end. "I am finishing up a masters degree and 10-year career in the Navy in several months and want to enter industry in the area of information systems and networking. My interest is working with an expanding company, to address its MIS and data communications architecture and infrastructure."

"What did you have in mind in calling me, Scott?"

"I was referred to you by Alli Harrison. She said you had been wrestling with the decision of what lines of business to be in for many years and of late were worried that the MIS and data communications infrastructures you had in place were not what you needed. I would like to meet with you, discuss your situation, and see if I can improve it to your and my betterment."

"Sounds good, Scott. We have plants in Missouri and Colorado. Any thoughts off the top of your head as to what this might mean as to architecture?"

"Well, without knowing the particulars, I would be hard pressed to give an opinion. Can we set up a time next Tuesday to meet?"

"Well, he's smart enough to avoid traps," Michael thought to himself. "Yes, how about you meeting me in my office at 10:00 A.M. on Tuesday, and I'll plan to spend the rest of the morning with you. I will call in my staff as we need them, but we will keep it informal."

INTRODUCTION

In this chapter, we describe networks and the models used to provide standards for connectivity. Both the logical and physical models of networks are presented as managers need to understand them. The standards and protocols needed to ensure proper movement of data play a large part in determining how well the network deals with traffic. Managers in our present network-centric environment must understand the concepts and terminology introduced in the chapter. It is important that all potential team members who will be making network decisions know the impact of the choice of alternative models, standards, and network configurations.

CONNECTIVITY—PROPRIETARY OR OPEN STANDARDS?

When a manufacturer develops a new capability, it is often based on that manufacturer's view of technology, architecture, and unique or proprietary standards. While the proprietary standards may allow that manufacturer's equipment to communicate with others in the product line, these standards generally preclude interoperation of "foreign" equipment, often by design. Thus, telecommunications managers who buy into a set of proprietary standards may have precluded the use of other manufacturers' equipment. The creator may have developed the standard because he or she believed it was the best way to do the job. If the proprietary standard is kept secret by implementing it in firmware within the equipment, other manufacturers cannot replicate it and are kept from communicating with the original equipment except as the original equipment allows or through conversion equipment. Thus, at various times in history, the decision to install Digital Equipment Corporation (VAX-based) or Burroughs equipment precluded the attachment of IBM equipment.

Therefore, when considering a network of computers there are several architectural approaches. If the proposed network is homogeneous, that is, all the same equipment, a single vendor may provide all the network protocol capability, including the electrically dependent and the application-dependent services. Also, the latter services may be obtained from vendors who will provide host-compatible software.

If, on the other hand, the network hosts are heterogeneous, there are two networking alternatives. One is to buy networking software from vendors who

Technology Note   7–1

A *system* is group of interrelated and interdependent parts working together to achieve a common goal. A cooperative system is a specialized type of system that requires at least two parties with differing objectives but with common goals to collaborate on the development and operation of a joint system in support of these common goals. Typically, each partner in a cooperative system develops and operates his or her own specific portion of the common system environment. Standards usually play a significant role in cooperative systems, and third-party facilitators are often involved.

Electronic data interchange (EDI) is the process of direct computer-to-computer communication of information in a standard format between organizations or parties (companies). As a result of this cooperation and communication, EDI permits the parties to perform and exchange information on a specific set of business functions electronically (purchasing, invoicing, notification, etc.) with a minimum use of paper, postage, and patience. The primary purpose of EDI is to provide a communications standard for the electronic transfer of common business documents between the respective computer systems of individual and diverse trading partners. As of 1992, over 31,000 U.S. companies had adopted EDI.

EDI is, by definition, a cooperative system. Its use presents a significant opportunity to lower the cost of doing business between trading partners, and, as a result, offers significant competitive advantage over those organizations not utilizing the technological opportunity.

When we say computer-to-computer communications, we mean that data are copied from the file or database of a program residing on one computer with its specific operating system, environment, and file structure. They are then moved to and stored in the file or database of a program residing on another computer with its specific operating system, environment, and file structure. Ideally, this is all done on computer command, without any human intervention *and* without either computer system knowing the features of the other system. That is to say, the sending computer does not know the nature of the receiving computer or its file structure and vice versa. The use of EDI does not require either party to know the nature of the other party's architecture or file structures. It requires only that, in addition to contractual arrangements between partners, the originating computer transforms its data to a specified EDI format. In like manner, the receiving computer will read the EDI-formatted data and transform it to its own file structure.

Information Window   7–1
The Quick Response Channels
for Textile and Apparel Companies

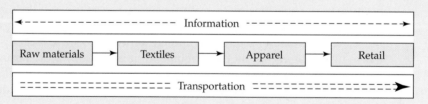

Quick Response is a combination of technology and partnerships. The *technology* aspects include bar code standards, bar code scanning, data processing, electronic data interchange (EDI), and electronic telecommunications. The *partnership* aspect means that trading partners, whether suppliers or customers, are seen by an individual entity as a possible alliance, not an adversary. It is questionable as to whether the technology or the partnerships have the greatest problems and opportunities. Each is vital to Quick Response; each takes effort and investment.

Quick Response has two facets: (1) to move information from the customer's point of contact in the retail store through the total textile-apparel channel and (2) to move goods efficiently throughout the channel to support the retail outlets. The object is information and goods movement in a dynamic and highly competitive market, while reducing costs and increasing sales through greater availability of merchandise for sale.

provide software to bridge from the one proprietary system to the other, such as from IBM's systems network architecture SNA to DEC's VAX-based software. These packages, if available, are usually limited to connect the major vendors. Another option is to buy software that provides a bridge into a standards-based environment. The **open architecture,** to be discussed next, lets the nodes interoperate, basing that interoperation on standard protocols.[1]

You may take the position that you are a decision maker and are not really concerned with the technology of architecture and connectability. But the decision maker *should* be concerned with the way that a vendor chooses to provide interconnectivity. It is a decision-making situation that has implications that reach beyond the present; it falls into a "pay me now or pay me later" category. If you, as the decision maker, choose to buy into a manufacturer's proprietary scheme, you are making a long-term decision and commitment. It means you must work within that vendor's scheme or standard, often to the exclusion of others. If, on the other hand, you choose an open systems standard that many vendors choose to meet, you will have many more choices later, and the competition for your business will be far greater. This is the tenet of interoperability: the ability to provide connectivity between equipment of different vendors without any special hardware or software interfaces.

ARCHITECTURE[2]

An **architecture** is a concept or plan that is implemented in a set of hardware, software, and communications products. The architecture specifies protocols, formats, and standards to which all hardware and software in the network must conform. *Network architectures* attempt to facilitate the operation, maintenance, and growth of the communication and processing environment by isolating the user and the application program from the details of the network. This was necessary to support distributed data processing with multiple computers in a network; the architecture should be open so that it can accommodate new technology. The purpose of network architecture in particular is to

- Provide an orderly structure for the communications network that ensures a specific level of compatibility.

- Provide isolation of the application systems from the physical hardware.

- Support faster development and easier maintenance of application systems by using system software utilities to perform communications functions.

- Be reliable, modular, and easy to use.

- Accommodate new devices and software for the network without changing the application systems.

In order to support our discussion and to assist in the definition of architecture, we typically use models that deal with **layers.** A layer or level evokes an orderly or logical grouping of functions. As long as the rules of the boundary between layers are honored, the intra-layer architectures are independent.

---

[1] For further discussion, see Richard W. Markley, *Data Communications and Interoperability* (Englewood Cliffs, NJ: Prentice Hall, 1990).
[2] For more on architecture, see Bennet P. Lientz and Kathryn P. Rea, *Data Communications for Business* (St. Louis: Times Mirror/Mosby, 1987); and Jerry Fitzgerald, *Business Communications* (New York: Wiley & Company, 1993).

FIGURE 7.2
Generic
Three-Level Model

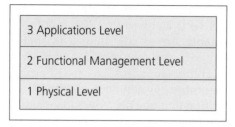

3 Applications Level
2 Functional Management Level
1 Physical Level

In addressing a model for open systems, we consider first the generic three-level model; then the TCP/IP model, the IBM SNA model, and finally the OSI model.

Without going into much detail, in the general model of Figure 7.2, the total system is partitioned into the physical or electrical domain at the bottom, the application or user interface level at the top, and the management of network functions in the middle. With such a model, as long as the standards of the interface boundary of each level are met, one level does not have to worry about the level above or below.

THE TCP/IP MODEL

The **Transmission Control Protocol/Internet Protocol** is one of the oldest networking standards, developed for the ARPANET (see Chapter 9 on the history of the Internet). Because TCP/IP is a file transfer protocol, consisting of the two layers TCP and IP, it can send large files of information across sometimes unreliable networks with great assurance that the data will arrive in an uncorrupted form. It allows reasonably efficient and error-free transmission between different systems, and, in many places, has become the standard of choice, especially when using the Internet. For example, TCP/IP is being used as the "transition standard" for the re-engineering of the U.S. Internal Revenue Service wide area network.

The Internet Protocol suite, commonly known as TCP/IP, is a de facto standard that is used to express the details of how computers communicate with each other. It is also a set of conventions for interconnecting networks and routing traffic. TCP/IP does not care about network hardware, carrier systems, or terminating off of or feeding onto interconnected networks. All it cares about is that it sees a corresponding suite of TCP/IP details at the far end, and it will pass the traffic as needed. It adapts for every form of long-haul data transport currently in use such as ATM, frame relay, X.25, private line, and dial up. The current Internet and the future information superhighway are and will continue to be based on TCP/IP. Network and machine operating systems such as MS Windows (9X, ME, NT, 2000, XP), Novell, Banyan, IBM (OS/2, VMS), DEC, and SUN all support TCP/IP because it transcends operating systems such as DOS, UNIX, or Windows.

TCP/IP utilizes a simple basic rule: "Act only as an envelope with a destination address and a return address. Ensure that the envelope gets to its destination safely and sealed. Don't worry about what is IN the envelope."

What Is TCP/IP?[3]

TCP/IP is the basic communication language or protocol of the Internet. Basically, it is a set of two communication protocols that an application can use to package its information for sending across a private network or the public Internet. TCP/IP

[3] Thanks to Justin Williams for help on this topic.

is a two-layer program. The higher layer, Transmission Control Protocol, manages the assembling of a message or file into smaller packets that are transmitted over the Internet and received by a TCP layer at the receiving end, which then reassembles the packets into the original message. The lower layer, Internet Protocol, handles the address part of each packet so that it gets to the right destination. Each gateway computer on the network checks this address to see where to forward the message. Even though some packets from the same message are routed differently than others, they'll be reassembled at the destination.

TCP/IP also can refer to an entire collection of protocols, called a TCP/IP suite. These include the World Wide Web's Hypertext Transfer Protocol (HTTP); the File Transfer Protocol (FTP); Terminal Emulation (Telnet), which lets you log on to remote computers; and the Simple Mail Transfer Protocol (SMTP).

History of TCP/IP

TCP and IP were developed by a Department of Defense (DoD) research project in the 1960s to connect a number of different networks designed by different vendors into a network of networks. The project was initially successful because it provided a few basic services everyone needed, including file transfer, electronic mail, and remote logon. In December 1968, the Advanced Research Projects Agency (ARPA) awarded Bolt Beranek and Bewman a contract to design and deploy a packet-switching network. The project was called ARPANET and four nodes were in place by the end of 1969 and connections to Europe were made by 1973.[4]

The initial host-to-host communications protocol used in ARPANET was the Network Control Protocol (NCP). NCP proved to be unable to keep up with the growing network traffic load. The Transmission Control Protocol (TCP) and the Internet Protocol (IP) were proposed and implemented in 1974 as a more robust suite of communications protocols. In 1983, the DoD mandated that all of their computer systems use the TCP/IP.

IP Addressing and Routing

IP addressing is the backbone of what TCP/IP sets out to accomplish. This allows for a node that has an IP address to interact with other nodes connected to a network. TCP/IP also supports routing, which allows for computers across different networks to communicate. Any computer that has an IP address is allowed to connect to other computers that have IP addresses.

IP Addressing and Subnetting

An IP address is made up of four sections for a total of 32 bits of information. Each of these sections is called an octet. Each octet maximum number is 255. The preceding refers to IPv4.

This IP address is referred to as a hierarchical address, as opposed to a flat or nonhierarchical address. A flat address would be a Social Security Number; that is, it does not show parental relationships like the telephone number. An example of a hierarchical addressing scheme is the telephone system. For example, the phone number 334.887.9999 can be broken down. The first three digits, the 334 prefix, shows that the phone number trying to be reached is in lower Alabama, that is, the

[4] Todd Lammle, *MCSE: TCP/IP for NT Server 4 Study Guide,* 4th ed. (San Francisco: Network Press, 2000).

area code for the phone system. The next three digits are the exchange within that area code, and the final four digits are the user code. This numbering scheme allows an organized way to route information across the Internet. The IP address is broken into two parts: the network address and the node address. These two parts are what gives IP addressing its layered structure.

The network address uniquely identifies each network. Every machine on the same network shares that network address as part of its IP address. For example, all IP addresses on Auburn University's campus have the network address of 131.204.xxx.xxx.

The node address is assigned to each machine or node on a network. This part of the address must be unique because it identifies a single machine. This number also can be referred to as a host address. So to continue with our example, in the complete IP address of 131.204.65.245, 131.204 is the network address and 65.245 is the node or host address.

The designers of the Internet decided to create classes of networks based on network size. For the small number of networks possessing a very large number of nodes, they created the rank Class A network. At the other end is the Class C network, reserved for the numerous networks with a small number of nodes. The Class B networks fit in between. The classes of networks are determined by the first octet of numbers in the IP address. Class A networks occupy 1–127, Class B networks occupy 128–191, and Class C networks occupy 192–223. For the IP address of 24.17.123.145, in a Class A network, 24 is the network address and the node address is 17.123.145. This allows for a small number of networks with a large number of nodes or computers. However, in a Class C network, with the IP address of 204.12.134.245, the network address will be 204.12.134 with a node address of 245. This division of networks allows for organized routing of information. For example, if a router gets a packet that is slated to go to the IP address of 131.204.65.245, the router will know that by looking at that first number, 131, that the packet will be routed to a Class B network. This cuts down on inefficient routing.

A problem arises if an organization has several physical networks but only one IP network address. This can, however, be handled by creating subnets. Subnetting is a TCP/IP software feature that allows for dividing a single IP network into smaller, logical subnetworks. This trick is achieved by using the host portion of an IP address to create a subnet address. It also can be thought of as the act of creating little networks from a single, large parent network. An organization with a single network address can have a subnet address for each individual physical network. Each subnet is still part of the shared network address, but it also has an additional identifier denoting its individual subnetwork number. For example, take a parent who has two kids. The children inherit the same last name as their parent. People make further distinctions when referring to someone's individual children, like "Kelly, the Jones's oldest, left for college." Those distinctions are like subnet addresses for people.

Back to the Auburn University example, the IP address is 131.204.65.245. Now, the network address is 131.204 because the first number, 131, falls within the Class B network. So, 65.245 is left. Now, on Auburn University's campus, there are more divisions between the different colleges. The Auburn College of Business has three subnets, 64, 65, and 66. So, we know that in 131.204.65.245, the 65 is the subnet address and the 245 is the node address, which is specifying a specific computer.

Disadvantages of TCP/IP

Finite Space

The major problem with the current TCP/IP suite is the total number of unique IP addresses that can be created. Using the bit numbering system, there can be a maximum or 2^{32} (roughly 4 billion) unique numbers. This sounds like quite a large number, but it is pretty small when you look at everything that is connected to the Internet. Soon, there will be toasters and refrigerators that will connect to the Internet. The Internet is growing too quickly to support the number of unique addresses. To combat this problem, a new IP version 6 is being created. Compared to the old IP version 4 (IPv4), the new IPv6 will be 128 bits long. That is the old IPv4 addressing squared—twice![5]

Maintenance

The use of TCP/IP on smaller networks is another drawback. TCP/IP requires a lot of overhead and therefore can slow up the speed of the network. "Overhead" in this context refers to the additional network control information, such as routing and error checking, that the protocol adds to data that the application layer needs to send across the network.[6] It would be easier to set up another type of protocol on a small to medium-sized network, such as NetBEUI or IPX/SPX.

Another problem with maintenance is the configuration of the devices that use TCP/IP. Someone will have to be in charge of distributing the IP addresses and staying in charge of who-got-what. This poses a large problem to IT managers. Some IT managers simply keep a spreadsheet of valid IP addresses. If a user wants a computer connected to the network, he/she will ask the IT manager. The IT manager will go to the spreadsheet and look for an IP address that is not taken and give that user the IP address. This leads to large problems and headaches on networks that are larger than about 20 people. To counter this there is another feature of TCP/IP called DHCP, Dynamic Host Configuration Protocol. DHCP allows for the user to just log onto the company network and the server will automatically assign that computer an IP address. This eliminates the hassles of keeping track of the IP address.

The TCP/IP protocol stack was established by DARPA in the late 1970s and is currently supported by every vendor of network products in today's marketplace. It also has been adopted by the federal government as the intermediate protocol until the full GOSIP (U.S. government implementation of OSI) standard can be implemented. Both the OSI and TCP/IP protocol stacks are similar and provide the same basic service, but TCP/IP packages the service a bit more simply. OSI is discussed in detail later in the chapter.

In the TCP/IP suite, each layer builds upon the layer below, adding new functionality. (See Figure 7.3.) The lowest layer, the **link layer,** is concerned with sending and receiving data using network hardware. We know that the IEEE 802 Committee has established the standards for generic Ethernet networks. Other protocols are the point-to-point (PPP) and serial line IP (SLIP) used when connecting to a network over an asynchronous dial-up link.

The **network layer** uses the Internet Protocol (IP) to send blocks of data (datagrams) from one point to another. IP is the major protocol of TCP/IP because each piece of data is sent over the network as an IP packet.

[5] http://www6.cs-ipv6.lancs.ac.uk/ipv6/documents/papers/bound/IPNG.htm.
[6] http://www.openvms.compaq.com:8000/72final/6556/6556pro_016.html.

FIGURE 7.3
The Simplified TCP/IP Protocol Suite Model (Stack)

Layers	Protocols and Standards
Application layer	FTP, SMTP, SNMP
Transport layer	TCP, UDP
Network layer	IP
Link layer	IEEE 802.x, PPP, SLIP

TABLE 7.1
IBM Systems Network Architecture (SNA)

IBM Systems Network Architecture (SNA) Layers[1]	General Responsibilities for the Layer
7 Transaction services	Provide network management services to the end user
6 Presentation services	Provide formatting and data compression services
5 Data flow control	Provides end-user control over the SNA session such as half-duplex or duplex communications
4 Transmission control	Establishes, maintains, and terminates SNA session
3 Path control	Creates end-to-end logical channels
2 Data link control	Transfers data reliably across a circuit
1 Physical control	Physically transmits serial and parallel data over a circuit

[1] Richard W. Markley, *Data Communications and Interoperability* (Englewood Cliffs, NJ: Prentice Hall, 1990), p. 117.

The **transport layer** is where the Transmission Control Protocol (TCP) is used by most Internet applications such as FTP, HTTP, and Telnet. TCP is connection-oriented and, therefore, the sender and receiver must establish a connection before data can be transferred. User Datagram Protocol (UDP) is a connectionless protocol and is less reliable except for small amounts of data.

The **application layer** uses a slightly more complex version of UDP called the Simple Network Management Protocol (SNMP). The Telnet application is a terminal emulation application that allows for workstation connection to a host as if it were a direct connection. The File Transfer Protocol (FTP) enables the workstation to interact with the host hard disk so that files may be copied and files can be uploaded to the host.

Conclusion

TCP/IP has had a dramatic effect on the Internet. It allows for an organized way of communicating across networks with different operating systems and hardware platforms. TCP/IP also has special features such as HTTP, FTP, Telnet, and SMTP. The benefits of TCP/IP completely outweigh the costs and disadvantages. These benefits are what people want on the Internet and this is why the Internet has grown exponentially over the last few years.

THE IBM SNA MODEL

Table 7.1 shows the IBM SNA model, which expands the generic three levels into seven levels. The same concept holds—partition the total system into manageable and homogeneous parts, honor the requirements of the boundaries—and you have to know the interworkings of only the level at which you are working.

THE OSI MODEL

A groundswell of interest in connecting heterogeneous computer systems has spurred demand for a set of standards that allow communication between dissimilar equipment. The **International Standards Organization (ISO)** and the Consultative Committee on International Telephony and Telegraphy (CCITT)—subsumed by International Telecommunications Union (ITU)—promulgated the Reference Model for Open Systems Interconnection in 1983. This model has become widely known as the **OSI (open system interconnection) model.** OSI was developed as a de jure (legally derived) standard to replace the IBM SNA de facto (commonly accepted) standard. OSI has currently evolved into de facto usage with fewer than seven layers.

The OSI model consists of seven layers that contain specific standards for each control level. The uppermost levels specify needs of the user as planned for the application, while the lower three levels concern communications in the physical realm, such as electrical parameters, circuit buildup and breakdown, message routing, and error detection and correction.

The layers in the OSI model provide a structured or modular approach to allow modification and development to be done at a particular level without impacting other layers. The layers are hierarchical in that lower layers provide services such as control information to the layer just above it. The layers are, however, specialized according to functions.

Business managers should be aware that the OSI model facilitates control, analysis, modification, replacement, and management of communication network resources because it provides reference standards. The adherence to OSI model standards makes software and hardware development far easier. This model has become important as the need for "enterprise computing" has increased. Systems managers have become much more concerned about **interoperability,** a term referring to the capability of two or more devices to transmit and receive data or carry out processes regardless of whether they are from the same or different manufacturers. This occurs without the user taking an intervening step; he/she does not have to "tweek" the devices. Increasingly, users expect to connect various devices and have them communicate without having to change hardware and software settings. Protocols, standards, and models such as the OSI seven-level model provide for interoperability and, ultimately, lower costs.

The OSI seven-layer model is the plan by which communications software is designed. The model facilitates control, analysis, upgradability, replacement, and management of the resources that constitute the communications network. The seven-layer OSI model is put into practice as software that handles the transmission of a message from one terminal or application program to another distant terminal or application program. Use of this open standards model makes it far easier to develop software and hardware that link incompatible networks and components because protocols can be dealt with one layer at a time. The user of such a model and its layers in design of network software and applications provides the developer with a clear roadmap. Often a module is constrained to the protocol of a specific level. This means that if the design meets the requirements of the interfaces between that level or layer and the ones below and above it, the designer is free to concentrate on only that task. Like most things in telecommunications, the OSI model was designed around the analog world, and as digital transmission becomes more dominant, analysts find this model too unwieldy. Because of its value as a reference model, we will continue to describe it.

Communications standards are established to ensure compatibility among similar communications services. This is the "how" of architecture.

Architecture is a concept or plan that is implemented in a set of hardware, software, and communications products. It is required to mask the physical configuration and capabilities of the network from the logical requirements of the users.

Architecture, standards, and layers allow the network to be changed without affecting the user; layer independence is like data independence in DBMS. Users want transparency and consistency.

Information Window   7–2
Benefits of Using an Open Systems Interface Architecture

I. Reduced Cost
  A. Allows use of any vendor's equipment designed to the standard.
  B. Limits the need for additional, third-party equipment for interface.

II. Greater Flexibility
  A. Allows for choice of any vendor's equipment meeting the standard.
  B. Encourages development of equipment due to large base of users.
  C. Consistent interfaces and protocols.

TABLE 7.2
Functions Provided by OSI Model Layers

Level	Layer	Function
7	Process (Applications)	Exists in host computer
6	Presentation	Exists in host computer
5	Session layer–Session control	Exists in host computer
4	Transport (Control)	Exists in host computer
3	Network (Control)	Exists in front-end processor (FEP)
2	Data link (Control)	Exists in FEP and/or controller
1	Physical (Link control)	Exists in terminal, modem

ISO-OSI model
The primary objective to provide a basis for interconnecting dissimilar systems for the purpose of information exchange.

In the description of the seven layers that follow, remember that the layers are like the floors of a tall building. The lowest layer is at street level, while the highest level is in the penthouse, or executive level. Ideas take place at the highest level and work their way down the floors until they come out the front door as messages that can be transported to another building. These physical messages enter the second building and make their way up the floors, being transformed along the way until they reach the highest (executive) floor as ideas.

Additionally, remember that in each layer, and on each floor of our buildings, there are different and specific tasks that take place. For example, messages are received physically on the ground floor, where they are handled by a department dedicated to receiving and transmitting physical messages. On each succeeding higher level, different groups or programs carry out unique functions to ensure the reliability of the ultimate message as it is delivered to the correct destination in its complete form. Table 7.2 displays a concise view of the seven layers of the OSI model.

Physical Layer

The objective of digital transmission is to send bits across the network. Regardless of where a message originates or which data code is used, a message must be reduced to an electrical or photonic signal of specified voltage or frequency and characteristics for transmission. The protocol in the **physical layer** ensures that when one node transmits a signal representing a logical 1, it is received and interpreted as a logical 1 at the next node. That is, this layer specifies the *electrical* or **photonic connection** between the transmission medium and the computer system. (See Table 7.3.) This layer, the lowest in the hierarchy, is basically a computer-to-computer protocol describing the conventions of the electrical or photonic circuits and mechanical system. If the network is circuit-switched, the physical layer also includes the procedures for establishing the circuit. *This layer typically deals with connection cable standards, pin assignments, voltages, current levels, impedances, and timing rates.*

Data Link Layer

The **data link layer** concerns itself with the *actual characters* and the sequence in which they are transmitted. It establishes and controls the physical paths of communications to the next node. This layer attempts to deliver error-free data over the circuit between adjacent computers that is established by the physical layer. (See Table 7.4.) *Within this layer are such things as error-detection methods, error-recovery methods, error-correction methods, methods for resolving competing requests for a shared communication link, and framing (data grouping) requirements for the data.*

Network Layer

The third layer defines *message addressing and routing methods.* When there are a number of nodes in the network and multiple paths from the source to the destination, the **network layer** routes the data from node to node. This layer also controls congestion if the network is overloading certain computers. (See Table 7.5.) *It does end-to-end routing of packets or blocks of information; collects billing, accounting, and statistical information; and routes messages.*

TABLE 7.3 **Physical Layer—Level 1**

What the Layer Does	What's Going On
• Physically establishes a connection when requested to do so by the data link layer (#2) • Physically transmits data as bits • Concerns itself with establishing synchronization of bit flow—duplex, half-duplex, point-to-point, multipoint, asynchronous, or synchronous transmission • Defines quality-of-service parameters	• Defines electrical standards and signaling required to make and break a connection on the physical link to allow bit stream from the DTE onto the network. • Specifies the modem interface between DTE and line • Concerned with voltage levels, currents, simplex/half- or full-duplex

TABLE 7.4 **Data Link Layer—Level 2**

What the Layer Does	What's Going On

• Segments bit stream into frames
• Coordinates data flow split over multiple physical connections
• Is responsible for error detection and correction
• Monitors flow of data frames and compiles statistics
• Ensures that data frames are in sequence
	• Defines standards for structuring data into
	    How machine knows where a frame starts
	    How transmission errors are detected, corrected
	    How polling and addressing are handled
	    How machines are addressed
	• Data link protocol used is High-level Data Link Control (HDLC). Normally located in host FEP
	• Whereas modems ensure that bits are accurately sensed for the communication line at the receiver, this layer groups bits into characters for processing
	• Responsible for error checking VRC, LRC, and CRC codes
	• ACK/NAK for receipt of good frames/blocks, and requesting retransmission if error found

TABLE 7.5   Network Layer—Level 3

What the Layer Does	What's Going On
• Routes packets • Establishes connections between transport layers on two computers that will communicate with each other • Controls flow; stops the flow of packets upon request from the transport layer • Maintains correct sequence of packets • Provides transport layer with acknowledgment that packet has been received correctly • Maintains quality of service • Is responsible for detecting and correcting errors • Is responsible for multiplexing several network connections to a single data link connection for maximum productivity • Handles internetworking, the movement of data from one network to another network	• Network addressing and routing • Generates ACK (positive acknowledgment) that entire message was received correctly • Breaks message from level 4 into blocks for level 2 • Decides on which communications circuit to send packet

TABLE 7.6   Transport Layer—Level 4

What the Layer Does	What's Going On
• Ensures that transport data protocol units arrive in proper order • Specifies grade of service, including acceptable error rates • Monitors status of connection • Establishes connections with another transport layer on a second computer • Detects and recovers errors	• Selects the transmission route between DTEs, comparable to postal system for letters • Handles user addressing; controls form of messages to compensate for speed mismatch • Prevents loss and duplication of entire message • Multiplexes several streams into one physical

Transport Layer

The **transport layer** is responsible for *maintaining a reliable and cost-effective communications channel* from a user's application software process in one computer to a user process in another. It is the highest layer concerned with the world external to its processor. The transport layer views the intervening network as a transparent entity that simply provides a service. The transport layer does not determine the route (the temporary or virtual channel chosen from multiple segments to create the virtual, or temporary, channel), but it ensures that a *reliable* channel exists between the computer processes.

This layer may break a long message or file into smaller segments at the source and reassemble it at the destination if it is required because of a network packet-size limitation. (See Table 7.6.) *The transport layer provides addressing to a specific user process at the destination, message reliability, sequential delivery of the data, and flow control of data between user processes.*

Session Layer

The **session layer** deals with the *organization of a logical session*. It organizes and synchronizes a period of interactive communication between user processes. That is, it establishes the connection between applications, enforces the rules for carrying on the dialogue, and tries to re-establish the connection if a failure occurs. In particular,

TABLE 7.7   Session Layer—Level 5

What the Layer Does	What's Going On
• Establishes and maintains transport connection with a certain designated quality of service • Organizes and synchronizes dialogues between presentation entities • Ensures the reliable transfer of data • Re-establishes transport connection if there is a transport connection failure • Expedites data transfer for high-priority items	• Sets term and conditions of session, such as who transmits first, how long, etc. • Establishes accounting functions for charging

TABLE 7.8 Presentation Layer—Level 6

What the Layer Does	What's Going On
• Selects the syntax to be used • Negotiates the syntax with its corresponding presentation layer on a second computer • Requests the establishment of a session • Encapsulates data in protocol data units	• Way data are formatted and presented to user at terminal • Application program talks to virtual terminal in this layer and this layer transforms to the real device

it authorizes the transport connection between user processes and maintains the continuity of the connection, for example, the order in which the applications are allowed to communicate and the pacing of information, so the recipient is not overloaded. For example, if the transport connection fails, the session layer provides a logical synchronization point so the activity can be resumed. (See Table 7.7.) *This layer provides access procedures, rules of half-duplex or full-duplex dialogues, rules for recovering if the session is interrupted, and rules for logically ending the session.*

Presentation Layer

The **presentation layer** is responsible for *formatting and displaying the data* to and from the application layer and deals with the transmission format of the data. The presentation layer may define how to compress the user data to improve data transfer rates or how to encrypt it for security. (See Table 7.8.) *The presentation layer provides transmission syntax, message transformations and formatting, data encryption, code conversion, and data compression.*

A major component of this layer is the concept of the *virtual terminal*. This concept allows the programmer at the application layer to send data to a universal virtual terminal where the layer will reformat the data to meet the presentation needs of the actual terminal. Such a capability relieves the application programmer of having to account for many possible terminal types.

Application Layer

Applications, from the OSI perspective, are *functionally defined by the user* and include such things as banking through ATM machines and airlines reservations. When the application involves cooperation between separated computers, the **application layer** focuses on unique communications services, such as file transfer, electronic mail, and remote terminal-entry protocols. (See Table 7.9.) *This layer, the highest in the hierarchy, provides user-oriented services such as determining the data to be transmitted, the message or record format for the data, and the transaction codes that identify the data to the receiver.* (See Table 7.10 for the entire seven-level model.)

TABLE 7.9   Process or Application Layer—Level 7

What the Layer Does	What's Going On
• Establishes authority to communicate • Identifies intended communication partners • Agrees upon level of privacy • Determines whether resources are adequate for communication • Decides upon an acceptable quality of service • Agrees upon responsibility for error recovery • Agrees upon responsibility for data integrity	• Services to user applications • Layer for data editing, file update, user thinking • Source and destination for data

TABLE 7.10   Summary of the Functions and Services Provided by OSI Model Layers

What the Layer Does	What's Going On
Level 7—Process (Application) Layer—Exists in Host Computer	
• Establishes authority to communicate • Identifies intended communication partners • Agrees upon level of privacy • Determines whether resources are adequate for communication • Decides upon an acceptable quality of service • Agrees upon responsibility for error recovery • Agrees upon responsibility for data integrity	• Services to user applications • Layer for data editing file update, user thinking • Source and destination for data
Level 6—Presentation Layer—Exists in Host Computer	
• Selects the syntax to be used • Negotiates the syntax with its corresponding presentation layer on a second computer • Requests the establishment of a session • Encapsulates data in protocol data units	• Way data are formatted and presented to user at terminal • Application program talks to virtual terminal in this layer and this layer transforms to the real device
Level 5—Session Layer—Session Control—Exists in Host Computer	
• Establishes and maintains transport connection with a certain designated quality of service • Organizes and synchronizes dialogues between presentation entities • Ensures the reliable transfer of data • Re-establishes transport connection if there is a transport connection failure • Expedites data transfer for high-priority items	• Sets term and conditions of session, such as who transmits first, how long, etc. • Establishes accounting functions for charging
Level 4—Transport (Control) Layer—Exists in Host Computer	
• Ensures that transport data protocol units arrive in proper order • Specifies grade of service, including acceptable error rates • Monitors status of connection • Establishes connections with another transport layer on a second computer • Detects and recovers errors	• Selects the transmission route between DTEs, comparable to postal system for letters • Handles user addressing, controls form of messages to compensate for speed mismatch • Prevents loss and duplication of entire message • Multiplexes several streams into one physical

TABLE 7.10 Continued

Level 3—Network (Control) Layer—Exists in Front-End Processor (FEP)

- Routes packets
- Establishes connections between transport layers on two computers that will communicate with each other
- Controls flow; stops the flow of packets upon request from the transport layer
- Maintains correct sequence of packets
- Provides transport layer with acknowledgment that packet has been received correctly
- Maintains quality of service
- Is responsible for detecting and correcting errors
- Is responsible for multiplexing several network connections to a single data link connection for maximum productivity
- Handles internetworking, the movement of data from one network to another network

- Network addressing and routing
- Generates ACK (positive acknowledgment) that entire message was received correctly
- Breaks message from level 4 into blocks for level 2
- Decides on which communications circuit to send packet

Level 2—Data Link (Control) Layer—Exists in FEP and/or Controller

- Segments bit stream into frames
- Coordinates data flow split over multiple physical connections
- Is responsible for error detection and correction
- Monitors flow of data frames and compiles statistics
- Ensures that data frames are in sequence

- Defines standards for structuring data into
  How machine knows where a frame starts
  How transmission errors are detected, corrected
  How polling and addressing are handled
  How machines are addressed
- Data link protocol used is High-level Data Link Control (HDLC). Normally, located in host FEP
- Whereas modems ensure that bits are accurately sensed for the communication line at the receiver, this layer groups bits into characters for processing
- Responsible for error checking VRC, LRC, and CRC codes
- ACK/NAK for receipt of good frames/blocks, and requesting retransmission if error found

Level 1—Physical (Link Control) Layer—Exists in Terminal Modem

- Physically establishes a connection when requested to do so by the data link layer (#2)
- Physically transmits data as bits
- Concerns itself with establishing synchronization of bit flow—duplex, half-duplex, point-to-point, multipoint, asynchronous, or synchronous transmission
- Defines quality-of-service parameters

- Defines electrical standards and signaling required to make and break a connection on the physical link to allow bit stream from the DTE onto the network
- Specifies the modem interface between DTE and line
- Concerned with voltage levels, currents, simplex/half- or full-duplex

OSI Summary

The subject of open systems architecture is somewhat removed from the decision of the manager, except that it provides an underpinning for his/her decisions. Realizing that upgrade and interconnect are inevitable, managers must choose

Information Window   7–3
The OSI Model

Here's a top-down look at each of the model's seven layers (see Figure 7.4):

- **Layer 7,** the application layer, is the server application (not the part that resides on the PC). This is the part referred to when discussing application integration projects, such as portals.

- **Layer 6,** the presentation layer, has codes for how the data will look when they are received. Pictures on the Internet are generally in GIF or JPEG files, which are examples of the presentation layer.

- **Layer 5,** the session layer, establishes communications between applications at the presentation layer.

- **Layer 4,** the transport layer, controls more advanced flow control functions, such as error checking. This is

the layer at which Transmission Control Protocol/Internet Protocol (TCP/IP) operates. Often shortened to IP, this is the foundation of the Internet.

- **Layer 3,** the network layer, connects two or more networks. It tells data which direction or route to take to a specific device.

- **Layer 2,** the data link layer, is the hardware dedicated to local area networking (LAN), such as the Ethernet network interface cards in a PC or server. Each bit of hardware will have a specific address.

- **Layer 1,** the physical layer, contains the wires, wireless technologies, and electricity that literally connect the computers involved.

Source: *Knowledge Management.* February 2001, Vol.4, p.45.

FIGURE 7.4   The OSI Model

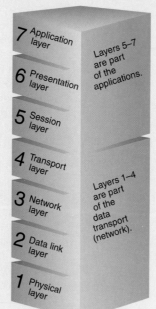

7 Application layer
6 Presentation layer
5 Session layer
Layers 5–7 are part of the applications.

4 Transport layer
3 Network layer
2 Data link layer
1 Physical layer
Layers 1–4 are part of the data transport (network).

equipment that will readily connect to that of other suppliers and that is designed for expansion and added features. Choosing a design that inhibits either of these attributes not only commits your organization to one vendor, it locks you into this one vendor's view of expansion and upgrade.

FIGURE 7.5 **Multiple-Layer Model Showing Translation of Communications**

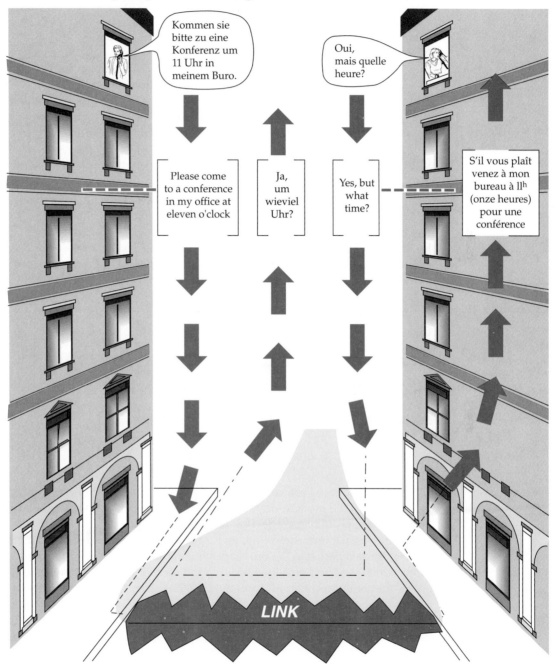

Figure 7.5 also gives an analogy of data moving down and up the seven layers. In this case, a telephone call with language translation is used. If the situation had involved data, the appropriate layers would have employed error detection and correction, security, encryption, compression, code/protocol conversion, communication channel continuity, and response in the event of a disruption.

TELECOMMUNICATIONS MANAGEMENT NETWORK (TMN)[7]

Definition

The telecommunications management network (TMN) provides a framework for achieving interconnectivity and communication across heterogeneous operating systems and telecommunications networks. TMN was developed by the International Telecommunications Union (ITU) as an infrastructure to support management and deployment of dynamic telecommunications services.

Overview

The telecommunications industry is seeing rapid and ongoing change. With emerging technologies, deregulation, and increased consumer demand, companies are presented with a wide range of opportunities and challenges. As companies unify their networks and systems, they must merge new technologies and legacy systems. This is no small task, as a company's networks may encompass analog and digital systems, multiple vendor equipment, different types of subnetworks, and varied management protocols.

Case 7-1

Transmission Control Protocol/Internet Protocol and Its Effect on the Internet

Jeannie Pridmore Sivel

ABSTRACT

Transmission Control Protocol/Internet Protocol (TCP/IP) is the communication protocol on which the modern-day Internet is built. It is a client/server-based protocol that is made up of layers. The TCP layer is responsible for packing the data in an acceptable format, error detection, and transmission. The IP layer is responsible for routing the data packet to the proper destination. TCP/IP is a robust communication protocol that was first developed for the Internet for military reasons. Today it not only is the communication protocol used on the Internet, but it is also the most used communication protocol package worldwide. The software is provided with all major operating systems. TCP/IP has helped the Internet grow. The software is so easy to use that most users do not even know that it is present and running.

INTRODUCTION TO TCP/IP

TCP/IP, Transmission Control Protocol/Internet Protocol, is a set of transmission protocols designed to allow cooperating computers to communicate and share resources. It was developed by researchers for ARPANET in the 1970s and

---

[7] http://www.iec.org/online/tutorials/tmn/

implemented in the 1980s. This protocol permits all computer types, regardless of hardware, to communicate and link together to build a network. It has become the basic communication protocol for the Internet.

TCP/IP is more appropriately a suite of protocols that includes TCP, IP, UDP (User Datagram Protocol), ICMP (Internet Control Message Protocol), and several others. TCP/IP is a client/server model based on the assumption that a large number of independent networks are connected together by the use of gateways. When transferring information, TCP/IP is only concerned that there is a corresponding TCP/IP suite at the other end of the connection.

TCP/IP, similar to other communication protocols, is comprised of layers. The TCP layer is responsible for delivery, error detection or lost data, and retransmission of the data until they are received and verified as complete and accurate. The IP layer routes data packets from node to node based on a byte destination address, the IP address. The current version, IPv4, has a 32-bit address size and operates on the network layer. ICMP operates at the same layer as IP. ICMP's purpose is to transmit information needed to control IP traffic.

TCP breaks a file into packets of manageable amounts of data. A header is placed in front of the packet and includes information such as the source port number, the destination port number, a sequence number, an acknowledgment number, and a checksum. TCP operates at the transport layer. UDP interacts with application programs at the same layer as TCP, but UDP does not have error correction or retransmission of corrupted or lost data packets.

Table 1 lists the four layers associated with the TCP/IP protocol suite and describes each.

The connections within the TCP/IP protocol suite are depicted in the figure below.

TABLE 1
TCP/IP Layers

TCP/IP Layer	Description
Application layer	Typically interaction with the network
Transport layer	Guarantee of data reliability
Network layer	Responsible for getting data to its destination
Physical layer	Communication with network hardware

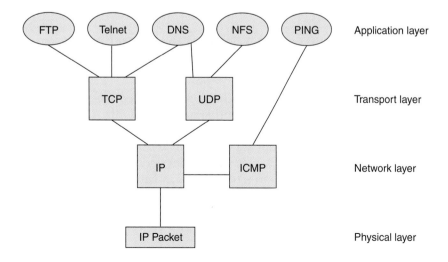

The TCP/IP protocol suite provides the lower levels needed to perform several functions:

1. File Transfer, FTP

2. Remote login and remote execution, Telnet

3. Computer mail

4. Hypertext Transfer Protocol, HTTP

EVOLUTION OF TCP/IP AND THE INTERNET

Even though TCP/IP and the Internet are two very different items, their histories are very much intertwined. In 1968, the U.S. Department of Defense funded an experiment to interconnect several different research networks that were designed by different vendors. In 1969, the Advanced Research Projects Agency network, ARPANET, was born. By 1973, it had connections throughout the United States and Europe.

The initial protocol was the Network Control Protocol, NCP. However, it did not take long to see that NCP had deficiencies and was unable to keep up with the growing network traffic. The military needed a more robust protocol. They needed a system that could recover from node or line failures. During battles, the destruction of a node or a communication line is normal. The military required a system that could maintain communications when a disaster strikes. In addition, a more robust communication protocol suite was needed to meet the needs of an open architecture network environment. This protocol suite became known as TCP and IP or simply, TCP/IP.

In 1983, the Department of Defense mandated the use of TCP/IP on all systems for all long-haul communications and split ARPANET into two systems: ARPANET and MILNET. ARPANET continued to be used for research; MILNET was used for military transactions. As these networks grew and others were added, the backbone of the Internet was developed, and the popularity of TCP/IP increased, so much so that by the time ARPANET was decommissioned in 1990, TCP/IP had succeeded in becoming the most used wide area network protocol worldwide.

THE INTERNET PHENOMENON

GROWTH

When ARPANET was founded in 1969, it consisted of four nodes. In 1983, when it was split, there were approximately 600 nodes. The introduction of the World Wide Web in 1994 took this growth pattern to a new level.

Currently, there are more than 200,000 interconnecting networks [4, p. 4]. It is estimated that a new network connection is made about every half hour, and that the Internet doubles in size every 10 months. The latest domain survey performed by Network Wizard counted 109,574,429 IP addresses that have been assigned a name. The figure below displays the exponential growth curve of Internet host users.

It is easy to see that the Internet, a global network of networks, has captured the world's imagination.

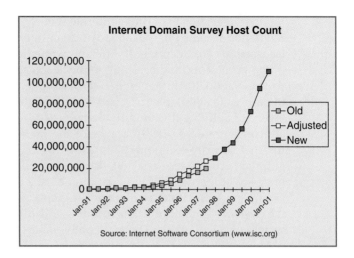

There are only a few basic tools that are needed to connect to the Internet. For example, a computer with a network interface card can connect directly to a local area network and thus the Internet. Now, in the Internet environment, software is given away free to help create interest. Every major computer operating system provides TCP/IP. If the computer does not have the program loaded, when direct access to the Internet is established, a copy of the TCP/IP program is provided to the node. This allows connecting and communicating on the Internet to be quick and easy.

TRIBULATIONS

The growth of the Internet has been very beneficial to most of the world's population. However, there are those who want to corrupt the Internet and its users. Society mostly thinks of these people as teenage boys locked away in their parents' basement who never see the light of day. In reality, these virus-creating hackers achieve billions of dollars in damage. In 1988, there were six security incidents. In 2000, there were 21,756 security incidents.

The Internet was designed to be an open network, and TCP/IP was designed to be the protocol for this friendly network environment. Security issues were only given a small amount of attention. As a result, several security concerns regarding TCP/IP have surfaced.

TCP/IP protocol lacks the ability to provide authentication, integrity, and privacy mechanisms to secure communications, a necessity for the world today. This is being addressed in many ways. In order to bolster security and privacy, many Internet users are adding firewalls to their current systems. Other users are placing additional secure protocol software on top of the TCP/IP program, such as Kerberos. Although this issue of security has received a lot of negative attention in the past couple of years, a formal approach to TCP/IP security is still missing. Further, no direction for providing authentication and integrity has been proposed.

FUTURE OF THE INTERNET AND TCP/IP

The Internet is growing at an amazing rate. As of July 2001, there were 31,299,592 Web servers, and TCP/IP will continue as the Internet standard protocol. However, security issues need to be addressed.

One suggestion to improve Internet security is to implement a Caller ID system. Every node on the Internet already has an Internet ID. With this type of system, all transactions are traceable. If a person wants to stay anonymous, then your computer's protocol could be set up to block access to them.

The National Institute of Standards and Technology is concerned with providing authentication, integrity, and confidentiality security services at the network layer, for both the IPv4 and IPv6, the next generation IP protocol. Current efforts are concentrated on IPv4 because of the high level of interest to rapidly handle Internet security technology issues. IPv6 security protocol will provide cryptographic security services that flexibly support combinations of authentication, integrity, access control, and confidentiality.

Implementing IPv6, a 128-bit address size, security protocol requires modifying the system's communication routines and a new system process that conducts secret key negotiations. The main deliverables of IPv6 are as follows:

1. Authentication.

2. Integrity.

3. Confidentiality.

4. Security Association Negotiation and Management.

The increase in the address size from 32 bits to 128 bits supports more levels of addressing hierarchy, allows for a greater number of addressable nodes, and provides simpler auto-configuration of addresses. IPv6 also introduces scalability of multicast addresses. Other changes include more efficient forwarding, less strenuous restrictions on option lengths, and more flexibility for introducing new options in the future.

SUMMARY AND CONCLUSIONS

TCP/IP has had a tremendous impact on the Internet. It is the basis for which all Internet communications take place. Its ease of use has helped to increase Internet clients. The drawback of this protocol includes security issues. At the time when TCP/IP was developed, the Internet was a friendly open network. The times have changed, and TCP/IP protocol will have to change with it.

In the future, TCP/IP will change with respect to security. It could end up as a read-only device. Nonetheless, TCP/IP protocol suite will adapt to meet today's need for higher security, and it will continue to be the communication protocol for the Internet.

REFERENCES

1. Carr, H. H., and C. A. Snyder. *Management of Telecommunications*. Burr Ridge, IL: Irwin/McGraw-Hill, 1997.

2. Cringely, R. X. *The Death of TCP/IP—Why the Age of Internet Innocence Is Over*. August 2, 2001. http://www.pbs.org/cringely/pulpit/pulpit20010802.html.

3. Internet Society. *A Brief History of the Internet*. August 4, 2000. http://www.isoc.org/internet/history/brief.shtml.

4. Kessler, G. C. *An Overview of TCP/IP Protocols and The Internet*. April 23, 1999. http://www.garykessler.net/library/tcpip.html.

5. Newton, S. E. *Introduction to the Internet Protocols*. January 20, 1994. Computer Science Facilities Group. Rutgers, The State University of New Jersey.

6. Protocols.com. *TCP/IP Suite*. December 2001.

7. Vigna, G. *Network Security Research*. http://www.cs.ucsb.edu/~vigna/listpub.html.

8. Wierzbicki, J. *The Internet, A Summary Introduction to TCP/IP, and Losing Underwear*. 2001. http://www.gamedev.net/reference/articles/article711.asp.

9. Yale University. *Introduction TCP/IP*. February 1995. http://www.yale.edu/pclt/COMM/TCPIP.HTM.

10. Zakon, R. H. *Hobbes' Internet Timeline v5.4* 2001. http://www.zakon.org/robert/internet/timeline/.

Case 7-2

TCP/IP Technical Overview

Steve Guendert

Transmitting data across computer networks is a complex process. The standard model for open systems networks is the Open Systems Interconnection (OSI) model. In the OSI model, network functionality is broken down into modules called layers. This simplifies and separates the tasks associated with data transmission. TCP/IP follows the OSI model very closely. Each layer is composed of code that performs a small, well-defined set of tasks. A protocol suite/protocol stack is a set of several such layers. It is usually a part of the operating system on machines connected to the network. In the remainder of this paper I will discuss protocol stacks in general, and then go into more specifics on the TCP/IP protocol stack. I will assume familiarity with the OSI model.

The TCP/IP protocol suite is named for two of its most important protocols: Transmission Control Protocol (TCP) and Internet Protocol (IP). It is the basic communication language or protocol of the Internet. The main design goal of TCP/IP was to build an interconnection of networks, also referred to as an internetwork or Internet, that provided universal communication services over heterogeneous physical networks. Basically, TCP/IP is a set of two communication protocols that an application can use to package its information for sending across a private network or the public Internet. TCP/IP is a two-layer program. The higher layer, Transmission Control Protocol, manages the assembling of a message or file into smaller packets that are transmitted over the Internet and received by a TCP layer at the receiving end that reassembles the packets into the original message. The lower layer, Internet Protocol, handles the address part of each packet so that it gets to the right destination. Each gateway computer on the network checks this address to see where to forward the message. Even though some packets from the same message are routed differently than others, they'll be reassembled at the destination.

PROTOCOL STACKS

A protocol stack is organized so that the highest level of abstraction resides at the top layer. For example, the highest layer may deal with streaming audio and/or video frames, while the lowest layer deals with raw voltages and/or radio signals. Every layer in a stack builds upon the services provided by the layer immediately adjacent to it.

Two terms are often confused: protocol and service. A protocol defines the exchange that takes place between the identical layers of two hosts. For example, in the TCP/IP stack, the transport layer of one host talks to the transport layer of another host using the TCP/IP protocol. On the other hand, a service is a set of functions that a layer delivers to the layer above it. For example, the TCP/IP layer provides a reliable byte-stream service to the application layer adjacent to it.

As a packet descends the model, each layer of the protocol stack adds a header containing layer-specific information to the data packet. A header for the network layer might include information such as source and destination addresses. The process of appending headers to the data is called encapsulation. During the process of de-encapsulation the reverse process occurs: the layers of the receiving stack extract layer-specific information as the packet progresses up the stack and process the encapsulated data accordingly. The process of encapsulation and de-encapsulation increases the overhead involved in transmitting data.

THE TCP/IP PROTOCOL STACK

The TCP/IP protocol stack comprises only four layers (the OSI reference model is seven layers). These four layers are the data link and physical layer, the network layer, the transport layer, and the application layer. I will discuss each layer in turn.

DATA LINK AND PHYSICAL LAYER

At the bottom of the OSI model are the data link and the physical layers, which consist of a network interface card and a device driver. The physical layer deals with voltages. The data link layer provides services such as framing, error detection, error correction, and flow control. Together they are responsible for getting raw bits across a physical link.

One important aspect of the Internet Protocol is that it has no restrictions about the physical medium over which it runs. This characteristic provides the TCP/IP protocol its adaptability and flexibility. For example, LAN technologies such as Ethernet, token ring, and FDDI all operate at the data link subnet layer. So do wide area networks such as ATM, X.25, and Switched Multimegabit Data Services

TCP/IP Model

TCP/IP Level	Description
Data link and physical layer	Physical layer: voltage
	Data link: framing, error detection and correction, flow control
Network layer	Routes packets to destination; moves data between hosts
Transport layer	Enables host-to-host communication
Application layer	End user interaction; formats data so they can be understood

(SMDS). Routers can interconnect all these different media technologies and the Internet Protocol can communicate over all of these lower-level subnetworks. Each of the subnetworks has its own internal addressing and framing formats. To accommodate these the subnetworks encapsulate IP packets with headers and trailer information according to the specific subnet protocol. This enables IP packets to be transmitted over just about any type of network media today.

NETWORK LAYER (INTERNET PROTOCOL)

The network layer protocol below the transport layer and above the physical and data link layer is known as the Internet Protocol (IP). It is the common thread running through the Internet and most LAN technologies including Ethernet. It is responsible for moving data from one host to another, using a variety of routing algorithms. Layers above the network layer break a data stream into chunks of a predetermined size known as packets or datagrams. The datagrams are then sequentially passed to the IP network layer.

The job of the IP layer is to route these packets to the target destination. IP packets consist of an IP header, together with the higher level TCP protocol and the application datagram. IP knows nothing about the TCP and datagram contents. Prior to transmitting data, the network layer might further subdivide it into smaller packets for ease of transmission. When all the pieces reach the destination, the network layer reassembles them into the original datagram.

The IP is the standard that defines the manner in which the network layers of the two hosts interact. These hosts may be on the same network, or reside on physically remote heterogeneous networks. IP was designed with internetworking in mind. It provides a connectionless, best-effort packet delivery service. It is called connectionless because it is like the postal service, rather than the telephone system. IP packets, like telegrams or mail, are treated independently. Each packet is stamped with the address of the sender and receiver. Routing decisions are made on a packet-by-packet basis. On the other hand, connection-oriented, circuit-switched telephone systems explicitly establish a connection between two users before any conversation takes place. They also maintain the connection for the entire duration of the conversation.

A best-effort delivery service means that packets might be discarded during transmission, but not without a good reason. Erratic packet delivery is normally caused by the exhaustion of resources, or a failure at the data link or physical layer. In a highly reliable physical system such as an Ethernet LAN, the best-effort approach of IP is sufficient for transmission of large volumes of information. However, in geographically distributed networks, especially the Internet, IP delivery is insufficient. It needs to be augmented by the higher-level TCP protocol to provide satisfactory service.

All IP packets or datagrams consist of a header section and a data section (the payload). The data section may be traditional computer data, or it may be digitized voice or video traffic. Using the postal service analogy again, the "header" of the IP packet can be compared with the envelope and the data section with the letter inside it. Just as the envelope holds the address and information necessary to direct the letter to the desired destination, the header helps in the routing of IP packets. The payload has a maximum size of 65,536 bytes per packet. It contains error detection and/or error control protocols like the Internet Control Message

Protocol (ICMP). To illustrate the idea of control protocols, let's use the postal service again. Suppose that the postal service fails to find the destination of your letter. It would be necessary to send you a message indicating that the recipient's address was incorrect. This message would reach you through the same postal system that tried to deliver your letter. ICMP works the same way. It packs control and error messages inside IP packets.

An IP packet contains a source and a destination address. The source address designates the originating node's interface to the network and the destination address specifies the interface for an intended recipient or multiple recipients (for broadcasting). Every host and router on the wider network has an address that uniquely identifies it. It also denotes the subnetwork on which it resides. No two machines can have the same IP address. To avoid addressing conflicts, the network numbers are assigned by an independent body. The network part of the address is common for all machines on a local network. It is similar to a postal code or zip code that is used by a post office to route letters to a general area. The rest of the address on the letter is relevant only within that area. It is used only to deliver the letter to its final destination. The host part of the IP address performs a similar function and can further be split into a subnetwork address and a host address.

The IP packet header also includes a Time to Live (TTL) parameter that is used to limit the life of the packet on the network. Imagine a situation in which an IP packet gets caught in the system and becomes undeliverable. It would then consume the resources indefinitely. The entire network could be brought to a halt by a blizzard of such reproducing but undeliverable packets. The TTL field maintains a counter that is decremented each time the packet arrives at a routing step. If the counter reaches zero, the packet is discarded.

TRANSPORT LAYER (TCP)

Two commonly used protocols operate in the transport layer: Transmission Control Protocol (TCP) and User Datagram Protocol (UDP), which provides more basic services. For the purposes of this paper we will assume the use of TCP.

The application data have no meaning to the transport layer. On the source node, the transport layer receives data from the application layer and splits them into chunks. The chunks are then passed to the network layer. At the destination node, the transport layer receives these data packets and reassembles them before passing them to the appropriate process or application.

The transport layer is the first end-to-end layer of the TCP/IP stack. This means that the transport layer of the source host can communicate directly with its peer on the destination host, without concern about how data are moved between them. These matters are handled by the network layer. The layers below the transport layer understand and carry information required for moving data across links and subnetworks.

In contrast, at the transport layer or above, one node can specify details that are only relevant to its peer layer on another node. For example, it is the job of the transport layer to identify the exact application to which data are to be handed over at the remote end. This detail is irrelevant for any intermediate router, but it is essential information for the transport layers at both ends.

APPLICATION LAYER

The application layer is the layer with which end users normally interact. This layer is responsible for formatting the data so that its peers can understand them. While the lower three layers are usually implemented as part of the OS, the application layer is a user process. The users do not see the data at this point. For example, email is the application layer, but it takes the client interface to show the email to the users. The interface is not a part of this application layer. Some application-level protocols that are included in most TCP/IP implementations include

- Telnet for remote login.

- FTP for file transfer.

- SMTP for mail transfer.

That, in a nutshell, is a brief overview of TCP/IP. For additional, more detailed information, please consult the sources used in this paper.

BIBLIOGRAPHY

1. Farley, Marc. *Building Storage Networks,* 2nd ed. Osborne/McGraw Hill, 2001, Berkeley, CA, pp. 387–423.

2. Lammle, Todd. *CCNA Study Guide.* Sybex, 2000, Alameda, CA, pp. 4–29.

3. Odom, Wendell. *Cisco CCNA Certification Guide.* Cisco Press, 2000, Indianapolis, IN, pp. 68–128.

4. Rodriquez, Adolpho, et al. *TCP/IP Tutorial and Technical Overview.* IBM Redbooks, IBM Corporation, International Technology Support Organization, Research Triangle Park, NC, August 2001, pp. 3–33.

Summary

Architectural models serve useful purposes. They provide a building-block approach to interconnectivity and interoperability. The models illustrate the various layers that must relate to one another in a data network and support standards that vendors should abide by. If layer boundaries match the model, one can make a change within a layer without impacting the other layers. Therefore, modification of the network or equipment enhancements are made easier.

In order to understand, design, and make interoperable complex systems, logical models are useful. For example, the original telecommunications model was seen as having three levels: physical, functional management, and applications. Future models contain the same functions but generally are separated into more levels to give greater detail.

ARPA created the first network system, which became the four-level TCP/IP model, as they developed what has become the Internet. IBM followed this with their seven-level Systems Network Architecture (SNA) model, which became the de facto model for many years.

The standards organizations wished to created a formal, vendor-independent model (e.g., open systems architecture). The seven-layer model was developed following the SNA model but separate from it. This was done in support of open systems for interoperability.

Key Terms

application layer, *250, 255*
architecture, *245, 251*
computer integrated
   manufacturing
   (CIM), *242*
data link layer, *253*
electronic data
   interchange (EDI), *244*
International Standards
   Organization (ISO), *251*

interoperability, *251*
ISO-OSI model, *252*
layers, *245*
link layer, *249*
network layer, *249, 253*
open architecture, *245*
open system
   interconnection (OSI)
   model, *251*

photonic connection, *252*
physical layer, *252*
presentation layer, *255*
Quick Response, *244*
session layer, *254*
Transmission Control
   Protocol/Internet
   Protocol (TCP/IP), *246*
transport layer, *250, 254*

Recommended Readings

Network Magazine
Computerworld

Discussion Questions

7.1. What are the implications for JL&S (or any business) of acquiring a facility in a different time zone?

7.2. What are the implications of buying non-interoperatable (proprietary) equipment?

7.3. What network architectures can be used in a LAN?

7.4. How is the OSI seven-layer model different from IBM's SNA model?

7.5. What is TCP/IP? What does TCP do? What does IP do?

7.6. At what level does the hub operate?

7.7. Which is the most important of the seven OSI layers?

Projects

7.1. Determine the architecture used in your school or organizational LAN.

7.2. Interview telecommunications managers and determine their beliefs as to the OSI layered model.

7.3. Call IBM and ask them if they are moving from their SNA model to the OSI model.

Chapter Eight

LANs, WANs, Enterprise Networks, and Network Equipment

CONTINUING CASE—PART 8

Carlton Has a Visitor

Carlton was pleasantly surprised to receive a call from an old friend and classmate from Georgia Tech, Fred Dye. He and Carlton discussed their varying paths since graduation and the direction of the businesses under JEI's umbrella. Fred was interested in working with the JEI organization and explained that he was in the business of setting up local area networks (LANs). He said that he was en route to Denver for a conference and would like to visit with Carlton and assess his needs for networks in the business. Carlton agreed that it would be a good opportunity for both to get reacquainted and for him to gain an insight about networks and their possibilities.

Fred arrived in Denver on the Red Eye Special, but allocated extra time to meet with Carlton. They spent the next afternoon together and reviewed the use of microcomputers by JL&S and JEI. Though Carlton had not begun to use a microcomputer personally, he had become used to seeing them in the offices of his colleagues. Neither of the classmates had worked with these machines in college, and Carlton had not had the time to become familiar with them since graduation. He did notice there were several makes and models around the office. Carlton reflected on the way microcomputers just seemed to appear. There had been no company initiative to introduce them—some enthusiastic employees had brought them in to do special tasks.

Bill used a word processor on his Tandy® computer to write his letters and Alli had brought her IBM/AT with her from college, spreadsheet included. She was the greatest proponent of the machine, always using it to make financial and marketing comparisons. It had been quite a task for her to convince Michael to allocate the funds to replace her personal machine with a JEI-purchased computer, but an effort well worth the energy. It allowed her to take her older AT home, where, to her surprise, it just seemed to collect dust. Carlton's father read a lot about PCs but never ventured out of the minicomputer arena. He seemed to relegate them to the "toy" category. He mentioned the IBM PC to Nowell once, but Nowell said they did not have the power and capacity he required. He did authorize the purchase of an Apple® IIe for the guards in Colorado Springs for better patrol scheduling and even got Matilda an IBM/XT for data entry. It contained a modem to attach to the JEI minicomputer and a printer for higher quality reporting than the DECWriter allowed. Another feature of the IBM PC that proved valuable to Matilda was that she could create files of data off-line, check them for accuracy, and then upload them instead of working with the minicomputer online. She moved to this mode, even though there was no connect charge to the JEI-owned computer, to give her greater control over the data entry process.

Carlton showed Fred a layout of the various JEI locations and the offices of those using microcomputers. Fred asked questions about the different lines of business and how the computer fit in each. Fred's view was that Carlton could gain substantial benefits by connecting the computers, that is, by installing networks. Carlton, however, wanted to know more about them and learn how to decide what sort of LAN to obtain, assuming he became convinced of their value. He first had to reconcile himself to all the microcomputers that he hadn't authorized in the first place.

After Carlton and Fred finished a fine dinner at Chez Henri, they continued their discussions of the need for LANs in Carlton's study. Carlton was interested in the potential of microcomputers in a networked environment. Fred believed microcomputers were going to be increasingly important for business, but their potential would be severely hampered unless they were connected to each other or to the firm's larger computers. Fred was very enthusiastic about LANs in general and the suitability for them in JEI's locations.

Fred explained he had supervised the installation of many different LANs in various production, service, and experimental settings. He said there was no "right" LAN solution for every environment, but that in certain situations, some solutions might be more right than others. Fred thought the nature of the work being done on microcomputers had to be evaluated as did the degree of skill the users had.

The overriding reason for implementing a LAN was a clearly recognized need to expand the computer environment beyond the stand-alone, desktop units that were presently deployed. Fred also pointed out that implementation of local area networking would not be readily accepted by many employees unless they believed it would meet a clearly recognized need. Of course, he added, there were always some real "computer jocks" who would welcome any new technology for its own sake rather than the work it was to facilitate! Most workers, though, needed to see personal benefits from using a LAN. Fred was sure that there was a direct relationship between ease of use of the networking features and willingness to expend efforts to use the network.

"But, Fred," interrupted Carlton, "didn't you say you are supposed to make the actual presence of a LAN transparent to the users? If they know they have greater capabilities but don't know where they reside, why would they balk at the new technology?"

"You are right," Fred responded quickly, "but still there may be much apprehension by the less skilled employees if you don't grease the skids. You know, let them know why you are giving them this new technology and how it will benefit them. Tying the connectivity of a network to actual tasks they do will get them to warm to the change very quickly."

Carlton and Fred discussed how to analyze the work and work group interdependencies that would suggest the usefulness of a network. They wanted to ensure that LAN deployment would increase productivity and quality before installation at any site. Carlton thought electronic mail and file sharing would be most needed. Specifically, he saw a need to be able to communicate between the various offices, especially Denver and the other Front Range offices.

"LANs tend to not stretch that far, from Denver to Colorado Springs," Fred told Carlton. "However, what we will be considering as we talk is putting LANs in Denver and Colorado Springs and connecting them with a communications line so that each group thinks the other group is right next door. We will create the same extension to Kansas City." (See Figure 8.1.)

In addition, Fred suggested that the sharing of expensive peripherals and automatic *backup* of data files would be important advantages of a LAN. Fred's comments about automatic backup of files struck a chord with Carlton as only last Tuesday Alli had lost a large file she had labored over for an entire morning. A telephone call had interrupted her thought process, and she had inadvertently responded to the "save" prompt with a "no."

Fred said there was a simple way to connect PCs that were close together, and several small offices used it. It was a low-cost alternative he referred to as a simple peripheral sharing or **serial port** net. Serial port LANs also were referred to as **zero slot** LANs. However, Fred told Carlton that, although they were very low priced, they had far less utility than traditional LANs. To further complicate the discussion, Fred pointed out that traditional LANs came in a variety of options. They were differentiated based on physical and logical layout, standards for moving data, server philosophies, cabling systems, speed, throughput capacities, standard adherence, operating systems, ability to connect heterogeneous computers, and, of course, price.

Fred had Carlton on the ropes now! The variety of options meant the LAN decision would be more complex than he had imagined. Carlton suggested the two of them discuss the options further so he would be able to understand the business.

FIGURE 8.1 **JEI's Network**

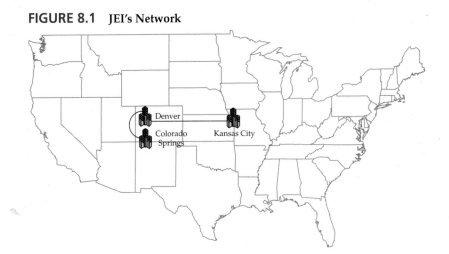

But Fred Was Not Finished, Yet!

Carlton had read about connecting microcomputers in the office and realized he knew very little about the underlying technology. That was alright at this point, as he was mainly trying to understand the business reasoning for connectivity. Fred had mentioned cost savings by sharing peripherals through connectivity. He had mentioned a **network server,** which he said is usually just another microcomputer dedicated to the function of providing service to all nodes (microcomputers and devices) on the network. The most common service is **file serving.** This means that each microcomputer on the LAN is assigned specific space or shares common space on the server's hard disk. Therefore, most **servers** would have very large disk capacity. As Fred had already pointed out to Carlton, the backup function could be carried out by the server. The **backup** function is usually done on a special tape unit that can provide off-hours backup of user files from either their or the server's hard drive.

File servers play an important role in electronic mail **(email).** They provide email storage and forwarding and routing to other networks. In addition, servers provide users transparent connection of LAN microcomputers to remote host computers as well as storing and sending users, print jobs to shared printers. Fred said this feature could be an important economic factor since stand-alone microcomputers had to have their own printers. Sharing of printers and any other peripherals could decrease even a small company's costs.

Carlton thought back to the first purchase of microcomputers by JL&S to track asset inventory such as radios, patrol vehicles, security, equipment, and so forth. In the JL&S case, Ed Walton set up the system, but as other security personnel found the application useful, they saw a need to procure other microcomputers and to try other applications. Insofar as they wished to use the same software, there was a need to purchase redundant copies. The LAN user could legally share copies of software with other users provided they purchased network versions of the software. Carlton saw this feature might reduce costs further. It could also end the controversy over which microcomputer database application to support by establishing a company standard that all locations would use. Carlton mused about the future—he imagined that JEI would have 100 microcomputers and all users wanted to run a specific software package, so he would have to purchase 100 individual programs to satisfy legal requirements. The total cost for a single application could approach $50,000 for a major product!

More information about LANs meant that Carlton needed some sort of checklist to help him make the decision that would best serve the business now and suit its future. There seemed to be several basic questions to ask and answer before deciding to purchase such an important segment of JEI's total information structure. He pulled out his notepad and started to list some of the more important questions.

1. Will the company's microcomputer applications be better in a network than stand-alone?

2. What kind of user training is needed? Is it going to take a significant amount of time and money to do the training?

3. Do we (JEI) need email?

4. What kind of resources will we have to devote to the procurement, installation, and maintenance of a network?

5. What network operating system do we need? How do we know this?

6. What sort of network interface card is appropriate?

7. What are the cabling choices? Is wireless "cabling" an option?

8. What is the likely rate of user demand now, and how is it expected to grow each year?

9. Should there be centralized control or distributed control?

10. What topology and protocol are best for use? How do I know this?

11. What characteristics differentiate vendors in terms of flexibility, maintenance, training, reliability, and so forth?

Carlton decided that his list was a good start and that now he needed to discuss each point with Fred. Some of the questions were about business, some were about the technology, and all had to do with getting the correct and cost-effective solution. He noticed in the latest issue of the computer magazine he received that there were a number of microcomputer networks readily available from mail order catalogs. Without answers to the above questions, he might as well throw a dart at an advertisement in the magazine as try to make a decision in any other way.

JL&S Finds Another Opportunity

"Carlton, who is Radio Mansion?" asked Michael as the two fished at the lake.

"Beats me, Dad. Why do you ask?"

"I was looking over a list of SII's customers yesterday, and Radio Mansion was near the top. I thought Gary might have mentioned it to you, that's all."

Radio Mansion was a retail electronics shop specializing in selling do-if-yourself electronics, especially piece parts to the home market. Realizing that competition was very intense for home music and video components, Radio Mansion quickly moved to components such as switches, wiring, and circuit protection. With time, their clientele began to ask for components for home security. Radio Mansion had since established a complete line of piece parts such as alarm sounders, wiring, switches, and intrusion and motion sensors. Ed Moto, the owner of Radio Mansion, had purchased a small desktop computer and installed an inventory management program. He used that program, from the keyboard and screen, as his point-of-sale interface. That way, he captured customer information as well as sales data, even though he had to enter it all through the keyboard. The computer support made ordering parts easier.

Ed spent time each Friday evening after the store closed creating purchase orders to SII and other vendors. He would use his inventory management system to print out the POs and place them in the mail. He generally tried to order at the discount break points, to reduce his cost per unit. Therefore he would receive case-lots of many parts and had developed the need for a small warehouse, even though many of these parts were slow movers.

Michael and Carlton met after lunch one day with Ed, after Michael noticed Radio Mansion's increasing orders to SII. After a short discussion of Ed's success and the amount of work it took to order and store his inventory, Michael and Carlton believed there was a great opportunity for Ed to reduce his manual data entry methods.

"Sounds like it's time for you to invest in **bar code** on your parts and a **wand** to read it at your counter," commented Carlton. The use of bar codes and wands or other types of readers at the point of sale is a popular sort of **online data input.**

"Yes," added Michael, "that will make his time use more efficient. Bar-code technology eliminates the requirement to key data by either data entry personnel or end-users. The wand reader is a specialized laser reader that can read the data from the bar code and send it directly to the computer for processing. But it seems to me that an even greater need is a way to replenish parts. Also, I'll bet you can save more by reducing your need for a warehouse."

"Yes," said Michael, "just-in-time as an inventory policy is where we are headed, but it is the total system that will make it all work. It seems to me, Ed, that you need three components. The first two involve using bar-code marking on your parts and a bar-code (wand) reader at your cash register. This becomes a **POS (point-of-sale)** system, capturing data quickly and easily. The third component of the total system is to pass this information on a frequent basis to any vendor who will supply in small quantities."

"Pardon my interruption, Dad," said Carlton, "there's a fourth component. Ed needs to employ the security services of JL&S both in the warehouse we will be dismantling and in his retail store. This will protect against future break-in as well as fire."

"Good point, Son. Make sure we help Ed with this protection. Meanwhile, it seems he needs to adopt a long-term strategy of electronic ordering of inventory."

"How do we do that?" asked Ed.

"Let's get Sarah Brown in here to help out on this," interrupted Carlton. "She is a recent graduate of the Masters of Science in Management program at California Polytechnic University, and we have just convinced her to join us at Kansas City. She is waiting for me in the outer office."

"I had worried for a long time about the cost of my warehouse, the insurance, and I even had a break-in recently," lamented Ed. "But how can I get rid of my inventory and still have the parts on the shelf, if I don't have inventory in the warehouse? And if I don't order in large quantities the cost will go up!"

"Just-in-time!" chimed in Carlton.

After introductions, Sarah began to explain, "The basic technology for communicating electronically with vendors is called *electronic data interchange* or *EDI.* First, you make contractual arrangements with your largest vendors, JL&S being the first, to place all of your orders electronically. Meanwhile, I will help you install EDI management software that takes inventory data from your computer and places it into a standard (EDI) data format. You transmit these data to us electronically once a week. We, as should the other suppliers, will agree to send you the parts by second-day air courier to guarantee shipment within 72 hours of receipt of your EDI request."

"But won't this cost a lot of money for shipping?"

"Doesn't your warehouse cost a lot of money for storage?" asked Michael. "Think in terms of incremental costs, and I believe you can see a net gain."

"OK, but won't I still need storage space?" asked Ed.

"Let's look at your store and see if we can't store all you need on the shelves," replied Michael. "I'll bet you have inventory in the warehouse only because of the discount rate, the seeming need to order large quantities, and the unpredictability of the suppliers. With the rapid data transfer of EDI and a good relationship with suppliers, you can be guaranteed when the goods will arrive."

"The point-of-sale system will allow you to be constantly aware of your inventory status," commented Sarah, "and then you will be able to see which items are moving fast."

"What will I need for POS and EDI to work?"

"For POS," Sarah cautiously commented, "you need only a wand reader at the register or computer, or POS terminal, and software in the computer that interprets the bar code. This is, of course, in addition to the actual coding stickers on the products. You will create these stickers on your printer from new software in the computer. For EDI, you need EDI management software for data manipulation, a modem to connect to the telephone network, and a **value added network (VAN)** for storing the data from your computer on its way to the computers of the various vendors."

"Then, after I deplete my existing inventory, I will order every week and receive the small orders on the following Wednesday?"

"Yes. In fact, you can order any day you wish, or you can have your inventory management system set to order at a specified reorder point, which should be just soon enough to replenish inventory before it is totally sold. This way, you set your inventory management system to automatically create the purchase orders, use the modem to make the call to the VAN, and store the EDI format data. Later, the suppliers will dial into the VAN and receive their data, updating their manufacturing control systems to ship the parts via second day carrier to arrive at your store within seventy-two hours."

"It seems too easy," replied Ed.

"It is easy and simple, once the total system is set up. This system is called **just-in-time (JIT)** inventory and is predicated on relationships and the technology of EDI. Make it all work and it works well. It takes an investment, but the investment pays off when there is a much higher probability of having the goods that the customers want to purchase. This higher level of sales is the greatest payoff. The reduced cost of inventory is an added benefit."

"I do have customers come to the store and not find what they want. Do you think this will give me more items in stock more of the time?"

"Definitely, Ed! Even the larger retail stores find that capturing the data by a POS system and sending them to the vendors for automatic replenishment helps produce higher levels of sales because they have what the customers want when they want it."

"Carlton," said Michael, as he picked up another handful of chips, "let's see just how many of our components and piece parts Radio Mansion might use and try them as our entry into supplying the retail market. While our Kansas City facility has concentrated on selling major components through SII and our original Front Range offices, it looks like we can find a ready outlet for some of the parts that we put into our larger assemblies, in addition to such components as motion, heat, and water sensors."

"Sounds great, Dad! We can increase our output of parts from Kansas City with little additional cost. It will mainly be a case of management and communications. If we can receive the orders electronically, we can update our MRP system in Kansas City, then have a smooth flow of orders to the lines. From this we can EDI our needs to our major suppliers."

"It sounds like I have introduced you to a way of increasing your production and sales without much human intervention," Michael told Carlton. "If you can get the electronic movement of data and update your manufacturing control programs, you can receive far greater efficiency in manufacturing and greater sales with little additional expense."

"As a point of reference," added Sarah, "the apparel and textile industry uses EDI and bar-code marking for an automatic replenishment system called **Quick Response.** This system uses standard telecommunications capabilities and computer processing of inventory to ensure that materials flow up the channel so stores will have the required items in stock. It has greatly enhanced their on-hand status."

Carlton and Sarah returned to Kansas City. They discussed the Radio Mansion task and the overall project of implementing EDI in JEI. Specifically, Sarah's task was to support Scott in JL&S's EDI efforts to an even greater extent. Scott, in continuing to develop the telecommunications architecture for JEI, would get SII involved and provide the connectivity and bandwidth to begin an outreach program to retail outlets. This new venture, according to

JEI's CEO, tied into their present lines of business and supported all their enterprises. The young engineer saw this as a wonderful opportunity because he could see how EDI could tie the parts of the system together and how EDI could be a major star in his future.

Carlton made a mental note to meet with Scott about the specific bandwidth and VAN requirements for any EDI venture they started. There were the considerations of the cost–benefit analysis as to direct connections, VAN store-and-forward, and use of broadband versus POTS connections. He knew he could start small as soon as the EDI requirements were finalized, but he could also see that this was a technology that could have direct benefits in dealing with suppliers and customers alike.

Information Window   8–1

Just-in-Time (JIT)—In a broad sense, an approach to achieving excellence in a manufacturing company based on the continuing elimination of waste (waste being considered as those things that do not add value to the product). In the narrow sense, just-in-time refers to the movement of material at the necessary place at the necessary time. The implication is that each operation is

closely synchronized with the subsequent ones to make that possible.

Source: Donald W. Fogarty, John H. Blackstone, and T. R. Hoffmann, *Production & Inventory Management* (Cincinnati, OH: South-Western Publishing Co., 1991), p. 826.

Technology Note   8–1

POS technology is most often associated with bar code. One of the early bar-code success stories was in the grocery industry with its adoption of the Universal Product Code (UPC) as the standard. The key to profits in the grocery industry is managing inventory, and the scanning of bar codes helped inventory management like nothing else ever had. Other retail industries, such as retail apparel, rapidly adopted bar code because of its great value in inventory management. Today, POS technologies are increasingly employed to co-opt customers into

assuming some of the sales transaction workload and allow internal redeployment of employees. More complex financial services are being added, and in the fast-food industry, new technologies are being employed. Some retail establishments are experimenting with self-service scanning technologies that may make the present concept of POS disappear. The capture and use of information have had a tremendous impact on operations and customer service.

INTRODUCTION

This chapter discusses local connectivity and extends to the ultimate wide area network, the Internet. The point of local connectivity is that the users are generally homogeneous in that they have similar needs. This is not the case for widely dispersed connectivity. The farther the users are from each other, the more their differences and certainly the differences in protocols and what is transported.

NETWORKS BY RELATIVE SIZE AND USE

Networks at the internal layer, whether analog or digital, connect the organization and give it a cohesive quality.

Topology has nothing to do with geographical coverage of the network. Topology, as previously discussed, is simply the physical connectivity pattern, for example, the arrangement of nodes and their connection to other nodes. We have become accustomed to referring to the networks by labels that reflect their relative size and, to some extent, their use. Thus, we have local area networks, or LANs, that frequently link work groups composed of relatively homogeneous users and wide area networks that connect the world. Figure 8.2 illustrates several levels or layers of data connectivity. We will use this reference of layers to show coverage and usage.

At the heart of the layers of connectivity is the machine that connects to other machines. Inside of the computer is its own high-speed network, the internal communications bus of the machine. Since it is the lowest or smallest geographic coverage network, we seldom consider it a network, but it does meet all of the criteria of a network. Outside of the computer, we consider several levels of organization **connectivity,** of organization usage of the network. In one sense, the titling and layering are artificial. We use the terms to give us a human reference.

The lowest level of connectivity is called the *internal layer* of the organization in Figure 8.2. Here we are concerned with limited distances and cohesive groups of people and machines. In the digital domain, as we will explain in the following pages, is the local area network. In the analog domain, an example of this internal,

FIGURE 8.2
The Onion Model of Network Connectivity

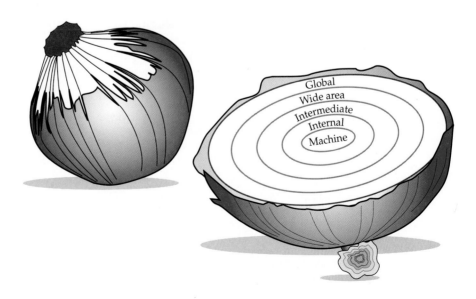

local area network
A group of machines connected in a relatively small area, where the uses are somewhat homogeneous. An example would be users of a functional area or all employees in a building.

Local area networks have essential parts, such as network adapter cards, cables, hubs, servers, and operating systems. Each of these will be discussed later.

Network adapter card provides an interface between the computer and the network operating system (NOS). The NOS in some protocols resides on the server.

Electronic mail is a driving force for the installation of LANs. Organizations are installing LANs to allow this communication, with resource sharing being of lesser consideration.

organizational connectivity is the PBX for voice[1] communications, either an exchange operated by the local Telco or customer premises equipment. Single PBXs support total organizational needs, up to their limit of lines, generally 10,000 lines.[2] Because this network has historically not been used for a large amount of data communications, we seldom consider it in the data connectivity layers. It is, however, one of the most pervasive internal layer networks with which you will come in contact and it readily can be used for data movement.

Wide area networks (WANs) are at the opposite end of the network continuum from LANs. They are networks that cover wide geographical areas. They go beyond the boundaries of cities and extend globally. The extreme of the WAN is the *global network.* In the middle, for areas within a city, networks are known as **metropolitan area networks (MANs).**

The first layer of data communications is the **local area network (LAN),** which provides connectivity over a limited distance, often thought of as covering an area of less than one kilometer in radius and connecting people within an organization, such as a campus, building, department, floor, or work group. LANs are normally privately owned, and thus, like the PBX (customer premise equipment), are non-regulated. LANs can be any of the topologies and protocols mentioned previously, with the bus and ring the most common topologies and Ethernet® CSMA/CD and token passing the most common protocols. Common bandwidths are 10 and 100 Mbps for bus and 4 and 16 Mbps for ring networks, each considered high bandwidths. Single channel *baseband* (digital) is the most common, though some use *broadband* (analog) for multichannel capacity to carry both data and voice.

Even though all telecommunications should be transparent to the users, the LAN has the greatest visibility and potentially greatest influence on them. During the short time since their introduction, microcomputers (Apple 1976, IBM 1981) have found their greatest value when connected to each other and to organizational data sources. In the early days of the 1980s, users went to great lengths to acquire microcomputers, often hiding them in organizational budgets when official approval to purchase was denied. As they discovered the value of this new resource, they realized quickly (usually in about six months) that the stand-alone microcomputer was missing something very valuable: organizational data. As the number of microcomputers in organizations increased, users searched for connectivity. An early form of resource sharing was via circuit switching of two or more microcomputers to a common printer. This is a non-LAN solution.

Users seeking connectivity first consider either point-to-point, or modem-to-modem, as a simple and inexpensive way of getting files from one machine to

[1] We can provide switched point-to-point and LAN data connectivity via organizational PBXs.
[2] Consider the groups of numbers of a telephone number, and you will be addressing the levels of Figure 8.2. Take our telephone at Auburn University, Alabama (USA): 01-334-844-4071. The digits "01" are the country code when dialing from outside of the public switched network covering the United States of America on the North American continent and Hawaii. This would be the widest layer, the international public switched voice network. Next is "334," the area code for the southern half of the state of Alabama. We have four LATAs, called calling zones, in the 205 and 334 area codes: Birmingham, Huntsville, Mobile, and Montgomery. The Montgomery LATA (334), the one in which the authors reside, has over 88 central offices, 66 of which are non-BOC exchanges. This is the intermediate layer of the public switched voice network. Next is the exchange number, "844," which is the exchange housed at and for the Auburn University PBX. This is the internal layer, and is one of several exchanges in our LATA (821, 826, and 877 are housed in the Auburn central office, and 705, 742 (cellular), 745, and 749 are housed in the Opelika central office). Finally, we have the nodes on the internal layer, my extension of "6522." In this case, there can be up to 10,000 nodes on this PBX as four digits can accommodate that many distinct users.

Information Window

8–2

The choice of a LAN is both technical and managerial. The technical choice is more structured and is vendor and cost driven. On the other hand, the managerial factors are more complex. For example, the intended use and scope of the LAN need to be determined. As a LAN grows, the managerial tasks become greater. One must avoid implementing a LAN on a piecemeal basis without the resources, including hardware, software, wiring, and people, to make the LAN work.

Pardon the interruption, but the nemesis of local area networks is the interference of interrupts on individual machines. Because modern personal computers are running multimedia sound and CD-ROMs, modems, tape backup, external drives, and more, the network adapter card is often in contention for the interrupt in the operating system that will give it the access required.

another. Then they move up to the local area network. The LAN seems like a dream compared to the simple point-to-point connection since even the inexpensive ones communicate at over 1 Mbps. Novice microcomputer users readily see the value of connectivity to communicate and share resources. Speed is not considered important in the beginning, partially due to a lack of experience and partially because 1 Mbps seems so fast. With experience comes a realization that speed is indeed important. This is more evident as LANs support hundreds of users vying for the same data path and set of resources.

The introduction of a LAN is a special case of the effect of technology on organizations. As the technology is routinized, that is, as it becomes a part of daily organizational life, people tend to grow dependent on it. Where telephone and desktop calculators were novelties at their introduction, they are now indispensable. The same has become true of the office computer. The office computer has become the *work station,* and it's rare to find a nonconnected workstation.

As with the choice of a mainframe computer and its operating system, the choice of a LAN and its speed and operating system will be felt for a long time. Organizations do not often change mainframes to the extent that a totally different operating system is used. When they do, it means changing all procedures and programs. Thus, the decision to adopt a given manufacturer's mainframe and a specific operating system is an important one with ramifications that extend far beyond the obvious (the same is true for servers). Because the selection of the LAN has similar considerations, you should not jump into the thick of things and select a LAN based on price or popularity. Small offices that connect a few nodes may find using the networking included in the Windows® operating system to suffice; this is an excellent choice if they share a small amount of data, a printer or two, and a small file server. However, as the office expands to 150 users, it may well outgrow the LAN. Windows® 2.1 Area 98 have a limit of 10 nodes on a Windows network; Window 2000 raised this to 25, which is still a constraint. This means that the demands of the users are greater than the capabilities of the LAN. This implies sub-LANs and bridges, or the installation of a different topology and protocol, such as a 100 Mbps Novell Ethernet bus to achieve the new speed (bandwidth) required. Changing LANs means you may not be able to use the same programs; you may have to have different servers (vendors qualify a select group of servers for their networks) and different procedures. While these alternatives are well accepted in the market, changing from one LAN to another requires investigation, expense, and disruption. Such a change means that the users will likely go through a degree of disgruntlement and loss of productivity. *The decision you make when choosing a LAN is a very long-term decision that has important consequences for the organization.*

An emerging trend to network PCs in the home is the *personal area network (PAN).* This trend is expected to have tremendous growth as more homes have multiple PCs and as they add XDSL or cable modem high-speed Internet access. Just as in the office, multiple computers in the home that are connected to share resources and information are more useful.

Backbone networks give structure to dispersed networks and nodes.

A **backbone network** is to LANs what a high-speed loop around a city is to the major streets that connect to the loop. That is, it is connectivity at a "higher" speed between LANs and major nodes, such as mainframe computers, Internet access points, and teleports. The backbone network is analogous to the backbone of a human in that it acts as a central structure of the organization. An example of such a network is the fiber optic backbone network (AU-NET) at Auburn University that connects all buildings at 1,000 Mbps to a central building, to the IBM mainframes, and to the Internet. With the backbone in place, departments can attach directly to it and communicate to the mainframes, other LANs, servers, and software or have a gateway to the Internet. The College of Business at Auburn University has

FIGURE 8.3   **Geographic or Layer Network Concept**

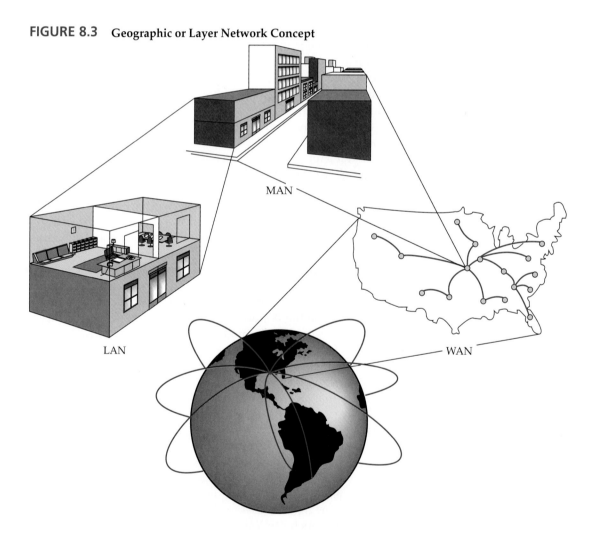

Global network

a 10/100 Mbps Novell Ethernet CSMA/CD bus for communications between the 250 staff, faculty, and doctoral students in the college, 1 Gbps fiber to communicate between wings of the building, and a gateway to AU-NET for communications to the rest of the campus and the world (through the Internet). The Internet, the international network of networks, is discussed in Chapter 9.

Remembering that the division between layers is to distinguish use, the next layer in scope is the *intermediate layer*. In Figure 8.3 showing a number of LANS, the intermediate layer would be the connection of the LANs into a corporate network, for example, a backbone. Each LAN has its own server for the operating system and shared resources for its groups of users, but each LAN is bridged or gatewayed to the other LANs for connectivity across a campus, division, or corporation.

A term used at the intermediate layer level is *metropolitan area network (MAN)*. As it implies, this is connectivity within a metropolitan-sized area, possibly providing services to many companies. For instance, the financial district of Denver or Chicago could take advantage of such a network to access commonly used resources. Such a network might be a fiber strand providing 10 to 100 Mbps connectivity by bus or ring topology for access to financial services or even to long-distance providers for voice service. A major form of MAN is the **fiber distributed data interface (FDDI)** network, based on optical fiber media, ring topology, and token-passing protocol, operating at 100 Mbps speed.

Just as a local area network provides internal connectivity to a small geographic area, and a metropolitan area network extends intermediate coverage to a wider area, *wide area layer* coverage is provided by *wide area networks* (WANs). WANs provide connectivity to larger and larger geographic areas, including the world. They can be privately owned and operated for internal use only, or they can be a common carrier resource, offered publicly. Privately owned WANs often have excess capacity that is sold or leased (brokered) to other organizations. WANs are long-haul, broadband, generally public access networks with wide geographic area, crossing rights-of-way, and are provided by common carriers. *Value added networks (VANs)* are a special form of WAN. They generally provide this wide area coverage and offer services in addition to connectivity in the form of added intelligence such as speed translation, store-and-forward messaging, protocol conversion, data handling, and packet assembly and disassembly. VANs are nonregulated because of the added services they provide. Their circuits may use switched and leased services on terrestrial circuits like wire or optic fiber or air media like microwave and satellite radio. They may offer speeds for casual connectivity or 56 Kbps to multimegabit rates for larger volume and constant traffic.

One form of WAN is a set of permanent circuits and channels onto which users are connected or into which they dial on an as-needed basis. This WAN provides connectivity between specified points by use of a specified (permanent) physical circuit. Another form is the **packet data networks (PDNs)**, which also provide connectivity to many points geographically. The PDN appears like a cloud with entry/exit points in many locations. The internal workings of the network are obscured from the users because of the way in which it provides connectivity. The first, and presently almost exclusive, way is by providing **virtual circuits** upon request. In this mode, commands from the requestor cause the network to establish a temporary physical channel for the duration of the communications. Each such setup will be different, based on the availability or busy state of the various linkages in the network, although there may be a preferred path, for example, the most direct route. The only time the specific arrangement of the virtual circuit is changed is when a link is disabled, at which time an alternate route is quickly established.

MANs give a city a competitive advantage. If you were a technologically oriented organization wishing to move to a new city, which would you choose, one with a MAN or one without one?

Wide area networks connect widely dispersed machines, possibly requiring intermediary machines to make conversion from one standard to another.

Information Window   8–3
Tradition versus Technology

On a vacation to Alaska, one of the authors walked to a mountaintop to sketch the scene. There, in deep concentration, was a native Alaskan holding a burning offering in his hands, giving thanks. To his side was a fellow tourist, trying to determine where he was with the aid of a global positioning system (GPS). The one knew instinctively his position in relation to the earth and its spirits; the other was lost.

In the second form of the PDN, the method of data transfer is the **datagram.** In this form, the data are packetized and sent over the network, much as a letter through the Postal Service. The major difference in this analogy is that the Postal Service letter has the total message therein where the datagram has only a portion of the message. A **packet assembler/disassembler (PAD)** receives the total data block, breaks it into predetermined-sized packets, adds the appropriate addressing, administrative, and error checking data to the packet, and places the packet onto the network. The intelligence of the network routes each packet to its destination, based on availability and busy state of each linkage at that moment. The virtual circuit is a *circuit-switched* network while the datagram is a **packet-switched network.** Circuit-switched networks take less overhead after setup, that is, no destination address is required, whereas each datagram must have a destination address.

Packet-switched networks have become very popular. Part of this is because standardizing of packets has allowed networks to become faster and faster.

VANs in general, and PDNs in particular, offer services that are reliable, are national and international in coverage, have low error rates, offer a variety of speeds, and are cost effective. Like the POTS for voice, they offer extensive data connectivity with shared cost.

Enterprise Systems

Several packaged software applications called enterprise systems promise to deliver significant business value for many industries. An evolution of these systems can be traced. In the 1960s, material requirements planning (MRP) was among the first of these systems. MRP was followed by manufacturing resource planning (MRP II), enterprise resource planning (ERP), supply-chain management (SCM), customer relationship management (CRM), and sales force automation (SFA) in order to fulfil enterprisewide business needs. By 1998, more than 60 percent of *Fortune* 1,000 companies had implemented ERP systems in the United States. Many of the ERP vendors are presently moving to provide real-time capabilities as part of their offerings so that rapid communication of important decision support information is available throughout the organization.

A typical ERP system consists of a set of separate, but integratible, modules. Each module addresses a particular business function. There are 14 common modules: financial accounting, controlling, enterprise control, investment management, treasury, personnel administration, personnel development, sales and distribution, material management, warehouse management, production planning, general logistics, quality management, and asset management. The ideal conceptual

ERP system would integrate all modules in an enterprisewide system, to include interorganizational partners.

In EMC's (a leading vendor of storage systems) vision, enterprise systems will reduce complexity of information management across the entire information system infrastructure. They advocate use of application suites that act as portals. By consolidating storage management, integrating functionality, and automating administrative services, EMC claims that higher service levels can be maintained. A high level of interoperability promises to integrate storage area networks (SANs), network attached storage (NAS), dense wove division multiplexing (DWDM), and directly connected storage into a single infrastructure.

Virtual Private Networks

Virtual private networks (VPNs) are an important category of network. A VPN uses a public network, such as the Internet, but includes software that is intended to make the members of the network very secure. The network acts as a tunnel inside the larger network. By using encryption techniques called tunneling, the data travel over a public network but cannot be read by it.

VPNs utilize strong encryption, authentication, and access control technologies to connect remote offices, business partners, and mobile employees via low-cost public Internet connections. Without VPNs, the employees and offices use a private, secure network. With VPNs, they can access the Internet via a telephone line, significantly reducing the cost of communications. By reducing the need for

---

Technology Note   8–2

Point-to-Point Tunneling Protocol (PPTP)—An open tunneling protocol developed by Microsoft, 3Com, Ascend, US Robotics (before it became part of 3Com), and others. It's supported out of the box by Windows NT and Windows 95, as well as remote access hardware from Ascend and 3Com. Novell's Border Manager also supports this protocol, as can other operating systems using PPTP software. PPTP is based on the Generic Routing Encapsulation (GRE) protocol, as outlined in RFCs 1701 and 1702.

Source: http://www.vpn.outer.net/Technologies/technologies.html.

Technology Note   8–3
VPN Made Simple and Personal

Virtual private networks (VPNs) don't have to be the private domain of the large organization. According to http://www.onsystems.com/ their product **Tijit** is a simple virtual private network (VPN) alternative for individuals and businesses. Tijit allows friends and family to network their computers together over the Internet. A Tijit user is able to share a picture or any other file on his home computer with his friends, family, or the entire Internet. Features include share-transfer of files; chat and instant message; secure private connections; and joining of communities to share files with others who share your same interests. VPNs may be established with MS Windows® operating systems.

expensive leased lines, VPN products can dramatically reduce corporate telecommunication expenses without sacrificing the security of dedicated private lines.

Peer-to-Peer Computing

We introduced peer-to-peer computing as a network on which all nodes are of equal status. The alternative is client/server architecture (C/SA), where one or more servers provide information to many clients.

In its new introduction of **peer-to-peer (P2P) computing,** each computer in the network gets information from every other computer rather than getting it from one large, central computer. The collective contents of the entire network are at the command of each connected computer. This is really nothing radically new; it's just search and share methodology. The concept is that data reside on individual computers rather than on central servers.

For example, under the normal search process, a company such as *AltaVista* sent out bots that visited websites and returned with information that was then catalogued into the mainframe database. When an individual queries the database, using the *AltaVista* search engine, the data search is what is presently on file. While such capabilities provide information from millions of computers, the data may be old or out-of-date.

P2P capabilities use distributed nodes on a network to make the search dynamic and up-to-date. *Napster* is an example of P2P. When a node logs into *Napster,* a new catalog is downloaded to *Napster's* centralized database. This keeps the database current.

One start-up firm, InfraSearch, plans to remake the entire Internet into a P2P network. The firm is issuing free software that will connect any computer to a P2P network. InfraSearch will provide server computers that will direct searches to the appropriate websites.

When consumers use the traditional search engine, they connect to a central index of Web content. This central index is updated by Web Crawlers and may be 24 hours to months old.

Using the P2P network, searchers seek the very latest information content on the other computers on the network. This includes the InfraSearch computers and both consumer and business computers on the network.

InfraSearch is just one of many firms seeking to capitalize on the new model of distributed computing represented by P2P. In late 2000, there were over 80 P2P start-up firms. In the new model, P2P enables the direct exchange of services (or data/information) between computers on the network. All of the servers and PCs that make up the network become peers and contribute part of their resources (processing power and storage) to the overall network computing effort. From the old client/server concept, we transform the clients into service providers instead of just consumers of services. The potential power of the P2P network lies in the capture of the unused MIPS of idle computers on the network so that supercomputer-type tasks can be performed. This is termed *grid computing.* Combined with P2P, grid computing needs to have the *distributed computing infrastructure* in order to achieve the promise of a dynamic, granular network where specific components of information can be rapidly located and efficiently shared.

Two specific uses of P2P have been by Intel and the governmental organization looking for life beyond Earth. Intel now uses the idle computers within its company to help with simulations of new products. It has indicated a saving of one-half billion dollars by using the desktop resource it already owns in preference to new mainframe processing.

Technology Note   8–4
Peer-to-Peer Computing

Peer-to-peer computing is defined as the sharing of resources (such as hard drives and processing cycles) among computers and other intelligent devices. Internet-based peer-to-peer applications position the desktop at the center of computing. This paradigm enables consumers to actively participate in the Internet rather than just surf it. This model also helps businesses capitalize on the power of desktop computers that are already in place in the enterprise environment.

Many consumers have likely heard of peer-to-peer networking applications such as Napster, but peer-to-peer computing involves much more than swapping music files. In fact, this compelling technology is on the rise today largely because of the advantages that peer networks offer in terms of collaborating on specific tasks.

Intel® Philanthropic Peer-to-Peer Program offers an ideal example of the value of peer-to-peer computing and demonstrates that peer-to-peer technology can dramatically accelerate the discovery of important medical breakthroughs. This effort is not only leading scientific computing into a new era, but also has helped launch the socially significant concept of PC philanthropy.

This project by United Devices began April 4, 2001, to use idle computers to compare potential helpful molecules against cancer-causing proteins. As of July 15, 2001, this project has signed up 491,916 members, with 789,060 computers, achieving over **two hundred million processing hours** (which is over 26,000 processing years). See www.ud.com.

Meanwhile, the search for extraterrestrial life uses P2P to take advantage of idle computers at home. By downloading software from www.seti.com, individuals make their idle computing cycle available for processing small packets of data from radio telescopes searching the heavens for life beyond Earth. The software returns the results of the data. The project has acquired the use of over three million computers, worldwide, with a combined processing power of **14 trillion floating point operations per second** and has garnered over **500,000 years of processing time** in the past year and a half.[3] A reminder that all of this is possible only with the connectivity of the Internet.

The discussion of peer-to-peer computing in Technology Note 8–4 emphasizes, as did SETI, what can be done when the task can be partitioned into similar, distributable tasks, as opposed to using a single-thread program on a mainframe or server. Because P2P distribution is enabled via the connectivity of the Internet, SETI has three mission processors and the United Devices product has 700 thousand processors working in unison. Because of the connectivity, the power of the distributed processing can be brought to bear, something that cannot be done without such connectivity.

The Internet as the Ultimate Wide Area Network

The Internet is a network of networks.

We generally think of WANs as privately owned networks, although they may be owned by a common carrier and made available for public traffic. With the introduction of the Internet, everyone has access to a wide area network. This TCP/IP protocol packet data network provides connectivity from almost anywhere to almost anywhere, at a moderate speed. Please see Chapter 8 for more detail on this technology and the organizational companion, the intranet.

[3] http://members.ud.com/dc/seti@home.htm.

The Real World   8–1
Who's Using Your Machine?

Wondering if your new Pentium 4–powered PC is moonlighting on the side? You should be. While your system is happily chomping away on 5 gigs of digital video, a freeloading interloper could be sucking excess processing power for its own dirty work.

Like a leech feeding off its host, a simple kernel of code can tap into your PC or Web server undetected, then use it to solve complex mathematical equations. The hack was devised by University of Notre Dame physicist Albert-László Barabási and computer scientists Jay Brockman and Vincent Freeh, along with Hawoong Jeong, a physicist from the Korea Advanced Institute of Science and Technology.

Such parasitic computing exploits the checksum—the error-detection scheme Net-connected computers perform on every data packet received to make certain it wasn't corrupted in transmission. The parasite covertly tucks bits of checksum data into each packet. As the host computer verifies these data with those of an arriving packet, it unwittingly crunches the equation embedded in the incoming checksum. When the checksum reports back to the sender, it carries with it a solution to the parasite's problem. Multiply this by hundreds of Web servers and networked PCs, and the Net could be doing a lot of people's busywork. "We could use all the idle resources on the Internet," says Jeong. "If this happens—and sooner or later it will—it means one really big supercomputer."

Sound familiar? It is. Parasitic computing works a lot like other forms of distributed computation (think Seti@home without user permission). Hackers can abuse parasitic code, but aside from slowing the network, they're not likely to do much damage, says Jeong. However, should a group need major tech muscle without a price tag, a parasitic assault may be the way to go. But Jon Howell, Microsoft Research computer scientist, warns: "Your problem must have a very high computation-to-communication ratio to be profitable." And if you don't want your hardware made slave *to* someone else's data crunching? The answer is simple: Unplug from the Net.—*Michael Behar*

Source: Michael Behar, "Who's Using Your Machine," *Wired,* December 2001.

Information Window   8–4

One of the authors recently attended a conference in San Francisco. While there, he walked to a waterfront restaurant for dinner. When the waiter approached, he reached into his belt and took out what appeared to be a communicator from Star Trek. When he asked for the drink and dinner order, he keyed them into the communicator. This sent the drink order directly to a printer at the bar and the dinner order directly to a printer in the kitchen. This reduced the trips the waiter made to each location to one instead of two. When the meal was over, the waiter printed the bill out near the table. While appearing more efficient for the waiter, the system had been installed to reduce traffic in the kitchen.

LAN PROTOCOLS

We said earlier that the three most used local area network (LAN) topologies were bus, ring, and star. Each tends to have its own protocol, and, thus, its own protocol standard. Originally, standards were created by companies inventing the protocol, as with several of the synchronous and asynchronous protocols noted earlier. With wider acceptance of a protocol, it generally comes under the stewardship of a standards organization, such as ANSI, CCITT, or IEEE (Institute of Electrical and Electronic Engineers). The following are IEEE standards for the protocols for the three most popular LANs.

IEEE 802.3 is the standard for the **CSMA/CD** (carrier sense multiple access/collision detection) baseband bus. This standard is used for Ethernet, Star-

TABLE 8.1   **Considerations for Choosing a Local Area Network**

Feature	Ethernet Bus	Token-Passing Ring	Star
Wiring	Present wiring, type 3	Special, often shielded	Present
Initial cost	Moderate	Higher	Lowest
Bandwidth, small number of users	Good, 9 Mbps	Good, 15.9 Mbps	Limited, 1–2 Mbps
Bandwidth, large number of users	Poor, 5–6 Mbps	Good, 15.9 Mbps	Poor, 1–2 Mbps
Installed base	High	Medium	Low
Choices	Large	Limited	Limited
Data packet size limit	1500 bytes	16,000 bytes	—
Overhead	High at high usage	Constant @ 4%	—

Information Window   8–5

Some considerations in selection of a LAN and LAN Operating System, not in order of importance:

- Ease of connectivity
- Vendor support
- Expandability
- Performance
- Ease of use

- Cost
- Flexibility
- Vendor profile
- Reliability
- Expense
- Security
- Portability
- Speed

lan, and IBM PC Networks, with Ethernet being the most popular. This protocol allows multiple nodes to connect along a central wire or coaxial cable, with no master–slave relationship; each node is of equal status. It calls for speeds up to 10 Mbps, with a maximum overall bus length of 2,500 meters and a maximum of 100 nodes, each of which generally cannot be more than 200 meters apart. CSMA/CD has good error detection.

IEEE standard 802.4 defines the **token-passing bus,** while **IEEE 802.5** defines the much more popular **token-passing ring.** The token-passing ring was championed by IBM, with their first entrant having a speed of 4 Mbps on shielded, twisted-pair were. Their speed increased to 16 Mbps in the early 90s with plans to move onwards to 100 Mbps. While IBM uses shielded twisted-pair wire for interference control, other vendors have found ways to use unshielded twisted-pair wire with good success.

Another standard of interest, *IEEE 802.6,* defines the protocol for the *metropolitan area network,* often using fiber distributed data interface (FDDI) transport. In the early 1990s, MANs ran as counter-rotating rings with speeds in the 100–300 Mbps range. This important standard set the foundation for connectivity within business centers, giving the connected companies increased speed among themselves and to selected services.

Table 8.1 lists some of the considerations in choosing a local area network.

WAN PROTOCOLS

X.25 Packet Data Network

X.25, in its most-used form, a virtual circuit, is basically a connection-oriented, packet-switching system that interconnects noncolocated local area networks

FIGURE 8.4 (a)   **Packet Switching**

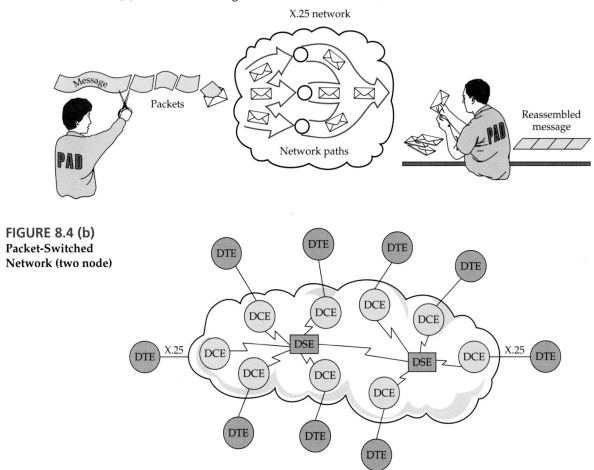

FIGURE 8.4 (b)
Packet-Switched
Network (two node)

or user terminals. X.25 is a publicly based network switching system run by most telephone operating companies. It acts the same way as the telephone system (see Figure 8.4): It makes a temporary physical connection (virtual circuit) between two locations, allows the conversation (in this case the transference of data) to occur, and upon completion breaks the physical connection so the middle carrier trunks can be used by someone else. And the good thing is you only pay for the time you use (much like a normal telephone bill). Other WAN protocols such as frame relay and ATM are discussed in a later chapter.

Technical

X.25 uses a switching system that utilizes end-user lines (connected to switch drop ports) and carrier trunks (connected to switch line ports). The switch then uses a series of matrix connection control systems that will connect a particular drop port to a specific line port for connection to the far end. The customer will always connect to this transport system by way of a PAD (X.25 packet assembler/ disassembler) or gateway (GW).

The user traffic may not take the same trunks two or more times in a row to get to a particular location; traffic direction is dynamic. That is why it is looked upon and diagrammed as a cloud.

FIGURE 8.5
X.25 Layers and
Frame Structures

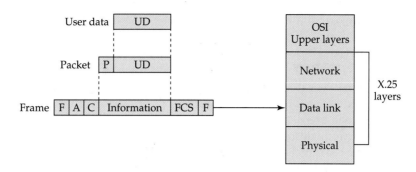

In referencing the OSI (open system interconnection) standard stack, X.25 is incorporated in the first three layers (refer to Figure 8.5).

1. Physical layer—incorporates specifications such as
    a. What type of wire medium (UTP, TP, STP, coax, etc.).
    b. What type of connections (RJ, V.35, RS-232, etc.) and end link transport speeds (2.4–56 Kbps).
    c. What the electrical voltages on the pins will be (spread of $+/-5$ to 25 volts DC).
    d. What the signaling will be (master, slave, clocking and synchronization, etc.).
2. Data link layer—describes specific data link protocol efforts such as
    a. Delimiting pointers for start and end of X.25 formatted packets.
    b. Packet numbering and accountability.
    c. Packet acknowledgement, error control, and flow control.
    d. SDLC or HDLC parameters.
3. Packet level (another name for the network layer)—controls
    a. Virtual network establishment between network switches.
    b. Network interface and DNIC (Data Network Identification Connection) addressing.
    c. Routing.
    d. Carrier interconnection flow control.

REPEATERS, BRIDGES, ROUTERS, GATEWAYS, AND HUBS[4]

With the rapid advancement of technology, there is always the question of how to stay connected or linked, in order to transmit information. This section examines how repeaters, bridges, routers, brouters, and gateways are used to link network segments and networks. It also examines how concentrators combine data from multiple channels into a single line for efficient transmission. The use of hubs to provide single or multiprotocol connections is viewed through past, current, and future trends.

Network Devices

With the rapid advancement of technology, there is always the question of how to stay connected or linked, in order to transmit information. This section examines how physical equipment is used to link network segments and networks. This

[4] Assistance on this part was provided in large part by Dafni Greene of Auburn University.

ranges from how hubs create networks to how concentrators combine data from multiple channels into a single line for efficient transmission.

Repeaters

A repeater is the simplest type of hardware that can be used to provide connection for network segments. A **repeater** is a device that receives a signal and regenerates it. When a repeater receives a signal, it forms a new signal that matches the old one at the appropriate amplitude. Since it creates a new signal, any distortion or attenuation that the old signal carried is removed. A repeater can receive electrical or optical signals.

This device operates at the first layer (physical layer) of the OSI model (see The Real World 8–2, page 299) and is transparent to data flow. Therefore the repeater is restricted to linking identical network segments. For example, a repeater can connect two Ethernet segments or two token-ring network segments. It cannot connect an Ethernet to a token-ring segment.

Repeaters are used mainly to extend the coverage of a network by extending the length of any one segment. Although several network segments can be connected via repeaters, there is a maximum distance limitation. For example, a coaxial bus-based Ethernet supports a maximum cabling distance of 2.8 Km, which cannot be extended any farther by using repeaters.[5]

Bridges

A **bridge** is a device that reads data frame addresses and uses this information to perform transmitting or translating functions. A bridge uses a combination of hardware and software to connect LANs that have the same or different data link layers, but the upper level protocols must be the same. A bridge operates at the second layer (data link) of the OSI Reference Model, as it is more powerful than a repeater. However, bridges are slower and more expensive to use than repeaters. There are two general types of bridges: transparent and translating.

Transparent bridges connect two LANs that use the same data link protocol. Since bridges operate at the data link layer, the physical layer does not have to be transparent. However, the majority of bridges are transparent at both layers.

A transparent bridge examines each frame that is processed at the data link layer. The bridge reads the source address of each frame and compares the address to a table of local addresses that it keeps separately for each network. If the address is not in the table, then the bridge will insert it (a process called *learning*). The bridge also examines the destination address of each frame and compares it to the table it has built. If the destination address matches an entry in the local address table, then the bridge simply repeats the frame because it belongs on the current network. If the destination address does not match, then the bridge transmits the frame to the other network (a process called **forwarding**). If a bridge compares addresses and realizes that a station has already received the message, then the frame will be discarded (a process called *filtering*).

There are two basic techniques that transparent bridges can use. The first one is called the **spanning tree protocol (STP).** This algorithm is used primarily in the Ethernet environment, and was invented to help overcome the problem of active loops. If networks are linked via bridges and form a loop topology, this can cause problems such as frame duplication and subsequent network saturation.

The STP protocol disables links and converts the loop into a tree topology. This creates a unique path for each node. The disabled nodes are on standby, and can

[5] Sanjay Dhawan, *Networking Device Drivers* (New York: Van Nostrand Reinhold, 1995), p. 70.

learn information from passing data, but are not allowed to transmit. If the network fails, the algorithm can reactivate the nodes and form a new tree. Although the STP protocol eliminates duplication, it will not be useful in situations where multiple paths are needed between networks.

The second transparent bridging protocol, called **source routing,** was developed by IBM for use with token ring networks. A portion of the information field in the frame is used to carry routing information. Discovery packets act as trail guides and determine the best path between the networks. A discovery packet travels to a bridge, and the bridge inserts the packet's ring number (from where the packet originated) plus the bridge's own identifier into the packet's routing information field (RIF). The bridge *floods,* or transmits the packet to all of the bridge's connections and avoids duplication by not retransmitting along the original connection. It is possible that the final destination will receive multiple copies of the discovery packet. The bridge at the destination point picks a path and transmits a response to the origin point. This is the path that will be used for the entire transmission session.

Since the two protocols discussed above had limitations, vendors came up with source routing transparent (SRT) bridges. This type of bridge supports both the spanning tree protocol and source routing protocol, and provides an added degree of flexibility. Ethernet and token ring networks may be connected through singular or multiple paths.

Translating bridges connect two LANs that use different data link protocols. For example, a translating bridge can be used to connect a token ring network to an Ethernet network. This is much more complicated because of frame and transmission rate conversion. It can become tricky because the networks have different format restrictions.

A translating bridge performs the same functions as a transparent bridge. However, instead of forwarding the data to the other network, the bridge must provide translation. This means that the frame must be converted to a different format and run at a different speed. The bridge will provide a buffer and negotiate the frame size and speed.

For example, Ethernet networks run at 10 Mbps while token ring networks typically run at 4 Mbps or 16 Mbps. This means that the data packets will be traveling at different speeds between the two networks and the bridge must provide a buffer. The second issue that occurs is the size of the frames. The maximum frame size on an Ethernet is 1,518 bytes while a token ring has a maximum frame size of 5,000 bytes (4 Mbps speed) or 18,000 bytes (16 Mbps speed). Bridges do not have the capacity to split and reassemble frames. Therefore, the only solution is to use software to configure workstations to use the smallest maximum frame size of each network. In the previous example, frames would be restricted to 1,518 bytes since that is the smallest frame size available.

Routers

A **router** is a device that chooses the best possible path for data frame transmission and uses software control to help prevent traffic congestion. A router operates at the third OSI layer, the network layer. Routers must be able to communicate using the same protocols at both the data link and network layers. However, it is possible for networks with different operating systems to use **multiprotocol routers** that are able to provide address translation. Of course, the networks must have similar upper-level protocols because it would be useless to route data to a destination point if the upper-layer protocols conflicted.

A router examines frames that are specifically addressed to the router. It looks at the logical address, which is typically an address assigned by a network administrator. Frames that are not addressed to the router are ignored.

Routers are very flexible because they have algorithms and protocols that allow them to select the best possible path to transmit data. If necessary, routers have the ability to split packets into fragments that will be reassembled at the destination point. This sometimes results in packets arriving out of order, but instructions are included for reassembly. Routers use flow control to try to prevent congestion. They have the capacity to monitor the bandwidth of the path, and will inhibit transmission as well as notify other routers to inhibit transmission if congestion occurs.

Routers are more powerful than bridges because they operate at a higher level in the OSI model. Unlike bridges, routers have the capacity to split and reassemble frames, as well as choose the best possible path for transmission. Bridges must examine all frames *(promiscuous mode)* while routers selectively examine frames *(nonpromiscuous mode)*. Of course, routers are slower than bridges and more expensive.

The two basic types of routing are called *static* and *dynamic.* The routing table is constructed by network personnel for **static routers.** Once the table is configured, the paths do not change. If a link is disabled, the router will issue an alarm. However, it will not be able to reroute traffic automatically.

Dynamic routers are able to make changes in the routing table and find an alternate path, if a link should become disabled. These routers can even rebalance the traffic load. Dynamic routers are constantly communicating with other routers, and any new information is used to update the address routing tables.[6]

Storage routers are used to help build and manage **storage area networks (SANs).** The storage router is a device that enables users to connect switched storage environments on a standard data network. They build a separate network infrastructure for the storage network. Cisco Systems has introduced a storage router that features optical *Fibre Channel*® and Gigabit Ethernet ports and 10/100 Base T ports. There are three protocols in use: Internet SCSI (iSCSI), Internet Fibre Channel Protocol (iFCP), and Internet Storage Naming Service (iSNS).

The devices support connection to Fibre Channel switches, SCSI devices, or both and will feature a Gigabit interface. These storage routers should facilitate the building of enterprise storage networks.

Brouters

A **brouter** is a hybrid device that performs bridging and routing functions. A brouter examines a frame and checks the destination address. If the frame is going to a different LAN, the brouter examines the protocol to make sure that it will be supported at the network layer. If it can be supported, the brouter simply performs routing operations. If the brouter does not support the protocol, the frame is bridged by using layer two information.

Brouters provide an additional level of flexibility compared to routers. However, connectivity does take place at a lower level in the OSI model. This happens because a frame that passes through a router that does not support network protocol is ignored, while a brouter will bridge the frame.

Brouters are slower compared separately to bridges or routers. However, if a system is using a combination of a bridge and router, then using a brouter as a

---

[6] Nathan J. Muller, *LANs to WANs* (Norwood, MA: Artech House, 1990), p. 212.

replacement should speed things up. A lot depends on the filtering and forwarding rates of the devices.

Gateways

A **gateway** is a device that uses software to connect networks with different architectures by performing protocol conversion. A gateway is the most complex device available that will connect networks. It operates at all seven layers of the OSI model, connecting networks that have different protocols, and performs an actual protocol conversion. A gateway can provide terminal emulation so workstations can emulate dumb terminals. It also provides for file-sharing and peer-to-peer communications between LAN and host. Gateways also provide error detection on transmitted data, as well as monitor traffic flow.

Gateways are very sophisticated and complicated to install. They are the most expensive devices that connect networks, as well as the slowest. Gateways normally are used to connect LANs to mainframes or connect a LAN to a WAN. It is possible to connect LANs with gateways, but typically other methods are used since gateways are both slower and more expensive than routers.

Hubs

Basically, a **hub** is a device that physically connects cables. Although a hub was originally a simple device, it has evolved over the years. Computer industry users refer to hubs in different ways. IBM refers to hubs as multistation access units (MSAUs). When referring to local area networks (LANs), a hub usually means the center or central node of a star topology. Sometimes vendors will refer to hubs as concentrators (not to be confused with the intelligent multiplexers). Because technology has increased at such a pace, creating a common terminology is very difficult.

ARCnet (Attached Resource Computer Network), developed in the 1970s by Datapoint, was one of the first networks to use hubs. ARCnet was basically a forerunner of Ethernet, and had a hybrid bus/star topology that used active and passive hubs. An active hub has the ability to filter noise from signals, boost signals, and split signals. With an active hub you can run cables to 2,000 feet. A passive hub can only split signals and has a distance limitation of 100 feet.

Modular Hubs

The initial hubs were called modular (or chassis) type units. Typically, they were placed in wiring closets. These units did an excellent job of providing connections. Small improvements were made such as adding slots for extra modules, but, overall, companies that manufactured hubs became complacent. Very little was done in research and development.

Modular hubs use a high-speed bus to link the various modules in the unit. These units are capable of providing single or multiprotocol links. This means that Ethernet, token ring, FDDI, and others can be mixed. If you run out of slots to provide links, then another modular unit can be connected via a bridge. Modular hubs provide a great deal of flexibility, especially when different backbone technologies have to converge.

In the early 1990s, companies started marketing stackable units. Although the **stackable hub** did not provide as many features as the modular unit, it filled a niche due to its competitive pricing. Stackable units are generally single protocol devices, which is great for connecting PCs of the same protocol that are on the same floor. Units are traditionally cascaded together through Ethernet running over a twisted-pair drop cable. Alternatively, some type of shared bus scheme may be used to allow information to flow between stacked units.

Switchable Hubs

In the mid 1990s, the hot topic was **switchable hubs.** While standard hubs may not be expandable, switchable hubs have ports that allow additional stackable hubs to be connected, thus expanding the total number of ports on that local device. Additionally, switchable hubs allow ports to be reassigned or turned on/off through software control. In the past, whenever ports needed to be reassigned someone would walk to the wiring closet and physically change the cables to the new port settings. Imagine how confusing that would be if you had to look at several hundred cables, and then change the right ones. Another feature that switchable hubs are using is remote monitoring (RMON). RMON allows remote devices to be managed from a central office. This technology allows users and resources to be placed in logical groups, even if physically separated. It also allows networks to be separated into small, independent segments. Each segment can run at full network speed, which gives the user dedicated bandwidth, and is a good method for splitting resources. For example, groups such as engineering or research and development can be given larger chunks of bandwidth because they often have a greater need for it.

Switching Architectures

There are two basic types of switching architecture or techniques. The first one is called **on-the-fly switching** (or *cut-through switching*). This type of switch begins to forward a frame before it receives the entire packet. Although it is quicker, this type of switch is more likely to suffer from errors because it detects errors by reading the end of each frame.

The second type of switch is called *buffered* (or *store-and-forward*). As the name implies, it places the data in a buffer until the entire packet is received. This allows it to make better routing decisions as well as have a better chance of detecting errors. At the same time, the price to be paid for waiting is a loss of speed.

ATM/Future Trend

The future of hubs seems to lie down the asynchronous transfer mode (ATM) path. (For more on ATM technology, please refer to Chapter 14.) Of course, businesses are slow to accept ATM because it is expensive. Since ATM employs a cell technology, most packet reading devices will have to be replaced. Although many people hope to switch/bridge LANs to ATM technology using the old methods, there may be some problems. One reason is that switching LANs to ATM involves using a LAN emulation protocol that makes an ATM network look like a LAN, which would allow bridging. This emulation protocol is slower than a native ATM protocol and would not allow maximum utilization of the bandwidth. The first ATM native protocol, classical IP (or RFC 1577) has become the predominant protocol for high-speed communications.[7]

Routing requirements are different for traditional routers compared to the LAN-to-ATM requirements. The first difference is that traditional backbones assume that network connections are shared, as opposed to an ATM link that is dedicated to a single device. Another problem is that traditional routers pass frames that need fragmenting to a slower exception path and transmit nonfragmented frames very quickly. Most of the traffic that flows through traditional routers is nonfragmented.

[7] Doug Green, "The Need for Routing in ATM Edge Devices," *Telecommunications,* March 1996, p. 36.

With the new ATM-to-LAN traffic, fragmentation needs to be the main function, not the exception. Otherwise, the full performance capability of ATM may not be realized.

Vendors have started to address the special needs of ATM switches. An *edge router* was created to provide ATM switches with routing and packet-to-cell conversion capabilities. It is also sometimes called an *edge path adapter (EPA)*. The **edge router** was specifically designed to work with ATM switches, using native ATM protocols. An edge router is able to support 30 MB of throughput as compared to traditional routers, which can only support between 7 MB and 12 MB at one time.

Network Connections Summary

The various devices that link networks are summarized in Table 8.2 and the characteristics of hubs are summarized in Table 8.3. The list starts with the simplest level and goes to the most complex. Of course, there is always a trade-off. Each time a device adds a layer of complexity, it suffers a loss of speed. The benefits of adding flexibility are costly. Therefore, when building a network, administrators must keep in mind that the more flexible networks will also be more expensive, as well as slower. However, sometimes the extra flexibility is a necessity.

TABLE 8.2 **Comparison of Linkage Alternatives**

	Connect	Function	OSI Model	Speed	Cost
Repeater	Similar segments	Regenerates signal Extends network length	Layer 1	Fastest	Least expensive
Hub	Nodes	Connection	Layer 1	Slow/medium	Least expensive
Bridge—Transparent	LANs with similar protocols, similar data link layers	Filters signal Decides if signal should be repeated or forwarded	Layer 2	Loses speed because extra layer is added	More expensive
Bridge—Translating	LANs with similar protocols, different data link layers	Filters signal Forwards signal or translates	Layer 2	Loses speed because extra layer is added	More expensive
Router	LANs with similar protocols, similar data and network layers (unless multi-protocol routers used)	Chooses best path Flow control Segments frame, transmits, and reassembles	Layers 1–3	Loses speed because of third layer that was added	More expensive as level of complexity increases
Brouter	LANs with similar protocols, similar or different data link layers	Performs both routing and bridging functions	Examines protocols at layers 2–3 Performs bridging at Layer 2	Depends on filtering and forwarding rate Can be faster or slower than bridges and routers	More expensive as level of complexity increases
Gateway	Networks with different protocols	Protocol conversion	Layers 1–7	Slowest	Most expensive

TABLE 8.3   Characteristics of Hubs

	Links	Function	Pros	Cons
Modular hubs	Multiple protocol	Physically connects cables	Can mix FDDI, Ethernet, etc.	Must physically change connections at the wiring closet
Stackable hubs	Single protocol	Physically connects cables, can add units by stacking	Able to fit more units in wiring closet because of smaller size	When connecting the stackables together, interference sometimes occurs (bleed over from the lines) Cannot mix different network segments
Switchable hubs	Multiple protocols	Uses software control to reassign ports Segments network into individual segments	Do not have to physically change connections in wiring closet Allows individuals to have full network speed	More expensive than modular or stackable hubs
ATM	LAN-to-ATM technology	New products allow ATM to be utilized more efficiently	Allows full performance of ATM to be realized	More expensive; ATM requires extra devices to utilize full potential

Conclusion

Repeaters, bridges, routers, and brouters are used to increase the effectiveness of data transmissions through networks. Gateways are used primarily to connect LANs to a mainframe or WAN. Hubs provide physical connections in wiring closets or remotely through software control. All of these devices are used to ensure that data are properly transmitted and translated between various nodes. In the future, much of the technology will have to be modified to satisfy the new requirements of ATM.

CLIENT-SERVER ARCHITECTURE

Client-server systems seem to be the way to distribute tasks to smaller, less expensive, distributed computers.

The basic construct behind **client-server architecture (C/SA)** is a client end and a server end that are distinguishable, yet interact with each other. At its roots, C/SA consists of two independent processing machines, in separate locations, each capable of performing operations separately, but operating with greater efficiency when operating together. A single server, the base machine around which the architecture is designed, can have multiple clients. The C/S environment differs from its predecessor, the mainframe-centered environment (legacy), in that much of the processing may now be performed by the client, which was previously (usually) a dumb terminal.

The advantages of client-server operations are significant. The ability to interconnect computers not only to share information but also to share the processing of information, creates a distinctive synergistic relationship transcending the capabilities of either machine in isolation. By combining the processing capacity and

The Real World
A Quick Look at Bridges & Routers

8–2

The devices used to interconnect networks are called bridges and routers. These internetworking devices can be hardware, or software-based. Software-based routers and bridges can be part of a server's operating system or also can be installed on standard computers to create dedicated, stand-alone devices. However, software-only bridges and routers must depend on the server's internal memory and CPU, which can degrade network performance. For maximum performance, a stand-alone solution is usually the best choice.

a. OSI seven layers

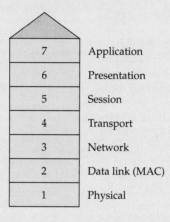

7	Application
6	Presentation
5	Session
4	Transport
3	Network
2	Data link (MAC)
1	Physical

b. Bridges

2	MAC
1	Physical

c. Routers

3	Network
2	MAC
1	Physical

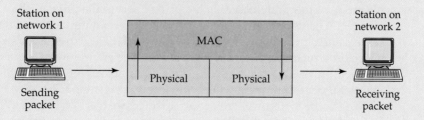

Station on network 1 — Sending packet

MAC

Physical   Physical

Station on network 2 — Receiving packet

(continued)

The Real World (Continued)   8–2
A Quick Look at Bridges & Routers

BRIDGES

A bridge operates at the data link layer (layer two) of the OSI architecture. Bridges can be used to connect networks with different addresses or to segment a network (segments having the same network address). When connecting networks with different addresses, a bridge acts as an address filter; it relays data between networks with different addresses based on information contained at the Medium Access Control (MAC) level.

Simple bridges are used to connect networks that use the same physical-layer protocol, and the same MAC and logical link protocols (OSI layers one and two). Simple bridges are not capable of translating between the different protocols.

Other types of bridges, such as transitional bridges, can connect networks that use different layer-one and MAC-level protocols: they are capable of translating then layering frames.

After a physical connection is made (at OSI layer one) a bridge receives all frames from each of the networks it connects and it checks the network address of each received frame. The network address is contained in the MAC header. Bridges examine the MAC header to read the network address and forward the packet appropriately.

SPANNING TREE AND SOURCE-ROUTE BRIDGING

The spanning tree protocol prevents problems resulting from the interconnection of multiple networks. In various bridging circumstances, it is possible to have multiple transmission routes exist, and to have an endless duplication and expansion or routing errors that will saturate the network with useless transmissions, quickly disabling it. Spanning trees are the method used to specify one, and only one, transmission route.

Source-route bridging is the other standard means of determining the path used to transfer data from one station to another. Stations that use source-routing participate in route discovery and specify the route to be used for each transmitted packet. Source-route bridges merely carry out each data packet when the packet is assembled by the sending station. Source-route bridging is important because it is a bridge routing method used on IBM token ring networks.

ROUTERS

Routers function at the OSI network layer (one layer higher than bridges). To communicate, routers must use the same network-layer protocol. And, of course, either the sending and receiving stations on different networks must share identical protocols at all OSI layers above layer three, or there must be necessary protocol translation at these layers.

Routers can allow the transfer of data between networks that use different protocols at OSI layers one and two (physical, Medium Access Control, and Logical Link Control). Routers can receive, reformat, and retransmit data packets assembled by different layer-one and layer-two protocols. Different routers are built to manage different protocol sets.

Source: "Bridge and Routers Tutorial," p. 22.

Legacy systems are mainframe-oriented and remain a mainstay of organizations that must process an extremely large number of transactions within a finite timeframe.

speed of a high-end micro-, mini-, or mainframe computer as a server and the cost benefits and end-user support of lower-cost microcomputer-based applications, end users can quickly and comfortably access data from remote sources.

The basis of C/SA is a network that connects the clients and the server(s). A simple mode of this architecture is the printer server that attaches to a LAN to serve all users (clients) on the LAN. A more complex configuration would have these servers and clients connected by way of a WAN. The extreme example is the use of a Web browser on the Internet. With such a Web environment, a query is made and the Web browser (a client) seeks out numerous servers to find the information, without the user knowing where the information came from. (See Figure 8.6.)

To date, the focus on client-server architecture has heralded the advent of a step forward from simple distributed processing or telecommunications links, revealing the novelty of the concept. Meanwhile, industry leaders like IBM furiously scramble to design integrative links to support C/S technology within many of the more dynamic and popular applications, from micro- to supercomputers.

FIGURE 8.6
Client-Server Architecture

Source: Adapted from Hindin, *Data Communication.*

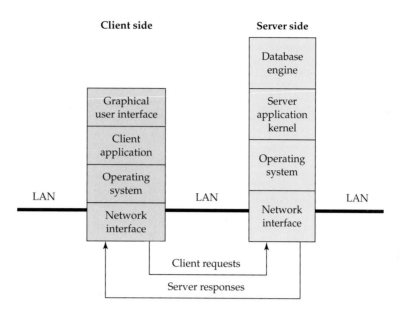

The Pointcast Network (PCN) is a great example of client-server architecture. You run the application (direct or as a screen saver) on your PC and it periodically requests information over the Internet from the PCN server, updating the data on your screen.

The concepts behind client-server technology are relatively new, and considered an extension of both the distributed and cooperative processing architectures of database management.

As a point of reference, *cooperative processing* is simply the sharing of computer processing tasks between two or more processors, either within or between computers. A similar operation, *distributed processing,* is the dispersion of data processing among computers in multiple sites. The client-server architecture is a logical extension of these two ideas, but takes the concept beyond either.

Figure 8.7 presents four typical client-server architectures that could be used in a company's implementation of the technology. The possible combinations and permutations of the applications and hardware represent a vast quantity of support that managers could have at their disposal. The needs of the company, coupled with the needs of the individual, drive the architectural design of the model and are restricted only by access to any outside information resources available and the resources of the firm.

C/S Fat and Thin Clients

The clients in C/S architecture have come to be called "fat" and "thin." **Fat clients** have large storage and processing power; therefore, they contribute to the high costs of C/S computing. **Thin clients,** on the other hand, frequently have no local storage and limited processing power. Some of them are completely server controlled, allowing users to download applications on demand. Thin clients can connect anywhere and do not need to be robust.

Five companies—IBM, Oracle Corporation, Netscape Communications Corp., Sun Microsystems, Inc., and Apple Computer Company—proposed a set of common specifications for thin clients called the *Network Computer (NC).* The NC Reference Profile is a list of established software specifications that should provide the framework for configuring the worlds of host-based, client-server, and Internet computing. With adequate bandwidth, it is possible, even preferable, to have all resources on the server and use the client as a "dumb terminal." This is reminiscent of the olden days of mainframes but provides greater security, sharing of resources, and ease of software update.

FIGURE 8.7   Models of Client-Server Implementation

Source: Adapted from McLarnon, *Software Magazine.*

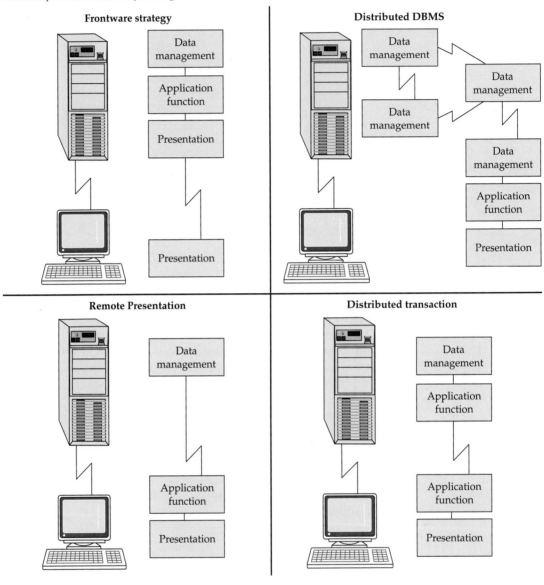

Case 8-1

Optical Switching

Randall Wood

Telephone usage first began in 1876. The first method of connectivity was direct connection of telephones to each other. A manual switch of mechanical connections, commonly called a switchboard, was brought on the scene in 1878. The switchboard required human operators and reduced the amount of wiring needed. [2]

Next out was the electromechanical switch. The step-by-step switch was the first switch of this sort and was invented by Alan B. Strowger in 1919. Strowger's switch required a rotary dial telephone, which created electrical pulses by opening and closing a contact in the telephone when its round dial was turned and released. The switch would then mechanically create a circuit based on the number dialed. Further improvements in electromechanical switching led to the development of the panel switch in 1921 and the cross-bar technology in 1938. The speed and reliability of these switches were, however, severely limited due to their moving mechanical parts.

Solid-state switches came into service in 1965 and were followed by digital switches in 1970. Digital switches, special-purpose computers, are faster and more reliable than their electromechanical counterparts. They also require less floor space, commonly called a footprint, at switch sites. New software capabilities also aided in the speed increase of these devices. [2]

Digital switches are widely used today and can handle large amounts of voice and data from several locations all at once. The amount of data that can be sent per unit time is called bandwidth. Long-haul connections of telephones or computers that require a significant amount of bandwidth are some of the major applications of these digital switches.

The most efficient medium for transporting data across these long distances is optical fiber. Since digital switches read and direct electrical digital data and the signal being transported is in optical form, there must be some method of making these devices communicate.

HOW AN OPTOELECTRONIC SWITCH WORKS

Whether data are originally in analog or digital form, they are all converted at the switch site to an optical form for long-haul transport. A digital receiver passes the electrical signal to a laser or light-emitting diode called an optical transmitter. The optical transmitter sends out pulses of a specific analog wavelength light. This signal can travel as far as 40 miles before it needs to be regenerated. At some point along the path, the signal will come to one or several switches. Upon reaching each switch, the signal must be converted back to an electrical form to pass through the switch.

An optical receiver first receives the optical signal. The signal is then converted back to its electrical digital equivalent. The digital signal is then electrically demultiplexed—split into several smaller electrical signals. Next, routing data called overhead are read from each data packet. Based on the routing data, each piece of data is switched to its desired destination. After the switching occurs, each newly directed data stream is electrically multiplexed—electrically combined—back into a larger digital signal. The new digital signal must then be converted back to an optical signal and sent along its way. Devices that perform these tasks are also called digital cross-connects and add/drop multiplexers. [5]

The conversion from digital to optical to digital seems like a tedious process. It, in fact, is much more tedious than just being able to keep the signal in optical form until it gets to the end-user switch. The extra equipment needed for conversion of signals also adds to footprint size.

Since data have to be converted back to digital form in an optoelectronic switch, the switch must be synchronized with other nodes on the network. That is, it must know when to start reading the data and is, therefore, referred to as bit rate dependent. Additional timing equipment is required at these switches to reduce the risk of bit errors.

The switch must also know how to read the data once it receives them. It would have to know what protocol to use in order to communicate with other nodes, which would call for the purchase of additional software for each site. The need for both synchronization and protocol gives rise to possible communication errors.

NEED FOR OPTICAL SWITCHING

Technological advances are allowing more electrical digital data to be multiplexed into the same time frame, thereby increasing bandwidth. This method is called time division multiplexing (TDM).

The optical fiber medium also has a tremendous bandwidth expansion capacity. Wavelength division multiplexing (WDM) and dense wavelength division multiplexing (DWDM) allow several optical signals of different wavelengths to be sent along a single fiber simultaneously.

Optical multiplexing or demultiplexing used in these technologies simply means the combination or separation of optical waves that are traveling on a fiber medium. As mentioned earlier, electrical or time division multiplexing refers to the combination or separation of electrical signals into or out of a particular time frame. However, the terms *multiplex* and *demultiplex* are used loosely with these technologies and at times must be taken out of context.

Optical couplers perform the necessary optical multiplexing and demultiplexing that make the WDM and DWDM technologies possible. New fiber and transmitter improvements are allowing more and more of these wavelengths to be placed on a single fiber. The current wavelength per fiber estimate of 160 is supposed to be achieved by 2001.

Receiving multiple wavelengths and performing a conversion on every one is often unnecessary. Some wavelengths travel through a switch the same way every time. Others need to be rerouted but have no need to drop off any segment of their data in the process. These wavelengths need not be converted from optical form to digital form and electrically demultiplexed. Allowing each of these wavelengths to remain in optical form would cut down on unnecessary conversions and equipment. Less equipment leads to less money required for each site, a smaller footprint, and less signal delay. [4]

HOW AN OPTICAL SWITCH WORKS

An optical switch requires no conversion of signal. The switch is usually constructed as a matrix with waveguides and crosspoints. A waveguide is a very small trench that guides the wave through the matrix. The waveguides cross paths at several points within the matrix called crosspoints. These switches also are called optical cross connects or optical add/drop multiplexers.

Optical signals traveling along optical fiber arrive at the switch. The multiplexed wavelengths on each fiber first need to be optically demultiplexed. Each individual wavelength is then directed to a particular waveguide insertion point. The wavelengths travel down their respective waveguides coming to each crosspoint.

If a wavelength is not to be switched, it will follow the straight path of its initial waveguide, passing each crosspoint, and will exit at the far end of the matrix. Each crosspoint, however, is a possible point of deflection. If the signal is to be switched, it will be deflected at one or more crosspoints within the matrix and exit at its desired location.

Since data are not taken out of optical form, optical switches are bit rate independent and protocol transparent. The purchase of expensive timing equipment and unnecessary software is eliminated with these devices. In addition, the lack of electrical conversion allows for the support of bit rates beyond the reach of practical optoelectronic systems.

TYPES OF OPTICAL SWITCHES

Several varying designs have resulted from the need for optical switching technology. Companies across the world have created numerous prototypes. The two main types of optical switches are the *mechanical mirror switch* and the *Champagne switch.*

The mechanical mirror switch contains tiny mirrors at each crosspoint. Each mirror is mechanically positioned and repositioned based on the desired path of the incoming wavelengths. Depending on the manufacturer, these mirrors can change position 200 to 400 times per second.

The Champagne switch is a relatively new design by Agilent Technologies. It has undergone extensive testing and is currently being tested by some of the company's partners for mass production. Agilent is a subsidiary of Hewlett-Packard and is currently the only company that has the capability and the rights to produce this switch.

Agilent decided to use a standard 32×32 matrix configuration. There are, therefore, 32 waveguides that cross paths with 32 more waveguides on each matrix. Additional matrix sizes can be created using this standard size as a building block. The matrix also can be subdivided to create several smaller matrices [3]

This switch has the capability of producing a tiny bubble at each crosspoint within the matrix and is thus referred to as the Champagne switch. It is based on total internal reflection from the sidewalls of waveguides etched at the crosspoints of a silica planar lightwave circuit matrix. The waveguides are normally filled with a refractive index-matching fluid to allow transmission across the trench to the next collinear waveguide segment.

If redirection of a signal is desired, a bubble will be formed and will displace the liquid at the necessary crosspoint. In the presence of a bubble, the light will undergo total internal reflection. The signal will then exit at the desired location. Actuators at each crosspoint have the ability to form and remove a bubble several hundred times per second. [1][3]

PROS AND CONS OF DIFFERENT OPTICAL SWITCHES

The obvious benefit of optical switches is the ability to keep the data signal in optical form as it passes through the switch. However, both types of switches have different characteristics and must be looked at individually.

MECHANICAL MIRROR SWITCH

As was the case with the older electromechanical switches, moving mechanical parts have a tendency to cause problems. Moving parts wear out over time. Wear leads to undesired changes in tolerances.

It is difficult enough to have each crosspoint's mirror reflect a signal at the precise angle desired without the tolerance inconsistencies. In fact, pointing accuracy better than 0.25 degree is required in a 32×32-size switch to achieve better than 10 dB insertion loss. The signal will not be recognizable if the loss gets too high. The possibility of a part breaking is always present as well. Durability and reliability seem to be shortcomings of this type of switch.

CHAMPAGNE SWITCH

The Champagne switch has no moving parts and thus seems to be very reliable. Through mass production and extensive testing and use of inkjet printers, Hewlett-Packard has proven the reliability of the inkjet technology used in Agilent's switch.

This switch requires little material; therefore, its switching matrix is only about 10 square inches in area. Since each bubble provides total internal reflection along each waveguide that intersects it, the switch produces very low losses. There is no threat of too much degradation of signal. [3]

FUTURE OF OPTICAL SWITCHING

Optical switching will take the place of optoelectronic switching for long-haul applications in the near future. Some optical switches are in place today and companies worldwide have plans to install them once they become more reliable and affordable.

Multiple wavelengths need to be present in order to get the most utility out of an optically switched network, but current DWDM transmitters are very expensive. They can cost 5 to 10 times more than regular optical transmitters. High initial costs and lack of the need to switch large amounts of data are enough to deter some communications companies from using optical switches in their networks. However, if future expansion is expected, purchasing these switches up-front is a wise investment.

Several optoelectronic switches remain in networks today. These switches may for the meantime be more reliable than the optical switch alternative. Optical switches are, nevertheless, being made more reliable everyday. It may not even be financially or physically practical to replace some of these switches immediately.

These situations may remain true for a short period of time, but they will only be temporary. As the prices of DWDM transmitters drop and the demand for more bandwidth increases, the demand for optical switches will increase. The switches will become more reliable and capable and will replace yesterday's switches. The worldwide network of the future will be entirely optical.

WORKS CITED

1. Agilent Technologies. *Tiny Bubbles—The Secret to Tomorrow's Broadband Networks.* http://www.agilent.com/Feature/English/02/.

2. Carr, Houston H., and Charles A. Snyder. *The Management of Telecommunications.* Burr Ridge, IL: Irwin/McGraw-Hill, 1997.

3. Fouquet, Julie E. *Compact Optical Cross-Connect Switch Based on Total Internal Reflection in a Fluid-Containing Planar Lightwave Circuit.* Agilent Laboratories. http://www.agilent.com.

4. Midwinter, John E. *Photonics in Switching.* Vol. I. San Diego: Academic Press, 1993.

5. Northern Telecom. *SONET 101: An Introduction to Basic Synchronous Optical Networks.* Richardson, TX: Northern Telecom, 1995.

Summary

Networks, at the various levels of interconnect and complexity, create the virtual organization. While this term is often used to mean an often temporary confederation of remotely located individuals, it also can mean the tight coupling of the formal organization. LANs provide the connectivity that homogeneous and closely colocated users require. MANs give connectivity to similar and nonsimilar organizations that require common access. WANs give a global reach to the individual organization and make it a part of other organizations.

The equipment used to create the desired connectivity is dependent on the architecture and the needs of the organization, virtual or real. Whatever infrastructure is created, it will be a significant expense. However, it is only by way of this expense, nay, this investment, that organizations can compete in the modern world.

Just as computers can be enhanced by connection to other computers, networks can vastly improve the effectiveness of organizations when the networks are connected. Every organization faces the task of which connectivity among networks to build and which alternatives to employ. A basic understanding of networking connectivity is vital for modern managers to be effective in making these choices. The alternatives have different costs and benefits; consequently, it is important for managers to evaluate the relative merits and costs of the choices.

Networks are composed of components to enable connectivity from small, local area to large, even global, networks. This chapter begins with a discussion of networks as to geography and security, from LANs to WANs and VPNs. It ends with descriptions of equipment from the simplest repeater and goes through routers to gateways.

In this chapter we discussed the idea of networks by their geographical distribution, whether they were local, metropolitan, or wide. In addition, we discussed value added networks, alternatives for moving data within networks, such as packet data networks, and enterprise systems along with virtual private networks. The emerging peer-to-peer computing model was covered. In order to move data on networks, we require specialized equipment; thus, we discussed these devices ranging from the simplest repeater to the most complex gateway. See Figure 8.8 for a depiction of the levels of an enterprise system.

Local area networks can be peer-to-peer or client-server architecture. The latter can be composed of fat or thin clients, whereas the LAN is generally composed of fat clients. In the process of discussion, we have placed the equipment in the proper position in the OSI model and provided comparison of network linkage alternatives.

FIGURE 8.8
Levels of Enterprise Systems

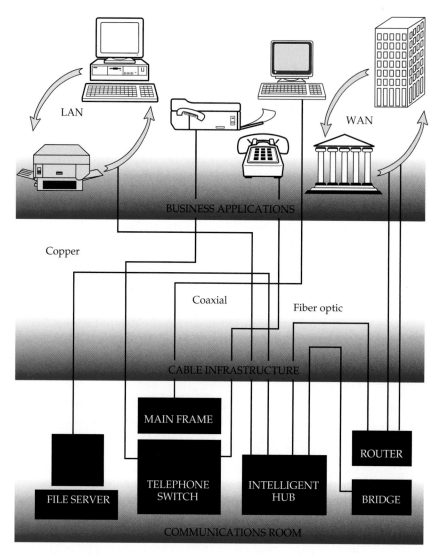

Key Terms

Recommended Readings

Communications Week

Network Magazine

Computerworld

Info World

Discussion Questions

8.1. Differentiate between a LAN, backbone network, MAN, and WAN.

8.2. What does a VAN do? What does it mean to say it is unregulated?

8.3. Differentiate between a datagram and virtual circuit on a packet data network.

8.4. Why is a PDN referred to as a cloud?

8.5. How are circuit-switched and packet-switched networks different?

8.6. How does a VPN work? What is their value?

8.7. Differentiate between a repeater, bridge, router, and gateway.

8.8. How does a switch add value over a hub?

Projects

8.1. Become a member of SETI or United devices P-2-P network. Determine the statistics to date.

8.2. Using a hub, create an N=4 Windows-based network.

8.3. In Project 8.2, make one node a server, one a thin client, and one a fat client.

Chapter **Nine**

The Internet Connects to the World; the Intranet Connects the Organization

CONTINUING CASE—PART 9

"Hey, Grandad, it's Steve. Got a minute?"

"Of course," replied Michael, leaning back in his chair to speak to his favorite grandchild on the phone. "What's up?"

"Well, I was wondering if you had an extra computer with a modem there at JEI, one that I could borrow for the weekend?"

"Well, I think the one on my desk is a good candidate, as Alli promises to get me a better one any day now. What do you have in mind?"

"I want to surf the Internet."

"Tell me more."

"Well, as you know, the Internet is just a network of networks, but it means that if I can get a computer and modem, I can get to lots of places with no cost. You know, like I showed you at school, where I could log into a local electronic bulletin board. I can now do the same to places in Europe and Japan."

"What do you mean without cost? As I remember, there is no such thing as a free lunch."

"Because the Internet is connectivity among networks, I can get connected to the computer at the *University of Denver*, since I don't have a regular Internet Service Provider account, like AOL. At school, where I am enrolled as a summer student, I can use the Internet to connect to other computers. The whole thing is something called a fixed-cost network, so there is no charge for using it."

"Why do you need to do this?"

"With the mainframe at U of D, I use their software to send email to anyone with an Internet connection as well as access websites and search engines."

"Tell me more about websites. Should JEI have one?"

"A website is just software running on the mainframe or a PC server that understands browser commands. With your computer and the mainframe's access to the Internet, I can input a website address and the programs will bring me the home page, that is the first page of the file at the location."

"What does it take to get to the Web page?"

"All it takes is to bring up your *Netscape*® browser, which is just a program on your computer, and type in the Web page address, called the *universal resource locator*, or *URL*. The whole system is designed so anyone can click to start the browser, type in the URL, and get to where they want to go."

"How do you know where you want to go?"

"That's easy! If you already know the address of a website, you type it in. If you don't know it, but just know the subject for which you are looking, say baseball scores, you use another program with the browser, called a search engine, to search for all websites that have 'baseball scores' in their header lines, up front."

"So I could search on something like 'security systems' and find our competition?"

"Yes, but since there are millions of computers connected to the Internet, and many of them have Web pages, you will get many thousands of hits, that is, pages with your subject. It's not bad, but you now have to look at all the sites and decide which ones are good for you."

"So I could search for competitors as well as suppliers! I have been noticing that salespeople have something on their business card that starts with http://www. I didn't have any idea what that was."

"You asked if I thought JEI should have a Web page. The answer is yes, definitely. Some companies create Web pages just to advertise their presence. Others list their services and let you email them for information. Still others will put a catalog on the site and let you order parts from it. This is what you might check out with your suppliers. If they have a website, you should be able to go there and order what you want without a salesperson or doing any paperwork."

"That's really interesting. It sounds like there may be some potential for us. Just how could JEI use a website?"

"First, JEI should have a site that shows all of its divisions, products, and services. You might have a description of the major ones on the home page and let people click on the area of interest. Say you have Lighting and Security, Risk Assessment, Computer Hosting, and Disaster Recovery. When the viewer clicked on, say, Lighting and Security, they would be taken to another page that shows the major areas within this area of JEI, that is, all of the products and services of JL&S. You could expand this to have an order form."

"Uhmmmn, sounds like a great idea!"

"And it is not an expensive one, Grandad. I have friends at U of D who can get you going and then you can see how far you want to go. The first one would be simple and give you and Dad a chance to think about the total idea. Then, when you know what you want to do, after looking at other sites, we can get some professionals to come in and make a killer site."

"Killer site?"

"Sorry, a really well-done site with graphics, email back to you for questions, and even a catalog of parts for your people at SII. You can allow SII special access and not let in regular people."

"Sounds great! Is there a catch?"

"Well, there is one. It seems that every time we create something good, someone tries to mess it up. This means that as you connect to the Internet, people called hackers could get into JEI's computer and do damage. Also, you can get viruses from programs you download from the Internet. The first case can be handled by putting in a firewall, which is just special software that watches out for bad people. We can handle the second by putting in virus check software on each machine."

"Hackers and viruses! I thought computers and the Internet were safe! Will a website not be a risky venture?"

"Well, you have a risk assessment division don't you?"

"Just like your father! You're right; I'll get them looking into the risk of a website and have your Dad investigate its value for all of our divisions."

"And, Grandad, this might be a new line of business under the risk assessment division. And you could hire me as a consultant!"

"If your Mom and Grandmom don't skin me alive, I'll use the consulting position to take over your allowance. I imagine that this will be great fun for you, but your primary job is to finish school. It looks like you will have a lot of ideas to draw upon from JEI, so you will want to include both business and engineering in your college program. That's a little ways away, so hunker down and work on the other stuff right now."

"You bet. Is it OK if I keep my ear to the ground for new ideas?"

"Of course, Steve, I need all the help I can get! Drop by the office and pick up the computer. Consider it a long-term loan, a part of your consulting contract."

"Yes, Sir!"

INTRODUCTION

The **Internet** is a phenomenon that started in the early 1970s and came to full bloom in the early 1990s. The allowance of commercial users at the beginning of 1994 accelerated an already rapid rate of growth and the introduction of the **World Wide Web (WWW)** that same year added even more accelerated use. The Internet has become a resource that is changing the way individuals and organizations communicate, operate, and share resources. The idea of using Internet technologies inside the organization, a phenomenon called the **intranet,** has given rise to another model for intra-organizational connectivity that is taking center stage.

The Internet and intranet are important to our study and use of telecommunications because of the ways they have changed our personal lives. To this point, we have discussed the value of connectivity among small groups and large populations. The Internet is the ultimate wide area network, giving us access to the world, its information, and its markets. The idea of the Internet is just an extension of simpler forms of connectivity, except that this "network of networks" has special tools, capabilities, and sources of information that are changing the way we live and do business.

Caveat: The Internet and its capabilities are changing on an almost daily basis. This is a discussion of Internet basics. Because of the rapidly changing technology, you will likely be knowledgeable of technologies and capabilities not covered here.

THE INTERNET—THE NETWORK OF NETWORKS

One of the authors received his first IBM microcomputer computer (a PC/AT [286]) in May 1985. The same year, his college installed an IBM token-passing ring network (see Chapters 5 through 8 for more on networks) and had connectivity to the IBM mainframe on campus. With this connectivity came access to **Bitnet,** a wonderful resource that gave the possibility of electronic mail to most universities.

A network is two or more nodes connected by one or more channels.

Bitnet was a network, supported by IBM, to give academic connectivity. With Bitnet and its counterparts, connected by gateways, academics could send email and, with some energy, files. We had connectivity, and we had access to the world.

The pathway to Bitnet began in 1969, when the U.S. governmental agency, Advanced Research Projects Agency (ARPA), set out to demonstrate the feasibility of a packet-switched network and subsequently created the **ARPANET (Advanced Research Projects Agency Network).** The experiment was very successful. This led to the creation of NSFNet by the National Science Foundation in 1986, for the purpose of connecting governmental research agencies and universities doing research. NSFNet absorbed the ARPANET in the late 1980s. Connected to or connected with each of the networks mentioned have been thousands of other networks, each privately administered. The secret has been that each network is administered as required, funded individually, and standardized to give connectivity among them all. Using TCP/IP (Transmission Control Protocol/Internet Protocol) and providing gateways among the networks has produced what we now know as the Internet—a network of networks.

The **Internet** is truly a network of networks. It provides connectivity and access to the world. The Internet's development and evolution are recent history, all of it occurring since Woodstock #1. Case 9-1, "The Role of Government in the Evolution of the Internet" by Robert E. Kahn, which appeared in the August 1994 issue of the *Communications of the ACM*, gives an excellent history of the evolution of the Internet and the involvement of several U.S. governmental agencies. The governmental agency experiment in packet-switched networks has grown and evolved to change our world. As of early 1994, there were 2.2 million connected computers from 56,063 registered networks, from 92 countries, with

The Real World   9–1
The Internet

General Definition—A vast global open information *metanetwork* (a network of networks) of computer hosts. (The means by which all the world's computers are able to communicate with each other.)

    Narrow Definition (IP Network)—A set of at least 25,000 of the 56,000+ registered Internetworks which are capable of routing Internet Protocol packets among themselves.

Broad Definition—The IP Internetwork plus all connected networks capable of routing traffic to a destination device or process.

Source: *The Internet Society*—A Presentation dated February 1994 distributed on CD-ROM Today® disk #1.

a network attachment growth rate of 12 percent per month. If you extrapolate the growth of the Internet connections, it is estimated that *everyone* on the planet Earth will be connected by the year 2004. Of course, it is not realistic to believe in such universal connectivity because of the poor technological sophistication in large parts of the world.

One of the main issues facing the government is how to close the gap in the "digital divide,"[1] a common phrase to describe the separation between those with access to the Internet and those without. Within the United States, the digital divide is not as serious as it appears at first glance. Initially considered race-based, it now appears that the digital divide is primarily income based. As the cost of computers and Internet access continue to decrease, this gap will get smaller. Efforts already have been made to place computers with Internet access in low-income area schools, libraries, and public housing, so that the young may learn essential computer skills. In 2000 the Clinton administration devoted $12.5 million to supporting efforts to boost the online population in lower-income segments.

The Internet is two things: technology and access. Figure 9.1 shows the T3 (45 Mbps) backbone network. From the original 45 Mbps backbone, evolving to early broadband speed (155 Mbps), will radiate T3 and T1 splines, giving connectivity among the tens of thousands of smaller network Internet service provider (ISP) points-of-presence, and individual access points.

What can you do on the Internet? There are books on this subject as well as files you can access free from the Internet. One such book is *Internet Essentials* by Lynda Armbruster, Que Publishers. As you will find there and in other books such as *Internet for Dummies,* you can sign up for ListServer to automatically send you text files on a large number of subjects, use File Transfer Protocol (FTP) to move files,

FIGURE 9.1
NSFNET T3 Backbone Service, Circa 1992

Source: Merit Network, Inc., October 1992.

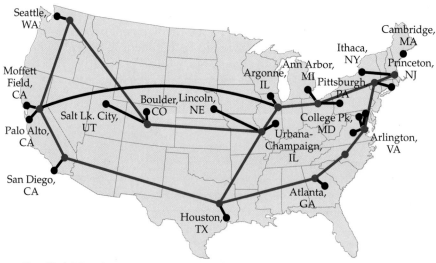

● = Core Nodal Switching Subsystem (CNSS)
● = Exterior Nodal Switching Subsystem (ENSS)

[1] Robert E. Kahn, "*Viewpoint*—The Role of Government in the Evolution of the Internet," *Communications of the ACM* 37, no. 4 (August 1994), pp. 15–19.

and Telnet to connect and log on to other computers as a guest user. These services are described below.

LISTSERV is the program that operates discussion groups on the Internet. Subscribers can send mail to this special program to be automatically distributed to each person on the list, a convenient way of communicating without human intervention. (*Note:* There is a LISTSERV from the White House.)

File Transfer Protocol (FTP) is a part of the Internet protocol suite of capabilities that enables a user to access files on a remote computer and move files between two computers connected to the Internet.

Telnet is a program that enables you to communicate with other computers and is typically used for remote access to host computers on which they have an account or to publicly accessible catalogues and databases.

Usenet started as a network on which to discuss specific topics and has expanded. Usenet newsgroups are broken down by topics, ranging from business to science to education.

Early users of the service, seeing a need for utilities that are easy to use and offer wide access to people and information, created a set of text-based software services. These are Archie, Gopher, Veronica, WAIS, WWW, Mosaic®, and WhoIS.[2] Many of these capabilities have been replaced by easier-to-use Web-based tools.

Archie is a collection of resource discovery tools, developed and maintained by McGill University, for locating files at hundreds of anonymous FTP sites by using a file name search. Archie also is available at other designated sites around the globe. If you are looking for a specific file, Archie can help you locate an FTP site that has it.

Veronica (Very Easy Rodent-Oriented Net-Wise Index to Computerized Archives) is a service that locates and indexes titles of Gopher items by keyword search. A Veronica search typically searches the menus of hundreds of Gopher services, perhaps all the Gopher servers that are attached to the Internet.

WhoIS provides information on registered users and network names, including their postal addresses. The main WhoIs database runs at the Network Information Center (NIC) with administrative and technical contacts for domains automatically registered when the applications are processed.

WAIS stands for Wide Area Information Server and is a client-server system developed to help users search multiple Internet sites at one time and retrieve resources by searching indexes of databases. WAIS searches are fast, and the results can either be scanned online or mailed to your network address.

Gopher is a menu-driven system developed at the University of Minnesota. The *Gopher* name was derived from Minnesota's nickname as the Gopher State, as well as the concept that the Internet search will "go for" files containing information you need. Gopher combines features of electronic bulletin board services and databases with parts of FTP, Archie, WAIS, and Telnet into one easy-to-use navigation tool. Gopher simplifies locating and retrieving ASCII text documents from various sources of information.

---

[2] Taken from *Internet Essentials* by Lynda Armbruster, Que Publishers.

The Real World
Webspeak Deciphered

9–2

The World Wide Web's technospeak is as sticky as the Web itself. Here's a translation of the worst of the jargon.

- **Browser.** Software that opens the door to the Web, allowing the display of text and graphics. **Mosaic** and **Netscape** are two popular browsers.

- **FAQ (frequently asked questions).** A grab bag of questions that new users of a website often ask—with answers, of course.

- **Hit.** A rough measure of a site's popularity; each hit represents one time that a file in the site is accessed.

- **Home page.** The opening screen of a website.

- **Hypermedia.** Video and sound files transmitted by way of the Web.

- **Hypertext.** Highlighted text linked to related pages in the same or other sites.

- **Search engine.** An electronic directory on the Web that searches for documents, pages, or sites based on key words. Yahoo! *(http://www.yahoo.com)* is an especially popular search engine.

- **Search provider.** An online service, university network, or corporate server that lets users connect to the Internet, which in turn is the gateway to the Web.

- **Website.** A collection of pages and files on the Web built around a common theme or subject.

- **Webmaster.** The authority figure responsible for maintaining and updating the information of a site. Like a sysop of an online bulletin board.

- **Universal resource locater.** A URL is the technical name of a Web address—*http://www. apple.com* is an example.

Source: John Simons, "Webspeak Deciphered," *U.S. News & World Report.*

The capabilities that follow are the result of transition from text-based to graphics and hyperlink-based interfaces, much like the movement from DOS to Windows. The basis of this movement is the software that allowed files to be retrieved and displayed with ease, for example, the World Wide Web (WWW) software developed by Tim Berners-Lee, who led a team at Switzerland's European Particle Physics Laboratory (CERN for short, for the name Conseil Européen pour la Recherche Nucléaire).

World Wide Web (WWW) retrieves resources as a powerful hypertext and hypermedia browser of databases. *Hypertext* is text with pointers to other text, and *hypermedia* also might involve images, sound, or animation, in addition to text. This public domain software goes beyond Gopher and WAIS as a global information system with an easy-to-use interface that provides access to almost all existing Internet-based information. The information appears on *home pages,*[3] providing access to individuals and organizations with only the click of a mouse button. Real World window 9–3 lists a very few home pages, oriented towards college financial aid.

HyperText Markup Language (HTML)[4] is one of the capabilities that is used like a word processor to create a WWW home page. HTML is a language;

[3] The term *home page* means the first page of an organization's information on the WWW. Many people use the term to mean any page in the hierarchy of information.
[4] The descriptions of HTML, HTTP, and the intranet that follow rely heavily on information from the WWW site of *JSB Computer Systems Ltd,* http://www.Intranet.co.uk; and the *Amdahl Corporation,* http://www.amdahl.com/doc/products/bsg/intra/concepts.html.

The Real World
WWW Sites for College Financial Aid

9–3

By late 1995, PC magazines and even *The Wall Street Journal* were giving WWW addresses for companies and services. Of immense value to college-bound students and their parents is the information that follows, taken from the September 1995 issue of *Computer Life*. All addresses start with http://

The Internet's Financial Information Page, a guide to the most up-to-date financial aid information on the Web—www.cs.cmu.edu:8008/afs/cs.cmu/ user/mkant/Public/FinAid/finaid.html

The Federal Information Exchange—lists assistance available from federal agencies—web.fie.com/web.fed/

Minority Online Information Service—gives information on federal scholarships and fellowships— web.fie.com/web/mol

Don't Miss Out: The Ambitious Student's Guide to Financial Aid—has details on grants and scholarships from colleges, state, and the federal government— www.infi.net/collegemoney/toc1.html

The Bookstore—supplies free loan applications— www.infi.net/collegemoney/bkorder. html

Student Financial Aid Information—maintains a calendar that shows you what to do and when to do it—www.wellsfargo.com/per/perstu/stuaid/index.html

The Foundation Center and the Princeton Review—are comprehensive guides to where to look for aid—fdncenter.org and www.review.com/faid/ 7000.html

Source: *Computer Life.*

a standard for creating multimedia, hypertext files; and a standard for serving these standardized files when they are requested. It allows the incorporation of text and images to make an impressive presentation. Where simple text, even with good fonts of varying sizes, is flat to view, images make pages pull you into them. Real World window 9–4 shows the result of a search on the Netscape® WWW browser for the initials "html", indicating home pages of help for use of this language. Your search will likely produce even more resources for your use.

HyperText Transfer Protocol (HTTP) is the standard used by the server and its clients, which will send HTML files over the Internet from the server to clients requesting them. Thus, browsers (*client* software that retrieves and displays the HTML file) like Netscape and Microsoft Internet Explorer use the command http:// on the WWW to access a home page, that is, a site with HTML documents. In a nutshell, the command "http" commands the browser to send the characters that follow the "//" to a network domain server, where a search is made of a database to find the characters and the attendant unique IP address. The address is queried and a file by the same name as the characters is returned to the browser where the HTML capability displays it.

Two standards discussed previously (HTML and HTTP) provide the basis for a whole new kind of access to computerized information. Creating multimedia files in a standard way allows client software to be built that not only can retrieve the files from an HTTP server, but also open them and display them as part of the request. And since the file can contain hyperlinks to other files (even when they reside on other computers), a user now has the ability to navigate information with a point-and-click interface from what appears to

Information Window   9–1

To distinguish between the Internet and the World Wide Web, a comparison to the Microsoft Windows® environment is useful. Computers use the *disk operating system (DOS)* to control the computer's actions. On top of this is placed the Windows® *graphical user interface*, which separates the operating system from the users, making the use of a computer a very easy action. In like manner, the Internet is connectivity between millions of computers. The WWW is the graphical user interface that allows graphical and easy use of this connectivity to access remote resources and information.

---

be standard textual documents. This technology takes away the complexity of accessing information on distributed computers.

Mosaic is the original hyperlink-based Internet information browser and World Wide Web client that provides transparent access to a number of resources, including anonymous FTP, WAIS, and WWW. A browser can recognize and manipulate a large range of data types and services, including multimedia-based resources such as sound and animation.

Netscape® is the original premier graphics and hyper-based Internet information presenter and browser that is the follow-up to Mosaic, developed by the same people.

Internet Explorer (IE)® is Microsoft Corporation's competitor to Netscape. One feature of these browsers is the access to search engines. That is to say, Netscape and IE include a "net search" button that takes the user to a page that includes access to several search facilities. Once the search engine is chosen, search words are included. The value of the search engine has spawned several dedicated capabilities, such as Alta Vista® and Google®. Real World window 9–4 shows the results of a search on "html".

Java is the programming language and environment designed to solve a number of problems in modern programming practice. It is simple, **object-oriented, distributed,** interpreted, robust, secure, architecture-neutral, portable, high-performance, **multithreaded,** and dynamic language. (See Case 9.4 for more on the Java language.)

Access to the Internet

If you are accessing the Internet personally, you have two choices. The first is through an online service, such as America Online®. While such online services began life providing access to their mainframe capabilities, they now have a major activity of providing connectivity to the Internet plus providing you a World Wide Web browser with search engines. These services initially marketed their capabilities and Internet access at a flat fee per month for a limited number of hours of access plus a charge per hour for access over the initial amount. These charges apply whether the user is accessing the mainframe capabilities or surfing the Internet. Most services have evolved to providing unlimited access for a larger fee.

The second method of access to the Internet is via an **Internet service provider (ISP),** such as *Earthlink.net*® or *Bellsouth.net*®. With these and other direct Internet

The Real World   9–4

Guide > Search for **html**

To track your stocks for free, check out the **Stocks** link under Infoseek Guide *News Update*.

 **Which Web server won?**

Click here to find out

Purveyor, the Premier Webserver

Titles 11 to 20 (of 100) ordered by *score · Previous 10 Titles · New Search*

WEB **Scott's Home Page**
-- *http://www.shepparton.net.au/~spade/ (Score 42, Size 16K)*
You are the 122nd vistior to my page. Thanks for visiting! I hope you are now enlightened!. (Here's some shortcuts for all you lazy people who couldn't bothered moving down to the section you want. Sheesh!). All about me!. Write to . . . (*See also Similar Pages*)

WEB **Mag's Big List of HTML Editors**
-- *http://sdg.ncsa.uiuc.edu/~mag/work/HTMLEditors/ (Score 42, Size 46K)*
I hope for this to be the most complete list of HTML editing tools around. If you know of a tool that is not on this list, or if you find incorrect or incomplete information here, please let me know . . I'm working on collecting other HTML . . . (*See also Similar Pages*)

WEB **HTML 2.0 Specification (Internet Draft)**
-- *http://www.mcis.duke.edu/HTML2.0.html (Score 42, Size 136K)*
HyperText Markup Language. Specification - 2.0. STATUS OF THIS MEMO. This document is an Internet draft. Internet drafts are working documents of the Internet Engineering Task Force (IETF), its areas, and its working groups. Note that other . . . (*See also Similar Pages*)

WEB **HTML 3.0 28th March 1995**
--*http://www.w3.org/pub/WWW/MarkUp/html3/html3.txt (Score 42, Size 372K)*
INTERNET DRAFT Dave Raggett, W3C Expires in six months email: HyperText Markup Language Specification Version 3.0 Status of this Memo This document is an Internet draft. Internet drafts are working documents of the Internet Engineering Task Force . . . (*See also Similar Pages*)

WEB **Running a WWW Service--4 HTML**
--*http://info.mcc.ac.uk/CGU/SIMA/handbook/handbook-4_HTML.html (Score 42, Size 24K)*
Part of a comprehensive manual, this section contains the basics on HTML and a number of good editing and conversion tools. (*See also* HTML, HTML authoring software, HTML conversion, HTML testing, HTML manuals, Style guides, *Similar Pages*)

WEB **Index of /~rayk/html/**
--*http://www.best.com/~rayk/html/ (Score 42, Size 9K)*
othlink.html size 2287 aproch.html size 914 vrnd01.html size 736 samhita.html size 1520 bsfwd.html size 8498 bs29-30.html size 4085 bs31-32.html size 6101 sidhanta.html size 4137 wait.html size 899 cait05.html size 405 prab012.html size 71014 . . . (*See also Similar Pages*)

WEB **HTML Working T. Berners-Lee ...**

providers, the fee is a fixed amount per month for either a fixed number of access hours or unlimited access. With its success, *Americal Online (AOL)*® has separated access into camps: AOL's private services plus Internet access and Internet access alone. The two major access providers, as of the end of 2001, were AOL and MSN (*Microsoft Services Network)*®.

If you are on a local area network in your organization, you will likely have a gateway to the Internet. This means you have access to the World Wide Web at LAN speeds, as constrained by the specific link to the Internet. At our university, the authors' computers are nodes on the College of Business 10/100 Mbps Ethernet LAN, which connects to the rest of the university by fiber-based Giga Ethernet. Initially we connected to the SURAnet via two T1 channels, which combined in Birmingham, Alabama, and then connected to a T3 link in Atlanta, Georgia, via a T1 circuit. This has evolved to our having two fiber links, each over 20 Mbps, to Atlanta, Georgia, where they access T3 or greater conduits to MAE East, in the connection point to the Internet backbone.

As we note in the following section, many companies and individuals have found the Internet an excellent place to conduct business. Other companies, such as magazine publishers, are in a quandary. Some find that they can place part of the magazine on online services or the Internet and attract readers to their paper copies. Others have found that they can provide an electronic version of their magazine for a fee and attract a new group of readers, either by providing material different than shown in the paper magazine, showing it earlier, or showing it more dynamically by video, audio, or multimedia. One feature of the WWW capability of the Internet is the cataloging (databasing) of home pages and their content. Automated agents, called robots, Web crawlers, bots, and spiders, intelligently search the WWW and record the headers of all home pages for which they are allowed access. This information is then placed in a database by the owner of the robot. A user may then choose a search facility (search engine) on the Internet, and put in search criteria, and then will receive a response as to what home pages exist in the database listing that match those criteria. Thus, as The Real World 9–4 illustrates, entering "html" as the search criterion in the Infoseek® search facility of Netscape® would return a listing of 100 home pages (numbers 11 to 20 are shown here). Not only are the names of the WWW home pages listed from the database, they are presented in such a way that clicking on the title takes you to

The Real World   9–5

A perfect example of utility achieved is Holiday Inn's website, the first in the hotel industry to offer online reservations. The site is a demonstrable cost cutter. Holiday Inn saves 75 percent on every reservation made through that medium as opposed to over the phone or through a global distribution system, like SABRE. More exciting, perhaps, is the fact that almost all of the bookings the company receives over the Net are new customers, the vast majority of them businesspeople.

Currently, the Holiday Inn site pays for itself but it should do more than that if usage increases. Director of Emerging Technologies Les Ottolenghi predicts that will happen as Web access becomes more ubiquitous.

Source: Webmaster by CIO Communications, Inc., 492 Old Connecticut Path, Framingham, MA, www.cio.com.

The Real World   9–6
The Hot Websites

Ranked by "hits"—how often any file in a website is accessed by a user—these sites are currently the most popular on the Web. All are free unless noted.

1. **Netscape** *(http://www.netscape.com)*. Home page of popular Web browser lists "What's Cool" sites.

2. **Yahoo!** *(http://www.yahoo.com)*. Looking for a particular website? Type in a key word and this search engine lists home pages of sites that include the same word.

3. **ESPNet** *(http://espnet.sportszone.com)*. Sports news and stats, updated daily. Chat with sportswriters and fans.

4. **Infoseek** *(http://www.infoseek.com)*. Search tool specializes in news wires, computer mags, and company profiles ($1.95 to $9.95 per month, plus fees).

5. **Pathfinder** *(http://www.pathfinder.com)*. Daily news plus articles from *Life*, *Entertainment Weekly*, and other Time Warner magazines.

6. ***Playboy*** *(http://www.playboy.com)*. Photos—yes, including the centerfold and other features—as well as interviews and articles.

7. **HotWired** *(http://www.hotwired.com)*. Cultural critiques and computer gossip from the creators of *Wired* magazine.

8. **Microsoft** *(http://www.microsoft.com)*. Information on the software giant and its multitude of programs. Upgrades to many of the programs can be downloaded.

9. **Silicon Graphics** *(http://www.sgi.com)*. An assortment of games, plus a gallery of graphics composed on the same kinds of powerful Silicon Graphics workstations that are used to create snazzy special effects in films.

10. **Lycos** *(http://www.lycos.com)*. This massive registry of websites is updated weekly.

Source: *U.S. News & World Report*.

that home page. Additionally, the search engine attempts to present them in order of relevance.

A final note on learning about the Internet. Since the early days of the Internet, a document has been available on the Internet that gives a good explanation of the features and services. The document is called *Zen and the Art of the Internet* by Brendan P. Kehoe. Search on this in order to learn more or just to see a different perspective. Though it is 35 pages in printed form, the file transfers quickly. This subset of the now-published book is somewhat dated, but remains quite useful.

Protocols[5]

Computers can't just throw data at each other any old way. Because so many different types of computers and operating systems connect to the Internet via modems or other connections, they have to follow communications **protocols.** The Internet is a very heterogeneous collection of networked computers and is full of different access protocols, including PPP, TCP/IP, and SLIP.

TCP/IP—Transmission Control Protocol/Internet Protocol

These two protocols were developed by the U.S. military to allow computers to talk to each other over long-distance networks. IP is responsible for moving packets of data between nodes. TCP is responsible for verifying delivery from client to server.

[5] Source: http://coverage.cnet.com/Resources/Information/Glossary/Terms/tcpip.html.

TCP/IP forms the basis of the Internet, and is built into every common modern operating system (including all flavors of Unix, the Mac OS, and the latest versions of Windows).

SLIP—Serial Line Internet Protocol

SLIP is a standard for connecting to the Internet with a modem over a phone line. It has serious trouble with noisy dial-up lines and other error-prone connections, so look to higher-level protocols like PPP for error correction.

PPP—Point-to-Point Protocol

PPP is the Internet standard for serial communications. Newer and better than its predecessor, SLIP, PPP defines how your modem connection exchanges data packets with other systems on the Internet.

MAE East, MAE West, and MAE Central

The United States MAE services (Metropolitan Area Ethernet) are Internet networks traffic exchange facilities located in various U.S. cities. The Internet backbone is supported by four vendors, MCI WorldCom being one. Technology Note 9–1 describes MCI WorldCom's view of MAE services.

Technology Note   9–1

BACKGROUND

In 1993, the National Science Foundation awarded MCI WorldCom the status of NAP (Network Access Point) to the NSFNet backbone in Washington, D.C. Prior to the awarding of this NAP status, MCI WorldCom and a small group of ISPs helped create an exchange "point" that eventually grew into what we currently call a MAE, or an Internet networks traffic exchange facility. Since then, MCI WorldCom has set up seven MAE sites nationwide where Internet service providers can establish peering relationships for the exchange of IP traffic.

Today, MCI WorldCom operates three of the major interconnect points for the Internet in the United States: MAE East, MAE West, and MAE Central. In fact, a major portion of the traffic that flows between ISP networks passes through MCI WorldCom MAE facilities.

MAE East is located in the Washington, D.C., metropolitan area and connects all of the major ISPs as well as European providers. MAE West is located in California's Silicon Valley providing a second interconnection point linking major ISPs in that area. Many are connected at MCI WorldCom in San Jose, while a smaller number (but individually larger in size) are connected at NASA Ames Research Center, home of the western Federal Internet

Exchange (FIX West). The two sites are linked together with multiple 155 Mbps (OC3) circuits. MAE Central is located in Dallas, Texas, and is the latest addition to our Tier-1 facilities. In addition to these Tier-1 facilities, MCI WorldCom has two tier-2 regional MAE sites in operation: MAE Houston and MAE Los Angeles.

WHAT IS A MAE?

A **MAE (Metropolitan Area Ethernet)** is the MCI WorldCom facility where ISPs connect to each other to exchange Internet traffic—an Internet networks traffic exchange facility. The easiest way to think of it is as a LAN switch where all the "pieces" of the Internet connect together in order to exchange traffic at high speeds. The MAE forms part of the "Inter" in Internet.

A MAE does NO routing of data. The routing function is performed by the routers that are normally connected to the MAE and that are owned and managed by the ISPs. In fact, the router is the only device that connects to a MAE. ISP hosts, as long as they act as routers, may occasionally be connected to switched ports at the MAE.

A MAE and other Internet traffic exchange points (e.g., NAPs and the CIX) are not connected to each other via dedicated links. If an ISP needs to have connections to

Technology Note (Continued)   9–1

multiple MAE locations, then the ISP will build its own backbone network.

TIER-1 AND TIER-2 MCI WORLDCOM MAE SITES

MCI WorldCom's MAE facilities are grouped into two categories: Tier-1 and Tier-2 MAE facilities. Tier-1 MAE locations are regarded as "national" connection points and have a combination of the following characteristics: One or more of the major ISPs (e.g., Sprint, MCI, UUNET, ANS, Netcom, BBN, PSI) connect to the MAE. There is a high-speed FDDI switch installed offering dedicated higher speed connections. The sites designated as Tier-1 MAE locations are MAE East, MAE Central, and MAE West. Generally, routers with very large routing tables are needed at Tier-1 MAE sites. Examples of these routers are Cisco 4700-M or Cisco 7xxx series routers.

Tier-2 MAE locations are regarded as "regional" connection points for regional ISPs and have the following characteristics: presence of regional or smaller ISPs with few or no major ISPs present and Ethernet switch and FDDI concentrator so lower speed or shared access services only. Existing sites designated as Tier-2 MAE locations are: MAE Los Angeles and MAE Houston. Generally, smaller routing tables are needed at Tier-2 MAE locations and so smaller routers are satisfactory. An example of this kind of router is a Cisco 4500-M.

Please note: Effective spring 1998 MCI WorldCom no longer sells access to the Tier-2 locations. These facilities remain active and in service; however, no new connections are being sold.

MAE SERVICES KEY BENEFITS

- Cost-effective way for ISPs to connect to other ISPs.

- Presence of multiple ISPs at a MAE.

- Low entry level requirements for an ISP to connect to a MAE.

- Colocation space for housing ISP equipment.

- MCI WorldCom's broad geographic coverage.

COMMON MISCONCEPTIONS RELATED TO MAE SERVICES

MAE services are not connections to the Internet. This is one of several common misconceptions related to MAE services. Following are more key points.

MCI Tier-1 and Tier-2 sites

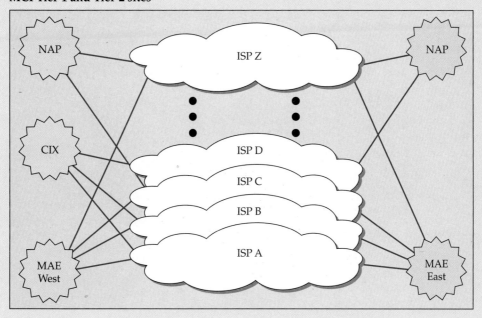

(continued)

Technology Note (Continued)   9–1

MAE services do not include peering agreements with any of the ISPs that are connected at a MAE. The ISPs must do the "peering" on their own. This involves negotiation and technical cooperation to enable the two ISP networks to pass traffic.

MAE services do not include transit with any of the ISPs that are connected at a MAE. Typically, a smaller ISP would become a customer of the ISP that provides the transit.

MAE services do not guarantee that there will be specific major ISPs at a MAE. While it is our objective to connect the key ISPs at a MAE, it is the decision of each ISP as to whether they interconnect at the MAE and with whom they negotiate peering.

MCI WorldCom does not provide IP addresses or AS (Autonomous System) numbers. IP addresses are provided by third parties on behalf of MCI WorldCom. These IP addresses only apply to physical ports at the MAE. AS numbers and IP Class addresses are provided by the InterNIC.

PEERING ARRANGEMENTS

It is a requirement for an incoming ISP to have peering or transit arrangements with the other ISPs connected to the MAE. MCI WorldCom cannot arrange peering. There is no single ISP in charge of the peering. Peering agreements are bilateral agreements between individual ISPs. Each ISP must negotiate independently and needs to contact individually every ISP with which they wish to peer. MCI WorldCom can and will only offer guidance (i.e., we can facilitate introductions to other ISPs). MCI WorldCom cannot provide peering.

COLOCATION

The MAE colocation facilities are a secure environment where ISPs may locate routing equipment for direct connection to the MAE. If the ISP customer takes colocation space instead of having the demarcation point extended to their premises, the Ethernet or FDDI port (demarcation) appears at the ISP's rack space. In the case of HSSI, the customer gets half rack of colocation as well as an extension to their premises. Colocation space is available on a first-come, first-served basis.

MAE MANAGEMENT

Management of a MAE is done via a dedicated Sun workstation. The MAE devices are managed using SNMP. The management workstation does not share a network segment with any service providers' router.

Custom applications run on the Sun management workstation to collect performance statistics on the MAE, monitor MAE equipment, and generate alarms. It also monitors connections and generates connection lists.

It is the responsibility of the ISP connected to the MAE to configure and manage their router equipment.

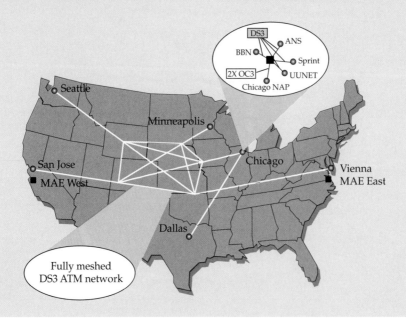

Technology Note (Continued)   9–1

SERVICE LEVELS AND LEAD TIMES

Service levels:

- Target mean time to repair = 2 hours

- Target availability = 99.99 percent, 24 hours per day, 7 days per week at all sites

Lead times:

- On-net (lit) building, no collocation: 30 calendar days

- Off-net building, no collocation: 45 calendar days

- Non-MCI WorldCom city, no collocation ICB

- Collocated equipment: 30 calendar days (dependent on space availability)

Source: http://www.mae.net/doc/maedesc/maedesc1.html.

Technology Note   9–2
NAP.net

WHO ARE WE?

Founded in July of 1995, our mission is to provide robust Internet connectivity to Internet service providers (ISPs) at affordable prices in an effort to develop a level playing field among the Internet community.

Our current network design and equipment selection are engineered to provide our customers with a fault-tolerant connection to the Internet utilizing multiple NAP connections and peering arrangements. Through this network our customers receive robust global transit. For those already connected at a NAP, virtual transit is available. Nap.net access services get you as close to the Internet as possible . . . right to the front door . . . by directly connecting you to the gateway for its national backbone. Our service is nonrestrictive . . . you control your content without limitations, restrictions, or inflated costs!

WHERE ARE WE?

Currently we connect to the "Net" at the Chicago NAP, MAE East, and MAE West. We have a point of presence at each of these locations as well as in Dallas and Seattle. Additional connections are continually being engineered.

Our routing equipment is deployed with the latest in technology releases. NAP.net is one of the first Network Service Providers to utilize true ATM DS3 connectivity to a NAP. Currently, our Chicago NAP connection is an OC3. At the meet points on the East and West coasts, we connect at the FDDI level (100 Mbps). All locations utilize ATM DS3 on ramps to our fully meshed DS3 ATM backbone. NAP.net's equipment has been installed with redundant power supplies and battery backup to ensure electronic survivability.

NAP.net's Tier-1 network includes extensive peering arrangements and backup connections to provide global connectivity continuously. Our outstanding network performance standards provide our customers with rock-solid national backbone network services.

SERVICES WE PROVIDE

Our services include

- Internet Connectivity:
  T1 (DS1).
  Ethernet: standard, measured.
  ATM DS3: full rate (FTS), rate shaped (STS), burstable (BTS), measured (MTS).
  Fast Ethernet.
  OC3.
  Virtual Transit—3 Mbps and up.

- MegaPOP service, which help ISPs to expand dial-up coverage without the high cost of hardware and line charges!

- News feeds.

- Secondary DNS.

(continued)

Technology Note *(Continued)* **9–2**
NAP.net

- Multicast routing (Mbone).

- IP addresses.

- Internic registration assistance for IPs, domains, AS numbers.

- Equipment colocation space in our facilities.

- Usage reports available for each customer, real time, online.

- Quality service performance that's measurable.

- Global IP transit, Tier-1 networking.

- Network Operations Center monitoring, 24 hours a day, 365 days a year.

- 100 percent port assignment via direct circuit connections for your circuit(s) only.

- Facility coordination for all your telecommunications needs.

- Technical support, 24 hours a day, 7 days a week.

- 120V/AC and 48V/DC, providing electrical stability at all times.

- Pricing—a value in comparison to any aggregated service provider.

- Nonrestrictive so you control your content and address without limitations or restrictions—fully resellable service.

   We do not compete with our customers (we are not a competing ISP).

Source: http://www.nap.net/who.html.

SPECIAL USES OF THE INTERNET

The Internet is like a 20-foot tidal wave coming and we are in kayaks. It's been coming across the Pacific for thousands of miles and gaining momentum and it's going to lift you and drop you.
Andy Grove

In its simplest definition, the Internet is connectivity among millions of nodes. This does not define how it is used; software defines how it is used. An example of this is, of course, the graphical interface of the World Wide Web. Another equally intriguing use is for telephone communications via Internet Phone® MSNetworking®. These applications, and others, use the multimedia sound card on computers to carry on long-distance phone conversations, at the price of Internet connectivity alone. Some foresee this as the pending doom of the long-distance providers. This is unlikely as the applications now stand. However, it is interesting to see that the addition of software on each end to the sound cards in the machines makes it a telephone circuit.

Because the Internet is "free" and because many organizations have their own IP networks, an obvious use is for voice telephone, that is, *Voice over IP (VoIP)*. The Cisco Systems corporation, consisting of some 30,000 people with many offices around the globe, utilizes VoIP for *all* internal voice needs. This gives greater control and avoids significant long-distance charges.

Similar programs provide forms of videoconferencing. You can use video and data or video and sound, requiring a video camera (for as little as $15 each) and software, along with the multimedia capability of both machines. Again, the Internet is the conduit; the software and hardware provide the capabilities.

BUSINESS ON THE INTERNET (ELECTRONIC COMMERCE)

By 1999, the number of Internet-connected computers had exceeded 200 million. The initial use of this resource was for colleague-to-colleague communications and file transfer. With time and the admission of commercial organizations to the Internet, things changed dramatically.

The explosive growth of the Internet has been fueled, in part, by a rush by companies to develop a presence there. Although many articles have been written about business on the World Wide Web, it was difficult to assess in the early days. By the end of 1995, many thousands of companies had been making money online. There appear to be four distinct revenue models for doing business on the Web.[6] Examples of each follow:

1. Direct selling or marketing of a firm's existing products or services.

2. Selling advertising space.

3. Charging fees for the actual content accessible on a WWW site.

4. Charging fees for online transactions or links.

Direct Selling

In the early days of Web marketing, small companies appear to have had more impact than large firms with comprehensive channels of distribution. Several small firms have found that the Web catapulted them into global distributors overnight while, in contrast, larger firms have found that the Web provided them with new niche market channels. Some large corporations such as Holiday Inn have found the Internet to be valuable in increasing reservations. While Holiday Inn is reluctant to reveal the impact on revenues (they were the first in the industry to secure online reservations on the Net), their website got over 7,000 visitors per week in the early days. (See Real World window 9–5 on page 320.)

Selling Advertising Space

In the area of selling advertising space on the Web, companies were spending about U.S. $10 million by 1995. Forrester Research predicted that over U.S. $2.2 billion would be spent annually by the year 2000. Automobile dealers have been initially

---

Information Window   **9–2**

National Semiconductor Corporation is an example of the power of using WWW home pages. The company hired a company to create an Internet presence for this manufacturer of computer chips. At the time that the pages went active that year, giving access to the company's total catalog of devices, National had exposure to 30 percent of the world's electronic engineers. These individuals would look at paper literature to specify components for systems in the design phase. Forty-five days after activation, the home pages were recording 5,000 inquiries per day, and the company had gained access to 70 percent of the world's population of electronic engineers. The charge to the home page developers was to make provisions for greater activity, as they expected inquiries to reach 50,000 per day in six months.

---

[6] Maddox, Wagner, and Wilder, "Making Money on the Web," *Information Week*, September 4, 1995.

Real World   9–7
Streaming Media 101, Part I: Bare Bones Technology

by Pamela Parker, Managing Editor of ChannelSeven.com and Internet Advertising Report 7/11/01

Amid the dreary doldrums of the online advertising business, a few bright spots do exist—arenas in which there's seen to be great potential for development and growth. Among those areas is streaming media, which can wow consumers with audio and video advertisements that arguably pack the emotional wallop of comparable radio and television spots.

Streaming media, then, is like radio or television. Then again, it's not. As part of **TurboAds.com**'s everlasting quest to demystify the latest online marketing vehicles—their capabilities and the technology behind them—we present **Streaming Media 101,** an exploration of this emerging form of rich media aimed at getting newcomers up to speed. Today, in part one, we get down to the bare bones—the basics of the technology.

Don't be scared. We're not going to make you learn super-techie terms that you'll never use, but understanding the difference between a server and a sniffer script might just make your job a little easier. Or, if all of this is old hat to you, this might be the ideal opportunity to educate your boss, co-worker, employee, or client about streaming.

Let's start at the beginning, with the stream itself. In the beginning—and instances of this still exist—there was the file download. If you wanted to watch a video or listen to a song, you had to download the entire file to your hard drive, and then play it locally. Some still advocate this type of experience, because the playback is usually smoother—you don't have to concern yourself with the vagaries of net congestion.

But downloading an entire file just takes so darned long, hence the development of streaming—a technology whereby the audio or video can be played as the file is downloaded. That content can be either live or pre-recorded, just like radio, television, or cable. Coincidentally, streaming is a big hit with people concerned about digital rights management, because the audio and video isn't actually stored on the user's computer. People have access to the content, but they don't actually own it and they can't copy it.

To make all this work, the audio or video content is first compressed using what's called a codec (short for compressor/decompressor) which makes it small enough to travel over the Internet. Then, when a consumer, using a streaming media player—the most common being **Real Player, Windows Media,** and **QuickTime**—requests that file, the appropriate file (that is, the one compressed in such a way to be decompressed by the user's particular type of player) is sent out across the Internet. The person's player decodes the file on the fly, and, voila, the audio or video plays.

An important thing to remember is that each stream is served up in response to an individual's request. That means it costs more—in terms of computer power—for each person who is listening or viewing. It's a very different proposition than radio or television, where you have the initial technology investment and then it doesn't matter how many people are receiving the signal.

There are advantages, though, over broadcast radio and television. As on the Internet, advertisements can be targeted to the individual that receives them. Different and serving systems have differing capabilities, but it's technologically possible to deliver an ad to that one individual that you know is dying to buy your product. Of course, you may not want to come up with creative for all of those particular individuals, but that's beside the point.

The other main advantage, of course, is interactivity. Once the prospective buyer receives the ad, he or she can click to buy the product or to seek more information.

Source: http://www.turboads.com/richmedia_news/2001 rmn/rmn20010711.shtml

---

provided presence on the Internet for $995 plus $500 per month for maintenance, a relatively inexpensive rate. (See Real World window 9–7.)

Charging for Content

In the emerging market, content providers have sold subscriptions, while counting on additional revenue from advertisers. Some daily newspapers have started charging for content. Among them are *The San Jose Mercury News* and *USA Today*. Several magazines have initiated online versions; however, advertising continues

Information Window   9–3

The *World Wide Web (WWW)*, a graphical portion of the Internet, began operation in mid 1994. In conjunction with browsers such as Netscape® and Mosaic,® it allows the user to navigate (surf) the Internet with little experience or knowledge of commands or locations. Users only have to click their mouse on a specified name or graphic, and the browser takes the user to that site. A site, or home page, is a graphical file: the interface for information.

Before the Web, there were electronic bulletin boards (BBS). The user would access a BBS directly via a POTS line.

The use of the BBS required a specific language, plus registration onto the BBS prior to usage, sometimes with a fee charged for time on the system. The Web uses a browser and does not require registration for access, though a site may require registration for access to databases, newspapers, stock quotes, and so forth. Thus, the Internet Web access and tracking of a FedEx package is just a change from the former direct dial into the FedEx BBS. However, the Web method is cheaper, easier, and faster for users.

to drive revenues. One obstacle to this area of Web business is the fact that many consumers are used to getting information from the Web free.

Charging for Service

Some businesses charge for providing services such as database searches, links, online marketplaces, and so on. One of the most successful of the early providers is Industry.Net, which offers an electronic marketplace service to manufacturers and suppliers. The clients can maintain an electronic "store front" for fees ranging from US $3,000 to US $8,000 per year. In 1995, Industry.Net earned about $28 million for the service. An additional service is an online catalog service with a planned online purchase order system, so customers can shop for specific products across manufacturers' sites. The catalog service costs from US $2,000 to US $500,000 for participants.

Another service is provided by Infoseek, a business that provides Internet database search service. The firm charges user subscription and transaction fees. Their revenues from this service are about $1.5 million per month. More money is made by selling advertising with sponsors' advertising banners appearing at the top of the page.

An aspect of enhanced onsite service has been employed by firms such as Federal Express, UPS, and even the U.S. Postal Service. They, for example, allow customers to track packages directly through their Web pages (http://www.fedex.com, http://www.ups.com, http://www.usps.com). Other firms that use the delivery services provide a link from your emailed confirmation of shipping to the carrier, so one only has to click on the URL and input the provided number. In a different vein, Sun Microsystems Inc. claims to have saved several millions of dollars by providing downloadable software program corrections (patches) and product literature via the Net. Microsoft will even install a program on your computer that either reminds you to go looking for updates or does it for you automatically. Many if not most mature technology providers post answers to frequently asked questions (FAQs) to give instant service while saving the company the cost of a help-desk person. These services are extremely valuable for customers who have nontraditional schedules.

There are several expansions of *electronic commerce* that are underway that promise a means of significant financial infrastructure via the Web. For example, many banks support banking. Many other services are being offered that seem to be only limited by the imagination of providers, as many have found by accessing the

The Real World   9–8
PC Computing

- **Sports** *(http://sports.yahoo.com)*
  Everything hard-core enthusiasts would want to know about mainstream sports from golf to tennis to auto racing to Major League Baseball, with stats updated daily. The site is filled with factoids but unfortunately shows few images of any kind. Recent stories included Al Unser Jr.'s disqualification from an Oregon car race, Pete Sampras's bid for his third consecutive Wimbledon victory, Betsy King's induction into the LPGA Hall of Fame, and the explosive growth of the PGA Senior Tour. Schmooze with sportswriters and fans.

- ALSO CONSIDER: **Endurance Training Journal** *(http://s2.com/etj/etj.html)*
  Training tips on cycling, running, and swimming—including pre- and post-workout stretching—and preparing for a triathlon. Cycling technique for hill climbing: If the hill is long, stay in the saddle; if it's short, stand on the pedals. Too bad the photos are decorative rather than instructive.

JUST FOR KIDS

- **CyberKids** *(http://www.mtlake.com/cyberkids)*
  All of the stories, poetry, and drawings in this online magazine are aimed at children—and are created by them, too. In one story by a 10-year-old, bears on bikes sell ice cream in the park; their helpers win a lifetime supply. A mystery written by an 11-year-old relates how a class led by "a teacher who makes learning fun"— one day she brings her poodle to class, for instance—

discovers local developers polluting a favorite pond. Both are charmingly illustrated.

- ALSO CONSIDER: **Family World** *(http://family.com)*
  Articles from 40 small parenting publications, such as *Seattle's Child* and Delaware's *Family Times*, offer very practical advice on such topics as how to get kids to walk without whining: Give them walking sticks.

BITS AND BYTES

- **HotWired** *(http://www.hotwired.com)*
  This online lifestyle magazine for the digerati from the creators of *Wired* magazine contains cultural critiques, computer industry news and analysis, chat sessions, and classified ads, with rich, colorful graphics and video clips throughout. Articles are refreshingly opinionated— HotWired doesn't think popular Web browser maker Netscape Communications, which recently announced an initial public offering, will fare well once Microsoft enters the online service realm. Video clips include a woman fighting a one-eyed monster from a Japanese cartoon. Later this week: the computer-generated animated "sketches" Merce Cunningham creates to choreograph his dances.

- ALSO CONSIDER: **c:/net.online** *(http://www.cnet.com)*
  Computer-product reviews, including CD-ROM picks and pans by syndicated computer columnist John C. Dvorak.

Source: John C. Dvorak, *PC Magazine*.

wrong site. In Denver, Colorado, Bronco fans can find details about schedules, players, and items for purchase, and even can converse with individual players via email: viewers of TechTV can get the latest download daily; and Dilbert fans can receive a cartoon each day and a newsletter each month.

What does it cost to get a World Wide Web presence (a home page)? The Forrester Research Company figures for July 1995 are listed in Table 9.1.[7] Obviously these prices are in a constant state of change because of evolution of the technology and the emergence of competition. The table shows the cost of creating a significant presence on the WWW. Academic institutions provide space for student pages free and Internet access providers often include page space for individuals as part of the monthly fee.

[7] *Webmaster*, June/July 1995.

TABLE 9.1
Cost of Creating
Web Home Page

Source: Forrester
Research, Inc.

Own WWW Site		Third Party Web Site	
Item	1st Year Costs	Item	1st Year Costs
Servers and software	$5,000–$20,000	Set-up fees	$2,000–$4,000
Highspeed link	$25,000–$40,000	Monthly charge	$300–$500
Personnel	$30,000–$60,000		Included
Total	$60,000–$120,000	Total	$5,000–$10,000

IBM's general manager for Internet Application Services has said, "Not being present on the World Wide Web will soon be the equivalent to not having a fax machine. In the not-too-distant future, not doing business on the World Wide Web will be equivalent to not doing business at all."[8]

The Internet business model is still evolving and assuming a "defined personality," according to Howard Anderson of the Yankee Group.[9] He views the Internet as an entity in which professional managers must find a balance between its quirky and chaotic nature and its application as a button-down business tool. He reported that in its early business use, the market was selling mostly access, despite the estimated 55 percent of the *Fortune* 100 using the Internet in some form.

One firm that had spectacular growth is Netscape®, which basically took free software and turned it into a company. As early as late 1995, there were over three million Netscape users and the stock was vastly oversubscribed on its initial public offering (IPO). Subsequently, Microsoft's Internet Explorer® has eroded Netscape's market share, helping result in a Department of Justice civil suit against the software giant.

AT&T offers three Internet businesses. The company has created **AT&T World-Net Services** to provide Internet access, navigation tools, and information directories. AT&T's *Hosting and Transaction Services* is a service designed to help businesses display, promote, and sell their products on the Internet. The third AT&T business is *Content Services and AT&T Interchange Online Network.* It is designed to work with content owners to provide tailored information and entertainment services to consumers, professionals, and businesses.

Direct Sales

A significant aspect of electronic commerce on the Internet is the idea of direct sales: the omission of middlemen in the marketing chain. In a non-Internet environment, IBM, for example, has direct sales, using (800) phone numbers and sales associates to help customers. This circumvents the intermediaries at the retail level. Taking it one step further IBM can place a home page on the Internet and let customers place orders there, bypassing even the sales associates and going directly to the warehouse for shipment. Dell and many other surviving PC manufacturers use this same model. This "disintermediation" gives the Internet a large impact on channels of distribution as well as causing significant price reductions.

Part of the Internet sales scheme involves informing the buyer of the transaction progress via email and using email to inform him/her of the buy-of-the-week. One

[8] Ibid.
[9] Howard Anderson, "Why the Internet Chews Up Business Models," *Upside*, 7, no. 8 (August 1995), pp. 22–37.

of the authors receives advertising emails each week from a shoe company, a book company, and a computer sales company, to name just a few. These emails are generally in full HTML graphic form, giving the look and functionality of a Web page inside the email client.

In markets where wholesalers and brokers are common, direct sales on the Internet have drastically changed the marketing chain. Additionally, the store is open 24 hours per day, from anywhere on earth. **Thus, electronic commerce is more than a different form of marketing and selling; it is a change in the players and the roles played.**

Tax on Internet Sales

As noted in Real World window 9–9, the consideration and effect of sales tax in general and a federally imposed tax in particular are of great concern in the United States. The concern is the value of the revenue generation from the tax as opposed to the inhibiting total sales effect of that tax. Historically, one state in the United States cannot tax the goods sold in another state. This was to inhibit the creation of barriers to trade but was based on physical transactions. When mail order became the first remote purchasing, followed by the first electronic sales of telephone orders, the tax assessors and collectors saw that they were losing tax revenue.

Security

One reason that the Internet has not been dominated by electronic commerce is the fact that many of the users are early adopters of the technology. Thus, the mass market has been delayed, awaiting mainstream acceptance. While many would

The Real World   9–9
Cox Internet Tax Bill Unanimously Approved:
House Judiciary Subcommittee Vote Means Taxes
May Not Hit in October

WASHINGTON (Thursday, August 2, 2001)—With expiration of the Internet tax moratorium just weeks away, the House of Representatives took action to extend it, just hours before adjourning for the August recess. House Policy Chairman Christopher Cox, author of the legislation to continue to prohibit discriminatory taxes on the Internet, was elated that the bill passed unanimously through the Judiciary Subcommittee on Commercial and Administrative Law.

"Today, with the end date for the moratorium just 80 days away, it is critical that we move to renew the ban on multiple and discriminatory taxes," stated Chairman Cox. "I commend Chairman Barr and his Subcommittee colleagues for taking this important step toward reassuring all Americans that government will not place special burdens on the new economy."

Chairman Cox's legislation—H.R. 1552, the Internet Non-Discrimination Act—mirrors the recommendation of the U.S. Advisory Commission on Internet Tax, and was endorsed by President George W. Bush during his campaign. It provides for a five-year extension of the existing Cox-Wyden Internet Tax Freedom Act, signed by President Clinton in 1998.

The Advisory Commission on Electronic Commerce was established in 1999 by Congress to conduct a thorough study of federal, state, local and international taxation of electronic commerce. For the last 10 months, 19 Commissioners have been deeply engaged in that endeavor.

Source: http://cox.house.gov/nettax/.

disagree, quoting the US$ billions in ecommerce, the problem with electronic commerce to many has been the perception of lack of a minimum level of security for transactions. For example, only a small percentage of individuals are willing to send their credit card numbers unprotected (unencrypted).

Online criminal activity has been estimated at US$10 billion per year. The cybercrooks always seem to be one step ahead of law enforcement. The lack of security has generated great concern.

A concern for security on the Internet takes a second dimension when users are accessing it via high-speed methods, for example, xDSL and cable modems. While the use of telephone/modem dial up continues to attract 128,000 new users a week worldwide, many users in North America, Japan, Korea, and Europe are switching to xDSL and cable modem, which means that (*a*) they are always connected and (*b*) they often have a static IP address. Both of these conditions allow intrusion from the Internet into the user's machine. Without this broadband always-on connection, the user is at far less risk on the Internet.

To combat intrusion, users are installing **firewalls.** *A firewall is a hardware and software combination that serves as a gateway between the user's or organization's internal network and the Internet.* A firewall allows the firm's employees to get out onto the Internet, but prevents unauthorized access into the protected network. The firm's publicly accessible Web pages reside outside the firewall service rather than on the protected network. Several firms offer network security programs. For example, IBM offers NetSP®, which provides a firewall between the internal network and the outside world. CheckPoint Software Technologies Ltd. markets Firewall I, a proven system. And, as we noted in an earlier chapter, ZoneAlarm is a free capability for personal use.

One consideration that makes the broadband connection of interest to the intruder is that it is available for secondary use. For example, entering through the Internet always-on portal, an intruder can deposit a hidden program. This may be done on dozens if not hundreds of computers. Then, on a command from the intruder's primary machine, or on a time command, these secondary machines commence simultaneous action, such as a **denial of service (DOS)** attack by instructing all computers to send a stream of messages to a target site, such as Yahoo.com®

Encryption, the scrambling of data to prevent disclosure, is an ability that needs to be available before the Internet will be considered secure enough for large-scale financial transactions. RSA Data Security, Inc., has a de facto standard in encryption technology. One of the most talked about encryption standards is the *Clipper Chip,* which was dictated by the U.S. government. The **Clipper Chip** was designed to permit a federal agency to decrypt encrypted messages, as required for national security. The government relaxed its encryption stance in 1995 after a French graduate student cracked the 40-bit encryption key used by Netscape in France. Security software vendors say that this incident points out the need for more impenetrable 64-bit or 128-bit keys. The debate between industrial need for security and the governmental agencies' need for detection continues. This tends to be a conflict between what is technically possible for security and what is politically mandated for security.

A final note on security: virtual private networks, discussed earlier, are a natural tool for the Internet. Use of this tunneling technology allows users who establish a network over this public connectivity to create a private and secure area. One form of this software is available free from AT&T under the name *Virtual Network*

Computing (VNC) (http://www.uk.research.att.com/vnc/). VNC is, in essence, a remote display system that allows users to view a computing "desktop" environment not only on the machine where it is running, but from anywhere on the Internet and from a wide variety of machine architectures.

Firewalls

With cable modems and xDSL service to the Internet, a new problem has surfaced. Because users are always connected with either of these capabilities, they are at more risk of intrusion via the Internet. The intrusions can range from people just looking around to actual theft and destruction of some Windows files. For example, two students using cable modems have had their *Windows* registry files stolen, necessitating the total reinstallation of *Windows*.

The goal of a firewall is to contain unrecognized users within a small area, called the *region of risk.* The region of risk describes what information and systems an intruder could compromise during access. The smaller the region of risk, the greater problems the firewall potentially causes for authorized users. The greater the region of risk, the greater the risk to the organization.

Caveat: Firewalls do not protect from all risk. For example, viruses attached to an email or document from authorized sources will not be stopped unless the firewall has the intelligence to inspect the message and look for viruses. Firewalls have no protection for disasters, which come predominately from acts of nature and mistakes of honest employees inside of the organization. This later is the domain of risk assessment and management, which take policies and backup provisions, not firewalls. Finally, a firewall is not intended to protect the violation of security and privacy from an authorized user.

The first line of defense for the always-on connectivity, although not of high security, is to turn off file and printer sharing. The next action against a variety of threats from the Internet is the firewall. Firewalls work by inspecting packets as

---

Technology Note   9–3

Firewall—A system designed to prevent unauthorized access to or from a private network. Firewalls can be implemented in both hardware and software, or a combination of both. Firewalls are frequently used to prevent unauthorized Internet users from accessing private networks connected to the Internet, especially intranets. All messages entering or leaving the intranet pass through the firewall, which examines each message and blocks those that do not meet the specified security criteria.

There are several types of firewall techniques:

Packet filter: Looks at each packet entering or leaving the network and accepts or rejects it based on user-defined rules. Packet filtering is fairly effective and transparent to users, but it is difficult to configure. In addition, it is susceptible to IP spoofing.

Application gateway: Applies security mechanisms to specific applications, such as FTP

and Telnet servers. This is very effective but can impose a performance degradation.

Circuit-level gateway: Applies security mechanisms when a TCP or UDP connection is established. Once the connection has been made, packets can flow between the hosts without further checking.

Proxy server: Intercepts all messages entering and leaving the network. The proxy server effectively hides the true network addresses.

In practice, many firewalls use two or more of these techniques in concert. A firewall is considered a first line of defense in protecting private information. For greater security, data can be encrypted.

Source: http://webopedia.internet.com/TERM/f/firewall.html.

The Real World   9–10
Guide to Securing Your Website for Business

INTRODUCTION

Businesses that accept transactions via the Web can gain a competitive edge by reaching a worldwide audience, at very low cost. But the Web poses a unique set of security issues, which businesses must address at the outset to minimize risk. Customers will submit information via the Web only if they are confident that their personal information, such as credit card numbers, financial data, or medical history, is secure.

VeriSign, Inc.,® the leading provider of trust services for electronic commerce and communication, offers a low-cost, proven solution for securely conducting business over the Web. By installing a VeriSign Server ID (available as part of VeriSign's Site Trust Services) on your server, you can securely collect sensitive information online, and increase business by giving your customers confidence that their transactions are safe.

This guide explains key issues related to Web security, describes the technologies VeriSign uses to address the issues, and provides step-by-step instructions for obtaining and installing a VeriSign Server ID. We invite you after read-ing this Guide to obtain your free trial Secure Server ID at www.verisign.com/server/trial/index.html or purchase one of VeriSign's Site Trust Services, which include either a full one-year Secure Server ID or a Global Server ID, at www.verisign.com/server.

A secure website can provide your business with powerful competitive advantages, including online sales and streamlined application processes for products such as insurance, mortgages, or credit cards. Credit card sales can be especially lucrative: according to independent analysts, cash transactions on the Internet will reach $9 billion by 2000, and $30 billion in 2005. No merchant can afford to ignore a market this large.

To succeed in this market, however, you must become fully aware of Internet security threats, take advantage of the technology that overcomes them, and win your customers' confidence. This section describes the benefits of e-commerce, and the specific risks you must address to realize the benefits.

Source: http://www.verisign.com/server/rsc/gd/secure-bus/.

"**Eighty-five percent** of Web users surveyed reported that a lack of security made them uncomfortable sending credit card numbers over the Internet. The merchants who can win the confidence of these customers will gain their loyalty—and an enormous opportunity for expanding market share."

they arrive at the computer, or at the firewall software in the computer. The effectiveness ranges from minimal to good, depending on the extent of the inspection, thus the speed of the process. Firewalls range in price (circa mid-2000) from free for *ZoneAlarm*® to $479 for *WebRamp 700*®. Newer cable modem systems are being designed so that all traffic from the cable modem termination system to the user is encrypted to ensure privacy and security.

Compression on the Internet

The technique of compression is discussed elsewhere. Because home pages on the World Wide Web often contain significant graphic images and video clips, and users move around large files, compression is important to the conduct of the Internet.

Comparison of the Internet and a Value Added Network

The Internet is a conduit and has resources only to the extent that they are attached to the conduit. The search engine resides either in your browser or in the home page of an organization that offers a search capability. It is the home pages that are attached that offer the services and appeal of the Internet.

On the other hand, value added networks (VANs) are both conduits and services. You may use a VAN to store a file and have another organization access the same VAN to retrieve that file. This is a primary method for EDI file transfer. In these cases, the VAN offers each party connectivity to its servers, which are services.

FIGURE 9.2   Brazil's National Research Network
*With more computers on the Internet than in all the rest of Latin America, Brazil is adding
to the infrastructure to woo users, despite high access cost.*

Source: *IEEE Spectrum.*

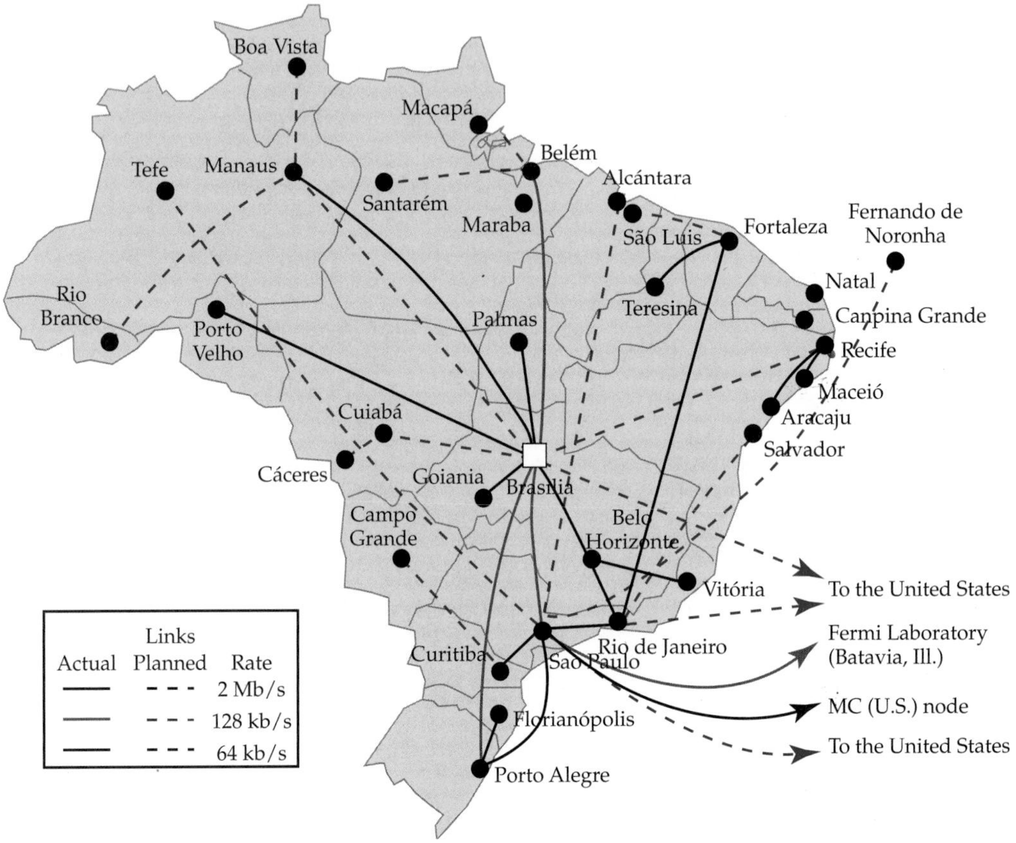

The Impact of the Internet in Underdeveloped Countries

The Internet is proving to be a boon for nations that have large land areas but relatively underdeveloped infrastructures. Thus, we expect to see large impacts in countries such as China and Brazil. The impact in Brazil is indicated by Figure 9.2 and the fact that the country is expending so much to provide connectivity.

During the time since the introduction of the WWW and its browsers, the world has seen not only industrialized nations take advantage of this capability but underdeveloped and developing countries gain global access and recognition. Just as a small 250 watt AM radio station can have a global presence on the Internet, developing countries can advertise to and communicate with the world. A negative aspect of this global visibility is that it may bring commerce that depends on nonexistent transportation services or may introduce ideas and practices not accepted by that country. Internet access by developing nations is a way to speed up the process only if they choose to provide the infrastructure. As of September 11, 2001, there was only one ISP in Afghanistan, a country that had less than one television set per 1,000 citizens.

SANS AND NAS[10]

The rise in importance of readily accessible, large storage has given rise to **network-attached data storage (NAS).** The needs based on growth of data stemming from the Internet, intranets, e-commerce, email, videoconferencing, voice recognition, Web-TV, and so on, cause additional attention to traditional server-based storage. The relative costs/benefits and impact on LANs, server-based storage, and network-attached storage (NAS) is compared to **storage area networks (SAN).**

There are two major storage management technologies evolving to provide organizations the ability to store and manage their valuable data: *network-attached storage (NAS)* and *storage area networks (SANs).* As organizations increasingly consider data as strategic, the ability to manage and store data has gained in importance. New business initiatives that create and use massive amounts of data have started to outgrow present infrastructure for storing and managing the data. Such business initiatives include data warehousing, data mining, customer relationship management, supply-chain management, and eBusiness.

SANs consolidate storage requirements into a common repository. (See Figure 9.3.) Usually the data come from a variety of platforms and go to a common platform. This requires SAN software. For the TC manager, the multiple connections and multiple devices mean that SANs create additional complexity.

SANs provide several benefits for businesses. They help satisfy the explosive demand for storage and use networking to enhance access to data. In addition, there is a means to manage more data with existing human resources. Many are now forecasting that IP networking will accommodate the greatest portion of the world's storage networking requirements. IDC predicts that disk storage capacity will grow by 86 percent per year, from 116,000 terabytes in 1998 to 2.6 million terabytes in 2003. Storage has become the biggest line item in IT budgets of many firms. The Gartner Group predicts that 80 percent of the world's storage will be connected to a SAN by 2004. We have a new player, the storage service provider (SSP), that will manage, store, and maintain customer's data.

> **A SAN** is a specialized network that deals with blocks of data. NAS is a specialized server, dedicated to serving files.—http://www.emc.com/news/in_depth_archive/08212000_san nas.jsp.

Information Window   9–4

SANs were introduced in 1998 with the goal of eliminating islands of server-bound storage. The idea was to free up the servers to do what they do best—process data—while managing information from a central location where it can be protected, shared, and mined. SANs also reduce much of the bulk server-to-server data movement that has been clogging corporate networks for years. The end result is a far more effective data network, where critical information is readily available and substantial savings are possible

Network-attached storage is an old idea that has gained new popularity with the rise of the Internet. If you've ever called up a file from a shared drive on Windows—the "G:\ drive," for example—then you've used a simple form of network-attached storage.

NAS allows multiple users to access the same files through the use of a specialized server. This arrangement holds a natural attraction for dot-coms, which need to send files (Web pages) to many users simultaneously.

IT Centrix, an independent IT efficiency consulting firm, concluded in August 1999 that centralized storage leads to a nearly 10-fold increase in productivity, when compared to the server-based distributed model; and the more information is generated, the greater the savings.

Source: http://www.emc.com/news/in_depth_archive/08212000_sannas.jsp.

[10] Information in this section was provided with assistance of Steve Guendert.

FIGURE 9.3
Storage Options

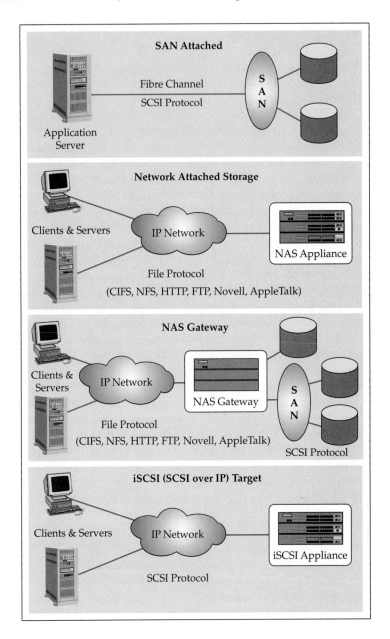

The NAS is basically a system for file sharing that should have the software and hardware preconfigured to make the network storage system. This concept and platform were invented for the Internet and therefore many see NAS as tailor-made for eBusiness.

eBUSINESS AND eCOMMERCE

Electronic commerce (eCommerce) is a dynamic set of technologies, applications, and business processes that link enterprises, consumers, and communities through electronic transactions and the electronic and physical exchange of goods, services, information, and capital. It is the exploitation of IT to deliver services and conduct

Technology Note   9–4

Experts say that data are doubling every year. The best place for much of these data is a **storage area network (SAN).** It helps large corporations and Web hosting companies store, protect, and retrieve their vast treasure troves of data instantly. It's much faster, easier, and more reliable than traditional server-attached storage.

A SAN is essentially a separate network of storage devices—hard drives, CD jukeboxes, backup tape drives—attached by high-speed fiber optic cable, running a protocol called *fibre channel.* Network hubs and/or switches connect the storage devices and servers.

SANs are not connected to a company's regular network. Instead, all storage and backup devices are connected to the separate SAN along with a company's servers. The servers make the connection between users and the stored data. The SAN uses fibre channel, a networking standard that typically moves data at 100 Mbps, but it will soon rise to 1 Gbps and then 4 Gbps.

SANs and fibre channel are an alternative to traditional server-attached storage systems based on the *Small Computer Systems Interface* (*SCSI*, pronounced "skuzzy") standard. In most cases, fibre channel moves data faster. It's also bidirectional, so it can send and receive data simultaneously; SCSI is one way. Fibre channel works over much longer distances, 10,000 meters versus SCSI's 75.

Source: Philip Zera, "The SANs of Storage Hold the Sands of Time," *Technology Investor*, November 2000, p. 28.

business. eCommerce improves commerce through the use of many core technology tools: the Web, electronic data interchange, electronic mail, electronic funds transfer, electronic benefits transfer, electronic catalogs, credit cards, smart cards, and other techniques. Therefore, eCommerce is not just about using the Web as a storefront. It involves shortening the supply chain, streamlining distribution processes, improving product delivery, reducing inventory-carrying costs, and many other measurable activities. In the business-to-business realm, eCommerce strategies allow businesses to leverage electronic alliances to speed the delivery of products and services to market.

IBM's practice has evolved to where eCommerce is different from **eBusiness (electronic business).** eCommerce involves buying and selling goods and services online, usually in the form of **B2C (business-to-consumers)** or **B2B (business-to-business).** This is opposed to the much larger concept of eBusiness, which is conducting business electronically, everything from sending email to advertising on the Web or creating an intranet so that your HR department can post online policies and procedures manuals. So, to IBM, eCommerce is a subset of eBusiness. For a tutorial, check out this website: http://idm.internet.com/features/Ecommercetut.html.

Electronic Payment Makes Electronic Commerce Work

The fast, electronic transfer of funds has speeded up commerce. It started with the *electronic funds transfer (EFT)* capability of the banking industry. Next, *electronic data interchange (EDI)* was added to allow for the transfer of standard business documents between computers as data files. One portion of this development was instructions to banks that resulted in EFT funds movement. With the advent of retail eCommerce, a form of EFT/EDI was required. The result was *Paypal®*.

Paypal and its competitors use the established credit card or bank check systems as their infrastructure. When the payee has established an account, all that is required to pay for a transaction, such as an auction purchase on *eBay®*, is to go to Paypal's website and provide the email address of the payee and payer and the amount. Paypal then moves the money from account to account and sends both parties an email of the transaction. This transfer takes place within an hour and requires no postage or physical instrument.

Mobile Commerce

M-commerce (mobile commerce) is often referred to as the next generation of eCommerce. It includes the selling of goods and services through wireless devices such as personal digital assistants (PDAs), cellular phones, and any other hand-held wireless device. The concept has taken hold in Europe where cellular phones and wireless PDAs have gained widespread popularity among Europeans of all ages. (See www.bluetooth.com.)

As of 2001, there were 700 million cellular users worldwide. According to the Gartner Group, sales of cellular telephones are projected to reach 700 million per year by 2004. PDAs and pagers should reach sales of 30 million and 10 million respectively. With this technology in place, IDC estimates that there will be a large increase in mobile and remote workers. They estimate there will be 55 million in the United States, 27 million in Western Europe, and 17.4 million in Latin America by 2004.

Ecash or Digital Cash

A facilitator of the mobile and electronic commerce revolution is ecash. **Ecash** or **electronic cash** allows an individual to make payment for purchases online through their checking account. Ecash differs from credit card and check payments online by allowing users to make small purchases, typically five dollars or less. Ecash or digital cash will enable users to make micro payments for goods such as colas or snacks from vending machines or merchants using their PDAs or cellular phones.

eBusiness Security

Corporate security has become a priority as firms build partnerships that span entire vertical industries and increasingly open their boundaries to a virtual exchange model. This means that Internet security has become a business imperative.

Despite the reports that over 60 percent of organizations have experienced some sort of security breach in the past two years (April 2000), 82 percent of network businesses do not use firewall protection. Some of the fault lies in the fact that about one-third of businesses do not recognize their data as a key business asset. As the B2B online trade becomes huge, firms will have to reevaluate the risks associated with loss of their data.

What are the threats? Some security experts believe that viruses are the biggest threat, followed by data theft and data manipulation. These experts also

Information Window   9–5

Although still in their infancy, these companies have seen some dramatic growth. Driveway, for example, grew from almost zero storage to 40 terabytes of EMC storage—enough to hold the equivalent of 1.5 billion sheets of printed paper—in just 30 days. And that promises to be just

the beginning. The average dot-com doubles its storage needs every 90 days.

Source: http://www.emc.com/news/in_depth_archive/06122000_virtual_storage.jsp.

see a requirement for all email to be encrypted. *Public key encryption* is a development that is becoming familiar. The most familiar form of public key encryption is PKI.[11]

PKI—Public Key Infrastructure

With increasing electronic business, the concept of electronic signatures promises to be the way of replacing paper for many legally binding documents such as purchase orders (POs), fund transfers, contracts, and so on. The infrastructure that supports digital signatures is **PKI (public key infrastructure).** The operation of PKI is shown below:

Source: Modified from The Burton Group and Digital Signature Trust (2000).

PKI—Public Key Infrastructure

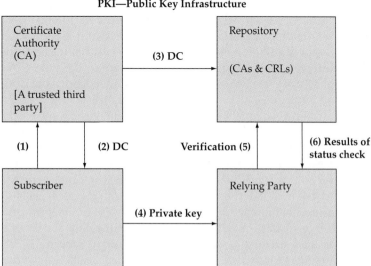

The process begins when a *subscriber* applies (1) to a *certificate authority* (CA) for a *digital certificate* (2). The CA returns the digital certificate (DC) to certify the authenticity of the *public key* it contains. The certificate authority publishes the certificate to a *repository* (3), which holds both the certificates and certificate revocation lists (CRLs). When the subscriber generates an electronic message, the subscriber "signs" it with a private key and sends it directly to a *relying party* (4). The relying party verifies the subscriber's message using the subscriber's public key, then goes to the *repository* to check the validity of the subscriber's certificate (5). The repository returns the results of the validity status check to the relying party (6).

The electronic signatures provision in S. 761, The Electronic Signatures in Global and National Commerce (E-sign) Act, took effect in October 2000. The act guarantees legal validity to digital signatures. The electronic signatures must be permanently attached to data and they must be nonreputiable, that is, no one can later deny the origin, submission, or delivery of a message or the integrity of its contents.

At present PKI is not required for simple business-to-consumer (B2C) transactions; however, for business-to-business (B2B) the value is there for both legal and dollar value considerations. Some forecasters believe that eventually all email will

[11] *Fortune* special issue, "Internet 2," October 2000.

require some sort of validation. The key elements include (1) authentication, (2) confidentiality, (3) integrity, and (4) nonrepudiation.[12]

Do You Need Secure Email?

With three trillion email messages per year, the question arises as to the need to secure the messages. Organizations wonder if they need to use encryption for this medium as they increase their use of it for official communications and even product ordering. Many believe that the medium is inherently secure due to the large volume and, thus, low probability of interception. Yahoo believed secure email has value as it introduced the service in late 2000. Netscape, meanwhile, developed a standard of its own.

Voting via the Internet

The U.S. presidential election of 2000 raised the question as to whether voting over the Internet was feasible. The answer is that it is technically feasible, but it is not (yet) politically feasible. What this means is that we have the technology to receive the vote of an individual from anywhere in the world over the Internet but the validity of that vote cannot yet be guaranteed. So, what does it take to cast the vote and what does it take to guarantee its validity?

Internet voting has the same requirement as any proper telecommunications-based system. It must have several elements. The first element is *identification*. This is the *validation* that the person accessing the application is authorized to do so and access is appropriate. The next element is *clarity of the interface*. This means that the user not only understands the layout of the computer screen (the interface) but is comfortable with it and the interface is nonambiguous. Next is *security*, that feature that ensures that neither the user nor anyone else can inappropriately access, view, copy, change, or destroy data in the system. If the data are about an individual, we must also add **privacy**, as security is not enough. Security is required first at the time of request for access; this is accomplished by identification. Then it is enabled by making sure that no one can electronically eavesdrop on the input device or data communications lines and intercept the information as it is entered or is in *transport*. Security of transport connectivity, for example, the network, is an ongoing problem as hackers and viruses abound. Finally, we must secure the data in *storage*, for example, the database or file. This ensures that the data cannot be lost due to a catastrophic event to the physical media, nor can it be accessed by an unauthorized person.

The industry believes that it can implement all of the above features that require Internet technology. However, the one feature that is not now present is validation, a nonambiguous, nonsharable, noncopyable, unique identifier for an individual. At this point in history, the closest we have is a biometric identifier. In the presence of a human, a surrogate of biometrics can be used, for example, one person determines the identification of another via a photograph. However, photographs don't work on the Internet, so there must be an electronic, nonsharable, noncopyable element similar to a fingerprint or retina or lens scan. Until then, the problem of identification will block Internet voting in most cases.

Challenges to Academic Honesty

One of the authors recently received a letter from the superintendent of The Virginia Military Institute, his alma mater. It contained the following comment:

---

[12] Modified from The Burton Group and Digital Signature Trust, 2000.

Incidentally, among the new challenges to our Honor Code, and to codes at other military academies, is a new species of what we might call Internet Crime—in which academic materials are downloaded, and then offered as original unattributed work.—*Josiah Bunting, Superintendent, VMI.*

The Internet, uniquely, allows the student or professional writer to easily search and copy material. It can then be presented as his/her own. It denies the originator his/her fair due. This is dishonest.

Pornography and Hate Groups on the Internet

New technology is often adopted for uses not acceptable to the general public. The existence of pornography and hate material on websites is of concern to citizens, parents, and lawmakers. While states and governments generally have the power to legislate within their domains, the Internet is global and is outside the reach of any specific state, government, civic, or religious organization. Regardless of the style (or form) of government, when the technology exists for reaching across borders, the influx of ideas cannot be suppressed. The U.S. government tried to impose its standards of morality on the content of the Internet in the Telecommunications Act of 1996; the act was found unconstitutional within three months. Nations, states, cultures, and other groups may wish to protect themselves from various influences, but find themselves limited by the very global nature of the Internet that provides the material.

One way individuals may protect themselves or their children from materials or actions they deem offensive or dangerous is to place a software barrier between the home or office computer and the Internet. On a LAN, this means software on the server that inspects the destination and/or content of the URL or email and applies rules of acceptable behavior. In the home, parents can place programs such as Net Nanny on each machine and create a file of restrictions, such as the child including his/her name on a URL or in email.

The Real World   9–11
Panel Agrees: Rethink Net Porn Laws

Internet porn may not be making headlines lately, but it hasn't gone away. And despite appearances to the contrary, neither has the latest law intended to keep adult material away from Net-surfing kids. The **Child Online Protection Act (COPA)** was passed two years ago after the Supreme Court overturned Congress's previous effort. COPA sought to make Net users give an adult ID before getting into commercial sites with adult materials.

The law has never gone into effect. A federal judge blocked it last year on constitutional grounds; in June, a federal appeals court upheld that ruling. (The Justice Department hasn't announced its next step; it could seek a Supreme Court review, proceed with a full trial, or let the injunction stand.)

One section of the law was not challenged: the creation of a 19-member commission to advise Congress on the best way to protect kids online. Even though funding was withdrawn after the injunction, commissioners were appointed—from free-speech advocates and execs at companies such as Yahoo and America Online to antiporn crusaders. For the past year, they've toiled in obscurity with no budget and little recognition.

Source: Leslie Miller, *USA Today*, October 17, 2000, available at http://www.usatoday.com/life/lds011.htm.

HOME NETWORKS AND INTRUSION

Consider that many people have computers at home and many of these people also have computers at the office. The office machines are generally networked, giving them access to shared resources. At home, in the 1980s, the machines were stand-alone devices, unless the owner purchased a modem for connectivity. In the 1990s, most machines were being delivered with modems installed and operational. These modems started at 2,400 bps and are now standard at 56 Kbps.

An evolving situation in the home, whether it is acting as a small office (SOHO) or not, is the presence of several computers, possibly one for entertainment and one or more work-related items. There is often just one good printer. Although each machine may have a modem (POTS or broadband connectivity), this environment necessitates sharing a phone line or even installing a separate line for modem access.

One option is to network the several computers. If the computers are using the Windows operating system, all one needs to make a network is to add network interface cards in each machine and a hub to connect them to give high-speed connectivity. This is a low-cost environment, one that can be installed by many home-owners.

Now that the several machines are connected, we would like for them all to have connectivity to the Internet through a single POTS line. The process, started when Windows 98 and Windows 2000 made it stable, is Internet connection sharing. Using the home network described, this technology sets one machine up as the server. This machine is the only one with direct connectivity to the Internet via modem and the only one that needs a modem. The other computers are set up as clients and the software allows them access to the modem via the network.

With only one machine in the always-on condition, it is necessary to go into the operating system and disable print and file sharing. This means that outsiders will have a more difficult time accessing your systems. However, if you have a network, this creates a problem because the other machines cannot share the resources of each other. So, in the case of multiple machines, or even one machine, you need a firewall. As we described earlier, this is software or hardware that acts as a shield to your computer or network.

One of the authors recently acquired DSL and installed *ZoneAlarm*® (www.zonealarm.com) as the firewall. This free software displays a small screen each time it detects and blocks someone on the Internet who attempts to enter your machine or just sends you an unwanted message or ping. During the first week of installation of DSL and *ZoneAlarm*, more than 50 suspicious messages were received each day. While they may have been harmless, it is an example of the attempts to find available machines for information or to access them. On the downside, this same author has had several students with always-on environments, two of whom have had intruders that stole their registry files, making Windows nonoperational. This means a total reload of the operating system was required.

As you provide more machines at home, connect them, and gain fast access to the Internet, you must be aware that you are inviting intrusion danger. Just as a surge protector or UPS is a vital protective device for hardware, a firewall is a vital protective item for software.

SUPERJANET—THE ACADEMIC NETWORK OF GREAT BRITAIN[13]

An example of a country that chooses the Internet as a way to support commerce and education is the United Kingdom. While its telephone infrastructure is as widespread as that in the United States, its POTS infrastructure does not support Internet access as well. In the early days, this would be seen as a problem, but as countries move to broadband access, this is of no consequence. Meanwhile, the following illustrates the UK's support of the research/academic infrastructure with telecommunications.

SuperJANET was conceived in 1989 as the strategic development path for a national network that could support the networking requirements of the UK research and higher education community in the 1990s. The preparatory work culminated in 1992 with the award of a contract worth £16M to British Telecom (BT) to provide a range of networking services over a four-year period that extends to March 1997. SuperJANET has several components which support different aspects of the project. The BT contract provides a national network with two components: a high-speed configurable bandwidth network serving up to 16 sites, initially using PDH technology to be replaced with SDH technology, and a high-speed switched data service (SMDS) serving 50 or more sites. The primary role of the PDH/SDH component will be to support the development and deployment of an ATM network. (SDH & ATM are covered in Chapter 14.) These components will be complemented by several high performance MAN (metropolitan area network) initiatives each serving an area where there are a number of sites closely located. The aim has been to provide a pervasive network capable of supporting a large and diverse user community.

The first milestone in the development of SuperJANET provided a pilot network serving Cambridge University, Edinburgh University, Imperial College, Manchester University, Rutherford Appleton Laboratory, and University College London. BT provided a 140Mbit/s PDH link to each of these sites as well as PDH connections for the universities of Glasgow and Nottingham. ULCC and Hammersmith Hospital were added to the network using a 34Mbit/s leased line and a dark fiber connection respectively, both provided by cable TV companies. The Hammersmith Hospital connection has become part of WESTNET, Super-JANET's first MAN, which also connects Queen Charlotte's hospital and was developed in collaboration with Videotron.

Switching equipment supplied on loan by Chernikeef/Cisco, Netcomm and GPT permitted the rapid development of the network. The network has two parts, an IP data network and an ATM network, both operating at 34Mbit/s. This illustrates the development strategy chosen for SuperJANET which aims to deploy a full-scale service data network very quickly to support widespread use and new applications and, in parallel, to introduce the new ATM technology.

The pilot network was used to support a preliminary demonstration of new applications; later the pilot IP network was transferred to full service and configured to provide a trunk network for JIPS, the JANET IP service. This development created an enhanced IP service for a large number of JIPS users and has helped to overcome some of the performance bottlenecks in the service.

The pilot ATM network has been extended to serve twelve sites and the scope of the video network. The principal vehicle used for the expansion of the data network was the SMDS service provided by BT. In addition some sites were connected via MAN initiatives.

The sites selected for connection to SuperJANET and the distribution of sites within the UK are shown in Figure 9.4. The universities of Birmingham, Cardiff,

[13] Extracted from the JANET site in England.

FIGURE 9.4   JANET Sites in UK

Source: http://www.scit.wlv.ac.uk/ukenfo/uk.map.html.

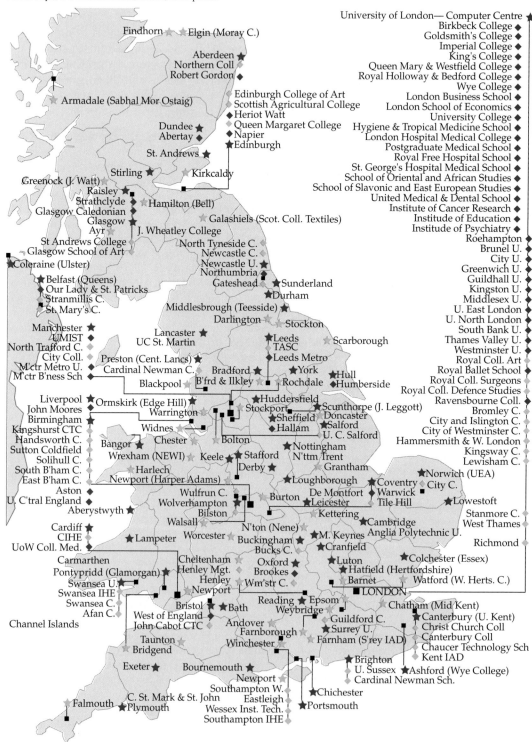

Glasgow, Leeds, Newcastle, and Nottingham have been connected to the PDH/SDH network in addition to the six sites connected during the pilot phase. The SERC has approved funding to provide PDH/SDH access for the Daresbury Laboratory. Aston, East London, LSE, Nottingham Trent, Strathclyde, and UMIST have been selected for MAN connections.

The Universities Funding Council funded the first year of SuperJANET. The Higher Education Funding Councils of England, Scotland and Wales approved funding to continue the project for the full four years. The funding councils support the connection of the universities. Later, funding was approved to connect the universities in Northern Ireland with contributions from the Department of Education in Northern Ireland, Queen's University Belfast, and the University of Ulster. The British Library funded to connect the Document Supply Centre at Boston Spa.

Source: Bob Cooper (Joint Network Team), R.Cooper@jnt.ac.uk.

THE INTRANET—USING INTERNET CAPABILITIES WITHIN THE ORGANIZATION

What Is an Intranet?

In simple terms, an *intranet* is the descriptive term used for the implementation of Internet technologies within a corporate organization, rather than for external connection to the global Internet. This implementation is performed in such a way as to transparently deliver the immense informational resources of an organization to each individual's desktop with minimal cost, time, and effort.

The impact of an intranet affects a corporation's operation, efficiency, development, and even its culture. To fully understand what is meant by the intranet, we need to look at several areas, namely

- Today's demands on business.

- The Internet and its technologies.

- The Internet versus an intranet.

- The intranet revolution.

Before investigating each area in detail, let's explore a single, simple example that puts the impact of the intranet in context.

Imagine this scenario. Your company has 20 sites and 1,000 people who need timely access to company news, corporate policy changes, human resource procedures—even simple, but crucial, documents such as phone books, product specifications, and pricing information. Normally, you use printed matter, such as employee handbooks, price lists, sales guides, and so on. This printed material is both expensive and time consuming to produce, as well as not contributing directly to the bottom line.

Once created, there is the question of distribution and dissemination. How can you guarantee that all your people have received exactly what they need? How can you be sure they have the latest and correct versions? How can you ensure that they even know that important policy details or other information has changed or is now available? The simple answer is, with printed technology, you can't.

Add to this the problem that, due to the changing nature of any organization in today's frenetic business world, the shelf life of any internal printed matter is reducing so rapidly that, in many cases, it is out of date before it reaches the people that need it. Many corporate hours are lost just confirming and verifying the validity of information.

Then we can start to consider the direct cost of preparation, typesetting, production, distribution, and mailing. Add labor costs and overhead and the fact that during any financial year most documents require reprint in ever-increasing frequencies.

For example, a standard price book may cost in the region of US $15 each to produce. Add the distribution cost, and multiply this by the number of people who need it, and then by the number of times per year it is produced. We can very easily see the substantial cost that is required to deliver just a single, accurate document to one of our employees to allow him/her to perform the job. But if you also add the hidden cost of the people verifying accuracy and quality of the information, the cost becomes even more astronomical. And this is just one document!

Today's cost-cutting environment demands that you do more for less. But you cannot eliminate these internal communications tools. In fact, we know that increased communication is absolutely essential within companies. Also, we know these increased demands on our busy staff mean they do not have the time to waste chasing down the correct price or product description. In today's competitive business arena, timely access to accurate information is crucial.

The above example assumed 20 sites and 1,000 employees, but in reality this problem is equally important to a single site with 20 people. Accurate, timely communication and information flow are essential in today's world.

The problem described above is not new. Attempts to exploit existing computer technologies were implemented, with different degrees of success. Implementations usually had built-in gross inefficiencies and expenses—for example, mail that resulted in the unnecessary stuffing of employee mailboxes, or client/server databases that put an inordinate and expensive load on the MIS teams who end up being responsible for the maintenance and update of the information.

The solution to the problem requires technology that

- Can deliver information on demand—as needed.

- Can guarantee the information is the latest and most accurate available.

- Ensures information can be held at a single source (although there is no need for that source to be the source of all information).

- Allows information to be maintained by the people who would normally maintain and prepare the original information.

The solution to this problem is provided by just one of the technologies available under the generic heading of the Internet. Different problems require different solutions, and the use of the full spectrum of Internet technologies within an organization will generate one of the biggest corporate IT revolutions.

The Internet and Its Technologies

There is abundant literature on the background and history of the Internet. Unfortunately, due largely to tremendous market hype, to many people the Internet and the World Wide Web, or more commonly simply the Web, are synonymous. Although the Web is an important piece of the Internet story, in reality the Internet is a series of components and layers of technology, each one meeting specific needs in a powerful and yet flexible way.

The main technology components of the Internet are

- Communications protocol—The ability to connect and communicate between networks and individual desktop devices.

- File transfer—The ability to transfer files between point-to-point locations.

- Mail—The ability to provide direct point-to-point communication between individuals or groups.

- Web browsing—The ability to provide hyperlinked, hypertext-based access to information on a one-to-many basis, on demand.

- Terminal emulation—The ability to access existing infrastructure applications.

- User interfaces—The ability to deliver the increasing technical complexity to the desktop in a transparent, seamless, and intuitive manner.

During the evolution of the Internet, a series of applications were created to meet the specific needs of each component area. Within each of these areas the survival of the fittest has brought several specific best-of-breed applications and standards— for example, the FTP protocol standard for file transfer, the Mosaic technology for Web browsing, the MIME standard for transparent distribution of all file formats, the HTML syntax as the language of the Web, and so on.

The Internet and the Intranet

Is the Internet actually competitive to the **intranet**? The answer is obviously a resounding No! To put it all in context, the *Internet* **continues to define the technologies available for external communication,** whereas an *intranet* **is the application of these technologies within your organization and centered around the corporate LAN.**

The individual component areas that make up the Internet are not necessarily new to corporations. In the context of the Internet, these mechanisms, methods, and technologies follow consistent standards that have a significant effect when applied within a corporate organization. In creating an intranet, there are several main reasons why the Internet technologies have such a dramatic impact on the scope of business networking applications. These include

- Universal communication—Any individual and/or department on the intranet can interact with any other individual/department and beyond to partners and markets.

- Performance—On an inherently high-bandwidth network, the ability to handle audio clips and visual images increases the level and effectiveness of communication.

- Reliability—Internet technology is proven, highly robust, and reliable.

- Cost—Compared with proprietary networking environments, Internet technology costs are surprisingly low.

- Standards—The adoption of standard protocols and APIs such as MIME, Windows Sockets, TCP/IP, FTP, and HTML delivers a fast-track series of tools that allow infrastructures to be built, restructured, and enhanced to meet changing business needs as well as allowing standards-based intercommunication between external partners, agencies, and potential customers.

The Intranet Revolution

Internet technologies are actually extremely well suited for developing internal corporate information systems: the intranets. In fact, Internet technologies are much more relevant and exploitable within a local LAN than over much slower, dial-up access routes associated with remote access to the Internet, although slow remote access is a viable use of this technology.

Within the early intranet adopters, the application of this hot technology was typically used as follows:

- Publishing corporate documents—Along with oft-mentioned human resource guides, these documents can include newsletters, annual reports, maps, company facilities, price lists, product information literature, and any document that is of value within the corporate entity. This is one area where significant cost control can be achieved as well as much more efficient, timely, and accurate communication across the entire corporate organization.

- Access into searchable directories—Rapid access to corporate phone books and the like. These data can be mirrored at a website or, via scripts, the Web server can serve as a gateway to back-end preexisting or new applications. This means that, using the same standard access mechanisms, information can be made more widely available in a simpler manner.

- Corporate/department/individual pages—Internet technology provides the ideal medium to communicate current information to the department or individual. Powerful search engines provide the means for people to find the group or individual who has the answers to the continuous questions that arise in the normal course of doing business.

- Simple groupware applications—With HTML forms support, sites can provide sign-up sheets, surveys, and simple scheduling. As intranet technologies continue to evolve, the press has been treating the technologies as alternatives to major groupware applications (e.g., Lotus Notes®) to the point that confusion has been caused as to the appropriateness of each area of technology. The intranet technology can be used to complement or serve as an alternative to groupware products. It is a matter of scale, cost, time scale, openness, and taste.

- Software distribution—Internal administrators can use the intranet to deliver software and updates on demand to users.

- Mail—Email has been termed a killer application. With the move to intranet mail products, with standard and simple methods for attachment of documents, sound, video, and other multimedia between individuals, email has become the communications method. Mail is essentially individual-to-individual, or individual-to-small-group, communication. With the emergence of Web technology, there are now better and more appropriate tools for one-to-many communication, which historically is where mail systems have been overburdened and overburdening to the point of reducing their effectiveness.

- User interface—The intranet technology is evolving so rapidly that the tools available, in particular HTML, can be used to dramatically change the way we interface with systems. There will be a significant debate, which will shortly hit the streets, that will pit graphical user interfaces (GUIs) *versus End User Comfortable Interfaces*. At the beginning of the 1990s, the industry was deluged with increases in productivity from GUIs. However, no one anticipated the converse loss of productivity by normal business users able to access the wealth of functionality provided by Windows. The GUI has been defined and refined by Microsoft as an iconic desktop. But, although this might be what technicians like—and like to believe it's what users like—it is definitely not the interface that most businesspeople are comfortable with. With HTML an

The Real World   9–12
Correspondence with Microsoft Corporation
on the Internet

Paul Kearns, postmaster@microsoft.com
Microsoft Corporation

Received: From COB-1/MAILQUEUE by charon.business.
auburn.edu via Charon 3.4 with IPX id 102.921022
132849.576; 22 Oct 92 13:29:39-0500

Subject: FW: Information about the.COM Network
to: tex@center.twc.auburn.edu
Date: Thu, 13 Aug 92 15:34:30 PDT
From: v-paulk@microsoft.com (Paul Kearns)
Cc: acctreq, rbowen, postmaster

>"how did you get a node on the.COM network?" I teach
telecommunications

>here at Auburn University and use the EDU network.
'.com' and '.edu' are both top level domains in the DARPA
Internet. Each top level domain represents the type of organization holding the Internet connection—commercial
or educational, respectively. Other top level domains are
'.gov' (governmental), '.mil' (military), and '.org', though
there are others. Each country name '.us' '.ca', '.fr', etc. is
also a top level domain.

Organizations specify which top level domain they belong
in when they request a domain from the NIC (Network
Information Center). Since you are an educational entity,
the people who connected you to the Internet requested
a domain in the '.edu' top level. We are a commercial site,
so we are in the '.com' top level domain.

End User Comfortable Interface can be built, only limited by the creator's imagination. The beauty of using intranet technologies for this is that it is so simple. Hitting a hyperlink from HTML does not necessarily take you to another page—it could ring an alarm, run a year-end procedure, or anything that a computer action can do. Microsoft's Windows®versions 3.x, 95, 98, ME, 2000, and XP created tremendous volumes of functionality, but most individuals probably only need 5 percent of the total functionality. The other 95 percent causes support pain, headaches, and disruption. Now, with the intranet tools, you can paint reality in HTML and make an in-context and uniform front-end to all computer-based resources. In doing so, not only can you create interfaces that users can use and appreciate, you also can remove the 95 percent functionality and access to elements that specific users don't need—getting rid of most of the headaches in one sweep.

Intranet technologies provide the tools, standards, and new approaches for meeting the problems of today's business world. The beauty of most of these technologies is that they are simple and, in their simple elegance, phenomenal power can be unleashed. Because these technologies are still moving from adolescence to maturity, there are still many rough edges. The route ahead, however, is being well-defined, and the new generations of intranet products designed specifically for corporate use will address these. *Communication is the key to business success.* Exploitation of intranet is the key to effective and efficient communications.

The Demands of Business Today

Competition has reached a new level of intensity in virtually all industries. Mere survival, let alone success, requires that a business perform at unprecedented levels of effectiveness. The new pressures on business include the following (we discuss this in detail in Chapter 16, but provide only a preliminary glance at this point):

- Shortened product lifecycles—Time-to-market is becoming an ever more significant factor on the ability to achieve market share, profitability, and even survival.

- Increased cost pressures—The need to control costs, with the corresponding desire to improve productivity, continues unabated with renewed emphasis on the productivity of the knowledge workers.

- Increased demand for quality and customer service—As competition builds, the increase in customers' expectations for responsiveness and personalized support is beginning to change the culture and operation of many industries.

- Changing markets—The only constant for business is that things will change. The need and ability to respond to ever-changing market forces continue to push the need to adopt and implement technology to be able to rapidly react.

- New business models—Constant change is now pushing into the very core of many corporations with corresponding new business models emerging for the way in which organizations and people work together. These include teleworking, virtual corporations, collaborative product development, and integrated supply chain management.

While each issue requires multifaceted strategies, the common link is the need to enable and expand communications within the organization, between partners, and out into the marketplace. The internal adoption of Internet technology to create the corporate intranet can make significant contributions to each of these critical areas.

Competitive Advantage through Intranets

Use of the corporate intranet can contribute to gaining and maintaining a competitive advantage. All employees may have updated and current information on a near-real-time basis. This reduces printing, mailing, and filing costs significantly. Salespeople in the field should be able to provide accurate, up-to-the-minute data, quotes, and terms to their customers.

Extranets

An extranet is an invitation-only group of trading partners conducting business via the Internet. http://www.misg.com/ misc/presentations/ geis_big/sld012.htm.

An **extranet** is a new technology that refers to an intranet that is partially accessible to authorized outsiders. Whereas an intranet resides behind a firewall and is accessible only to people who are members of the same company or organization, an extranet provides various levels of accessibility to outsiders. Users can access an extranet only if they have a valid username and password, and the user identity determines which parts of the extranet they can view. Extranets are becoming a very popular means for business partners or customers to exchange information, particularly in B2B usage. Extranets solve some common problems in using EDI in that they are very user-friendly and easy to keep and run. FedEx and UPS allow customers access to parts of their intranets via the extranet so that customers can check on the status of shipped parcels. Extranets are a natural evolution taking advantage of the Internet infrastructure and previous Internet investments to focus communications to exchange information and share applications with business partners, suppliers, and customers.[14]

[14] Source: http://webopedia.internet.com/TERM/e/extranet.html.

Case 9-1

The Role of Government in the Evolution of the Internet

Robert E. Kahn

From its origins as a U.S. government research project, the Internet has grown to become a major component of network infrastructure, linking millions of machines and tens of millions of users around the world. Very little of the current Internet is owned by, operated by, or even controlled by governmental bodies. Most of the funding for Internet services comes directly from private sources, although the educational community in the U.S. receives most of its research funding from governmental sources. Increasingly, however, the provision of Internet communication services, regardless of use, is being handled by commercial firms on a profit-making basis.

The situation raises the question as to the proper long-term role for government in the continued evolution of the Internet. Is the Internet now in a form where government involvement should cease in its entirety so as to allow private sector interests to determine its future trajectory? Or is there still an important role for government to play in the future? This case concludes that there are a series of important contributions for government to make and a few areas where government involvement will continue to be essential to the long-term well-being of the Internet. In fact, as the Internet continues on its commercial and international trajectory, the role of government will continue to be essential, and may expand to include more involvement by governments around the world.

INTERNET ORIGINS

The Internet originated as part of an ARPA research project on internetworking in the early 1970s. At that time, ARPA had demonstrated the viability of packet switching for computer-to-computer communication in its flagship network, the ARPANET, which linked several dozen sites and perhaps twice that number of computers into a national network for computer science research. Extensions of the packet-switching concept to satellite networks and to ground mobile radio networks were under development by ARPA, and segments of industry (but notably not the traditional telecommunications sector) were showing great interest in providing commercial packet network services. At least three or four distinct computer networks were likely in existence by the mid-1970s and the ability to communicate between them was highly desirable if not essential.

In a well-known joint effort, circa 1973, Vinton Cerf (then at Stanford) and I (then at ARPA) collaborated on the design of an internetwork architecture that would allow packet networks of different kinds to interconnect and machines to communicate across the set of interconnected networks. The internetwork architecture was based on a protocol which came to be known as TCP/IP. During the period between 1974 and 1978, four successively refined versions of the protocol were implemented and tested by ARPA research contractors in academia and industry with the fourth version eventually being standardized.

The TCP/IP protocol was used initially to connect the ARPANET (based on 50kbps terrestrial lines), the Packet Radio Net (PRNET—based on dual rate 400/100kbps spread spectrum radios), and the Packet Satellite Net (SATNET—based on a 64kbps shared channel on Intelsat IV). The initial satellite earth stations were in the U.S. and U.K., but subsequently additional earth stations were activated in Norway, Germany, and Italy. Several experimental PRNETs were connected including one in the San Francisco Bay area. At the time, there were no personal computers, workstations, or local area networks available commercially and the machines involved were mainly large-scale scientific time-sharing systems. Remote access to time-sharing systems was made available by terminal access servers.

The technical tasks in constructing this initial ARPA Internet revolved mainly around the configuration of "gateways" (now known as routers) to connect different networks together and the development of TCP/IP software in the computers. These were both engineering intensive tasks which took considerable expertise to accomplish. Although industry would later offer commercial gateways and routers by making TCP/IP software available for some workstations, minicomputers, and mainframes, initially these capabilities were unavailable. They had to be hand crafted by the engineers at each site by obtaining components from wherever they could be had.

In 1979, ARPA established a small Internet Configuration Control Board (ICCB) consisting primarily of members of the research community to help with this process and to work with the ARPA in evolving the Internet design. This process was also important in that it brought a wider segment of the research community more directly into the decision-making aspects of the Internet project which, until then, had been almost solely undertaken by ARPA. The ICCB was chaired by ARPA. The ICCB met several times a year and as the interest in the ARPA Internet grew, so did the interest in the work of the ICCB.

During this early period, the U.S. government (mainly ARPA) funded network R&D, supported the various networks in the ARPA Internet (they leased various components, bought others and contracted out the day-to-day operational management) and maintained responsibility for overall policy. In the mid-to-late 1970s, experimental local area networks and experimental workstations developed by the research community were connected to the Internet by dint of engineering expertise at each site. In the early 1980s, commercial workstations and local area networks became available that were Internet compatible, and the task of getting connected to the Internet was significantly eased.

In addition to R&D contracts, U.S. government contracts were issued for various infrastructure purposes such as to fund groups to maintain lists of hosts on the network and their addresses and to take responsibility for assignment and registration of host names and addresses. The government funded other groups to monitor and maintain the key gateways between its networks, in addition to support for the networks themselves. In 1980, the U.S. Department of Defense adopted the TCP/IP protocol as a standard. By the early 1980s, it was clear that the internetwork architecture that ARPA had created was a viable technology for wider use in defense.

EMERGENCE OF THE OPERATIONAL INTERNET

The Department of Defense had become convinced that for its use of networking to grow, it needed to split the ARPANET into two separate networks. One of these networks, to be known as MILNET, would be used for military purposes and mainly link military sites in the U.S. and perhaps around the world. The residual portion of the network would continue to bear the name ARPANET and continue to be used for research purposes. The use of the TCP/IP protocol would still allow computers on the MILNET to talk to computers on the new ARPANET, but the MILNET network nodes would be protected by virtue of locating them in protected sites, rather than in research labs and on university campuses. If problems should develop on the ARPANET, the MILNET could quickly be disconnected from it by simply unplugging the small number of gateways that connected them. In fact, these gateways were outfitted so that they could limit, if desired, the interactions between the two networks to the exchange of email.

By the early 1980s, the ARPA Internet was known simply as the Internet and the number of connections to it continued to grow. Recognizing the importance of networking to the larger computer science community, NSF began supporting a set of computer science researchers to connect to the emerging Internet via an effort called CSNET. This allowed new research sites to be placed on the ARPANET and be paid by NSF, and allowed new research sites to be connected via a commercial network (Telnet) which would be gatewayed to the ARPANET. A capability for supporting dial-up email connections was also provided. In addition, access to the ARPANET was informally extended to research colleagues at numerous research sites, thus helping to further diffuse the networking technology within the community. Also during this period, other federal agencies with computer-oriented research programs (notably DOE and NASA) created their own "community networks."

Although TCP/IP had been declared a defense standard a few years earlier, it was one of many standards (although the only one that dealt explicity with internetworking of packet networks) and its use was not yet mandated on the ARPANET. However, on January 1, 1983, TCP/IP become the standard for the ARPANET, replacing the older host protocol known as NCP. This step was also necessary for the ARPANET-MILNET split which was to occur about a year later. With the use of TCP/IP now mandatory on the ARPANET, the rationale for connection of local area networks was evident and the growth of users and networks accelerated. It also led to a rethinking of the process that ARPA was using to manage the evolution of the network.

ARPA replaced the ICCB as a mechanism for dealing with network evolution with the Internet Activities Board (IAB). The IAB was to be constituted similarly to the old ICCB, but the many issues of network evolution were to be delegated to initially 10 task forces charted by the IAB and reporting to it. The chair of the IAB was selected from the research community supported by ARPA. Having previously assumed responsibility for overseeing the process that was used to evolve the Internet protocols, ARPA began to delegate the responsibility for certain aspects of the standards process to the IAB.

Following the CSNET effort, NSF and ARPA worked together to expand the number of users on the ARPANET, but they were constrained by the limitations placed by defense on the use of the network. By the mid-1980s, however, network connectivity had become sufficiently central to the workings of the computer science community that NSF became interested in broadening the use of networking to other scientific communities. The NSF supercomputer centers program provided a major stimulus to broaden the use of networks by providing limited access to the centers via the ARPANET. At about the same time, ARPA decided to phase out its network research program, only to reconsider this decision about a year later when the seeds for the subsequent High Performance Computer Initiative were planted by joint actions taken by the administration and then-Senator Gore.

In this period, NSF formulated a strategy to assume responsibility for the areas of leadership that ARPA had formerly held and planned for the fielding of an advanced network called NSFNET. NSFNET was to link the NSF supercomputer centers with very high-speed links, then 1.5Mbps and to provide for access from members of the U.S. academic community to the NSF supercomputer centers, as well as to one another. (For a brief period in the mid-1980s, there was a small initial NSFNET which linked the supercomputer centers with 64Kbps lines.)

In 1990, the last node of the ARPANET was decommissioned by ARPA. Replacing it was the NSFNET backbone and a series of regional networks funded in various ways, with most funded by the U.S. government or started with government funding and soon thereafter to be self-supporting. The effort by NSF greatly encouraged and expanded the involvement of many other groups in providing network services as well as using them. It followed as a direct result of the planning for the High Performance Computing Initiative which was being formed at the highest levels of government. Defense still retained the responsibility for control of the Internet name and address space, although it continued to contract out the operational aspects.

The Department of Energy (DOE) and the National Aeronautics and Space Administration (NASA) are heavy users of networking in the support of their respective missions. In the early 1980s, they built HEPNET (high energy physics net) and SPAN (space physics analysis net) based on the Digital Equipment Corporation's DECNET protocols. Later, DOE and NASA respectively developed ESNET (energy sciences net) and NSI (NASA science internet) to support both TCP/IP and DECNET services. These initiatives were early intrumental influences in the development of multiprotocol networking technology which was subsequently embraced by the Internet.

International networking activity was also expanding in the early and mid-1980s. Starting with a number of X.25 networks as well as international links to ARPANET, DECNET, and SPAN, the networks began to incorporate open internetworking protocols. While initially the thrust was based on the use of OSI protocols, the same forces that drove the U.S. to use TCP/IP (such as its availability in commercial workstations and local area networks) also caused a growth in the use of TCP/IP internationally.

The number of task forces under the IAB continued to grow and, in 1989, the IAB consolidated its various task forces into two groups: the Internet Engineering Task Force (IETF) and the Internet Research Task Force (IRTF). The IETF was given responsibility for the "near-term" Internet developments. The IETF was responsible for generating options for consideration by the IAB structure as Internet standards. The IAB structure, with its task force mechanism, had opened up the possibility of getting broader involvement from the private sector without the need for government to pay directly for their participation. The U.S. government role continued to be limited to oversight and to provide financial support which facilitated the convening of the IETF in plenary session several times per year and sponsorship for many of the IRTF participants. By the early 1990s, even that mechanism needed to be augmented by the charging of nominal attendance fees to cover the out-of-pocket costs of the meetings.

The opening of the Internet to commercial usage was a significant development in the late 1980s. The initial step was to allow commercial email providers to use the NSFNET backbone to communicate with authorized users of the NSFNET and other federal research networks. Regional networks, initially established to serve the academic community, had taken on nonacademic customers as an additional revenue source in their efforts to become self-sufficient. NSF's Acceptable Use Policy, which restricted backbone usage to traffic within and in support of the academic community, together with the growing number of nonacademic Internet users, led to the formation of two privately funded and competing Internet carriers, both spin-offs from U.S. government programs. They were UUNET Technologies, spun off from a DOD-funded seismic research facility, and Performance Systems International (PSI) which was formed by a subset of the officers and directors of NYSERNET—the NSF-sponsored regional network in New York state and lower New England.

Beginning in 1990, the growth in the Internet (fueled significantly by the enormous growth on the NSFNET and including significant commercial and international growth) averaged upwards of 10% per month for months at a time. NSF also helped to stimulate this growth by funding incremental as well as fundamental improvements in Internet routing technology, as well as by encouraging the widespread distribution of network software from its supercomputer centers. Interconnections between commercial networks (and other networks) are handled in a variety of ways including the use of the Commercial Internet Exchange (CIX) which was established, in part, to facilitate packet exchanges among commercial services providers.

Recently, the NSF decided that further funding for the NSFNET backbone was no longer required. It also embarked on a path to make the NSF regional networks self-supporting over a several-year period. To assure the continued availability of network access to the scientific research community, NSF made competitively chosen awards to several parties to provide network access points (NAPs) in four cities. NSF also contracted with MCI for a very high-speed backbone service (initially at 153Mbps) linking the NAPs and several other sites. It also funded a routing arbiter to oversee certain aspects of traffic allocation in this new architecture.

The Internet Society was formed in 1992 as a private sector effort to help promote the evolution of the Internet. As a professional society, it has individual members but the bulk of its initial support comes from industrial contributions. In 1992, the IAB was reconstituted as the Internet Architecture Board, which became part of the Internet Society. It delegated its decision-making responsibility on Internet standards to the leadership of the IETF, known as the Internet Engineering Steering Group (IESG). While not a part of the Internet Society, the IETF is the mixing bowl in which the candidates for future protocols emerge. The Internet Society now maintains the Internet standards process, and the work of the IETF is carried out under its auspices.

ISSUES FOR CONSIDERATION

As the Internet continues to grow, the roles of the various participants in developing and evolving standards naturally come under closer scrutiny. When the financial implications of Internet standard decisions were relatively small, the current standards process that emerged from the research community proved entirely satisfactory. As the financial impact of such decisions becomes increasingly significant, the nature of the standards process will continue to change accordingly to allow more direct industrial involvement in the decision-making process. How this will ultimately play out is yet unclear: However, the vitality of the current process derives from the broad involvement of the many communities that have a stake in the Internet. Unlike typical standards processes that form consensus decisions and then proceed to implement them, the Internet process works essentially in reverse by a kind of grass-roots mechanism. Internet standards are those that have been tried, found by actual trial and error to be desirable and the resulting standards developed as a result of widespread implementation. No better model of a standards process has yet emerged that is as dynamic and agile to allow more direct involvement by industry.

Further, with the widespread internationalization of the Internet, scores of countries now have fundamental interests in its evolution. Within the U.S., the Internet is seen in many quarters as the starting point for the National Information Infrastructure. Around the world, there is growing recognition that the set of NIIs (assuming each country commits to developing one) should be compatible with each other along some yet unknown dimensions. Who should take the lead in making this compatibility occur? Is this a role for the private sector, for governments acting together, or for some hybrid approach? There is clearly a role for government here, at least to provide oversight, support and guidance if not active participation.

Independent of the resolution of these issues, a further concern is the viability of any entity that has no individual or organization with overall responsibility for its evolution. It seems fair to say that many of the traditional carriers would prefer this capability to be provided as a turnkey service by them on an end-to-end basis. Industry surely has within itself the capacity to provide many of the necessary capabilities, but history shows that a government role was necessary to make it happen in the first place. What guarantees are there that the same degree of vitality in its future evolution will take place if market forces alone determine what new capabilities are added to the Internet? Furthermore, the Internet offers distinct possibilities for providing bypass mechanisms to conventional service offerings by the regulated carriers. These possibilities create the potential to make it more difficult for the regulated carriers to compete effectively in those areas and also make it hard for the relevant government regulatory bodies to ignore.

Finally, the carriers can only go so far in providing Internet services. Ultimately, the communication pathways must enter the users' machine, pass through layers of software and end up in applications programs. The computer industry along with the many vendors of computer-related equipment must play a role in determining how this segment of the Internet will evolve. The nature of innovation in technology almost surely guarantees that many new technological options will continue to be generated from many different sources and make their appearance throughout the Internet. Thus, it appears inherent that no single entity can possibly be in charge of the overall Internet. A key to the success of the Internet is to insure that the interested parties have a fair and equitable way of participating in its evolution, including participation in its also evolving standards process. A proper role for governments would be to oversee the process to make sure it remains fair and equitable and evolves so as to meet public needs across a wide spectrum.

An international infrastructure such as the Internet will ultimately require countries to deal with many of the details that are now taken for granted. For example, Internet names and addresses may take on additional legal meanings in the various countries as they rely on the Internet to a greater degree. Trademark of Internet names and addresses is only one aspect of concern. Contracts of all sorts may have Internet names and addresses embedded within them. Countries need to gain a sense of acceptance for names and addresses without necessarily assuming responsibility for day-to-day operation of this aspect of the Internet. Computer viruses know no national boundaries. If a major security attack should involve multiple countries, how will those countries work together to respond to such a challenge?

Finally, the ability to conduct network-based business between countries will require the resolution of many legal issues including intellectual property protection, the formalization of legal contracts online and the ability to deal with associated customs and trade-related matters. At its core, many of these legal issues require the use of encryption technology which has been perhaps the most closely held of all the network-oriented technologies. How can this kind of capability be made available in the international arena in ways that are acceptable to the national authorities? More generally, how can other controversial issues which are likely to arise in the future be effectively discussed and resolved? Various subsets of these kinds of problems have arisen in the context of other international public networks including the telephone network and are thus not unique or entirely new. As the Internet continues to grow, many of the approaches developed in that context may be directly or indirectly applicable to the Internet. Some combination of public and private sector involvement will likely be required to deal with these problems more generally.

It seems uncontested that governments have a fundamental role to play in the funding of advanced research and development which can push the frontiers of technology and knowledge. Often, this will involve the development and use of pilot projects or testbeds to try out ideas and concepts in actual working prototype environments. It also seems clear that governments must provide the necessary oversight to insure the standards process is fair and equitable. Governments must also take responsibility for helping to resolve problems which arise where independent decision making by multiple countries (e.g., in legal, security or regulatory matters) introduces further internetworking problems. In the case of the U.S. national infrastructure development, the U.S. government must provide the leadership in many dimensions, including the removal of barriers where they inhibit and can be removed, the insertion of legal, security or regulatory mechanisms where the national interest so dictates, and the direct stimulation of public interest sectors that require and merit government assistance (for instance research, education, or certain network aspects of public health, safety, and universal access). Other nations may find similar incentives for government involvement as well.

Two final observations seem appropriate to make. First, it will be essential to separate the process by which standards are selected for the Internet from the process by which the options are generated in the first place. The current situation is almost ideal: standards are selected by a process akin to ratification only after independent design and implementation processes have produced viable working options. This separation needs to be maintained.

Second, the most important use of the Internet, and indeed the NII, will be to allow individuals to communicate with each other and to rapidly access the information they require or desire. In may cases, this information will consist of intellectual property of others. There is also the opportunity for every user of the Internet to become a potential provider of information services, thereby vastly increasing the amount of information available. How much of this information may be deemed valuable in a literary or business sense remains to be determined, but much of it may be important in many other contexts. It is essential that we sensitize individuals to the value of intellectual property, and the need to protect it accordingly; this will also have the side benefit of encouraging others to develop and make available intellectual property of their own. A combination of ethics, technology and law is needed to insure the effective development of this important aspect of the network in the future.

CONCLUSIONS

Over a span of some 20 years, the role of the U.S. government in the evolution of the Internet has gone from that of complete provider to involved participant. While the U.S. government took the lead in virtually every aspect of the Internet in the early days, it currently plays a more limited role. It is now a major funder of network R&D, and it provides a significant oversight role in the evolution of the Internet. Within the U.S., it provides direct support or even control for several key aspects of the Internet operation, such as the registration of names and addresses and insuring adequate backbone connectivity: it continues to stimulate the architecture of the Internet along healthy new directions.

However, the role of the U.S. government in the Internet has been steadily declining for several years, particularly as the private sector and international interest in the Internet has increased. In the final analysis, though, there is a major continuing set of rules and responsibilities for governmental bodies to undertake (both in the U.S. and around the world). Governments must architect the way in which different countries cooperate on various aspects of the Internet and its use and they must continue to provide the oversight role in its evolution, both nationally and internationally. Other governments can, but need not, play the leadership role that the U.S. government has traditionally done in the U.S. Without such a role in the U.S., however, it is doubtful the NII will become a reality on its own. Without government involvement on an international basis, it is unlikely that a global information infrastructure will emerge or that the Internet will evolve in as vital and dynamic a way as has heretofore been the case.

If one takes a long enough perspective, network and computer technology may be seen to still be in its infancy, and many of the current uses of the technology reflect past practices carried out more effectively in new environments. The real challenge to society will be for the public and private sectors to work together in harnessing the yet untapped potential of new and increasingly powerful technology in the network-based setting of the NII, and to nourish and incubate the powerful, even revolutionary new ideas that have not yet been uncovered.

Source: Robert E. Kahn, "The Role of Government in the Evolution of the Internet," *Communications of the ACM* 37, no. 8 (August 1994), pp. 15–19.

Case 9-2

NREN and Its Present State in Relation to Internet2

Teresa Lang

WHAT IS NREN?

Today, the **National Research and Education Network (NREN)** is the **National Aeronautics and Space Administration's (NASA)** research wide area network (WAN). The network uses gigabit technology capable of moving data at 622 megabits per second and is part of a national effort to develop innovative networking technologies. NASA uses the NREN to test applications that are under development. Once the new networking technology is tested and complete, NASA plans to use it to improve the design of air and space vehicles, permit Earth system modeling, and provide access to vast databases.

Most recently, the NREN has been used to prototype applications linking high-speed network users with high-end computation resources, including the ability to view images that have been created and stored at remote sites. NASA expects the emerging technologies developed and tested with the assistance of the NREN will significantly benefit their overall networking applications.

The technologies currently under development include multicasting, quality of service, gigabit networking, hybrid networking, adaptive middleware, and traffic engineering. NREN evaluates the alternative approaches to implementing these technologies and prototypes solutions in context specific to NASA applications. [1]

WHAT IS INTERNET2?

Internet2 is a closed membership research network. This membership consists of universities, the U.S. government, and some private-sector businesses. Those working in academia are using the network to build applications for teaching and research and establishing digital libraries. Businesses are working with and incorporating the new networking protocols and software into their future products with plans to use them in commercial applications.

Internet2 actually consists of two interconnected networks. The first one is called Abilene, has a transfer rate of 2.4 gigabits per second, and was built by Cisco and Nortel. The second network was commissioned by the National Science Foundation and is called the very-high-performance backbone network system (VBNS). The VBNS has a transfer rate of 2.4 to 40 gigabits per second, or 64 times faster than NASA's NREN.

The two networks evolved separately and are now interconnected to one another as well as to research networks around the world. Although the two networks are interconnected with one another, neither is connected to the commercial Internet. The commercial Internet is the network referred to by the general public as "the Internet." [2]

A goal of Internet2 is to provide better and more appropriate networking capabilities to support the research and educational activities of the nation's major universities. Internet2 functions as a closed system, available only to members for experimenting with new network technology, new collaboration technology and new instructional technology.

Internet2 is used to prototype new quality-of-service controls, multicast techniques, and network-based videoconferencing. It also is used to facilitate improvements in commercial networks by sharing newly developed technology with both the education community and the private sector. As a result, networks are expected to become more flexible and efficient due to advances made with Internet2. [3]

FROM NREN TO INTERNET2

So, both NREN and Internet2 are working toward some of the same advances in technology. Then why are there two initiatives working toward the same end?

NREN was first established in the early 1990s, and was further empowered with federal funding when Congress passed the U.S. High Performance Computing Act of 1991. (This is when Vice President Gore took credit for the Internet.) The Act was developed and passed with the intent of coordinating government, industry, and the academic community toward the development and use of emerging technologies.

The 1991 Act established the Federal Networking Council, which included the National Science Foundation (NSF), the Department of Defense (DOD), the Department of Energy (DOE), NASA, and other agencies. The Council was to develop and establish the NREN.

The NREN ended up to be a federal program composed of two parts. The first part involved research on high-speed networks, and the second part was the aggregation of the federal research networks.

The Information Infrastructure Act of 1993 clarified the use of the term "the network" referred to in the NREN section of the High Performance Computing Act of 1991. In the 1993 Act, "the network," previously considered to be the NREN, was defined to be the Internet—the same Internet that the general public uses today, but before it was turned over to the private sector for commercial use. This in effect left the NREN without a purpose or identity.

For awhile after this, NREN was known as the Interim Interagency NREN, or IINREN. It included the NSFNET backbone, and all the networks allowed to use the backbone for research and education purposes. The NREN changed from technology innovation to the furtherance of the development of the present reality. [4]

The term *NREN* today refers to what is now part of the technology research continuing at NASA, one of the original agencies involved in the project. It is used to connect scientists all over the country.

NASA's NREN is still under development in coordination with Qwest Communications International Inc. It is due for completion in 2002 and will connect at least seven installations. When complete, NREN will provide multicasting and quality-of-service features that allow engineers to collaborate on projects.

Multicasting is also called point-to-point transmission. It is the simultaneous delivery of IP packets to multiple endpoints. This technology allows a collection of different applications to efficiently distribute large data sets to many different sites.

Quality of service is the commitment of resources to specific applications to ensure that performance limitations such as bandwidth, latency, jitter, and packet loss are maintained within acceptable ranges. This technology facilitates efficient sharing of resources among several users while giving preferential treatment to selected applications when the resources are limited.

Middleware is an adaptive technology that enables distributed multimedia applications to adapt to available CPU and network resources. [1]

Although the focus and the definition of NREN changed in the early 1990s, the initiatives to develop faster, more efficient networks continued.

The NSF transferred the responsibility for the Internet, as the general public now knows it, to the private sector in 1995. The Internet had grown so quickly that the NSF could no longer maintain it. So it was turned over to the private sector for commercial use and profit.

The Internet continued to grow and usage increased. This continued to the point the Internet became so clogged that universities and scientists were unable to effectively use the Internet to achieve their research goals. So the NSF (one of the original agencies involved in developing the first Internet) began searching for ways to improve networking capabilities to assist scientists and the academic community.

In 1997, work began on the Next Generation Internet (NGI). The federal government once again supported the effort with funding, and coordinated an effort to develop advanced research networks at six agencies. These agencies included the Defense Advanced Research Projects Agency (DARPA), Energy Department, NASA, the National Institutes of Health, the National Institutes of Standards and Technology, and NSF.

The federal government has three objectives for approving funding for the Internet2 initiative. The first is to connect universities and/or national labs at speeds 100 to 1,000 times faster than the Internet. The second is to provide a test bed for next-generation network technology. The third is to demonstrate how advanced networks will enable future scientific research, national security, distance education, environmental monitoring, and health care. [3]

A goal of NGI is to maximize the potential for fiber-optic cables. Researchers are working to create smarter vehicles to take advantage of the capacity already available and perfecting videoconferencing technology.

The NSF entered into a five-year agreement with MCI WorldCom to build a national network called the very-high-performance backbone network system (VBNS). [5]

Two years after the inception of VBNS, several universities came together and formed the University Corporation for Advanced Internet Development (UCAID). This group serves as an alliance for the academic researchers, hardware and software vendors, and service providers involved in the project. UCAID first called this initiative Internet2 and the network Abilene. The initiative shares much of its focus with that of the NGI's initiative, and the combined efforts have become known as Internet2 (although UCAID claims to be the "official Internet2").

UCAID worked out a five-year deal with Qwest Communications in which they donated a national OC-48 (2.4 gigabit/s) network to UCAID called the Abilene network. Cisco System Inc. provided the routers and Nortel Networks Corp. provided the switches for the research network.

The VBNS runs an OC-12 (622 megabit/s) IP over an asynchronous transfer mode (ATM) backbone. It will run dual technology with one backbone based on ATM and the other IP over Synchronous Optical Network (Sonet). [6]

These fast networks are separate from the "public or commercial Internet" and therefore allow researchers to do experiments that large ISPs aren't willing to do on their own networks. Commercial networks are expected to be reliable in a way that the research backbone doesn't have to be. Internet2 also gives vendors and service providers the chance to test and experiment with new technology before putting it on the market. [6]

INTERNET2 TODAY

October 4, 2001, Internet2 was used for the world's largest virtual Internet video-conference event. The conference was scheduled to take place in Austin, Texas, on October 1–3; however, due to travel complications related to the World Trade Center and Pentagon tragedy on September 11th, the conference was to be canceled. Instead of canceling, organizers held the event via videoconferencing from Ohio State University using Internet2. [6]

In a September 24, 2001, press release, Auburn University announced it is now connected to "the next generation of the Internet," Internet2. In fact, Auburn has been connected for almost a year. [7]

REFERENCES

1. NASA Research and Education Network, NASA. October 9, 2001, *at* http://www.nren.nasa.gov/about/overview.html.

2. "A History of Internet2." *Internet World*, October 1, 1999.

3. NERO Web pages, Oregon State University. October 9, 2001, *at* http://www.cs.orst.edu/~pancake/internet2/internet2/html.

4. Kahin, Brian. "Whatever Happened to the NREN?" *Telecommunications* 28, no. 9 (May 1994), p. 28.

5. Dean, Joshua. "Gazing into the Internet's Future." *Government Executive* 33, no. 10 (August 2001), p. 64.

6. "Megaconference III Cancelled in Austin; Goes Virtual from Columbus, Ohio." *PR Newswire*, October 4, 2001.

7. Emmons, Mitch. "Internet2 Ties Research Community Together at High Speed." *Auburn University News*, September 24, 2001.

Case 9-3

Understanding Firewalls

Drew Hicks

FIREWALLS?

A firewall controls access between two networks or between a node and the outside world. Usually, the first place a firewall is installed is between your local network and the Internet. This software or hardware prevents the rest of the world from accessing your private network and the data on it. Try to think of a firewall as a comprehensive way to achieve maximum network privacy, with the secondary goal of minimizing the inconvenience authorized users experience when accessing the network. The ultimate firewall is created by not connecting your network to the Internet.

Implementing a firewall is a difficult task that requires a balance of security with functionality. For example your firewall must let users navigate both the local network and the Internet without too much difficulty. However, it must securely contain unrecognized users in a small area. This is called the region of risk. **The region of risk describes what information and systems a hacker could compromise during an attack.** The greatest risk would be connecting your network to the Internet without a firewall; the entire network becomes the region of risk.

Other than containing your region of risk, one must understand the numerous limitations of firewalls. Firewalls cannot defend against viruses. For example, a firewall on a large network with a high volume of incoming and outgoing packets will be asked to examine each and every packet with no chance of stopping thousands of incoming viruses. Firewalls cannot protect your data from disasters. The only way to protect data from disaster is to implement risk management, which includes backing up data to safe locations, various forms of RAID. Finally, a firewall will do nothing to guard the confidentiality of data on the internal network.

TYPES OF FIREWALLS

In order to choose the most practical firewall to meet the needs of a wide range of users, you must understand the different types of firewalls. There are three basic types: network-level, application-level, and circuit-level.

A *network-level firewall* is typically a screening router that examines packet addresses to determine whether to pass the packet to the local network or to take blocking action, such as denying access to the system or passing it to a protected area, called the honey pot. Since the packet includes the sender's and recipient's IP addresses, the firewall uses the information from each packet to manage the packet's access. This is done by instructing the screening router to block packets with a file that contains the IP address from restricted areas (blacklisting).

Depending on how the screening router file is constructed, the network-level router will recognize and perform specific actions for each request type. For example, a router could be programmed to let Internet-based users view your Web pages, yet not let those same users use FTP to transfer files to or from your server. A screen router can consider the following information before deciding to send a packet through: source address of incoming data, destination address, data's session protocol (TCP, UDP, ICMP), source and destination application port, and whether the packet is the start of a connection request. A properly installed network-level firewall will be very fast and almost transparent to users.

An *application-level firewall* is a host computer running proxy-server software. Proxy servers communicate for network users with the servers outside the network. In other words a proxy server controls traffic between two networks. In some cases, a proxy server manages all communications of some users with a service or services on the network. This is how most of the security on websites is controlled today. When using an application-level firewall, your local network does not connect to the Internet. Instead, the traffic that flows on one network never interacts with traffic on the other network because the two network cables do not touch. The proxy server sends a copy of each approved packet from one network to the other. Application-level firewalls mask the origin of the initiating connection and protect your network from Internet users who may be trying to hack into your network.

As with screening routers, you can configure proxy servers to control which services you want your network. For example, you can direct clients to perform FTP downloads, but not perform FTP uploads. Unlike a router, you must set up a different proxy server for each service you provide. Application-level firewalls provide an easy means to audit type and amount of traffic on a site. They also make a physical separation between your local network and the Internet, which makes them a great choice for security. However, because a program must analyze the packets and make decisions about access control, application-level firewalls tend to reduce network performance.

A *circuit-level firewall* is similar to an application-level firewall in that both are proxy servers. The difference is that circuit-level firewalls do not require special proxy-client applications. As named, a circuit-level firewall creates a circuit between a client and a server without requiring that either application know anything about the service. In other words, a client and a server communicate across a circuit-level firewall without communicating with the circuit-level firewall. Circuit-level firewalls protect the transaction's commencement without interfering with the ongoing transaction. The main advantage of the circuit-level firewall is its ability to provide service for a wide variety of protocols. Unlike the application-level firewall, the circuit-level firewall can be used for HTTP, FTP, or Telnet without changing your existing application or adding new application-level proxies for each service. In addition, circuit-level firewalls only use one proxy server, making maintenance a snap.

SECURITY RATINGS

The Department of Defense (DOD) provides the *Orange Book* for further specifics of network security. The *Orange Book* describes four general divisions of security, with each security division having classes resulting in seven security-rating classes.

- Division D Security Rating—The Class D1 security rating is the lowest rating of the DOD's security system. Essentially, a Class D1 system provides no security protection for files or users (Windows 95).

- Division C Security Rating—Classes in the Division C security provide discretionary (need-to-know) protection and provide audit capabilities for tracking users' actions and accountability. There are two subcategories, C1 and C2.

- Division B Security Rating—Division B secure systems must have mandatory protection, instead of discretionary protection as in Division C. Mandatory means that every level of system access must have rules. In other words, every object must have a security rating attached. The system will not let a user save an object without a security rating attached. Division B security is broken down into three subcategories, B1, B2, and B3.

- Division A Security Rating—Division A security ratings are the highest ratings the *Orange Book* provides. Division A only contains one secure class, A1. The use of formal security verification methods characterizes Division A. Formal security methods assure that the mandatory and discretionary security controls employed throughout the system can effectively protect classified information the system stores or processes. Division A security ratings require extensive documentation to demonstrate that the system meets all security requirements in all aspects of system design.

CONCLUSION

A firewall combines hardware and software, which you design to protect your network from unauthorized access. You can use different types of routers to provide simple security, and as a foundation for your firewall. You can use firewalls to protect your network from without and to protect internal departments from other departments.

You must use virus protection software to protect against viruses, because a firewall will not stop viruses by itself. Before you design a firewall, develop a security plan outlining the type of access your employees and users have. The three main types of firewalls are network-level, application-level, and circuit-level firewalls. The Department of Defense *Orange Book* defines seven levels of operating system security. You should ensure that your system has a security level of C2 or higher for maximum protection.

Case 9-4

The Java Language:

A White Paper

INTRODUCTION

The Java programming language and environment is [sic] designed to solve a number of problems in modern programming practice. It started as a part of a larger project to develop advanced software for consumer electronics. These devices are small, reliable, portable, distributed, real-time embedded systems. When we started the project, we intended to use C++, but we encountered a number of problems. Initially these were just compiler technology problems, but as time passed we encountered a set of problems that were best solved by changing the language.

JAVA

Java: A simple, object-oriented, distributed, interpreted, robust, secure, architecture neutral, portable, high-performance, multithreaded, and dynamic language. One way to characterize a system is with a set of buzzwords. We use a standard set of them in describing Java. The rest of this section is an explanation of what we mean by those buzzwords and the problems that we were trying to solve.

We wanted to build a system that could be programmed easily without a lot of esoteric training and which leveraged today's standard practice. Most programmers working these days use C, and most programmers doing object-oriented programming use C++. So even though we found that C++ was unsuitable, we designed Java as closely to C++ as possible in order to make the system more comprehensible.

Java omits many rarely used, poorly understood, confusing features of C++ that in our experience bring more grief than benefit. These omitted features primarily consist of operator overloading (although the Java language does have method overloading), multiple inheritance, and extensive automatic coercions. We added auto garbage collection thereby simplifying the task of Java programming but making the system somewhat more complicated. A good example of a common source of complexity in many C and C++ applications is storage management: the allocation and freeing of memory. By virtue of having automatic garbage collection the Java language not only makes the programming task easier, it also dramatically cuts down on bugs.

Another aspect of being simple is being small. One of the goals of Java is to enable the construction of software that can run stand-alone in small machines. The size of the basic interpreter and class support is about 40K bytes; adding the basic standard libraries and thread support (essentially a self-contained microkernel) adds an additional 175K.

OBJECT-ORIENTED

This is, unfortunately, one of the most overused buzzwords in the industry. But object-oriented design is very powerful because it facilitates the clean definition of interfaces and makes it possible to provide reusable "software Ics." Simply stated, object-oriented design is a technique that focuses design on the data (=objects) and on the interfaces to it. To make an analogy with carpentry, an "object-oriented" carpenter would be mostly concerned with the chair he was building, and secondarily with the tools used to make it; a "non-object-oriented" carpenter would think primarily of his tools. Object-oriented design is also the mechanism for defining how modules "plug and play." The object-oriented facilities of Java are essentially those of C++, with extensions from Objective C for more dynamic method resolution.

DISTRIBUTED

Java has an extensive library of routines for coping easily with TCP/IP protocols like HTTP and FTP. Java applications can open and access objects across the net via URLs with the same ease that programmers are used to when accessing a local file system.

ROBUST

Java is intended for writing programs that must be reliable in a variety of ways. Java puts a lot of emphasis on early checking for possible problems, later dynamic (runtime) checking, and eliminating situations that are error prone.

One of the advantages of a strongly typed language (like C++) is that it allows extensive compile-time checking so bugs can be found early. Unfortunately, C++ inherits a number of loopholes in compile-time checking from C, which is relatively lax (particularly method/procedure declarations). In Java, we require declarations and do not support C-style implicit declarations.

The linker understands the type system and repeats many of the type checks done by the compiler to guard against version mismatch problems. The single biggest difference between Java and C/C++ is that Java has a pointer model that eliminates the possibility of overwriting memory and corrupting data. Instead of pointer arithmetic, Java has true arrays. This allows subscript checking to be performed. In addition, it is not possible to turn an arbitrary integer into a pointer by casting.

While Java doesn't make the QA problem go away, it does make it significantly easier. Very dynamic languages like Lisp, TCL and Smalltalk are often used for prototyping. One of the reasons for their success at this is that they are very robust: you don't have to worry about freeing or corrupting memory. Programmers can be relatively fearless about dealing with memory because they don't have to worry about it getting corrupted. Java has this property, and it has been found to be very liberating.

One reason that dynamic languages are good for prototyping is that they don't require you to pin down decisions early on. Java has exactly the opposite property: it forces you to make choices explicitly. Along with these choices comes a lot of assistance: you can write method invocations and if you get something wrong, you are informed about it at compile time. You don't have to worry about method invocation error. You can also get a lot of flexibility by using interfaces instead of classes.

SECURE

Java is intended to be used in networked/distributed environments. Toward that end, a lot of emphasis has been placed on security. Java enables the construction of virus-free, tamper-free systems. The authentication techniques are based on public-key encryption. There is a strong interplay between "robust" and "secure." For example, the changes to the semantics of pointers make it impossible for applications to forge access to data structures or to access private data in objects that they do have access to. This closes the door on most activities of viruses.

ARCHITECTURE NEUTRAL

Java was designed to support applications on networks. In general, networks are composed of a variety of systems with a variety of CPU and operating system architectures. To enable a Java application to execute anywhere on the network, the compiler generates an architecture neutral object file format—the compiled code is executable on many processors, given the presence of the Java runtime system. This is useful not only for networks but also for single system software distribution. In the present personal computer market, application writers have to produce versions of their application that are compatible with the IBM PC and with the Apple Macintosh. With the PC market (through Windows/NT) diversifying into many CPU architectures, and Apple moving off the 68000 towards the PowerPC, this makes the production of software that runs on all platforms almost impossible. With Java, the same version of the application runs on all platforms.

The Java compiler does this by generating bytecode instructions which have nothing to do with a particular computer architecture. Rather, they are designed to be both easy to interpret on any machine and easily translated into native machine code on the fly.

PORTABLE

Being architecture neutral is a big chunk of being portable, but there's more to it than that. Unlike C and C++, there are no "implementation dependent" aspects of the specification. The sizes of the primitive data types are specified, as is the behavior of arithmetic on them. For example, "int" always means a signed two's complement 32-bit integer, and "float" always means a 32-bit IEEE 754 floating point number. Making these choices is feasible in this day and age because essentially all interesting CPU's share these characteristics. The libraries that are a part of the system define portable interfaces. For example, there is an abstract Window class and implementations of it for UNIX, Windows and the Macintosh.

INTERPRETED

The Java interpreter can execute Java bytecodes directly on any machine to which the interpreter has been ported. And since linking is a more incremental and light-weight process, the development process can be much more rapid and exploratory.

As a part of the bytecode stream, more compile-time information is carried over and available at runtime. This is what the linker's type checks are based on, and what the RPC protocol derivation is based on. It also makes programs more amenable to debugging.

HIGH PERFORMANCE

While the performance of interpreted bytecodes is usually more than adequate, there are situations where higher performance is required. The bytecodes can be translated on the fly (at runtime) into machine code for the particular CPU the application is running on. For those accustomed to the normal design of a compiler and dynamic loader, this is somewhat like putting the final machine code generator in the dynamic loader. The bytecode format was designed with generating machine codes in mind, so the actual process of generating machine code is generally simple. Reasonably good code is produced: it does automatic register allocation, and the compiler does some optimization when it produces the bytecodes. In interpreted code we're getting about 300,000 method calls per second on a Sun Microsystems SPARCStation 10. The performance of bytecodes converted to machine code is almost indistinguishable from native C or C++.

MULTITHREADED

There are many things going on at the same time in the world around us. Multi-threading is a way of building applications with multiple threads. Unfortunately, writing programs that deal with many things happening at once can be much more difficult than writing in the conventional single-threaded C and C++ style.

Java has a sophisticated set of synchronization primitives that are based on the widely used monitor and condition variable paradigm that was introduced by C.A.R. Hoare. By integrating these concepts into the language they become much easier to use and are more robust. Much of the style of this integration came from Xerox's Cedar/Mesa system.

Other benefits of multithreading are better interactive responsiveness and real-time behavior. This is limited, however, by the underlying platform: stand-alone Java runtime environments have good real-time behavior. Running on top of other systems like UNIX, Windows, the Macintosh, or Windows NT limits the real-time responsiveness to that of the underlying system.

DYNAMIC

In a number of ways, Java is a more dynamic language than C or C++. It was designed to adapt to an evolving environment. For example, one major problem with using C++ in a production environment is a side-effect of the way that code is always implemented. If company A produces a class library (a library of plug and play components) and company B buys it and uses it in their product, then if A changes its library and distributes a new release, B will almost certainly have to recompile and redistribute their own software. In an environment where the end user gets A and B's software independently (say A is an OS vendor and B is an application vendor) problems can result. For example, if A distributes an upgrade to its libraries then all of the software from B will break. It is possible to avoid this problem in C++, but it is extraordinarily difficult and it effectively means not using any of the language's OO features directly.

By making these interconnections between modules later, Java completely avoids these problems and makes the use of the object-oriented paradigm much more straightforward. Libraries can freely add new methods and instance variables without any effect on their clients. Java understands interfaces—a concept borrowed from Objective C which is similar to a class. An interface is simply a specification of a set of methods that an object responds to. It does not include any instance variables or implementations. Interfaces can be multiply inherited (unlike classes), and they can be used in a more flexible way than the usual rigid class inheritance structure. Classes have a runtime representation: there is a class named Class, instances of which contain runtime class definitions. If, in a C or C++ program, you have a pointer to an object but you don't know what type of object it is, there is no way to find out. However, in Java, finding out based on the runtime type information is straightforward. Because casts are checked at both compile-time and runtime, you can trust a cast in Java. On the other hand, in C and C++, the compiler just trusts that you're doing the right thing. It is also possible to look up the definition of a class given a string containing its name. This means that you can compute a data type name and have it easily dynamically linked into the running system.

SUMMARY

The Java language provides a powerful addition to the tools that programmers have at their disposal. Java makes programming easier because it is object-oriented and has automatic garbage collection. In addition, because compiled Java code is architecture-neutral, Java applications are ideal for a diverse environment like the Internet. For more information send mail to **java@java.sun.com.**

Source: The Java Language: A White Paper, from java@java.sun.com.

Case 9-5
TCP/IP Protocol and Its Effect on the Internet

Justin Williams

WHAT IS TCP/IP?

TCP/IP, Transmission Control Protocol/Internet Protocol, is the basic communication language or protocol of the Internet. Basically, it is a set of two communication protocols that an application can use to package its information for sending across a private network or the public Internet. TCP/IP is a two-layer program. The higher layer, Transmission Control Protocol, manages the assembling of a message or file into smaller packets that are transmitted over the Internet and received by a TCP layer at the receiving end that reassembles the packets into the original message. The lower layer, Internet Protocol, handles the address part of each packet so that it gets to the right destination. Each gateway computer on the network checks this address to see where to forward the message. Even though some packets from the same message are routed differently than others, they'll be reassembled at the destination.

TCP/IP also can refer to an entire collection of protocols, called a TCP/IP Suite. These include the World Wide Web's HyperText Transfer Protocol (HTTP); the File Transfer Protocol (FTP); Terminal Emulation (Telnet), which lets you log on to remote computers; and the Simple Mail Transfer Protocol (SMTP).

HISTORY OF TCP/IP

In the 1960s, TCP and IP were developed by a Department of Defense (DoD) research project to connect a number of different networks designed by different vendors into a network of networks. The project was initially successful because it provided a few basic services everyone needed, including file transfer, electronic mail, and remote logon. In December 1968, the Advanced Research Projects Agency (ARPA) awarded Bolt Beranek and Bewman a contract to design and deploy a packet-switching network. The project was called ARPANET and four nodes were in place by the end of 1969 and connections to Europe were made by 1973. [1]

The initial host-to-host communications protocol used in ARPANET was the Network Control Protocol (NCP). NCP proved to be unable to keep up with the growing network traffic load. The Transmission Control Protocol (TCP) and the Internet Protocol (IP) were proposed and implemented in 1974 as a more robust suite of communications protocols. In 1983, the DoD mandated that all of their computer systems would use the TCP/IP protocol suite for long-haul communications.

FEATURES OF TCP/IP

HTTP

The HyperText Transfer Protocol (HTTP) is the set of rules for exchanging files (text, graphic images, sound, video, and other multimedia files) on the World Wide Web. The Web can be defined as the following: all the resources and users on the Internet that are using the HyperText Transfer Protocol. Essential concepts that are part of HTTP include the idea that files can contain references to other files. HTTP allows for the transferring of files using the HyperText protocol, called HTML files. A major feature of HTML files is the ability to link between files.

FTP

The File Transfer Protocol (FTP) allows a user on any computer to get files from another computer or to send files to another computer. Security is handled by requiring the user to specify a user name and password for the remote computer. Provisions are made for handling file transfer between machines with different character sets, end-of-line conventions, and so forth. FTP is a utility that you run any time you want to access a file on another system. You use it to copy the file to your own system. You then work with the local copy.

TELNET

Telnet's specialty is terminal emulation. It allows a user on a remote client machine, called the Telnet client, to access the resources of another machine, the Telnet server.

Telnet achieves this by dressing up the client machine to appear like a terminal directly attached to the local network. This projection is actually a software image, a virtual terminal that can interact with the chosen remote host. These emulated terminals are of the text-mode type and can execute refined procedures like displaying menus that give users the opportunity to choose options from them. Telnet's capabilities are limited to running applications or peeking into what's on the server. It can't be used for file-sharing functions like downloading files.

SMTP

Simple Mail Transfer Protocol allows users to send messages to users on other computers. Originally, people tended to use only one or two specific computers. They would maintain "mail files" on those machines. The computer mail system is simply a way for you to add a message to another user's mail file. There are some problems with this in an environment where microcomputers are used. The most serious is that a microcomputer is not well suited to receive computer mail. When you send mail, the mail software expects to be able to open a connection to the addressee's computer in order to send the mail. If this is a microcomputer, it may be turned off, or it may be running an application other than the mail system. For this reason, mail is normally handled by a larger system, where it is practical to have a mail server running all the time. Microcomputer mail software then becomes a user interface that retrieves mail from the mail server.

IP ADDRESSING AND ROUTING

IP addressing is the backbone of what TCP/IP sets out to accomplish. This allows for a node that has an IP address to interact with other nodes connected to a network. TCP/IP also supports routing, which allows for computers across different networks to communicate. Any computer that has an IP address is allowed to connect to other computers that have IP addresses.

IP ADDRESSING AND SUBNETTING

An IP address is made up of four sections for a total of 32 bits of information. Each of these sections is called an octet. Each octet maximum number is 255. Therefore, there will never be an IP address of 342.200.12.567.

The IP address is referred to as a hierarchical address, as opposed to a flat or nonhierarchical address. An example of a hierarchical addressing scheme is the telephone system. For example, the phone number 334.887.9999 can be broken down. The first three digits, the 334 prefix, show that the phone number trying to be reached is in lower Alabama, that is, it is the area code for the phone system. The next three digits are the exchange within the area code, and the final four digits are the user code. A flat address would be a Social Security Number; for example, it does not show parental relationships like the telephone number. The hierarchical numbering scheme allows an organized way to route information across the Internet. The IP address is broken into two parts: the network address and the node address. These two parts are what gives IP addressing its layered, hierarchical structure.

The network address uniquely identifies each network. Every machine on the same network shares that network address as part of its IP address. For example, all IP addresses on Auburn University's campus have the network address of 131.204.xxx.xxx.

The node address is assigned to each machine or node on a network. This part of the address must be unique because it identifies a single machine. This number also can be referred to as a host address. So to continue with our example, in the complete IP address of 131.204.65.245, 131.204 is the network address and 65.245 is the node or host address.

The designers of the Internet decided to create classes of networks based on network size. For the small number of networks possessing a very large number of nodes, they created the Class A network. At the other end is the Class C network, reserved for the numerous networks with a small number of nodes. The Class B networks fit in between. The classes of networks are determined by the first octet of numbers in the IP address. Class A networks occupy 1–126, Class B networks occupy 128–191, and Class C networks occupy 192–223. For the IP address of 24.17.123.145, in a Class A network 24 is the network address and the node address is 17.123.145. This allows for a small number of networks with a large number of nodes or computers. Whereas, in a Class C network, with the IP address of 204.12.134.245, the network address will be 204.12.134 with a node address of 245. This division of networks allows for organized routing of information. For example, if a router gets a packet that is slated to go to the IP address of 131.204.65.245, the router will know that by looking at that first number, 131, that the packet will be routed to a Class B network. This cuts down on inefficient routing.

A problem arises if an organization has several physical networks but only one IP network address. This can be handled, however, by creating subnets. Subnetting is a TCP/IP software feature that allows for dividing a single IP network into smaller, logical subnetworks. This trick is achieved by using the host portion of an IP address to create a subnet address. It also can be thought of as the act of creating little networks from a single, large parent network. An organization with a single network address can have a subnet address for each individual physical network. Each subnet is still part of the shared network address, but it also has an additional identifier denoting its individual subnetwork number. For example, take a parent who has two kids. The children inherit the same last name as their parent. People make further distinctions when referring to someone's individual children, like "Kelly, the Jones's oldest, left for college." Those distinctions are like subnet addresses for people.

Back to the Auburn University example, the IP address is 131.204.65.245. Now, the network address is 131.204 because the first number, 131, falls within the Class B network. So, 65.245 is left. Now, on Auburn University's campus, there are more divisions between the different colleges. The Auburn College of Business has three subnets, 64, 65, and 66. So, we know that in 131.204.65.245, the 65 is the subnet address and the 245 is the node address, which is specifying a specific computer.

DISADVANTAGES OF TCP/IP

FINITE SPACE

The major problem with the current TCP/IP suite is the total number of unique IP addresses that can be created. Using the bit numbering system, there can be a maximum of 232 (roughly 4 billion) unique numbers. This sounds like quite a large number, but it is pretty small when you look at everything that is connected to the Internet. Soon, there will be toasters and refrigerators that will connect to the Internet. The Internet is growing too quickly to support the number of unique addresses. To combat this problem, a new IP version 6 is being created. Compared to the old IP version 4 (IPv4), the new Ipv6 will be 128 bits long. That is the old Ipv4 addressing squared—twice! [5]

MAINTENANCE

The use of TCP/IP on smaller networks is another drawback. TCP/IP requires a lot of overhead and therefore can slow up the speed of the network. "Overhead" in this context refers to the additional network control information, such as routing and error checking, that the protocol adds to data that the application layer needs to send across the network. [4] It would be easier to set up another type of protocol on a small-to-medium-sized network, such as NetBEUI or IPX/SPX.

Another problem with maintenance is the configuration of the devices that use TCP/IP. Someone will have to be in charge of distributing the IP addresses and staying in charge of who-got-what. This poses a large problem to IT managers. Some IT managers simply keep an Excel spreadsheet of valid IP addresses. If a user wants a computer connected to the network, he/she will ask the IT manager. The IT manager will go to the spreadsheet and look for an IP address that is not taken and give that user the IP address. This leads to large problems and headaches on networks that are larger than about 20 people. To counter this there is another feature of TCP/IP called DHCP, Dynamic Host Configuration Protocol. DHCP allows for the user to just log onto the company network and the server will automatically assign that computer an IP address. This eliminates the hassles of keeping track of the IP address.

CONCLUSION

TCP/IP has had a dramatic effect on the Internet. It allows for an organized way of communicating across networks with different operating systems and hardware platforms. TCP/IP also has special features such as HTTP, FTP, Telnet, and SMTP. The benefits of TCP/IP completely outweigh the costs and disadvantages. These benefits are what people want on the Internet and this is why the Internet has grown exponentially over the last few years.

REFERENCES

1. Lammle, Todd. *MCSE: TCP/IP for NT Server 4 Study Guide.* 4th ed. San Francisco: Network Press, 2000.

2. http://whatis.techtarget.com/WhatIs Definition Page/0,4152,214173,00.html.

3. http://www.python.org/~rmasse/papers/tcpip/.

4. http://www.openvms.compaq.com:8000/72final/6556/6556pro_016.html.

5. http://www6.cs-ipv6.lancs.ac.uk/ipv6/documents/papers/bound/IPNG.htm.

Case 9-6

German Federal Law for Data Protection

TABLE OF CONTENTS

22. Election

23. Legality

24. Control through the Federal Agent

25. Appeal through the Federal Agent

26. Additional Duties of the Federal Agent

Third Section: Data Processing of Private Agencies and Public
For Profit Agencies

   First Subsection: Basic Rights of Data Processing

27. Application

28. Data Storage, Transmission, and Use for Own Purposes

29. Businesslike Data Storage and Purposes of Transmission

30. Businesslike Data Storage and Purposes of Transmission in Anonymous Form

31. Special Purpose Connections

32. Reporting Duties

   Second Subsection: Rights of Affected Parties

33. Notification of the Affected Parties

34. Information Provided to the Affected Parties

35. Correction, Erasure, and Barriers to Data

   Third Subsection: Agent for the Data Protection Oversight Agency

36. Summoning of an Agent

37. Duty of the Agent

38. Oversight Agency

Fourth Section: Special Regulations

39. Related Purposefulness for Personal Data which Underlies a Professional or
    Office Secret

40. Processing and Use of Personal Data through Research Institutions

41. Processing and Use of Personal Data through the Media

42. Data Protection Agents of the Broadcasting Institutions of the Federal Law

Fifth Section: Ending Regulations

43. Penalty Regulations

44. Fines Regulations

Case 9-7

Network-Attached Storage (NAS)

Steve Guendert

INTRODUCTION

Storage devices that optimize the concept of file sharing across the network have come to be known as network-attached storage, or NAS for short. NAS architectures utilize the mature Ethernet IP network technology of the LAN. Data are sent to and from NAS devices over the LAN using TCP/IP. NAS technology began as an open systems technology in 1985, when it was introduced by Sun Microsystems as NFS, or the Network File System. NFS was an integral element in the growth of network computing, as it allowed Unix systems to share files over a network.

Prior to discussing NAS in detail, just as it was important to have an overview level of knowledge of fibre channel, it is important to have an understanding of TCP/IP. This also will be important for the following section on iSCSI and emerging technologies. The next section below is an overview of TCP/IP.

TCP/IP TECHNICAL OVERVIEW

Transmitting data across computer networks is a complex process. The standard model for open systems networks is the Open Systems Interconnection (OSI) model. In the OSI model, network functionality is broken down into modules called layers. This simplifies and separates the tasks associated with data transmission. TCP/IP follows the OSI model very closely. Each layer is composed of code that performs a small, well-defined set of tasks. A protocol suite/protocol stack is a set of several such layers. It is usually a part of the operating system on machines connected to the network. In the remainder of this paper I will discuss protocol stacks in general, and then go into more specifics on the TCP/IP protocol stack. I will assume familiarity with the OSI model.

The TCP/IP protocol suite is named for two of its most important protocols, Transmission Control Protocol (TCP) and Internet Protocol (IP). It is the basic communication language or protocol of the Internet. The main design goal of TCP/IP was to build an interconnection of networks, also referred to as an internetwork or Internet, that provided universal communication services over heterogeneous physical networks. Basically, TCP/IP is a set of two communication protocols that

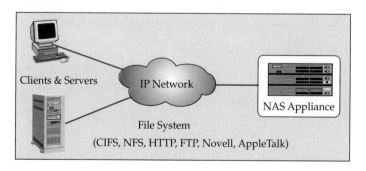

Clients & Servers

IP Network

NAS Appliance

File System
(CIFS, NFS, HTTP, FTP, Novell, AppleTalk)

an application can use to package its information for sending across a private network or the public Internet. TCP/IP is a two-layer program. The higher layer, Transmission Control Protocol, manages the assembling of a message or file into smaller packets that are transmitted over the Internet and received by a TCP layer at the receiving end that reassembles the packets into the original message. The lower layer, Internet Protocol, handles the address part of each packet so that it gets to the right destination. Each gateway computer on the network checks this address to see where to forward the message. Even though some packets from the same message are routed differently than others, they'll be reassembled at the destination.

PROTOCOL STACKS

A protocol stack is organized so that the highest level of abstraction resides at the top layer. For example, the highest layer may deal with streaming audio and/or video frames, while the lowest layer deals with raw voltages and/or radio signals. Every layer in a stack builds upon the services provided by the layer immediately adjacent to it.

TCP/IP MODEL

Two terms are often confused: protocol and service. A protocol defines the exchange that takes place between the identical layers of two hosts. For example, in the TCP/IP stack, the transport layer of one host talks to the transport layer of another host using the TCP/IP protocol. On the other hand, a service is a set of functions that a layer delivers to the layer above it. For example, the TCP/IP layer provides a reliable byte-stream service to the application layer adjacent to it.

As a packet descends the model, each layer of the protocol stack adds a header containing layer-specific information to the data packet. A header for the network layer might include information such as source and destination addresses. The process of appending headers to the data is called encapsulation. During the process of de-encapsulation the reverse process occurs: the layers of the receiving stack extract layer-specific information as the packet progresses up the stack and process the encapsulated data accordingly. The process of encapsulation and de-encapsulation increases the overhead involved in transmitting data.

THE TCP/IP PROTOCOL STACK

The TCP/IP protocol stack comprises only four layers (the OSI reference model is seven layers). These four layers are the data link and physical layer, the network layer, the transport layer, and the application layer. I will discuss each layer in turn.

TCP/IP Level	Description
Data link and physical layer	Physical layer: voltage Data link: framing, error detection and correction, flow control
Network layer	Routes packets to destination, moves data between hosts
Transport layer	Enables host-to-host communication
Application layer	End-user interaction, formats data so they can be understood

DATA LINK AND PHYSICAL LAYER

At the bottom of the OSI model are the data link and the physical layers, which consist of a network interface card and a device driver. The physical layer deals with voltages. The data link layer provides services such as framing, error detection, error correction, and flow control. Together they are responsible for getting raw bits across a physical link.

One important aspect of the Internet Protocol is that it has no restrictions about the physical medium over which it runs. This characteristic provides the TCP/IP protocol its adaptability and flexibility. For example, LAN technologies such as Ethernet, token ring, and FDDI all operate at the data link subnet layer. So do wide area networks such as ATM, X.25, and Switched Multi-megabit Data Services (SMDS). Routers can interconnect all these different media technologies and the Internet Protocol can communicate over all of these lower-level subnetworks. Each of the subnetworks has its own internal addressing and framing formats. To accommodate these the subnetworks encapsulate IP packets with headers and trailer information according to the specific subnet protocol. This enables IP packets to be transmitted over just about any type of network media today.

NETWORK LAYER (INTERNET PROTOCOL)

The network layer protocol below the transport layer and above the physical and data link layer is known as the Internet Protocol (IP). It is the common thread running through the Internet and most LAN technologies including Ethernet. It is responsible for moving data from one host to another, using a variety of routing algorithms. Layers above the network layer break a data stream into chunks of a predetermined size known as packets or datagrams. The datagrams are then sequentially passed to the IP network layer.

The job of the IP layer is to route these packets to the target destination. IP packets consist of an IP header, together with the higher-level TCP protocol and the application datagram. IP knows nothing about the TCP and datagram contents. Prior to transmitting data, the network layer might further subdivide it into smaller packets for ease of transmission. When all the pieces reach the destination, the network layer into the original datagram reassembles them.

The IP is the standard that defines the manner in which the network layers of the two hosts interact. These hosts may be on the same network, or reside on physically remote heterogeneous networks. IP was designed with internetworking in mind. It provides a connectionless, best-effort packet delivery service. It is called connectionless because it is like the postal service, rather than the telephone system. IP packets, like telegrams or mail, are treated independently. Each packet is stamped with the address of the sender and receiver. Routing decisions are made on a packet-by-packet basis. On the other hand, connection-oriented, circuit-switched telephone systems explicitly establish a connection between two users before any conversation takes place. They also maintain the connection for the entire duration of conversation.

A best-effort delivery service means that packets might be discarded during transmission, but not without a good reason. Erratic packet delivery is normally caused by the exhaustion of resources, or a failure at the data link or physical layer. In a highly reliable physical system such as an Ethernet LAN, the best-effort approach of IP is sufficient for transmission of large volumes of information. However, in geographically distributed networks, especially the Internet, IP delivery is insufficient. It needs to be augmented by the higher level TCP protocol to provide satisfactory service.

All IP packets or datagrams consist of a header section and a data section (the payload). The data section may be traditional computer data, or it may be digitized voice or video traffic. Using the postal service analogy again, the "header" of the IP packet can be compared with the envelope and the data section with the letter inside it. Just as the envelope holds the address and information necessary to direct the letter to the desired destination, the header helps in the routing of IP packets. The payload has a maximum size of 65,536 bytes per packet. It contains error detection and/or error control protocols like the Internet Control Message Protocol (ICMP). To illustrate the idea of control protocols, let's use the postal service again. Suppose that the postal service fails to find the destination of your letter. It would be necessary to send you a message indicating that the recipient's address was incorrect. This message would reach you through the same postal system that tried to deliver your letter. ICMP works the same way. It packs control and error messages inside IP packets.

An IP packet contains a source and a destination address. The source address designates the originating node's interface to the network and the destination address specifies the interface for an intended recipient or multiple recipients (for broadcasting). Every host and router on the wider network has an address that uniquely identifies it. It also denotes the subnetwork on which it resides. No two machines can have the same IP address. To avoid addressing conflicts, the network numbers are assigned by an independent body. The network part of the address is common for all machines on a local network. It is similar to a postal code or zip code that is used by a post office to route letters to a general area. The rest of the address on the letter is relevant only within that area. It is used only to deliver the letter to its final destination. The host part of the IP address performs a similar function and can further be split into a subnetwork address and a host address.

The IP packet header also includes a time-to-live (TTL) parameter that is used to limit the life of the packet on the network. Imagine a situation in which an IP packet gets caught in the system and becomes undeliverable. It would then consume the resources indefinitely. The entire network could be brought to a halt by a blizzard of such reproducing but undeliverable packets. The TTL field maintains a counter that is decremented each time that the packet arrives at a routing step. If the counter reaches zero, the packet is discarded.

TRANSPORT LAYER (TCP)

Two commonly used protocols operate in the transport layer. One is Transmission Control Protocol (TCP) and the other is User Datagram Protocol (UDP), which provides more basic services. For the purposes of this paper we will assume the use of TCP.

The application data have no meaning to the transport layer. On the source node, the transport layer receives data from the application layer and splits them into chunks. The chunks are then passed to the network layer. At the destination node, the transport layer receives these data packets and reassembles them before passing them to the appropriate process or application.

The transport later is the first end-to-end layer of the TCP/IP stack. This means that the transport layer of the source host can communicate directly with its peer on the destination host, without concern about how data are moved between them. These matters are handled by the network layer. The layers below the transport layer understand and carry information required for moving data across links and subnetworks.

In contrast, at the transport layer or above, one node can specify details that are relevant only to its peer layer on another node. For example, it is the job of the transport layer to identify the exact application to which data are to be handed over at the remote end. This detail is irrelevant for any intermediate router, but it is essential information for the transport layers at both ends.

APPLICATION LAYER

The application layer is the layer with which end users normally interact. This layer is responsible for formatting the data so that its peers can understand them. While the lower three layers are usually implemented as part of the OS, the application layer is a user process. The users do not see the data at this point. For example, email is the application layer, but it takes the client interface to show them the email. The interface is not a part of this application layer. Some application-level protocols that are included in most TCP/IP implementations include

- Telnet for remote login.

- FTP for file transfer.

- SMTP for mail transfer.

That in a nutshell is a brief overview of TCP/IP.

HOW DOES NAS WORK?

By making storage devices LAN addressable, the storage is freed from its direct attachment to a specific server, and any-to-any connectivity is facilitated using the LAN fabric. This may sound very similar to the previous discussion on SAN. The primary distinction between NAS and SAN rests on the differences between data files and data blocks. NAS transports files; SAN transports blocks. NAS uses file-oriented delivery protocols such as NFS for Unix servers and CIFS (Common Internet File System) for Microsoft servers, whereas SAN uses block-oriented delivery protocols such as SCSI. File I/O is a high-level type of request that, in essence, specifies only the file to be accessed, but does not directly address the storage device.

A file I/O specifies the file. It also indicates an offset into the file. For example, the I/O may specify "Go to byte 1567 in the file (as if the file were a set of contiguous bytes) and read the next 256 bytes beginning at that position." Unlike block I/O (SAN) there is no awareness of a disk volume or disk sectors in a file I/O request. Inside the NAS appliance, the operating system keeps track of where files are located on disk. The OS issues a block I/O request to the disks to fulfill the file I/O read and write requests it receives.

Because data blocks are the raw materials from which files are formed, NAS also has a block component; however, this is typically hidden in the NAS enclosure and to the outside world the NAS device is a server of files and directories.

NAS accomplishes the primary goal of storage networking: the sharing of storage resources through the separation of servers and storage over a common network. Much like SAN-based storage, NAS overcomes the many limitations of parallel SCSI and enables a more flexible deployment of shared storage. When designed with redundant configurations/architectures, NAS also can provide highly available, nondisruptive storage access.

In principle, any user running any operating system can access files on the remote NAS storage device. In addition a task such as backup to tape can be performed across the LAN enabling sharing of expensive hardware resources, such as automated tape libraries, between multiple servers.

NAS BENEFITS

NAS offers a number of benefits, which address some of the limitations of directly attached storage devices (DASD) and also overcome some of the complexities associated with SANs.

- **NAS exploitation of the existing infrastructure:** Because NAS utilizes the existing LAN infrastructure, there are minimal costs of implementation. Introducing a new network infrastructure such as a fibre channel SAN can incur significant upfront hardware costs. In addition, new skills must be acquired and a project of any size involving a SAN will need careful planning and monitoring to bring to a successful completion.

- **Simple implementation:** Since NAS devices attach to mature, standard LAN infrastructures and have standard LAN addresses, they are typically (according to vendors) extremely simple to install, operate, and administer. This "plug-and-play" operation results in low risk, ease of use, and far fewer operator errors. This equates into a lower total cost of ownership (TCO).

- **Reduced total cost of ownership (TCO):** Because of its use of existing LAN network infrastructures, and of network administration skills already employed in many organizations, NAS costs may be substantially lower than for directly attached or SAN attached storage.

- **Resource pooling:** A NAS appliance enables disk storage capacity to be consolidated and pooled on a shared network resource at a great distance for the servers and clients that will share it. Consolidation of files onto centralized NAS devices can minimize the need to have multiple copies of files spread across distributed clients. Thus, overall hardware costs can be reduced.

- **Improved manageability:** By providing consolidated storage, which supports multiple application systems, storage management is centralized. This enables a storage administrator to manage more capacity on a NAS appliance than typically would be possible for DASD.

- **Scalability:** NAS appliances can scale in capacity and performance within the allowed configuration limits of the individual appliance. However, this may be restricted by considerations such as LAN bandwidth constraints and the need to avoid restricting other LAN traffic.

- **Connectivity:** LAN implementation allows any-to-any connectivity across the network. NAS appliances may allow for concurrent attachment to multiple networks, thus supporting many users.

- **Heterogeneous file sharing:** Remote file sharing is one of the basic functions of any NAS appliance. Multiple client systems can have access to the same file.

- **Enhanced choice:** The storage decision is separated from the server decision, thus enabling the buyer to exercise more choice in selecting equipment to meet the business needs.

NAS DRAWBACKS

On the flip side, NAS is not the perfect storage network solution. Below are some of the "others" to counter the benefits outlined above:

- **Consumption of LAN bandwidth:** Ethernet LANs are tuned to favor short burst transmissions for rapid response to messaging requests, rather than large continuous data transmissions. Significant overhead can be imposed to move large blocks of data over the LAN. This is due to the small packet size used by messaging protocols. Because of the small packet size, network congestion may lead to reduced or variable performance. So the LAN must have plenty of spare capacity (and a willing network manager!) to support implementation.

- **Data integrity:** The Ethernet protocols are designed for messaging applications, so data integrity is not of the highest priority. Data packets may be dropped without warning in a busy network and have to be resent. Since it is up to the receiver to detect that a data packet has not arrived and to request that it be resent, additional network traffic can be created.

- **Proliferation of NAS devices:** Pooling of NAS resources can occur only within the capacity of the individual NAS appliance. As a result, in order to scale for capacity and performance, there is a tendency to grow the number of individual NAS appliances over time, which can increase both hardware and storage management costs.

- **Suitability for database storage:** Given the fact that their design is for file I/O transactions, NAS appliances are not optimized for the I/O demands of some database applications. They do not allow the database programmer to exploit "raw" block I/O for high performance. As a result, typical databases such as Oracle and IBM DB2 do not perform as well on NAS devices as they would on DASD, SAN, or iSCSI.

- **Software overhead impacting performance:** TCP/IP is designed to bring data integrity to Ethernet-based networks by guaranteeing data movement from one place to another. The trade-off for reliability is a software-intensive network design that requires significant processing overheads that can consume more than 50 percent of available processor cycles when handling Ethernet connections. This is not normally a drawback for applications such as Web browsing, but it is an issue for performance-intensive storage applications.

- **Impact of backup/recovery applications:** One of the potential downsides of NAS is the consumption of substantial amounts of LAN bandwidth during backup and recovery operations. This may impact other user applications. NAS devices may not suit applications that require very high bandwidth.

Summary

One of the major phenomena of the early 1990s was the stabilization and wide acceptance of the Internet. What started as a research tool and evolved into a communications medium for academics and governmental agencies became a major commercial vehicle. Companies have found ways to ensure security on the world-wide conduit, as they established home pages for visibility, shopping malls to purchase from, and databases of their catalogues for total access to the latest literature. This has been fueled in part by the World Wide Web and its user-friendly browsers, led by Netscape and Microsoft's Internet Explorer. Other companies have added plug-in applications to Netscape, making the home pages of greater interest and amusement.

In the mid-1990s, the Internet concept spread to the internal organization, and the concept of the intranet received wide and rapid acceptance. Companies realized that an Internet presence was invaluable and that these same tools could be of great value inside the organization as a single repository for company literature in an easy-to-use format. Now there could be a telephone directory that is always up-to-date and not dog-eared. Organizations could place operating procedures and training manuals in a place so authorized people could pass through the firewall from the outside, or access them internally, and get access to organizational documents they need. This has exploited the great potential for knowledge transfer and training and side-stepped political battles. Information that once was the property of a department (with access at their control) now can be viewed and used by any authorized employee.

The United Kingdom, like the United States, has taken large strides to network the country. In the case of JANET and SuperJANET, the plan was overt, starting with academe and research agencies, much as in the United States with ARPANET and Bitnet.

Key Terms

Advanced Research Projects Agency Network (ARPANET), *313*
application gateway, *334*
Archie, *315*
AT&T WorldNet Services, *331*
Bitnet, *313*
business-to-business (B2B), *339*
business-to-consumer (B2C), *339*
Child Online Protection Act (COPA), *343*
circuit-level gateway, *334*
Clipper Chip, *333*

denial of service (DOS), *333*
distributed, *318*
electronic business (eBusiness), *339*
electronic cash (ecash), *340*
electronic commerce (eCommerce), *338*
encryption, *333*
extranet, *352*
File Transfer Protocol (FTP), *315*
firewall, *333*
Gopher, *315*
HyperText Markup Language (HTML), *316*

HyperText Transfer Protocol (HTTP), *317*
Internet, *313*
Internet Explorer (IE), *318*
Internet service provider (ISP), *318*
Internet2, *361*
intranet, *312*
Java, *318*
LISTSERV, *315*
Metropolitan Area Ethernet (MAE), *322*
middleware, *362*
mobile commerce (M-commerce), *340*
Mosaic, *318*

Discussion Questions

9.1. What technology is required to create an intranet within an organization?

9.2. What is the more direct equivalent to JANET in the United States?

9.3. What technology did we not discuss that is applicable for accommodation of those with special needs?

9.4. What are the ways you can access the Internet from your community? Do you have a home page?

9.5. What have you purchased on QVC or the Home Shopping Network on TV, and what have you purchased via the Internet? How were the purchases different?

Projects

9.1. Access the Internet's World Wide Web and search for a topic of interest to you, such as healthcare; sportscars; *Sports Illustrated*; CAD/CAM; travel; museums such as the Louvre; skiing; lodging in Boone, North Carolina; stock prices.

9.2. Get a free trial to one of the online services and search for the same topic and compare with the services of a simple ISP.

9.3. Find an organization with an intranet and determine the problems or issues involved with creating one.

9.4. Look in the preface of this text and send the author(s) email, commenting on the approach of the book.

9.5. Read the paperback book, *The Cuckoo's Egg*, by Cliff Stof. Discuss how the intrusion might differ today.

9.6. Contact local companies and determine who has firewalls and extranets. Do they believe they work?

Chapter **Ten**

Business Applications of Telecommunications

CONTINUING CASE—PART 10

JEI's Vision and New Ventures

Information Management

Based on their talks about JEI's direction, Michael hired Dana Hood as a risk analyst to not only give him a new line of business but also to give him greater management of his own firm. In the process he gained professional management and, for the first time, realized he needed to hire other professionals. Dana was a proponent of information resource management, organizational computing, and enterprise (front-line) information systems. Michael saw a need for risk analysis among his friends' firms. Dana was able to give him a sense of the firm's organization and to dispel his uncomfortable feeling by giving him plans that included telecommunications architecture. Both agreed that she would focus on information technology (IT) planning:

- Information systems risk analysis.
- Information systems architecture.
- Telecommunications architecture planning.
- Business continuity planning.

Michael decided that leasing warehouse space on a business-continuity basis had a lot of merit. The idea of collecting large monthly fees for the sites on the chance that the customer wouldn't need them was inherently appealing. He developed a plan with Dana to (1) catalog available space in Denver and Colorado Springs that would be suitable and (2) begin to approach existing and potential customers to

- Lease space in one of the cataloged warehouses as a "cold site" for customers to occupy during time of disaster.
- Lease the contingency to provide telecommunications into JEI's computer systems during the time the customer's system was down, similar to a reciprocal backup agreement.
- Lease the ability for his customers to move their IS operations into a "hot site" warehouse space and continue operations.

Then Michael realized that a disaster that struck Denver also was likely to strike Colorado Springs. It was like the Pacific Stock Exchange in San Francisco having a backup site in Los Angeles. He needed to have greater diversity for his clients. Telecommunications could offer this diversity and safety. For example, he needed to have data communications channels to sites remote enough that a local disaster would not affect that site. Michael made a mental note for Dana to find such sites and high-speed data communications channels.

As he thought about this new diversity, he realized that these same data communications channels could be used for data backup. While many organizations use tape backups and store them offsite, he could offer them data channel backup paths, which means data are immediately stored and available from a remote location, making the backup safer than if stored locally.

Back at the Bank

The cataloging of space was an area that Dana saw as ideal for a database management system (DBMS). She also perceived a need for a DBMS for JL&S's inventory. The first client that Michael approached was his own bank. Very soon after he began to tell his friend John Keller about what he could offer, John responded with a different possibility.

"Michael," John started, "I think your idea of contingency planning is great, and one we should talk more about. First, though, I have an immediate problem I would like to discuss. After we talk about this, let's talk about a disaster plan. Actually, the two needs will join together very nicely."

"What is it, John?"

"The federal examiners are insisting that we keep a set of tapes containing duplicate data in a safe place in case of destruction of the original data. We have been placing our backup tapes in the vault each Friday evening. Not only are we running out of space in the vault, the examiners believe an offsite location for the tapes is far better. Can you provide me a safe location for these tapes?"

"I have not thought about this exact problem until now, but there is a small vacant warehouse that I've been considering in addition to my inventory that is very secure and should be ideal for such storage.

Let me make arrangements for leasing the building and set up a space for your tapes. I think I can do this today or tomorrow, and we can move your data the day after tomorrow. As I remember, the space I am thinking about is about 4,300 square feet, of masonry construction, and large enough to offer safe storage of tapes and other business records to many businesses."

"Fine, check back with me tomorrow morning, and I will personally take the tapes to your location as soon as the space is ready. At that time, we can discuss more about the disaster planning you have in mind."

Michael leased the vacant warehouse and created a data vault out of a 40' by 30' concrete block maintenance area. He installed a steel door and chicken wire for magnetic shielding and protected it with his highest-quality security systems for fire, smoke, water, and intrusion. The shelving in place was ideal for their needs, so he began storing the bank's tapes. The bank now delivers computer tapes each Friday of all transactions that occurred in all systems on their computer. The bank had thought that storing their backup tapes in the vault, or at an offsite location, would satisfy the auditors. This view was soon to change.

Michael answered the phone as he returned from lunch. It was John Keller again, who said in a very anxious voice, "Michael, the auditors are due to arrive next week, and I have not installed the edicted EDP Contingency Plan, required by the Comptroller of the Currency's Revised Bank Circular #177. I had thought I would be in compliance with the backup copy of my data, but I have just been told that the auditors will impose sanctions if I do not have an adequate contingency plan when they arrive. I need to talk to you about your new services."

"Sure, John, I can get the paperwork started tomorrow on leasing some space on a contingency basis and your use of my computer as a backup. Then we can start developing your disaster plan.

Dana Hood, a new member of my staff, has a lot of experience in this area. I am sure we can create a plan within a week to keep you out of trouble."

"Great! What I need in the plan is (1) provisions for offsite backup of critical data files, which we already have; (2) provisions for backup hardware; (3) copies of my critical software that are either resident on the backup hardware or can be migrated to it quickly; (4) procedures (documentation) on how to move to the contingency system; (5) a supply of forms and supplies in a secure offsite location; and (6) a plan for alternative means for processing transactions."

"I know we can do all of this in the time you have. Is this a one-time task or is it recurring?"

"After we set up my contingency plan, I have to have it reviewed by the auditors and certified by my board of directors annually. It looks like you and I will be seeing a lot of each other in the coming week."

Michael smiled. At last, here was a new venture that was clearly related to the existing business. Carlton would continue to operate his security line and Michael could concentrate on how it all fit together. He would need to hire new managers for the Contingency Operations and for the Data Entry and Operations function, which he had been handling up until now. The organizational chart for JEI, after hiring Chris Tonkas for Contingency and Gerry Brown for Computer Operations (known as Johnson Information Systems), looked like that in Figure 10.1.

JEI Considers Offshore Manufacturing

Carlton and Doug sat in the plush office on the top floor of Johnson Control's office tower, overlooking the city. They were reviewing the year's performance and the variety in their product line and thinking about the future.

FIGURE 10.1　Organization Chart for JEI

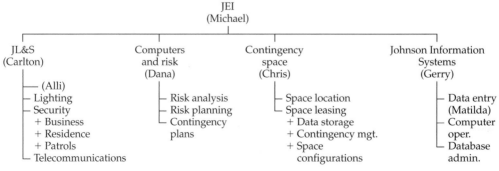

Doug asked, "Have you ever thought about beginning a line of products for the low-end market, Carlton?"

"Why should we do that when we have established a reputation for top quality?"

"Well, we do produce the very best controls here. Now that we have contained costs, we are selling all our controls at a profit. JL&S uses about 10 percent of them, and we sell the rest to noncompeting companies in the same market. Alli's predictions were very good as to the total market for our high-quality controllers, especially the part about the limit of the market. As you and I have discussed, we are presently producing just below where we think saturation would be. Meanwhile, we have employed the unused space for manufacturing new lines of sensors for fire, water, smoke, and intrusion. That gives us products for sensors, processor-based circuit boards, control boxes into which boards are mounted, touchpads for entry of codes, cipher locks, and the software design needed for the controls."

"Why would we want to go after the low end of the market?"

"I receive at least four calls a week asking if we have a lower-priced line of controllers that can be used for the low-end home security market. These buyers are very cost conscious; they don't want all the features and don't demand the reliability of our premiere products. Also, they don't expect the product to last more than 10 years, or have a **mean time between failure (MTBF)** of more than five years. I know we have always tried to produce a product that will last a minimum of 15 years with an MTBF of 10 years and even then have a failsafe characteristic. But I wonder if we are missing a significant part of the market. Let's ask Alli about our potential market."

Filled in on the discussion, Alli joined her two colleagues. "How does $200 million this year for the total home market and $1 billion before the end of the decade sound?" Alli asked as she settled down in an easy chair with a cup of fresh coffee.

"How much of a market do you think we are missing, *and* do you think entering the lower-quality market will hurt our image in our primary market?"

Alli answered, "First of all, we must use a different product name and logo, possibly not even tying it to our other products. If we do this properly, I think we could be looking at total sales of over $1 million in parts to VARs during the next calendar year, at profit margin of 20 percent on sales *if* we can get the controllers manufactured at 60 percent of what we make our best parts for now."

Carlton responded, "How can we make a controller for 40 percent less cost?"

"We could go global for low labor and use the latest manufacturing technology. There are many places where labor is both skilled and of lower cost than here. Additionally, we can design the products for manufacturability, to have less capability than our present line, and make them for a very specialized market. We would need to make sure that we are not engineering or manufacturing high-risk junk, but equipment with limited capabilities and a known lifetime. It would probably open new markets for our JL&S high-end products as well as the new low-end product line we are considering."

"Why make something with a known short lifetime, Alli?" asked Doug.

"Contrary to what you engineers think, part of the market does not want to pay for things that will last forever. Take home builders in particular. They want to be able to tell prospective buyers that they have installed a high-quality home protection device, but they must keep the costs down. If the builders spend $1,000 on a home security system, they probably get $2,000 impact from it. If they spend $2,000, which is what our present line would cost, they would get about the same impact. The home market cannot differentiate adequately between the levels of quality. Both would be reliable within the design parameters, and neither would fail unsafe, but our best line would work longer and do more than a new, more modest line of products."

"So, where could we build these devices at a 40 percent reduction in cost? Any ideas for a location?"

"Personally I would like Mexico or Malaysia," answered Alli with a smile. "They both have wonderful beaches, and I know I would have to keep close tabs on costs. Each has advantages as far as transportation facilities. While Mexico is close to us, Malaysia has superior air transport. Because we will be dealing with high-value, low-weight circuit boards, air transport is a natural. Malaysia already has a large number of facilities that specialize in electronic component assembly and air transport to the customer. Of course, there are several other factors we must consider. Some of the relevant factors are listed here (Figure 10.2). These factors are for international site selection and are somewhat different from the standard domestic models."

FIGURE 10.2 **Some Considerations for International Job Site Selection**

- Inexpensive labor.

- Favorable tax levies.

- Skilled labor and productivity.

- Proximity of commercial air services and transportation infrastructure.

- Fully developed telecommunications services.

- Land and building cost avoidance.

- Incentives and inducements.

"Don't they have a lot of circuit board manufacturing companies in Malaysia?" asked Carlton. "If they do, we might be able to use them initially as a pilot and then build a manufacturing facility of our own later. Tell you what, Alli, you run some more numbers based on a design I want Doug to make. The two of you make sure we are building a low-cost, safe, and reliable product. While Doug completes the design and creates a breadboard model, Alli, you estimate costs and market potential better and begin your investigation of possible sites. Go ahead and plan on making trips to the top three locations. Don't forget to consider Europe, especially Ireland and Scotland. Be sure to contact some of their representatives at the Atlanta World Trade Center."

Three months later, Doug and Carlton had completed the design of the new line of sensors and control boards. The breadboard models were fully tested and resting snugly in Carlton's new attaché case. Alli recommended Scotland as the prime location due to existing manufacturing facilities, favorable tax considerations, and a ready supply of skilled labor. Although Mexico and Malaysia both had advantages, ranging from distance to Denver and air transport, Scotland was picked initially because of its proximity to the European market, which Alli discovered to be ripe for both their new products and their existing ones. Thus, going global for manufacturing would enter JEI into new sales markets and give them diversity in case of changing economic conditions in the U.S. market. The availability of telecommunications services at low costs (services at the lowest total cost in Europe from British Telecom International) played a significant role in the decision, given that the firm would primarily rely on telecommunications to manage remotely.

The trio were met at London's Gatwick Airport by Gray Walton Hume, who took them by British Rail to Edinburgh, Scotland. Gray had made arrangements to show them three plants close to the city with the requisite manufacturing facilities. After they completed their plant visits and then looked over several vacant facilities, Carlton raised the question of telecommunications.

"I know for sure that all three of the plants we visited have excellent telephone capabilities, but I am not sure of the warehouses. Just what do you have in mind?" asked the Scotsman.

"We have found that we can have a high level of control without having a manager in place if we have good communications. This means voice communications for the people we do employ and reliable data communications between computers. In this case, I am most interested in data circuits so we can communicate our requirements to this facility and receive frequent updates on the availability of finished goods. The optimum would be access to an X.25 packet-switched network."

"Well," replied Gray, "let me call my third cousin, Oscar McVeigh Carr, the local contact for British Telecom, and I will quickly find out if we have such an ability."

On the return trip aboard British Caledonian Flight 43, Doug slept while Alli and Carlton discussed what they had seen. "I like the first plant, Carlton," Alli commented as she signaled the steward for a fresh drink. "I don't think we actually need to invest in a facility of our own, such as one of the vacant warehouses we saw, if the manufacturing people can meet our quality demands and production schedule. Do you think they can?"

"I was very impressed with their training program for the production employees, as well as their use of surface mount technology for our processor-based circuit boards. They seemed impressed with Doug's design, said it was the first time someone took design-for-manufacturability into consideration. They said they should be able to tool up for it in less than half a day. My prime concern is their ability to test the finished product."

"Well, Carlton," Alli replied, "I think I have great news in that regard. Gray struck out at British Telecom but did introduce me to Steven Caldwell, the local manager for CompuServe®, who assured me that he can connect us in Edinburgh to his satellite-based T1 global packet-switched network. He further said we have major access to their network at T1 speeds in Denver and Kansas City, and we have 9.6 or 2.4 Kbps access in each of the other cities where we have offices. With this type of capability, we can have the plant upload data on each completed unit from the computer-based test stations. With these data we not only will know finished inventory, but can act as our own quality control department. For example, we can receive the data in Kansas City for initial check and then shuttle it directly to the JEI computer in Denver to perform a second level of analysis on all units and thorough analysis on a statistical sample. With the type of data circuit that CompuServe can provide, we can act as if we were onsite. All we have to decide on is how to inform the production line when they are out of tolerance."

"And we can use that same data circuit to give them our requirements. Sounds like we can use Doug's MAPICS program for scheduling and inventory control. Can CompuServe act as our consultant for EDI?"

"That's what they promised. They have EDI management software on the CompuServe network, so we don't even have to develop the software to translate from MAPICS to the scheduling program in Scotland or from the test stations to our JEI computer."

"And what about our CAD files?"

"I was thinking about that also. You know that shipping a CAD file allows them to have the same design that we have, but the files are quite large."

I think that we can accommodate the size with T1 speed. If CompuServe had said something less, we would be in a bind and have to use air mail. This way we can make changes and implement them in the production line quickly. We can even view the same version of a release and discuss it on the phone."

"Speaking of mail," commented Carlton as he sipped his third cup of coffee, "did you discuss electronic mail with the Scottish plant?"

"Yes, I did," replied Alli.

"Cost?"

"We can afford it! I'm sure it will be cost-effective, given our dispersion."

"Will we have protocol problems?"

"No, they said they can handle any major protocol and can even connect to us through a PAD on our LAN without a connect fee. This way we pay only for the number of packets transmitted, and we can operate constantly."

"Do we need to hire an onsite manager to work with the factory supervisor?" asked Carlton.

"No, I don't think so. Let's do this the same way you manage the Boulder office and we have always managed Colorado Springs."

"You mean by having adequate data communications we can manage remotely?"

"Right. And with this facility in Scotland, we also can ship new releases to the manufacturer and even instructions to the robotics controllers on the line."

"Alli, did you ask Mr. Hume about problems with transnational movement of data?"

"Yes, and he said their rules provided for that when our company established a manufacturing facility or contract manufacturing in their country."

"What about voice communications between Kansas City and Edinburgh?"

"Well, we can at least go satellite. I don't like the time delays involved, but it gives us an initial connection."

Alli glanced over at Doug as he continued to sleep. "I'll bet he's dreaming about the new design right now," she thought.

BUSINESS APPLICATIONS

There are a number of telecommunications-based applications important to our study that don't fall conveniently into one of the chapters of the book. For example, automated teller machines are a major force in the banking industry that use simple modem communications. To place them next to the discussion on modems masks their real value, that of making banking a 24-hour process. Thus, we discuss some of these applications in this section.

While there are many business telecommunications applications that could be discussed here, we discuss only a few in the following pages, in the real-world examples, and in the cases at the end of the chapter. Businesses are continually finding new ways to solve business problems or exploit opportunities via the use of telecommunications technology, and the applications describing them here are examples.

The right technology is the one that provides the resolution to the business problem or opportunity with the best fit for the organization's future needs.

It is becoming increasingly evident that assessing any technology decision must be done not with a view to merely automate something or "throw some technology" at the problem, but with a view to examine alternate ways in which a process may be accomplished using different technology solutions and then to pick an appropriate solution. The same is true of business telecommunications solutions as well. *Bringing technology to bear on a process yields richer dividends if one is willing to consider re-engineering the process.*

Don't acquire technology; acquire business solutions.

Since there are multiple vendors and alternative technologies for business applications, telecommunications managers must become aware of the choices and perform analysis of the relevant trade-offs. For example, most analysts will expect to find significant cost differences as well as technical differences associated with a specific business application. Of equal importance is the long-term effect of the solution selected, that is, the ability of that solution and its technology to blend with existing as well as future technologies and solutions adopted. In other words, don't choose a solution that will constrain the organization to a proprietary architecture or a specific vendor. Be aware of expandability, multiple sources of peripherals, and compatibility among vendors' equipment. The telecommunications manager needs to thoroughly understand the technical and management implications of the choice for the business.

Level of quality and level of service are driving forces when it comes to choosing between competing vendors' solutions.

From a management perspective, the primary focus is on the *level of quality* and the *level of service* rather than on the technology itself. Managers must ask what the impact and implications are for the business or organization choosing a particular technology. Also, the question of what will be the impact on customers, suppliers, or partners should be answered. Since the management decision today is likely to have long-term implications, it is essential for the telecommunications manager to evaluate the decision within the framework of the expected environment at the end of the forecasted life of the technology. What will be the firm's structure, and how will the technology fit the evolving architecture?

Above all, the manager must evaluate the impact on the firm's business over the expected life of the technology. Again, what service levels and quality levels are needed to support the business? It is important for the telecommunications manager to have a broad understanding of the business and the business needs rather than simply evaluating a technology for its inherent capability. *The value of any telecommunications technology is measured in its contribution to the firm's business objectives.*

The business applications we describe in this chapter may include reference to a brand name or specific vendor; however, there are competing sources and technologies available. A rational evaluation and selection must be made.

CONTROL OF DISPERSED OPERATIONS

For many years, managers have desired to decentralize or disperse parts of the business. One of the problems facing these managers is the management control of the **dispersed operations.** Various means of control have been used over the years, and some examples help illustrate the efficacy of telecommunications in achieving the desired control. We have seen how JL&S has employed telecommunications for controlling dispersed locations. Now let's compare their methods with those of a different type of organization.

In one case with which the authors are familiar, a corporation owning several fast-food franchises used only voice communications with the dispersed stores. They had cash register tapes collected for the entire week at the end of business each Friday. The tapes were mailed to corporate headquarters where data entry clerks keyed the sales data into a computer. The system was slow and prone to error; however, the corporate managers were reluctant to change the system.

In contrast, another corporate holder of multiple fast-food stores employs telecommunications to transmit all data from its local stores each day. The local transactions are stored until the end of the business day, then sent as batch files for processing overnight. Each store receives a summary the next day, and management at headquarters is kept up-to-date on each store's performance on a daily basis. Thus, management control is far superior to that in the first case. Both corporate management and local store managers get information in a timely manner, in this later case. The data from transactions are captured at the point of sale without the necessity for re-entry, making them more accurate.

An extension of this concept is real-time capture and transmittal to corporate headquarters. Management must consider the cost-effectiveness of this alternative. This could be achieved with relatively low-speed modems with a continuous circuit or, better, a packet-switched circuit. The management issues and implications outweigh the technical issues involved.

GLOBAL LOGISTICS

As we have emphasized, managers must think globally. Most large firms have a global component. For example, Ford Motor Company has a satellite-based network encompassing all of its dealers. This interactive system replaces the parts catalog, allowing direct entry and retrieval of parts information and ordering on a worldwide basis. Parts not available locally can be found at their nearest source and shipped from there. Meanwhile, in the automobile service bay, the mechanics use this satellite-based system to help diagnose any unusual problems for the vehicle being serviced by accessing a centralized database and expert system.

The Boeing Company used a global network to coordinate the logistics for building the Boeing 777 jetliner. Boeing established a tracking system to ensure that all parts are delivered when and where they are needed. This ranged from delivery of engines from the United Kingdom or the eastern United States to delivery of wing components from other Boeing manufacturing facilities in the Seattle, Washington, area. The logistics (transportation) manager tracks origin and size of every component of the airplane as well as preferred and required delivery modes (air, sea, rail, truck). Global telecommunications is essential in ensuring that this system effectively links more than 3,000 domestic (U.S.) suppliers and 300 non-U.S. sources located in 23 countries.

SERVICE BUREAU

The following business application is one of historical perspective and importance. What started out as a place for paper transactions is now done electronically from hidden sources. You will remember that this was an important event in Michael Johnson's professional life.

Even low-speed modems can provide adequate connectivity for many environments. The use of the technology may not be appropriate from a management standpoint.

Telecommunications can replace or negate the need for a paper or CD-ROM parts catalog, instruction manual, and training books.

Telecommunications can replace or negate the need for a large warehouse.

Service bureau provides timeshare computer-based services for clients.

**Timesharing
as multitasking**
A computer operating
system technique that
provides the
interleaving of two or
more programs in the
processor. Only one
program runs at a
time, but they take
turns quickly.

Personal timeshare
Prodigy®,
CompuServe®,
America Online®,
Delphi®, and other
online services offer
computer-based
timeshare services in
the home and
business.

A **service bureau** is a concept that had great popularity and promise in earlier days of MIS, primarily before the advent of low-cost telecommunications. The premise of this service was that many smaller companies had the desire to have computer-based systems but did not have the ability to manage a large computer or did not want the financial responsibility associated with buying or leasing and running a mainframe computer. The giants of the computer industry, IBM and Control Data, both had the ability and resources for such a capability and created a business of providing fee-based services to other companies. One method of operation was for the smaller company to bring the data forms to the bureau. Bureau personnel performed data entry, directed processing, and created the output reports to be picked up by the client. Other companies, such as banks and insurance companies, began to provide a similar service by taking advantage of nighttime excess capability of their mainframe computers. In some cases, enterprising individuals would approach several companies that had small amounts of excess capacity, combine these capacities, and sell the service. In this case, the selling organization had no resources, only those they leased and resold.

With the advent of economical telecommunications capabilities, the service bureaus provided the services by way of dial-up and leased telephone lines. Commercial *timeshare services* were provided by companies such as Boeing Computer Service (BCS), McDonnell-Douglas (McAuto), and Computer Services Corporation (CSC). Timeshare means a business can have at its disposal almost unlimited computer processing and storage, output report printing or printing at their premises, fee-based programming services, and the use of a wide variety of royalty-based programs. For example, a company could contract with McAuto to lease a video display terminal, a 100-line-per-minute line printer, a 4,800 bit-per-second modem, mainframe processing, blocks of disk storage, and a variety of accounting, finance, inventory, and engineering programs. There would be a monthly fixed fee for equipment and a variable charge for processing, storage, and program use. The computer services from a bureau are an expense as opposed to being an incurred liability.

With the advent of higher-speed communications, significant portions of the information systems function can be provided by a timeshare company, though it appears that the computer is on the company's premises. All the client would see would be the video terminals (or terminal emulation via personal computers) and output devices such as laser printers. This is one form of outsourcing. All processing would be done elsewhere. All of this, obviously, is made possible by telecommunications.

The services that began with the service bureau and evolved into timeshare services have now evolved to be called the **application service provider (ASP).** The concept was named during the 1990s explosion of dot-com companies as they outsourced their IT requirements due to financial and labor constraints. About the same time, services developed for Web-hosting and server-hosting. This was all made possible by the existence of wideband private and public networks.

As these services merged, they became application providers and began to offer more capabilities, ranging from server care-and-feeding to dedicated applications. We note that these companies potentially offer all of the capabilities that a competitive organization requires.

An example of the need to outsource to an ASP was made clear as *Victoria's Secret* moved to Web-cast their new fashions. The first time this was done, the company chose to use internal resources, which promptly froze when the number of people wishing to gain access exceeded the capability of the servers. The next year, the company moved the Web-cast to a hosting company in order to support the expected two million global viewers.

AUTOMATED TELLER MACHINES (ATMs)

Automated teller machines (ATMs), based on telecommunications and online data, have changed the way we use banking services. It may be the beginning of info-dollars.

A very familiar telecommunications phenomenon and personal service that surfaced in the 1980s is the **automated teller machine (ATM)** that provides 24-hour banking services (Figure 10.3). Each ATM is the property of and connects to a specific financial institution. (As early as January 1988, there were 3,000 ATMs in the

FIGURE 10.3
Automated Teller Machine (ATM)

Bank-in-a-box
If you have access to your deposited cash 24 hours a day via ATM, why not have access to your account information via online access?

state of Hawaii.) Most ATMs are directly connected to their control nodes via dedicated, leased phone lines. Input of requests to these machines is via a telephone-like touchpad. Instructions are via video screens, from locally stored instructions, and identification is through a magnetic card reader and key pad. The results of the transactions are printed at the ATM, where money may be disbursed and deposited. ATMs cost many tens of thousands of dollars to install, have $25,000 or more in available cash, and must be audited (money counted) twice a business day. ATMs are also called *cash machines,* as that is a primary function. Figure 10.4 discusses and displays the interconnections of one ATM network, the AVAIL network in Georgia. Although this is an early configuration, it is representative of the connectivity.

Just in case you wondered, as of the end of 2001, there were approximately 273,000 ATMs in the United States.

When a customer makes a purchase with a debit or credit card, the data surrounding the transaction are typically processed remotely. For example, a customer purchases a bird feeder at Wal-Mart with her VISA® card. The transaction is transmitted via telephone lines or satellite to the card processing location. There, the appropriate sales data are recorded in the database for the customer's account.

FIGURE 10.4
The AVAIL Network in Georgia

AVAIL is a medium-to-large bank-transaction network, owned by 11 for-profit institutions, serving 210 institutions, with some 1,600 ATMs connected to the 36 bank processors. AVAIL processes 2.5 million transactions/month.

Southern Bell, AT&T MicroTel provide leased circuits, mostly twisted-pair. Most circuits are digital, but not all, such as Savannah. Digital circuits run at 4800 or 9600 bps. Backup to digital circuit via dial-up analog circuit.

AVAIL has a switch, connected to 36 bank or 3rd-party processors. AVAIL does not attach to ATMs.

AVAIL has direct-line connections to HONOR in Florida, ALERT in Alabama, RELAY in the Carolinas, MOST in Washington, DC, PLUS (global) network, CIRRUS global/national, and Armed Forces Financial Network (global).

Minimum print capability for reports, so customers dial in for download.

Automated audit trail. Logs all transactions. Gets audited by Feds, but not a regulated industry. Routinely have 3rd-party audit.

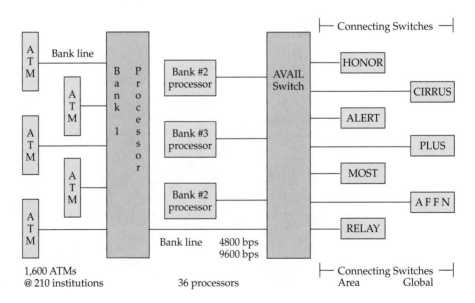

Information Window   10–1

The Society for Worldwide Interbank Financial Telecommunication (SWIFT) in Brussels, Belgium, is a customer-owned organization that originated when 240 banks collaborated to develop a standardized method of transferring funds across national borders. The business is providing financial network messaging service for the global banking community. There are now over 5,300 financial institutions and branches that use SWIFT's services. Operations cover customer sites and installations in 130 countries around the world. The SWIFT network transmits 2.7 million messages and moves US $1.5 trillion in funds daily.

ELECTRONIC SERVICES FROM HOME

Access to Online Services

Computers in the home—As of the mid-1990s, 46% of the homes in the United States had computers, 26% had modems, and 11% had access to online services. This was just prior to direct Internet access.

The first dial-in computer-based services available to noncommercial customers, for example, users at home, were electronic bulletin boards (BBS). Enterprising people would dedicate a computer and one or more phone lines with modems and, for a fee, allow users to dial in and download files or become part of a conference, for example, an email-based chat session. The advent of CompuServe® and Prodigy® brought a new capability: access to a mainframe that contained a variety of services, ranging from games and **online shopping** to stock quotes and online chat groups. America Online® (AOL) joined and surpassed both in subscribers, now touting in excess of 25 million subscribers. Each service has the goal of having the best and most user-friendly interface in the hope that customers will continue to pay the monthly fee and stay connected. With the success of AOL, dozens of other Internet service providers (ISPs) came on the scene, only to disappear in the competition. AOL, like Prodigy and CompuServe, provided primarily services from its own computers, mainframe and servers. With the advent of the WWW, AOL moved, slowly, to offer access to the Internet. Other ISPs such as *MSN*®, however, used a model that had little or no content on their servers and just gave good access to the Internet.

Two technologies have fueled the wish to be online and computer use from home. First, modem speed has increased over the past 10 years from 2.4 Kbps to 58 Kbps, making the online experience more enjoyable, especially with the increase of convergence, for example, text, images, sound, video, and so forth. The extension of this evolution has been broadband access via DSL and cable modems. (See Figure 10.5.) Second has been the appearance of the World Wide Web, which, with its convergence of text, graphics, sound, and video, offers great reasons to be connected.

FIGURE 10.5
Transfer Times for a 10 Mb File

Source: Cable Alabama Data Services.

28.8 Kbps	46 minutes
56.0 Kbps	23 minutes
ISDN 128 Kbps	10 minutes
T1 1.54 Mbps	52 seconds
Cable modem 10 Mbps	8 seconds

Financial organizations such as Charles Schwab®, Ameritrade, CSFB, and Datek® began offering financial information and online stock trading via dial-up access. In some early cases, the service provider did not allow access via the Internet because of security concerns; this has changed and now almost all financial service providers provide access via the Internet. Institutions like *The Wall Street Journal* provide news and stock information.

With low cost and high-speed access, a new brokerage client was born, the "day trader." This individual, using either his/her own equipment or renting it from an access provider, believes he/she can outguess the minor swings of the market on an hour-by-hour basis. The news media have shown individuals making U.S.$2,500 within 15 minutes on the swing of a stock. They also reported the shooting rampage of a day trader in Atlanta, Georgia, who was not so lucky.

Banking

Online banking assumes a secure connection. The early concern of Internet banking concentrated on security.

Meanwhile banking from home via dial-up access allows access to information and transactions, such as paying bills and moving funds from checking to savings, or getting stock quotes. Each has significantly changed the banking industry, giving the customer more choices and making the institution a 24-hour accessible convenience.

Where the first access to bank accounts was via direct modem dial-in, this moved quickly to access from the Internet. As early as the late 1980s, C&S Bank in Atlanta (now a part of Bank of America) members who subscribed to Prodigy online service could dial into their C&S account, access information, and pay bills. The extra charge of $5.00 per month often was less than the postage for the bills. Access via the Internet now means that the Internet will help redefine the nature of competition in banking, as access via the computer is as readily available as a local phone call to the Internet provider.

Shopping

The idea of shopping at home is an old one, but the process changed drastically with the evolution of technology in the home. Sears Roebuck popularized catalog shopping; you (anxiously) received your new catalog and placed orders by mail. Eventually, Sears, and others such as L.L. Bean, used the telephone to replace or supplement the mail order form, giving faster service and a more personalized interface, the human associate at the company. Where the original mail order business relied on the customer sending a check or money order, the new telemarketing mode relies on the credit card infrastructure.

The late 1990s saw the widespread home ownership of computers. With the availability of high-speed access such as via CATV to the Internet and the WWW, online services via home access will grow explosively.

Taking this evolution one step farther, using the television at home as a live, dynamic catalog brought home shopping to a new level. Now customers can sit in the living room, watch one of several shopping channels (e.g., QVC®, Home Shopping Network®, etc.), place a phone call on an (800) area code, and provide a credit card number or a shopping channel account number, and the goods are sent out. Placing this same shopping environment on the Internet allows customers to cruise QVC and the Home Shopping network via a computer, see videos of merchandize, use their credit cards for purchases, and have merchandise shipped to the door.

TELECONFERENCING

Desktop teleconferencing by way of POTS, ISDN, or Internet access makes use of small inexpensive cameras and the multimedia system onboard many computers to make this technology feasible at a low cost.

Teleconferencing means having a conference over a distance. Its earliest and most primitive form is called a telephone conference call, or *audio conferencing*. At the lowest level, several people talk on phones at each end of the circuit using two or more telephone numbers. At a higher level, each end has a speakerphone in a conference room and everyone can hear and talk with everyone in both rooms. This latter mode can be expanded to include people in more than two rooms, and even connect individuals outside of any of the rooms, for example, by using a cellular phone regardless of location. InterCall in West Point, Georgia, sets up thousands of telephone conference calls each business day, each with hundreds of participants.

Videoconferencing

Teleconferencing reduces costs but, more importantly, makes more coordination possible.

This is the visual mode of teleconferencing, simply using two-way video and audio channels between two or more sites. The initial installations use two analog television channels with a TV camera at each of two sites and two TV receivers at each site, one showing that site and one showing the remote site. This now has been expanded to use digital channels, more than two sites at a time, and equipment that automatically switches to whichever site is active, based on audio levels. For example, the IEEE organization wished to have an organizational meeting of several chapters located in Birmingham, Alabama; New Orleans, Louisiana; Jacksonville, Florida; Atlanta, Georgia; and Nashville, Tennessee. Instead of four sets of participants traveling to one site, they all used teleconferencing facilities of BellSouth Corporation. This system used T3 (45 Mbps) and T1 (1.544 Mbps) channels and provided video and audio connectivity among the five sites. Each site had two monitors and one camera. Switching was automatic, and everyone could see themselves and the speaking site.

Where **videoconferencing** once meant a very high expenditure for fixed facilities (several hundreds of thousands of U.S. dollars) and high connect charges, the costs of both have dropped dramatically. With the introduction of ISDN and the ability to move low scan (15 frames per second) color video images and audio on the two 64 Kbps ISDN channels, we have had videoconferencing to the desktop for several years. (Remember that AT&T offered video telephones in New York in the early 1960s and introduced them again in the late 1980s.) PictureTel® (www.picturetel.com/home.asp) sells podiums with TV camera and monitor that operate on ISDN lines for about US $20,000 each, allowing any conference room with ISDN to become a switched video teleconferencing room. No special lighting is required, and any room can be connected to any other so-equipped room via ISDN.

Since the early hype about the savings potential of videoconferencing systems, there was a takeoff in sales with the growth increase of 30,000 systems in 1994 to 250,000 in 1996. Part of this growth has been spurred by steadily declining hardware prices. Part was due to perceived risk due to Operation Desert Storm. In 1995, one could procure high-quality systems for less than $30,000 versus about $250,000 for a cumbersome and lower-quality system in 1983. Desktop kits can now transform a personal computer into a system for under $1,000, and transmission rates are now only two to five times the rates for POTS. Cost savings have been reported to make the video teleconferencing investment pay off in as little as eight months.

The heaviest users of videoconferencing seem to be firms that need to confer across divisions of geography, language, and history. Several firms have found new uses for videoconferencing technology. The Northrop Corporation reported

Technology Note 10–1
Maximum Performance

The system's single PCI codec card is an application accelerator that delivers maximum performance with minimum reliance on the PC processor, thereby freeing the host PC for other tasks. The codec also facilitates easily configured videoconferencing over ISDN via an onboard basic rate interface (BRI) or over IP-based networks via the PC network interface card (NIC).

Source: www.picturetel.com.

Information Window 10–2

The components of a typical group videoconferencing system shown are

Camera—Each location has a video camera that can be zoomed, panned, and tilted from a local or remote control panel.

Control pad—There is a control pad for dialing the connection, controlling volume, and controlling camera movement.

Monitors—Dual TV monitors and picture-in-picture can allow simultaneous viewing of the party/parties at the other location, one's own image, and a document.

Graphics camera—The graphics camera shows line close-ups of documents and graphics.

Compression/decompression—This unit, called a codec, is the brains of the system. The codec converts the compressed outgoing sound and pictures into digital data for transmission. It also decompresses incoming voice, image, and video. Without the use of compression, videoconferencing would require T3 circuits, not fractional T1 circuits or POTS lines.

Phone link—The video calls usually are transmitted via high-quality phone links, such as ISDN. Full-color, full-motion video, even with compression, requires high bandwidth.

that about 40 percent of its videoconferences link the company with subcontractors and suppliers. Hewlett-Packard is using videoconferencing as a substitute for physical visits to key corporate customers.

How does videoconferencing work? There are differences, such as group systems that work for television-based systems versus desktop systems that work on camera-equipped PCs. The major components are shown in Information Window 10–2. Videoconferencing works with *any* channel that will connect the two systems and provide adequate digital bandwidth. Thus, the Internet is a candidate for videoconferencing. There will be delays, making the picture and audio jumpy, but it does work.

Data Conferencing—Collaborative Work

Data conferencing
can use text-only or
text-over-video.

New products that allow **data conferencing** using only one regular phone line with a standard modem promise to further lower the costs of remote conferencing. Data conferencing application software from *PictureTel*® costs $249 (circa 2001) and allows two or more users to exchange data and simultaneously edit (collaboratively work on) documents while talking during a conference call. This software is now being bundled by computer and OS vendors. While this technology is a version of early 1990s voice-over-data, it allows much better communications than in the past.

Chat and Instant Messenger

Many people wish to communicate in real time to have the greater richness of immediate response. This capability has existed from the earliest days when people dialed into a variety of services and joined a chat room. For example, there are a variety of multiuser chat rooms on AOL; many are subject specific and some for a specific portion of the population such as AARP's group. The authors have used this "immediate" mode for assistance from a help desk.

A communications mode between the immediacy of chat and the uncertain reponse time of email is the *instant messenger*. This is a variation of email that displays a window on a user's computer showing when desired nodes (your buddy list) are active. If the destination node is active, the user can send a short, but immediate message. Originally developed by engineers in Israel as ICQ, this capability has spread like few technologies as users, especially the younger ones, wish to be always available when on the computer.

Email Conferencing

Email conferencing is already well established. The time delays tend to negate the ability for real-time negotiations.

We have made the assumption so far that all of the conferencing must be in real time (i.e., the reception and response take place with all participants online at the same time, such as chat sessions on America Online or Yahoo). This is often not necessary, which means that use of simple electronic mail, with the attendant delays, is data conferencing. Another form is the forums on bulletin boards, where each participant in turn logs on, downloads or reads the progress since last log-on, and leaves a response. This gives a living history of the discussion by allowing the user to see what has been said to date.

Why Use Teleconferencing?

Teleconferencing changes the way you interact with others.

The obvious reason for using audio or video teleconferencing is that people can meet together without the time and expense of traveling. It is simply an extension of a simple phone call, where more than two people meet. When the meeting involves the need for graphic presentation or person-to-person interaction that includes nonverbal information exchange, such as facial expressions and body language, videoconferencing becomes the choice. When the participants must travel great distances (more than an hour) and stay overnight, then the expense of the travel becomes measurable. Thus, our first consideration for teleconferencing is *cost avoidance*, where the costs are measurable and comparable with the expense of the videoconference equipment and connect time.

The (fixed and variable) expense of videoconferencing has been an inhibitor to the use of this technology for many years. As the cost of the equipment has decreased, digital channels have become more common and cheaper, and compression techniques allow for narrower bandwidth. Video teleconferencing has at last moved to a more feasible technology.

An unusual incident that spurred the interest in and use of teleconferencing in the early 1990s was Operation Desert Storm, often called the Persian Gulf War. With this military action came a fear that terrorists might strike at U.S. airlines, making air travel riskier. Now it was not just a dollars-versus-dollars comparison determining the use of teleconferencing, but a human-life-versus-travel-dollars comparison. Having this occur at a time when technology and connect costs were decreasing also helped encourage the use of teleconferencing. The fear of terrorist actions has encouraged teleconferencing as an alternative to air travel. Since September 11, 2001, many people and organizations have looked anew at the cost and risk of air travel, prompting some to opt for teleconferencing.

The most important reason for using teleconferencing, however, may not be out-of-pocket travel expenses and opportunity costs of being away from the office and on the road. It may be that with easy visual connectivity, managers can have meetings with no more notice than if the participants were in the next building. This means that finance officers from the various divisions of a corporation can meet weekly instead of monthly to coordinate their activities. Managers can meet with your design team, suppliers, and sales personnel on a frequent, even ad hoc, basis, and have them all participate in the development process. It may be the ability to have easy, multiple, people-to-people coordination and involvement that is the greatest value of teleconferencing.

TELECOMMUTING

Telecommuting can mean working at home, a remote office, or out of your car.

Telecommuting, in its simplest definition, means working at the office without having to go to the office. Say you are an airlines reservation representative or a travel agent. You would usually drive your car or take public transportation to a building where you work. Your car requires a parking space, gas and oil, maintenance, taxes, washing, and insurance. The building must have been built, financed, and taxed; is heated and cooled; and has furniture. The trip to and from the office may take 15 to 115 minutes, which is usually considered idle, unproductive time.

Telecommuting can save money, but more importantly it reduces unproductive time and the risk of exposure of that travel time.

The alternative, telecommuting, is to **work at home.** The employer pays to have two extra POTS phone lines (or one ISDN line) run to a worker's home. When a request for service comes to the now-vacant office, the CO, ACD, or PBX switch forwards the call to the home. The second phone line connects a personal computer to the computer providing travel information. Clients do not know where the agent is as to state, city, or bedroom or living room.

Having employees work at home is becoming a solution for societal problems of congestion and pollution. It may be imposed by law.

The concept of telecommuting promotes the idea that many people do not need to travel to an organized building to do their job. Customers do not care where the phone is answered as long as it is answered quickly, the connection is clear, and the response is adequate. The environment benefits if you stay at home and avoid the use of carbon-based fuels that produce pollution. Your company benefits if you stay at home and don't require space, heating, cooling, desk, cafeteria, and so forth. Your city or state benefits if you stay at home and avoid congestion on existing highways, so they can avoid building more highways in the future. The oil companies and car manufacturers, however, may not want you to stay at home. Do you think you should stay home?

The technology now exists to allow more and more people to telecommute. This means that more people, such as parents with small children whom they wish to care for and individuals with physical disabilities, can have jobs. The downside is that when workers stay at home they are removed from the social environment at the office. If the environment they are missing is perceived as positive and they need such, telecommuting is not a wonderful thing. Otherwise, it has many advantages. (See Figure 10.6.)

FIGURE 10.6
Advantages and Disadvantages of Telecommuting

1. **Advantages**
   a. Organization
      i. Reduces overall cost due to
         (1) Less office space
         (2) Lower overhead
         (3) Less parking space
         (4) Lower heating and A/C bills
         (5) Fewer desks and telephones
         (6) Less inclement overtime pay
      ii. Employees tend to work more hours
   b. Employee
      i. Less travel and expense of travel to/from work
      ii. People are more productive at home
      iii. Distractions of office (water cooler) are reduced
      iv. More time with family
      v. Higher morale
   c. Environment
      i. Decreases number of vehicles on road—less congestion
      ii. Decreases number of vehicles on road—less pollution
      iii. Lower fuel consumption
2. **Disadvantages**
   a. Organization
      i. Loss of office synergism and teamwork
      ii. Less direct control by managers due to loss of contact
      iii. Distractions by home environment
      iv. Cost of telecommuting equipment
   b. Employee
      i. You are never away from work
      ii. You are alone and away from the office social setting

Telecommuting does not, by definition, mean working in the home. It may mean having small offices located on the outskirts of larger cities where a group of employees work. The point is that the large centralized office can be dispersed to smaller offices that are closer to the employees' living areas; have lower requirements for parking, heating, and so forth; and, in general, have lower costs and increased productivity. Managers should ask what environment reduces costs for the organization and the employee and increases productivity.

A recent Authur D. Little study estimated that replacing 10 to 20 percent of traditional commuting, business travel, shopping, and information transmission with telecommuting and other remote computing implementations could result in societal benefits of US $23 billion a year. The annual savings would include elimination of

- 13 million business trips.

- 600 million truck and airplane delivery miles.

- 1.8 million tons of regulated pollutants.

- 3.5 billion gallons of gasoline.

- US $500 million in maintenance costs for the existing transportation infrastructure.

- 3.1 billion hours of personal time.

Telecommuting Guidelines

David Morrison, a management consultant, recommends the following guidelines when establishing an effective telecommuting program:

1. Plan your activities in detail, determine the business reasons for telecommuting, and involve all participants in the planning.

2. Run a pilot program with a small group to iron out the wrinkles prior to full implementation.

3. Use care in selecting participants. Use the program for productivity, not for reward or punishment. Realize that some people need the supervision of the office and others want the social environment found there.

4. Keep lines of communication open between managers and participants. Be sure participants are actually performing as intended.

5. Build good work habits for the remote workers by encouraging habits for each worker that reinforce positive behavior. For some this means a specific time and place for remote working, while others can be more flexible.

6. Encourage participants to stay connected to each other to avoid isolation and alienation.

7. If you have a large number of participants in the remote work program, the organization should consider a full-time facilitator to support the participants. This person should perform periodic follow-up with all participants and evaluate them for continuation.

A problem may arise if a telecommuting employee is terminated unless contractual arrangements are clear as to repossession of equipment.

8. You should discuss with your legal staff whether a contract is required with the participants to ensure that employees do not lose benefits such as worker's compensation and that the organization receives the expected results. Also, there should be clear terms relinquishing company equipment upon termination.

9. You should have a training program to ensure that participants are aware of such things as security of organizational data they create or download, backing up computer-based data, and care of organizational equipment.

10. Realize that electronic mail is important and that online services can provide a central point of contact for all participants.

11. The organization should consider the extent that standardized equipment and software are required. If there is a significant sharing of text files and spreadsheet data, single word processor and spreadsheet programs may be required. Most likely, the same operating and basic computer system would be chosen.

The case at the end of the chapter on **distance learning** extends our discussion of teleconferencing. It shows a specific use of the technology, that of corporate training. More importantly, the case highlights the organizational implications of the *use* of technology: shifting the locus of activity and also the locus of control and organizational influence.

COLLABORATIVE OR GROUP PROCESSES

LANs and WANs provide natural environments for applications that allow people in dispersed locations to do collaborative work as if they were colocated. (See Figure 10.7.) Work flows among people as they participate in creation and revision

FIGURE 10.7
**Alabama
Supercomputer
Network**

Source: Alabama
Supercomputer Authority.

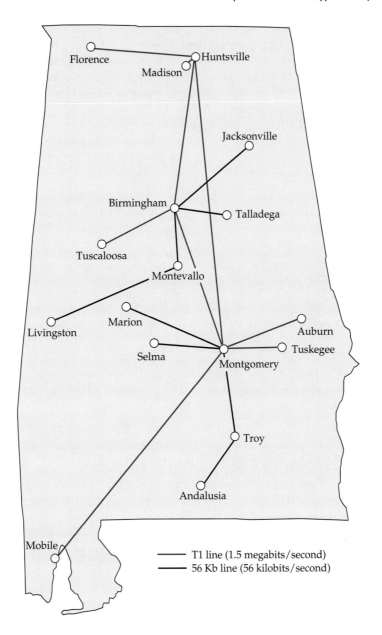

of documents: they collaborate. These networks provide the environment for such applications as Lotus Notes®, which provides connected storage space and communications by which individuals can share information and work together.

Workflow and Work Groups

The rapid growth of networked computing has led to a proliferation of products that are called *workflow technologies*. The concept of workflow includes several features. Some workflow systems are designed to speed electronic distribution of documents to work groups. Often, the application of workflow processes such as described above are considered "tactical" applications of re-engineering. This involves analyzing, compressing, and mechanizing the business process and involves the way people in work groups perform steps as a task. The use of the network allows much faster collaborative work, thereby reducing cycle times for those firms using the workflow systems.

Some of the basic workflow tools use a standard electronic mail engine as their transport. The proliferation of email has generated a great deal of demand for these systems where ad hoc workflow environments exist and will not allow highly structured approaches.

Most client-server software vendors now include workflow engines in their latest revisions. The idea is to provide the ability to view the corporate process as well as the work group involved in the process. There appear to be several categories of workflow tools:

1. *The Business Process Re-engineering or Definition Methodology.* This method captures more details and takes advantage of some of the **business process re-engineering (BPR)** tools.

2. *The Process Design Mapping Tool.* This is a process mapping tool that employs graphical capabilities for process design that shows people, paperwork, and objects flowing through the system.

3. *The Workflow Development Environment.* This allows customers to decide how users in the work groups access their workflow assignments.

4. *The Workflow Builder.* These are tools to allow users to code workflow applications.

5. *The Workflow Management Engine.* The engine manages the actual running of the process to ensure data flows over the network to the right persons in the work group.

6. *Learning Applications.* These are workflow applications that teach members of the work group as they perform tasks. These applications are sometimes termed Electronic Performance Support Systems (EPSS).

Regardless of the sort of workflow tools, they can significantly improve business operations. They are a network use that can pay off for any business using work groups to process flows of work in the organization.

ELECTRONIC DATA INTERCHANGE (EDI)

EDI requires telecommunications, agreements, and a willingness to trust.

We defined a *system* in Chapter 1 as a group of interrelated and interdependent parts working together to achieve a common goal. A *cooperative system* is a specialized type of system that requires at least two parties with different objectives but common goals to collaborate on the development and operation of a joint system in support of these common goals. Typically, partners in a cooperative system develop and operate their own specific portions of the common system environment. Standards usually play a significant role in cooperative systems, and third-party facilitators are often involved.

EDI strengthens the nature of partnerships.

Electronic data interchange (EDI) is, by definition, a cooperative system. EDI is the process of direct computer-to-computer communication of information in a standard format between organizations or parties (companies) that, as a result of this communication, permits the receiver to perform a specific set of business functions (e.g., purchasing, invoicing). The primary purpose of EDI is to provide a communications standard for the electronic transfer of common business documents between the respective computer systems of individual and diverse trading partners. That is to say, EDI uses existing communications technology and takes data from an existing computer-based information system (CBIS) and places it into another CBIS. No new equipment is required, just data standards and EDI management software. EDI provides a significant opportunity to lower the cost of doing business between trading partners, strengthens the partnership, and has other effects on the parties involved. As a result, EDI offers significant competitive advantage to those organizations utilizing the technology.

Background

Float is the "extra" time that an item is in the system. It is wasted time. EDI reduces float.

To demonstrate the potential for EDI to improve the information and paperwork flow within and between organizations, consider the following scenario. The purchasing department at Company A decides to procure a particular product from supplier Company B. In order to accomplish this task, the Company A purchasing department creates a purchase order. Typically, this process consists of either manually typing the necessary information on the company's unique purchasing form or computer generating the form through some mode of online entry. The purchase order document is then forwarded to Company A's mail room for subsequent pickup by a mail service (Postal Service or other carrier). The document is taken to the local mail service office where local mail is removed and the residual forwarded to a central sorting site for routing to the mail service office closest to the supplier. At the local mail service office, the document is placed in a vehicle for transport and delivered to supplier Company B's mail room. The mail room at the supply company sorts the inbound mail and delivers the purchase order to the order department where it is likely to be keyed into an order processing system. The order processing system triggers the creation and/or delivery of the product or service and the generation of a corresponding invoice. Whether the invoice is manually generated or computer printed, it requires distribution to the mail room for pickup. Some invoices may require envelope stuffing either before or at the mail room. The invoice is then transported to the local mail company pickup office and to the central sorting site, and again routed to the office closest to Company A for delivery. The invoice is then received by the mail room of Company A, sorted, and distributed to the ordering department for verification of receipt of service or merchandise. The invoice may be keyed in and is then marked for payment and forwarded back through the mail room to the accounts payable department and keyed for payment. The notification of recently received merchandise might also be input into some computer-based inventory or other asset management system.

In this example, it is important to note the number of opportunities for the document to be delayed, mishandled, or lost. In addition the same basic information has to be keyed and verified (or potentially corrected) a large number of times. Of great importance is the *time* required to complete the process.

EDI Scenario

EDI is standards that allow business to be conducted electronically instead of by paper.

EDI is the direct computer-to-computer communication of information in a standard format that permits the receiver to perform a specific business function. Consider the foregoing purchasing example within an EDI framework. Figures 10.8(a) and 10.8(b) show the points of the transaction in question. In an EDI environment, the purchasing agent at Company A would simply enter the purchasing information into Company A's micro or mainframe computer, or a computer-based inventory or scheduling system would generate a purchase automatically, an action

FIGURE 10.8(a)
The Integrated
Electronic Business
Cycle

Source: *EDI World*, May 1996.

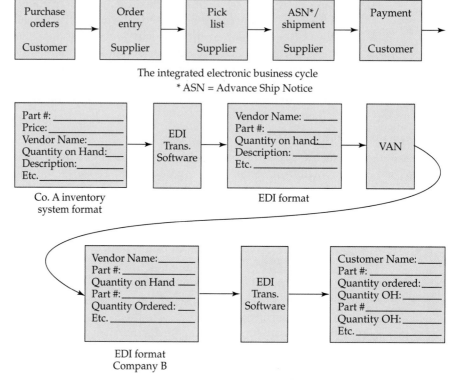

The integrated electronic business cycle
* ASN = Advance Ship Notice

FIGURE 10.8(b)
An EDI Model

unlikely to occur without EDI. The system would electronically forward the purchase order on a predetermined schedule to supplier Company B's computer, after EDI management software or software created by the MIS department had converted the stored format data to EDI format. The receipt of the electronic purchase order after conversion by Company B's EDI management software would create an automatic update of the order entry system triggering the generation and/or delivery of the product or service by the supplier. As a result of the rendering of the product or service, Company B would electronically generate, translate, and transmit a corresponding EDI invoice to the purchasing company's computer. Verification of merchandise received becomes a check-off process and inventory and accounts payable files or databases are automatically updated.

Although each partner company may be fully automated within their own company environment, each step in the manual intercompany transfer process takes a significant amount of time and has an opportunity for error (e.g., either lost paper or incorrectly keyed information). The old adage that "time is money" is appropriate, particularly if the purchased item is to be utilized as a component in a subsequent product offered for sale. A new adage might be "delay is at least expensive, if not a lost sale." Figure 10.9(a) shows some of the uses of EDI in business transactions. A Real World window later in the chapter illustrates how UPS uses EDI-based tracking.

EDI, along with the use of electronic funds transfer (EFT), allows two or more organizations with differing computer systems to communicate their needs in real time, without much, if any, human intervention. (See Figure 10.9[b].) Just-in-time inventory methods rely heavily on EDI, allowing a manufacturing system to request delivery of parts and make them available on the factory floor when

FIGURE 10.9   Financial EDI vs. EDI

a. Example standard business transactions that can use EDI

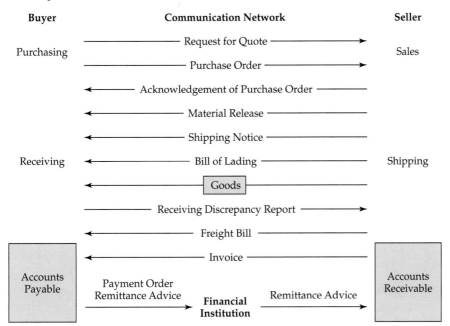

b. The payment process using EDI and EFT

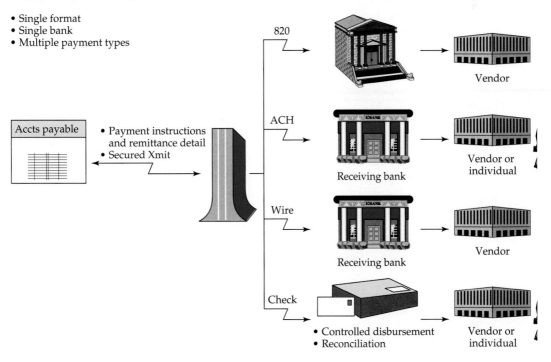

FIGURE 10.10
Parties and Their
Interactions with
EDI

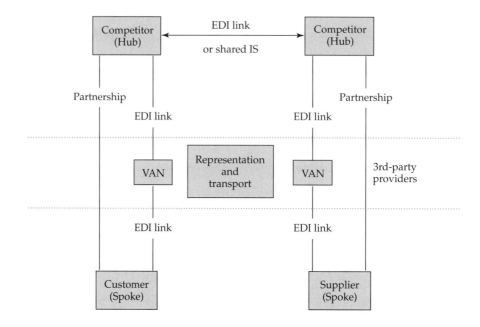

Benefits of the
Use of EDI
1. Improved customer service
2. Improved accuracy of data
3. Reduced clerical errors
4. Faster access to information
5. Decreased administrative costs
6. Reduced delivery times
7. Improved cash flow

needed. This negates the need for warehouses and stockpiles of expensive goods. It all relies on common standards and a telecommunications network.

While EDI appears to offer great advantages, there are several problems that must be addressed. For example, the standards used vary both by industry and internationally. While the X.12 ANSI standard is designed to be universal, industries such as grocery and transportation began developing a standard before X.12 came into being. Meanwhile, EDIFACT was developed in Europe and has differences from U.S. standards. There is also a need for EDI translation (management) software for both sender and receiver(s). The value added network (VAN), while considered an added expense, provides the interface between differing operating systems. The VAN also provides store-and-forward capabilities. The VAN can be replaced by a direct connection, including the Internet; however, they will not have store-and-forward capabilities.

There are three levels of players in the arena of EDI. As Figure 10.10 shows, relationships exist between sources, destinations, and third-party providers. The alliances made in this environment change the nature of business. For example, the means of transportation change with many small packages sent just-in-time by UPS® instead of one large shipment by a freight carrier.

ENTERPRISE APPLICATIONS DEPEND ON TELECOMMUNICATIONS

ERP, enterprise resource planning, attempts to integrate organizational components through networked software.

As mentioned in chapter 8, applications such as ERP, SCM, CRM, and other enterprisewide capabilities are absolutely dependent on telecommunications connectivity. Most organizations that implement these applications employ a client-server architecture. Thus, the telecommunications considerations of reliability, level of service, redundancy, and so forth, are vital to keeping the organization operational. These systems are, by nature, distributed systems that cannot exist without connectivity.

SCM, supply chain management, focuses on all components of the logistics chain for manufacturers.

CRM, customer relationship management, goes hand-in-hand with competitive advantage.

ENHANCING CUSTOMER SUPPORT

Customer Relationship Management (CRM)[1]

Customer relationship management (CRM) is a business-driven strategy aimed at optimizing revenue, profitability, and customer satisfaction by recognizing that the only lasting competitive advantage comes from the strength of the customer relationship. Such a customer-centric business architecture needs to be matched by an information technology (IT) infrastructure that puts customer information at the center, for easier information sharing, data management, and high-speed communication among diverse business systems.

In today's intensely competitive world, customers are more demanding, customer satisfaction rarely guarantees loyalty, and, especially in the Internet age, competitors are just a click away. The strategic objective of CRM is to build relationships with profitable, desirable, loyal customers. Loyal customers are typically less sensitive to price. Marketing to loyal customers is far less expensive than acquiring new ones. CRM recognizes valued customers for their exceptional loyalty, understands each customer's value to the business over the life of the relationship, and rewards the customer by personalizing the relationship and tailoring services to exact customer needs.

IT is a crucial element in achieving CRM's goals. The IT part of CRM can be defined as a computer-enabled process that begins with acquisition of knowledge about customers, proceeds with in-depth analysis of their needs, then uses the analysis to drive profitable interactions. The key element is that businesses have to dynamically balance customer value and supply-chain costs to provide exceptional services to loyal customers while appropriately satisfying all other customers' needs. Businesses provide real-time, differentiated responses to customers according to their loyalty, lifetime profit potential, requirements, and cost to serve.

CRM involves capturing and integrating all customers' data from everywhere in the organization, analyzing and consolidating them into information, and then distributing the results to various systems and customer contact points across the enterprise. This approach goes beyond merely automating customer contacts with front-office applications in marketing, sales, call centers, and customer service. This approach creates a complete view of the customer, proving direct feedback to operational systems and offering executives the decision support they need to make better and faster decisions. Such an architecture for business intelligence makes information about the customer operational, turning analysis into action and ultimately into revenue and profit.

The implementation of CRM entails a fundamental change in the culture and operations of an organization. It also means addressing the infrastructure requirements for its implementation on the Internet. A four-step roadmap can be considered:

1. Transform core business processes.

2. Build new applications.

3. Run a scalable, available, safe environment.

4. Leverage knowledge and information.

---

[1] Contributed by Ken Liang.

CRM application suites are sold by vendors such as Siebel, Clarify, Vantive, and others. ERP vendors such as Oracle, SAP, and Baan also are active in CRM. Comparing CRM to ERP sheds light on CRM's unique focus. ERP does result in operational efficiencies and lower costs, but when every business has it, ERP does not create the competitive advantage. CRM, on the other hand, turns the attention outside the enterprise to the customer. Better knowledge of customers through CRM improves customer retention and acquisition. CRM accelerates profitable sales by identifying the most profitable customers and segments for focused marketing, product bundling, cross-selling, and up-selling. CRM significantly enhances customer loyalty and boosts performance, while at the same time erecting formidable barriers to competition. These are huge opportunities for businesses to create a sustainable competitive advantage.

Application Service Providers (ASP)

The idea behind application service providers is to host and lease applications, negating an organization's need to create/acquire, install, store, and maintain them. It is possible *only* by sufficient bandwidth between the organization and the ASP to move the data and receive the results.

The ASP Model

An ASP takes software applications, hosts them on powerful servers, makes them network-accessible, and provides users seamless access, resulting in a pay-as-you-go outsourcing option for IT.

The answer to the question in Real World 10–2 may be yes, but there is a condition! You must have connectivity and enough bandwidth to pass the data and output to make it all work as if it were on your own server.

Services from ASPs range from the simple to the complex. At one end is a building into which you place your equipment, such as servers. The ASP provides security, an environment, power, and possibly bandwidth. In this case, the renter does all the work. Next, the ASP might take care of backup and migration of data. Following that it may load applications to the server and even be responsible for updates. Then the ASP may own the servers. Finally, the ASP might offer capabilities and applications in addition to the dedicated renter's server. All the while, the ASP is responsible for the environment, security, and reliable bandwidth. Remember, this is not contingency backup; this is the primary function of the organization. It is a form of outsourcing.

The Real World   10–1

"You rent it. You don't fix the roof. You don't worry about the plumbing. And when you aren't using it you don't have to pay. Know any software like that? Owning a business is great. Owning and running its information technology can be a costly distraction. Interliant, the most experienced ASP, will lighten your load and save you money. We'll host and manage your critical applications for you, over secure networks, with cost based on actual usage."

Source: Advertisement by Interliant in September 2000 issue of *eCompany.*

The Real World   10–2
Repent! The End of Software Is Near!

Is it time to throw away your CD-ROM and embrace Web-based services? Yes and no.

There was a time when, if someone was talking about software, you knew what they meant: Software was the stuff you installed from a CD-ROM onto the hard drive of a PC, or server. But as more and more applications turn into services available over the Internet, the definition of software is getting awfully fuzzy—so much so that people are talking about the "end of software." Application service providers (ASPs) now lease Web access to the pro-

grams that you used to have to buy in shrink-wrapped boxes. And new programs are increasingly designed to be used only over the Web. When even Microsoft in late June (2000) announced its Microsoft. net strategy of delivering services instead of packaged applications, I began to wonder if the software on my hard drive or on my company's server would soon be a thing of the past. Will you and I need nothing but a browser to do all our work?

Source: David Kirkpatrick, *eCommerce*, September 2000.

The Real World   10–3

Geoworks' Mobile ASP™ (application service provider) is a robust, sophisticated, and customizable mobile information solution for organizations that lack the time or resources to develop such services in-house.

Source: Geoworks ad, *M-business magazine*, November 2000.

Business-to-Business

Business-to-business (B2B) constitutes the majority of electronic commerce volume. Frequently businesses are able to re-engineer their supply chains and establish stronger partnerships through B2B applications. B2B applications range over a wide variety of areas. For example, there are uses that connect to all parts of a firm's value system such as suppliers, transportation, sales and marketing, service, and so forth. Cisco Systems is often cited as an example of success using B2B. Cisco uses its extranet for online sales and electronic purchasing, resulting in several economies. Their customers find that they can get access to prices, configuration suggestions, order status, invoice checking, and technical support. Cisco saves in marketing expenses, administrative costs, and lower customer service costs. In addition, they achieve improved customer service and happier customers—all contributing to increased sales.

The frenzy of enthusiasm for B2B has caused vendors to recast ERP as extended ERP that helps the firm transform to an eBusiness by providing enterprisewide planning for B2B. This effort is aimed at exploiting the Internet for core business functions. Most firms attempt to measure the benefits of eBusiness. The areas that they track are customer service, knowledge of customer preferences, marketplace presence, brand recognition, supply-chain efficiency, and cycle times with their supply-chain partners.

Business-to-Consumer

The business-to-consumer (B2C) part of electronic commerce was at first perceived to be the locus of action. Here was a chance for even small firms to establish a virtual storefront equal to those of the largest corporations. Another great advantage was the idea of disintermediation that could occur as the dot-coms often had no inventory, no warehouses, no wholesalers, but used drop-shipment from the manufacturer directly to customers. Thus, the B2C firm could operate with a fraction of the costs of a traditional store. Benefits also include increased sales and revenues, expansion to global markets, as well as finding new sources of revenues.

Bandwidth Brokerage

A company that began to broker electricity and natural gas used its expertise in the area of bandwidth. Enron, in its heyday, both sold unused bandwidth on their own network as well as provided unused bandwidth on networks owned by others. By being able to route traffic from congested networks to those having excess capability, Enron was able to help companies manage their bandwidth demand and sold space on high-speed networks as a commodity, for example, a bandwidth utility, offering short-term access to high bandwidth as opposed to long-term contracts. Global Crossing used the Enron exchange to sell its bandwidth as opposed to being its own marketing agent. Both of these firms succumbed to accounting problems.

Wireless Applications

Many of the applications that are mentioned previously can be supported or complemented by wireless technology. (See Chapter 3.) While many wireless appliances have not reached the same bandwidth as wired media, wireless has a specific advantage of untethering the user.

Originally wireless was overhyped and too expensive; however, prices continue to fall. Handheld devices are generally smarter and more powerful than they were just a few years ago. Wireless infrastructures now have sufficient return on investment to lead even small organizations to display them.

The greatest of wireless capabilities, circa 2002, is to coordinate activity of people in the field. This allows personnel more time to spend with customers and less time at a stationary, wired workstation or telephone. Many firms have gleaned substantial payoffs from building wireless networks.

Information Window   10–3

BandwidthOnCall is all about establishing a channel and neutral marketplace for connecting buyers and sellers of high-speed network bandwidth. We offer this interactive quotation service using the latest in B2B Internet technologies that go well beyond a simple RFQ matchmaking exchange. We invite buyers to submit their requirements to the top "Tier 1" bandwidth providers and then create an open forum for discussing the buyer's "need for speed,"

availability and costs of Telco lines from T1 to OC48, terms, and the service level agreements (SLAs). BandwidthOnCall facilitates tapping into 21st century networks by streamlining the negotiation process and saving both sides money and time.

Source: http://www.bandwidthoncall.com.

Technology Note 10–2 gives several examples of the use of wireless capabilities. The following is a use of a specific technology, for example, global positioning system (GPS), as a business application.

Business Uses of GPS

The next time you see a Sears truck, notice the round, white antenna on top. This is a GPS antenna and is used to show the driver where s/he is and give direction to the next assignment. Large trucking firms have installed GPS as well as two-way communications to allow the trucks to know where they are and the route to their destination; to ask specific questions of the controller; and to provide status information.

GPS-based equipment exists to place on personal vehicles, taxis, and other company vehicles. With this equipment in place, the user or company knows (*a*) the mileage driven for records and (*b*) where the vehicles have gone and when the drivers are spending too long at a specific site.

Finally, and more personally, upscale cars are being delivered with GPS-based mapping for business and pleasure. This allows the driver to know where s/he is at

Technology Note   10–2
Where the Wireless Web Works

Businesses flocked to wireless projects as their cost fell by more than 50% in the past two years. Here's what companies are doing:

	PROBLEM	PROJECT	PAYOFF
Workers on the move: The rollout of data networks helps companies improve customer service by getting info to reps more quickly.	**Pepsi Bottling Group's 700 technicians phoned in to get service-call data—and faxed back billing info.**	Now a wireless network sends details to the service rep's handheld. The device zips billing data to the office.	**Service response time cut by 20%. Errors from the old fax system gone. Correct parts ready for pickup.**
Wireless workplaces: Offices are setting up systems that transmit data from the Web or a company's intranet to employees moving about the workplace	**Staff at St. Luke's Episcopal Hospital in Houston spent too much time on administrative tasks. Handwritten records had potential for errors.**	A wireless network for three of the hospital's floors lets staff check charts, lab results, and patient data, wiping out handwriting errors.	**Staff on the networked floor cut time spent on data entry 30%. The respiratory therapy group cut staff by 20%, saving $1.5 million a year.**
Smart machines: Wireless devices in plants and warehouses can automatically collect data from other computers around them, speeding up work flow and eliminating paperwork.	**Office Depot's 2,000 drivers sorted through info from 40-plus deliveries daily. This led to data-entry errors and slowed inventory tracking.**	Drivers' handheld devices automatically transfer customer data to the company's Web site when they return each evening.	**No more handwritten bills, which reduced customer complaints about missed deliveries by more than 10% last year.**

Data: Gartner Inc., International Planning & Research, Cahners In-Stat Group, Venture Development Corp.

Source: "Where the Wireless Web Works," *Business Week*, February 18, 2002.

all times, ask directions for a specific address, or ask for directions over the entire United States. (A nephew of one of the authors used this system on his Acura to find the home of a stray dog he found, taking the address from the collar.)

Utility Companies Enter the Telecommunications Business

Until the passage of the Telecommunications Act of 1996, companies outside of the official telecommunications industry were not allowed to offer or compete in this field. Because of the deregulation of the industry, The Southern Company, an electrical utility, offers many user-friendly, time-saving telecommunications features in its product *Southern LINC*®. Southern Linc features:

Instant LINC—With the touch of just one button, your unit becomes a two-way radio. Our most popular feature, you'll find yourself using this one all the time in either Private or Group mode.

Private Instant LINC—Sometimes what you have to say isn't for everyone's ears. Just switch to Private Instant LINC, and you can speak to any individual you choose. Nobody else will hear a word, thanks to the inherent privacy of digital technology.

Group Instant LINC—One of our best time-savers. Why talk to people one at a time when you can get the same message to them all at once? When you use Group Instant LINC, you can spread the word to everybody in a designated talk group—no matter where they are in our coverage area.

Programmed Names—Scroll through programmed individuals or groups right on the display screen, stop on the name or group you want and press a button, and you can speak to that person immediately via Instant LINC.

Numeric and Text Paging—Southern LINC paging allows anyone to send a numeric page directly to your handset. Plus, numeric pages or text messages of up to 140 characters can be sent from this website's Send-a-Page feature or from Internet email by addressing the email to your Southern LINC phone number followed by the Southern LINC Internet extension page.southernlinc.com. Best of all, you can respond with one-touch call-back if a phone number is given in the message. And if your unit is off or you're out of the coverage area, messages are stored for up to seven days and delivered as soon as you power back up. For detailed instructions please reference the Guide to Southern LINC Services.

Voice Mail—One-touch message retrieval. Automatic call back. Record multiple greetings. Receive faxes. Send the same message to multiple Southern LINC users simultaneously. All of these great features are available with our voice mail system.

Call Alerts—If you need to let someone who's away from their unit know that you're trying to reach them, get their attention with the Call Alert feature. An audible beep and display message will prompt them to call you once they return.

Phone Service—You knew at some point we had to mention that our handset gives you reliable phone service. Just switch to phone mode anywhere in our coverage area and reach anyone within the United States. Plus, you'll enjoy call waiting, call forwarding, call hold, speed dialing, and our optional state-of-the-art voice mail system.

Personal Toll-Free Service—Get a low-cost, toll-free number for your Southern LINC handset and save your customers who are outside your local calling area or the Southern LINC territory money and hassles. Plus, you'll enjoy free Caller ID when you subscribe to Personal Toll-Free Service.

NEW Informance SolutionsSM—Using the latest Motorola Internet-ready handsets, Informance Solutions gives you access to email, allows you to receive and

Information Window   10–4

The telecommunications sector has a dual role: it is a distinct sector of economic activity and it is an underlying means of supplying other economic activities (for example, electronic money transfers). The annex says governments must ensure that foreign service suppliers are given access to the public telecommunications networks without

discrimination. Negotiations on specific commitments in telecommunications resumed after the end of the Uruguay Round. This led to a new liberalization package agreed upon in February 1997.

Source: www.wto.org

---

respond to business information, provides you access to information on the Internet, lets you send job orders directly to employee handsets and reroute them to take advantage of changing employee availability and location, displays visual tracking of vehicles, and much, much more.[2]

Elimination of Telecommunications Trade Barriers

The U.S. entry into the World Trade Organization Agreement (WTO Agreement) in February 1997 had the effect of liberalizing the provision of switched voice telephone and other telecommunications services in scores of foreign countries. These new rules mean that it is far easier for foreign affiliated carriers to enter the U.S. market for provision of international services.

MILITARY USES OF TELECOMMUNICATIONS

The military has always relied on communications for command and control. This information can now come via laser channels from ground-based, airborne, or satellite stations.

A discussion of the uses of communications by the military is not unusual. The telegraph messages of the U.S. Civil War were replaced with radio communications in World War II (WWII). The use of radar in WWII gave units advanced warning (information) of the attack of enemy aircraft. Unit radios were in use in that war and came into greater use in the Korean War. With entry into the Vietnam conflict, the lieutenant commanding a platoon had a personal radio, as did some men under his command. The twisted-pair land lines for the EE-8 field phones of WWII are replaced by fiber cable, microwave antenna, and satellite communications. Shipboard communications and computers rely on satellite. With the maturing of laser and satellite capabilities, and with the increasing awareness of the possibilities by military commanders, changes continue.

What is the potential telecommunications bandwidth of a laser beam?

The military use of technology often heralds and precedes the commercial and personal use of the same technology, but in a different way.

Laser-based data communications is being tested between aircraft to provide a reasonably secure channel of 1.2 Gbps for video and data. Initially, the services are not using compression in the channels and, thus, can carry about 10 video signals. The objective is to develop this technology because of its bandwidth and inherent security. It is also seen as a medium for satellite to aircraft data channels. The biggest problem at the present time is air-to-ground transmission.

Laser binoculars are field glasses that have an IR laser transmitter and receiver built in (made by Sony). Thus, if the two people can see each other, they can talk via the microphone, earphones, and IR channel. Again, the channel is line-of-sight

---

[2] http://www.solinc.com/Pages/1.1_feat_func.asp.

and reasonably secure, as the interceptor would have to be able to intercept the transmission directly or a part of it that was bounced off of a structure. Power levels are extremely low.

The U.S. Army is a heavy user of space. Although this sounds a bit strange, the Army uses space communications, such as satellite, to a great extent. When the Army entered the future battle area in Operation Desert Shield and Desert Storm, the commanders were offered GPS receivers. They refused! Later, as these satellite-tracking position indicators began to be used by a few units, the commanders realized that, for the first time in history, the higher commands could know exactly where all of their resources were located, at any time. This was a revelation to these seasoned leaders.

How did military commanders in the 1700s and 1800s get weather data?

The next revelation was the availability of weather data. Instead of having high command in the continental United States receive the weather satellite data from the National Oceanic and Atmospheric Administration (NOAA) satellite, process it, refine it, filter it, and pass it down the chain of command, the commanders could receive the same satellite data in the field, with no filtering and no time delay. Again, a historical first.

Another consideration of the Army is the use of existing digital satellites to provide commanders in the rear area video of the action at the front. Now, on a large monitor, by using such capabilities as Hughes DirecTV, GPS, and NOAA weather satellites, the commander can see the action, know where all resources are located, and have the weather overlaid. Information is power!

Finally, satellite communication of voice and data has come into its own. You don't have to be a Navy Seal guarding the battleship *Missouri* (movie *Under Siege* with Steven Segal) or an Army Special Forces Unit in the jungle (*Predator* with Arnold Schwarzenegger) to understand the concept and value of satellite communications on the ground for voice and data. The units in the field and the commanders, wherever they are, have access to satellites. Communications channels are always available.

What are the primary information sources for a business organization?

Information warfare is a focus in all branches of the military that has taken on new importance in recent decades and is rapidly assuming a central place in modern military thinking and planning. According to the *Cornerstone of Information Warfare*, quoted in the July 1996 issue of *Air Force Magazine*, "Information Warfare is any action to deny, exploit, corrupt, or destroy the enemy's information and its functions; protecting ourselves against those actions; and exploiting our own military information functions." Information warfare or information dominance has become the fifth pillar of the USAF's core competencies, along with control of the air, control of space, global mobility, and the ability to project power precisely.

Students of telecommunications and military strategy alike would come to the above conclusions quickly. The aim of military actions for thousands of years has been to negate the enemy's ability or willingness to continue the conflict. As we found in Desert Storm, if the enemy is denied information as to the whereabouts of opposing resources, the side with information has an unbeatable advantage. Therefore, primary targets at the onset of the Persian Gulf War in 1991 were telephone exchanges, power stations, command-and-control nodes, and other vital information communications links. The same was true of the resources in Afghanistan after September 11, 2001.

In closing this section on the military uses of telecommunications, especially the part on information warfare, we should realize that the military units and their need for information have a lot in common with all organizations. The military's vision of competition and having a competitive advantage seems extreme when compared with business and other organizations, but remove the specific mechanisms of destruction and the aims are the same, for example, to use information for the advantage of the organization's goals and objectives. This often means new ways to use old technology as well as inventive uses of new technologies. In peace time, the military must compete for scarce resources with other units of government. Nonmilitary and nongovernmental organizations do the same, but they compete for resources and customers in the world-at-large. Each organization must have information to be competitive and if they can deny or distort information to their competitors, they will be more effective. Refer to Case 10-4 for one of the latest uses of telecommunications technology by the military.

The Real World 10–4
UPS Using Package-Tracking Applications— System Brings Up-to-Date Information to Employees and Customer

Paramus, NJ. To collect package-location information from trucks and log that information into its corporate databases in New Jersey, United Parcel Service Inc. uses TotalTrack distributed package-tracking applications. UPS is trying to push applications out to people in the field as much as they can, according to Marc Dodge, systems manager of telecommunications at the UPS location here. "We look at a new application and try to put as much of the processing power as we can in the hands of the users," he said.

Using IBM mainframes, OS/2 clients and database servers, and Novell Inc.'s NetWare file servers, TotalTrack is just one part of UPS's UPSNet, which is a collection of about 50 internally written distributed applications on several computer networks throughout the country. Many of the applications and computer systems have been in operation since the mid-1980s, Dodge said.

The purpose of the package-tracking system is to centralize package information on the mainframes, where it can be accessed from a number of locations, thereby giving customers as well as employees up-to-date information. The company estimates that its volume of air traffic has risen by 25 percent over the past year, at least in part because of TotalTrack's ability to give customers this type of immediate information.

Joseph Lawless, manager of distributed systems at UPS, said that it's hard to gauge just how much the client/server system has improved tracking performance since much of the work was previously done using manual data entry.

Package information is uploaded from handheld delivery devices used by UPS drivers to log in package information. Drivers can plug their handheld systems into an adapter, which makes a cellular call that dumps package data into the UPS network. Data are transmitted to one of two locations—Paramus or Mahwah—via Tandem Computer Systems front-end processors. There are normally two processors that collect data from calls. In December, UPS added a third processor to take excess traffic from the cellular network, Lawless said.

Package data in their final form reside in a DB2 database on the mainframe, but the tracking applications and related file and print applications are on PC servers running OS/2 and Novell Inc.'s NetWare respectively. Customers and employees use software to download package information and other related UPS information from the distributed LANs.

Application integration is not completely seamless, and PC users seeking package information must toggle between applications to receive some information. But the custom design calls for a minimum of keystrokes, Dodge said. Over 56,000 UPS PCs connect to the servers via token ring LANs and on the wide area using IBM's 6611 router and several bridges.

The OS/2 PC servers connect to the mainframe database via LU6.2 connections to CICS. An example of OS/2-based applications are those that govern logistics to hub buildings, which are the places where packages are sorted. Some buildings can handle up to 80,000 packages, Dodge said. UPS has designed its own applications for package counting, location information, trailer loading information, and other logistic details. A logistical mistake in package sorting can literally cause a jam in the facility.

Source: Margie Semilof, *Communications Week.*

Case 10-1

Distance Learning—The Real Impact

Margaret Barham

INTRODUCTION

Distance learning is the current high-tech buzz word in corporate training. The ability to transmit a training session to multiple sites to provide training to a large number of individuals without requiring the costs or lost time associated with travel is a very attractive cost-saving proposal. Distance learning can be very broadly defined to include the familiar videocassettes mailed to training locations, executable computer files to be used with personal computers with sound boards, broadcast television to satellites at the remote company locations with various mechanisms used to permit interactive participation, or video teleconferencing with interactive participation by attendees. It is only the last two options that truly take advantage of recent advances in telecommunications and permit the attendee to ask questions, thus providing the "feel" of being in a class.

These programs are frequently being sold to management as cost savings [(Department of Energy [DOE] Central Training Academy Distance Learning Brochure)] without considering the other potential impacts. There are several areas, in addition to costs, that could have a significant impact on the local business unit.

STANDARDIZATION

The organization employing distance learning can use this as a tool to develop standard training modules for staff at remote locations that will

1. Address compliance issues related to mandatory training.

2. Facilitate transfer of staff among various sites.

3. Provide a mechanism for transferring organization knowledge and/or culture.

4. Develop standard prerequisites for training modules.

5. Develop training modules based on job task analysis that drives standardization of job assignments.

SHARED RESOURCES—REDUCTION OF SITE TRAINING STAFF

One of the standard benefits of telecommunications in all applications is the ability to share resources and expand the application of limited resources. The resources shared by distance learning are the professional trainer(s) and the subject matter expert(s).

1. The organization can rely on a reduced number of subject matter experts to develop training modules.

2. The site training staff would no longer require the level of expertise necessary to develop the training modules but would supply site-specific information and administer the exams.

3. The number of training staff at each site could be reduced.

POTENTIAL LOSS OF LOCAL CONTROL

The drawback from a local perspective would be the potential or perceived loss of control over the training program. The implementation of the distance learning program could maintain local control through permitting the local organization to determine which training modules to obtain from the central organization as supplements with the ability to develop and use local training modules as desired. The alternative is to have the overall training program developed by the central organization with local organizations providing support and implementation. The perception of local training managers would likely be the attempt to implement the second method since central organizations tend to expand areas of authority and consolidate control and influence. For example, the Department of Energy operates various sites throughout the country, and these sites must each provide a wide range of required training. The training requirements are generally outlined in DOE Orders that must be followed by all sites. Therefore, the impetus would be to standardize these courses and eliminate local variation to ensure the training meets the requirements and to facilitate documentation of compliance. The following are probable perceptions of the local training organizations:

1. The site training organizations would no longer have control over the content of the training modules.

2. Even if the central organization requested input from the local training organizations, this input into the content could range from significant to none, and the decision would still be made at the central level. Also, smaller organizations would be concerned that their input would be overridden by that of the major sites.

3. The implementation of the standard prerequisites could limit the flexibility of local training staff to evaluate individuals' job experience or related education/training to reduce attendance at unnecessary training classes.

4. Reliance on standard job task analysis and roll-up to standard job descriptions reduces the local capability to define jobs based on the workload and/or skills of individuals.

5. Site-specific issues might not be addressed or, worse yet, addressed inadequately or incorrectly.

SHIFT IN FOCUS FROM EDUCATION TO TRAINING

The reliance on job task analysis results in a training focus. Keen (*Competing in Time,* page 235) makes a strong case for differentiation between education and training. This is not just appropriate for telecommunications but applies to other professions. The focus on training limits the flexibility of the company in that staff are task trained and not as able to adjust to changing conditions. Education provides the knowledge base to analyze, evaluate, and develop cost-beneficial solutions. Training provides task-oriented knowledge that is generally not transferable.

BARRIERS TO SUCCESSFUL IMPLEMENTATION OF DISTANCE LEARNING

As a local manager responsible for development of training programs that are being moved under the control of a central organization that is starting to implement a distance learning program, I will tend to resist the change until I have been convinced that the potential negative impacts outlined above will not be the ultimate results of the change.

The tendency of innovations is to expand the applications. Once an organization has invested capital in deploying the hardware necessary to support distance learning there will be organizational prodding to expand the use of the system. This will lead to expanding the role of the central organization in the training from supplemental courses offered to a limited number of professionals, to required training that all employees must complete.

As an example, the DOE Central Training Academy proposal includes a limited number of courses in safeguards (security and nuclear materials control and accountability) as the initial offering. These courses currently have somewhat limited participation mainly due to the cost of sending individuals to Albuquerque, New Mexico. One factor that limits the participation but is also a very attractive feature is the specialized nature of the courses. These courses are designed to provide an opportunity for professionals from the various sites to meet in a classroom situation and provide additional input into the course from other than the prepared materials. This type of training/education interaction is difficult to generate through distance learning. It will require coordination and attention to the class registrants to maintain the cross-fertilization provided by scheduling participants from various backgrounds. Distance learning also requires some adjustment by the class participants; they must become comfortable talking to a camera or transmitting comments using a keyboard. Another factor is that participants frequently view these trips as a reward and look forward to meeting with others in the same profession both during and after the class. Some classes have out-of-class assignments, and the distance learning will force participants to work only with those from their home location. The use of teams of individuals from different locations provides a great opportunity to broaden the view of individuals who have only worked at a single site. Another factor is class attendance. When the Central Training Academy has given courses at various sites, the individuals who work at that site are at somewhat of a disadvantage in that routine (or somewhat less routine) problems may interfere with their ability to attend the full day. One of the benefits of travel is the removal from the routine work location, which permits an individual to focus on the training being provided.

To continue the DOE example, the issuance of new DOE Orders related to required training has led to a proliferation of training modules for each individual working on a DOE site and additional training for individuals working with nuclear materials. These training modules are currently developed by site staff and have led to large training organizations both within the Training Department and within the responsible operating Departments. The Nuclear Materials Control and Accountability Department has a Training Coordinator who is responsible for developing training modules for individuals handling accountable nuclear materials, and the Health Physics Department has a group assigned to developing and providing training for radiation workers. The future of these types of positions could logically be questioned if the distance learning program expanded to include required training based on the DOE orders. The resistance to dismantling empires is significant and must be addressed to permit full utilization of the concept of distance learning and the maximum cost reduction based on elimination of duplication of effort at the various sites.

There is need for careful consideration of which classes should be offered through distance learning. Classes designed to last all day with additional evening assignments may be impractical. Distance learning may need to subdivide the material into smaller segments that can more easily be scheduled into a regular work week.

CORPORATE/ORGANIZATION BENEFITS FROM DISTANCE LEARNING

For a corporate planner or executive, the potential benefits from developing a comprehensive distance learning program are significant. The use of technology to provide opportunities for staff at remote locations to meet in training classes on a routine basis will go a long way towards developing a corporate viewpoint. One of the problems of organizations with multiple locations is that staff loyalty is frequently centered around the local facility, not the overall organization. It is a challenge for the organization to instill a sense of belonging among diverse facilities. Several mechanisms for exploiting the capabilities of distance learning to provide more than a reduction in travel costs are discussed below.

1. Provide a sense of community among staff with similar functions at diverse facilities through grouping for distance learning. All accounts payable staff could be in a defined group who would attend distance learning for all topics, not just accounting. For example, at the DOE, all staff must attend General Employee Training, Defensive Driving, and Carcinogen Awareness Training. If these were offered through Distance Learning to groups of individuals working in related functions, the more frequent contact would facilitate development of personal relationships that help foster the sense of corporate community.

2. As Distance Learning is more fully applied, individuals become more comfortable with the concept and start thinking of other business uses for the technology. The introduction of successful, affordable technology consistently leads to development of novel applications by end users.

3. Careful planning and phased implementation with consideration of local concerns can mitigate many of the barriers identified in the previous section. The overall program should identify the long-range goals including areas of training that will continue to be site specific.

SUMMARY AND CONCLUSIONS

The current methods of evaluating distance learning do not consider the full range of potential impacts, positive and negative. The reductions in travel-related costs are easily measured but represent only a small portion of the impact. The overall distance learning program and its implementation must be planned and designed to maximize the benefits of the technology. The simple replacement of a distance learning training class for a locally provided training class will not maximize the benefits nor address the barriers to effective implementation.

The development must include steps to analyze which training is more appropriately offered through the distance learning; to determine which should continue to be site specific; and to develop mechanisms to provide early and continuing participation by the distributed parts of the organization. This will permit standardization of training, more effective use of training expertise, and the ability to develop closer ties within a distributed corporation/organization.

Those implementing the distance learning program must consider the impact on routine work schedules and, if necessary, decrease the length of individual training classes. Most remote training is from three to five days to minimize travel costs. Without the travel cost factor, classes can be broken into smaller segments, which will decrease the impact on routine operations and permit students to better assimilate the materials. Another implementation factor to consider that will provide the opportunity to develop multisite relationships is to define training groups, which include individuals from various sites, for a series of classes. This will foster the development of personal relationships among class participants at remote sites and tend to broaden the perspective of those individuals.

Case 10-2

How Email Works

Mark A. Braun

INTRODUCTION

Electronic mail, or email, is a form of communication heavily utilized in today's "high-tech" world. Email is familiar to many people and is typically a preferred form of communicating one-on-one or one-on-many due to its asynchronous nature, that is, email does not require real-time communication and therefore can transfer information very efficiently. Standard email is quickly becoming a preferred form of communication, with millions of email messages being transferred per minute nationally. In addition to standard email, other forms of email also exist such as bulletin boards and chat rooms. There are many advantages and disadvantages associated with email that can be debated endlessly. Regardless of its merits or deficiencies, email, like the telephone or radio, is here to stay. This case analysis will describe how email works from a technical perspective.

HISTORY

An engineer named Ray Tomlinson sent the first email message in 1971. Mr. Tomlinson worked for BBN, a company contracted by the U.S. Department of Defense to build the ARPANET. The ARPANET is the precursor to the Internet. Late in 1971, Mr. Tomlinson was experimenting with a software program called SNDMSG that he had written to allow programmers working on ARPANET computers to leave messages for each other. SNDMSG only worked locally, but allowed the exchange of messages between users who shared the same machine. Users could create a text file and deliver this file to a "mailbox." The mailbox was a file with a particular name with the feature of allowing users to append text to the end of the file. Hence, a contiguous number of messages could be received and reviewed by the owner of the mailbox. At the owner's command, the mailbox could be purged.

In addition to SNDMSG, Tomlinson also was working on an experimental file transfer protocol called CYPNET to enable transfer of files among linked computers. Tomlinson adapted CYPNET to use SNDMSG to deliver messages to mailboxes on remote machines through the ARPANET. This linked capability led to the designation of the "@" symbol to distinguish between messages addressed to mailboxes on a local machine from those headed onto the network. The first email message to traverse the ARPANET was sent between two machines sitting side-by-side at BBN in Cambridge, Massachusetts.

SIMPLE EMAIL SYSTEM

Email is simply a text message. Originally, all email messages were comprised of text only and were therefore on the order of bytes in size. However, the advent of attachments to email has provided the capability to send data such as bit maps, video, sound and so forth. The size of emails with attachments can vary by orders of magnitude from bytes to megabytes. The fundamental elements that enable the creation and transfer of email are the email client and server.

The email client is software that enables the user to manipulate email. The four primary functions performed by the email client are (1) display of all email messages in the mailbox utilizing header information such as the sender, the subject, time, and date; (2) selection of a message header from the mailbox list to display the content of the email message; (3) the capability to create new email messages including addressee, subject, and body; and (4) addition of attachments to sent messages as well as saving attachments from messages received.

Popular brand name email clients are *Microsoft Outlook*®, *Novell GroupWise*®, and *Pegasus*® among others. This software can run stand-alone or on a network server. If email is accessed via the Internet, the email client is a Web page running on the respective mail provider's server. America Online is an example of a Web-based email provider. Regardless of where the client resides, once a client can be accessed, email can be sent and received.

The email client connects to an email server to transfer and receive messages. The server is a computer running software applications that constantly monitor specific ports waiting for incoming email traffic. The server is also capable of transferring email, based on a specific address to another server utilizing a second port.

A simple email server would store a list of email accounts uniquely identifying each person who can receive email on the server, for example, **mark.** In addition, it would have a text file for each account to store email messages, for example, **mark.txt.** Given this structure, when a person "sends" an email, the email client connects to the email server and transfers the address of the recipient (**mark**), the name of the sender (e.g., **roger**), and the body of the message. The server, in turn, would format this information and append it to the bottom of the **mark.txt** file. Other information such as the time, date, and subject line is typically stored as well. As more email is received for **mark,** the server appends this information to the bottom of the file in the order it is received. Access to email for **mark** requires the client to connect to the server and request a copy of the **mark.txt** file. The email client receives and manipulates the contents of the **mark.txt** file and provides a graphical user interface to perform the four basic email functions described above.

ACTUAL EMAIL SYSTEM

Most email systems consist of clients and two different servers running on a server machine. A Simple Mail Transfer Protocol (SMTP) server processes outgoing mail; incoming mail is processed by a Post Office Protocol version 3 (POP3) server. The ports discussed in the previous section assigned to these applications are port 25 for SMTP and port 110 for POP3.

When email is sent, the email client communicates with the SMTP server to facilitate the proper transfer of the message. Depending on the destination of the message, the SMTP server connected to the client's host may communicate with other SMTP servers to actually deliver the email. To describe this process, consider sending an email message via the Internet from **roger** to **mark.** The client for **roger** is located at **houston.com** whereas the client for **mark** is located at **snyder.com.** When **roger** sends an email, **roger's** client connects to the SMTP server at **houston.com** using port 25. A simple set of text commands and responses are exchanged to enable the transfer of the addresses of the sender and recipient as well as the body of the message. The **houston.com** SMTP server uses the recipient's address, **mark@synder.com,** and decomposes it into the recipient name (**mark**) and the domain name (**snyder.com**). The domain name is equivalent to an Internet protocol (IP) address that uniquely identifies the address of the domain's server. In this case, the recipient's domain is different from the sender's domain. Consequently, the SMTP server at **houston.com** connects to a Domain Name Server (DNS) to determine the IP address of the recipient. The DNS replies with one or more IP addresses (or none) for the SMTP server(s) at **snyder.com.** Once the IP address is received, the **houston.com** SMTP server connects to the SMTP server at **snyder.com** via port 25. Once connected, another simple set of text commands and responses are exchanged between servers to properly identify the source and destination as well as transfer the text message. The **snyder.com** SMTP server recognizes the destination of the message is **mark** and subsequently transfers the message to the POP3 server at **snyder.com.** The POP3 server puts the message in **mark's** mailbox for access from the client.

In the scenario described above, if the SMTP server at **houston.com** cannot connect to the SMTP server at **snyder.com,** the message is placed in a queue at **houston.com.** The queue is monitored and a retry to send the message is attempted at some periodic interval. After a prescribed period of time, for example, four hours, a message is sent to the sender indicating a problem has occurred and the email message was undelivered.

In addition to connection problems, other forms of errors can occur when transferring email either within a LAN or via the Internet. If the host or "user id" is not valid, the SMTP server will not be able to determine the proper address to transfer the email message. This can be determined when the SMTP server communicates with another SMTP server in the LAN, the DNS, or the destination SMTP server outside the LAN. If a valid address cannot be determined due to an invalid host or user id, the SMTP server will send a message back to the originator's email client indicating the destination address is invalid. This type of message is typically returned to the sender in a short period of time. Consequently, if the sender does not receive an "invalid destination" type message within a few minutes, the sender can safely assume a valid address was used. Again, connection problems can occur that require "time-out" periods prior to a return message transmission, as stated above.

In order to retrieve or view the email message sent by **roger,** the email client at **snyder.com** connects to the POP3 server at **snyder.com** using port 110. An account name and password are typically required to gain access. Given this information, the POP3 server at **snyder.com** opens **mark's** text file and enables access utilizing a very simple set of text commands. The email client may request a copy of all email messages to the client's host, thereby enabling the POP3 server to delete the messages from the server and free up memory.

Attachments to email text can be transferred and received as well. Typically, attachments are objects produced by some type of application such as a word processor, spreadsheet, or graphics application. Attachments are usually not simple text data. As a result, an encoding/decoding process is required to format the data for transfer within the email message. The object produced by the application is typically a binary file. Since email is text or ASCII-character based, an encoding process converts every three bytes from the binary file into four text characters. This is done by taking six bits at a time and adding decimal value 32 to the value of these six bits to create a text character. This process essentially creates a text-encoded version of the original binary object. This information would be appended to the email's text body using the keywords "begin" and "end." Subsequent to transfer, the destination email client would decode these data to recreate the binary object. This encode/decode process was originally done "by hand" using a program called *uuencode* and *uudecode*. However, most email clients today automatically perform this function.

SUMMARY

The transfer and processing of email is functionally a very simple process. Email requires a client and server to facilitate the proper formulation, transfer, receipt, and viewing of messages including attachments. Regardless of destination, client-server communications enabling this data transfer is fundamentally the same. A remote destination simply requires additional communications among multiple SMTP servers. Although the merits of email can be debated, it is clear that this form of telecommunication is firmly embedded into today's society and it will continue to be used into the foreseeable future.

REFERENCES

1. "The First E-mail Message." *Pre Text Magazine,* www.pretext.com, October 2000.

2. "Computers & the Internet." www.Howstuffworks.com, October 2000.

3. "E-Mail." *A Practical and Authoritative Guide to Contemporary English, The American Heritage Book of English Usage,* 1996.

4. "Harness: E-Mail: How It Works." *www.learnthenet.com,* October 2000.

Case 10-3

The Truth about Telecommuting

Stacy Sthole

WHAT IS TELECOMMUTING?

Telecommuting is essentially working for a company from the privacy of your own home or car. Telecommuting, also known as telework, has grown rapidly in the past year and is expected to increase to 39 million full- and part-time employees working at home by the year 2004. In the past telecommuters usually had a stand-alone PC, a phone, and a fax machine to keep in touch with their office. Today, technology allows for a lot more than just a stand-alone PC. Some telecommuters have DSLs to improve the speed of communication with their company along with cell phones and other gadgets to keep in touch.

ADVANTAGES AND DISADVANTAGES

Employees who telecommute have several benefits that may include setting their own hours and prolonging the life of their car. Family life is important and several telecommuters enjoy being able to go to ball games or field trips with their children. Some telecommuters say that their productivity increased once they started working from home, which allows them to focus on work and not what is going on in the office. Another advantage of being a telecommuter is being able to move or live wherever you wish. Since you do not have to drive into work everyday, you could live several hours or even several states away from the actual location of the company.

Disadvantages for the employee are hard to find, but one drawback seems to be the fact that if you are not careful, you may end up working around the clock. Another drawback could be less raises and promotions if you work 100 percent at home, for example, out of sight, out of mind. To guarantee success, you must combine commuting and telecommuting.

Employer advantages may include increased productivity, no cost lengthening of the workday, less office space, and tax credits for telecommuting workers. Employee morale seems to go up; therefore, customer satisfaction will increase.

Disadvantages for employers could include security issues, home and work conflict, expensive technology, and lack of face-to-face interaction with customers.

TELECOMMUTING LIABILITIES

Companies that are considering or already allow telecommuting should make sure coverage is sufficient. Companies should consider workplace safety, information theft, equipment theft or damage, and discrimination as liability issues.

WORKPLACE SAFETY

OSHA will not inspect employees' homes, but remember that employees may claim injury and employers must investigate or pay based on state workers' compensation laws. If an employee, however, develops carpal tunnel syndrome, you more than likely will not be responsible. The best bet is to let them know of the dangers and offer to pay for ergonomically correct equipment.

INFORMATION THEFT

Employers are still responsible for electronic and paper files regardless of location. Even though the courts have not ruled on this topic, employers should take the necessary steps to ensure safety to prevent theft. By installing a firewall to the home computer and securing client papers, employers are staying one step ahead.

EQUIPMENT THEFT OR DAMAGE

Employers should make sure that the employee has homeowners insurance, if the company is paying for the equipment. If the employee does not have coverage, then the employer must add it to the current business policy.

DISCRIMINATION

As an employer, you must have good reason why one employee is able to work from home and another is not. Put these policies in writing to help avoid being sued for discrimination.

TAX ISSUES

Working at home while living in one state and the employer maintains an office in another state can cause a major tax headache. There are two types of tests to determine which state can tax the income of a telecommuter. The first test is the *physical presence test*. The physical presence test states that the employee's income is taxed according to where the work actually took place. For example, if the employee spends 55 percent of the time telecommuting, then the income is taxed 45/55 (45 percent to the employer's state and 55 percent to the employee's state). The second test focuses on the reason for telecommuting, *the convenience versus necessity test.* According to this test, the state in which the employer resides and works can tax the employee's income only if it is the employer's necessity that the employee works from home. Courts have ruled not enough office space at the employer's location is not a necessity. If this test is used and the telecommuter works from home only 30 percent and the necessity test fails, then all of the income is taxed in the state in which the employer is located.

The only problem with these two tests is when the employer's state and the employee's state use different tests and the states will not allow a tax credit for the taxes paid to the other state.

TELECOMMUTING PROGRAMS

Los Angeles County government started a telecommuting program in 1989 to reduce smog and traffic congestion. LA County telecommuting program is strictly voluntary and all participants are given a training course and must sign an agreement about the rules.

The employers in Virginia are given a grant of $3,500 per worker to help with the cost of the initial process of telecommuting.

A pilot program was kicked off in Los Angeles, Denver, Washington, and Southeastern Pennsylvania this past May to help improve the quality of the air. Participants will be able to earn air-pollution credits. Companies use a computer program called Teletrips. Teletrips calculates the reductions in auto emissions each day the employee works at home. The government can put these calculations into an equation to find out if the area is meeting the federal air-quality standards.

TELECOMMUTING TIPS

To make telecommuting successful, the telecommuters must make sure they have the motivation to get up in the morning. If you work from home, you need to be able to separate work life from home life. One way to do this is to install a separate phone line in your office for business use only. To ensure that telecommuting will be effective, you must have a good working relationship with your manager and stay in contact with him/her often. Another way to make working from home a success is for you to have a high-speed Internet connection, that is, cable modem, DSL, or ISDN.

CONCLUSION

Telecommuting is a fast-growing industry of workers in today's businesses. There are disadvantages and advantages to both the employee and the employer. You must remember to take into consideration liability and tax issues before deciding whether to telecommute or not.

REFERENCES

1. Boyd, J. "IT Favors Telecommuting." *Internet Week,* no. 876 (2001), pp. 10–11.

2. Godinez, V. "Internet Survey Offers Advice to Telecommuters." *The Dallas Morning News*, 2001.

3. Hillburg, B. "House Lawmakers Look to Ease Rules for Working at Home." *Daily News* (Los Angeles), 2001.

4. Horowitz, B. "Telecommuting: What New York State Nonresidents Should Know." *CPA Journal* 7 (2001), pp. 60–62.

5. Kanaley, R. "Number of Telecommuters in U.S. Jumps 20 Percent over Past Year." *The Philadelphia Inquirer,* 2001.

6. McKay, M. "Telecommuting Increases in Popularity for America's Work Force, Surveys Show." *The Record,* 2001.

7. Sandlund, C. "Telecommuting: A Legal Primer." *Business Week,* 2001.

8. Simon, D. "Telecommuting: Which State Is the Employee In?" *CPA Journal* 7 (2001), pp. 59–60.

Case 10-4
Land Warrior Wireless LAN

John Matlock

Land Warrior is the U.S. Army's attempt to network soldiers on the battlefield. Although much more than simply electronics, it uses an integrated system of information technologies connected by data communications to enhance soldier mission capabilities. Data communications begin with a personal area network and expand through a wireless local area network to a tactical Internet. The personal area network connects a computer, GPS, and a helmet-mounted display on the individual soldier. The wireless LAN uses the IEEE 802.11b standard with a modified protocol to connect soldiers (moving nodes) of the infantry rifle company in a peer-to-peer mesh network.

The mission of Land Warrior soldiers is to get close to the enemy by means of fire and maneuver in order to destroy or capture enemy soldiers to repel their assault by fire, close combat, and counterattack. Capabilities of infantrymen have evolved throughout history via technological advancements such as bronze, gunpowder, and aircraft. Information technology is finally becoming available to further enhance the dismounted soldier in close combat. The Army's vision for the infantry soldier is to significantly improve his mission capability with a fully integrated soldier system. This integrated system provides overmatching lethality, enhanced survivability, and situational awareness on the electronic battlefield. The soldier will use this system in all environments of conflict. The system seamlessly integrates with other soldiers and their weapon systems.

Integral to this system is the use of telecommunications and data communications through the wireless local area network (WLAN). This network enhances the soldiers' ability to shoot, move, communicate, and remain tactically aware. This system creates the potential to change the fight by enhancing squads and platoons with significantly greater decentralized capabilities. Data communications begin at the soldier level and progress through the squad, platoon, and company network. Information sharing through these communication systems continues through the battalion and higher levels.

The fully integrated soldier system includes subsystems for protective clothing, individual equipment, weapon systems, a computer, software, and communications. Data communications combine these subsystems with a personal area network to integrate their capabilities. The integrated helmet assembly provides an 800 by 600 pixel color display and an image intensification display for night operations. The helmet-mounted display enables a soldier to view real-time information including the current threat. The view on this display provides each soldier with the common tactical picture. The daylight video sight enhances lethality, survivability, and information sharing. The weapon system includes a daylight video sight that allows the user to sight in on targets without positioning himself directly behind or adjacent to the weapon. This indirect view capability allows the gunner to engage targets from behind protective cover while exposing only the weapon. The daylight video sight camera allows soldiers to transmit pictures of the current situation. He can pass real-time pictures of potential terrorists or enemy activities.

The computer radio subsystem consists of several information technologies that operate through the personal area network. This system operates in the suspend mode to conserve battery power until communications become active. The personal area network contains two computers. The first computer sits on the small of the back and contains a mobile Pentium III processor running at 500 MHz. This system includes a keyboard and a flat panel display. The operating system is Microsoft Windows 2000. Applications include Oracle 8i Light databases. The second computer sits on the chest for accessibility. The individual user controls his network assets with this machine. The operating system is Microsoft Windows CE. This machine contains the mouse for controlling helmet-mounted display images and a push-to-talk device for voice communications. This network uses the same type of PCMIA card available commercially for laptop computers except that the antenna is separated. The global positioning system enables the soldier to know his exact location and the location of his comrades at all times. The GPS system includes an integrated navigation system to plan and execute foot movement routes. The host controller box (hub) and the cell batteries reside in a pouch within the protective clothing. The two computers communicate via universal serial bus (USB) connections through this hub to form the personal area network.

The WLAN enables soldiers to understand the situation before and during contact. The system on each soldier is a node. All nodes in the network may be in constant motion, making this system a moving wireless network. Soldiers can receive or pass real-time threat updates using the wireless LAN. This system enables the soldier to communicate via voice or data to all other soldiers in his unit. This capability significantly increases situational awareness by allowing each networked soldier access to updated information on the enemy and friendly situation. All nodes across the environment share information to create and update a common picture. Each soldier transmits pieces of information available to him. Information from multiple sources collects in common databases that each soldier can access to assess the big picture. Leaders can access this collected information to track the status of the enemy situation, mission progress, supply levels, and personnel issues.

The scope of coverage for the WLAN is the infantry rifle company. The company network contains 152 nodes, one for each member of the company. The organizational structure of the company includes a headquarters element, a mortar section, and three platoons. Each platoon contains its own headquarters element and three nine-man squads. WLAN radio transmission range is 1.3 km for the soldier and 5 km for leaders at the squad-leader level and above. The nine-man rifle squad is the lowest level of a LAN. Each member with his computer operates as a node. The platoon network consists of three squads communicating through the platoon radio transmitter operator (RTO) to the platoon leader. Each platoon leader can transmit to communicate with the company commander and the leaders of adjacent platoons.

The WLAN is an ad hoc network, using the IEEE 802.11b protocol. This standard allows transmission of data at rates of up to 11 Mbps and 1.8 GHz. The network architecture is peer-to-peer (P2P) where all nodes are of equal status. Mesh topology allows each user to access other nodes to obtain updated information. This system provides capability for multicast addressing for individuals and groups. Expected simultaneous group connections are six nodes at a time. Transmissions are full duplex.

The communications platform handles basic packet routing. Two soldiers (nodes) in direct communication will pass packets directly in the passive mode. If the recipient is not in direct communication, the sender's packets travel in the hybrid route discovery mode by hopping from one reachable node to another enroute to the recipient. The system determines the viable number of hops for retry operations and uses an intelligent packet hop-counting process. Each node maintains a common routing table for voice and data packets. A leader can set priorities within this table for important recipients such as subordinate leaders. Beyond these prioritized addresses, the table tracks which addresses are reachable at any given time. The wireless LAN computer handles message-level routing and retry. If the sender's computer does not receive an acknowledgement (ACK) that the recipient has received the message, it automatically retransmits the message. Line access methods such as carrier sense multiple access with collision detection (CSMA/CD) for Ethernets or collision avoidance (CSMA/CA) for Wi-Fi are not used since collisions are not a problem while using retry. The system reduces or eliminates background beacon messages. The system keeps track of whom it can see. Instead of transmitting messages to all nodes, packets hop (are routed) through one reachable node to the next enroute to the intended recipient.

The user can transmit both voice and data over the same medium. The current requirement is for real-time routing for VoIP. Group VoIP relies on multicast addressing. This system uses inherently multicast protocol. A leader can select a predefined address group to communicate in an intercom mode.

REFERENCES

1. Greenway, John R., Major General Retired. *The Soldier Is the System*. Military Information Technology Online, www.mit-kmi.com/Archives/5_3_MIT/5_3_Art3.cfm.

2. Murray, John. *Land Warrior v1.0 Wireless LAN Communications Notes*. San Jose, CA: Pacific Consultants, www.pacificconsultants.com, May 3, 2001.

3. Program Management Office for Soldier Systems. *Available at* www.pmsoldiersystems.army.mil/public/default.asp.

4. Wireless Ethernet Compatibility Alliance. *Available at* www.weca.net.

Case 10-5

Implementing Information Technology for Competitive Advantage: Risk Management Issues

Ronald E. McGaughey Jr., Charles A. Snyder, and Houston H. Carr

INTRODUCTION

Competitive advantage is the ability to excel in the marketplace due to price, product, service level, or performance. Examples of the use of information technology (IT) in this role have been widely reported; some are now legendary. What is neither widely known or legendary is that many firms took large risks to be industry leaders. American Hospital Supply gave customers access to its database and American Airlines stretched the frontiers of computer capabilities with its cooperative timesharing venture with IBM. If customers had not been ready to accept and use direct database access or if computers were not capable of carrying the workload, we would not be lauding these companies for their exploitation of IT.

We tend to equate risk with something external to us; that is, natural disasters present the risk of power disruption or worse. Less obvious is the risk inherent in the adoption of a new computer-based system or the distribution of data processing and data storage across a country or world via telecommunications networks. The implementation of IT involves significant risk, both from external sources and from the technology and process of implementation.

THE NATURE OF RISK

According to Webster's Dictionary (1989), *risk* is "the possibility of loss or injury; also, the degree of the probability of such loss." The four components of risk are threats, resources, modifying factors, and consequences. (Please refer to Exhibit 10.1.) *Threats* are the broad range of forces capable of producing adverse consequences. *Resources* consist of the assets, people, or earnings potentially affected by threats. *Modifying factors* are the internal and external factors that influence the probability of a threat becoming a reality, or the severity of consequences when the threat materializes. *Consequences* have to do with the way the threat manifests its effects upon the resources and the extent of those effects. Threats to IT resources follow the same logic and have been the subject of recent discussion [1, 13, 14, 17, 21].

Risk becomes loss when there is some adverse change in existing or expected circumstances. Change produces the uncertainty inherent in risk. No one can be sure if and when change will take place, nor can one be certain about consequences of change. From an organizational standpoint, change may be internal or may take place in the environment. Because internal change is to some degree controllable, a firm may respond to the risk associated with internal change in a proactive fashion. External change is uncontrollable[1] by the firm, requiring

EXHIBIT 10.1
The Components of Risk

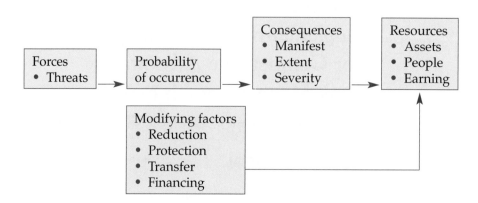

---

[1] By definition, external changes take place in the environment and affect the organization (system) but are not controlled by it.

responses that may be reactive. To the degree that change can be anticipated, a proactive response is preferred. An organization should deal with different types of risk in different ways.

According to Crockford [1], the major categories of risk are:

- *Fire and natural disasters*—the most obvious threats to company property and earnings. Examples of recent disasters are the telephone office fire in Hinsdale, Illinois; the flood in Chicago, Illinois, that disrupted power and telephone service in the financial district; the earthquake in San Francisco, California, that destroyed power and telecommunications service; and the storm called Hurricane Hugo that played havoc with the Eastern U.S. Coast. (See Loch, Carr, and Warkenton [11] for a discussion of threats to information systems.)

- *Accident*—death or injury to key personnel and/or damage to assets, reputation, and so forth.

- *Political and social*—from change. They are sometimes interrelated.

- *Technical*—associated with adopting or not adopting technological change.

- *Marketing*—receptiveness to an organization's products and promotional efforts.

- *Labor*—current and future availability of suitable human resources.

- *Liability*—risks associated with the organization's responsibility for its products and actions.

Risks can also be categorized as insurable and uninsurable risks. *Insurable risks* can be underwritten, transferring the cost of adverse consequences to an outside party. A company can buy insurance to cover liability risks caused by fire or natural disasters and losses resulting from accidents. Organizations must find other ways of coping with *uninsurable risks,* such as implementing an obsolescent technology.

Risks can also be categorized as historical or new. *Historical risks* are associated with events that have occurred and may continue to occur. Data are often available for analyzing these. *New risks* and the events that cause them may have happened before, but did so without being observed. They pose some unique challenges for those responsible for managing risk. Risks range from improbable to highly probable and from inconsequential to highly significant.

The four primary methods of handling risks are:

- *Reduction*—taking action to eliminate the risk or to reduce its severity. Example: removing hazards to workers.

- *Protection*—using physical means to accomplish the same objective as reduction. Example: installing sprinkler devices.

- *Transfer*—arranging for someone else to carry all or part of the risk burden. Examples: purchasing product liability insurance; pushing the responsibility for carrying inventory onto suppliers or customers.

- *Financing*—providing for risk in the normal operating budget. Examples: self-insurance plans, and less common financing methods, such as contingent lines of credit.

RISK MANAGEMENT

Risk Management is the science and art of recognizing the existence of threats, determining their consequences on resources, and applying modifying factors in a cost-effective manner to keep adverse consequences within bounds. Decision making with regard to risk should focus on identifying, measuring, and handling them.

Strategies for handling risk necessarily address one or more of the components of risks: threats, resources, modifying factors, and consequences. The appropriate strategy depends on the nature of the risk and situational variables that influence the organization's range of choices; that is, financial limitation may influence the feasibility of certain strategies, such as self-insurance. In developing risk management strategies, an organization should use a systematic approach for identifying, classifying, and understanding risk.

RISK ANALYSIS, IS, AND IT

There are risks involved in any decision. Normally, the magnitude of the risk of introducing new investments is positively related to the resources required. IS risks are positively related to reliance on IS support. Nosek pointed out that companies are seeking higher payoff, higher risk systems to optimize their management of information resources. As organizations become more dependent on IS, the need to assess and manage risks becomes more important.

Recent authors have advocated the use of information technology to gain competitive advantage. They devote little attention to the risk of failure or the risk associated with disruption of critical IS support. Wiseman discussed supplier risk and suggested that legal risk was an issue facing organizations using strategic information systems. Thus the risks accompanying IT investments in pursuit of competitive advantage have mostly been ignored.

Organizations should realistically assess the risks involved in their IT investment decisions and integrate risk management into IS planning and control. The process of IT risk assessment can be facilitated by employing some existing frameworks; one such allows a systematic review of the IT investment at various critical organizational processes or functions.

THE VALUE CHAIN

Value chain analysis provides a useful framework for evaluating the strategic significance of new information technology. The value chain can show how and why information technology is changing the way companies operate internally, and the relationship between firms that are a part of the chain—the company, its suppliers, its customers, and its rivals.

The chain is made up of "value activities," which endow company products—goods or services—with value that entices customers to buy the products. Customer perception is reflected in the price that customers are willing to pay. To gain competitive advantage over rivals, a company must create value at a lower cost, create products that are more valuable than competitors' products, or some combination of these.

Value activities are divided into primary and support. *Primary activities* include the creation, marketing, and delivery of products to buyers, with support and service after the sale, including inbound logistics, operations, and outbound logistics. *Support activities* provide inputs and infrastructure that make the primary activities possible; they include human resource management, technology development, and procurement. The firm's infrastructure supports all the activities in the value chain; they can be broken down into more detailed activities. Linkages connect the interdependent activities.

IT can affect any of the activities by improving efficiency or effectiveness or by fundamentally changing the activity. IT can change industry structure and the rules of competition, create competitive advantage by giving firms the means of outperforming rivals, and spawn new businesses.

Products, processes, and the nature of competition are increasingly influenced by IT; as a consequence, the information component of products has increased. Much more information can now be made available. Not only are products and processes transformed by IT; the nature of competition itself can be reshaped.

Porter and Millar [7] suggest that senior executives follow five steps in positioning their firms to take advantage of new opportunities:

1. Assess information intensity in terms of the value chain and the product.

2. Determine the role of IT in industry structure.

3. Identify and rank the ways in which IT might create competitive advantage, the internal and external linkages, the value system components, competitive scope, and new or existing products.

4. Investigate how IT might spawn new businesses.

5. Develop a plan for taking advantage of IT based on the first four steps.

Snyder first suggested that the value chain might be of value in IT risk analysis. This concept was further elaborated on by Rainer, Snyder, and Carr. Steps three and four in the process were modified to include risk analysis—the evaluation of alternatives identified in step four and five should include an evaluation of risks. The plan should include provisions for handling the risks associated with alternatives selected for implementation.

RISKS ASSOCIATED WITH IT

The risks associated with IT strategic planning are largely speculative. They are those that offer the potential for gain or loss. Product differentiation through IT might increase the appeal of a product, thereby increasing sales revenue. The potential exists for gain or loss and the risks involved are speculative risks.

Thus risk management must focus on both planning and risk control. *Pure risks* present only the prospect of loss, that is, the risk of failure of a computer-based information system, such as an airline reservation system. Before the system was installed it possessed *speculative risk;* this changed to pure risk once the organization became dependent on the technology.

Risk analysis can and should be conducted as a part of strategic IT planning. As the firm uses value chain analysis to identify ways to use IT for competitive advantage, it should also assess the riskiness of alternatives explored. In addition, the value chain should help identify exposures to risk inherent in a firm's use of IT.

APPROACHES TO RISK ANALYSIS

The focus of risk analysis can be quantitative, qualitative, or both. Selection of an approach should be guided by the nature of the risks. *Quantitative approaches* generally translate risks into numbers, often financial, using probability theory. *Qualitative approaches* attempt to explain risks using descriptive variables. Quantitative approaches include: Annualized Loss Expectancy (ALE), the Courtney method, the Livermore Risk Analysis Methodology (LRAM), and Stochastic Dominance. Some use the Delphi Technique to quantify risk. Qualitative approaches include: Scenario Analysis, Fuzzy Metrics, and Questionnaires. The Delphi Technique is sometimes used here also.

The approaches are useful primarily for evaluating pure risks. They do not consider payoff—only losses. However, risks identified in value chain planning for IT are speculative; therefore the methods of pure risk assessment may be inappropriate.

In evaluating speculative risks, an attempt is made to identify and quantify the benefits and costs associated with a particular alternative. Discounted cash flow techniques generally capitalize cash flows at an appropriate rate to recognize the time value of money. Probability estimates are assigned to the range of possible outcomes. Some subjective judgment is necessarily associated with this activity. These provide a means to arrive at an expected value of the alternative. Selection criteria include the rate of return provided by the alternatives, the net present value (NPV), the payback period, etc.

THE VALUE CHAIN AND RISK ANALYSIS

When managers use the value chain to decide how to use IT for competitive advantage, they should decide whether the risks are speculative or pure. The approach to their evaluation and management should be appropriate for the type of risk.

If the risks are speculative, financial management approaches may be appropriate. For example, the expected rate of return could be calculated, with outcomes identified and the probability of that outcome assessed. The expected return (mean) and standard deviation for each alternative can then be calculated. A higher mean is generally preferable, because it provides higher expected profits, but the standard deviation is a measure of dispersion, and greater dispersion means greater risk. The coefficient of variation, calculated by dividing the standard deviation by the mean, normalizes the dispersion for better comparison.

IT costs can be difficult to estimate, but a greater problem is in estimating the benefits. Approaches like value analysis may prove useful.

For all pure risks, the threats and the IT resources must be identified, the internal and external factors that influence the probability of the threat becoming a reality must be identified and understood, and the potential impact (consequences) must be assessed. The firm then must decide how to reduce the effect.

Once pure risks are identified and evaluated, decisions must be made about how to handle them. Management should set priorities: this will help managers in planning for and controlling pure risks.

Often, graphical tools have been recommended for clarification where traditional techniques have been inadequate. For example, Shoval and Lugasi developed a graphical tool for cost–benefit analysis so that risk and uncertainty would be brought into the computer selection process.

PROPOSED TOOLS FOR IT RISK ANALYSIS

Two matrices are proposed for use in IT risk analysis: the speculative risk grid in the early stages of planning and the pure risk grid for setting priorities for management.

THE SPECULATIVE RISK GRID

The speculative risk grid is a simple tool that can help managers evaluate the early stages of planning, where initial screening of alternatives takes place, and that can act as a supplement to conventional quantitative approaches. The two dimensional matrix can help managers get an overview of the relative risks of alternatives. Alternatives identified in value chain analysis, or some other approach, can be placed on the grid based on probability of loss and the potential for gain or loss. (See Exhibit 10.2.)

The potential loss and gain for each alternative is ranked. The potential for loss is assigned a value that is negative (-5 for very large potential loss to -1 for small potential loss). The rank values for loss and for gain should be multiplied by their respective probabilities (the probabilities for loss and gain need not sum to one in this matrix). The results should then be added. The placement factor will be used along with the probability of loss to determine where the alternative will be placed on the grid:

Placement Factor = ([potential loss × prob. of loss]+[potential gain * prob. of gain])

Because the potential for loss is often overlooked in assessing alternative uses, the probability of loss is used to determine placement on the grid. Placement of alternatives can especially help management in the early stages of IT planning. Pooled judgment can be used in developing the estimates needed to calculate the placement factor.

Ideal placement is in Quadrant IV on the grid. This represents low risk and a positive expected outcome (plotting factor > 0) for the organization. Because emphasis is placed on the downside risk—placement of alternatives on the grid is based on the risks of loss rather than gain—the approach is conservative.

The following example shows how the grid could be used:

> Building Supply Company is considering an electronic link between its price database and the construction companies it serves. This would assist construction companies in the job bidding process, since many now use CAD systems and computer systems that assist in costing out projects. It would eliminate the need for telephone calls to

EXHIBIT 10.2
The Speculative Risk Grid

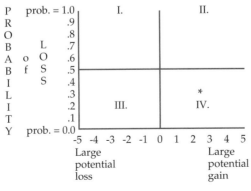

Outcome

check prices and would also reduce the time that sales personnel spend on the telephone—they could then provide better service to customers. Building Supply managers believe that the electronic link will encourage the construction companies to buy from them rather than competitors and that it will increase switching costs. Managers also believe that the "high-tech" image will predispose customers to buy from Building Supply. A positive outcome of 4 is assigned. Managers express concern that competitors may gain access to prices and undercut the Company, thereby taking away some business. They also fear that a disruption in the electronic link might cause a loss of customer goodwill. Potential negative outcomes are ranked at 2. The probability of the positive outcome is estimated to be .7 and the probability of the negative outcome is estimated at .3 (the probabilities need not sum to 1.0 because they will not always be mutually exclusive outcomes). The plotting factor is calculated as follows:

$$([\text{Pt. loss} * \text{Pb. loss}] + [\text{Pt. gain} * \text{Pb. gain}]) = \text{PF} ([-2*.3] + [4*.7]) = .67$$

This case alternative falls into Quadrant IV. It appears to be promising with regard to potential outcomes (positive plotting factor) and it is not very risky. It could be better evaluated when compared to other alternatives placed similarly on the speculative risk grid.

THE PURE RISK GRID

In managing pure risks, the focus is on identifying threats, the consequences of threats, and means of handling the associated risks. The threats can be identified and ranked in importance on a scale of 0 (insignificant negative consequences) to 10 (extreme negative consequences). The Y axis represents the likelihood (stated as a probability) of the threat materializing and the X axis represents the consequences (based on rank of importance) of the threat. (See Exhibit 10.3.)

The threats should be identified and each placed on the grid based on the likelihood of occurrence and probable consequences. Those that fall into Quadrant I are most important to deal with because they are likely to occur and have substantial negative consequences. Plans for monitoring, control, and handling them should have high priority. The following example shows how the grid might be used:

> The Beach Company is located in southeast Florida. The corporate mainframe that serves all locations nationwide is at that location. The system is the cornerstone of the company's excellent customer service value chain analysis highlighting the importance of the computer system. If the corporate mainframe is disabled, locations nationwide would be unable to place orders to the regional warehouses,

EXHIBIT 10.3
The Pure Risk Grid

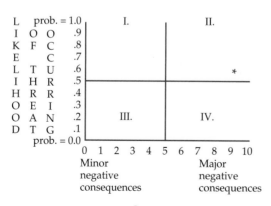

Consequences

thereby preventing prompt delivery of products to customers. Manual backup systems could be used, but service to the customer would be disrupted. For a company that built its reputation on customer service, poor service could destroy its customer loyalty and therefore cannot be tolerated, even for a short time. Assessment of threats to the system reveals that a hurricane could knock out the corporate mainframe and restoration of service could take a long time. Since hurricanes are a threat to coastal Florida for several months every year, negative consequences are ranked 9 in importance and the probability of the threat materializing is ranked 0.6.

This case falls into Quadrant II, suggesting that it should be viewed as a high priority threat that warrants management's attention and exploration of appropriate means of dealing with the threat.

The pure risk grid can help an organization to establish the relative importance of the risks identified by some other approach. Then more detailed analysis should be done on the various pure risks.

SUMMARY AND CONCLUSIONS

Risk management strategies should be integrated with strategic IS planning. The identification, classification, and understanding of IS risks can be aided by use of value chain analysis. Just as it can help a firm identify alternative uses of IT that may offer promise for competitive advantage, it can also help identify IT risks which should be considered in evaluating alternative uses of IT. The value chain can also help determine where exposures to pure risk exist with regard to current IT.

Some tools are useful for evaluating speculative risks, and some for pure risks. Firms should use appropriate tools and IT managers should be familiar with the tools and approaches for risk analysis and know when and how to apply them.

Evaluating speculative risks involves special challenges, because costs and benefits are often difficult to quantify. New approaches are needed. The speculative risk grid was introduced and described. Pure IT risks are not particularly difficult to identify. Numerous quantitative and qualitative tools are available for evaluating them in order that appropriate means of handling risks might be prescribed. It is important to set priorities, so that those most critical risks can be addressed first. The pure risk grid was introduced to show how it can help managers set priorities regarding pure risks.

Source: Reprinted from *Information & Management*, no. 26 (1994), pp. 273–280.

REFERENCES

1. H.M. Behesti and M.R. Mattson. "Computer Based Management Information Systems and Risk Management." *Focus on Management*, Vol. 1, No. 3 (1989), Society for Advancement of Management, 2331 Victory Parkway, Cincinnati, Ohio 45206.

2. J.I. Cash; F.W. McFarlan; and J.C. Mckenney. *Corporate Information Systems Management* (1988), Irwin: Homewood, IL.

3. N. Crockford. *An Introduction to Risk Management* (1980), Woodhead-Faulkner Limited: Cambridge CB2 3PA.

4. E.A.C. Crouch and R. Wilson. *Risk/Benefit Analysis* (1982), Ballinger Publishing Company: Cambridge, MA.

5. N.A. Doherty. *Corporate Risk Management* (1985), McGraw-Hill Book Company: New York.

6. A.L. Froman. "Technology as a Competitive Weapon," *Harvard Business Review* (January–February 1982), 97–104.

7. G. Gonnella. "Making Expensive Decisions." *Information Center* 4:10 (October 1988), 32–35.

8. B. Ives and G.P. Learmonth. "The Information System As A Competitive Weapon," *Communications of the ACM* 27(12), (1984), 1193–1201.

9. H.R. Johnson and M.R. Vitale. "Creating Competitive Advantage with Interorganizational Information Systems," *MIS Quarterly* 12:2 (June 1988), 152–165.

10. P.G.W. Keen. "Value Analysis: Justifying Decision Support Systems," *MIS Quarterly* 5:1 (March 1981), 1–15.

11. K.D. Loch; H.H. Carr; and M.E. Warkentin. "Threats to Information System Security: Management's Perceptions Reflect Yesterday's Environment," *MIS Quarterly* 16:2 (June 1992), 173–186.

12. A.H. Mowbray. *Insurance: Its Theory and Practice in the United States* (1930), McGraw-Hill: New York.

13. J.D. Newton. "Developing and Implementing an EDP Disaster Contingency Plan for a Small National Bank." Unpublished Master's Thesis (1987), Auburn University, Alabama.

14. J.D. Newton and C.A. Snyder. "Risk Analysis for Computerized Information Systems," Proceedings Southern Management Association, Orlando, FL (November 1985).

15. J.T. Nosek. "Organization Design Strategies to Enhance Information Resource Management," *Information and Management* 16:2 (Feb 1989), 81–91.

16. M.E. Porter and V.E. Millar. "How Information Gives you Competitive Advantage," *Harvard Business Review* (July–August 1985), 149–160.

17. R.K. Rainer, Jr.; C.A. Snyder; and H.H. Carr. "Risk Analysis for Information Technology," *Journal of Management Information Systems* 8:1 (Summer 1991), 129–148.

18. J.A. Senn. "New Strategies for Gaining Competitive Advantage," *SIM SPECTRUM* 3(4), (1986), 1–6.

19. P. Shoval and L. Yaacov. "Computer Systems Selection: The Graphical Cost-Benefit Approach," *Information and Management* 15:3 (Oct. 1988), 163–172.

20. C.A. Snyder. "Information Technology Risk Management Methodologies," (1989), Unpublished research paper presented at the Fourteen Symposium on Operations Research (Extended abstract in Proceedings), Ulm, Germany.

21. P. Tate. "Risk! The Third Factor." *Datamation* (April 15, 1988), 58–64.

22. C.A. Wiseman. *Strategic Information Systems* (1988), Irwin: Homewood, IL.

Summary

In this chapter, we discussed a few business applications that employ telecommunications. As mentioned at the outset, we can not cover all business application types in a single chapter. We have provided some examples in the continuing case, the chapter itself, the end-of-chapter cases, and in The Real World windows rather than simply provide a "laundry list."

It is important that we note once again that managers must understand telecommunications requirements from a business perspective. The temptation to try to exploit a particular telecommunications technology must be resisted as it is business needs that must be the overriding factor.

Managers must evaluate the implications of buying one technology versus another from the business point of view. *What are the positive features and what are the constraints imposed by a choice? What will be the long-term impact of a choice to solve today's problems or seize a present opportunity?* If managers keep these principles in mind, the choices should become more rational and ones the organization can live with over time.

We have investigated how organizations use telecommunications to exert control over their dispersed operations—now that many are globally dispersed. Increasingly, managers are finding that telecommunications makes control of dispersed operations far more effective and efficient, and is often indispensable.

We have seen the application of telecommunications technology to both local (limited area) and global businesses that are very complex. Many firms have found that global networks can afford them control over far-flung operations, so they can operate as if dispersed operations are colocated with their operations. The Ford Motor Company example describes only a small part of their extensive use of telecommunications to perform business activities better. The Boeing Company example indicates that very complex projects can be accomplished on a global basis.

The capabilities that started as a service bureau evolved to timeshare and on to application service provider due to advances in connectivity and bandwidth. These capabilities have enabled businesses to take advantage of competitive resources not in their possession.

One of the business applications that nearly everyone is quite familiar with is the automated teller machine (ATM) used by banks worldwide. The use of ATMs has proliferated, and today most of them are networked for more utility. Advantages of the ATM accrue to both the banks and their customers.

Also discussed was the topic of electronic services from the home. Access to online services has become routine and a burgeoning business application area. Shopping networks and the emerging area of communications on the Internet show explosive growth.

The business applications of teleconferencing with emphasis on video, data, and email conferencing were covered. These applications have great impact on organizations, emphasizing more collaborative work. Collaborative work has become more important as firms employ teams both internally and externally.

Telecommuting has been a use of telecommunications for some time. We pointed out that there are many advantages to telecommuting, although managers should be aware that there are also some disadvantages. With concerns about the environment and effective use of time, telecommuting has had far more emphasis recently.

One business application that is associated with electronic commerce is electronic data interchange (EDI). Many firms have found that EDI has contributed to their businesses by helping eliminate paper, shortening cycle times, reducing floats, removing sources of errors (e.g., re-entry of data), and so on.

We also have covered some interesting military applications of telecommunications. Part of our rationale is that many of the applications initiated by the military later migrate to business as managers become aware of their potential to solve business problems.

Remember, however, that managers must keep the business objectives salient and not allow fascination with technology to unduly influence their decisions. The business impact and implications of a telecommunications choice have to be considered.

Key Terms

application service provider (ASP), *396*
automated teller machines (ATM), *397*
bandwidth brokerage, *416*
business process re-engineering (BPR), *408*
customer relationship management (CRM), *413*

data conferencing, *402*
dispersed operations, *394*
distance learning, *406*
electronic data interchange (EDI), *408*
email conferencing, *403*
float, *409*
global logistics, *395*
information warfare, *420*
mean time between failure (MTBF), *391*

online banking, *400*
online shopping, *399*
service bureau, *396*
telecommuting, *404*
teleconferencing, *401*
timesharing, *396*
videoconferencing, *401*
work at home, *404*

Recommended Readings

EDI World—A periodical about the uses of electronic data interchange.
Info World—An information systems publication that discusses both mainframe and microcomputer resources.
The technical section of *The Wall Street Journal* and *Business Week*—The issues appear several times a year and highlight current uses and advances in technology.

Discussion Questions

10.1. What are the implications for JL&S (or any business) of acquiring a facility in a different country?

10.2. Should banks use ATM services as a no-cost enticement for customers or as a charge for service?

10.3. Discuss the relative merits of a bank providing electronic access to your account.

10.4. If a firm chooses to implement EDI for competitive advantage, how can it assure the advantage will last?

10.5. Discuss how telecommunications enables management to achieve control of dispersed operations. Compare a business organization, the military, a government, a religious organization, and a political party. Are there any significant differences in the use of telecommunications for achieving management control?

Projects

10.1. Visit a Wal-Mart, Sears, Kmart, Neckermann, or other large chain store and determine their use of EDI:

    a. What standards do they use? Who are their major partners? Do they use a VAN or direct connection?

    b. How has the use of EDI contributed to the competitive advantage of the partners?

10.2. Visit any retail merchant and determine

    a. How credit card transactions are processed.

    b. What telecommunications technologies are involved in the total transaction processing process.

10.3. *a.* Determine the number of ATM installations in your community.

    b. Who are the network providers?

    c. What costs the bank most: ATM, check processing, or teller transactions? What costs the customer the most?

10.4. *a.* What online services are available in your community?

    b. Who are the Internet access providers in your community?

Chapter **Eleven**

How Do Legislation and Regulation Affect Telecommunications?

The case is intended to follow chronologically with the technology being used. At this point in the case, we must step back in time to the 1980s as we will be discussing events that took place in this era, the divestiture of the Bell Operating Companies from AT&T and other legal matters that strongly affected and continue to influence the field of telecommunications.

Additionally, the reader is reminded that the case is contrived, based on the personal knowledge of the authors. As in many factual cases, the case shows that personal relationships drive business deals. We do not advocate this form of decision making nor are we recommending any vendor. At this point in history, IBM was the dominant vendor in the computer industry and the major provider of systems to small businesses.

CONTINUING CASE—PART 11
A Time of Change for JEI

Michael had to contain his enthusiasm about his newfound understanding of how a business could be organized, with the help of a computer. It was not the computing power of the computer; it was the power to organize and explore the data and operate with remote sites that appealed to his business sense.

Michael had been quite successful over the four months since buying the IBM System 34. He had learned about the system and had taught Carlton how to use it to run the business. Michael had been careful not to interfere with Carlton, but then Michael had lots to keep him busy. During this time, he had created a new structure for his business, with JEI as the parent and JL&S as the operations division, as well as convincing 12 small businesses to let him provide their accounting needs on his computer. He made the sale for JL&S and let Carlton arrange for the phone line and modem leases and installation. Carlton really liked all this technology and tended to spend more time on it than the old core business.

Michael then began to consider the organization of JEI. The parent company owned and operated the computer but let JL&S provide contact with the public. Michael saw himself as the person to look to the strategy of the total organization and let Carlton tend to the operations of JL&S. Clients who needed computer support kept coming to JEI while JL&S continued to win lighting and security contracts.

A Change Was Coming

As Michael learned more about telecommunications, he came to appreciate the legal arena for this technology. Each time he added new lines or equipment, he was told that the charges for the service were set by the Colorado Public Utilities Commission. This seemed normal, as he knew that the state regulated many areas, like transportation and power. As he started to pay more attention to his possibilities for expansion, he realized he would most likely come into contact with more legal and regulatory requirements. One was the implication of expanding beyond the Colorado state boundaries. Should he do that, he would be involved in interstate commerce, at which time federal regulations and agencies would have their say.

Michael's first introduction to the impact of federal regulation had been through AT&T. He had always used them for long distance services, as they had that monopoly. He also knew that monopoly was at jeopardy, as there were stories in the news of helping U.S. telecommunications competitiveness by making some dramatic changes. Although he could not see how the U.S. government would be successful, he kept abreast of what was happening in the court case of the U.S. Justice Department versus American Telephone and Telegraph (AT&T) as the federal government sought to disassemble one of the world's largest corporations. AT&T had been accused of **antitrust** violations, again. With time, Michael noticed that AT&T was not fighting the same battle; this time, AT&T saw value in negotiating with the courts and gaining access to additional lines of business.

Through all of the news coverage, and as the Justice Department pursued its case with greater and greater zeal, Michael became concerned how the AT&T case would affect JEI. He had discussions with his Bell representative and felt that he would not see much difference in business operations if the case went against AT&T. It seemed that there might be some difference in how long-distance calls would be handled and little had been said about who could manufacture equipment, but this did not seem to make much difference to Michael. After all, what was important to him was the local telephone network and that would not change. For all he knew, he could continue to call on his friends at the local Bell Company for help and installation of equipment.

Later, Michael noted with some dismay the news that AT&T had agreed to what was being called a "consent decree." This was the second time AT&T and the Justice Department had tangled over antitrust, with AT&T agreeing to specific changes. In the latest case, AT&T consented to divest itself of the Bell System. This was to end the antitrust suits that had become serious during the Ford administration.

Michael read in 1982 that U.S. District Court Judge Harold Greene had decreed that AT&T must "divest" its local telephone companies. Since the effective date was not to be until January 1, 1984, Michael decided it wouldn't be a great deal of concern for him as he was too busy with his new computer ventures.

Michael had a call from Betty Ann Tavenner of AT&T, requesting an appointment to go over the current and anticipated changes in the way JL&S and JEI received telecommunications service. Further, she said that the reorganized company would be called American Bell. When Betty Ann visited Michael, she informed him that there was a great deal of turmoil as the personnel of the company found out whether they would be assigned to the **Bell Operating Company (BOC)** or to American Bell. Michael was told that the BOC would be his local service provider; however, American Bell would be only one choice for long-distance service. Betty Ann urged Michael to continue to use American Bell for long-distance service, and told him that no action would be required on his part unless he wished to choose an alternative long-distance carrier.

Michael was visited the next day by Reiner Stone of the Mountain Bell Company. This time he was informed that Mountain Bell would be his local exchange carrier (LEC), that is, his local telephone company, and that all of his billing would come from them. A big change would be which company was able to provide what service. By the time Reiner left

his office, Michael was confused about the impact of these changes on his business.

On April 13, 1983, Michael heard the announcement that the new parent or regional holding company of Mountain Bell was to be called US West. He wondered what a name like that really meant—there was no mention of the old Bell System, telephone, or even telecommunications in the new name. To complicate Michael's telecommunications picture even further came the announcement that despite his previous understanding that AT&T would keep long-distance, he would still be billed for long distance by Mountain Bell if he made toll calls within their area.

A few weeks later, Michael was informed that Judge Greene, not so affectionately referred to as "The Bell Buster," had refused to allow AT&T to use the name American Bell, so Michael would get new business cards from any representative from that organization with whom he had contact. Soon a new logo was announced and it struck Michael that it appeared remarkably like the "death star" used in a popular film of the time. He mused, "Perhaps it's fitting because it seems to be the death of a great company and a lot of good business relationships."

On November 21, 1983, however, divestiture of local companies officially began and Michael started to feel uneasy with the thought that the changes might impact his businesses. The press had a field day with the changes and the new terms as AT&T was reorganized and regional holding companies assumed control of the local service. Michael was somewhat confused to see that there were 22 Bell Operating Companies (BOCs) operating under seven regional holding companies, as he had always considered AT&T ("Ma Bell" or "The Phone Company") as a monolith.

January 1, 1984

Michael greeted the new year with his family as usual. The next day he returned to the office. That afternoon, he received a call from Carlton who said that when he called the telephone office for a new line and telephone, Harry Peterson told him that the line would be installed as usual but he would have to get his own telephone instrument. It had something to do with divestiture.

"It doesn't make sense, Dad. All I want to do is continue business as usual, but the people at the telephone company say the rules have changed.

They said they would still be able to lease some equipment, but we would have to purchase our old phones or go out and purchase new phones."

"What do you think all this means, Carlton?"

"I don't know, but what I do know is that I have received three phone calls today from people selling modems. They say theirs are just as good as the ones we lease from the telephone company and a lot cheaper. I know I am an electrical engineer, but they never taught us how to make a cost-versus-benefit analysis of telecommunications equipment. What is the meaning of figuring out return on investment, anyway?"

"I'll explain that later. Meanwhile, you might get a copy of an economic analysis book on capital investments. Let me call the telephone company and try to get things straight. I'll call you back later."

Michael spent the next hour on the phone with Harry at the telephone company. Harry explained that as of January 1, AT&T and the Bell System were separate companies and provided separate and noncompeting services. In the process Harry moved from working for Mountain Bell, one of the new 22 Bell Operating Companies (BOCs), to US West, one of the seven Regional Bell Operating Companies (RBOCs). The outcome of all of the information he received was that he, Michael, not the telephone company, was now responsible for making telecommunications decisions for JEI and JL&S. Where he used to make one call to Mountain Bell for local and long-distance telephone and telecommunications support, now he would have to work with several vendors and make the final choice himself. Occasionally, he could use the local telephone company as one of the vendors, but they were not allowed to manufacture equipment. His local service would still be provided by the local telephone company, Mountain Bell in this case, but he would have to choose a long-distance carrier. He could still have AT&T provide long-distance services, but he could also choose another carrier. Michael's stomach started to feel queasy as he realized that he would have to spend much more time on his telephone and telecommunications needs than before. He had been comfortable in relying on Harry at the telephone company; now he had to learn more technology than ever before. He now had more choices about more technology than he ever realized possible.

Michael found that, with divestiture, he would find a new concept of *local access and transport areas (LATA)* that would directly affect the operations of JL&S in different parts of Colorado and beyond. His AT&T contact told him the reason Colorado Springs was in a separate LATA from Denver had to do with the areas served by a 4ESS switch, which made it a "natural" division under the divestiture guidelines. (See Figure 11.1.) Of course, what it really meant was that now two carriers would be

FIGURE 11.1 **JL&S Long-Distance Calls Cross LATA Boundaries**

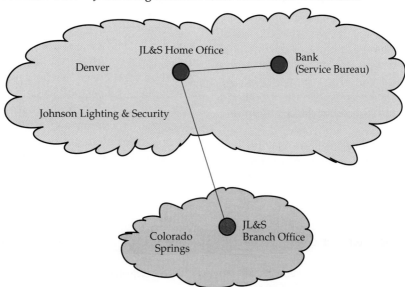

involved in telecommunications between Denver and Colorado—Mountain Bell and the *IXC (Inter-eXchange Carrier)* Michael chose to select.

Michael further learned that he would be dealing with two companies for any call that crossed LATA boundaries. He was told that in those instances, the Local Exchange Carrier (LEC), Mountain Bell in this case, would route the calls to the IXC point-of-presence (POP), where the call would be handed off for transmission to the IXC's POP in the destination LATA. There it would be handed off to the LEC for the "last mile." Michael was to have this point reinforced with the multiple bills that would now be coming to JL&S and JEI from the LEC and IXC.

Access Charges

After divestiture, the FCC mandated **access charges** so that every telephone customer would pay a tariff for having access to the public network. The access charges were designed to replace the subsidies to local service that had been paid from long-distance profits. Since competition in long distance was now allowed, prices were likely to be driven down towards costs. Thus, the regulators decided to shift the cost of subsidizing local service away from long-distance profits to all telephone customers. The access charges were to be pooled and allocated to all LECs for the local service subsidy.

Further confounding Michael's ability to grasp the changes were the telecommunications industry deregulation and the resulting confusing array of new products, services, and vendors. For example, Michael received more advertisements and product pitches about telecommunications than he had time to read and comprehend. He thought that Judge Greene had destroyed a good arrangement with the most reliable telephone company in the world and had made a sound and somewhat stable system very confusing and chaotic.

All of a sudden, Michael realized that he was staring at a Chinese wood block print on the wall (Figure 11.2) as he thought. A friend, Kuong Jih, had given him this print and said the characters were very important. While many such prints had the characters for good luck, long life, and happiness, this one had the characters for *crisis*. The special meaning here was that the Chinese create the word *crisis* out of the characters for two words, *danger* and *opportunity*. That was exactly what the Modified Final Judgment and Divestiture had presented

FIGURE 11.2   **The Chinese Characters for Crisis**

to him, the possibility of danger in the form of uncertainty *and* the opportunity of capitalizing on the changes.

Michael smiled again, as he realized that he had a symbol for his new venture, JEI. It was the Phoenix, the mythical bird that rises out of its own ashes. JEI would be great only if he could turn his back on the limitations of his past JL&S vision, take advantage of the danger and opportunity of a new direction, and develop a new vision and architecture that would not only build a greater business but also create a true competitive advantage. From this chaos in telecommunications could come opportunity. To allow his Phoenix to fly, he must develop objectives for JEI and prepare a strategy for flight.

Summary

As we continue to track the evolution of JL&S, we show how a business grows and the important influence that telecommunications can have. The clouds of change that were on the horizon for Michael and Carlton were not obvious for most small businesses. The impact of the changes has fundamentally altered the U.S. telecommunications picture. You are presently living with the continuously evolving results of these actions, whereas Michael was just becoming aware of them. The changes that JL&S and JEI experienced have not ceased, but continue as the formerly stable environment has become quite dynamic.

INTRODUCTION

In this chapter, we will address the laws that have caused major change in the telecommunications industry. One of the major events of the 1980s continues to be of interest today: the divestiture of the Bell Operating Companies from AT&T. It is important that you understand the history of the legal battle that led to the breakup of a very successful corporation, the one that had brought universal telephone service to the United States.

In the preface, we said, "This is a book about the use and management of telecommunication resources that support the business of the organization, for example, business telecommunications." Part of the management of the resource relates to the legal environment. *Legal* means the rules or laws under which we must operate and *environment* means that part outside of our organization over which we have minimum or no control but which controls us. Thus, we must be concerned with the actions and acts of the various federal and state legal and governing agencies.

This chapter is about management and control of the telecommunications industry. We discuss the major regulatory agencies, laws, and regulations that affect the industry and users. This discussion extends to the continuing deregulation and possible re-regulation within the industry. We restrict our discussion to those aspects of the regulatory environment that affect the business users of telecommunications. Finally, we address finding cheaper and better ways of providing telecommunications services that bypass the recognized providers.

These subjects are of vital concern as we live the history of regulation and deregulation in the form of the most significant change in the U.S. telecommunications industry, the breakup of AT&T and its divestiture of the Bell System. This topic begins with a brief discussion of the rationale for regulation of the telecommunications industry.

Caveat

The telecommunications industry has been dependent on standards and standardization from the very beginning. AT&T was such a significant player in the days prior to divestiture (to be explained in this chapter) that this single company often created the telecommunications standards. Whether AT&T was the standards-creating agency or AT&T followed the standards set by others, these standards were vital to the telecommunications industry for voice interconnectivity. We develop the subject of standards further in a later chapter.

REGULATION

Regulation Means to Control

Regulation should be an enabler, not an inhibitor!

If you are sitting in a room that is being heated or cooled automatically, you are in the midst of a control system: a system with **regulation.** The thermostat senses the ambient temperature and constantly compares it to the standard set by a person.

When the temperature falls below the standard, in the case of heating, the heater is activated to raise the temperature. With a cooled environment, the operation is reversed. In any case, the thermostat, a second-level feedback mechanism, uses information about the environment, compares it with a standard, creates an error signal (deviation in a positive or negative direction from the standard), and takes action to reduce the error signal to zero.

In the field of electrical engineering, we regulate a voltage so it will stay within predetermined limits. The power company (a regulated electrical utility) produces electrical power from generators to be nominally 110 volts at the wall or light socket, and regulates it to be within 108 and 112 volts. (See Figure 11.3.) As the voltage level drops below 105, the condition becomes a *brownout*, and a television picture may shrink unless it has its own voltage regulation circuit. In order to avoid the problems of brownout, the power company regulates its output through the use of feedback and the comparison of this feedback to a set standard. As with the thermostat, deviation from the standard produces an error signal that triggers an adjustment to return the output to within standard limits. Just as the power company self-regulates and controls the quality of its output, telecommunications

FIGURE 11.3   **Regulation through Feedback**

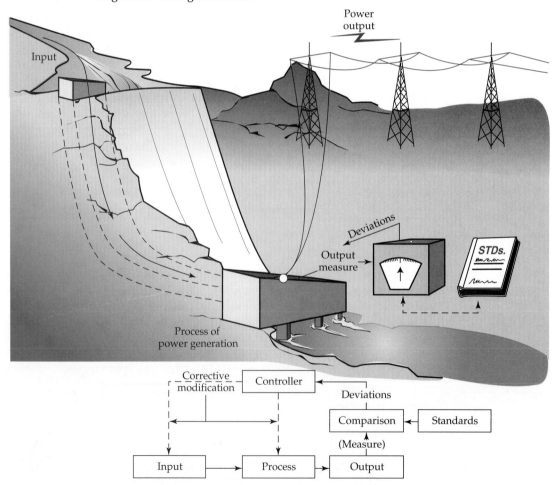

companies regulate and control the nature and quality of their products and services. (See Figure 11.3.)

At the time in history when AT&T was growing, the general public and the federal government were concerned about the wrongdoings of big business. Their apprehension was that big business, in general, and in time AT&T in particular, would have enough power to take any actions they wished, to the detriment of small businesses and consumer welfare throughout the country. The concerns here were *monopoly* and *antitrust*.[1] As we show in the history of AT&T and the telecommunications industry, the ideas of enforcing antitrust legislation have evolved to become more accommodating, allowing firms to continue to exist but with voluntary restructuring.

MONOPOLY

Monopoly is generally considered a bad practice. It can be achieved by superior performance or a proprietary product.

When a **monopoly** exists, it means that a person or organization has exclusive right to or control of a territory, product, or service. The term *monopoly* is viewed by many much like a four-letter word. If a company gains a monopoly, it means that there is no competition. In other words, there is a *single* seller and no close substitute. Monopoly is fair and legal when a company produces a product that truly has no equal, or keeps ahead of its competitors to the extent that users cannot find substitutes for the original product. This is termed a *complete monopoly*. Even in such a situation, we tend to condemn the circumstance because of the ability of the monopolist to (unfairly) set prices. We prefer to have choices, with prices established through competition. Monopoly is considered bad and illegal when the monopolist has created the situation through unfair tactics, such as buying up all of its competitors, bankrupting its competitors through unfair practices, or making illegal contributions to politicians to influence regulations.

There are such situations as **natural monopolies,** however, and they are considered appropriate and good under certain conditions. The basic considerations for a natural monopoly, or public utility, are (1) the capital expenditure to create the entity is large; (2) having redundant facilities, as would be the case in competition, would unduly drain the resources of all competitors (wasteful duplication); and (3) the service is required by many firms and individuals. This *has been* the usual case in local cable television systems and was the case in the early days as well as present days of telephone service. Monopolies were granted to local telephone companies, often AT&T subsidiaries, to avoid wasteful duplication while protecting the public interest through regulation. Thus, federal rulings and local decrees provided AT&T and other local telephone companies monopolies for telephone service. This lasted, though often contested and legally tested, until the mid 1960s.

There are two ways to handle natural monopolies: (1) nationalize them and have full government operation or (2) regulate them as privately owned industries. The

[1] You should be aware that all countries do not have the same view of competition, monopoly, and antitrust. The history of the United States of America has been to protect the small company from the ravages of the large company. Further, laws disallow collusion between companies, even when it appears to be in the common good, and keep a separation between the private sector and public (governments and financial institutions) organizations. Such appears not to be the case in other countries such as Japan. For example, there appears to be overt action to foster large companies as well as cooperation between large corporations, the financial industry, and the government in order to make Japanese industries more competitive on a global scale.

United States populace, through its government, chose to regulate rather than nationalize.

The rationale behind regulation of the telecommunications industry is to avoid possible abuse of uncontrolled monopolistic power and guarantee consumers benefits from economies of scale that the natural monopoly positions allow companies to achieve. This practice has a downside feature of stifling progress by protecting the status quo. With a regulated monopoly, there is a government-erected barrier to entry; thus, there is no competitive pressure to sustain the technical innovation that initiated the industry and led to the monopoly.

DEREGULATION

Deregulation returns the control of the industry to the market forces of competition, generally followed by changes in prices.

The intent of deregulating a portion of the U.S. telecommunications industry was to provide better, more economical service and new, more flexible products to telecommunications customers and to open the market to competitive forces. The sentiment came because some believed that AT&T seemed to be stifling the industry. Whether AT&T was overtly trying to keep the status quo in telecommunications or just keep their financial books in order, the end result was seen as a sluggish telecommunications industry during a time of rapid changes globally.

Technological Progress from an Accounting Viewpoint

Depreciation is an accounting consideration to account for value under tax laws. It severely impacts the ability of owners to replace aging equipment.

Whenever a large capital plant, that is, lots of money for lots of expensive equipment, is required, such as a telephone or cable television (CATV) system, the installer of the system must have time to recoup the investment and make a reasonable profit. For example, when either a local Bell Operating Company or an independent telephone operator installed a new switchboard or computer-based switch, the prices charged for telephone service had to reflect repayment for the new equipment. The Western Electric Company, the former manufacturing arm of AT&T, designed and manufactured equipment of high quality, usually designed to last 20 years. This concept tends to ignore the pace of technological change. For example, suppose a local telephone company installed a step-by-step switch in 1965 and expected it to last until it was fully depreciated and replaced in 1985. During this time, crossbar and solid state switching became the norm, and even they were soon replaced by digital switches. If the company was depreciating the older switches over a 20-year time frame, it would not be economical to replace them in the early 1970s for crossbar technology, the late 1970s for solid state switches, and mid-1980s for digital switches. While the accountants were happy with 20-year depreciation, due to the quality of the equipment and the tax structures, the customers wanted newer technology. (The telephone companies, being monopolies, are allowed a return on investment; they receive a higher return if they have a higher investment in equipment. Thus, there was a counterincentive to replace the older equipment.)

Telephone Service

AT&T provided total telephone service to much of the United States. This included local service in large cities (Atlanta or San Francisco) where installation was relatively easy, highly profitable long-distance service, and rural service (Carson County, Wyoming) where there may be one or fewer telephone customers every country mile. Having the total system, AT&T could **cross-subsidize** the rural service with revenue from long-distance and business services, where fees could be higher than "normal." This differential pricing for service was allowed by the agencies responsible for overseeing AT&T because it allowed the development of universal service[2] to portions of the populace not otherwise economically feasible.

Potential telecommunications competitors began dogging the heels of AT&T and the independent telephone operators. Such companies saw that there was high profit in portions of telephone service, due to the differential pricing for services, especially long-distance service. They petitioned to be allowed to compete in these areas. This was a good deal for the new entrants and the customers serviced in competition. The new entrants, however, will usually single out the highly profitable areas only and leave the low-profit areas for the telephone company. So not only was the business of AT&T being assaulted because it contained profitable areas, AT&T would potentially be left with only the low-profit business lines even though they had created the telecommunications industry as we know it today.

Part of the result of breaking apart AT&T has been to make each service self-reliant. That is, local service fees must pay for local service. There is no cross-subsidization of local service from long-distance service. As a result, long-distance rates have decreased since divestiture went into effect and the cost of local service has increased—in some cases of each as much as 35 percent.

The closest we get to cross-subsidization of local service by long-distance in the United States is the access fee collected by the local telephone company for connection to the long-distance network. This is a fixed monthly charge and is designed to make up part of the revenue lost by the local operators at divestiture. A second source of income for the local service providers is fees charged to long-distance providers for passing their charges to the local customers.

To maintain universal service, the Bell Operating Companies (BOCs) were required to subsidize residential customers by increased fees from business customers and access fees to long-distance services after their divestiture. This provided additional incentive for bypass by business customers.

This is not to say that AT&T was without fault. The question of the breakup of one of the world's largest companies is not simple. It is not simple for AT&T, the government, or the customers. What follows took a number of years to evolve, and the end is not in sight. The result of this evolution is a change of perception from one where technological and economic considerations were conducive to natural monopoly to the point where we have encouraged competition in all aspects of telecommunications.

With the separation of the Bell Operating Companies, AT&T was forced to change in order to survive in a (for the first time) competitive market. The process of change for AT&T proved to be a painful one, and the company made many false starts. Twelve years later, the company continued to change as it voluntarily divided into three separate companies **(trivestiture)** to better control the business and meet competition. The difficulty in adjustment is covered in a *Fortune* article noting that AT&T had a total earnings during the 12-year period of US $12 billion, while General Electric, a company of comparable size, had US $44.6 billion in earnings.

On January 1, 1984, the Bell System was separated—divested—from the AT&T Corporation. At that time, the Bell System became seven separate companies, all worth about US $40 billion and all listed on the NYSE, as was AT&T. These seven

[2] AT&T vice president Kingsbury was instrumental in the concept of *universal service*. He believed that AT&T should create a public telephone network that would access *all* parts and homes in the United States. Without such a goal, rural service would never have become a reality without government subsidy.

The Real World   11–1

NEW YORK—OCTOBER 25, 2000—AT&T today announced plans to create a family of four new companies, each operating under the "AT&T" brand, committed to uniform standards of quality and continuing to bundle each other's services through intercompany agreements.

Under the company's restructuring plan, which it expects to complete in 2002, each of its major units will become a publicly held company, trading as a common stock or a tracking stock. AT&T shareowners ultimately would own stock in four businesses, each a leader in its industry.

AT&T Wireless is one of the fastest-growing wireless companies in the United States. *AT&T Broadband* is the largest cable TV and broadband services company. *AT&T*

Business is the leading enterprise communications and networking company. And *AT&T Consumer* is the premiere consumer communications and marketing company.

Upon completion of the company's plan, AT&T Wireless and AT&T Broadband will be represented by independent, asset-based common stocks. AT&T Consumer will be represented by a tracking stock of AT&T. AT&T's principal unit will be AT&T Business. Each of the four companies will be individually accountable to customers, investors, employees, and other constituencies who will be able to evaluate their performance against comparable companies.

Source: http://www.att.com/press/item/0,1354,3420,00.html.

Bell Companies, called **Regional Bell Operating Companies (RBOCs),** had one or more Bell Operating Companies, or Baby Bells, under them, providing local service. Meanwhile, AT&T kept Western Electric, Bell Labs, long lines, the systems business, and their computer business. Since that time, several things have happened.

First, the RBOCs missed the value and creativity of Bell Labs, the organization that produces more inventions and patents than any other in the world, and created their own unit, called BellCore. Next, AT&T recognized that the company still had three distinct types of business and decided to voluntarily split into three companies: AT&T, Lucent, and NCR. Subsequently, Lucent has spun off Avaya. Finally, some of the RBOCs have seen fit to merge with each other or other companies, for example, Bell Atlantic took over NYNEX and has subsequently merged with GTE and become *Verizon;* SBC Communications, Inc., now owns Pacific Bell and Ameritech. US West has been acquired by Qwest. BellSouth and SBC have merged their cellular business in a firm called *Cingular.®*

Each of the RBOCs and AT&T saw the value of wireless capabilities and either created or acquired a major holding in that arena. In order to compete nationally and globally, the RBOCs created nonregulated divisions doing business primarily in foreign countries. Meanwhile, several RBOCs "absorbed" their Bell Operating Companies, some for name recognition; for example, BellSouth took over all operations of South Central Bell and Southern Bell and does business only as BellSouth.

Because in the United States, we have chosen to regulate the telecommunications industry, it is useful to examine a feature of this industry that results from regulation. This feature is the *tariff.*

TARIFF

A **tariff** is a list of regulated telecommunications services and rates to be charged.

A tariff is a list of regulated telecommunications services and rates to be charged. Carriers may not offer services without first filing an application for the new service. This application is called a **tariff.** The tariff describes the service in detail, gives the rationale for offering it, and lists the price and basis for charging customers. For example, a tariff for telecommunications services would be composed of charges as follows:

1. Charge for time (long-distance call, based on time and distance).

2. Flat rate for full-time use (leased line).

3. Monthly minimum (phone bill).

4. Amount of data sent (packet data transmission).

In the United States any change in a tariff must be done through the application to the affected regulatory body(s) and accompanied by public hearings. Thus, change may take a long time and may have to be justified to many constituencies.

The regulations affecting the telecommunications industry in the United States have been influenced or imposed by several major legislative acts, laws, decisions, or decrees, which are discussed below. Their importance is not just historical; they have shaped and continue to shape the basis on which business decisions are made.

BYPASS

Consider how cellular bypasses not only the local Telco but also the long-distance provider.

IXC
Interexchange carrier = long-distance provider.

LEC
Local exchange carrier = the local telephone service provider.

To use a system that goes around what would be considered normal telecommunications services is called **bypass.** To see how this might work, let's develop a scenario of greater and greater bypass. (See Figures 11.4 and 11.5.)

Initially, you are using the local Telco for all of your local services and have a designated **interexchange carrier (IXC)** for long-distance services. This means that all of your phone instruments connect via local loops to the CO switch. If you needed to expand your number of instruments, and thus lines, you would contract for more of each from the **local exchange carrier (LEC).** Suppose, though, that you purchased a PBX and decreased the number of lines from your facility to the CO switch. You have started bypass as you have substituted your own equipment for the LEC services.

With time, you began to have a fairly large amount of data transfer, using POTS and modems. As the transfer level rose, you leased a hardwired, switch-bypassed circuit from the LEC between two remote points in your organization for less noise and greater bandwidth. Because you were only bypassing the CO switch but did

FIGURE 11.4
Levels of Bypass

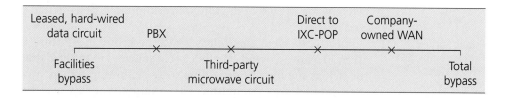

FIGURE 11.5
Technologies Used in Bypass

Telco facilities	Digital termination systems
Fiber optics facilities	Teleports
Microwave and satellite	Private T1s
Shared Tenant Services (STS)	Private WANs
Common carrier WANs and VANs	Cellular telephone
Private Communications Systems	
Alternate local loop providers (CATV)	

not reduce any LEC services, you incurred no reduced charges, but, in fact, increased your costs. In any case, you bypassed the CO switch for technical reasons.

Next, you incurred a significant amount of long-distance expense, and your IXC provider said they would reduce their charges if you would connect directly to their point-of-presence (POP) in the central office, circumventing the LEC switch. This is bypass of the LEC facility, though you would be using their local loop. Further, they would bill you direct. This form of bypass is for reduced cost.

The next step of this bypass, again for cost, would be to run directly to a POP of the IXC outside of the CO switch. You would have to install a circuit to the POP, from either a specific data path or from your PBX for internally switched circuits, but you have an opportunity to have a conditioned line, that is, wider-bandwidth, lower-noise channel. Again, the primary reason for bypass is cost.

As your intercompany data traffic rises, a third party approaches you to set up a microwave or satellite system between your facilities, bypassing both the LEC and the IXC. Because of the wide dispersion of your operations, you opt for the satellite system, installing VSAT[3] antennas at each facility and leasing transponder time. This gives you data communications, and voice communications once digitized, anywhere in the footprint of the satellite transponder. You might do this step for both cost and bandwidth reasons.

With success of the satellite system, you decide to expand that system to include all facility-to-facility voice and data communications. Now you use the LEC for local services only, passing all intercompany communications over your company network. The IXC is now used only for out-of-company long distance services. See Figure 11.4 for the levels of bypass and Figure 11.5 for the technologies used in bypass.

Legal Consideration of Bypass

Shortly after divestiture, the topic of bypass became of great importance to local Telcos. They feared a loss of the greater part of their revenue stream from their largest and most reliable customers. When companies had phone bills in excess of $40,000 per month, per division, they were interested in services that would reduce this expense. Articles in the trade journals voiced doom for the LECs as alternatives to their services became apparent.

In one study with which the authors are familiar, the cause for alarm was indeed warranted. Within one state's boundaries, the major telephone provider found that in excess of 55 percent of the firms that were surveyed in the mid-1980s already were using bypass of the LEC. An additional 8 percent had plans or were committed for bypass.

Public Service Commissions (PSCs) are the state regulatory agencies that agree to tariffs and assign franchises.

Not only were the Telcos concerned, but the **Public Service Commissions (PSCs)** were involved. The Telcos commented to the PSC that universal service was at risk as the bypass providers were skimming the cream of profits, leaving the low-profit service community to the Telcos. Not only was the cross-subsidy of long distance lost, but further revenue and profit were being drained by bypass. The Telcos told the PSCs that their very existence was at risk. Further, as revenues dropped, the ability to invest in new equipment and services dropped. The Telcos were installing very expensive switches and artificially stretched out depreciation because of the prescribed long lifetime of the assets. To be competitive, the Telco needed to depreciate old equipment much faster to modernize plant and

---

[3] Very small aperture terminal devices are antennas under 36 inches in diameter. Some overnight delivery companies are using them (12-inch size) on the top of trucks for constant communications via satellite.

equipment. In the meantime, many providers of bypass services were new in business, with questionable experience and low funding. They were also less regulated than the Telcos and could offer more incentives to potential customers than could regulated Telcos.

A specific, but not so obvious, form of bypass that was of great concern for LECs was the use of cellular telephone systems. It was possible for conversations to occur within or across cells or total cellular systems without any connection to or intervention by the CO switch, thus reducing the impact of the switch. For this reason, the FCC ensured that one of the two cellular licenses for any area went to the local Telco. In spite of this, the cellular provider has the ability to redefine local and long-distance service. For example, one cellular provider in Alabama provides connection to Columbus and Atlanta, Georgia, without going through an IXC and without the equivalent IXC charges. Meanwhile, another cellular provider has a local area that provides local calls to a distant city where the same calls would be toll calls when provided by the LEC.

JEI and Their Use of Bypass

You will remember that Michael leased an FX line from Denver to Colorado Springs. This was a cost consideration for his customers and a management consideration for Michael. He was not bypassing either LEC or their CO; he was providing a service that bypassed their need to make a long-distance call. So, the only advantage was that of expense. Today, he could have done the same with an 800 number. This later mode would be a pure variable cost to him for each phone where the FX line was a fixed cost.

Michael chose to not purchase a PBX and, instead of this form of bypass of the CO switch for additional lines, he stayed with LEC services. In this case, Centrex services had no effect on bypass considerations as they were an alternative LEC service.

When he contracted with Kelly Rainer to use his microwave system for communications to Fort Collins and Greeley, he was contracting directly for bypass services. Because he stayed within the LATA, he bypassed the "long-distance" (toll trunk) services of the LEC. On the occasion when his "phone" stopped working, Carlton would question where the problem was. The LEC pointed to the instrument as the culprit, and the instrument maker pointed to the LEC, all of which frustrated Carlton with service. Added to pressure from escalating local costs and the inability to understand the billing system was the slow rate of technological improvement. As people changed jobs after divestiture, many appeared to be inept. All of these factors led customers to consider bypass services.

REGULATIONS, DEREGULATION, AND DIVESTITURE

As we continue this chapter, we address the laws that have caused change in the telecommunications industry. One of the major events of the 1980s continues to be of importance today: the divestiture of the Bell Operating Companies from AT&T. It is important to understand the history of the legal battle that led to the breakup of a very successful corporation, the one that had brought universal telephone service to the United States. *While the legal environment described herein is peculiar to the United States, the implications of legislation, regulation, and the power of governance are applicable to all nations.*

THE MAJOR ACTS OF LAW

In the United States, Congress sets laws at the federal level, and state legislatures must operate within the overriding laws. States, however, set their own restrictions, as long as they do not run counter to the federal statutes.

Listed below are the major laws that affect the evolution of the U.S. telecommunications industry. They have a basis in history, in the *Sherman* and the *Clayton Acts*.[4] The Sherman (Antitrust) Act of 1890, the cornerstone of antitrust polity in the United States and the first and most basic antitrust law, resulted from a variety of social, economic, and political factors that came together at the end of the 1800s. Its primary tenets are that

(a) Every contract, combination in the form of trust or otherwise, or conspiracy, in restraint of trade or commerce among the several States, or with foreign nations, is hereby declared to be illegal . . . (b) Every person who shall monopolize or attempt to monopolize, or combine or conspire with other person or persons, to monopolize any part of trade or commerce among the several States, or with foreign nations, shall be deemed guilty.

The next major antitrust legislation, The Clayton Act of 1914, was a result, at least in part, of Congress's dissatisfaction with Sherman Act enforcement. When the U.S. government in the form of its Congress or Department of Justice believes an organization is conspiring or is acting to restrain trade, the power of these acts is brought forth. Sometimes, other laws are enacted to allow for a controlled form of monopoly, as was the case of the **Graham Act.**

Graham Act

This act, in 1921, recognized and legitimized AT&T's natural monopoly and the monopolies of independent Telcos in their region, and exempted the telecommunications industry from the provisions of the Sherman Antitrust Act. The U.S. Congress decided that the redundant services that would ensue from competition would not be logical or in the public interest. Thus, they were treated as *natural monopolies* and similar to the railroads. After all, the telegraph lines were constructed along the railroad rights-of-way. This rationale led to the **common carrier** service concept being applied to the telecommunications industry. Each of the common carriers serves a specified area under a franchise granted by the appropriate government body. The common carrier controls the system and must provide system facilities to the qualified public at a stated rate. The ferry boat is often cited as an example of a common carrier service. The operator of the ferry boat had to provide services at a standard fare to anyone of the public who had the fare and wished to use them. Today, common carriers in the telecommunications industry fall into two broad classes: the interexchange carriers and the local exchange carriers. More will be said about them later.

Common carriers are regulated.

Communications Act of 1934

Beginning in 1910, the Interstate Commerce Commission regulated wire communications. Congress created the **Federal Communications Commission (FCC),** by the **Communications Act of 1934.** As noted in the act, the agency was created

For the purpose of regulating interstate and foreign commerce in communication by wire and radio so as to make available, so far as possible, to all the people of the United States a rapid, efficient nationwide and worldwide wire and radio and communication service with adequate facilities at reasonable charges.

[4] David L. Kaserman and John W. Mayo, *Government and Business, The Economics of Antitrust and Regulation* (Fort Worth: The Dryden Press, 1995).

The FCC is composed of a board of governors appointed by the president of the United States. It and its technical staff have the power to regulate all interstate telecommunications facilities and services as well as international traffic within the United States. This commission has control of the radio and television broadcasting industries. When the transmission is broadcast in the public domain, as with radio, television, microwave, and satellite facilities, the FCC allocates and regulates the frequency spectrum and power transmitted. With circuits such as wire, coaxial, and optical fiber, the commission regulates types of service and rates through tariffs within their interstate or international domain. Where the latter circuit is within a state boundary, a local state agency (discussed later) has authority.

In the United States of America, tariffs within a state are handled by state agencies, called **Public Utility Commissions (PUCs)** or **Public Service Commissions (PSCs).**[5] When the services described in the tariff cross a state boundary, the FCC is involved. This separates the state and federal authorities. In many other countries, however, one agency does both jobs. This agency, the **PTT, or Postal, Telephone, and Telegraph,** office or administration, governs telecommunications services and pricing within the total country. Thus, in a country other than the United States, a telecommunications company often has to have the approval of the single PTT agency. In the United States, the company may have needed the approval of the FCC and each of the affected state PUCs. This could amount to 51 applications for tariff if the service is nationwide.

> U.S. companies wanting to provide telecommunications in countries outside of the United States generally have to have the approval of the country's PTT.

Suits and Consents

While AT&T had a granted monopoly, this status did not go uncontested. The first incident, before the creation of the FCC, was in 1912. The federal government became concerned with AT&T's pressure on independent operators. Out of this came agreements by AT&T as to its conduct. Of greater significance was the *Kingsbury Commitment,* by the vice president of AT&T, noting a commitment by AT&T to **universal service.** From this, AT&T was committed to quality, reasonably priced communications service nationwide. This set the rationale for cross-subsidization of services that was used until divestiture.[6]

> **universal service**
> A vision that everyone in the United States should have equal access to telephone service.

AT&T Consent Decree: 1949–1956

A consent decree is akin to an out-of-court settlement; it is an agreement between the parties, the Department of Justice and AT&T in this case, in lieu of a court pronouncement. The **AT&T Consent Decree** of 1956 limited Bell System companies to the telephone business. It further limited the activities of Western Electric to the manufacture of equipment exclusively for the Bell System companies. Finally, it kept AT&T and Bell systems out of data-processing activities. While this would seem unacceptable today, it would have been difficult to predict the future of computing

---

[5] Some states use the title Public Service Commission (PSC) instead of Public Utilities Commission (PUC). In some states, the commission members are elected; in other states they are appointed to office. Further, some states combine the industries over which the commissions have power.

[6] As noted earlier, the original cross-subsidization was the application of higher-than-warranted charges for long-distance services as well as services to the business community. The extra income was used to support installation and services to the nonprofitable rural communities. With divestiture, the revenue to the LEC from long distance was stopped. However, a substitute revenue has been allowed in the form of connect charges by the LEC to the long-distance network (network access charge). The consumer, of course, pays these charges. These revenues go into an administered pool to provide continued support to universal service. The disproportional charges to business continue.

equipment in the early 1950s. Looking backward, as AT&T did at the time of divestiture, a different course of action might have been even more profitable for AT&T.

Carterfone Decision of 1968

This court case came about as the only way to allow non–Western Electric equipment to be connected to the Bell network. Up to this point in time, you had to lease equipment from the Bell System or, as in the case of modems, use a nonhardwired acoustic coupler to make the connection. AT&T's rationale for this was that to allow "foreign" equipment would degrade and place the network at risk.

Additionally, since all equipment was leased from the local telephone company, the tariff for local service included type of service and quantity of connected devices. The telephone company, in some instances, tested local circuits during off hours to detect the presence of nonleased and foreign equipment, that is, extra telephones. Thus, if you had a second telephone instrument or a business telephone, you paid a greater fee.

The outcome of this decision was the attachment of nontelephone company devices to the telephone network. However, in the early days of this decision, AT&T had the right to inspect the equipment and require that it be modified as required to match their specifications.

The FCC decision allowed the Carter Electronics Corporation of Dallas, Texas, to connect its mobile radio system to the Bell network after a long battle with AT&T. The FCC concluded that the interconnecting device would not adversely affect the network. This decision opened the door for a major new industry: the interconnect industry.

The telephone network interface box defines the point of service responsibility.

The present status of this decision is that the local telephone company has authority only to the outside of the premise wall. The customer, therefore, may connect any type and quantity of devices to their side of the *telephone network interface box*[7] installed by the telephone company. If the premise devices fail, however, the customer can choose to have them repaired or replaced at their own expense, or the telephone company will perform the repair, primarily to the premise wiring, at a fee.

In the Home

The telephone made by Western Electric for the Bell System prior to 1984 was engineered and manufactured to be rugged and reliable, though, in the early days, not decorative.

Do you have a Princess® telephone?

The effect of the **Carterfone Decision** is obvious in the business environment. It means that the telecommunications manager may connect any telecommunications device to the premise side of the interface box. With divestiture also came the requirement that this same telecommunications manager make all the decisions as to what equipment he or she needed on the premises.

Much the same environment exists in the home. The homeowner may connect a variety of devices to the premise side of the interface box without consultation or consent of the local Telco. This is how one is able to buy three extension telephones at the drug or discount store for as little as $11 each and plug them into the home (premise) wiring, along with a $29 telephone answering machine. There is also the option of adding additional wiring to a home, extending the telecommunications

---

[7] Connecting things to the POTS is now rampant. Most homes have several telephones and an answering machine. One of the authors has developed a device to be attached to a telephone. Though the Carterfone Decision allows such a connection, the device being developed must be certified by Underwriters Laboratory® for safety and the FCC for EMI radiation. In addition, there is a circuit inside that isolates it and ensures that the device will not adversely affect the network.

capabilities of the premises. An additional item for which the customer now has responsibility is the wiring itself. Let us explain by example.

After a thunderstorm the telephones in the home of one of the authors did not work. The Telco repair number and the computer's expert system guided us through a series of questions. At the end, an order was created to dispatch a repairman to the house.

The repairman came to the house, unplugged the house telephone wiring from the telephone network interface box, and plugged in a working telephone, at which time he received a dial tone. This indicated that the fault was on the residence side of the box, that is, repair was the customer's responsibility. Since the fault had not been isolated, the choices available were to pay the Telco to fix the problem or find someone else to do the job. The local Telco, South Central Bell (now BellSouth), was called and did the job, finding a shorted wire under the house, for a cost of $200. After the repairman left, it was a simple task to call the Telco and add premise wiring insurance to the telephone bill for $1.50 per month.

The purpose here is not to complain about the Telco's charges for repair. The point is that now the homeowner, like the business owner, must make all decisions about telecommunications services. This is a result of divestiture.

MCI Decision

MCI has gone from an upstart company, believing it could compete with AT&T, to one of the Big Three long-distance providers.

In the late 1960s, Microwave Communications Incorporated (later called MCI), petitioned the FCC to be allowed to compete in the long-distance market or, more specifically, in exclusive full-time intercity telecommunications links to organizations. This was not a new service, as AT&T and the Bell System had such services for many years. What MCI wanted was not only to provide the service, point-to-point, but also to be allowed to connect their service to the AT&T and Bell System public-switched network. They realized that communications between specific cities were highly concentrated and highly profitable, and, thus, professed that competition was in the public interest.

The result of this decision required phone companies to interconnect MCI and other long-distance carriers to local customers. Such companies tended to offer services to only high-density routes such as large city routes. Until 1968, AT&T was the exclusive long-distance provider. In the late 1980s, there were 450 such providers. In many cases, the providers[8] leased the circuits from AT&T and resold the service to customers at a lower price than offered by AT&T.

You should quickly realize the value and profit potential of such long-distance service. If it were not so, why would Sprint®, MCI WorldCom®, and AT&T advertise so extensively on television? Long-distance service is a big business, and it all started with the **MCI Decision.** Even though AT&T continues to control a significant portion of this service, the competition is fierce and increasing.

---

[8] Hotels are a special case of providing long-distance services. Generally, when you make a call from a hotel/motel room, you pay a premium for using their equipment. You will pay a premium even when you use a credit card. You have two choices to avoid this premium: (1) go out of your room to a pay phone, though this may be operated also by the hotel/motel, or (2) establish service with AT&T to use their (800) service. Generally, hotels/motels do not attach a fee to (800) services. AT&T will create an account by which you call them via an (800) number and then are attached to their IXC network. A unique feature of this service, other than the ability to avoid local fees, is that the IXC charge is fixed by minutes of the call, regardless of the distance called, as is usual. In many cases, this will actually save money in IXC charges in addition to local fees.

Computer Inquiry I (CI-I)

Regulated companies and industries have certain privileges, but also have constraints. Regulated monopolies enjoy protection but often wish to extend their protection into unregulated portions of business. Conversely, regulation agencies often believe their jurisdiction should include what are now unregulated portions of business. Such was the case in 1971 when the FCC considered whether the data-processing industry would come under their auspices. The outcome of this inquiry (CI-I) was that the telecommunications industry would remain regulated, but the data-processing industry would not. This would have a significant impact on AT&T's willingness to accept the consent decree. As a side note, it may well have been this decision that spurred the rapid development of the computer industry.

Open Skies Policy of 1971

The question is not "if" you can place a satellite in orbit, but "where" you can place it.

The first Atlantic telegraph cable was laid in 1866, providing the first real-time "data" telecommunications between the United States and Europe. In 1956, the Transatlantic cable was laid, providing voice telecommunications between the continents of North America and Europe. With the placing of the first military satellite transponder in orbit in 1958 and the first commercial transponder in geo-synchronous orbit in 1963, further national, transnational, and transcontinental telecommunications circuits were created. The question arose as to what extent these facilities and circuits should be regulated. In the **Open Skies Policy** of 1971, a ruling was made that anyone could enter the communications satellite business. Thus, if a person or firm has the money and there exists an opening in the particular part of the sky where you wish to place a transponder, any person or business can place a satellite[9] in orbit and use or rent its channels.

U.S. Department of Justice Antitrust Suit

The United States Department of Justice filed an antitrust suit against AT&T because of that company's domination of the local and long-distance telephone networks. The antitrust trial began in 1980, and for six months the DOJ put forth its case, contending that AT&T had violated the Sherman Act through a series of pricing and access strategies designed to destroy the incipient competition in long-distance services and equipment manufacturing. The Justice Department deemed that this domination constituted an *unfair monopoly* and believed this monopoly was having a detrimental effect on the U.S. telecommunications environment. Out of this suit and the **Computer Inquiry II (CI-II)** discussed below came the consent decree of 1982 between the U.S. Department of Justice and AT&T, called the **Modified Final Judgment** in which AT&T would reorganize by divesting the *Bell Operating Companies (BOC)*. The BOCs were permitted to engage in any economic activity they chose, except (1) interexchange (long-distance) service, (2) the provision of information services, and (3) the manufacture of telecommunications

---

[9] In the early 1990s, homes received television signals three ways: (1) air medium broadcast, using a home-mounted antenna; (2) CATV, using coaxial cable; and (3) satellite reception. The latter could be obtained two ways: (a) for about $2,500 to $5,000 you would have a 10+ foot steerable antenna installed and receive signals from over 13 satellite transponders; (2) for about $1,500, you could have a three-to-five-foot fixed disk installed that received signals from only one transponder. In the mid 1990s, Hughes Communications began providing services from a new satellite, using a $750+, 18-inch antenna and amplifier, with digital, compressed signals. The Open Skies Policy has changed the nature of competition in the television market.

products or customer premise equipment. The BOCs also were required to provide nondiscretionary access to the local exchange ("equal in type, quality, and price") to all interexchange carriers and information service providers. AT&T retained its manufacturing arm, Western Electric; its research facilities, Bell Labs; and its long-lines division, by which it competed with emerging companies to provide long-distance services. Judge Harold Greene presided over the breakup of the largest company in the United States and continued to direct telecommunications policy in the United States for a number of years. His decisions affected the ability of the BOCs to have a monopolistic market and to compete for other services.

Computer Inquiry II (CI-II) in 1981

This is one of the most important reviews of the telecommunications industry. The result specified

1. Computer companies could transmit data on an unregulated basis.

2. The Bell System was allowed to be in the data-processing (DP) market.

3. Customer premises equipment and enhanced services were deregulated.

4. Basic communications services would remain regulated.

5. No cross-subsidization of product lines was permitted.

6. Enhanced services, that is, where some processing of the information being transmitted or some value was added, were not regulated.

7. LEC customers had equal access to all long-distance companies (IXCs).

8. The BOCs would deal in basic services, which would be tariffed and regulated, and excluded from the transportation of information and the manufacture of equipment.

9. The *Modified Final Judgment of 1982* was produced.

How many phone books do you have in your community?

The fact that BOCs could not compete in the information business has led to increasingly vigorous efforts to overturn this provision. Meanwhile, the BOCs were restricted from moving the *Yellow Pages*® into an electronic form, inviting new entrants to appear. These efforts and resources had significance in the creation of the Telecommunications Act of 1996, to be discussed later.

MODIFIED FINAL JUDGMENT AND DIVESTITURE

The breakup of AT&T was effective on January 1, 1984. (Did George Orwell miss this one?) AT&T negotiated a settlement of the long-standing (since 1974) antitrust suit so that it could retain long-distance and manufacturing capabilities in exchange for divesting the operating companies and be released from the 1956 restriction on entering the consumer computer business. While the agreement on the surface was a corporation bending to industry and governmental pressure, behind the scenes at AT&T the executives were taking a truly realistic view of their future. It is reported that the decision to divest was the result of Charles Brown, CEO, and a few top executives spending five long, hard days in a smoke-filled room.

The breakup of AT&T was the most wrenching change to take place in the U.S. telecommunications industry. By all accounts, AT&T was the premier telephone company in the world, and the services provided were the best deployed anywhere. At the time of divestiture, AT&T was the largest corporation in the United States with over a million employees and earnings that would be greater than most countries' GNP. Naturally, many customers of the company were concerned with the divestiture and the potential impact on the availability and quality of services to their businesses. Of no small concern was the potential impact on the research arm of AT&T, Bell Laboratories. Bell Laboratories had gained the reputation as the world's best research organization, and its list of patents was and remains phenomenal. Many were worried that the changes to the Bell System would hinder the flow of inventions from this great institution to the point that the national competitiveness and defense might be jeopardized.

Divestiture separated 22 **Bell Operating Companies (BOCs),** known as the Bell System, from AT&T, and grouped them into seven **Regional Bell Operating (or Holding) Companies (RBOCs).** In other words, the Modified Final Judgment separated from AT&T the local public-switched voice networks. It affected the long-distance network to the extent that it allowed unrestricted competition. There were other phone companies (local network), such as GTE, Continental Telephone, United Telephone, and 1,375 other local exchange carriers/companies (LECs) providing local service. The RBOCs were:

- NYNEX Corporation

- BellSouth

- US West

- American Information Technology (Ameritech)

- Bell Atlantic

- Southwestern Bell

- Pacific Telesis (PACTEL)

Caveat: If you find the name of a company herein that no longer exists, such as South Central Bell, please realize that name changes in this evolving environment are the norm. We have tried to be current, but keeping up with name changes in the telecommunications industry is much like changing a tire on a moving vehicle.

Local Access and Transport Areas (LATA)

How many LATAs are there in your state?

At the time of divestiture, the physical United States was divided into areas of about equal geographic or population size, called **local access and transport areas (LATAs).** One hundred sixty-five (165) such areas were defined in the continental

The Real World 11–2

Eleven years after AT&T was forcibly split into pieces by the federal government, it is breaking up again—without a shove from anyone.

AT&T Corp. yesterday stunned the business world with a plan to divide itself into three independent, publicly traded companies, in effect jettisoning an ailing computer unit and a potent equipment business to focus on its communications mainstay.

Source: *The Wall Street Journal,* September 21, 1995.

Have you switched IXCs this year? Why?

United States, Alaska, Hawaii, and Puerto Rico. Service intra-LATA is provided by one or more LECs. Service across LATA boundaries must be carried by an IXC. Previously both services were provided by AT&T's Bell System. With the higher-priced long-distance and business services, the system could move money from profitable areas to less or nonprofitable areas, such as remote local service (farms) in order to provide universal service at a reasonable price. With divestiture came a separation of local and long-distance service and the prohibition of cross-subsidization. The only transfer of funds from IXC to LEC is through the network access charge[10] and payments from the IXC for LEC services.

Caveat: Our reference to local (LEC-provided) services and long-distance (IXC-provided) services refers to landline or wire-based service, that is, local loops connected to a CO switch and to the POP of an IXC. Meanwhile, a major form of bypass of this system is cellular telephone, which defines its own local calling area, often extending across LATA boundaries. In this case, the LEC is the local cellular provider. That company, not the wire-based LEC, provides the wireless local loop, at least part of the switching, and defines the local (toll-free) calling area. Cellular service is like measured service (also called *area calling service*) for wire-based systems; that is, you pay a fee for each minute of the call. Unlike the wire-based system, both the caller and the called pay for cellular connections. Both systems have discount periods and may have an amount of calling minutes included in the base fee, giving what is called "free time."

More Caveat: Just when you thought you were getting it all straightened out, the rules change. During late 1995, regulators changed the definition as to who can provide *local long distance.* This is a toll call within LATA. Until that time, all in-LATA calls were the purview of the various LECs who had franchises within the LATA. However, with the change of rules, AT&T, as the first IXC, was allowed to provide local long distance within LATA, in addition, of course, to cross-LATA long-distance service. *This is not the last change, in case you were wondering.*

Information Window   11–1

At the same time the U.S. Justice Department was conducting its antitrust suit against AT&T, it also was conducting an aggressive antitrust suit against the *International Business Machines Company (IBM)*. In dealing with the U.S. Justice Department, IBM developed and brought to bear the most formidable computer-based information ever seen in the judicial system. The system was so significant that the Justice Department had to ask IBM for a copy of their system in order to understand the information being presented. IBM honored the request and conducted a very aggressive court defense of itself and the data-processing field. Unlike AT&T, IBM was not found in violation of antitrust statutes, and the data-processing industry would continue to be immune from federal regulation.

[10] Every LEC customer pays the network access charge, running about $3.50 in the early 1990s. LEC customers may choose a specified IXC, resulting in automatic connection of that IXC when direct distance dialing (DDD) is chosen. Customers wishing to restrict their ability to incur IXC charges (not make long-distance calls) may choose to remove an IXC designation from their account. They can continue to receive long-distance calls and make collect and credit calls, just not use IXC-charged direct distance dialing without special considerations. That is to say, with designation, dialing a "1" makes the IXC connections; without designation the caller has to dial the IXC access number first. Access to AT&T from any phone with any IXC designation is possible by dialing 10288.

Information Window   11–2

Some of the problems associated with divestiture involved the division of assets of the old Bell System. The simplified rules were "sole or predominate use" of the assets. For example, if a particular telephone cable carried more than 51 percent of inter-LATA traffic, AT&T would have ownership of that cable. Even manholes were divided up based on the percent of owned cables going through them.

The human resources, or employees, of the firm were generally assigned based on their work. This meant that the vast majority would be staying at their old jobs even if this meant that they might change companies but stay in the same location; however, some people had to change both work and companies as well as physical location.

The engineers had an immense job of reviewing blueprints of thousands of facilities, along with the files and usage records, to determine disposition of assets. Some of this work began in the summer and fall of 1982. AT&T had formed a divestiture staff that issued divestiture implementation guidelines to detail what had to be done, but not how to do the job.

Within Mountain Bell, telephone engineers used yellow and pink felt-tip markers to designate ownership, with yellow for Mountain Bell and pink for AT&T. Later they used nearly a ton of plastic tape and stickers to mark offices that had both companies' assets.

Local Exchange Carriers (LECs)

The **LEC** is the local phone company. The LEC in place at the time of divestiture is referred to as the incumbent LEC (ILEC) and any arrivals are called competitive LECs (CLECs). These companies provide public-switched telephone service (the local network) within LATAs, but inter-LATA telephone traffic must be carried by long-distance carriers such as AT&T, MCI, and Sprint (called interexchange carriers [IXCs]). The LECs are responsible for the circuit from the premise (office or residence) wall (network interface box) to the wiring frame via the local loop. They also provide switching of the local network and connection to the long-distance network through the point-of-presence of the IXC. Even after divestitute, this was a protected market. Now there are several competitors for both the local loop and switching. Cable TV companies in some areas are being allowed to provide local loop to the residence, and cellular companies not only provide a wireless local loop, but also provide switching outside of the CO. So if your home or office call does not go through, you have to consider the following for repair:

- Instrument manufacturer.
- Local loop provider.
- IXC.
- Remote local loop.
- Interior wiring.
- Switching provider.
- Remote switching.
- Remote instrument manufacturer.

Local Exchange Competition

When the Bell System was divested from AT&T, there became a distinct separation between local and long-distance telephone service. Local service remained regulated and the more profitable long-distance service became unregulated and invited many

The Real World
Lawsuits Challenge Telecom Act

11–3

The U.S. Supreme Court last week heard the first of several arguments that could lead to huge dips and spikes in the relative fortunes of regional Bells, competitive carriers, cable companies, wireless providers, and the Internet itself.

The high court is reviewing 10 lawsuits grouped into three cases that challenge the Telecommunications Act of 1996, marking the culmination of litigation that has characterized the law until now. Carriers trying to compete with the regional Bells said the landmark law's formulas and the lax enforcement of its penalties have let the incumbents maintain a near monopoly on local service.

If a lawsuit focusing on the prices that the established carriers can charge their competitors for sharing infrastructure tips the regional Bells' way, "prices would go through the roof," said Charles Hunter, general counsel of the Association of Communications Enterprises. The regional Bells maintain that the cost of building their infrastructure should be considered when determining how much the competitors should pay when sharing the lines.

On October 2, the Supreme Court heard arguments in a separate case about the rights of telecommunications companies to attach their equipment to power companies' utility poles. Established telephone companies hope the justices will conclude that when cable providers offer high-speed Internet service, they should be regulated. The Bells said regulations have been burdensome to them, and are a key reason why cable providers have a 70 percent market share in bringing broadband to the home.

"If we were all operating under the same set of rules, the market would determine which among the competitors would win the hearts and minds of customers," said Lawrence Sarjeant, general counsel of the U.S. Telecom Association, which represents the large established carriers.

The Supreme Court will hear arguments on the pricing case this week. Arguments in a third case, focusing on whether federal courts can review regulations set by state regulators, are scheduled to be heard December 5.

THE SUPREMES TAKE ON TELECOM ACT

The U.S. Supreme Court is reviewing issues that could shape telecom policy for years to come. They include

1. **Formula used to calculate fees charged by incumbents to competitors known as Total Element Long Run Incremental Cost**
   Five cases consolidated: *Verizon Communications v. the Federal Communications Commission, WorldCom Inc. v. Verizon Communications, FCC v. Iowa Utilities Board, AT&T Corp. v. Iowa Utilities Board, General Communications Inc. v. Iowa Utilities Board*
   Scheduled: October 10
   Issue: Are FCC accounting rules fair, as applied to rates charged by incumbent telecom companies to would-be competitors?

2. **Utility pole attachments**
   Two cases consolidated: *FCC v. Gulf Power Co., National Cable and Telecommunications Association v. Gulf Power Co.*
   Heard: October 3; decision expected within four months
   Issue: Which tariffs should utility companies apply to telecom companies that use their poles for Internet and wireless services?

3. **Telecom Act jurisdiction**
   Two cases heard in tandem: *Mathias v. WorldCom Technologies Inc., Verizon Maryland Inc. v. Public Service Commission of Maryland, U.S. v. Public Service Commission of Maryland*
   Scheduled: December 5
   Issue: Who is the final authority in solving Telecom Act–related disputes: state public utility commissions or the FCC?

Source: Bill Scanlon, with contributions by Max Smetannikov, "Lawsuits Challenge Telecom Act," *Interactive Week*, October 11, 2001, http://techupdate.zdnet.com/techupdate/stories/main/0.14179,2817162,00.html.

competitors. The local providers, that is, the Bell Operating Companies, petitioned to be allowed into long distance. The response from the federal judge overseeing divestiture was that this could happen when other competitors entered the local market, providing greater competition locally as had happened in the long-distance market.[11]

[11] The Telecommunications Act of 1996 provides that ILECs may provide inter-LATA service when CLECs provide sufficient local service. As of 2002 two states have certified that this environment exists and the ILECs are allowed to provide inter-LATA long-distance service.

So, how does local competition happen? What would cause a company to want to compete with the **ILEC (incumbent local exchange carrier)?** Initially, this meant running wired local loops to homes and offices. Then the cable companies realized that they already passed these homes with coaxial cable and "all they had to do" was allocate bandwidth for telephony and they were in the local market. But what about companies such as AT&T? How would they get into the local market again? Running UTP is a very expensive alternative.

A primary way to become a **CLEC (competitive local exchange carrier)** is to do it wirelessly, for example, cellular telephone. While the tower and equipment for each cell cost $100K to $400K, they can be installed quickly and require no wires to the user premises. Thus, the user can receive local service wirelessly, and many cellular companies are including roaming into other service areas and free long distance.

THE TELECOMMUNICATIONS ACT OF 1996

The Telecommunications Act of 1996 will

- Allow Bell Operating Companies to offer long-distance service.
- Free long-distance carriers to offer local service.
- Permit cable companies to offer telecommunications services.
- Let telecommunications carriers provide video programming.
- Make online service providers restrict access to indecent material. (This has already been tested in court and overturned.)

In January of 1996, the U.S. Congress passed and the president signed into law the **Telecommunications Act of 1996.** This was the first major telecommunications action since the Communications Act of 1934 (47 U.S.C. §151). While there was great interest, and subsequently demand, for telecommunications services, the new law changed the rules (the playing field) to make possible more services than ever before, by more participants, in more ways, and with new technologies.

The potential for change made possible by the new telecommunications act is significant as it allows new services to be offered by new providers, providers previously denied entrance to specific parts of the industry. This creates not only enhanced offerings but turmoil. Consider the implications to the simple telephone bill that resulted from the divestiture of the Bell Operating Companies from AT&T. What was once a straightforward instrument, now seemingly took a CPA to interpret, or to translate as some would say.

With local telephone services provided by either the local exchange carrier, the cable company, a new cable or exchange carrier, or the long-distance carrier, or even the power utility, the potential for turmoil was great.

The Telecommunications Act of 1996, supposedly designed to deregulate the U.S. telecommunications industry, obviously has far-reaching implications. One analyst, ignoring the social implications, noted, "The bill will result in a complete redefinition of the industry as we know it today." The following U.S. legislation is specifically called out in the Telecommunications Act of 1996:

- Elementary & Secondary Education Act of 1965 (20 U.S.C. § 8801).

- Higher Education Act of 1965 (20 U.S.C. § 1141).

- Americans with Disabilities Act of 1990 (42 U.S.C. § 12102(2)(A) and 42 U.S.C. §12181(9)).

- Section 104, Nondiscrimination Principle, Section 1 (47 U.S.C. §151).

- Section 502, Obscene or Harassing Use of Telecommunications Facilities under the Communications Act of 1934.

- Cable Act Reform (47 U.S.C. §522(6)(B)).

- Cable Service Provided by Telephone Companies, Title VI (47 U.S.C. §521).

In addition, the **Telecommunications Act of 1996** allows (electric) utility companies to provide phone and cable service. Most electric utilities have an extensive telecommunications infrastructure installed to serve utility management and, by using their transmission towers, they have valuable rights-of-way.

NYNEX and Bell Atlantic lost little time in announcing their intended merger after passage of the Telecommunications Act of 1996.

Could an IXC bypass your LEC and provide long-distance service to your home? Could your CATV provider?

AT&T, in addition to local, long-distance, and wireless services, has entered the training delivery service. Via satellite, they will provide the delivery of one-to-many delivery points, using the 10" VSAT disk for one-way video and two-way audio.

- Provision of Telecommunications Services by a Cable Operator, Section 621(b) (47 U.S.C. §541(b)).
- Library Services and Construction Act (20 U.S.C. §335c).
- Eligible Telecommunications Carriers, Section 214 (47 U.S.C. §214).
- The Public Utility Holding Company Act of 1935 (15 U.S.C. §79).
- Securities Exchange Act of 1934 (15 U.S.C. §78a).
- Section 201, Broadcast Spectrum Flexibility (47 U.S.C. §335).
- Section 304, Competitive Availability of Navigation Devices (47 U.S.C. §548).

The Telecommunications Act of 1996 marked the beginning of a new era in deregulation for the U.S. telecommunications industry. This act promises to have widespread impact on the telecommunications infrastructure of the 21st century. The act basically ended several government rules that were designed to keep barriers between local and long-distance calling, wireless services, cable television, and radio and television broadcasting. This act is likely the harbinger of things to come in many other countries.

While it's still too early to assess the real impact of the first major U.S. telecommunications legislation since the Telecommunications Act of 1934, it is clear that it has had the short-term effect of precipitating a frenzy of mergers, restructuring, and deal making that promise to rearrange several industries. For example, telephone companies, CATV operators, information technology providers, film studios (content providers), broadcasters, and utility companies appear to be entering each other's businesses. There have been several so-called megadeals, some of which have fallen by the wayside and some of the original RBOCs have disappeared as a result of mergers. The Bell Atlantic bid for takeover of TCI (TeleCommunications, Inc.) fell through. AT&T, however, did take over McCaw Cellular Communications, Inc., in a US $11.5 billion deal. Many other deals have been initiated that may result in companies that will be able to offer a full line of electronic communications, ranging from the network to content provision. Many firms are beginning to market "bundles" of communications.

Many analysts believe that this legislation will drive prices down and, more importantly, will provide the incentive for the major players to build the broadband infrastructure that will constitute the "Information Superhighway." Some predictions are that the expansion of capabilities will bring on a new era of electronic commerce with buyers and sellers, producers and consumers, suppliers, and so forth, interacting on the "I-way."

Some analysts believe that long-distance resellers (firms that buy excess capacity from IXCs and resell it to consumers) will be a way for the BOCs to get into the long-distance business. Some BOCs already have the network in place within their territories to handle long distance without use of any other firm's services or facilities. Analysis showed one BOC that 90 percent of their long-distance traffic remained within their territory; thus, they simply had to get approval from the regional agencies, and they were in the long-distance business. This possibility existed because they had already installed the infrastructure necessary to handle the traffic.

In the aftermath of the act, AT&T moved aggressively to position itself to reenter the local service arena. AT&T also entered direct television broadcasting; positioned itself to take advantage of the McCaw Cellular purchase; offered unlimited Internet access for a low cost, with the offer free for its long-distance customers for one year,

The Real World   11–4

Cingular Wireless, a joint venture between SBC (NYSE: SBC) and BellSouth (NYSE: BLS), provides wireless voice and data service to more than 19 million customers in 38 states, the District of Columbia, and two U.S. territories. SBC and BellSouth share control of Cingular Wireless. Cingular operates in 42 of the top 50 markets in the United States. For more about Cingular Wireless, visit our website at http://www.cingular.com.

Based in Bellevue, Washington, VoiceStream Wireless Corp. is a major nationwide provider of communication services in the country and operates using the globally dominant GSM technology platform. VoiceStream and its affiliates own licenses to provide service to over 220 million customers. VoiceStream is a member of the North American GSM Alliance LLC, a group of U.S. and Canadian digital wireless PCS carriers. The GSM Alliance helps provide seamless GSM wireless communications for their customers in more than 5,500 U.S. and Canadian cities and towns as well as international service. VoiceStream has roaming agreements with more than 125 of the major operators worldwide providing service in 70 countries. It is now a part of Deutsche Telekom's T-mobile International as Deutsche Telekom bought VoiceStream. For more information, visit the website at http://www.voicestream.com.

Source: http://www.bellsouthcorp.com.

and so forth. (Use their (888) area code for IN-WATS and get a listing free on the Internet.) The goal was to be the premier deliverer of a whole range of services—local, long distance, wireless, entertainment—according to the AT&T chairman.

It was also clear that AT&T would not move into these arenas uncontested. Not only would there be competition from its former offspring, the BOCs, but the major long-distance carriers as well. The entire landscape of telecommunications was thrown into a state of flux with new developments taking place at a frantic pace—because of the Telecommunications Act of 1996.

Telecommunications Consolidation

After two decades of deregulation and accompanying consolidation, scores of media companies were, by 2002, reduced to six global conglomerates. The media companies were AOL Time Warner, News Corp., Sony, Viacom, International, and Disney. The local telecommunications companies were reduced to four majors: Qwest, BellSouth, SBC, and Verizon.

THE TELECOMMUNICATIONS INDUSTRY INFRASTRUCTURE

From the beginning of the telegraph until about the middle of the 1990s, the telecommunications industry consisted of distinct players working in specific technologies and providing services through separate and distinct networks. The phone companies provided voice services via the POTS network; CATV provided video entertainment via their private coaxial cable networks; long-distance providers had their private networks. With the evolution of the industry, the Telecommunications Act of 1996, and the opportunities in the global market, the industry changed. Companies saw value in providing services outside of their speciality, making singular networks work for all forms of transport, and even getting into content in addition to the transport itself. Meanwhile, countries that had been heavily regulated, like the United States and Brazil, either reduced regulations or privatized government-controlled businesses, while in other countries the government agencies made alliances with foreign private companies. While companies may be regulated in their home country, they are free to compete in other countries. Thus, the BOCs have major activities in other countries whereas they would have been restricted in the United States.

In anticipation of deregulation and the globalization of the market, the major players positioned themselves for what they believed the new market to be by forming alliances, merging, and making acquisitions. Some of these alliances were between public and private organizations. Many analysts believe that the provision of the network services and access was going to be priced near cost, so profits would be more akin to commodity margins. Thus, mergers and alliances make sense to give companies new markets, such as content as opposed to only transport, and higher profits. The downside of this is that a company can become stretched beyond its core competencies. Thus, you will find some companies that will concentrate on core competencies while others diversify into allied fields.

The implication of this for you, the reader, is that the environment is anything but dull. It is evolving and offers great opportunities for victory and defeat. As Michael notices, it is a time of crisis, and crisis in the Chinese view is a combination of opportunity and danger.

Copyright Legislation

Copyright, in the United States, is an attempt to maximize the intellectual resources available to all. People who create works—literature, art, software programs, music, and others—are given a limited right to keep people from making unauthorized copies of their work. This allows them to sell copies for a profit and provides a financial incentive to create more works.

In exchange for this, the public demands a number of concessions, primarily the following three:[12]

1. Fair use is the right to make unauthorized copies of works for certain protected purposes—mainly for academics, reporting, or criticism. When a student quotes a book in a high school paper, she is making a fair use, and can't be stopped by the copyright owner.

2. First sale is the right to sell a copy over and over again, once it is made, as long as you don't make any new copies. When you read a book, then sell it to a used book store to be bought and read by someone else, you're exercising your rights under first sale.

3. Limited time—copyrights are granted for a limited time. After that time expires, the work goes into the public domain—it can be copied and used by anyone, for any reason.

The Digital Millennium Copyright Act (DMCA)[13]

The DMCA, passed in 1998, prohibits the circumvention of copy protection and the distribution of devices that can be used to circumvent copyrights—even if their users don't do anything illegal once they've broken the security. Software makers, Hollywood, and the music industry make up the core proponents of the law.

[12] Source: http://www.anti-dmca.org/faq_local.html.
[13] Source: http://news.cnet.com/news/0-1003-200-7079519.html?tag=tp_pr.

Why Did Congress Pass the DMCA?[14]

The **World Intellectual Property Organization (WIPO)** drafted an international treaty that requires signatory nations to enforce particular rights in their own national laws. Some believed further U.S. legislation was necessary to implement U.S. adherence to the treaty. **The result was the DMCA.** It is sometimes referred to as the WIPO Treaty Implementing Legislation.

Please refer to http://www.educause.edu/issues/dmca.html for further information on this law.

The 1998 enactment of the **Digital Millennium Copyright Act (DMCA)** represents the most comprehensive reform of U.S. copyright law in a generation.[15] The DMCA seeks to update U.S. copyright law for the digital age in preparation for ratification of the WIPO treaties. Key among the topics included in the DMCA are provisions concerning the circumvention of copyright protection systems, fair use in a digital environment, and online service provider (OSP) liability (including details on safe harbors, damages, and "notice and takedown" practices). Resources on these and other topics are included below.

Internet Regulation

The European Cybercrime Treaty and the Hague Convention on Jurisdiction and Enforcement of Judgements in Civil and Commercial Cases are to be subject to ratification in 2002. The first allows criminal sanctions for computer hacking and the latter could force one country's laws to be applied to other countries, where the two countries are signatories.

Nontelecommunications Acts That Affect Telecommunications

We discuss later in this chapter the *Americans with Disabilities Act* of 1990. This legislation, which seems an extension of the Civil Rights Acts of the 1950s and 1960s, has a portion specifically aimed at the use of telecommunications for those with special needs. Thus, it is not only the technology legislation that affects the use of the capabilities.

The Real World 11–5
Cyber-rights Coalition Slams European Anti-hacking Treaty

A coalition of 28 international cyber-rights organizations have criticized a European draft treaty on cybercrime. The treaty could broaden European and U.S. law enforcement powers online by outlawing networks equity tools and requiring companies to keep extensive logs of the traffic on their systems, reports MSNBC.

The Council of Europe's Draft Cybercrime Treaty, authored by the 41-nation body in consultation with the U.S. Department of Justice, could be signed as early as December. The current draft of the treaty attempts to level the legal playing field throughout Europe by standardizing computer crime statutes and requiring signatories to cooperate with one another. The treaty would make it illegal to write or possess hacking software and even includes aiding and abetting rules that appear to make the publishing of software vulnerabilities or exploits illegal.

Source: Adam Turner, "Cyber-rights Coalition Slams European Anti-hacking Treaty," *Fairfax IT,* October 26, 2000, at http://it.mycareer.com.au/breaking/20001026/A8830-2000Oct26.html.

---

[14] Source: http://www.anti-dmca.org/faq_local.html.
[15] Source: http://www.educause.edu/issues/dmca.html.

The Real World   11–6

The treaty is called the Hague Convention on Jurisdiction and Foreign Judgments in Civil and Commercial Matters, and is being negotiated under the little-known Hague Conference on Private International Law. The treaty is complex and far reaching, but is effectively unknown to the general public.

The general framework for the convention is as follows:

1. Countries which sign the convention agree to follow a set of rules regarding jurisdiction for cross-border litigation. Nearly all civil and commercial litigation is included.

2. So long as these jurisdiction rules are followed, every country agrees to enforce nearly all of the member country judgments and injunctive orders, subject only to a narrow exception for judgments that are "manifestly incompatible with public policy," or to specific treaty exceptions, such as the one for certain antitrust claims.

3. A judgment in one country is enforced in all Hague convention member countries, even if the country has no connection to a particular dispute.

4. There are no requirements to harmonize national laws on any topic, except for jurisdiction rules, and, save the narrow Article 28(f) public policy exception, there are no restrictions on the types of national laws that are to be enforced.

5. All "business-to-business" choice of forum contracts are enforced under the convention. This is true even for non-negotiated mass-market contracts. Under the most recent drafts of the convention, many consumer transactions, such as the purchase of a work-related airline ticket from a website, the sale of software to a school, or the sale of a book to a library, are defined as business-to-business transactions, which means that vendors of goods or services or publishers can eliminate the right to sue or be sued in the country where a person lives, and often engage in extensive forum shopping for the rules most favorable to the seller or publisher.

6. There are currently 49 members of the Hague Conference, and it is growing. They include: Argentina, Australia, Austria, Belgium, Bulgaria, Canada, Chile, China, Croatia, Cyprus, Czech Republic, Denmark, Egypt, Estonia, Finland, Former Yugoslav Republic of Macedonia, France, Germany, Greece, Hungary, Ireland, Israel, Italy, Japan, Republic of Korea, Latvia, Luxembourg, Malta, Mexico, Monaco, Morocco, Netherlands, Norway, Peru, Poland, Portugal, Romania, Slovakia, Slovenia, Spain, Suriname, Sweden, Switzerland, Turkey, United Kingdom of Great Britain and Northern Ireland, United States of America, Uruguay, and Venezuela.

Source: http://www.cptech.org/ecom/jurisdiction/ whatyoushouldknow.html.

Transnational Data Flow

The transmission of data and information across national borders has become an important issue. It is important from a financial viewpoint because data, like material, have value, and countries want to tax them. In such a case, the PTT must define quantity and value. Other issues are the different views of security and how it is enforced, who has access to information, and the definition of privacy, among others. Thus, because countries view these issues differently, the movement of data across borders, or **transnational data flow,** is not as simple as leasing a satellite channel and placing ground stations.

The results of countries placing their regulations and restrictions is most likely the stifling of information flow and is counterproductive to effective operations. Actions such as the European Community effort, where national boundaries are transparent when it comes to goods movements, apply also to data, giving companies in these countries the ability to move data as freely as other resources.

Value-Added Carriers

VANs are common carriers who are not regulated.

Value-added carriers, also called **value-added networks (VANs),** provide public transmission services of an enhanced nature, often packet switching. Changes in the regulatory environment led to the development of new types of common

The Real World   11-7

Under the *European Union's General Data Protection Directive* approved on October 24, 1995 (to be acted upon by member countries), personal data are defined as data relating to the natural person such as an identification number or references to physical, physiological, mental, economic, cultural, or social factors. Before this directive, the various countries in the EU and, indeed, across all of Europe had vastly varying definitions of privacy and opinions of private protection versus the public good. For example, Sweden has a stronger view towards the public good where the other countries value the protection of the individual over the public.

Hong Kong has adopted a law closely modeled after the EU's Directive. The objective is to protect the individual's right to privacy with respect to personal data. This occurred in 1995 and the impact of the change of ownership of Hong Kong in 1997 is not known.

Privacy in the United States of America always has been an important issue, although laws similar to the EU Directive have not been enacted. Individuals do have rights as to use of data about them, but it is not unusual for one to find his/her name has been sold to a mail list without consent. More importantly, individuals have the right to see information (e.g., credit history) about themselves and paths exist for correction of incorrect data. This law and its rules are not as rigid as in the EU. As U.S. organizations deal with EU organizations, the EU laws will take precedence. For a U.S. organization to not abide by the stricter laws could have severe consequences.

Privacy is becoming an important issue as countries cooperate to work towards transnational data flow.

Companies outside the EU doing business with organizations within EU jurisdiction must abide by the EU privacy laws, or else.

carriers such as VAN carriers. Value-added carriers may lease their channels from other carriers but add value by providing additional services such as store-and-forward, protocol conversion, and mail boxes. When an organization begins considering the use of wide area telecommunications, it should first contact a VAN for consultation and services available.

Satellite Carriers

Companies such as RCA, Western Union, AT&T, American Satellite, and ITT have placed transponders in orbit and provide both analog and digital communications links. These capabilities allow across and between continental audio (voice), video (television), and data services.

International Carriers

Common carriers specializing in telecommunications services between countries, often across bodies of water, are called international carriers. Originally, this meant use of wire-based circuits. This was replaced by microwave and satellite channels and, most recently, with optic fiber–based channels.

International record carriers (IRCs) provide *gateway* facilities for transnational communications. They may provide simply channels, translation gateway services, or other value-added services, internationally, including expertise in multiple government regulations.

Standards-Making Bodies

These organizations, though often comprised of voluntary members, become an important contributor as the industry is now global. The standards that are met in a country are defeating to standards of other countries that don't match. In order to interoperate across national boundaries, countries, like companies, must cooperate, giving rise to the standards-making organizations.

National Customs

What is the best way to develop telecommunications in an undeveloped country—high regulation, low regulation, or government ownership?

The focus of this chapter has been the effect of governing bodies on the field of telecommunications. Other chapters will discuss the management issues surrounding telecommunications projects. These two environments take place within the cultural environments of the country in which the technology is used. Just as each country has different regulation standards and laws, each culture has customs as to interrelationships between people. These customs come into play when working with governmental personnel, in such cases as processing licenses and presenting tariffs. Some cultures will embrace technology and others will hold it at arm's length. For example, Japan relies heavily on face-to-face discussions, using the telephone to make appointments for such meetings, while managers in the United States will spend hours on the telephone for the same discussion. Also, technologically advanced countries can adapt to new technology faster than less developed countries can. This is not a criticism; it just means that it is important to be sensitive to both the culture of the country in which a capability is placed and the nature of the people who use such technology. For example, credit and telephone calling cards are as common as the use of currency in the United States, but countries in Asia will use currency-equivalent telephone cards that must be purchased with cash and used as cash for long distance. While this latter practice is also used in the United States, it is primarily for financial incentive reasons as opposed to cultural ones.

SPECIAL PEOPLE WITH SPECIAL NEEDS

Up to this point, all of our discussions have been about the technology, with no thought as to the ability of the operator. Let's stop for a moment and think about those parts of the technology with which the operator must interface. Additionally, let's ask ourselves whether this technology might, as in the case of Michael Johnson's grandson's friend, help with the special needs of our population.

To put this problem in perspective, it is estimated that approximately 17 percent of the U.S. population requires some kind of assistance in the use of facilities and capabilities that most people take for granted. Thus, when we use the term *millions*, we do not exaggerate! The accommodation technologies provide assistance in the three major categories of vision, hearing, and mobility.

Telecommunications versus Computer-Based Capabilities

The natural inclination at this point is to describe a great number of computer-based capabilities that aid those with special needs. An example is the enlargement of text on the monitor of a personal computer. Because this is a telecommunications text and not a computer text, we will leave computer-based capabilities to others and concentrate on only those capabilities that are related to the field of telecommunications.

Telecommunications Interface

Telephone

The hearing impaired need an interface that enables them to use the telephone. If you must rely on the telephone, you must be able to hear what it relates to you. A person who is partially deaf can be helped by an amplifier in the telephone or the use of an amplifier in a hearing aid. You will notice more public phones with built-in amplifiers, which help thousands of people who need slight amplification.

However, a totally deaf person cannot rely on this instrument since it offers no visual cues, and the person cannot detect the sounds. Thus, there must be a different mode of help, one that does not rely on sound. The answer comes in the form of technology with human help. The technology is the **TDD,** which means *telecommunications device for the deaf,* which is a machine that employs "graphic communications in the transmission of coded signals through a wire or radio communications system."[16] (See the telecommunications portion of the law in Case 11-5 of this chapter.) It is a small panel with a typewriter-like keyboard, display, and modem. With this small (purse-size) terminal, the user can replace a private or public telephone (plugs are available on public phones) and send typed messages to people with a similar device. (Software can emulate this on a microcomputer.) If either the sender or receiver requires this aid but doesn't have it, a capability exists, called *telecommunications relay services (TRS),* that can help. With this service, required of all long-distance providers by the ADA of 1990, a special operator intervenes who has the TDD and can relay the typed message to the hearing person and vice versa. This service is also available for visually impaired people who could not use a TDD.

Television

A telecommunications service that may require an aid for a user who is hearing impaired is television. Again, part of the information is relayed by sound. In this case, an earlier technology, *closed captioning,* provides the answer. All television sets of 13-inch size or greater now come with circuitry built in to display the text that accompanies many programs. (The text must be keyed in at the TV station, as no technology to date can do this automatically, which incurs an extra expense.) With this service, the hearing-impaired user can read what would normally be heard. For some programs, where dialog is occurring, such as in a daytime soap opera, the texts are color coded for the person speaking.

A second accommodation for television is for the visually impaired. As strange as it might seem for a blind or nearly blind person to watch a visual medium, our society relies extensively on this medium for news and entertainment. While much of the information of a television program can be gained by sound alone, some stations provide additional information about the visual source. The technology is called *Descriptive Video Services.* This service uses one channel of the stereo signal provided via the SAP (second audio program) encoding scheme to provide an audio description of the scene when the sound portion of the program is quiet. This allows the viewer to have more information than would usually be received visually.

Mobility

We described earlier the technology of telecommuting, an ability to work at a place other than a formalized office environment. Consider the possibilities of this technology for a person who has problems getting around, whether from missing or defective limbs, obesity, or lack of motor control. Now, these individuals can be accommodated in their home or remote office. This means travel is reduced, and they can be productive in a familiar environment. With the addition of a computer, an additional telephone line(s), and perhaps a fax machine, the mobility-impaired individual has a way to be part of the working world, without having to travel in it.

ADA of 1990 (S. 933) Excerpt—Sec. 102. Discrimination. (a) General Rule.—No covered entity shall discriminate against a qualified individual with a disability because of the disability of such individual in regard to job application procedures, the hiring, advancement, or discharge of employees, employee compensation, job training, and other terms, conditions, and privileges of employment.

---

[16] Americans with Disabilities Act of 1990, Title IV, Telecommunications, Public Law 101–336, July 26, 1990, Section 401, amending the Telecommunications Act of 1934 (enclosed in this chapter as Case 11-5).

THE AMERICANS WITH DISABILITIES ACT OF 1990

Public Law 100–336 was enacted to expand the rights of disabled individuals in their access to employment opportunities, services, telecommunications, public access, and transportation. As the U.S. Congress came to realize that over 40 million citizens require some form of accommodation, this act was passed. This law creates a legal environment to encourage employers and providers of public services to accommodate those with special needs. It illuminates the level of need and makes accommodation more clearly a social duty. Computer-based systems and telecommunications have much to offer. As we move to 200 to 500 channels of television in the home via hybrid-fiber coaxial channels and the use of computer-based navigators, we must realize that many thousands of viewers will need some extra consideration. The same technology that makes this entertainment and learning environment possible can make this accommodation available.

Case 11-1

History of Antitrust Law

Rama Ayyagari

At the turn of the century, after the Industrial Revolution, the United States was subject to new economic forces that required stricter regulation by the government. As it became feasible and economically beneficial to form larger and larger companies, the ideal competitive capitalist marketplace became threatened. The Sherman Act of 1890 sought to alleviate that threat by outlawing trusts: "Every contract, combination in the form of trust or otherwise, or conspiracy, in restraint of trade or commerce among the several States, or with foreign nations, is declared to be illegal." At first it was applied broadly, outlawing any trust, but later was interpreted to restrict only trusts that were anticompetitive.

The Sherman Act and the later Clayton Act (which sought to strengthen the Sherman Act) forbid tying. The case of tying is most often disputed by challenging whether two products are tied, or whether they are one product. This is pertinent to the Microsoft/DOJ case where Microsoft claims that Windows and Internet Explorer are really one product.

Since the Sherman Act, the courts have been working out what constitutes an unfair use of monopoly power. The courts today believe that monopolies in and of themselves are not harmful. However, they are in a unique position to indulge in certain anticompetitive practices.

By creating antitrust law, the government successfully curtailed the worst abuses of monopoly power. The applicability of 20th century law to the 21st century economic order is being tested by recent government action against the largest of the software giants, Microsoft Corporation. This paper examines the Microsoft antitrust case and its historical precedents. I will consider the legal and economic implications of monopoly power in the software industry and evaluate several possible resolutions to the Microsoft case. [1]

BACKGROUND

Investigations into Microsoft's (MS) behavior began in 1989, but it was not until October 1997 that the Department of Justice filed a lawsuit against Microsoft. The claim was that by tying the use of Windows 95 operating system to the use of Internet Explorer, MS was abusing its dominant position and trying to force Netscape out of business. Other allegations were that MS put pressure on PC makers to favor IE over Netscape. Judge Thomas Penfield Jackson finally ruled in June 2000 that Microsoft had indeed broken U.S. laws and that it should be split in two. [2]

THE ALLEGATIONS

In its current lawsuit against Microsoft, the U.S. Department of Justice (DOJ) and many states allege that Microsoft monopolized the market for PC operating systems and leveraged this monopoly power in markets for complementary goods such as the market for browsers. There are three main types of allegations of DOJ and the states against Microsoft:

1. Monopolization of the market for operating systems for PCs.

2. Anticompetitive bundling of Internet Explorer with the Windows operating systems.

3. Anticompetitive contractual arrangements with various vendors of related goods. [3]

In 1995, Microsoft signed a consent decree with the Department of Justice. This decree prohibited, among other things, Microsoft from making license agreements that were contingent upon the licensee entering other license agreements with Microsoft. This was meant to address Microsoft's practices of using its operating system's dominance to crack open other markets, and to forestall such practices in the future.

In October of 1997, responding in part to the complaints of Netscape and its lawyer Gary Reback, the Department of Justice announced that it was filing a petition to find Microsoft in contempt, alleging that it had violated that consent decree.

The Department of Justice claimed that Microsoft was forcing computer manufacturers to license their Internet Explorer Web browser as a condition of licensing the Windows operating system. Another part of the DOJ's petition was that the nondisclosure agreements Microsoft forced its partners to sign were overly broad and improperly discouraged these partners from bringing potential abuses to light.

Microsoft claimed that Internet Explorer was a crucial part of Windows, and thus not subject to the separate licensing stipulation of the decree.

Microsoft first became involved with the U.S. government in July of 1990, when the Federal Trade Commission began investigations of Microsoft after the company announced plans to jointly develop operating systems with IBM. When these plans dissolved, the FTC refocused their efforts towards Microsoft's general business and marketing tactics. Two years later, the four-member FTC team voted 2–2 on a proposal to instigate a legal injunction against the company. Six months later, the team reached another deadlock, thereby ending their interest and involvement in the legal issues concerning Microsoft's business practices.

DOUBLE ROYALTIES: AN ANTICOMPETITIVE PRICING TECHNIQUE

One provision of the 1994 consent decree signed by Microsoft and the Department of Justice limits Microsoft's licensing agreements with personal computer manufacturers. In the years preceding the decree, Microsoft had a practice of offering large discounts to PC manufacturers (up to a 40 percent price reduction) if the company would pay Microsoft a royalty for every computer the manufacturer sold, regardless of whether the machine had a Microsoft operating system installed or not. The alternative was to pay Microsoft "per processor" royalties with no discount.

"This is unfair for several reasons, the first being that consumers, in effect, pay Microsoft when they buy another product, and the second being that it would be uneconomical for an OEM to give up the 60 percent discount in favor of installing a less popular OS on some of its computers."

The conclusion of the decree is that Microsoft may only charge a computer manufacturer for each copy of an operating system installed and shipped on a PC. Furthermore, Microsoft's general contract liberties are restricted by the decree: the company is allowed to author contract terms that last at most one year.

APPLICATIONS DEVELOPMENT FOR RIVAL OPERATING SYSTEMS

The other major provision of the consent decree restricted Microsoft from obliging applications developers into contractual agreements that eliminated the possibility of developing applications for rival operating systems. Some claimed that Microsoft was using unfair tactics to leverage companies into producing applications only for Microsoft operating systems. If this were the case, by stating that Microsoft's "testing agreements with applications software developers would not preclude their working with other producers of operating systems, so long as confidential information was not revealed," would encourage competition.

The software industry possesses several features that suggest that software—especially operating system software—is a natural monopoly, meaning that the natural tendency of the market will be for a single firm to emerge as dominant. In particular, the software industry is characterized by increasing returns to scale and positive network externalities. Furthermore, Microsoft has developed monopoly power in the personal-computer operating system market and leveraged that power to develop large market share in desktop applications and PC server software.

IN DEFENSE OF MICROSOFT

On their Press Page Microsoft provides an extensive white paper in their own defense. The arguments presented there, and others put forth by Microsoft and their supporters, tend to fall under these broad divisions:

- Don't punish success.

- Microsoft is good for consumers.

- Standards are good for the industry.

- Government interference is bad.

DON'T PUNISH A CAPITALIST SUCCESS

It's inevitable that a successful company accused of monopolistic policies will throw up its hands and say "that's the whole point of business." Microsoft characterizes itself as a corporation that attained success through good products and shrewd tactics, whose future success is far from determined.

For Microsoft, these tactics include their relentless product shipping schedule, dogged if unspectacular technological improvement, brilliant marketing, and effective forging of corporate alliances. Microsoft has been a success for 18 years in a fiercely competitive and fast-moving field, a field in which "products are conceived, marketed, and buried in the span of a senator's term," as Gates said during the recent hearings. It is anticapitalistic and a waste of taxpayer money to hound a company as successful as Microsoft.

Hand-in-hand with this is Microsoft's claim that they're really not the giant that they're made out to be. In this industry, their line goes, you're only one or two mistakes away from complete disaster. They point to IBM's fall from dominance. As far as gross revenues, Microsoft is far behind (hardware) giants IBM and Hitachi, and not too far ahead of Sun and Oracle. Amazingly enough, they quote a statistic saying that Microsoft was responsible for only 13 percent of the operating system revenues in 1996. What this conveniently leaves out, of course, is that the majority of computer users sit down to an operating system made by Microsoft.

CONSUMER OUTLOOK

Microsoft is always quick to point out the rapid rate of improvement and cost in the computer industry, and in Microsoft products. The consumer reaps the benefits of constant competition and innovation. Every year, you can buy faster computers for less money, and software with more and more features. Microsoft contends that their practices are beneficial to consumers, who get a wide variety of products at ever-falling prices. A more concrete example can be seen in the so-called browser wars. Because of Microsoft and Netscape's fierce battle to attract more users to their respective World Wide Web browsers, consumers have been rewarded. The products were developed extremely rapidly, even for software, with new features adopted at every turn. At this time, both are available on almost every possible platform and offered free to anyone who cares to download them.

STANDARDS

There is probably no industry in which agreed-upon standards are as important as the computer industry. The proper interaction of software and hardware, software and other software, and computers with other computers via networks depends on many sets of standards and protocols. One crucial area is the ability of application programs to work with the operating system and use the computer effectively. While many of their competitors would hesitate to put it in so many words, Microsoft's dominance in the operating systems arena has created effective standards and furthered the development of application software.

There they detail the process of creation and support of the Win32 API, the application programming interface that allows other software to fully use the features that Windows provides. Although it is perhaps a disturbing fact, were the operating system market more rich in competitors than it is, software companies would have to spend more time ensuring that their products worked on all systems, and less creating new and better versions.

POSSIBLE SOLUTIONS

Following are the benefits and detriments of four different courses of action that the court could take with respect to Microsoft:

1. Avoid any sort of government intervention.

2. Rule that Microsoft must alter its selling conditions so that OEMs have the option to install Windows without Internet Explorer.

3. Split Microsoft into an operating system company and an applications company.

4. Make personal-computer operating systems into a regulated legal monopoly.

NO GOVERNMENT INTERVENTION

One possibility—the one that Microsoft supports—is for the court to rule that Microsoft may continue to operate as it has been, including Internet Explorer as an integral part of the Windows operating system.

This option has the advantage of letting the market regulate itself rather than substituting government short-sightedness or stupidity for competition. It gives consumers the benefits that come from tightly integrated software products, and it avoids the pitfall of discouraging successful innovation by penalizing a company that grew to become a market leader through good business sense, capable product development, and creative innovation.

This option has the disadvantage of allowing Microsoft to continue leveraging its dominance in the operating system market sector to drive out competition in other related market spaces through anticompetitive practices. Supporters of non-intervention must contend with the specter of a future Microsoft behemoth whose powerful reach has spread across nearly every personal-computing software market. Given the peculiar economics governing the software industry, taking no action to curtail Microsoft seems dangerously likely to lead to the destruction of any meaningful competition in PC software.

SPLIT MICROSOFT'S OPERATING SYSTEMS BUSINESS FROM ITS DESKTOP APPLICATIONS BUSINESS

In the case of AT&T in the late 1970s, the federal courts decided that allowing one company to deal both in long-distance telephone service and in the natural monopoly of local telephone service provided too great an opportunity for anticompetitive practices. The courts split AT&T up into a long-distance carrier and seven regional local telephone service companies. A similar course of action is possible in the Microsoft case: Microsoft could be split into two separate businesses, one of which creates operating systems and the other of which creates applications programs.

This option has the advantage of eliminating Microsoft's opportunity and incentive to use anticompetitive practices to use its monopoly in operating systems to gain market share in application markets. Microsoft formerly claimed to have an organizational "Chinese wall" in place that prevented Microsoft applications developers from getting early access to changes being made to the Windows operating system, but now everyone, including Microsoft, admits that no such firewall exists. Splitting Microsoft into two separate companies would effectively create such a firewall.

This option would have the disadvantage of doing away with the operational efficiency benefits that Microsoft is able to glean from being vertically integrated, benefits that are passed on to the consumer in the form of low prices and tightly integrated software products that work together well. Another disadvantage of splitting Microsoft is arguably that it would be unfairly punishing a successful company whose main "fault" has been that it makes better software and markets it more shrewdly than its competitors. This remedy might appear excessive given the nature of the offense.

REGULATE OPERATING SYSTEMS AS A NATURAL MONOPOLY

In *MCI Communications Corp. v. American Telephone and Telegraph,* the federal courts ruled that local telephone networks constituted an "essential facility" to which competitors must be allowed access even if no anticompetitive practices were involved in acquiring the facility. In the AT&T case, the government recognized that telecommunications networks constituted a natural monopoly and decided to grant an official monopoly on the operation of such networks, introducing extensive regulation on the business practices allowed to telecommunications companies operating as common carriers.

The government could take similar action in the Microsoft case, identifying personal-computer operating systems as an essential facility for developing application software and regulating access to that facility (e.g., access to the code base, knowledge of upcoming OS enhancements). The fact that operating systems, like telecommunications networks, can be considered a natural monopoly is an argument in favor of government regulation of the OS market. Regulation is a frequently adopted policy in the case of natural monopolies. Public utilities such as electric power are one example of this.

This option would have the advantage of severely reducing the ability of Microsoft to gain an unfair advantage in software application markets simply because of its control of the operating system market. As the AT&T case proves, breaking up a large, successful company and regulating one part of its operations as a natural monopoly does not necessarily operate as a grave impediment to continued innovation in that field.

This option is not without its disadvantages, however. For one thing, valuable synergies between the operating system and applications that are possible because of Microsoft's vertical integration would be eliminated. Furthermore, the rapidly changing nature of the personal computer market means that the division between operating systems and applications, which, as the Microsoft case illustrates, is already blurred, is likely to become even more unclear in the future. Effective regulation of such a complicated and evolving industry by a technologically incompetent government is unlikely to produce results that are beneficial to consumers in the long run.

In addition, the lack of technical knowledge among policy makers and people in the legal system is a contributing factor to the confusion and controversy surrounding the Microsoft antitrust case.

REFERENCES

1. http://cs-education.stanford.edu.

2. http://news6.thdo.bbc.co.uk/hi/English/static/in_depth/business/2000/ Microsoft/court.stm.

3. http://www.stern.nyu.edu/networks/ms/old.html.

Case 11-2

Microsoft, Feds Reach a Deal

Joe Wilcox,
Staff Writer, CNET News.com
November 2, 2001, 12:00 PM PT

WASHINGTON—Microsoft and the Justice Department on Friday settled their acrimonious antitrust battle, an agreement that many called a victory for Microsoft and that could run into resistance from state attorneys general.

The proposed deal would impose relatively mild restrictions on the software maker compared with earlier rulings in the three-year-old case, focusing largely on tweaking Microsoft's competitive behavior.

Among other provisions, the company promised to refrain from contracts and related activities that compel other companies to do its bidding. The Windows operating system, at the heart of a court ruling that branded Microsoft a monopolist, would emerge largely unchanged, and Windows XP—once a focal point of further proceedings—will be free of any significant restrictions.

The settlement with the federal government, however, is not the final word in the three-year-old case. The 18 states that are part of the lawsuit have until Tuesday to respond to Friday's proposal, which will then be reviewed by U.S. District Judge Colleen Kollar-Kotelly.

If approved, some analysts said the agreement could greatly benefit computer manufacturers, which would have the freedom to substitute non-Microsoft applications on Windows, including Web browsers, e-mail clients, media players and instant-messaging applications.

Microsoft Chairman Bill Gates described the agreement as "fair" and necessary, despite the restrictions on his company.

"While the settlement goes further than we might have wanted, we believe that settling this case now is the right thing to do to help the industry and the economy to move forward," Gates said. "This settlement will help strengthen our economy during a difficult time and ensure that our industry can continue delivering innovation."

Gates added: "We recognize that the success of our products has created concerns. This settlement addresses those concerns in a fair ... manner, enabling Microsoft to continue innovating and pushing technology forward."

During a Friday-morning news conference, Attorney General John Ashcroft called the proposed settlement "strong and historic" and said that it would end "Microsoft's unlawful conduct."

Ashcroft said that a competitive software industry is vital to the U.S. economy and that effective antitrust enforcement is crucial to preserving competition in the high-tech arena.

"With the proposed settlement being announced today, the Department of Justice has fully and completely addressed the anticompetitive conduct outlined by the Court of Appeals against Microsoft," he said.

One of the settlement's enforcement mechanisms would be a technology-oversight team installed at Microsoft with access to Windows source code, the Justice Department revealed during the press conference.

WHAT WILL THE STATES DO?

One complicating factor is that the 18 states that are co-plaintiffs in the landmark case are not yet onboard. The judge gave them until Tuesday to decide whether they would back the agreement.

Tom Miller, Iowa attorney general and one of the leaders of the state coalition, emphasized that he and his peers had "taken an active role" in the negotiation and mediation process ordered by Kollar-Kotelly.

"While there have been some promising developments in the mediation over the past few days," he said, "the states have not joined today in the settlement agreement reached between the Department of Justice and Microsoft. As elected law enforcement officials, we believe that it is imperative that we fully assess the specific language of the agreement."

Friday's agreement, which is less onerous than the final proposal submitted during last year's failed settlement discussions, has some legal experts and high-tech trade organizations crying foul. The settlement, they say, lacks the bite warranted by an appeals court ruling in June that upheld antitrust claims against Microsoft, most notably that it illegally maintained a monopoly in Intel-based operating systems.

The new proposal puts forward "a very mild remedy," said Emmett Stanton, an antitrust lawyer with Fenwick & West in Palo Alto, California. "What of Microsoft's monopoly maintenance conduct is actually being remedied? If they're not opening up the APIs, (and if) the tie-in agreements are not in place, what's going to be different? It doesn't sound like Microsoft is giving up very much."

Many of the provisions of the settlement reflect changes already made by Microsoft.

Besides the provision regarding competing applications, the proposal submitted Friday requires that Microsoft disclose server protocols to ensure that it cannot make Windows desktop software work better with its server software than with that of competitors.

In addition, the company agreed not to retaliate against PC manufacturers or software developers for supporting some kinds of competing products. To help enforce this provision, Microsoft agreed to license Windows to computer makers uniformly, rather than offer better pricing only to some, for a period of five years.

Microsoft also is prohibited from engaging in exclusive contracts that would prohibit software developers or PC makers from using competing products.

The proposed settlement would be in effect for five years, with the possibility of a two-year extension.

"Each of these things is capable of being evaded, which Microsoft has successfully done in the past," said Bob Lande, an antitrust professor with University of Baltimore School of Law. "I don't have any confidence that these provisions are going to be effective."

Lande criticized the agreement for not offering enough means of enforcement and for failing to ensure that there are no shenanigans.

"So you're going to let (PC makers) take off the Microsoft media player and put in another media player if they want?" he asked. "But what if every five seconds a notice pops up and says, 'Are you sure you wouldn't like the Microsoft media player?'"

Jonathan Jacobson, an antitrust lawyer with Akin, Gump, Strauss, Hauer & Feld in New York, described the settlement as "pretty odd."

"It appears to do nothing more than what is utterly obvious from the Court of Appeals decision," he said. "It seems that what's missing here is one of the basic principles of antitrust remedies, which is that following a finding of antitrust law violations the defendant be fenced in from perpetuating the unlawful conduct. This decree seems not to do that."

NOT A DONE DEAL

While Microsoft and the Justice Department may have reached an agreement in principle, the settlement is not a done deal until approved by Kollar-Kotelly after holding a Tunney Act hearing. That law emerged from a Nixon-era settlement with ITT that critics charged was politically motivated.

"The judge is required to review the public comments received, and she is permitted to undertake any evidentiary proceeding she wants, to make sure entry of the decree is in the public interest," said Glenn Manishin, an antitrust lawyer with Kelley Drye & Warren in Vienna, Va. "The whole point of this Tunney Act is to make sure there aren't any backroom, smoke-filled deals like there were with the ITT deal in the late 1960s."

Opponents of the settlement are likely to question the extent to which politics played a role in the agreement. The Justice Department has gone from advocating a breakup of Microsoft under the Clinton administration to accepting a much milder settlement at the behest of Assistant Attorney General Charles James.

"The obligation of Judge Kollar-Kotelly is to determine whether the settlement is the product of political influence or an objective appraisal of antitrust policy and precedent," Manishin said.

Despite the appeals court ruling, recent action by the Justice Department raises the specter of political maneuvering, critics charge. In September, with little consultation with the 18 states, the agency unexpectedly took breakup and the tying claim—whether Microsoft illegally integrated Internet Explorer into Windows 95 and 98—off the table.

"In no respect did the White House seek to shape or influence the outcome," Ashcroft said during the Friday press conference.

JUDGE COULD BE OVERRULED

Whatever Kollar-Kotelly does with the settlement, there is no guarantee that an appeals court would not later overrule her. In 1995, U.S. District Judge Stanley Sporkin refused to sign an earlier consent decree hammered out between the Justice Department and Microsoft.

"Sporkin got reversed because he relied on evidence that wasn't in the record before him," Manishin said.

A federal appeals court later replaced Sporkin with U.S. District Judge Thomas Penfield Jackson, Kollar-Kotelly's predecessor responsible for the landmark antitrust case.

After the two sides failed to settle before an earlier deadline, Kollar-Kotelly appointed Boston University law professor Eric Green to mediate the talks.

Lawyers for the Justice Department, Microsoft, and 18 states were expected to deliver the proposed settlement to Kollar-Kotelly during a 6 A.M. PST status hearing.

There, the states were expected to ask the judge for more time to review the proposed settlement, which would be presented in the form of a consent decree, said sources familiar with the matter. About five states, among them California, led the coalition seeking more time to review the document and weigh continuing the case without federal trustbusters.

WILD CARDS

The states remain wild cards in the case. They could oppose the settlement during the Tunney Act hearing or pursue the case independently of the Justice Department.

"But that could be very tough to do," said Andy Gavil, an antitrust professor at Howard University School of Law.

One problem: The Justice Department could oppose the states' continuation. Some states also lack the will they once had to fight the case, particularly given pinched economic resources with a recession looming.

If the states do carry on the fight, they will likely rally around the appeals court's unanimous June decision upholding the eight separate antitrust violations against Microsoft.

"Just one (violation) is serious enough under antitrust law," Manishin emphasized.

Throughout the case, the states were the strongest advocates of breaking up Microsoft. But after the appeals court ruling, the Justice Department unexpectedly removed breakup from the remedy.

"Once you, as a practical matter, took breakup off the table, the question is what kind of conduct-remedies would a court impose?" said Fenwick & West's Stanton. "Part of the trade-off is, do you want some remedies sooner or some different ones much later on?"

With breakup no longer an option, the Justice Department may have decided to get as much as it could now rather than waiting.

"Tougher remedies might not get imposed for another six months or a year, another appeal or another generation of Windows," Stanton said. "If the trade-off is softer, milder (restrictions), but . . . in place now," that could have been more appealing to the federal government, he said.

The states now face a similar dilemma as they plot their next move. If they go it alone, they could appear before Kollar-Kotelly in March for a remedy hearing.

No matter what happens next, Microsoft's legal problems stemming from the case won't disappear.

"They were found to be a monopoly," said Gavil, who noted that the finding and supporting evidence could be used in a host of civil lawsuits pending against Microsoft. "It's not over yet."

Source: http://news.com.com/2100-1001-275317.html?legacy=cnet.

Microsoft Deal May Be Changed

Microsoft Corp. and the U.S. Department of Justice are weighing the possibility of modifying the controversial settlement they reached last year in the long-running antitrust case.

In a joint filing to a federal judge, lawyers for the two parties said that in light of roughly 30,000 opinions about the proposed deal received during a legally mandated public-comment period, they might propose changes, although they did not commit to doing so. If any are made, they will be submitted to the court by February 27.

Microsoft spokesman Jim Desler cautioned that any modifications would be "refinements" rather than wholesale changes to the agreement.

Of the 30,000 public comments received, the Justice Department said that roughly 7,500 were in favor of the settlement, roughly 15,000 opposed, and roughly 7,000 expressed no clear opinion.

The department said that 2,900 of the comments were substantive critiques of the agreement, with 45 of those being in-depth analyses. Another 2,800 were form letters or e-mails.

The filing comes as a U.S. District Court judge is deciding how to proceed in determining whether to approve the proposed settlement. Under federal law, she must decide whether the agreement—which has been attacked by Microsoft rivals, consumer groups, and many antitrust scholars as being inadequate—is in the public interest.

Judge Colleen Kollar-Kotelly had recently asked the two sides whether they planned to amend the agreement and for advice on how to proceed.

Microsoft and the Justice Department urged her to hold a one-day hearing in which only the company, federal prosecutors, and representatives of nine states who joined in the agreement would present arguments and answer questions. The Justice Department argues that opponents of the agreement are adequately represented in the lengthy public comments that will be provided to the court.

If the court believes other parties should be represented, the hearing should still be limited to one day, Microsoft and the Justice Department said.

The judge can order broader hearings of almost any nature and will hold a hearing tomorrow to discuss the issue further. The issue is complicated by the fact that hearings are scheduled to begin in March before Kollar-Kotelly on behalf of nine states and the District of Columbia that did not sign onto the federal agreement and are pursuing tougher sanctions against Microsoft.

The nine states and Microsoft's rivals have urged the judge not to rule on the settlement deal until after those hearings are concluded. Microsoft and the Justice Department want her to rule as soon as possible.

Source: February 10, 2002. http://news.com

Case 11-3

China's Telecommunications Industry Today

Yajiong Xue and Xuan Xie

The communication industry in China, particularly the telecommunications industry, has witnessed rapid growth over the last decade. In 1989, teledensity in China was 1 percent; today it is 19 percent. The telecommunications sector has grown to become one of China's pillar industries. With its population of 1.26 billion, the People's Republic of China is set to become the world's biggest national telecommunications market.

According to a rough estimation, the business volume of China's telecommunications industry in 2001 reached 350 billion Yuan RMB (around US$43 billion), a 16 percent increase compared with the amount in 2000. [1] In addition, China has built one of the largest public telecommunications networks in the world, including the world's second largest mobile and fixed-line networks. China plans to invest in its telecommunications infrastructure with the equivalent of US$500 billion by 2005. It is the fastest-growing market in the world and already has the second most wireless subscribers. Chinese officials forecast a 20 percent annual growth in telecommunications through 2005.[1]

China's telecommunications market became more liberalized in 1998—the year when the Ministry of Information Industry (MII) was created. The objective for the MII is to regulate China's telecommunications industry independently and efficiently.[1] The MII is now a superagency overseeing telecommunications, multimedia, broadcasting, satellites, and the Internet.[2]

CHINA VOICE COMMUNICATIONS MARKET

By the end of December 2001, the capacity of switches in China had reached 210 million wireline users and 220 million mobile phone users. The optical communications channel had reached 1.5 million kilometers. GSM networks had almost covered the whole country and CDMA networks had been set up to enlarge volume and market. International roaming was established in 76 countries and regions.

China increased long-distance call lines by 590,000, leading the total capacity to 2.56 million lines. The total length for long-distance fiber cable is now 303,000 kilometers, increasing by 17,000 kilometers from the beginning of the year.[3] There were 60 million new cellular phone subscribers in 2001 with 35 million new fixed-line telephone subscribers (see Table 1). The number of mobile users in China became the largest in the world (14 percent), which draws the world's attention. Whereas the mobile phone usage in China is very low relative to its population, by around 2005, when the world is expected to boast about one billion mobile phones, it is entirely plausible that a quarter of them will be in China. Its market is growing so fast that every three months China adds enough subscribers to equal the entire Australian mobile-phone population. [3]

CHINA DATA COMMUNICATIONS MARKET

The first email ever sent from the PRC was delivered on September 20, 1987, through the China Academic Network (CANet) from Beijing to Germany. [5] Since then, China's datacom networks have grown drastically although it was still far behind the developed countries.

Table 2 summarizes the major findings of the nationwide Internet survey conducted by China Network Information Center (CNNIC) during the last five years. From October 1997 to July 2001, the figures increased tens of times; however, the

TABLE 1
Penetration for Voice Communications in China

Telephone	179 million subscribers, 13.9% of total population
Cellular phones	145 million subscribers, 11.3% of total population

Source: *China's Telecommunications Industry in 2001.* See Reference 4.

TABLE 2
**General Situation
of China's Internet
Development**

Source: *Semiannual Survey
Report on the Development
of China's Internet.* See
Reference 6.

Date	October 1997	July 1998	July 1999	July 2000	July 2001
Computer hosts in China	299,000	542,000	1,460,000	6,500,000	10,020,000
Internet users in China	620,000	1,175,000	4,000,000	16,900,000	26,500,000
Total number of domain names registered under ".CN"	4,066	9,415	29,045	99,734	128,362
Total bandwidth for international connection	25.41 Mbps	84.64 Mbps	241 Mbps	1,234 Mbps	3,257 Mbps

diffusion of the new technology is still highly limited if China's huge population is considered.

As it joined the World Trade Organization and has more opportunities to participate in global markets, China is working actively to fund fiber-optic research and development and foster domestic companies that can become suppliers of the fiber-optic equipment that serves as the foundation for China's communications infrastructure.[7]

MAIN ACTORS IN CHINA'S TELECOMMUNICATIONS SECTOR

Established in 1998, the Ministry of Information Industry (MII) bureaucracy plays an important role in China's telecommunications sector. Recently, its associated enterprise China Telecom restructured into four independent companies responsible for fixed-line services, mobile, paging, and satellite communication services. This signaled an end to the state's total monopoly over telecommunications. Domestic and foreign-investment companies have started to engage and compete in the telecommunications industry.

The new approved telecommunications regulations loosely divide China's telecommunications operations into two categories: (1) basic telecommunications business, referring to business that provides public network infrastructure and the transmission of public data and basic voice communications services, and (2) value-added telecommunications business, referring to business that provides telecommunications and information services by using the public network infrastructure.[1] According to the China–U.S. WTO (World Trade Organization) Agreement, after China entered the WTO, foreign firms could take 50 percent ownership of value-added services in two years and 49 percent for mobile and fixed-line services in five and six years, respectively.[8]

The MII announced that the value-added telecom services, related to the Internet, eCommerce, intelligent networks, and paging services, would open first and widest to foreign investment and competition upon China's WTO entry. But foreign capital would be permitted to own only 49 percent of the shares now and 50 percent in two years. The new rules will level the playing field, giving domestic firms more chances to develop, and grant Chinese investors majority control over Internet businesses, which they are expected to exercise within the as-yet-unwritten rules of the MII.[2]

SUMMARY

China's modernization is now inextricably linked with the global phenomenon of the telecommunications industry. With almost 20 percent of the global population, China possesses unique characteristics in building its telecommunications infrastructure. China will certainly be able to adjust and perfect its own development models, becoming a main actor in the world's telecommunications market.

REFERENCES

1. *Chance on China.* www.iflr.com, March/April 2001. *Available at* www.corporatlocation.com, last visited December 31, 2001.

2. *PRC Ministry/Commission Profile: In-Depth Version.* January, 2001. http://www.chinaonline.com/Last visited January, 25, 2002.

3. "China's Telecommunication Industry Reports Rapid Growth." *Asiainfo Daily China News,* July 19, 2001.

4. *China's Telecommunications Industry in 2001.* China Data Com, www.cndata.com/cnnews/news/yjyw/article4263.asp, December 28, 2001. Last visited January 3, 2002.

5. Qiu, J. L. "Virtual Censorship in China: Keeping the Gate Between the Cyberspace." *International Journal of Communications Law and Policy,* no. 4 (Winter 1999/2000).

6. *Semiannual Survey Report on the Development of China's Internet.* China Internet Network Information Center, http://www.cnnic.net.cn, last visited January 1, 2002.

7. Richards, K. "China's Expanding Valley of Fiber Optics." *Lightwave* 17, no. 12 (2000).

8. Zhang, B. "Assessing the WTO Agreements on China's Telecommunications Regulatory Reform and Industrial Liberalization." *Telecommunications Policy* 25 (2001), pp. 461–483.

9. Brahm, L. J. *China's Century: The Awakening of the Next Economic Powerhouse.* Singapore: John Wiley & Sons (Asia) PTE Ltd., 2001.

Case 11-4

Telecommunications Bill of 1996

SECTION 1. SHORT TITLE; REFERENCES.

(a) Short Title—This Act may be cited as the "Telecommunications Act of 1996".

(b) References—Except as otherwise expressly provided, whenever in this Act an amendment or repeal is expressed in terms of an amendment to, or repeal of, a section or other provision, the reference shall be considered to be made to a section or other provision of the Communications Act of 1934 (47 U.S.C. 151 et seq.).

SEC. 2. TABLE OF CONTENTS.
The table of contents for this Act is as follows:

TITLE III—CABLE SERVICES

Sec. 301. Cable Act reform.

Sec. 302. Cable service provided by telephone companies.

Part V—Video Programming Services Provided by Telephone Companies

Sec. 651. Regulatory treatment of video programming services.

Sec. 652. Prohibition on buy outs.

Sec. 653. Establishment of open video systems.

Sec. 303. Preemption of franchising authority regulation of telecommunications services.

Sec. 304. Competitive availability of navigation devices.

Sec. 629. Competitive availability of navigation devices.

Sec. 305. Video programming accessibility.

Sec. 713. Video programming accessibility.

TITLE IV—REGULATORY REFORM

Sec. 401. Regulatory forbearance.

Sec. 10. Competition in provision of telecommunications service.

Sec. 402. Biennial review of regulations; regulatory relief.

Sec. 11. Regulatory reform.

Sec. 403. Elimination of unnecessary Commission regulations and functions.

TITLE V—OBSCENITY AND VIOLENCE

Subtitle A—Obscene, Harassing, and Wrongful Utilization
of Telecommunications Facilities

Sec. 501. Short title.

Sec. 502. Obscene or harassing use of telecommunications facilities under
the Communications Act of 1934.

Sec. 503. Obscene programming on cable television.

Sec. 504. Scrambling of cable channels for nonsubscribers.

Sec. 640. Scrambling of cable channels for nonsubscribers.

Sec. 505. Scrambling of sexually explicit adult video service programming.

Sec. 641. Scrambling of sexually explicit adult video service programming.

Sec. 506. Cable operator refusal to carry certain programs.

Sec. 507. Clarification of current laws regarding communication of obscene
materials through the use of computers.

Sec. 508. Coercion and enticement of minors.

Sec. 509. Online family empowerment.

Sec. 230. Protection for private blocking and screening of offensive material.

Subtitle B—Violence

Sec. 551. Parental choice in television programming.

Sec. 552. Technology fund.

Subtitle C—Judicial Review

Sec. 561. Expedited review.

TITLE VI—EFFECT ON OTHER LAWS

Sec. 601. Applicability of consent decrees and other laws.

Sec. 602. Preemption of local taxation with respect to direct-to-home services.

TITLE VII—MISCELLANEOUS PROVISIONS

Sec. 701. Prevention of unfair billing practices for information services provided over toll-free telephone calls.

Sec. 702. Privacy of customer information.

Sec. 222. Privacy of customer information.

Sec. 703. Pole attachments.

Sec. 704. Facilities siting; radio frequency emission standards.

Sec. 705. Mobile services direct access to long distance carriers.

Sec. 706. Advanced telecommunications incentives.

Sec. 707. Telecommunications Development Fund.

Sec. 714. Telecommunications Development Fund.

Sec. 708. National Education Technology Funding Corporation.

Sec. 709. Report on the use of advanced telecommunications services for medical purposes.

Sec. 710. Authorization of appropriations.

SEC. 3. DEFINITIONS.

   (a) Additional Definitions.—Section 3 (47 U.S.C. 153) is amended—

      (1) in subsection (r)—

         (A) by inserting "(A)" after "means"; and

         (B) by inserting before the period at the end the following: ", or (B) comparable service provided through a system of switches, transmission equipment, or other facilities (or combination thereof) by which a subscriber can originate and terminate a telecommunications service"; and

      (2) by adding at the end thereof the following:

      (33) Affiliate.—The term 'affiliate' means a person that (directly or indirectly) owns or controls is owned or controlled by, or is under common ownership or control with, another person. For purposes of this paragraph, the term 'own' means to own an equity interest (or the equivalent thereof) of more than 10 percent.

      (34) AT&T consent decree.—The term 'AT&T Consent Decree' means the order entered August 24, 1982, in the antitrust action styled United States v. Western Electric, Civil Action No. 82 0192, in the United States District Court for the District of Columbia, and includes any judgment or order with respect to such action entered on or after August 24, 1982.

      (35) Bell operating company.—The term 'Bell operating company'—

      (A) means any of the following companies: Bell Telephone Company of Nevada, Illinois Bell Telephone Company, Indiana Bell Telephone Company, Incorporated, Michigan Bell Telephone Company, New England Telephone and Telegraph Company, New Jersey Bell Telephone Company, New York Telephone Company, US West Communications Company, South Central Bell Telephone Company, Southern Bell Telephone and Telegraph Company, Southwestern Bell Telephone Company, The Bell Telephone Company of Pennsylvania, The Chesapeake and Potomac Telephone Company, The Chesapeake and Potomac Telephone Company of Maryland, The Chesapeake and Potomac Telephone Company of Virginia, The Chesapeake and Potomac Telephone Company of West Virginia, The Diamond State Telephone Company, The Ohio Bell Telephone Company, The Pacific Telephone and Telegraph Company, or Wisconsin Telephone Company; and

      (B) includes any successor or assign of any such company that provides wireline telephone exchange service; but

(C) does not include an affiliate of any such company, other than an affiliate described in subparagraph (A) or (B).

(36) Cable service.—The term 'cable service' has the meaning given such term in section 602.

(37) Cable system.—The term 'cable system' has the meaning given such term in section 602.

(38) Customer premises equipment.—The term 'customer premises equipment' has the meaning given such term in section 602.

Telecommunications Bill Of 1996

TITLE I—TELECOMMUNICATION SERVICES
Subtitle A—Telecommunications Services

SEC. 101. ESTABLISHMENT OF PART II OF TITLE II.

(a) Amendment.—Title II is amended by inserting after section 229 (47 U.S.C. 229) the following new part:

PART II—DEVELOPMENT OF COMPETITIVE MARKETS

SEC. 251. INTERCONNECTION.

(a) General Duty of Telecommunications Carriers.—Each telecommunications carrier has the duty—

(1) to **interconnect directly** or indirectly with the facilities and equipment of other telecommunications carriers; and

(2) not to install network features, functions, or capabilities that do not comply with the guidelines and standards established pursuant to section 255 or 256.

(b) Obligations of All **Local Exchange Carriers.**—Each local exchange carrier has the following duties:

(1) **Resale.**—The duty not to prohibit, and not to impose unreasonable or discriminatory conditions or limitations on, the resale of its telecommunications services.

(2) **Number portability.**—The duty to provide, to the extent technically feasible, number portability in accordance with requirements prescribed by the Commission.

(3) **Dialing parity.**—The duty to provide dialing parity to competing providers of telephone exchange service and telephone toll service, and the duty to permit all such providers to have nondiscriminatory access to telephone numbers, operator services, directory assistance, and directory listing, with no unreasonable dialing delays.

(4) **Access to rights-of-way.**—The duty to afford access to the poles, ducts, conduits, and rights-of-way of such carrier to competing providers of telecommunications services on rates, terms, and conditions that are consistent with section 224.

(5) **Reciprocal compensation.**—The duty to establish reciprocal compensation arrangements for the transport and termination of telecommunications.

(c) Additional Obligations of Incumbent Local Exchange Carriers.—In addition to the duties contained in subsection (b), each incumbent local exchange carrier has the following duties:

(1) Duty to negotiate.—The duty to negotiate in good faith in accordance with section 252 the particular terms and conditions of agreements to fulfill the duties described in paragraphs (1) through (5) of subsection (b) and this subsection.

The requesting telecommunications carrier also has the duty to negotiate in good faith the terms and conditions of such agreements.

(2) Interconnection.—The duty to provide, for the facilities and equipment of any requesting telecommunications carrier, interconnection with the local exchange carrier's network—

(A) for the transmission and routing of telephone exchange service and exchange access;

(B) at any technically feasible point within the carrier's network;

(C) that is at least equal in quality to that provided by the local exchange carrier to itself or to any subsidiary, affiliate, or any other party to which the carrier provides interconnection; and

(D) on rates, terms, and conditions that are just, reasonable, and nondiscriminatory, in accordance with the terms and conditions of the agreement and the requirements of this section and section 252.

(3) Unbundled access.—The duty to provide, to any requesting telecommunications carrier for the provision of a telecommunications service, nondiscriminatory access to network elements on an unbundled basis at any technically feasible point on rates, terms, and conditions that are just, reasonable, and nondiscriminatory in accordance with the terms and conditions of the agreement and the requirements of this section and section 252. An incumbent local exchange carrier shall provide such unbundled network elements in a manner that allows requesting carriers to combine such elements in order to provide such telecommunications service.

(4) Resale.—The duty—

(A) to offer for resale at wholesale rates any telecommunications service that the carrier provides at retail to subscribers who are not telecommunications carriers; and

(B) not to prohibit, and not to impose unreasonable or discriminatory conditions or limitations on, the resale of such telecommunications service, except that a State commission may, consistent with regulations prescribed by the Commission under this section, prohibit a reseller that obtains at wholesale rates a telecommunications service that is available at retail only to a category of subscribers from offering such service to a different category of subscribers.

Case 11-5

Americans with Disabilities Act of 1990

TITLE IV—TELECOMMUNICATIONS

SEC. 401. TELECOMMUNICATIONS RELAY SERVICES FOR HEARING-IMPAIRED AND SPEECH-IMPAIRED INDIVIDUALS.

(a) TELECOMMUNICATIONS.—Title II of the Communications Act of 1934 (47 U.S.C. 201 et seq.) is amended by adding at the end thereof the following new section:

State and local governments.
47 USC 225.

"SEC. 225. TELECOMMUNICATIONS SERVICES FOR HEARING-IMPAIRED AND SPEECH-IMPAIRED INDIVIDUALS.

"(a) DEFINITIONS.—As used in this section—

"(1) COMMON CARRIER OR CARRIER.—The term 'common carrier' or 'carrier' include any common carrier engaged in interstate communication by wire or radio as defined in section 3(h) and any common carrier engaged in intrastate communication by wire or radio, notwithstanding sections 2(b) and 221(b).

"(2) TDD.—The term 'TDD' means a Telecommunications Device for the Deaf, which is a machine that employs graphic communication in the transmission of coded signals through a wire or radio communication system.

"(3) TELECOMMUNICATIONS RELAY SERVICES.—The term 'telecommunications relay services' means telephone transmission services that provide the ability for an individual who has a hearing impairment or speech impairment to engage in communication by wire or radio with a hearing individual in a manner that is functionally equivalent to the ability of an individual who does not have a hearing impairment or speech impairment to communicate using voice communication services by wire or radio. Such term includes services that enable two-way communication between an individual who uses a TDD or other nonvoice terminal device and an individual who does not use such a device.

"(b) AVAILABILITY OF TELECOMMUNICATIONS RELAY SERVICES.—

"(1) IN GENERAL.—In order to carry out the purposes established under section 1, to make available to all individuals in the United States a rapid, efficient nationwide communication service, and to increase the utility of the telephone system of the Nation, the Commission shall ensure that interstate and intrastate telecommunications relay services are available, to the extent possible and in the most efficient manner, to hearing-impaired and speech-impaired individuals in the United States.

"(2) USE OF GENERAL AUTHORITY AND REMEDIES.—For the purposes of administering and enforcing the provisions of this section and the regulations prescribed thereunder, the Commission shall have the same authority, power, and functions with respect to common carriers engaged in intrastate communication as the Commission has in administering and enforcing the provisions of this title with respect to any common carrier engaged in interstate communication. Any violation of this section by any common carrier engaged in intrastate communication shall be subject to the same remedies, penalties, and procedures as are applicable to a violation of this Act by a common carrier engaged in interstate communication.

"(c) PROVISION OF SERVICES.—Each common carrier providing telephone voice transmission services shall, not later than 3 years after the date of enactment of this section, provide in compliance with the regulations prescribed under this section, throughout the area in which it offers service, telecommunications relay services, individually, through designees, through a competitively selected vendor, or in concert with other carriers. A common carrier shall be considered to be in compliance with such regulations—

"(1) with respect to intrastate telecommunications relay services in any State that does not have a certified program under subsection (f) and with respect to interstate telecommunications relay services, if such common carrier (or other entity through which the carrier is providing such relay services) is in compliance with the Commission's regulations under subsection (d); or

"(2) with respect to intrastate telecommunications relay services in any State that has a certified program under subsection (f) for such State, if such common carrier (or other entity through which the carrier is providing such relay services) is in compliance with the program certified under subsection (f) for such State.

"(d) REGULATIONS.—

"(1) IN GENERAL.—The Commission shall, not later than 1 year after the date of enactment of this section, prescribe regulations to implement this section, including regulations that—

"(A) establish functional requirements, guidelines, and operations procedures for telecommunications relay services;

"(B) establish minimum standards that shall be met in carrying out subsection (c);

"(C) require that telecommunications relay services operate every day for 24 hours per day;

"(D) require that users of telecommunications relay services pay rates no greater than the rates paid for functionally equivalent voice communication services with respect to such factors as the duration of the call, the time of day, and the distance from point of origination to point of termination;

"(E) prohibit relay operators from failing to fulfill the obligations of common carriers by refusing calls or limiting the length of calls that use telecommunications relay services;

"(F) prohibit relay operators from disclosing the content of any relayed conversation and from keeping records of the content of any such conversation beyond the duration of the call; and

"(G) prohibit relay operators from intentionally altering a relayed conversation.

"(2) TECHNOLOGY.—The Commission shall ensure that regulations prescribed to implement this section encourage, consistent with section 7(a) of this Act, the use of existing technology and do not discourage or impair the development of improved technology.

"(3) JURISDICTIONAL SEPARATION OF COSTS.—

"(A) IN GENERAL.—Consistent with the provisions of section 410 of this Act, the Commission shall prescribe regulations governing the jurisdictional separation of costs for the services provided pursuant to this section.

"(B) RECOVERING COSTS.—Such regulations shall generally provide that costs caused by interstate telecommunications relay services shall be recovered from all subscribers for every interstate services and costs caused by intrastate telecommunications relay services shall be recovered from the intrastate jurisdiction. In a State that has a certified program under subsection (f), a State commission shall permit a common carrier to recover the costs incurred in providing intrastate telecommunications relay services by a method consistent with the requirements of this section.

"(e) ENFORCEMENT.—

"(1) IN GENERAL.—Subject to subsections (f) and (g), the Commission shall enforce this section.

"(2) COMPLAINT.—The Commission shall resolve, by final order, a complaint alleging a violation of this section within 180 days after the date such complaint is filed.

"(f) CERTIFICATION.—

"(1) STATE DOCUMENTATION.—Any State desiring to establish a State program under this section shall submit documentation to the Commission that describes the program of such State for implementing intrastate telecommunications, relay services and the procedures and remedies available for enforcing any requirements imposed by the State program.

"(2) REQUIREMENTS FOR CERTIFICATION.—After review of such documentation, the Commission shall certify the State program if the Commission determines that—

"(A) the program makes available to hearing-impaired and speech-impaired individuals, either directly, through designees, through a competitively selected vendor, or through regulation of intrastate common carriers, intrastate telecommunications relay services in such State in a manner that meets or exceeds the requirements of regulations prescribed by the Commission under subsection (d); and

"(B) the program makes available adequate procedures and remedies for enforcing the requirements of the State program.

"(3) METHOD OF FUNDING.—Except as provided in subsection (d), the Commission shall not refuse to certify a State program based solely on the method such State will implement for funding intrastate telecommunication relay services.

"(4) SUSPENSION OR REVOCATION OF CERTIFICATION.—The Commission may suspend or revoke such certification if, after notice and opportunity for hearing, the Commission determines that such certification is no longer warranted. In a State whose program has been suspended or revoked, the Commission shall take such steps as may be necessary, consistent with this section, to ensure continuity of telecommunications relay services.

"(g) COMPLAINT.—

"(1) REFERRAL OF COMPLAINT.—If a complaint to the commission alleges a violation of this section with respect to intrastate telecommunications relay services within a State and certification of the program of such State under subsection (f) is in effect, the Commission shall refer such complaint to such State.

"(2) JURISDICTION OF COMMISSION.—After referring a complaint to a State under paragraph (1), the Commission shall exercise jurisdiction over such complaint only if—

"(A) final action under such State program has not been taken on such complaint by such State—

"(i) within 180 days after the complaint is filed with such State; or

"(ii) within a shorter period as prescribed by the regulations of such State; or

"(B) the Commission determines that such State program is no longer qualified for certification under subsection (f)".

(b) CONFORMING AMENDMENTS.—The Communications Act of 1934 (47 U.S.C. 151 et seq.) is amended—

(1) in section 2(b) (47 U.S.C. 152(b)), by striking "section 224" and inserting "sections 224 and 225"; and

(2) in section 221(b) (47 U.S.C. 221(b)), by striking "section 301" and inserting "sections 225 and 301".

SEC. 402. CLOSED-CAPTIONING OF PUBLIC SERVICE ANNOUNCEMENTS.

47 USC 611.

Section 711 of the Communications Act of 1934 is amended to read as follows: 47 USC 611

"SEC. 711. CLOSED-CAPTIONING OF PUBLIC SERVICE ANNOUNCEMENTS.

"Any television public service announcement that is produced or funded in whole or in part by any agency or instrumentality of Federal Government shall include closed captioning of the verbal content of such announcement. A television broadcast station licensee—

"(1) shall not be required to supply closed captioning for any such announcement that fails to include it; and

"(2) shall not be liable for broadcasting any such announcement without transmitting a closed caption unless the licensee intentionally fails to transmit the closed caption that was included with the announcement.".

TITLE V—MISCELLANEOUS PROVISIONS

SEC. 501. CONSTRUCTION. 42 USC 12201.

(a) IN GENERAL.—Except as otherwise provided in this Act, nothing in this Act shall be construed to apply a lesser standard than the standards applied under title V of the Rehabilitation Act of 1973 (29 U.S.C. 790 et seq.) or the regulations issued by Federal agencies pursuant to such title.

(b) RELATIONSHIP TO OTHER LAWS.—Nothing in this Act shall be construed to invalidate or limit the remedies, rights, and procedures of any Federal law or law of any State or political subdivision of any State or jurisdiction that provides greater or equal protection for the rights of individuals with disabilities than are afforded by this Act. Nothing in this Act shall be construed to preclude the prohibition of, or the imposition of restrictions on, smoking in places of employment covered by title I, in transportation covered by title II or III, or in places of public accommodation covered by title III.

(c) INSURANCE.—Titles I through IV of this Act shall not be construed to prohibit or restrict—

(1) an insurer, hospital or medical service company, health maintenance organization, or any agent, or entity that administers benefit plans, or similar organizations from underwriting risks, classifying risks, or administering such risks that are based on or not inconsistent with State law; or

(2) a person or organization covered by this Act from establishing, sponsoring, observing or administering the terms.

Case 11-6

A Comparison of Privacy and Security in Great Britain, China, Afghanistan, and the United States

Brent Fox

INTRODUCTION

Restriction of free thought and free speech is the most dangerous of all subversions. It is the one un-American act that could most easily defeat us all.—Justice William O. Douglas

Much has changed since September 11, 2001, in Americans' perspective on privacy and security. Many of us would have written our congressmen for some of the things that they are now pushing, but our perspective has changed. The most recent extension of the law is attempting to target individuals to wiretap, rather than the phones themselves. Even the most radical civil rights groups find this hard to discredit. The e-monitoring that people once faced at work from their employer may now extend into their living room. This paper looks at the policies of Great Britain, China, the United States, and Afghanistan towards privacy and security. Given the recent tragedy, this paper will probably be obsolete before it is turned in.

GREAT BRITAIN

Great Britain is the most intrusive of the Big Brothers. England is no stranger to attacks by radical religious fundamentalists. Britain's ongoing differences with Northern Ireland have forced the country to lessen citizens' privacy in order to provide them with security. A recent article in *USA Today* found that Britain has more video surveillance cameras than any other country in the world. The typical resident of London is caught on camera between 8 and 300 times each day. [1] Parliament does not believe that is enough. In the past month, the government announced that they would spend $120 million more on cameras, many with face-recognition. These cameras will be linked on a network that allows them to communicate.

The limiting of civil liberties is nothing new in Britain. Since the 1970s the government has limited free speech and trial by jury. [2] The government even went as far as banning any media in support of the Irish Republican Army. Although this monitoring seems drastic in the United States, British citizens don't seem to mind. "Our lives are being monitored to an extent that would have seemed inconceivable back in 1984 and scarcely anyone seems to give a damn about it," said BBC commentator John Humphries.

To further the lack of privacy, Britain is now collecting and storing DNA taken during police investigations, at a rate of one million per year. [3] The government intends to, as some think, have a DNA database of all of the citizens in the country, innocent or guilty. It is obvious that of all of the countries studied, Brits have the least amount of privacy. Developments in technology such as databases and networks will extend the reach of the law even further, allowing these sources of information to communicate among one another. Great Britain is a perfect example of how terrorists can put people in enough fear to sacrifice freedom for perceived safety.

CHINA

Growing up in the United States, we were taught the evils of Communism, especially how these citizens had no privacy from their government. According to what I have researched, our history teachers were not that far off. China is now in the process of requiring citizens to replace their identification cards, driver's licenses, employee cards, and passports with a Digital Biological Information Passport. [4] This card will have a large amount of biological information, as well as their personal information, that will identify the Chinese. Since the Chinese government controls much of the media, this press release seemed positive about the new technology, but it is obviously propaganda to any rational-thinking human being.

Another example of Chinese propaganda from the state-controlled press is this statement: "For the previous half century, the Chinese people, led by the Chinese government, had unswervingly probed into and fought for the elimination of poverty and backwardness, the building of a rich, strong, democratic and civilized country, and the achievement of the lofty ideal of complete human rights." [5] Those of us who remember Tiananmen Square find this achievement very hard to believe and no further credence to the Xinhua News Agency will be given in this paper. The fact of the matter is, we don't know how much monitoring the Chinese government does of its citizens. The government controls the press and the freedom of the press is what alerts most countries to officials' misdoings. That is one reason I chose to write about China, to show the possibilities of monitoring without the government being held accountable. It is obvious that the Chinese government uses the media to control what citizens think and the biological cards are one example of turning the scales far toward security and far away from privacy.

THE UNITED STATES

The right of the people to be secure in their persons, houses, papers, and effects, against unreasonable searches and seizures, shall not be violated, and no Warrants shall issue, but upon probable cause, supported by Oath or affirmation, and particularly describing the place to be searched, and the persons or things to be seized.

The fourth amendment to the Bill of Rights is one of the most powerful statements our forefathers made in regard to the balance of privacy and security. They enlisted several checks and balances with the judicial branch in order to protect citizens' right to privacy. Even the fourth amendment has become loosely interpreted with new technology and the latest terrorist attacks. As previously mentioned, employers can monitor almost anything their employees do. Network administrators are more powerful than even George Orwell predicted. They can read your email, look at the websites you frequent, even watch you at your desk. This may soon become closer to reality for the government if citizens' panic takes over their reason. The most specific privacy issues now being faced are wiretapping, encryption, biometric identification technology, government surveillance, and the development of national databases. [6]

A group composed of both conservatives and liberals is now lobbying against these issues. The group's official stance stated, "Our most basic and fundamental freedoms are under attack unlike any time since the Revolutionary Era." While this is truly unsettling, it is now up to the American citizens to decide if they would rather be safe or private.

In the words of Benjamin Franklin, "They that give up essential liberty to obtain a little temporary safety deserve neither liberty nor safety." Those are harsh words from one of our country's founders. Mr. Franklin's perspective was on both sides of the fence, as the colonies had very little privacy from King George and his new country had entrusted citizens with certain unalienable rights. Unless American citizens stand up for their rights in the midst of terror, they could forever lose the freedoms for which our founding fathers laid their lives on the line.

AFGHANISTAN

Does anyone really know privacy and security in Afghanistan? We have all heard of the ability of Osama bin Laden to escape any type of monitoring that anyone has. Next we should ask what about the rest of the Afghan citizens. Does it really matter? Most of the citizens of the state do not even have a rotary phone, much less Internet access. I suppose you could monitor what they draw in the sand or write in the caves, but the fact is that most people in the Middle East do not have the technology that we are accustomed to in the civilized world. Only the very rich have access to technology and many use satellite phones because the phone companies have not run phone lines through the desert and mountains.

Even if companies would do this, and the people could afford it, and the people would be interested in using it and learning how, the oppressive government in most of the Middle East states would not allow it. The few facts available show that telecommunications in Afghanistan is virtually nonexistent. There is about one phone per thousand and one television per 300 people. There is only one ISP in Afghanistan and, by now, their infrastructure is probably in pieces. Afghanistan will have to start from the ground up to rebuild their telecommunications. As of now, the privacy is an afterthought and the only security concern is for their own lives.

CONCLUSION

I'm sure this paper is quite different to the ones completed in the past due to the September 11th attacks. I started the paper with the most advanced in monitoring citizens and ended with a country that wouldn't know what to do with technology such as fiber if they had it. The coming months will be very interesting for this topic, as the United States inches herself closer to less privacy for the perception of more security. The final sentence of this paper, from one of the wisest of men to lead this great country, warns of that occurrence.

> *A society that will trade a little order for a little freedom will lose both, and deserve neither.—Thomas Jefferson*

REFERENCES

1. Ellen Hale. "Many Britons Smile on Spread of Candid Camera." *USA Today,* September 26, 2001.

2. T. R. Reid. "England Finally Enacts Bill of Rights." *The Washington Post,* October 3, 2000.

3. Stephen Robinson. "Stop Them Taking Liberties." *Daily Telegraph,* July 5, 2001.

4. "China Invents Biological Identity System." Xinhua News Agency, October 7, 2000.

5. "50 Years of Progress in China's Human Rights." Xinhua News Agency, February 17, 2000.

6. Thomas Edsall. "Attacks Shift Balance of Power, Alliances Among Interest Groups." *The Washington Post,* September 19, 2001.

Summary

The one characteristic that exemplifies the global telecommunications industry and environment is change. It is questionable as to whether the change in technology or the change in regulation and deregulation has had the greatest effect. While it would

The Real World   11–8
Phone Competition Is Hot-Wired in Chile

Beyond the wrangling in Washington over how to phrase the sentences in the new telecom bill lies a juicier question: What happens to cozy competitors when anyone with a digital impulse can suddenly crash into a market?

Check out Chile, unquestionably the wildest telecom market in the world. Last year all restrictions on entry into the long-distance business were removed at a stroke. The result: What BellSouth's Chilean manager calls "This awful, stupid competition" that squashed prices 99 percent. The phone wars in the United States look like a lawn party by comparison.

Want in? In Chile, it's simple: Just rent space on the networks of Chile's two newly privatized telephone companies (or build your own), and you're in business. Now get ready for competing in hyperdrive. Here, callers can switch phone companies on a call-by-call basis simply by dialing a three-digit prefix. The phone companies are bombarding the country with ads touting prices, so callers can clip and save on the fly.

More than half a dozen Chilean companies have jumped into the fray, along with three Baby Bells: BellSouth, which was already a cellular phone provider in Chile; SBC (a.k.a. Southwestern Bell), which spent more than $300 million to buy a stake in VTR, a major Chilean operator; and Bell Atlantic, which made a smaller investment in Iusatel, a Mexican company.

As a result, the price of off-peak calls from Chile to the United States fell from $1.50 a minute in late 1994—just before competition began—to about a penny a minute early last year. Prices have eased upward a bit, but they are still around 20 cents to 25 cents a minute—the lowest in the world for international long distance.

The torrid one-upsmanship also has spilled into the courts, with the phone companies spitting out lawsuits like machine-gun bullets. (Most allege unfair competition.) "The guys making money here are the lawyers and the ad agencies," says Iusatel general manager Gaston Periera, formerly of Bell Atlantic.

The Baby Bells don't want to live through anything like this in the United States, nor is it likely they will have to: Market entry will be gradual and regulated. Still, the hot Chilean market can provide a cautionary tale to U.S. telephone companies, especially to one that hasn't entered the dance down south: AT&T. Barely more than a year ago Entel, once Chile's state-owned long-distance carrier and now private, had 100 percent of the market. Today its share is 40 percent.

Source: Andrew Kupfer, "Phone Competition is Hot-Wired in Chile," *Fortune.*

Privatization of telecommunications is a strong force in countries that tried government ownership and experienced limited growth.

be possible to forecast the time when most countries will have eased regulation, that time is not in the near future. Country-based regulation is a fact of life, one that must be understood, not just tolerated, to be competitive. United States citizens, through their representatives in Congress, view certain industries as very important to public service and national interests. These industries tend to be candidates for dishing out abuse and unfair practices. From this view has come the regulation of the railroad, airline, trucking, and telecommunications industries, to name just a few. The creation of a regulatory agency for telecommunications means that self-regulation was not considered sufficient, so an outside governmental agency was established to act in the public's behalf. Thus, the environment in which telecommunications companies operate has significant influence on the systems and interfaces of these companies. To ignore the importance of regulation, and the evolving deregulation, is to bury your head in the sand.

The divestiture of AT&T was one of the most profound and important events impacting telecommunications in the United States. Rules governing the components of AT&T continue to evolve, and the effects continue to be felt. One impact felt in all companies is that telecommunications managers are now responsible for all technical and business decisions that impact the enterprise's communications needs. Vendors can help, but no vendor can do what AT&T once did for the enterprise. Variety, flexibility, and growth have replaced what was viewed as stability. The major implications for managers are that the regulatory environment and government actions impact telecommunications decisions. Managers must incorporate these factors into their processes as a regular facet of their management tasks.

The two major U.S. legislative acts of the 1990s dealing with telecommunications have been the *Telecommunications Act of 1996* and the *Americans with Disabilities Act of 1990*. One opened up competition in the local and long-distance telephone markets. The other provided accommodation for people with challenged conditions. Technology has the potential to accommodate social needs.

Key Terms

access charge, *452*
Americans with Disabilities Act of 1990, *481*
antitrust, *449*
AT&T Consent Decree, *463*
Bell Operating Company (BOC), *450*
bypass, *459*
Carterfone Decision, *464*
common carrier, *462*
Communications Act of 1934, *462*
competitive local exchange carrier (CLEC), *472*
Computer Inquiry I (CI-I), *466*
Computer Inquiry II (CI-II), *466*
cross-subsidization, *456*
depreciation *456*
deregulation, *456*
Digital Millennium Copyright Act (DMCA), *476*

divestiture, *468*
Federal Communications Commission (FCC), *462*
Graham Act, *462*
incumbent local exchange carrier (ILEC), *472*
interexchange carrier (IXC), *459*
international record carriers (IRCs), *478*
local access and transport area (LATA), *468*
local exchange carrier (LEC), *459*
MCI Decision, *465*
Modified Final Judgment, *466*
monopoly, *455*
natural monopoly, *455*
Open Skies Policy, *466*
Postal, Telephone, and Telegraph (PTT), *463*
privatization, *507*

Public Service Commission (PSC), *460*
Public Utility Commission (PUC), *463*
Regional Bell Operating Company (RBOC), *457*
regulation, *453*
satellite carriers, *478*
tariff, *458*
Telecommunications Act of 1996, *472*
telecommunications device for the deaf (TDD), *480*
transnational data flow, *477*
trivestiture, *457*
universal service, *463*
value-added carriers, *477*
value-added network (VAN), *477*
World Intellectual Property Organization (WIPO), *476*

Recommended Readings

Yale Journal on Regulation
Journal of Regulatory Economics

Telecommunications Policy
Public Utilities Fortnightly

Discussion Questions

11.1. How has regulation impacted communications between personal computers?

11.2. Discuss the pros and cons of a telecommunications provider having a natural monopoly.

11.3. How have deregulation and divestiture impacted the concept of *universal service?*

11.4.   Why would the U.S. Justice Department want to break up AT&T?

11.5.   Was the breakup of AT&T, from what Michael could tell, a blessing or a bane?

11.6.   Can you cite any instances or examples of firms seizing the opportunity of the postdivestiture environment? How did they exploit the turbulence?

11.7.   Divide the class into teams with one team debating the *pro* divestiture position and the other debating the *con* position. List the major points made by each team. Discuss the points as they impact a business like JEI.

11.8.   In the decades that have passed since the Modified Final Judgment and the separation of the Bell Operating Companies from AT&T, does the judicial organization continue to inhibit the progress of the BOCs and RBOCs?

11.9.   What has been the impact of the U.S. Telecommunications Act of 1996 on costs of (*a*) local service, (*b*) cable TV, and (*c*) long-distance rates?

11.10. Compare the telecommunications industry before and after the Telecommunications Act of 1996.

11.11. Discuss the impact of the Telecommunications Act of 1996 on (*a*) competition, (*b*) mergers and partnerships, and (*c*) services.

11.12. What is the corollary of the Telecommunications Act of 1996 and regulatory and privatization acts in other countries?

11.13. How does SAP work? How does closed captioning work? Why do all new TV sets over 13-inches diagonal have closed captioning?

Projects

11.1.   Get data from the IBM website about the Systems 3x and their replacement, the AS/400, and determine the next likely replacement system. Include IBMs Web-sphere.

11.2.   Again, look in your telephone directory. This time, who is your LEC, what LATA are you in, and what other LECs are in the LATA? What LATAs join you?

11.3.   Bring a telephone bill to class and analyze the component parts.

11.4.   List the alternative IXC providers in your area. Can you do manual least-cost routing to various providers?

11.5.   Invite a member of your LEC to the class to discuss the impact of divestiture and deregulation on businesses.

11.6.   Divide the class into teams and brainstorm the desired uses for telecommunications that are either inhibited or prohibited by regulation.

11.7.   Investigate the history of ISDN tariffs (first in 1987 by Illinois Bell) and the present status.

11.8.   Contact your state PSC/PUC and determine the last tariff filed and any pending tariffs. Describe the services they provide.

11.9.   Research the last 10 tariffs approved by the state PSC/PUC, document their history, and show the time required to get a tariff approved.

11.10. Get the state position on the latest tariff from the PSC/PUC. Get the position on the issue from the LEC. Discuss the impact of the difference of points of view on the customer.

11.11. Interview five local businesses and determine the extent that bypass is either being used, planned, or considered. Interview your LEC and determine how bypass is affecting their business.

11.12. Provide a chronology of key legal/judicial events from 1940 to the present that have affected the telecommunications environment in the United States.

11.13. Divide the class into teams and have each team investigate one area of the Telecommunications Act of 1996, report on its implications, and provide evidence of its impact.

11.14. Divide the class into two teams. Have the teams debate the position that reconsolidation in the telecommunications industry is restoring the sort of competitive constraints that existed prior to the AT&T divestiture.

11.15. Determine the major telecommunications provider companies that have failed in the past two years. What is the impact on businesses that were their customers?

11.16. Contact your local state agency responsible for aiding people under the ADA of 1990 and determine what telecommunications devices they support and recommend.

Chapter Twelve

Management of Voice and Data Systems in Organizations

CONTINUING CASE—PART 12

Time to Call Home

"This is your captain, again," came the announcement over the aircraft's speakers. "We are within 15 minutes of landfall on the Eastern Seaboard of the United States. For those of you who have waited so patiently, the Air Fones® are now operational."

Alli reached for the phone on the back of the seat in front of her and removed the handset. She slipped a credit card into the slot and, upon receiving a dial tone, dialed the JEI headquarters number in Denver. "Hi, Michael," she said cheerfully, "we are on our way home."

"With good news I trust."

"The best! We have a manufacturing site with superior telecommunications and won't have to have an onsite manager. We'll fill you in tomorrow morning, after a good night's sleep. This jet lag is a killer."

"Well, happy landing to you all," replied Michael. "Where are you now?"

"We are about 15 minutes east of Maine. We wrote up a short summary of our contacts. Want me to fax it to you now?"

"That would be great!"

Alli reached under the seat and brought up her laptop computer. She started the fax/modem software and tagged the report for sending. Then she ran a cable from her machine to the port on the back of the phone set, pressed the initialize button, and watched the computer perform handshaking with the fax machine at JEI. Instead of her report being fed into the machine, however, a response appeared on her fax screen, showing her a menu of options.

"Hmmn," thought Alli, "the boss has installed a new bit of technology. This looks like a fax-back service. Pressing 100 will give me a menu of reports I can receive from the machine, without involving any of our staff. I'll ask for a general description of JEI services, then send my fax to Michael."

After pressing 01, the JEI sheet appeared on her screen. She saved it to a file and selected *receive* on the menu. Her computer began sending the report to Michael. When the fax had been sent, she hung up the phone and settled back for the rest of the flight home.

Carlton Helps Dwayne Once More

Carlton picked up the phone. It was Dwayne Aldridge from Denver, calling for Michael.

"It's for you, Dad. It's Dwayne."

"Hey, Dwayne, it's good to hear from you. What's up? Did the squirrels burn down another warehouse?"

"No, I have an interesting opportunity, and I thought I would ask you for advice. I have a distributor in Hong Kong who comes in contact with a lot of unusual furniture items. They are often made in home factories, inside the People's Republic of China. By the time he can get a photographer there and mail me a photo, someone has already capitalized on the idea. He tried fax, but the quality is poor. Can you think of a way to shorten the time by which he sends me a good picture of a new item?"

"Hey, do I have an idea for you! Do you have a digital camera?"

"I get several technology catalogs, and I planned to get one soon."

"Great. Be sure to get a large memory and then you can take a lot of photos."

"The next time your contact hears of a new furniture item, have her go to the source and take several pictures of it. Then have her go to your office, where you have a reader for the pictures and a contract with *Wireless and Cable* for T1 service. Your contact puts the disk in the reader and sends the pictures to us at our Denver office. We'll call you when we receive them and give you a disk copy; we can even print them out on our color printer. Then, if you like them, you get on the phone and get your contact to get you a quantity."

"You mean you can transmit pictures on a telecommunications line?"

"Exactly! You could do this by fax, as you know, but this way they are in color and of excellent quality."

"I tried fax but the quality was not what I wanted, and color is important. With what you describe, I could get a jump on the competition!"

"Call this number at *Wireless and Cable* and make a deal."

"Helping out a friend, Dad?" asked Carlton.

"Hey, he rents two of our warehouses in Denver. We want to retain our customer focus, and this helps him pay the rent. Dwayne has really grown since the fire, and we have a good customer in his retail chain. Who knows where solid customer relationships can lead us in the future?"

Michael Considers the Consequences of Offshore Manufacturing

Michael had gone to the lake for the first time since his staff had returned from Scotland. Their excitement and enthusiasm during the debriefing were contagious. As opposed to many of his ventures, this one was following a good business course. He found Alli's predictions of the new market potential exciting, and he knew he needed both the manufacturing capability and the low cost that Scotland offered. The clincher was that Carlton would be able to manage scheduling, production, and quality at the Scotland plant without having to be there, through telecommunications. His company was maturing rapidly through the use of connectivity in and among their facilities in the United States, and the Scotland plant could simply extend the technology they understood.

Carlton let the screen door slam, interrupting his father's thoughts. "Sorry to disturb you, Dad, but I was wondering what you thought of our Scotland deal?"

"You all did an excellent job, Son! You have developed a firm business plan, Alli has a great marketing plan as usual, and Doug is a first-rate manufacturing engineer. The connectivity you and Scott have designed into the total operation is the real glue that will hold it together and make it work, and work profitably. The only question is whether we need a manager onsite at start-up."

"Well, Dad, I have a deal for you. Margie thinks a short stay in Scotland would be great, so I would like to take a short leave of absence from Kansas City and become the temporary site manager in Scotland. I was thinking that three months would be sufficient to stabilize production and finalize our design. Doug can run things in my absence, and we can keep in close touch by email. Also, let's have Scott expand the website to include the manufacturing capability in Scotland when it goes on line. What do you think?"

"Has Margie packed yet?"

"She is doing so as we speak."

"Then have a good and productive trip!"

Carlton Needs a Service Level Agreement

Carlton had been in Scotland for a month when he realized that the operation needed better coordination with local vendors and some way to tell them what he expected and to measure their performance. His father had done this many times for JEI, so he gave him a call.

"Hey, Dad, what is the instrument you use to contract with telecommunications providers and hold them to the requirements?"

"It's called a service level agreement. I learned quickly that I needed to get my service providers in line with my thoughts and a way to hold them to their commitment. The SLA details the service to be provided and under what circumstances. For example, the company that connects the bank to the backup site has to be up 99.4 percent of the time, must have a continuous data rate of 56 kbps, allow bursty traffic of 10 percent of the norm, and have error rates of less than 1 in 10 million bits. We measure all of these parameters and meet with the provider once a month to review his performance. Why do you ask?"

"I need to set up data service through Gray Hume. He talks a good story and I want to be sure he does what he says. Do you have an SLA that you could fax or email me to go by?"

"No problem, Son, I have one that I just executed with the local phone company. We have a committed information rate, which is what you probably need. It should be easy to use the SLA and just change the name and parameters."

"How about sending it as a file and I can use my word processor to make the changes."

"I'll have Scott send it within the hour. Anything else you need?"

"Yes, there is, now that you mention it. What is the software program you use to map the networks? I am at a point where I can start doing it here."

"It's called *netViz*®; you can go to www.netviz.com and order a CD. The file is too large to download at your speed."

"I remember it was easy to use and had database features that will allow us to show our total configuration. What do you use for capacity management?"

"I use *netViz*® for the most part there also, although I use a spreadsheet to have a listing of just the equipment. I need to add all of our bandwidth in this spreadsheet also as I think I am running out of bandwidth in some places."

"Great, I'll get on the website and order the CD and start putting all of my equipment in a spreadsheet."

Michael hangs up the phone and ponders his success in hiring Scott. Scott has been very effective in mapping the network and ensuring performance called out in SLAs. He enjoys the periodic meetings as it supports his belief that he has a good infrastructure. As he considers this experience, he realizes that Scott might add even more value by promoting him to chief information officer for JEI. "I'll ask Carlton about this the next time we talk."

INTRODUCTION

This chapter discusses the organizational side of the management of voice and data systems. It and the following chapters describe telecommunications strategy, give a management overview of the operational side of the organization, and discuss the phases of the development life cycle of telecommunications projects. While this chapter focuses on the management of the organization, the next chapter addresses the decision methodology of project management and telecommunication system implementation.

Deregulation removes government control, allowing market forces to be effective.

The deregulation of the telecommunications industry has given businesses many more choices, opportunities, and problems.

The **environment** of a system is that part which impacts or influences the system, but over which the system has minimal or no control.

Where is the **boundary** that separates the system from its environment?

During the time we have watched Michael and his ventures in business, many forces have been at work shaping what is now the modern global telecommunications industry. Initially, most U.S. companies had only a single telecommunications vendor to deal with—AT&T. Since deregulation and divestiture, companies have dozens of telecommunications vendors. Realizing this, organizations are taking steps to not only manage their communications capabilities, but to understand the importance of this asset and its ability to influence competition. Additionally, they are attempting to include considerations for communications in their strategic planning. Deregulation of the telecommunications industry has given businesses many more choices, opportunities, and problems. *Choices* come from multiple vendors offering a great variety of goods and services from which to choose. *Opportunities* abound in how companies use these goods and services in bringing to fruition their visions of communications and to enhance their competitive advantage. *Problems* also abound because of the available choices, limited resources, rapid obsolescence, and fierce competition.

To reflect for a moment, telecommunications at the beginning of the second half of the 20th century meant analog voice communications, that is, the telephone. LECs continued to make extensive use of human operators, switches were electromechanical, and long-distance communication was special and expensive. As the new millenium began, human intervention in voice communications was rare, most communication beyond the local switch was digital, and data were rapidly overtaking voice in importance, expense, and revenue generation. The recognition that voice and data can be integrated into the same circuit or channel is at hand as we move to all digital circuits for greater control, an absence of noise, and greater speed (wider bandwidths).

As the second half of the 20th century began, mainframe computers were just beginning to gain wide acceptance. Even then, they were used in stand-alone, batch modes. Now, mid- and micro-sized computers abound, with distributed processing[1]

---

[1] Distributed processing is a means of placing several smaller computers near the activities that they support as opposed to having one larger centralized processor. In like manner, the storage of data can be distributed.

Competitive advantage means you have a disproportionally larger share of a market because the customer is able to positively differentiate your product or services.

and data storage requiring significant data communications facilities to connect everything. What this means is that not only computing and data storage must be attended to, but also that communication paths between them must be planned, installed, and maintained. In other words, we have changed our view of what we are managing. **We are learning that the operations department must focus primarily on running a communications network, not a stand-alone computer.**

Along with a change of corporate attitude as to what is a necessary evil and what is an asset comes a change in view of customers and suppliers. Where once we dealt with suppliers (vendors) in a purely adversarial manner (get as much and give as little as possible), enlightened companies now consider them partners in their total enterprise. This includes frequent exchange of data and even access to private databases. We have done the same with customers, realizing that we are to them what our suppliers are to us. As we can tighten the total channel from the supplier of raw materials to the ultimate consumer, sending information "down" the channel and goods "up" the channel in response to consumer demands, the total system works better and more efficiently. As we develop partnerships in the channel, we may exclude competitors, and even gain some loyalty. All of this requires a change of attitude, legal commitments, and a superior and stable communications capability. Where paper "floated" along, now electronic orders, invoices, and receipts move quickly. Where companies once "lived on the float," they now prevail on lower costs and greater sales that result from having the information required to place the right goods where they are wanted in a timely manner with a minimum of inventory and cost.

The Real World   12–1
The 12 Worst U.S. IT Disasters

Incident	Date	Data Centers Affected
1. Nationwide Internet virus	May 16, 1988	500+
2. Chicago flood	April 1992	400
3. New York power outage	August 13, 1990	320
4. Chicago/Hinsdale fire	May 8, 1988	175
5. Hurricane Andrew	September, 1992	150
6. Nationwide Pakistani virus	May 11, 1988	90+
7. San Francisco earthquake	October 17, 1989	90
8. Seattle power outage	August 31, 1988	75
9. Chicago flood	August 13, 1987	64
10. East Coast blizzard	March 1993	50
11. Los Angeles riot	April/May 1992	50
12. World Trade Center disaster	September 11, 2001	40

As a footnote, a *Disaster Protection Plan* brochure from Wang noted that, "In 1992, Hurricane Andrew—the largest and costliest disaster in U.S. history—caused destruction of over $6 billion, *five times* the damage caused by Hurricane Hugo in 1989."

Quick Response,
a rapid replenishment method in the textile and apparel industry, provides a competitive advantage to its users by use of telecommunications technology.

We have to view technology, and especially telecommunications technology, as an investment and a way to gain and maintain **competitive advantage.**[2] Our ultimate aim is to give customers more reasons to do business with us than with a competitor. Partnerships work to achieve this with suppliers, and having the right goods at the right time does this with the ultimate customer. To gain competitive advantage, organizations are spending a significant amount of money on communications and other computer-based equipment. For example, to install Quick Response (see Information Window 12–1), one retailer has spent in excess of $180 million over a three-year period to upgrade computers and point-of-sale terminals, put in a standard barcode system with readers, and move sales data down the channel to the suppliers. This retailer has 45 stores in the Southeast, with one store alone having over a million SKUs (stock keeping units).

Information Window 12–1
Quick Response in the Apparel and Textile Industry

Quick Response is a program in the apparel and textile industry used to gain and maintain a competitive advantage. It is a management philosophy encompassing strategy, partnerships, and technology to create information channels and merchandise replenishment systems to have the right product on the shelf at the right time with minimum inventory. Quick Response seeks competitive advantage through satisfying changing customer preferences. This means *having what customers want when they want it.*

Quick Response is a combination of technology and partnerships. The *technology* aspects include barcode standards, barcode scanning, data processing, electronic data interchange (EDI), and electronic telecommunica-

tions. The *partnership* aspect means that trading partners, whether suppliers or customers, are seen by an individual entity as a possible ally, not an adversary. It is questionable whether the technology or the partnerships have the greatest problems and opportunities. Each is vital to Quick Response; each takes effort and investment.

Quick Response has two facets (see figure below): (1) to move information from the customer's point of contact in the retail store through the total textile-apparel channel and (2) to move goods efficiently throughout the channel to support the retail outlets. The object is information and goods movement in a dynamic and highly competitive market, while reducing costs and increasing sales through availability of merchandise for sale.

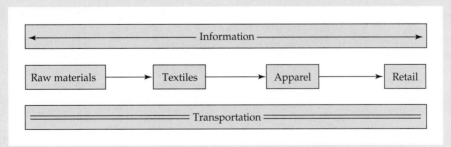

[2] Although the term *competitive advantage* is usually associated with for-profit companies, we could apply this term, as a concept of doing business better, to any organization. While an army, church, or federal agency has no commercial competitor, each dollar allocated to the organization does have competition in the form of alternate uses. Thus, the application of technology to not-for-profit organizations is important to minimize cost and maximize customer service, just as in for-profit, private sector organizations.

PRESSURES TO USE TELECOMMUNICATIONS

Why are some companies moving ahead rapidly, changing their view of voice and data communications, while others are dragging their corporate feet? In many organizations, control of voice communications and data communications resides in totally different parts of the organization. The telephone operators, once under

---

Information Window   12–2
Video Teleconferencing for the IEEE at BellSouth

Members of the IEEE organization gathered in Nashville, Atlanta, New Orleans, Jacksonville, and Birmingham to discuss plans for the coming year. They gathered at the offices of South Central Bell or Southern Bell (parts of BellSouth, the RBOC, before they were renamed with the RBOC name) that housed video teleconferencing equipment. In some cases, the channel was a DS3 (45 Mbps) circuit for full-duplex video and audio conferencing. In most instances, they used a DS1 (1.544 Mbps) for full-duplex, color, full-motion video and audio. Each site had two 26-inch TV sets, one on themselves and one at the site that was voice activated. When a person began to speak, the equipment switched the video and audio to that site without human intervention.

Of note is the use of twelve 64 Kbps channels in each direction for full-duplex transmission. They achieved full-motion, color video with only 768 Kbps, which is about a 60-to-1 compression ratio. Meanwhile, the conference room next door had point-to-point videoconferencing using a basic rate ISDN dial-up circuit.

The Real World   12–2
Web Telephones: The Internet's Version of CTI

One of the most interesting by-products of the advances in PC-based computer-telephony integration (CTI) technology is its head-on collision with the Internet. The result is a product called the Web telephone. Web telephones allow two people to converse in real time over the Internet, rather than via a telephone carrier. A half-dozen of these products are now available. Most of them are aimed at the consumer market, but a few are aimed at businesses. These include the WebPhone from NetSpeak Corp., in Boca Raton, Florida (http://www.netspeak.com); WebTalk from Quarterdeck Corp., in Marina del Rey, California (http://www.quarterdeck.com); and Revolutionary Software Inc.'s Intercome for OS/2.

These packages work in one of two ways: Users either agree to log in to the same telephone server at the same time to conduct a call (following the "chat" paradigm), or users exchange IP addresses and use them to make spontaneous or prearranged calls. For users that have dynamically changing IP addresses, products in the latter category, such as WebPhone, can use a host address to make a call, query for the current IP address, and route accordingly. Eventually, some of these products, such as WebPhone, will add store-and-forward capabilities for voice messaging and unified message boxes, says John Staten, chief financial officer of NetSpeak.

CTI vendors also are beginning to announce products that perform voice messaging over the Internet. In March, CallWare Technologies Inc. introduced an Internet component for CallWare voice messaging users. This allows users to send and retrieve messages over Internet or intranet links. The company says this add-on is supported by the same PBX systems—from vendors such as AT&T, Mitel Corp., Northern Telecom Inc., and Siemens Rolm Communications Inc.—that currently support its other CallWare voice messaging products.

Source: Julie Bort, "Web Telephones: The Internet's Version of CTI," *INFOWORLD*, http://www.infoworld.com.

the administrative function, dealt with the simple idea of enabling or facilitating voice communications. As technology replaced people in this function, computer-based hardware continued the same service until the organization began to realize the importance of voice communications and the data-processing organization realized the importance of data communications. At that point, each function viewed their domain—voice or data—as important. Enlightened organizations have seen the need to bring these two functions together, generally under the control of the MIS organization. The basis for this structure is that telephone and voice communications are largely understood by most people in the organization and are seen as an investment as opposed to a cost; technology has replaced people in voice communications; voice can be treated just as data, once digitized; and there is a need to combine voice and data on the same lines for control and lower cost. In reality, we want to include and combine *all* forms of data communications, including video, imaging, fax, on digital circuits. In today's environment, with the convergence of voice and data, organizations *must* combine voice and data organization structures. As voice moves to IP technology this change becomes obvious. In the environment of convergence, managers have found that it is far easier for data communications people to learn voice than the other way around.

CIO (chief information officer)
The top IT management executive.

Managers are realizing the importance of controlling all information resources and have even designated an executive to manage this area. The **chief information officer (CIO),** a position at the same level as the vice presidents of finance, sales, and operations, has been created in many organizations to control the information resource from a total organization perspective. Part of the reason for having an executive as manager is the overriding business reason for telecommunications in achieving the organization's goals. As we discuss below, the telecommunications organization must be run like a business.

A BUSINESS WITHIN A BUSINESS

What **business functions** will you not find in a telecommuncations group?

The telecommunications organization, like its parent MIS organization, has the same functions as its parent (see Figure 12.1). Consider for a moment the organization of Johnson Lighting and Security Company. We have shown that a portion of Michael's evolving firm installs security and lighting devices. This is the *operations function,* which is comparable to the factory in a production company. He also has a *marketing function* that analyzes the environment and works with potential customers for new business. His *administrative group* keeps track of inventory,

**FIGURE 12.1
Functions of a
Business**

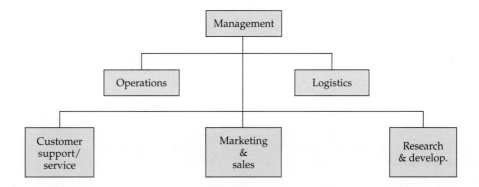

funds, and accounts. *Customer support,* a highly important group in any service organization, works with customers once the installation is complete, resolving problems, performing contract maintenance, and providing information back to JL&S about additional customer needs. While JL&S and JEI are not yet deep into *research and development,* that function will become more important with time.

Because we have said that the telecommunications function is a business within a business, just as is MIS, we would expect to find the same functions that any business has. The most obvious is the operations function of installation and operation of the network. Before that can happen, there must be marketing to customers to determine needs, research and development to plan for and engineer these needs, customer support once new equipment is installed, and administration to keep track of it all. As we will show, not all of these functions require the same level of technical ability. All, though, are required.

Information Window 12–3
Porter and Millar Value Chain

The value chain (Porter, Porter and Millar) is helpful in that it provides a partitioned view of the *activities* that produce value for a firm. (See Figure 12.2.) The *primary activities* in this model are inbound logistics, operations, outbound logistics, marketing and sales, and service. One can see that these activities are similar to functions of any business. In addition there are *support activities* that must exist for effective performance of the primary activities. The support activities include the firm's infrastructure, human resource management, technology development,

and procurement. While the entire value chain should be viewed holistically, the partitioning allows managers to view the extent of telecommunications deployed in each of the activities.

This examination can reveal areas that could benefit from the implementation of upgraded capabilities. The model is also useful in benchmarking one's own organization with competitors. Many firms now believe that information technology (including telecommunications) is mission critical.

FIGURE 12.2 **The Value Chain Model**

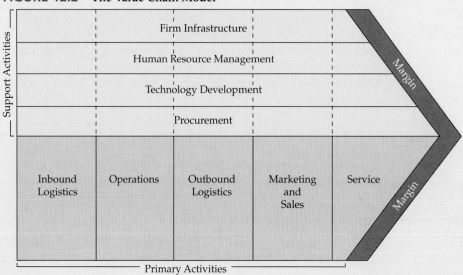

To put the business-within-a-business theme into perspective, consider the phases many telecommunications groups go through. First the group is tolerated as a group of mechanics that install and move telephones and modems. This is the *operations phase.* Then the value of data and telecommunications is realized, and the group and MIS become an *information utility.* Data and communications are viewed like electrical power. Finally the organization realizes the potential of the groups, and they become a *coordinated business resource.* (See Information Window 12–4.)

business within a business

What advantages can be achieved by viewing the telecommunications organization as a business within the overall business?

Telecommunications should be treated like a full-fledged business, in support of the parent organization; it is this support that gives it purpose. That is, the telecommunications organization, its products, and its services are not self-evident and telecommunications projects are not undertaken for their own sake, but are in support of some activity within the company. Telecommunications and MIS projects are always undertaken to support or solve a business problem or opportunity. Thus, when projects are anticipated, the classical functions of management—planning, organizing, staffing, directing, and controlling—must be considered. These views must be applied to both the telecommunications group and projects undertaken.

Planning requires a perspective of the timing and life of the project, and the level of the organization being supported. Planning involves preparing to deal with events and including other facets of organization to make the plans come to fruition. The three levels of planning are as follows:

Information Window   12–4

THE OPERATIONS ERA

- Concerned with providing reliable telephone and telex services inside the firm.

- Central planning is rare.

- Responsibility for communications is scattered among a number of people and budgets: data and voice communications are separate.

- People take for granted that the telephone system works. In moving from strategy to cables and boxes, from abstraction to physical system, if the boxes do not work, the strategy is irrelevant.

THE INTERNAL UTILITY

- Telecommunications is a technical function; attention is focused on providing facilities as needed and on controlling costs.

- Largely a reactive strategy.

- Disrupted in early 1980s due in part to Bell System divestiture.

- Controlled costs by tracking them and charging them out.

- Realized that phone calls should be transmitted in digital form, and that in some state all information—telephone calls, computer data, pictures, documents, and diagrams—could share the same highway instead of needing separate, incompatible facilities.

- The *telecommunications utility* is complex to plan, implement, operate, and advance.

THE COORDINATED BUSINESS RESOURCE

- Depends on management enlightenment: the recognition at the top of the organization that the topic is no longer an internal utility that is an expensive subset of the firm's administration and operations but a function that is part of the company's business infrastructure.

- Telecommunications operations become a business issue when the business is online.

- You want the technology to be as stable as a utility, so you can depend on it and use it in nonutilitarian ways.

Source: Adapted from Peter G. W. Keen, *Competing in Time* (Cambridge, MA: Ballinger, 1988), p.15.

Process functions of management
- Planning
- Organizing
- Staffing
- Directing
- Coordinating and control

The closer the event is, the easier it is to plan for, such as daily events.

The more strategic the activity, the greater is its impact, and the smaller the ability to accurately predict its outcome.

- *Operational* planning deals with the day-to-day operations of the organization and its resource usage. Supervisors organize and oversee the daily activities of their people to accomplish actions in support of the organization's product or service. To do this, they plan for the day's or week's activities. The time horizon of organizational planning as noted is immediate, often spanning only days or weeks.

- *Tactical* planning deals with a longer timespan and pays particular attention to the acquisition of resources for future operations. The time horizon may lengthen to a year and is concerned with personnel acquisition and training, inventory purchase and storage, and funds acquisition. It is budget-oriented and closely linked with the equivalent planning of the parent organization.

- *Strategic* issues are those that charter the direction of the organization. They answer questions such as "what business should we be in," "where should we build a new facility," and "who are present and future competitors?" The time horizon of strategic thinking is from one to five years. Strategic planning, a prime function of upper management, prepares for the future. Because the telecommunications group supports the strategic planning of the parent organization, telecommunications management should be included in the parent's plans. The more the telecommunications function knows about the vision, direction, and plans of its parent, the better it is able to support these plans with architecture, reserve capability, and trained personnel.

Caveat: The idea of a strategic planning time horizon being up to five years is a historical one: that is to say, this is the time span traditionally used or used with traditional organizations. As one telecommunications executive noted. "How can I make a five-year plan? I cannot forecast well enough to make a one-year plan." In the voice and data communications industry, technical changes occur so rapidly that we do not have the luxury of believing we can plan five years hence or depend on our present competitive advantage lasting 12 months without change. If you are dealing with Internet-based business, change is even faster.

The next function of management is that of **organizing.** Organizing for projects includes several considerations, the main of which is establishing relationships among the entities of the organization. Some projects, such as additional telephones in the office or factory, are of operational importance, while others that are used for vendor negotiations may be more tactical in nature. The creation of new networks that will change how the organization competes or supports its personnel are of

Frank and Ernest

strategic importance. While every project must be justified, the manner of this justification will relate to the importance and time orientation of the outcome.

When considering telecommunications and MIS projects, managers must consider the costs and the benefits. Benefits may be either tangible and measurable or intangible and nonquantifiable. For example, many strategic projects relate to the future nature of business and are visionary. Thus, while the cost may be readily apparent, the benefits may not be as they deal with highly intangible outcomes, such as different methods of conducting business.

The management function of **staffing** relates to the classical acquisition, retention, and training of qualified personnel who can plan, define, install, operate, and maintain technology in support of business problems and opportunities. The level of staffing, that is, the number and quality, depends on the complexity of the voice and data systems resource and the extent to which their operation and maintenance are provided by vendors or outsourced. As the organization gains total control of the telecommunications resource, it requires more and better qualified personnel.

Do telecommunications managers lead, orchestrate, or simply organize?

The first such member of a telecommunications group is the *telecommunications (TC) manager,* the person with an ability to grasp technical subject matters and business needs. Although he/she need not personally be a technician or former technician, he/she must be able to converse with and stand his/her ground with the technical people. This person will interpret business needs and direct other people and vendors to develop a telecommunications plan.

Caveat: There has been a temptation historically to place a person in the position of telecommunications manager based on political connections or promotability as opposed to credentials that meet the demands of the position. As shown in Figure 12.3, filling this position with one who only checks the long-distance charges and keeps the telephone directory up-to-date is a misallocation of resources.

The next group of staff members is the *designers and implementers* of telecommunications capabilities. These engineers find solutions to business problems and

FIGURE 12.3
The TC Manager as a Bill Verifier

The Real World   12–3
Leadership Is Not Managership

"Managers are not leaders automatically. Managers manage systems, finances, computers, equipment. But *leaders lead people,* people with hopes, dreams, and ambitions, just like the leaders. Without people, the high-tech systems and equipment of managers will utterly fail." General H. Norman Schwarzkopf, Commander of U.S. Forces, Desert Storm.

opportunities and design networks and capabilities to support the solutions. Once implemented, the *network operations staff* operates them on a daily basis, with help from the *technical support staff.* This latter group needs to be technically competent and experienced as they must be able to define problems and resolve them quickly. The last members of the group are the *administrative support staff,* who take care of accounting, inventory, and general administrative tasks. In some cases, *consultants* will be hired to complement the other members of the group on a short-term basis.

How do we reconcile the need to control resources and the need to effectively use them?

The management function of **directing** involves the supervisory task of getting people to successfully perform the required tasks. The primary skill is dealing with people to get complex jobs done; the requirement is for leadership.

Finally, the telecommunications manager performs the function of **controlling** the telecommunications resources of the organization. This means inventory management of equipment, circuits, and networks. The concern is not just the inventory of physical parts but also the inventory of what is really important about telecommunications: communications circuits and channels, now referred to generically as bandwidth. Equipment must be acquired and funded and the costs must be charged or allocated. Some costs are obvious as are their allocation, such as when a circuit or piece of equipment is obtained specifically for a given function or project. Other costs must be allocated based on use or some other criteria. Some believe that no service should be seen as a free good, so chargeback for use, based on some criteria such as amount of data transferred or permanent bandwidth, is in order. The problem of such chargeback is that it may actually inhibit use if the method is wrong.

Security means the right people have access and all others do not.

Another aspect of control is *security,* against the threat of theft or intrusion into the network. The first deals with physical locks and accountability, and the latter deals with software locks and training. In either case, because of the importance of telecommunications and information systems capabilities, **disaster recovery** is an important aspect of security and control. It deals with the ability to continue operations upon the catastrophic interruption of organization facilities, such as the terrorist attacks in New York and Washington on September 11, 2001; the San Francisco earthquake; Hurricanes Andrew, Hugo, and Opal; or the blizzard of 1993. A secure telecommunications capability is one that works continuously, reliably, and without intrusion. (See the section on risk assessment later in this chapter for more on disaster planning.)

Adequate disaster recovery capability is the diference between continued success and failure.

Security of the data accessible via the network:
- Encryption
- Access
- Passwords
- Firewalls

Computer Telephony Integration (CTI)

Computer telephony integration (CTI) is the fusing of telephone operations with computers. It has as its focus the management of voice telephony. CTI employs the

CTI can receive the Caller ID information of an incoming call (between rings one and two) and use that information to look up the customer or vendor in a database. This information can be displayed on a computer screen when the call is answered.

power of the computer and advances in telephony to enable telecommunications managers to exert management control over voice. One aspect of the management is over the routing and additional data about the incoming call. Another aspect is that of management reporting and control of long-term voice activity.

CTI falls into the following categories:

1. *Interactive voice response.* These systems use telephone keypads as the data-entry interface for performing standardized call functions with a database, that is, verifying account balances.

2. *Call center.* Many inbound calls are received and intelligently routed to real people. The interactive voice response system may be used to gather initial information, or Caller ID information may be used to pull information from a database and send it to a customer service representative.

3. *Interactive fax.* This involves using fax machines as nodes on a network of fax servers to send automated responses, fax broadcasting, or fax-on-demand.

4. *Messaging.* Messaging is a store-and-forward system. It includes voice mail, fax mail, and email. With "unified messaging" each user has a single inbox where all types of mail can be accessed.

5. *Outbound systems.* The computer generates outbound calls with predictive dialing. The calls are transferred to a human if answered.

6. *Audio-text systems.* This application allows voice and data to travel over POTS lines during the same call. It requires proprietary equipment at both ends for data transmission.

Today, much of CTI has gone into the client-server arena. For example, Microsoft included its client-side Telephone API[3] (TAPI) with every copy of Windows 95. The server-side TAPI is embedded in the Windows NT server. Novell's version, Telephony Services API (TSAPI) is also available. There are many vendors in the CTI arena.

There are several tools available for CTI applications. Telecommunications managers should ensure that the tool chosen will support current software and telecommunications equipment investments. Bandwidth is of great importance if universal or unified messaging is used. Based on the lower costs and ease of use of new systems, CTI will likely be an essential part of the organization's telecommunications architecture.

TELECOMMUNICATIONS STRATEGY ISSUES

telecommunications strategy
What is the purpose of a TC strategy?

For the organization's telecommunications **strategy** to succeed, managers must understand the major telecommunications strategy issues. In today's environment, among the major issues of telecommunications strategy are the integration of computing platforms across the organization to support organizational objectives and functions. For example, a multidivision organization may have different vendor equipment at its distributed locations, yet require the same processing of data for customer service. These same platforms often must communicate with vendors'

---

[3] API = Application Program Interface.

Information Window   12–5

During hurricanes, especially the memorable occurrences of Andrew, Hugo, and Opal, companies learned about disaster planning and recovery. In reviewing of disaster plans, organizations learn quickly that all facets of this protective venture are not high technology. For example, of great importance is mapping emergency evacuation routes for personnel, determining how to get personnel back to work, and ensuring sufficient supplies, such as fuel for power generators. The technology of backup generators fails without fuel.

Information Window   12–6

Copper wire is valuable: During 1961, one of the authors was stationed in the Philippine Islands with the U.S. Air Force. His unit, the Ground Electronics Engineering Installation Agency, installed radio and wire communications facilities. One afternoon, his unit installed a 500' length of communications cable in a trench near the State Department area. This cable was 200 pair, twisted-pair copper wire, in a lead sheath. At the end of the day, the work detail covered the trench with dirt and went home. Shortly thereafter, some inventive locals arrived on the scene. They dug small holes at each end of the newly laid cable, cutting each end from the cable it was attached to. They then made a loop of one end and attached it to a brace of water buffalo, which obediently pulled the cable out of the ground without disturbing the earth. The next day, the Air Force discovered that, for some reason, the new circuit did not work.

Why would someone steal copper wire? Unlike the glass in fiber optic cable, which has no intrinsic value, copper as well as the lead sheath were valuable resources, salable on the open (black) market. Thus, as in the Philippines in the sixties, the theft of copper wire for resale and profit often disrupts communications services.

Samina-SCI, a U.S. contract manufacturing company, relies on EDI for all customer orders and ordering of billions in parts. Without EDI, they could not operate.

platforms to effect such strategies as JIT. In the latter case, EDI allows application-to-application transfer of data. However, for intra-organizational functions on diverse platforms, the telecommunications environment may have to solve this problem directly to allow the various applications to communicate to each other.

The telecommunications strategy should point to an architecture that will support organizational functions. It should not constrain either the organization or the evolution of technology in support of its functions. These issues are even more important in an era in which client-server computing has become the norm. For example, if the telecommunications strategy and the resultant architecture were firmly in place to support directly connected applications, then client-server applications would find a foreign environment. However, if the strategy and architecture had been designed to encompass client-server, its ultimate adoption would entail no major obstacles. In this case the strategist either would have paved the way for evolution to client-server applications or would have imposed obstacles to them. These are the issues that have caused the evolution into open systems architecture, where vendors design to public specifications as opposed to proprietary standards.

Telecommunications for Competitive Advantage

The vast majority of strategic information systems are dependent on telecommunications. Strategic information systems planning must encompass new market strategies and new technologies (for example, the firm's intranet).

There are several cases cited in the information system literature and in Chapter 10 about firms gaining competitive advantage through employing information technology. Several of these cases are well-known. Other cases may not have had the exposure of American Airlines or American Hospital Supply, but are significant nonetheless.

The Boeing Company's design system established for the Boeing 777 aircraft has been cited as a key competitive feature. This system has global links with subcontractors and, in addition, a parts logistics system that connects to customers. The airlines can obtain information regarding parts availability to support their maintenance efforts.

Federal Express, a package and mail service, has used its telecommunications network to support the claim: "Absolutely, positively overnight delivery and we'll tell a customer at any point in the delivery process where the package is, whether it has been delivered, and who signed for it." Federal Express, now called simply FedEx, obtained a competitive advantage through its ability to add value with information distributed globally. Competitors such as United Parcel Service (UPS) were forced to emulate FedEx's system. UPS reportedly spent US$1.4 billion in this effort to regain its competitive position.

United Services Automobile Association (USAA) has been a leader in relying on information technology for its customer (member) services. It has used telecommunications and computer systems to expand its products and services. USAA has made extensive use of CTI, imaging, and so on, to become an often-cited example of gaining advantage via information technologies.

There are many other instances of firms making use of telecommunications for competitive advantage. One factor that seems certain is that today's competitive advantage will likely erode as competitors emulate the success of innovators. This means that managers should continuously seek opportunities to exploit telecommunications technologies to keep ahead of the pack.

TELECOMMUNICATIONS PROJECTS

Telecommunications projects, by their very nature, mean distributed nodes/sites, often with wide geographic requirements. Even small organizations tend to spread out and telecommunications allows them to communicate at a distance while working in a centralized mode. When the distances expand, time becomes a consideration as communications between New York and Denver or San Francisco have different constraints. Thus, when developing a widespread telecommunications

Information Window   12–7

The parents of a friend of the authors have an electroplating business. Their parents started in a single building, but soon expanded down the street to a second location. The first telecommunications unit to help them was, of course, the telephone, so they could speak across the distance without walking anywhere. Next, they installed fax machines to transport documents. The point to be stressed is that even a small Mom-and-Pop business finds telecommunications capabilities vital.

capability one must consider not only the local busy (peak) time but also the peak times at all other pertinent locations.

Telecommunications-intensive systems become nonoperable when the telecommunications portion becomes dysfunctional.

Remember that most medium-to-large information systems have a telecommunications component; thus, we call them *computer-based, telecommunications-intensive information systems*. When designers consider the responsiveness of the information system, they must consider the responsiveness of the total system. Here we mean (1) the time it takes the computer processing the request to acknowledge the request for work, (2) the other tasks that share the processor, (3) the length of time of processing, and (4) the telecommunications processing and delay times. Thus, for a transaction that looks up a part number and prints the price and description on a terminal screen, a responsive system must be able to

- Quickly receive the request (not wait in an input queue).

- Have enough of the processor's time (while sharing with other tasks).

- Process the request quickly (0.1–0.5 second).

- Have a "fast enough" telecommunications line to move the required data back to the requesting terminal quickly.

- Perform the above within a time that is reasonable to the user.

Just as the response time of the system is composed of the response times of the individual parts, so is the reliability of the system composed of the reliability of individual parts. Thus, a reliable, responsive system must be composed of reliable, responsive parts.

Early Internet access providers found their services growing at 5 percent per week.

When considering new telecommunications facilities in addition to those required for new information systems applications, several facts must be taken into account. (1) Data communications traffic is growing at 40 to 50 percent per year, compounded. We are in an area where the need for data circuits, or pipelines, is doubling every other year. (2) An unusual situation occurs when installing a new facility of any kind, and a telecommunications facility is no exception—that is referred to as the *superhighway (or freeway) effect.* The creation of a good resource results in significantly greater use of the resource than predicted, simply because it is perceived as valuable. Thus, when designing a new network, the designer must understand the effect of providing a resource that may be its own worst enemy, due to the high demand it causes. Because of the increased utilization, the useful lifetime of the resource is reduced. (3) New facilities must work with the old. This constraint is called backward/downward compatibility. (Remember that every new release of your PC's operating system has to continue to run old programs.)

freeway effect How does a new TC capability attract greater use than first anticipated?

As we discuss in detail in the next chapter, telecommunications projects generally follow a life cycle, much like information systems. We will explore the MIS-familiar **SDLC (systems development life cycle).** As with SDLC in information systems, the more time and energy spent in analysis and design, the less will have to be spent actually installing and maintaining the facility, and the more maintainable the end product will be. In the area of purchasing components for telecommunications from a multitude of vendors, one heuristic says that the number of operational problems in a communications network increases as the square of the number of vendors. When there was only one vendor, that is, AT&T, to deal with, there was one problem $(1 \times 1 = 1)$. If you kept AT&T as your IXC (1) but added Sprint (1) and MCI (1) for least-cost routing, added a BOC as a LEC (1), bought your instruments from GTE (1), and installed a PBX from Nortel® (1), your problems grew to 36 $(6 \times 6 = 36)$. Adding one additional vendor, for maintenance, runs this number to 49. Although the level of standardization at the voice communications level makes this situation exaggerated, the point is that with variety comes complexity.

By the way, when you are part of a telecommunications project, or just have to explain one to a senior manager, remember that **the more senior the manager the smaller the tolerance for technical details.** While we hope these same senior managers will become educated enough to be able to intelligently make technical decisions and not leave these to the engineers and other "techies," they will want a minimum of technical data on most occasions. Thus, when you are talking about putting in a data communications line between two sites to exchange financial data on cash management, and the vice president of finance asks how fast a line you need, what do you say? You might say we will put in a 9,600 bits-per-second line, using a dial-up connection because that will transfer about 1,000 characters a second, or take about two seconds to move a page of text. (A page is $66 - 6 = 60$ lines/ 2×80 char/line $= 2,400$ char/page.) If their eyes don't roll back into their heads, you might say that this same line will move 20 pages of text in a minute, which in this case is adequate. However, should the business wish to move more data in the same amount of time, you would have to move to either a leased line or dial-up data line, at say 58 Kbps, which is offered by the local phone company. The point here is that we rounded the data to put them into accurate, although not precise, units. These are units that a senior manager will understand, and we did not use technical jargon.

Requests for proposal/quotation are made to vendors of services that request or give information. In the case of an *RFP (request for proposal)*, a company defines and tells a vendor what functionality or service it wants, when, and what it must do. The response from the vendor is a *proposal* in which they say what they will provide, how (designed, off-the-shelf, or purchased from another vendor), when, at what cost, and under what special conditions. Special conditions include discounts contingent on total annual purchases, deviations from the original RFP specification, added features, and warranty.

RFP/RFO
What is the major difference between an RFP and an RFQ?

A *request for quotation (RFQ)* is similar to an RFP except it just requests cost information because the data requested are often about existing (off-the-shelf) equipment. Again, the responsive *quote* will say what, how much including discounts, deviations, sources, and timing. In the case of either an RFP or RFQ, the aim is to get vendors to tell what they will do, for what dollars, when, and under what circumstances. It may be off-the-shelf equipment with or without discount, or it may mean a totally engineered system. In any case, vendors are expected to perform enough engineering to reduce their risk and to give sufficient detail to remove any concern you have as to their ability to perform the task. Additionally, large projects call for progress payments, the incremental payment of funds for completion of incremental work. Whenever RFPs/RFQs are issued, it is important to specify a standard response format for ease of comparing the responses and selecting the best alternative.

Many people will consider vendors as adversaries, as each is viewed as wanting to extract as much of your money with as little effort as possible. In reality, they are often experts in their field who have the ability (via free consulting, handbooks, and computer programs) to help you design a link or network. Often they will provide free assistance to gain a competitive advantage over their competitors. In many cases, vendors are becoming "partners" and are actively involved in assisting organizations to solve their business problems. The vendors recognize that a good customer is very valuable and a mutually profitable relationship is to their advantage over the long term.

THE MANAGEMENT OF TELECOMMUNICATIONS

There are two sides to the management of telecommunications. One side is managing the technology; the other is managing the organization. In both cases, the objective is to have an organization and equipment in place that will support the voice and data communications needs of the parent organization. Given that, we now will look further at the organization that supports the technology.

If you stop for a moment and consider what skills you would find in a telecommunications group, you would expect to see those who design and install the new equipment and facilities, others who make the existing telecommunications infrastructure work, and people who take care of all the nontechnical details. Thus, you will find a group with a lot of diversity, ranging from telecommunications engineers to purchasing agents. Since design comes before operations, let's look at the design function first.

Our Objective

cost-effective
Often the most innovative uses of telecommunications will have mostly intangible benefits.

The two primary objectives of network management are (1) to satisfy systems users and (2) to provide cost-effective solutions to an organization's telecommunications requirements. (See Figure 12.4.) Telecommunications resources are installed to allow greater communications and sharing of resources, to provide strategic links to suppliers and customers, and to enable centralization of decision making in a decentralized organization. Often, these applications allow you to stay in business and to remain competitive. (This may be the cost of doing business, as opposed to having a proper cost-to-benefit ratio.) Thus, you must be able to defend such applications with accounting-oriented people who demand a specified ROI. In a globally competitive market, you must have adequate telecommunications to even have a positive return on anything. It is very important to document both tangible and intangible benefits so the organization may succeed. Value-added approaches can be of benefit in assessment of the value of new systems. Often convincing evidence of the value of new telecommunications systems can be made by a careful accounting of the intangible benefits expected.

FIGURE 12.4
Objectives of Network Management

I. **User satisfaction**
   A. **Performance**—predictable transaction response time
   B. **Availability**—all necessary components are operable when needed
      1. Operational considerations—out of service for maintenance
      2. Mean time between failure
      3. Mean time to repair
         a. Repair facility
         b. Alternatives
   C. **Reliability**—probability that system will continue to function
      1. Error characteristics of medium
      2. Stability of hardware and software
      3. Complexity of system
      4. Backup components and redundancy
II. **Provide cost-effective solutions to organizations' TC requirements**
   A. **Planning**
      1. Install required features now and upgrade later
      2. Install with future in mind
   B. **Modularity** of equipment as opposed to upgrading from line to line

THE ORGANIZATIONAL SIDE OF TELECOMMUNICATIONS MANAGEMENT

Design and Implementation of New Facilities and Services

The first group to consider is the most engineering-oriented; these are the individuals who design new facilities. You might never come in contact with one of these people unless you are on a project that is increasing an existing capability or planning for a new facility. Then you will work with this group as they strive to determine the requirements of the new system, design additions to existing capabilities, and make sure it all works together. These people do not work in a vacuum as they must know everything about the present installed plant. They must know present equipment, wiring, circuits, terminals, switches, and vendors who might interface with or maintain them.

The designers start with the total requirement for the new or improved telecommunications capability and end up engineering and planning for the detailed physical components. If, for example, the objective is to increase the chance of getting a WATS line between 2:00 PM and 4:00 PM, the designers might do something like this:

- Look at the present number of WATS lines.

- Chart the traffic by zone of users, by time of day.

- Either look at the records for attempts to access a line or put a recorder on the system to document the unsuccessful attempts to access.

- Make an estimate of the cost and benefit of several levels of increased service.

- Make a recommendation.

This example is an easy one as the change involves a change of service from the IXC provider. What does this group do if you want to add VoIP or an IP VPN, be able to communicate via EDI to a supplier or customer, or upload large files across continents? In each case, the designers will determine the service change, define and investigate the alternatives, and present their recommendations. Once a plan of action is set, the designers will engineer or buy the required capabilities and install them.

Network Diagramming and Design Tools

In the client-server world, it has been common for new applications to place a crippling load on the network, slowing both the new and existing applications. Simply adding more servers and LAN segments will not necessarily solve the problem. The older methods of prediction about the impact of new applications were mostly seat-of-the-pants estimates. Problems have arisen because, in many instances, unmonitored LAN construction has created large Web networks with segments connected by simple bridging.

Especially in client-server environments, corporate networks have grown far too complex for any single manager to understand the true impact of changes. Now many network managers resort to simulation, software that can give you a graphic view or a working model of the network, to determine the impact of changes to their networks. Several software programs are available that can show LAN managers the traffic flow on their networks and assess the impact of adding applications and new users. The software allows "what-if" scenarios to be performed, for example, the impact of adding nodes, routers, servers; splitting the network into segments; and so forth. This capability is important as organizations move to scale their client-server applications up to serve the entire enterprise.

The simulation helps with capacity planning, that is, planning the network with the bandwidth to support the anticipated applications but without acquiring unneeded capacity. In the past, most networks were built on an ad hoc basis as the LANs were relatively low-cost and played a relatively minor role. As LANs have become an essential component in the organization's computing strategies, the lack of accurate measures of net performance and the piecemeal architecture of networks become significant roadblocks. Many of the networks beg for redesign or replacement in order to support client-server applications. One factor that makes networks more difficult to model than mainframe computers is the "bursty" nature of traffic, the mode where traffic is random in occurrence and highly variable in structure. The terminals in mainframe computing usually generate predictable and easily measured traffic, but network traffic varies greatly and often follows no pattern. Because processing is occurring at both the client and the server locations it is far harder to get a clear picture of an application's impact on overall network performance. Several vendors provide LAN simulation products. The products usually cost over US$10,000 and require both an understanding of the network and a fair amount of training.

In addition to simulation packages, there are several network diagramming tools available. These tools make it easy to document networks and visualize future configurations. Network diagramming software allows one to design and construct a diagram of the network quickly. Information about each device can then be input into a database that can be used as the basis for reports. Thus, these programs become very useful in network management tasks. Some popular products are *netViz*® (see Figure 12.5) *SysDraw*® the *Network Illustrator*®, *Visio Technical*®, *Visio Shapes*® for Network Equipment, and *ClickNet Professional*®.

Falling in between network simulators and diagrammers are *network designers* such as *NetSuite Professional Design*®. Network designers help the network manager by indicating whether the design of the network has the right physical configuration to work.

FIGURE 12.5
Example of netViz®

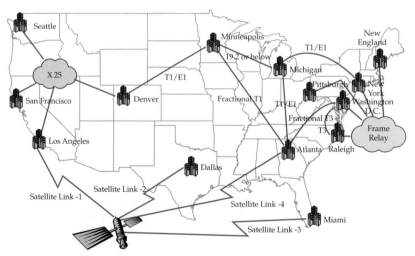

ABC Electronics' Corporate Network

Since the tools listed on page 532 are rapidly evolving as demand increases, it is important for network managers to assess the latest tools and their features. Professional publications publish product comparisons on a regular basis.

Network Operations and Technical Support

Once the designers have engineered new capabilities and have seen the installation to completion, these capabilities are turned over to the group who cares for them on a day-to-day basis. These are the people called when something does not work, and who perform routine and emergency maintenance to keep the system operational. They upgrade hardware and software, answer calls at the help desk, and work when you don't so maintenance does not interfere with normal service.

The service level described above is fine if you are in a business that operates for 8 to 12 hours a day. The operations and support group has people on duty to answer trouble calls and fix equipment. They have spare modems and can move telephones. Additionally, a group of the people work at night and on weekends to perform maintenance that necessitates bringing the system down. Much of this later work is totally transparent to the users. In fact, if the maintenance is done right, there will be no downtime and no need for trouble calls during the day. However, since equipment tends to fail in spite of the best of preventative maintenance, you do need repair personnel.

Now what happens in the situation where you are in a 24-hour-a-day business that must have its systems operational at all times, such as an airline reservation system, the phone company, or an emergency division of a hospital? You either must have sufficient redundancy built in so a failed part has a backup part that takes over the function automatically, or you must tolerate down time. When does Total System Services, Inc., of Columbus, Georgia, perform telecommunications and computer maintenance on their network and mainframes that handle VISA® and MasterCard® credit checks all day and all night?

Caveat: One of the most important characteristics of a system, any system, is reliability. Organizations want the system to operate when they need it, and they want it to operate properly. Additionally, they want a minimum of delays. For this to occur, the firms need sufficient capacity to have the minimum delay, and they need to use a stable design of good hardware and software so that breakdown is infrequent. The measure of frequency of breakdown, or interruption of service, is called **mean time between failures (MTBF).** The hard drive on a personal computer has an MTBF of 250,000+ hours, which, at 1,000 hours for a six-week period, means it should work continuously for thirty years before failure. (This is on an average basis, of course.) The higher the MTBF figure for any given

MTBF
Why is it important to know the MTBF of TC system components?

Information Window   12–8

Good design and good equipment, or good repair facilities—you can pay me now or pay me later, but you will pay!

Although this advertising theme started with some other product, it is equally applicable to telecommunications systems.

piece of equipment or system, the higher the cost. Therefore, you either need good design and good equipment, or good repair facilities. This is where the technical support group fits in.

Administrative Support

Just in case you think telecommunications groups are all peopled with engineers and "techies," ask yourself how they buy equipment, pay their bills, keep track of all their equipment, and do other such administrative tasks. With administrative people, of course! These are the nontechnical people who have such jobs as

1. Ordering and purchasing communications products and services.

2. Receiving equipment.

3. Inventorying equipment.

4. Checking and paying communications bills.

5. Determining chargeback methods to users, that is, who pays for what?

6. Coordinating adds, moves, and changes of equipment, including maintaining blueprints of present installations, handling the paperwork to make changes, and so forth.

7. Preparing and publishing a phone directory, whether it be paper or electronic.

8. Registering new telecommunications users for telecommunications access and for computer applications access, that is, maintenance security.

9. Training users.

10. Maintaining telecommunications procedures.

11. Providing telephone operator services.

The administration group performs the type of work that business administration graduates are qualified to perform. While it takes an engineer or engineering-trained person to do design and heavy-duty troubleshooting, much of the other work takes a more broadly trained and educated person. Both functions are very important if the total system is to be reliable. (See Table 12.1 and Figures 12.6 and 12.7.)

Final Thoughts

If you get a feeling that we are trying to separate the management of the telecommunications function from the telecommunications capability, you are right. The capability of telecommunications tends to be very hardware and engineering oriented, and requires people with special skills and inclinations. The management of the telecommunications function is much like the management of any specialized group of people—it takes the same organization and planning skills to direct the people and achieve the goals and objectives. As with any group of technical people, those in charge need to understand the technology at a high level, but not necessarily at a detailed level. For example, the manager of the telecommunications group needs to be able to understand what his/her designers and installers do, but not necessarily how they perform the tasks in detail.

TABLE 12.1   Telecommunications Job Categories for a Small-to-Medium-Size Organization

Position	Education	Duties
Technical		
Design engineer	BS or MSEE	Performs the analysis and engineering required to design and create the new or enhanced capability. This includes selection of media, protocol, and architecture and involves network maps that show components and capabilities that will support the organization. Works with Telco and vendors on new design and changes.
Operations and troubleshooting	Technical training plus vendor certification	Works with the system on a daily basis to keep it operational. Maintains and repairs system parts as required, generally using troubleshooting guides and component replacement. Installs hardware and software for system and end users. Works with Telco and vendors on daily operations.
Webmaster	Technical plus design	Creates, maintains, and continuously updates the organization's presence on the Internet, for example, WWW pages and interface design, database, etc.
Network administrator (involves management *and* technical duties)	BS plus network engineering certification	Concerned with the daily operation of LANs and WANs, especially the volume of traffic, speed of response, storage of data, and migration of data to avoid bottlenecks.
Management		
Chief information officer (CIO)	MBA	Overall responsibility for the total telecommunications capabilities of the organization, paying particular attention to the future needs as contained in the strategic plans. Maintains strategic linkages with vendors and partners.
Telecommunications manager	BS/BA plus MBA	Ultimate responsibility for telecommunications architecture and the organizational implications of any change or new capability. Directs the activities of all other members of the telecommunications group. Evaluates possible vendors and providers.
Administration	BS/BA	Performs the administrative functions required to support other functions, such as databases of assets, chargeback for services, and management reporting. Responsible for procurement of systems components, change configuration, and problem management.

FIGURE 12.6
Telecommunications Group Activities

I. System creation and upgrade
 A. Design and configuration
  1. Node equipment
  2. Media & bandwidth
  3. Software
  4. Tariffs
 B. Testing
  1. Initial
  2. Continuous
  3. Reporting
 C. Diagnosis
  1. Meeting spec
  2. For problems
  3. Fine-tuning
 D. Documentation
  1. Assets (database)
  2. Operations
  3. Repair

II. Operations
 A. Monitoring
 B. Control
 C. Diagnostics
 D. Problem reporting system
 E. Repair
 F. Documentation

III. Administration
 A. Personnel
  1. Attract & retain qualified personnel
  2. Training
 B. Asset management
 C. Purchasing
 D. Chargeback for asset usage

FIGURE 12.7
Telecommunications
Job Categories for a
Large Size
Organization

Source: Keen & Cummins.

I. Planning and development
  A. Director, telecommunications planning
  B. Manager, network planning
  C. Data network design technician
  D. Voice network design specialist
  E. Business applications development specialist
II. Service and support
  A. Director, network services and support
  B. Data communications service manager
  C. Help desk technician
  D. LAN service manager
  E. Office automation applications specialist
III. Operations
  A. Director of network operations
  B. Network security manager
  C. Data network operations manager
  D. LAN manager
  E. Voice systems technician
  F. Voice network operations technician

THE TECHNICAL SIDE OF TELECOMMUNICATIONS MANAGEMENT

Critical success factors (CSF) are those few things that must go properly for the organization to be successful.

This part of telecommunications management is concerned with *network management (or operations)*—the set of activities required to keep the communications network operational and reliable. These are the day-to-day tasks that must be done to keep the capability up and running and to keep the users satisfied. It is the tip of the iceberg that everyone sees, the part that must go right[4] for telecommunications, as it is installed, to be successful.

The scope of network operations responsibilities includes everything from the user's terminal to the mainframe, from a microcomputer to the shared network printer on the LAN, from the transmitting computer to the receiving computer, and from the supplier's modem to the customer's modem. While the network operations group may not be responsible for all of the equipment, they are the ones who are the point of help and must be able to work with such equipment as

A. User workstations

B. Modems

C. Line concentrators

D. Front-end processors

E. LANs/WANs

F. Network operating systems

G. Cluster controllers

H. Communications lines

I. Multiplexers

J. Communications software

K. Network management software

L. Hubs, routers, bridges

---

[4] John Rockart introduced **critical success factors (CSFs).** These are the few things that must go right for an organization to be successful. Reliable network operations have become a CSF for any organization that relies on telecommunications in the conduct of business.

When a call comes to the telecommunications help desk, or technician's cell phone, or an alarm sounds on the trouble board, or the network operating system displays a message on the operator's terminal or wireless PDA, someone from the network operations group must respond. These are the people who take the heat, the ones who keep it all together with spit and baling wire,[5] experience, and tenacity.

Consider that computer and communications networks in many companies are growing at a rate of 15 to 50 percent per year compounded. If your organization is expanding and taking on new markets, customers, and competitors, you may double your telecommunications capability every other year. The budget for this group and its equipment tends to be increasing, with an average communications budget for companies in the United States growing 10 to 20 percent per year. With this type of physical and fiscal growth, not only will you need to pay attention to telecommunications evolution, you will have a fair amount of visibility. To be more specific, it is important to manage the telecommunications capability because

- It is an expensive asset or resource.

- Competition is often impossible without it.

- It can create, maintain, or counter a competitive advantage.

- It may define how you do business.

- It may be your primary link to suppliers and customers.

Caveat: Early in the book we described what we called *computer-based telecommunications-intensive information systems.* Because computer-based information systems in organizations are so intertwined with telecommunications, you often cannot separate them. While there is one group of people who worry about software problems and another group who worries about telecommunications problems, the total system is vital[6] for the ongoing operations of the organization. Neither part is more important than the other, and neither part works without the other. This is a symbiotic relationship.

As the organization uses and relies on telecommunications, it tends to define how it does business and competes. *SABRE*® is one of the two most extensive airline reservation systems for reservation agents and airline asset management. It was created initially to schedule maintenance and to load the aircraft. It quickly became the premier method of competition for its creator, generating more profit than the carrying of passengers. Consider American Airlines without their *SABRE*® reservation system. The day they lost the pointers to their database system (of 1,100 disk drives), they operated and competed completely differently than the day before or the day afterwards. When the 800 service to Delta Airlines that ran through the central office in one part of Atlanta, Georgia, failed due to a lack of DC power, they were forced to operate and compete differently. Each of these companies depends on their telecommunications-intensive information systems to operate and compete. Without a part of the system, they have to change what they do and how they do it. As technology changes, the organization must be aware of the

---

[5] Please forgive these metaphors, but as is often the case, historical, colloquial references serve best. With the introduction of the hay baler on U.S. farms came the wire used in the machine to hold the bales together. The wire found many uses, from the barn to the kitchen, as it fixed so many things. Alas, the wire has been replaced by twine and gone is this wonderful resource, but not the metaphor.

[6] The definition of vital is "necessary for life."

changes and adapt. *SABRE*® is now threatened by Delta and other competitive systems such as *ORBITZ.com*®. While AA made *Micro-SABRE*® available from *America Online*® and other online sources, Delta along with most airlines has placed its reservation capability on the Internet. The Internet reservation capability has fundamentally changed the way that airline reservations are made, dramatically reducing the role of travel agencies.

Network Operations

This is the management of the physical network resources. Personnel in the group work in activation of components, lines, and controllers, rerouting traffic when circuits fail, and execution of normal and problem-related procedures. These people, in larger organizations, tend to sit in "control rooms" and watch system monitors (see Figure 12.8). While larger mainframe network monitoring and operating systems, such as IBM's NetView®, have intelligence in the system to do much of the control, humans are still needed to direct unusual actions. For example, IBM's NetView was originated as a mainframe-based capability that could manage several other mainframes and the networks attached. The operator had access to all resources on the total network. When a node failed, the system would generally be designed to intercept the message to the operator and try to execute reinitialization procedures, as contained in an expert system's lookup table. If this failed, the message was passed on to the operator for action. This environment encompasses large networks and possibly many mainframe computers.

One view of a network operator is a person sitting at a monitor in a control room, sending out commands to components on the network through the terminal keyboard. (See Figures 12.9 and 12.10.) The other view is the LAN network administrator, who spends most of his or her time working with users and checking on

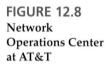

FIGURE 12.8
Network Operations Center at AT&T

Information Window   12–9

Imagine a room with 100 servers, such as would be normal for a server farm like Rackspace (www.rackspace.com). Would you want 100 monitors? Monitors cost about $100 each, take up a lot of space, use power, and give off heat that must be handled by the environmental control unit. The answer is to have only as many monitors as you would have servers or computers active at any one time. This can be done by using KVM switches. These Keyboard, Video, Mouse boxes allow a number of computers to be connected and use one keyboard, one video monitor, and one mouse. All this environment requires is a cable from the KVM switch to each computer; the one keyboard, mouse, and video monitor connect directly to the switch.

FIGURE 12.9
Sprint's Network Control Room

equipment in closets. Both are responsible for the physical wired network, the cards in microcomputers, modems, terminals, and anything that can stop or go bad. In reality, either of these roles can be supported remotely with telecommunications equipment. Just as a programmer can dial into the mainframe from home for a late-night problem resolution, the network operator or administrator can dial into the network to take action.

Considerations of Network Project Management

Project management requires

- Strong leadership
- Coordinating
- Planning
- Budgeting

FIGURE 12.10
Network Administration at Sprint

The Real World   12–4

Note that in Figure 12.8 there is a screen allowing operations center personnel to view breaking news from a national news TV broadcaster such as CNN. The reference to CNN and its activity during the Gulf War prompted some memories. I was an officer during Desert Shield and Desert Storm, working command and control at a major installation in the Northwest. We had CNN coverage in the command post and found that in addition to getting the information out quickly, CNN had a very good track record for accuracy of their information. We essentially got the news from CNN, then verified its legitimacy via military intelligence channels. By the time I retired in 1994, CNN access was standard for almost every command and control facility on every base in the Air Force.

Source: Retired U.S.A.F. officer.

- Scheduling

- Administration

For large-scale projects, it is important to use a *work breakdown structure (WBS)* (see Figure 12.11) so that every team member is allocated specific job functions, budget, and personnel resources at the proper time and place for execution of the

FIGURE 12.11
**Project
Management Tasks**

Even the smallest project requires expertise, information, and support from many people in the organization. A large-scale project may require the melding of a multidisciplinary team of people with varied skills, knowledge, expertise, and organization roles. In order to improve the success of a project, helpful management tools, utilities, and models can be found.

Several tasks need to be done:
1. Definition of scope of the project.
2. Assembling of a team:
    a. What expertise (knowledge)?
    b. What information is needed?
    c. What skills are needed?
    d. Source of team members.
3. Criteria
    a. Knowledge, expertise, experience.
    b. Access to information.
    c. Support skills (persuasion, negotiation, research, communications skills).
    d. Commitment.
    e. Reliability.
    f. Benefits to team member.
    g. Importance of reallocating teams.
4. Project plan
    a. Purpose.
    b. Parameters and goals.
    c. Deadlines.
    d. Key elements.
        i. Breakdown.
        ii. Assignments.
    e. Resources.
    f. Problems/obstacles.
    g. A time line (schedule for each task).
    h. Accountability.
    i. Feedback reporting.
    j. Tools.
5. Implementation
    a. Team delivers.
    b. Leader guides.
6. End project
    a. Reports.
    b. Lessons learned.
    c. Disband team (with appraisals).
7. Review and evaluation

project. Most network projects involve teams; consequently team leadership and management become essential skills. Project leaders need clear goals and vision and need to foster open communications, provide mutual trust and support, and ensure that teamwork is a part of performance appraisal. Some other items a project leader must understand are

• Team roles and responsibilities.

Project management's purpose is to manage and control *resources* to achieve a quality product, on time and within budget.

- Time reporting.

- Budget tracking.

- Issues and risks.

- Change process.

- Communications.

- Action items summary.

- Unplanned activities.

- Meeting and status reports.

Often projects fall behind schedule. In these cases, project managers need to be familiar with "crunch-time" alternatives. An understanding of project management techniques such as PERT can help identify where resource reallocation can return the project to planned schedule.

Project managers must be aware of *political considerations,* for example the differing views of different powerful people. Project managers who ignore this part of project execution are always at peril.

Network Management Software

There are now scalable network management systems to give network managers real-time total visibility to everything on the network, no matter how sophisticated or dynamic it is. The distributed nature of modern networks requires remote monitoring of LANs across WAN connections. In order to understand and resolve network issues before they impact, it is essential to have a real-time view of activity. Some capabilities, called *sniffers,* allow the administrator to see the level of traffic by circuit and node, balking, and collisions. S/he even can inspect packets. These applications are valuable in recording and reporting for SLA (service level agreement) compliance. In choosing network management, it is important that the overhead does not add significant traffic so that it impacts user performance on the network. Network management software becomes vital to those organization that require 24 × 7 reliability since their telecommunications infrastructure undergirds their business. One source for network management software is www.chevin.com.

SNMP and CMIP

A problem arises when the total network contains several gatewayed networks of differing protocols. The problem is one of providing information about one network to another. To facilitate this exchange of management data among network nodes, network management protocols are essential. Two such protocols are **Simple Network Management Protocol (SNMP)** and **Communications Management Information Protocol (CMIP).**

SNMP is an application layer protocol that outlines the formal structure for communication among network devices. It is the mechanism that enables network management by defining the communications between a manager and an object (the item to be managed). SNMP is for use in an environment in which multiple management stations control the different manageable devices remotely over the network. It is composed of four components, containing details of how every piece of information regarding managed devices is represented, defines the hardware and software elements to be monitored, and contains a control console to which network monitoring and management information is reported. SNMP allows network managers to get the status of devices and to set or initialize them. It is a simple protocol with a limited command set. With limited provisions for security and lacking a strict standard base, there is some inconsistency among different vendors' implementation.

CMIP

The International Standards Organization has defined the Communication Management Information Protocol (CMIP), which is a more complex protocol for exchanging messages among network components. Though more recently developed than SNMP for the seven-layer OSI model, it has the potential for better control and ability to overcome SNMP limitations. There is, however, no interoperability between SNMP and CMIP.

Problem Management

This is the process of expeditiously handling a problem from its initial recognition to its satisfactory resolution. A typical scenario is when a call comes to the help desk. The person on duty listens to the problem and makes an entry in the log, noting the problem, equipment, person calling, and to whom the problem resolution was assigned. This gives a historical picture of the network and can show problem trends. If the network operator cannot clear the problem personally, the problem is further assigned to a technician, who checks with the caller for any clarification, diagnoses the equipment, makes the repair when possible, and clears the log entry.

With many vendors supplying equipment for a telecommunications system, a problem may have to be referred to one of them for resolution. This can lead to finger pointing, as one vendor points to another's equipment as the offending apparatus. The network operations group should try to resolve the problem with the parties involved. Failing this, the problem should be escalated to a higher management level, within or outside of the organization. The first priority is to get the network operational; the second is to be sure the correct agency makes the repair or funds the resolution. Through all of this, the group must apply management to the problem environment to assure speedy resolution and documentation of problems and actions.

Performance Measurement and Tuning

Service Level and Service Agreements   The network environment has historically been composed of one or more large mainframe computers and their connecting circuits and equipment, supplying service to functional departments within an organization. In this environment, the question arises as to the service level that will be provided; that is, what will the network operations group guarantee to their customer? Suppose you are the manager of the accounting department that relies completely on mainframe-resident programs. You must have these programs, your[7] stored data, and the connecting network. You are a customer of this data services environment and, in an environment of competition for your money,

Sprint has a room in which they monitor all aspects of the network. Central to the room is a television set showing CNN (Cable News Network), which is to Sprint the best early warning system available for potential problems that may affect their networks, such as riots, earthquakes, and other disasters.

---

[7] Yes, it is *your* data. Just as money you place in a bank account is yours and the bank is just the regulated custodian, the data in your files and databases are yours and data services is the custodian.

would seek out a vendor who would guarantee you a specified level of service at a low price. Here the term *service* means that the total system, computers and networks, is operational and reliable during a specified percent of the time, with a stated response time. For example, you agree to a system that is available 99 percent of the time from 7:00 AM through 6:00 PM, Monday through Friday, with a response time for a simple transaction of 1.5 seconds, 95 percent of the time, and for complex transactions of 4.5 seconds, 90 percent of the time. If you want a higher service level, given that was possible, you would likely pay an increasingly higher price for incremental increases. In each case, you are discussing a *service level*. To receive this level of service, you would negotiate a *service agreement* with data services.

Measurements   For the operations group to show that they are meeting specified service agreements, or any particular environment, they continuously, or periodically, measure parameters of this service. These parameters include transaction times, response time, circuit and processor utilization (busy time), queue lengths, equipment failures, circuit errors, transaction mixes, and overall service levels. With such parameters, data services can not only demonstrate their performance but take actions to improve service by tuning present resources and by adding equipment, circuits, and computing power. For example, database administration uses the usage history of databases to migrate the most-used data closer to the disk heads and seldom-used data to off-line storage. The telecommunications operations group could move circuits so high-usage customers do not compete for the same resource (for example, the same port on the front-end processor or same communications line) and service requests are balanced across individual resources. As individual usage increases, resources are dedicated, such as provision of a high-speed line, distributed controller or processor, or local processor.

Management Reporting   This means that the operations group takes their measurements and reports to the customer and their own management the activity and success of the telecommunications capability. Much of the management reporting will be by exception. That is, a report is produced only when the system or parameter goes out-of-bounds. If a circuit is expected to be operational 98 percent of the time from 6:00 AM through midnight and records for this month show 98.5 percent and last month, 98.6 percent, then this statistic would not need to be shown. If a historical operational statistic has been 90 percent with a 98 percent requirement, and the system makes 97 percent this month, it may be well to show this to let others know the situation is improving and closer to meeting the promised, or required, level of service. Further, if it can be shown why the former level was low and equipment has been installed or procedures instituted that have achieved the new level, it is best to let this be known.

Remember that most repetitive historical data are boring, so statistics should be reported by exception or by trend graphs. If the situation is improving, show a year's worth of data with a band of acceptability drawn in. Also, if you are reaching the limit on capability, show that along with the trend. For example, if the trend of busy time on a circuit has been increasing for 16 months and a reasonable projection shows that the circuit will be saturated or that unacceptable queues will develop within four months, use the graph of historical data to (1) alert management to this situation, (2) defend yourself if the case warrants, or (3) propose additional equipment to ward off the situation when it affects the company's competitive position or its ability to service customers.[8]

One advantage of having a PBX and automatic call distribution capability is that these systems gather data continuously and can generate management reports on demand. These reports can show circuit utilization, delays, balking, response times, and overall service.

Configuration Control   Because telecommunications capabilities change, an accurate knowledge of what is installed and its location is very important. The maintenance of records that track all equipment, media, and circuits is an administrative task that requires less technical skill but no less dedication. This task often falls by the wayside as more important tasks take precedence and as time passes. Take, for example, a college campus that has evolved over two centuries, such as the University of Georgia. When they began the planning for a new AT&T System 85 switch in 1987, it became more practical to lay all new wiring than to depend on records documenting existing wiring. Given that some of the wiring on campus was over four decades old, some circuits were lost due to the age and condition of documentation. At the end of the $2 million contract for excavation, new conduits, new wiring and fiber circuits, and a complete inventory and wiring diagram database existed. This is now considered a valuable resource and is something every organization should have and keep up-to-date. A portfolio of all information technology systems, capabilities, and projects should be maintained and be available to the CIO.

Configuration management gives data to use in cost allocation and information for expansion and improvements. Documentation must include not only a database of equipment, but an inventory of circuits, channels, and bandwidth, showing all equipment and points of high risk that may require special attention or redundant resources. The point of configuration management is to support design, evolution, repair, and maintenance.

Risk management is the analysis and actions taken to ensure that the organization can continue to operate under any foreseeable conditions.

Change Management   When projects are implemented to add to or change existing configurations, it is vital to support change management. **Change management** provides monitoring of all changes to the installed network in a planned, coordinated way. When the environment is highly dynamic and users are requesting changes rapidly, lack of coordination of changes can lead to disaster. Change management includes a process for approving requests and documenting them to always know the installed environment. The person in the position of change coordinator needs to understand the nature of this technology. It is a good job for a MIS graduate who has gained an understanding of the network.

risk management
Since we can't achieve 100 percent security from all possible losses, why is risk management an important TC topic?

Risk Assessment and Management   In the use of any technology, process, or methodology, someone should determine where things are likely to go bad. Managers must think about objectives, the system and procedures they have installed to achieve the objectives, and the weak points in the equipment, staffing, and procedures.

Risk management is the science and art of recognizing the existence of threats, determining their consequences to resources, and applying modifying factors in a cost-effective manner to keep adverse consequences within bounds.

---

[8] Here is where combined knowledge of technology and business will pay off. It is the technology that is reaching its limit, but it is the effect on the business that is important. An engineer trying to sell the case for more bandwidth will not be as successful as you will be in asking for additional equipment to support growing business needs.

Risk assessment and analysis involve a methodological investigation of the organization's resources, personnel, procedures, and objectives to determine points of weakness. Finding such points, managers overtly manage the risk by passing it to someone else (insurance or outsourcing the task) or strengthening the weak points by making changes or building redundancies.

We have mentioned the problems caused by the terrorist attacks on the World Trade Center; Hurricanes Hugo and Andrew on the East Coast of the United States; the San Francisco earthquake on the West Coast; and the Hinsdale, Illinois, central office fire. These are well-publicized, significant acts of nature, accidents, or acts of terrorism. Just as significant but somewhat less expected were the results of the major snowstorm in the city of Birmingham, Alabama, in early March of 1993. Over 13 inches of snow came to that southern city, and business halted. The city planners had not ever considered the possibility of a blizzard. The city had absolutely no snow removal equipment. If risk assessment had been complete and in place, it would have considered, before the event, which telecommunications systems needed to function in spite of the snow and, of equal importance, how to protect telecommunications equipment vulnerable to water damage from the run-off as the snow melted.

Unexpected events have caused some planners real headaches. A college in Texas placed its academic mainframe computer in the basement of a low-lying building, just above the sanitary sewer level, and the rains came. Talking about stinking grades at exam time! On the other hand, a commercial timeshare firm that knew the risk of low-lying areas for its mainframe in Chicago placed it on the fifth floor of a ten-story building. Snow fell, crushed the roof, and flooded the computer despite its lofty positioning.

A large company in south Georgia, which relies heavily on computer and telecommunications technology had a well-thought-out disaster recovery plan when Hurricane Opal hit in 1995. The plan to call the appropriate personnel to work depended on telephone communications, which were destroyed by the storm. The only way to bring in the required personnel was to drive to a radio station and make an announcement.

A less obvious problem to assess and manage is what to do when someone in an office goes on vacation, is sick, or goes on medical leave. Hopefully, there are provisions for a replacement with like skills, trained and with adequate documentation to do the job. What about a labor strike? These possible problems are less consequential than acts of nature, but more likely to happen.

Finally, what about everyday network and computer operations? We have seen mainframe computers brought to their knees by a 100-millisecond flicker of the power because there was no surge protection and no uninterrupted power supply (UPS). Does the file server on your organization's LAN have redundant components, or does it have a backup server for mission-critical functions? (We discussed LANs and file servers in Chapter 6.) Are there alternate, redundant lines from your PBX to the CO in case of an attack by a marauding backhoe? One telecommunications-dependent firm has buried the telecommunications trunks on their premises in deep trenches and then poured concrete on top to protect against such digging.

Risk management is the analysis and subsequent actions taken to ensure that organizations can continue to operate under any foreseeable conditions, such as illness, wars, accidents, labor strikes, hurricanes, earthquakes, fire, power outages, heavy rains, oppressive heat, or flu epidemics. Telecommunications capabilities support all facets of the company; therefore, risk analysis and management are always in order.

Disaster Planning   The beginning of risk management is assessment, which leads to management on a continuous basis. A specific point is the creation of a *disaster plan* in case of a catastrophic occurrence. If organizations depend on telecommunications-intensive computer-based information systems, like banks, stock exchanges, and airlines, what do they do in case of a total power outage, telephone line cuts, and fires? A disaster plan requires procedures that occur every day to allow recovery after a disaster and permit the organization to continue operations. For a bank, the daily operations involve placing backup copies of data and programs in an absolutely safe place. The disaster plan provides the place, procedures, and equipment to make use of those data for continued operations. Disaster plans are often referred to as "business continuity plans" for good reason. (See the two cases at the end of the chapter for examples of **disaster planning.**)

Quality of Service

Service Level Agreement

A service comprises a set of broadly repeatable functions and processes. In the area of information technology and telecommunications, outsourcing has become an industry trend that has expanded geometrically over the past three years. The ubiquitous environment of the Internet and World Wide Web has fostered the connectivity of wide-area networks to local-area networks, with thin-client architecture evolving a pay-as-you-go business application clientele. Factors such as total cost of ownership, speed of deployment, focus on core competencies, scalability with flexibility, and qualified IT manpower are driving the different outsourcing model options. One constant among the IT outsourcing models, which range from application service providers (ASPs), through Internet service providers (ISPs), to virtual private networks (VPNs), is the level of services agreed upon between a client and the service provider, or **service level agreement (SLA).** An SLA can be summarized as a series of commitments by a vendor to a customer. Unfortunately the SLA is a very complex document to qualify, quantify, and manage.

What is an SLA?   "An SLA is, in effect, pricing. You ask for a certain commitment for a certain price," says Ellen Van Cleve, datacom director for a *Fortune* 500 company and vice president of the Communications Managers Association (CMA).

Information Window   12–10
Why Managed Hosting

Rackspace® servers are customized, dedicated servers (also called outsourced servers or managed Web servers). This means that your server is made just for you. You choose the components that you need today and maintain the server software. We monitor and maintain the server hardware, routing equipment and network connectivity.

Rackspace also provides customized support, which helps new users get acclimated with their Web server. We also provide online help resources and 24×7 fanatical technical support with every package we sell.

Wondering how this compares with the alternatives out there? We have put together answers to some of the most commonly asked questions about managed servers, virtual hosting, colocation, and "roll your own" (RYO) data centers to show you how we measure up.

Source: http://www.rackspace.com/whyrs/why_managed_hosting.php.

To clarify what services are described and how those services are measured is the challenge of an effective SLA, and SLAs cover an assortment of data services: frame relay networking, leased lines, Internet access, Web hosting and outsourcing, and specific end-user applications from analytical and vertical integration to collaborative and personal-specific.

"There is nothing special about an SLA. It's a legal contract like any other," says David Simpson, founding partner in a San Francisco law firm specializing in telecom contracts. As with all contracted documents, negotiations between client and service provider determine the technology agreement and verification that promises made are kept. Table 12.2 suggests five tips to use when negotiating SLAs.

SLA commitments are made to convince skeptical customers to employ specific services in an atmosphere of collaboration and partnership, so what is the challenge to creating a SLA? As with any negotiated document, standards and the interpretation of standards are determined by the individual negotiators. With respect to SLAs, the concept of standardization across the IT and telecom industry is a desirable and attainable goal. Any negotiated SLA should address each of the following basic questions equally to form a robust contract between the service provider and client:

- What is the provider promising?

- How will the provider deliver on those promises?

- Who will measure delivery, and how?

- What happens if the provider fails to deliver as promised?

- How will the SLA change over time?

An SLA Model   The SLA should be a legally binding service agreement negotiated between two legal entities that stipulates the what, where, when, how, why, and recourse of outsource business services over a specified segment of time. Many methodologies and resulting models have been created to convey the intent of the SLA. One simplistic model employed to work with an outsourcing team involved in the preparation of outsourcing agreement documentation has two broad components of agreement clauses and schedules. Agreement clauses provide structure, management, interpretation, obligations, financial terms, warranties, liabilities, resolution processes, intellectual property issues, and termination arrangements. Schedules provide high-level detail about particular agreement aspects or arrangements such that schedules further define, quantify, and extend the level of an agreement clause.

Enhancing Customer Support

The two sides of customer care involve the SLA to protect the client and customer service on the part of the provider. Customer relations management may involve computer telephony integration and building and mining customer knowledge

TABLE 12.2
SLA Negotiation Tips

1. Figure out the worth of the service.
2. Know the carrier's net design.
3. Access your carrier's partnerships.
4. Include corporate counsel.
5. Invest in validation tools.

bases. The point, for the provider, is to maintain a competitive advantage in the eyes of the client.

Committed Information Rate (CIR)

One should not simply lease a medium from a vendor. The object of acquiring a medium is not to simply have the medium but to have the desired functionality. Specifically, the objective is to have a given, reliable service. A **committed information rate (CIR)** is an agreement where the vendor guarantees a specific service and states penalties. For example, the vendor may run a T1 line from your server to the ISP, but you agree in the CIR to either six DS-0s or a bandwidth of 384 Kbps, 22 hours per day, with the proviso that you will be allowed to exceed this bandwidth for bursty traffic on a limited basis. Additionally, the CIR will state whether the additional packets will be discarded or whether you will pay additionally for them. As time passes, the organization may choose to rewrite the CIR to expand the bandwidth, with new guarantees.

Internet and Intranet Considerations

Since the Internet and intranet technologies have become such important phenomena, there must be special attention afforded to their management. As more businesses rely on the Internet and intranet applications, they need to have people who can ensure that adequate security is maintained for their internal data. As the chief technology officer for one of the largest U.S. banks said, "We have a new source of adversity; for example, a computer hacker with a US$3,000 computer is seeking to transfer millions from our bank." This comment illustrates the critical importance of firewalls to prevent unauthorized access to company data when the organization is using the Internet for electronic commerce access. The electronic environment presents a new era of vulnerability, and consideration of it must be included in risk management planning and calculations.

Information Window   12–11
So What Is a Service Level Agreement (SLA)?

- It is a contract or contracts.

- It is an understanding between a service provider and their customer.

- It sets expectations for performance.

- It defines the procedures and reports needed to track compliance.

An SLA should contain

- The service to be performed.

- The performance expectations of the service provider.

- The process of reporting problems with the service.

- The time frame for problem resolution.

- The process for monitoring service levels.

- The penalties for noncompliance.

- Escape clauses (for both parties).

Source: http://www-1.ibm.com/servers/eserver/iseries/asp/pdfs/sla_ap.pdf.

The Real World   12–5
Disaster Recovery, Coast to Coast

The recent Deep Freeze on the East Coast and other problems drove as many companies to disaster-recovery sites as the more dramatic Los Angeles earthquake.

In the Los Angeles area, Comdisco Disaster Recovery Services Inc. reported that five customers were using its disaster recovery business, while SunGard Recovery Systems Inc. reported one customer needed its services. On the East Coast, SunGard, Wayne, Pennsylvania, had one company using its services in Atlanta because of a water-main break, one in Philadelphia because of the freeze, and seven others in the region ready to use its services because of power outages, the company said.

A spokeswoman for Rosemont, Illinois–based Comdisco said 17 clients in the Middle Atlantic region and four in Atlanta alerted Comdisco they might have to use its facilities. Public Service Electric and Gas Co. in New Jersey began shutting power off to customers late Wednesday to prevent a total blackout because of the heavy demand. In Washington, the mayor threatened to fine any nonessential business that opened on Thursday, also because of a power shortage.

Among those companies that turned to SunGard and Comdisco because of the Los Angeles earthquake, none were using the services to back up mainframe computers. Comdisco said its customers needed other kinds of backup, such as telephones and PCs.

Corporate Telecommuting Center, Valencia, California, announced a new disaster-recovery service the day of the earthquake. But according to one CTC customer, the service was apparently knocked out. "No one is out there," said Arthur Southam, president of CareAmerica Health Plans, Chatsworth, California. Calls to CTC were unanswered.

Source: John T. Mulqueen, "Disaster Recovery, Coast to Coast," *Communications Week.*

Some considerations for the Internet and intranet environment are

- Selection of network browsers and authorization to use.
- Network services.
- Access devices.
- Employee use.
- Managing WWW presence—Webmaster.
- Resource allocation.
- Transaction security.

According to a *Datamation* article, some factors applicable to the decision whether to host a World Wide Web site yourself or choose an outside service provider are

1. How many hops do you need to make to connect to your service provider? Fewer is better.

2. How does the service provider connect to the Internet backbone? How fast is the connection? Directly, at multiple points, and through T3 lines (or fiber optics) are best.

3. Is your line actively monitored and is maintenance provided on a 24 × 7 basis? Yes to both questions should be the answer.

4. What is the measured throughput over your line at peak periods? With how many others are you sharing your line speed? You should approach at least 70 percent of nominal line speed, and the sum of shared line speeds should not exceed three

The Real World   12–6
Intranets Flourish Due to Easy Development

On top of the oft-cited benefits of cross platform deployment and an easy user interface, IS managers are enjoying shorter development cycles and easier management with Web-based applications.

Now that nearly every vendor has Web enabled its development tools, the reality is approaching the hype as users around the globe rush to deploy intranets.

According to a worldwide survey of large IS organizations, users have quickly become enamored with internal Web-based applications because they are easy to use, easy to build, cost effective, and immediate, and don't have strings attached. The initial wave of intranet applications ranges from online phone and mail directories to documentation of company policies.

"You don't have to worry about software distribution, version control, and keeping software up to date," said Willi Weiers, manager of the systems technology center at Post AG, Germany's postal service in Darmstadt, Germany.

Intranets also eliminate dependency on paper, keep employees informed, enhance internal exchange among employees, and make collaborative work across time zones a reality, users said.

"By eliminating paper systems, I have really seen an increase in the amount of communications between employees," said John Stevens, a database administrator at Boeing Co., in Seattle. "We are implementing tons of intranets, probably in the hundreds."

However, the ease with which employees can publish data worldwide requires IS to carefully consider data access policy and security, users report.

Moreover, the networking complexity introduced by intranets is making the job of network administrators harder, users said.

"Our network administrators didn't have a lot of UNIX and Internet networking experience, so the workload was initially really heavy," said Randy Jew, network specialist at Pacific Gas and Electric Co., in Cupertino, California.

And although analysts warn of hidden costs and management burdens, the acceptance of intranets in a short time among users is remarkable in an industry notorious for hype and exaggeration.

"I think this is the first time in the history of data processing that a new technology has gained that degree of acceptance," said Werner Schwaiger, data processing specialist at BMW AG, in Munich, which in December started deploying its first intranets.

Source: Torsten Busse, "Intranets Flourish Due to Easy Development," *INFOWORLD.*

to five times the speed of interconnection to the backbone; for example, a T1 direct connection to a backbone should not be shared by more than three to five T1 lines.

5. What firewall is provided? You want a product that rates high in effectiveness.

6. What is the operating system? A debate exists between the use of Windows NT, UNIX, OS/2, or MacIntosh, and the answer may depend on your specific case. Also, there are AS/400 and MVS servers.

7. What Web server is provided? There are many choices, such as Netscape's Communications Server® and Microsoft's Internet Information Server®, which led the way. Check the competing choices thoroughly.

8. What authoring tools are provided? There are lots of choices, and you are not limited to a single product. In this arena, you need to evaluate your needs and fit the appropriate project.

9. What tool for counting activity is provided? To count hits, you need a product or should develop your own. You need the information so you can perform economic analysis. Good tools are available, and some provide the information needed to assess the effectiveness of your presence.

SECURITY ISSUES FOR MANAGERS

Managers must be aware that security is a major responsibility for the total telecommunications infrastructure of their business. Often, this also includes the security of their links to suppliers, customers, and other partners. In addition, many organizations have employees who telecommute, who travel or take computers to their homes and connect to the firm from just about anywhere. Since information and its transport media are everywhere in the organization and almost everywhere the employees go, the security issue is pervasive and very broad in scope.

The manager must examine the threats to security in order to determine appropriate safeguards. Each category of threat has safeguards that may be considered as alternatives. In the final analysis, there must be a reliance on trust. Total security would mean that no one could have access. The manager is responsible for ensuring that procedures exist that put proper controls in place so that trust remains the final and not the total item relied upon. What are some security threats? The following list provides a start (see Table 12.3):

TABLE 12.3   Security Threats

Threat	Source or Target	Consequences	Primary Defense
Users	Internal, mobile	Majority of security a control problem	Controls for prevention and deterrence; training
Programmers	Internal	Bypass, disability of security mechanisms	Properly designed control and supervision audits
Hardware	Internal	Failed protection mechanisms lead to failure	Control, detection, limitation, and recovery procedures
Databases	Internal	Unauthorized access, copying, theft	Passwords, intranet, VPN
Systems software	Internal	Failure of protection, information leakage	Controls, audits
Operators	Internal	Loss of confidential information, theft, insecure	Proper access controls, partitioning of data
Radiation (interception)	External, remote	Interception of confidential data	Shielding, access control
Spoofing	External	Fraud	Authentication
Hacking	External	Intrusion, destruction of resources	Firewall, passwords
Denial of service	External	Stoppage of real work	Firewall, honey pot, VPN
Crosstalk	External	Leakage of confidential data	Shielding, separation
Wiretaps (eavesdropping)	External	Loss of data	Procedural controls, audits
Environmental hazards	External	Disruption of service, loss of resources	Precaution/management controls, BC plans
Criminal attacks	External	Theft of resources	Control procedures and prosecution
Power outages	Internal	Disruption of service, loss of business/reputation	UPS, generators
Viruses, worms, Trojan horses	External	Disruption of service, loss of resources	Firewall, procedures
Access	External	Loss of data, sabotage to equipment	Proper authentication and control procedures, physical barriers, biometric controls.

User threats: The greatest threat is from human error or inadvertent acts on the part of users. These threats may be the result of improper training, poor system design, inadequate procedures, programming flaws, and/or carelessness. Sometimes there are overt acts on the part of users that become security threats; for example, willful entry of erroneous data, fraudulent identification, bypass of proper authorization and authentication, and other intentional security breaches.

Programmers: At times, programmers bypass or disable security mechanisms, install insecure systems, and circumvent established procedures.

Hardware can have flaws that make data vulnerable to loss or interception. Hardware and its software must work together to ensure they do not contribute to lack of security.

Databases contain confidential and often private data. Access must be closely controlled to prevent unauthorized copying, destruction, and theft.

Systems software The various network components that are controlled by systems software need to be constructed so that there is little risk of data leakage. Fail-safe protection mechanisms are required.

Operators can be considered as a special class of users. Procedures should be devised to prevent implementation of insecure systems, unauthorized copying, and theft.

Radiation (interception): With many media, we are concerned with radiation that can be intercepted by unauthorized persons.

Spoofing: The use of fraudulent source or return address, preventing the recipient from taking actions.

Hacking: A form of attack that poses threats of data destruction, fraud, spread of viruses, and so forth.

Denial of service: Attacks aimed at disabling or degrading systems connected to the Internet to the extent that legitimate users are prevented from accessing them.

Crosstalk: Loss of data/information because of radiation between wires.

Wiretaps (eavesdropping): The unauthorized interception of data from transport media.

Environmental hazards: Natural occurrences such as flood, earthquakes, tornadoes, hurricanes, severe snow and sand storms, fires, climate control system failure, explosions, act of war, and so on.

Criminal attacks: Deliberate attacks on computer and telecommunications systems that range from data tampering to fraud.

Power outages: Power failure, strong power fluctuations, and brownouts that prevent normal operations.

Viruses, worms, Trojan horses: Applications created to perform unwanted acts; software attacks that can destroy or damage data or software by attaching to other computer programs.

Access: The restriction of unauthorized persons to the system resources. Usually access control includes authorization and authentication.

What are some common means of countering threats? This is a list of some defense measures:

- Physical controls:

  Secure (locked) facilities.

  Guards.

- Procedural controls:

  IDs and passwords (authentication).

  Segregation of duties.

  Supervision.

- Surveillance.

- Detection:

  Audits.

  Audit trails.

- Containment of loss.

- Recovery.

- UPS.

- Redundant facilities.

- Correction.

- Encryption.

Some controls such as *physical controls* are concerned with protection of the physical property. We often visualize this as placing critical assets in locked vaults, perhaps with armed guards. With even the most secure physical environment, there must be some human access. Consequently, we have *access controls* that allow access only by authorized people. In order for access controls to be effective, there must be specific *authentication* measures in place and enforced. These measures are part of the procedural controls.

KERBEROS

Kerberos is an authentication protocol developed at MIT that lets clients and servers reliably identify each other's identity before allowing a network connection.[9] (*Kerberos* got its name from the three-headed dog from Greek mythology that guarded the gates of Hades.) The idea behind Kerberos is to provide security to an open, distributed computer network where a single computer can access the resources of any other computer on the network. Kerberos provides a system that has had extensive public review for secure authentication and message integrity as well as confidentiality between clients and servers. This protocol is likely to have increased importance as grid or distributed computing gains popularity.

---

[9] For detailed information on Kerberos, go to http://web.mit.edu/kerberos/www/.

The Kerberos protocol uses secret key cryptography (symmetric key cryptography). In this system two principals share a secret key to encrypt and decrypt their messages. The trusted third party (the key distribution center [KDC]) provides the secret key for the principals to share. In this arrangement, the private key is never shared, unlike in the asymmetric key cryptography or public key cryptography system where a principal has both a public and a private key.

Case 12-1

Putting a Stop to Spam: A Little Understanding of SMTP Can Help Alleviate the Spam Nuisance Factor

Rik Farrow

Freeloading commercial e-mailers do more than fill your mailbox with unsolicited e-mail; they also steal server time and network bandwidth, and have even crashed mail servers. And if your mail server can be used as a relay for spam, you may find your site "blackholed" (cut off from sending e-mail to many sites), in addition to receiving thousands of angry e-mail messages from spam victims.

It used to be easy to track down spammers. And all it took to block spam were firewall or mail server rules that denied access from the spammers' domain. Spammers today use commercial tools designed to hide the source of the spam, and they use third-party sites as relays so the spam won't be blocked before it reaches its victims.

Simple Mail Transfer Protocol (SMTP) not only makes spam possible but also allows it to be tracked back to its source. All it takes is the ability to read and understand e-mail headers and some knowledge about how SMTP works. By denying spammers access to relay sites, network managers and administrators can help to stem the tide of Unsolicited Commercial E-mail (UCE).

SMTP

SMTP (RFC 821) is really simple. Like many Internet protocols, the commands are sent as text and can be entered manually with tools such as Telnet or netcat (utilities that perform functions such as debugging and exploration). This simplicity isn't an accident, since keeping things simple made debugging early Internet servers much easier.

This same simplicity makes it easy to spoof e-mail, something spammers commonly do. A complete SMTP exchange requires only five different SMTP commands. The HELO command begins the exchange, and is customarily followed by the name of the system sending the e-mail. The MAIL FROM command sets the name of the sender. Notice that any e-mail address may be used here—there's no authentication of the sender. Multiple RCPT TO lines, each with a valid destination mail address, may follow the MAIL FROM line. Finally, the actual e-mail message follows the DATA command.

Spoofing e-mail requires the perpetrator to essentially lie twice. The first lie involves using someone else's e-mail address (or a completely fictitious one) with the MAIL FROM command. When you receive the e-mail, the address used with the MAIL FROM command appears in the mail headers after the word "From," often as the very first line.

The second lie is changing the message header. The message header has its own From: line, but this one has a colon after the word "From." Again, the sender can put anything he or she wants here, as the mail server pretty much ignores the content of the e-mail—that is, everything that follows the DATA command up until the single dot that terminates the e-mail message.

REVEALING HEADERS

If you can't trust most of what you see in mail headers, how can you detect spam, other than by ridiculous subject lines that refer to making money or increasing the size of some body part? The answer lies in a header line that the spammer (and e-mail spoofer) cannot change—the Received: line.

Mail servers add Received: lines anytime they handle e-mail. The Received: line includes a variety of information, not all of which can be spoofed—and this is the key (see Figure 1).

An example Received: line begins with "from mailserver.bildoze.com (mail1. bildoze.com [162.42.150.115]) by mail.acme.com." The last part of the Received: line contains the name of the mail server that received this message, and you can trust that this is accurate—if it is your mail server that received the message. The name "mailserver.bildoze.com" is the server name used in the HELO command, and is easy to spoof. The name found in parentheses, "mail1.bildoze.com," may be included by the receiving mail server and is based on a reverse name lookup of the actual source IP address, which is found inside the square brackets. Not all mail servers perform the reverse DNS lookup, so you won't always see a name in front of the sender's IP address. But because the receiving mail server knows the sender's IP address, you can trust this information.

When the name following "from" is different from the name within parentheses, or is different from the name obtained by nslookup (a utility that performs DNS lookups) or Sam Spade (see Table 1) on the IP address, someone is spoofing SMTP. The hostname portion can be different, as servers can have multiple names (such as "mailserver" and "mail1," as shown in the example above). But the domain name (bildoze.com) must be the same, and when the name supplied by the HELO

FIGURE 1   Received: lines are added by mail servers that relay or deliver e-mail. This example, taken from some Unsolicited Commercial E-mail (UCE), shows that the name "plain" was used in the HELO message, but the actual source IP address was 12.99.89.82, which resolved to 82.mubb.snfc.snfccafj.dsl.att.net. The open relay used was netf5000.sitico.com.cn, which is running Microsoft Exchange version 5.5.

```
Received: from plain
  ([12.99.89.82]) by
  netf5000.sitico.com.cn
  with SMTP (Microsoft
  Exchange Internet Mail
  Service Version
  5.5.1960.3) id R9ZHFWFT;
  Sat, 1 Sep 2001
  05:18:07 +0800
```

TABLE 1
Resources

- At the Mail Abuse Prevention System (MAPS) site, **www.mailabuse.org,** you can subscribe to access various services for blocking sites that relay or distribute Unsolicited Commercial E-mail (UCE). Go to **http://mail-abuse.org/rbl/.**
- A very useful page for help in interpreting mail headers is **www.stopspam.org/ e-mail/headers/headers.html.**
- For an explanation of third-party relaying, go to **http:/mail-abuse.org/tsi/ar-what.html.**
- Another site dedicated to stopping mail abuse, with a relay tester that you can use, is **www.abuse.net/relay.html.**
- Check out Sam Spade for IP address lookup and more at **http://samspade.org/t/.**

message is different from the one found by an actual DNS lookup, the e-mail you're looking at has been forged.

You might see many Received: lines in an e-mail header, so you must determine which one should be used to check for forgery. In many cases, the last Received: line was the first one added by a mail server, and this one will show evidence of forgery. But spammers have taken to adding fake Received: lines as part of the message header to make picking out the actual sender more difficult. Here is where understanding the rest of the Received: line comes in. Each Received: line contains not only a "from sender" part, but also a "by receiver" clause, and the next line up in the chain should show that the receiver has become the sender, as mail is relayed to the recipient. If this isn't the case, the Received: line has been forged.

RELAYING

Spam would be relatively easy to block if it all came from a list of well-known servers. You could configure your firewall to block access from any address in these networks, or do the same thing with your e-mail server. And many sites, including some very large ones such as AOL, have already done this. But this hasn't stopped the spammers. Instead, they've started using other people's mail servers to relay their spam.

Any mail server can be a relay. Relaying used to be quite common in the early Internet and was even required by some transport protocols, such as Unix to Unix Copy Program (UUCP). Today, relaying is something that an ISP might do for its customers, and that some large organizations might want to do for some of their members when used with authentication.

Remember the RCPT TO command in the SMTP protocol? To relay mail, the spammer provides many RCPT TO lines, all with e-mail addresses that don't belong to the same domain as the mail server. (See Figure 2.) The relay mail server dutifully delivers each e-mail, a process that involves using DNS to look up the correct Mail Exchanger (MX) records, then connecting to the server using the SMTP protocol, and finally delivering the mail. Relaying makes it possible for someone using a slow, dialup link to reach millions of targets because the relay mail server does the lion's share of the work.

Of course, using someone else's server to relay mail is a form of theft. Spammers use mail servers as relays without authorization. Using a mail server as a relay has crashed mail servers, and may cause the loss of legitimate e-mail. Sites that unwittingly assist in spam delivery may then find themselves added to a blackhole

FIGURE 2 **Mail from the system client1.bildoze.com to sales.acme.com goes through (in this case) two mail servers, which each act as relays. Each relay adds a Received: line. These mail servers must relay only for their own domain, and not act as open relays.**

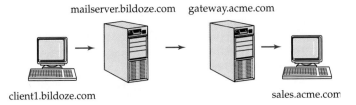

list—a list of sites known to be spam relayers. If your site gets blackholed, no one at your site can successfully send e-mail to sites that subscribe to that blackhole list.

Blackholing has been successful in reducing the number of sites that will act as spam relays. It has also incurred the wrath of spammers, who have hired lawyers to attack the blackhole sites (see Table 1).

Spammers have tools for automatically locating open relays. According to the Mail Abuse Prevention System (MAPS, www.mailabuse.org) site, the number of open mail relays has declined from around 50 percent in 1996 to less than 20 percent in 1999. That's still a very large number of potential relays, but things have gotten better. In the mid-1990s, some popular firewall products actually worked as mail relays. Today, some firewalls can be configured to block spam.

You can test your site's public mail servers by connecting to port 25 (the SMTP server port) and attempting to relay mail. The key is to use an e-mail address in the RCPT TO command that doesn't belong to the mail servers domain. You must do this from a system that's outside of your domain, or you can use a relay tester, such as the one found at www.abuse.net. You should get error messages, beginning with a 5, such as "`553 Requested action not taken: mailbox name not allowed.`"

NO RELAYING

Sendmail, the most commonly used mail server software for Unix/Linux systems, disables relaying by default. Microsoft Exchange and Lotus Notes may have relaying enabled, and it appears that most of the relay servers used in the spam that I receive arrive courtesy of an Exchange server (this information is also contained in the Received: line where you can detect the forgery). Version 4.0 of Exchange won't perform relaying without patches. Version 5.0 can support relaying if routing is enabled, which is required for supporting POP clients. Version 5.5 (and Service Pack 1) provides more control over who can use Exchange for relaying. I strongly suggest that you read the Release Notes and configure Exchange so that only users within your domain can use Exchange for relaying.

Take a few minutes to check and see if your company's site can be used as an open relay for spam. Consider joining organizations that provide real-time support for blocking spam. UCE/spam is more than a nuisance—it's widespread, unauthorized use of servers and networks. Compared to other Denial of Service (DOS) attacks, spam is the most common. But fortunately, you can take action to avoid being a victim.

Source: Rik Farrow, "Putting a Stop to Spam," *Network Magazine*, November 2001, pp. 80, 82.

Case 12-2

Disaster Recovery

Denise Johnson McManus

A disaster recovery plan is a series of procedures to restore normal data processing following a disaster, with maximum speed and minimal impact on operations. A comprehensive plan will include essential information and materials for necessary emergency action. Planned procedures are designed to eliminate unnecessary decision making immediately following the disaster. Disaster recovery planning begins with preventative measures and tests to detect any problem that might lead to a disaster. If this planning process is completed, the chance of experiencing a total disaster is lessened. The severity of a disaster determines the level of recovery measures. [1] Disaster classifications are helpful in organizing procedures for a disaster plan. There are nine essential and required steps for a successful implementation of disaster recovery planning, which are displayed in Table 1.

The key to beginning a successful disaster recovery plan is to gain a commitment from top-level management and the organization. To obtain the required support, the CEO and top managers need to understand the business risk and personal liability if a disaster recovery plan is not developed and a disaster occurs. Although many companies have excuses for not developing a plan, a corporate policy should be mandated requiring disaster recovery planning. The corporate policy would assist in defining the charter for contingency planning, while encouraging cooperation with internal and external staff. Unfortunately, very few organizations have a corporate policy on disaster recovery. Therefore, it is imperative that corporations begin developing a disaster recovery plan immediately.

FINANCIAL RISK

Furthermore, statistics indicate that if a company's computers are down for more than five working days, 90 percent will be out of business in a year; however, this can be avoided if a coherent disaster recovery plan is developed and implemented.[5, p. 65] "The disaster recovery process generally is much longer than the duration of the disaster itself."[2, p. 27] The company experiences immediate problems from the disaster and continues to experience difficulties for several months. The inability to communicate with customers and suppliers is devastating, which

TABLE 1
Disaster Recovery Planning Process

1. Obtaining top management commitment.
2. Establishing a planning committee.
3. Performing risk assessment and impact analysis.
4. Prioritizing recovery needs.
5. Selecting a recovery plan.
6. Selecting a vendor and developing agreements.
7. Developing and implementing the plan.
8. Testing the plan.
9. Continuing to test and evaluate the plan.

can prevent the company from staying in business. Therefore, an effective disaster recovery plan directly affects the bottom line, staying in business.

Disaster recovery planning costs are feasible and can be budgeted. Not only can they be allocated across many business units, but they also can be amortized over many years. Many costs must be considered when developing the disaster recovery plan. Not only the time invested by the team members, but also implementation costs must be considered when developing the budget. Table 2 displays a hypothetical mid-sized business model example. The initial cost of contingency planning would include startup costs and development of the plan. After the initial development has been completed, the yearly cost would be $60,000.[4, p. 44] Although $60,000 seems expensive, Table 2 reveals that one day of lost business equals $90,000. Thus, the cost of the contingency plan can be recovered quickly, if a disaster should occur.

Costs are a major concern for disaster recovery plans. Some of the costs incurred for disaster recovery plans include costs of insurance; fees for hot-site backup, stockpiled equipment, supplies, forms, redundant facilities, or cold sites; communications networks for recovery purposes; testing; training; and education. These costs are often used as the excuse, for top-level management, not to develop and implement a plan. Budgetary constraints are one of the main obstacles in disaster recovery planning. Not only will the company incur monetary losses, but also possible loss of customer confidence, should the business be affected by a disaster.

Since most organizations are very dependent on computer systems to support vital business functions, such as customer support, the need for a disaster recovery plan is critical. Financial and functional losses increase rapidly after the onset of an outage. Corrective action must be initiated quickly, and disaster recovery methods should be functioning by the end of the first week of an outage. Loss of revenues and additional costs rise rapidly and become substantial as the outage continues. The financial costs vary between industries, but all industries show progressive increase as the length of outage continues.

Furthermore, if the financial impact to the business does not warrant the financial support of the corporate executives, an analysis of The Foreign Corrupt Practices Act of 1977 should get the required attention and support of the officers. The Act deals with the fiduciary responsibilities, or "standard of care," of the officers, which may be judged legally. "In the legal publication 'Corpus Juris Secundum' the 'Standard of care' is defined as follows: 'A director or officer is liable for the loss of corporate assets through his negligence, fraud, or abuse of trust.'"[4, p. 43]

However, the most convincing reason for having a business disaster recovery plan is that it simply makes good business sense to have a company protected from a major disaster. Additional reasons to have a recovery plan include a potential for

TABLE 2
Budgeting a Disaster Recovery Plan

Daily	Normal No Plan	Disaster No Plan	Normal with Plan	Disaster with Plan
Revenue	$100,000	$ 0	$100,000	$ 100,000
Expenses	− 80,000	− 80,000	− 80,164	− 80,164*
Outages/expenses	0	− 10,000	0	− 3,000
Contingency plan	0	0	0	− 5,000
Profits	$ 20,000	$−90,000	$ 19,836	$ 11,836

* Calculation based on $60K/365 days = $164/day.

greater profits and reduced liabilities to the company and the employees. Thus, a formal or informal risk review provides a powerful argument for recovery planning. It tells you where your needs are not met, and helps you determine the critical areas that must have backups. Recovery from a major disaster will be expensive. However, the inability to recover quickly and support primary business functions would be significantly more costly and destructive to the company.

PLANNING

The process of developing a recovery plan involves management and staff members, as displayed in Table 3. Each member of the disaster recovery team has a specific role that is defined in the plan. Disaster recovery planning is a complex process. The corporation must utilize a structured approach in determining the scope, collecting the data, performing analysis, developing assumptions, determining recovery tasks, and calculating milestones. The issues displayed in Table 4 must be considered during the planning process. This highly interactive process requires information from throughout the organization. The plan requires continuous revision. It is out of date whenever a change occurs in the organization, the software, or the equipment.

The process of building a plan is extremely valuable to the company. The purpose of identifying problems and developing a recovery process forces the organization to examine the impact of a disaster on the company and the business. Thus, the end result should be a plan that can be utilized for all levels of disasters. Recovery from a major disaster requires the efficient execution of numerous small plans that comprise the master plan. These subplans include acquiring hardware, reinstalling communication lines, and many other functions. Recovery managers select the plan, assign responsibility, and coordinate resources to execute the plan.

CONCLUSION

In a society where individuals are linked to each other through media technology, many individuals have experienced or witnessed the vast devastation of a disaster. Many disasters that have occurred in the United States in recent years

TABLE 3
Disaster Recovery Team

1. Top management.
2. Functional and operations managers.
3. Service providers.
4. Recovery team.
5. Disaster recovery coordinator.
6. Outside vendors.

TABLE 4
Recovery Planning Issues

1. Unanticipated interruption of routine operations.
2. Identification of key risks and the exposure to risk.
3. Identification of consequences if existing plan fails.
4. Identification of recovery strategy.
5. Identification of test and evaluation process.

have driven many companies to recognize the importance of disaster recovery planning. A disaster recovery plan appears to be a cost-effective, but underutilized, tool. Organizations that have prepared for an extended outage through insurance and a contingency plan reported significantly lower expected loss of revenues, additional costs, and loss of capabilities. In the last six years, a disaster has been reported somewhere in the United States and the world approximately every year. The size of the disaster is not the determining factor of staying in business; it is the disaster recovery plan that will determine if the doors will stay open or closed. "Smart companies make it their business to have a disaster recovery plan in place." [2, p. 32] "If a disaster does strike, being prepared can make the difference between a smooth recovery and a slow terrifying struggle to survive." [2, p. 32]

BIBLIOGRAPHY

1. Collins, Mike. "Motorola ISG Disaster Recovery Plan for Huntsville Facility." Policy and Procedures, February 28, 1995. (Typewritten).

2. Howley, Peter A. "Disaster Preparedness Is Key to Any Telecommunications Plan." *Disaster Recovery Journal* 7 (April/May/June 1994), pp. 26–32.

3. Lewis, Steven. "Disaster Recovery Planning: Suggestions to Top Management and Information Systems Managers." *Journal of Systems Management* 45 (May 1994), pp. 28–33.

4. Powell, Jeanne D. "Justifying Contingency Plans." *Disaster Recovery Journal* 8 (October/November/December 1995), pp. 41–44.

5. Preston, Kathryn. "Disaster Recovery Planning." *Industrial Distribution* 83 (December 1994), p. 65.

Case 12-3
Wireless Worksheet

Net managers wondering whether wireless is the way to go need hard facts if they're going to make informed decisions. That means knowing how much they have to lay out for equipment and services, how much wireless will save their companies, and how long it will be before the up-front investment pays for itself. To help corporation networkers crunch the numbers and build a wireless business case, *Data Communications* has come up with these basic worksheets.

Wireless Costs

CLIENT COSTS (per user)

- End-user device _____
- End-user modem _____
- Client software _____
- Training _____
- Installation _____
- Other (specify:_____) _____

Subtotal

x number of users _____

Line 1 (Total Monthly Costs) _____

SERVER COSTS

- Server _____
- Server software _____
- Landline installation _____
- Other (specify:_____) _____

Line 2 (Total Server Costs) _____

MONTHLY RECURRING COSTS

- Fixed fees for wireless service _____
- Usage charges (estimated) _____
- Landline links to network _____
- Maintenance _____
- Other (specify:_____) _____

Line 3 (Total Monthly Costs) _____

Line 4 (Line 1 + Line 2 + Line 3 = Total Wireless Costs) _____

Wireless Gains (Mobile Workers and Support Staff)

Determine the number of mobile employees and support staff, as well as the number of days they work each month. Then determine how much time they spend on tasks that could be replaced with wireless technology.

Average cost of commuting time (× number of end-users) _____/month

Dollar value of time mobile reps are in office doing paperwork that could be replaced with wireless entry _____/month

Dollar value of time clerks spend entering paperwork that could be replaced with wireless entry _____/month

Estimated salary eliminated by attrition or layoffs _____/month

Revenue gains (e.g., selling warranties on site after service calls, collecting money on site with credit cards) _____/month

Estimated sales increase from wireless (e.g., benefits of immediate access to inventory database) _____/month

Amount saved via wireless applications (e.g., telemetry, utility readings) _____/month

Cost of errors in order entry (include time spent by sales rep, service rep, clerk) _____/month

Overtime eliminated on loading with wireless _____/month

Line 5 (Total Expenses) _____

Miscellaneous

Dollar value of eliminated office space _____/month

Dollar value of eliminated phone lines _____/month

Dollar value of eliminated parking spaces _____/month

Value of PCs eliminated/replaced with mobile devices ($8,000 is average annual figure for buying and maintaining 1 PC) _____/month

Line 6 (Total Miscellaneous) _____

Line 7 (Total Wireless Gains) _____/month

To determine payback period in months, divide Line 4 by Line 7 _____

To determine net monthly gain by going wireless, subtract Line 3 from Line 7 _____

Wireless Data: Now or Later?

COSMOPOLITAN MAGAZINE HELPS ITS READERS figure out if they've found the man of their dreams or the boyfriend from hell. *Smart Money* quizzes aging baby boomers so they can tell if they're on the road to retirement or ruin. *Data Communications* can't do anything about your love life—or your bank account. But we've come up with an even dozen questions to help you decide if it's time to devote some of your wireline attention to wireless opportunities. Just circle the appropriate answers and tally up your score to find your cable-cutting quotient.

1. How competitive is your industry?
(a) Extremely   (b) Very
(c) Somewhat   (d) Not at all

2. How often do salespeople take orders at customer sites?
(a) Daily   (b) Weekly
(c) Monthly   (d) Never

3. While in the field or away from the desk, how often could sales people make use of the corporate database?
(a) Daily   (b) Weekly
(c) Monthly   (d) Never

4. While in the field or away from the desk how often could *other* employees (like service reps) make use of the corporate database?
(a) Daily   (b) Weekly
(c) Monthly   (d) Never

5. How much time do field employees spend commuting each day?
(a) More than 2 hours
(b) 1 to 2 hours
(c) 30 to 60 minutes
(d) Less than 30 minutes

6. How often do clerks need to enter orders after they've already been taken by sales reps in the field?
(a) Daily   (b) Weekly
(c) Monthly   (d) Never

7. How often could field sales or service reps benefit from checking customers' credit while at their sites?
(a) Daily   (b) Weekly
(c) Monthly   (d) Never

8. How much time do field employees spend on paperwork each week?
(a) More than 10 hours
(b) 5 to 9 hours
(c) 1 to 4 hours
(d) Less than 1 hour

9. How many field workers already use a laptop, PDA, or palmtop?
(a) All   (b) Most
(c) Some   (d) None

10. How important is it that company executives have constant access to e-mail and corporate databases?
(a) Extremely   (b) Very
(c) Somewhat   (d) Not at all

11. How important is instant access to information to employee safety?
(a) Extremely   (b) Very
(c) Somewhat   (d) Not at all

12. How important is Internet access to your employees while they're on the road?
(a) Extremely   (b) Very
(c) Somewhat   (d) Not at all

Scoring: Score each answer using the following scale. Add up the grand total to find out whether thin air is a workable transport:
(a) = 4   (b) = 3
(c) = 2   (d) = 0

Cable-Cutting Quotient
35–48 What are you waiting for? Call a few wireless providers or a systems integrator today. Wireless should save your company some cash and make employees more efficient.
25–34 Put wireless near the top of your to-do list—you'll probably see a return on investment. Figuring out your payback period should help you get an idea of how much you stand to save.
9–24 If you've got a gut feeling that wireless might help your company your instincts could be on the money. Get a couple of quotes from service providers and run some numbers to see if you stand to save.
0–8 Forget it for now. Unless you see an overwhelming single need (like employee safety for police officers or a nomadic CEO who insists on constant connectivity), wireless won't do you much good at the moment.

Source: *Data Communications,* May 21, 1996, pp. 45, 47.

Case 12-4

Leveraging Technology in Plant Maintenance

David W. Heglar

This article examines the use of technology in responding to increasing demands on limited personnel resources—specifically in an expanding manufacturing facility with a large maintenance workforce.

In 1995, a Wilmington manufacturing facility began an expansion that doubled its capacity—increasing both the numbers and types of equipment supported by the maintenance staff. Although the amount of production and support equipment doubled, the maintenance staff increased by only 10 percent due to a focus on increasing utilization through technology. In addition, the shift from manual tracking, dispatch, and monitoring systems to automated systems provided increased information on the status of equipment and allowed for more complete cost information to be utilized by the plant management in making capital allocation decisions.

TABWARE

In 1995, the Maintenance Department began the implementation of a computerized maintenance management system. The brand chosen for implementation was Tabware® by the Flour-Daniels Corporation, a software package that operates on an ORACLE® 8-I database. The system was implemented in a modular fashion, with the initial installation focusing on scheduling and information tracking of maintenance activities. In 1997 the system was expanded with plant trades charging time to individual work orders—resulting in the ability to assign labor costs directly to jobs—allowing maintenance management to focus engineering efforts on the jobs that required the most trades resources. Redesign of tasks, reengineering of problem equipment, and targeted preventive maintenance all reduced the requirements of trades resources—removing the need to add personnel. In 1998 the ability to charge parts to individual work orders was enabled at the Wilmington facility. This provided total cost of maintenance for individual pieces of equipment and was integrated into the design and purchasing process for upgrades in the facility. In 2000, real-time access reporting was implemented in the Tabware system, allowing the ability to query the maintenance database on cost information via a Web-based link anywhere in the facility. Department managers, engineers, and technicians are able to track similar machines' performance, research maintenance changes, and review parts usage by area of plant, time of day, shift, and a multitude of other factors to gain better information on equipment performance. Today these data are being used in troubleshooting production issues, in designing new machines, and in focusing engineering resources on the costliest areas of each production department to constantly reduce the total manufacturing costs of the product.

COMMUNICATIONS

The ability to effectively utilize maintenance resources in the plant environment requires communication of problems to the maintenance staff. In the early 80s, maintenance personnel utilized numeric pagers to respond to production issues. This resulted in delays—from the system delays of the pager company to finding a phone in the facility to contact the area requiring support. In 1986 the plant installed a 450 MHz radio system, utilizing seven repeaters to support the production communities, security, maintenance, and engineering. Following expansions in 1992 and 1996, plant growth resulted in the need for additional communication capabilities. Limited frequency availability in the 450 MHz bands, interference issues in the plant, and security concerns associated with the 450 MHz system led the plant to switch to a five-repeater, digital, trunking 900 MHz system from Motorola® (www.motorola.com). The new system incorporated phone access capability and the expandability of up to 300 talk groups or separate channels. In addition to the expanded capabilities internal to the plant, the system was chosen to support community objectives; being similar to local emergency management systems, talk groups were allocated to the local fire, police, and emergency management services to act as backup channels in the event of system failure of the county emergency management system. This partnering with the local EMS also supports communications between responding EMS, fire, and police to events in the plant by allowing communication to internal personnel during the initial response.

In 2000 the plant fire alarm and monitoring system was upgraded to include alphanumeric paging capability. This upgrade ties equipment alarms of critical equipment and fire alarm points directly to pagers for automatic paging of response personnel internal to the plant. In addition to the 1,657 fire points and 9 spill alarm systems in the plant, critical facilities equipment (chillers, air compressors, water pumps, HVAC systems) automatically inform key personnel anywhere in the plant of alarms via pagers. This system is comprised of a Notifier® Fire Alarm System coupled via a serial port to Motorola's Air Apparent® monitoring system (www.emergin.com) and outputting through a 25-watt repeater mounted on the roof of the security building. As critical equipment is identified, alarms are tied in via monitoring modules to the Notifier Fire Alarm System and then added to the pager system database. Currently the plant is using 30 pagers to equip emergency response and maintenance personnel, reducing the response time to critical plant systems to less than two minutes following an alarm condition. This has reduced equipment downtime and prevented collateral damage due to slow response to alarm conditions—saving material and labor dollars in the facility.

HANDHELD DEVICES

Moving forward with technology, the advent of the handheld device has provided a number of opportunities. In 2000 the maintenance department began utilizing Palm Pilots® to eliminate repetitive entries on inspections. Using inspection software from Breeze Software (www.breezesoftware.com)—an application that allows for creating inspection forms for the Palm device—safety and housekeeping inspection forms were created that loaded on the Palm. The inspection is conducted with the data entered in the field as the inspection occurs, and then the results are downloaded into the database, eliminating the need to enter the data twice. Utilizing this software package for tracking housekeeping activities, forms were designed for assigning nightly cleaning activities. These are loaded at the end of every day and left for the night contract cleaners, who perform the assigned tasks and check off the activities in the Palm®; the following morning the information is uploaded to the database, providing complete cleaning history of the plant. This tracking system has allowed the reduction of the contract cleaning staff by 30 percent, with no noticeable impact to the cleanliness of the plant.

The maintenance department has begun testing of two Palm VII® handhelds, working to integrate the Tabware® work-order system with the Internet connectibility of the Palm to send work orders directly to the on-the-job tradesman. The purpose of this capability is to interconnect the problem machine directly to the tradesman, so that when a problem occurs, the work order is automatically generated, sent to the tradesman anywhere in the plant, and combined with a parts list to allow immediate response. Currently five machines are connected to the total system as a test, with multiple alarms generating separate work orders through the Tabware system and sending them out via the email server to the Palm address.

LAPTOP DEVICE

The plant is exploring setting up a LAN based on the 802.11b protocol to allow expanded access to equipment documentation and drawings for trades. The technology being utilized in this test is Enterasys's RoamAbout® technology (www.enterasys.com/roamabout/indoor.html), which is an IEEE 802.11b direct sequence spread spectrum (DSSS) wireless network solution. Currently the tradesman must go to an area computer to pull up needed information on down equipment, resulting in back-and-forth trips during troubleshooting or the wasteful printing out of paper copies of documentation that are then thrown away following the job. Utilizing the proposed system, the tradesman will be able to bring up documents and drawings, research past history of the machine, and find parts all while being at the machine requiring repair. This will result in reduced man-hours and increased utilization of the trades resources. The system has been installed and was in testing by the Computer Information Technologies group for implementation with maintenance in quarter 1 of 2002.

CONCLUSION

Telecommunications is allowing the leveraging of personnel resources inside of production facilities as well as on the road. Utilizing automated systems, older technologies such as pagers, and the newest handheld and radio LAN technologies, large gains in utilization are possible. Focusing on the value-added tasks of maintenance—time on tools and reducing or eliminating travel time, data entry time, and accessing information time—the ability to support a rapidly expanding plant was achieved with a minimal increase in personnel. An added benefit to the increased technology was valuable information, which the company has turned into a competitive advantage, by continually reducing the costs of maintenance and increasing the uptime of equipment—through design, repair, and replacement.

Case 12-5

Business Continuity Best Practices

Greg B. Zimmerman

INTRODUCTION

A business continuity plan covers both the hardware and software required to run critical business applications and the associated processes to transition smoothly in the event of natural or human-caused disaster. To plan effectively, you need to first assess your mission-critical business processes and associated applications before creating the full business continuity plan. While the mechanics are different, most information technology organizations follow the same basic methodology. That methodology, along with real-world cases experienced during the September 11 World Trade Center attacks, will be examined in this paper.

Business continuity, also called disaster recovery, can be defined as "the uninterrupted session or flow of information technology within a commercial enterprise or establishment." The following topics represent a common methodology for business continuity:

- Management awareness.

- Planning.

- Assessment and auditing.

- Priority.

- Strategy.

- Management approval.

- Testing (pre- and production).

- Implementation.

- Periodic reports and audits.

While this is not a comprehensive list, it does contain elements found in almost every business continuity plan. Of course, certain components could be added or eliminated, depending on the nature of the business. These components can be molded into the project management model (planning, testing, implementation, and analysis).

PLANNING

Most of the work falls into the planning stage. Like any good project, you should plan your work and work your plan. Management awareness is the first and most important step in creating a successful business continuity plan. To obtain the necessary resources and time required from each area of your organization, senior management has to understand and support the business impacts and risks. Several key tasks are required to achieve management awareness.

One of the first steps is determining the types of disaster that could strike. This analysis should cover effects on communications with suppliers and customers, the impact on operations, and disruption on key business processes. This prestudy should be completed in advance of the business continuity planning process, knowing that it will require additional verification during the planning process. The following are examples of possible disasters:

- Fire.

- Weather (storms, extreme heat, extreme cold).

- Water.

- Earthquake.

- Chemical accidents.

- Nuclear accidents.

- Crime.

- Airplane crash (loss of key staff).

- Avalanche.

WTC example
Major damage to the U.S. military's proprietary IP network was caused by water used to fight the massive fires.

The possibility of each scenario is dependent on factors such as geographical location and political stability. The organization should assess the impact of a disaster on the business from both a financial and a physical perspective by asking the following questions:

- How much of the organization's resources could be lost?

- What are the total costs?

- What efforts are required to rebuild?

- How long will it take to recover?

- What is the impact on the overall organization?

- How are customers affected; what is the impact on them?

- How much will it affect the share price and market confidence?

Senior management needs to be involved in the business continuity planning process, and should be aware of the risks and potential impact on the organization. Estimate on costs and time to recovery should be studied initially. Once management understands the financial, physical, and business costs associated with a disaster, it is then able to create a strategy and verify that this strategy is implemented across the organization. Management acceptance can be easy to gain if presented with numbers from the Gartner Group. The Gartner Group has estimated that two out of five businesses that are struck by a disaster will cease operations within five years.

WTC example
Oppenheimer Funds was located in the World Trade Center. Management awareness and sponsorship of business continuity was raised to a higher level after the World Trade Center bombings of 1993.

In addition, the senior management has to accept and sponsor the business continuity project, as well as provide financial and human resources for the project. With this executive sponsorship, communication to the masses needs to be generated for acceptance by the general population. It is key that the business understands that the business continuity committee has complete acceptance and backing from the executive level. Often times, this is announced at a town hall or enterprisewide broadcast by a senior executive.

The true planning begins in the business continuity planning stage. During the business continuity planning stage, you should identify the mission-critical, important, and less-important processes, systems, and services in the network and put in place plans to ensure these are protected against the effects of a disaster. Key elements of business continuity planning include the following:

- Establish a planning team.

- Perform risk assessments and audits.

- Establish priorities for your network and applications.

- Develop recovery strategies.

- Prepare a current inventory and documentation of the plan.

- Develop verification criteria and procedures.

A planning team should be created to manage the development and implementation of the business continuity strategy and plan. This team should include representatives from all sectors of the business. This team will be responsible for all business continuity activities and planning, and for providing regular monthly reports to senior management.

Prior to beginning, the planning team needs to thoroughly understand the business and its processes, technology, networks, systems, and services. The business continuity planning team should prepare a risk analysis and business impact analysis that includes the most probable disaster situations. The risk analysis should include the worst-case scenario of completely damaged facilities and destroyed resources. It should address geographic situations, current design, lead-times of services, and existing service contracts. The analysis should provide financial details on replacing damaged assets, procuring additional headcount, and creating business continuity service agreements with key vendors.

PRIORITIZATION

Prioritization of risk is the next key step. Priorities should be based on the following levels:

WTC example
Oppenheimer Funds turned to networking to cope with the crisis. Their backup tapes were immediately recovered from the off-site storage facility and transferred to an Oppenheimer data center in Denver. Network redundancy and secondary network paths allowed the parent company in Springfield, Massachusetts, to access key corporate data.

- **High risk:** Network or application outage or destruction that would cause an extreme disruption to the business, cause major legal or financial ramifications, or threaten the health and safety of a person. The targeted system or data require significant effort to restore, or the restoration process is disruptive to the business or other systems.

- **Medium risk:** Network or application outage or destruction that would cause a moderate disruption to the business, cause minor legal or financial ramifications, or provide problems with access to other systems. The targeted system or data require a moderate effort to restore, or the restoration process is disruptive to the system.

- **Low risk:** Network or application outage or destruction that would cause a minor disruption to the business. The targeted systems or network can be easily restored.

The business process prioritization is important to identify the key systems, applications, and networks that accompany them. However, without connectivity between them, it is almost useless. Connectivity between branches, offices, and even countries should be analyzed to determine priorities as well. The site priorities and location of key services contribute to a fault-tolerant design, with flexibility and redundancy built into the network infrastructure, and services and resources spread over a wide geography.

STRATEGY

After a thorough prioritization process is completed, a recovery strategy should be created to cover the myriad of scenarios that could be experienced. No strategy can cover every individual situation that occurs. For this reason, the strategy could contain groups of common scenarios. Such groups could be total loss, partial loss, or partial damage. Each group should address key components such as people, facilities, network services, communications equipment, applications, clients and servers, support and maintenance contracts, additional vendor services, lead time of Telco services, and environmental situations. The recovery strategy should include the expected down time of services, action plans, and escalation procedures and also should determine parameters, such as the minimum level at which the business can operate, the systems that must have full functionality (all staff must have access), and the systems that can be minimized.

It is important to keep the system inventory up-to-date and have a complete list of all locations, devices, vendors, used services, and contact names. The inventory and documentation should be part of the design and implementation process of all solutions. Business continuity documentation should include

- Complete inventory, including a prioritization of resources.
- Review process structure assessments, audits, and reports.
- Gap and risk analysis based on the outcome of assessments and audits.
- Implementation plan to eliminate the risks and gaps.
- Business continuity plan containing action and escalation procedures.
- Training material.
- A communication plan for disaster situations.

TESTING

Once a draft of the plan is created, a verification process should be created to prove the disaster recover strategy and, if the strategy is already implemented, review and test the implementation.

It is important that the plan be tested and reviewed frequently. It is recommended that the verification process and procedures be documented and a proof-of-concept process created. The verification process should include an experience cycle; business continuity is based on experience and each disaster has different rules. Business continuity consultants can and should be used to develop and prove the concept, and product vendors should be consulted to design and verify the plan.

WTC example
The bond desk of Morgan Stanley Dean Witter did not exist after the attacks. However, a brilliant strategy that included this function as a high priority had the bond desk functioning in another location two days later with alternate employees.

WTC example
Several companies, including Morgan Stanley Dean Witter and United Airlines, used externally hosted websites to communicate necessary information to employees during the attacks. Employees were aware of the communications plan and knew to utilize these websites in the case of a real disaster.

WTC example
Shipping giant FedEx has reviewed and restructured its business continuity plan after reports that their Memphis hub may have been targeted. Plans include immediate shifting of the hub functions to one of their other locations.

IMPLEMENTATION

Some key decisions will have to be considered: How should your plan be implemented? Who are the critical staff members, and what are their roles? Leading up to the implementation of your plan, try to practice for business continuity using roundtable discussions, role playing, or disaster scenario training. Again, it is essential that your senior management approves the business continuity and implementation plans and communicates the importance to the organization.

Redundancy and backup services form a key part of business continuity, and these services should be reviewed to make sure they meet the criteria for the business continuity plan. Network recovery can be defined as the ability to recover from any network failure or issue whether it is related to a disaster, link, hardware, design, or network services. A high-availability network design is often the foundation for business continuity and can be sufficient to handle some minor or local disasters. Key tasks for redundancy planning and backup services include the following:

- Assess the strengths and weaknesses of your network; identify gaps and risks.

- Review and verify your current backup services.

- Implement network redundancy and backup services.

It is recommended that the business assess the strength of your network keeping in mind the following three levels of availability: general-use networks, high-availability networks, and 24 × 7 network environments. Doing so helps prioritize risks, sets requirements for higher levels of availability, and identifies the mission-critical elements of your network. The following areas of your network should be examined (keep in mind that this list is not exhaustive):

- Network links:
  - Carrier diversity.
  - Local loop diversity.
  - Facilities availability.
  - Building wiring verification.
- Hardware strength:
  - Power, security, and disaster.
  - Redundant hardware.
  - Mean time to repair or replace.
  - Network path availability.
- Network design:
  - Layer 2 WAN design.
  - Layer 2 LAN design.
  - Layer 3 IP design.

WTC example
As in the U.S. military example mentioned earlier, secondary routes were utilized to keep the IP services available around the world immediately.

- Network services:
  - DNS strategy.
  - DHCP strategy.

A business continuity plan should include a secondary services strategy, which needs to be consistent throughout the whole organization. Secondary scenarios are important to provide higher availability and access to main sites and/or access to existing parallel business continuity sites during a disaster. All system and application backup strategies depend upon network connections. Disaster handling requires communication services, and the impact of a disaster could be greatly limited by having available communications services.

Having support services from major vendors in place adds a strong value to business continuity planning. The services divisions of major IT vendors such as IBM, Compaq, and Hewlett-Packard offer work space recovery options. More specialized services are provided by disaster recovery specialists Comdisco, SunGuard, and Rentsys. Key questions regarding vendor support include

WTC example
Thirty-five companies affected by the WTC attacks are using Comdisco (a disaster recovery giant) to provide office space and IT hot sites. Most of the customers have required office space at Comdisco facilities in Queens, New York, or across the Hudson River in New Jersey. Customers are having backup tapes that were stored in off-site locations brought to the Comdisco hot sites for restoral.

- Are support contracts in place?
- Has the business continuity plan been reviewed by the vendors? And are the vendors included in the escalation processes?
- Can the vendor react quickly to additional hardware, software, and support needs?
- Does the vendor have sufficient resources to support the business continuity plan?

CONCLUSION

While having a business continuity plan in place does not ensure 100 percent success, it does provide a framework for disaster recovery. Key factors are communication, planning, funding, and testing. No one can forecast when disaster will strike, but with proper planning, experience will be gained that will assist in the execution of the continuity process.

WTC example
Because of the catastrophic nature of the disaster, several companies have turned to hosting services provided by Unisys.

REFERENCES

1. Barnes, J. *A Guide to Business Continuity Planning*. New York: John Wiley & Sons, 2001.

2. Bowen, T. S. *Be Prepared: Disaster-Recovery Plans Essential to Success*. CNN.COM, August 1999. Available at http://www.cnn.com.

3. Butler, J., and P. Badura. *Contingency Planning and Disaster Recovery: Protecting Your Organization's Resources*. Stamford, CT: Computer Technology Research Corporation, 1997.

4. Chen, A., and M. Hicks. "How to Stay Afloat." *Smart Business Magazine*, October 2001. Available at http://www.smartbusinessmag.com.

5. Doughty, K. *Business Continuity Planning: Protecting Your Organization's Life*. New York: Auerbach Publishers, 2000.

6. Gibson, S. "Disaster Recovery." *Smart Business Magazine,* September 2001. Available at http://www.smartbusinessmag.com.

7. Hall, M., and M. Solomon. "Navigating a Nightmare." *Computerworld* 35, no. 38 (September 17, 2001), pp. cover, 61.

8. Hiatt, C. J. *A Primer for Disaster Recovery Planning in an IT Environment.* Hershey, PA: Idea Group Publishing, 2000.

9. Hiles, A. *Business Continuity: Best Practices.* Brookfield, CT: Rothstein Associates, 2000.

10. Jones, E. D. *Business Continuity Self-Assessment Checklist.* Brookfield, CT: Rothstein Associates, 2000.

11. Rothstein, P. J. *Disaster Recovery Testing: Exercising Your Contingency Plan.* Brookfield, CT: Rothstein Associates, 1995.

12. Schwartz, E.; P. Krill; E. Scannell; and E. Grygo. "U.S. Attack: IT Disaster Recovery Revs into High Gear." *InfoWorld,* September 2001. Available at http://www.infoworld.com.

13. Toigo, J. W. "E-Business and Disaster Recovery Planning: More Art than Science." *Enterprise Systems,* December 2000. Available at http://www.esj.com.

14. Toigo, J. W. *Disaster Recovery Planning: Strategies for Protecting Critical Information Assets.* Upper Saddle River, NJ: Prentice Hall, 1999.

15. University of Arkansas. *Disaster Recovery Plan, Disaster Preparation (DRPDR003),* March 2000. Available at http://www.uark.edu.

16. Wrobel, L. A. *Disaster Recovery Planning for Telecommunications.* Norwood, MA: Artech House, 1990.

Summary

This chapter is about the management of the organizational and technical sides of telecommunications technology. The organizational aspects of telecommunications management reflect, in one sense, a classical management environment. That is, you must attract, train, and retain competent people, some with special skills. The senior telecommunications managers must be a part of the management and executive teams to be informed of the strategic plans for the organizations, if they are expected to support those plans. The group must understand the business of the organization to understand the sources and uses of projects they will be expected to manage. As the environment changes, bringing new controls and competitors, those responsible for the strategic direction of the organization must be in a position to detect the changes and take appropriate actions, preferably in a proactive as opposed to reactive stance.

The management of the technical aspects of telecommunications involves the engineering tasks for design and installation of capabilities, daily operation, maintenance, and repair. In all cases, the management implications of any addition or change must be analyzed lest it lock the organization into a future that is highly constraining. The architecture adopted must allow for evolution and interoperation of multivendor equipment. The protocols must be designed to nonproprietary standards that fit into existing capabilities and must evolve to accept future expansions. An organization that has ignored the potential of the Internet and intranet capabilities will be at a marked disadvantage in the competitive world.

Some of the management issues relate to knowing what you already have and what the organization needs to stay competitive. Other issues relate to the risk of natural disasters and the organization's ability to continue operations. All issues relate to how telecommunications supports the business of the organization. Proper management of people and technology solves business problems and takes advantage of business opportunities. Most importantly, the telecommunications group can provide a vital element of competitive advantage for the organization. Without it, the organization faces an uncertain future.

Key Terms

change management, *545*
chief information officer (CIO), *519*
committed information rate (CIR), *549*
Communications Management Information Protocol (CMIP), *542*
competitive advantage, *516*
computer telephony integration (CTI), *524*
configuration management, *545*

controlling, *524*
critical success factors (CSF), *536*
directing, *524*
disaster planning, *547*
disaster recovery, *524*
mean time between failures (MTBF), *533*
organizing, *522*
Quick Response, *517*
request for proposal/ request for quotation (RFP/RFQ), *529*

risk analysis, *546*
risk assessment, *546*
risk management, *545*
service level agreement (SLA), *547*
Simple Network Management Protocol (SNMP), *542*
staffing, *523*
strategy, *525*
systems development life cycle (SDLC), *528*

Discussion Questions

12.1. What are some significant factors for consideration in backup for critical telecommunications capabilities?

12.2. Does JEI itself need a business continuity plan?

12.3. What would be the impact of loss of telecommunications capabilities on JEI's business?

12.4. How vulnerable is JEI in each of its major business processes?

12.5. List and discuss the major disasters that have occurred over the past 10 years. What have been their effects on businesses in the area?

12.6. Discuss the pros and cons of having MIS and TC under the same manager. Would it be better or worse to separate them?

12.7. What are the pros and cons of outsourcing the management of your TC capabilities?

12.8. What are the minimum contents for an RFP? Why is it important to have a thoroughly reviewed RFP before submitting it to potential providers?

12.9. Why is an RFP more difficult to create and more important than an RFQ?

12.10. What is the impact of the MTBF of components of a system on the reliability of the system?

Projects

12.1. Look up the topic of *Information Technology Risk Analysis and Management* and find a model. Discuss this model in class.

12.2. Go to your community's financial institutions and determine what sort of business continuity planning is employed. Determine any regulations or laws that require continuity planning for these institutions. Do you consider the plans adequate?

12.3. Investigate, in your community, the existence of organizations that provide backup data storage, hot sites, cold sites, shared installations, and so forth. What does it cost to use these services? What is the role of telecommunications in providing these services?

12.4. Investigate the Pacific Stock Exchange, located in California. Where exactly is it located, and where is the backup site? What power and telecommunications facilities does it have? How safe is it?

12.5. Investigate 10 companies in your local community, perform risk analysis, and rank them in terms of risk of loss of computing and telecommunications capabilities. What is your estimate of the MTTB (Mean time to belly-up) for each?

12.6. Divide the class into groups, each group finding an organization with a telecommunications group. What are the qualifications of its members?

12.7. Interview the manager of a telecommunications group and determine the most important job qualifications of the various individuals of the group. How is the organization meeting its rapidly changing staffing needs, through internal staffing, external consulting, or "growing their own"?

12.8. You are the manager of an organization, recently given the responsibility to form a new TC group. Write an advertisement to hire members for your group.

12.9. Find a business and categorize it based on Keen's stages of TC management. Give your reasons for your categorization.

12.10. Interview local business managers responsible for controlling the TC resources of their organization and determine the major TC issues. Why are they considered issues?

12.11. Determine if your school has documented its telecommunications assets. If so, is the documentation accurate?

12.12. Propose an architecture for JEI and draw it with netViz.

Chapter **Thirteen**

How Do You Manage Telecommunications Projects? SDLC for Telecommunications

CONTINUING CASE—PART 13

Scott Sets up a Project

Michael walked into Scott's new office and sat in an easy chair. "All settled in, Scott?"

"Yes, and the office is great! I really love the view of the mountains."

"Yes, they do soothe you like nothing else."

"Michael, I was wondering if you had reviewed the telecommunications projects recently. You told me when I was hired that you had assumed this task as JEI CEO. Although I will take over this task now, I was wondering if you had a feel for our progress."

"It's been about two months since I looked at the portfolio of projects, so it's a good time to review them anew. It'll be good to have a fresh view of the prioritization we have and our progress. How about making that your first priority?"

"Right! I'll give you a status update on Friday at our weekly meeting. Will Carlton be here for that, or is he still in Scotland?"

"He'll be in Scotland for several more weeks, but you can email him the briefing."

Scott gathered the folders for the telecommunications projects from Michael's desk. He then called each of JEI's managers to be sure he had them all. The folders included both those in process and those awaiting action. He reviewed each of the active projects and marked their progress on a chart showing their present status as to SDLC (systems development life cycle) stage. Scott saw that the company had several projects that were backlogged. One of his first tasks was to list these projects and determine their priority so that the firm's resources would be allocated to the most important systems first. As

he looked at the status in Figure 13.1, he pondered the priorities as Michael had them noted and thought about each. Michael had the Scotland bandwidth project as the most important task, and he agreed, as an internal data communications infrastructure and access to adequate external bandwidth were required before the facility could go online.

Scott saw that the second priority was the finalization of the ERP system with JIT at Kansas City. It would be possible, with adequate bandwidth, to make Scotland a part of these capabilities and not have to have a separate, stand-alone capability. The other projects were less urgent, although important to JEI's future. The communications to the security patrols needed their new capabilities to give them wider coverage and faster response time. Additionally, the new system would give the walking patrols 9-1-1 capability in case of fire or medical emergency. He wanted to get this online but had not decided if it was of highest priority for the backlog items.

Scott looked at the backlog for quite a while. He kept being drawn back to the upgrade of the PBX in Denver to go beyond least-cost routing and include Voice over Internet Protocol. With the wide area network that JEI now had installed, it would be possible to send much of the voice traffic over their own bandwidth. Additionally, each site has good Internet access, so that is at least a consideration.

Scott reached for the phone to call Sarah when she walked into the office. "Great timing, Sarah, I was just about to call you."

FIGURE 13.1 JEI Project Status

Project	Location	Phase	Priority
Access to increased bandwidth	Scotland	Analysis and general design	1
ERP and JIT	Kansas City	Detailed design and implementation	2
In-plant network	Scotland	Detailed design and implementation	3
Upgrade of LAN	Denver	Investigation and feasibility study	4
Upgrade of PBX to VoIP	Denver	Backlog	
Upgrade STS infrastructure	Kansas City	Backlog	
Install ERP and link to KC	Scotland	Backlog	
Upgrade security radios	Denver and CS	Backlog	

"I heard you had a great office and wanted to see if you needed help in decoration."

"I think I am in pretty good shape, thanks to my wife's enthusiasm for decorating."

"What did you have to talk about, new CIO?"

Scott blushed a bit as she said his new title. "Well, I would like to get a backlogged project active. How about your taking the task as project manager for the PBX upgrade to VoIP? It'll be great experience for you in project management and we need the outcome."

"Great, Boss! Who do I get on my team?"

"Well, first you need to talk to Alli about what she had in mind and write up a single-page description of the project. Is it just solving a problem of high long-distance charges or is it an opportunity of using VoIP as a competitive advantage? Then, let me know who you think will be good additions to the team and I'll send out a memo. Once that is done, you can call a gathering of the team and determine the feasibility of doing the job. Be sure we have all of our bases covered; I am most concerned with the state of present PBX technology to VoIP, so let's get a consultant here if we need to."

"I'll go see Alli today and have a project description on your desk tomorrow. May I use the JEI conference room for the rest of the week?"

"Check with Michael's administrative assistant."

Sarah met with Alli; they detailed out the task as well as they could, or at least what they thought could be done. They began by determining the logic behind the proposed improvement and listing anticipated business benefits from adding the capabilities. Thus, they had a much better feel for the way in which enhanced PBX capabilities would support JEI's business needs. Sarah created the memo, including the names of the team members she wanted.

When Sarah convened the team, she set up a strawman schedule, with a feasibility study being next. The team spent the major part of a week determining what products were on the market, the cost of the enhancement, and operational and maintenance considerations for VoIP. Next, they performed the systems analysis for the system, going much deeper into the requirements and capabilities of VoIP. They went to Supercomm exhibits first and then visited several vendors to hear the quality of VoIP over a private network and over the Internet. She told each vendor what she wanted to achieve and promised to send them an RFP by which they could propose a solution for the project.

Returning home with a good understanding of the alternative solutions, the team sent out the request for proposals to the vendors they visited and began to make the design drawings for the enhancement. For the most part, the enhancement would be the addition of a small amount of equipment and a software upgrade. Sarah believed that it would be a good time to include an uninterruptable power supply and other surge protection to the system. They also determined that the PBX was running at about maximum capabilities, so they included the addition of lines to the project.

Two weeks later, the proposals arrived from the participating vendors and the team set about making a decision for a final design. Sarah presented the team's recommendation to the management team that met each Friday and got the go-ahead to purchase the equipment and software. She created an installation plan so that ancillary equipment and services, such as additional cooling and space, would be available upon the arrival of equipment. Sarah also made up a test plan in preparation of the installation of equipment.

As the equipment arrived, the team tested each piece as best they could. Then they installed all the equipment and software and began a systems test. The test went well and within a week the team was ready to implement the capability and allow usage by Alli's department. When Alli was satisfied that the enhancement worked as desired, all of JEI was told of the new capability, although in reality the PBX now had the installed intelligence to make the routing decision with a subsequent lowering of cost. Sarah met with this team one last time to make a review of the project and the extent to which they were successful in meeting the objectives. This satisfied the project and meant that the people doing maintenance would include new enhancements in their routine inspection. At each stage of the project, Sarah's team was careful to fully document their actions, updating JEI's configuration maps and database. Consequently, at the end of the project, they had a repository with detailed documentation to provide to the CIO. This documentation should prove of great value whenever the next enhancement is called for.

INTRODUCTION

In this chapter we continue the discussions begun in Chapter 12 concerning how projects originate and are carried through. Specifically, in this chapter we will discuss the *systems development life cycle (SDLC)* of a telecommunications project, the stages involved, and the activities and deliverables of each stage. Use of the SDLC approach is borrowed from the development of computer-based systems as telecommunications design and implementation follow much the same course of definition, design, and discovery.

The management of telecommunications, like the management of an organization, starts with a mission and vision, is activated with implementation, continues with operation and maintenance, and ends with disposal. The vision must come from upper management, as it defines its business, customers, and ways of competing. From vision must come a set of objectives that bring vision to fruition. The objectives, like vision, come from the strategic and executive level of management. After objectives comes a strategy to make the objectives operational, then comes planning for the operational actions.

One set of tasks from the executive suite to the factory floor is contained in Figure 13.2.

VISION

Vision is the guiding view of the future from the executive level.

Vision translates the **mission** of the company and its objectives into a clear picture of simple principles. Vision is a picture of the future, an easily understood statement about a practical and desirable, if not fully predictable, goal. It should include an indication of values, by answering the question, "what's important around here?"[1]

The Real World   13–1
Date with Disaster

L.A.'s Cedar Sinai, a 1,000-bed private hospital, lost half its network when the earthquake struck and electric power went out. Fortunately, the hospital recovered 70 percent of its 3,000-plus network devices, including routers, bridges, and controllers, within 18 hours, and 90 percent were restored after 48 hours.

NEW YORK AND CALIFORNIA DOMINATE DISASTERS

Disaster incidents by state (percentage based on 2,436 outages since 1982).

California	18.4%	New York	26.0%
Pennsylvania	3.5%	Connecticut	2.2%
South Carolina	1.4%	D.C.	4.1%
Illinois	14.2%	Florida	5.6%
Maine	3.6%	Texas	3.7%
New Jersey	4.5%		

Source: "Date with Disaster," *Information Week.*

---

[1] Peter G. W. Keen, *Shaping the Future* (Cambridge: Harvard Business School Press, 1991), p. 19.

FIGURE 13.2 Mission, Operating Philosophy, and Vision

Source: Adapted from Collins and Huge, "Management by Policy." Milwaukee, WI: ASQC Quality Press, 1993, p. 81.

Mission—explains the scope of the business and why the business exists

    → **Operating Philosophy**—explains how the values, beliefs, guiding principles, and mission will be followed

        → **Vision**—provides strategic direction in 5 to 10 years

            → **Objectives**—describes what end results you are trying to achieve

                → **Strategy**—explains how the vision will be attained

                    → **Long-Range Plans**—describes three- to five-years, horizon

                        → **Annual Plan**—executes the strategy for this year

                            → **Financial Plan**—displays the budget to make it happen

OBJECTIVES

Strategy leads to **architecture** leads to **planning** leads to **development**.

From **objectives** will come an idea of the major function of the organization, who its customers are, and what activities it will be involved in. These activities will affect the functioning of the MIS and telecommunications activities.

STRATEGY

Strategy is the overall plan for achieving organizational objectives.

Strategy means large-scale, future-oriented plans for interacting in a competitive environment to optimize achievement and organizational objectives. Strategy is the organization's game plan that reflects the company's awareness of how to compete, against whom, when, where, and for what.

ARCHITECTURE

System architecture is the overall design plan for the entire system. Architecture will support or inhibit future actions.

The **architecture** reflects the technical strategy. It is roughly like a city plan, a mixture of fixed main routes, zoning regulations and ordinances, and procedures for extending and modifying existing buildings and expanding or adding roads. [Keen] It is a model of the desired end result that is used to guide the efforts that should achieve the end result (see Figure 13.3). Architecture should be defined during the planning stages and refined throughout the life cycles of the system. According to James Martin,[2] there are three "enterprise architectures": *information systems architecture, business systems architecture,* and *technical architecture.* Each of these is described below:

> **Information systems architecture** is the aggregation of data, functions, and their interaction that represents business requirements. This architecture is represented by data models such as entity-relationship diagrams and by functional decomposition diagrams accompanied by definitions, matrices, and detailed process definitions and diagrams.

[2] IE-EXPERT (Version 4.0).

FIGURE 13.3
TC Architecture Must be Congruent with and Provide Support to Organizational Strategy

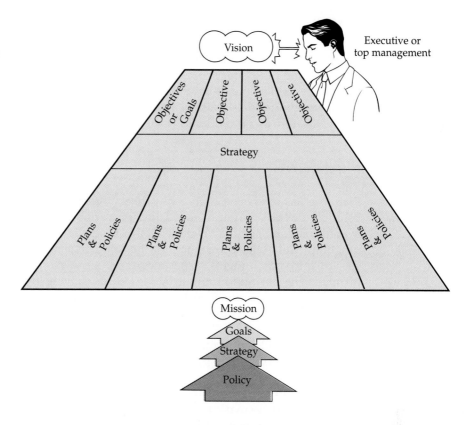

Business systems architecture is the aggregation of individual business applications and descriptive characteristics of business systems. This architecture should show dependencies between business systems and define the category of each business system. Examples of categories are strategic planning, monitoring, control, and transactions.

Technical architecture is the defined collection of technologies and components. This includes high-level descriptions and definitions of the required technological infrastructure for systems development. Usage information, policies, and statistics that apply to the technologies should be included.

Network architecture is the set of conventions or standards that ensure all the other components are interrelated and can work together. This technical architecture is the overall design blueprint for creating and evolving the network over changes in time, technology, uses, volumes, and geographic locations. The architecture has to reflect the business vision. There are a number of often-conflicting criteria for selecting the standards, scale and type of technology, and technical policies for the selection of vendors and equipment. [Keen]

Network architecture is a primary part of any computer-based system because of distributed departments, processing, and data storage. This portion of the total information systems architecture specifies structure descriptions, relationships of network senders and receivers, logical paths, protocols, and communication functions that manage and support the transfer of information. Previously, an information systems developer might consider the transfer of computer digital data, but today the consideration of networks must include voice, images, text, and data.

Architecture is a specification that determines how something is constructed, defining functional modularity as well as the protocols and interfaces that allow communications and cooperation among modules.

POLICY

Policy is the specific guidelines for execution of a strategy.

A **policy** is the set of mandates and directives from the top of the firm summarized by the ground rule, "This is how we do things around here." It addresses questions of authority and accountability. Policy is not the same as planning. It sets the criteria for planning and establishes the ground rules for it. Both are needed to define the architecture that provides the framework for using the technology.

PLANNING

Planning is the act of establishing the means of attaining strategic objectives.

Planning has long been cited as a primary function of top managers. In reality, planning can be thought of as existing on various levels: at the top level where overall company planning is done; at the middle level where intermediate plans, programs, and budgets are made for the company; and at the project level where specific projects, budgets, schedules, and technical performance targets are planned. The devolution might be viewed as moving from plans directly concerned with organizational goals, through functional planning areas, to the specific work package level. Thus, planning levels move from the general to the specific and from long to intermediate time horizons.

CEOs are challenging their staffs to create 10-year telecommunications plans. Staffs are not successful in putting together 5-year plans, much less 10-year plans, that work financially and strategically. This is extremely difficult due to the dynamic nature of the industry/market and the explosion of broadband technologies. The industry/market is accelerating as opposed to stabilizing. Video and bandwidth requirements drive the change. You have to balance short-term and long-term goals.

Planning for telecommunications may seem an impossible task because of the rate of change in technology and the uncertainty surrounding the move to Net-based business. Gary Hamel has this to say in the February 5, 2001, issue of *Fortune:* ". . . any company hoping to survive the tsunami of innovation and change that the Web threatens to unleash will need more than a digital business plan." He sees a need for "habitual and radical innovation."

For telecommunications, long-range planning involves architecture. Mid-level planning determines components that fit the architecture. At the lower levels, planning details the configuration, features, procedures, and training for specific operations.

IMPLEMENTATION

Implementation is the process of doing or executing a planned course of action.

He who rejects change is the architect of decay. The only human institution which rejects progress is the cemetary.—Harold Wilson

Implementation is the action phase of the planning process. Often implementation involves adaptation to changes that have occurred after the planning decision was made; consequently the entire planning cycle may be considered dynamic and iterative to the extent that the environment dictates. One can easily visualize the dynamic nature of the process by considering this example. A great deal of strategic, intermediate, and operational level planning had been done before implementation on D-Day of the Allied forces invading Europe near the end of World War II. Because of the dynamic and volatile environment, military commanders

The Real World
Revolution at Ford

13–2

At the Ford Motor Company, the basic designs and parts of cars are being designed on a global scale—and the designers and production experts are now all working together regardless of their physical location. Using technologies such as videoconferencing, computer networking, and computer simulation, designers around the world work simultaneously on the same drawing, and crash test-ing and product management are done without the need to build expensive prototypes. Using the information technology for these purposes, Ford has reduced project approval time for a new automobile design by more than 75 percent.

Source: "Revolution at Ford," *The Economist.*

at the implementation levels had to make many adaptive decisions. Similarly, telecommunications managers must be prepared to make adaptive decisions in the dynamic telecommunications environment of today.

TELECOMMUNICATIONS DESIGN AND IMPLEMENTATION

Change is a part of all life, including business life. The telecommunications environment is characterized by rapid and significant change.

With change comes the need (and opportunity) to enhance present facilities and install new capabilities.

Systems analysis and design is the process of systematically creating systems to achieve some organizational objectives.

Telecommunications systems contain all components and capabilities needed to move information reliably to serve organizational needs.

The one thing you can depend on in life and in business is change. You can expect telecommunications and computer vendors to change equipment capabilities, users to change their needs and expectations, and the environment to change in terms of the complexion of competition. With change comes the need to enhance present facilities and install new capabilities. A simple way of looking at this from a telecommunications standpoint is that it often means more bandwidth between points or to new points. Of course, new standards and advances in hardware can spur the need to enhance telecommunications facilities and capabilities. If there are no digital channels, firms will be installing or enhancing the ability to transmit digital data on analog circuits, or they must create digital channels. If they have digital data circuits, they will increase their transfer ability (bandwidth) with faster circuits or more circuits, or by multiplexing existing circuits. All of the changes will require network analysis and design.

Telecommunications networks that are put together in a piecemeal fashion are rarely adequate. The process of determining needs, analyzing alternatives, delineating system specifications, and designing the system that will properly serve the organization is usually referred to as *systems* **analysis and design.** Through the past 20 years, the principles of analysis and design have been refined in the realm of computer-based systems so that there are several standardized approaches and methodologies. Network analysis and design also have been subject to some refinement, however, not nearly to the extent that computer-based or management information systems (MIS) have. Because of the maturity of the systems and analysis process and methodology of MIS, we will use that *system's development life cycle* as a reference for our investigation of network analysis and design.

Network Analysis and Design

This is the process of understanding the requirements for a communications network, investigating alternative ways for implementing the network, and selecting the most appropriate alternative to provide the required capacity. Because it is so very important to understand the business problem or opportunity for which the enhanced or new network capability is being installed, much of this chapter discusses the process of analysis, design, and implementation of such capabilities. At this point, it is important to understand that the better you define the problem[3] and describe its solution, the easier your life will be in the future as you operate, maintain, and change the capability under consideration.

Telecommunications systems include hardware, software, procedures, data, and people.

Telecommunications systems contain all components and capabilities needed to move information or data to serve organizational needs. The components include hardware, software, procedures, data, and (most importantly) people. The system connects the components to the telecommunications network, with each geographic location containing one or more nodes.

Network Implementation

Implementation is the process of installing and making the network operational. After you have determined what to do and how to do it, this is the "then do it" stage. In many respects, implementation is the easiest part. With proper planning, all you have to do is put the components where they go, test them, and turn them on. We will talk more about this later.

Sources of Requests for Projects

There are several reasons for projects, which is to say several sources of change. For example, one source of recommendations for change is the *telecommunications group* itself, specifically the network operations staff. These people, as they work with the network and handle problems daily, see (1) better and more cost-effective ways of doing the present jobs, (2) present capabilities being taxed to their limits, and (3) worn-out equipment being called upon to perform too long.

Information pipeline or conduit is a description of a circuit, channel, or path, using the analog of data flow to fluid flow.

If the firm is moving data and digitized voice from site to site and the data must wait as the pipeline[4] is filled during normal work (business) hours, you can readily state the implications of these delays and recommend improvements. Possibly your organization requires greater bandwidth on existing circuits, new and redundant circuits, or fiber instead of microwave or satellite channels. Being the closest to the network, the network operations people have the greatest knowledge of what is needed, based on the present requirements. Their major limit often is restricted knowledge of what new requirements are desired from a business needs perspective. Thus, the telecommunications group should be kept aware that they *should* recommend enhancements and additions to make sure that present service is adequate, efficient, cost-effective, and reliable.

Functional areas that presently use the telecommunications capabilities, the user groups, can offer opportunities for change. As the production managers see the

---

[3] Most of the time we assume the solution to a problem. In business, taking advantage of an opportunity may be of greater value and uses the same process as solving a problem. We will use problem definition and solution also to include defining and creating a solution to take advantage of an opportunity.

[4] The term *pipeline* is often used to describe a data channel. The larger a water or oil pipeline, the more fluid can flow. In like manner, the wider the bandwidth (higher the speed) of a data circuit, the more data can flow. Thus, the digital channel is a pipeline for data. Because we can visualize physical pipelines and most data circuits look the same, the data pipeline concept is quite useful.

Information Window   13–1

The people in the functional areas are the telecommunications department's customers. If the telecommunications specialists get to know these customers and what they do, it will stop being a surprise when they ask for something new or better. In fact, if specialists do their jobs right and really get to know what their customers do, together they can arrive at what the customers need or can use to make their jobs easier or more profitable.

EFT (electronic funds transfer) is the transfer of funds via electronic (signal) surrogates over a data network.

value of communicating with their suppliers to ensure that inventory is kept at a minimum and arrives when required, they may see how they need similar channels of communications with their customers. The finance department may want to move to **electronic funds transfer (EFT),** allowing more efficient handling of funds, at a lower cost, by moving monies through a network as opposed to checks through the mail. The sales and marketing department may see competitors providing laptop computers to their representatives and request information on this equipment and the telecommunications channels to support them. This may mean more in-WATS (area codes 800, 888, 877, etc.) lines, or it may mean a dedicated digital network. **The people who are the closest to the operation of the company know the most about their operations and processes.** As they become educated in communications and telecommunications, they are in the best position to request capabilities and enhancements to improve their business processes.

Because *senior managers* are chartered with working at the strategic level, looking into the future, they should request information about possibilities that can address future problems and opportunities. Even if they are in the functional areas mentioned above, they will have a different view of the nature of business than their subordinates who deal with day-to-day operational problems. These managers consider long-term and far-reaching concerns. Senior managers should look at

- Who *will* our customers and competitors be next year, and the next?
- Who *should* our customers be?
- How *should* we operate?
- How *should* we compete?
- What *should* we be doing?

The last group of people to make demands that require new facilities or recommend new capabilities are customers, vendors, suppliers, and governmental agencies. This first cluster, *customers,* deserves and demands a lot of your company's attention. Firms that listen to customers and can fulfill requirements using telecommunications technology create partnerships and exclude possible competitors. Because telecommunications has the ability to define competition and customer service, telecommunications managers should expect comments and suggestions from customers that will cause change and require new or enhanced capabilities.

Technology vendors will persist in showing you their latest products. If, however, your firm has formed partnerships with them, you will be working as allies. As allies or partners, vendors will help develop the products that will assist you. Increasingly, firms forge *partnerships* with *suppliers.* This often entails sharing access to databases, ERP systems, and so forth.

Finally, *governmental agencies* create demands that may need to be met with technology. One of the latest cases is electronic filing of tax data. Be aware that when you work with governmental agencies, even though they may seem to be demanding expenditures from you unfairly, you may find them to be new customers. Meeting government demands may show you different and better ways to do the jobs you are doing.

CAPACITY PLANNING

What is the effect of
not performing
capacity planning?

Network administrators need to be able to predict bottlenecks when adding new capabilities. The task involves forecasting computer (CPU, I/O, and memory) requirements and LAN and WAN bandwidth to accommodate the capabilities.

Usually, the planners need to gather data on current capacity and usage for nodes, servers, and media, and forecast the impact on computing and bandwidth in light of business growth and the new applications. Next, there is a need to model the solutions at the required performance level. Then the solution needs verification at the forecasted levels.

Unfortunately, there is no tool or suite of tools that does the entire task. Some firms, for example, American Airlines, have created labs to simulate nodes, servers, and bandwidth on the network to create an environment nearly identical to the real one so modeling and volume testing can be accurate. Some network management tools, such as Distributed Sniffer System® from Network General Corporation, do provide net traffic statistics. Ameritech Network Services (ANS) uses this tool to monitor LAN and WAN traffic in a five-state area. Other vendors offer tools as well. TrendTrack®, LANAlert®, and Spectrum® are examples.

The Institute for Computer Capacity Management has provided three elements needed for capacity planning: workload characterization, forecasting, and performance prediction. Each is discussed below.

Workload Characterization

- Obtain user views of the business model and an idea of the number of users and types of transactions currently and likely for the future.

- Collect data daily; do trends weekly, monthly, quarterly, and annually to reveal monthly and seasonal cycles.

- Create a baseline of the current workload for forecasting.

- Categorize nodes by type based on equipment and function to obtain information on the number of servers and their locations. Identify the feeder and major switching centers.

Forecasting (Estimating Future Workload)

- Determine the desired end result capability.

- Estimate the growth rate of the system. Don't underestimate! Be sure to reflect new users, increased use by current users, and additions, especially at the client level. FileNet always forecasts 25 percent to 45 percent more growth than their customers estimate.

- Determine and factor in applications that are planned or are under development.

Performance Prediction (Recommend a Configuration)

- Build a model.

- Size test workloads to peak periods rather than average or sustained demand.

- Document all assumptions and calculations and double-check.

- Fit calculations into a long-range plan rather than being content with the immediate capability additions.

- After installation, evaluate actual versus predicted performance and adjust both the network and the capacity planning system.

- Perform capacity planning at, at least, annual intervals.

A METHODOLOGY FOR DESIGNING, DEVELOPING, AND IMPLEMENTING TELECOMMUNICATIONS CAPABILITIES

SDLC (systems development life cycle) is a formal development process composed of logical phases that guide systems development from concept through implementation, operations, and maintenance.

The process of design and development of enhanced or new capabilities follows a formal development process. The process includes the members of technical services interacting with requesters and users, as well as a significant amount of work that does not involve them. One process of creating and maintaining a telecommunications system is based on the MIS life cycle approach, called the **systems development life cycle (SDLC).** As shown in Figures 13.4 and 13.11, the SDLC is composed of the major **phases** of problem definition, feasibility, systems analysis, design, procurement, implementation, test evaluation and review, and maintenance and change. This approach represents a systems view to solve problems.

In recent years, systems analysts have been concerned with the topic of *network modeling.* The move to client-server architecture has been a major reason for this concern. Some graphical tools have evolved to aid in the design task. We will examine network modeling briefly in the following section.

NETWORK MODELING

Network modeling is a method to document the parts of the system.

Network modeling has been defined as a diagrammatic technique that is employed to document the system in terms of the users, data, and processing locations. Frequently, it is useful to focus on *logical* or *essential* network modeling, that is, the modeling of the network requirements independent of the actual implementation. In the process of design, these models will be converted to implementation models that specify the particular system.

Using the netViz® software package, several diagrams of the telecommunications system can be displayed to help the designers and managers get a picture of the system. Several presentations are employed to assist in the process.

In Figure 13.5 created with netViz, we see JEI's overall logical network between its major sites. Next is a geographic view of the network from the owner's perspective (Figure 13.6). This gives a clear picture of the overall connectivity.

FIGURE 13.4   Process Flow, Sources, and Process Outputs of the TC SDLC

Source: Adapted from Powers, Cheney, & Crow, *Structured Systems Development*, 2nd ed. Boston, MA: Boyd & Fraser Publishing, 1990, p. 43.

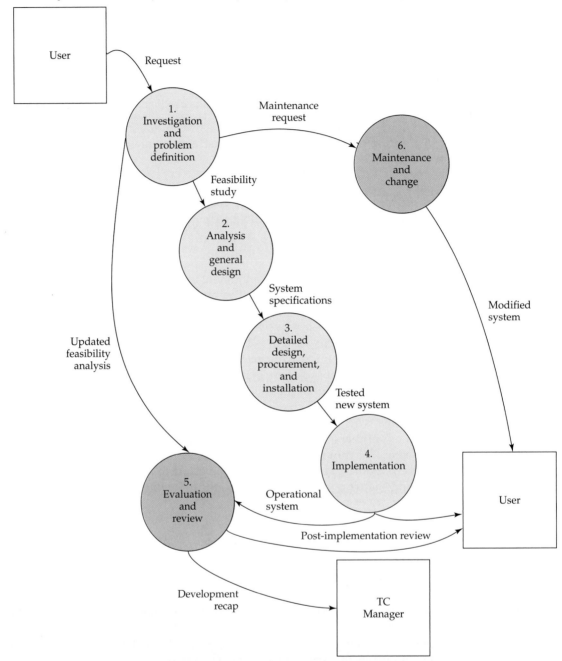

The system designer's view (Figure 13.7, p. 593) is more detailed and provides basic information needed to solve the basic technological connections.

Another view of the system is the network topology DFD (data flow diagram) in Figure 13.8, p. 594. The next example (Figure 13.9, p. 595) shows netViz-created network topology. Figure 13.10, p. 596 provides a logical order data flow for JEI.

FIGURE 13.5 **JEI and Its Subsidiaries**

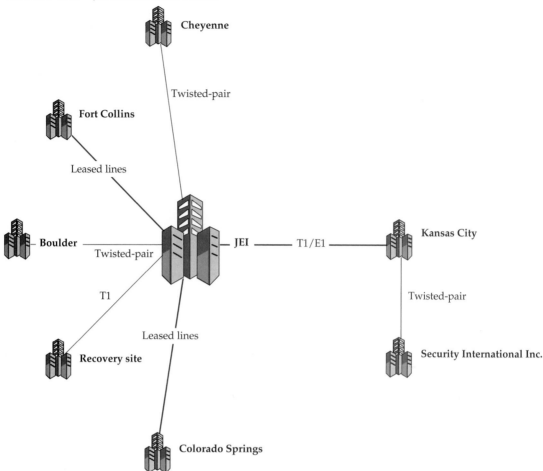

Formal development is an approach to satisfying the requestor's telecommunications requirements that relies predominantly on the various groups within data services to supply the tools, resources, and expertise required. Typically, it is implemented using a life cycle approach—specific tasks occur at specific places in the total life of the system. Development is partitioned into activities with defined roles and responsibilities for users and data services personnel. Activities have *specified end products,* and the life cycle is subject to frequent formal review. Formality may ease political problems because roles and responsibilities are defined. Partitioning of tasks facilitates management of development. Figure 13.11, p. 596 shows the macro phases of the systems development life cycle and the relative amount of time or effort required for each. The discussion that follows breaks each of these larger phases into smaller tasks for discussion. These are the tasks during the life of a telecommunications project where specific actions take place and specific and often-visible outcomes are produced. Remember that a telecommunications project may concern only wider bandwidth or it may be part of a larger information system project and involve programmers as well as members of the telecommunications group.

FIGURE 13.6   **System Owner's View of the Network**

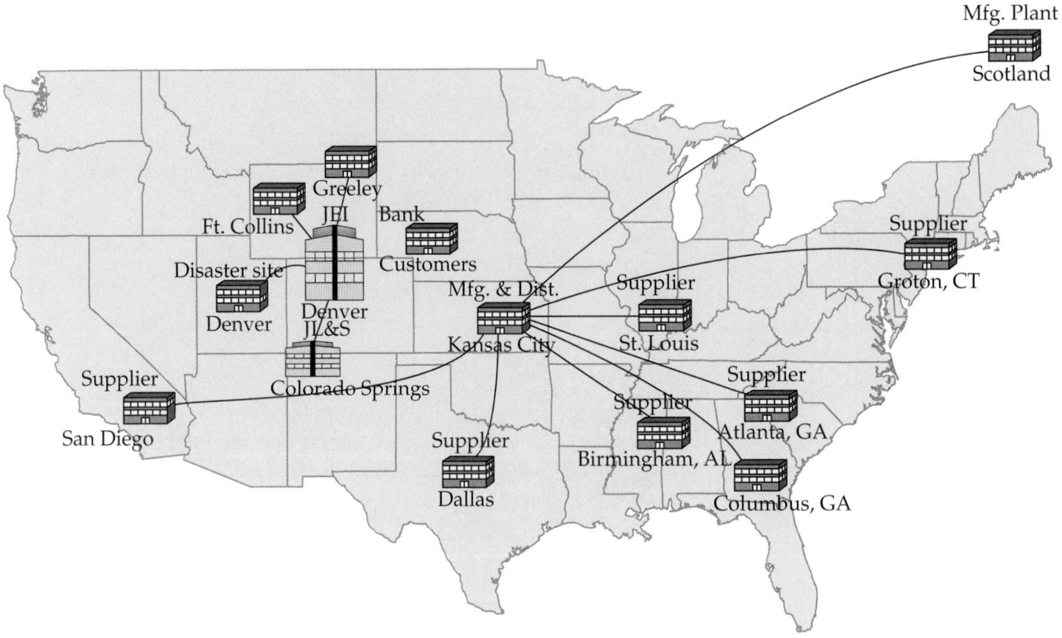

PHASES OF TELECOMMUNICATIONS ANALYSIS AND DESIGN

The Request

TC projects
A problem, opportunity, or threat triggers a telecommunications analysis and design project.

The beginning of a telecommunications project is the request for change, quite often called the *problem definition* stage. This is where one of the groups discussed previously requests an enhancement or addition that requires a change in the system or network. The request will usually be in writing to make it formal. This starts a project.

Projects really get under way with the development of a statement of the problem/opportunity at hand.

I. Problem Identification, Definition, and Objective Statement

Any project to install a new telecommunications capability begins with a statement of the problem, opportunity, or threat at hand. The process should not begin with the statement, "The boss said do it, so here goes." It should begin, after a problem, opportunity, or threat has surfaced, with a technical and user-oriented discussion and description of the object of investigation. The effort can start as a request from users for quicker response from a remote site, a statement by management that it will be necessary to support a remote site with significant data transfer, or a member of a technical staff noting that a present capability has outlived its usefulness and should be replaced because of greater capabilities available, and so forth. In any case, a team of people should be assembled to identify, discuss, and describe the problem, opportunity, or threat and a proposed solution. See Table 13.1, p. 599 for deliverables for this phase.

A systems development team is a group of people who perform the tasks involved in the various development phases. Team membership will likely change as the group moves forward.

FIGURE 13.7   **System Designer's View of the Network**

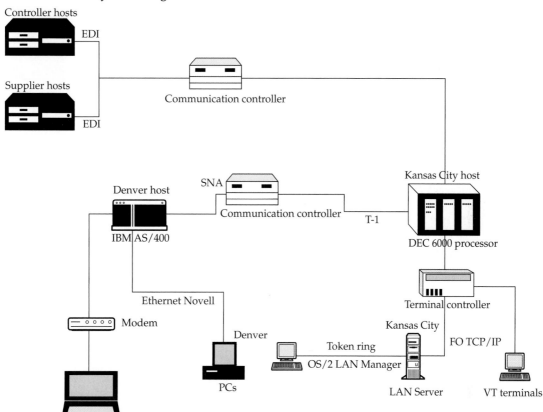

Team Composition

The **project team** should be composed of members of groups who will have a vested interest in the outcome of the project, that is, the stakeholders.

reason for TC systems
TC systems are built, not for the sake of the system, but to solve business problems.

Champions are required for most new ideas, lest the idea die from the weight of organizational inertia.

While it would be assumed that the development team assembled will discuss and describe a proposed solution, remember that the solution will be for a user-defined business need. Therefore, the team should be composed of people who not only can implement the capability technically, but can understand why the capability was requested and can use it effectively. For these reasons, the team should be composed of a leader, person(s) competent in the specific technology to be utilized, interested user(s), Telco and IXC representatives, and a consultant if the complexity of the system warrants.

Before discussing the team leader, let's discuss the concept of a **champion.** If we were discussing leading-edge technology or technology that would drastically change the nature of competition, structure of business, or the way jobs are performed, you should readily see the need for someone to champion the cause. A champion is one who strongly believes in the crusade at hand and spends much of his/her time educating colleagues and marketing the idea. (If the capability to be enhanced or added is considered somewhat mundane, you might question the need for such interest.) There must be at least one person who strongly believes in the capability, preferably from a business standpoint. If such is not the case, the support for the idea may soon wane or even disappear. In the case of

FIGURE 13.8   **Network Topology DED (about 1989)**

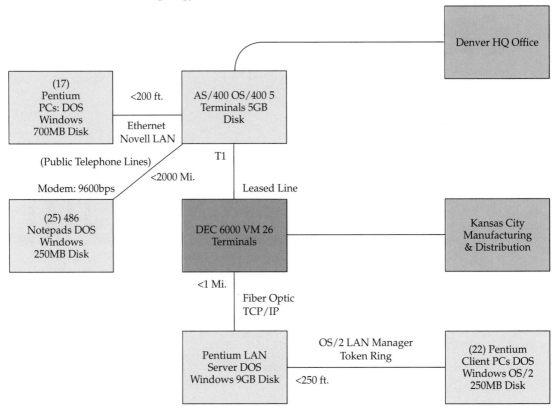

telecommunications technology, it may be an interested user who is the champion, and not the team leader. Furthermore, the level of interest may mean that the capability is included in the overall architecture of the organization. In either case there must be a champion for the business case early on so that the architecture will support all capabilities.

The **team leader** must be technically competent to organize an effective, efficient solution and understand the business need.

Team Leader   The end result of a telecommunications project will be a new or enhanced business-supporting capability. For this reason, the team leader should be a person who will ultimately own or utilize the capability. Because of the technical nature of telecommunications capabilities and the fact that the telecommunications capability may well be transparent to the ultimate users, the team leader will generally be someone from the telecommunications group, for example, one of the telecommunications specialists. In the rare case of the change of the total telecommunications system or the addition of several million dollars in enhancements, the leader may well be a member of upper management. The purpose of the team leader in the problem definition stage is to be sure that all participants understand and agree on the task. The leader will be responsible for organizing the schedule of meetings and tasks, and producing the deliverables necessary to achieve the end results. The first deliverable is usually a white paper describing the problem, opportunity, or threat to be addressed.

FIGURE 13.9   JEI's Subsidiaries and Suppliers (early 90s)

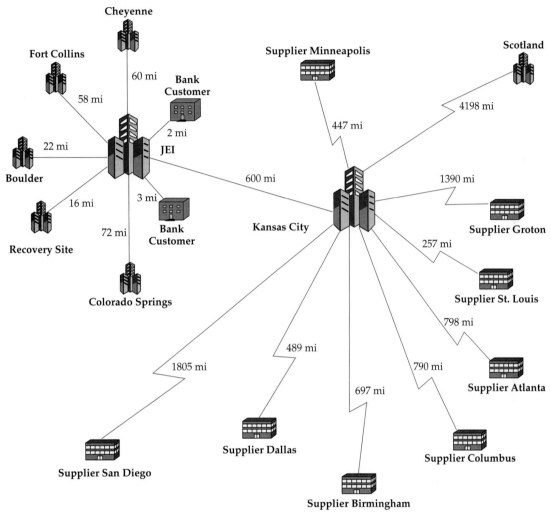

Technical specialists are required to design and implement the specific engineering details of the project.

Technical Specialist(s)   At the initial meeting only one technical specialist may be required as it is desirable to keep the group small. The technical representative provides the expertise to discuss the technical realities of the project. He or she acts as the in-house consultant on present capabilities and advises how technology can be enhanced or added to achieve the project goals. With complex projects, several technical specialists will likely be required to ensure all technical facets of the project will be covered.

interested users The persons for whom the system is built should be included to ensure a proper solution.

Interested User   If the project resulted from a request from a user, the user or someone with a similar interest or competency will be valuable in describing the end desired result of the project. While the user may not initially understand the technical solution, involvement in the project during its life should result in an understanding of the technical features of the project and the ability of the technology to solve the business problem. As users understand the technology itself, they can apply it better and more appropriately.

FIGURE 13.10
Order Data Flow

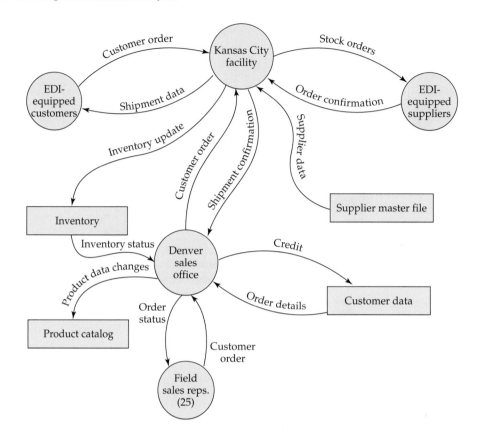

FIGURE 13.11
Time/Effort
Duration of SDLC
Phases

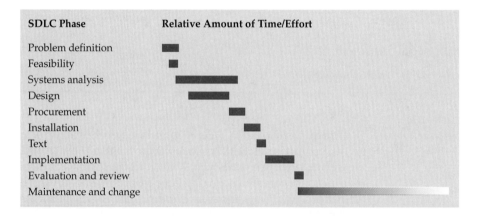

SDLC Phase	Relative Amount of Time/Effort
Problem definition	
Feasibility	
Systems analysis	
Design	
Procurement	
Installation	
Text	
Implementation	
Evaluation and review	
Maintenance and change	

Telco and IXC
representatives and
consultants provide
valuable experience
and specific area
knowledge.

Telco and IXC Representative   When the project involves an enhanced or different interface with the LEC/CLEC or long-distance network, a Telco or IXC representative can be very valuable, even necessary, at this stage of discussion. At this phase, they participate at no cost and can provide a valuable view in addition to specific information on their capabilities and associated costs. After the implications of the Telecommunications Act of 1996 have taken full effect, the vendor may be the same for local and long-distance services.

Information Window   13–2
Composition of a Telecommunications Project Team

- Leader
- Person(s) competent in the specific technology to be utilized
- Interested user(s)

- Telco and IXC representatives
- Consultant

ILEC is the incumbent LEC (i.e., the Baby Bell) and CLECs are the competitive LECs, formed to compete in the local area. There has been a recent (2001) tendency for CLECs to consolidate.

risk
Every project has associated risk of some undesirable outcome. It is useful to assess risks and plan for management of them.

There is risk in implementing new projects, and there is risk in not implementing them (opportunity costs).

Asking the right questions is a valuable part of the analysis and design phase.

Consultant   If the project is of significant magnitude, money for a consultant may be well spent. Even though consultants entail out-of-pocket costs, they should bring valuable and specific experience without having specific vendor bias. They are hired on the basis of having worked on similar projects and created solutions to similar problems.

Risk Analysis and Management

We discussed risk analysis and management earlier, making an assumption that we were encompassing risk in the management of the overall telecommunications capability. When you enhance or add to the total telecommunications capability, questions should be asked to determine the level of risk you are adding. With the addition of capabilities comes added complexity, which also increases the risks.

Preliminary Determination of Requirements

When addressing the potential telecommunications project, the team should ask and answer several questions. You might consider these questions as the first-cut **requirements specification** and a part of the preliminary feasibility study. You must, however, have another feasibility study (which we will call the updated feasibility analysis) *after* you conduct the analysis stage in which you determine what the requirements really are and the technology needed to implement the solution.

1. *What is the purpose of this project?* What is the changed telecommunications system supposed to do for the organization? What applications will be affected? What are the strategic implications of *not* having the systems? In Michael's case, the telecommunications system will be used to move clients' data to the backup sites, to move information and data between the various nodes of JEI for required management control of operations, and to link JL&S to the Kansas City manufacturing site, as well as several other applications. The purpose should be clearly stated.

2. *How many nodes are to be connected?* What are the points that need connecting in order to serve organizational purposes? It is important to note that customers, suppliers, and vendors may also have nodes that must be considered. What is the distance between the nodes? Do connections cross LATA and/or national boundaries?

3. *What is the volume of traffic between nodes?* What is the traffic volume within a particular time? For a PBX, how many lines are making how many calls? For a data

network, what is the volume of data being moved, in megabytes per minute? The expected volume should be carefully derived and stated as it will define the end result.

4. *What is the mix of voice and data usage?* The volume within a time period needs to be classified by voice, data, video image, and fax. Peak loads need to be assessed.

5. *How time-sensitive are the messages transmitted?* Can you allow queues to develop because of high demand relative to capacity? What is the consequence of delay? What is the consequence of not having a WATS line available?

6. *Can you create the solution with existing bandwidth, or do you need to create new bandwidth? What excess bandwidth should you create as a result of this project?* When any capacity that has a volume parameter, such as the bandwidth of a channel, is enhanced or added, there should always be some extra included, a reserve amount. First, you need some safety in your estimate of the need. Second, this is the least expensive time to create growth capability, to generate a reserve that can be used for future needs. The cost of adding such expansion capability now is slight in comparison with the cost of adding it later. *A heuristic is: add 20 percent more bandwidth than you presently need and then add another 20 percent.* Forecasting expected volume, users, and so on, for the presumed life of the system gives a "rough-cut" of the minimum needs. By adding a safety factor, the future needs should be accounted for. In considering the amount to put in as a safety factor, look at the incremental cost of adding 25 percent or twice the number of fiber strands. If the incremental cost is acceptable, the safety should be added.

7. *What is the risk to the total telecommunications capability of adding this project and what is the risk of not adding the project?* Adding this project will increase capability and complexity. Not completing the project will leave the organization with the present level of capability. Which involves the greater risk?

8. Geographic dispersion of nodes must be considered. *Where are the users located?* How far is it between the points that must be connected? Are there transnational data flows involved? Each dimension is important for the project.

Vendor equipment is the least variable component of the overall cost equation.

As you progress through the project, you will deal with entities, events, and considerations that can impose risk on the ultimate outcome. Although the existence of vendors is of great concern and will involve significant amounts of time and analysis, the least variable component of the overall cost equation is the vendor equipment. If this is true, then what are the more variable components? They are

- System parameters
- Labor issues
- Topology
- Power
- Structures
- Rights-of-way

It is necessary to address risk initially and throughout the project. Part of the risk involves not completing the project within budget. A greater risk may be due to not completing the project by the project need date.

Information Window   13–3
Considerations of a TC Project

- Purpose?
- How many nodes?
- Geography—How dispersed are the nodes?
- Volume of traffic between nodes?

- Mix of voice and data usage?
- Time-sensitivity of messages?
- Existing bandwidth or new?
- Risk?

TABLE 13.1
SDLC Phase I
Deliverables

Phase	Deliverable
Problem definition	White paper describing the problem to be solved or the opportunity to be capitalized upon by the telecommunications capability and the objective of the project.

II. Preliminary Investigation and Feasibility Study

This phase of the project will most likely occur at the first meetings of the team. Its purpose is to understand the purpose of the project and to ask very specific questions as to its viability. Specifically, it is necessary to find out if you can, and should, do the project, before you determine details about the task at hand. Table 13.3 lists the deliverables to the phase.

Technical Feasibility

The **feasibility phase** is an assessment of whether a project is doable, based on several criteria, each of which must be met.

Technical **feasibility** is the analysis performed to determine if the planned computer and telecommunications facilities are available for the solution. Can we technically build the systems given the current environment and state-of-the-art technology? All too often, we assume that the answer is yes. It is vital to examine the technology carefully and determine if indeed the enhancement or addition is technologically possible given the present capabilities resources, and skills. Although networks are readily available, the organization may not have the personnel to work with them. Network administrators are more than programmers with new titles. On the other hand, if your needs call for extreme bandwidth for data movement, such as 10 Gbps for CAT or CAD imaging, these technologies are just entering the market.

Behavioral Feasibility and Implications

behavioral impact of TC systems
Even the most elegant technical solutions require willing humans to make them work.

Behavioral feasibility and implications refer to the impact of the new system on operators and users. The implication of a new MIS system is that of a harbinger of change and is often viewed as a replacer of jobs. Telecommunications may be totally transparent to the ultimate users, but not to the members of the telecommunications group. If the project changes the way users do business, we must realize that change to people's jobs and human relationships is an important behavioral issue and questions such as the ones that follow must be addressed. For example, for users, the installation of telecommuting may have a negative effect on the social environment. Changing the operating system from IBM-compatible to Apple-compatible may have severe emotional consequences for the technical staff. Thus, the organization should ask itself

- Are the users able to adapt to the changes brought on by the new system?

- How will the system change the flow of work, the nature of work, the interactions of the people, and the ability to serve the customer?

- Will personnel be able to learn to use the system easily?

- Will fear of replacement of personnel be an issue?

Economic Feasibility

Economic feasibility is more than just the cost of the project. It is the cost versus benefit of completion, and the opportunity cost of not completing the project on time.

Economic feasibility considers the question "Can we afford the application?" What are the costs of building, operating, and maintaining the system in view of organizational resources? Before one can determine the feasibility in all seven areas, one must understand the purposes of the telecommunications system. This implies an analysis of the problems and the tasks. The analysis will be done in great detail during the systems analysis phase (which follows feasibility analysis), but a reasonable amount of analysis must be done during feasibility to ensure that the task is indeed economically feasible. In part, this is because at the end of the feasibility analysis stage, the reviewing analyst or team will most likely be required to give preliminary cost and schedule estimates. A fixed-cost figure for the project may be demanded to attain a cost–benefit ratio or a return-on-investment value. Again, the team will have only a basic idea of the task but will be required to give fairly accurate schedule and cost estimates. This may mean that if you are designing a new local area network for an organization that has yet to be defined, you must be able to estimate the cost of the project prior to the analysis phase and the definition of the organization. Will there be 20 nodes or 200, one file server or five, what will traffic be like, and, thus, which network operating system is best?

Information Window   13–4

Many comments about the behavioral reaction to technology have focused on the change brought about by the introduction of computers to replace manual processes. An example of telecommunications that has both a well-received and rejected impact was an instance of telecommuting during pregnancy leave for women in Britain. The participants were provided in-home terminals, by which they could continue working while waiting for or attending to the new baby. In some cases, the women loved the flexibility and welcomed the ability to work remotely and on their own schedule. They related to this new environment so well that they said they wished to continue it even after the arrival of the child so they could care for the child and other children in the home while continuing to work on their own schedule. However, other participants stated that they couldn't wait to get back into their organizational environment where there was a great opportunity to interact personally with fellow workers. They missed the collegial interaction so much that they eagerly awaited the time they could return (physically) to the office and this social environment. They felt a very real void because they lacked the intimate conversations with others in the on-the-job location. Thus, what was welcomed in one case was rejected in another.

The range of the true estimate depends on the phase in which the estimate is made.

As unfair as this may seem, it is a reality. Another reality is that the range of this estimate should be considered good to only plus or minus 50 percent. (See Table 13.2.) Thus, management should realize that a project estimated during the feasibility phase to cost $100,000 will cost somewhere between $50,000 and $150,000. It will not be until the completion of the systems analysis stage that the estimate can be more precise. Even in the design phase the range of accuracy will likely remain at 10 percent.

For every investment in telecommunications technology, managers need to evaluate the benefits expected as returns for the costs. In this regard, it should be noted that initial expense is not the appropriate cost. There should be an estimate of what has become customary to label as total cost of ownership (TCO) for the outlays. This means that there is a need to determine the costs over the life of the technologies. These costs include initial equipment costs, training costs, maintenance, software, licenses, installation, power, and so forth, that the system requires. The benefits usually will be evaluated in tangible and intangible categories. Tangible benefits are those that can be objectively measured. Examples include personnel savings, time reductions, direct returns on investment, and so on. The intangible benefits are more difficult to quantify; however, they can be significant. If a system changes the way business is done, how decisions are made, and customers' perceptions, these may be vital to company success even if not easily measured.

Part of the economic consideration of installing the project is the *opportunity cost;* for example, the fact that the organization has limited recourse and the resources applied to the project in question cannot be applied elsewhere. If we need a PBX expansion, two new networks, and a new modem pool, and have only enough people to do one project, what is the implication of choosing a particular project relative to the value of the other projects?

Operational Feasibility

Operational feasibility addresses the question of the ability to operate the telecommunications system in the organization's environment. Do we have the requisite employees with the right skills? Do we have the people to design, install, operate, and maintain the network? You need one group to design and install the equipment, but a different group to operate and maintain the systems. For the former, you can develop the group or you can hire the work done. In the latter case, you can develop and train the group or you can **outsource** the task to an operations and maintenance group, such as EDS. Many times you can operationally install a capability and not have or be able to attract and retain the people to operate and maintain the system. This factor is so important some analysts separate it into a human resources feasibility category. Do we have the appropriate facilities to properly house equipment and staff? Do we have, or can we create, procedures to make

TABLE 13.2	SDLC Phase	Cost Variance
Cost Estimate Variance by SDLC Phase*	Feasibility analysis	±50%
	Systems analysis	±20%
	Systems design	±10%
	Installation and test	± 5%

*These figures are not based on research but on the experience of the authors.

the system operable and reliable? The answers to these questions will determine the success of the project. If you allow management to edict that you have the operational ability because you outsource the design and installation, but they don't provide the resources for continuous operation, you are at great risk.

Time Feasibility

Completing a project within budget is of little consequence if the project is not completed on time.

We now arrive at the question of the project schedule. We must know if the organization can build and implement the telecommunications system on time for it to meet the intended need. The analysis and design of the system must precede the implementation and operation of the system, and all of this requires time. If the system must be available by a certain date, there is a definite lead time required. If sufficient time to finish the project is not available, other considerations are of little value. If the project *must* be completed on time, alternatives must be found. As an example, if the organization was starting operations in a new manufacturing building in 30 days, requiring 50 telephones, you only had 22 ports left on the PBX, and it takes six months to upgrade the PBX, what should you do?

Regulatory Feasibility

Regulatory feasibility determines if the end result is permissible under law.

The organization must determine if the proposed telecommunications system is within the provisions of the existing regulatory environment and whether the regulations will inhibit it. Does the telecommunications system comply with appropriate FCC and state PSC regulatory rules? If a global network is involved, the regulations of the various nations (PTTs) must be complied with as well. Examples of regulatory impact might be in obtaining right-of-way, obtaining FCC permits for microwave links and radio frequencies, determining that tariffs exist to support the services needed, and other licenses, permissions, and so forth.

Since the telecommunications environment has historically been heavily regulated, and constantly changing, this issue of feasibility cannot be ignored. The Telecommunications Act of 1996 has become law. The result of this act has yet to be fully seen. Not only will the regulatory environment affect progress, but changes in the laws will provide additional alternatives. As CATV adds a digital channel, it may provide an excellent network around a city that has no other digital channels. New competitors will offer new options for managers and the regulatory constraints on each must be ascertained.

Ethical Feasibility

Ethical behavior is a part of good business behavior.

A recurring theme in the academic world is the ethical implications of business processes and practices. This includes the general areas of information systems and technology because of the ability to gather, store, retrieve, report, and transmit information about individuals and organizations. In the purest sense, telecommunications technology is exemplified in the cable television system supplying news and entertainment to millions of homes. The technology is amoral: it is without morality or ethics. Its use, however, is subject to considerations of both. Thus, when a project creates or extends telecommunications capabilities, the team must at least consider the ethical implications of the result of the project. There are no hard-and-fast rules for guiding the team in this area; they must rely on their own code of conduct and decide if the new capability will invade privacy, violate security, or cause harm to the organization, its members, its customers, suppliers, and vendors, or the environment. While we are sensitive to privacy and security of the organization's papers and property, we also must be sensitive to the effect of projects on the personal lives of its members and the environment.

Project Management

Project management allows complex projects to be dissected and controlled, efficiently and effectively allocating scarce resources.

Once feasibility analysis has been completed, and the team has given or received approval to begin development of the project, some form of **project management** must be applied. The personnel of the telecommunications group may use a simple cardex file or a computer program for this. The objective is to describe the tasks involved, the personnel to be used, the resources required, the sequences of events, and the time required for each event. Significant programs with a large number of events and people may require a computer-based project management capability. PERT or critical path techniques may be valuable for complex projects.

The intent of project management is to control the progress and costs of the program. Another intent is to gain customer concurrence of major milestones of effort. For example, at different times during the systems analysis phase, at the end of design, at the completion of implementation and testing, and finally at cutover, the team will ask the customer organization's management to sign off on completed tasks. The intent is to have agreement between the team and the customer as to what has been done. If the work were being accomplished under a contract with an outside firm, these sign-off instances would be accompanied by progress payments. Internally, it just gives an indication of milestones completed.

Project management is required in order to complete the development on schedule and within budget. The project team leader can go far in accomplishing these objectives with adequate definition and management of the project.

TABLE 13.3
SDLC Phase II
Deliverables

Phase	Deliverable
Feasibility analysis	Report based on the technical, economic, ethical, behavioral, operational, regulatory, and time feasibility of developing and utilizing the proposed capability. Preliminary cost estimate of the project.

III. Systems Analysis—Detailed Understanding and Definition

The systems analysis phase is the phase in which the system's specification is defined.

This stage has gained greater importance as technicians, users, and management alike have realized that the more we know about the task, up-front, the better the capability can be designed, created, and maintained. Management often agrees only hesitantly with this view because the more time spent in analysis, the later the "real work" (procurement, implementation, and test) begins.

Systems analysis picks up where feasibility analysis left off and has the specific objective of providing sufficient information in the form of a system specification so that a correct and complete design can be created and maintained. This involves extensive interaction with the requester to determine what is available now; what new capability, change, or enhancement is desired; and what the end result should be. Here the technical experts may converse at length with users, managers, and executives. This is neither an easy nor a trivial task, because each participant uses a different point of reference and often a different form of communication. For example, users are looking for the end result, while technicians are considering the technical means of the solution. Deliverables for this phase are shown in Table 13.4, p. 606.

System Specification

The system specification should provide information about the final system in sufficient detail for development of either requests for proposal (RFPs) or requests for quote (RFQs). Therefore, the system specification needs to be as specific as possible so vendors can make proposals or quotes for the project. While the final details will be done later, there must be sufficient detail for the overall system blueprint at this stage. If the specification is too general, the vendors will interpret it differently and the resulting proposals will not be easily compared. It is also advisable to provide vendors with a specified format for their proposals so the comparisons can be easily done. For example, if a specific protocol is required to be compatible with the existing telecommunications architecture, this fact must be stated clearly. If existing networks are token ring, to require a token-ring proposal, the specification must state this or else proposed systems may be very complex and not fit your needs.

During systems analysis you must determine as much about the capability as you can. Specifically, you need to know the following to create an adequate system specification:

A. Requirements specification

    1. Capacity

    2. Queuing possibility

    3. Expansion versus use of present bandwidth

    4. Future growth

    5. Geographic requirements

    6. Reliability

    7. Peak and busy hours

    8. Response

    9. Availability

B. Network map and equipment list

C. Present and anticipated applications

D. Simulation

Prototyping

Prototyping is a means of rapid development of a system that is iterative in its refinement stages.

A method of creating computer-based systems rapidly is called **prototyping.** This method results in a good approximation of the ultimate capability. If the telecommunications enhancement or addition is not transparent to the users, a prototype may be valuable. For example, if the project is to install a totally new data path between the central mainframe and a remote site, it would be possible to use a modem and dial-up telephone lines to demonstrate, or prototype, the end result. The demonstration would be slow, but would have all of the other characteristics of the ultimate capability. At times, the prototype may actually suffice for the desired capability, as the true amount of traffic is determined. Prototyping is an interative process and involves the interaction of users with the team as the system evolves to meet their needs. This interaction and user involvement are real strengths of the prototyping approach.

Simulation

Simulation is a means of testing a system design based on the performance of a model that reflects the real system.

As the telecommunications project or installed base becomes more complex, **simulation** of the present or enhanced capability is of significant value. While a prototype shows the capabilities of a new computer program, simulation shows the results of increased traffic and enhanced capabilities. This entails software into which the characteristics and parameters of the system can be stored so a simulation of that system can be exercised. Transaction generators can approximate the predicted traffic, allowing the software to gather statistics about node and channel busy levels, delay times, and overall throughput. Although network measurement and simulation may entail a sizeable outlay of capital, they give viability to the system not possible by any other means.

A very basic form of simulation, one that does not require significant resources, is a computer-based program that allows you to draw the proposed capability in order to document and visually represent the final result. Some programs also will allow for dynamic activity on the system, giving an idea if the system will support the intended outcome. Our use of netViz® to show diagrams of JEI's network is an example of this type simulation.

Make-or-Buy Decision

Make-or-buy decision comes after a complete systems analysis phase. It is a standard management decision on procurement of systems, software, and so on that involves analysis of the alternatives.

When developing a telecommunications capability, a question that should be addressed at the end of system analysis is whether to build the system with in-house programmers or purchase the capability from an outside vendor. Telecommunications capability, whether hardware, software, or media, will generally be purchased. The only question is whether to *outsource* the task for design and implementation and even operation and maintenance. When an organization is first entering telecommunications on a significant scale, such as for global communications, it is often a good move to buy the capability and have the vendor even operate the capability and perform maintenance. The end result incurs out-of-pocket costs, but provides an operable, reliable, and maintainable capability in a minimum of time and at a reasonable cost.

Architecture

Architecture is a specification that determines how something is constructed, defining functional modularity as well as the protocols and interfaces that allow communications and cooperation among modules.

Architecture, as previously discussed, is a specification that determines how something is constructed, defining functional modularity as well as the protocols and interfaces that allow communications and cooperation among modules. Specifically, *network architecture* specifies structure descriptions, relationships of network sender, and receivers, logical paths, and communication functions that manage and support the transfer of information. The consideration of networks should include voice, images, video, and data. Hopefully, the organization has established an overall telecommunications architecture, and this project must comply with it. If not, the total task is far greater and includes a decision on the overall environment and its standards. This is a point where a consultant could be of great value.

Planning

Once the team understands the system requirements, they and other members of the parent organization must attend to details that will come into play at the time of installation of the equipment. Specifically, plans must be made for the physical placement of the equipment, installation of the media, documentation for all who must use the equipment and resultant capability, and training for those who need it.

Physical placement means that the industrial engineers or the members of the telecommunications group must ensure that tables, closets, or shelves exist to hold the equipment; that electrical power is available; and that the environmental conditions are correct. Often buildings have telecommunications equipment closets that do not provide adequate cooling for the equipment installed. It sounds simple, but someone must check these items or the system will not work when it arrives, or it will fail later.

Because telecommunications projects use physical paths for voice and data flow, new *circuits and channels* will likely be installed. This involves allocating existing twisted-pair wires or laying additional pairs, coaxial cables, or fiber strands. This can all be done in the period of preparation for the arrival of the node equipment. The circuits and channels should be tested as they are installed even though they will be tested again upon the arrival of the node equipment.

Documentation is the act of creating a history of the system's development so that future modifications or understanding is simplified. If not properly performed, there is a high probability of problems and increased costs later.

Documentation ranges from having a place to assemble the vendor-supplied technical material to creating new, user-oriented manuals and brochures that explain what the users need, in their language. Part of this is a library function; part is a writing function. It is easy to delay documentation but this temptation must be avoided. Documentation provides a necessary history and should be accurate and up-to-date. Inadequate or nonexistent documentation can make system maintenance and upgrade a real challenge!

Finally, *training* will be required, and someone must determine who needs it, at what level, how, and when. A training plan should be developed by those who will deliver the training. The users should be told of the training they will need and a preliminary schedule developed. Training should be scheduled so users will put their new knowledge into action without significant delay or the effectiveness will be lost. Frequently vendors will include training for some of the technologies and new equipment. The organization should take advantage of vendor-provided training if available.

A test plan is created as part of systems analysis so that the system can be proved later.

After the equipment is installed, **testing** will be performed. Thus, a *test plan* must be developed, including a schedule of testing. Although this plan is to be used only after the equipment arrives, someone must think through what is to be done, by whom, how, and when.

TABLE 13.4
SDLC Phase III Deliverables

Phase	Deliverable
Systems analysis	Specification of requirements, defined strategy and architecture, and, where practical, a prototype or simulation of the system. An updated cost estimate of the project, a make-or-buy decision, and test plans.

IV. Investigation of Alternatives

Alternatives are the different ways a single project can be designed and implemented.

After the team has completed the systems analysis phase, several questions must be addressed. Deliverables for this phase are shown in Table 13.5.

- First, after all of the information has been gathered during systems analysis, is the change to be an expanded capability or a new capability?

- If the change is an added node, can the network accommodate the addition, will enhancements be required, or will a new network be required?

- Can we lease part of the enhancement, must we build it all in-house, or can we contract it out to a third party (make-or-buy)?

- Are there alternatives in media? Does the consideration of growth potential (reserve) impact this choice?

- What are the cost and schedule implications for each alternative?

- Will the cost fit the budget and required return on investment?

TABLE 13.5
SDLC Phase IV
Deliverables

Phase	Deliverable
Alternatives	Statements of the alternatives available, the cost and value of each, and a recommendation as to the best alternative.

V. General Network Design

Network design is the overall plan for a network that indicates components, connectivity, etc.

The design of the new system, based on the requirements gathered during the systems analysis stage, involves the creation, on paper, of the system parts and interactions. The system specification is the basis for design. This phase of activity generates the initial configuration of the system. Much like a bridge, design entails the creation of engineering drawings from which the parts would later be made and the bridge constructed. Deliverables for this phase are shown in Table 13.6. We must take into account such considerations as

A. Physical circuits

B. Logical channels

C. Availability

D. Response

E. Capacity

    1. Primary channels

    2. Redundancy

    3. Excess capacity (growth)

F. Human resources skills required and sources

G. Training required and sources

H. Location of equipment and requirements

    1. Electrical, including grounding and UPS

    2. Cooling

    3. Lighting

    4. Support

I. Maintenance requirements

There are increasingly sophisticated design tasks on the market that will assist in the design task. These should aid in documenting and visualizing the final capability.

TABLE 13.6
SDLC Phase V
Deliverables

Phase	Deliverable
Network design	Diagram showing the components of the project change as they relate to the overall telecommunications capability.

VI. Selection of Vendors and Equipment

RFIs are requests for information. They are sent to vendors in order to solicit information not readily available from published sources.

A major portion of enhancing and adding to a telecommunications network is the purchase of equipment from vendors. Assuming either the design and development must be obtained from vendors or the operations and maintenance are to be outsourced, equipment and software must be obtained from vendors. If the design just calls for additional modems of a standard type, you only have to go to an approved catalog and place an order. However, major changes will require submission of *requests for proposal (RFPs)* and *requests for quote (RFQs)*. The best sources are determined after evaluation of their proposals and quotes. Deliverables for this phase are shown in Table 13.7.

RFPs and RFQs officially ask vendors for statements of task and cost. Involving vendors early allows them to have greater accuracy in their proposals and quotes.

There is a whole field of study concerning the procurement of goods and services. It is desirable that the vendors would be rated and ranked on a list of characteristics. There are surveys published by such magazines as *Network Magazine* and *Infoworld* that show vendor ratings. Such sources can be quite valuable in the rankings of vendors. First, the technical response of each vendor should be rated based on engineering merits, the capability, reliability, and maintainability of the equipment. Next, the vendors should be rated as to experience, reliability, and reputation. Then, taken altogether, the equipment–vendor combinations should be ranked and a recommendation based on technical and corporate merit should be recorded. For example, the project team is working on an assignment to select a new server for a network expansion. Requests for proposal (RFPs) have been sent to a number of vendors and the team has received six responses, including the specifications of their candidate server and its cost. The team might develop a spreadsheet as in Table 13.8, allowing a final decision to be justified on the composite score of each vendor.

TABLE 13.7
SDLC Phase VI
Deliverables

Phase	Deliverable
Vendor and equipment selection	Rating and ranking of vendors, by equipment or service to be purchased. Recommendations based on technical and corporate merit.

VII. Calculation of Costs

Estimation of costs is part science and part art.

Estimating is the process of predicting what the system will cost when it is complete. During the feasibility phase, the team is required to make such a prediction based on minimal information. Now that the team has reached a much later point in the project, they should have as much information as they will ever have assembled and, thus, the process tends to be more of a calculation than an estimation. Rating and ranking of alternatives and vendors is based on the technical merit of the solution, technical and corporate merit of the vendors, and cost of the proposed

TABLE 13.8 **Spreadsheet to Score Vendors**

Criteria	Weight	Vendor A	Vendor B	Vendor C	Vendor D	Vendor E	Vendor F
Reliability	20%						
Cost	30%						
Features	10%						
Maintainability	10%						
Reputation	5%						
Service	10%						
Performance	10%						
Other	5%						
Total Score	100%						

solutions. Deliverables for this phase are shown in Table 13.9. As in the feasibility phase, in estimating costs, the following must be considered at a minimum:

A. Hardware

    1. Procured hardware

    2. Media

    3. Upgraded hardware

B. Software

C. Personnel

D. Supplies

    1. Installation

    2. Ongoing

E. Maintenance

F. Conversion (from existing systems)

TABLE 13.9
SDLC Phase VII
Deliverables

Phase	Deliverable
Cost	Calculation of the cost by alternative vendor. Recommendation of final configuration.

VIII. Presentation to Technical and Management Group on Recommendation

Include technical managers *and* business managers in the presentation and they will be ready to make better decisions when required.

When all of the alternatives and vendors have been rated and ranked, it is time to report to the management groups that will likely make the final decision. It would be a mistake to only present the team's finding to the technical managers because the business managers, the ultimate users, must understand the implications of the solutions from both a technology and a cost standpoint. The team should assure that senior management, not the engineers, make the final decision as to the enhanced or added capability. Senior managers need to understand the business value of what they are buying, especially the value of the overt growth potential. When senior management understands the technology, they should more readily include it in their strategic planning. Deliverables for this phase are shown in Table 13.10.

TABLE 13.10
SDLC Phase VIII
Deliverables

Phase	Deliverable
Presentation to management	Report to senior management about recommendation of final configuration.

IX. Final Decisions and Design

After the presentation to management, the final decision as to vendors, capabilities, and a configuration will be made. It is time to put aside all other alternatives and finalize the design based on the decisions. New facilities are mapped onto old facilities, an inventory of the prospective new facilities and capacities (old minus deleted plus new) is made, and preparation is begun for the arrival of the new equipment. It is now time to place the orders. Once the detailed design has been generated, the organization is committed to this configuration. If you don't understand the implications of these decisions, you may live to regret them. Additionally, casting your lot with the wrong vendor or the wrong system can have severe and long-term repercussions. Deliverables for this phase are shown in Table 13.11.

Documentation of network design and implementation is a part of configuration control.

TABLE 13.11
SDLC Phase IX
Deliverables

Phase	Deliverable
Final design decision	Updated design with pending changes.

X. Procurement—Order Hardware, Software, and Services

After the new capability is designed, the hardware and software selected, and vendors chosen, it is time to create purchase orders for any products or services to be provided by vendors. This function may be provided by the parent organization, or there may be a person in the administrative portion of the telecommunications group, or the MIS group, who does this. In any case, the company usually has forms and procedures so there is no question as to the fairness of the selection or ambiguity of the order. It is important to document this process in the event a losing vendor questions the process. The deliverables for this phase are shown in Table 13.12.

procurement
Most telecommunications projects involve procurement of equipment, software, or services.

TABLE 13.12
SDLC Phase X
Deliverables

Phase	Deliverable
Procurement	Purchase orders for equipment selected.

XI. Preparation for Implementation

Plans for installation that were made during analysis need to be executed. The areas to house the equipment should have been provided with space, cooling, electrical power, lighting, and security. Since system documentation now exists, a training plan is approved, and installation and test plans are done, the organization is ready for the equipment to arrive. The plan should detail all of the preceding facets so that no confusion will exist when the equipment arrives. Deliverables for this phase are shown in Table 13.13.

TABLE 13.13
SDLC Phase XI
Deliverables

Phase	Deliverable
Preparation for implementation	Plans for the space, cooling, electrical power, lighting, and security needs at implementation time.

XII. Installation of Equipment

The plan may call for acceptance testing of each piece of equipment as it arrives or to accept it based on final testing at the shipper's facility. Since the additional media should already be installed, the equipment that is arriving only needs to be attached to the media. It is desirable to test each interface point upon installation. In some cases, the vendor performs installation and testing as part of the contract. Deliverables for this phase are shown in Table 13.14.

TABLE 13.14
SDLC Phase XII
Deliverables

Phase	Deliverable
Equipment installation	Receive, test, and install the pieces of equipment.

XIII. System Testing

System testing, based on a detailed test plan, determines whether you have an adequate design.

During this stage, the system is tested as a total entity. Where parts were tested upon acceptance, the intent of the testing stage is to ensure the integrity of the total capability that has been changed and to demonstrate that the planned changes are, in fact, in place. Once the pieces are all together, a test plan and test data are required. Deliverables for this phase are shown in Table 13.15.

The *test plan*, developed at the end of the systems analysis phase, should show a schedule for exercising the pieces and the paths of the system, in progressively more rigorous form. Initially, point-to-point connectivity is checked, then end-to-end connectivity. Transaction generators can be used to create transactions at a specified rate in order to demonstrate the reliability and integrity of all parts and paths of the system. The ultimate purpose is to determine bottlenecks, level of queuing, balking, and the system's ability to handle heavy workloads. It is not until the system passes the test requirements that it can be placed into productive use. Until then, enhancement and additions should be kept separate from the in-place system where possible. When segregation is not possible, testing when the system is idle or off-line is necessary.

Don't forget the FCC and UL compliance for certification of the total project.

Part of the test process is to ensure that components and circuits, when installed, meet the required FCC, Underwriters Laboratory (UL), and local electrical, structural, and electromagnetic radiation standards. While all equipment provided by vendors will have gone through a certification program, the entire system must meet the same FCC and UL requirements as to radiation, interference, and safety.

TABLE 13.15
SDLC Phase XIII
Deliverables

Phase	Deliverable
Testing	A demonstration that the system with all enhancements and additions performs as expected, end-to-end, with integrity and reliability, under prescribed loads.

XIV. Training

Training may involve only the telecommunications group as the end results of many telecommunications projects are to remain transparent to the user.

We noted in the systems analysis phase that training would be required for all persons who must use the enhancement and additions. In many cases, these enhancements and additions will be totally transparent to the ultimate users of the system. Thus, neither training nor documentation will be required for them. However, system descriptions and documentation for the telecommunications group must be updated to show the present state of the system. Manuals from vendors will be placed in the telecommunications library, and group documents will be updated to show changes. Deliverables for this phase are shown in Table 13.16.

Members of the telecommunications group will usually receive training in-place at the vendor's site. Training should cover the new equipment and capabilities, including troubleshooting and repair methods. Training on any new test equipment and media used also should be included. At times, the vendor will provide onsite training.

TABLE 13.16
SDLC Phase XIV
Deliverables

Phase	Deliverable
Training	Training documentation, primarily for the telecommunications group personnel. This includes equipment operations and systems procedures.

XV. Implementation

Implementation goes smoothly *only* if everything else was done properly.

Cutover methods are the means adopted to change from the existing system to the new system; sometimes referred to as "conversion."

Once the system has been installed and tested, it is placed in a production status and available to the users. There is much that has been done up to now to prepare for this stage, such as collection of appropriate user documentation, preparation for training, placement of new equipment, and formulation of plans for switching over to the new system after an appropriate period of use. Deliverables for this phase are shown in Table 13.17.

Cutover

Additions to the existing system can be brought into use in several ways. Depending on the extent of the enhancements and additions, the telecommunications group can use the following:

1. **Pilot**—bring the new system up for only a small group of users and applications and let them test it in a real mode. This assumes that the system can be duplicated or that a group of users can be segregated. While this mode is com-

mon for computer-based systems, it may not be possible for telecommunications systems.

2. **Parallel**—introduce the new system and keep the old system active as it was. Again, this is common in computer-based systems but may not be possible with telecommunications systems as the expense of two systems may be too large.

3. **Phased**—this occurs when portions of the new capability are added in sequence. This is quite possible for telecommunications systems as new media are added, new concentrators and modems arrive, and new servers are placed into use.

4. **Phase-in, phase-out, and modular**—this approach is similar to phased. In this case, the switch to a new capability is frequently keyed to transactions so that from a key date, all new transactions use the new systems. The modular approach is a combination of phased and pilot approaches. This mode is useful if the new capability is applicable to business units in an incremental manner.

5. **Cold turkey**—this occurs when the system is changed and brought online all at once with other considerations. For example, if the system in question was a new PBX, it could be introduced as a pilot or it could be brought online cold turkey, disabling the old system totally. This cutover method has the greatest risk but least expense if all goes well.

Maintenance of old and new systems is a problem if old systems are preserved. In telecommunications, this is seldom the case, as removed portions are discarded or salvaged. However, when reliability is vital, new systems may be installed to replace old ones, but the old ones are retained and maintained as backup capabilities. This is expensive, but may be advisable for critical systems.

TABLE 13.17
SDLC Phase XV
Deliverables

Phase	Deliverable
Implementation	Installed system as defined in specification.

XVI. After-Implementation Cleanup and Audit

Audit to see if you did what you planned to do. Then brief management.

When all of the enhancements and changes have been installed and brought into productive use, it is time to clean up, place everything back into inventory that is not in use, and audit your performance. The question to be answered is, "*How well did we do?*" The point is to learn from the experience. So review what was planned, what was actually accomplished, and how it all went. What mistakes were made and what can be learned from them? What successes were achieved and how can these be institutionalized? Deliverables for this phase are shown in Table 13.18.

After the project is reviewed, gather technical and business management and present the findings. Emphasize what the enhanced system will do, mainly from a business standpoint but a little from a technical point of view. The managers should know what the system can do for them, and they should learn more and more about the technology in place so that future system changes will be easier.

It is important that the new system description be provided to the chief information officer or chief technology officer for inclusion in the portfolio of information technologies. This will ensure that the portfolio is up-to-date.

TABLE 13.18
SDLC Phase XVI
Deliverables

Phase	Deliverable
Cleanup and audit	Paper describing the project, process, and product. Briefing to management on the enhancements, including additional training in the technology.

XVII. Turning System Over to Maintenance Group

After implementation, turn the capability over to the maintenance group, having created a system that *you* would be willing to support.

This stage follows the implementation and acceptance of the system. As the enhanced system is used, problems are uncovered, new views of the system's potential use become apparent, and new possibilities may be realized. Problems require quick correction, and changes and extensions need to be considered. While the maintenance personnel are likely to have been a part of the group that created the new system, the system must be placed in a maintenance status. The maintenance and change stage may entail numerous small system enhancements, each of which must work within the total system. This phase will last until the next project makes yet another change to an evolving telecommunications system. Frequently, system component enhancement will be made during this phase. Deliverables for this phase are shown in Table 13.19.

TABLE 13.19
SDLC Phase XVII
Deliverables

Phase	Deliverable
Maintenance and change	The system is the deliverable.

Case 13-1

Application Service Providers

Kelly Ammons

An application service provider, or ASP, in the simplest terms rents software. **An ASP is any company that remotely hosts software applications and provides access and use of it to its clients over a network for a recurring fee.** ASPs provide Web-based access to a range of business applications on a pay-as-you-go subscription basis.

With the advent of the application service provider, the cycle of computing trends has come full circle. The introduction of outsourced Web-based shared resource business applications has returned us to the days of service bureaus and time-sharing.

Application service providers have emerged due to the growth of the Internet and the promise of open communications. ASP outsourcing differs from the traditional mainframe-based time-sharing. ASP outsourcing utilizes client-server architecture and relies on secure, cost-effective packet data communications.

The most common features of an ASP include

- An ASP owns and operates a software application.

- An ASP owns, operates, and maintains the servers that are required to run the application.

- An ASP makes the application available via the Internet in a browser or through some type of thin client.

- An ASP charges either on a per-use basis or on a monthly/annual fee basis.

The ASP market is around two years old. It has already grown rapidly and is expected to continue to grow. Scott Heinlein of TeleChoice.com indicates that the ASP market projections range from $7.8 billion to $48 billion by 2003. There are many established ASPs, and more emerge daily. According to WebHarbor.com, there are more than 300 active ASPs. Corio, FutureLink, ServiceNet, and Usinternetworking are a few of the better-known ASPs.

ASP DRIVERS

Numerous internal factors drive the ASP model. First, an ASP allows applications to be implemented in days or weeks compared to months for the implementation of in-house or consultant-built applications. Secondly, it allows a company to focus on its core competencies instead of focusing on its IT backbone that supports the company. The ASP model also allows for scalability. A company can start small and easily expand its applications by using an ASP. The ASP also competes on price because it is considerably cheaper to rent software applications than to buy those applications.

A number of external factors drive the ASP model. One factor is the shorter application cycles of software. The application cycle of software is the amount of time between new versions of the same software. By the time a company gets their system implemented and tested, a new release is being marketed. Secondly, the Internet shows the importance of time-to-market and scalable IT infrastructures. The Internet allows users to stay informed and take advantage of the quick pace provided. Applications must be implemented quickly in order to successfully compete in the Internet's quick-paced environment.

Thirdly, locating and retaining skilled IT personnel can be a challenge. Skilled IT personnel are highly recruited and expect extensive compensation packages in addition to exciting job assignments. It is difficult to find them and even more difficult to keep them. ASPs are responsible for implementing and maintaining the software that they lease to their customers. By using an ASP, companies can take advantage of computer applications without needing the extensive IT staff to support it.

Finally, network improvements also have driven the growth of the ASP market. Increased bandwidth allows for software applications to be transferred over a network quickly. These improvements allow for a seamless blend of remotely managed shared environments and locally managed individual environments.

APPLICATION SERVICE PROVIDERS' BEST PRACTICES

In order to add value, ASPs should be based on the following "best practices":

- **Availability**—Some ASPs are delivering 99 percent uptime.

- **Security**—In order to gain customers, ASPs must be able to guarantee that a company's data and applications are secure.

- **Networked storage**—This should include disaster recovery.

- **Management**—ASPs should be able to decrease headaches associated with managing applications.

TYPES OF ARCHITECTURE

There are three types of application hosting architecture: Web server/browser-based applications, thin client-server, and Java-based applications. Each type has its strengths and weaknesses.

The Web server/Web application can deliver an application to any browser. The common interface lowers training costs. This is best used when dealing with forms to fill out, workflow, and group scheduling. The downside is that it is difficult to manage the individual desktop experience. Security and the bandwidth requirement also limit this application.

The thin client can deliver to most client types with low bandwidth connections. It is possible to support individual users on dial-up connections or offices on dedicated data services. It provides built-in management and administration. The thin client can be used for any Windows application.

The Java architecture is platform independent and does not require installation on a desktop computer. It also can be used for any Windows application. This architecture falls short on performance and also requires large amounts of bandwidth to download applications.

TYPES OF SERVICE

ASPs offer three types of service offerings. The first are core or basic services. These are services such as application updates and upgrades, continuous monitoring of the applications, support and maintenance of the network and servers on which the application runs, and, finally, customer support. ASPs also offer managed services including all core services plus additional services and guarantees around support, security, application performance, and data redundancy. These managed services include data security, technical support, and daily backup of the application and its data.

ASPs also offer extended services. These include all managed services plus professional services such as application configuration and extension, strategy and planning, and training and educational support.

TYPES OF APPLICATIONS

There are essentially six types of applications that can be offered by an ASP. First are *analytical applications.* These include applications to analyze business problems such as financial or risk analysis. Second are *vertical applications,* which are industry-specific applications, such as patient billing in health care or claims processing in the insurance industry. *Enterprise relationship management applications* also can be offered by an ASP. These include accounting, human resources, materials management, and facilities management. *Customer relationship management applications* include sales force automation, customer service, and marketing applications. A fifth type of applications is *collaborative applications.* These applications include groupware, email, and conferencing applications. The last type of applications is the *personal applications*. These include office suites and other consumer applications.

SWOT ANALYSIS

A SWOT analysis of the ASP model identifies the strengths, weaknesses, opportunities, and threats associated with the ASP model.

STRENGTHS

An ASP provides the leasing company the latest technologies with lower risks and lower total costs. Midsize firms that could not afford high-end software solutions used by larger competitors are able to do so through ASPs. Firms can get a fully functioning, large application such as ERP, which could cost millions of dollars to implement, without paying for development, installation, hardware, or software. Firms just pay a monthly fee that amortizes the ASPs' costs over time.

A basic package of a basic application starts at $30 per month per person with the fee increasing with the complexity of the application. This fee can increase drastically for the more complex applications such as a human resource application that can cost $1,800 per month per person. Usinternetworking has said its average customer pricing of applications ranges from $40,000 to $100,000 per month. These costs are lower than the cost to buy the software and accompanying hardware and also hire and train an IT staff on the new applications.

An ASP deploys applications quickly. ASPs can deploy basic services such as office applications throughout the company in a few hours. More complex applications such as creating an eCommerce platform can be implemented within days. Even the most complex applications such as ERP can be deployed within weeks. An ASP can decrease implementation time by over half.

The ASP also provides all the supporting technology such as networks, hardware, and supporting software and is responsible for any maintenance required within the application. ASPs provide constant updates on software.

ASPs are able to connect processes across a company even when employees are in different locations without the need for expensive intranets. ASPs also can connect a company with its trading partners with lower costs and commitments. Finally, a company is able to take advantage of more complex applications without hiring an expert IT staff to support the applications.

WEAKNESSES

One weakness of ASP usage is that the leasing company has little control over the applications. Many are also uneasy about a company having control over a large part of their operations. A company's internal IT staff has no direct control in fixing any problems that are associated with the applications. A company must rely on a third party, the ASP, to correct problems quickly and efficiently. Sometimes an ASP's sense of urgency may not match that of the company.

Many ASPs provide little customization. The ASP offers commodity versions of flexible software that allows the ASP to install applications faster and cheaper that appeal to a greater audience. This may work for small and midsize companies that are less complex and have fewer employees to adapt to the new software. Larger companies with complex functions, many computer systems, and numerous employees need to be able to customize their applications for a smoother transition.

Connection speed is critical to the ASP application. Companies with less than high-speed connections must incur added expenses by investing in newer, faster technology in order to take advantage of an ASP application. Bottlenecks within network can degrade real-world performance. The quality of technology for efficient network delivery of leased applications is critical to the success of the ASP and the leasing company. The presence or absence of a WAN or high-bandwidth Internet connection determines the way an ASP can provide the hosted applications.

Using an ASP provides no equity and potentially harsh consequences for opting out of a contract before it expires. A company's management must work with its IT staff to ensure that the most feasible and appropriate application is rented from the ASP.

OPPORTUNITIES

Bandwidth continues to increase at a quick pace. This increased bandwidth makes it possible to lease more complex applications without the time delay caused by inadequate bandwidth.

As more applications are leased, there is a continued decrease in operational expenses due to the decrease in information technology personnel needed and the decrease in hardware that would be purchased if the applications were bought and run in-house.

It is predicted that the ASP market will undergo a market shakeout. It is predicted that more than 60 percent of all ASPs will disappear by the end of 2001 due to poor service or market consolidation. Many of the less-established and less-reliable ASPs will go out of business. A shakeout would make it easier for a company to find a dependable ASP that can provide the services that the company needs.

THREATS

If a market shakeout does not occur within the ASP industry, it will become increasingly difficult to find a reliable ASP through the hype created by numerous ASP companies. The market is evolving so quickly that it is difficult to understand what an ASP can offer the leasing company. Many leasing companies will decide to lease software in order to solve problems that cannot be solved by software applications.

ASPs gain significant control over important information within a business. Security remains an important issue in determining the value added by renting applications. A company that plans on leasing software should make sure that the ASP is reliable and also can guarantee that the company's information is secure.

GUIDELINES TO CHOOSING AN ASP

A company should follow a few guidelines when choosing an ASP. The first is adequate security. A company should make sure that its information is safe from hackers, employees of the ASP, and, most importantly, competitors. Secondly, with the prediction of a shakeout of ASPs, a company should be concerned with the consequences of the ASP going out of business. Will the company be able to continue business, can it quickly find a replacement service, and can it gain access and possession of its data. A company also should be concerned with the frequency with which the ASP backs up data. It is also important to know how easily these data can be accessed.

A company must define the business processes that are to be outsourced and be clear on the objectives that should be accomplished by the ASP. A company also should check the track record of the ASP. Many new ASPs do not have the experience or validity to handle the objectives that need to be accomplished.

CONCLUSION

A company should decide to use an ASP based on the bandwidth available within the company, the type of application that is to be leased, the size of the company and number of users affected by the new application, and the amount of money available for the application.

A company should make sure that the ASP conforms to "best practices" such as sufficient uptime, security, network storage, and efficient management of the application. Using an ASP that does not provide these characteristics can cost the company more than the cost of implementing the application in-house. It is important that the company research and ask the appropriate questions to determine if the ASP is reliable and if it provides the services needed by the company.

BIBLIOGRAPHY

1. Corbett, Michael F. "E-Sourcing the Corporation." *Fortune Magazine,* March 2000.

2. Gillan, Clare, and Meredith McCarty. "ASP's Are for Real . . . But What's Right for You?" An IDC White Paper. International Data Corporation. July 1999.

3. "How ASPs Deliver Value: Next Generation Portals for Business Applications." Giotto ASP White Paper. May 3, 1999.

4. Koch, Christopher. "Monster in a Box?" *CIO Magazine,* May 2000.

5. Koch, Christopher. "ASP & Ye Shall Receive." *CIO Magazine,* May 2000.

6. Ward, Lewis. "How ASPS Can Accelerate Your E-Business." *E-Business Advisor,* March 2000.

7. www.aspnews.com.

Case 13-2

The Effect of the Internet on Securities Purchases/Trading

Andy Echols

The slogans say it all; from E-trade's "Your Broker is Obsolete" catch phrase to Datek's "The Rules are Changing" battle cry, it is apparent that drastic changes are occurring within the securities trading business. The Internet has opened the door for online trading, which consequently diminishes or even eliminates the need for conventional stockbrokers who normally would charge around $300 to $500 per stock transaction. It is revolutionizing how business is conducted in the securities exchange industry. The firms that can meet the technological demands of high-capacity online trading create a significant competitive advantage over online rivals. The biggest brokerage firms, names such as Merrill Lynch and Charles Schwab, have had to substantially alter or tear up their business plans in order to compete with the advances in technology. Eighty percent of the brokerages offer online services today, with the other 20 percent quickly to follow suit. The Internet has sparked an intense battle for market share between online brokers and traditional brokers. Interestingly, the structure of the trading market seems to have reached a medium where online firms are creating physical presences and traditional firms are developing online services. The victors appear to be the customers who are enjoying an array of financial services at significantly lower prices, as well as continuously expanded market information from the Internet. However, online trading also creates problems, which must be addressed.

LOWER TRADING COSTS

Online brokers have found a cheaper way, through new technological efficiencies, to offer an old service. Online brokers are able to charge one-tenth to one-twentieth the fee of their full-service counterparts. The lower prices of trades are a direct result of the lower cost structure of firms offering online trading. Traditional stockbrokers cannot compete or find it quite difficult to compete with online discounters on price. This leaves investors asking themselves what might justify the higher brokerage fees charged by full-service brokers. The Internet technologies result in the virtual firms that do not need branch offices, which reduces overhead costs. Online brokers can disseminate information and quotes via the Internet resulting in savings of paper, printing, and postage costs. This also frees up the broker to focus on more important tasks other than transmitting quotes or research to investors. Thus, the arrival of advanced networking technology has altered the economics of stock trading.

Another reason the prices per stock trade continually decline is that the low barriers to entry result in difficulty in maintaining a competitive edge among online traders. In 1997 there were 17 firms that offered online trading. Currently, more than 75 online-trading brokers are vying for traders' e-Business. [1] The competition among the online firms has pushed the cost for some online trades below $10. Comparing this cost to the traditional brokerage rates will provide astounding quantitative evidence as to the Internet's impact on securities trading.

CHANGE IN BUSINESS MODELS

Traditional brokers are reworking their pricing structures to become more competitive. The average commission price for online trades has decreased from an average of $52.89 in 1997 to about $14.00 per online trade. [2] Online trading has put pressure on the established exchanges to either change their ways or risk being left behind. All indications are that online trading will continue to bring in more customers. As more and more people become comfortable with using the Internet and disclosing confidential information, online trading will increase.

The trend to Internet technologies reflects a substantial movement toward greater connectivity, speed, and efficiency. New research suggests that almost a third of all stock trading will take place on the Internet by the year 2002, an incredible 18 million accounts. In 2002, experts estimate online accounts will hold approximately $688 billion in assets, up from 3 million accounts and $120 billion in assets in 1998. [2]

Many of the traditional brokerages have moved into the online market, while conversely the online firms are opening physical locations. This new business plan, into which most of the large, traditional brokerages such as Charles Schwab and Merrill Lynch have evolved, is termed "clicks and bricks." Now the successful online firms, such as Datek Online, E-trade, and Ameritrade, are using this approach. While the online firms will have nowhere near the physical presence of the traditional brokers, they believe that a physical presence is critical to survival. Charles Schwab opens 50 percent of their new accounts at their branches. Among other services, the online firms can use the physical locations to focus on education seminars and hands-on demonstrations of the online services. [3] Now it appears the Internet upstarts, which forced traditional brokers to offer Internet trading, are starting to look a lot like their adversaries.

The Internet also has a wide variety of resources for investors to get the latest financial and stock-related news, press releases, and company announcements. Some of the resources for this type of information include Pcworld.com, WSJ.com (*The Wall Street Journal*), CNETNews.com, and the *Financial Times*. In addition, most publicly traded corporations maintain their own websites that include sections for investor news. Also, investors can easily access their online accounts 24 hours a day and see their portfolios in real time. Moreover, there are many chat forums on reputable websites designed for enthused investors. The forums allow investors to share and receive insight into stock and market trends that they otherwise would not be able to have.

Other advantages to online trading are

- **Faster trade executions**—Investors who use online brokerages find their trades are executed much more efficiently and quickly compared to making a phone call to their stockbroker. With the Internet, investors can make trades almost instantaneously (e.g., within a minute or so), without needing to wait until their stockbroker is available on the phone.

- **More informed investment decisions**—Online brokerages offer a wide variety of analysis tools to aid the investors. Investors have the option of using an unassisted online brokerage such as E-trade, Datek Online, and Ameritrade or can pay more and use brokerages such as Merrill Lynch and Charles Schwab to offer trading advice. Either way, investors have access to an abundance of information including graphs, analyst predictions and recommendations, and historical data.

LEVELING THE PLAYING FIELD

Another consideration of online trading is the accessibility of the stock market to those who could not afford a broker and thus did not have the information necessary to trade stocks. "The masses out there obviously want this, and you can see it by the popularity of the ECNs [electronic communications networks]," said Tony Kafeiti, online supervisor at Castle Online. Kafeiti thinks online trading is growing because it allows small investors to take a more hands-on approach, and also the online houses don't show preferential treatment towards larger traders, something the established houses are notorious for. "They've leveled the playing field," Kafeiti said. Currently investors can jump into the stock market with as little as a few hundred dollars, whereas before a few hundred dollars would hardly cover the brokerage fee. Since the rules are more even for all investors, many observers feel it has led to a true democratization of the stock market. "They're giving individual investors the tools and the timing that were formerly accessible only to professionals," said Alan Ackerman, who works for a New York brokerage firm. [4]

Online trading has attracted new players such as younger investors into the stock market. Younger investors feel comfortable making online trades because they are more up-to-date on technology and because they grew up on it. Many of these younger investors would be unable or unwilling to pay the hefty commission attributed to traditional stockbrokers.

PROBLEMS WITH ONLINE TRADING

TECHNOLOGICAL PROBLEMS

There have been numerous systems breakdowns, and a year ago the Securities and Exchange Commission (SEC) suggested that capacity requirements for e-brokers should be mandated. "Based on the number of complaints we have gotten, we are still seeing problems with the firms' operational capabilities," said SEC Commissioner Laura Unger. However, Datek Online and National Discount Brokers believe that the industry will solve the problem itself since the online firms that want to compete and retain customers will upgrade and get their operations houses up to speed. "If a brokerage firm doesn't have sufficient capacity, the customer will go someplace else," said a Datek spokeperson. Many of the online firms believe monitoring capacity capabilities is necessary, but are concerned SEC regulations would be too rigid and unworkable. The number of systems outages at online firms has decreased as firms are developing more experience and creating more effective systems. [5]

Datek Online has recently leased a fiber-optic infrastructure from Metromedia Fiber Network, Inc., giving them the required bandwidth to execute a mass number of trades faster and more reliably during peak trading periods. The unmetered, fixed-cost bandwidth enables Datek to add capacity as needed and provides an unshared private communications network that is effective and secure. By offering virtually unlimited, unmetered bandwidth at a fixed cost, Metromedia Fiber Network is eliminating the bandwidth barrier and redefining the way broadband capacity is sold. [6]

FRAUD

With the benefits and potential of the Internet from technological innovation, investors need to be alert for frauds. Like never before have scam artists had the access to communicate with a mass of investors. Cost is no longer an inhibitor as anyone with $800 can purchase a computer with a modern and have access to the mass of people. With 200 million users on the Internet, a number of creative scams will surface. Through automated gathering software, fraudsters can obtain specific information on targeted investors with seemingly personalized pitches. Fraudsters have cost people millions by spreading false information about companies and buying or selling the stock to make a profit.

Fraud remains at the forefront of potential problems with online trading. But the biggest problem revolves around the perception of security on the Web. It is commonly believed Web fraud is running rampant, thus deterring many potential online investors. However, statistics show the Internet to be the least vulnerable of several commerce vehicles. There are effective preventative measures to minimize the possibilities against fraud, which include not allowing maintenance functions, such as address changes, or redemptions to take place through a website.

OVERCONFIDENCE

Another potential fallback to online trading is that inexperienced investors overestimate their ability to predict profitable and solid stocks. Some experts believe that cheap and accessible trading could be detrimental to inexperienced traders. Investors who have become involved in online trading make on average 12 times as many trades compared to investors using traditional stockbrokers. While that could lead to greater profits, the market has historically rewarded investors who stay with stocks over an extended period of time. Researchers have found that the new online investors trade more actively, more speculatively, and less profitably than they did before. [7]

The Internet has propelled online trading to alter the model of securities trading. Online trading has been a nightmare for full-service brokers, who are losing clients to online competitors and seeing themselves belittled in television advertisements. Thus, the full-service brokerages are forced to cut prices, which greatly benefits the investors. However, recently we are seeing another shift as many of the mainstream online brokerages are creating a physical presence in the investing world as well. The constant for all of the modern brokerages is that they will offer online trading. Online trading offers a vast amount of resources available on demand 24 hours a day. Investors have access to graphs, charts, and expert analysis that predict the movements of the stocks. Now small investors have the resources and timing that was once only available to the stockbrokers. While there are problems with capacity, fraud, and validity of investing information, the credible firms and websites should be able to address and correct these problems. The benefits of online trading far outweigh the hazards. Online trading will continue to gain trading market share not only for the low price but also because of the freedom. As Charles Schwab puts it, online trading is the "ultimate empowerment of the individual."

WORKS CITED

1. Snow, David. "Picking an Online Broker." *Available at* www.techtv.com/money machine, February 2000.

2. Perlman, Jay. "Securities Fraud and the Internet." *Available at* www.fool.com/specials/2000/sp000223fraud.htm, February 23, 2000.

3. Fugazy, Danielle. "Online Brokerages Go from Clicks to Bricks." *Securities Data Publishing,* June 5, 2000.

4. Prial, Dunstan. "Brokers Taking Back Seat: Alternative Exchanges Revolutionizing Stock Market Trading." *Business News,* September 13, 1999.

5. Schroeder, Mary. "Online Brokers to SEC: Leave Capacity to Us." *Securities Data Publishing,* October 1, 2000.

6. "Metromedia Fiber Network to Provide Optical Backbone for Datek Online." *Business Wire, Inc.,* October 18, 2000.

7. Barber, Brad, and Terrance Odean. "Taking Sides: How Online Trading Exploits Investors." *Crain Communications Inc. Investment News,* October 9, 2000, p. 10.

Summary

This chapter has covered a large amount of management material that applies specifically to the analysis, design, development, and operation of telecommunications capabilities and the projects that create them. Much information exists about this area for computer-based systems, but far less exists for telecommunications. There are two points to remember in the final analysis. First, *telecommunications capabilities serve the parent organization in reaching its vision, goals, and objectives.* They do not exist in their own right, but to serve an organization or business purpose. The people that support this technology must have the same goal. Second, *the design and development of a telecommunications system takes time, talent, and vision.* Technology, money, and people are involved. All of the factors must be managed. People management and technology management must be merged for the network to be successful.

As the organization progresses through the SDLC of a project to expand or add new capabilities or equipment (see Table 13.20), the team members must always keep in mind that the system does not exist in and of itself. The end result of this project must blend with the total existing system and fit the future needs and planned evolutionary path of the total system. This is why we keep referring to the implication of your actions. Are you following the tenets of the architecture you created? Are you choosing equipment, systems, or vendors that will fit the plan or have dire consequences? Do you indeed have a vision and plan that is compatible with the firm's? These are not idle questions; they determine your organization's ability to compete in the future. This ability may be the basis for your career.

The chapter that follows again discusses technology, broadband digital technology specifically. Its value and use should only be considered within an understanding of the path that the telecommunications group is taking in supporting the organization in its vision. Among the most important phases of the SDLC is the feasibility phase because so many variables are brought to bear at one point in time.

TABLE 13.20
Summary of Deliverables of Macro Phases and Effort of SDLC

SDLC Phase	Deliverables at End of Macro Phase
Problem definition	White paper—problem definition
Feasibility	TBEOTRE feasibility, preliminary cost
Systems analysis	Specification, architecture, prototype, updated cost
Design	Design showing components
Procurement	Purchase orders
Installation	Installed parts, training, documentation
Test	Tested system
Implementation	The system
Evaluation	Determine if problem is solved
Maintenance and change	Insure system kept correct over its life

Analysis is vital to ensure that the particulars of the proposed system are adequate. The overall implications and impact of the technology and its installation must be considered. The development team must keep this point salient as they proceed throughout the project—failure to do so is almost certain to lead to suboptimal decisions and impose constraints that will prevent the telecommunications system's investment from yielding the best returns for the organization.

Key Terms

alternatives, *606*
analysis and design, *585*
architecture, *582*
audit, *613*
champion, *593*
cold turkey, *613*
cutover, *612*
documentation, *606*
electronic funds transfer (EFT), *587*
feasibility, *599*
implementation, *584*
information pipeline, *586*

information systems architecture, *582*
mission, *581*
network architecture, *583*
network design, *607*
network modeling, *589*
objectives, *582*
outsourcing, *601*
parallel, *613*
phases, *589*
pilot, *612*
planning, *584*
policy, *584*

procurement, *610*
project management, *603*
prototyping, *604*
requirements specification, *597*
risk, *597*
simulation, *605*
strategy, *582*
systems development life cycle (SDLC), *589*
testing, *606*
vision, *581*

Recommended Reading

Zackman, John. "A Framework for Information Systems Architecture." *IBM Systems Journal* 26, no. 3 (March 1987).

Discussion Questions

13.1. Should the project team members be the same over the entire project timespan? Why or why not?

13.2. How would you find a champion for a TC project? What would you look for?

13.3. What are some of the considerations for the make-or-buy decision? What are the advantages and disadvantages of "make" and "buy"?

13.4. When is feasibility analysis performed, and why is it important to update the feasibility analysis after the analysis and design phases? In other words, why do feasibility analysis at least twice?

13.5. If a telecommunications vendor is willing to provide a "total systems solution," why is it necessary for the business to bother with project analysis and design?

Projects

13.1. Go to organizations and determine if they are increasing or decreasing their outsourcing activities. What is influencing their decisions?

13.2. Find a business that has brought up a new TC system and find out what cutover methodology was used and why. What problems were encountered and would another cutover method have helped?

13.3. Put together a team to develop a cable TV system for your school or a local community. Develop a total system, using the SDLC approach.

13.4. Find a systems approach to decision making and compare the steps to the phases of the TC SDLC. What are the similarities and differences?

13.5. Interview a representative from the ILEC or a CLEC to determine the assistance they provide organizations in determining TC system requirements.

13.6. Interview a representative from the IXC to determine the assistance they provide organizations in determining TC system requirements.

13.7. Find an organization adopting a client-server computer architecture and determine the telecommunications system's impacts.

13.8. Draw a network diagram to show the locations/connections in an organization, such as your school, college, or local firm. Use netViz in this project.

13.9. Interview a network manager and determine how he/she has documented the networks of the organization. Determine the degree of the existing documentation.

Chapter **Fourteen**

Bandwidth for the Office

CONTINUING CASE—PART 14

Work at JEI

Sarah has finished her project on the enhanced PBX. JEI and the Boulder facility now had access to Voice-over-IP and costs were expected to reduce by one-half within three months. Although the primary channel would be over the Internet, as JEI had no IP WANs, it was a step in the right direction. Sarah received a note from Michael lauding the project and the enhanced capabilities. Sarah was pleased to get the recognition for a job well done from the company's elder statesman and founder. Michael saw this as not just a cost reduction exercise but cost reductions leading to competitive advantage. At the same time, Sarah had said that people are complaining about the network in the Denver office being slow. She said this is the fault of the staff as they have increased convergence by sending larger files, sound, video, and fax. Michael decided these uses were valuable and chose to increase the speed of the Denver LAN and the bandwidth among the facilities. Since JEI installed Category 5 cabling when they first put in the Ethernet bus, they could increase the bandwidth from 10 to 100 Mbps with only a change of cards. This movement from Ethernet to Fast Ethernet should solve the problem for the immediate future at a very low cost. He told Sarah to purchase the necessary equipment and see if any software change would be required.

Sarah placed an order for 10/100 NICs. She then looked into the various ways to increase bandwidth to the remote facilities. DSL technologies would not work as they are for short distances, so she was forced to turn to other technologies. She contacted her LEC representative and found that they can provide bandwidth within the LATA but she must work with her IXC to cross LATAs, which was the case outside of Denver and Boulder. Sarah called AT&T and asked about options. After a business lunch, where she described her needs, the AT&T representative recommended a low-cost trial installation of 56K X.25 between Denver and Colorado Springs. This would give JEI a chance to test out increased bandwidth with a mature technology with no commitment for long-term usage. AT&T could have them operational in a week and they could see whether this met their needs. This packet data network would provide good bandwidth for data and could

even be used for large file transfer during off hours. She wished they could use the PDN for voice but was told by AT&T that the delays were excessive for voice.

After several months of trial, Sarah found that the speed was appropriate but the users had to schedule large file movement for after hours. As she had been told that the delays in X.25 were too large for voice traffic, she had not pursued that further. Even though they had installed VoIP, it was used primarily over the Internet and she wanted a more reliable and more secure network for voice. Again, she contacted her AT&T representative, who recommended that she consider frame relay. It was an easy and low-cost upgrade from X.25 and JEI could go with either the same bandwidth or an increased amount. Additionally, frame relay had lower and predictable delays and was, therefore, suitable for voice.

With experience using an X.25 packet data network and later frame relay, Sarah recommended the migration to frame relay at a bandwidth of 512 Kbps between the two cities plus adding Boulder. This speed and the lower delays in frame relay allowed them to include several channels of voice as well as data plus the inclusion of graphics. Sarah negotiated with the representative and AT&T agreed to a low-cost trial period. The PBX was changed to make the frame relay network the primary VoIP route when possible. The frame relay server was set up to give voice priority, creating more voice channels as the need arose. Michael and Sarah reviewed the results of the trial. The capability worked well. Michael asked Sarah to direct AT&T to make the installation permanent and to expand the frame relay capability to the other U.S. facilities outside of Denver. This speed was sufficient for their needs because the statistical MUX managed the voice-versus-data demands. Now the various divisions had no hesitation to coordinate on any detail. Michael was approached by a large customer in Cheyenne about joining the frame relay network. Due to the size of his annual purchases and because this was the first customer to migrate to 100 percent EDI and EFT, Michael asked Sarah to instruct AT&T to make the connection.

Alli asked Sarah to check out higher bandwidth for communications to the Scotland facility as they were sending a lot of data between their ERP/MRP systems and those in Kansas City. Sarah queried several international carriers by way of an RFI, in which she indicated JEI's basic requirements. After considering the responses, she choose AT&T due to their fiber-based network to the UK. She called the AT&T representative to her office and asked about alternatives. The AT&T representative told her that she could expand JEI's frame relay capability to Scotland by using ATM to carry the frames. AT&T could establish a point-of-presence at JEI's Denver office and carry the traffic to Scotland by way of London. They charged by the volume of data, not by distance. The committed information rate would be 256 Kbps with allowance to 512 Kbps with no additional charge. They could burst to 1 Mbps if required, with an attendant 10 percent surcharge for the bandwidth over 512 Kbps. This appeared to be a good solution to Sarah and she had AT&T make up a service level agreement for Michael to sign. Sarah then approached Michael to purchase additional network monitoring equipment so she could determine if AT&T was meeting its service level. She was already monitoring the Denver LAN and now she could view the traffic level to all divisions, including Scotland. She had a committed information rate from the frame relay network over ATM of 128 Kbps with bursts to 512 Kbps at no additional cost. Sarah believed the network was really coming together and would meet JEI's needs for the near future as well as fitting into the overall telecommunications architecture.

"Hi, Boss, Sarah here. I've got the data on higher bandwidth to Scotland. Want me to bring it up?"

"No, not right now. I'm on my way to the off-site data backup facility. Scotland did you say? Did you realize that the link to Scotland would be complicated because it represented transborder data flows?"

"Uhmmn, we didn't discuss that. I guess the AT&T representative thought it was OK. I'll expand the feasibility analysis to include a review of the regulations governing the movement of data between sovereign nations that might have an impact. Since it's the UK and the United States, I don't expect problems, but it must be cleared. I'll let you know at the Friday staff meeting."

JEI Considers Wireless

"Hey, Sarah, how many of our facilities in Denver do we have connected with high bandwidth?"

"Well, Michael, we just installed frame relay to the major facilities but the backup site is on wire-based T1 and the warehouses are on POTS lines as they only require security notification. Why do you ask?"

"I thought we should consider higher speed and I want to expand our backup business. It seems to me that the LEC said they could only provide T1 to the backup site and warehouses because they had no other media. What other options are there?"

"Well, all of these facilities are within wireless range. We could put in a wireless microwave system and increase the speed to 45 Mbps, if need be. Fortunately, we can take advantage of the terrain of the front range, all the way to Colorado Springs if necessary. Want me to check out prices?"

"Yes. See what the installation schedule would be also; I would like to talk with some potential customers next week and ask them about possible services to them. In particular, I would like to use our experience in bank transaction backup to bring most of the banks in Denver on board. See if you can find a wireless T1 solution from each bank in Denver to our office building and then use either the DPN or a wireless solution to the data vault. Next, see if we can do the same in Boulder and then Colorado Springs. And, if we are as successful as I hope, you will need to check on the size of the backup servers."

"Will do, Boss, anything else?"

"Yes, ask Doug if our backup facility has multiple telecommunications lines. We installed backup power at the beginning, but I think we opted for just one phone line. Since we started with truck delivery, we were not concerned with communications transport and we may have let that feature slip through the crack. Carlton mentioned something about R-A-D-E for reliability of servers."

"That's R-A-I-D, Boss, **redundant array of inexpensive disks.** Be sure we have at least RAID 1, which means the server has a mirrored hard drive. I'll ask for a staff briefing about this technology and our risk of going down. My guess is that we will want a higher level of redundancy, but that can be used to market the service. The bankers love nothing better than safety and reliability."

INTRODUCTION

The book started with an introduction to voice and data technologies, followed by their uses. We next explored the regulatory and legal arena, followed by a discussion of the management of the telecommunications organization and its projects. We now enter, again, the area of technology with a discussion of bandwidth alternatives and emerging bandwidth technology. As the need for bandwidth increases, the competing broadband technologies become more important.

Where Are We Coming From?

In order to see where we need to go, let's review for a moment where we came from and where we are today. In Chapters 5 and 6, we discussed LANs and WANs, using several media, topologies, and protocols. The slowest analog medium was POTS twisted-pair, supporting data communications at 33.6 and 56 Kbps actual, carrying 115 Kbps effective with compression. With **switched-56** service, we can have a bandwidth of 56 Kbps, and we can have 64 Kbps with a single B channel on ISDN, up to 128 Kbps if using two B channels combined. Going beyond this speed, such as fractional T1 or even full T1 circuits, we need special, often dedicated, circuits.

When twisted-pair is used internally for LANs, the bandwidth of 10 Mbps using 10BaseT Ethernet protocol and 16 Mbps with token-passing protocol rises to 100 and 1,000 Mbps with 100/1,000 BaseT, TX, and FX FastEthernet. These circuits are not public-switched capabilities, but internal networks. If we are not a part of a network and want to move data faster than the inherent speed of the public switched network, we have to connect to a network. Even then we would often be restricted to the connection speed. This means that we should evaluate broadband technologies, particularly switched circuits that will give bandwidth in excess of those of fractional T1 circuits.

In this chapter we discuss the competing broadband technologies. These protocols and media compete for preeminence as the standard for carrying the high volume of *video, voice, image,* and *data* (VIVID) traffic in the next century. We introduced ISDN earlier and now refer to it as **narrowband integrated services digital network (NISDN)**, although the marketplace would just call it **ISDN (integrated services digital network)** or **BRI ISDN (basic rate interface ISDN)**. The technologies we discuss here will provide a standard, as does ISDN, but with traffic bandwidths that are orders-of-magnitude larger. While the total bandwidth of basic rate ISDN is 128 Kbps and primary rate ISDN is 1.436 Mbps (23 * DS0), the *broadband technologies of this chapter begin at 1.544 Mbps*, or T1 speed, and aim for the gigabit-per-second range. These technologies are vital to nations and organizations as we continue expanding global competition.

The insatiable appetite for more bandwidth continues unabated. This market is growing at about 40 percent per year ($66 billion by 2003) and the Internet market is growing at about 60 percent per year ($56 billion by 2003). The market outside the United States is twice as large and is growing twice as fast. The new market dynamics are discussed.

Caveat: In these two chapters (Chapters 14 and 15), we discuss a variety of bandwidths and sometimes drop below the T1 standard, still calling it broadband. The T1 barrier is not a firm, fixed point. For example, when we discuss wireless speed, we consider speeds above 384 Kbps as pretty fast and may call them broadband. We will include a broader discussion of xDSL to help dispel the confusion caused by the

There is *no* right technology. You choose the one(s) right for your environment.

With the advent of the broadband technologies to be discussed here, the seven-layer ISO model has been revised due to need.

variety of DSL technologies, for example, IDSL, ADSL, VDSL, SDSL, HDSL, as xDSL will become a popular choice for Internet access in the next few years.

CONVERGENCE

Convergence, in its simplest form, means bringing together two or more technologies. We see it first in an insurance company that uses ACD to route the call and Caller ID to bring up the caller's file to be displayed on the computer at the time the phone rings. While this is specifically CTI (computer telephony integration), it shows that as we converge, we need either more processing or more bandwidth, or both.

On networks, convergence may arrive as did email. First email meant low bandwidth text messages. Next came browser formats with graphics. Then, voice was added, and now video is being added. The more we converge various formats, for example, audio, graphics, video, and data, the more bandwidth we require.

Bandwidth on the Internet

Let's use activity on the Internet as an example of increasing needs for bandwidth because of convergence. When some users first began to experience the Internet, circa 1990, much of the information was textual or binary data, such as an executable file. Thus, bandwidth required for file transfer was moderate. Let's say you were downloading a moderate-sized .exe file of 400 Kbytes, obviously not a Windows file of any capability. The modem was probably a 14.4 Kbps model. Do the math, and you will see that in this environment even this task took a while, and we assume no retransmissions. What if the file was a more usual Windows file at 3 to 60 Mbytes? When the user moves into Windows files, especially multimedia, the size of the files grows, but fortunately they often come with good **compression.** Examples are .GIF images, .ZIP files, .WAV sound files, or movies in .AVI or .MOV format. Still, the size of the transmitted file has increased over its DOS ancestor. If the user is really into multimedia, he/she is downloading not only still images, but audio and video clips. Even with MPEG compression for video, the files are very large. Meanwhile, in the professional world they are moving **computer-aided design (CAD)** files of multimegabytes and medical images of the same size.

> **Compression** has a strong influence on the effect of any bandwidth; therefore, a narrowband channel with good compression can emulate a broadband channel without compression.

Just the addition of more users on any network, such as has happened on the Internet, causes the traffic to increase substantially. If they are sending email, these small packets add up quickly to the need for more bandwidth or the mail will be delayed. If the users are clients accessing servers, as on the World Wide Web, that adds more traffic, especially since much of the traffic on the Web is graphics and images.

The backbone of the Internet was basically a T3 (45 Mbps) channel in the mid-1990s. As the support for this backbone was transferred to the commercial world, vendors discussed higher-speed (broader-bandwidth) channels for the backbone as well as for access links. The discussion of these technologies occurs later in this chapter. The objective in this portion of the chapter is to develop an understanding of the need for bandwidth.

The Parts of the Problem

This chapter and the next present higher-speed, for example, broader, bandwidth service to the business arena and the home environment. Figure 14.1 illustrates the areas of interest and raises some problems as well. For example, where does the small office/home office (SOHO) fit as it brings the technologies of the office to

FIGURE 14.1
Bandwidth Coverage for Chapter 14

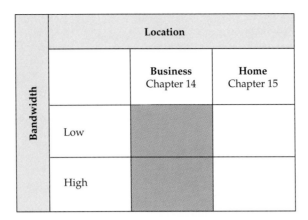

FIGURE 14.2
Industry Convergence

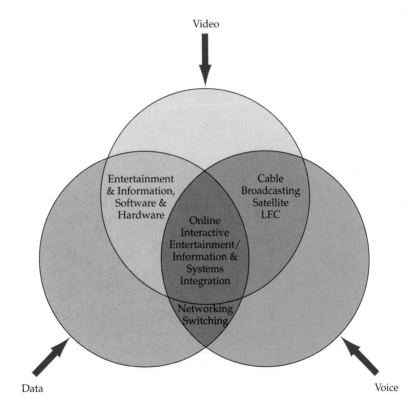

the home? How about wired versus wireless as they are competing technologies for both environments? While there is not a definitive break between the two environments, we believe their separation is appropriate to simplify discussion.

Lower-Speed Bandwidth for the Office

Convergence of technologies is a major cause for the need for greater bandwidth.

When organizational units wish to communicate by *video, voice, image,* and *data* (one company uses the catchword VIVID) using data communications, they have to create, lease, or buy transport media or channels. (See Figure 14.2.) As channels are established between points of source and destination, there must be a trade-off between the ability to move the requisite data within the time allowed and the cost

The Real World
Bill Gates on the Future (circa 1994)

14–1

"There are basically two domains where you can look to get a clue about the future. One is what I call low-bandwidth interactive: online services and the Internet. The second is high-bandwidth, the sort of bandwidth you get with CD-ROM, which is much faster than anything you get from online services. Too may people are having this big debate about whether the future in home devices is going to be more like the PC or the TV. The answer is you're going to have both; people will have networks in their home, and the TV and PC will be some of the many peripherals on that network."

Source: *Wired*.

of this capability (i.e., capability versus cost). When the requirements of source-to-destination paths change, the additional considerations of adding capacity to existing paths, procuring more paths, or switching paths arise.

Organizations that must move files or messages between a number of sources and destinations would seem to have no problem when the files are only a few thousand characters per day or week. This situation presently calls for low-cost, medium-speed modems and paths from the local and long-distance voice network providers. For example, suppose you were a fast-food enterprise with 15 restaurants in the southwestern United States and you wanted to have the individual managers report on the day's sales each night. This could be accomplished by providing modems and switched telephone paths between each restaurant's computer and the headquarters. If each transaction required a data transfer of total sales data only, then each manager would be required to transmit a single number of approximately eight digits ($90,000.00), which would require less than a second on even a 300-baud connection.[1] If each restaurant transmitted total sales by category, for example, 20 categories of food products with a six-digit identifier for the product and a field of six-digits (123.56) designating total sales, you would need to transmit $20 \times 12 = 240$ bytes = 2,400 bits. (Add 10 percent for overhead and you have $2,400 + 240 = 2,640$ bits total.) This could be done with a 2400 bps modem and a switched phone line in slightly more than one second for the actual data transmission and *8 to 28 seconds for call setup and breakdown*, with a reasonable cost for the phone line. The total movement of data from the 15 restaurants to the home office would take less than one-half hour's time (minimum of one minute per call) until the number of restaurants exceeded 30. The next level of data transfer (bandwidth) occurs when the stores choose to transmit sales by item within category (see Table 14.1). In the following example, remember that file format, delimiting, and control add 5–10 percent overhead to the other bandwidth. This is omitted from the calculations for *convenience*.

If, however, you were operating a department store chain with 15 retail stores, you would have different data communications needs, depending on whether you were reporting each night the total sales, sales by department, sales by category within department, or sales by SKU (SKU means *stock-keeping unit* and is a unique 14-digit number for each vendor, style, size, and color combination). For the latter SKU situation, you may well be reporting megabytes of data from each store nightly. Moderate-sized retail stores can easily stock 15,000 SKUs, with large ones

Overhead associated with data transmission adds 10 percent to the bandwidth for format, framing, control bits, delimiters, and communications protocol.

---

[1] For simplicity, we assume 10 bits per character as used in asynchronous protocols like Xmodem, using 8 bits for data, one for stop, and one or none for parity.

such as Dillards® having over one million SKUs. Having 15,000 SKUs would require moving 300,000 bytes of data each night: 15,000 × (14 bytes for SKU nr + 4 bytes quantity + 2 bytes extra). This translates into the transfer of three million bits of data from each store each night (10 bits per character/number using asynchronous protocols and assuming no repeat transmissions due to noise on the line), requiring a 2,400 bps modem just over 20 minutes each (see Table 14.2). In this case, a 20-minute phone call would be considered expensive, especially when it is made 30 nights per month from each of 15 stores. (20 minutes × 15 stores × 30 nights/month = 9,000 minutes/month = 150 hours/month.) Standard modems now transmit at 56 Kbps using compression to increase the effective transfer rate in excess of 60 Kbps. This would reduce the length of the phone call to under 50 seconds each, still using POTS and IXC switched lines. But it still requires 6.25 hours per month.

At this point, you should begin to understand the reason behind the push for broadband data communications is because as the amount of time to upload data increases

TABLE 14.1
Bandwidth Estimates

Number of Data Points	Characters/ Point	Total Characters	Total Bits	Time on 2400 bps Modem
1 = Total sales	8 = 12,345.78	8	80	< 1 sec
20 = Sales by category	6 ID + 6 value	240	2,400	~ 1 sec
100 = 5 per category	6 ID + 6 value	1,200	12,000	~5 sec

TABLE 14.2
Bandwidth Estimates

Number of Data Points	Characters/ Point	Total Characters	Total Bits	Time on 2400 bps Modem
1 = Total Sales	8 = 12,345.78	8	80	< 1 sec
20 = Sales by department	6 ID + 6 value	240	2,400	~1 sec
100 = 5 per category	6 ID + 6 value	1,200	12,000	~ 5 sec
15,000 SKUs	14 SKU + 4 nr + 2	300,000	3,000,000	~ 20 minutes

Information Window   14–1

When we purchase a modem, we make the assumption that it will communicate at the stated speed, for example, 33.6 Kbps or 56 Kbps. For most modems, the physical device does perform as expected. However, this *does not* mean that you will be transferring data at this speed. When you connect to a POTS line, neither the Telco nor the IXC guarantees a data bandwidth. Since the local loop is designed to transport analog voice communications, the LECs cannot eliminate noise as with digital channels. Therefore the analog loop cannot be guaranteed to carry data. While most IXCs use digital channels and, therefore, provide the full bandwidth they received from the POP, Telcos generally make no attempt to provide full bandwidth when it comes to data.

Even if the analog bandwidth of the POTS line is 300–3,000 Hz as expected, noise on the line can cause the modems to degrade to a speed of far less than their advertised rate. (This ignores the fact that service providers like online services may be providing low-speed modems.) LECs are now realizing that data are a significant portion of the traffic on their network and are creating tariffs to guarantee, at an increased price, specified *analog* data bandwidth.

The one place you can find wider bandwidth, because it is part of the tariff, is in ISDN. In this service, the circuit is divided into two 64 Kbps channels. Meanwhile, the serial port on your computer may be restricted to 32.4 Kbps. The way to maximize the amount of bandwidth over ISDN is to install an ISDN card in the computer as opposed to using the serial port.

so does the phone bill. (See Table 14.3 for representative long-distance charges.) This situation worsens if the stores choose to use a centralized warehouse and a centralized computer, as the point-of-sale terminals would be communicating real-time with the centralized computer. In this case we would have to move a packet of data with each sale of an SKU as it happens. Additionally, there are the accounting records, management reports, marketing information, and so forth, that most be moved each day or week. The above examples show how the need for digital speed is fueled.

Returning to the Dillards department store example, in one store, we see 20 point-of-sale registers, each of which handles an average of 10 customers per hour; each customer has an average of three items. The bandwidth requirements are shown in Table 14.4.

This example shows that even a retail store with 20 POS terminals can operate real time with very low bandwidth asynchronous communications. Doubling the number of terminals or the quantity of items per customer or the rate of customers per hour, or all three, would not tax this system. Where the need for greater bandwidth comes into play is with a convergence of needs, for example, bandwidth for other functions such as management reports, software downloads, voice communications, or even videoconferencing. Since we are considering continuous data circuits between each store and the headquarters, and since we also have many phone calls between these entities each day, let's move voice communications from the POTS and IXC lines to the new leased lines we installed for data transfer.

In our example, we really need only a slow dial-up POTS line for our daytime data needs; however, as you undoubtedly know from experience, the time to make the POTS connection to the centralized computer with a modem, handshaking, and other startup protocol, plus the time to tear down the line, will add a significant amount of overhead time, in this case, tens of seconds for a 1/3-second data requirement. Thus, we move to a continuous circuit, such as a 9.6 Kbps X.25 *packet-switched network*, or even a continuous 56 Kbps circuit. The X.25 system would handle all of the data needs, but not the software download and the voice communications. For software downloads at night, the X.25 running at 56 Kbps would

TABLE 14.3
Representative MCI WorldCom Business Long-Distance Charges (circa 1995)

Distance (Miles) Anywhere in U.S. for Business	Cost Daytime	Cost All Other Times
0–55	27 cents	19 cents
56–292	28 cents	19 cents
293–925	29.59 cents	19 cents
926 and above	30 cents	19 cents

TABLE 14.4
Bandwidth Requirements for POS

Item	Quantity	Transfer Speed
		2.4 Kbps
Bytes per SKU	20	
SKUs per customer	3	
Bytes per customer	60	
Bits per transaction	600	0.29 sec
Transactions per hour per POS terminal	10	
POS terminals	20	
Hours per day	10	
Bits per day transferred	1,200,000	500 sec

suffice; however, we really need more continuous bandwidth during the working day; for example, we need fractional T1 circuits if we are to include voice. (Remember that a **T1** channel has a total bandwidth of 1.544 Mbps and is inherently divided into 24 DS0 channels with 8 Kbps left for control. Thus, a fractional T1 is one or more of these channels.)

If we lease a single T1 subchannel, we have 64 Kbps with which to work. This would be adequate for either data or voice. Using ADPCM, we need 32 Kbps per voice channel; with one level of compression, we can go to 16 Kbps per phone channel. So, from this example, if we leased as little as one T1 DS0 subchannel per store, we could potentially support all of our POS terminals, the movement of data, and two voice channels, simultaneously and continuously. During off hours, we could support software downloads. If these requirements increased due to more voice channels and other requirements to, say, a quarter T1 circuit, we would divide the bandwidth for data and voice. With 15 stores, each requiring 1/4 T1 bandwidth, the total bandwidth requirement is just under four T1 circuits. If possible, we would negotiate four T1 circuits and spread them around our region; otherwise we would have to lease 15 individual fractional (1/4) T1 circuits. And remember, these are full-time leased circuits, which means that, because the data and voice traffic are not constant, we can give priority to voice and data for management reports during times of low POS traffic and reverse the priority during rush business hours, giving us an effectively higher data transfer rate akin to the functioning of a statistical MUX.

As the voice and data communications between the stores and the central node increase, each would move towards needing a full T1 circuit, especially as they realize the value of videoconferencing, which may require a 1/4 T1 (386 Kbps) channel each way for full-color, moderate motion. However, managers of such a total organization know its bandwidth requirements will increase and need to understand what the market will offer. Continuing to buy or lease permanent or virtual circuits becomes expensive; even when the near-term offerings of switched high-speed circuits are available. Even when the traffic within the total organization will support a private network, as for large corporations such as Texas Instruments, EDS, and J. C. Penney, the demand for bandwidth is taxed as new needs for data communications, and thus more bandwidth, become salient requirements.

Thus, we come to the consideration for broad bandwidth. As we migrated from simple uses in the examples above to more complex examples, we went from 2.4 Kbps to 1.544 Mbps bandwidth. Now suppose you have more stores with more POS terminals, more videoconferencing, and more files being moved. You need more bandwidth. *How much more* is the question.

Information Window 14–2
Bandwidth

- Analog TV channel = 6 MHz.

- Digital TV channel = 1.2–8 Mbps compressed.

- One analog TV channel, digitized, can hold 3–10 digital channels.

- Commercial digital teleconferencing calls for 1/4 T1.

- Personal videoconferencing can be achieved over ISDN BRI.

Part of the answer to how much bandwidth is enough has been addressed by SouthTrust Bank and Bruno's Grocery. The $22 billion SouthTrust has 500 branch banks and 60–70 stand-alone ATMs and was using X.25 over 9.6 Kbps digital circuits in the late 1990s for all data communications. They believed this speed was adequate as long as the traffic was text and there were no software downloads. However, at the end of the decade, they switched to 56 Kbps circuits to include multimedia and software download. Meanwhile, Bruno's transfers 30 megabyte files from each of 256 stores each night on 9.6 Kbps lines. They are going to frame relay (to be explained later in the chapter), which will ride on 56 Kbps or 64 Kbps, or 1.544 Mbps channels.

DIGITAL SUBSCRIBER LINE (DSL)

If your organization is the owner of an extensive twisted-pair copper network, such as the Telco's extensive POTS local loop network, you would want to take advantage of it delivering broadband services, ranging from Internet access to video-on-demand. **Digital Subscriber Line (DSL)** is a technology that provides digital communications over twisted-pair copper from 64 Kbps and T1 to 6.0 Mbps and beyond over repeaterless local loops of up to 18,000 feet in length. (See Table 14.5 for a comparison of bandwidth versus distance for 24-gauge wire.) The initial DSL technology in use was ISDN, using a bandwidth of 160 Kbps for BRI and delivering two 64 Kbps bearer channels plus a 16 Kbps delta channel to homes and offices. This was the original *digital local loop*, giving the users a digital domain and ISDN switching, and providing a switched digital communications network. As with all DSL capabilities, ISDN provides digital channels over an analog circuit. That is, ISDN and all DSL technologies use modems at each end.

Downstream data rates depend on a number of factors, including the length of the copper line, its wire gauge, the presence of bridged taps, and cross-coupled interference. Line attenuation increases with line length and frequency, and decreases as wire diameter increases. Ignoring bridged taps, DSL will perform as shown in Table 14.5. It is predicted that 80 percent of the residences and offices in the United States can be accommodated via DSL due to the presence of 24 AWG and 26 AWG gauge twisted-pair wire in the local loops.

DSL technology is rapidly being developed and new capabilities are emerging. For example, we describe ADSL below as having a bandwidth of 64 Kbps to 9 Mbps downsteam and 640 Kbps upstream at distances of up to 18,000 feet. As noted in Table 14.6, VDSL (very-high-data-rate DSL) permits data rates over much shorter lines, transmitting up to a SONET (described below) STS-1 (51.84 Mbps) signal downsteam and proposing to send between 1.6 Mbps and 2.3 Mbps upstream. Further variants address a 19.2 Mbps upstream, as well as a symmetric bidirectional data rate.

Caveat: As noted, DSL is dependent on distance and wire size. The defined customer service area (CSA) for DSL for good speed is 12,000 feet. If the distance is reduced to 9,000 feet the speed in the new protocol can approach 30 Mbps. At 1,000 feet, it can achieve STS-1 speeds of 51.85 Mbps. Thus, as the attached central office moves closer to the user, available unshared bandwidth will increase.

High-Data-Rate Digital Subscriber Line (HDSL)

DSL depends on the use of a pair of matched modems. HDSL initially required four modems and four wires (two lines) to deliver up to 2048 Kbps (E1) speed and is

TABLE 14.5
Practical Limits on 24-Gauge TW Pair

Designation	Bandwidth Limit (one way)	Distance Limitation
DS1 (T1)	1.544 Mbps	18,000 feet
E1	2.048 Mbps	16,000 feet
DS2	6.312 Mbps	12,000 feet
E2	8.448 Mbps	9,000 feet
$\frac{1}{4}$ STS-1	12.960 Mbps	4,500 feet
$\frac{1}{2}$ STS-1	25.920 Mbps	3,000 feet
STS-1	51.840 Mbps	1,000 feet

TABLE 14.6
Copper Access Transmission Technologies

Source: http://www.adsl.com/adsl/dsl_tut.html.

Name	Meaning	Data Range	Mode	Application
V.22, 32, 42	Voice band modems	1.2 Kbps to 28.8 Kbps	Duplex	Data communications
DSL	Digital Subscriber Line	160 Kbps	Duplex	ISDN service Voice and data communications
HDSL	High-data-rate Digital Subscriber Line	1.544 Mbps 2.048 Mbps	Duplex Duplex	T1/E1 service Feeder plant, WAN, LAN access, server access
SDSL	Single-line Digital Subscriber Line	1.544 Mbps 2.048 Mbps	Duplex Duplex	Same as HDSL plus premises access for symmetric services
ADSL	Asymmetric Digital Subscriber Line	1.5 to 9 Mbps 16 to 640 Kbps	Down Up	Internet access, video-on-demand, simplex video, remote LAN access, interactive multimedia
VDSL, BDSL, or VADSL	Very-high-data-rate Digital Subscriber Line	13 to 52 Mbps 1.5 to 2.3 Mbps	Down Up	Same as ADSL plus HDTV

The Real World   14–2
ADSL Forum, Kim Maxwell, Chairman

The ADSL Forum was formed in late 1994, with 50 members, to help the telecommunications community understand and apply this revolutionary technology. Focusing first on ADSL, the Forum promotes the concept of copper access for broadband services and develops practical solutions for system problems engendered by ADSL and VDSL networks. The Forum pays particular attention to the near term, when ADSL will be deployed along a migration path toward ATM, but before ATM becomes widely distributed.

Copper lines can be used now, for video-on-demand, Internet access, remote LAN access, and multimedia access. As a consequence, solutions must be developed now for wiring, premises distribution, terminal interfacing, link protocols, and network management, all in conjunction with evolving network paradigms.

Source: http://www.adsl.com/adsl/adsl_for.htm.

ADSL at the time of deployment in 1997 had a planned adaptive rate mode from 500 Kbps to 6 Mbps, depending on the line length. **What is this—narrowband, broadband, or both, or neither?**

often used in the delivery of T1 services, such as connecting PBXs, cellular antenna sites, routers, and IXC access points. HDSL is often referred to as a repeaterless T1 line, though the actual bandwidth may be between 56 Kbps and T1. Unlike ADSL described below, HDSL is symmetric with the rated speed in both directions. It is used by Internet providers to the home due to its symmetry and good bandwidth unless the end node is a server that must deliver significant bandwidth upstream, although access to the Internet is definitely an asymmetric environment with very narrow upstream needs and high downstream bandwidth needs.

HDSL requires two lines. SDSL, which is HDSL over a shorter length, uses only one line, so it will run over POTS and offers T1 symmetric services for the residence. This may have a short life, however, as second-generation ADSL chips incorporate upstream rates up to 1.5 Mbps.

Asymmetric Digital Subscriber Line (ADSL)

ADSL allows video-on-demand and other broadband communications on twisted-pair.

ADSL provides 1.2 Mbps to 6.0 Mbps digital bandwidth on an analog twisted-pair (POTS) line.

Asymmetric Digital Subscriber Line (ADSL) converts existing twisted-pair telephone lines into access paths for multimedia and high-speed data communications. ADSL transmits more than 6 Mbps to a subscriber and as much as 640 Kbps in both directions. Such rates expand existing access capacity by a factor of 50 or more without new cabling. ADSL can literally transform the existing public information network from one limited to voice, text, and low-resolution graphics to a powerful, ubiquitous system capable of bringing multimedia including full motion video, to everyone's home this decade.[2]

Description of ADSL

Is there a difference between choosing from among 200 channels at your TV set-top or receiving one channel that is switched on command at the source?

JPEG is a standard for compression of photographs.

MPEG is a standard for compression of video material.

LECs can provide video-on-demand with the existing media and ADSL protocol.

An ADSL circuit connects an ADSL modem on each end of a twisted-pair telephone line, creating three information channels: a high-speed downstream channel, a medium-speed duplex channel (thus the name asymmetric), and a POTS channel. The POTS channel is split off from the digital modem by filters, thus guaranteeing uninterrupted POTS, even if ADSL fails. The high-speed channel ranges from 1.5 to 6.1 Mbps, while duplex rates range from 16 to 640 Kbps. Each channel can be submultiplexed to form multiple, lower-rate channels. Figure 14.3 depicts a representative delivery method.

ADSL divides the downstream channel logically into 256, 4 KHz channels, each of which is modulated and can carry as many as 60,000 bps. Noise will make some of these channels inoperable or the signal-to-noise ratio will limit the bit rate, giving an effective bandwidth that is dependent on the distance traveled, ranging from 1.544 Mbps at 18,000 feet to 51.840 Mbps at 1,000 feet (see Table 14.5). The upstream arrangement is 32 channels of 4 KHz each.

The primary use of ADSL is for repeaterless T1 channels, especially for Internet access. This environment generally requires a 20:1 or better factor of downstream to upstream data rates. Therefore it would be possible to provide the full ADSL circuit to the home with 6 Mbps downstream and 300 Kbps upstream, which would make the 28.8 Kbps modem comparable to the 300 baud acoustic coupler modem of olden days.

ADSL allows the use of the installed POTS network to provide high-speed Internet access and limited video-on-demand offerings. As the lines of the network are the most difficult and expensive portion of the total network to install, any scheme

[2] Tutorial from ADSL Forum, Kim Maxwell, Chairman. *Available at* http://www.adsl.com/adsl/adsl_tut.html.

FIGURE 14.3   **Asymmetric Digital Subscriber Line (ADSL)**

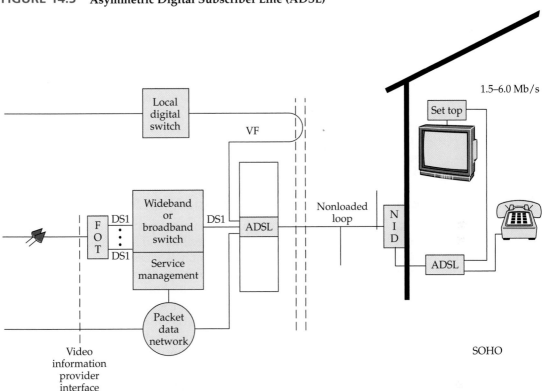

The Real World   14–3

Currently available. The Amati Communications Overture 8 ADSL/DMT modem offers transmission speeds up to 6.144 Mbps downstream and 640 Kbps upstream, using discrete multitone (DMT) modulation. This traffic can be carried over existing copper lines without interference with regular telephone service. The unit can be connected directly to a LAN, Internet, or corporate network to boost traffic transmission rates.

Source: From "Product Reference Guide" in *Telecommunications.*

While providing sizeable digital bandwidth, ADSL can't compete with CATV's simultaneous multichannel capability.

that provides digital bandwidth to the home with only the addition of black boxes at each end means that service could be provided very soon. The actual time of delivery is much more dependent on regulation than on technology.

COMPETING BROADBAND TECHNOLOGIES

Digital Subscriber Line (DSL), including ISDN, is technology that brings digital communications to the office or home using existing POTS lines. BRI ISDN delivers it in two 64 Kbps channels and ADSL ups the bandwidth as high as 9 Mbps, both with a distance restriction of 18,000 feet. The technologies discussed next truly

Information Window   14–3

Caveat: This field is rapidly advancing. The material for these technologies comes from the latest journals and books, vendors' presentations at conferences, and discus-sions with people in the field. Because of the many sources of information, we use footnoting extensively, giv-ing credit where credit is due.

ISDN has modems, but uses transceivers and not carrier-based modulation. There is analog–digital conversion, but the operation converts incoming digital signals into line pulses in such a way that timing can be recovered from the line signal at the receiver. Thus, ISDN and HDSL are transceivers and VDSL and ADSL are modems.

CCITT is the International Telegraph and Telephone Consultative Committee, an international standards group.

BISDN—broadband ISDN— involves ISDN standards with transmission rates higher than 1.544 Mbps.

begin the movement to broadband, that is, multimegabit speeds. They are listed in the order of appearance in the market.

Broadband Integrated Services Digital Network (BISDN)

With the advent of low-cost, high-data-rate optical fiber transmission channels; high-speed, low-cost microelectronic circuits; and high-quality video monitors and cameras comes the demand for broadband services. In recognition of this demand, the **International Telegraph and Telephone Consultative Committee (CCITT)** began standardization of a concept known as **broadband integrated services digital network (BISDN)** in 1988. The CCITT simply defines BISDN as "a service requiring transmission channels capable of supporting rates greater than the primary rate (T-1)." BISDN also can be defined as an all-purpose, all-digital network that will meet the diverse needs of users by providing a wide range of services. Such services include high-speed data services, video phone, videoconferencing, high-resolution graphics transmission, and CATV services, along with such narrowband ISDN services as telephone, data, telemetry,[3] and facsimile. BISDN services can be broken into two categories: communications and distribution (Table 14.7). *Communications services* are services in which there is a two-way exchange of information either between two subscribers or between a subscriber and a service provider. They can be divided into conversational, messaging, and retrieval services, as well as all current telephone network services. *Distribution services* may be classified as noncontrollable or controllable, so they may or may not operate under the control of the user. The information transfer is usually unidirectional, from service provider to subscriber. Therefore, BISDN and its wide assortment of services provide many opportunities and choices for subscribers. [14, 27, 29, 43]

Frame Relay

Frame relay was initially introduced in the late 1980s as an additional packet-mode bearer service for NISDN. *Frame relay can be defined as "an ISDN frame-mode service based upon fast packet switching."* In simplistic terms, it can be thought of as "relaying" variable-length units of data, called frames, through the network. It is a connection-oriented technology that supports variable-length packets at medium- to high-speed data rates. [4, 27, 29]

Frame relay is now rapidly being deployed across the United States. Although it was introduced in the 1980s, it wasn't used much until later. Frame relay received

---

[3] *Telemetry* is a data link to a remote sensor. Telemetry is used for testing aircraft or in the space program, where a link exists from the craft to the ground controller. Until the mid-1990s, telemetry used radio channels. Laser channels are being developed due to their inherent security and wider bandwidth.

TABLE 14.7
BISDN Services [27]

Category	Service Class	Type of Information
Communications	Conversational services	Moving pictures (video) and sound • Sound, • Data, • Document
	Messaging services	Moving pictures (video) and sound • Document
	Retrieval services	Text, data, graphics, sound, still • Images, moving pictures
Distribution	Without user individual presentation control	• Video • Data • Text, graphics, still images • Moving pictures and sound
	With user individual presentation control	Text, graphics, sound, still images

FIGURE 14.4
Frame Relay Frame Format

Flag	Frame relay header	User data field	FCS	Flag

its big boost from the public support by Novell and IBM in the LAN and mainframe environments.

Description of Frame Relay

permanent virtual channel (PVC)
Networks create virtual channels by lookup tables. These can become permanent by always being active.

Since frame relay provides connection-oriented point-to-point service, it is offered as a **permanent virtual channel (PVC)** service. The PVC must be reliable and mostly error-free because error correction and flow control functions are only performed at the end users' customer premises equipment (CPE). Each node in a frame relay network only has to perform three tasks: ensure the frame is valid, ensure the frame possesses a known destination address, and relay the frame toward the destination. If any problem develops while processing a frame, the frame is discarded. The intended receiver must detect any missing frames, notify the sender, and wait for retransmission. [21, 27, 29]

Currently, frame relay access speeds range from 56 Kbps to 1.544 Mbps (T1). CompuServe and British Telecom offer public frame relay service at speeds as low as 9.6 Kbps, however. In addition, speeds of 34 Mbps and 45 Mbps (T3) are under consideration. As higher-than-modem speeds are being demanded with Internet access, BellSouth has begun to offer frame relay services in larger cities like Atlanta. [15, 26, 50]

Frame relay uses variable-length frames, which are similar to the LANs it interconnects. The format of a frame (as shown in Figure 14.4) consists of a beginning and ending flag, a frame relay header, a user data field, and a frame check sequence (FCS). [21, 27]

The flags are used to delimit the beginning and end of the frame with the bit pattern 01111110. The frame relay header (two to four octets) contains the address as well as the congestion control bits. The user data field consists of any integral number of octets of information and conforms to the ISDN's Link Access Procedure on the D channel (LAPD), which establishes a maximum frame size of 262 bytes. Finally, the frame check sequence (FCS = two octets) contains the remainder from the cyclic redundancy check (CRC) calculation that is used to detect bit errors. [27, 29]

Advantages of Frame Relay

First, frame relay provides higher performance than traditional X.25 packet switching because error correction and flow control are not performed at every node, as in the X.25 network. This reduces the amount of packet-handling equipment in the network, which controls communication costs. Frame relay service has the potential to be an economical alternative to private lines offering the same bandwidth. In addition, frame relay achieves higher performance because the nodes spend less processing time looking for errors. *As a result, frame relay provides lower delays, higher throughput, and better bandwidth utilization than the X.25 packet-switching network.* The single access line with multiple permanent virtual circuit features seems a big technical advantage as well as a potential cost advantage. [20, 26, 27, 29]

Frame relay has strong management implications of low technical risk and low implementation cost, plus interfacing with X.25.

Second, frame relay is generally a simple software upgrade from most X.25 devices (proven technology), so the investment in currently used equipment is protected. If more than a simple upgrade is necessary, the start-up cost for frame relay equipment is relatively low. *Thus, frame relay has the advantage of not only possessing a low technical risk, but a low implementation cost as well.* [8, 27]

Third, frame relay supports numerous applications, such as block-interactive data applications, file transfer, multiplexed low-bit rate, and character-interactive traffic. Block-interactive data applications consist of high-throughput, low-delay applications, such as high-resolution graphics, videotex, and CAD/CAM. Multiplexed low-bit rate applications multiplex multiple low-speed channels onto a single high-speed frame relay data channel. Character-interactive traffic describes low-throughput, low-delay, low-volume traffic, such as text editing. [27]

Finally, frame relay is supported by a number of firms and standards organizations. For example, Cisco Systems, Digital Equipment Corp. (now Compaq), Northern Telecom (now Nortel), and StrataCom formed the Frame Relay Forum in 1990. Then, in 1991, WilTel Inc. became the first carrier to deliver end-to-end frame relay service on a public network. As of 2002, more than 300 companies had joined the Frame Relay Forum. [27, 30]

Disadvantages of Frame Relay

Even though performing error correction and flow control only at end points is an advantage of frame relay, these savings can create some potential disadvantages. If an error occurs, the time to correct the error is longer than in an X.25 network operating at the same speed. Also, frame relay requires a mostly error-free transport network. This bases frame relay on the use of PVCs, which limits flexibility. [13, 27]

Another problem is that frame relay suffers from longer delays at the switching points than cell-based systems. A receiving switch waits until the entire data unit is received before forwarding it to the next switch. This delay makes frame relay unsuitable for voice or steady-flow traffic that requires real-time processing. The problem is compounded by frame relay's low switching rate; its current top switching rate is 1.544 Mbps (T1), while ATM switches have rates in the gigabit-per-second range. [29, 35]

Finally, frame relay is more difficult to manage as the network grows. As it uses permanent virtual channels, the number of PVCs grows with the net, causing management problems.

Frame Relay versus X.25

X.25 was designed to provide error-free delivery using high-error-rate links. Frame relay takes advantage of the new, lower-error-rate links, enabling it to eliminate

The Real World 14–4
Boost the Performance of Your Network

Frame Relay from BellSouth Business Systems will enable you to . . .

- Establish transparent connections among LANs in multiple locations . . . allowing you to easily communicate across diverse boundaries without complex commands.
- Exchange data in error-free, digital form at 1.5 megabit per second speeds . . . whenever you need faster transport or to expand your private line network.
- Add new end-point users for a fraction of the cost of adding expensive hardware, software and dedicated lines . . . it's as simple as adding a telephone line.
- Achieve superior LAN interconnection performance utilizing your existing system . . . you don't have to make commitments to new system architecture and equipment.
- Send high-speed "bursts" of data between multiple locations . . . independently addressed and switched without prior establishment of a network connection.

When it comes to economical LAN connectivity, faster speeds, and superior performance . . . Frame Relay from BellSouth Business Systems is your solution.

Source: BellSouth Business Systems. © 1994 BellSouth Business Systems, Inc.

FIGURE 14.5 **Frame Relay BellSouth Ad**

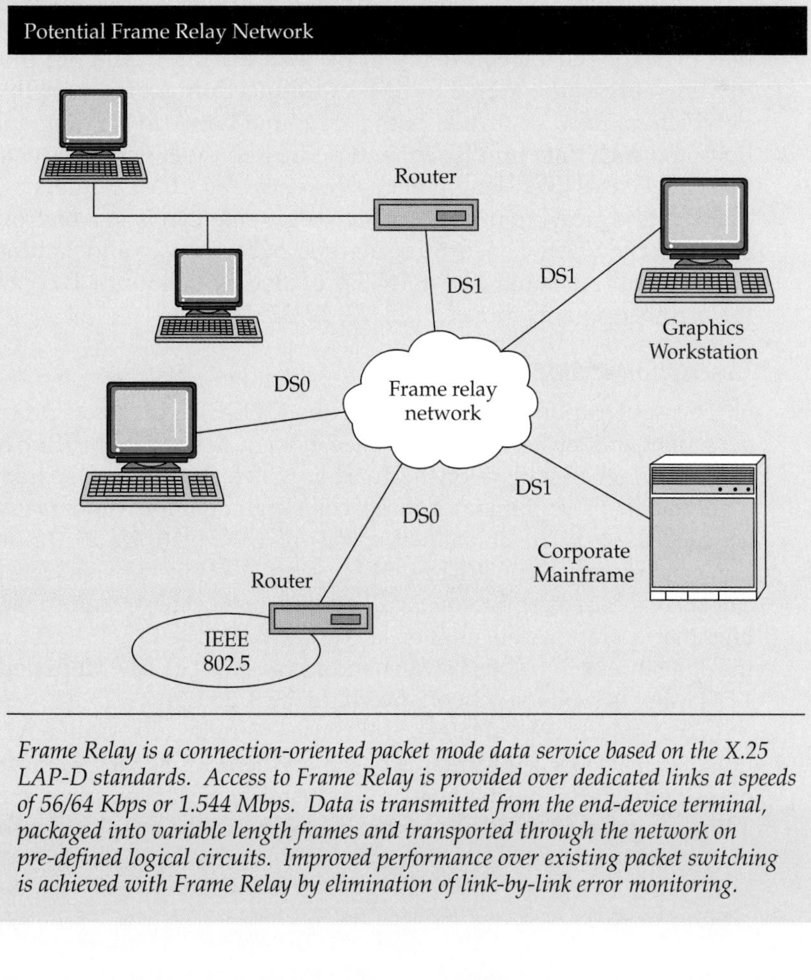
Potential Frame Relay Network
Router
DS1
DS1
Graphics
Workstation
DS0
Frame relay
network
DS1
DS0
Corporate
Mainframe
Router
IEEE
802.5
Frame Relay is a connection-oriented packet mode data service based on the X.25 LAP-D standards. Access to Frame Relay is provided over dedicated links at speeds of 56/64 Kbps or 1.544 Mbps. Data is transmitted from the end-device terminal, packaged into variable length frames and transported through the network on pre-defined logical circuits. Improved performance over existing packet switching is achieved with Frame Relay by elimination of link-by-link error monitoring.

many of the services provided by X.25. The elimination of functions and fields, combined with digital links, enables frame relay to operate at speeds 20 times greater than X.25.

X.25 is defined for layers 1, 2, and 3 of the OS1 model, while frame relay is defined for layers 1 and 2 only. This means that frame relay has significantly less processing to do at each node, which improves throughput by an order of magnitude.

X.25 prepares and sends packets, while frame relay prepares and sends frames. X.25 packets contain several fields used for error and flow control, none of which is needed by frame relay. The frames in frame relay contain an expanded address field that enables frame relay nodes to direct frames to their destinations with minimal processing.

X.25 has a fixed bandwidth available. It uses or wastes portions of its bandwidth as the load dictates. Frame relay can dynamically allocate bandwidth during call setup negotiation at both the physical and logical channel level.[4]

Switched Multimegabit Data Service (SMDS)

First available in 1991, SMDS is a high-speed, connectionless (datagram), cell-oriented, public, packet-switched data service developed to meet the demands for broadband services. Bellcore (now Telcordia) standardized **switched multimegabit data service (SMDS)** in 1989 as a metropolitan-area network (MAN) construction plan in order to accommodate high-speed data switching services inside the local access and transport areas (LATAs) of the regional Bell operating companies (RBOCs). GH-speed refers to the six data rates (ranging from 1.17 Mbps to 34 Mbps) presently offered by SMDS. **Connectionless** is a type of communication in which no fixed or virtual path is required between sending and receiving stations and each data unit is sent and addressed independently. *Cell-oriented* means that SMDS uses fixed-length packets or cells. Also, SMDS refers to a service that is aimed at the growing market of interconnecting LANs in a metropolitan area. For example, the STAR Consortium, a group of businesses and Samford University in Birmingham, Alabama, uses SMDS provided by BellSouth to connect the LANs of the member organizations. [1, 25, 27, 29, 32]

Description of SMDS

SONET's main purpose is high-speed, high-reliability, serial digital transmission over optical fiber cable.

ATM is a variation of packet-switching technology that transmits fixed-length units of data (called cells) at very high speeds.

SMDS uses Distributed Queued Dual Bus (DQDB) as an access protocol between the subscriber and the network. DQDB technology, defined in the IEEE 802.6 MAN standard, provides all stations on the dual bus with knowledge of the frames queued at all other stations. This eliminates packet collisions and improves data throughput. SMDS accessed the network initially at speeds of 1.17, 4, 10, 16, 25, 34, and 155.52 Mbps. Lower access speeds of 56 Kbps, 64 Kbps, and their increments were defined later. As a result of these access speeds, SMDS providers must have high-capacity switches and lines that operate at data rates of T1, T3, and SONET's OC-3 (155.52 Mbps). Note that the difference of 374 Kbps between the access speed of 1.17 Mbps and the T1 speed of 1.544 Mbps is used for network overhead. [3, 8, 25, 29]

Like ATM (discussed later), SMDS uses 53-byte cells. Unlike ATM's cell format, however, SMDS's cell format is based on the IEEE 802.6 specification. The differences occur in the 5-octet header. For instance, SMDS employs the CCITT's E.164 addressing system so addresses are analogous to the telephone numbering system.

[4] http://www.rad.com/networks/1994/fram_rel/frame.htm.

The Real World   14–5
Boost the Performance of Your Network

CDS from BellSouth Business Systems will enable you to . . .

- Establish transparent connections among LANS in multiple locations . . . allowing you to easily communicate across diverse boundaries without complex commands.

- Exchange data in error-free, digital form at 1.5 megabit per second speeds . . . whenever you need faster transport or to expand your private line network.

- Add new end-point users for a fraction of the cost of adding expensive hardware, software and dedicated lines . . . it's as simple as adding a telephone line.

- Achieve superior LAN interconnection performance utilizing your existing system . . . you don't have to make commitments to new system architecture and equipment.

- Send high-speed "bursts" of data between multiple locations . . . independently addressed and switched without prior establishment of a network connection.

When it comes to economical LAN connectivity, faster speeds, and superior performance . . . Connectionless Data Service from BellSouth Business Systems is your solution.

Source: BellSouth Business Systems. © 1994 BellSouth Business Systems, Inc.

FIGURE 14.6   SMDS BellSouth Ad

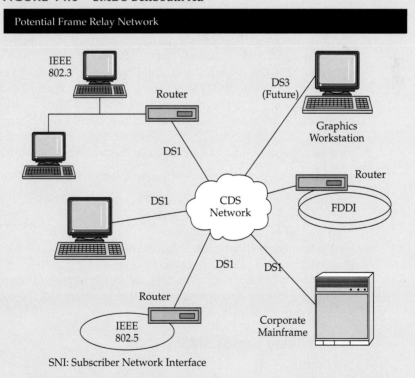

SNI: Subscriber Network Interface

CDS is BellSouth Business Systems' name for Low-Speed SMDS. A service functionally equivalent to SMDS, CDS is offered at rates from 56 Kbps through 1.5 Mbps. CDS uses a frame-based protocol known as Data Exchange Interface (DXI) for access to the BellSouth Business Systems network.

ATM, on the other hand, does not currently use E.164 addressing. Despite the differences in the headers, SMDS will run over ATM switches that will provide wide-area networking for BISDN. Therefore, SMDS networks can become components of the BISDN networks that will be implemented later. [21, 29, 35, 37, 38, 39]

Advantages of SMDS

Since SMDS is a public network, it provides any-to-any connectivity with no theoretical distance limitation. SMDS subscribers can send data to any endpoint on the SMDS network. This is especially attractive to businesses that need to communicate with many other organizations, such as customers, suppliers, and business partners. Because SMDS enables subscribers to achieve mesh connectivity with fewer access lines and less network equipment than point-to-point private lines, SMDS makes the connection of widely scattered LANs economical. However, the real cost advantage of SMDS may lie in usage-based pricing in which a subscriber pays a minimum fee for leasing the access line, plus a per-byte charge for data transmitted. [3, 25, 32, 37]

SMDS is based on a single set of standards defined primarily by Telcordia. This allows multivendor equipment to interoperate on the same network. By the mid 90s, SMDS was deployed in 35 areas nationwide; all major metropolitan areas in the United States scheduled access. Many RBOCs or their replacements sell SMDS service. BellSouth, for instance, offers T1 SMDS service in Atlanta, Birmingham, Charlotte, and Nashville and T3 SMDS over ATM. Thus, SMDS also operates transparently with different technologies, like ATM and frame relay. [2, 3, 8, 25]

SMDS offers enhanced network services, such as call screening, call verification, and call blocking. It supports common protocol architectures, such as TCP/IP (Transmission Control Protocol/Internet Protocol), Novell, AppleTalk, DECnet, **SNA (Systems Network Architecture),** and **OSI (Open Systems Interconnection)**. SMDS allows subscribers flexibility in selecting different access speeds for each of their sites and in defining specific user groups. It also makes adding or dropping sites as simple as adding or dropping a telephone number. Finally, SMDS provides bandwidth on demand, so a subscriber with a 10 Mbps access speed can burst to 34 Mbps for specified increments of time as long as the average bandwidth utilization is 10 Mbps. [3]

Disadvantages of SMDS

One major disadvantage is that SMDS cannot easily handle delay-sensitive traffic, such as voice and video traffic. SMDS's overhead can be described as moderate to high. Its use for delay-sensitive traffic is hindered because SMDS cannot guarantee the timing of cell arrivals. As mentioned previously, 374 Kbps of the 1.544 Mbps bandwidth on a T1 line is devoted to overhead. [25, 40]

Another problem with SMDS is its implementation cost. These initial costs include the implementation of new SMDS switches and the modification of SMDS access equipment. [8]

Frame Relay versus SMDS

Similarities

Frame relay and SMDS are both services that provide wide-area connectivity for LANs at moderate-to-high data rates. Both are fast packet-based data services that perform packet assembly and disassembly, error checking, and flow control only at the endpoints. Since frame relay and SMDS are *data* services, neither is well-suited for voice, video, or other delay-sensitive traffic. For this reason, both services are designed to interface with ATM, which integrates data, voice, and video. For instance, frame relay frames can be encapsulated into the payload portion of ATM cells. This process converts frame relay packets into cells at the network entrance, moves the cells through the network, and reconverts the cells back into frames at the network exit. With this approach, a carrier can offer both frame relay services as well as cell-based services such as SMDS and ATM. (As previously mentioned, SMDS uses ATM-like 53-byte cells and operates over ATM switches.) [21, 23, 35, 38]

Differences

Frame relay is **connection-oriented** (point-to-point), whereas SMDS is *connection-less* (point-to-multipoint). Connectionless (datagram) service provides any-to-any connectivity without establishing a logical connection before the exchange of information. Thus, connectionless service is more flexible, but is more difficult to manage and troubleshoot. Frame relay and SMDS also differ in transmission rates. SMDS may operate at the OC-3 (155.52 Mbps) rate, while frame relay currently reaches T1 speeds with the possibility of T3 (45 Mbps) speeds in the future. Thus, SMDS is more appropriate for applications such as large file transfers. Frame relay, however, works well for low-volume applications like electronic mail. Another difference between frame relay and SMDS is in the units of data to be transported. Frame relay uses variable-length packets or frames. SMDS, on the other hand, uses fixed-size, 53-byte cells. These differences can be important to users as they determine the service that best meets their business needs or requirements. [25]

Competitive access providers (CAPs) provide service competing in the LEC area.

It appears the SMDS deployment may not continue because frame relay is readily available and being deployed by firms who believe it is a logical step to ATM. RBOCs and CAPs are deploying ATM.

Synchronous Optical Network (SONET)

Synchronous optical network (SONET) was conceived by R. J. Boehm and Y. C. Ching of Bellcore (Bell Communications Research, now Telcordia) and proposed as an optical communications interface standard to the ANSI (American National Standards Institute) T-1 Committee at the end of 1984. ANSI standards have been published for SONET rates and formats; optical parameters; and operation, administration, maintenance, and provisioning (OAM&P) communications. By 1988, an international version known as *synchronous digital hierarchy (SDH)* was adopted by CCITT in Recommendations G.707, G.708, and G.709. Since then, a significant effort has been made to harmonize the difference between SONET and SDH. Thus, SONET and SDH now use the same basic structure and are designed to interoperate at 155.52 Mbps and higher transmission rates. [10, 29, 43, 46]

SONET's main purpose is high-speed, highly reliable, serial digital transmission over optical fiber cable. SONET provides carrier mechanisms to flexibly supply multiplex, and manage transmission rates beyond T1 and T3 speeds. Therefore, SONET provides a means for taking advantage of the high-speed digital transmission capability of optical fiber. [46]

Description of SONET

SONET transmission rates are multiples of a basic signal rate of 51.84 Mbps. This 51.84 Mbps rate is referred to as synchronous transport signal 1 (STS-1) when an electrical signal is used or optical carrier 1 (OC-1) when an optical signal is employed. Higher rates are formed by combining multiple OC-1/STS-1 signals to form an OC-n/STS-n. This is accomplished by interleaving bytes from n OC-1/STS-1 signals that are mutually synchronized. As previously mentioned, SONET

TABLE 14.8
SONET/SDH Rates

SONET Level	SDH Level	Line Rate (Mbps)
OC-1/STS-1		51.84
OC-3/STS-3	STM-1	155.52
OC-9/STS-9	STM-3	466.56
OC-12/STS-12	STM-4	622.08
OC-18/STS-18	STM-6	933.12
OC-24/STS-24	STM-8	1,244.16
OC-36/STS-36	STM-12	1,866.24
OC-48/STS-48	STM-16	2,488.32
OC-192/STS-192	STM-64	9,953.28

and SDH interoperate at SDH's lowest defined rate of 155.52 Mbps, which corresponds to OC-3/STS-3 (three OC-1/STS-1 signals equal 3 × 51.84 Mbps = 155.52 Mbps). Table 14.8 lists several SONET rates and the equivalent SDH rates. [9, 27]

In addition to the rates listed in Table 14.8, SONET supports transmission speeds of 13.27 Gbps (OC-256) and higher. Therefore, SONET defines both high-speed transmission over fiber and a consistent multiplexing scheme, which makes the design of SONET multiplexers very straightforward. [27, 28]

Advantages of SONET

SONET's advantages stem from three areas. First, SONET defines a multiplexing standard for combining lower-speed digital channels into high-speed digital transmission signals. This allows SONET equipment to support future SONET interfaces as well as T1 and T3. Thus, the amount of network equipment for each node is significantly reduced and multiplexing is simplified. [9, 18, 22]

Second, SONET defines standard optical interfaces for interconnecting fiber terminals from different vendors. This allows network owners to purchase and deploy fiber optic equipment from different vendors without a concern for compatibility. "Mid-Span Meet" refers to this interconnect capability of SONET, which provides increased flexibility for network designers when adding equipment to the network or when interconnecting different carrier networks. Business decisions about SONET should take this compatibility feature into consideration. [17]

Third, SONET defines a set of network management protocols. These protocols allow the network to be monitored, reconfigured, and maintained from a central point. Therefore, a technician located hundreds of miles away could create access links in minutes. In addition, the network management protocols can set up loopbacks, order bit-error-rate tests, or collect performance statistics. [17, 18]

An additional benefit of SONET is a flexible payload structure that can accommodate most types of digital signals. As a result, SONET can transport services such as bursty asynchronous data, high- and low-speed synchronous data and voice, and on-demand services (e.g., videoconferencing). This flexibility allows for broadband services such as BISDN. One function of SONET is as the transmission medium for BISDN. Notice in Table 14.8 that OC-3, OC-12, and OC-48 are speeds defined by BISDN. In BISDN, SONET performs such functions as mapping cells into transmission systems and extracting the cell. Also, even though ATM can be supported by any digital transmission hierarchy, ATM cells are optimized when transported within the SONET payload. Therefore, BISDN employs SONET as the transmission medium and ATM as the switching technology. [9, 19, 21, 34]

Finally, SONET equipment has been deployed since 1989, making it a more stable standard than more recent entrants. This should lead to a longer product life, more

Committed information rate (CIR) means you have a channel that may be priced at a mileage rate, but you are guaranteed a data bandwidth on a continuous rate and possibly a burst rate. This is a *level of quality*.

competition, and reduced equipment prices. For example, MCI WorldCom installed SONET equipment operating at OC-48 on a 150-mile route in Texas in 1992. In early 1993, Sprint announced plans to build an all-SONET global network. These and other deployments will only improve network connectivity for businesses. Michael Finneran, president of dBrn Associates, Inc., an independent consulting firm, believes "SONET will play a major role in improving how business customers are connected to public network services." [9, 10, 18, 21, 36]

Disadvantages of SONET

SONET is specifically intended for local exchange (LEC) and interexchange (IXC) carriers. Thus, most business users only will see the impact of SONET indirectly. More importantly, these business users are at the mercy of the LECs and IXCs to supply SONET services. Additionally, SONET equipment is expensive. These costs have deterred many LECs and IXCs from investing heavily in SONET, so the entire network was not SONET-compatible. [17, 21, 46]

Asynchronous Transfer Mode (ATM)

When first defined in the late 1980s, BISDN was based on a switching technology known as **asynchronous transfer mode (ATM).** In 1990, the ATM standard was formally adopted for BISDN services. ATM is a variation of packet-switching technology that transmits fixed-length units of data (called cells) at very high speeds. The speeds presently specified range from 155.52 Mbps to 2.488 Gbps. ATM switches are predicted to run at rates of 100 Gbps or faster. ATM standards are developed by the CCITT, ANSI, and the ATM Forum, the latter a union of over 100 telecommunications equipment makers and telecommunications carriers.[5] [5, 41]

Description of ATM

The most difficult part of broadband technologies is the management of delay and congestion.

ATM, for the most part, can predict delays.

Quality of service and service assurance for voice on broadband are just becoming available.

ATM, using a technique called cell switching, breaks all data into cells, or packets,[6] and transmits them from one location on the network to another over fiber-optic paths connected by switches. The 53-byte size cell consists of a 5-byte header and a 48-byte information payload, which results in a bandwidth efficiency of 91 percent (see Figure 14.7). The use of a 53-byte cell reduces the queuing delay for high-priority cells since the wait behind a low-priority cell is decreased. Also, the fixed size means that the processing can be done by a simple hardware circuit that allows faster processing speeds. Another important advantage of the 53-byte cell is that small cells meet the low delay requirements necessary for voice data. Remember that with usual packet switching, packets can be of varying sizes with each packet containing its own unique address information. Thus, more processing overhead is involved in reading the address and determining the length of each packet. ATM combines the best features of packet and circuit switching. [9, 11, 16, 27, 43]

ATM is a connection-oriented transfer service. However, ATM is very flexible and can accommodate both connection-oriented and connectionless network services. Two types of ATM connections exist: *virtual channels (VCs)* and *virtual paths (VPs).* A virtual channel describes the connection between ATM end-user equipment, while a virtual path refers to a group of VCs that all have the same endpoint. Once the virtual channels are established, routing tables are created that route the cell to the appropriate output link. The use of VCs and VPs simplifies the network architecture, increases network performance and reliability, and reduces processing and connection setup

---

[5] Unfortunately, ATM is also a widely employed acronym for automated teller machine.
[6] Please refer to Chapter 5 for the format of the X.25 packet.

FIGURE 14.7
53-Byte ATM Cell
(Bullet)

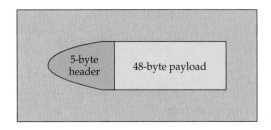

Information Window   14–4

Connection-oriented transfer services are communications where a true physical or a permanent or temporary virtual path is established for data transfer. The POTS is a prime example of such a service.

Connectionless services are a type of communications in which no fixed or virtual path is required between sending and receiving stations and each data unit is sent and addressed independently.

time. Data are broken into fixed-size cells at one point, transmitted to the destination as quickly as possible, and reassembled in the original order. [11, 27, 29, 43]

Advantages of ATM

One of ATM's advantages lies in its scalability. First, ATM will operate on different physical media, moving from unshielded twisted-pair to optical fiber cable. Second, ATM is media independent and allows 150 Mbps, 600 Mbps, and 2.4 Gbps links on the same network. Finally, ATM switches provide bandwidth-on-demand, so users can send as much data as they have within a specific amount of time and pay accordingly. ATM's fixed cell size can be rapidly handled by routers, and there is less delay for voice and video. [12, 31]

Another advantage is ATM's ability to support different kinds of traffic, such as voice, video, and data, either separately or in multimedia applications. Likewise, ATM is both distance and protocol independent, while serving local and wide area requirements. Thus, ATM allows the user to mix and match channels[7] of varying bandwidth and data types. These advantages lead to a wide variety of applications such as high-speed LAN interconnection; computer disaster recovery; supercomputer access; medical imaging; and multimedia for distance learning, collaboration, and concurrent engineering. ATM is viewed as a unifying technology for LANs and WANs as well as for multimedia applications. The scalability and flexibility of ATM mean that the technology can provide the sort of unification that was heretofore impossible. In order to increase user satisfaction and productivity and decrease network operating cost, network managers should be aware of these potential applications available through ATM. (See Figure 14.8 for the ATM process.) [12, 14, 33, 52]

Many companies, such as Adaptive, AT&T, BBN, Fujitsu, Hitachi, IBM, Cisco Systems, Digital Link, Fore Systems, NetExpress, Proteon, Siemens Stromberg-Carlson, StratCom, Telco Systems, and Wellfleet, are producing ATM switches. Also, AT&T,

---

[7] ATM is asynchronous, sending cells of data that are not synchronized to each other. Synchronous communications requires dedicated (though virtual) channels for each speed of transmission. Because of the nature of ATM, it can accept the synchronous communications at varying speeds, place them into standard cells, and intermix them on the same ATM circuit.

FIGURE 14.8   ATM Process

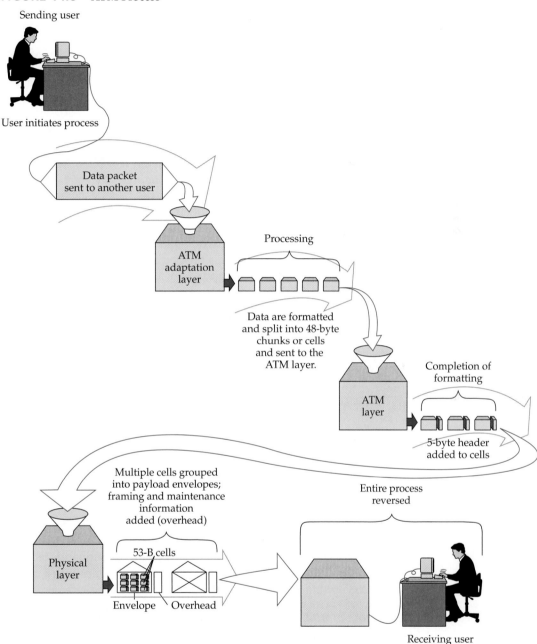

MCI WorldCom, Metropolitan Fiber Systems, Sprint, and WilTel plan to use ATM switches within their networks. Strong support for ATM services also comes from the ATM Forum, which was formed in 1991 as an industry consortium of ATM service providers and vendors. With this support, ATM services became available in the United States in 1994. As Tom Super, vice president of Research & Development for NYNEX Science & Technology Inc., explained [27]:

> ATM technology is ultimately going to displace all other switching technologies. As a connection-oriented, cell-switching technology, ATM promises to be the

Isochronous communications is the accommodation of asynchronous transmission over a synchronous link, where filler bits are inserted to keep the circuit synchronized.

dominant global networking technology of the 1990s and early 2000s because it is equally suitable for LAN and WAN environments, for data, voice and image applications, and for private and public networking. It handles both isochronous and bursty traffic. While efficiently allocating bandwidth-on-demand and guaranteeing bandwidth for delay-sensitive applications, ATM manages to combine the benefits of both packet switching and circuit switching. I expect ATM should be a force in the private network marketplace . . . and in the public arena. [47]

Disadvantages of ATM

One of the drawbacks of ATM technology is the expense. Tom Nolle, president of CIMI Corp., a consulting and research group, believed that ATM technology would not be cost-justifiable in the United States until the year 2000. ATM is a new transfer technique, so its standards are still evolving and product stability is not ensured. Finally, ATM creates a new set of problems for network designers and planners. For example, network designers and planners must determine when ATM will meet their needs, and then find the correct combination of commercially available ATM carrier services and equipment. Network managers must examine the compatability expense when addressing the impact on their networks of MANs and WANs. As of 2002, ATM has proven neither as popular nor as cost-effective as predicted. This may be because competing technologies have become more cost-effective. [27, 42, 51]

ATM Has Various and Scalable Bandwidth

One of the benefits of ATM is the scalability of the bandwidth. At the lower end is ATM running at T1 speeds. As the following comparison shows, the T1 domain is understood and prices show a competitive environment. Moving up from 1.5 Mbps, we find IBM's 25 Mbps for LAN-to-LAN switching, or even for a star LAN. The next step, though it might be missed, is 51.84 (STS-1) Mbps, but more likely is the OC-3 bandwidth.

The assumption is that ATM will use fiber as a medium. (T1 channels are often on twisted-pair copper circuits.) However, a company in Huntsville, Alabama, has established a 155.52 Mbps ATM network using coaxial cable. Thus, while we might wish to migrate quickly to fiber channels, the move is not mandatory for ATM.

Broadband Integrated Services Digital Network (BISDN) Technology

In the beginning of this section on competing broadband technologies, we described BISDN as a generalized, if not generic, description of broadband. The term also is used to denote a specific form of the technology.

Description of BISDN

In order to provide the services that require large bandwidth, BISDN is based on transmission speeds and capacities at the 155.52 Mbps, 622.08 Mbps, and 2.488 Gbps levels. These bit rates derive from CCITT G Series Recommendations for *synchronous digital hierarchy (SDH), synchronous optical network (SONET)* standards of the T1 Committee, and the CCITT I Series Recommendations that support the concept of *asynchronous transfer mode (ATM)*–based BISDN. Therefore, the transmission medium over which BISDN will operate is described by SDH/SONET with ATM employed as the switching mode. [29]

BISDN also differs in several ways from ISDN. First, ISDN uses the existing telephone network infrastructure of copper wires, whereas BISDN uses optical fiber

Information Window

Pros and Cons of T1 ATM

14–5

DEFINITION

T1 ATM is targeted for entry-level ATM customers who are not ready to invest in T3 lines that can cost as much as eight times the cost of T1 lines (even though the speed differential is 30 times higher), but runs on the same media, using different boxes.

PROS

- T1 lines are relatively inexpensive, allowing customers who are unable to afford or justify more expensive T3 lines to start setting up ATM WANs.

- T1 ATM can carry LAN, voice, and video traffic from remote sites to an ATM-based campus; frame-relay-to-ATM connections can carry only LAN traffic.

CONS

- ATM is tariffed much higher than frame-relay; frame-relay-to-ATM interworking specifications make frame relay access to central ATM networks more attractive than T1 ATM access.

- Voice-over-frame-relay standards should make the transport of multiple data types over frame-relay more competitive against ATM.

cable. Second, because ISDN is primarily a circuit-based network, it only performs packet switching on the D channel. BISDN, however, uses only packet switching. Finally, ISDN channel bit rates are prespecified, whereas BISDN uses virtual channels without any prespecified bit rate. The only limitation on BISDN rates is the physical bit rate of the user-to-network interface. [16]

Advantages of BISDN

As a point of reference, ISDN's data rates are inadequate for many applications of interest. For instance, a 50-megabyte file takes about five minutes to move at T1 transmission speeds. This same file can be moved in 2.5 seconds at 155.52 Mbps. Also, with local area network (LAN) speeds in the broadband range (e.g., 10 or 100 Mbps Ethernet buses, 4 and 16 Mbps token rings, and 100 Mbps **fiber distributed data interface [FDDI]** protocols), higher speeds are needed for LAN-to-LAN interconnection. BISDN provides the solution to these problems. BISDN can be used to interconnect LANs over wide areas at speeds equal to or greater than today's LAN speeds. Thus, BISDN solves the problems by providing high data rates over a distance. [7, 28]

Several fields are emerging as the possibilities of BISDN are realized. For instance, teleradiology transmits medical imagery among hospitals, physicians, and patients, which requires large bandwidth due to the size of the data files. BISDN makes large file transfers quick and easy. Other commercial applications of BISDN include broadband video telephony, broadband videoconference, video surveillance, video/audio information transmission service, high-speed telefax, video mail service, and broadband videotex. [28, 43]

Finally, in addition to providing various services, BISDN can reduce the costs of operating a network. This cost reduction is the result of BISDN's ability to integrate a broad mix of services so the network operator can handle special services in a

The Real World
Ethernet Goes Metropolitan

14–6

Wide area Ethernet promises to be as easy, cheap, and useful as office Ethernet, but the reality is likely to be substantially more complicated, predicts Peter Judge.

Everyone knows about Ethernet—it's cheap, goes together like Legos, wires up your office building, and is more reliable than most of your office colleagues. But it stops at the office walls.

And we all know about wide area networks (WANs)—they are mysterious and expensive packaged-up services you get from telecoms carriers to link offices together. They keep going wrong, and if you ask how they actually work, they turn out to be a pile of promiscuous protocols sprawled on top of each other—"IP on ATM on Sonet," or the like.

Promising to clear all this up is wide area Ethernet, giving IT managers something as easy, cheap, and useful as office Ethernet, but linking offices together. So it's no wonder that wide area Ethernet is one of the remaining hot spots in a fast cooling network industry—especially metropolitan area Ethernet, as the metropolitan area is the next step out from the campus, and the next logical step if Ethernet is going to expand.

The metropolitan area is also the main bottleneck, where service providers have a shortage of bandwidth. Most of them have plenty of capacity between cities, but within those cities they have trouble reaching businesses with fibre.

But WANs—and metropolitan area networks (MANs)—are different from office networks. Firms own their office networks, and probably just carry data on them. MANs are owned by service providers, and shared by various customers, as well as by various kinds of traffic, including voice. Service providers' metropolitan networks are mostly based on Sonet/SDH, which uses a double ring to provide almost-immediate recovery from any fibre breaks, and a time-division system to set up connection-oriented paths, which make sure that a firm's voice traffic doesn't get held up by someone else's data traffic.

Now, there are some service providers out there, such as Yipes in California, that are happy to offer Ethernet-style data-only services using Ethernet, but most service providers want to keep their existing mix of data and profitable voice services. So they are happy to adopt Ethernet in metropolitan networks, but only if they can duplicate the features of Sonet.

And this is not simple at all. Ethernet uses the spanning tree protocol to explicitly rule out the rings that providers want for reliability. And it doesn't offer connection-oriented services. So obviously enough, the Ethernet that finds its way into service provider networks won't be the office Ethernet, but something more complex.

There is currently an argument between vendors who support something called Resilient Packet Ring (RPR), which is a modified Ethernet to replace Sonet/SDH, and those who want pure Ethernet. It's not edifying—RPR is still at the working group stage at the Institute of Electrical and Electronics Engineers (IEEE), which has not even reached agreement on requirements for RPR let alone the technical implementation, while the advocates of "pure Ethernet" are obviously bluffing. They have to be adding proprietary technology since pure Ethernet simply won't do the job.

Metropolitan Ethernet will not be like office Ethernet because firms won't own it—their service provider will. But because IT managers want office Ethernet between sites, that is what service providers will offer them. But it will be Ethernet as a "service." IT managers will not see Ethernet frames and IP packets as the wide area dial tone or the underlying protocols. They will be the usual orgiastic mess of WAN stuff—Ethernet on MPLS on RPR, or whatever.

Source: http://www.zdnet.co.uk/itweek/columns/2001/34/judge.html.

more standardized manner. Thus, the need to build service-specific transmission and switching systems is minimized. [49]

Disadvantages of BISDN

The main disadvantage or drawback to BISDN is an economic issue. The cost of BISDN, at the present time, is greater than that of ISDN. This situation should improve, however, as the cost of technologies such as optical fiber cable continues to decline. Another consideration is that BISDN only began to be commercially available in the mid-to-late 1990s. Thus, BISDN's capabilities are yet to be proven in action. [24, 48]

WIRELESS TECHNOLOGIES

All of the above technologies are wired media. The area of wireless broadband has made significant advances in the past few years and will continue to do so. The advantages are (*a*) much faster installation, (*b*) movability, and (*c*) far simpler right-of-way access. Consider the following scenario: You are a multidivision company in downtown Atlanta (or another large city), with offices in Buckhead, the Hartsfield Airport area, and on highway 400 in Marietta. (For those not familiar with Atlanta, these buildings would be several miles apart and, more importantly, have high congestion around them, which would make running wired media a real challenge.) Thus, the right-of-way problem is solved by use of line-of-sight wireless technology when the bandwidth is suitable.

Cellular

Cellular telephones operate from omnidirectional radio towers, located in cells of two to five miles in diameter. Although higher speeds of and above 384 Kbps will not be available until generation 3 of most cellular protocols, the infrastructure exists for fixed wireless lower broadband transport. A building that requires connectivity installs one or more cellular attachments and the cell systems do the rest. A significant advantage of this technology is that it can be moved without interference with the signal.

A specific market for cellular-based broadband service, especially Internet access, is being developed to hotels. We are seeing data ports appearing for wired access and wireless access will take its place. Thus, a businessperson can enter a hotel and have fee-based access to a laptop or palm device.

Microwave

This is tried and true technology that has a proven track record. While it does require FCC registration for frequency spectrum allocation, the installation is simple and the protocols are stable. Thus, two facilities that can see each other can install microwave wireless broadband capability.

Satellite and VSAT

Though both rely on a stationary orbiting transponder, these are tried and proven technologies. Rare would be the car dealership that does not have a VSAT antenna on its roof. Satellite service is common for cable TV companies and digital channels are not increasing in number. Direct Broadcast Service television and data are provided by DirectWav with more offerings on the horizon.

LMDS/MMDS

These technologies operate at broadband data rates and can provide omnidirectional access within 25 miles from the central transmitter. While the central tower is a bit pricy the receiving units are simple wire-frame microwave antennas with low-cost node equipment. Licences for the various bands can be purchased, or the service could be leased from a common carrier.

Wireless T1

A number of companies have created various forms of wireless transmission with ranges up to four miles that will carry T1 bandwidth. One form requires FCC registration for spectrum and the other form uses spread spectrum and public bands. Both forms can quickly create a wireless channel on rooftops or walls for US$20,000 or less and offer reasonable security.

BROADBAND TECHNOLOGIES, SO WHAT?

With the growing use of LANs in the business environment and with LAN speeds in the gigabits-per-second range, the need has arisen for LAN interconnection over wide areas and at high speeds. Services such as frame relay (data), SMDS (data), and BISDN (data, voice, video, image, graphics, fax, etc.) provide high-speed LAN interconnection, which improves communications and the sharing of information across an organization, between an organization and its suppliers, and between an organization and its customers. In addition, all of these services can be supported by ATM switches. Similarly, SMDS and BISDN are both designed to operate over SONET transmission facilities. Therefore, broadband technologies will provide multiple services, so network managers must select the services that match their requirements. This task may be especially difficult since many analysts predict that the complexion of the broadband services landscape will change. [6]

Many analysts predict that frame relay loses market share to SMDS as users demand bandwidth. Eventually, SMDS also loses market share to BISDN as SONET use grows. William Stallings says, "The growing use of SONET in the coming years will thus help smooth the way to BISDN." Since both frame relay and SMDS can interface with ATM/BISDN, another likely scenario maintains that frame relay, SMDS, and BISDN will coexist and be widely available from the service providers. For example, BellSouth plans to purchase eight Fetex-150 ATM switches from Fujitsu in order to offer SMDS, frame relay, and cell relay services. Since ATM switches can support frame relay, SMDS, and BISDN, ATM appears to be the eventual winner in high-speed networks. [2, 12, 44]

The Real World   14–7
Bandwidth Is Tight. ATM Sounds Nice.
But It Also Sounds Pretty Darn Expensive.

Everyone is talking about ATM as the answer for speeding up busy networks. But there are two good reasons why business hasn't stampeded en masse to the ATM solution. It costs a lot. And to get there, you have to rip out everything you have.

Well, with all respect to the status quo, IBM now unveils the new 25 Mbps ATM Workgroup solution. It comes complete with workstation adapters, giving you an immediate boost in bandwidth with plenty of room to grow in the future. And it all comes at the refreshing low price of US $495 per connection.

Source: Advertisement in *PC Magazine.*

Network managers must closely monitor the changes and developments in broadband services, so the proper combination of services may be acquired in the most cost-effective manner. These broadband services might present some problems for network managers but, at the same time, create many opportunities. From high-speed LAN interconnection, to videoconferencing, to large file transfer, to multimedia applications, broadband services are at the center of a firm's ability to obtain and maintain a competitive advantage through telecommunications. With the greater bandwidth and flexibility provided by frame relay, SMDS, BISDN, ATM, and SONET, new applications exist for firms to exploit and gain an advantage over competitors who do not realize the benefits of broadband telecommunications capabilities. Therefore, those managers who ignore the opportunities presented by broadband technologies risk placing their firms at a competitive *dis*advantage.

BISDN's Role

BISDN is a connection-oriented packet service based on ATM cells. These cells can be transmitted in the traditional packet-switching mode or in the payload of a SONET envelope. Since ATM cells are optimized when transported using SONET, several ATM manufacturers have announced products that use SONET as the physical transport for ATM cells. Therefore, BISDN offers ATM over SONET as a common transport platform. [4, 10, 41, 44]

The goal of BISDN is one network capable of supporting multiple services, such as frame relay and SMDS, on the same platform. This would allow two frame relay users to connect to one another over a BISDN (ATM/SONET) backbone network or a frame relay user to connect to an SMDS user over the BISDN (ATM/SONET) backbone network. Currently, however, frame relay and SMDS are implemented on service-specific platforms, such that frame relay networks are built using frame relay switches and SMDS networks are built using SMDS switches. (Table 14.9 shows a comparison of various broadband technologies.) [23]

TABLE 14.9
Comparison of the Broadband Technologies

Features	X.25	Frame Relay	SMDS	SONET	ATM	BISDN
Service	X	X	X			
Switching					X	X
Connection-oriented		X			X	X
Connectionless (datagram)	X		X			
Fixed packet			X		X	X
Variable packet		X		X		
Data	X	X	X			
Data + Transmission				X		
Media				X		
Suitable for real-time processing	No	No	No	Yes	Yes	Yes
Compatability		X				X.25
			X		X	Frame relay
		X			X	SMDS
					X	SONET
		X	X	X	X	ATM
			X			BISDN

Information Window 14–6

ANSI	American National Standards Institute	NISDN	Narrowband Integrated Services Digital Network
ATM	Asynchronous Transfer Mode		work
BISDN	Broadband Integrated Services Digital Network	OC-*n*	Optical Carrier
CCITT	International Telegraph and Telephone Consultative Committee	OSI	Open Systems Interconnection
		RBOC	Regional Bell Operating Companies
CRC	Cyclic Redundancy Check	SDH	Synchronous Digital Hierarchy
DQDB	Distributed Queued Dual Bus	SMDS	Switched Multimegabit Data Service
FDDI	Fiber Distributed Data Interface	SNA	Systems Network Architecture
IEEE	Institute of Electrical and Electronics Engineers	SONET	Synchronous Optical Network
IXC	Interexchange Carrier	STM-*n*	Synchronous Transport Module
LAN	Local Area Network	STS-*n*	Synchronous Transport Signal
LAPD	Link Access Procedure-D Channel	TCP/IP	Transmission Control Protocol/Internet Protocol
LATA	Local Access Transport Area	VC	Virtual Channel
LEC	Local Exchange Carrier	VP	Virtual Path
MAN	Metropolitan Area Network		

Case 14-1

Toward a Needs Assessment Model for Telecommunications Managers

Jeffrey S. Harper, Robert G. Little, and Charles A. Snyder

INTRODUCTION

The past decade has been an unsettling time for many organizations. Technological change, changes in market demands, deregulation of many service industries, and competitive globalization have had substantial impact on the way firms do business. [5]

Many organizations have turned to information systems (IS) in an effort to maintain a viable business posture. Organizational information technology (IT) investments continue to grow at a rate substantially greater than economic growth, indicating the importance of IT to business managers. Effective implementation of an organization's information architecture can compress time and space and permit sharing of scarce corporate expertise. [22]

Information technology has become integrally linked to strategic planning in today's organizations. As managers have developed an awareness of this link between IT and competitive positioning, telecommunications (TC) technologies have become an important component in the business plan. The ability of firms to overcome many of the disadvantages associated with the geographic dispersion of national or international organizations through the use of the connectivity provided by TC is widely recognized. TC technologies, such as networking and electronic data interchange, also have been shown to positively contribute to organizational competitiveness. [4, 10, 12] Unfortunately, most firms are behind on linking TC and strategies.

The telecommunications industry has seen a plethora of new TC technologies, products, and services. Managers are experiencing the time compression of technological cycles between product generations. The rate of new product offerings has contributed to an ever-decreasing life cycle of systems, effectively reducing the period a system can be expected to be in service to just a few years. [8] As a result, decision space has become more confusing.

Managers of today's firms find themselves in the difficult position of trying to support their organization with telecommunications products and services offered by a complex and highly technical market. Although some TC managers are quite sophisticated, many others lack the rudimentary skills and knowledge necessary to confront current TC issues. In a proprietary study with which the authors are familiar, many of the TC managers interviewed were found to be without the TC knowledge, background, and, unfortunately, concern necessary to ensure strategic alignment with TC capabilities. Research has indicated that responsibility for TC-related activities may be only one of several job duties required of the individual. For example, a facilities management or maintenance manager may oversee TC activities. Further, TC and IS activities may be separated, reflecting the organization's separation of data processing and data communications from voice communications. [17] In such instances, the manager may feel overwhelmed by his or her own lack of ability to fully assess TC needs in the face of the myriad of TC products and services available and an ever-growing number of vendors willing to supply different combinations of these products and services. Recent deregulation of the TC industry will further muddy the waters and cause more confusion as the result of even more choices available to the TC manager.

While there are exhaustive sources for analysis and design for IS, these sources are generally intended for modernizing or upgrading computer-based systems. As such, they do not necessarily target networking or other TC technologies. There is a need for a parallel, systematic process for TC.

This paper is intended as a first step in building a normative model for guiding managers that endeavor to align their organization's TC capabilities with the firm's business strategies. The first phase of this normative model appears to be a needs assessment, similar to the requirements analysis phase of the traditional analysis and design process for IS.

Although researchers have given the telecommunications field considerable attention in recent years, needs assessment is rarely mentioned and never defined. For the purposes of this study, the term *needs assessment* is defined as *an integrated set of procedures that provide the basis for an action plan, whereby user needs can be efficiently addressed in a cost-effective manner consistent with organizational goals and objectives*. The purpose of this paper is to identify the component elements and structure of a needs assessment process that can be used by TC managers.

METHOD

The study includes four phases. In the first phase, we asked a focus group of managers with TC responsibilities in different organizations questions relating to how they went about determining what products and services to use. The purpose of this phase was to determine if any type of structured needs assessment process was currently in place. The second phase consisted of a combination of (1) a cross-field review of the literature on needs assessments and (2) semistructured, personal interviews of managers with TC responsibilities in different organizations through a sample of convenience. In the third phase, the findings of the literature review and personal interviews were synthesized in order to provide a basis for the fourth phase—the development of a needs assessment process that can be used by TC managers. Figure 1 depicts the research method applied to this study.

REVIEW OF LITERATURE

A survey of current publications identified the existing documentation on and common characteristics of needs assessments across multiple disciplines. A keyword search of a large business publications database produced a listing of 37 articles that made mention of the term *needs assessment.* Of these, 18 were not applicable to this study because the term *needs assessment* was only superficial, not an integral part of the article. Therefore, 19 articles from a variety of industries or functional areas were used in this study. These articles dealt with needs assessments to different extents. In 14, the needs assessment was the primary focus of the article, while in five needs assessment was mentioned as a peripheral, support, or secondary issue. Eleven of the articles were applicable to business in general, while eight were directed toward such diverse fields as health care, real estate, military operations, education, manufacturing, high-tech industries, public safety management, and training and development.

To ensure that no pertinent elements addressed in the literature were inadvertently omitted, the authors reviewed the articles independently. Their separate inputs were then synthesized to form a consolidated listing of the important factors of a needs assessment. Disagreement on classification was resolved through discussion to arrive at a consensus.

INTERVIEWS WITH TC MANAGERS

Interviews with managers with TC responsibilities were conducted to match the key issues identified by practitioners with the generic listing of the common elements of a needs assessment. The title, responsibilities, and a description of the employer organization for each of the individuals interviewed are shown in Table 1.

FIGURE 1
**Depiction of
Research Method**

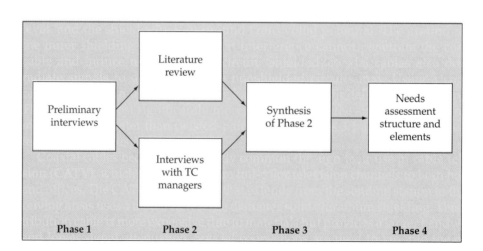

Each interview was conducted at the manager's office. Table 2 lists the open-ended questions each manager was asked concerning his or her telecommunications responsibilities.

Information from the interviews and literature review were subjected to content analysis in an attempt to identify common themes that would be useful in developing an exploratory needs assessment model that would be applicable to TC managers. The themes were then grouped to indicate a series of chronological steps indicating a model that would be appropriate in performing a needs assessment. Conclusions concerning the model and implications of the study were discussed.

FINDINGS

The preliminary interviews were conducted to determine if a needs assessment was currently being used by the TC managers. In each case, the managers indicated they usually reacted to a request for additional services or capabilities from organization members, frequently relying on a major vendor to supply a (hopefully) cost-effective solution. The managers rarely attempted to anticipate future needs, opting instead to satisfy current requests only. There was no indication a structured or systematic procedure for needs assessment was available.

TABLE 1
Characteristics of Interviewees

Title	Responsibilities	Employer Organization
Executive vice president for administrative support services	Management of 85-person department responsible for supplying administrative (i.e., MIS, accounting, scheduling, personnel, clerical, etc.) services to the Engineering Production function	High-tech contractor, aerospace division, 900+employees housed in seven buildings. Corporate office located in another U.S. region.
Dean of financial affairs	Management of 37-person staff covering business office, facilities/maintenance, MIS	Two-year junior college of approximately 5,500 students and 100 faculty.
Office manager	Management of 11-person staff responsible for all business functions and clerical support	Regional law firm operating in three cities. Home office: seven lawyers, six support staff. Branch #1: four lawyers, three support staff. Branch #2: three lawyers, two support staff.
Dean of academic affairs	Management of 83 faculty and 12 faculty support staff	Upper-level public senior college with approximately 3,300+students.

TABLE 2
Open-Ended Interview Questions

- What are your TC responsibilities?
- Do you use some sort of structured format to assist you in deciding when and what TC services/products to implement? If not, what procedure do you now use?
- Do you see a use for a structured needs assessment?
- What are some of the things you think a needs assessment should include?

Other fields typically use needs assessments as a basis for action plans. A total of 11 industries or functional areas were represented by the needs assessment literature. Table 3 lists the articles addressing each of these industries/functional areas. Our review of the literature identified several factors that were listed as important elements of a successful needs assessment. Table 4 categorizes these factors by the 11 industry or functional areas represented in the literature. *Interviews with users/customers* was listed most frequently as an important element in a needs assessment (7 of the 11 categories). This finding is consistent with our interviews with TC managers and vendors.

The second most frequently identified elements were *use of questionnaires* and *issuance of a formal report*, each included in 6 of the 11 categories. *Use of questionnaires* referred to surveying employees across organizational levels and functions, while *issuance of a formal report* was considered as a necessary and concluding element to inform management of findings and recommendations. Neither of these elements was mentioned by the majority of our interviewees. However, one manager did mention that she felt some method of capturing the full spectrum of employee needs would be especially beneficial in her particular situation.

The next most frequently mentioned elements were *group discussion* and *determination of priorities*. These factors were mentioned in the literature for 4 of the 11 categories. *Group discussions* were identified as an important way to involve individuals with differing backgrounds in the needs assessment process, thereby ensuring all points of view are considered. *Group discussion* also was mentioned as an effective way of generating alternatives when new products or services are considered.

Determination of priorities refers to rank-ordering needs so that resources may be allocated in a manner consistent with budgetary constraints. Several interviewees stated that cost–benefit analysis was performed on individual project proposals; however, comparisons between project proposals were not usually conducted. Rather, each individual project was evaluated on its own merits, regardless of its impact on other projects.

Use of outside consultants, compilation of data, attaining management commitment, analysis of results, determination of user/customer needs and requirements, and *positive return on investment* were identified as important factors in 3 of the 11 categories. *Use of outside consultants* was considered important because the organization sometimes

TABLE 3
Publications Representing the 11 Industry/Functional Areas

Industry/Functional Area	Publication Reference(s)
Government agency	[8, 11]
Human resource management/training	[13, 16, 20, 23]
Industry association	[14]
High-tech industry	[1, 6]
Health care	[21, 24]
Education/training	[19]
Real estate/facility management	[2]
Corporate training	[3, 7, 9]
Industrial sales	[18]
Professional association	[15]
Educational institution	[25]

TABLE 4 Needs Assessment Factors across Industry/Function Categories from Review of Literature

	Gov't Agency	HRM/ Training	Industry Assocs.	High-Tech Industry	Health Care	Education/ Training	Real Estate/ Facility Mgmt	Corporate Training	Industrial Sales	Profess'l Associations	Educational Institutions	Total
Interviews	x		x		x	x		x				5
Group discussion	x				x	x			x			4
Formal report	x	x			x			x	x			5
Outside consultants	x			x	x							3
Hard data			x									1
Expectations								x				1
Prior research				x					x			2
ID data sources				x					x			2
Data compilation	x			x					x			3
Use of statistics				x					x			2
Needs vs. strategic plan		x					x					2
Internal vs. external sources		x			x							2
Assessment goals		x							x			2
Management commitment		x					x				x	3
Methodology		x				x						2
Assess. control and administration		x										1
Analysis of results		x			x		x					3
Review of job functions			x			x						2
Interview providers/ vendors			x									1
Test system before use			x					x				2
Technical audit			x									1
Available funding							x					1
Continuous assess't cycle					x					x		2
Technol. risks/ opportunities							x					1

(continued)

TABLE 4 Needs Assessment Factors across Industry/Function Categories from Review of Literature—*continued*

	Gov't Agency	HRM/Training	Industry Assocs.	High-Tech Industry	Health Care	Education/Training	Real Estate/Facility Mgmt	Corporate Training	Industrial Sales	Profess'l Associations	Educational Institutions	Total
User needs/requirements					x	x	x					3
Competitor information		x										1
Priorities determination	x				x			x			x	4
Nature of problem									x	x		2
Collaboration/partnership			x									1
Current results vs. expectations						x						1
Positive ROI				x			x		x			3
Questionnaires	x	x			x	x		x		x		6

lacks expertise in a technical area, skill in conducting a needs assessment, or the necessary objectivity to make difficult choices. Interviews confirmed that many TC managers prefer to rely on trusted vendors to supply solutions to user needs. Each TC manager interviewed stated that often his or her first action in response to a request for a new product or service was to contact a vendor for assistance in determining how best to deal with the request.

The literature considered *compilation of data* an important part of any needs assessment. The premise here appears to be more information makes for a better decision. This element includes organizing and synthesizing data into pertinent information so that informed judgments can be made. The interviewees made no mention of how or when they gathered and complied data.

Attaining management commitment includes two aspects. First, management must be convinced that a needs assessment is necessary. Second, management must agree that the findings and recommendations of the completed needs assessment will receive appropriate consideration in the decision-making process. Because none of our interviewees currently use a needs assessment methodology, management commitment was not at issue.

Another important factor identified in the literature, *analysis of results*, deals with the implementation of the findings of the needs assessment. Cost–benefit analysis, *positive return on investment*, user satisfaction surveys, and analysis of strategic "fit" with the organization's mission, vision, values, and goals are some of the more prominent methods of analysis mentioned in various articles. Procedures currently used by the TC managers we interviewed seldom included these types of analyses. Because the managers usually selected the first acceptable alternative presented to them, fulfillment of needs and strategic "fit" were assumed. One TC manager, however, indicated that he had experienced a situation where two implementations for separate departments conflicted with each other. The implementations were incompatible and not interoperable, causing suboptimization from a total organizational perspective. Each implementation had seemed like a fine idea when considered separately.

Determination of user/customer needs and requirements can be accomplished through *questionnaires, interviews,* or *group meetings,* three items already discussed. This determination is one of the primary foci of the needs assessment; however, our interviewees cautioned us that *user needs and requirements* often can be a never-ending "wish list." The TC manager must ensure *user needs and requirements* must be aligned with organizational goals through a *determination of priorities.*

The review of literature also identified other items considered important to the needs assessment process. However, these factors were listed in only one or two instances, as compared with the above factors that were identified as important across three or more categories of industry/function. These included *uses of hard data, identify expectations, identify data sources, compare needs vs. strategic plan, assessment goals, assessment control and administration, review of job functions, technical audit, available funding, current results vs. expectations,* and *continuous assessment cycle.*

STEPS IN THE NEEDS ASSESSMENT PROCESS

Further analysis of the needs assessment literature identified a series of sequential steps involved to complete the entire process. Table 5 lists the steps involved in a needs assessment. We have included the factors identified in the above section in the appropriate step.

TABLE 5
The Steps of a
Needs Assessment

Performing a needs assessment includes the following steps:
- Define objectives and scope of the assessment.
  Attain management commitment
  Assessment goals
  Determination of priorities
  Identify expectations
- Identify users, products, and services to include in the assessment.
  Identify data sources
  Use of outside consultants
- Determine user needs/requirements.
  Interviews with users/customers
  Review of job functions
  Use of questionnaires
  Group discussions
- Evaluate needs with respect to organizational goals.
  Compare needs vs. strategic plan
  Available funding
- Measure current resource allocation to product/service delivery.
  Assessment control and administration
  Technical audit
  Current results vs. expectations
- Analyze the data.
  Use of hard data
  Compilation of data
  Positive return on investment
- Include key findings in the decision-making process.
  Issuance of a formal report
  Continuous assessment cycle

CONCLUSIONS AND IMPLICATIONS

Table 5 identifies a seven-step process that can be used by a TC manager as a basis for determining appropriate *proactive* actions associated with providing TC products and services to his or her firm. We have associated the key elements identified in the literature and through our interviews of TC managers with the appropriate step of the assessment.

Additional research to validate the procedure for needs assessment as identified here is warranted. From a telecommunications perspective, many important elements listed in each step may be further defined and expanded. A study linking strategic direction to product and service alternatives would be helpful, as well.

This study indicates TC managers pursue a generally reactive strategy to implementing new products and services. TC managers can become proactive in their actions. The needs assessment instrument is one tool that can be of assistance in this endeavor.

REFERENCES

1. Bacon, G.; S. Beckman; D. Mowery; and E. Wilson. "Managing Product Definition in High-Technology Industries: A Pilot Study." *California Management Review* 36, no. 3 (1994), pp. 32–56.

2. Brown, R.; P. Lapides; and E. Rondeau. "Corporate Policy Is Part of RE/FM Planning." *Facilities Design and Management* 13, no. 7 (1994), pp. 50–53

3. Cline, E., and P. Seibert. "Help for First-Time Needs Assessors." *Training and Development* 47, no. 5 (1993), pp. 99–101.

4. Dearing, B. "The Strategic Benefits of EDI." *The Journal of Business Strategy* 11, no. 1 (1990), pp. 4–6.

5. Dowling, M.; W. Boulton; and S. Elliott. "Strategies for Change in the Service Sector: The Global Telecommunications Industry." *California Management Review* 36, no. 3 (1994), pp. 57–88.

6. Durkin, N. "Total Research Quality Management Process at Vista Chemical Company." *Industrial Engineering* 26, no. 1 (1994), pp. 30–31.

7. Fitz-Enz, J. "Yes . . . You Can Weigh Training's Value." *Training* 31, no. 7 (1994), pp. 54–58.

8. Gallelli, J. "Changes in Public Safety Technology Management." *Communications* 31, no. 4 (1994), p. 80.

9. Goldstein, I. *Training in Organizations: Needs Assessment, Development, and Evaluation.* Pacific, Grove, CA: Brooks/Cole Publishing Company, 1993.

10. Grover, V. "An Empirically Derived Model for the Adoption of Customer-Based Interorganizational Systems." *Decision Sciences* 24, no. 3 (1993), pp. 603–640.

11. Hubble, L., and R. Green. "State Training Needs Assessment." *The Public Manager* 21, no. 2 (1992), pp. 33–36.

12. Kaufman, F. "Data Systems That Cross Company Boundaries." *Harvard Business Review* 44, no. 1 (1966), pp. 141–155.

13. Kaufman, R. "Auditing Your Needs Assessment." *Training and Development* 48, no. 2 (1994), pp. 22–23.

14. Kavanaugh, E. "Get Computer Literate." *Association Management* 46, no. 4 (1994), pp. 42–45+.

15. Macenski, A. "A Vision for the Future." *Professional Safety* 39, no. 5 (1994), pp. 7, 56.

16. McClelland, S. "A Systems Approach to Needs Assessment." *Training and Development* 46, no. 8 (1992), pp. 51–53.

17. McCreary, Jerry Dale. "Alternative local telecommunications services: an experimental study of telecommunications manager's decision making processes." Unpublished doctoral dissertation, Auburn University, AL, 1994.

18. Monoky, J. "Want to Satisfy Your Customers' Needs?" *Industrial Distribution* 83, no. 6 (1994), p. 79.

19. "More Than 75 Ideas to Strengthen Your Educational Programs." *Association Management* 46, no. 11 (1994), pp. 60–64.

20. Rinholm, B. "Training for New-Product Staff Should Be 'Customer-Driven.'" *Marketing News* 28, no. 9 (1994), p. E11.

21. Roberts, C., and S. Shortell. "Are Today's Hospital CEOs Prepared to Lead Networks?" *Hospitals and Health Networks* 68, no. 15 (1994), p. 12.

22. Sankar, C.; U. Apte; and P. Palvia. "Global Information Architectures: Alternatives and Trade-offs." *International Journal of Information Management* 13, no. 2 (1993), pp. 84–93.

23. Schultz, J. "Align HR to Serve the Customer." *Personnel Journal* 74, no. 1 (1995), pp. 61–64.

24. Trocchio, J. "The Hows and Whys of Conducting a Community Needs Assessment." *Trustee* 47, no. 3 (1994), pp. 6–7+.

25. Wiggins, L. "Rutgers Expands Its Horizons." *Planning* 60, no. 4 (1994), p. 23.

Case 14-2

A New Look at Broadband Technologies

Jack Jackson

BACKGROUND

In order to explore new technologies in broadband that promise to have a dramatic impact on our future, it is first important to define broadband. Textbooks define broadband as transmission equipment and media that can support a wide bandwidth: an analog path that may be frequency-division multiplexed to create several channels; a high-speed digital path that may be time-division multiplexed to create multiple channels. [1] Simply stated, broadband technologies enable providers to deliver Internet and other telecommunications services in greater quantities and with faster speeds. Such services include high-speed data services, video phone, videoconferencing, high-resolution graphics transmission, and CATV services, along with such narrowband ISDN services as telephone, data, telemetry, and facsimile. [2] Thus, for this investigation of broadband technologies, we will define it as the enabler to provide convergent telecommunications service to customers.

MARKET OPPORTUNITIES

Broadband has become such a hot topic that *Fortune* magazine recently devoted almost an entire issue to its future infrastructure and potential uses. As *Fortune* points out, starting with the first deployments of fast online access a couple years ago to the next generation of wireless networks, the investment in broadband technologies amounts to over a trillion dollars. AT&T, for example, has spent $100 billion acquiring cable television lines in a bid to sell continuous streams of voice, video, and Net services. [3] Broadband investment is not only in the domestic market as evidenced by British cellular companies that pledged $35 billion to license airwaves for a new kind of speedy wireless service. [4]

The potential market for broadband service is enormous. Today, more than 100 million people are connected to the Internet; there are over one billion Web pages and 75 million host computers. The communications industry is experiencing rapid innovation and change. The industry is expected to grow 8 to 10 percent annually, which is three to four times the growth of the economy. Commerce on the Internet, barely a blip a few years ago, could surpass $300 billion by 2002. Wireless phones have gone from being a novelty to a necessity. It took radio 30 years to reach 50 million people. It took 13 years for TV to do the same. But the World Wide Web reached twice as many users in half the time. In four years, experts project 250 million users around the world. [5] The need for speed and new services has never been greater.

MARKET STRATEGIES/DELIVERY STRATEGIES

There are primarily three different means of delivering broadband services: via cable, Digital Subscriber Line (DSL), or fixed wireless. Each has its own set of advantages and disadvantages as well as risk and potential reward.

Most cable operators began experimenting with high-speed data services in the mid-1990s, but coaxial cable networks then were built to broadcast information in only one direction; connecting to the Internet means upgrading networks to accommodate two-way traffic. Today, broadband cable is actually a mix of coaxial cable and fiber (hybrid fiber-coax). You connect your computer to a special cable modem; data travel from your house along a coaxial cable that runs to a neighborhood node, where it connects with fiber. From there data travel to a head end, where signals are processed for fast transmission or delivery. [6]

Cable operator's like AT&T have a strong lead over their phone company counterparts. By the end of the year, there will be about 4 million cable-modem subscribers, compared with 1.7 million telephone company DSL subscribers. Cable services have faster speeds than DSL and fixed wireless, advertising speeds of three million bits per second, which is about 50 times faster than a 56K dial-up modem. [7] One drawback of cable modems, however is that if many homes in a neighborhood share the coaxial part of the network, it can significantly slow down traffic. It is also very expensive for providers to build the infrastructure. For example, AT&T is spending an additional $2.5 billion to upgrade its cable lines for telephone and broadband services.

Qwest Communications CEO Joseph Nacchio is taking a different approach, providing broadband services through traditional twisted-pair copper wires with a technology known as Digital Subscriber Lines (DSL). Developed over a decade or so ago (pre-Internet), DSL ships data and voice traffic across a phone line to a box at the central office known as a DSLAM. The DSLAM and the terminator at the residence convert the analog line to digital, pump up the capacity of the copper line to the customer, and route traffic between the Internet and the home.

The predominance of copper wires gives DSL an advantage over cable as far as access is concerned, but there are several drawbacks. Customers who live more than three miles from the central office can't get the service; the DSL signal degrades if it has to travel long distances on copper. Companies are trying to fix this problem by augmenting copper wires with fiber-optic cables and remote switches in distant neighborhoods, a kind of hybrid fiber/copper. DSL likewise can be limited through electromagnetic interference. DSL does not match the speed of cable modems but the investment is much less with already a mostly installed infrastructure and customer base. On the positive side, the DSL from the central office to the residence is a dedicated line and the bandwidth is not shared. Sharing occurs only at a point of mixing channels.

Sprint is attempting to take advantage of the third main avenue to providing broadband services: through fixed wireless networks. The technology, known as multipoint multichannel distribution system, or MMDS, allows customers to send and receive fairly robust streams of data between a central broadcast tower and small antennas affixed to their homes. Information from the Internet flows across fiber to Sprint's local head end; from there it is routed—sometimes via fiber, sometimes via microwave—to the big central tower, where data are transmitted to the intended home antennas. [8] A cable links the home antenna to a special modem for the service.

One major drawback with fixed wireless is that buildings, trees, or hills sometimes block the signal between the tower and the home antennas. Also, like the cable networks, fixed wireless is shared and multiple users can slow access. Existing fixed wireless systems are not as fast as their wired counterparts but within a few years it is estimated that speeds will be improved to 2.4 million bits per second or about 42 times the speed of a 56K modem. With these speeds the portable advantages of wireless can be quickly realized (i.e., mobile commerce). Another method of fixed wireless is via satellite, which solves some of the issues mentioned above but has some inherent speed and access problems as well.

Broadband service does not begin and end with the three means mentioned above. Cable modems, DSL, and fixed wireless are now the most common means of delivering broadband but can be surpassed by newer technologies. There is already much talk of using Ethernet technology, which is a well-established computer-networking technology that could be expanded over fiber-optic cables.

AT&T'S BROADBAND STRATEGY

AT&T's broadband strategy is based on the idea of convergence. Convergence is the coming together of technologies to provide one solution for a single customer. By providing a range of high-speed voice, data, Internet, cable TV, and wireless services, carriers hope to gain added customer loyalty, higher profit margins, and increased competitiveness. AT&T is among the carriers that believe IT managers want a partnership with a one-stop shop, so the long-distance company is recasting itself as an integrated communication service provider. "AT&T's strategic direction is any place, any distance, any way, any time," says Mike Jenner, AT&T's VP and general manager of IP Network Services. [9]

To fulfill this vision, AT&T is building infrastructure, buying competitors, and entering partnerships. By early next year, for example, AT&T will deliver local phone service over cable through a partnership with cable TV company Insight Communications Co. As the local exchange carrier, AT&T will install and maintain the needed switching equipment in Insight's markets. [10]

AT&T is currently the nation's largest broadband services company, providing television entertainment services to about 16 million customers across the nation. AT&T's centerpiece product offering is AT&T@Home, which is a revolutionary new service provided via broadband technology that enables customers to enjoy the Internet with easy access to the hottest content at unprecedented speeds. [11] Subscribers receive 24-hour unlimited access to the Internet, a high-speed cable modem, a customized browser, a menu of local community content, three private email addresses, 15 megabytes of Web space for personal home pages, remote email from any Internet connection, and access to news and chat groups. [12]

CEO C. Michael Armstrong described AT&T's strategy recently in a speech. "Our Internet and telephone customers will get better service and better performance at equivalent or lower prices. Our broadband customer's Internet connection is always available and always on, more like TV or radio. Customers get almost instantaneous access to any Web page. No more jokes about 'point-click—and wait.' " [13]

NEW BROADBAND TECHNOLOGIES—WIRELESS

Broadband's capabilities, especially increased speed, are creating opportunities for new services that eventually will change the way we work and live. These new services range from entertainment offerings to enhanced tools for business.

One major area that wireless broadband technology will impact dramatically is the concept of M-commerce. The "M" stands for mobile commerce and it is the equivalent of eCommerce over mobile wireless technologies. M-commerce allows the marketplace to be more dynamic and to have no physical barriers. Many M-commerce services will spread rapidly across the planet once third-generation (3G) wireless technologies allow much larger chunks of data, including video, to be downloaded at greatly enhanced speed. [14]

A new technology, ultra-wideband, uses wireless technology for a variety of services including detecting burglars or finding earthquake survivors behind walls, determining a golf ball's distance from the hole, or sending high-speed data among home computers. A company named Time Domain based in Huntsville, Alabama, is commercializing this technology.

Ultra-wideband uses extremely low-power radio pulses and sends at such a low power and across a broad frequency range—and because the pulses are so short (half a billionth of a second)—receivers listening for transmission at specific frequencies perceive them as mere background noise, as low-level signals that exist almost everywhere and that are almost universally ignored as long as they don't interfere with reception. Time Domain's system sends out 40 million pulses a second. Delaying or advancing a pulse by a few trillionths of a second defines it as a 1 or 0, creating a short-range data carrier capable of transmitting up to 10 megabits a second or more. [15]

Other uses emerge from the fact that pulses moving at the speed of light travel about one foot in a billionth of a second. By measuring the delay in the arrival of an expected pulse, distance from the transmitter to receiver can be determined, making UWB an ideal position locator. [16]

NEW BROADBAND TECHNOLOGIES AVAILABLE BY CABLE MODEMS AND DSL

What impact will cable modems and DSL technologies have on the economy? According to a report issued by *Research* (April 1999), "Broadband will propel consumer spending to $20 billion per year. Overall spending will increase by 19 percent annually over the next five years, from $9.9 billion in 1999 to $19.9 billion in 2003." [17]

Both cable modems and DSL offer a plethora of new services, including increased ability to telecommute, interactive distance learning, telemedicine, film/video on demand, broadcast-quality audio/video conferencing, and online collaborative work teams.

Currently 24.7 percent of U.S. households conduct business from home according to a U.S. IDC Report Residential Telecom Survey. With increased Internet access and higher speeds through broadband this number could grow dramatically over the next several years.

Distance learning also can be greatly enhanced through broadband technologies. Instead of waiting several days to receive videotapes via the mail, Auburn University MBA outreach students could access Webcasts via the Internet in real time or whenever time allows. Collaboration tools could be used more frequently to connect outreach students with in-class students for a richer learning experience. These technologies all exist today and broadband provides the ability to make it a reality.

Even companies like NBC are looking to get into the broadband market to provide a wide range of services via DSL. NBC's Internet division, NBCi, will invest $70 million in Telocity for a nearly 20 percent stake in the company.

The Telocity system, which allows users to plug a standard telephone wire into a traditional telephone jack to receive DSL signals, potentially eliminates the need for telephone companies to dispatch technicians to install high-speed equipment for each new high-speed subscriber. In the process, it gives NBCi a way to establish itself as a portal of choice on a computerlike system that over time could evolve into a new breed of digital media server for the home.

The Telocity box, for instance, could be programmed to store music files downloaded from the Web to play on an in-home stereo system. "Clearly, we've been looking for an environment to deliver a high-quality video experience," NBCi President and Chief Operating Officer Edmond Sanctis said. "As we think about convergence, this goes toward the idea of becoming a gateway into the home." [18]

CONCLUSION

There are numerous examples that highlight the potential broadband technologies have to reshape our lives and the global economy. In my research I have tried to explain the underlying technologies, discuss the market potential, describe one company's approach, and provide examples of new services associated with broadband.

All of this points toward the concept of convergence where broadband technologies are enabling different services to be bundled and new partnerships to form. As the AT&T example demonstrates, the investment in broadband is enormous; however, I get the feeling that the payoffs will be equally enormous.

REFERENCES

1. Houston Carr and Charles Snyder, *The Management of Telecommunications* (Burr Ridge, IL: Irwin/McGraw-Hill, 1997).

2. Ibid.

3. Stephanie Mehta, "The Trillion Dollar Bet," *Fortune*, October 2, 2000.

4. Ibid.

5. C. Michael Armstrong, "Telecom and Cable TV: Shared Prospects for the Communications Future," *Speech*, November 2, 1998.

6. Mehta, "The Trillion Dollar Bet."

7. Ibid.

8. Ibid.

9. Candee Wilde, "Telcos Answer Customers' Calls for More Services," *Informationweek.com*, August 21, 2000.

10. Ibid.

11. Chris Bona, "AT&T Cable Services Showcases High Tech Internet & Video Products at the Chicago Auto Show," AT&T Press Release, February 8, 2000.

12. Ibid.

13. Armstrong, "Telecom and Cable TV."

14. Mehta, "The Trillion Dollar Bet."

15. Robert Poe, "Super-Max-Extra-Ultra-Wideband!" *Business2.0.com,* October 10, 2000.

16. Ibid.

17. "The Promise Land of Broadband," *available at* http://ipservices.att.com, October 14, 2000.

18. Steven Vonder Haar, "News," *Inter@active Week*, December 20, 1999.

Summary

This chapter makes the transition from what we now use for data communications to what we will be using in the very near future. As organizations realize they need to use data communications more for VIVID applications and as they accept convergence of these technologies, their need for higher bandwidth will become apparent. While banks and grocery stores can now manage 500 branches with 9.6 Kbps X.25 digital channels, they will need to migrate to broader bandwidth in order to move from text-only applications to software download and multimedia applications.

DSL and ISDN allow LECs and IXCs to use existing infrastructures while moving from an analog to a digital environment and to provide bandwidth beyond modem speeds. ADSL has the potential to bring bandwidth in excess of T1 to the home and office, even moving this local-loop-based technology to 30 Mbps bandwidth. This capability will make possible more offerings and potentially change the way businesses communicate and conduct business. Change begets change.

The standards for the truly high bandwidth technologies exist, but the hardware to support them is just emerging. Some hardware does exist, but the cost is still too high to encourage a large-scale move to that offering. Thus, it is not the technology pull that will cause the shift, but rather the convergency push that will make organizations adopt the faster speeds. Organizations that require broadband capabilities but can live with the inherent delays will probably move to the more reliable features of X.25, frame relay, and SMDS. With time, the cost of ATM on SONET will fall and the need for shorter delays will increase, making these the technologies of choice. During the transition, the IXCs will make the investment in ATM over SONET and share these costs with a broader base of customers. One present customer for this bandwidth is the Internet, those millions of people without supervision who wish to send multimedia files around the world in seconds or even play interactive computer games with competitors from any part of the globe.

The next chapter extends this subject of broadband technologies to and within the home. The home environment uses some of the office technologies, especially for SOHO. In addition, the trend towards telecommuting makes the home connectivity an integral part of many business decisions. Entertainment presently uses other technologies but will migrate to the same ones discussed above.

Key Terms

Asymmetric Digital Subscriber Line (ADSL), *640*

asynchronous transfer mode (ATM), *651*

basic rate interface ISDN (BRI ISDN), *631*

broadband integrated services digital network (BISDN), *642*

committed information rate (CIR), *651*

competitive access providers (CAPs), *649*

compression, *632*

computer-aided design (CAD), *632*

connection-oriented, *649*

connectionless, *646*

convergence, *632*

Digital Subscriber Line (DSL), *638*

fiber distributed data interface (FDDI), *655*

frame relay, *642*

high-data-rate Digital Subscriber Line (HDSL), *638*

integrated services digital network (ISDN), *631*

International Telegraph and Telephone Consultative Committee (CCITT), *642*

isochronous communications, *654*

narrowband integrated services digital network (NISDN), *631*

Open Systems Interconnection (OSI), *648*

overhead, *634*

permanent virtual channel (PVC), *643*

redundant array of inexpensive disks (RAID), *630*

switched-56, *631*

switched multimegabit data service (SMDS), *646*

synchronous optical network (SONET), *649*

Systems Network Architecture (SNA), *648*

T1, *637*

Discussion Questions

14.1. Why should a packet-switched network be considered in moving data?

14.2. What are the necessary characteristics of a global network that has large CAD files to transfer? What if the files are needed in color and 3-D?

14.3. What are the regulatory issues faced by telecommunications managers who are building global networks? What are possible cultural issues?

14.4. What are the broadband choices that corporate communications managers need to consider today?

14.5. List the broadband options and evaluate them from a cost-per-Mbps standpoint.

14.6. What are the emerging applications that might be considered bandwidth-hungry?

14.7. If an organization wishes to have teleconferencing and multimedia communications between three domestic locations and one in Mexico, what are the bandwidth needs?

14.8. What are the major issues that the telecommunications manager needs to be concerned with in making the broadband technology choices for a firm?

14.9. What changes in the telecommunications industry are driving the demand for further bandwidth?

14.10. How can EDI be impacted by the deployment of ATM technology?

14.11. What are the implications of free bandwidth?

14.12. Is JEI likely to be satisfied with VoIP over frame relay?

Projects

14.1. Refer to current issues of *Communications Week, Network Magazine,* and so on, and bring diagrams of global networks to class. Compare the networks and provide your evaluation as to their (1) reliability, (2) cost versus expense, (3) appropriateness, (4) technology, (5) adaptability, and (6) utility.

14.2. Evaluate the risks faced by a firm with a multinode global network. Classify the risks and highlight any special risks that result from a firm's global nature.

14.3. Why should telecommunications managers build dedicated global networks? Evaluate the advantages/disadvantages of outsourcing the networks versus building your own.

14.4. What are the present drivers that influence locating facilities outside the United States? Evaluate economic, technological, regulatory, and telecommunications-related factors.

14.5. Visit a hospital and determine how broadband telecommunications are employed. What applications demand the greatest bandwidth in medicine? Determine if "telemedicine" is practiced and the technologies that are applicable.

14.6. Contact both your LEC and an IXC and determine broadband alternatives that are tariffed.

14.7. Find a firm that has implemented a client-server LAN-based environment and access the changes in telecommunications traffic attributable to larger applications, increased routing, and network management. What bandwidth changes were required for these changes?

14.8. With firms undergoing business process re-engineering (BPR), there is frequently an increased emphasis on work-group communications. Locate a company that has undergone BPR and determine what problems or challenges in communications were encountered and the firm's solutions. What does the telecommunications manager plan for the network that required increasing use of broadband?

14.9. Research the Ford Motor Company's use of broadband in its global teleconferencing system. What technologies are presently employed and what are the bandwidth requirements now and planned for the future? Determine the history of this system and the reported results obtained by its use.

14.10. Write a short report on the evolution of the information superhighway. Include the origin of such metaphors as *road-kill, speed bumps, tollbooths, super-hypeway*, and *pit stops*. What would the model of the information superhighway look like from the perspective of telecommunications vendors, the CATV industry, and the user community?

Problems

The homework doesn't have some of the data fields you should use, which are the same as in the examples in Chapter 14. Use 8 bytes for sales when only total sales are sent; otherwise use 6 bytes for sales by category, SKU, and so forth. Use 6 bytes for the number of items and use the SKU size as in the book, for example, 14 bytes. In other category-type fields, use numbers only and choose the number of bytes you need for the field. In Problems 14.5 and 14.6, it asks for speed of modem. Use standard speeds and choose the lowest you can allow.

Hint: Always draw the data fields and the data lines.

14.1. We have a bidirectional circuit on fibre. We wish to create telephone channels for 100 employees. We will use statistical multiplexing, which means that we need only 45 channels to serve the 100 employees. Using ADPCM, how much digital bandwidth do we need?

14.2. Regional headquarters of *Arby's* wants to receive data each night from each franchise as to the *total dollar value of sales* it made for that day. (For all of these questions, disregard setup time for the circuit.) How long will it take each franchise to send the information? (Designate the data fields; use a 28.8 Kbps mode.) _____ seconds for each franchise. _____ seconds total for the region with 13 franchises.

14.3. Now the regional manager of *Arby's* wants each franchise to send nightly the *total sales by each of six categories* of foods. How long will it take each franchise to send the information? (Designate the data fields; use a 28.8 Kbps mode.) _____ seconds for each franchise. _____ seconds total for the region with 13 franchises.

14.4. Moving right along, now send the *total sales for each of the 17 items within each of the six categories*. How long will it take each franchise to send the information? (Designate the data fields; use a 28.8 Kbps mode.) _____ seconds for each franchise. _____ seconds total for the region with 13 franchises.

14.5. *Big Lots* has a number of stores in the United States. Until now, they have used cash registers and sent tapes in at the end of the week. The regional headquarters then moved the data from the tapes to the computer. Now the Southeast Region wants each of the 127 stores in its region to be connected at the end of the day and upload data for total sales and units sold for each of 7,564 items (SKUs), if there were sales within that SKU. (Prices vary by store.) How long will it take each store to send the information? (Designate the data fields; use a 28.8 Kbps mode.) _____ seconds for each franchise. _____ seconds total for the region.

14.6. As a trial, the regional manager wants the store in Auburn to have its two POS registers working online with the computer in Atlanta. What speed modem or circuit will be required if the average for each register is 14 customers per hour during peak times, with an average of nine items per customer? Same data requirements apply as in Problem 14.4. _____

14.7. The *Dillards* store at the mall wants to have interactive transactions with all terminals in the store and the central regional computer. The store carries

17,500 SKUs and has 21 terminals in the store; prices are stored in the computer and must be retrieved for the customer receipt. During peak hours there are an average of nine customers per terminal per hour, and each customer has an average of seven items. What speed modem or circuit will be required? _____

14.8. A clean twisted-pair copper wire circuit has been installed from the cable television provider to your home. Divide the circuit into its theoretical maximum of 250 analog POTS-wide channels and operate each with a 14.4 Kbps modem equivalent. Can you deliver a digitized television channel of 4 Mbps to your home? If so, how many channels? _____ No _____ Yes = _____ channels

14.9. The cable television provider, the phone company, or the electric utility has installed a fiber cable to your home to provide television. Initially they will offer digitized standard channels with HDTV later. The protocol of the fiber is SONET and the switching protocol is ATM. Using the OC-3/STS-3 rate, the overhead associated with ATM, and a bandwidth of 4 Mbps per channel, and assuming no delay though switching or transfer on SONET, how many channels can this circuit deliver simultaneously? _____ channels

References

1. Aber, Robyn. "An SMDS Glossary." *Business Communications Review,* June 1992 supplement SMDS, pp. 30–31.
2. Aber, Robyn. "SMDS Service One Year after Kickoff." *Business Communications Review*, June 1993, pp. 51–54.
3. Aber, Robyn. "SMDS Solves Users' Needs." *SMDS Today: Networks in Action*, pp. 2, 5–6, 8, 10, 14.
4. Ali, M. Irfan. "Frame Relay in Public Networks." *IEEE Communications Magazine*, March 1992, pp. 72–78.
5. Bell, Trudy E. "Telecommunications." *IEEE Spectrum*, January 1991, pp. 44–47.
6. "Broadband Transition." *Communications News*, October 1993, p. 6.
7. Byrne, William R.; George Clapp; Henry J. Kafka; Gottfried W. R. Luderer; and Bruce L. Nelson. "Evolution of Metropolitan Area Networks to Broadband ISDN." *IEEE Communications Magazine*, January 1991, pp. 69–70ff.
8. Chen, Tai. "Frame Relay, SMDS, and HSCS: Comparing Features and Performance." *Telecommunications*, May 1992, pp. 19–20, 22.
9. Cheung, Nim K. "The Infrastructure for Gigabit Computer Networks." *IEEE Communications Magazine*, April 1992, pp. 60–68.
10. Ching, Yau-Chau, and H. Sabit Say. "SONET Implementation." *IEEE Communications Magazine*, September 1993, pp. 34–40.
11. Clarkson, Mark. "All-Terrain Networking." *Byte*, August 1993, pp. 111–114, 116.
12. Clarkson, Mark A. "Hitting Warp Speed for LANs." *Byte*, March 1993, pp. 123–124, 126, 128.
13. Cox, Tracy; Frances Dix; Christine Hemrick; and Josephine McRoberts. "SMDS: The Beginning of WAN Superhighways." *Data Communications*, April 1991, pp. 105–108, 110.
14. Crowl, Steve. "ATM for Multiservice Wide Area Networks." *Business Communications Review*, February 1993 supplement ATM, pp. 11–15.
15. Dagres, Todd. "Frame Relay's Day Will Dawn." *Business Communications Review*, April 1993, pp. 28–32.

16. Delisle, Dominique, and Lionel Pelamourgues. "B-ISDN and How It Works." *IEEE Spectrum*, August 1991, pp. 39–42.

17. Finneran, Michael. "The Impact of SONET on Network Planning." *Business Communications Review*, June 1992, pp. 51–55.

18. Finneran, Michael. "SONET: Access to the World." *Business Communications Review*, July 1993, pp. 62–63.

19. Frame, Mike. "Broadband Service Needs." *IEEE Communications Magazine*, April 1990, pp. 59–62.

20. Garciamendez-Budar, Edsel. "The Emergence of Frame Relay in Public Data Networks." *Telecommunications*, May 1992, pp. 24, 26, 28, 30, 32.

21. Gasman, Lawrence. "The Broadband Jigsaw Puzzle." *Business Communications Review*, February 1993, pp. 35–39.

22. Giancarlo, Charles. "Making the Transition from T3 to SONET." *Telecommunications*, April 1992, pp. 17–20.

23. Gupta, Sudhir. "Interworking: Frame Relay, SMDS, and Cell Relay." *Telecommunications*, February 1993 supplement InteNet, pp. 51–52, 57.

24. "Industry Outlook: Multimedia and the Future of Communications." *Telecommunications*, April 1992, p. 10.

25. Johnson, Johna Till. "SMDS: Out of the Lab and Onto the Network." *Data Communications*, October 1992, pp. 71–72, 74, 76, 78, 80, 82.

26. Karpinski, Richard. "The Bell Tolls for LEC Data Strategies." *Telephony*, February 1, 1993, pp. 34, 38, 40.

27. Kessler, Gary C. *ISDN*. 2nd ed. New York: McGraw-Hill, 1993.

28. Kleinrock, Leonard. "ISDN—The Path to Broadband Networks." *Proceedings of the IEEE*, February 1991, pp. 112–117.

29. Lee, Byeong Gi; Minho Kang; and Jonghee Lee. *Broadband Telecommunications Technology*. Norwood, MA: Artech House, Inc., 1993.

30. Lowe, Sue J. "Data Communications." *IEEE Spectrum*, January 1992, pp. 39–41.

31. McQuillan, John. "Keeping ATM's Promise of Scalability." *Business Communications Review*, October 1993, pp. 10, 12.

32. McQuillan, John. "SMDS: Home Run or Strikeout?" *Business Communications Review*, July 1990, pp. 14–15.

33. McQuillan, John. "Why ATM?" *Business Communications Review*, February 1993 supplement ATM, pp. 1, 3.

34. Miller, Thomas C. "SONET and BISDN: A Marriage of Technologies." *Telephony*, May 15, 1989, pp. 32–35, 38.

35. Mollenauer, James F. "The Impact of ATM on Local and Wide Area Networks." *Telecommunications*, March 1993 supplement InteNet, pp. 35, 38–39, 42–43.

36. O'Brien, Bob, and Dolores Kazanjian. "Sprint Plans All-SONET Network." *Telecommunications*, March 1993, pp. 9, 10.

37. Schriftgiesser, Dave. "SMDS: A Phone Service for Computers." *Business Communications Review*, June 1992 supplement SMDS, pp. 4–9.

38. Schriftgiesser, Dave, and Roger Levy. "SMDS vs. Frame Relay: An Either/Or Decision?" *Business Communications Review*, September 1991, pp. 59–63.

39. Sinnreich, Henry, and John F. Bottomley. "Any-to-Any Networking: Getting There from Here." *Data Communications*, September 1992, pp. 69–72, 74, 76, 78, 80.

40. "SMDS Now, ATM Later?" *Data Communications*, June 1992, p. 18.

41. "SMDS, SONET and ATM." *Business Communications Review*, June 1992 supplement SMDS, p. 7.

42. Smith, Gail. "Planning for Migration to ATM." *Business Communications Review*, May 1993, pp. 53–58.

43. Stallings, William. *ISDN and Broadband ISDN*. 2nd ed. New York: Macmillan Publishing Company, 1992.

44. Stallings, William. "The Role of SONET in the Development of Broadband ISDN." *Telecommunications*, April 1992, pp. 21–24.

45. Strauss, Paul. "Virtual LANs Pave the Way to ATM." *Datamation*, August 15, 1993, pp. 20–22, 24.

46. Stuck, Bart. "Can the Carriers Deliver on SONET's Full Potential?" *Business Communications Review*, June 1993, pp. 44–48.

47. Super, Tom. "InfoVision: Visions of the Information Age." *Visions of the 21st Century: An RBOC Perspective*, November 20, 1992.

48. Toda, Iwao. "Migration to Broadband ISDN." *IEEE Communications Magazine*, April 1990, pp. 55–58.

49. White, Patrick E. "The Role of the Broadband Integrated Services Digital Network." *IEEE Communications Magazine*, March 1991, pp. 116–119.

50. Williamson, John, and Steven Titch. "Gazing Toward the Broadband Horizon." *Telephony*, October 5, 1992, pp. 34–39.

51. Wilson, Carol. "ATM: Hype or Happening?" *Telephony*, October 5, 1992, p. 60.

52. Wyatt, John C. "ATM Technology: The Emerging Opportunities." *Telecommunications*, November 1992 supplement InteNet, pp. 43–45.

Chapter **Fifteen**

Bandwidth for the Home

CONTINUING CASE—PART 15

Michael Gets Internet Access at the Cabin

Michael sat on the porch of his cabin and wished he had Internet access there so he could, as he did at home, receive stock quotes and send and receive email. He had purposely not installed a telephone at his hideaway so there was no way to dial into any service. For many years, he was cut off from all of civilization when he went to his retreat, but now civilization had moved closer. While he still had a lot of space around his cabin, the neighbors just a few miles away had not only telephones but cable service. They could get analog and digital television as well as Internet access. Michael loved his isolation but wished for connectivity some of the time.

As the CEO of JEI sat with his quiet thoughts, Carlton drove up in his new SUV. "Hi, Dad, what're you thinking about?"

"Oh, kind of wishing I had Internet access for stock quotes and email. It's nice to have the isolation up here but I am spending more time here now and miss the convenience of access."

"Well, we have several choices. You could use your cell phone and laptop computer, but that would be slow and expensive. Then you could break down and get wired telephone service and be able to use the 56K modem in the laptop. It is possible that the phone company can even provide DSL here, as I remember there is a small subcentral office just about three miles away. You could talk to the cable company and see if they will bring cable to you. You enjoy TV and opted to go DirecTV satellite service but you could downgrade to cable. They used to offer DirectPC but you need a phone line to use it. I know that cable would be a television step down, but it would provide Internet access. Finally, Hughes has announced DirectWAY, bidirectional satellite Internet service. I don't know the cost or bandwidth, but it's access and I think it is fairly fast. With it, you could still have your satellite TV, which comes off of a different satellite, and have Internet access. That is if you can convince Mom to let you have two satellite antennas on the cabin. What do you want to do?"

"I like the idea of DirectWAY as it leaves me remote and still gives me access. Whom do I contact to find out the particulars?"

"I'll have Sarah look into it. She's a DirecTV customer also and has DSL from the phone com-

pany, so she's up on most of the technology of access."

Two days later, Sarah walked into Michael's office, followed by a guy with a Circuit City uniform and a cart with several boxes. She smiled from ear to ear as she saw the question mark on Michael's face.

"What's all this?" Michael asked.

"This is Carlton's Father's Day gift to you. He told me to go ahead and get the DirectWAY equipment and sign you up for Internet access. I had the boxes delivered here to show you, but I'll have Steve take them to the lake this afternoon and set them up. He said he was planning on going up there anyway and he seemed really interested in this technology."

"I should have known that my son had something up his sleeve when he mentioned all the options. Go ahead and let my grandson set it up and play with it this afternoon. I plan to spend the night there and will be ready for a lesson."

Steve took the DirectWAY boxes to the lake, aimed the antenna, and set up the equipment. He, his dad, and his grandfather all used the same cellular service and it had good service at the lake. He placed the call, gave the service representative his father's business credit card number, and was up and running in no time. He was surprised at the good speed he obtained and was downloading shareware software when his grandfather walked in, earlier than he expected him. "Just couldn't wait, huh?"

"OK, hotshot, get me onto Charles Schwab's site and let me see my portfolio. Then you can explain what you are doing and how I can do it. I'm no dummy, you know."

Michael and Steve spent most of the evening working on the computer with the new access. About one-half the way through, Steve clicked on JEI's website, just to surprise his grandfather. "Want to leave the staff a message?" he asked, pointing to the email icon.

"Uhmmn, I think I will. Wait a minute, can I get to the office email system instead?"

"Certainly," imitating Grocho Marx. Steve brought up a VNC client. Since he had installed a VNC server on Michael's machine at JEI, he was attached in no time.

"What did you just do?" asked Michael.

"I am using a program by *AT&T* called VNC (virtual network connection). I installed it on your computer at the office and created a password. You just click on this icon (pointing to the screen) and click OK, as it already has the IP address of your machine. The access packet is uploaded to the DirectWAY satellite, down to the Hughes earth station, and onto the Internet. Did you see your computer ask for a password? I put in my middle name for a password; think you can remember it?" he said smiling.

"Then I can operate my machine as if I were at my company desk."

"Right. So, if you forget to bring a file with you, you can download it this way. The access is not very fast, so I'll get Sarah to put remote access software (RAS) on the server that will allow any of your management staff to log in from home, or the cabin. The main server is where the email server is located. RAS will make it seem as though you are there in person, whereas VNC is slower."

"And what about eBay for your grandmother?"

"Not a problem. Hughes is your ISP, so you just use your *Netscape*® browser. Here, I'll put eBay in your desktop so it will automatically start the browser and go to Grandma's *My eBay*® page. You have the eBay password, but the page will stay active as long as the browser is active. Here, I'll put a Yahoo icon also, so you can get to stock research there as well as on the Schwab site. You use Yahoo to pay bills, right?"

"You have a great memory, Steve. How about printing from the websites."

"Just do what you usually do. Just pretend you are at the office or home and you're in business."

"Do you have *AOL's Instant Messenger* installed?"

"It's right here and I have copied your buddy list from home, so you're ready to go. See, Dad is on his machine at home. I guess we had better not send him a note as I am sure he thinks we both are in bed by this hour. Mind if I stay up for a while and play *Quake* with my friends over the Internet?"

"Fine, but I'm off to bed. Turn out the lights when you are through."

Michael went fishing the next day, taking his cell phone as usual. He didn't want to be in touch, but he felt safer with this along. As he fished, the cell phone gave a chirp, not a ring but a chirp. He looked at the screen and it said "text message." He didn't know what that meant, but pressed OK and, sure enough, there was a text message waiting. Michael clicked on the message and read, "HI G, INSTALLED SHORT MESSAGE SERVICE ON UR PHONE. COOL, RITE. STEVE."

Michael continued to fish and wondered what short message service (SMS) was. He thought it was great that he could receive a text message on his phone because this meant getting just the message and not spending a lot of time talking. Wondering how he could use it within JEI, he called Sarah, getting her voice mail. "Sarah, please have a presentation for Friday's staff meeting about short message service on cell phones and how we can use it for JEI business." He put the phone down and concentrated on fishing.

Back Home

"How was the fishing, dear?"

"Great, not only do I have a limit of rainbows, but Steve came up and installed Internet access. We had a ball."

Michael settled down in his home office and logged into his stock account. Although he used the same laptop computer at home as at the lake, he wished he was not confined to his office to get connectivity. He picked up the phone and called Sarah. "Hey, is there a way I can put an Internet connection point in both my home office and den?"

"I can go one better than that. Let me get you an 802.11b wireless adaptor and wireless NIC and you can get connected anywhere in the house, or on the patio for that matter."

"What's 802.11b?"

"Not to worry; it is just a standard for wireless connectivity. It's quite fast and you are connected as soon as you are within range and your computer is on."

"On the patio, that's great."

"Yes, in the kitchen, den, office, and anywhere within the limit of the wireless adapter."

"Wish I had that convenience for my PDA, or can it work with the same system?"

"No, but I can install *Bluetooth* on your laptop and PDA and they can communicate to synchronize your calendar and address book. With your laptop connectivity, you can synchronize with the office. By the way, I got the new memory for your PDA and MP3 software so you can use it to carry around the music you like. It comes with good ear buds, so you and Bach can fish together. You can even listen to the Schubert Trout Quintet."

"Did you get my new digital camera?"

"It's in the mail. With the connectivity at the lake, home, and office, you can send everyone photos of the fish you catch, or show us how long the one was that got away."

"I've been thinking about the advantages of wireless capability. Can we make the cabin wireless?"

"No problem. Since Steve connected you to satellite, I'll get a second wireless adapter for the lake so you can be connected in the cabin, on the porch, and on the dock. I fear you motor too far out on the lake to stay connected. Then again, you aren't worried about connectivity when you and Mr. Bach are fishing, right?"

"You are very right. I will need my cell phone so I'll keep it along for security. Did Steve tell you to put remote access software on the server so the management staff can get to email and other services?"

"Yes, I received his email today and the software is on order. We are using a firewall on the server, but it is smart enough to get the encrypted email through to a remote computer. I probably should take your laptop to the lake and check it out. Tomorrow is supposed to be warm and sunny, so I'll go then, if that's alright with you?"

"Always looking for sunny, and sunning, weather. Yes, that's fine. You can get the laptop at the office and be sure it all works. The refrigerator is stocked with food and drink as usual, so have a great time."

INTRODUCTION

This is a companion chapter to the preceding one, which discussed medium to high bandwidth to the office. Now we explore bandwidth to the home. The settings and demands are different, so the technologies are different at the higher range. In both cases, we explore the need for bandwidth and the present solutions for both wired and wireless media.

THE PARTS OF THE PROBLEM

This chapter presents higher-speed, for example, broader, bandwidth service to the home environment. Figure 15.1 illustrates the areas of interest. We discuss the home entertainment and small office/home office (SOHO) areas, and see that

---

The Real World   15–1

Evidence of the importance of computers and telecommunications is seen in the number of articles appearing in premier business publications such as *Fortune, Business Week,* and *The Wall Street Journal.* The *Fortune* issue of July 8, 1996, had as a cover story "Gates (Microsoft) & Andy Grove (Intel)—*Mr. Software and Mr. Hardware Brainstorm Computing's Future.*" Of even greater interest are Andy Groves's comments on the Internet:

"The Internet is like a 20-foot tidal wave coming and we are in kayaks. It's been coming across the Pacific for thousands of miles and gaining momentum and it is going to lift you and drop you. We're just a step away from the point where every computer is connected to every other computer, at least in the U.S., Japan, and Europe. It affects everybody—the computer industry, telecommunications,

the media, chipmakers, and the software world. Some are more aware of this than others.

"As exciting as that is though, there's one big problem—telecommunications bandwidth."

Bill Gates concurs: "Bandwidth bottlenecks. No question, that the biggest obstacle to where we'd like to take the PC . . . low-cost interactive bandwidth—not just to businesses but also to homes—is going to come very slowly. Sure, if you look 20 years out, you're going to have a lot. But in the next five years, the percentage of homes that will have better than plain old telephone lines won't go beyond 20 percent to 30 percent, even in the U.S."

Source: Brent Schlender, "A Conversation with the Lords of Wintel," *Fortune.*

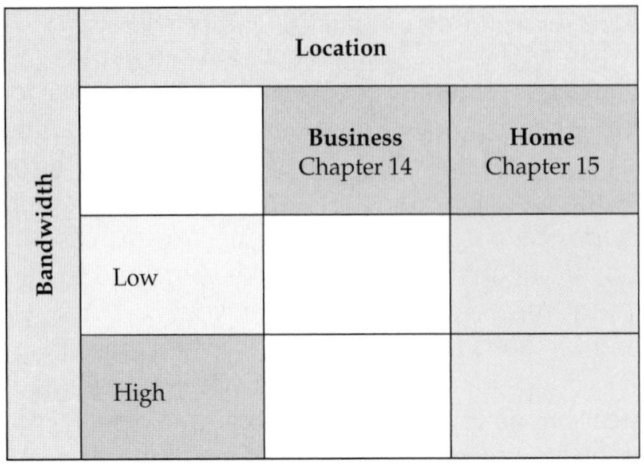

FIGURE 15.1
Bandwidth
Coverage for
Chapter 15

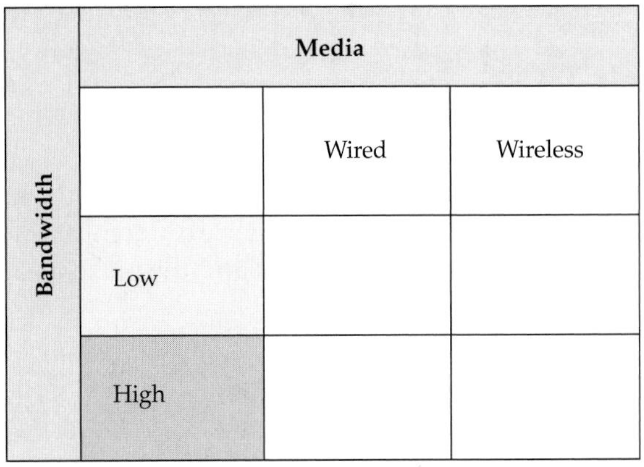

Location		
	Business Chapter 14	**Home** Chapter 15
Low		
High		

(Bandwidth axis on left)

FIGURE 15.2
Options for the
Home

Media		
	Wired	Wireless
Low		
High		

(Bandwidth axis on left)

many of the solutions are different to the home than to the office. Again, wired versus wireless solutions are giving the homeowner various options. (See Figure 15.2.)

DIGITAL HOME

It is a small step from the home office to the concept of the digital home. Just as networking gained ground in the office, it now has become more commonplace in the home. Many new homes are being built with networking as an integral part of the building. People are seeking to build links to every piece of electronic gear in the home, for example, PCs, set-top boxes, stereos, handheld devices, and so forth. Some of these devices require high bandwidth. For example, interactive TV, online services, and remote multiple-player game consoles demand faster speeds.

In addition to devices mentioned above, many envision the home where every gadget will be interconnected. This includes heat, air conditioning, security, refrigeration, stove, whirlpool bath, coffee pot, alarms, and so forth.

History of Bandwidth to the Home

The history of digital bandwidth to the home has evolved greatly. Until recently, connectivity from a home meant a modem over POTS lines. While the speed of the modems has increased over the past two decades, the technology has remained the same: the modulation of an analog signal to carry digital bits. The constraint imposed by the voice spectrum of POTS has limited the information-carrying capacity. The first new technology, Integrated Systems Digital Network (ISDN), was introduced in 1987 and provided two DSO channels, capable of providing the home, or office, 64 or 128 Kbps. Partially because of the significantly higher cost to the home ($80 per month as opposed to $20 per month) and partially due to the reluctance of ISPs to allow this higher bandwidth, ISDN was never fully accepted in the home for Internet access and to no large degree for the SOHO.

In the time since ISDN was introduced, the U.S. population has become accustomed to the quality of cable TV and has demanded more and more channels. This form of entertainment saw its first competition in the middle 1970s with the advent of large antennas in the home and expensive analog direct satellite broadcast. While the service was just a stepchild of the service of the cable provider, the introduction, in the 1990s, of digital Direct Broadcast Service (DBS) was in direct competition to cable. Now, both cable and DBS are seen as possible new services, specifically data and higher-than-modem-speed Internet access.

Bandwidth for the Home

We have addressed the various technologies and alternatives for the business office; now we move to an examination of the needs for the home. Do we have similar needs there? Can we see a need for bandwidth in the home that may emulate a commercial need? Well, how about cable TV? There may be 50 channels of analog TV for an analog bandwidth of 300 MHz (50 channels at 6 MHz each = 300 MHz). Fifty to sixty analog TV channels are about the effective analog bandwidth for the **coaxial cable** feeding homes when low-bandwidth coax is used, for example, 350 MHz. However, the alternative coax provides 550 MHz or 750 MHz, enabling a greater number of channels. (Where the authors live, the local cable provider, until recently, carried 47 channels to the area. The limiting factor was that part of the installed circuits were old and restricted the whole network to that bandwidth. The cable company changed these old circuits and added six more channels. Their plans called for using three of the channels for analog programming and carrying nine compressed digital channels on the remaining three channels. Thus, by changing technology, they were able to increase the effective carrying capacity of the medium.)

How will you choose a channel from 300 or a movie from a library of 15,000?

The home market is being told that they can have, not just 50 channels but 100, 200, or even 500 channels of entertainment as a predecessor of true **video-on-demand** (see below). Thus, the initial push for greater (analog) bandwidth in the home seems to have come from cable television.

More Digital to the Home

Of great interest in this home environment are the VSAT (very small aperture terminal) satellite providers to the home. *Hughes DirecTV*®, DBS, and *The Dish Network*® sell an 18″ satellite antenna and decoder/amplifier that gives access to over 150 basic channels plus premium and pay-per-view channels of high-quality entertainment, delivered in a true digital environment. These providers, able to take advantage of totally new equipment rather than having to upgrade and be downward compatible with existing equipment, provide their signal in digital format, giving higher quality video and CD-quality sound.

Cable and satellite providers of video entertainment have seen another market niche, very-high-quality, uninterrupted music such as Digital Music Express®

(www.dmxmusic.com) and Syrus (http://www.siriusradio.com/servlet/snav?/servlet/index.jsp) and XM satellite radio and other music providers. Depending on just how the provider creates the music "channels,"[1] one may receive from 6 to 60 channels of digitized, CD-quality music, without interruption for announcements or advertisements, plus some 30 channels of normal TV audio and radio programming. In the home, this may require another set-top box to tune to the channel that is carrying the specific *type* of music desired unless the provider is allocating cable or satellite spectrum. For reception in a truck or automobile, additional equipment includes a receiver/decoder and an antenna. Some units connect to the receiver in the vehicle; others rebroadcast the received signal on an unused FM channel.

As the demand grows for more TV channels and the use of that resource for Internet access, providers are moving to use the higher frequency channels to carry digital signals. A 6 MHz analog cable channel can carry 27 Mbps, suitable for three NTSC channels for one HDTV channel or one HDTV and one NTSC. The objective, besides providing more channels, is to compete with DBS digital quality, using the existing cable resource.

broadband
Debate continues as to where broadband starts; is it T1, or T3, or OC-3? The concept of broadband originated with analog CATV FDM on coax. In the digital world, we are moving toward OC-3 (155.51 Mbps) as the new definition.

If present technology allows for three digital channels on one analog channel and the consumer market demands 150 channels, the only change to the system that carries 50 analog channels would be the digital interface equipment. However, if the demand jumped to twice that (300 channels) or even three times that (450 channels), we exceed the bandwidth for most of the coaxial cables that run from the street to the residence. Thus, if the need was to deliver 300 channels simultaneously to the residence for multiple TV sets, we need more bandwidth. However, if we can change the rules, such as deliver *only* channel(s) from the street to the residence that are actually watched, then the bandwidth from the street to the home reduces drastically. Considering that technology now exists that can deliver six compressed digital TV channels over twisted-pair, you can see that alternative technologies can substitute for traditional high-bandwidth circuits.

Bandwidth via Coaxial Cable

Video-on-Demand

Video-on-demand
gives the user choice, based on storage of movies and other programs at the source.

There has been a lot of hype over **movies-(video-)on-demand**, being able to watch *any* movie or video when you want it. This is of concern when one thinks about trying to choose from among 100, 300, or 500 channels of entertainment. The concept of channel surfing now ceases to be fun because it takes 42 minutes to watch each channel for 5 seconds to choose a program from among 500 channels. Yes, there would be some redundancy, but the point remains that humans do not do a good job of choosing movies at the video store, much less choosing from 500 alternatives every 30 minutes. For this reason, satellite providers and more and more cable providers are dedicating a channel to give information on what is coming up by way of a program guide. Some providers charge for this service, but most provide information by channel for the next seven days and include the intelligence that helps in programming the VCR for recording.

Additionally, DBS offers search engines to determine when a type of program will be available. Video digital recording services, such as *TiVo*,® go one step further

---

[1] Music channels are created in two ways on CATV. One is to timeshare one channel with all or part of the music channels provided. The other is to spread the channels across the TV spectrum, using space between existing TV channels.

and find the programs a customer specified and automatically record them in digital format on a hard drive. The TiVo service also records the habits of the viewer and (*a*) recommends programs as well as (*b*) records programs that should match the viewer's preferences. While these services do not require bandwidth above that necessary to transport the channel, they provide the ability to help viewers watch what they wish. As the technology and service mature, the requirement for great bandwidth is likely to develop also.

Thus, we come to the concept of (*a*) providing a large number of *movies on-demand* when you want them, for a fee, or (*b*) providing *all desired entertainment on-demand*. This former concept is almost available at this time with satellite and cable providers allocating specific channels for pay-per-view and providing the viewer a schedule of first-run movies. The desired movie or other entertainment is selected and the reverse channel (generally POTS) tells the provider to charge your account. This is referred to as **near video-on-demand.**

Near video-on-demand gives the user access to a large library of films, but requires human intervention.

Near video-on-demand either provides programming on multiple schedules or, as in the case of hotels, requires a person to load a selected program. True video-on-demand allows watching any program that has been presented to date (over, say, the past three years), plus most movies, at any time you want. The 6:00 AM news can be watched at 3:00 PM, the movie *Casablanca* is available any time, and even the first Super Bowl can be called, as the user desires. Given that this means large storage problems for the providers, it also means that there must be a channel from the provider's database of programs to *each* television set in the service area. Each logical channel has to carry only one TV channel, which can be compressed digitally, but this means possibly hundreds of thousands, even millions, of channels being demanded. (See Table 15.1 for the media and forms by which we receive TV signals at this time.)

TABLE 15.1
Methods of Transporting Television

Transport	Digital	Analog	Quality	Cost	Requirements
Coaxial cable		X	Good	Low	Analog encoder/decoder
	X		Superior	Moderate	Digital encoder/decoder
Fiber cable	X		Superior		Same as digital coax
		X	Good		Same as analog coax
T1 on twisted-pair	X		Moderate	High $19–$80K	Expensive due to high compression and wide variety of components
ISDN on twisted-pair	X		Poor	High	Same as T1
Satellite	X	X	Superior	Competitive	Purchase or lease antenna and decoder/amplifier
Broadcast radio		X	Good	"None"	Only need receiver
LAN (Ethernet, frame relay, FDDI)	X		Good		Encoder/decoder on desktop

Information Window   15–1

Full-color, full-motion (standard NSTS) television requires about 27 megabytes of data per second, uncompressed. However, MPEG compression techniques can reduce this to about 1.2 megabytes per second. This allows a 74-minute, full-color, full-motion movie to be recorded on a 4.5-inch compact disk.

Measuring Bandwidth

Since coaxial cable goes to most homes in large and medium-sized U.S. cities, providers would like to continue to use this resource. Suppose the provider could send to the home only the channels(s) that the home was watching. If there were three TVs active, that would mean just three 6 MHz signals. Transmission of three 6 MHz signals is possible over twisted-pair wire in digital form, as we will see in the following section! The problem is that we would have to carry the signals to the pole near the home, then switch them to the home or switch them at the source. Now we can see the need for broadband, as we send the large number of signals to the curb and need the ability to switch the individual signals to the home.

Two scenarios could provide the desired video-on-demand. The first calls for a high bandwidth loop around a city, providing hundreds, if not thousands, of individual channels at any one time, providing, in our case, up to three of these channels to a residence. This can be done with a SONET ring, which requires a significant investment. The alternative is to provide STS-1 SONET/ATM from the source to each home. This provides 51.84 Mbps, enough for two HDTV channels or eight NTSC channels. With this bandwidth and switching at the source, plus larger servers containing the programming of the past three years and all movies, homes could receive just the program they wished, when they wished it. Besides the increased bandwidth investment, this would require a pay-per-view strategy for *all* programs. For example, watching the nightly news, which may be on-demand or on-schedule, may have a price of 10¢ as there would be advertisements included. Watching an older show might cost 25¢–50¢ and watching a third-run movie, without commercials, might cost $2.00. Choosing a first-run movie could be offered at a price of $5.00 without interruption, or $1.00 if the viewer will view a commercial chosen for that socio-economic area of town. With sufficient bandwidth and switching, video-on-demand is possible and economically feasible.

SOHO CONSIDERATIONS

More people are working out of their homes, or small satellite offices, because of the size and nature of their businesses or due to the need for special accommodation. This is the domain of the **small office/home office (SOHO).** People who work in SOHOs realize the value of connectivity, both fixed and mobile. Few home office workers would be without pagers and cellular phones and most want at least a second phone line for fax or Internet access.

POTS and Broadband Internet Access

Our discussion above is about entertainment and is an extension of existing broadcast and coaxial or satellite-based entertainment television. The next area we examine is that of voice and data. For the home with only one, or at most two, telephone line, POTS does a good job. When the residence becomes a SOHO, the need may rise to more voice lines, fax, and high-speed data lines, which may include Internet access. The following addresses the alternatives available for these requirements, in a wired mode. Wireless access follows.

Bandwidth via UTP—Digital Subscriber Line (DSL)

If an organization is the owner of an extensive twisted-pair copper network, such as the Telco's extensive POTS local loop network, it would want to take advantage of it by delivering broadband services, ranging from Internet access to video-on-demand. Digital Subscriber Line (DSL), covered in detail in the previous chapter, converts existing twisted-pair voice telephone lines into access paths for high-speed data communications *and* digital voice. DSL transmits more than 6 Mbps to a subscriber and as much as 640 Kbps in both directions when the destination is within 18,000 feet of the source central office. Such rates expand existing access capacity by a factor of 50 or more without new cabling. DSL can literally transform the existing public voice network from one limited to voice, text, and low-resolution graphics to a powerful, ubiquitous system capable of bringing multimedia, including full-motion video, to everyone's home. It is predicted that 80 percent of the residences and offices in the United States can be accommodated via DSL due to the presence of 24 AWG and 26 AWG gauge twisted-pair wire in the local loops.

Remember that ISDN is a form of DSL, providing two DSO channels with a maximum, but guaranteed, bandwidth of 128 Kbps. This is sufficient for one voice channel and one data channel for the home or SOHO. When more bandwidth is required, SOHOs can move to pure DSL and have expanded ability. From an entertainment standpoint, it is possible to deliver full-color, full-motion television on a POTS line using DSL with MPEG compression.

For the business venture operated from the home, for example, SOHO, DSL has another value. It can provide high-speed data paths and Internet access as well as multiple voice channels. This latter technology is called **Voice-over-DSL,** where the bandwidth is divided into multiple voice channels and a data channel. Thus, a SOHO could have 12 voice channels (using 768 Kbps) and still have over five megabytes for data. Because this requires only one POTS local loop, the cost should be much less.

HFC and FTTC for the Home

The technologies of **hybrid fiber coax (HFC)** and **fiber to the curb (FTTC)** were introduced in Chapter 3. These are fiber-based broadband alternatives for the home, originally designed for cable television. For either, a fiber circuit carries the TV or data to each neighborhood. One format is a SONET ring, running at speeds of 622 Mbps and higher. In the neighborhood, providers run either fiber to the home or coaxial cable for the home. The former gives greater bandwidth while the latter is less expensive. As the bandwidth availability increases, the services provided can increase.

Wireless Considerations

Wireless is a strong competitor to the coaxial cable, UTP, and fiber media for three reasons. First, the cost for the last mile is less. Second, installation can be much quicker and less expensive. Finally, the end node can often move without special considerations.

Cellular to the Home

Cellular providers have already recognized that they are in a good position to compete for Internet access to the home as soon as they can get their bandwidth up to about 386 Kbps. Considering that cable Internet access is often priced at $40 per month and DSL is priced at $50 per month, cellular has an opportunity to gain a revenue stream from existing towers in the $35-per-month range, a cost comparable to that of many present cellular phone customers (circa 2002). Originally, cell phones could transmit and receive only 9.6 Kbps. As generation three technology is installed, the bandwidth should move quickly to 386 Kbps for either stationary or moving destinations. Thus, a SOHO could have a fixed reception point for cellular data and Internet access. It is further expected that this bandwidth will move to the 2 Mbps range within a short time, providing even greater bandwidth than cable or DSL, with mobility. Therefore, access from a laptop, palmtop, or desktop should be fast and reliable.

How much do you spend on telecommunications services each month? Add it up and be surprised.

MMDS and LMDS

The MMDS and LMDS technologies, covered in Chapter 3, offer service similar to cellular, but are designed for stationary point-to-many-point service. Originally designed for educational television, they are now used for commercial cable TV and high-speed data. The range of the central tower is about 25 miles and the receiving unit requires a 36″ parabolic antenna that is line-of-sight to the tower. Licenses are required for services, but installation can be quick as opposed to the laying of cable or fiber.

Some providers claim that new fixed wireless services can deliver DSL speeds. During the early deployment, many adopters have said that many problems exist. They cite transmission latency of as much as 30 seconds or longer and ping times over 1,000 milliseconds. Multipoint Multichannel Distributions Systems (MMDS) promise to fix these problems. Companies providing MMDS claim 256 Kbps of upstream, but early adopters say they typically get about 128 Kbps. Next-generation equipment is seen as overcoming these problems. Also, greater capacity can be achieved by replacing the supercell structures' single tower with smaller antennas and smaller cells.

Data from Satellite

It is believed that Microsoft and others are planning low orbit satellites for high-speed Internet access. The demise of the Iridium venture may slow the deployment of this technology. Meanwhile, Hughes has created *DirecPC*® and *DirectWAY*® as one-way and bidirectional data access. Both use different satellites than entertainment *DirecTV*® and offer 400 Kbps download speed or better. This gives the home without a cable, DSL, or cellular system available data (e.g., Internet) access at a good speed. For example, farmers in west Texas were early in adopting *DirecTV*® as a replacement of large TV antennas. They followed suit by implementing *DirectWAY*® for Internet access.

Bluetooth and IEEE 802.11a/b

Within the home, the environment has evolved to the presence of a number of devices requiring connectivity; some are already wireless compatible. Handheld and laptop devices may already have IR ports for connectivity to other IR devices. These same devices also may have long-distance connectivity to the Internet, via cellular or other technology. In the home, per se, the need is short-distance connectivity, often with machines requiring different protocols. **Bluetooth** is an attempt to allow any wireless device to connect to any other wireless device. This technology is designed for short distances and bandwidth of about 700 Kbps, both parameters being suitable for a home environment. Thus, users at home or a SOHO would be able to use a USB port and a Bluetooth hub or an internal Bluetooth card and have connectivity within a building environment.

The second wireless method of connectivity is with devices that meet the **IEEE 802.11a/b** specification. The first was 802.11b, with a bit longer range and much higher bandwidth, for example, 11 Mbps. This mature technology would allow SOHO wireless LAN with high speed. IEEE 802.11a parameters call for a bandwidth of 51 Mbps, offering a path for video conferencing and other high-speed needs.

TELECOMMUTING

Broadband, both to and from the home, is likely to gain importance as telecommuting's popularity increases. Many people are embracing the idea that work from home or a SOHO offers more advantages than commuting to an urban office. If their work involves movement of large data files, especially those containing lots of images or video, greater bandwidth is in demand.

With higher bandwidth, many of the old constraints will disappear. As broadband becomes widely available to the home, there should be a greater incentive for new applications to emerge from the SOHO. For example, a person with disabilities who lived at his mother's home discovered the ability to convert his SOHO into an ASP, providing, first, a currency-converter that could perform instant conversions of any currency into another. This entrepreneur became independent and, in a way, released from the constraints formerly imposed by illness. This sort of venture should spread as more people understand that Web service can have a new meaning and can emanate from a new location—the home.

INTERNET ACCESS

Web-Based Learning

High bandwidth access to the Internet promises to revolutionize the way people can learn. With Web-based learning programs, anyone with Web access can obtain sophisticated instruction about nearly any topic. This may mean life-long learning opportunities for people with disabilities, and gaining education and training from places too remote for normal travel.

Bandwidth for the Home—CPE for the Home/SOHO

Such networking providers as *Cisco Systems*®, *D-Link*®, and *3Com*® have started to market DSL bridges and routers to their enterprise and small business product offerings. Large corporations have started to outfit their telecommuters and new remote offices with both broadband voice and data capabilities. This means that the residence and SOHO are beginning to have significant CPE (customer premises equipment) installed. Most of the CPE will be bridges and routers, but integrated access devices (IADs) also will play a role.

Video Porn

New technology brings capabilities that are undesirable to many in society. From a telecommunications standpoint, the first was the use of the telephone for verbal phone sex, people communicating about this subject. Next came still photos on the Internet as modems increased in speed. Text and still photos are not necessarily large files and offer subject material that may be worth waiting for, in the mind of the viewer. With greatly increased bandwidth, it will be possible to have movies at the viewer's computer. With lower bandwidth, files can be downloaded over, say, 15 minutes' time and played at home. With increased speed, .AVI movies can be streamed to the home. While initially the movies may be only a portion of the screen, in the near future the quality level of the 15-frames-per-second (FPS) scenes will increase to 30 FPS and enlarge to fill the screen. Technology is amoral and the content is subject to societal moral standards, not the conduit.

Copyright Infringement

With higher bandwidth it is possible to send larger and larger files. With compression, the files are made smaller. A major event in this arena was the advent of the MP3 compression protocol, allowing an 80+ Mbyte music file to be reduced to about 2.5 Mbyte. This made it feasible to share music over the Internet. *Napster*® took this one step further and established an ability to find the music you wished and download it from the source. While Napster was only an information-sharing resource, with the actual files coming from some 3,500 personal servers, the music industry and federal government held Napster accountable for copyright infringement and required Napster to remove any copyrighted material that the holder requested to be removed. As we will see in the next section, this same idea has moved to video material.

Video Compact Disk Movies (V-CD)

The first medium to record movies from broadcast television or make a copy of a professional VHS tape was VHS tapes at home. This medium has a very large bandwidth and it is only the recording ability of VHS that limits the quality of the copy.

   The next form of high-quality movie was the DVD. Movies on cable TV are about the same quality as VHS and on direct broadcast satellite (DBS) are somewhat above that of VHS and are in digital form. A technology is available that allows a full VHS movie to be recorded onto a **video compact disk (V-CD).** MPEG2 compression provides the space and the resultant copy is in VHS format. This makes it possible to copy a broadcast movie and store it on a single V-CD. Personal servers are storing movies in V-CD format and making them available for personal downloading. Each movie requires one or more CDs for storage as they are 700 Mbyte or larger. Again, as with Napster, copyright infringement becomes an issue.

The Real World   15–2

The Moxi Media Center, designed to replace TV set-top boxes, is slightly larger than a VCR. The unit receives satellite or cable-TV signals and contains a personal video recorder to pause or store live television, a DVD and music CD player, an Internet connection, and a hard drive that can store thousands of songs. It can be attached to a computer network so entertainment and data can be received on any TV or PC in the house.

Source: *Business Week,* March 4, 2002.

Online Banking and Bill Paying

For years, banks have provided the ability to have bill payments drafted from customer accounts, using EDI and electronic funds transfer. This capability is evolving into total online banking or bill payment. This supports the ability to send checks electronically either on an as-need basis or on a periodic schedule. Bandwidth makes this process easier.

Online Auctions

While online auctions such as *eBay*® and *uBid.com*® can be easily accessed and utilized via 56K modems, the customer's experience is much more robust with higher bandwidth. One author began using eBay on 56K modem but lost interest. With the installation of DSL, he is now an avid user, taking full advantage of the excellent search engine to find items of interest. Higher bandwidth makes this experience as well as other activities of greater interest and enjoyment.

Audio, Still Photos, and Video File Download

With the introduction of the MP3 compression protocol, audio files were available in a size that could be downloaded in a reasonable time, especially with broadband to the home. Where a .WAV file of music might be 80 Mbytes in size, MP3 files are only 2+Mbtyes. This encouraged download, which encouraged demand for broadband. This applies also to **digital camera** or scanned photos, using .JPG format.

The evolution of music and still photographs to video requires significantly larger files and download times. People wishing to gain access to this medium must have a broadband connection. DSL and cable modems become a natural solution to the need for bandwidth.

Interactive Video Chat

Two of the newest technologies for home use, as an evolution of email, are *short message service (SMS)* and *instant messenging (IM)*. SMS tends to be cell phone–based and is very popular as more than 22 *billion* text messages are sent from cell phones to other cell phones each day, worldwide.

Instant messenging is a function of connected machines and is based on a buddy list, people to whom you correspond/chat often. The list shows who is online and sending a short text message is as simple as clicking on the buddy's name and typing. As you are able to chat interactively with a select group of "buddies," the natural extension of this text-only format is to add audio or, even more desirable, video. This is happening and promises to gain great acceptance *when* broadband access from the home to the Internet is available. Considering that instant messenging uses very short, text-only messages, it requires little bandwidth. Video, on the other hand, will be a bandwidth hog.

As a final thought on wireless connectivity, the future of PDAs and palmtops lies in devices with cellular wireless technology built in. *Samsung®* and *Nokia®* already have produced handheld devices that contain PDAs and cellular capabilities in a single instrument.

Web-Based Gaming

Video gaming started with *Pong®* and *Atari®* and were designed as stand-alone devices for single players. As the environment moved to more powerful gaming machines and PCs, the environment has moved to multiple players and remote competition. *Doom®* offered a mode where gamers could play against each other on the same machine or over a network. Microsoft's strategy with their *X-Box®* is that the future is in Internet-based gaming where opponents play each other over any distance. Where Doom passed only small bytes of data, the X-Box will require higher bandwidth, providing yet another reason for pushing broadband to the home.

Information Window   15–2

One of the authors has *BellSouth DSL FastAccess®* in his home. (The second author lives too far to receive DSL.) Using his POTS line and an *Alcatel Home®* DSL modem between the wall jack and the NIC in his computer, he has download speeds of about T1. Because he has a second computer, a router is attached to the DSL modem. The router acts as a (hardware) firewall and a hub, connecting the second computer via cat 5 cable to the first and to the DSL modem. Both machines are running *ZoneAlarm®* for added protection since the machines have file and print sharing allowed so each machine can see the other. Both machines are running the United Devices (www.ud.com) program and automatically use the DSL modem to return results on cancer research. (See Figure 15.3.)

FIGURE 15.3

Just how fast is FastAccess DSL?
FastAccess DSL can download a 3.8MB music file in as fast as 20 seconds. Download times with a 56k and a 28.8k modem are so slow it's staggering: more than 9 and 17 minutes respectively.

Check out how much music you can download in 5 minutes.

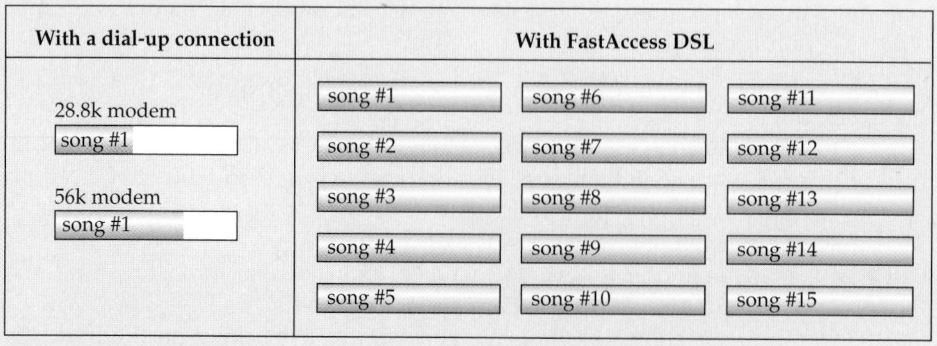

With a dial-up connection	With FastAccess DSL		
28.8k modem	song #1	song #6	song #11
song #1	song #2	song #7	song #12
56k modem	song #3	song #8	song #13
song #1	song #4	song #9	song #14
	song #5	song #10	song #15

With BellSouth FastAccess DSL, you can download 15 songs faster than you can download 1 song with a dial-up connection.**

Source: BellSouth advertisement.

VOICE-ENABLED DSL

A valuable asset is voice-enabled DSL over POTS lines or fixed wireless bandwidth, providing the SOHO with both (multiple) voice lines and data lines. For voice-enabled DSL, technology at each end of the wire digitizes the transmission (like ISDN) and creates several channels, depending on the requirements. The standard telephone line still exists but the wideband channels are divided into multiple voice and data channels. Thus, a single wire can have, for example, three voice lines and two data channels. More sophisticated environments could have the use for any given bandwidth dynamic, meaning that data needs have all the bandwidth until there is a need for choice, at which time the allocation changes.

NEITHER HOME NOR OFFICE

We are spending more time in our vehicles. Until telecommuting becomes the norm, travel is the norm. Cars now have as many as 40 computers or microprocessors onboard. The near future technology will be to add a bus to the vehicle and move the sensor data around the vehicle. A display, on the dashboard or steering wheel or

---

The Real World   15–3
Digital Satellite Radio for Your Car

In 1981, *MTV*®'s "Video Killed the Radio Star" entered our houses for the first time. With an exclamation of "totally cool, dude" and a flip of our feathered hair, we welcomed the new experience of watching music on cable television. The next exciting development was digital radio over cable that gave us an enormous selection of music with just a click of the TV remote.

Now the idea of digitally transmitting radio—CD-quality sound broadcast over channels arranged by genre or subject—has taken one more step into the future. It's available in your car.

"Conventional radio just doesn't have the demand to support a whole channel dedicated to Hindi music," say Charles Robbins, corporate affairs spokesman for *XM Radio*®, a Washington, D.C., satellite radio company. Robbins describes initial media, retail, and customer response to satellite car radio as "wildly enthusiastic."

If you're not convinced that a wide variety of channels is worth $9.95 a month when FM and AM are free, Robbins offers other advantages including less than seven minutes of commercial advertising per hour and no static or fade-out as you are always within the satellite's range.

By the time you read this newsletter, the XM service should be available throughout the United States. While the technology is still in its infancy, you'll need to purchase a satellite-ready adapter for your current stereo or buy a whole new stereo system to access the XM service or its closest competitor, *Sirus*® ($12.95 a month). We recently found XM-ready 50-watt *Pioneer*® systems for $189 and SM-ready 60-watt *Alpines*® for $329 (installation not included on either model).

As with digital radio offered by cable providers, users will have access to more information than provided by traditional radio (song titles, album information, and artist names, for example). They also will have the freedom to surf a world of channels, catching a *BBC News*® or *CNN Headlines*® broadcast between sets of experimental music or Latin jazz. Like traditional radio, the channels are manned by programmers (digital DJs) who decide what you hear and when.

Both XM and Sirus have negotiated deals with car companies to offer the satellite tuners as purchase options. Companies from *Ford*® to *Porsche*® are already planning to include satellite-ready radios in future models. So, stay tuned.

Source: Mapquest.Com newsletter, no. 38 (January 24, 2002).

projected onto the driver's windshield, will combine the data and give the driver exception reports. GPS is already being added to vehicles, for navigation assistance/maps, or in the combination with satellite/cellular communications, such as *On-Star*® to offer assistance in the car. **Digital satellite radio,** as embodied in *Sirus*® and *XM*® radio, brings 100 channels nationwide. Microsoft has invested in its *Windows CE*® operating system, intending it to be the heart of all of this data movement and control. The final extension of this will be the vehicle that receives data from the road and drives itself, avoiding accident situations.

Case 15-1

In-Home Wireless Networking

Chris Dillard

INTRODUCTION

Multiple-personal-computer (PC) homes are becoming almost as commonplace in today's society as multiple-television homes. Providing signal to each television in a home was not an issue for broadcast television, and was planned for by the cable television industry when they installed coaxial cable jacks in practically every room. With more homes containing multiple computers, the need to share, or network, those computers and their peripherals has rapidly expanded. Networking allows for the sharing of data files, peripherals (printers, scanners, etc.), and broadband Internet access, including Digital Subscriber Line (DSL) and cable access.

Home PC users interested in networking have a variety of options available to accomplish their goal. These options may be broken down at their most basic level into wired and wireless. Wired networking may include connecting PCs with Ethernet cable and network interface cards (NICs), or with existing phone lines. Each of these wired methods provides reliable and fast connections but does not provide for much mobility. Most wired Ethernet home networks utilize the 10BaseT protocol providing speeds up to 10 Mbps, while phone line–based networks reach speeds up to 1 Mbps. The newest generation of wireless networks can run at speeds up to 11 Mbps and allow for less cable clutter and more mobility. Wireless networking will be the topic of this discussion.

WIRELESS CONSIDERATIONS

The increased popularity of wireless home networks can be attributed to reduction in costs, ease of installation, reliability, and mobility. Costs of wireless equipment have dropped significantly over the last two years, and are now competing with traditional wired networking equipment. Wireless networking allows for the creation of a home network where it is impractical or difficult to run cables, without a reduction in speed.

The wire in a traditional wired network, which ensured fast, reliable connections, could also be its weak link. Cabling or recabling a home can be an expensive and time-consuming process. Improperly spliced or accidentally cut cables can result in a crippled network, and these cable faults are not always easily found.

Installing a wireless network alleviates the potential for cable faults and the inconveniences of drilling through walls and hiding cable.

Potential problems to consider when installing a wireless network include radio frequency interference, security, and speed. Radio waves can be susceptible to noise generated by large appliances, degrading the network's performance. Security is also an issue given the broadcast range and interoperable hardware available for wireless networks. Walls and distance can decrease the speed of your network, potentially degrading the quality of some applications such as streaming video.

STANDARDS

For computers to communicate with one another on a network, they must adhere to the same standards. While all wireless networks work on the same basic principle of communicating between PCs via radio signals, the speed at which they transmit data and the frequencies they use differ, depending on which standard is used. For a technology to become standardized, its specifications must be published, with vendors agreeing to follow the published standards. [1] The Institute of Electrical and Electronics Engineers (IEEE) determines Ethernet's standards, following a process that includes allowing vendors and the public to comment upon proposed standards. IEEE 802.11, IEEE 802.11b, Bluetooth, and HomeRF are four standards utilized in the wireless home networking industry; however, 802.11b has moved to the forefront. These standards do not work with one another, and all adapters on the network must use the same standard in order to communicate.

All standards call for adapters to use a small segment of the 2.4-GHz radio spectrum. Adapters may use one of two spread-spectrum technologies to increase efficiency and security: frequency-hopping spread-spectrum (FHSS) or direct-sequencing spread-spectrum (DSSS). FHSS sends part of each data packet across several adjacent radio frequencies, one right after another, until the entire message has been sent. DSSS divides the radio band into three equal parts and spreads the entire data packet across one of those sections. Direct sequence adapters encrypt and decrypt data, causing any unintended recipients to only hear white noise. FHSS provides some data transfer security in the speed at which the hopping signals change frequency, because most radios cannot follow them. FHSS has been abandoned in favor of DSSS.

Carrier Sense Multiple Access/Collision Avoidance is the principal medium access method employed by wireless networks. Most wired Ethernet networks utilize collision detection; however, because wireless networks are utilizing half-duplex radio transceivers, which are not capable of transmitting and receiving simultaneously, collision detection is not possible. The transmitting system "listens" to the channel before transmitting a data packet to ensure the channel is clear, and if so the packet is sent. The receiving system sends an acknowledgment, or ACK, packet back to the sending system when received. If the sending system does not receive the ACK within a certain amount of time, the original packet is retransmitted.

IEEE 802.11

Completion of the 802.11 wireless standard in 1997 was an important step in the progression of wireless networking technologies. The standard was created to increase interoperability between differing brands of networks, as well as to improve performance. Increased interoperability allows customers to purchase equipment from a variety of vendors without having to be tied to their particular standard. IEEE 802.11 is capable of 2 Mbps data transfer rates in a noise-free environment using DSSS and may fall back to 1 Mbps using FHSS in noisy environments.

IEEE 802.11B (WI-FI)

The wireless standard 802.11b, also known as Wireless Fidelity (Wi-Fi), provides wireless networks with the same speed capabilities as not only its wireless competitors, but also its wired Ethernet counterpart. Using DSSS, 802.11b delivers data at a rate of 11 Mbsp and advertises an indoor range of 300 to 500 feet. [2] IEEE 802.11b also allows for a smooth transition from 802.11, because they share the same underlying protocol. IEEE 802.11b is capable of the same file and Internet sharing as 802.11, but adds applications such as streaming video and shared MP3 audio, which both consume a large amount of bandwidth.

WECA (Wireless Ethernet Compatibility Alliance) was recently formed to provide compliance and standards for the wireless network industry. WECA has created the Wi-Fi^{TM} logo as a seal of approval for products that have successfully passed interoperability testing for that standard. [3] It is hoped the Wi-Fi logo will assure customers their products will work together.

An additional benefit of the 802.11b standard is the introduction of wireless networks in public places, such as airports. Currently, these connections are only available in some premium-traveler clubs, but may soon enter the public waiting areas if successful.

The next generation of the IEEE 802.11 family, 802.11a, is set to appear later in the year. This standard will broadcast in the 5 GHz frequency range and provide data transfer speeds of 54 Mbps. Drawbacks for current 802.11b users considering a move to this new standard include initial increased equipment costs and backwards incompatibility. [1]

BLUETOOTH AND HOMERF

Bluetooth is a standard similar to 802.11b, but products utilizing each are not interoperable. This standard also broadcasts in the 2.4 GHz frequency range, but utilizes FHSS rather than DSSS. Bluetooth was not intended for true home PC wireless networking, but rather for smaller devices such as personal data assistants (PDAs) and mobile phones. FHSS is cheaper to implement than DSSS and is more power efficient, but its range is limited to about 30 meters and it only has a data transfer rate of about 1 Mbps. Microsoft recently announced that Windows XP will not include native support for Bluetooth, but will include support for 802.11b. [4]

HomeRF was developed by the HomeRF Working Group, which included companies such as Intel and Proxim. HomeRF broadcasts in the 2.4 GHz range, transmits data at 1.6 Mbps, and has an indoor range of 300 feet. HomeRF failed to gain the popularity of 802.11b because of its slower data transfer speed and shorter range, and subsequently lost the backing of Intel. The next generation of HomeRF, Symphony HomeRF, advertises speeds of 10 Mbps and greater interference resistance than 802.11b. [5]

SETTING UP A WIRELESS NETWORK

Ease of installation, transfer speeds, software support, and costs are important aspects to consider when deciding on a wireless home network. With most DSL and cable connections only transferring data at about 1.5 Mbps, any speed bottlenecks will occur because of the Internet connection itself. If software support does not allow for a simple, effective installation and integration of the wireless network, the benefits of a simple hardware installation will be lost.

Setting up a wireless network means physically connecting your Internet connection and PC or laptop to a device that sends radio signals to separate workstations. The separate workstations, or systems, are equipped with internal or external network adapters, which receive signals from and send signals to another peer system, or the central device. The connection allows for not only Internet connection sharing but also file and peripheral sharing.

In the simplest of wireless networks, two systems each has a wireless adapter installed and functions in a peer-to-peer network topology. The systems may consist of two PCs, or a PC and a laptop. The peer-to-peer network is referred to as operating in an "ad-hoc" mode, and does not utilize a central access point, or router. A network consisting of a central access point and remote systems containing network adapters is operating in "infrastructure" mode.

Wireless network users have a variety of vendors and hardware options to choose from. Desktop systems can be equipped with a wireless network interface card (NIC) ($40–$200), a PC card adapter ($80–$150), and PCI PC card reader bay ($50–$100), or a universal serial bus (USB) adapter ($100–$175). Laptops are generally equipped with PC card adapters but are also capable of using USB adapters.

Access points ($100–$400) act as a transceiver, control encryption on the network, and can act as a bridge, or router, to a wired 10/100BaseT Ethernet network. Access points can benefit the network by improving range. An access point mounted in a central location receives data from each system and can resend the data to all systems within its range. Access points function similar to cellular phone towers. When a wireless adapter is detected within its range, the user is identified and network data are transmitted to and from that user. A hardware access point can support up to 64 users. If multiple access points are located within a home, a PC or laptop will lock onto the one providing the strongest signal.

SECURITY

Wireless home network users are understandably concerned about security given radio waves penetrate walls, and most network standards broadcast a few hundred feet. Although DSSS offers a degree of security through its frequency switching technology, it is primarily used to optimize data transmission and should not be relied on as the sole source of security. [1] If a network is operating based on the 802.11b standard, it would be possible for a hacker with a laptop to join the network, given the laptop contained an 802.11b PC card adapter.

One method available for Windows operating system users would be to restrict file and printer sharing to network users who possess an authorized password.

Another security feature that is required by the IEEE's Wi-Fi standard is Wired Equivalent Privacy (WEP). WEP encrypts each data packet before transmission, whether the network is wired Ethernet, wireless Ethernet, or a hybrid. Each wireless network user is assigned a set of keys based on a key string passed through the WEP encryption algorithm. Network access is denied to anyone who does not have an assigned key. Standard encryption uses a 40-bit key, but many vendors are providing hardware with 64-bit to 128-bit encryption. Although encryption/decryption will increase security, it also will slow down the overall speed of the network.

CONCLUSIONS

For the home PC user interested in connecting multiple PCs, laptops, or peripherals, a wireless network offers an attractive solution. Competitive costs, easy installation, widely adopted standards, improved speed, and reliability are making wireless networks increasingly competitive with wired solutions. The next generation of wireless standards, software, and hardware should only tighten the gap of the competition. Future network standards will add telephony and multimedia support to the existing standards, opening the door for video-on-demand, audio-on-demand, voice-over-Internet-provider (IP), as well as high-speed Internet access.

REFERENCES

1. Needleman, Ted. "Wireless Networking." *Laptop*, September 2001, pp. 48–60.

2. Waring, Becky. "Wireless Home Network Wars." *PC World*, April 2001, pp. 42–45.

3. Champness, Angela. "IEEE 802.11 DSSS: The Path to High Speed Wireless Data Networking." Wireless Ethernet Compatibility Alliance, www.wirelessethernet.org, October 2001.

4. Denton, Chad. "Shed Your Network Cables." *Smart Computing* 12, no. 8 (August 2001), pp. 92–95.

5. Waring, Becky. "Wireless Comes Home." *PC World*, July 2001, pp. 119–127.

Case 15-2

Broadband in the Home

Mark Bryant

INTRODUCTION

With the advancing capabilities of the Internet and the need for high-quality digital data, video, and voice services, consumers want more bandwidth than their typical dial-up modem can handle at home. They want high speed at a reasonable cost, and an always-on connection that doesn't tie up their phone line. The solution is broadband technology and it is growing rapidly as more and more consumers discover this service in their area.

According to the FCC, there were 375,000 subscribers to broadband services as of late 1998. This total consisted of at least 350,000 cable users and 25,000 DSL users. By the end of 1999, the number of subscribers tripled to over a million. Approximately 875,000 subscribed to cable and 115,000 to DSL, with the remaining consisting mostly of wireless and other media. Cable companies have increased their subscribership threefold and exchange carriers have increased their DSL subscribership fourfold. Fifty-nine percent of the zip codes in this country have at least one subscriber to broadband technology, and 91 percent of the country's population lives in those zip codes. [1]

There are three broadband services that are widely available to home consumers: cable, DSL, and wireless. Information about each service will be introduced along with the basics of transmission. Each of these services also will be described and evaluated according to availability, cost, and speed. Having knowledge about each service will help consumers make better decisions on which broadband technology is right for them.

CABLE

A cable modem is a device that allows high-speed data access via a cable TV network. To offer highspeed Internet services, a cable operator creates a data network that operates over its hybrid fiber/coax (HFC) plant. The following diagram provides a high-level look at a typical large-market cable network, including a regional cable head-end (typically serving 200,000 to 400,000 homes), that feeds distribution hubs (each serving 20,000 to 40,000 homes) through a metropolitan fiber ring. At the distribution hub, signals are modulated onto analog carriers and then transported over fiber-optic lines to nodes serving 500 to 1,000 homes. From the node, these signals are carried via coaxial cable to the home. [2]

A splitter at the side of the home segments coaxial cable lines serving the cable modem and TV outlets. Cable modems may connect to an Ethernet card in the PC with Category 5 cabling and RJ-45 connectors, or through a Universal Serial Bus (USB) port. A device called a cable modem termination system (CMTS), located at the local cable operator's network hub, controls access to cable modems on the network. Traffic is routed from the CMTS to the backbone of a cable ISP. [3]

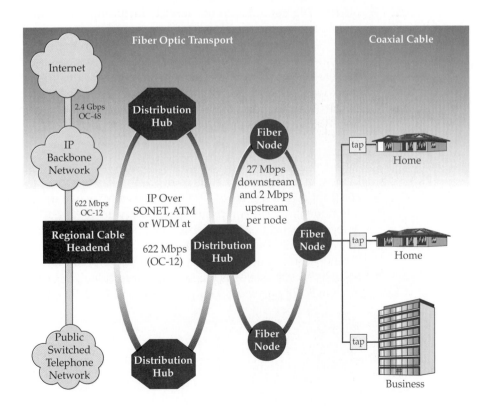

TRANSMISSION

The cable architecture was originally designed to transmit data in one direction—downstream. To offer Internet services, a cable company must upgrade the system to also transmit upstream. Because of this, a cable modem sends and receives data in two slightly different fashions. The preferred downstream modulation technique, 64 QAM, offers up to 27 Mbps per 6 MHz channel. Data can be placed in a 6 MHz channel adjacent to TV signals on either side without disturbing the cable television video signals. Typically, it is placed in the 50 MHz to 750 MHz portion of the spectrum.

In a two-way activated cable network, the upstream data are transmitted in the 5 to 42 MHz spectrum. Because cable is an RF network, it is vulnerable to transient problems "within the network" from RF interference. Since cable networks are tree and branch networks, noise gets added together as the signals travel upstream, combining and increasing. Most manufacturers use QPSK, or a similar modulation scheme, in the upstream direction, because it is a more robust scheme than higher-order modulation techniques in a noisy environment. The drawback is that QPSK is "slower" than QAM. [2] Upstream transmissions may therefore compete with others in the area and get delayed (suffer high latency) due to noise-fighting techniques, and cable companies may prohibit any kind of constant upstream use. [4]

AVAILABILITY

Cable is the most available service for broadband technology in the home because homes are typically already wired with coaxial cable. Many cable companies are offering high-speed Internet service, including Time Warner with Road Runner and AT&T with Excite@Home.

Cable companies have been reluctant to open their wires to unaffiliated ISPs, claiming they've invested too much in the system to lease the lines to other companies. ISPs have filed lawsuits to gain access to the lines, and they've won some local cases, which the cable companies have appealed. AT&T has recently softened its stance, announcing that it's willing to share its lines with other ISPs, though that won't likely happen until 2002. [5]

COSTS

In most markets, service costs from $30 to $40 a month, although in some areas the cheapest access will cost $70. Companies may waive the installation fee and lease the modem, which is typically proprietary. In 1996, CableLabs, an industry technology organization, developed an open standard for cable modem products called DOCSIS (Data Over Cable Service Interface Specification). The standard was developed to ensure that cable modem equipment built by a variety of manufacturers is compatible, as is the case with traditional dial-up modems. [3] If the cable modem is not provided, it may cost as much as $200, but prices continue to decline.

SPEED

Cable modem speeds vary widely, depending on the cable modem system, cable network architecture, and traffic load. In the downstream direction, network speeds can be anywhere up to 27 Mbps, an aggregate amount of bandwidth that is shared by users. Few computers will be capable of connecting at such high speeds, so a more realistic number is 1 to 3 Mbps. In the upstream direction, speeds can be up to 10 Mbps. [2] However, noise and other interference usually limits the speed between 64 Kbps and 1 Mbps.

DSL

DSL (Digital Subscriber Line) utilizes more of the bandwidth on copper phone lines than what is currently used for plain old telephone service (POTS). By utilizing frequencies above the telephone bandwidth (300 Hz to 3,200 Hz), DSL can encode data to achieve higher data rates than would otherwise be possible in the restricted frequency range of a POTS network. In order to utilize the frequencies above the voice audio spectrum, DSL equipment must be installed on both ends and the copper wire in between must be able to sustain the higher frequencies for the entire route. There are many different kinds of DSL that differentiate on speed and bandwidth allocation that are beyond the scope of this paper.

TRANSMISSION

On the consumers' end, a DSL modem modulates digital information from the computer to send it along the local loop. The data travel through a network

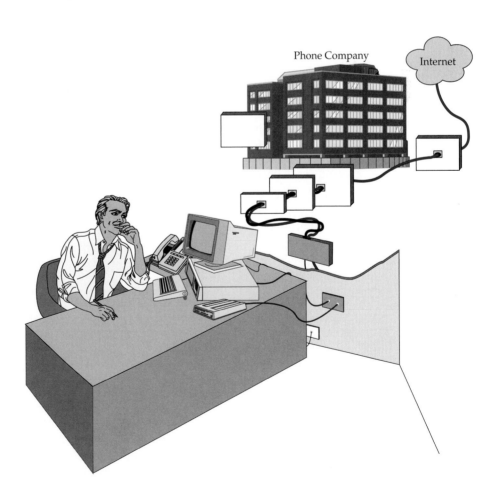

interface device, to the main distribution frame, and to a splitter. These signals are then translated by a Digital Subscriber Line Access Multiplexer (DSLAM) located at the phone company's nearest central office and sent to an ISP (which is frequently the phone company itself) to get out to the Internet. [6]

Typically, the DSLAM connects to an asynchronous transfer mode (ATM) network that can aggregate data transmission at gigabit data rates. At the other end of each transmission, a DSLAM demultiplexes the signals and forwards them to appropriate individual DSL connections. [7] The farther away the consumer is from the central office, the slower the connection will be, along with more line distortion and signal deterioration.

AVAILABILITY

DSL is not as widely used as cable, but it is available in many areas. If one lives more than two miles (or about 18,000 feet) from the nearest central office, he/she can't get DSL at all. According to the industry trade group ADSL Forum, about 60 percent of U.S. telephone customers live within areas that could support DSL. [8] One can contact the local phone company or use "Telco Exchange's DSL Pricing and Availability" Web page. Internet service also is needed, and most phone companies double as ISPs. [8] FreeDSL is a company offering free hardware and setup with no monthly charge for service. For the service, users must agree to provide personal information for demographic use and to have a small navigational bar containing advertising always visible while connected. [7] Speed also is limited to 144 Kbps, but may be increased with a monthly fee.

COSTS

In most markets, service costs from $45 to $60 a month, and can even get as high as $100. There is usually a fee for installation. The phone company must come out to check the phone line and condition it for service. They will have to install a splitter, or a consumer may install microfilters at the phone jack itself. If the equipment is not included, a modem may cost as much as $200, but prices continue to decline.

SPEED

DSL provides speeds up to 8 Mbps downstream (to the user) and up to 1 Mbps upstream, depending upon line length and loop and line conditions. Typically, however, downstream speeds are usually 256 Kbps to 1.5 Mbps and upstream is constrained between 64 Kbps and 640 Kbps. G.Lite (also known as DSL Lite, split-terless ADSL, and Universal ADSL) is essentially a slower DSL that doesn't require splitting of the line at the user end but manages to split it for the user remotely at the telephone company. This saves the cost of what the phone companies call "the truck roll." G.Lite, officially ITU-T standard G-992.2, provides a data rate from 1.544 Mbps to 6 Mbps downstream and from 128 Kbps to 384 Kbps upstream. G.Lite is expected to become the most widely installed form of DSL. [7]

WIRELESS

Wireless access technology takes shape in a number of different forms such as via a satellite TV service provider or a cellular phone network. Wireless systems can provide access to a large number of subscribers in a relatively large area. Although line-of-sight (LoS) clearance is required for wireless technologies to operate properly, new technology advances and substantial use of spectrum engineering systems are lessening the effects of this potential limitation. One major problem with wireless technology is rain fade (or attenuation). The signal attenuation caused by rain and climate varies greatly by region, but equipment advances are enabling service providers to make it less of an issue.

TRANSMISSION

The most commonly used wireless technology is MMDS (multipoint multichannel distribution system). The following diagram provides a high-level look at a typical broadband fixed wireless network, including a fixed wireless head-end that connects to a central antenna that broadcasts data directly to home and business locations, or to smaller cell sites, which in turn reach remote pockets of businesses or residences. Data are either sent back upstream from customers over wireless frequencies or through traditional dial-up telephone modem connections.

The fixed wireless head-end is the control point for the broadband access network. This switch/router also connects to a wireless cable modem termination system (CMTS) that coverts data from a wide area network (WAN) protocol, such as packet over SONET, into digital signals that are modulated for transmission over the wireless network. These signals are then converted into wireless microwave frequencies through a transceiver and broadcast through an antenna to customer homes. Content and application servers are typically located at the fixed wireless head-end, as are network management and operations support systems.

An antenna and transceiver at the home receive the incoming data signal and transmit it over in-home coaxial cable lines to a broadband modem. The modem connects to an Ethernet card in the PC with Category 5 cabling and RJ-45 connectors or a Universal Serial Bus (USB) interface. [9]

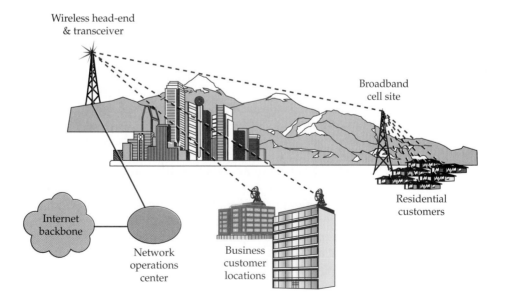

Wireless head-end & transceiver

Broadband cell site

Residential customers

Internet backbone

Network operations center

Business customer locations

AVAILABILITY

Wireless technology is growing slowly because transmitting towers have to be built; the infrastructure is not already in place like cable and POTS. A consumer must be within a 30-mile radius of the tower in order to receive the wireless signal. The FCC also has begun the process of opening additional spectrum bands for fixed wireless applications, including 25 MHz at the 4.6-GHz level and a huge block of 1.4 GHz at the 40-GHz level. Companies such as AT&T, MCI WorldCom, NextLink, WinStar, Teligent, and Sprint have all secured spectrum for the deployment of advanced point-to-multipoint systems. [10]

Currently, wireless technology is available in larger metropolitan areas. American Telecasting Inc. (ATI) has launched service in Denver and Colorado Springs, Colorado plus Portland, Oregon. CAI Wireless Inc. has launched in Rochester, New York, and in New York City. CS Wireless Inc. has deployed high-speed Internet service in Dallas, Texas. People's Choice TV (PCTV) has launched its SpeedChoice service in Phoenix, Arizona and Detroit, Michigan while DirectNET is offering service commercially in Ft. Lauderdale, Florida. [9]

COSTS

In most cases, a point-to-multipoint wireless connection costs less than one-tenth what it would cost to run wire to the same site. But this may be insignificant because most homes are well wired. In most markets, service costs from $40 to $80 a month plus a fee for installation and a transmitter.

SPEED

Just like wired cable, a 6 MHz wireless television channel can support 27 Mbps of downstream data throughput using cable modems with 64 QAM technology. A telephone line will still have to be used for upstream, which may be limited to 33.6 Kbps using a typical dial-up connection. Work is still being done on migrating to a full two-way wireless data delivery, which would be limited to 1 Mbps upstream. [9]

CONCLUSION

With the advancing capabilities of the Internet and the need for high-quality digital data, video, and voice services, consumers are finding that they now have a choice in high-speed connections via cable, DSL, or wireless technology. Benefits include fast data-transmission rates and an always-on connection at an affordable price. In comparing the three currently available broadband technologies, a consumer will find that they all offer similar benefits. Companies are moving fast to promote their technology as more and more consumers subscribe to high-speed service. Availability of service in the consumer's area will be the main factor in selecting a service. Because speeds may vary for each service and are very similar, price per month and installation charges will be the mitigating factor on selecting among competing services in a given area. Having knowledge about each service will help consumers make better decisions on which broadband technology is right for them.

The following chart compares the three major broadband services according to availability, costs, typical performance, and some pros and cons for each service.

Source: "Bandwidth on Demand," http://www.pcworld.com/current_issue/article/chart/0,1925,9499+4+0,00.html.

Service	Availability	Typical Monthly Cost	Typical Maximum Performance (downstream/ upstream)	Pros	Cons
Wireless	Widespread	$50 (for 100 hours)	400 Kbps/ 33.6 Kbps	Good downstream speed, available to anyone with a clear view of the southern sky.	Uses dial-up for upstream connections; installation is complex.
Cable	Limited	$30–$65	15 Mbps/ 33.6 Kbps– 2.5 Mbps	Where available, it's currently the cheapest way to get a continuous high-speed connection	You can't choose your ISP; shared-node system may lead to security and speed problems.
DSL	Very limited	$49–$1,200	144 Kbps–8 Mbps/ 64 Kbps–8 Mbps	Turns your ordinary phone line into a fast connection that's always on.	Still very sparsely deployed and often costly; most versions require installation by a technician.

REFERENCES

1. "FCC Issues Report on the Availability of High-Speed and Advanced Telecommunications Services." *Available at* http://www.fcc.gov/Bureaus/Common_Carrier/News_Releases/2000/nrcc0040.html.

2. "Cable Modem FAQ." *Available at* http://www.cabledatacomnews.com/cmic/.

3. "Cable Modem Primer." *Available at* http://www.cable-modem.net/tt/primer.html.

4. "DSL vs. Cable." *Available at* http://www.dslreports.com/faq/faq - 129.

5. "Cable Modems." *Available at* http://www.pcworld.com/heres_how/article/0,1400,14281,00.html.

6. "The $1 Trillion Bet." *Fortune*, October 9, 2000, pp. 125–134.

7. "DSL Guide." *Available at* http://whatis.techtarget.com/WhatIs_Definition_Page/0,4152,213915,00.html.

8. "DSL." *Available at* http://www.pcworld.com/heres_how/article/0,1400,14129,00.html.

9. "Wireless Broadband." *Available at* http://www.cabledatacomnews.com/wireless/.

10. "Beyond T1/E1 1999–2000 Volume 1, U.S. Residential Markets." *Available at* http://www.cir-inc.com/reports/t1e1v1/exec.html.

Summary

This chapter discussed what seems to be separate applications of broadband technologies: linkages to the home and SOHO. Much of the impetus for delivery of broadband has come from the telecommuters who demand higher bandwidth in the home. Some people believe that the distinction between office and home may be blurring as the tendency to be always connected grows.

DSL and ISDN allow LECs and IXCs to use existing infrastructures while moving from an analog to a digital environment and to provide bandwidth beyond modem speeds in the home and SOHO. ADSL has the potential to bring bandwidth in excess of T1 to the home and office, even moving this local-loop-based technology to 9 Mbps bandwidth. This capability should make possible more offerings to the home and potentially change the way businesses communicate and conduct business. Change begets change.

As we see more bandwidth to the home, we also see a need for new CPE in the home environment. The provision of bridges and routers may become more commonplace as high-bandwidth applications need to be shared between home and office. Corporations appear likely to be driving this trend for their telecommuting employees.

We discussed the major drivers for higher bandwidth to the residence. The Internet may well be the major driver. As people demand faster Internet access and discover more uses, there should be corresponding efforts by providers to offer more choices and more reliable broadband to the home.

The next chapter attempts to put a rational perspective on the future. The last two chapters have given you the foundation for that journey since much of the future will be bandwidth driven. As with all management decisions, the choice of which of these technologies to adopt will have significant implications as to the ability to compete.

Key Terms

Bluetooth, *693*
broadband, *688*
coaxial cable, *687*
digital camera, *695*
digital satellite
   radio, *698*
fiber to the curb
   (FTTC), *691*

hybrid fiber coax
   (HFC), *691*
IEEE 802.11a/b, *693*
movies-on-demand, *688*
near video-on-
   demand, *689*
small office/home office
   (SOHO), *690*

video compact disk
   movies (V-CD), *693*
video-on-demand, *688*
Voice-over-DSL, *691*

Discussion Questions

15.1. What other broadband options exist for Michael to provide service at the lake cabin?

15.2. If Michael installs IEEE 802.11b wireless at the lake, how far out can he go on the lake and still stay connected?

15.3. When will Michael run out of bandwidth on DirectWAY® at the cabin?

15.4. Do you need a router as well as a hub in a home or a SOHO network?

15.5. Would it be appropriate to use a switch instead of a hub for a home or SOHO network?

15.6. Can you use the extra in-wall telephone pairs for a network in the home or SOHO?

15.7. What minimum connectivity do you need to a SOHO?

15.8. How could you use DSL in a SOHO?

15.9. Could DSL deliver TV? NTSC? SDTV? HDTV? If so, how many channels?

15.10. Compare and contrast email, online chat rooms, instant messaging, and short message service.

15.11. Is ISDN a viable alternative for a SOHO?

15.12. If building a new home with a SOHO, how should it be wired? Or should it be wired?

15.13. What are the major limiting factors for telecommunications in the SOHO?

15.14. Is the bandwidth available to the home a major obstacle for telecommuters?

15.15. Discuss the "ideal" home network configuration.

15.16. What is the current status of converging business and home broadband availability?

15.17. Discuss the ramifications of government regulations on the availability of broadband to the home.

Projects

15.1. Determine if vendors in your area are offering fiber to the home. If yes, what services are offered? What costs are involved?

15.2. Determine if video-on-demand is offered in your area. What services? What is the cost?

15.3. Research the firewall alternatives for a SOHO.

15.4. Are cable TV providers using MMDS/LMDS in your area? What services and distances?

15.5. Determine the present level of telecommuting and trends in your state/province. Graph the present usage and extrapolate the trends for five years.

15.6. Determine the attitude in your community towards pornography and hate sites on the Internet. What recommendations do these same people offer?

15.7. Determine the attitudes in your school or community for music sharing via Napster. Are these the same as for movie sharing by way of video-CD?

15.8. Determine the impact on a local photo processor of digital cameras and the sharing of images via the Internet. What future do you find for the photo processor? For Eastman Kodak and Fuji Films?

15.9. Determine the telecommunications technology offered by a local car dealership for vehicles. What is coming online next?

15.10. Contact a major department store and determine their participation with online catalogs. What bandwidth does the home require to take advantage of this service?

15.11. Configure a SOHO with two PCs, a notebook, two printers, a digital camera, a Web camera, a scanner, and a copy machine. What telecommunications equipment is needed? Draw the topology.

15.12. Contact the LEC and determine the costs of DSL connectivity; compare to the cable modem provider's cost. Evaluate the data rates and reliability of each provider.

15.13. Determine the cost and performance differences in configuring a wired SOHO as in Project 15.11, above, with a totally wireless alternative.

15.14. If a telecommuter needs to transfer large graphics files, what are the minimum requirements for setting up a SOHO to ensure acceptable data rates? What are the issues, costs, and alternatives that should be considered?

15.15. Research the status of high-bandwidth-to-the-home solutions from competing vendors in (*a*) the United States, (*b*) the EU, (*c*) Latin America, (*d*) Asia, and (*e*) Africa. What are the trends? Outline the implications for economic growth and development. Rank order the regions by bandwidth available per capita.

Chapter **Sixteen**

Epilogue

CONTINUING CASE—PART 16

Michael Plans for Retirement

Michael called a meeting of all of his officers in early May. He wanted to review the development of the company over the past few years and lay out his vision for the future. As he sipped his coffee prior to the meeting, he mused about how the firm now represented a family of companies that were very capable in their markets. He realized that one thing that gave them a competitive edge was fast access to relevant information that provided constant contact with their customers and suppliers.

He observed that today's communications network was a far cry from his first telephone in the Denver office. Now, there were paging; wireless PDAs; cellular telephone; mobile connectivity: broadband access at home, the cabin, and the office; and an entire array of telecommunications technologies that made his business capable and competitive.

The firm had become very profitable and appeared to be on course for continued growth. Michael was now ready to pass the reins to Carlton; he wanted to make greater use of his lake cabin and to remove himself from an active role in JEI. Until recently, Michael had found the thought of parting to be emotionally difficult, but he had come to understand the change to be just another venture in his life. He was leaving a vibrant and profitable company with a good customer base, excellent relations with suppliers, and a set of technologies that were a firm underpinning for the future. He had done well with his little lighting company, and it was time to enjoy his retirement and allow his son to add his vision to JEI.

"Where's the sugar?" asked Alli as she poured her coffee.

"I have it over here on the coffee table," replied Carlton, as he sat down on the sofa.

"Let me tell you something right away," said Michael, a bit nervously. "I spent the weekend at the lake and finally came to the conclusion that it is time for me to retire and turn the company over to you. Specifically, I plan to step down as CEO at the end of the month and turn over the running of JEI to Carlton."

"Boss," interrupted Alli, "why?"

"I have worked with JL&S, JEI, SC, and SII for long enough. I would like to travel some, plus I think the company is at a point where we should go public and

issue stock in an IPO (initial public offering). This will give us greater exposure and return a fair amount of wealth to us all. I have been talking with my stockbroker about how to go public with a stock issue, and he feels we would do very well, financially. Since each of you holds at least 10 percent of the present stock, you will end up with a large number of shares, which you can cash in or hold, as you wish. Meanwhile, I plan on retaining financial control of the company, but give effective control to Carlton."

"Any other news, Dad?" replied Carlton, after almost spilling his coffee.

"You are definitely ready to run the company, Son; you just have to get used to my chair. I'm sure you are prepared to put your brand on operations and keep JEI moving forward."

"Who would take the other positions?" asked Alli.

"Good question! I don't want to specify JEI's organization. That will be Carlton's job, possibly with a few suggestions from me. What I think we really need to do is determine what type of company we are now and where we want to be in the future, then create the executive structure to support it."

"What is your vision?"

"It seems to me that our strength has always been our customer orientation. Alli, you do a great job in marketing, but it is always tempered by an ability to support the customer when the goods are delivered. We need to determine how we can put together a team-based management structure that always views the customer's needs, applies them to our ability to produce a quality product on a time schedule that meets our sales efforts, and follows up often with our customer base to supply solutions to new needs."

"Will that change our manufacturing locations?"

"We have been very successful with our manufacturing facilities in Kansas City and Scotland, but we are being pressured to tighten our costs even more. Mexico and the Far East have always been appealing from a cost-of-labor standpoint, but the imperative is quality products on a firm delivery schedule. With telecommunications, we can go anywhere; with design-for-manufacturability and the correct manufacturing technology, we can even manufacture here at home."

"What about our nonmanufacturing lines of business, Dad?" asked Carlton. "It seems to me that we have concentrated on manufacturing and installation for the past year and have not done as much in the area of risk services."

"Good point, Mr. Chairman!" replied Michael. "I am turning the reins over to you, so over the next few months you can align the company with your vision. Why don't I keep my fingers in the risk services department? There has been a lot of publicity of natural disasters lately, and the market for risk assessment and disaster recovery is growing."

Michael Reviews Risk Services

The weeks went by quickly as Michael settled into active retirement. Carlton became accustomed to his new role and only called his father three times for advice. Michael had cleaned out his desk and moved to a smaller office in the JEI building. It was still on the executive floor, but he knew he must not interfere with his son's running of the company. Michael enjoyed his free time and spent six weeks traveling in Europe with his wife. They did make a side trip to the manufacturing facility in Scotland, but only to see if the business still tugged at Michael. While there, he discussed possible use of the Internet for the WAN as opposed to the carriers now being used. He thought the Internet would provide a great way to begin their teleconferencing at a low startup cost and a virtual private network would be secure for the data.

Back from Europe, the former chairman of JEI began to spend more time at the office, rethinking risk services. Dana Hood, his risk services manager, suggested setting up three divisions. The first would handle disaster planning and assessment consulting; the second would handle disaster recovery with mobile systems to clean up and restore customer sites; and the third would expand the data vaulting service. Michael had seen possibilities for JEI's risk services, but had not seen the market mature as he had hoped. He now wanted to direct his son's company's efforts in this arena, restructuring the division into risk analysis and planning consulting, disaster recovery, safe data storage (data vaulting), and disaster recovery sites. He reasoned that with the increasing concern for terrorist actions, there was an expanding market for such services. And, in

Dana, he had an enthusiastic cohort for the expansion of JEI's disaster recovery and risk management business.

Michael knew that disaster recovery or business continuity now meant several things. First, it meant planning for such an event. Next, it meant the immediate resumption of operations for a client when a storm, fire, flood, or sabotage made facilities unusable. One way to cope was to have leased contingency facilities, either open space as cold sites or computer-supported hot sites. Now, he thought, was the time to consider bringing facilities to the client by way of mobile facilities when disaster struck. His customers needed two things: computer support and telecommunications facilities. He could put together an 18-wheel rig with power generation, a medium server, several client workstations, and good voice and data communications onboard. Additionally, he could configure two small offices for clients and one for his personnel. This capability would be leased on a contingency basis, and the client would pay full fees once it reached the disaster site.

As he thought of the truck-mounted facilities, he realized that what clients needed was either to recover their own facilities and continue business, possibly with remote computer support, or move to new temporary facilities with computer support. Thus, the trailer had to primarily provide the telecommunications connection to JEI's or other computers, not have a large computer per se. He would also need telephone facilities on the rig as a way to help the client's management get organized. With the mobile rig in place, JEI's team would move into the storm-, fire-, or flood-ravaged building and start the cleanup of facilities. Often it would mean just arranging with local utilities for power, water, and telecommunications. Sometimes, it would mean bringing power from the mobile rig into the building and hooking up his mobile telecommunications capabilities. With mobile power in the rig, a very small PBX could connect to the nearest working central office by landline, cellular, or satellite connections; JEI could get a business up and operating quickly. Often, the next step in recovery was to pump out the water and clean the office area of the mud, soot, salt, or debris of the storm, fire, or flood. This was the job of the cleanup crews. The worst problem as far as JEI was concerned was the recovery of paper documents. Michael discovered there were companies specializing in freeze-drying paper documents for recovery and decided he would defer to them for this service. He would, therefore, actively encourage clients to move towards imaging of documents so he could telecommute the resultant files to his data vaults along the Front Range. He had leased two worked-out gold mines in Colorado and found them perfect for highly secure data storage. He had installed redundant, secure telecommunications to each mine and could now eliminate the daily truck schedules formerly necessary to physically transport the data tapes and disks to storage. In addition, he had adequate standby power generation capability in place in the event the power grid was knocked out by the disaster. With the improved telecommunications, JEI could provide backup data storage to a client anywhere. The connectivity could be by landline, by way of broadband fiber networks, or by satellite links. In either case, he could now expand his data storage services nationally, or even worldwide, which would give him a natural entry to the same clients for risk assessment and disaster recovery planning. To do this, he must ensure RAPS: reliability, access, performance, and security.

Michael saw that many of his ventures had been "targets of opportunity," as his old Air Force buddy Reade Sidner once commented. Fighter pilots were given two duties in World War II. The first was to escort bombers to the target and ward off any enemy fighters. The other was to escort the bombers, but if unopposed, seek out any target of opportunity, as an offensive measure of defense. So it had been with JEI. They seemed to stumble onto new opportunities. It was now time to change the nature of this venture with capitalization on the correct telecommunications technology.

Broadband Technologies

Carlton attended one of the many reunions of his alma mater, this time keeping an eye open for new talent for JEI. He had kept up with his reading in engineering and was finding more and more references to broadband technologies. It was not a new subject; broadband integrated services digital network, SONET, and ATM had been in the engineering news for several years. But the competing technologies were settling down, and the broadband industry was maturing to the point where users like JEI could have access to much broader bandwidth pipelines.

After the reunion, Carlton met with his division chiefs and the subjects of high-speed telecommunications and standardization came up. For the first time, the question arose as to whether JEI should move to higher-speed circuits. Because of the importance of broadband technology to the data storage line of business, that product line had developed quite an expertise in the various technologies. When asked whether they were ready to start marketing their expertise, Dana noted they were not quite ready to do this and asked if JEI could wait for a bit. Next, Carlton asked Sarah Brown about the need for standardization.

"What do you mean?" asked Sarah, who continued to have overall telecommunications responsibility.

"It seems to me that we should strive for the same topology and protocol wherever possible. The Kansas City factory and office building operate on an Ethernet bus, the headquarters here operates on a token-passing ring, and SII installed an inexpensive star network. Would it not be better if we all went to the same capability? We really should revisit our telecommunications architecture to ensure we can remain consistent in the overall plan."

"We have gateways on each network that connect them all via the WorldCom network and the Internet," replied Sarah. "It seems OK to have done what we did, assemble what we had into a cohesive whole, as long as we consider problems we might face in the future. Do you think it worth the expense to change out all of the cards, controllers, and gateways in the headquarters and at SII just to have consistency?"

"Well, maybe not, but it would make your job easier!"

"Well," sighed Sarah, "Specialty Controls in Kansas City continues to use DEC minicomputers as JEI in Denver moves to an IBM AS/400 small mainframe. JEI does processing for offshore manufacturing and SC supports SII's offices. To date, the differing architectures have not been a problem, but then the offices have been kept autonomous where possible. As new acquisitions are considered, topologies and protocols of LANs and operating systems of mini- and mainframe computers will be important."

"Let's not take the easy way out, however. As we upgrade our LANs, let's be sure to consider our real needs and the system architecture, and do the same when we upgrade our small mainframes. Possibly in time we will migrate any one facility to a different topology and protocol and, perhaps, move all processing here to headquarters, now that we have good telecommunications services among the facilities. One thing is for sure, we continue to need greater and greater bandwidth on the LANs and the WAN that Sarah looks at constantly. Alli, how is the teleconferencing task coming among our divisions?"

"Great!" replied the new president of JEI. "I am in negotiations with a vendor on video cards for several of our PCs, and we already have the broadband access to WorldCom's network. I just have to settle on the actual bandwidth we want. We can work with as little as 386 Kbps, but it is at 15 frames per second, which seems jerky after a while. I am trying to see if they have a variable bandwidth and if our cards are smart enough to change to a higher frame rate as the picture becomes more dynamic. In any case, Sarah is working with the vendor and believes the price will be reasonable if we keep our conferences short. I was even approached by a satellite vendor offering a 1/2 T1 channel between 8:00 PM and 4:00 AM CST for less cost than the 386 Kbps channel on WorldCom at that time. That is late for most of our offices, but it would be a great way to have a quarterly meeting with all of our personnel plus even some of our largest customers. You might note that we could fit Scotland into this time frame also. I'll let you know what I find."

"And how is EDI coming, Sarah?"

"Great! We have 94 percent of our suppliers and 70 percent of our customers on EDI. The ones onboard are transmitting all of our business forms on EDI. Additionally, 99 percent of our customers and vendors are using email. We are finding this is less costly than voice communications and allows customers and vendors in other time zones to let us know of problems or questions."

"Well, people, security is still a good business!" chimed in Carlton. "Selling off the lighting division was a good idea and allowed us to expand SII quicker than we expected. Once we found that we could use pager technology effectively as part of the security alert capability, we have really shot ahead of our competitors. Manufacturing overseas remains a challenge, but I think teleconferencing will be of great value there. I find many of our offshore vendors like face-to-face dealings. We have tried to work with them using data and voice communications for too long. Alli, I think you should become

less sensitive about the cost and more attuned to how teleconferencing will give us an edge with both our vendors and our larger customers."

"Fine. Have you thought about picking up the cost of ISDN or DSL in our homes and letting us telecommute some each week? I for one could use the quiet as I work on strategy."

"I think that is a great idea! Sarah, get us costs on ISDN and DSL in all of the homes and offices of the executive and management staff, and let's get remote control software and teleconferencing hardware at home and the office. Be sure to put a PC with all the bells and whistles at the lake for Dad and me. I don't want us to have to rely on his laptop.

"Alli, did you get all of our cellular phones upgraded?" Carlton continued.

"Yes, and I will be issuing all of you PDAs with wireless modems and 802.11b connectivity. Hopefully, we'll be able to combine the cell phones and the PDA very soon."

"What about SII, Doug?"

"You know, Boss, I was wondering about how JL&S and SII should work together. Although SII has a great presence, we have been very successful with the name recognition of the JEI sticker. Alli, where do we do the best, manufacturing or retail sales and installation?"

"That depends on whether you mean dollar volume or contribution, but do you know what may be an even hotter issue, Carlton?" asked Alli.

"I give up, what?" replied Carlton.

"We have developed an expertise in telecommunications to support our various lines of business. In some cases, telecommunications is our business, or at least a major part of it, as in disaster recovery. It seems to me we could take advantage of this knowledge and start offering more telecommunications services to other businesses in, say, the Denver and Kansas City areas."

"What do you mean?"

"Well, it's similar to the situation in the past when we started offering computer services. We ran twisted-pair and optic fiber to give us the bandwidth we needed. Why not approach the city fathers and get permission to use their underground conduits to provide fiber cable access to each major business building in the business district. Then we could approach businesses and offer them the broadband pipelines for services ranging from local loop access and long-distance voice to intercity data communications. We already have VSAT and could add a large earth station to eventually become a teleport. But now we could be an alternate access provider and compete with the LEC also."

"I am with you! The idea is so obvious we should have thought of it before. Who do you have we can put on the task?"

"Hey, remember me," chimed in Doug. "I thought we were going to wait on offering broadband services. I am not sure I can support this amount of change."

"I know it will stretch you a bit, Doug," replied Carlton, "but we must strike while the iron is hot! Sarah can help you on this part time, but I want her to continue on voice and data system strategy. She has a colleague, Denise Alonso, who is a whiz with broadband. Denise formerly was a consultant for AT&T, so she has great experience. She can work up the technical details for you, Doug, and Alli can help her with the financial analysis. We will then need to have someone in marketing to contact customers."

"I am way ahead of you!" replied Alli. "Let's set up a task force with the people we need and get ready to hit the street running! I think time is of the essence, so let's not let this one sit. As I read the present environment, there is going to be a window of opportunity for us to enter a lucrative market for low incremental costs. Considering the trouble CLECs have had, we may be able to seize a sizable percentage of local exchange customers by offering the proper incentives. Doug, I know Michael is putting a lot of pressure on you to go with risk services, but we need to get on this also. Can you handle them both or do we need to hand broadband off to someone else?"

"Let me keep oversight responsibility for a while. If it gets too large, I will quickly let you know. The two subjects are too closely aligned to separate just now."

"Well, if we are going to talk about change," interrupted Sarah, "we need to have a multitier phone/fax answering system for SII. If a call is a voice call, the computer becomes a voice response system and lets the caller respond to questions to show the firm's interest. The result is that the system either connects the caller to one of our marketing specialists or engineers, gives a recorded response, or records a message from the caller. If the call is a fax, the response is a list of possible fax documents on our products and services. The caller then inputs

the number of the requested item, and it is immediately faxed back. This way, SII is available for query 24 hours per day." Sarah pulled out her project portfolio notebook and asked each of the officers to provide her with a short project description and priority so that she could bring the portfolio up-to-date.

"I like that idea," responded Carlton and Alli at the same time. "Sorry, Boss," Alli blurted out, "but I really like this idea. It is very important that a caller believes his/her request was heard. You know, Doug has set up 800 information numbers for all products made by all JEI divisions. Let's add fax-back and ACD to them also. This gives customers an information source that the competition hasn't got. Thus, any customer has a convenient means of obtaining information about any product as well as a conduit for providing product feedback to us."

"However," she continued, "I would like to suggest one change for the SII installation that will require some thought. If the caller really needs to speak to a person and it is after normal business hours, say late at night, what would be the effect of automatically transferring the call to our manufacturing plant in Scotland and letting one of the engineers take the call, personally? Scotland is awake when we sleep, so there would always be a person on call."

"Outstanding!" replied Carlton. "Why don't you look into this prospect on your next trip there? You are still planning on visiting all of our facilities this month, right?"

"My bags are packed as we speak."

"Hey, while you are there, ask them how the Internet is serving them as a WAN and whether we need to find an alternate path. I don't want slow speed to cause a bottleneck."

"Speaking of bottlenecks, Boss," commented Dana, "part of my investigation of risk has been here at JEI headquarters. As we have grown, we have created operating procedures and other documentation that everyone needs to access electronically. I found several copies of a few documents, each with a different date on it. We all need to work from the same copy. Why don't I create an intranet onto which we can place all of these documents, plus a few that are sitting in your desk drawer?"

"Great idea," Carlton replied. "How about moving our World Wide Web page from the Internet provider and placing it on the intranet. This way, we have better control over it, the cost is reduced, and we can use the intranet for both internal and external needs."

"Got you there," Dana replied, "I will get a server and an Internet IP address and start moving the home pages next week. I figure I can make all of our JEI stuff secure with passwords and a firewall but allow our customers access to everything else. I also will put all of the fax-back documents on it plus a database of all of our products."

"Super," commented Michael, listening in near amazement. "I forgot about competing via the Internet because the last time we talked about it security seemed to be a large issue. Since you have such good ideas on this, how about another problem we have?"

"What's that, Michael?" asked Dana.

"Doug has come up with a neat bit of software that our SII offices can use to demonstrate our systems to customers. The software is in the early stages, and we need to be able to deliver it and frequent updates to each of the several dozen SII offices, quickly. Any ideas on how to do this?"

"Uhmmn, I think I know how we can do it," Dana replied. "We have started to use VSAT, so let's ensure that all offices have this capability, use the commercial satellites, and transmit to all concerned."

"Great, and would you find out about running Giga-Ethernet between all the buildings here in Denver? We could upgrade our telephone and data circuits at the same time. Also, look into Giga-Ethernet long haul; you know, a WAN. This would avoid protocol conversions."

Michael continued to listen, feeling more secure in his staff and leaving the operation in their capable hands. Yes, he would work on risk assessment and management, but his primary goal was to set the strategy, hire personnel, and leave the details to them. His wife had already selected their next trip to the Maya ruins in Mexico and he knew now he could leave with no fears. A long way from Oak Street, JEI was stable and successful and Michael knew it.

INTRODUCTION

Telecommunications value is the ability to facilitate and add value to the business.

Some equate keeping up with the field of telecommunications to changing a tire on a moving vehicle.

There is a blurring of the lines that traditionally separated the home, office, and business.

The voice industry is changing and broadband is a driver.

Competition is coming for the LECs, leading to multiple providers that look alike. LECs will differentiate by value-added content.

In closing this book on the management of telecommunications, there is a tendency to make predictions. Considering the fast-changing nature of the field of voice and data communications, we would make such predictions at our peril. Instead, we address forces, in both the general area of technology and the specific field of voice and data systems, that will cause change. Voice and data systems will continue to evolve and will change the nature of how we conduct business, wage war, and live our lives. Take the following as a guide, a set of guideposts, and not a specific picture of the years ahead.

As you read this text, you experienced the telecommunications changes in the home, office, and business. The information superhighway (the Internet) goes to most neighborhoods. Your CATV provider may already be providing local loop services to the central offices, and your LEC may be competing in the area of information services. An alternative to the LEC may be offered by a *competitive access provider* (*CAP*). The major IXCs continue to advertise and compete for a large amount of voice and data transport dollars, and video rental store owners have a difficult time sleeping with the advent of pay-per-view movies via CATV and satellite. Consider the following questions: Who provides local public-switched voice network access? The overall telecommunications environment is changing even more and at a greater rate in the United States since the signing of the Telecommunications Act of 1996. What is the LEC's business outlook.

How many television channels do you receive, and what is the medium for delivering them to you? Who is the provider: CATV or DBS, LEC, or other? Do you have digital satellite radio? Do you live in a smart home or work in a smart office where security is computer-based? Are you using HDTV? Do you use a CD-ROM,

Information Window   16–1

It's out of my calling area: The wife of one of the authors tried to call from the Auburn, Alabama, calling area (LATA) to her parents in the Mobile, Alabama, calling area (LATA) using AT&T as the IXC. After the number was dialed (on a Touch-Tone phone), there was no sound of the call going through. She did this several times. When she finally got through, her parent answered the phone but there was no sound of her voice. The author called the local operator and related the problem, expecting her to realize that it might be the local switch, the remote switch, or the IXC connection. The response was, "It's out of my calling area. You will have to call AT&T, Sprint, or MCI." The operator was pleasant, but stuck to the story. Even in one's home one has to be a telecommunications manager, working with the LEC, IXC, and instrument manufacturers.

Bandwidth is to the future what storage was to PC and software.

DVD, or VCR for movies? What is your audio storage medium: cassette, compact disk, mini-CD, or DAT or DCC tape? Have you ever needed medical assistance via telemedicine where your doctor consulted with a remote expert? How much of your world is virtual and how much is real? How much do you pay for all of the telecommunications services? Is the television image two-dimensional or 3D, virtual reality? Are you connected to a games channel; is it interactive and multimedia, and does it include virtual reality? Does your car have GPS navigation, *On-star*®, or some other personal assistance device, and was it an option or standard feature? Do you still have a citizen's band (CB) radio in your car? Do you have a printer and/or a facsimile machine in your car? Has the distinction between your home office and your business office blurred? What can you get besides cash (e.g., traveler's checks) from your bank's ATM? Does your television come to you via cable or direct satellite broadcast? Is your cellular telephone digital or analog? What does your pager do, your PDA, your laptop, your fax, and your interactive multimedia CD-ROM-based entertainment? Is your PDA wireless connected and contain a cell phone and MP3 player? The technologies for the home are advancing as fast as the technologies specifically designated for the office and business. Each technology calls for and requires dollars, and frequently the dollars purchase more and more capability as the pace of new products continues to accelerate and their price decreases.

At the office, you may have a desktop, laptop, network computer, or integrated workstation. The computer should be as easy to use as the telephone, and the workstation should integrate voice communications. Can you use teleconferencing at your desk? Do you use Caller ID on incoming calls and connect the ID to your customer database? Does your company use a PBX, and does it have a hierarchial voice response system? Does your organization practice **bypass?**

Global competition means global communications.

Are you using twisted-pair copper, coaxial cable, optical fiber, wired media, or wireless in the form of *Firewire*, IEEE 802.11b, MMDS/LMDS, cellular, or satellite circuits? When it comes to disaster recovery, wireless has completely different considerations than wired. How does your firm access the Internet?

Electronic commerce includes technologies such as electronic document interchange (EDI), facsimile, email, Quick Response, JIT, bar coding, the Internet, and imaging.

How do you keep current on this fast-changing technology? Have you visited Comdex, SuperComm, Networld/Interop, NCF, or other technology conferences? What journals and magazines do you read to understand voice and data systems technology? Are you involved in distance learning, teleconferencing, or telecommuting? Are you overcoming environmental problems, such as pollution and traffic congestion, via telecommunications connectivity?

It is useful to analyze the capability of your personal computer, at the office or at home. How much RAM, speed, and storage capacity does it have? Another way to address this concern is to determine what connectivity you have, therefore indicating what RAM, speed, storage, and processing power you really need locally. Are you still worried about which operating system is the best or are you using a processor that can run them all? What difference does it make in your architecture? What LANs does your firm use, and what are their topologies and protocols? Is bar coding important to your organization? Are high-speed networks important? Does imaging play an important role in your organization?

Who are your customers and your competitors? How do you access and support your customers? Are you using customer relationship management (CRM)? How do you gain and maintain a competitive advantage in the global community? Do you employ enterprise resource planning (ERP) systems? Analyze the technology that is now routine for competing and your ability to access it ahead of the market. Do you maintain connectivity to suppliers? Does your organization use supply-chain management (SCM)?

It is quite popular to ask questions such as these in order to assess one's use of computer technology. Most of the capabilities and services addressed by the questions are not possible without broadband telecommunications. In the next section, we look at factors that provide pressure to adopt technology, especially voice and data systems, and those that inhibit this movement. The previous questions should have set the stage to address this focus.

As bandwidth becomes cheaper, the applications and the technology will dramatically change at home, office, and business, particularly as multiple providers supply capability.

THE FORCES DRIVING THE ADOPTION OF TECHNOLOGY

One way to think about future events is to look at the pressures, advances, and changes that cause technology to be adopted. The following is a list of such forces generated by a Delphi technique among faculty members in our academic department.

1. Shortening of product development cycle times.

2. Increasing global competition.

3. Increasing customized production versus mass production.

4. Emphasis on quality.

5. Customer orientation.

6. Proactive versus reactive adaptation.

7. Increased use of collaborative work.

8. Decentralization of functions with centralized control.

9. Work teams (cross-disciplinary versus specialized functions).

10. Constant environmental change: economic, regulatory, and technological.

11. Constant organizational change and development.

12. Just-in-time (perhaps evolving to "last minute")—flexible manufacturing.

13. Partnerships with suppliers and customers (EDI).

14. Deregulation, which leads to increasing competition.

15. Decrease in cost-performance ratio of information technology.

16. Increased information technology familiarization through experience, education, and training.

17. Enhanced media exposure to technological advances, for example, AOL and WWW on television, newspapers; technology issues in *The Wall Street Journal*; and so on.

18. Deployment of greater bandwidth.

19. Growing number of generic types of technology available.

20. Different technologies that can be combined to form an increasingly large number of configurations, which allows customers to find just the right combination for their needs.

21. Standardization (especially global), which works to reduce switching costs and the risk of trying a new technology.

22. Improvement in choices—after some 30 years of making information technology adoption choices, decision makers are beginning to get good at it.

23. Growing wage differential between developed and less-developed countries. Developed countries must substitute technology for labor in order to compete with low-wage countries.

The Constraints to the Adoption of Technology

Not all pressures are in favor of the adoption of new technologies, especially telecommunications. The following is a list of constraints to adoption that were generated by the same Delphi experience. When you consider the inclusion of a provision for regulating decency in the U.S. Telecommunications Act of 1996, the first item on the list becomes very relevant.

The Real World   16–1

Three fundamental trends are shaping the communications needs of enterprises and the solutions Avaya provides:

- Desire for **access** to and from any device, anywhere, for any transaction. Increasingly, enterprises are creating fast, effective linkages with customers, consumers, employees, and suppliers.

- Drive towards **virtualization.** Enterprises are exploiting communications technology to create flexible, "virtual" resources and capabilities.

- Demand for operational **performance.** Volatile markets, global instability, and rapid technological change require enterprises to reduce costs and strengthen security, while increasing throughput.

Source: Avaya 2001 Annual Report.

1. Ethical considerations—the Internet spreads pornography and hate literature and allows access to indecent materials.

2. Security concerns—credit card numbers have greater exposure to theft on the Internet.

3. Privacy concerns—more databases are connected; the government has more personal information.

4. Human resistance to change—the use of checks is not decreasing despite the proliferation of ATMs.

5. Regulation—the FCC continues to dictate broadcast standards.

6. Complexity of technology—telephones can be difficult to use; the telephone bills are hard to read; choices are greater.

7. Workforce literacy and skills inadequate to absorb new technologies at a fast rate.

8. Insufficient supply of qualified labor necessary to implement technology effectively, for example, IT skills crisis.

9. Insufficient ability to increase market share enough to absorb higher output (productivity increase) provided by new technology, making it difficult to justify the capital costs of purchasing such technology (particularly a problem when technology also is adopted by major competitors, thus creating excess product/service supply relative to existing product/service demand).

10. Short-term results from management perspective for realizing expected gains from investment in new technology.

Some organizations may have a high propensity to take risks (low risk aversion) and become early adopters of technologies; others may have great risk aversion. Those who are risk averse are likely to be laggards in adopting new technologies. Managers should realize that there are risks associated with both extremes. The early adopter may bet it all on a technology that fails, while the laggard may never be able to catch up to a successful early adopter.

TECHNOLOGY AND APPLICATIONS TRENDS

Voice and data systems technologies and the applications they support continue to change at a very rapid pace. These changes are needed to support the fundamental changes in organizations and the shifts in the way we do things in general. Leaders in information technology are focusing on several roles telecommunications technology played in organizations. They understood that voice and data systems technologies are becoming the enabler in shaping the distributed enterprise, and they are trying to keep pace with the increasing rate of change and the more competitive global marketplace. Some of the centers of attention are the Internet and electronic commerce, distributed systems management, and enterprise networking, which are discussed below.

Doing Business on the Internet

In the mid-1990s, the Internet was a lightning rod attracting attention as the initial manifestation of the information highway. The World Wide Web was seeing the generation of business home pages at a phenomenal rate. Businesses were rushing to establish an Internet presence in order to stake a claim and to extend their overall communications reach. While the explosive growth of the Internet continued unabated, some critics doubted the ability of this aging technological infrastructure to keep pace with demands. Others, however, saw in the Internet the prototype of a new world of networks that was about to forever change the way business would be done. Electronic commerce appeared to have found a new and irresistible channel. The efficacy of a network of networks was just beginning to be exploited with predictions of retail sales via the Internet of more than $4 billion early in the new millennium. Electronic commerce did not mean just EDI anymore. Electronic commerce via the Internet was off and running.

The widespread popularity of the Internet led to a rapid proliferation of so-called dot.com firms with exuberant financial backers in the late 1990s. Many of these firms failed as the U.S. and world economies went into recession. The surviving eCommerce companies appeared to be those with sound business plans. Despite the contraction in the number of firms, there was continued growth in actual eBusiness transactions.

Rare would be the business today that does not have a Web presence. If they are in retail sales, they most likely have a sales site. Those working further up the food chain most likely have websites for business-to-business transactions. An example of the use of the Internet is the increasing retail sales each of the last four Christmas seasons (as of 2002).

Distributed Systems Management

As business systems become enterprisewide and more complex, the management of these distributed systems becomes increasingly difficult. Trends such as client-server environments presented many new challenges. The clients in this architecture often became "fat" and overloaded their servers. Managers faced very difficult tasks in performing capacity planning, disaster management, and so forth, that were essential to meeting the expectations of both top management and users. The trend towards more client-server installations will exacerbate this problem unless new technologies are implemented to handle demands. As organizations become increasingly dependent on enterprisewide distributed systems, their management will be a priority. Distributed systems require management all the way from customer contact representatives to back-office knowledge workers. Managers must keep abreast of the telecommunications requirements of distributed systems or be doomed to experience system failures.

Distributed systems can be outsourced as well as being corporate-owned assets. The dot.com experience of the 1990s showed that outsourcing is a very valuable strategic objective, as the need for corporate servers and processing was reduced. Passing applications to ASPs and storage to server farms means greater reliability, possibly faster access, and definitely lower liability as the accountability moves from the balance sheet to the expense column.

Enterprise Networking

The distributed enterprise is absolutely dependent on a well-integrated, dependable, open communications infrastructure. This infrastructure not only must span the organization internally, but must reach out seamlessly to customers, suppliers, and partners as well. Managers must understand the choices in building the telecommunications infrastructure, the factors involved in deploying high-speed links, internetworking, evaluating and preparing for the implementation of new broadband applications, and their implications for competitive advantage. The rapid deployment of ATM and SONET means that the managers must understand how to take advantage of the technologies or be left to play catch-up.

The trend to move data via the Internet gains momentum daily. This trend may alter the marketplace for many vendors as use continues to grow. For example, many firms now find that they can use the Internet for EDI as a replacement for VANs. Much of what we do can be delivered by the publicly available infrastructure. As firms become more comfortable with transactions via the Internet, their use of this resource will continue to grow. It appears that the networks of enterprises will be more Web-based, and tend to change the structure of the organization so it will not resemble the command-and-control hierarchies of the past. Of course, as Internet use increases, there will be pressure to modernize and improve the capacity of the Internet so that the infrastructure can support more uses and users.

It appears rather certain that nearly everything and everybody will be connected and that there will be more collaborative activity—among both knowledge workers and smart devices. Geography will no longer set limits on where innovation, work, or transactions happen.

Scalable, pervasive networks and new wireless technologies should eventually enable people to reach any other person or device. The infrastructure should evolve to the point that it will no longer be a limitation.

The **virtual workplace** will be more and more commonplace as "telework" gains popularity. Many employees will employ mobile computers, wireless connections, and so on, and will be "in the office" whenever and wherever they hook up to the network.

The concept of a virtual hospital is gaining acceptance. There were more than 50 medical centers in the United States offering telemedicine services at the beginning of this millennium. Improvements in the technologies of data compression, image quality, satellite, and fiber optic transmission should continue to bolster this trend.

Advanced networks are providing high bandwidth and low latency, which should provide steps in the direction of scalable networks. As soon as ubiquitous, high-speed, dial-up bandwidth is widely available, scalable networks can emerge.

The addition of "smart devices" is anticipated. The installation of intelligent agents as network brokers will likely be developed to insulate users from the underlying complexity of the networks.

Technology trends such as inexpensive lasers, fiber optics, compact disk–based multimedia, and conversion to digital communications that helped shape the 90s should evolve further. One development that is expected to have high impact is micro electrical mechanical systems (MEMS) technology. This technology is anticipated to lead to several new uses of sensors of many types combined with telecommunications links.

Telemedicine

Telemedicine (also referred to as "telehealth" or "e-health") allows health care professionals to use "connected" medical devices in the evaluation, diagnosis, and treatment of patients in other locations. These devices are enhanced through the use of telecommunications technology, network computing, video-conferencing systems, and coder-decoders (CODECs). Specialized application software, data storage devices, database management software, and medical devices capable of electronic data collection, storage, and transmission are all key components of the telemedicine infrastructure.

Telemedicine customarily uses two methods to transmit images—data and sound—either "live," real-time transmission, where the consulting professional participates in the examination of the patient while diagnostic information is collected and transmitted, or "store and forward" transmission, where the consulting professional reviews the data whenever time is available. Many programs employ both transmission capabilities to maximize efficient use of resources appropriate to the medical services being provided.

AMD is the worldwide leading provider of "connected" medical devices, peripherals, and software used in telemedicine. With more than 2,000 installations in over 40 countries, AMD brings a wealth of experience and expertise to your telemedicine program. AMD provides complete device and software solutions, backed up by expert integration, customer service, and training support.[1] One may find additional material at the following Web locations:

Telemedicine Information Exchange (TIE):	http://tie.telemed.org/.
The American Telemedicine Association:	http://www.atmeda.org/.
Telemedicine Today Magazine:	http://www.telemedtoday.com/.

Nanotechnology

Nano, Greek for dwarf, is a hybrid science: the modeling, measurement, and manipulation of matter on the nanoscale. This deals with substances that are 1 to 100 nanometers across. Nanoscale electronics, of concern to us, turn single molecules into a switch, conductor, or other circuit element.

IBM built an entire logic circuit on a carbon molecule 1.2 nanometers wide (it takes 80 thousand of these nanotubes side-by-side to be the diameter of a human hair). HP has created circuits by manipulating molecules chemically to form components and paths at this molecular size. Thus, as **nanotechnology** evolves, it

---

The Real World   16–2
What Is the Semantic Web?

As Tim Berners-Lee is the first to acknowledge, today's World Wide Web can be a difficult place to get things done. Your search engine can't tell the difference between a Zip Code and phone number. To a computer perusing a travel site, a departure time of "09:05A" could just as easily mean 09.05 Australian dollars. On the **Semantic** **Web,** words will be tagged in a language called XML, so computers can tell what they mean. And smart software programs called "agents" will be able to grasp both the meaning and context.

Source: *Business Week*, March 4, 2002, p. 98.

---

[1] http://www.americanmeddev.com/about_telemedicine.cfm.

promises very small devices that can be imbedded into other objects and systems to sense, manipulate, and transport data.

Universal Description, Discovery, and Integration

Universal Description, Discovery, and Integration (UDDI) is a set of specifications that were designed to help firms publish information about themselves, their Web service offerings, and the required interfaces for linking with those services. UDDI combines an electronic "white pages" that list basic contact information, electronic "yellow pages" with details about the company and the company's electronic capabilities for trading partners, and "green pages" with standards and software interfaces to comply with an order to execute electronic functions using XML as their common language. UDDI was jointly developed by Ariba, IBM, Intel, Microsoft, and SAP.

Wireless and Mobile Technologies

Wireless technologies should continue to proliferate. Even though one fiber optic strand has more bandwidth than the entire radio spectrum, fiber will never be used to the exclusion of radio. Many believe that wireless is the driving force in technology of this decade. Personal communication systems (PCS) will continue to expand rapidly.

Mobile positioning satellites will be employed by automobile manufacturers, boat builders, and others to provide custom services such as alerting emergency agencies, provision of navigation assistance, and others. The technologies for such communications will be designed into the products. As an example, an award-winning product at a recent consumer electronics show was a walkie-talkie with GPS and mapping built in, allowing one user to transmit a map of his/her location.

Better, Faster, Cheaper

Technology should provide faster and cheaper ways to deliver data, text, graphics, audio, and video. Some refer to the idea of telecomputing as a medium of human communication. This form of networked intelligence provides vast new business opportunities.

Two-way videoconferencing promises to be widely used in medicine and education as the technologies of broadband media and compression are widely deployed. Higher-speed microcomputers enable networks to an extent unimaginable. Movement towards standardization and demands for interoperability should help in achievement of a true worldwide network. This should further underline the globalization of business.

In the telecommunications arena, networks will have increasing bandwidth capability; DSL, frame relay, and ATM will proliferate rapidly. Much of the old POTS network will need to be converted so that digital transmission will become the standard, otherwise IP telephony will replace it. While the old POTS infrastructure is likely to remain for some time, technological enhancement will enable the system to cope while the newer technologies are implemented and eventually supplant POTS.

Business telecommunications promises to be very dynamic as managers will be faced with integration of wireless applications. Wireless has found great acceptance and continues to grow with the advent of *Bluetooth, Firewire*, IEEE802.11b, IEEE802.11a, wireless LANs, direct satellite delivery of data, and so forth. The main business reasons for this growth are the opportunities and problem solutions found in the wireless technologies.

One of the most important forces in furthering business telecommunications is the emphasis on customer and partner relationships. We continue to see customer access to the firm increasing. Likewise, firms have noted the efficiencies of having connections to suppliers and partners. In effect, the form of the business organization has changed dramatically. Both customers and suppliers are now linked to the business for better functioning and service as well as competitive advantage. Often we see the existence of virtual LANs connecting the important players.

In the world of the consumer, telecommunications appears to be assuming an increasingly important role. Consumers demand such services as remote banking, shopping, and customized services that, in turn, demand more sophisticated voice and data systems. As more consumers have high-speed Internet access, this demand will likely increase.

Cost Trends

Cost of the appliances and computer chips that enable networks will likely continue to fall as they become commoditylike. Computer chips continue to be developed that vastly outperform their predecessors and at better cost/performance ratios. These chips allow for convergence of technologies into a single unit, for example, a palmtop that contains a cell phone, an MP3 player, and a digital camera.

The recent trend toward deregulation in many nations is driving competition with an expected lowering of costs for services as the vendors battle for market share. Although the opening of competition may see rates temporarily rise, the longer-term trend should be to push prices of many services to a point just above their costs. An example is long-distance telephone service. It will soon have such a competitive structure that it may develop into a fixed-cost commodity.

Equipment costs are likely to vary considerably as new technologies protected by patents can be high. However, cost of equipment in the highly competitive marketplace should trend downward as the demand attracts more competitors. As many of the new technologies are widely deployed, their costs should drop. Examples are *Palm Pilot*®, *Handspring*®, and *Blackberry*® coming to the market individually only to quickly evolve into strong competition.

We expect the content carried by the networks to be a higher profit margin area. Many telecommunications providers are scrambling to add content and/or make alliances with content providers because of this.

NTT's I-Mode and Microsoft's X-Box Point the Way

The Japanese NTT's wireless architecture called i-mode, supporting DoCoMo, provides wide bandwidth between mobile devices. I-mode is the platform for mobile phone communications that has revolutionized the way nearly one-fifth of the people in Japan live and work. Introduced in February 1999, this remarkably convenient, new form of mobile service has attracted over 28 million subscribers. With i-mode, cellular phone users get easy access to more than 40,000 Internet sites, as well as specialized services such as email, online shopping and banking, ticket reservations, gaming, and restaurant advice. Users can access sites from anywhere in Japan, and at unusually low rates, because their charges are based on the volume of data transmitted, not the amount of time spent connected. NTT DoCoMo's i-mode network structure not only provides access to i-mode and i-mode-compatible content through the Internet, but also provides access through a dedicated leased-line circuit for added security.[2]

On another front, Microsoft's X-Box game machine is designed to support Internet-based, global play between competitors or colleagues. The niche in the larger gamer market seems to be storage (hard drive) and (more importantly) high-speed connectivity. These two personal technologies point to the future, one that is wireless, personal, and connected.

Between Email and Chat

Two phenomena sweeping the world are SMS and IM. *SMS (Short Message Service)* is prevalent outside of the United States and moves text messages from one cell phone to another. Estimates of 17 *billion* SMS messages are being sent each day, at a charge of 17 cents each. SMS is often preferable to a voice call as it takes far less time for the recipient to get the message.

The alternative of SMS (although it is slowly catching on) for the United States is *IM (Instant Messenging)*. This involves, for the time being, software in your desktop that determines when the members of your *buddy list* have an active email client. The IM capability can send very short messages that pop up on the recipient's systems, without the overhead of traditional email. A response is short, quick, and easy. New versions, coupled with good bandwidth, allow for the transmission of video to the buddy. This system has propagated to many ISPs and is free. A major challenge for U.S. providers is to make this a cash stream, as is done outside of the United States with SMS.

Legislative and Regulatory Trends

The Telecommunications Act of 1996 was the harbinger of great change in the United States. Many other nations also are making fundamental changes to their laws and regulations that will cause the environments for telecommunications to be forever altered. Many countries have now allowed the entry of domestic and foreign firms to compete with their PTTs, formerly monopolistic providers of telecommunications. The relaxation of regulation means that more firms will be going abroad. European and Asian telecommunication firms will be active in the Americas and vice versa.

The trend towards deregulation should spur more competition globally and possibly influence more common standards. The networks that exist must be adapted so they can interact as a more common infrastructure for international or global interoperability.

[2] See http://www.nttdocomo.com/.

In order for all nations to benefit from the explosive developments in telecommunications, it will be necessary for the trend towards deregulation to continue. *Legislation must be an enabler and not an inhibitor.* It should facilitate networking rather than impose barriers.

CONVERGENCE

We have traced the business use of telecommunications in the case as well as viewed its historical development to provide a better understanding of the basis of today's systems. One of the factors that is changing everything is **convergence.**

Technological Convergence

The convergence of technologies is rapidly taking place—the most obvious is the convergence of computing and telecommunications, which has been accelerated seemingly by business applications. Firms see the potential of combining the power of computer-based information systems and telecommunications networks. Some of the driving forces are the Internet and intranet evolution; the World Wide Web has been the greatest change stimulus in modern times. The biggest impact has probably been the power of electronic mail over a global network. This factor has allowed a new era in collaborative work to begin.

The idea of collaborative applications and their main component, groupware, has been rapidly adopted by many firms worldwide. Groupware involves the sort of convergence that was mentioned earlier. Specifically, groupware includes computer-based applications, databases, messaging, Web access, and directories. Some observers such as Eric Hahn of Netscape feel that groupware and the Internet are two sides of the same coin. Several other collaborative applications are also major drivers for changing the face of telecommunications. Among them are workflow, knowledge sharing, and learning. With adequate bandwidth, the Internet and intranet evolution should see full-motion video, imaging, EDI, and so on, incorporated into business applications on a very widespread scale.

Several factors seem to be assisting the convergence. One of the major ones from the computing side is the seeming free fall in hardware prices and dramatic improvement in processing and storage capabilities. Coupled with these facts is the object-orientation evolution—characterized by the Java revolution. Common object request broker architecture (CORBA)–enabled applets should provide a way for firms to distribute software and run fully enabled corporate applications over the Internet. Again, convergence has occurred in this instance.

Real-time enterprises are based on the notion that when something is happening, the firm wants to react to it fast. The ingredients for real time include advancements of Web service standards, more competition among middleware messaging vendors, and new real-time applications. Firms are using real time to better combine business processes and workflow—cutting both time and expense. For example, The Limited, a clothing retailer, has moved from what they termed "rear view mirrors" of historical data, transferred in batch mode, for crucial business decisions to real time. They now are able to have stores on the U.S. West coast react to early indications of East coast sales and can rejigger floor sets to emphasize the fast-selling items before stores open in the West. Retail, manufacturing, and B2B market sections with integrated supply and distribution chains can share data across applications with quick handoff of vital information to the points where it is most needed in the enterprise.

Government and Convergence

The role of government in oversight of the world of convergence is controversial. How much control should be exerted? (Government ownership, regulation, or privatization?) If we have truly global connectivity, how can one nation impose its standards on others? (The differing laws of various countries about privacy are a prime example, although such collaborative actions at the Hague Conference may change this.) Some of these issues have become obvious as the Internet has grown. (But at least one country is installing an in-country intranet and filters to and from the Internet so it can "protect its citizens.") The most anyone can predict is that there will be several issues confronting nations, and most are ill-prepared to deal with them because of their global nature.

As long as the present trend towards deregulation (and privatization) continues around the world, it seems certain that the telecommunications environment will be volatile. The advent of new competitors in provision of local exchanges, the falling of old exclusive PTT barriers, and the entry into telecommunications by nontraditional competitors (e.g., electric and gas utilities) promise a very exciting environment. Competition promises to add new telecommunications providers, such as CATV and utilities. The CATV firms propose to offer Ethernet-speed cable modems for Web access. In addition, there are new firms seeking to provide satellite access to the Internet, such as Hughes *DirectWay*®.

Convergence Comes at a Price

The development of de jure standards surrounding the Internet promises to encourage electronic commerce. The consumer should be made comfortable with authorization and encryption standards so the concept of digital cash can be exploited. One author, who is active on eBay, pays for most purchases via *PayPal*®, which is electronic mail–based to move funds and inform the seller of the transfer. Efforts underway promise to provide a higher level of comfort to most consumers. Clearly, the comfort for both businesses and consumers is related to their perceptions of security.

Assisting the trend towards collaborative work is the availability of bandwidth to support real-time audio and video. Increasingly, the Internet will be used for this sort of virtual workgroup collaboration even in the multinational environment.

The issues of security, risk, and risk management will remain a major focus. The electronic environment ushers in a new era of vulnerability. One such is information warfare for both the military and industrial entities. Thus, network managers must be able to perform proper risk analysis and risk management as a critical part of their jobs.

The complexity and accelerating pace of change of the evolving telecommunications environment call for a systems approach. Managers must be aware that the behavior of the total entity is more than simply the sum of the parts. Therefore, managers need to study the systems and obtain an understanding of how they behave.

The rapid pace of change has great implications for the human resources involved in telecommunications. The trend towards organizational downsizing has resulted in what some refer to as a loss of tribal knowledge. This means that telecommunications managers must pay more attention to proper documentation of all systems from the macro-level architecture down to the micro-level implementation. The result of an economic recession in the United States in 2000–2001 and further recession resulting from terrorist actions, for example, September 11, 2001, brought this home to many.

Some will argue that in the evolving organization, the value of experience is declining because of the pace of change. This is true *if* employees do not have a continuous learning environment. One of the factors that impacts the telecommunications organization is a shortage of knowledge and skills in the technologies at the leading edge of development (refer to Appendix A). This trend is likely to continue as "hot" technologies continue to be applied. If telecommunications managers are implementing a hot technology, they must face the risk of the loss of expertise because other firms seek that expertise. This is especially relevant when dealing with new "handcrafted" systems. The mobility of the human resources with expertise can be a real burden. Therefore, managers should look outside for systems management assistance. It is vital that telecommunications managers design-in management at the introduction of new technologies.

Graduate students were given a task to list those things that would change their lives when they had free computing, global connectivity, and low or no-cost high bandwidth. Please refer to Appendix B for the results to date to see if you agree.

INFORMATION WARFARE

Information warfare strategies, like physical warfare strategies, are designed to hinder or disable military forces, disable industrial infrastructures and manufacturing capabilities, or disrupt civilian and government economic activity in order to put an aggressor or a target country at a disadvantage.

Source: Michael Erbschloe, *Information Warfare, How to Survive Cyber Attacks* (New York: McGraw-Hill, 2001).

Wars have historically meant the clash of men and weapons ranging from stones and spears to rifles, cannons, and bombs. The beginning of the 21st century saw a different kind of war emerging: nation states allied against called terrorist actions. Terrorism is now faceless, nation-independent, using any weapon available against perceived evil in the minds of the terrorists. An extreme example has been the attack on the United States of America in the form of a small group of terrorists, hijacking commercial aircraft and crashing them into the World Trade Center in New York City, in rural Pennsylvania, and into the Pentagon in Washington, DC, on September 11, 2001.

Large countries have become dependent on information technology and aggressors will likely use this dependence as a war target. With the connectivity of the Internet, the attack can come from anywhere. The attackers do not have to have high funding, just good knowledge. The form of the attack, that is, the nature of **information warfare,** could be sending viruses or other forms of software to military or commercial sites for the purpose of disrupting or disabling systems on which companies and nations depend. Examples would be disabled or overloaded POTS switches and network servers.

Companies and nations become more vulnerable as they gain greater dependence on information technology. Therefore, these entities must take a defensive posture and perhaps an offensive capability to stop or punish attacks, giving future aggressors reason to pause. As this is just an extension of a concern for security and privacy, it should be an obvious task.

The Real World   16–3
The Computer Wins Its Spurs on Afghan Battlefield

The war in Afghanistan revealed significant advances in the U.S. armed forces' ability to gather information and use it quickly to strike at an enemy. The so-called "sensor-to-shooter" gap had been narrowed considerably.

"I think there was immense progress," says Nick Cook, aerospace consultant to *Jane's Defence Weekly*. Before Afghanistan, the Pentagon's target was to be able to fire a weapon within 10 minutes of spotting a target. "Now people are thinking of shorter periods than that."

According to President George W. Bush: "Our commanders are gaining a real-time picture of the entire battlefield, and are able to get targeting information from sensor to shooter almost instantly."

Gathering information about an enemy and using it to hit him before he can hit you is perhaps the oldest goal of military strategy. Before radios and aircraft, it could take months. But the 10-minute target emerged after the Gulf war because defense chiefs were unhappy

that they could not hit Iraqi missile launchers in the time it took to pull one out of a hiding place, fire a Scud, and hide it again.

In theory, advanced sensors, digital communications, and precision weapons make it possible to reduce the gap to seconds. In practice, it is not so easy.

The Kosovo campaign in 1999 showed U.S. weaponry was good at hitting fixed targets such as buildings and bridges, but less good at hitting moving targets: very few Serb tanks were destroyed.

The mix of technology, information, and human decisions that should make it happen is known by one of the defense world's more complex acronyms: C4ISTAR—command, control, computers, communications, intelligence, surveillance, target acquisition, and reconnaissance.

The challenge for modern commanders is to synthesize the mass of data available from many sources into a picture of the battlespace that they can understand—and

The Real World (*Continued*)   16–3
The Computer Wins Its Spurs on Afghan Battlefield

especially one that gives them confidence that targets are correctly identified.

A second element is to circulate information across a network including anyone who might need it, including commanders in and outside the theater of war, and aircraft in the air and ships at sea. Then, command and control must be structured so as to give quick authorization to hit a target and give an order to fire a weapon.

Using digital and Internet technology to do all this is known as "network-centric warfare." It is a central thrust of Pentagon policy and a favorite theme of Vice Admiral Arthur K. Cebrowski, appointed by Donald Rumsfeld, the defense secretary, to spearhead the planned Bush-era transformation of U.S. military capabilities.

Though not a weapon in itself, defense experts see network-centric warfare as a "force multiplier" enabling much more effective and quick use of the formidable U.S. arsenal. It also makes U.S. forces less vulnerable to attack, because damage to one headquarters or ship will not disable the whole network.

Commanders in Florida ran the campaign in Afghanistan using data from an extensive bank of sensors ranging from satellites to human eyes. They received images from satellites, U-2 spy planes, Joint Stars battlefield surveillance aircraft, Awacs early warning aircraft, a British Canberra photo-reconnaissance aircraft, and Predator and Global Hawk spy drones.

To these pictures were added signals and electronic intelligence gathered by U.S. Rivet Joint and British Nimrod R1 aircraft, and eyewitness reports of U.S. and other special forces soldiers operating alongside anti-Taliban forces.

Most of the data feeds arrive at an operational headquarters separately. Bob Hoffa of Northrop Grumman says: "It's like looking at a variety of TV screens and watching four different football matches at the same time."

Experts say there is a long way to go in overcoming this first barrier: massaging the data into a coherent picture.

Second, the quality of images needs further enhancement so commanders have no doubt in their minds when

(*Continued*)

The Real World (Continued)   16–3
The Computer Wins Its Spurs on Afghan Battlefield

selecting targets. The next generation of sensors will allow much more accurate identification.

Third, the mass of real-time data has to be rapidly communicated. Bandwidth is a limiting factor, and will become more so as the number of unmanned spy planes multiply. More high-speed datalinks between aircraft are also needed.

Fourth, the role of human beings in the information chain needs study. Pilots of advanced fighters have on-board computers that sift information and make decisions for them. They know a missile is heading towards them, but they do not know how they know. Network-centric systems will do the same for all the information coming to commanders.

Thomas K. Adams, a former officer writing in the U.S. Army *War College Quarterly*, said: "The explosion of avail-able information inevitably results in information overload and flawed decision making . . . soon it becomes obvious that the slowest element in the process is the human decision maker."

Yet each strike must go through an authorization process, sometimes reaching up to the highest level. Targets have been lost while necessary approvals were sought—but some officers would argue this is better than giving a mistaken order that might kill innocent people.

For commanders, this could become more rather than less awkward. In the world of network-centric warfare, the president may be watching the same pictures that they are.

Source: Alexander Nicoll, "The Computer Wins Its Spurs on Afghan Battlefield," *Financial Times*, February 6, 2002, p. 3.

Case 16-1

Information Warfare: The New Front Line

David P. Goode

The September 11, 2001, terrorist attacks on the United States served as a wake-up call to American policy makers and citizens alike that our geographic positioning between friendly nations and oceans along either coast no longer safeguards us. Just as the world has become a global marketplace, a global community, it also has become a global battleground. Many of our enemies exist within our own borders, and those elsewhere may have access to technology that is essentially limitless, allowing them to strike at the heart of our infrastructure without ever being detected. Information technology has become the great equalizer between the "have's and have-not's" of the world. No longer is sheer strength in size and numbers an assurance of military and diplomatic dominance. In fact, many of the factors that traditionally have been cited as reasons for strength now stand out as areas of vulnerability. Those with large communications infrastructures stand to lose the most from the threat of information warfare. This report will look at the dangers of information warfare, its various forms, and what steps might be taken to safeguard our technological infrastructure.

TRENDS IN INFORMATION WARFARE

There are some very simple reasons why the United States is hesitant to employ various malicious forms of information warfare. First and foremost, America does not want to provoke an attack upon itself. The ironic reality of this new form of warfare is that it tends to inflict more damage upon the powerful, complex infrastructures that traditionally have been advantageous to a nation. Essentially, the United States doesn't want to "do unto others what can be done more easily unto (itself)." The more technologically advanced a country, the more vulnerable it is to the techniques of information warfare. It is no secret that the United States is heavily dependent on its technological infrastructure; therefore, any successful attack could be potentially devastating. The civilian and military sectors alike share in their vulnerability to attack on the country's information networks. Although the military spends a considerable amount of effort protecting its infrastructure within its institutional boundaries, it remains heavily dependent on the civilian information infrastructure. Nearly every aspect of the military industry depends on civilian information networks, whether it is through the national electric power grid, dependency on civilian transportation systems, or its reliance on the civilian sector for its basic communications ability. About 95 percent of military communications travel over the same phone networks used to fax contracts to other sites. The national electric power grid powers American military bases. Pentagon purchases are paid for via the federal banking network. Soldiers are transported under the guidance of civilian rail and air traffic control systems. Each of these information nodes represents a substantial vulnerability for the military in times of crisis.

The increasing flow of information, the evolution of the global market, and the creation of the Internet are all factors in creating the modern global village.

International corporations rather than nations are becoming the main actors in our society. With these changes, it's inevitable that we change the way we wage war. The catastrophic events in New York City in September highlight the fact that warfare is shifting more and more toward civilian targets. This trend likely will continue as information warfare plays a greater role in future conflicts. It is a basic tenant of warfare that the priority of a target is determined by its value to the other side. There is nothing more valuable in modern warfare than the flow of information gained through the use of digital technology. Thus, it is no surprise that military leaders have begun to shift their focus away from traditional methods of war fighting to deal with this new threat. With the increased digitization of the battlefield, it only makes sense to take measures to protect against attacks from outside interference. It is important to note, however, that information warfare is not confined to the battlefield. In fact, the civilian sector is more likely to be the source and the target of this type of attack. A major reason is that there is an inherent vulnerability in information technology infrastructures worldwide. The pace of development for cyber-security measures has not kept up with technology, creating an opportunity for would-be attackers to exploit sources of weakness. In both the military and civilian sectors, it's apparent that Western society has become heavily dependent on the digitized flow of information. Computers control nearly all of our vital national systems, to include power and water supplies, air traffic control, financial, and so forth. Further, we've come to rely on IT more heavily for our everyday lives than do the people of other countries. The unfortunate fact is that a day will come in our future when we will be faced with an attack on the very things we rely upon the most for our daily operations.

Potential Weapons

- Computer viruses that could be fed into an enemy's computers.
- Back doors and trap doors built into the system by the designer to allow the ability to sneak back into the system.
- Trojan horses, or malicious code inserted into programming to perform a disguised function.
- Worms that can self-replicate and use up a system's resources.
- Chipping, or slipping booby-trapped computer chips into critical systems sold by foreign contractors to potentially hostile third parties.
- Logic bombs that may lie dormant for years until they wake and attack the host system.

THE PERFECT WEAPON

Information warfare and terrorism have emerged as perfect bedfellows in the information age. The aim of terrorism is not to destroy an armed enemy head on, but to circumvent its strengths and undermine its will to fight. Terrorism accomplishes this by targeting the most vulnerable points in the society and disrupting daily life. By interfering with our most essential systems (power, water, etc.), the terrorists can use a technological assault to create mass confusion and loss of morale. While technology to operate and maintain information networks is expensive, the technology required to attack them is relatively cheap. It is interesting to note that over 60 percent of university degrees in computer science are given to students from developing countries, with the vast majority being from Muslim countries. The reality of the terrorist threat hits home when you look back at the Desert Storm conflict in the early 90s. During the Gulf War, according to the Pentagon, a group of Dutch hackers offered to disrupt the U.S. military's deployment to the Middle East for $1 million. Saddam Hussein turned down the offer, maybe to the benefit of the United States. The results could have been catastrophic for the deployment. The relatively inexpensive and mobile nature of information warfare lends itself very well to terrorists' use. Many would agree that it is the perfect terrorist weapon.

"This threat arises from terrorist groups or nation-states and is far more subtle and difficult to counter than the more unstructured but growing problem caused by hackers. A large, structured attack with strategic intent against the U.S. could be prepared and exercised under the guise of unstructured "hacker" activities . . . there is no nationally coordinated capability to counter or even detect a structured threat."
— Defense Science Board,
The Pentagon

Another way potential evildoers might choose to exploit information technology is through use of the Internet. It's long been thought by those within political circles in Washington that Osama Bin Laden has used the Internet to disseminate instructions to operatives in the field. Because the Internet spans geographical, cultural, and economic boundaries, its potential for outreach is tremendous. It's thought that the Internet will replace most other forms of media in the future, with the others merging into the Web. The dangerous potential of this technology in the hands of terrorists lies primarily with their ability to target the masses effectively by tailoring their disinformation to different sectors of the population—thus, the ultimate propaganda tool.

A VITAL RESOURCE

Information warfare entails more than simply exploiting information technology to gain an advantage on a battlefield. A more vital area of focus is that of protecting information systems critical to the functioning of our society. Being the most technologically advanced country in the world has its disadvantages—namely, we're the most vulnerable to attacks on our information structure. Within the military itself, nearly every aspect of daily operations is maintained by a complex structure of information networks. The Defense Information Systems Agency (DISA) recently opened a "continuity-of-operations" center in Slidell, Louisiana. The center stands ready to solve computer and communications problems encountered by design or accident that take place at any of the military's 16 main computer centers. Also, DISA has recently awarded several large computer security contracts and its biggest contract ever for antivirus software. The RAND Corporation, a Washington-based defense think tank, has recently developed exercises to explore a variety of threats and counteroptions available to the defense sector in the event of a massive information warfare strike. The scenario goes like this:

THE ATTACK: A three-hour power blackout in a middle-eastern city has no reasonable explanation; computer-controlled telephone systems in the United States "crash" or are paralyzed for hours; misrouted freight and passenger trains collide, killing and injuring many passengers; malfunctions of computerized flow-control mechanisms trigger oil refinery explosions and fires . . . electronic "sniffers" sabotage the global financial system by disrupting international fund-transfer networks, causing stocks to plunge on the New York and London exchanges. In America, local automatic teller machines begin randomly crediting or debiting thousands of dollars to customers' accounts; as news spreads across the country, people panic and rush to make withdrawals. Television stations in the Middle East lose control of their programming and a misinformation campaign of unknown orchestration sows widespread confusion. Computerized dial-in attacks paralyze the phone systems at bases where U.S. troops are scheduled to begin deployment; various groups flood the Internet calling for massive rallies to protest U.S. war preparations; computers at U.S. military bases around the world are stricken—slowing down, disconnecting, crashing.

This exercise highlights the dangerous potential of a massive information attack and how it might detrimentally affect our vital resources. Some key factors to remember in the battle against information warfare are

1. Waging information war is relatively cheap—acquiring "weapons" does not require vast financial resources or state sponsorship, only computer expertise and access to major networks.

2. Boundaries are blurred in cyberspace—traditional distinctions (public versus private, warlike versus criminal behavior, etc.) tend to get lost in the chaotic and rapidly expanding world of cyberspace.

3. Opportunities exist to manipulate perception in cyberspace—a misinformation campaign can galvanize public support or opposition using the Internet.

4. Information war has no front line—the battle takes place in the shadows. The political battlefield is anywhere networked systems have access. As the United States relies more heavily on complex, interconnected network control systems for necessities, its vulnerability remains.

THE NEXT STEP

There is currently debate in the United States, which faces the most immediate threat, on what steps need to be taken to protect against information warfare, and what part the government should play in protecting civilian networks. The civilian networks are controlled by private interest groups, some of them internationally owned. Therefore, the question of how the government would regulate them is complex. However, the vulnerability and ease of manipulation of some networks are weak links in modern society, and their exploitation by hostile elements threatens all elements of society. One suggested solution is to require organizations with a dependence on sensitive information technology to fulfill certain security criteria before being issued a government license. However, it must be noted that although such measures will provide a minimum level of protection against tampering, there is no such thing as 100 percent security. The solutions are certain to lag behind the potential threat until the threat becomes reality. At present, the cost of protection is higher than the cost of the attack. Until an attack on a major system actually happens, organizations are unlikely to take security measures as seriously as they should. Information technology is clearly changing the landscape of political discourse and advocacy. It offers new and inexpensive methods for collecting and publishing information, for communicating and coordinating action on a global scale, and for reaching out to policy makers. It supports both open and private communication. Advocacy groups and individuals worldwide are taking advantage of these features in their attempts to influence foreign policy. When technology is used in a normal, nondisruptive way, it can be an effective tool for activism, especially when combined with other media. However, with regards to cyberterrorism, few conclusions can be drawn about its potential impact on foreign policy, as there have been no reported incidents that meet these criteria. What can be said is that the threat of cyberterrorism is influencing policy decisions related to cyberdefense at both a national and an international level. It's important to realize that no government or private entity is likely to be able to completely protect its systems from information attacks. In regard to the civil sector, it may be optimal for system owners to bear the costs of protection, given the government's inability to make any guarantees. The government, on the other hand, should limit itself to protecting its own systems, enforcing laws against hacking and abuse, promoting interoperability and security standards, and investing in research and development related to information security. Deterrence implies the ability to identify attacks and determine the parties responsible and the will to retaliate. Prevention implies the ability to identify potential attackers, define and recognize whatever warning signals of a pending attack might be present, and use offensive information warfare techniques to disable attack assets. Although there is no easy solution to fighting the battle against information warfare, the most important step is to realize that the front line has moved to our front door, and that information systems may be the prime target of those who wish to see our demise in the future. With that said, the United States must remain vigilant in our efforts to promote security of our information infrastructure, provide protection for the systems that comprise that network, and aggressively pursue those who use technology to disrupt our way of life, our freedom.

REFERENCES

1. Alberts, D. S., and R. E. Haynes. *The Realm of Information Dominance: Beyond Information War.* Washington, DC: National Defense University, 1995, pp. 560–565.

2. Allard, K. "Data Transforms Warfare." *Defense News,* 11, no. 9 (1996).

3. Anthes, G. H. "Net Attacks Up, Defenses Down." *Computerworld,* January 1996, pp. 71–72.

4. Arquilla, J. J., and D. F. Ronfeldt, "Cyberwar and Netwar: New Modes, Old Concepts, of Conflict." 1999. [On-line]. *Available at* http://www.rand.org/publications/randreview/issues/RRR.fall95.cyber/.

5. Campen, A. D., D. H. Dearth, and R. T. Goodden. *Cyberwar: Security, Strategy, and Conflict in the Information Age.* Fairfax, VA: AFCEA International Press, 1996.

6. Denning, D. "Activism, Hacktivism, and Cyberterrorism: The Internet as a Tool for Influencing Foreign Policy." [On-line]. *Available at* http://www.terrorism.com/documents/denning-infoterrorism.html.

7. Khalilzad, Z.; J. P. White; and A. W. Marshall. "The Changing Role of Information in Warfare." [On-line]. *Available at* http://www.rand.org/publications/MR/MR1016.

8. Pollitt, M. M. "Cyber Terrorism: Fact or Fancy." FBI Laboratory [On-line]. *Available at* http://www.cs.georgetown.edu/~denning/infosec/pollitt.html.

9. RAND Research Review. "Information Warfare: A Two-Edged Sword." 1995. [On-line]. *Available at* http://www.rand.org/publications/randreview/issues/RRR.fall95.cyber/.

10. Shahar, Y. "Information Warfare: The Perfect Terrorist Weapon." 2000. [On-line]. *Available at* http://www.ict.org.il/articles/infowar.htm.

11. Stein, G. J. "Information Warfare in 2025." August 1996. [On-line]. *Available at* http://www.au.af.mil/au/2025/volume3/chap03/v3c3-1.htm-Executive%20Summary.

12. Waller, D. "Onward Cyber Soldiers." *Time*, August 24, 1995, pp. 38–46.

13. Wood, R. J. *Information Engineering: The Foundation of Information Warfare.* Maxwell AFB, AL: Air War College Research Report, 1995. Available from Air University Library, Maxwell AFB, Alabama.

Appendix A

Ten Technologies for 2002 to 2007

J. Fenn

A survey of Gartner analysts selected 10 high-impact technologies, including biometric authentication, speech recognition and Web services, that enterprises should evaluate.

Gartner analysts from a range of disciplines proposed and ranked information technologies (see Note 1) that are not yet widely adopted and that will have the biggest impact on enterprises between 2002 to 2007—e.g., through rapid growth of consumer or corporate adoption, high return on investment (ROI) or changed business processes. The following technologies gained the highest number of votes (see Note 2), and so represent technologies that planners should include in their portfolios. Many will also play a key role in driving and supporting the major IT-enabled trends of the next decade (see "Emerging Trends 2002 to 2007: Fulfilling Expectations," COM-15-1072).

BIOMETRIC AUTHENTICATION

Core Topic
Emerging Trends and Technologies: The Future of Technology, Business and Society

Security technologies have gained increased prominence since the Sept. 11 terrorist attacks, and biometrics (e.g., fingerprint, voice, iris or face recognition) are a key contender for applications requiring strong authentication. Most of the real adoption during the next five years will come from government applications (e.g., immigration, social security, surveillance), while corporate adoption will continue to grow slowly until the biometric readers (e.g., cameras, fingerprint readers, high-quality microphones) are routinely embedded in the hardware (e.g., laptops).

SPEECH RECOGNITION

Key Issue
Which emerging and embryonic technologies should early adopters be examining for competitive advantage?

The major growth area for speech recognition will be in call center automation, where its role as a more flexible and user-friendly alternative to Touch-Tone supports straightforward cost justifications through reduced call volumes to human operators. Although the capabilities of speech recognition will still be constrained to task-specific applications (e.g., call routing, stock trading, travel reservation, order status), there is still significant potential for the use of speech to expand beyond the early adopters.

WEB SERVICES

Web services are software components that can be accessed over public networks using generally available protocols and transport (i.e., SOAP over HTTP). Web services technologies are becoming an integral requirement in infrastructure and tool markets and, by 2005, will start to become a crucial tool for business in general by enabling enterprises to focus on their core competencies while outsourcing other functions through the Web services model (see "How Web Services Mean Business," COM-13-5985).

PORTALS

Portals provide access to and interaction with relevant information, applications and business processes, by select targeted audiences, in a highly personalized manner. The next generation of portals will continue to play a key role in enterprise IT initiatives as a focal point of integration for multiple data sources and applications (see "Next for Portal Products: The Portal Application Server," SPA-14-5721).

ALWAYS-ON WIRELESS DATA AND COMMUNICATIONS DEVICES

Always-on, or at least instantly available, access to data and communications is becoming increasingly prevalent through a range of wireless devices—personal digital assistants (PDAs), smart phones—and through voice portals on ordinary mobile phones. As user interface, bandwidth and cost hurdles are overcome, service providers will learn through experience what are the services and transactions that will form the basis of the long-anticipated m-commerce opportunities.

CONVERGED NETWORKS

The ultimate goal of networking is convergence—a single network infrastructure to handle all applications: voice, data, video and multimedia. Much of the journey toward achieving this goal will be achieved during the next five years, including voice and data being handled to a large degree on a single network (see "Emerging Network Technologies for the Decade," T-14-0296). Special-purpose networks will still be necessary for video and content delivery until around 2010, when a single advanced IP network will handle the majority of the world's communications needs.

DIGITAL WALLETS AND INTEREST PORTFOLIOS

Digital wallets (e.g., Microsoft Passport and Gator) provide a single place for users to store personal information to ease online tasks such as form filling, authentication and one-click shopping. Growth will be driven by user requirements for coherent and secure management of their online identities (e.g., single sign-on), and by vendor initiatives such as Microsoft requiring users to register for Passport to gain access to other online services.

WIRELESS LAN

Wireless LANs are migrating from the domain of emerging technologies into a mainstream networking option. Corporations with a need for flexibility in how their users access networks on campus are finding that wireless LAN technologies provide a satisfactory price/performance ratio (see "Wireless LAN: The Next Killer Application," HARD-WW-DP-0032). For the next five years, wired access will still offer a bandwidth premium, so both approaches will continue to be used in tandem.

PRIVACY MANAGEMENT TECHNOLOGY

As online purchases and transactions become a mainstream part of society's behavior patterns, many consumers will wish to maintain the anonymity provided by cash purchases in the physical world. This will provide opportunities for third-party intermediaries to act as a buffer between buyers and sellers of goods and services (perhaps evolving from the digital wallet providers), and for technologies that offer personalization and other enhanced services without sacrificing privacy.

INSTANT MESSAGING

Instant messaging (IM), the ability to spontaneously communicate with friends and co-workers in a conversational manner, has grown to become a heavily used and highly useful business tool (see "Instant Messaging: The Sleeping Giant," AV-14-0650). IM represents a new medium for business communication and collaboration—one that is complementary to traditional forms of communication, particularly e-mail and voice. By 2003, IM services will be found in 70 percent of enterprises (0.8 probability), installed, for the most part, by users for interpersonal communication. By 2005, IM will surpass e-mail as the primary way in which consumers interact with each other electronically (0.7 probability).

BOTTOM LINE

Enterprises of all levels of technology aggressiveness should evaluate the role that speech recognition in the contact center, Web services, portals, always-on wireless devices, converged networks, wireless LANs and IM will play, as these technologies will have a high penetration or provide tangible benefits in many applications by 2007. Type A (leading-edge) enterprises should also evaluate whether biometric identification, digital wallets and privacy management technology will be relevant to their business operations, as these technologies will continue to mature but fall into a higher-risk category in terms of user adoption.

NOTES

1. **Retrospective on Technologies for 2000 to 2010**—In April 2000, Gartner published its first analysis of technologies prioritized by Gartner analysts. The selection criterion was similar (i.e., technologies that will be transformational within the next 10 years but are not generating the level of activity or attention that they warrant within user enterprises), but the time frame was longer (2000 to 2010).

   The following technologies from the April 2000 report were also in the top-ranked technologies this time:

   • Wireless Web technologies (always-on wireless data and communications)

   • Biometric identification

   • Speech recognition

   • Webtops (personal portals)

   The following technologies were selected in the April 2000 report as becoming significant after the 2007 date used this time:

   • Display technologies

   • Embedded miniature computers

   The following technologies selected in the April 2000 report were not ranked highly enough this time to make the top rankings:

   • Content-based retrieval

   • Natural-language processing

   • Bluetooth (wireless personal area networks)

   • XML

   • Pattern recognition

   • E-cash

2. **Methodology**—Using a modified Delphi method, a group of Gartner analysts from a cross-section of technology and business areas created a list of high-impact technology areas. Each analyst then voted for up to 10 of the technologies that will be of highest impact within 10 years, with the emphasis on those that are currently undervalued.

Appendix B

The Ways That High Bandwidth Will Change Your Life

Question: What would be the effect of free computing, global connectivity, and low- or no-cost adequate bandwidth?

- **Assumption #1:** Items are positive. You can also include negative consequences.

- **Assumption #2:** This list is based on the fact that 100 percent of the world would have instantaneous access to the complete knowledge of mankind (as opposed to only about 8 percent now). The sharing of information is going to be the basic reason for major advancements and changes.

TRAVEL

- With unlimited bandwidth, there would be more telecommuters, because there would be no reason to travel to work. Bandwidth-intensive line-of-business applications would no longer restrict workers to traveling daily.

- With less people traveling to work every day, fuel conservation would be improved.

- There would be a sharp reduction in air travel for business/military/government meetings. The use of video teleconference centers (VTC) would become much more effective, secure, and available.

- Professional/global: Virtual tours and online conversations with individuals in other areas will enhance travel to different countries and cities.

- Less travel will mean lower levels of emissions from automobiles and aircraft.

- Less travel means that people will not have to live as close to their physical place of employment.

- People would become lazy because they could do so much stuff without leaving the house.

- With unlimited bandwidth, there is no need for real offices—you can have virtual offices.

- People can work anyplace.

- Airlines would provide wireless communications devices for their passengers at no extra charge.

- The number of work-at-home professionals would be on the rise.

- There would be increased ability for remote management of large systems with remote support staff.

- There would be a major change in the way business is done—more working from home, the car, virtually anywhere.

- Road infrastructures would change drastically—as the opportunity to telework will reduce the two-hour commutes that many people currently deal with.

- More professional/business people will work from remote locations instead of commuting to offices.

- Multiple vehicle locations could be tracked in real time (traffic congestion).

SECURITY

- Information warfare will become more and more important as we rely more and more on information technology.

- Security would become a necessity. Hackers would have more avenues for attack.

- Global/business: The military will be overwhelmed with "how to deal with security."

- Security consulting companies will be in short supply.

- With global connectivity, everyone would be exposed to hackers.

- Hacking will become more predominant and easily done.

- A long list of passwords will be needed.

- Wars are fought by destroying information systems and never firing a single bullet.

- Faster encryption technology improvements will be made.

- New encryption technology will evolve.

- Locks will become more technological. The physical (easily cracked) lock will become obsolete, and electronic (more secure) locks will become the standard.

- More people will be online (safety in numbers, as far as online banking, etc.).

- A long list of passwords for logon purposes would be needed.

- Inclement alarm systems will provide more timely alerts.

PRIVACY

- There will be less privacy as people integrate computers and networks more and more into their lives. More and more personal information will be traveling across the networks allowing a detailed record of whereabouts and actions.

- There will be less privacy for government as well as corporate data. There may be many firewalls or any other safety features; however, data being accessible to virtually everyone and anyone will have tremendous complications.

CONVERGENCE

- There would be an integration of all data providers: no more separate phone companies, cable companies, and ISPs. One company, possibly a government-sanctioned monopoly, would provide every data need of a home or business, with one fiber optic cable.

- Telephone, TV, and Internet will be combined on one device.

- Telephone, television, movies, and music will be absorbed into computer-based services.

- Individual/personal: Home satellite dishes (i.e., DirecTV) will be upgraded and become the standard for sending and receiving on the Internet.

- All telephone, cable, satellite, and other space/air will be combined.

- There will be one wire coming into our house. This wire will have the Internet, TV, phone, and even power (wait until the power companies start to be ISPs; they have the largest wire system in the United States).

- Media will be combined into a single wireless household system.

- All information will be easily accessible. With total connectivity, the challenge will be converting information into usable knowledge.

- Total integration of all aspects of communications could be achieved—by combining voice, Internet, radio, and television.

- Individual/personal: Once high-speed processors have become second nature in everyone's home and bandwidth is unlimited, the flat wall-panel TV would become mainstream, thus resulting in the convergence of TV and Internet. This would change the way we watch, surf, and produce entertainment and information. TV and the Internet have already made attempts to merge with the onset of Web TV. However, Web TV's platform was too limited for the advanced Internet user.

- More and more devices will become voice-command-driven (TVs, VCRs, phones, maybe cars).

- Technologies (television, telephone, radio, and Internet) would converge into one data stream.

- Business/personal: Unlimited bandwidth would eventually spur the complete integration of wireless technology into almost every product in our lives. Bluetooth or some other similar technology would make this happen, thus allowing everyday life to become "easier": our refrigerator would order milk when the weight was too low, our electric meter would automatically send the signal to the power plant for billing, and our fast-food order would be ready for pickup before we actually go through the drive-through.

- Business/individual: Assignment of *one* personal IP number. This number will be your contact address for everything (phone/videoconferencing, website, etc.). The hassles of having three different phone numbers will end.

- Professional/personal: A true distributed system would be developed where a user's profile can be taken anywhere (i.e., your desktop, applications, etc. can be accessed from any computer; users take their personal computers with them—virtually).

- Home will no more remain just a home. It may become an office, a laboratory, a commercial enterprise, or anything an enterprising person can think of. In other words the SOHO dream would become reality.

- Professional/business: Offices in the workplace will be reduced to a "box" that fits over your head like a large helmet.

- Events from around the world could be seen (instead of TV).

- Better compatibility between various consumer electronic gadgets such as palmtops, digital cameras, cell phones, and so forth.

- The use of separate cable, telephone, and snail-mail delivery media could be merged into one integrated medium that could surpass the quality and effectiveness of the existing systems.

COMMERCE

- More people would be able to shop from home.

- There would be a reduction in traditional brick-and-mortar businesses.

- It would save time and cost, which makes the whole world competitive.

- It makes the whole world one marketplace.

- All companies—even one-person companies, from the individual craftsman who makes fishing flies to painters—would utilize the Internet for reaching customers.

- A global, or Internet, currency would be adopted.

- There would be more worldwide eCommerce.

- With the increase in telecommunications capability will come the combination of the world stock markets onto an electronic exchange.

- Businesses will become more and more integrated.

- As increased bandwidth becomes available, "gadgets" become more cost-effective for the personal consumer.

- Overall consumer costs would be lowered.

- Boundaries of international markets will collapse, and there would emerge a 24-hour global market that will be as volatile as the international money markets. This will have profound implications for the global business community as it will be a whole new way of doing business.

- Power companies may be able to disconnect specific nonessential loads, such as being able to shut down a specific house when no one is inside.

- Business: Advertising will be turned upside down. The money used to pay an advertiser to contact consumers will be diverted directly to the consumer (many companies have tried this but unsuccessfully). Technology will allow consumers to remove nearly all ads from their view (TV, computer, phone); thus, consumers will begin to demand compensation for their time.

- Every person will consider him/herself to be his/her own company, responsible for his/her own growth and promotion. We already see this in the management people, but this will move down to every person—blue collar, and so on. The knowledge of how much a job pays will be so accessible that pay will become more homogenous as low-paying areas will move up, and so forth.

- The music industry would drastically change to distribute most/all goods over the Internet. Same for all electronic media goods: all software, rental movies, and music will be sold online; retail stores will only have physical goods.

- There will be increased specialization and niche marketing.

- Demand for immediate financial information will increase and become the norm.

- Business/personal: Increased computing power and unlimited bandwidth will cause software companies to eventually move to purely Web-based applications. Currently, Web-based applications are increasing in use, but years from now it will probably become the most efficient means of producing, updating, and delivering quality software.

- Virtual corporations formed from strategic alliances of major companies will become very popular.

- Small and medium-sized online businesses will be able to compete more effectively.

- Global markets will be readily available to online businesses and users.

- Any company or business without a website is considered out of date.

- People would have more and more methods for earning and saving money.

- One could feasibly have access to all types of software by logging on to a central "rental" company without having to buy the full package.

- Users pay for software only when they use it.

- More information for strategy planning would be available.

- There will be universal electronic money.

- Application programs would go over the Internet.

- As more shopping is shifted from a physical store to an e-store, shipping companies (UPS, FedEx, USPS) will grow at unbelievable rates. They also will invest billions of dollars into technology.

- The idea that a customer will be required to go to a store, push products around, wait in line, and carry their products home will be replaced. In the new system, the customers will be required to do nearly no work and will have products delivered directly to their home.

- Global/business: Companies will share market strategies to obtain a niche in particular areas.

- Business/personal: Selling of products and services will become unlimited.

- There will be increased mergers between cable companies and ISPs.

- Buying trends will change. Some retail sales will increase, while other forms of retail will be completely wiped out.

- There will be increased competition for JIT delivery companies.

COMMUNICATION

- We will have unlimited wireless access to the Internet with the ability to find out information about any subject at any time.
- We will be able to speak to anyone on the planet with real-time translation capability through a wearable translation system with bone mike–type interface.
- There will be real-time communication.
- Telecommunications: There would be danger to traditional phone companies.
- The use of telephones would be cut down.
- It would promote globalization within a corporation by allowing better connectivity between foreign offices. We would be able to more easily share data and allow for better communications, such as video conferencing and lowering communications costs.
- It would promote globalization for smaller companies by allowing them access to a more global marketplace rather than their local area.
- It would help in the transportation of large data.
- Telephone with video will become common in business.
- It would improve capabilities to conduct meetings over videoconferencing networks.
- There would be smaller cell phones carrying more bandwidth.
- There will be more voice-driven communication devices.
- More companies would adopt VPN technology.
- The use of satellite telecommunications would become the dominant means for transmitting data around the world. This would result in greater demands for increased transmission rates that relay satellites could transmit and the effectiveness of on-orbit technology.
- The traditional phone company as we know it would be eliminated as all telephone would go to voice over IP.
- It would give a new depth to teleconferencing within the military. We could all sit behind our desks at our own computers and conference at any time, even if outside the continental U.S. (OCONUS).
- More corporations will use virtual private networks as a means of communication and moving information among their various locations.
- There would be easy data communications, with full utilization of wireless connectivity.
- Business/personal/enterprise: There would be a savings in time and cost for communication.
- Space communications will become unrestricted.

- Scientists will use global communications to combine efforts for best solutions.
- You will be able to open pet doors when not at home by using wireless communications.
- Wide area telecommunications service (WATS) would increase.
- The PC would be used as a phone for calling home.
- There won't be problems sending huge files.
- The idea that a *wire* must be attached to an appliance (computer, PDA) will be archaic.
- The integrated house would be a computerized system.
- Services such as video conferencing would become highly effective.
- It would be a paperless world in every aspect.
- Business/personal: Business can be done anytime, anywhere.
- We would have more and more email accounts and spend more and more time checking each of them every day.
- Networks would not limit us.
- There will be real-time exchange of information.
- Individual/personal: Home networks: Mom, Dad, brother, and sister each would have his/her own computer; and each computer would be on a "home" network.
- You will be able to monitor and adjust settings on appliances programmed to cook dishes at your home from remote locations.
- Continued ERP development will give rise to corporations that will control/own their entire supply chains.
- Appointments/scheduling/meeting arrangements will be made by agents (instead of secretaries).
- Downloading will become effortless as to time and equipment required.
- Global/business/personal: It would be a pencil-less world.
- Business/personal/enterprise: It would be an accurate, fast data process.

ENTERTAINMENT/NEWS

- It will be easy to download MP3 files.
- There would be a consolidation/elimination of movie rental and theater stores.
- There would be more free entertainment and give-away software.
- You would be able to view any movie any time you wanted.
- You would be able to hear any song at any time you wanted.

- A totally wired house could be controlled by a remote control.

- Movie theaters as we know them would be eliminated and we would have personal subscriptions/PPV of new-release movies.

- Video games could be played in almost real time.

- There would be interactive games with multiple players.

- Feedback for what TV shows are popular will be automatic.

- More live shows could be downloaded.

- With unlimited bandwidth in the home, many TV channels will be watched simultaneously (i.e., *Back to the Future 2*).

- Business: Production of graphic design will have to change for entertainment purposes because of the onslaught of digital recording. HDTV and other digital technologies will make the pictures so precise that previously used stage design techniques will become too "phony" looking on the new TVs. New forms of lighting, stage design, makeup, and so on will need to be developed to keep up the realistic effect that is achieved on today's programs.

- The PC becomes an all-in-one entertaining tool.

- Songs would not take as long to download.

- It would change the way we watch, surf, and produce entertainment and information.

- Users will be able to experience virtual reality in many walks of life; for example, simulation of flying an airplane, taking a cruise in the Mediterranean, or taking a train trip across the nation.

- Global/personal: Television will be available throughout the world.

- Some athletic contests can be held online for players in different countries.

- We can work a little bit and communicate with our colleagues during vacations.

- Individual: There would be free entertainment.

- There would be access to real-time programming (video and audio) from all over the world.

- Individual/professional: PCs will become all-in-one entertaining and working tools.

- Individual: People will pay more attention on tech-related news than any other types of news.

SOCIAL/BEHAVIORAL

- There will be physical isolation.

- Physical human contacts will be reduced to the barest minimum.

- Workers would suffer longer work hours due to overload of information and the boss knowing how to, and being able to, get hold of you constantly.

- There will be more time to do other things.

- There will be the potential softening of nationalism and religious segmentation.

- For executives and managers, information overflow will occur. Managers will have to change the way they think in order to use all information efficiently.

- There will be ubiquitous porn.

- There will be a degradation of culture (literature, philosophy, etc.) with an emphasis on entertainment for the masses.

- There will be increasing technological addictions (virtual reality, Internet surfing).

- Scheduling of dinner plans, meetings, dates, and so forth will be negotiated through agents. It may develop to the point when a person doesn't even know what they have planned for the day until they ask the computer.

- Global/personal/business: The "distance" between people will be longer (because of less oral communication).

- There will be less oral communication between people.

- In the simplest form, the rise of this capability will eliminate the isolationist and create a unified world that is linked together by the instantaneous relay of information.

- One will be able to attend church services at home.

- The world would become more unreal than ever.

- There would be a widening of the digital divide (the difference between those who have technology and those who don't).

- There would emerge a global pool of knowledge that would be accessible to all irrespective of the part of globe people live in. This will lead to better diffusion of different cultures and hence global harmony [seems farfetched but it is possible].

- Business: Blue-collar jobs will be eliminated by mass computerized automation and use of robots.

- It will make people more lethargic as one would not be required to leave the home to do anything. This may have lasting sociological implications for the human race.

- There would be an information explosion.

- Information will emerge as the real power.

- Professional/personal: The disabled will be able to access abundant information by use of technological advances and online computing.

- Global/personal/business: Use of online computing will contribute to lower fuel consumption due to less driving.

- Increase in computers (and computerlike machines) will continue to demand more and more electrical power (look at California now).

- As more and more electronic devices are built and operated, the *fuel* of business will no longer be gasoline; it will be electricity. Electricity prices will continue to rise.

- The fascination that something is digital will diminish. People will begin to forget there ever was anything but digital.

- Individual: The disaster caused from computers will destroy people's lives.

- Business/personal/enterprise: Everything is controlled by computers.

- Individual/business: Computer-related crimes can be untraceable.

- Individual: Virtual dating will be the order of the day.

PROCUREMENT

- By allowing bids to be solicited from a far greater number of sources, prices ultimately will be lowered to consumers. It also would allow for the consumer to search for the best prices.

- There will be server-based applications: pay for application access, rather than a personal copy.

- A fundable trend will develop that customers can negotiate every step of a purchase/transaction, and have *all* the terms coincide with their delivery times, dates, and locations.

RESEARCH

- Further education resources by allowing better access to research and educational materials. It would open opportunities for individuals who before did not have the means to obtain their desired education. It also would help with research by allowing them to collaborate on a single project from many locations around the world.

- Business: Distributed computer firms will continue to develop. The wasted CPU cycles on any computer will be converted into effective cycles. (Groups such as SETI and www.distributed.net are using this resource, but only if it is donated to them. More are used for encryption analysis or raw data analysis.)

- There will be atomic/organic computing.

- There will be more high-tech technology tracking or investigation.

- There would be an unprecedented amount of parallel processing capability to aid in the solution of complex scientific mysteries.

- There would be access to all the electronically stored knowledge in every library in the world.

- Less time would be spent obtaining information.

- It would be easier to do research and obtain access from anywhere (no longer use books).

- Technology will lead to greater specialization. Technology also will allow the use of a specialized skill over a greater area (e.g., surgical skills, diagnosis, etc.).

MEDICAL

- Doctors will be able to make better diagnoses over the phone.

- Holography will be used.

- There will be increased medical advances due to the ability to utilize increased bandwidth to perform research.

- Business/personal: Medical operations will be assisted online for those without expertise.

- Technical medical procedures will be performed using online support.

- Emergency medical procedures will be directed online.

- Doctors will attend to their patients from home.

EDUCATION

- More distance learning will take place.

- The number of physical books at the library will decrease.

- Students can attend school from the home using videoconferencing; Auburn University's outreach program abandons videotape and outreach students can attend class in real time over a network or download the video later.

- The average person's reading/learning speed will increase because they will have no choice but to be bombarded with tons of information at one time.

- There will be a greater opportunity for education.

- There will be a decrease in global illiteracy due to interactive, distance education.

- Individual/education: Education would become more available to people, regardless of nationality, location, or socioeconomic level. By allowing everyone unlimited access and computing power, people will be able to attend colleges or other forms of education through a virtual environment. That is already taking place today, but these programs are often extremely expensive. Thus, only the people who can afford to go are able to. By leveling this playing field, more and more people will be able to attend because it will not cost as much for the school or institution to use the technology.

- Individual/enterprise: The point when real computer education begins will continue to be at an earlier age. Children will learn to write and type at nearly the same time.

- Professional/education: No longer will technical continuing education be an option for teachers; it will be a necessity.

- Individual/business/enterprise: Education resources will be unlimited.

- Educational instruction opportunities will become unlimited; for example, studying cultures and languages through interactive online learning, hands-on simulated design projects with immediate feedback, networking capabilities to interact freely with different markets.

- Educational opportunities would be enhanced enormously.

- Individual/enterprise: Virtual classical music lessons will be offered online.

- Telelearning will be on a huge scale—to the point that professors will contract to a virtual university and live where they want to (I recommend Kure Beach, North Carolina, for a nice small town on the coast). In 5 to 10 years many under-grads will get degrees and only go to campus like today's outreach students do—for a short period to meet residency requirements.

- Capabilities throughout the WWW would be practically boundless, and dis-tance learning might really escalate. We could attend live, interactive classes from our homes or even work.

- There would be more online training tools.

- People could learn other languages easier with the global aspect.

- Individual/personal/enterprise: People will be self-taught about everything through computers.

- MIS: Professors will no longer teach in the classroom setting.

- Children will learn foreign languages via use of computer and contact with for-eign teachers in other countries.

- The means by which schools could educate students would be greatly enhanced by the ability to gain an unlimited amount of information. This would in essence eliminate the cultural biases and ignorance that students today develop.

- One may initiate a learning process (now that all the bottlenecks will have been removed) that has never been seen before in the history of mankind.

- Children will be required to learn computers prior to pre-school.

- Professional/business: Athletic training will become interactive virtual reality online.

- There will be the ability to attend class at any time anywhere in the world.

ARTIFICIAL INTELLIGENCE

- More AI software will be required to manage business.

- There would be artificial intelligence as in the movie AI.

- Houses will become much more intelligent. Lights, heating, and music will be tailored to a person. A house will become sensitive to a specific person and adjust the environment.

- Intelligent software agents will become very popular, helping individuals and organizations to process data and information.

LAWS/REGULATIONS

- Continued Internet growth will result in the development of "world" laws. Individual government laws are difficult (if not impossible) to enforce on the WWW.

- Tax preparation will be completely Internet-based. Obtaining W-2, stock, mutual fund, and other account information will all be delivered to tax preparation software via the Internet.

- Agents or other software will continue to develop and become useful. Being able to say, "find me the best TV for $500" will become the norm. Agents will filter/process data into usable information/knowledge.

- As increased bandwidth becomes available, it becomes more difficult to regulate and secure.

- Business/personal: Daycare centers will be monitored online by state officials.

- Computers will be utilized more in situations requiring an unbiased observer, such as referees.

- Computers also will be used to regulate areas such as air and car traffic.

- A new career field in cyber laws will evolve.

- Auditing approaches must change.

- Intellectual property rights and protection will increase.

- There will be increased government regulation.

- Individual/business: Federal and state governments will find it mandatory to enact restrictive laws dealing with viruses.

- There will be standardization and increased governmental control of domains, servers, and so forth, perhaps to assist in control of viruses, but more likely to help in some form of taxation still yet to be invented/implemented.

- There would possibly be an increase in taxation of such delivery methods.

NAVIGATION

- Traffic and emergency vehicles will utilize the Internet. A fire truck may be able to dynamically view traffic conditions and alter traffic lights in order to reach a destination faster.

- Cars will be controlled by satellite (every car will have its own axis so no traffic jam or accident could happen).

- There would be total interconnectivity of farm equipment: auto-seeding systems, irrigation systems, remotely sensed (satellite) imagery, variable rate nutrient applicators, and so forth used in conjunction to optimize yields and communicate with the main office.

- Tracers will be put on children's bikes to show their present location via a map.

- There would be online traffic information for fire trucks and ambulances.

STORAGE

- Storage capacity will increase. People will demand huge servers with unlimited information available (e.g., every sports statistic in history), because they will have the bandwidth to download it all.

- There will be the ability to segregate large data centers across a wire for space, business continuity, disaster recovery, resource sharing, and system administration.

- Filing cabinets will be replaced with RAID drive towers.

- This would make my tasks in the Air Force easier. I could send and receive any documents, files, or programs without having to burn CDs or Zip disks. It would certainly make briefings considerably less complicated.

- There would be cental storage, SAN.

TRASH

- Funny thing is, we are talking about landlines mostly. What about when increased bandwidth becomes available in wireless fashion?

- The same concept will occur perhaps with computer gaming.

- Bandwidth continues to increase. FTTC (fiber to the curb) will become a reality.

- People around the world could communicate in real time.

- In cold weather, you will be able to crank your car with a remote device without even going outside.

- Business: Information for a complex could be centralized.

- Business: There could be a reduction in personnel for a complex.

- Long distance would go away.

- Most people don't have to go to the hospital.

- There would be more bandwidth and smaller facilities.

- A business's computer system and another business's computer system will dissolve.

- There will be no delay for Auburn tapes.

- TV and the Internet have already made attempts to merge with the onset of Web TV.

- There would be data everywhere and not a thought to think.

- Business exists ubiquitously.

- Textile improvements through the use of carbon nanotubes will decrease the weight of body armor to one-half the current weight of soft armor (Kevlar) and with monolithic boron carbide plates providing soldiers protection from armor-piercing ammunition.

- Doctors will be able to diagnose cancer or other disease within an individual's body years prior to its occurrence, allowing preparation to combat the ailment.

- People will be able to purchase a new body part (e.g., heart, kidney, etc.) that is made up of that person's own DNA.
- Internet phones will be available.
- eCommerce will increase.
- Interactive voice response (IVR) will increase.
- There will be the ability to chat in real time (MSN, ICQ).
- There will be genetic advances.
- Life expectancy will increase by hundreds of years.
- There will be the ability to live on Mars.
- We will be able to stop the aging process.
- There will be more special methods of earning money.
- The bandwidth of a single voice channel would be changed. With unlimited bandwidth, there would be no need to limit a voice channel to kHz.
- Innovations: It would help to make goods and services available in areas where they were once unattainable.
- There is concern over the copyright issue.
- There would be lower overall consumer costs.
- There would be high demand for JIT delivery.
- There would be increasing bandwidth requirements.
- Bionics would develop.
- Telepathy would be developed.
- Missile defense system of the United States would improve.
- The plasma bomb, the most harmful arm ever, would be developed.
- There would be light speed vehicles.
- There would be germ bombs.
- Military technology would protect the country.
- Business models must be found that would still make money.
- Computers would need to be adapted to withstand higher bandwidth.
- Students could take final exams online so that they can have longer breaks.

Summary—Telecommunications and YOUR Future

As we complete this text, it has been 60 years since Prosper Eckert and John Mauchly launched ENIAC, the first large-scale electronic computer. Like many of the discontinuous events that change the way we work and view the world, the ENIAC didn't generate much interest among business managers. Yet it was a breakthrough that has altered the competitive balance of the marketplace and transformed business and government. The networking of computers has expanded and altered markets on a global basis. Now the convergence of computers and telecommunications has again transformed markets and organizations.

Nowhere has this been more evident than in the meteoric rise of the Internet. The Internet connects global communities, provides a forum for all sorts of debates, and allows small firms to market their wares anywhere in the world. The Internet has altered the balance of global competition and has enabled small firms to play on the same field as their larger, more resource-rich competitors. The Internet promises to further the impetus towards the use of information technology for businesses that extends beyond internal use to external uses such as marketing, customer service, and partnering. The shift is from a technology focus to an information management focus.

Today, more than a half-century after the birth of the large-scale computer, and a scant 20+ years after the commercial introduction of the microcomputer, technology has progressed remarkably. Still, the benefits of exploiting the technology by effective management remain largely unrealized. This is your challenge for the future.

It is a great time to be alive, to experience the changes that are occurring, many of which are being fueled by and are fueling the technology of telecommunications. If you understand the technology and the world of change, you are in a far better position to control your own destiny.

As we close this venture into the management of business telecommunications, we leave you at the beginning of your personal adventure. As you grasp and understand the technology, you are in a far better position to understand its use in supporting business decisions. You must keep learning and not rest on your laurels, or developments in this field will soon pass you by. It is an exciting time, for Carlton, Alli, and JEI, and for you!

Take this book as the beginning of your adventure into a world that is changing rapidly. But remember: *Change is not your enemy; lack of information is.* With a solid understanding of the material in these chapters, you are well prepared to face the telecommunications challenge that will have a profound influence on you and your world. Seize all opportunities that come your way to extend the knowledge you have gained here. Seize new technologies as ways to enhance the competitive advantage of your organization. And above all . . . Carpe Diem (Seize the Day!) . . . and let *your* adventure begin!

The Real World   16–4
The FitLinxx Global Fitness Network

The FitLinxx Network is a combination of computers and network connectivity to gather information from exercise machines in facilities such as gyms. It provides its members with a single, consolidated view of their workout information. Exercise information from a member's use of a "facility" (YMCA, commercial club, hospital, rehabilitation center, etc.) or manually logged over the Internet is integrated into a single record accessible from either location.

Beneath the covers, the FitLinxx Network is a heterogeneous collection of technologies and protocols used to acquire, transport, and aggregate fitness data. Custom hardware attaches to equipment in a facility to acquire data as a member exercises. That data is stored in facility servers, simultaneously being transferred to other facilities and central locations, including a website. The network is a global distributed processing system; each facility operates independently, while central systems monitor and manage information amongst facilities and central locations.

The key components of the in-facility FitLinxx system are the server, kiosk, management station, strength training partner (TP), and cardiovascular (CV) network adapter (CNA). The kiosk and management station are PCs providing the user interface to the system for members and fitness staff, while the TP and CNA are custom devices to interface to exercise equipment. The TP provides a touch-screen guiding members through a workout and monitors the equipment electronically. CV adapters communicate with CV equipment using RS-232 and the industry standard CSAFE protocol originally developed by FitLinxx (*http://www.fitlinxx.com/csafe*).

Facilities are wired in a star topology using ethernet (10BaseT). Both NETBEUI and IP serve as layer 3 protocols. A facility has a common ethernet, but in all but rare instances any data exchange involves only the server and one other component.

The server is the network's in-facility focal point. It provides core services (file sharing, database) to the other components and monitors the facility on behalf of central systems. Kiosks and management stations provide access to member data stored on the server. TPs retrieve member workout details from the server to guide the member, and subsequently update workout results. The server maintains constant communication with CNAs to record member workouts.

The facility serves as the "edge" of the network. Member data also flows over the wide-area to propagate to other facilities a member may belong to, as well as being made available on a website. Disaster-recovery backups are retrieved and archived centrally, as is monitoring information used to manage the overall network. Software upgrades and patches are deployed in a controlled manner to all facilities without any facility intervention, and usually off hours.

This integration of the individual facility networks into a global network is the responsibility of a 7×24 network management system. This system is comprised of redundant "scheduler" machines, a cluster of "execution" machines, and warehouse storage machines. To ensure ubiquitous and economical access, facility connections use analog modems. Sites are accessed using PPP, and both NETBEUI and IP protocols.

The scheduler is the heart of the system. It manages a queue of all tasks needing execution, including schedules, resources and constraints for each task, dispatching tasks to execution machines. The scheduler and execution machines are loosely coupled—the scheduler may be stopped at any time without affecting active tasks. Execution machines may be removed from service at any time, or additional machines added to pick up load, and the scheduler dynamically adjusts.

Permanent scheduler tasks include workout data replication to the web and other facilities, disaster recovery backups, facility configuration auditing and alert monitoring. Tasks are used to distribute and install software upgrades, execute one-time database patches, or retrieve files from a facility for aid in problem troubleshooting. Tasks use special software to optimize traffic over the low-bandwidth dialup connections, managing in aggregate hundreds of GBs of remote data, and optimizing performance when attempting to troubleshoot a problem remotely.

Source: David Bolen, CTO, FitLinxx.

Key Terms

bypass, *721*
convergence, *731*
electronic commerce, *721*
information warfare, *733*

nanotechnology, *727*
Semantic Web, *727*
telemedicine, *726*

Universal Description,
   Discovery, and
   Integration (UDDI), *728*
virtual workplace, *726*

Recommended Readings

Zachman, John. "A Framework for Information Systems Architecture." *IBM Systems Journal* 26, no. 3 (March 1987).

PC Computing, Network Edition—A biweekly computer magazine.

Discussion Questions

16.1. What sort of mergers and alliances have occurred in the telecommunications industry? What is the present trend? How do telecommunications providers differentiate themselves one from another?

16.2. How have the barriers to entry into the telecommunications industry changed over the past 10 years? What is the likely trend for the coming 10 years?

16.3. Is competition in the local loop arena an incentive for providers to deliver superior service at a lower cost?

16.4. How does EDI combine with business processes to generate electronic commerce?

16.5. What are the benefits that a firm can obtain by providing customers a toll-free customer hot-line?

16.6. How does a client-server computer system architecture impact the firm's telecommunications requirements?

16.7. Should Michael have retired earlier? Has his lengthy tenure inhibited the adoption of advanced telecommunications technology?

16.8. Discuss the aspects of the "war on terrorism" following the attacks on the United States on September 11, 2001, that demonstrate network-centric warfare.

Projects

16.1. Interview three high-bandwidth user firms and determine their telecommunications planning horizons. What are their major concerns in telecommunications planning?

16.2. Find a geographically dispersed firm that has connected remote sites, vendors, and customers, and possible mobile computer users and telecommunications. Diagram the connectivity and label the paths to show bandwidth and equipment. What are the ballpark costs of the network?

16.3. Survey vendor offerings to determine relative costs of switched and leased digital services using separate access lines and equipment for voice, video, and data, versus products offering integration to use a single set of access lines.

16.4. Investigate how remote users can gain LAN access in their corporate network. Contrast leased lines and modems with integrated options. What are performance and cost differences?

16.5. Interview cellular providers and determine what enhanced features they offer their customers. What do they forecast for their territories in terms of enhanced service use, data transmission, competition, and growth rates?

16.6. Contact a representative of the LEC and determine their plans for broadband technology deployment in your area. Ask what the major applications are that drive the LEC to make the investment in those technologies. What emerging opportunities does the LEC rank as most important? What is the extent of use of desktop video, Internet access, distance learning, and telemedicine?

16.7. Outline a plan for JEI's future telecommunications architecture. Determine an appropriate level of IP reliance.

16.8. Research the potential impact of information warfare on businesses.

Glossary[1]

5ESS Electronic switching system—AT&T digital switch at the CO; an electronic switching computer for central office functions.

10BaseT (Ethernet) The nomenclature of the medium and protocols that use unshielded twisted-pair wiring, in a baseband mode, operating at 10 megabits per second. This is the most-installed medium and protocol of the mid-1990s as most buildings have wiring installed that will support it (IEEE 802.3).

100BaseT (Fast Ethernet) 100 Mbps Ethernet, using category 5 cabling.

100BaseT-4 100 Mbps Ethernet, using four-line category 3 cable.

100BaseTx 100 Mbps Ethernet, using optic strands.

800 area code In-WATS—an area code where the recipient pays all charges. *See WATS.*

1000BaseFx (Giga-Ethernet) 1000 Mbps using category 6 or FX cable.

1000BaseT Giga-Ethernet; 1000 Mbps using category 6 or FX cable.

A

access charge The charge LEC customers pay to access an IXC connection. After divestiture, the FCC mandated "access charges" so that every telephone customer would pay a tariff for having access to the public network.

acknowledgment (ACK) A character sent from the receiving unit to the source, confirming that a packet of data was good.

acoustic Refers to sound waves in an air medium. The maximum human acoustic (hearing) ability is in the range of 20 cycles per second (hertz) to 20,000 hertz.

acoustic coupler A device that provides the ability to transmit and receive messages using the standard telephone line without an electrical connection.

adaptive differential pulse code modulation (ADPCM) The standard that measures only the difference in adjacent values and, thus, requires less bandwidth. It measures the signal just like the PCM method but transmits the difference between successive measured values instead of the value itself.

address Part of the header of a block of synchronous data that notes the destination of that block.

advanced mobile phone service (AMPS) The original analog cellular telephone protocol. A cellular equivalent to POTS.

Advanced Research Projects Agency Network (ARPANET) The first wide area network, developed by the Defense Department's ARPA agency. The precursor of the Internet.

air-medium radio Radio (electromagnetic radiation) uses the air/space medium for a channel.

alternatives The choices available, including the cost and value of each.

American National Standards Institute (ANSI) Standards group composed of industries and agencies.

American Standard Code for Information Interchange (ASCII) A binary coding convention. Seven-bit codes define 128 characters; eight-bit codes define 256 characters. The exact codes in a code set depend on the use of that code. Most microcomputers use ASCII codes. IBM mainframes and some PC software use EBCDIC.

Americans with Disabilities Act of 1990 (ADA 1990) Stipulates that individuals with disabilities that can be accommodated will be considered without prejudice for jobs, advancement, and facilities.

amperage The strength of an electric current expressed in amperes.

amplifier For analog signals, repeaters are used to increase the signal strength. *See repeater.*

amplitude The distance from the trough to the top of the crest of the signal; the greater the amplitude, the "louder" the signal.

[1] Assistance in creation of this glossary was provided by Denise Johnson McManus, Ph.D.

amplitude modulation (AM—radio) Using the variation in amplitude in the carrier wave to carry information.

analog (to) One thing is an analog of another if it represents the former, as electrical waves represent acoustic waves.

analog (wave) A signal in the form of a continuous wave.

analogous Similar to.

analysis and design The process of determining needs, analyzing alternatives, delineating system specifications, and designing the system that will properly serve the organization, usually referred to as systems analysis and design.

antitrust The prohibition of trusts, cartels, or similar business monopolies that operate in restraint of trade.

application gateway The way a software capability accesses the network.

application layer The highest layer in the OSI hierarchy. It provides user-oriented services, such as determining the data to be transmitted, the message or record format for the data, and the transaction codes that identify the data to the receiver.

application service provider (ASP) A company that delivers and manages applications and computer services from remote data centers to multiple users across a wide area network. (Source: WWW.aspindustry.org)

Archie An early, DOS-based program for finding files on the Internet.

architecture A specification that defines how something is constructed, defining functional modularity as well as the protocols and interfaces, which allow communications and cooperation among modules. It is a concept or plan that is implemented in a set of hardware, software, and communications products. It reflects the technical strategy.

area calling service The tariffed service offered by LECs that makes up the area for local calls. Sometimes includes measured service.

area code The three digits used to direct the call to the geographic area in which the exchange of the destination resides.

artificial intelligence (AI) The capability of computers to learn and mimic human actions.

Asymmetric Digital Subscriber Line (ADSL) Digital technology on analog POTS lines, providing high bandwidth. The circuit is digitized and divided into a telephone channel and one or more data channels.

asynchronous Protocols and systems that have no synchronism between cells or characters. In character-based communications, one character is sent at a time with start and stop bits to signal the receiver where a character begins and ends. With cell-based systems, the cell is of fixed length and format.

asynchronous transfer mode (ATM) A switching technology used by BISDN. It is a variation of packet-switching technology that transmits fixed-length units of data (called cells) at very high speeds. The speeds presently specified range from 155.52 Mbps to 2.488 Gbps, with future predictions of 100 Gbps or faster. *See also automatic teller machine.*

AT&T Consent Decree The agreement by AT&T to cease specified activities. In 1956, AT&T was limited to the telephone business.

AT&T WorldNet Services Internet access service provided by AT&T.

Attachment Unit Interface (AUI) The portion of the Ethernet standard that specifies how a cable is to be connected to an Ethernet card.

attenuation A characteristic of electrical and photonic signals is that they diminish or weaken as they travel away from their source. For example, the light from a flashlight is blinding at the bulb but is barely visible a mile away.

audio Relating to sound frequencies in the range of 20 to 20,000 Hz.

audio conferencing Use of audio devices to aid in meetings where participants are not all at the same location.

audit A detailed post-implementation evaluation of the project.

automated call distribution (ACD) A computer-based system of managing telephone calls.

automated teller machine (ATM) Provides 24-hour banking and puts the banking industry into a real-time mode. It is also called a bank-in-a-box.

automatic repeat request (ARQ) An error-correcting technique wherein an NAK is sent if the block was determined by the receiving unit to have errors, resulting in a retransmission of that block.

AVAIL A large bank transaction network.

B

backbone network   Connectivity at a "higher" speed between LANs and major nodes, such as mainframe computers. A backbone network is to LANs as a high-speed loop around a city is to the major streets that connect to the loop. The backbone network is analogous to the backbone of a human in that it acts as a central structure.

backup   To make a copy of a file or disk for recovery.

bandwidth   The data throughput capability of a channel. In digital circuits it is measured in bits per second, denoting the speed of transmission. For analog channels, it is the difference between the highest and lowest analog frequencies, measured in hertz (Hz), of a transmission channel.

bandwidth brokerage   The matching of sources and requirements to sell excess bandwidth.

bar code   An optical tag that uses vertical bars to represent numbers. Bar-code technology eliminates the necessity to key data by either data entry personnel or the end-users because codes can be easily read by scanners. *See wands.*

baseband   Narrow band circuit, generally not subdivided into channels. Often describes a digital circuit.

basic rate interface ISDN (BRI ISDN)   The residential/office configuration of ISDN generally configured with two 64 Kbps B channels and a 16 Kbps D channel, plus 16 Kbps for administration, for a total bandwidth of 160 Kbps.

batch processing   Computer-processing mode where jobs are entered into a queue as a whole block and wait their turn for complete access to the computer.

baud   A unit of signaling speed equal to the number of discrete conditions or signal events per second. In modems, it refers to the number of changes of the analog signal per second and is generally not the same as bits per second.

Baudot code   A code of five digits using two shift characters to represent 58 characters.

Bell Operating Company (BOC)   One of 22 LEC corporations carrying the Bell System name and logo resulting from divestiture. A BOC is an LEC, but an LEC does not have to be a BOC. There are 1,300 independent phone companies other than the BOCs.

Bell System   Referred originally to AT&T, which was comprised of the Bell Operating Companies, Western Electric, Bell Labs, and AT&T Long Lines. It is now only the Bell Operating Companies.

binary   The basic numbering system used by digital computers. That is, every piece of data that a computer processes or stores is encoded into a series of 1s and 0s in accordance with some standard convention, called a code.

bit   A binary digit, the basic building block for digital representation of data.

bit rate   The information transfer rate usually expressed in bits per second (not to be confused with baud). Bit rate specifies bandwidth.

Bitnet   The early, IBM-supported wide area network for academics.

bits per second (BPS)   The measurement of digital speed.

block check character (BCC)   The data field in the message trailer containing error detection characters. The larger the BCC field, the greater the probability of error detection.

Bluetooth   A wireless protocol that allows multiple wireless devices to transfer signals over short distances.

bridge   Intelligent devices that connect networks using the same protocol.

broadband   Transmission equipment and media that can support a wide bandwidth. An analog path that may be frequency-division multiplexed to create several channels; a high-speed digital path that may be time-division multiplexed to create multiple channels.

Broadband Integrated Service Digital Network (BISDN)   A service requiring transmission channels capable of supporting rates greater than the primary rate. It also can be defined as an all-purpose, all-digital network that will meet the diverse needs of users by providing a wide range of services: high-speed data services, video phone, video conferencing, high-resolution graphics transmission, and CATV services, including ISDN services such as telephone, data, telemetry, and facsimile. BISDN employs SONET as the transmission medium and ATM as the switching technology.

broadcast   Simultaneous transmission to a number of stations.

brouter   A device that functions as a bridge and a router.

browser   A computer program that provides a graphical user interface for the World Wide Web.

bus   A transmission path or channel where all attached devices receive all transmission at the same time.

bus network   A multiple-point network with no master–slave, as all nodes are considered equal although one node may have the network operating system software resident.

bus topology   A single communications line, or channel, to which many nodes are connected. Each node on the network is of equal status; there is no master and no slave; the failure of one node has no effect on other nodes; faults may be difficult to locate; additions are easy.

business process reengineering (BPR)   The restructuring of basic business processes for greater efficiencies.

business-to-business (B2B)   The conduct of transactions electronically between businesses.

business-to-consumer (B2C)   The conduct of transactions electronically between a retailer and a customer.

bypass   When an organization circumvents the standard telecommunications provider, such as the LEC, to get a telecommunications service.

byte   The combination of bits to hold one character; usually a group of eight bits.

C

cable   A group of wires or other media bundled or packaged as a single line. A coaxial circuit is referred to as a cable, although it generally has only a single circuit.

cable modem   A terminating device for CATV that uses the coaxial cable as a high-speed conduit for data, generally for access to the Internet.

cable, or community, television (CATV)   A system for distributing TV from a central point (the headend) that typically is based on coax cables and is able to carry 50–100 television channels.

call waiting   The ability to switch from the active voice circuit to another circuit, that is, to change lines. The key system allows a user to switch between two active phone conversations by placing one call on hold

with one button and activating the other line with another button. Call waiting allows this at the switch.

Caller ID   Provides information between the first and second ringing signal that notes the calling party.

capacity   The bandwidth of the channels. The greater the bandwidth, the greater the capacity.

carrier frequency   The basic high-frequency signal onto which the true information signal is modulated.

carrier sense   The protocol's ability to listen to a multiple-user channel and determine if it is presently unused.

Carrier Sense Multiple Access/Collision Detection (CSMA/CD) protocol   A scheme used on the Ethernet bus networks to ensure that transmissions do not interfere with each other, that is, collisions are handled gracefully.

carrier wave   A high-frequency signal onto which the information is modulated.

Carterfone Decision   A milestone decision that allowed the connection of (foreign) non-AT&T equipment to the switched-voice network. The FCC allowed the Carter Electronics Corporation of Dallas, Texas, to connect its mobile radio system to the Bell network after a long battle with AT&T.

category 3 wiring   Unshielded twisted-pair 24–26 gauge wiring, with a mild twist, for example, the type used to wire most buildings.

category 5 wiring   Unshielded twisted-pair 24–26 gauge wiring with a mild to severe twist to reduce interference. Much more costly than category 3 wiring.

cathode ray tube (CRT)   A specialized type of monitor developed for radar that displays via dots.

cell   A fixed-length packet in an asynchronous transfer mode (ATM) system.

cellular blocking   Failure of a cellular phone to gain access due to lack of available frequencies.

cellular radio   A radio-based telephone service.

cellular (radio) telephone   A means of dividing wireless radio telephone coverage areas into cells for reuse of frequencies.

central office   The terminal point of all local loops and the location of the switch that connects the users to the network.

centralized computing   The concentration of computing services in a single point; often used with mainframes.

Centrex   A group of services provided by the Telco as a specially priced service, giving the view that you have your own PBX. The LEC maintains the equipment and charges the customer for this service. Both are regulated by state and federal bodies.

Centrex vs. PBX   The comparison of a private switch and a LEC switch that is configured for a client.

champion   The individual who avidly supports a new technology.

change management   Organizes the process of making changes to an installed capability. Because of the complexity of telecommunications systems, a lack of change management will lead to the inability to have configuration management.

channel   A communications path between nodes.

channel bandwidth   The range of hertz or the bps within a channel.

chief information officer (CIO)   The top information executive. A position at the same level as the vice president of finance, sales, and operations is being created in many organizations to control the information resource from a total organization perspective. In some organizations, the position has greater scope, and the title is chief technology officer (CTO)—the top technology management executive.

chief technology officer (CTO)   An officer who is concerned with the applications of all technology within the organization.

Child Online Protection Act (COPA)   An act in the United States directed at protecting children when they are accessing the Internet.

circuit   A (physical) path over which a signal can travel. Some media include paths in both directions, either simultaneously or one direction at a time.

circuit-level gateway   A device for connection of networks at the circuit level.

circuit media   Vary in expense, bandwidth, and immunity to noise. Circuit media are the "physical" paths of circuits, which may be subdivided into channels. The same media discussed previously (twisted-pair wire, coaxial cable, microwave, omnidirectional radio, and satellite channels) can be used for transmitting either analog or digital signals.

circuit switching   The temporary establishment of a connection between two pieces of equipment that permits the exclusive use until the connection is released, for example, a POTS call.

cladding   A layer of material surrounding the glass core of a fiber optic strand.

client   The user or using computer that takes advantage of facilities or services of the server computer in a client-server architecture (C/SA) system.

client-server architecture (C/SA)   An extension of cooperative computing and distributed computing, where two or more computers cooperate to perform a task.

Clipper Chip   An attempt to permit U.S. government agencies to decrypt encrypted messages in the 1990s.

CO switch   Central office equipment that makes telephone connections without human operators. This sets up a path from the sender to the receiver. *See central office.*

coaxial cable   Called "coax," a shielded wire that performs the same function as twisted-pair, but provides broader bandwidth and more protection from interference. A coaxial cable is similar to a pair of copper wires except that one wire is a braided or solid sheath that encompasses (shields) the other wire.

code   The representation of characters by numbers or bit patterns.

code division multiple access (CDMA)   A cellular protocol based on spread spectrum technology designed to increase the efficiency of the channel.

code length   The number of bits in a code character.

codec   A device that converts analog signals to digital signals or vice versa.

cold site   Sometimes called a shell site, it consists of prepared facilities without any equipment.

cold turkey   A switch-over process when the system is changed and brought online all at once without other considerations. This involves the greatest risk but least expense if all goes well.

collision   The interference of one transmission with another, when both are in contention for the use of the channel; when two nodes transmit simultaneously.

committed information rate (CIR)   The specified guaranteed bandwidth that will be delivered, regardless of the bandwidth of the channel or circuit.

common carrier   Any company that provides a service to the public. AT&T is a common carrier of long-distance services.

common management information protocol (CMIP) An ISO standard protocol for exchange of network management commands and information between devices attached to a network. *See also SNMP.*

communicate The transfer of information between parties.

communications The process of transferring information from a sender to one or more receivers via some medium.

Communications Act of 1934 Created the Federal Communications Commission (FCC) to regulate radio, telegraph, and other future telecommunications services.

Communications Management Information Protocol (CMIP) One of the standards used to note the status of a node on the network.

competitive access providers (CAPs) A provider of POTS services other than the ILEC.

competitive advantage The ability to gain a disproportionately larger share of a market because of cost leadership or product or service differentiation.

competitive local exchange carrier (CLEC) A LEC that enters the market to compete with the ILEC in provision of local telephone services (since the Telecommunications Act of 1996).

compression A process (hardware- or software-based) to reduce the amount of data communicated or stored by coding redundant data; it makes a data stream smaller by encoding schemes, by having single characters represent larger groups of redundant characters. Compression reduces the bandwidth required.

CompuServe Graphics Interchange Format (GIF) A format used with still graphics that includes compression.

computer-aided design (CAD) The use of a computer for the creation of automated industrial, statistical, biological design, and so forth.

computer inquiry An investigation by an agency of the U.S. government to determine if specific practices were subject to regulation.

Computer Inquiry I (CI-I) Determined that continued regulation of the communications industry was appropriate but that the data-processing industry would not be regulated. This may be the decision that spurred the rapid development of the computer industry.

Computer Inquiry II (CI-II in 1981) One of the most important reviews of the telecommunications industry. *See divestiture and Modified Final Judgment.*

computer-integrated manufacturing (CIM) The application of information and manufacturing tech-

nology, plans, and resources to improve the efficiency and effectiveness of a manufacturing enterprise through vertical, horizontal, and external integration.

computer telephony integration (CTI) The use of computer applications and telephone signals, such as Caller ID, to aid in customer service. The capability of voice and computer networks.

concentration The process of combining multiple messages into a single message for transmission.

concentrator Any device that combines incoming messages into a single message or places them onto a single line.

conditioned line A communications line on which the specifications for amplitude and distortion have been tightened by adjusting the electronic parameters.

conducted wire A wire that is suitable for carrying an electrical current.

configuration control The inventory of all resources. It is vital to ensure that you know what resources are presently available and the relationships that exist among them. Configuration management gives you data to use in cost allocation and information for expansion and improvements.

configuration management The logical management of resources on a network.

connect time The amount of time that elapses while the user of a remote terminal is connected to a time-share system.

connection-oriented Communications where a true physical or a permanent or temporary virtual path is established for that data transfer. The POTS is a prime example of such a service.

connectionless A type of communications in which no fixed or permanent path exists or is created between sending and receiving stations, and each data unit is sent on its own to traverse the network.

connectivity The communications path between two or more nodes.

consent decree An agreement by an organization to a government regulatory agency or a court to cease a specific practice in exchange for some consideration by the entity to which the consent is made. A consent decree is like an out-of-court settlement. The 1956 decree limited Bell System companies to the telephone business. AT&T consented to divest itself of the Bell System in the Modified Final Judgment and limited it to the voice communications industry.

contention A situation in which two or more nodes compete for use of the same channel.

contingency planning   Preparing to deal with unexpected events; a plan to continue business in the event of unforeseen adverse occurrences.

control   A project involving feedback to determine if the goals and objectives of a project are being met.

controlling   To exercise supervision over a process or resource to ensure performance according to plan.

convergence   The bringing together of multiple media such as voice, video, and graphics.

coordinating   To perform the necessary steps in the proper sequence to keep the business operating as normal.

critical success factors (CSF)   Those (few) things that must go properly for the organization to be successful.

cross-subsidization   Charging extra for one service in order to support another. AT&T could cross-subsidize the rural service with revenue from long-distance and business services, where fees could be higher than "normal."

crosstalk   A radiation of signal from one circuit to another. Signals inadvertently transferred (induced) between elements (wires) of a cable. The result appears as noise.

customer premises equipment (CPE)   The instruments and equipment on the customer's site.

customer relationship management (CRM)   Establishing processes and software to ensure that customers are satisfied and remain loyal.

Customer Service Area (CSA)   The distance from the central office that can be serviced without engineering, for example, the 12,000-foot length for DSL.

cutover   The different methods to bring additions or modifications to the system online. The methods: pilot, parallel, phased, phase-in, phase-out, modular, and cold turkey.

cyclic redundancy check (CRC)   A standard used for error detection in synchronous communications.

D

data   Facts about the activities of the organization.

data circuit-termination equipment (DCE)   The functional units that establish, maintain, and release the connection and provide any data conversion between the DTE and the transmission line.

data communications   That part of telecommunications that relates to movement of data between machines, usually computers.

data communications equipment (DCE)   Equipment that connects a node with a channel; the device that terminates a data transmission connection.

data conferencing   The sending of files back and forth to conference.

data link   The physical means of connecting one location to another for communications.

data link layer   The OSI layer with the actual transmissions of characters and the sequence in which they are transmitted.

data-sharing model   An expansion of the communications model to incorporate sharing of data between people or devices.

Data Signal Format One (DS-1)   A standard; any medium that carries 1.544 Mbps speed with 24 DS-0 (64 Kbps) channels plus 8 Kbps for control. *See T1.*

Data Signal Format Zero (DS-0)   A standard for a data channel having a bandwidth of 64 Kbps.

data terminating equipment (DTE)   The end nodes that use data communications, often with DCE as intermediaries. DTEs talk to DTEs.

data transfer rate   The average number of bits, characters, or blocks per unit of time.

datagram   One mode of data transfer for the X.25 packet network, analogous to the U.S. Postal Service in that datagrams find their way around the network.

decibel (db)   A measurement of change in signal strength, based on a logarithmic scale.

decision support systems (DSS)   Computer-based capabilities used to aid in solving unstructured problems.

decode   The process of reconversion of the message so the receiver can understand it. Changing a digital signal into its analog form or another type of digital signal.

demodulation   The process of retrieving intelligence (data) from a modulated carrier wave, for example, the reverse of modulation.

denial of service (DOS)   Intentionally sending a large number of requests to a node to attempt to saturate it and logjam its operation.

dense wave division multiplexing (DWDM)   The use of multiple waves on a single fiber strand.

depreciation   An accounting process of charging long-term expenses as a cost; used to offset revenues for tax purposes.

deregulation   The removal of control previously exercised by a governmental agency. Returning the control of the entity to the free market.

design-for-manufacturability Considering the capabilities of the manufacturing facility when creating the design for maximum output and quality products.

destination The final receiver.

dial A process that signals the network by sending pulses or tones to the CO equipment where they are interpreted and the proper circuit is established.

dial tone The sound on the handset indicating that the switch is ready to accept information for connection of a call.

dialing Originally it meant the use of a circular rotary dial to send pulses to the switch; now the term is used to mean any method of sending a signal to a switch or PBX to gain access.

differential phase shift keying (DPSK) A modulation technique in which the relative changes of the carrier signal phase are coded according to the data to be transmitted.

digital Binary (bistate) codes to represent data, which means that the data are encoded into a series of 1s and 0s in accordance with some standard convention, called a code. Noise on a circuit appears much like digital data.

digital camera A camera that uses digital storage instead of film.

digital circuit A circuit expressly designed to carry the pulses of digital signals. It, however, may utilize analog and modem technologies, for example, ISDN.

Digital Millennium Copyright Act (DMCA) An attempt internationally to thwart copyright infringement.

digital PBX A privately owned telephone switch that is digital-based instead of analog-based.

digital satellite radio A satellite-based service to provide radio-type programs such as talk and music channels.

digital signal processor (DSP) A microprocessor especially designed to analyze, enhance, or otherwise manipulate sounds, images, or other signals.

Digital Subscriber Line (DSL) Use of high-speed modems on existing twisted-pair POTS line to provide a digital environment.

digital-to-analog (D/A) converter A device that converts a digital value to a proportional analog signal.

direct broadcast satellite (DBS) The transmission of commercial television from satellite directly to the home.

direct distance dialing (DDD) The user-dialed long-distance number sequence without operator intervention or assistance.

directing A prime task of management, involving the issuing of instructions for the execution of plans.

disaster The results of severe adverse conditions, such as the damage from a flood.

disaster planning A contingency plan for continuance of operations in the event of unforeseen adverse occurrences, often called business continuity planning.

disaster recovery Provides alternatives for continued operations and recovery from damage. Recovery and planning are vital to modern organizations as they rely on computers and telecommunications for continued operations. It is an important aspect of security and control.

discrete Digital; nonanalog or noncontinuous.

dispersed operations The opposite of centralized; decentralized resources.

dispersion The tendency of photons in a light pulse to spread out as they travel in any medium.

distance learning The provision of course work to remote locations via telecommunications.

distortion The tendency for signals to change from their originated form appears naturally as a result of the environment through which the signal must pass. Noise and distortion must be countered in order to pass data correctly.

distributed Decentralized, scattered resources.

distributed computing A type of information systems architecture that divides the processing tasks between two or more computers that are linked by a network.

distributed data processing (DP) Data processing in which some or all of the processing, storage, and control functions are situated in different places and that depends on telecommunications.

divestiture The separation of the Bell System from AT&T. The result of the Modified Final Judgment.

DoCoMo Means "anywhere" in Japanese; an NTT subsidiary and Japan's biggest mobile service provider, with over 31 million subscribers as of June 2000.

documentation To log and compile the required information, rationale, and steps to perform a task.

dogma Hype and rhetoric are not recognized; assumed to be true and complete.

downloading The transmission of a file of data from a mainframe or other host computer to a microcomputer.

dual-tone-multifrequency (DTMF)   A method of signaling a desired telephone number by sending tones on the telephone line. Each code is composed of two (dual) tones.

dumb terminal   A terminal that has little or no memory or processing power and is not programmable.

duplex   Bidirectional circuit capability.

dynamic router   A device (*see router*) that determines the best temporary route for a packet based on present conditions.

dynamic routing   A technique used in data networks by which each node can determine the best way for a message to be sent to its destination.

E

echo   The reversal of a signal, bouncing it back to the sender, causing interference.

echo suppressor   A device that permits transmission in only one direction at a time, thus eliminating the problem caused by the echo. Such devices add complexity to circuits and can cause interference with signals.

edge router   A router on the edge of an enterprise network.

effective compression   Equal to the channel's native bandwidth, minus the effects of noise, plus that gained due to compression.

electrical   Direct or alternating current used to carry a signal on a conductive medium.

electromagnetic   Rapidly varying (high-frequency) current used to carry another signal.

electromagnetic interference (EMI)   Analog radio-like radiation that interferes with other devices.

electronic   Use of solid state devices, for example, to amplify or switch.

electronic bulletin board systems (BBS)   Using a PC connected to a publicly accessible, often fee-based server.

electronic business (eBusiness)   Conducting business electronically, involving everything from sending email, advertising on the Web, or creating an intranet so that your HR department can post online policies and procedures manuals.

electronic cash (ecash)   Using email or its equivalent to pay bills where no physical money changes hands.

electronic commerce (eCommerce)   A dynamic set of technologies, applications, and business processes that link enterprises, consumers, and communities through electronic transactions and the electronic and physical exchange of goods, services, information, and capital.

electronic data interchange (EDI)   A set of standards for computer-to-computer communications of standardized business documents.

electronic funds transfer (EFT)   Allows more efficient handling of funds at a lower cost by moving monies through a network as opposed to checks in the mail.

electronic mail (email)   Allows users to communicate electronically with other users as if two typewriters were connected by a channel. Email adds a new dimension to the office environment, replacing paper copies and reducing time of transmittal.

electronic performance support systems (EPSS) Special systems designed to capture knowledge of experts so that the relevant knowledge may be called on by a person who needs just-in-time expert advice. Some knowledge management (KM) systems employ EPSS.

email conferencing   Using email in a back-and-forth mode to conference, that is, non-real-time chat.

encode   The process of preparing a message for efficient transmission. Encoding means to change the idea or information into symbols during transmission; also, the transforming of a digital signal into an analog signal.

encryption   Transformation of data from the meaningful code that is normally transmitted to a meaningless sequence of digits and letters that must be decrypted before it becomes meaningful again.

enterprise information systems   The aggregation of data processing, functions, and their interaction across the entire organization.

equal access   A part of the Modified Final Judgment that specified that LECs must provide all of the IXC access equal in type, quality, and price to that provided to AT&T.

equipment life span   The useful time during which equipment will meet its intended purpose. In the past, the expected life of IT equipment was 10–20 years. Presently it is 3–5 years. While the equipment may easily last several times that number of years, its technological usefulness does not.

error   A discrepancy between a computed, observed, or measured value or condition and the true, specified, or theoretically correct value or condition.

error correction   Changing erroneous characters back to the intended value.

error detection   The techniques used to ensure that transmission and other errors are identified.

Ethernet   The trade name designated by the creators of CSMA/CD protocol.

Ethernet protocol   The most used network operating system protocol using CSMA/CD (carrier sense multiple access/collision detection) management (IEEE 802.3 standard) at 10 Mbps over unshielded twisted-pair wire (10BaseT). Ethernet was developed in 1980 by Xerox, DEC, and Intel.

exchange   The first three digits of the seven-digit phone number is the exchange destination. One or more exchanges reside in the switch in a central office.

executive information systems (EIS)   Computer-based systems designed specifically for high-level managers.

expert systems (ES)   Expert knowledge embedded in a computer program so that the program can make decisions.

Extended Binary Coded Decimal Interchange Code (EBCDIC)   An eight-bit mainframe-originated code used on IBM PCs.

external modem   A device that sits on the desk and plugs into an electrical outlet for power and connects to the computer through a cable that fits into a standard socket called a serial port on the back of the computer.

extranet   An invitation-only group of trading partners conducting business via the Internet.

F

facsimile   The transfer of any document one could put on a copier. It senses and transmits spots of light and dark.

Fast Ethernet   Ethernet running at 100 Mbps.

fat client   A desk-top node that is capable of storage and processing. It usually has excess capacity and overhead.

feasibility   A phase in the SDLC analysis to determine the feasibility of a project, including technical, behavioral, economic, operational, time, regulatory, and ethical feasibility categories.

Federal Communications Commission (FCC)   The appointed federal body governing most interstate communications activities. It has a board of governors, appointed by the president of the United States, with control of the radio and television broadcasting industries. The FCC regulates all types of tele-communications service and rates through tariffs.

fiber distributed data interface (FDDI)   A network based on optical fiber media, ring topology, and token-passing protocol, operating at 100 Mbps; a major form of MAN.

fiber optic cable   Very small one-way glass strands that have the largest bandwidth of any media used.

fiber optic circuits   Use a laser or light-emitting diode (LED) at the source end and a light detector at the receiving end. There must be a light-to-electrical signal conversion at each end.

fiber to the curb (FTTC)   Bringing fiber strands from the source to the curb outside of the residence or office.

file server   A dedicated computer on a network that shares its disk space with other nodes.

File Transfer Protocol (FTP)   A standard created to move files over the Internet.

file upload   Transmitting a file to the host site, or from another device that is connected via a network.

firewall   Software or hardware that protects node(s) from intrusion from the Internet.

FireWire standard external bus (IEEE 1394)   A wire-based standard for fast digital transfer.

fixed node   A node that is not intended to move.

fixed wireless   A wireless mode that is not intended to be mobile.

float   The time funds are in transit between payment and receipt.

foreign exchange   A leased line from a local Telco or long-distance carrier, or both, from the firm's location to the switch of a distant central office.

format   The message format of the protocol defines the location and amount of true data contained in the message and the overhead necessary to ensure that the destination receives the data as they were sent.

forward channel   In full-duplex, when the primary movement of data is in one direction, the circuit can either be switched half-duplex or allocate the greater bandwidth to the source-to-destination (forward) direction and a minimum bandwidth to the reverse (response) channel. This makes the forward channel fast and the reverse channel slow.

forwarding   The act of sending a received message to another node.

fractional T1   Use of one or more DS-0 channels of a T1 channel.

frame relay   An ISDN frame-mode service based upon fast packet switching. In simplistic terms, frame relay can be thought of as "relaying" variable-length units of data, called frames, through the network.

frequency   The number of oscillations of a signal per second; the number of repetitions or cycles that occur within a second of time is termed hertz. It is the pitch of the signal.

frequency division multiplexing (FDM)   The division of a transmission circuit into two or more channels by splitting the frequency band carried by the circuit into narrow bands to become distinctive channels.

frequency modulation (FM)   Uses variation in the frequency of the carrier wave to carry information. In FM radio, the analog music and voice signal varies the frequency, not the strength (amplitude), of the carrier wave.

frequency shift keying (FSK)   Frequency modulation of a carrier by a signal that varies between a fixed number of discrete values.

front-end processor (FEP)   A small computer that sits between remote devices and the host mainframe, relieving the host of tasks, such as line control, message handling, and code conversion.

full duplex   A circuit that allows data to be sent and received at the same time—a simultaneous two-way circuit or channel. This method requires two paths, that is, two twisted-pair circuits, or division of the communications channel into two parts.

Full-Duplex Ethernet (FDE)   Bidirectional Ethernet protocol.

G

gateway   Intelligent devices that connect networks that use differing protocols, thus requiring protocol conversion.

General Packet Radio Service (GPRS)   A standard for wireless communications that runs at speeds up to 150 kilobits per second.

geosynchronous orbit   A satellite orbit that exactly matches the rotation speed of the earth, generally placing it at an altitude of 22,500 miles above the surface.

giga   One billion. A gigahertz is one billion Hz.

Giga-Ethernet   Ethernet running at 1000 Mbps.

global area network (GAN)   The extreme of the WAN.

global logistics   Movement of goods, services, and so on between locations worldwide.

global positioning system (GPS)   Satellite-based portable device to determine location, altitude, and speed.

Global System for Mobile Communications (GSM)   The most popular mobile technology in Europe; currently expanding within the United States.

Gopher   A software system to make navigation around the Internet easier.

Graham Act   The act of 1921 that recognized and legitimized AT&T's natural monopoly and the monopolies of independent Telcos in their regions, and exempted the telecommunications industry from the provisions of the Sherman Antitrust Act.

groupware   Software that allows groups of people to communicate and work together simultaneously.

guard channel   The space between the primary signal and the edge of the analog channel.

H

hacker   Individual who enjoys exploring the connected world, especially the unauthorized invading of the computers of others, for fun or mischievous intent.

half-duplex   Transmission in either direction on a specific channel, one direction at a time.

Hamming code   A data code that is capable of being corrected automatically by including sufficient redundancy that allows the true data to be detected through errors.

handshake   The initial process of a communications session whereby two units determine the speed of transmission and other parameters and, therefore, the receiving node knows when to sample the line to detect a bit.

Hayes-compatibility   Equipment that has the same protocol and configuration of the standard established by Hayes.

header   The part of a block of synchronous data that contains information about the message, such as its destination, source, and block number.

hertz (Hz)   The technical term for analog frequency, that is, cycles per second. The greater the hertz, the higher the pitch of an audible signal.

high-data-rate Digital Subscriber Line (HDSL) An early form of DSL that is bidirectional, running at about T1 speed. It is often used to create T1 circuits.

high definition television (HDTV) High-quality television; digital at 19.6 Mbps in the United States; analog in Japan.

high-level data link control (HDSL) A bit-oriented data link protocol. A protocol standardized by ISO.

hot site Sites in disaster recovery that are set up with equipment already installed.

hub Network equipment that connects multiple nodes.

hybrid fiber/coax (HFC) The combination of coax and fiber optic circuits, allowing for high bandwidth to the neighborhood and coax to the residence, giving a good balance between cost and existing media.

hybrid network Some combination of any or all of the types of networks.

hype Emphasize the good; downplay the bad; repeat the message.

HyperText Markup Language (HTML) Computer application/language for creating pages for the World Wide Web. A browser is required to display the page.

HyperText Transfer Protocol (HTTP) The software capability that provides the graphical user interface for the WWW.

I

IEEE 802.11a/b Protocols for wireless, open architecture communications.

implementation The action phase of the SDLC where the system is made operational and turned over for use.

impulse noise A sudden spike on the communications circuit, often originating from inductive sources such as a refrigerator or air conditioner. The most encountered noise in PC telecommunications.

incumbent local exchange carrier (ILEC) The LEC that existed before competition was allowed after divestiture of AT&T.

information Processed data that enhance the recipient's knowledge. Subjective versus objective because of processing for a user.

information pipeline A channel.

information systems architecture The aggregation of data, equipment, applications, functions, and their interaction, which represents the business requirements.

information warfare Use of tactics to deny the enemy his or her data while protecting your own. Often applies to a military environment but can be in commerce also.

infrared Light below the visible range used in some wireless communications.

integrated services digital network (ISDN) A hierarchy of digital switching and transmission systems with high data rate transmission channels, high speed, and high quality using digital capabilities. Digital telephone, providing a digital circuit, composed of multiple channels.

intelligent terminal A terminal that has onboard memory and processing, and/or can be programmed.

interactive voice response (IVR) A system that provides an audible response to a keyed entry.

intercom Provides intercommunications within an organization, often by special telephones or specialize PBX operations.

interexchange carrier (IXC) Provider of telecommunication services across LATA boundaries. A long-distance carrier.

interface A shared boundary; the interface of the computer is the display on the monitor.

interference The intrusion of an unwanted signal. One signal's interruption of, mixing with, or replacing another.

inter-LATA Long-distance telephone calls between LATAs, which must be handled by IXCs.

internal modem A modem installed interior to a computer, attached to the system bus, providing greater speed as opposed to use of the serial port.

international record carriers (IRCs) Communications carriers that provide gateway facilities for transnational communications.

International Standards Organization (ISO) An international organization tasked with standards.

International Telegraph and Telephone Consultative Committee (CCITT) A standards body for communications technologies.

Internet A network of networks. The ultimate WAN, connecting people over most of the Earth. Global connectivity.

Internet Explorer (IE)   Micosoft's browser.

Internet service provider (ISP)   An organization that provides access to the Internet at the retail level. It receives service from a wholesale services provider.

Internet2   A specialized Internet accessible only via research and academic organizations.

interoffice communications   Ways that information gets around the office.

interoperability   The capability of two or more devices to transmit and receive data or carry out processes regardless of whether they are from the same or different manufacturers.

intranet   Implementation of Internet technologies within a corporate organization. An internal, corporate Internet.

inward WATS (800 or 888 service)   Capability that allows callers to call a long-distance number toll free. Long distance, for example, 800 and 888 area codes, where the receiver pays the charges.

IP telephony   Use of the Internet Protocol to carry voice traffic over the IP network.

ISO-OSI model   A model for the creation of telecommunications equipment. Its primary objective is to provide a basis for interconnecting dissimilar systems for the purpose of information exchange.

isochronous communications   The accommodation of asynchronous transmission over a synchronous link, where filler bits are inserted to keep the circuit synchronized.

information technology (IT)   All equipment, processes, procedures, and systems used to provide and support information systems within an organization.

International Telecommunications Union (ITU)   The successor to the CCITT.

J

Java   A computer language developed by Sun Microsystems that is platform independent.

Joint Photographic Experts Group (JPEG)   A standard for formatting and compressing still images.

just-in-time (JIT)   In a broad sense, an approach to achieving excellence in a manufacturing company based on the continuing elimination of waste. In a narrow sense, just-in-time refers to the movement of material to the necessary place at the necessary time, negating large storage quantities.

K

key instrument   An upgraded standard telephone that has access to more than one POTS or PBX line.

key system telephone   An upgraded telephone handset that has the basic ability to switch incoming calls.

kilo   One thousand; 1 kilohertz is 1,000 hertz.

knowledge management (KM)   The management and control of an organization's intellectual capital.

L

laser   A device that produces a pure intense light. For telecommunications purposes, the light is the carrier frequency that can be modulated or pulsed to carry information.

layers   Architecture, standards, and layers allow the network to be changed without affecting the user; layer independence is like data independence in DBMS.

leased circuit   A circuit that is owned by a common carrier but leased to another organization.

least-cost routing   The process whereby a PBX chooses between several IXC services and chooses the lower-cost route.

legacy systems   Older applications running on mainframes.

light-emitting diode (LED)   A semiconductor device that converts electrical energy to light; used for very-low-power numeric displays and status lights.

line access   The method that the sender node uses to gain access to send a message. The simplest method of access, though the most expensive in overhead, is polling, involving one master node and several slave nodes.

line conditioning   A means for providing higher-quality communications on a channel or circuit by adjusting parameters, thus reducing noise.

line termination equipment   The equipment that terminates local loops (wiring frame) and then connects them to the switch that makes the loop-to-loop connections.

line turnaround   A protocol for half-duplex transmission in which one modem stops transmitting and becomes the receiver, and vice versa. Although there is time required for turnaround, this allows the full bandwidth of the channel to be used in each direction.

link layer   *See data link layer.*

liquid crystal display (LCD)   Called a "flat screen display," this device is thin and has far lower voltage, power, cooling, and space requirements than a CRT display.

LISTSERV   Software to manage Internet mail.

local access and transport area (LATA)   A geographically defined area in which LECs operate and across which IXCs operate. Inter-LATA calls are carried by long-distance carriers such as AT&T, WorldCom, and Sprint (called specialized common carriers [SCC]).

local area network (LAN)   Connectivity among two or more nodes closely located, often thought of as covering an area of less than one kilometer in radius and connecting people within an organization, such as a campus, building, department, floor, or work group. LANs are privately owned; thus, like the PBX (customer premises equipment), they are nonregulated.

local calling area   Those telephone exchange prefixes to which a caller on flat-rate service can call without a toll.

local exchange carrier (LEC)   The local telephone company. The company providing local telephone service. This company operates one or more exchanges in the local calling area and provides service within LATAs. LECs are BOCs, GTE, Continental Telephone, United Telephone, and 1,375 other small Telcos.

local loop   The connection from the telephone instrument to the switching equipment, located at the Telco's CO. It is a pair of wires that are in reality a single (conducted) wire that forms an electrical path, a loop from the telephone to the connect point at the switching equipment.

local multipoint distribution service (LMDS)   A microwave technology used to distribute data and TV signals from a single point to many points up to about 25 miles.

long-distance calls   Calls outside of the local service area.

M

mainframe computer   A large computer that can process large programs or a very large number of transactions quickly. Users can access via terminal or via a network.

management   The control of the work of others.

management information systems (MIS)   All systems and capabilities necessary to manage, process, and use information as a resource to the organization.

material requirement planning (MRP)   A software system that provides the capability to schedule the materials required to build the end product.

MCI decision   Legislation that ended AT&T's monopoly in long-distance services.

mean time between failure (MTBF)   *See MTBF.*

measured rate service   A method of charging for local calls based on the number of calls, their duration, and the distance.

medium   The means of movement of signals from node to node; the physical evidence of the path.

mega   One million; 1 megahertz is 1,000,000 hertz.

mesh network   A network configuration in which there are one or more paths between any two nodes.

message   The content of what is being sent across the line.

Metropolitan Area Ethernet (MAE)   Internet networks traffic exchange facilities located in various U.S. cities.

metropolitan area networks (MAN)   Connectivity within a metropolitan-sized area, often providing services to many companies.

metropolitan optical network (MON)   A MAN using optical fiber.

microcomputer   A small-scale, or personal, computer.

microwave   Terrestrial and satellite technology that provides communications via line-of-sight high-frequency radio waves. They use micro or short wavelength radio waves and parabolic antennas to constrain the direction and radiation of the signal, thereby giving greater distance and lower susceptibility to noise.

microwave radio   Omnidirectional radio operating in the short (micro) wavelength frequencies.

middleware   Software that connects two other applications.

milli   One-thousandth; a millisecond is 1/1000 of a second.

minicomputer   A midrange computer that is between the mainframe and the microcomputer in size and processing power.

mission   A statement of the scope of the business and why the business exists.

mobile commerce (M-commerce)   The buying and selling of goods in a moving Internet environment.

modem (MOdulator-DEModulator)   A piece of equipment that transforms digital codes to analog form (and vice versa) that can be carried by the voice telephone system.

Modified Final Judgment   The outcome of the U.S. Justice Department's (CI-II) antimonopoly court case against AT&T, whereby AT&T divested itself of the Bell System Companies (BOCs).

modulation   The process by which a signal's characteristic is varied according to the characteristics of another signal. *See AM and FM.*

monitor   In telecommunications it is software or hardware that observes, supervises, controls, or verifies the operations of a system.

monopoly   The exclusive right to or control of a territory, product, or service.

Morse code   The standard code developed by Samuel Morse using dots and dashes (long and short signals) to represent characters.

Mosaic   The first browser; it evolved into Netscape®.

Motion Picture Experts Group (MPEG)   A standard for formatting and compressing video/moving images.

movable node   A node that may be in one of several places, but not constantly moving.

movies-on-demand   Movies that you want, when you want them.

moving node   A connected device such as a PDA that remains connected while being transported.

MTBF   The mean or average time before or between failure of equipment or components.

multicasting   To transmit a single message to a select group of recipients.

multiple lines   Having more than one phone line.

multiple-station access unit (MAU or MSAU)   A wiring hub in a token ring LAN.

multiplexer (MUX)   A device that interleaves two or more data streams to be carried on a single channel.

multiplexing   A function that allows two or more data sources to share a common transmission medium so that each data source has its own "channel."

multipoint circuit   A circuit with several nodes connected to it.

multipoint microwave distribution system (MMDS) (also know as multichannel multipoint distribution system)   A microwave technology used to distribute data and TV signals from a single point to many points. Range is about 25 miles.

multiprotocol router   A router that can work with different protocols.

multithreaded   The ability of an operating system to execute different parts of a program, called threads, simultaneously.

N

nanotechnology   A field of science whose goal is to control individual atoms and molecules to create computer chips and other devices that are thousands of times smaller than current technologies permit.

narrowband integrated services digital network (NISDN)   Standard ISDN incorporating two DS-0 channels.

narrowcast   Where broadcast (radio) stations send a single message simultaneously to all listening receivers, narrowcast servers send an individual message to each receiver.

National Aeronautics and Space Administration (NASA)   The governmental agency of the U.S. government tasked with all space operations.

National Research and Education Network (NREN)   A high-speed network; the predecessor to Internet2.

National Television Standards Committee (NTSC)   A standard for present (non-SDTV or HDTV) television.

natural monopoly   A competitive structure where (1) the capital expenditure to create the entity is large, (2) having redundant facilities would unduly drain the resources of all competitors (wasteful duplication), and (3) the service is required by many firms and individuals.

near video-on-demand   The appearance of video-on-demand in a pay-per-view arrangement; often a service provided by a hotel.

negative acknowledge character (NAK)   A transmission control character transmitted by a station indicating that the block of data received contains errors.

Netscape   A browser to operate as the graphical user interface for the World Wide Web; the successor to Mosaic.

Netware Network operating system (NOS) software for a LAN produced by Novell.

network One or more channels that provide connectivity between two or more nodes. An interconnected group of systems or devices that are remote from one another.

network accessible storage (NAS) A specialized server, dedicated to serving files.

network architecture The set of conventions or standards that ensure all the other components are interrelated and can work together. This architecture is the overall design blueprint for creating and evolving the network over changes in time, technology, uses, volumes, and geographic locations.

network-attached data storage (NAS) A server that is dedicated to nothing more than file sharing.

network control program (NCP) Software that controls the operation of a front-end processor or communications controller.

network design The process of understanding the requirements for a communications network, investigating alternative ways for implementing the network, and selecting the most appropriate alternative to provide the required capacity.

network interface card (NIC) A circuit card in a microcomputer that provides the electrical interface to a network.

network layer(s) The third layer of the OSI model that defines message addressing and routing methods. This layer does end-to-end routing of packets or blocks of information; collects billing, accounting, and statistical information; and routes messages.

network modeling The process of drawing or simulating a network in various configurations.

network operating system (NOS) The software that manages a network.

network server A computer that is dedicated to the function of providing service to all nodes (microcomputers and devices) on the network.

node An end point or switching point in a group of devices that can communicate with each other.

noise Any unwanted signal that interferes with the desired signals.

O

object-oriented A special type of programming that combines data structures with functions to create reusable objects.

objectives The desired end results.

off hook Means the device is in use.

off line When a telephone or computer node is not connected.

office automation systems (OAS) Use of technology in the office.

offshore manufacturing In the United States, to manufacture products in a country other than the United States, generally outside of North America.

omni-directional radio Transmit in all directions.

on hook The telephone device is not actively connected to the circuit and, thus, the device is available for calling. The term comes from the days when a hook held the earpiece of the telephone.

on-the-fly switching Switching from one cell to another as the node moves.

online The state of being connected, usually to a computer, not requiring any intervention for access.

online banking Using banking services on the Internet as opposed to the physical bricks-and-motor.

online data input Inputting data to a device that is connected to a network as opposed to a disk medium.

online services *America Online, CompuServe, MSN,* and others—online communications systems that can be utilized to communicate around the world via personal computer. While providing Internet access, these services offer specific computer-based services from their own mainframes.

online shopping Retail purchases on the Internet.

open architecture Equipment and software design that lets the hosts interoperate, basing that interoperation on standard protocols.

Open Skies Policy 1971 legislation that allows anyone to launch and operate geosynchronous satellite-based communications.

open systems interconnection (OSI) model Consists of seven layers that contain specific protocols for each control level.

operating system The central control program that governs a computer hardware's operation.

Optical Carrier 3 (OC-3) An optical standard with speed of three times SAS-1 = 155.52 Mbps.

Optical Carrier 12 (OC-12) An optical standard with speed of 622 Mbps.

optical fiber A communication medium made of very pure, very thin glass or plastic fiber that conducts light waves.

organizing The task of defining relationships.

Orthogonal Frequency Division Multiplexing (OFDM) More efficient use of spectrum.

out-of-band signals Signals outside of the frequency range allowed for a voice signal.

outsourcing Buying as opposed to making systems or services.

overhead The financial burden that supports ancillary operations as opposed to line operations. Overhead operations do not touch the organization's product but support it. Resources that must be used to enable a process.

P

packet A unit of digital data with a set number of bytes, including some that act as an address code.

packet assembler/disassembler (PAD) A device that receives the total data block; breaks it into predetermined-sized packets; adds the appropriate addressing, administrative, and error checking data to the packet; and places the packet onto the network. The process is reversed at the destination.

packet data network (PDN) Provides connectivity to many points geographically. The network appears like a cloud with entry/exit points in many locations. Internal working is obscure to users as it provides connectivity in two ways: (1) almost exclusive use is by providing virtual circuits upon request; commands from user cause the network to establish a physical channel for the duration of the communications; (2) the second method of data transfer is datagrams, where the data are packetized and sent over the network, much as a letter through the U.S. Postal Service.

packet filter A resource that opens and inspects incoming packets to determine if it should discard or pass them.

packet-switched network *See packet data network (PDN).*

packet switching A transmission technique that is designed to cut costs and maximize use of digital transmission facilities interspersing packets (blocks) of digital data from many customers on a single communications channel.

pager A radio-based alerting device, generally capable of receiving textual information.

parallel Circuits that use concurrent movement of all bits in a byte. In a parallel circuit the number of wires from sender to receiver is equal to or greater than the number of bits for a character.

parallel port The Centronix port on a computer usually used with the printer. Data travel in parallel over eight lines as opposed to serially over a single line.

parity bit The binary digit appended to a group of binary digits to make the sum of all the digits either always odd (odd parity) or even (even parity).

parity checking Bit-level error detection in an asynchronous protocol.

path The route between any two nodes of the network.

peer-2-peer (P2P) computing The distribution of computers over a wide area, often by the Internet, and using them for a common problem, such as is done with *SETI* and *United Devices*.

peer-to-peer The ability of two computers to communicate directly without passing through or using the capabilities of another computer.

peripheral equipment Equipment that works in conjunction with a communications or computer system but is not integral to them.

permanent virtual channel (PVC) A fixed connection using a lookup table that indicates the specific route to take over a PDN, time-after-time.

permanent virtual circuit (PVC) A full-time connection between two nodes in a packet-switching network, created by static entries in a table.

personal area network (PAN) Wireless connectivity of equipment on the person and to nearby equipment for synchronization.

personal communications Various communications devices that usually are carried easily and employ radio as their technology. Pagers are an example of personal communications devices.

personal communications system (PCS) A small personal communications device that initially has digital cellular communications and may include paging and electronic mail.

personal computer (PC) A microcomputer.

personal digital assistant (PDA) A portable (pocket-sized) device that offers the functionality of a notebook and clock, and when connected with a modem, access to paging and the Internet.

personal identification number (PIN)   A secret identifier known only to the individual as a means of security. It may be used in addition to a password.

personal timeshare   *MSN, CompuServe, America Online*, and other online services offer timeshare services in the home and business.

phase   An attribute or parameter of an analog signal that describes its relative position measured in degrees.

phase modulation   Modulation in which the phase angle of the carrier is the characteristic varied.

phase shift   The offset of an analog signal from its previous location. This is a way to achieve phase modulation.

phase shift keying (PSK)   A modulation technique in which the phase of an analog signal is varied.

phase shift modulation   The encoding of digital information on an analog wave by rapidly switching the phase angle of the carrier.

phases of SDLC   Problem definition, feasibility, system analysis, design, procurement, implementation, test, maintenance, and change.

photonic   Using light as the data carrier on a transparent medium. Infrared systems use space as the medium and light as the carrier. Fiber optic cable uses glass or plastic as the medium and light waves as the carrier.

photonic connection   Connecting a fiber strand to connect light waves.

physical layer   The lowest layer of the OSI model, dealing with electrical properties.

pilot   A means to bring a new system up in the cutover phase for only a small group of users and applications and let them test it in a real mode.

plain old telephone service (POTS)   The simple telephone service provided by the local exchange carrier. The local loops that connect the CO switch and residence and office telephones in a star network.

planning   The preparation for the future, thought of as existing on various levels from the top level where overall company planning is done; middle level—intermediate plans, programs, and budgets, schedules, and technical performance targets are planned. Planning levels move from the general to the specific and from long to intermediate time horizons.

point of presence (POP)   The location within a LATA at which customers are connected to an IXC.

point-of-service or -sales (POS)   Systems that automate the sales transactions data to a large extent. The universal product code (UPC) and bar codes are technologies used by POS.

point to point   Single communications devices at both ends of a single communications link.

Point-to-Point Protocol (PPP)   The Internet standard for serial communications. *See SLIP.*

policy   The small set of mandates and directives from the top of the firm summarized by the ground rule "This is how we do things around here."

polling   An access method that involves the master node asking, in turn or based on a priority listing, each slave if it has messages to transmit or if it is ready to receive a message the master is holding for it. With this method of line access, collisions are not possible because the slave must have the attention of the master to transmit and two slaves cannot have access at the same time.

port   A connector on a node.

portable   Any device that is small and easy to move from one location to another, such as a laptop computer.

portable telephone   A telephone that operates exactly like a POTS instrument except it uses radio transceivers in lieu of wire from the base to the hand instrument.

Postal, Telephone, and Telegraph (PTT)   An office or administration that governs telecommunications services and pricing within the total country.

presentation layer   The layer of the OSI model that is responsible for formatting and displaying the data to/from the application. The presentation layer provides transmission syntax, message transformations and formatting data encryption, code conversion, and data compression.

prioritization   The process of ranking the importance or precedence of a list.

privacy   The right and ability to have information about one's person secured.

private branch exchange (PBX)   A multiple-line business telephone system that resides on the company premises and either supplants or supplements the LEC local services.

privatization   A movement to spur competition by eliminating or curtailing government ownership.

process layer   *See application layer.*

processing   Manipulation of data in a node.

procurement   The purchase of goods and services from suppliers.

project management   The administration, organization, and direction of the parts and resources of a project.

project team   A group of people organized for the purpose of completing a project.

protocol   Rules of communication. A protocol is a standard or set of rules or guidelines that govern the interaction between people, between people and machines, or between machines.

protocol analyzer   Test equipment that examines the bits on a communications circuit to determine whether the rules of a particular protocol are being followed.

protocol converter   Hardware or software that converts a data transmission from one protocol to another. *See gateway.*

prototyping   A quick and easy method used to create an approximation of the ultimate capability.

proxy server   A server that sits between a client application, such as a Web browser, and a real server. It intercepts all requests to the real server to see if it can fulfill the requests itself. If not, it forwards the request to the real server via proxy.

public key infrastructure (PKI)   A system of digital certificates, certificate authorities, and other registration authorities that verify and authenticate the validity of each party involved in an *Internet transaction*, the sale of a good or service over the Internet.

Public Service Commission (PSC)   *See Public Utility Commission.*

public-switched network (PSN)   A network that provides circuits switched to many customers. *See POTS.*

public-switched telephone (voice) network (PSTN)   *See public-switched network.*

Public Utility Commission   The by-state agencies in the United States that establish tariffs within a state. Some states use the title Public Service Commission (PSC). In some states, the commission members are elected; in other states they are appointed to office.

pulse code modulation (PCM)   The standard for transforming voice analog signals to digital representation using 8,000 samples per second and eight-bit codes to represent signal amplitude. This requires a bandwidth of 64,000 bps.

punched paper tape machine   A device that creates feed holes and code holes in paper tape to represent information.

Q

quadrature amplitude modulation (QAM)   A technique using a combination of phase and amplitude modulation to achieve high data rates while maintaining relatively low signaling rates, that is, high bps on a low or moderate baud rate.

quality of service (QoS)   A statement/measure of the nature of the data transmission rates, error rates, and other service provided.

Quick Response   A combination of technology and partnerships in the textile and apparel industry. The technology aspects include bar-code standards, scanning, data processing, and electronic data interchange (EDI).

R

radio   A device that employs electromagnetic radiation for wireless transmission and reception of communications.

radio frequency interface (RFI)   *See EMI.*

radio telegraph   A mode of communications that uses a radio channel for telegraph purposes.

real time   The actual time during which a physical process transpires. Information received in time to affect the decision at hand.

receiver   The destination of communications.

reciprocal backup agreement   An agreement between companies with very similar equipment and operating systems to back each other up in case of disaster.

redundant array of inexpensive disks (RAID)   Use of multiple smaller and less-expensive storage devices as a single entity to provide reliability and security from failure.

regeneration   The remaking of a perfectly shaped signal from a weak and misformed signal. Where analog channels simply amplify the attenuated signals, digital channels utilize signal regeneration or recreation to overcome attenuation and noise.

regenerator   A device that recreates (only) the desired signal, in perfect and amplified form.

Regional Bell Operating Company (RBOC) or Regional Bell Holding Company (RBHC)   The original seven parent corporations to which BOCs belonged as a result of the 1984 divestiture: NYNEX

Corporation, BellSouth, U.S.West, American Information Technology (Ameritech), Bell Atlantic, Southwestern Bell, and Pacific Telesis (PACTEL).

regulation　The control of a process or output so that it is kept within limits. This involves comparison against a standard via the use of feedback. Regulation for organizations means that a regulatory agency is created by some higher governing body to oversee the conduct of the organization.

remote job entry (RJE) terminal　A terminal attached to a computer via a telecommunications line.

repeater　Also called an amplifier. By convention, devices that amplify analog signals are called repeaters, whereas devices that regenerate and amplify digital signals are called regenerators, though they could be referred to as regenerative repeaters.

request for proposal and request for quotation (RFP/RFQ)　Formal request to vendors for a formal response describing the proposed makeup and possible costs for a specific set of goods and services.

requirements specification　The document that states what system will be created; produced in the systems analysis phase.

reverse channel　The secondary channel in a full-duplex circuit, generally of low bandwidth.

rhetoric　Simplify the message to fit time and complexity constraints.

ring network　A network in which each node is connected to two adjacent nodes. The protocol most often used with the ring topology is the token-passing protocol (IEEE 802.5).

ring topology　Nodes are connected in a circle; each node has a downsteam and an upstream neighbor.

risk　The possibility and probability of an undesirable event causing loss or injury and the level of consequence.

risk analysis　A methodological investigation of the organization, its resources, personnel, procedures, and objectives to determine points of weakness.

risk assessment　The process of analyzing present operations and proposed additional capabilities to determine the risk to continued operations. *See risk analysis*.

risk management　The way risk is avoided, minimized, or transferred. The analysis and subsequent actions taken to ensure that you can continue to operate under any foreseeable conditions, such as illness, labor strikes, hurricanes, earthquakes,

power outages, heavy rains, oppressive heat, or epidemics of the flu.

rotary dial telephone　Third-generation telephone instrument where the switch is signaled via pulses created by the rotating dial.

router　A piece of hardware or software that directs messages towards their destination, often from one network to another.

RS-232-C　A specification for the physical, mechanical, and electrical interface between data terminal equipment (DTE) and circuit-terminating equipment (DCE). A specification for a port and cable for serial communications.

S

satellite　A transponder in an orbiting vehicle in space that repeats microwave signals from and to earth stations.

satellite carriers　Common carriers offering geosynchronous satellite services: RCA, Western Union, AT&T, American Satellite, and TTT.

security　The denial of unauthorized access to protect resources from access, change, copy, or destruction.

Semantic Web　The idea of having data on the Web defined and linked in a way that they can be used by machines, not just for display purposes, but for automation, integration, and reuse of data.

sender　The originator or source of communications.

serial　Bits of the character follow each other sequentially down a single channel.

serial line Internet protocol (SLIP)　A standard for connecting to the Internet with a modem over a phone line.

serial port　The connection on a node (computer) that transfers the data sequentially on two wires from/to devices such as modems and PC mice.

server　A device on a LAN that provides shared access to file space or print capability.

service bureau　A timeshare service providing computer-based services for clients.

service level agreement (SLA)　A set of performance objectives reached by consensus between the user and the provider of a service.

session layer　The OSI layer that deals with the organization of a logical session. This layer provides access procedures, rules of half-duplex or full-duplex dialogs, rules for recovering if the session is interrupted, and rules for logically ending the session.

shared resource   Assets such as a printer that are used, in turn, by multiple users on a network.

shared tenant services   The sharing of services (provided by the owner) among several tenants in a building or campus.

shielded twisted pair (STP)   UTP with an extra shielding layer for noise reduction.

shielding   A protective enclosure that surrounds a transmission medium. It is designed to protect and minimize electromagnetic leakage and interference.

signal system no. 7 (SS7)   A signaling system used among telephone company central offices to set up calls, indicate their status, and tear down the calls when they are completed.

signal-to-noise ratio   The relationship between the level of the desired signal and the level of the undesirable noise.

Simple Network Management Protocol (SNMP)   A protocol for exchanging network management commands and information between devices on a network.

Simple Object Access Protocol (SOAP)   A lightweight protocol for exchange of information in a decentralized, distributed environment.

simplex   Transmission on one preassigned path, one-way circuit or channel, like AM or FM radio, air-broadcast TV, and cable television.

simulation   A program that shows the results of increased traffic and enhanced capabilities of a new computer program, or any new project, by use of mathematical models to represent external systems or processes.

slave station   A node that operates under the control of a master or control node.

small office/home office (SOHO)   An office at home or one having limited facilities.

smart terminal   A terminal that is not programmable but has memory capable of being loaded with information.

SMDS interface protocol   Uses distributed queued dual bus (DQDB) as an access protocol between the subscriber and the network.

software defined network (SDN)   A bulk pricing offered by telephone companies designed for businesses

or others who make a large number of calls. Standard-switched telephone lines are used to carry the calls.

solid wire   A single thread of wire of the size, or gauge, stated. It is the least expensive to make but its stiffness increases as the size increases.

source   The originator of communications, that is, the sender.

source routing   Use of information contained within each data frame as opposed to using interval tables.

spanning tree protocol (STP)   A link management protocol, it is part of the IEEE 802.1 standard for media access control bridges.

spectrum   The frequency bandwidth of an analog channel. The spectrum of a telephone channel is 4 kHz.

spread spectrum technology   A radio transmission technique in which the frequency of the transmission is changed periodically, increasing quality and security.

stackable hub   A hub that can be attached to another, making it appear as a single node.

staffing   The attracting, retaining, and training of the human resources needed for continued operations.

stand-alone   A device that is not connected to another device, such as a personal computer that is not on a network.

star network   The topology used to connect a central node to each outlying node of a network in a star network. In this topology, all circuits radiate from a central node, point to point. It is used in low-cost slow-speed data networks.

start of header (SOH)   The first character of the header of a block of synchronous data.

static router   A router that uses a nonchanging table for switching.

statistical multiplexer (stat-MUX)   A device that multiplexes based on volume of traffic. It allocates channel space or time based on historical need, providing bandwidth on demand.

statistical multiplexing   Sharing the bandwidth based on historical need.

statistical time division multiplexing (STDM)   A technique that combines signals from several nodes based on need for bandwidth.

step-by-step (Strowger or stepper) switch   Use of a rotary dial on the instrument to send out electrical pulses that stepped a series of switches according to the telephone number, setting up a path between sender and receiver. The switch and rotary phone came into use in 1919. The switch was invented by Almon B. Strowger.

stop bit The bit that indicates the end of a character in asynchronous communications.

storage A means of holding data.

storage area network (SAN) A high-speed subnetwork of shared storage devices; a machine that contains nothing but a disk or disks for storing data.

storage-attached network (SAN) A specialized network that deals with blocks of data. NAS is a specialized server, dedicated to serving files.

store-and-forward An application in which input is transmitted, usually to a computer, stored, and then later delivered to the recipient.

stranded wire A single wire that is composed of a group of smaller solid wires. The objective of stranding is to make the wire flexible and easy to handle, while having the same electrical properties as a single strand of the same equivalent size.

strategy Large-scale, future-oriented plans for interacting with a competitive environment to optimize achievement and organizational objectives. It is the organization's game plan that reflects the company's awareness of how to compete, against whom, when, where, and for what.

stress testing Placing a heavy load on a system to see if it performs properly.

subchannel The result of subdividing the bandwidth of a channel, which itself may be the division of a circuit.

subsidiary communications authorization (SCA) A subchannel within the assigned FM frequency (channel) of a radio station.

switch Any mechanical, electromechanical, digital, or photonic device that opens or closes circuits; changes parameters; or selects paths or circuits.

switchable hub A specialized hub that designates bandwidth to individual nodes as opposed to just sharing it across all nodes.

switched-56 A dialup data service that guarantees full-duplex 56 Kbps bandwidth.

switched multimegabit data service (SMDS) A high-speed, connectionless (datagram), cell-oriented, public, packet-switched data service developed to meet the demands for broadband services.

switched virtual circuit A temporary connection between two nodes established only for the duration of a session in a packet-switching network.

synchronous Communications that are block-of-data oriented and must have the transmitter and receiver synchronized.

synchronous communications Sending data as a block as opposed to a character (asynchronous). *See packet.*

synchronous data link control (SDLC) A bit-oriented data link protocol developed by IBM.

synchronous digital hierarchy (SDH) BISDN is based on transmission speeds and capacities at the 155.52 Mbps, 622.08 Mbps, and 2.488 Gbps levels. These bit rates derive from CCITT G series recommendations for synchronous digital hierarchy, synchronous optical network (SONET) standard of the T-1 Committee, and the CCITT I series recommendations, which support the concept of asynchronous transfer mode (ATM)–based BISDN. The transmission medium over which BISDN will operate is described by SDH/SONET with ATM employed as the switching mode.

synchronous optical network (SONET) Uses the same basic structure as SDH and is designed to interoperate at 155.52 Mbps and higher transmission rates. SONET's main purpose is high-speed, high-reliability, serial digital transmission over optical fiber cable.

Synchronous Transport Signal 1 (STS-1) A standard with speed of 51.840 Mbps.

system A group of interrelated and interdependent parts, working together to achieve a common goal.

System 36 An IBM minicomputer that is an upgrade from a System 34 and one level below a System 38. This series evolved into the AS/400.

systems development life cycle (SDLC) A means of putting a project's development activities into a rational sequence so that systems development can take place consistently. It involves a series of phases that take the project from conceptualization through implementation.

systems network architecture (SNA) A seven-layer communications architecture developed by IBM.

T

T1 A standard; any medium that carries 1.544 Mbps speed with 24 64 Kbps (DS-O) channels plus 8 Kbps for control; same as DS-1.

T3 A standard; any medium that has approximately 45 Mbps bandwidth, for example, 44.736 Mbps, equal to 28 T1 channels.

target specification The documentation from the systems analysis phase, detailing the new system in sufficient detail so as to be designable and buildable by others.

tariff A regulated telecommunications service and rates to be charged.

T-carrier system A family of high-speed, digital transmission systems, designated according to their transmission capacity.

technology Devices and systems (including programming and methodology) that perform new tasks. From the Greek *tekhnikos*, meaning *method*.

Telco An abbreviation meaning the local telephone service provider; the telephone company.

telecommunications Communications via electronic, electromagnetic, or photonic means over a distance. From the Greek *tele*, meaning *at a distance*.

Telecommunications Act of 1996 Legislation by the U.S. Congress making significant changes to the Telecommunications Act of 1934.

telecommunications architecture The structure of the telecommunications infrastructure.

telecommunications device for the deaf (TDD) A keyboard device that plugs into a telephone jack and allows the nonhearing person to send and receive phone calls visually.

telecommunications systems All components and capabilities needed to move information, or data, to serve organizational needs. Components include hardware, software, procedures, data, and (most important) people.

telecommunications technology All systems and capabilities used to communicate over a distance.

telecommunications utility The environment where voice and data communications are treated just like power and water.

telecommuting Using telecommunications to work from home or some other location instead of on the business's premises. It allows you to work at the office without going to the office.

teleconferencing A meeting at a distance. The oldest form is audio conferencing—telephone conference call.

telegraph A device consisting of a long-distance loop of wire that has an electric storage battery for energy, a key to open and close the circuit, and a sounding unit that responds to the electrical current with a noise. This is the earliest electrical transmission of data.

telemedicine Use of broadband data communications to assist medical personnel in treating patients at a distance.

telephone The device that converts voice (acoustic) signals into (analogous) electrical signals for transmission, and reconverts them into acoustic (voice) signals at the receiving end.

telephone number prefix The first three digits of the seven-digit telephone number.

telephone service Service provided by the LEC and the IXC for use to call anywhere.

telephone system The public-switched voice network; goes almost everywhere.

telephony Transmission of speech or other sounds. A general term used to denote all voice telecommunications.

teleprocessing The processing of data at a distant or remote location by using data communications circuits.

teletypewriter A typewriter-like device for creating the codes used in the telegraph system. It replaced the code-skilled operator with machine encoding and decoding as well as providing the first form of message storage (tape) for the telegraph.

Telnet A terminal emulation capability that allows a person to log onto a distant computer over TCP/IP networks.

terminal A point at which information can enter or leave a communications network.

testing The process to determine bottlenecks, level of queuing, balking, and the system's ability to handle heavy workloads.

thick Ethernet Any Ethernet operating on traditional 0.4-inch coaxial cable.

thin-ax (thin Ethernet) Small, thin coaxial cable of 0.25-inch diameter.

thin client A user node that has no storage and very limited processing.

time division multiple access (TDMA) A cellular telephone protocol designed to make more efficient use of the spectrum by dividing available transmission time on a medium among multiple users.

time division multiplexing (TDM) A technique for the division of a transmission channel into two or more subchannels by allotting the time slots of a common channel to several information sources. Unlike FDM, which is simultaneous (parallel), TDM is sequential (serial) transmission.

timeshare A computer system operating technique that provides the interleaving of two or more programs in the processor, for example, multitasking. Only one program runs at a time, but they take turns quickly.

timeshare service Services that are shared by a number of clients. Generally, computer-oriented services such as almost unlimited computer processing and storage, output report print or printing at their premises, fee-based programming services, and the use of a wide variety of royalty-based programs.

timesharing Use of a resource by multiple concurrent users on a time-allocation basis.

token A small data packet used to control conflicts and congestion with token-passing protocol.

token-passing protocol The protocol most often used with the ring topology (IEEE 802.5). In this operating system, a small data packet, called a token, continuously passes around the ring from node to node. The use of the token ensures that there will be no collisions on the network.

toll The charge to use a telecommunications channel or service. A tariff.

toll charge The charge associated with a call that is beyond the local calling area.

topology The physical layout and connectivity of a network. It refers to the way the wires, or more specifically the channels, connect the nodes; protocol refers to the rules by which data communications take place over these channels.

touchpad A small 12-key terminal attached to the CO switch. The DTMF touchpad uses a tone for each column and one for each row, two per code. This is a total of 7 tones to create 12 codes.

Touch Tone Signals sent in "dialing" that involves 7 (DTMF) tones to create 12 distinct codes.

traffic The movement, volume, and speed over a communications link. As the level of traffic increases, the probability of a circuit being busy increases.

transaction processing system (TPS) Computer-based systems that run on a timely basis, gathering and storing the data of the organization.

transceiver A radio that contains both a transmitter and a receiver.

translating bridge A bridge that connects LANs that use different data link protocols.

Transmission Control Protocol/Internet Protocol (TCP/IP) A set of transmission protocols for interconnecting communications networks such as the Internet.

transnational data flow The movement of data across national boundaries. Because some nations treat data as a resource, much like materials, the movement of data across their national boundaries is restricted, for example, tariffed.

transparent bridge Interconnection devices used on CSMA/CD LANs to make decisions on frame forwarding.

transparent mode A mode of binary synchronous text transmission in which data, including normally restricted data link control characters, are transmitted only as specific bit patterns.

transport To carry; the object of voice and data communications.

transport layer The OSI layer responsible for maintaining a reliable and cost-effective communications channel. The transport layer provides addressing to a specific user process at the destination, message reliability, sequential delivery of the data, and flow control of data between user processes.

transport model A model concerned with the addresses, reliability, and delivery of data via a channel.

tree network A form that creates a network of networks. It connects the individual networks so that the total system works together while giving the individual network independence. There is no single point of failure.

trellis code modulation A specialized form of quadrature amplitude modulation (QAM) that codes the data so that many bit combinations are invalid. It is used for high-speed data communications.

trunk line When the sender is connected to one central office (CO) and the receiver to another, the call goes between the two COs via a trunk line or trunk cable.

twisted-pair copper wire A circuit of copper wires as a loop with a single wire going from the sender to the receiver and back.

U

ultrahigh frequency (UHF) A band of frequencies above VHF in the range of 440–900 megahertz.

unicode A standardized coding system that has 2^{16} points that can be used to represent the characters of all languages.

uninterruptable power supply (UPS) A battery-operated device for protection against unstable voltage, power outages, and power surges.

Universal Description, Discovery, and Integration (UDDI) A Web-based distributed directory that enables businesses to list themselves on the Internet and discover each other, similar to a traditional phone book's Yellow and white pages.

universal product code (UPC) A printed bar code on retail goods that is used with POS.

universal serial bus (USB) The capability for higher-speed data transfer than the standard serial port. USB1.1 operates at 12 Mbps; USB2.0 operates at 480 Mbps.

universal service The provision of high-quality voice communications to homes and offices in all of the United States. The vice president of AT&T, Kinsbury, stated belief in and commitment to universal service.

unshielded twisted pair (UTP) The standard wiring used for telephony and much of data communications. *See twisted-pair copper wire.*

Usenet A worldwide bulletin board system that can be accessed through the Internet or through many online services, supporting forums, called newsgroups, that cover every imaginable interest group.

V

V.32 *bis* A CCITT standard for transmitting data at 14.4 Kbps, full-duplex on a switched circuit.

value-added carriers Telecommunications common carriers providing additional services, such as store-and-forward, thus making them unregulated.

value-added network (VAN) A common carrier that has additional services and is, therefore, not regulated.

value area networks (VAN) A special form of WAN that generally provides wide area coverage and offers services in addition to just connectivity in the form of

added intelligence such as speed translation, store-and-forward messaging, protocol conversion, data handling, and packet assembly and disassembly. VANs are nonregulated because of the added services they provide.

vertical redundancy check (VRC) Used for parity bit error detection with asynchronous communications.

Very Easy Rodent-Oriented Net-Wise Index to Computerized Archives (VERONICA) A DOS-based program for finding information on the Internet.

very high frequency (VHF) A band of frequencies in the 200–400 MHz range.

very small aperture terminal (VSAT) Small satellite earth stations, ranging in size from 18 to 36 inches in diameter.

video compact disk movies (V-CD) The storage of a video program on a CD as opposed to a DVD via compression.

video-on-demand *See movies-on-demand.*

videoconferencing Use of television to connect conference participants visually and audibly. This is simply the use of two-way video and audio channels between two or more sites.

VINES Network operating system (NOS) software for a LAN produced by Banyan.

virtual circuit Exists on protocols where there are multiple paths from sender to destination. The network operating system or router selects a temporary path for the duration of the communications. This is one mode for data transfer in an X.25 packet network.

virtual private network (VPN) A capability on the Internet that connects multiple users in a secure environment.

virtual telecommunications access method (VTAM) IBM's primary telecommunications access method.

virtual terminal A concept that allows an application program to send or receive data to or from a generic terminal definition. Other software transforms the input and output to correspond to the actual characteristics of the real terminal being used.

virtual workplace Using the network for the resources you would expect in the standard workplace; working at home with the access as if in the office.

vision Determining the mission of the company, including broad statements about philosophy and goals. Vision is a picture of the future, an easily understood statement about a practical and desirable, even if not fully predictable, goal.

Voice-enabled DSL (VeDSL) A Digital Subscriber Line that is channelized to carry multiple voice channels, providing voice and data to the SOHO.

voice mail An intelligent answering machine that stores voice messages for the receiver.

Voice-over-DSL Transport of voice conversations over a DSL circuit.

Voice over Frame Relay Transmitting digitized voice over a frame relay WAN by controlling the inherent delays.

Voice over Internet Protocol (VoIP) Transporting digitized voice over a network that incorporates Internet Protocol.

voice spectrum The 300 to 3,000 Hz band used on telephone equipment for the transmission of voice and data.

voice telephone Standard POTS instrument.

voltage The electrical potential in computers and telecommunications equipment, equivalent to water pressure.

W

wand A specialized laser reader that can read the data from the bar code and send it directly to the computer for processing.

WhoIS A capability to determine the human identification of a user ID or IP address on the Internet.

Wide Area Information Server (WAIS) A client-server system to help users search multiple Internet sites and receive resources.

wide area networks (WAN) At the opposite end of the network continuum from LANs. They are networks that cover wide geographical areas. They go beyond the boundaries of cities and extend globally. The extreme of the WAN is the global area network (GAN).

wide area telecommunication service (WATS) Bulk discount pricing of long-distance services.

WiFi IEEE 802.11b protocol, operating at 11 Mbps.

wired Connected by physical wires or fiber.

wireless Connectivity using radio or IR technology.

wireless communications Communications in which the medium is not wire or cable, but is broadcast by radio or infrared waves.

wireless telegraphy A radio-based telegraph that ushered in the age of wireless communications, allowing overwater, ship-to-ship, and ship-to-shore telegraph communications. It uses radio waves to send telegraph messages through an air medium (wireless telegraphy by Guglielmo Marconi, 1886).

wiring frame A terminal point in the central office for all local loops.

work at home (WAH) By use of telecommunications, the user is able to work at a home office instead of traveling to a formal, urban office.

workload generator Computer software designed to generate transactions or other work for a computer or network for testing purposes.

World Intellectual Property Organization (WIPO) An international organization dedicated to promoting the use and protection of works of the human spirit.

World Wide Web (WWW) The graphical interface portion of the Internet.

X

X.12 A set of standards for electronic data interchange.

X.25 A standard for packet-switched networks.

X.400 A standard for the transmission of electronic mail.

XMODEM An often-used PC-to-PC asynchronous communications protocol.

Z

zero slot Simple way to connect PCs via serial port connections. Such connectivity was referred to as zero slot LANs.

Abbreviations

ACD   Automated call distribution

ACK   Acknowledge

ADA   Americans with Disabilities Act of 1990

ADPCM   Adaptive differential pulse code modulation

ADSL   Asymmetric Digital Subscriber Line

AI   Artificial intelligence

AM   Amplitude modulation

AMPS   Advanced mobile phone service

ANSI   American National Standards Institute

ARPANET   Advanced Research Projects Agency Network

ARQ   Automatic repeat request

ASCII   American Standard Code for Information Interchange

ASP   Application service provider

ATM   Asynchronous transfer mode

ATM   Automatic teller machine

AUI   Attachment Unit Interface

B2B   Business-to-business

B2C   Business-to-consumer

BBS   Electronic bulletin board system

BCC   Block check character

BISDN   Broadband Integrated Service Digital Network

BOC   Bell Operating Company

BPR   Business process reengineering

BPS   Bits per second

BRI ISDN   Basic rate interface ISDN

BTW   By the way

CAD   Computer-aided design

CAP   Competitive access provider

CATV   Cable, or community, television

CCITT   International Telegraph and Telephone Consultative Committee

CDMA   Code division multiple access

CI-I   Computer Inquiry I

CI-II   Computer Inquiry II

CIM   Computer-integrated manufacturing

CIO   Chief information officer

CIR   Committed information rate

CLEC   Competitive local exchange carrier

CMIP   Common management information protocol

CMIP   Communications Management Information Protocol

CNA   Certified Novell Administrator

CNE   Certified Novell Engineer

CO   Central office

COPA   Child Online Protection Act

CPE   Customer premises equipment

CRC   Cyclic redundancy check

CRM   Customer relationship management

CRT   Cathode ray tube

C/SA   Client-server architecture

CSA   Customer service area

CSF   Critical success factors

CSMA/CD protocol   Carrier Sense Multiple Access/Collision Detect

CTI   Computer telephony integration

CTO   Chief technology officer

D/A   Digital to analog

db   Decibel

DBS   Digital broadcast satellite

DCE   Data circuit-termination equipment

DCE   Data communications equipment

DDD   Direct distance dialing

DMCA   Digital Millennium Copyright Act

DOS   Denial of service

DP   Data processing

DPSK   Differential phase shift keying

DS-0   Data Signal Format Zero

DS-1   Data Signal Format One (*see* T1)

DSL   Digital Subscriber Line

DSP   Digital signal processor

DSS   Decision support system

DTE   Data terminating equipment

DTMF   Dual-tone-Multifrequency

DWDM   Dense wave division multiplexing

EBCDIC   Extended Binary Coded Decimal Interchange Code

EDI   Electronic data interchange

EFT   Electronic funds transfer

Email   Electronic mail

EIS   Executive information systems

EMI   Electromagnetic interference

EPSS   Electronic performance support systems

ES   Expert systems

FCC   Federal Communications Commission

FDDI   Fiber distributed data interface

FDE   Full-Duplex Ethernet

FDM   Frequency division multiplexing

FEP   Front-end processor

FM   Frequency modulation

FSK   Frequency shift keying

FTP   File Transfer Protocol

FTTC   Fiber to the curb

GAN   Global area network

GIF   CompuServe Graphics Interchange Format

GPRS   General Packet Radio Service

GPS   Global positioning system

GSM   Global System for Mobile Communications

HDSL   High-data-rate Digital Subscriber Line

HDSL   High-level data link control

HDTV   High definition television

HFC   Hybrid fiber/coax

HTML   HyperText Markup Language

HTTP   HyperText Transfer Protocol

Hz   Hertz

IE   Internet Explorer

IEEE   Institute of Electrical and Electronic Engineers

IEEE 802.11b   WiFi

IEEE 1394   FireWire standard external bus

ILEC   Incumbent local exchange carrier

IR   Infrared

IRC   International record carrier

ISDN   Integrated services digital network

ISO   International Standards Organization

ISP   Internet service provider

IT   Information technology

ITU   International Telecommunications Union

IVR   Interactive voice response

IXC   Interexchange carrier

JIT   Just-in-time

JPEG   Joint Photographic Experts Group

Kbps   Kilo bits per second

KM   Knowledge management

LAN   Local area network

LATA   Local access and transport area

LCD   Liquid crystal display

LEC   Local exchange carrier

LED   Light-emitting diode

LMDS   Local multipoint distribution service

MAE   Metropolitan Area Ethernet

MAN   Metropolitan area networks

MAU or MSAU Multiple-station access unit

Mbps Mega bits per second

M-commerce Mobile commerce

MCSE Microsoft Certified Systems Engineer

MHz Megahertz

MIS Management information systems

MMDS Multipoint microwave distribution system, also known as multichannel multipoint distribution system

Modem MOdulator-DEModulator

MON Metropolitan optical networks

MPEG Motion Picture Experts Group

MRP Material requirement planning

MTBF Mean time between failure

MUX Multiplexer

MUX Multiplier

NAK Negative acknowledge character

NAS Network accessible storage

NAS Network-attached data storage

NASA National Aeronautics and Space Administration

NCP Network control program

NIC Network interface card

NISDN Narrowband integrated services digital network

NOS Network operating system

NREN National Research and Education Network

NTSC National Television Standards Committee

OAS Office automation systems

OC-3 Optical Carrier 3 (155.52 Mbps)

OC-12 Optical Carrier 12 (622 Mbps)

OFDM Orthogonal Frequency Division Multiplexing

OSI Open systems interconnection

P2P Peer-2-peer

PAD Packet assembler/disassembler

PAN Personal area network

PBX Private branch exchange

PC Personal computer

PCM Pulse code modulation

PCS Personal communications systems

PDA Personal digital assistant

PDN Packet data network

PIN Personal identification number

PKI Public key infrastructure

POP Point of presence

POS Point-of-service or -sales

POTS Plain old telephone service

PPP Point-to-Point Protocol

PSC Public Service Commission

PSK Phase shift keying

PSN Public-switched network

PSTN Public-switched telephone (voice) network

PTT Postal, Telephone, and Telegraph

PUC Public Utility Commission (*see* PSC)

PVC Permanent virtual channel

PVC Permanent virtual circuit

QAM Quadrature amplitude modulation

QoS Quality of service

RAID Redundant array of inexpensive disks

RBHC Regional Bell Holding Company

RBOC Regional Bell Operating Company

RFI Radio frequency interface

RFP Request for proposal

RFQ Request for quotation

RJE Remote job entry

SAN Storage area networks

SAN Storage-attached network

SCA Subsidiary communications authorization

SDH Synchronous digital hierarchy

SDLC Synchronous data link control

SDLC Systems development life cycle

SDN Software defined network

SKU Stock Keeping Unit

SLA Service level agreement

SLIP Serial line Internet protocol

SMDS Switched multimegabit data service

SNA Systems network architecture

SNMP Simple Network Management Protocol

SOAP Simple Object Access Protocol

SOH Start of header

SOHO Small office/home office

SONET Synchronous optical network

SS7 Signal system no. 7

STDM Statistical time division multiplexing

STP Shielded twisted pair

STP Spanning tree protocol

STS-1 Synchronous Transport Signal 1

TCP/IP Transmission Control Protocol/ Internet Protocol

TDD Telecommunications device for the deaf

TDM Time division multiplexing

TDMA Time division multiple access

TPS Transaction processing system

UDDI Universal Description, Discovery, and Integration

UHF Ultrahigh frequency

UPC Universal product code

UPS Uninterruptible power supply

USB Universal serial bus

UTP Unshielded twisted pair

VAN Value-added networks

VAN Value area networks

V-CD Video compact disk movies

VeDSL Voice-enabled DSL

VERONICA Very Easy Rodent-Oriented Net-wise Index to Computerized Archives

VHF Very high frequency

VIVID VIdeo, Voice, Image, and Data

VOD Video on demand

VoIP Voice over Internet Protocol

VPN Virtual private network

VRC Vertical redundancy check

VSAT Very small aperture terminal

VTAM Virtual telecommunications access method

WAH Work at home

WAIS Wide Area Information Server

WAN Wide area networks

WATS Wide area telecommunications service

WIPO World Intellectual Property Organization

WWW World Wide Web

Index